Cognitive Neuroscience of Language

David Kemmerer

Ψ **Psychology Press**
Taylor & Francis Group

NEW YORK AND LONDON

First published 2015
by Psychology Press
711 Third Avenue, New York, NY 10017

and by Psychology Press
27 Church Road, Hove, East Sussex BN3 2FA

Psychology Press is an imprint of the Taylor & Francis Group, an informa business

© 2015 Taylor & Francis

Every effort has been made to contact copyright holders. Where this has not been possible, we would be pleased to hear from the parties concerned.

Library of Congress Cataloging in Publication Data
Kemmerer, David L.
Cognitive neuroscience of language / by David Kemmerer.
pages cm
Includes bibliographical references and index.
1. Cognitive neuroscience. 2. Language acquisition. I. Title.
QP360.5.K455 2014
612.8′233—dc23
2014017766

ISBN: 978-1-84872-620-8 (hbk)
ISBN: 978-1-84872-621-5 (pbk)
ISBN: 978-1-315-76406-1 (ebk)

Typeset in Galliard
by Book Now Ltd, London

Contents

Detailed Contents

Preface

Welcome to *Cognitive Neuroscience of Language*. During the past few decades, research on how our brains enable us to perceive and produce language has been advancing at a dramatic pace. As a result, the field now contains a wealth of fascinating findings about this uniquely human capacity. Broadly speaking, the purpose of this book is to give students, teachers, researchers, and clinicians a solid, accessible introduction to this material. More narrowly, the text has been deliberately designed for use in courses offered to graduate students and upper-level undergraduate students. Although much of the content is inherently challenging, no previous knowledge of either neuroscience or linguistics is required, since technical terms and important principles from both disciplines are explained along the way. In fact, during the roughly three-year period when I was writing the book, I used the accumulating chapters in my own courses at Purdue University, and many students with little to no background in the neurobiology of language managed to perform quite well, emerging with a deep appreciation of the current state of the art in this exciting field of study.

The book begins by discussing human functional neuroanatomy and brain mapping methods (Part I) as well as classical and progressive aphasia syndromes (Part II). The subsequent chapters then build on that background by focusing on the following topics: the perception and production of speech (Part III); the processing of language in written and signed modalities (Part IV); the meanings of words for objects, actions, and abstract notions (Part V); and the formulation and comprehension of complex expressions, including grammatically inflected words, complete sentences, and entire stories (Part VI). Substantial space is devoted to elaborating recent discoveries about the neural substrates of these central aspects of language. But in order to keep the length of the book within manageable limits, several other topics are not covered, such as development, rehabilitation, bilingualism, figurative language, conversation, and co-speech gesture.

A distinctive feature of the text is that almost all of the chapters in Parts III–VI draw upon prominent theoretical models that characterize the various linguistic domains at both cognitive and neurobiological levels of analysis. In addition, these chapters illustrate how the different components of the models are supported, and in some cases challenged, by experiments employing diverse brain mapping techniques. A special effort has been made to describe these experiments in considerable detail, providing information about their goals, methods, results, and implications. The rationale for such an in-depth approach is that it may help students understand not only how empirical studies are conducted, but also how they contribute to the dynamic interplay between theory and data.

A website with supplementary material is available at www.psypress.com/cw/kemmerer. Here teachers and students will find PowerPoint slides for each chapter as well as internet links and test questions.

Acknowledgments

I am extremely grateful to my editors, Paul Dukes and Fred Coppersmith, for recognizing the potential of my original proposal and gradually bringing this book to fruition. They shepherded the manuscript through countless drafts while skillfully orchestrating a complicated review process.

I would also like to acknowledge the assistance of the following scholars, each of whom provided valuable feedback on batches of several chapters: Joana Acha, Sheila Blumstein, Jonathan Brennan, Eva Fernández, Christopher Grindrod, Nancy Hedberg, Greg Hickok, Li Hsieh, Edith Kaan, Laura Kertz, Ellen Lau, Filip Loncke, Michele Miozzo, Raksha Anand Mudar, Jodi Tommerdahl, and Matthew Wagers.

In addition, I am indebted to the following people for serving as expert reviewers of single chapters: Juliana Baldo, Larry Barsalou, Mike Bonner, Rutvik Desai, Karen Emmorey, Jack Gandour, Lisa Goffman, Argye Hillis, Brad Mahon, Alex Martin, Loraine Obler, Maria Piñango, David Poeppel, Liina Pylkkänen, Meredith Saletta, and Stephen Wilson.

Many other individuals helped me keep the project moving forward by answering questions, sending papers, and providing encouragement. I'm grateful to all of them: Daniel Abrams, Sharon Ash, Marina Bedny, Jeff Binder, Richard Binney, Anjan Chatterjee, Oren Civier, Evelyn Ferstl, Ed Fox, Guido Gainotti, Murray Grossman, Paul Hoffman, Matt Lambon Ralph, Lotte Meteyard, Silke Paulmann, Steve Pinker, Friedemann Pulvermüller, Brenda Rapp, Jamie Reilly, Myrna Schwartz, Peter Sörös, Cindy Thompson, Michael Ullman, Cosimo Urgesi, and Dirk Wildgruber.

Special thanks goes to my mentor, collaborator, and friend, Dan Tranel, who taught me how to not only survive, but thrive, in the competitive world of cognitive neuroscience.

And last but certainly not least, I thank my wife and soul mate, Natalya Kaganovich, for her inspiration, reassurance, love, and companionship.

PART I

Fundamentals

The Human Brain

1

Introduction

In our scientifically advanced, 21st-century societies, we routinely encounter ideas and images—in magazines, newspapers, books, TV programs, and of course the Internet—informing us that the amazing richness of our mental lives emerges from the equally amazing complexity of our physical brains. It is therefore easy to forget that as organs go, the human brain doesn't really look all that special, at least not when observed with the naked eye. After all, it's just a three-pound hunk of rounded, furrowed flesh about the size of a small cantaloupe and with the consistency of cold butter. It doesn't pump like the heart, nor does it expand and contract like the lungs. In fact, it doesn't seem to do much at all, which is no doubt why it was dismissed as a relatively unimportant part of the body throughout much of recorded history.

For example, an ancient text dating back to 1700 BC indicates that when the Egyptians mummified their dead, they carefully preserved the heart but threw away the brain, which suggests that they didn't believe it would be of much use in future incarnations. Similarly, around 335 BC, one of the greatest figures in ancient Greek philosophy, Aristotle, placed the heart at the top of his hierarchy of bodily organs, but assigned the brain the lowly function of serving as a radiator to cool the blood. The radical conceptual shift that was necessary to realize that the brain, rather than the heart, has preeminent status did not take place until the late 1600s, when Thomas Willis, a pioneering physician working in Oxford, England, conducted a series of brilliant experiments that led him to infer that all of our perceptions, thoughts, feelings, memories, and actions arise from the coursing of special forces along the multifarious pathways of the nervous system (for a captivating account of Willis's life and times, see Zimmer, 2004). Near the end of the next century, in 1791, Luigi Galvani discovered that those forces are actually electrical impulses, and another hundred years later, in 1889, Santiago Ramón y Cajal argued that the impulses operate as information-bearing signals that are passed between independent cells arranged in fantastically complicated networks.

After these groundbreaking insights had been made, serious research on the human brain was finally poised to take off. A number of major developments occurred during the first half of the 20th century, and then the pace of progress accelerated dramatically, one might even say meteorically, during the second half. Most importantly, during the 1970s and 1980s, not only did neuroscientists begin to forge productive interdisciplinary collaborations with scholars in the closely related fields of psychology, linguistics, and artificial intelligence, but they also gained access to several new techniques for measuring both the structure and the function of the brain with unprecedented precision. These advances generated a wealth of exciting new findings with far-reaching theoretical and clinical implications, and to stimulate further investigation and promote public awareness, U.S. president George H. W. Bush officially declared the 1990s to be the "Decade of the Brain." Since then, our understanding of how the brain creates the mind has continued to deepen, and today it is common knowledge that although the fragile organ lodged inside our skulls may appear to be just a messy glob of goo, it is actually the most complex computational device in the known universe.

This chapter provides an overview of the general organization of the human brain. The primary aim is to establish the biological background necessary to tackle the material on the neural substrates of language that is covered in Chapters 3–16. There are three main sections: The first focuses on the anatomical, physiological, and representational properties of neurons. The second section describes several subcortical structures—specifically, the brainstem and thalamus, the hippocampus and amygdala, and the basal ganglia and cerebellum. Finally, the third section concentrates on the architecture of the cerebral cortex, which is the wrinkled outer mantle of the brain that underlies our most intricate mental processes.

Neurons: The Basic Signaling Units of the Brain

Toward the end of the 19th century, it was widely believed that the multitudinous cells of the brain are physically fused together to form a gigantic net or reticulum that functions in a holistic manner. In 1889, however, Santiago Ramón y Cajal, who was mentioned above, argued that brain cells are in fact discrete units that may touch one another without actually joining. To bring into sharp relief the anatomical structures of individual brain cells, he frequently used a staining technique called the silver nitrate method, which had been invented by one of his contemporaries, Camillo Golgi. And because he was a gifted artist, he was able to produce many exquisite drawings of what he perceived through his microscope (Figure 1.1).

Being a talented writer as well, he once described brain cells as having "delicate and elegant forms, the butterflies of the soul" (DeFilipe, 2009). In 1891, one of his strongest advocates, Heinrich Wilhelm Gottfried Waldeyer-Hartz, christened these cells "neurons," and over the course of the next few years, Cajal made several ingenious discoveries about them. First, he inferred that neurons connect with each other only in particular places, referred to later as "synapses." Second, he inferred that neurons connect with each other in principled, rather than indiscriminate, ways. And third, he inferred that electrical signals travel through neurons in only one direction, thereby giving rise to the possibility of systematic information flow through circuits. Together with the pivotal claim that neurons are independent structural and functional elements, these insights constituted the foundational bedrock of modern neuroscience, and they rapidly gained broad endorsement. Remarkably enough, Cajal's most conspicuous critic was none other than Golgi, whose histological technique had paved the way for his major findings. In 1906, both Cajal and Golgi

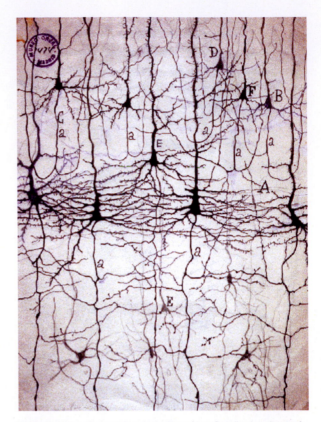

Figure 1.1   One of Santiago Ramón y Cajal's drawings of brain cells.

received the Nobel Prize in Physiology or Medicine, but Golgi used the occasion to renew his attack on Cajal. Indeed, Golgi steadfastly maintained the reticulum theory until his death in 1926. Cajal's own reflections on the shared Nobel Prize include the following poignant remark: "What a cruel irony of fate to pair, like Siamese twins, united by the shoulders, scientific adversaries of such contrasting character" (quotation from Kandel, 2006, p. 68).

Cajal's central claim that brain cells are discrete units was ultimately confirmed once and for all in 1955, when the invention of the electron microscope allowed researchers to demonstrate that in the vast majority of cases, a tiny gap does in fact exist between the connecting branches of neurons. Since then, high-resolution imaging techniques have steadily improved, and today the neuroscience literature is filled with astonishingly detailed images that often combine scientific revelation with stunning beauty (Eisenstein, 2009; Schoonover, 2010). For example, the Brainbow method uses fluorescent proteins, originally derived from the DNA of a glow-in-the-dark jellyfish, to label distinct neurons with a rich palette of over 150 separate colors (Figure 1.2; Lichtman et al., 2009). At

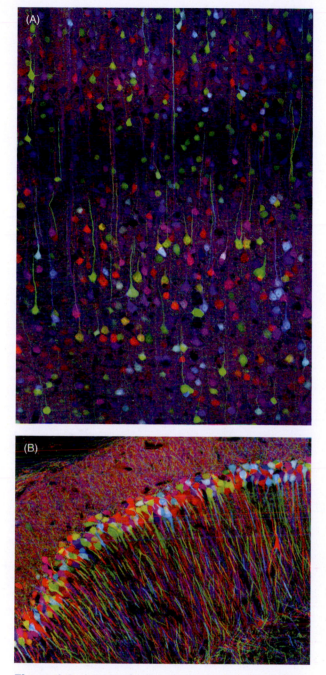

(A)

(B)

Figure 1.2 Images of cells in the hippocampus formation of a mouse that has been genetically engineered to express the Brainbow transgene. Each neuron has a unique color. (A) The cerebral cortex of the mouse. (B) The hippocampus of the mouse. (*Source:* Livet, Weissman, Sanes, and Lichtman. Harvard University.)

because the labeling is random, but efforts are under way to extend the technique so that different *types* of neurons can be tagged with different *ranges* of hues— for instance, reds and oranges for one kind of neuron, yellows and greens for a second, and blues and violets for a third. If this project succeeds, it will be possible to visualize the structural organization of the nervous system in an entirely new way (see also Shen, 2013, and Underwood, 2013).

From a different perspective, one of the most innovative approaches to not only studying human neuroanatomy, but also conveying the results to a broad audience, is currently being pursued by a team of researchers at The Brain Observatory, which is based at the University of California, San Diego. They are creating an on-line resource called the *Concise Digital Atlas of the Human Brain,* and the following website already allows one to inspect several differently stained sections of the same brain at multiple levels of magnification, with the greatest resolution being 0.4 micrometers per pixel: http://thebrainobservatory.ucsd.edu/. Thus, one can start out by scrutinizing the images from a bird's-eye view, so to speak, where the contours and compositions of large-scale structures are plainly visible, with handy labels on an adjacent figure; and then one can gradually zoom in on particular regions, getting closer and closer and closer, until the whole screen is ultimately filled with individual neurons, like the stars in a clear night sky. It's not for nothing that Jacopo Annese, the director of the website, envisioned it as "the brain's Hubble telescope."

Altogether, the human brain contains nearly 100 billion neurons whose connecting fibers, if laid end to end, would stretch for about 150,000 kilometers. Even the cerebral cortex taken by itself holds about 30 billion neurons with 1 million billion connections, and if we were to count one of those connections every second, it would take 32 million years to cover them all. Needless to say, we are dealing here with a biological machine of unimaginable complexity. So to reduce the situation to a more manageable scale, let's take a look at some of the most basic anatomical, physiological, and representational properties of neurons. (For a technical discussion of "the human brain in numbers," see Herculano-Houzel, 2009.)

Anatomy

The major structural characteristics of neurons are shown in Figure 1.3. Like all of the other cells in our bodies, neurons have a central region that contains the nucleus. What distinguishes neurons from other cells,

present, the main virtue of this promising approach is that the various hues help researchers disentangle neurons in the dense jungle of the brain. Its main limitation is that the colors themselves are meaningless

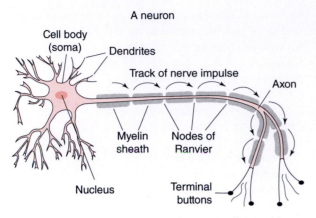

A neuron

Cell body (soma)

Dendrites

Track of nerve impulse

Axon

Myelin sheath

Nodes of Ranvier

Nucleus

Terminal buttons

Figure 1.3 Basic components of a neuron. (Adapted from Ward, 2010, p. 18.)

however, is that their forms are uniquely designed for signal transmission. They tend to resemble trees, with branching roots to receive incoming messages, and a long trunk with a bushy crown to pass messages on. The branching roots are called **dendrites**, from the Greek word for "tree," and the long trunk is called the **axon**, from the Greek word for "axle." The axon is encased by **myelin sheaths**, which are fatty substances that provide insulation to protect and accelerate signal propagation. These sheaths are about 1 millimeter long, and they are separated by small spaces called the **nodes of Ranvier**, where signals are rapidly rejuvenated in a manner described below. The axon splits into many segments that end with **terminal buttons**, which relay information to downstream neurons. Finally, the tiny clefts between the terminal buttons of message-sending neurons and the dendrites of message-receiving neurons are called **synapses**, from the Greek *syn-* ("together") and *haptein* ("to clasp").

Although all neurons have the anatomical features just described, they vary greatly in size and shape. Regarding size, some neurons, like those in the middle layers of the retina, span only a fraction of a millimeter, whereas others, like those that extend from the spinal cord to the toes, transverse a distance of up to

a meter. And regarding shape, a wide variety of forms have been observed under the microscope, inspiring a host of vivid names like "pyramidal," "granular," "stellate," "chandelier," "basket," "fork," etc.

Due to their connectivity patterns and response profiles, some types of neurons are known to be specialized for certain aspects of sensory or motor processing. But the higher up in the brain one goes, the more mysterious the disparate kinds of neurons become. Still, there are several cases in which significant progress is being made. An excellent example involves a distinctive class of cells called von Economo neurons that have been the focus of increasing attention in recent years for the following reasons (e.g., Allman et al., 2010; Seeley et al., 2012; Evrard et al., 2012; Butti et al., 2013). They are found in only a few brain regions that are well-established as contributing to emotional processing, self-awareness, and social cognition, most notably the anterior cingulate and the anterior insula (both of which are discussed later). They are altered in many neuropsychiatric disorders that involve impairments of these mental capacities, like autism and schizophrenia. And they are present in large quantities in several other socially complex mammalian species, including apes, elephants, whales, and dolphins. These findings suggest that von Economo neurons play a very special role in interoception (i.e., the sense of one's internal bodily state) and in the affective, and perhaps also the communicative, relationships between individuals. The precise nature of that role, however, has yet to be determined (for some recent proposals see Allman et al., 2005, and Critchley & Seth, 2012).

Physiology

Neurons crackle with electricity, and this lies at the heart of their basic adaptive function—signal transmission. To gain a rudimentary understanding and appreciation of the energetic lifestyle of neurons, just picture a representative cell, like the one shown in Figure 1.4. Imagine that its dendrites are receiving lots—indeed, hundreds if not thousands—of inputs from other neurons. These inputs take the form of electrical currents that move toward the cell body through a process called **passive conduction**. At the base, or "hillock," of the axon, all of the signals are effectively summed up, and if the total exceeds a certain threshold, the neuron fires. That is to say, it generates what is technically

Dendrites Richly branching neural structures that receive signals.

Axon An elongated branching neural structure that transmits signals.

Myelin sheaths Fatty substances that insulate the axon to facilitate signal propagation.

Nodes of Ranvier Small spaces between myelin sheaths where signals are renewed.

Terminal buttons Axonal endpoints.

Synapses Gaps between the terminal buttons of transmitting neurons and the dendrites of receiving neurons.

Passive conduction The passive flow of electrical currents from the dendrites to the body of a neuron.

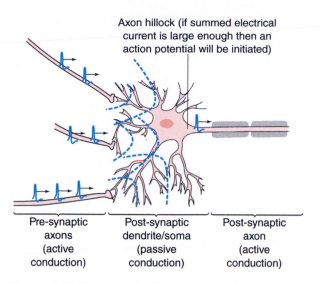

Axon hillock (if summed electrical current is large enough then an action potential will be initiated)

Pre-synaptic axons (active conduction)   Post-synaptic dendrite/soma (passive conduction)   Post-synaptic axon (active conduction)

Figure 1.4   Passive and active conduction of electrical signals. (Adapted from Ward, 2010, p. 19.)

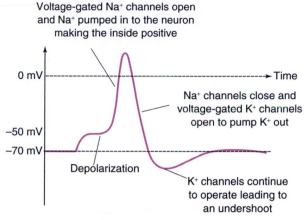

Voltage-gated Na^+ channels open and Na^+ pumped in to the neuron making the inside positive

0 mV — Time

Na^+ channels close and voltage-gated K^+ channels open to pump K^+ out

−50 mV

−70 mV

Depolarization

K^+ channels continue to operate leading to an undershoot

Figure 1.5   The action potential. (Adapted from Ward, 2010, p. 20.)

referred to as an **action potential**, which is an impulse that gets propagated down the axon through a process called **active conduction**.

The nature of the action potential is illustrated in greater detail in Figure 1.5. In general, both the cytoplasm inside a neuron and the fluid outside it are rich in positively and negatively charged particles, or "ions." However, the default state of a neuron is such that the net charge inside it is more negative than the net charge outside it, with the resting intracellular potential usually hovering around −70 millivolts (mV). If, at any given time, the total dendritic input is positive enough to raise the inner level to about −50 mV, a critical threshold is crossed and a remarkable cycle of changes is suddenly triggered. First, miniature gates in the cell membrane open up, allowing certain positive ions, chiefly sodium (Na^+), to rush in so that the electrical balance quickly reverses, or "depolarizes," becoming more positive inside than outside. This is the action potential, also known as a spike, and, importantly, it is always an all-or-nothing affair, never a matter of degree. Immediately afterward, the sodium channels shut down and other doors open up, allowing certain positive ions, chiefly potassium (K^+), to be pumped out. The outward flow of K^+ not only restores the predominantly negative

voltage level inside the cell, but causes it to briefly go even lower than −70 mV. This temporary "hyperpolarization" prevents another spike from occurring straight away and ensures that the impulse travels forward rather than backward along the axon. Bear in mind, though, that this whole process is extremely fast, lasting only 1 millisecond. (For an instructive video that dynamically portrays all of the key aspects of the action potential, see www.youtube.com/watch?v=ifD1YG07fB8.)

We noted above that myelin sheaths significantly increase the speed with which an axon can transmit a current. Whereas an unmyelinated axon may send a signal at a rate of less than 1 meter per second, a thickly myelinated one may do so at a rate of 10–100 meters per second. Even a well-myelinated axon, however, would not be able to propagate an impulse very far if it were not for the nodes of Ranvier. These small spaces between myelin sheaths are essential for signal transmission because they enable the action potential to be perpetually renewed. In short, at each node, the complete cycle of Na^+ inflow and K^+ outflow is repeated, and this sequential process of signal rejuvenation, referred to earlier as active conduction, allows the impulse to traverse the entire length of the axon without fading away (see Figure 1.3).

When the impulse reaches the terminal buttons of the axon, it must cross the synaptic cleft, which has a width of only 20 nanometers (i.e., 20 billionths of a meter). In the vast majority of cases, this process involves the release of specialized chemicals called **neurotransmitters** that bind to particular receptors on the postsynaptic neuron, like a key fitting into a lock. If the presynaptic neuron is excitatory, the released

Action potential   Also known as a spike, this is a sudden change in the electrical properties of a neuron such that the net charge inside its axon shifts from negative to positive.

Active conduction   The recurrence of spikes at the nodes of Ranvier, allowing the signal to traverse the entire length of the axon without fading away.

Neurotransmitters   Specialized chemicals that carry signals across the synaptic cleft.

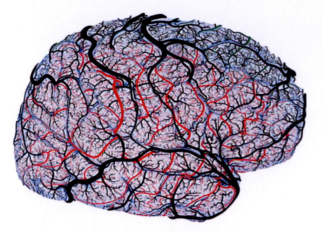

Figure 1.6   The vascular system of the brain. Colored vessels are arteries, tapering off into arterioles and capillaries, whereas black vessels are veins. (From Huettel et al., 2004, p. 138.)

neurotransmitters make the postsynaptic neuron more likely to fire, but if the presynaptic neuron is inhibitory, the released neurotransmitters make the postsynaptic neuron less likely to fire. Whether the target cell ultimately does or doesn't fire depends largely on how all of the other myriad inputs to it are summed up, as described above. It is crucial to note, however, that the relative "strengths" of individual excitatory and inhibitory connections are by no means rigid; on the contrary, they are highly plastic, and this adjustability is one of the most powerful cellular mechanisms by which brains are able to continuously modify and update themselves on the basis of experience.

The integrative and signaling activity of neurons does not come for free; instead, it requires substantial energy consumption. The human brain, to put it bluntly, is a metabolic pig. Although it comprises a mere 2–3 percent of total body weight, it devours about 20 percent of the oxygenated blood flowing from the heart. This oxygenated blood reaches the brain via a network of large vessels called **arteries**, each of which can be 4–10 millimeters in diameter (Figure 1.6). These arteries branch into smaller vessels called **arterioles**, with diameters in the range of 20–50 micrometers, and they in turn branch into even smaller vessels called **capillaries**, which are only about 10 micrometers thick—not much wider than a single red blood cell. Within the dense meshwork of the capillary bed, the arrival of freshly oxygenated blood provides the

Arteries   Large vessels that carry oxygenated blood from the heart to the rest of the body, including the brain.

Arterioles   Small arteries.

Capillaries   Very small, thin-walled vessels where oxygen is extracted.

fuel supply that is vital for neural activity. The deoxygenated blood then flows out of the brain and back to the heart through **veins** (Figure 1.6). As we will see in Chapter 2, these properties of the vascular system are exploited by two of the most commonly used techniques for determining which brain regions are engaged when people perform various cognitive tasks—positron emission tomography (PET) and functional magnetic resonance imaging (fMRI).

Representation

Having reviewed the major anatomical and physiological characteristics of neurons, we can now address, at least in a very simplistic manner, the question of how suitably organized networks of these cells manage to create our multifaceted mental worlds, representing everything from single colors to glorious sunsets, pure tones to symphonies, and basic tastes to tiramisu, as well as supporting the sophisticated abilities that are the main focus of this book—namely, producing and comprehending language. We noted above that whenever a neuron fires, it's always an all-or-nothing affair, never a matter of degree. Neurons vary greatly, however, in the precise *rate* at which they fire, and this is how they code information. All neurons have a baseline firing rate that they maintain, within certain limits, when they are neither excited nor inhibited beyond a critical threshold. But if the environment happens to contain the particular type of stimulus that a given neuron is tuned to represent, that neuron's firing rate will increase significantly above its baseline level. Moreover, the better the match between the stimulus and the neuron's unique tuning properties, the faster the neuron will fire. It's as if the neuron's firing frequency indicates how confident it is that its preferred stimulus is present.

One of the most interesting ways in which assemblies of neurons can capture complex patterns of information is by being configured in multilayered hierarchies. In the visual system, for example, it is well established that object recognition depends on a long progression of synaptic connections that extend through numerous stages of processing, with early stages representing elementary features of shape and subsequent stages representing increasingly complex combinations of those features. The essential aspects of this type of hierarchical coding scheme are shown in Figure 1.7, which portrays a little caricature of a "table detection" network. At the lowest level there are two cells that code for "vertical edge" and "horizontal edge," respectively. At the next level there is

Veins   Vessels that carry deoxygenated blood back to the heart.

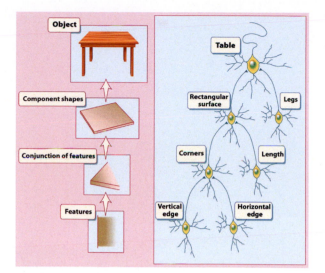

Figure 1.7 Hierarchical coding by neurons. Neurons that represent elementary features project to multiple layers of higher-order "conjunctive" neurons that capture increasingly complex patterns of information. (From Gazzaniga et al., 2009, p. 223.)

a cell that codes for "length," as well as a cell that receives convergent input from both of the cells at the first level, thereby enabling it to combine the features of horizontal and vertical edges to derive the more complex feature of "corners." At the third level there is a cell that codes for "legs," as well as a cell that receives convergent input from both of the cells at the second level, thereby enabling it to combine the features of corners and length to derive the more complex feature of "rectangular surface." And lastly, at the fourth level there is a single cell that receives convergent input from both of the cells at the third level, thereby enabling it to combine the features of rectangular surface and legs to derive the ultimate object representation—"table." (For an illustration of a similar neural network, only designed for the auditory recognition of vocal calls, see Figure 5.2 in Chapter 5.)

The table detection network in Figure 1.7 is only an instructional toy, but it does exemplify some important principles of hierarchical coding that seem to be implemented by real brains, especially in the cerebral cortex. In fact, there is substantial evidence that nested tiers of neural assemblies underlie the representation of complex patterns of information not only in the visual system, but also in the other perceptual systems. As information flows from lower to higher tiers in each modality-specific system, neurons record increasingly complex combinations of features, and at the most central levels of representation, which are found in various higher-order association areas, information from different modalities is integrated, giving rise to neurons with amazingly

specific tuning properties. For example, one study identified a single cell in the anterior medial temporal region that responded robustly to photographs of the television host Oprah Winfrey, as well as to presentations of her written and spoken name (Quiroga et al., 2009). Although this neuron also responded to pictures of the actress Whoopi Goldberg, it did so to a much lesser degree, and it did not respond at all to pictures, written names, or spoken names of nearly 100 other familiar people. Thus, the neuron seems to capture a special set of multimodal features that are, at least to a large extent, unique to Oprah Winfrey. (For further theoretical discussion, see Quiroga, 2012; and for another example of a highly selective cell, see Box 10.2 in Chapter 10.)

A final point is that hierarchical coding networks are not limited to bottom-up feedforward connections that allow sensory signals to be matched with knowledge stored in long-term memory. They also contain top-down feedback connections that allow perceptual processes to be guided by internally generated priorities and predictions (Mesulam, 2008; Meyer & Damasio, 2009; Clark, 2013; for a dramatic illustration see the following video of the Charlie Chaplin hollow mask illusion: www.youtube.com/watch?v=QbKw0_v2clo). Interestingly, these top-down connections from central to peripheral brain regions also allow relatively fine-grained sensorimotor representations to be reconstructed in the absence of external input. This is what happens when we dream at night and when we deliberately conjure up various sights, sounds, smells, and so forth in our imaginations.

Navigating the Neural Landscape

Before surveying some of the major large-scale structures in the brain, it is worthwhile to introduce a set of anatomical terms that provide a spatial coordinate system or frame of reference for specifying, in three dimensions, the planes of particular sections and the locations of particular regions (Figure 1.8). First of all, when the brain is sectioned, or sliced, it is typically done so along one of three planes. If this is done in a manner that separates the left side from the right side, the resulting view is **sagittal**. If it is done in a manner that separates the front from the back, the resulting view is **coronal**. And if it is done in a manner that separates the top from the bottom,

Sagittal   A section that separates the left and right sides of the brain.

Coronal   A section that separates the front from the back of the brain.

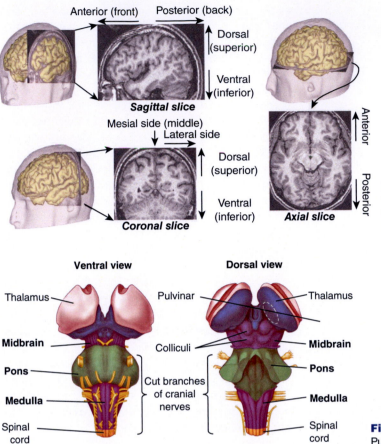

Sagittal slice

Coronal slice

Axial slice

Figure 1.8   The main planes in which the brain is viewed, and the main directional terms that are used to refer to regions. (From Dehaene, 2009, p. xii.)

Ventral view

Dorsal view

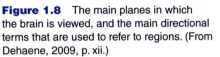

Thalamus

Midbrain

Pons

Medulla

Spinal cord

Pulvinar

Colliculi

Cut branches of cranial nerves

Thalamus

Midbrain

Pons

Medulla

Spinal cord

Figure 1.9   Brainstem and thalamus. (From Purves et al., 2008, p. 19.)

the resulting view is **horizontal** (also sometimes referred to as axial or transverse). In addition, when it is necessary to indicate the relative positions of structures seen from a certain vantage point, the following terms are frequently used. Structures toward the front of the brain are referred to as **rostral** or **anterior**, whereas structures toward the back are referred to as **caudal** or **posterior**. Structures toward the top of the brain are referred to as **dorsal** or **superior**, whereas structures toward the bottom are referred to as **ventral** or **inferior**. And lastly, structures toward the outer left or right side of the brain are referred to as **lateral**, whereas structures toward the midline are referred to as **medial**.

Horizontal   A section that separates the top from the bottom of the brain.

Rostral/anterior   Toward the front of the brain.

Caudal/posterior   Toward the back of the brain.

Dorsal/superior   Toward the top of the brain.

Ventral/inferior   Toward the bottom of the brain.

Lateral   Toward the outer left or right side of the brain.

Medial   Toward the midline of the brain.

Building the Brain from the Bottom Up

When you look at a human brain, most of what you see is its convoluted outer covering—the cerebral cortex. But beneath that impressive dome there are numerous subcortical structures, some of which are described below.

Brainstem and Thalamus

The **brainstem** lies at the base of the brain and is continuous with the spinal cord (Figure 1.9). Anatomically, it has three major sectors—the medulla, the pons, and the midbrain—each of which houses many nuclei. Taken together, these nuclei maintain bodily homeostasis by regulating such basic functions as heart rate, blood pressure, breathing, and degree of wakefulness. Damage can cause coma or even death, depending on which

Brainstem   A set of three vertically aligned structures—the medulla, pons, and midbrain—that lie at the base of the brain and are essential for the regulation of bodily homeostasis.

structures are destroyed (see Damasio, 2010, for an intriguing hypothesis about how the brainstem contributes to consciousness). The brainstem is also the portal for the cranial nerves, which receive sensory input from, and send motor output to, the head and neck. Some of these nerves are essential for the perception and production of speech, as discussed toward the end of Chapter 6.

The **thalamus** is a large egg-shaped structure that sits on top of the brainstem (Figure 1.9). There are actually two of them—the thalami, one in each hemisphere—but we will typically use the singular term to refer to the generic structure. Although the word *thalamus* derives from the Greek expression for "inner chamber," it is not hollow. Nor is it a homogeneous entity; instead, it is divided into many separate nuclei that collectively handle a massive amount of traffic in the brain. The thalamus is sometimes called the "gateway to the cortex" for the following reasons. First and foremost, almost all forms of perceptual input, the sole exception being the sense of smell, pass through a specific nucleus in the thalamus before being routed on to the appropriate cortical region. To take a few examples, signals originating in the retina pass through the lateral geniculate nucleus before reaching the primary visual cortex, and signals originating in the cochlea pass through the medial geniculate nucleus before reaching the primary auditory cortex. In addition, all of the signals coming from the basal ganglia and cerebellum pass through particular thalamic nuclei before reaching their cortical targets, and most of the signals coming from the amygdala do too. It is noteworthy, however, that the thalamus is not just a hub for relaying information up to the cortex, since it also receives a great deal of feedback from the cortex. In fact, every distinct area in the entire cerebral cortex has reciprocal (i.e., bidirectional) connections with a specific part of the thalamus, and these cortico-thalamo-cortical loops promote reverberatory cycles of activity that may facilitate attention, short-term memory, and the coordination of different brain regions underlying multifaceted mental representations. For recent overviews of the involvement of the thalamus in language, see the special 2013 issue of the journal *Brain and Language* devoted to this topic (volume 126, issue 1).

Hippocampus and Amygdala

The **hippocampus** is named after a giant seahorse (in Greek *hippo* means "horse" and *kampos* means

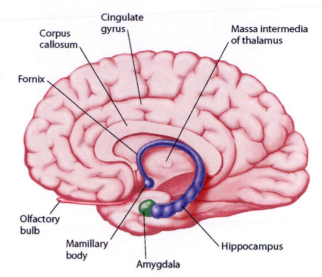

Figure 1.10 Hippocampus and amygdala. (From Gazzaniga et al., 2009, p. 81.)

"sea-monster"), but it looks more like a long, curved sausage (Figure 1.10). Like the thalamus, there are actually two of them—the hippocampi, one in each hemisphere—but again we will generally stick with the singular term. Composed of many different fields of neurons, the hippocampus resides deep within the temporal lobe. An extension from its posterior end arches upward and forward and takes on a new name, the fornix, which itself terminates in a small nucleus called the mammillary body. All of these structures, as well as some surrounding ones, play crucial roles in the establishment of long-term declarative memories—that is, memories that can be verbally retrieved and reported more or less easily, including factual information about the world (e.g., the current president of the United States) and autobiographical information about your own life (e.g., where you went to high school).

Basically, the hippocampus receives a huge amount of convergent input from the cerebral cortex, and it processes that input by registering the spatiotemporal relations among all the elements that constitute particular episodes of experience. It retains these complex patterns, and very gradually, over a period that may last for years, it transfers them back to the original cortical areas, where they are laid down in a quasi-permanent fashion as strongly weighted synaptic connections among widely distributed populations of neurons. This whole process is called memory consolidation, and much of the evidence for it comes from research involving

---

Thalamus A large egg-shaped structure (one in each hemisphere) that sits on top of the brainstem and routes input from the sensory periphery, as well as from the basal ganglia, cerebellum, and amygdala, up to the proper cortical areas. It also maintains reciprocal interactions with every part of the cortex.

Hippocampus A sausage-shaped structure (one in each hemisphere) that lies deep in the temporal lobe and is essential for the establishment of long-term declarative memories.

brain-damaged patients who have suffered hippocampal lesions (Squire & Wixted, 2011).

The most famous of these patients, HM, became profoundly amnesic after both of his medial temporal lobes were surgically removed in 1953, when he was 27 years old, in a last-ditch attempt to alleviate epileptic seizures that had become excessively debilitating (Corkin, 2013; Eichenbaum, 2013). Following the operation, his seizures abated, but he was unable to recall anything that had happened to him since he was 16. Even more dramatically, from the time of the surgery until his death in 2008, over five decades later, he could not remember even such simple things as his last meal, where he lived, or his own age. In addition, he had great difficulty learning the meanings of new words, which suggests that the hippocampus is essential for this linguistic process. (See Ullman, 2004, for a thoughtful discussion; see also Duff & Brown-Schmidt, 2012, for data regarding the contribution of the hippocampus to on-line language use.) Despite his severe amnesia, however, HM could still hold information in short-term memory and learn new motor skills, indicating that these abilities rely on other brain mechanisms. After HM died, his full name was revealed—Henry Molaison—and his brain was frozen to about −35°C and then sliced into 2,401 paper-thin sections during a 53-hour procedure that the general public was able to watch via several web cameras. These tissue sections have been archived for future investigation.

The **amygdala** lies at the anterior tip of the hippocampus (Figure 1.10). Its name derives from the Latin word for "almond," reflecting its nut-like shape. As with the thalamus and hippocampus, it comes as a pair—the amygdalae, one in each hemisphere—but we will usually employ the singular term. This structure has a complex internal organization consisting of several nuclei characterized by different input/output connectivity patterns and associated functions. For our purposes, though, what matters most is that it has been reliably implicated in emotional processing. More precisely, the amygdala is crucial for rapidly assessing the salience and significance of stimuli, or what one might simply call their personal value (Pessoa & Adolphs, 2010). It is particularly sensitive to potentially dangerous situations, as indicated by the sorts of deficits displayed by individuals who have suffered amygdala damage.

For example, patient SM, whose amygdala did not develop normally in either hemisphere, is not only impaired at recognizing expressions of fear in other

> **Amygdala** An almond-shaped structure (one in each hemisphere) that rests at the anterior tip of the hippocampus and plays a key role in emotional processing.

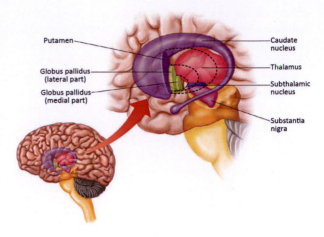

Figure 1.11 Basal ganglia and cerebellum. Dashed lines indicate the borders of nuclei that have been cut away. (From Banich & Compton, 2011, p. 117.)

people's faces, but is also unable to experience fear herself (Feinstein et al., 2010). When a team of researchers took her to the Waverly Hills Sanatorium, which is reputedly the scariest haunted house in the world, she led the group the whole way and reacted to the monsters by laughing, smiling, and trying to talk to them. In an amusing reversal of roles, she even startled one of *them* by poking him in the head! Similarly, when the researchers took her to an exotic pet store, they had to restrain her from getting too close to the poisonous snakes and spiders. Consistent with these findings is the striking fact that even though SM's life history has been filled with traumatic events, including occasions when she was held up at knife-point and gun-point and explicitly threatened with death, she never recalled feeling afraid. Angry and upset, yes, but never deeply distressed.

Taken together, these and many other discoveries about the amygdala demonstrate that it is indispensable for promoting adaptive behavior in threatening situations. As we will see in Chapter 7, there is also some evidence that this subcortical structure contributes to the perception of emotional prosodic patterns in speech, not only when they are threatening, but more generally when they are subjectively relevant, contextually novel, or acoustically salient.

Basal Ganglia and Cerebellum

The **basal ganglia** consist of several tightly integrated nuclei that are located near the thalamus (Figure 1.11). There is one set in each hemisphere, comprising the following structures: the caudate and putamen, which are collectively referred to as the striatum; the globus pallidus, or pallidum, which has both a lateral part and a medial part; and the subthalamic nucleus. The substantia nigra—a small midbrain body that generates dopamine, an important neurotransmitter—is also sometimes grouped together with the basal ganglia because it projects heavily to the striatum.

Setting aside many complexities, the operation of the basal ganglia can be characterized roughly as follows (Surmeier, 2013). The striatum continually receives signals from most of the cerebral cortex, and it recognizes in those signals familiar situations, like when one walks up to the front door of one's favorite restaurant. The striatum then sends this information along two parallel routes through the other components of the basal ganglia. One of these routes can be thought of as the "go" pathway because its job is to implicitly learn what types of actions are adaptive in certain situations (e.g., push the door), whereas the other route can be thought of as the "no-go" pathway because its job is to implicitly learn what types of actions are maladaptive in certain situations (e.g., don't pull the door). The outputs of these two pathways essentially consist of recommendations for what to do and what not to do, and they are projected up to the frontal cortex, via the thalamus, for more careful consideration.

As the example involving the restaurant suggests, the basal ganglia underlie the unconscious acquisition, selection, initiation, and cessation of what are colloquially called habits and more formally called procedural skills. Moreover, the basal ganglia serve these functions not only at the level of overt behavior, but also at the level of covert thought. It is therefore not surprising that basal ganglia disturbances have negative consequences not only for motor control, as in Parkinson's disease and Huntington's disease, but also for cognitive control, as in obsessive-compulsive disorder and schizophrenia (Bradshaw, 2001). With respect to language, the basal ganglia have been implicated in many aspects of both production and comprehension, and some of these findings are discussed in later chapters (see especially Chapters 6, 7, 13, 14, and 15).

The **cerebellum** occupies a space posterior to the medulla and pons (Figure 1.11). Although its name derives from the Latin word for "little brain," it actually contains two-thirds or more of all the neurons in the entire brain, and some of its most distinctive cells—Purkinje neurons—have prodigious dendritic arbors that receive signals from up to 200,000 other cells. The cerebellum has several subdivisions, most of which contribute, in various ways, to regulating muscle tone and ensuring that movements are executed fluidly, with appropriate timing and coordination. Damage to the cerebellum often disrupts postural balance and causes arm and hand actions to become jerky and tremulous. In addition, lesions affecting certain sectors of the cerebellum frequently impair articulatory control, giving rise to a unique type of dysarthria that is discussed in Chapter 6. Interestingly, recent research suggests that, like the basal ganglia, the cerebellum facilitates not only movement but also cognition (Schmahmann, 2010).

The Cerebral Cortex

We turn now to the most highly evolved part of the human brain, the cerebral cortex, which consists of two fairly symmetrical hemispheres. The term *cortex* derives from the Latin word for "bark," "rind," "husk," or "shell." This mantle covering the rest of the brain can be thought of as a layered sheet of neurons, about 2–4 millimeters thick, that has been crumpled up to fit inside the cranium but actually occupies about 2,000 square centimeters of surface area, so that if it were unfolded and flattened out, it would cover roughly the same amount of space as three-and-a-half sheets of 11 × 8.5 inch printing paper (Van Essen et al., 2012). As mentioned above, the cortex contains approximately 30 billion neurons, and each of them makes contact with at least 1,000 other cells. The cell bodies reside within the cortex itself, and because they appear grayish (with hints of reddish brown reflecting capillaries), cortical tissue is sometimes referred to as **gray matter**; in contrast, most of the axons project out beneath the cortex, and because they are a pale creamy color (due to myelinization), the tissue under the cortex is sometimes referred to as **white matter**. The vast synaptic space of the cerebral cortex provides the massively interactive computational matrix that subserves our most sophisticated mental processes, including the majority of linguistic operations. The following discussion addresses several aspects of cortical architecture: its division into lobes; its gyral–sulcal organization; its cytoarchitectonic organization; its connectional organization; its implementation of sensory, motor, and higher-order cognitive functions; and its implementation of linguistic functions.

Basal ganglia A set of interconnected nuclei—the caudate, putamen, globus pallidus (or pallidum), and subthalamic nucleus—that reside near the thalamus and are essential for the unconscious acquisition, selection, initiation, and cessation of habitual behaviors in both motor and cognitive domains.

Cerebellum A large structure lodged behind the medulla and pons that is necessary for balance and the on-line temporal control of movements. It has also been implicated in cognition.

Gray matter Cortical tissue consisting primarily of neuronal cell bodies.

White matter Subcortical tissue consisting primarily of myelinated axons.

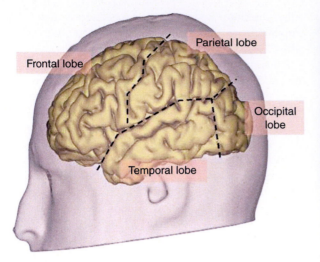

Figure 1.12   The four visible lobes. (From Dehaene, 2009, p. xii.)

The Major Lobes—Visible and Hidden

Geographically, each cerebral hemisphere is divided into five "cortical continents"—four visible lobes, plus a fifth that is hidden from view. The four lobes that can easily be seen are the **frontal, parietal, temporal, and occipital lobes** (Figure 1.12). The borders between them are based primarily on anatomical landmarks, especially certain sulci (the nature of which is described in the next subsection). The frontal and parietal lobes are separated from each other by the central sulcus. The temporal lobe is separated from the frontal and parietal lobes chiefly by the lateral sulcus, more commonly known as the sylvian fissure. And the occipital lobe is separated from the parietal and temporal lobes by a somewhat arbitrary line connecting the parieto-occipital sulcus on the brain's dorsal surface with the preoccipital notch on its ventrolateral surface. Note that another somewhat arbitrary line, extending perpendicularly from the one just mentioned to roughly the posterior end of the sylvian fissure, helps separate the occipital lobe from the temporal lobe. Finally, the fifth lobe, which is hidden from view, is called the **insula**, a name based on the Latin word for "island." As shown in Figure 1.13, it is a large swath of cortex that faces laterally but lies at the very bottom—or, more technically, at the greatly expanded fundus—of the sylvian fissure.

> **Frontal, parietal, temporal, and occipital lobes**   The four visible lobes of each cerebral hemisphere, demarcated chiefly by prominent anatomical landmarks.
>
> **Insula**   The hidden lobe of each cerebral hemisphere, oriented laterally but buried deep within the sylvian fissure.

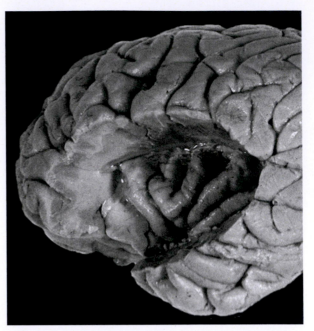

Figure 1.13   The exposed left insula of a human brain. (Courtesy of the Digital Anatomist Project at the University of Washington: www9.biostr.washington.edu/da.html.)

Gyral–Sulcal Organization

Perhaps the most salient feature of the cerebral cortex is that it is folded into many convolutions. The raised bulges are called **gyri**, and the deep grooves are called **sulci**. This complex configuration is adaptive for several reasons (Bullmore & Sporns, 2012). As noted above, it squeezes a great deal of surface area into a relatively small three-dimensional volume; in fact, as much as two-thirds of the cortex lies within the sulci. In addition, it significantly reduces the amount of axonal wiring that is required, and hence also the distances across which signals must be conducted. Interestingly, recent research suggests that the axonal fibers projecting to gyri are much denser than those projecting to sulci, not only in humans but also in chimpanzees, macaque monkeys, and a range of other mammalian species (Nie et al., 2012; see also Chen et al., 2013). These findings support the view that during brain development gyral–sulcal patterns are biomechanically caused by stiff axons constantly "pushing" harder against certain regions of the cortical surface than others so that, given the physical constraints imposed by the skull, the disproportionately pushed regions expand outward to form convex gyri, and the other regions bend inward to form concave sulci.

> **Gyri (singular = gyrus)**   The raised bulges of the cerebral cortex.
>
> **Sulci (singular = sulcus)**   The deep grooves of the cerebral cortex.

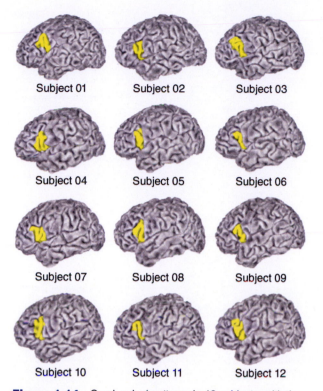

Figure 1.14 Gyral–sulcal patterns in 12 subjects, with the pars opercularis of the left inferior frontal gyrus highlighted in yellow. (Unpublished data from Javier Gonzalez Castillo and David Kemmerer.)

A very important aspect of cortical anatomy is that, while the same major gyri and sulci are usually exhibited by all normal human brains, their precise shapes and sizes vary substantially, as illustrated in Figure 1.14 (see also Juch et al., 2005). Although some of this variation can be attributed to environmental factors, the vast majority of it appears to be genetically influenced, as indicated by research showing that the morphology of cortical convolutions, as well as the surface area of specific regions, is more similar in monozygotic (identical) than dizygotic (fraternal) twins (Bartley et al., 1997; Peper et al., 2007; Chen et al., 2012).

So what are the major gyri and sulci of the human brain? Figure 1.15 presents almost all of them from both lateral and medial perspectives, and Figure 1.16 presents just the gyri from ventral, dorsal, rostral, and caudal perspectives. The abbreviations in these diagrams are linked with the corresponding full names in Table 1.1, which is organized according to lobe. Figure 1.17 presents two additional structures that are not depicted in the previous figures because they reside within the sylvian fissure on the dorsal surface of the temporal lobe, a region that is sometimes called the supratemporal plane. These

structures are, first, Heschl's gyrus (HG, also known as the transverse gyrus), and second, the planum temporale (PT). Both of them are highly pertinent to language because they play essential roles in speech processing, as described briefly below and more extensively in Chapter 5. The numbers in Figure 1.17 stand for Brodmann areas, which we discuss next.

Cytoarchitectonic Organization

Crosscutting the gyral–sulcal topography of the cerebral cortex is another type of structural arrangement, namely **cytoarchitectonic organization**, which has to do with the presence/absence, packing density, and layering of the various types of cells in a given area (Zilles & Amunts, 2010, 2012). Earlier we noted that the cortex is a large sheet of neurons about 2–4 millimeters thick. It might be more useful, however, to think of it as a multilayered cake, since cytoarchitectonic studies have shown that it is composed almost entirely of six different layers of cells stacked on top of each other (Figure 1.18). Each layer is characterized not only by the morphological properties of the cells within it, but also by their connectional properties. Thus, layers I, II, and III typically communicate with other cortical areas; layer IV typically receives input from the thalamus; layer V typically sends output to subcortical motor structures; and layer VI typically sends output to the thalamus. Perpendicular to these horizontal layers are vertical columns, each of which measures roughly 0.4 millimeters in diameter and consists of roughly 100 neurons that are representationally tuned to respond to similar features of the external environment or internal milieu. These columns have been argued to constitute the basic functional units of the cortex (Mountcastle, 1997; Jones, 2000; Buxhoeveden & Casanova, 2002; Tanaka, 2003).

Although the layered organization of the cortex is fairly uniform across its vast extent, there are many discontinuities marked by shifts in the thickness and composition of the six tiers. Based on such boundaries, during the first half of the 20th century several scientists created maps that portray the cortex as a mosaic of cytoarchitectonically distinct areas, like patches on a quilt. To be sure, these parcellation schemes have much in common, but at the same time they vary substantially in the precise number and configuration of cortical areas, largely because of differences between the researchers in their favored methodologies and in their

Cytoarchitectonic organization Similarities and differences between cortical areas with respect to the presence/absence, packing density, and layering of various cell types.

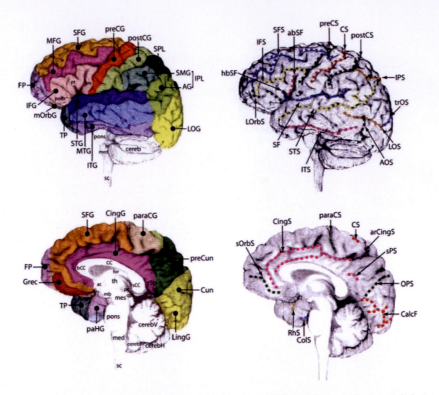

Figure 1.15 Major gyri and sulci of the brain from lateral (top) and medial (bottom) views. Gyri are labeled on the two left images, and sulci are labeled on the two right images. Abbreviations are linked with full names in Table 1.1 (From H. Damasio, 2005, pp. 18–21.)

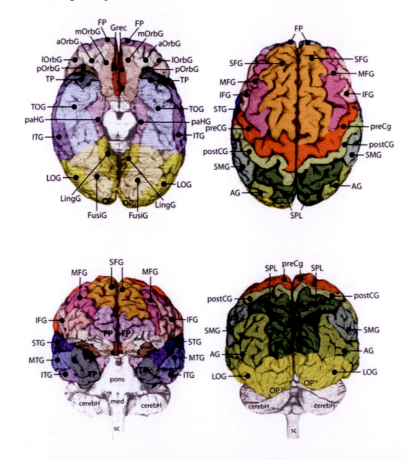

Figure 1.16 Major gyri of the brain from ventral (top left), dorsal (top right), rostral (bottom left), and caudal (bottom right) views. Abbreviations are linked with full names in Table 1.1 (From H. Damasio, 2005, p. 23.)

Table 1.1 Abbreviations and Full Names of the Gyri and Sulci Shown in Figures 1.15–1.17

Gyri		Sulci	
Abbr.	**Full Name**	**Abbr.**	**Full Name**
Frontal Lobe		**Frontal Lobe**	
preCG	Precentral gyrus	preCS	Precentral sulcus
SFG	Superior frontal gyrus	SFS	Superior frontal sulcus
MFG	Middle frontal gyrus	IFS	Inferior frontal sulcus
IFG	Inferior frontal gyrus (three sectors: porb = pars orbitalis; pt = pars triangularis; po = pars opercularis)	hbSF	Horizontal branch of the sylvian fissure
		abSF	Ascending branch of the sylvian fissure
		LOrbS	Lateral orbital sulcus
FP	Frontal pole	sOrbS	Suborbital sulcus
Grec	Gyrus rectus	CingS	Cingulate sulcus
OrbG	orbital gyri (four sectors: aOrbG = anterior; lOrbG = lateral; mOrbG = middle; pOrbG = posterior)		
CingG	cingulate gyrus		
Parietal Lobe		**Parietal Lobe**	
postCG	Postcentral gyrus	postCS	Postcentral sulcus
SPL	Superior parietal lobule	IPS	Intraparietal sulcus
IPL	Inferior parietal lobule	OPS	Occipito-parietal sulcus
SMG	Supramarginal gyrus	sPS	Subparietal sulcus
AG	Angular gyrus	arCingS	Ascending ramus of cingulate sulcus
preCun	Precuneus		
paraCG	Paracentral gyrus		
CingG	Cingulate gyrus		
Temporal Lobe		**Temporal Lobe**	
HG	Heschl's gyrus	SF	Sylvian fissure
PT	Planum temporale	STS	Superior temporal sulcus
STG	Superior temporal gyrus	ITS	Inferior temporal sulcus
MTG	Middle temporal gyrus	RhS	Rhinal sulcus
ITG	Inferior temporal gyrus	ColS	Collateral sulcus
TP	Temporal pole		
paHG	Parahippocampal gyrus		
TOG	Temporo-occipital gyrus		
Occipital Lobe		**Occipital Lobe**	
LOG	Lateral occipital gyrus	LOS	Lateral occipital sulcus
FusiG	Fusiform gyrus	AOS	Anterior occipital sulcus
LingG	Lingual gyrus	trOS	Transverse occipital sulcus
Cun	Cuneus	CalcF	Calcarine fissure
OP	Occipital pole		

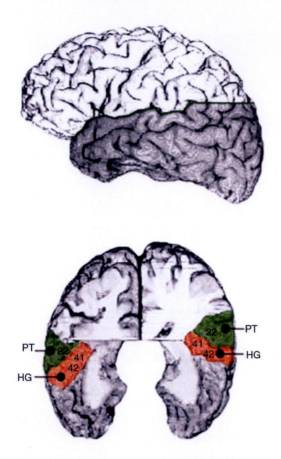

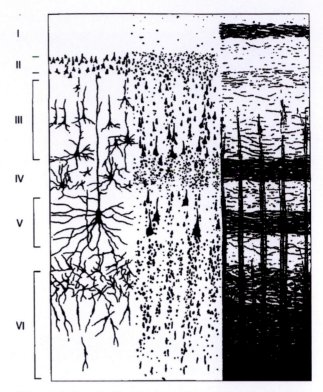

Figure 1.18 Idealized cross-section of the cortex showing its organization in six layers, as revealed by a Golgi stain highlighting entire cells (left), a Nissl stain highlighting cell bodies (middle), and a Weigert stain highlighting myelinated axons (right). (From Gazzaniga et al., 2009, p. 71.)

Figure 1.17 Heschl's gyrus (HG) and the planum temporale (PT). To reveal these structures, the superior temporal gyrus has been "unroofed" by removing the frontal and parietal lobes above the sylvian fissure and above a straight line drawn from the end of the sylvian fissure to the edge of the brain, as shown in the image on top. (From H. Damasio, 2005, p. 27.)

abilities to detect transitions between areas (for a comparison of six approaches see Zilles and Amunts, 2010).

The most famous map was published in 1909 by Korbinian Brodmann, a German neurologist who liked to dissect brains in his kitchen sink. In its original format, this map was a drawing of the lateral and medial views of the left hemisphere of a schematized human brain, segregated into 43 cortical areas that were numbered consecutively according to the order in which they were identified. The numbers ranged from 1 to 52, but 12–16 and 48–51 were omitted because, as Brodmann explained, he had previously used those numbers to designate certain areas in the brains of other mammalian species, and he could not find homologous areas in the human brain. The 43 Brodmann areas (BAs) are presented from lateral and medial perspectives in Figure 1.19 and from ventral, dorsal, rostral, and caudal perspectives in Figure 1.20.

Since the 1980s, BAs have been used quite frequently, in conjunction with labels for gyri and sulci, to refer to particular cortical regions, especially when interpreting data from functional neuroimaging experiments. It should be borne in mind, however, that Brodmann's map has several weaknesses. For one thing, it completely lacks information about areal boundaries inside sulci. In addition, like the other early 20th-century maps, it is based on subjective observations, and it ignores neuroanatomical differences between individuals. In recent years, a growing number of technologically advanced investigations have begun to overcome these limitations by developing observer-independent, probabilistic demarcations of cytoarchitectonic areas in both gyri and sulci (Zilles and Amunts, 2010, 2012; see also Van Essen et al., 2012). In some cases, these state-of-the-art studies have led to the retention, albeit with considerable refinements, of areal contrasts originally proposed by Brodmann. For example, in the frontal lobe the distinction between BAs 44 and 45—these being the two regions that collectively compose Broca's area, which is one of the major computational hubs for language—has been supported and given a more solid foundation (Amunts et al., 1999). In other

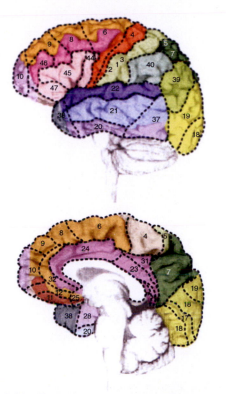

cases, however, new work has challenged Brodmann's classifications and gone beyond them. For example, in the parietal lobe the distinction between BAs 39 and 40—two regions that, like Broca's area, make important contributions to language—has been seriously questioned, and essentially the same cortical territory has been carved up into no less than seven more fine-grained areas (Caspers et al., 2006). More generally, each hemisphere of the human brain is currently estimated to have between 150 and 200 distinct areas (Van Essen et al., 2012). Despite these signs of progress, however, and mostly for the sake of simplicity, many researchers still follow the long-standing tradition of employing Brodmann's system. We will do so too in the chapters ahead.

Finally, it is worth asking whether cytoarchitectonically defined areas can be used as a structural guide to the functional organization of the cortex. For some low-level sensory and motor areas, the answer appears to be "yes." To take a straightforward example, in the occipital lobe BA17 corresponds directly to the primary visual cortex. For most other areas, however, the issue is complicated. One problem is that, as indicated above, the cytoarchitectonic structure of the cortex is still being explored, and in some sectors the correct parcellation has not yet been determined. For instance, continuing with the occipital lobe, even though BA18 is already known to contain some cellular subdivisions (Amunts et al., 2000), its complete

Figure 1.19 Brodmann areas, with the lateral view of the left hemisphere shown on top, and the medial view of the right hemisphere shown on bottom. Colors indicate gyri as in Figure 1.15. (From H. Damasio, 2005, pp. 24–25.)

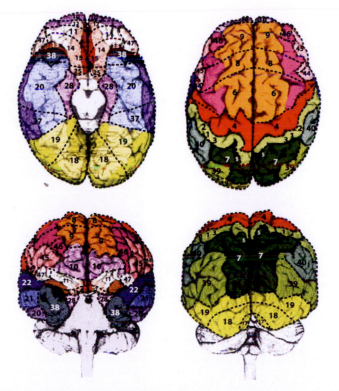

Figure 1.20 Brodmann areas from ventral (top left), dorsal (top right), rostral (bottom left), and caudal (bottom right) views. Colors indicate gyri as in Figure 1.16. (From H. Damasio, 2005, p. 26.)

architecture is far from understood, and the subdivisions that have been identified so far do not map easily onto the much larger number of functionally separate zones that exist within the region, zones that are well established as subserving different aspects of visual processing (Orban et al., 2004; Wandell et al., 2007). Another concern is that even when the configurations of particular areas have been strongly validated, it can be extremely difficult to ascribe to them unique computational functions that are capable of accommodating all the relevant experimental data. For instance, returning to BAs 44 and 45 in the frontal lobe, although there is abundant evidence implicating both of them in many kinds of linguistic processing, they have also been associated with some nonlinguistic tasks, and their specific roles remain quite elusive—a point that will become increasingly clear as this book unfolds. It may be the case that both areas do in fact have idiosyncratic functions that are closely tied to their idiosyncratic cellular compositions, and if so, the exact nature of those functions may be discovered in the coming years. Presently, however, the precise "job descriptions" of BAs 44 and 45, and of the vast majority of other BAs too, are not well characterized, but are rather the topic of ongoing research. The upshot is that, at the current stage of inquiry, it is advisable to treat BAs as being, for the most part, structurally rather than functionally defined regions.

Connectional Organization

The multifarious regions of the cerebral cortex do not operate in isolation. On the contrary, they are massively interconnected with each other, and most if not all of our complex mental processes, including those involving language, require the dynamic, cooperative interplay of signals among the widely distributed components of large-scale cortical networks (Mesulam, 2000; Bressler & Menon, 2010). These signals are carried by bundles of axons that course through the white matter along particular pathways, like highways between cities.

By far the biggest and busiest fiber tract in the human brain is the **corpus collosum**, which houses more than 100 million axons interconnecting the two hemispheres. It lies beneath the cingulate gyri and is abbreviated "CC" in the medial view of the brain shown in Figure 1.15. Beginning in the 1940s, a radical and rarely used type of surgical intervention for some patients with severe epilepsy was to cut the corpus collosum, thereby creating a kind of firewall to prevent seizure activity from spreading across the hemispheres. For many decades, these

so-called split-brain patients have provided neuroscientists with extraordinary opportunities to scrutinize the behavior of each hemisphere independently of the other, and a great deal has been learned in this manner about the hemispheric lateralization of various mental abilities (see Wolman, 2012, for a recent retrospective essay about this research; see Gazzaniga, 2000, 2005, for more technical reviews).

Fiber tracts that interconnect different cortical areas within the same hemisphere are often referred to as association pathways or **fasciculi**. As an illustration, Figure 1.21 depicts the arcuate fasciculus of the left hemisphere (Catani & Mesulam, 2008). This tract, which is essential for a wide range of linguistic functions, was once thought to consist of just one thick band of axonal cables, but many neuroscientists now believe that it can be decomposed into three separate branches or segments that undergird a network comprising the following regions: "Broca's territory," which, for purposes of this analysis, occupies not only the posterior inferior frontal gyrus (BAs 44 and 45), but also the adjacent portions of the middle frontal and precentral gyri; "Wernicke's territory," which occupies the posterior portions of the superior and middle temporal gyri; and "Geschwind's territory," which occupies the supramarginal and angular gyri. As the figure indicates, the "long segment" of the arcuate fasciculus, which corresponds more or less to the classic portrayal of the tract, links Broca's territory with Wernicke's territory; the "anterior segment" links Broca's territory with Geschwind's territory; and

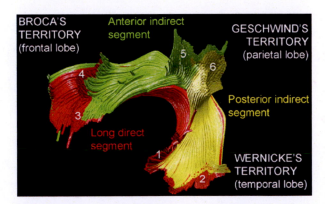

Figure 1.21   The arcuate fasciculus of the left hemisphere. 1 = posterior superior temporal gyrus; 2 = posterior middle temporal gyrus; 3 = posterior inferior frontal gyrus; 4 = posterior middle frontal gyrus and the adjacent portion of the precentral gyrus; 5 = supramarginal gyrus; 6 = angular gyrus. (From Catani & Mesulam, 2008, p. 957.)

Corpus collosum   The large white matter tract that interconnects the two hemispheres.

Fasciculi (singular = fasciculus)   White matter tracts that interconnect different cortical areas within the same hemisphere.

the "posterior segment" links Wernicke's territory with Geschwind's territory. The general layout of these white matter segments has been gaining acceptance, but it is noteworthy that the anatomical details regarding their cortical termination points are still being elucidated (for reviews see Friederici, 2009; Dick & Tremblay, 2012; Axer et al., 2013; Gierhan, in press; see also Glasser & Rilling, 2008; Saur et al., 2008, 2010; de Schotten et al., 2011; Margulies & Petrides, 2013).

Three other language-related fasciculi are shown in Figure 1.22 (Catani & Mesulam, 2008). The inferior fronto-occipital fasciculus links inferior frontal areas with occipital areas; the inferior longitudinal fasciculus links temporal areas with occipital areas; and the uncinate fasciculus links orbitofrontal areas with anterior temporal areas. The likely contributions of these and other pathways to various linguistic functions are discussed later (e.g., see Figure 15.4 and the accompanying text in Chapter 15). In the current context, the main point is simply that they are among the many long-distance fiber tracts that tie together the diverse cortical regions that are necessary for producing and understanding utterances.

How are the images shown in Figures 1.21 and 1.22 generated? They are the outcome of studies employing a method called **diffusion tractography**. In short, this technique, which is a special application of magnetic resonance imaging (described in Chapter 2), involves measuring the passive movements of water molecules along the lengths of axons in the white matter of the brain so that the directions of fiber tracts can be reconstructed for references see, e.g., Johansen-Berg & Rushworth, 2009; Chanraud et al., 2010; Dell'Aqua & Catani, 2012). While the approach is by no means immune to error, it has been progressively improving in recent years, and further enhancements are under way (Figure 1.23). In fact, one of the most rapidly evolving lines of investigation in contemporary neuroscience involves the mapping of what is now called the "human connectome," an expression originally coined by Sporns et al. (2005; see also the following website: www.humanconnectome-project.org/). Just as the human genome consists of the entire sequence of genes characterizing our species, so the human connectome consists of the entire matrix of connections characterizing our brains. Carefully tracing all of those nerve fibers, even at the macro-level of long-distance fasciculi, is obviously a hugely ambitious

> **Diffusion tractography** A method for measuring the passive movements of water molecules along the lengths of axons in the white matter of the brain so that the directions of fiber tracts can be reconstructed.

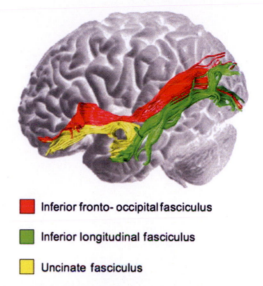

■ Inferior fronto- occipital fasciculus
■ Inferior longitudinal fasciculus
■ Uncinate fasciculus

Figure 1.22 The inferior fronto-occipital, inferior longitudinal, and uncinate fasciculi of the left hemisphere. (From Catani & Mesulam, 2008, p. 958.)

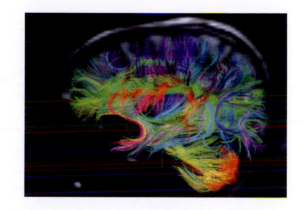

Figure 1.23 Brain connectivity revealed by a technique called diffusion spectrum imaging. (From Bardin, 2012, p. 394.)

enterprise, and no one expects the project to produce a wiring diagram like the one you might see for the flow of electricity in a house. But the field is moving forward at an extremely fast pace, and remarkable discoveries with both theoretical and clinical significance are undoubtedly on the horizon. For some recent studies and perspectives, see the special 2013 issue of the journal *NeuroImage* (volume 80) and the special 2013 issue of the journal *Trends in Cognitive Sciences* (volume 17, issue 12).

Sensory, Motor, and Higher-Order Systems

Having reviewed several aspects of the structural organization of the cerebral cortex, we turn now to some of the most well-understood properties of its functional

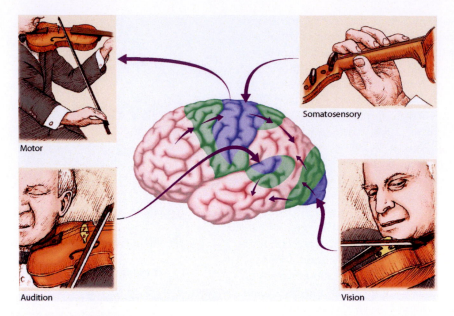

Motor

Somatosensory

Audition

Vision

Figure 1.24   Lower-level (blue) and higher-level (green) sensory and motor systems of the cerebral cortex. (From Gazzaniga et al., 1998, p. 72.)

organization. We begin by considering the major sensory and motor hierarchies that allow us to perceive and act on our environments. Then we briefly discuss a few high-order cortical systems before shifting to an overarching perspective on the language network in the last part of the chapter.

As shown in Figure 1.24, and as mentioned above, visual information from the outside world enters the cortex in the occipital lobe, specifically in the primary visual cortex, an area that has three additional names: BA17, V1, and striate cortex. The location of this area in the illustration is somewhat misleading, however, because it actually resides in the calcarine fissure on the medial surface of the occipital lobe (see Figures 1.15 and 1.19). The primary visual cortex has a very fine-grained **retinotopic organization**, which is to say that it preserves the detailed spatial layout of input from the retina, with the consequence that adjacent columns of neurons on the cortical surface represent simple features emanating from adjacent points of space in the visual field. Moreover, the primary visual cortex in each hemisphere represents the opposite side of the visual field, such that the region in the left hemisphere represents everything to the right of the central point of fixation, and the region in the right hemisphere represents everything to the left of that

point. In both hemispheres, the primary visual cortex projects forward through a dense array of other occipital areas that become increasingly specialized for extracting information about particular attributes of visual stimuli, such as form, color, motion, and depth. Then, near the anterior edge of the occipital lobe, the flow of processing splits into two separate streams. One stream extends into the ventral temporal lobe and is sometimes called the "what" pathway because it is devoted to recognizing objects on the basis of their shapes, colors, and apparent textures. The other stream extends into the posterior parietal lobe and is sometimes called the "where" pathway because it is devoted to representing the locations of objects both in relation to each other and in relation to the viewer, or, more precisely, the viewer's body parts. The latter stream is also sometimes called the "how" pathway because it subserves the kinds of visuomotor transformations that are necessary to program object-directed actions—for example, converting the position of a coffee mug encoded in eye-centered coordinates into its position encoded in hand-centered coordinates so that one may reach out and grasp it efficiently.

Figure 1.24 indicates that the cortical gateway for auditory information lies in the posterior part of the superior temporal gyrus, but again this is rather misleading because the primary auditory cortex actually resides in Heschl's gyrus, which is buried in the sylvian fissure, and which houses BAs 41 and 42 (see Figure 1.17 and Box 1.1; see also Box 5.2 in Chapter 5). This region has

Retinotopic organization   A form of cortical representation that preserves the spatial arrangement of signals from the retina.

Box 1.1   Born for Phonetics?

Expertise is often associated with both structural and functional changes in the brain. For example, London taxi drivers have a larger hippocampus than ordinary commuters (Maguire et al., 2000), and musicians have more gray matter in certain auditory, motor, and visuospatial areas than non-musicians (Gaser & Schlaug, 2003). Similar effects have also been found for language, with even more far-reaching implications. In a recent study, Golestani et al. (2011) conducted a series of neuroanatomical analyses of two groups of subjects: 17 individuals with 1–9 years of formal training in phonetic transcription; and 16 age- and gender-matched controls. Significant differences were discovered in two regions. First, compared to the control subjects, the phoneticians had greater surface area and greater overall volume in the pars opercularis of the left inferior frontal gyrus, this being the posterior portion of Broca's area, a region known to contribute to phonological processing (see Chapters 5 and 6). Interestingly, the amount of tissue that was observed in this territory increased in direct proportion to the amount of training that the phoneticians had received, which suggests that the neural plasticity was the result of transcriptional experience (Figure 1B1.1). Second, compared to the control subjects, the phoneticians not only exhibited a larger amount of gray matter in Heschl's gyrus bilaterally (Figure 1B1.2), but were also more likely to have a "split" or "duplicated" Heschl's gyrus in the language-dominant left hemisphere (Figure 1B1.3). Remarkably enough, unlike the effects in Broca's area, these effects bore no relationship whatsoever to how much training the phoneticians had received, making it likely that they reflect genetic rather than environmental factors. In support of this interpretation, Golestani et al. (2011) refer to several studies which suggest that the gyral patterns of the early auditory cortices develop *in utero* between the 31st and 36th weeks of gestation and are fully stabilized by the age of 7. Hence, it is possible that the unusual patterns displayed by the phoneticians were in place well before their formal training began. Indeed, as Golestani et al. (2011, p. 4219) point out, such patterns "may make it more likely for individuals to become phoneticians or to work in other domains requiring detailed auditory processing." That is to say, some people may be neuroanatomically predisposed to become experts at speech perception. Or, to put it even more simply, they may be born for phonetics.

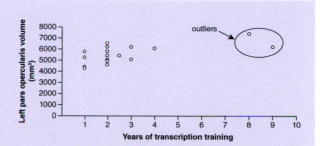

Figure 1B1.1   Scatter plot showing relationship between phonetic transcription training and left pars opercularis volume. (From Golestani et al., 2011, p. 4218.)

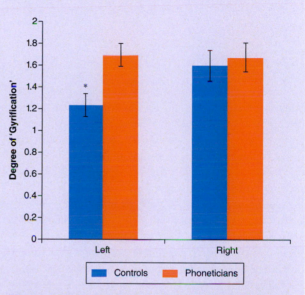

Figure 1B1.2   Differences between phoneticians and controls in the volumes of the left and right Heschl's gyrus (referred to here as the transverse gyrus). (From Golestani et al., 2011, p. 4217.)

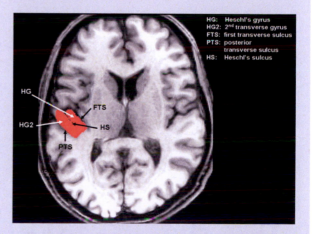

Figure 1B1.3   A subject with a "split" or "duplicated" Heschl's gyrus in the left hemisphere. (From Golestani et al., 2011, p. 4215.)

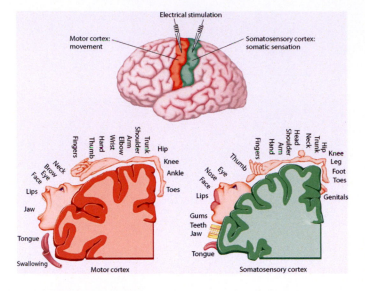

Figure 1.25 Somatotopic maps in the somatosensory and motor cortices. (From Gazzaniga et al., 1998, p. 75.)

a **tonotopic organization**, which means that cortical columns that are adjacent in anatomical space respond preferentially to sound frequencies that are adjacent in auditory space. It also exhibits hemispheric asymmetries, since the left primary auditory cortex has a much stronger representation of input from the right ear, and the right primary auditory cortex has a much stronger representation of input from the left ear. More complex auditory computations are carried out by a host of other cortical areas further up the perceptual hierarchy. These areas are located in the planum temporale (see Figure 1.17) and in portions of the superior temporal gyrus, superior temporal sulcus, and middle temporal gyrus. All of them contribute in various ways to the analysis of speech, music, and other kinds of environmental sounds.

The third sensory modality shown in Figure 1.24 is for somatosensory information. Signals about the felt shape and texture of objects, as well as about temperature, pressure, and pain, are initially processed at the cortical level in the postcentral gyrus, which contains BAs 1, 2, and 3. Although these BAs have different functions, they are often regarded as collectively constituting the primary somatosensory cortex, also referred to as S1. Perhaps the most salient property of this region is that it has a rich **somatotopic organization**, such that the surface of the body is mapped out along its vertical extent. As illustrated in Figure 1.25, this representation is, for the most part, upside down, with disproportionately large amounts of

cortical territory devoted to the most sensitive parts of the body, these being the hands, feet, lips, tongue, and genitals. Note that although the spatial layout of the body is mostly preserved in the map, there are some discontinuities. In particular, the face area is not beside the neck area but is instead below the hand area, and the genital area is not beside the upper leg area but is instead below the foot area. Note also that, as suggested by the electrode drawings in Figure 1.25, direct stimulation of specific sites in the primary somatosensory cortex typically induces feelings in the corresponding body parts. In addition to processing signals originating from receptors in the skin, the primary somatosensory cortex also processes signals originating from receptors in the muscles and tendons. The latter signals carry proprioceptive information about the relative positions of one's body parts in space and about the forces acting on them at any given time. The primary somatosensory cortex, however, only processes these myriad inputs in rudimentary ways. More sophisticated analyses are conducted by regions in the posterior and inferior sectors of the parietal lobe, as well as in the insula.

As shown in Figures 1.24 and 1.25, the detailed map of the body's surface in the postcentral gyrus is paralleled by a closely matching map of the body's musculature in the precentral gyrus (see also Figures 11.6 and 11.7 in Chapter 11). This is the primary motor cortex, which corresponds to BA4, also known as M1. It serves as the final cortical "command station" for executing actions, and as suggested by the electrode drawings in Figure 1.25, direct stimulation of particular points on this map usually elicits involuntary twitches of the corresponding body parts. Numerous higher-level motor programming regions reside in BA6, anterior to BA4. In the current context, though, it is sufficient to make just

Tonotopic organization A form of cortical representation that reflects the linear relations between sound frequencies.

Somatotopic organization A form of cortical representation that captures the layout of the body.

one main distinction, specifically between the premotor cortex, which occupies the lateral sector of BA6, and the supplementary motor area, which occupies the medial sector. Ignoring for now many subtleties, it is generally believed that the former region contributes more to externally than internally triggered actions, as when one quickly hits the brake after seeing a streetlight turn red, whereas the latter region contributes more to internally than externally triggered actions, as when one gets up from a chair after deciding to go out for a drive.

The sensory and motor systems summarized above constitute the major cortical "portals" through which we perceive and act on the world, but of course they account for only a small part of our mental lives. As neuroscientific research has progressed during the past few decades, it has become increasingly clear that other cortical areas mediate various aspects of more advanced cognitive capacities by participating in large-scale networks that are distributed across multiple lobes of the brain. At least half a dozen cortical systems of this nature have now been identified, two of which are as follows. First, the "executive/supervisory network" depends on certain regions in the lateral prefrontal cortex (BAs 9, 10, 44, 45, and 46) and inferior parietal cortex (BAs 39 and 40) (e.g., Jung & Haier, 2007; Vincent et al., 2008). It typically comes into play in psychologically demanding situations that require reasoning, planning, troubleshooting, multi-tasking, overcoming habitual responses, and keeping information in an activated state. Second, the "mentalizing network" is supported by a set of areas that include the medial prefrontal cortex (BAs 9 and 10), posterior cingulate (BAs 23 and 31), and temporoparietal junction (intersection of BAs 22, 37, and 39) (e.g., Saxe, 2006; Frith & Frith, 2006, 2010). It plays a key role in social interaction, since it is engaged whenever one tries to understand the overt behavior of animate agents—most importantly, other people—in terms of covert mental states such as beliefs and desires. Both of these large-scale networks facilitate the use of language for thought and communication, but the neural system that actually underlies the core components of language is anchored in a number of mostly separate areas, as discussed below.

Language-Related Regions: Broca's Area, Wernicke's Area, and Beyond

Because most of the chapters that lie ahead are devoted to elaborating the many nuances of the neurobiology of language, it is worthwhile to get a general sense of the "big picture" here at the outset. It has been known since the second half of the 19th century that the human brain has a fairly strong left-hemisphere dominance for language, with two main regions grounding the network (Figure 1.26).

Both of these regions have already been mentioned, and as described in greater detail in Chapter 3, both of them are named after their founders. The first one, **Broca's area**, is typically treated as comprising the posterior sectors of the inferior frontal gyrus—specifically, the pars opercularis, which corresponds roughly to BA44, and the pars triangularis, which corresponds roughly to BA45 (Amunts & Zilles, 2012). The second one, **Wernicke's area**, is widely regarded as including the posterior third of the superior temporal gyrus, but many scholars believe that it extends further into adjacent temporal and/or parietal regions, hence covering not only posterior BA22, but also portions of BAs 21, 37, 39, 40, 41, and 42 (see Bogen & Bogen, 1976, and the supplementary material in Raushecker & Scott, 2009; see also the discussion of Wernicke's aphasia in Chapter 3). According to the traditional model, these two regions form the following very simple network: Broca's area represents the "motor images" of words and is essential for speech production; Wernicke's area represents the "auditory images" of words and is essential for speech perception; and the two regions communicate via the arcuate fasciculus (for further discussion of this classic approach see Figure 3.3 and the accompanying text in Chapter 3).

Needless to say, our understanding of the neural substrates of language has advanced tremendously since the late 19th century, and modern theories now treat Broca's and Wernicke's areas as being multifunctional "epicenters"

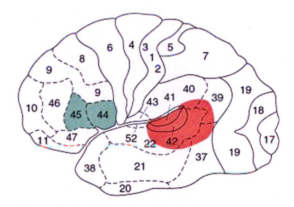

Figure 1.26 Broca's area (green) and Wernicke's area (red). (From Kaan & Swaab, 2002, p. 351.)

Broca's area A classic anterior language-related region typically treated as comprising the pars opercularis (roughly BA44) and pars triangularis (roughly BA45) in the inferior frontal gyrus.

Wernicke's area A classic posterior language-related region widely regarded as including the posterior third of the superior temporal gyrus; many scholars, however, believe that it extends further into adjacent temporal and/or parietal regions, hence covering not only posterior BA22, but also portions of BAs 21, 37, 39, 40, 41, and 42.

or "hubs" in a far-flung network that encompasses many other frontal, temporal, parietal, and occipital regions in the left hemisphere, as well as several regions in the right hemisphere. Within this sort of framework, complex linguistic processes, like producing and comprehending sentences, are accomplished by synergistic interactions among entire communities of cortical areas, with particular areas contributing to the overall task in more or less specific computational ways that have yet to be fully determined. This type of approach is exemplified by the model shown in Figure 1.27, which comes from a 2010 article entitled "The anatomy of language: A review of 100 fMRI studies published in 2009," by Cathy J. Price, a leading cognitive neuroscientist at University College London (for an even more impressive review see Price, 2012; see also Friederici & Gierhan, 2013). In the current context, we don't need to worry about the many functional–anatomical facets of this framework, since all of these complexities are discussed at length in later chapters, together with in-depth considerations of the kinds of experimental studies that generate the relevant findings. For present purposes, the key point is simply that Price's model provides a nice illustration of the level of detail at which the large-scale cortical network for language is being investigated and characterized in many contemporary approaches. As we move forward, we will encounter several theoretical schemes that are variations on this one.

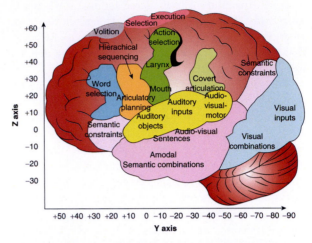

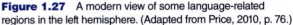

Figure 1.27 A modern view of some language-related regions in the left hemisphere. (Adapted from Price, 2010, p. 76.)

Summary and Key Points

- There are roughly 100 billion neurons in the human brain, about 30 billion of which are in the cerebral cortex.
- Basic anatomical properties of neurons:

  - *Soma* = cell body.
  - *Dendrites* = tree-like branches that receive signals from many other cells.
  - *Axon* = a single long segment that splits toward the end to transmit signals to many other cells.
  - *Myelin sheath* = fatty substance that insulates the axon to facilitate signal propagation.
  - *Nodes of Ranvier* = gaps between myelin sheaths that enable the signal to be rejuvenated.
  - *Terminal buttons* = Endpoints of the axon where chemical neurotransmitters are released.

- Basic physiological properties of neurons:

  - In the default resting state, the balance between ions inside and outside the membrane of a neuron is –70 millivolts (mV)—more negative inside than outside.
  - If the summed dendritic input is strong enough to raise the inner potential to about –50 mV, gates in the membrane open up, allowing sodium (Na^+) to rush in so that the electrical balance reverses, becoming more positive inside than outside.
  - Then the sodium gates close and other gates open up, causing potassium (K^+) to be pumped out of the cell so that the current inside returns to negative.
  - This whole cycle is called an *action potential* or a *spike,* and it is always an all-or-nothing affair, never a matter of degree.
  - Action potentials are repeated at the nodes of Ranvier, allowing the signal to traverse the entire length of the axon.
  - Due to their tremendous metabolic demands, neurons consume about 20 percent of the oxygenated blood flowing from the heart. This fuel supply reaches the fine-grained capillary bed in the brain, where individual capillaries have a diameter of only about 10 micrometers.

- Basic representational properties of neurons:

  - Neurons that represent elementary features of the external environment or internal milieu project to multiple layers of higher-order "conjunctive" neurons, which represent increasingly complex patterns of information by registering combinations of features.
  - Such hierarchically organized representational networks are commonly found in the cerebral cortex, and signals typically flow through them in both directions—bottom-up and top-down.

- Navigational terms:

  - *Sagittal* = a section that separates the left and right sides of the brain.
  - *Coronal* = a section that separates the front from the back of the brain.
  - *Horizontal* = a section that separates the top from the bottom of the brain.
  - *Rostral/anterior* = toward the front of the brain.
  - *Caudal/posterior* = toward the back of the brain.
  - *Dorsal/superior* = toward the top of the brain.
  - *Ventral/inferior* = toward the bottom of the brain.
  - *Lateral* = toward the outer left or right side of the brain.
  - *Medial* = toward the midline of the brain.

- Major subcortical structures:

  - The *brainstem* has three main parts—medulla, pons, and midbrain—all of which contain nuclei essential for the regulation of bodily homeostasis, including cardiac and respiratory functions.
  - The *thalamus* routes all sensory signals (except smell) to the appropriate cortical areas, as well as all signals from the basal ganglia and cerebellum, and most signals from the amygdala. It also maintains bidirectional "loops" of activity with every cortical area.
  - The *hippocampus* plays a critical role in the gradual process of consolidating long-term declarative memories—i.e., transferring them to the cortex for permanent storage.
  - The *amygdala* contributes to emotion by rapidly registering the personal value of stimuli, especially stimuli that may be dangerous.
  - The *basal ganglia* have several parts—putamen, caudate, globus pallidus, subthalamic nucleus, and substantia nigra—that collectively underlie the unconscious acquisition, selection, initiation, and cessation of adaptive vs. maladaptive thoughts and behaviors—what we sometimes call habits.
  - The *cerebellum* is necessary for controlling muscle tone and ensuring that movements are executed fluidly, with appropriate timing and coordination. Like the basal ganglia, it also facilitates cognition.

- Major aspects of cortical organization:

  - The cortex has five *lobes,* four of which are visible—frontal, parietal, temporal, and occipital—and one of which is hidden—the insula.
  - The cortex has many *gyri* and *sulci*—i.e., raised bulges and deep grooves.
  - The cortex has many *cytoarchitectonic areas*—i.e., areas distinguished by the presence/absence, packing density, and layering of cell types. The most widely used parcellation scheme involves the *Brodmann areas.*
  - Different cortical areas in the two hemispheres are interconnected by the *corpus collosum.*
  - Different cortical areas in the same hemisphere are interconnected by *fasciculi.*
  - Visual information is processed initially in the occipital lobe.
  - Auditory information is processing initially in the temporal lobe.
  - Somatosensory information is processed initially in the parietal lobe.
  - Motor programming is handled predominantly by the frontal lobe.
  - Linguistic processing depends on a large-scale network of mostly left-lateralized cortical areas extending across all of the lobes.

Recommended Reading

- Carter, R. (2009). *The human brain book.* London: DK. Written by Rita Carter, who is an award-winning medical journalist, in consultation with Chris and Uta Frith, who are both world-class cognitive neuroscientists, this book combines clear and lively prose with stunning graphics to convey a wealth of fascinating information in a visually entertaining way.
  More technical details about the human brain can be found in the following cognitive neuroscience textbooks:

- Baars, B.J., & Gage, N.M. (2010) *Cognition, brain, and consciousness: Introduction to cognitive neuroscience,* 2nd edition. San Diego, CA: Academic Press.
- Ward, J. (2010). *The student's guide to cognitive neuroscience,* 2nd edition. New York: Psychology Press.
- Banich, M.T., & Compton, R.J. (2011). *Cognitive neuroscience,* 3rd edition. Belmont, CA: Wadsworth.
- Purves, D., Cabeza, R., Huettel, S.A., LaBar, K.S., Platt, M.L., & Woldorff, M.G. (2012). *Principles of cognitive neuroscience,* 2nd edition. Sunderland, MA: Sinauer.
- Gazzaniga, M.S., Ivry, R.B., & Mangun, G.R. (2013). *Cognitive neuroscience: The biology of the mind,* 4th edition. New York: Norton.

Brain Mapping Methods

2

Introduction

In every scientific field, the limits of what can be learned are heavily constrained by the tools that happen to be available for observing and measuring the phenomena of interest. So when technological advances take place in methodology, they often lead to revolutionary new discoveries. For example, after the telescope was invented in 1608, it only took astronomers a few years to gather enough data about the movements of celestial bodies to cast serious doubt on the traditional geocentric view that the sun revolves around the earth, and support instead the opposite heliocentric view that the earth revolves around the sun. Similarly, in the modern world of high-energy physics, the creation of bigger and better particle accelerators, like the Large Hadron Collider, has allowed researchers to gain progressively deeper insights into the subatomic structure of matter.

The same principle clearly applies to the rapid rise of cognitive neuroscience during the past few decades, since the spectacular evolution of this field can be attributed largely—not entirely, but largely—to major technological breakthroughs. In terms of overall impact, the most significant innovation was undoubtedly the development of functional magnetic resonance imaging (fMRI) in 1991. This technique is by far the most frequently used method for investigating the functional organization of the human brain, and as shown in Figure 2.1, the number of papers either reporting new fMRI studies or reviewing selected sets of such studies has steadily increased and now exceeds 2,500 per year. In light of so much productivity, it is hardly surprising that Peter Bandettini, an influential researcher who works in the Section on Functional Imaging Methods at the National Institutes of Mental Health, recently remarked that "fMRI has been one of the greatest methodological success stories in science in the past 20 years" (2012, p. A4).

It is important to realize, however, that even though fMRI currently dominates the field, it is by no means the only way to explore the neural substrates of cognitive capacities in general, or of linguistic capacities in particular. Several other approaches are also available and used quite widely. Moreover, like fMRI, all of them owe a great deal to recent technological advances. Still, it cannot be overemphasized that none of the sophisticated instruments in the cognitive neuroscientist's toolkit is an ideal "brainoscope." Instead, each method has unique strengths and weaknesses, and for this reason researchers often draw upon data from different combinations of approaches, with the ultimate goal of achieving the greatest possible convergence of results so that specific hypotheses and theories can be bolstered or, as the case may be, challenged (Shallice & Cooper, 2011).

This chapter describes four classes of methods that are commonly used to examine how various aspects of linguistic knowledge and processing are implemented in the brain. The overarching aim is to provide enough background information about these methods to allow readers to understand and appreciate, at least in a rough sense, the sorts of procedures that were used in the many experimental studies that are summarized in subsequent chapters of this book. The first section focuses on neuropsychology, which involves using behavioral and lesion data from brain-damaged patients to determine not only which mental abilities can be impaired independently of others, but also which neural structures are necessary to support them. The second section focuses on functional neuroimaging, which includes fMRI as well as PET (positron emission tomography), and which uses blood flow as a proxy for neural activity to identify which brain regions tend to be engaged

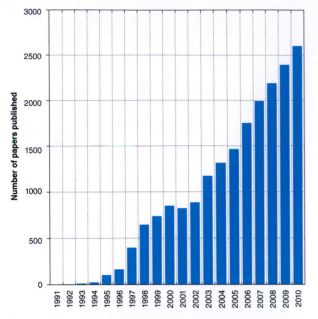

Figure 2.1   Based on a literature search using Scopus, with the search terms "fMRI" or "functional MRI" and limiting the papers to only articles or reviews, this graph shows a very steady increase in papers published since 2001. (From Bandettini, 2012, p. A4.)

in healthy individuals when they perform particular types of cognitive tasks. The third section focuses on electrophysiology, which measures correspondences between neural activity and mental processes in two major ways—by directly stimulating specific sites, and by recording electrical signals either intracranially or at the surface of the scalp. The fourth section focuses on transcranial magnetic stimulation, which involves delivering brief pulses to specific brain regions, thereby either facilitating or disrupting their operation, depending on the parameters of the protocol. Finally, the fifth section concludes the chapter by comparing the chief merits and shortcomings of all four classes of methods.

Neuropsychology

A little "insider" joke in cognitive neuroscience goes something like this: Brain damage is always bad for you, but if you're lucky, it will be bad for you in theoretically interesting ways. This quip nicely captures the essence of the research-oriented branch of neuropsychology, which involves taking advantage of otherwise unfortunate cases of brain damage by using them to make new discoveries about the complex design of the normal system. In the domain of language, neuropsychological investigations usually pursue one or both of two general aims: first, to carve the language faculty at its joints, so to speak, by

determining which of its components can be selectively disrupted; and second, to identify reliable links between specific linguistic deficits and specific lesion sites. The former goal is concerned mainly with understanding the cognitive architecture of language, whereas the latter goal is concerned mainly with understanding its neural architecture. These two types of research are sometimes carried out separately, but they often go hand in hand. The following overview addresses both lines of inquiry, beginning with cognitively oriented issues and then shifting to neurally oriented ones. Before proceeding, though, it is important to emphasize that neuropsychological studies frequently have significant implications not only for theoretical efforts to characterize the organization of language in the mind/brain, but also for clinical efforts to diagnose and treat patients' impairments. Indeed, acquiring accurate information about a given patient's linguistic disorder and underlying neuropathology is often an integral part of developing an appropriate intervention strategy.

Single and Double Dissociations

Back in the early 19th century, many people believed that the brain operates as a cohesive, indivisible unit, with each part contributing equally to every ability. One of the chief proponents of this "equipotentiality" view was a physiologist named Marie-Jean-Pierre Flourens, who wrote in 1824 that "all sensations, all perceptions, and all volitions occupy the same seat in these (cerebral) organs" (quotation from Gazzaniga et al., 2009, p. 4). It did not take long, however, for this theory to be overturned by observations of neurological patients who displayed selective impairments of particular mental capacities as the direct result of lesions in particular brain regions. Indeed, the most influential study of this nature was Paul Broca's famous demonstration of a causal connection between an impairment of speech production and damage to the left inferior frontal gyrus (see Chapter 3). This report, which appeared in 1861, is often regarded as marking the birth of scientifically based neuropsychology, and ever since then researchers have been systematically exploring the myriad ways in which brain injuries can "fractionate" the mind, disrupting certain abilities independently of others and thereby revealing the hidden componential architecture of the cognitive system (Shallice, 1988; Rapp, 2001).

In modern neuropsychological investigations, the most valuable forms of behavioral data are dissociations, of which there are two main types. The following discussion elaborates both of them initially in abstract terms and then with concrete examples. The first type is known as a **single dissociation**, and it occurs when a patient is administered two different tasks and performs significantly worse on one than the other. Dissociations of this type invite the inference that the patient's lesion has selectively disrupted some mental representations and/or computations that are required by the poorly executed task but not by the better executed task. It is crucial to realize, however, that this kind of conclusion is not always warranted, because in some situations a single dissociation may not really reflect a disturbance of specific mechanisms that are necessary for only one of the two tasks, but may instead reflect a disturbance of more general processing resources that are shared by the two tasks but demanded more by one than the other. In simpler terms, the more affected task might just be inherently harder than the less affected task, and the patient's brain damage might have induced abnormal sensitivity to this difference in difficulty.

Fortunately, this sort of concern can be mitigated in several ways. One is to ensure that the two tasks are matched on as many variables as possible and that they elicit comparable accuracies and reaction times from healthy control subjects. An even more powerful solution, however, is to obtain the second type of dissociation, which is known as a **double dissociation**. In most cases, this happens when two different patients display diametrically opposed patterns of performance on two different tasks—for instance, when patient A performs significantly worse on task X than on task Y, and patient B performs significantly worse on task Y than on task X. Such a finding further reduces the likelihood that either patient's performance might be due to differences in task difficulty, and it strongly suggests that each task requires at least some unique mental structures and/or operations that could be selectively disrupted in such a manner that the ability to accomplish each task could be impaired independently of the other. Double dissociations are, in fact, the holy grail in neuropsychological research, since they often provide compelling evidence that two tasks rely on at least partially segregated cognitive mechanisms.

To get a firmer handle on these theoretical issues, let's take a look at a topic that has received substantial attention not just in neuropsychology, but in cognitive neuroscience more broadly—namely, the linguistic

distinction between nouns and verbs (for reviews and perspectives see Shapiro & Caramazza, 2003b; Mätzig et al., 2009; Kemmerer & Eggleston, 2010; Pillon & d'Honincthun, 2010; Vigliocco et al., 2011; Crepaldi et al., 2011; Kemmerer, 2014). For the sake of argument, suppose you gave a patient two word retrieval tasks—one in which he had to name pictures of objects with the most appropriate nouns, and another in which he had to name pictures of actions with the most appropriate verbs. If he performed significantly worse on the object-naming task than on the action-naming task, this would constitute a single dissociation, and it might lead you to infer that his injury has compromised certain mechanisms that are essential for producing nouns but not essential for producing verbs. Would such a conclusion be justified? Not necessarily. For example, if the target nouns in the object-naming task were significantly longer and less frequent than the target verbs in the action-naming task—like *orangutan* vs. *walk*—it would certainly be possible that the patient had more trouble accessing nouns than verbs simply because the object-naming task was more challenging than the action-naming task, and the patient's injury exacerbated his sensitivity to this difference in difficulty.

But now let's push this hypothetical scenario one step farther. Suppose you had designed your experiment quite meticulously by matching the two sets of target words for length and frequency, and by showing that most normal individuals produce both kinds of responses with comparable correctness and speed. Would it then be legitimate to assert that the patient's disproportionately lower score on the object-naming task than on the action-naming task reflected a selective disturbance of mental representations and/or computations that are uniquely required for noun retrieval? The basis for such a conclusion would definitely be stronger. It would be greatly reinforced, however, if you could also demonstrate that another patient, tested with the very same materials, exhibited the exact opposite dissociation, this being significantly worse performance on the action-naming task than on the object-naming task. For you would then have the equivalent of neuropsychological gold—a double dissociation—and you would be able to support an argument to the effect that the two patients' impairments most likely affected non-overlapping cognitive mechanisms. In particular, you would have evidence that, in the context of your two naming tasks, the first patient probably had an impairment of mechanisms essential for noun but not verb production, whereas the second patient probably had an impairment of mechanisms essential for verb but not noun production.

Single dissociation   Patient A performs significantly worse on task X than on task Y.

Double dissociation   Patient A performs significantly worse on task X than on task Y, and patient B performs significantly worse on task Y than on task X.

Table 2.1   Examples of Large (30%+) Dissociations Between Nouns and Verbs in Picture-Naming Tasks (% Correct)

Patients with Worse Noun than Verb Retrieval			Patients with Worse Verb than Noun Retrieval		
Case	Nouns	Verbs	Case	Nouns	Verbs
Mario	7	88	BW	98	60
HY	35	85	FDP	96	50
HF	49	83	LK	93	63
EA	42	82	LR	92	40
ZBL	41	78	EM	90	59
SK	47	77	TB	88	37
ML	38	75	UB	87	48
SF	27	73	FC	87	30
EBA	12	72	RE	83	35
RG	29	64	MB	83	35
PV	13	58	JH	80	47

Data from Mätzig et al. (2009).

Although I have presented this example in the form of a thought exercise, in actuality robust double dissociations between nouns and verbs in picture naming tasks have been documented in a number of experimental papers. This is nicely illustrated by Mätzig et al.'s (2009) review of the relevant literature, since they identified 63 patients who displayed noun–verb dissociations in which the difference in accuracy between the two categories of words was at least 30 percent (see Table 2.1 for a sample of scores). These findings suggest that the two abilities that we have been considering—naming objects with appropriate nouns, and naming actions with appropriate verbs—do in fact depend on at least partially distinct cognitive mechanisms that can be selectively disrupted. It is important to note, however, that noun-related and verb-related picture naming deficits can reflect problems at any of several different levels of representation and/or computation, including visual, conceptual, grammatical, and phonological (Laiacona & Caramazza, 2004; Laine & Martin, 2006; Rohrer et al., 2008). Hence, the precise nature of the disturbance for any given patient can only be elucidated through careful investigation.

This is exemplified in an especially striking way by Rapp and Caramazza's (2002) in-depth study of patient KSR. Once in a blue moon, remarkable double dissociations are manifested by individual brain-damaged patients. In this particular case, the behavioral pattern involved a complex interaction between the variables of grammatical category and output modality, such that the patient had significantly more trouble with nouns than verbs in oral production, but significantly more trouble with verbs than nouns in written production. This peculiar pattern showed up across several tasks, including a sentence completion paradigm involving noun–verb homophones. For each item, KSR was presented with a "carrier sentence" signaling the category of the target word—e.g., *Give me the . . . (fish); I want to . . . (fish)*—together with a picture of the corresponding object or action. As shown in Figure 2.2, she produced spoken nouns much less accurately (40 percent) than spoken verbs (80 percent), and she produced written verbs much less accurately (50 percent) than written nouns (90 percent).

How can such an unusual performance profile be explained? Rapp and Caramazza (2002) considered the following two accounts, among others. One possibility is that the meanings of nouns and verbs are segregated within the semantic system, and although both types of concepts are still intact for KSR, she has two impairments—one affecting the projections from compartmentalized object concepts (typically encoded by nouns) to the phonological output lexicon, and another affecting the projections from compartmentalized action concepts (typically encoded by verbs) to the orthographic output lexicon

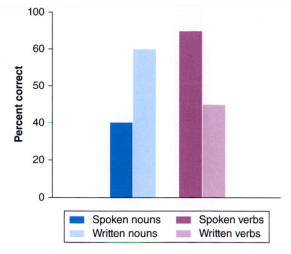

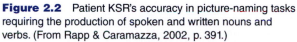

Figure 2.2 Patient KSR's accuracy in picture-naming tasks requiring the production of spoken and written nouns and verbs. (From Rapp & Caramazza, 2002, p. 391.)

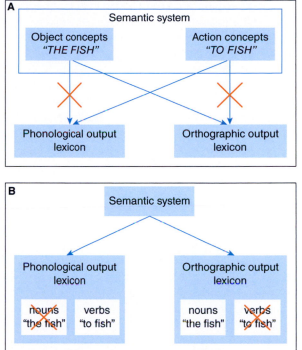

Figure 2.3 Two alternative accounts of KSR's performance profile. (A) An account that assumes segregation of word meanings according to conceptual category within the semantic system. (B) An account that assumes segregation of word forms according to grammatical category within the output lexicons. See text for details.

(Figure 2.3A). An alternative possibility, however, which is somewhat more radical, is that the forms of nouns and verbs are segregated within the phonological and orthographic output lexicons, and KSR has two impairments—one affecting the compartmentalized forms of nouns in the phonological output lexicon, and another affecting the compartmentalized forms of verbs in the orthographic output lexicon (Figure 2.3B). In the current context, we don't need to worry too much about which of these accounts is more plausible. Instead, what matters is the more general notion that detailed neuropsychological studies like this one can uncover surprisingly fine-grained disorders that impose nontrivial constraints on theories about the organization of the normal linguistic system.

Before moving on, I would like to make two final points. First, although I have elaborated the nature of single and double dissociations by concentrating rather narrowly on the noun–verb distinction, this has only been for illustrative purposes. As indicated in later chapters, neuropsychological investigations have greatly enhanced our understanding of all the different subdomains of language. Second, attentive readers will have noticed that throughout the discussion of the noun–verb distinction, I have focused on the details of behavioral patterns and have not mentioned anything specific about lesion data. This is partly because appreciating the logic of dissociations does not really require one to deal directly with the brain (Caramazza, 1992; Caramazza & Coltheart, 2006), and partly because the intricacies of visualizing lesions and relating them to behavioral deficits are described

further below. Before getting to those topics, however, it is worthwhile to address the methodological issue of how patients should be grouped for research purposes.

Groups and Individuals

Historically, there has been some tension in the neuropsychological community over the following question: Is it better to study groups of patients or single cases? This controversy was rather intense during the 1980s, but since then it has become increasingly clear that both types of approaches have merits and shortcomings.

One of the main benefits of group studies is that they allow researchers to test hypotheses about correlations between disturbances of particular mental abilities and lesions in particular brain regions. After all, if a certain type of deficit is thought to reliably result from damage to a specific area, it is necessary to conduct studies that include large numbers of patients both with and without the impairment of interest and both with and without the injury of interest.

An important concern about group studies, however, is that they are limited by how carefully the behavioral criteria for group membership are formulated. Although some patients are obviously more similar than others, the fact of the matter is that every patient is as unique as a snowflake, with an idiosyncratic set of symptoms brought about by an idiosyncratic distribution of brain damage. And for this reason it is essential that group studies specify as clearly as possible the type of impairment that serves as the main behavioral factor for sorting patients.

Indeed, this methodological issue lies at the very heart of the criticisms that were mounted against the group study approach back in the 1980s, primarily by Alfonso Caramazza and his colleagues (Caramazza, 1984, 1986; Caramazza & Berndt, 1985; Badecker & Caramazza, 1985; Caramazza & McCloskey, 1988; McCloskey & Caramazza, 1988; Caramazza & Badecker, 1989, 1991; Miceli et al., 1989). During that period, many investigations focused on groups of aphasic patients who were classified as belonging to certain syndromes, with a **syndrome** being defined as a collection of symptoms that tend to co-occur statistically. For example, a number of studies enrolled patients with the syndrome known as Broca's aphasia, and the researchers who conducted those studies basically treated the patients as being alike for experimental purposes. Caramazza and his colleagues argued, however, that it was not valid to assume that patients diagnosed in terms of loosely formulated syndromes had essentially the same disorders, because the specific symptoms that were taken to constitute the general syndromes could all be shown to dissociate from each other. For instance, as described more fully in Chapters 3 and 14, Broca's aphasics often have the following symptoms: impaired production of syntactically complex sentences; impaired comprehension of syntactically complex sentences; worse retrieval of verbs than nouns; markedly disrupted closed-class elements (i.e., tiny morphemes that serve grammatical functions, like the article *the,* the preposition *of,* the plural suffix *-s,* and the past-tense suffix *-ed*); and apraxia of speech (i.e., an impairment of complex articulatory coordination). Crucially, however, not every Broca's aphasic manifests all of these symptoms; on the contrary, the various symptoms can appear in a wide range of combinations across patients, and they can also fractionate into even more fine-grained deficits that likewise dissociate from each other across patients (for additional details see Chapter 14). For these reasons, Caramazza and his colleagues

Syndrome A collection of symptoms that tend to co-occur statistically.

claimed that syndromes such as Broca's aphasia lack both empirical integrity and theoretical utility. Not surprisingly, though, the advocates of syndrome-based studies attempted to defend their approach, and several rounds of heated debate ensued, leading to papers with provocative titles like the following: "Clinical syndromes are not God's gift to cognitive neuropsychology: A reply to a rebuttal to an answer to a response to the case against syndrome-based research" (Caramazza & Badecker, 1991).

Given the controversy surrounding syndromes, one might think that a more profitable strategy for designing group studies would be to sort patients very strictly in terms of the presence or absence of particular, well-defined symptoms. Even then, however, questions may arise as to how narrowly symptoms should be characterized. We noted above, for example, that while a symptom like worse retrieval of nouns than verbs in picture naming tasks may initially seem to be quite restricted, it can actually have several different causes, including a disturbance at the level of word meanings, a disturbance at the level of word forms, or a disturbance at the level of the interface between word meanings and word forms. As a consequence, any two patients who display that particular symptom may appear superficially to have the same deficit but actually have distinct underlying dysfunctions.

It is not hard to see that this line of thinking leads naturally to a philosophy that tends to prioritize individual case studies over group studies. And, to its credit, the single case approach has generated many powerful insights about the organization of the mind/brain, not just in the domain of language, but in other realms of cognitive neuroscience too. For instance, as indicated in Chapter 1, research on patient HM has contributed tremendously to theories about the role of the hippocampus in long-term memory, and, likewise, research on patient SM has contributed tremendously to theories about the role of the amygdala in emotional processing. At the same time, however, it remains true that group studies are extremely useful—and, in the long run, indispensable—for testing hypotheses about the universality of specific brain–behavior relationships.

Visualizing the Brain: The Basic Mechanics of Magnetic Resonance Imaging

In order to relate deficits in particular linguistic abilities to lesions in particular brain regions, it is necessary to demarcate as precisely as possible the anatomical boundaries of the damaged tissue. Back in Broca's time, one could not examine a patient's brain until after he or she died. But thanks to modern structural neuroimaging techniques, researchers can now obtain remarkably clear and detailed pictures of a patient's brain *in vivo*.

Although the first technique of this kind was computed axial tomography (CT or CAT), the most commonly used method today is **magnetic resonance imaging (MRI)**. The physics and data processing behind this type of brain scanning are quite complicated, but the basic points are fairly accessible and can be summarized as follows. Like the rest of the body, the brain consists mostly of water. Every water molecule contains two hydrogen atoms, and because the protons in the nuclei of these atoms are constantly spinning about their principal axes, they create tiny magnetic fields. Normally, the orientations of the protons, and of the associated magnetic fields, are random. What an MRI machine does is manipulate those orientations by creating a very powerful magnetic field, measured in tesla (T) units. Whereas the gravitational force of the earth creates a magnetic field of only 0.001 T, MRI scanners create fields that range from 0.5 T to more than 10 T. Most scanners currently used for human research are 1.5 T or 3 T, but some are as strong as 7 T. Needless to say, no metal objects are allowed in such environments, especially those that are on or in the bodies of people!

So how does a scanner affect the orientations of hydrogen protons so that brain images can be obtained? There are three key steps (Figure 2.4). First, when a person is placed in the machine, a small fraction of the protons—only a few per million—become oriented in a direction parallel to the magnetic field. Second, a radio wave is rapidly passed through the volume, causing the aligned protons to absorb some of this energy and shift their orientation by 90 degrees in a predictable manner. Third, when the radio wave is turned off, the protons release the energy as they rebound back into alignment with the magnetic field. This last phase is called relaxation, and it is critical for structural neuroimaging because it generates the signals that are picked up by the detectors surrounding the head. Different tissues in the brain, like gray versus white matter, vary in the density of hydrogen, and this in turn leads to measurable differences in the relaxation rates of protons. As a result, fine-grained anatomical contrasts can be discerned, and highly detailed three-dimensional brain images can be constructed. The spatial resolution—that is to say, the clarity or precision—of these pictures depends on the strength

Magnetic resonance imaging (MRI) The most common method for obtaining structural images of the human brain *in vivo*.

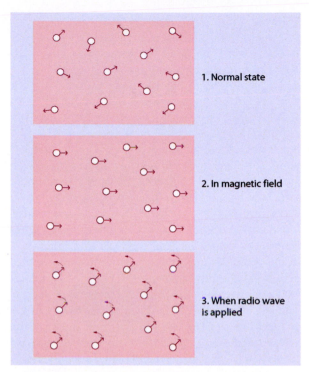

Figure 2.4 Basic principles of MRI. In their normal state, the tiny magnetic fields of hydrogen elements have random orientations. When an external magnetic field is imposed, some of the elements become aligned with it. The application of a radio wave causes the elements to shift 90 degrees, and when that wave is turned off, the elements relax back into alignment with the external magnetic field, emitting a detectable signal in the process. Different organic tissues, like gray vs. white matter in the brain, can be visualized because they have different densities of hydrogen. (From Gazzaniga et al., 2009, p. 132.)

of the magnetic field as well as on several other factors, but even a 1.5 T scanner can reveal structures at a scale of 1 millimeter or less, and scanners that are 3 T or higher can identify anatomical features at a scale of fractions of a millimeter. Although MRI is often used to visualize the brains of healthy individuals, its most valuable application undoubtedly involves the identification of lesions in brain-damaged patients, as described below.

Types of Brain Damage

Despite being lodged inside a thick, hard skull and covered by a tough layer of protective material, the human brain is a fragile organ that is vulnerable to many types of damage, some of which are due to outside forces, and some of which are due to internal ones. The kinds of disturbances that most often give rise to linguistic impairments are briefly outlined below.

Stroke

A **stroke**, also known as a cerebrovascular accident (CVA), occurs when the blood supply to a particular part of the brain is interrupted. There are several types of stroke, but the most common involves ischemia, which happens when a blood vessel in the brain becomes obstructed by a clot, thereby depriving all of the downstream tissue of oxygen. Sometimes the clot forms within the blood vessel that eventually gets clogged. In such cases, the ischemic stroke is classified as thrombotic. In other situations, however, the clot originates in a different part of the circulatory system—usually in the heart or in the large vessels of the upper neck and chest—and when it travels up into the brain where the arteries branch out and taper off into increasingly smaller arterioles and capillaries, it eventually gets stuck. In such cases, the ischemic stroke is classified as embolic.

If the afflicted tissue includes certain sectors of the brainstem that are essential for basic life functions, the person will most likely lose consciousness and die within minutes. If, however, the territory is restricted to certain cortical and white matter regions that support specific cognitive capacities, the person will survive, but those capacities will be compromised. For example, because the posterior cerebral artery supplies occipital areas that subserve fundamental aspects of visual perception, strokes that occlude various branches of that artery usually induce various kinds of visual impairments. Similarly, because the middle cerebral artery supplies perisylvian areas that subserve core linguistic operations, strokes that occlude various branches of that artery usually induce various kinds of linguistic impairments. For many stroke patients, the deficits can be partially or completely alleviated if blood flow is rapidly restored to the deprived tissue through one or another type of treatment (for an example see Box 3.3 in Chapter 3). If, however, circulation cannot be re-established quickly, the tissue will eventually die and become absorbed, leaving a cavity that gets filled with cerebrospinal fluid.

As an illustration, Figure 2.5 shows the brain of a profoundly aphasic patient who suffered a stroke involving some of the anterior branches of the left middle cerebral artery. This 3D image is based on an MRI scan, and the damaged areas are depicted in the darkest shades of the gray scale. It is apparent from the lateral view of the left hemisphere that this patient's lesion is centered in the heart of Broca's area, with some extension both anteriorly into the orbital sector of the inferior frontal gyrus

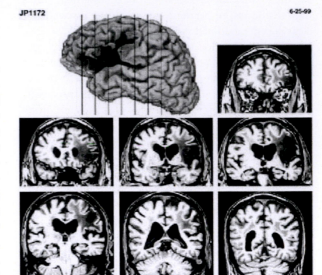

Figure 2.5   Lesion site of a stroke patient. The damage is centered in the heart of Broca's area but extends anteriorly into the orbital sector of the inferior frontal gyrus and superiorly into the mid-lateral sector of the precentral gyrus. As shown in the coronal sections, the damage included some of the white matter underneath the inferior frontal, middle frontal, precentral, postcentral, and supramarginal gyri. (From Kemmerer & Tranel, 2003, p. 426.)

and superiorly into the mid-lateral sector of the precentral gyrus. It is also apparent from the coronal sections that the lesion includes the anterior insula as well as a large swath of white matter beneath the inferior frontal, middle frontal, precentral, postcentral, and supramarginal gyri. (*A caveat:* The two symmetrical dark holes that lie toward the midline of the brain in most of the coronal sections do not reflect damaged areas, but instead reflect normal ventricles, which are fluid-filled chambers that provide a cushion for the brain.) As a result of his stroke, many of this patient's linguistic abilities were severely impaired (see the investigation reported by Kemmerer & Tranel, 2003; see also the discussion of this patient in Chapter 11).

Traumatic Brain Injury

The most frequent form of brain damage suffered by people under 40 years of age is **traumatic brain injury (TBI)**. There are two main types of TBI. First, a closed head injury occurs when a person sustains a sudden blow to the head that damages the brain while leaving the skull

Stroke Interruption of the blood supply to a particular part of the brain.

Traumatic brain injury (TBI) Brain damage caused by external forces that may leave the skull intact (closed head TBI) or penetrate the skull (open head TBI).

intact. Car accidents and sporting accidents are common causes of such devastating events. Second, an open head injury occurs when both the brain and the skull are penetrated by an object such as a bullet or a piece of shrapnel. In recent years, the most widely publicized case of an open head injury is probably Gabrielle ("Gabby") Giffords, who was forced to resign from her seat in the U.S. House of Representatives after being shot in the head on January 8, 2011, in an assassination attempt near Tucson, Arizona. Although she has managed to recover some of the mental and physical abilities that were impaired by the violent attack, she remains seriously disabled.

As an example of a TBI, Figure 2.6 depicts the brain of a man who was the unfortunate victim of an automobile accident. The damage was restricted to the left perisylvian territory, affecting Broca's area, the inferior precentral and postcentral gyri, the anterior supramarginal gyrus, most of the superior temporal gyrus, and the posterior middle temporal gyrus. The lesion is remarkably superficial, however, being almost completely confined to the cortical tissue and sparing most of the underlying white matter. In fact, even in some of the cortical regions that exhibit abnormal signals on the MRI scan, there may be some preservation of neural function. If so, this would help explain the patient's somewhat unusual neuropsychological profile: Although he was severely aphasic, he had no

motor or sensory deficits whatsoever (see the investigation reported by Kemmerer et al., 2007).

Neurodegenerative and Infectious Diseases

Whereas the types of brain damage caused by strokes and TBIs have abrupt onsets, those caused by **neurodegenerative and infectious diseases** are progressive in nature. A frighteningly large number of such disorders have been documented, all of which involve gradual atrophy (i.e., tissue loss) in specific regions, or sets of regions, in the brain. In fact, recent research suggests that many of these disorders target particular networks of areas that, in the healthy brain, have strong functional–anatomical connectivity and significantly correlated gray matter volume (Seeley et al., 2009). Ten disorders that have deleterious consequences for language are listed in Table 2.2. The first seven affect language in mostly indirect ways by impairing certain aspects of perception, memory, cognition, and motor control that are necessary for the efficient production and comprehension of words and sentences. The last three, however, are all variants of primary progressive aphasia (PPA) that directly target core components of the language circuitry. As described in detail in Chapter 4, these syndromes are characterized by close correspondences between, on the one hand, distinctive patterns of slowly worsening language deficits, and on the other hand, distinctive patterns of regionally specific atrophy.

The mostly nonoverlapping distributions of cortical atrophy that are commonly found in the three PPA syndromes are shown in Figure 2.7 (see also Figure 4.3 in Chapter 4). In the nonfluent/agrammatic variant the tissue loss is centered in the left inferior frontal cortex; in the semantic variant it is centered in the anterior temporal lobes bilaterally; and in the logopenic variant it is centered in the left temporoparietal territory. The images in the figure reflect the application of a special form of MRI called **voxel-based morphometry (VBM)**, which is ideally suited to determine the locations and magnitudes of atrophy in patients with neurodegenerative or infectious diseases (Whitwell, 2009). Basically, the technique involves dividing the brain into thousands of tiny cubes called **voxels**, each of which is a volume element that extends a short distance in each of three dimensions (just as a pixel is a picture element that extends a short

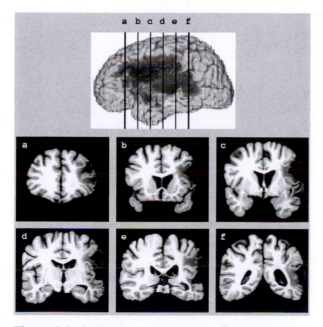

Figure 2.6 Lesion site of a patient who suffered a closed head TBI. The damage was restricted to the left perisylvian territory and was remarkably superficial, being almost completely confined to the cortical tissue, with little involvement of the underlying white matter. (From Kemmerer et al., 2007, p. 80.)

Neurodegenerative and infectious diseases Disorders that lead to progressive atrophy (i.e., tissue loss) in specific regions, or sets of regions, in the brain.

Voxel-based morphometry (VBM) A form of MRI that involves measuring regional differences in gray and white matter concentrations between groups of subjects.

Table 2.2   Ten Neurodegenerative and Infectious Diseases that Affect Language

Disorder	Type	Affected Brain Regions
1. Alzheimer's disease	Degenerative	Medial temporal areas; lateral temporoparietal areas; posterior cingulate/precuneus
2. Parkinson's disease	Degenerative	Dopaminergic cells in substantia nigra
3. Huntington's disease	Degenerative	Caudate and putamen in basal ganglia
4. Corticobasal syndrome	Degenerative	Primary and higher-order sensoriomotor cortices in frontoparietal regions
5. Amyotrophic lateral sclerosis	Degenerative	Motor neurons
6. Multiple sclerosis	Possibly infectious	Demyelination, especially of fibers near ventricles
7. Herpes simplex encephalitis	Infectious	Ventral, medial, and polar temporal areas; amygdala; hippocampus; insula; anterior cingulate
8. Nonfluent/agrammatic variant PPA	Degenerative	Inferior frontal cortex (left)
9. Semantic variant PPA	Degenerative	Anterior temporal lobes
10. Logopenic variant PPA	Degenerative	Superior temporal and inferior parietal areas (left)

PPA = primary progressive aphasia.

distance in each of two dimensions). Then the relative concentrations of gray and white matter in each voxel are calculated. Areas of atrophy in a pathological group of subjects can be identified by comparing their results with those of a healthy control group.

Tumors

Finally, lesions can also arise from tumors, which are masses of tissue that grow abnormally and serve no physiological purpose. There are several types of tumors, classified according to how they develop and whether they are likely or unlikely to recur after surgical removal. The most common type of **tumor** is called a glioma. Such tumors usually originate in the white matter and expand outward, thereby either destroying or displacing neurons (Figure 2.8). The rate at which they grow is highly variable, however, with some developing quite slowly and escaping detection for years, and others developing quite rapidly and inducing dramatic disturbances. There has recently been some debate as to whether neuropsychological studies involving tumor cases allow valid inferences to be drawn about the localization of particular mental capacities, but most experts lean toward the view that these kinds of studies can generate valuable insights, as long as a host

Voxel A three-dimensional volume element.

Tumor A mass of tissue that grows abnormally and serves no physiological purpose.

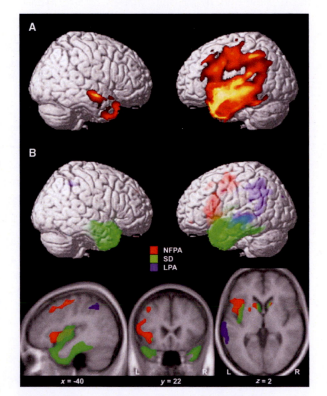

Figure 2.7   Cortical thinning in primary progressive aphasia (PPA) as measured by voxel-based morphometry. (A) Areas significantly atrophied in all patients vs. controls. (B) Areas of significant atrophy in each clinical subgroup versus controls. Red = nonfluent progressive aphasia (NFPA); green = semantic dementia (SD); purple = logopenic progressive aphasia (LPA). (From Gorno-Tempini et al., 2004.)

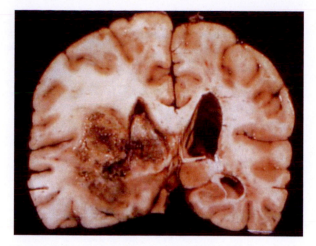

Figure 2.8 Post-mortem view of a malignant glioma that infiltrated the white matter of the right parietal lobe. (From Gazzaniga et al., 2009, p. 136.)

of potential complications are carefully avoided (see the 2011 clinical neuroanatomy "Discussion forum" in the journal *Cortex*, volume 47, issue 8).

An instructive example in the linguistic domain is a study by Kinno et al. (2009), which found that a group of Japanese-speaking patients with gliomas infiltrating Broca's area had significantly worse comprehension of passive sentences like *The square-person is being pushed by the circle-person* than of active sentences like *The circle-person is pushing the square-person* (note that the original stimuli consisted of Japanese sentences that were paired with scenes in which stick-figures with either square or circular heads acted on each other). Importantly, the patients' lesion sites overlapped with an area that was engaged significantly more by passive than active sentences in a separate fMRI study in which a group of healthy subjects performed the very same comprehension tasks as the brain-damaged patients. From a methodological perspective, this matters a great deal because the consistency between the neuropsychological data and the fMRI data supports the idea that reliable inferences about brain–behavior relationships can in fact be drawn from tumor cases (see Chapter 15 for further information about the role of Broca's area in sentence comprehension).

Relationships Between Behavioral Data and Lesion Data

As noted earlier, detailed case studies can reveal not only that certain cognitive capacities can be impaired independently of others, but also that those selective deficits are associated with certain lesion sites. Large-scale group

studies are needed, however, to determine whether the deficit–lesion correlations found in individual patients can be generalized to larger populations. This section describes two ways in which such group studies are often conducted. It also makes a few cautionary points that must be borne in mind when exploring structure–function relationships from a neuropsychological perspective.

Lesion Overlap and Subtraction Analysis

Sometimes the primary goal of a group study is to identify the neural basis of a particular type of deficit. A frequently used technique for conducting this kind of study is **lesion overlap and subtraction analysis** (Rorden & Karnath, 2004). Although such investigations have many steps, three of them are key. First, two groups of patients are recruited, one that exhibits the deficit of interest and another that does not. As emphasized above, it is essential that the deficit is clearly defined and that the patients are carefully examined to ensure that they either do or do not manifest it. Second, in separate procedures for each group, the contours of the patients' lesions are reconstructed in the common space of a standard brain template, and the degree to which the lesions overlap is calculated at every voxel. Third, the lesion overlap map for the patients *without* the deficit is subtracted from the lesion overlap map for the patients *with* the deficit, in order to pinpoint the areas of damage that are linked specifically with the deficit.

This technique can be illustrated by summarizing a study by Tranel and Kemmerer (2004) that sought to identify the neural basis of impaired knowledge of the meanings of locative prepositions, these being words like *in, on, around, through, above,* and *below,* which are used to refer to various kinds of spatial relationships between entities. Four tasks were administered to 78 brain-damaged patients with focal lesions (mostly due to stroke) distributed throughout the left and right cerebral hemispheres. As shown in Figure 2.9 and described below, all of these tasks required the patients to process the types of spatial concepts that are encoded by locative prepositions, but they differed in other ways:

- *Naming* ($N = 80$ items): For each item, the participant is shown a spatial array of objects and is asked to orally name the location of one object relative to another.

Lesion overlap and subtraction analysis The superimposed lesion sites of patients without a particular deficit are subtracted from the superimposed lesion sites of patients with the deficit, so that the resulting brain map reveals the areas of damage that are linked specifically with the deficit.

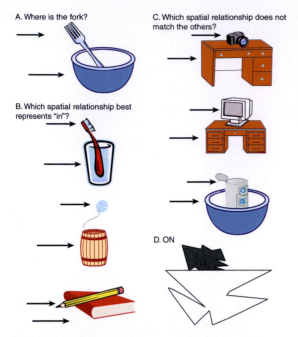

Figure 2.9   Examples of stimuli used by Tranel and Kemmerer (2004) to evaluate knowledge of the meanings of locative prepositions. (A) Naming task. (B) Matching task. (C) Odd One Out task. (D) Verification task. In the real stimuli in (A)–(C), the upper arrow is red and indicates the "figure" object whose location is at issue, whereas the lower arrow is green and indicates the "ground" object that serves as a point of reference. (From Tranel & Kemmerer, 2004, p. 725.)

- *Matching* (*N* = 50 items): For each item, the participant is shown three spatial arrays of objects together with a preposition and is asked to choose which array best represents the meaning of the preposition.
- *Odd One Out* (*N* = 45 items): For each item, the participant is shown three spatial arrays of objects and is asked to choose which one involves a type of relationship that is different from the other two.
- *Verification* (*N* = 44 items): For each item, the participant is shown a spatial array of abstract shapes together with a preposition and is asked to decide whether the preposition correctly describes the array.

Overall, the 78 patients displayed a complex pattern of associations and dissociations across the four tasks, such that some patients failed none of them, others failed just one, others two, others three, and others all four. Given this variability, the researchers first formed two groups of patients in the following manner: They reasoned that the patients who failed all four tasks (*N* = 6) most likely had impaired knowledge of the meanings of locative prepositions, whereas the patients who failed only one task (*N* = 9) most likely had unimpaired knowledge of those meanings (but perhaps had

idiosyncratic disturbances involving certain processes uniquely required by certain tasks). Next, the researchers created separate lesion overlap maps for the two groups of patients. And finally, they contrasted the map for the impaired group against the one for the unimpaired group. This subtraction revealed that defective knowledge of the meanings of locative prepositions was associated specifically with damage in just a few areas of the left hemisphere, most notably the cortex and underlying white matter of the inferior frontal, inferior parietal, and posterior superior temporal regions, as indicated by the warmly colored voxels (yellow-to-red spectrum) in Figure 2.10. It is important to note that because the analysis included patients both with and without the deficit of interest, the results provide strong evidence that lesions affecting the areas just mentioned are *more likely than not* to bring about the deficit. Thus, the study serves as an instructive example of how the lesion overlap and subtraction technique can be used quite effectively to connect particular types of linguistic disorders with particular areas of brain damage.

Voxel-Based Lesion–Symptom Mapping (VLSM)

Another method for identifying the lesion correlates of various disorders is **voxel-based lesion–symptom mapping (VLSM)** (Bates et al., 2003). In this approach, the first step is to administer a task of interest to a sample of patients with widely distributed lesions. Then the patients' lesion sites are transferred to a standard brain template, and for each voxel two groups of patients are formed—

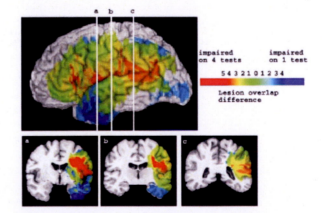

Figure 2.10   Results from Tranel and Kemmerer's (2004) neuropsychological study of locative prepositions, illustrating the lesion overlap and subtraction method. The lesion overlap map of the 6 patients who failed all 4 tasks was contrasted against the lesion overlap map of the 9 patients who failed only 1 task. The color bar indicates the number of lesions in the subtraction image at each voxel, and the white lines indicate the planes of the coronal sections depicted below. (From Tranel & Kemmerer, 2004, p. 740.)

those who have lesions at that voxel, and those who do not. Finally, at all of the voxels where the numbers of patients in the lesioned and non-lesioned groups exceed a certain threshold, statistical *t*-tests are used to compare the behavioral data of the two groups. The resulting *t*-values provide continuously varying measures of the degree to which decreasing task performance is tied to the presence vs. absence of damage in particular brain regions. In other words, VLSM allows researchers to identify the neural underpinnings of deficits, and to quantify those brain–behavior relationships in an analogue manner, without having to initially classify patients according to whether they do or do not have the relevant impairment.

This technique is nicely exemplified by Wu et al. (2007), who used it to explore the same type of linguistic disorder discussed above, namely impaired knowledge of the meanings of locative prepositions. In this study, 14 patients with left-hemisphere lesions were given a battery of tasks, one of which required them to match simple sentences containing locative prepositions (e.g., *The circle is above the square*) with one of four pictures. The patients' accuracies ranged from 43 percent to 100 percent, with a mean of 85.6 percent. Using VLSM (or, more precisely, a somewhat modified version of it), the researchers identified, on a voxel-by-voxel basis, the exact brain areas where significant behavioral differences emerged between patients with versus without a lesion the given site. As shown in Figure 2.11, these areas turned out to be fairly consistent with those that Tranel and Kemmerer (2004) found to be associated specifically with impaired knowledge of prepositional meanings in their lesion overlap and subtraction analysis. Needless to say, the fact that the two approaches led to similar results is encouraging, since it suggests that both of them are valid techniques for investigating deficit–lesion correlations.

A Few Caveats About Neuropsychological Research on Structure–Function Relationships

Now, because the human brain is a fantastically complex computational system containing a plethora of highly interactive components, it should come as no surprise that attempting to understand it from a neuropsychological perspective—or from any other perspective, for that matter—is far from straightforward (Catani et al., 2012). Here are three cautionary points that are worth keeping in mind:

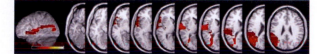

Figure 2.11   Results from Wu et al.'s (2007) neuropsychological study of locative prepositions, illustrating the voxel-based lesion-symptom mapping (VLSM) method. Colored areas indicate regions where patients with lesions performed significantly worse than patients without lesions. Brighter colors represent a greater number of patients with lesions at the given voxel. (From Wu et al., 2007, p. 1549.)

- In order to infer a causal relationship between an impairment of a particular ability and damage to a particular region, it is necessary to demonstrate not only that patients with the deficit tend to have lesions at that site, but also that patients with lesions at that site tend to have the deficit.
- The types of deficit–lesion correlations manifested by stroke or TBI patients in the chronic period—i.e., more than six months after lesion onset—can be somewhat different from those manifested by such patients in the acute period—i.e., less than six months after lesion onset. This is because acute patients with relatively small lesions often recover rapidly, due to intact areas "taking over" the affected functions (e.g., Jenkins & Merzenich, 1987; Grefkes & Fink, 2011).
- Some impairments may be attributable not so much to areas of damage that are visible on conventional MRI scans, but rather to other areas that are structurally intact but dysfunctional for either of the following reasons. (1) **Hypoperfusion**: They still receive enough blood supply to survive, but not enough to operate normally (e.g., Fridriksson et al., 2002; Hillis, 2007b). (2) **Diaschisis**: They depend on axonal input from the site of structural damage, and that input is no longer available (e.g., Sharp et al., 2004; Gratton et al., 2012).

All three of these issues can be clarified by considering a recent debate regarding the neural basis of apraxia of speech (AOS), a disorder of articulatory programming that was mentioned above in the context of Broca's aphasia and that is discussed at greater length in Chapter 6. Very roughly, AOS affects high-level motor aspects of the orchestration of speech, leading to distortions of consonants, vowels, and prosody while sparing the strength

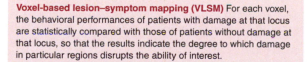

Voxel-based lesion–symptom mapping (VLSM) For each voxel, the behavioral performances of patients with damage at that locus are statistically compared with those of patients without damage at that locus, so that the results indicate the degree to which damage in particular regions disrupts the ability of interest.

Hypoperfusion A brain area receives enough blood supply to survive, but not enough to operate normally.

Diaschisis Even though a brain area is structurally intact, it is dysfunctional because it no longer receives axonal input from a different area that has been damaged.

and tone of the relevant muscles of the articulators (lips, tongue, jaw, and palate). Patients generally know what they want to say and how it should sound, but cannot accurately coordinate their articulators to produce the desired output (see Table 6.4 and the accompanying text in Chapter 6). For example, when asked to repeat the word *catastrophe* five times, one patient said, "catastrophe, patastrophe, t-, catastrophe, katasrifrobee, aw sh-, ka-, kata-, sh-, sh-" (Ogar et al., 2006, p. 343).

In 1996, Nina Dronkers, a high-ranking researcher at the University of California in Davis, published a landmark paper showing that 25 chronic stroke patients with AOS had 100 percent lesion overlap in just one left-hemisphere region—specifically, the superior anterior sector of the insula—whereas none of 19 chronic stroke patients without AOS had damage there (Dronkers, 1996; the lesion data are depicted in Figure 2.12, which is reproduced as Figure 6.23 in Chapter 6). It is important to note, however, that this study has three limitations related to the points made above. First, although it provides evidence that AOS is reliably associated with damage to a particular part of the insula, it does not indicate whether damage to that region usually gives rise to AOS. This leaves open the possibility that the seemingly causal link between AOS and insular damage may be misleading, and that the real neural basis of AOS may involve damage to some other area(s). Second, all of the patients in the study were chronic, so it is conceivable that acute patients may exhibit somewhat different deficit–lesion correlations. And third, the study focused exclusively on areas of structural damage, thereby allowing for the possibility that other areas which are still intact may nevertheless be dysfunctional and hence potentially implicated in AOS.

In 2004, another high-ranking researcher, namely Argye Hillis at Johns Hopkins University, conducted a follow-up study of AOS that addressed all three of the limitations of Dronkers's (1996) investigation (Hillis et al., 2004b). First, 80 stroke patients were selected not according to behavioral criteria, but rather according to their sites of structural damage, with 40 patients having lesions that included any part of the left insula and 40 having lesions that spared that territory. Second, the patients were evaluated for AOS when they were still highly acute, within 24 hours of stroke onset. And third, the patients were scanned with imaging techniques that identified not only areas of tissue damage, but also areas of hypoperfusion (i.e., significantly reduced blood flow). So what were the results? Contrary to Dronkers's (1996) study, abnormalities in the main region of interest, that being the superior anterior sector of the left insula, turned out not to be significantly related to AOS. Specifically, among the 29 patients who had either

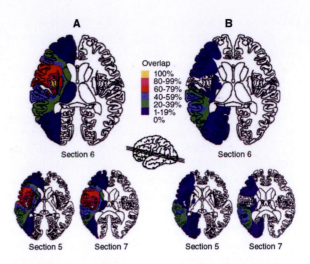

Figure 2.12 Comparison of lesion overlap in patients with and without chronic apraxia of speech. (A) Overlapping the lesions of 25 patients with apraxia of speech yields a common area of infarction (yellow) on section 6 of the reconstruction program (top of figure). This region represents an area of 100% overlap, that is, all 25 patients with this articulatory planning disorder have lesions that include this one area of the insula. In the bottom row are shown the neighboring sections either below (section 5) or above (section 7) the critical slice. (B) Overlapping the lesions of 19 patients without apraxia of speech shows infarctions over much of the left hemisphere as in the previous group. However, a comparison of section 6 in the two groups reveals that not one of these 19 patients without apraxia of speech has a lesion in the same region of the insula as those who do exhibit the disorder. (From Dronkers, 1996, p. 159.)

damage or hypoperfusion in that region, only 12 (41 percent) exhibited AOS; moreover, among the 51 patients who did not have either damage or hypoperfusion in that region, 19 (37 percent) did in fact exhibit AOS (Table 2.3). Further analyses revealed that AOS was actually associated with abnormalities in Broca's area, since 26 (87 percent) of the 30 patients who had either damage or hypoperfusion in that region manifested the speech disorder, and only 5 (10 percent) of the 50 patients who lacked such abnormalities did not manifest it (Table 2.4).

Why, then, did Dronkers (1996) find such a close link between AOS and insular damage? Hillis et al. (2004b) suggest that this may have happened because, among all the regions in the brain, the insula is one of the most vulnerable to stroke, due to its unique anatomical placement relative to the middle cerebral artery (e.g., Caviness et al., 2002; Payabvash et al., 2011). It is also noteworthy that, in keeping with Hillis et al.'s (2004b) results, 60–79 percent of Dronkers's (1996) chronic patients with AOS had damage to Broca's area, and the remaining patients may well have had hypoperfusion in that region. Still, the precise neural underpinnings of AOS remain controversial, as shown by a number of more recent studies

Table 2.3 Relationship Between Abnormalities in the Superior Sector of the Anterior Insula and Acute Apraxia of Speech

Apraxia of Speech	Damage or Hypoperfusion in the Superior Sector of the Anterior Insula	
	Present	Absent
Present	12	19
Absent	17	32

Source: Hillis et al. (2004b, p. 1483).

Table 2.4 Relationship Between Abnormalities in Broca's Area and Acute Apraxia of Speech

Apraxia of Speech	Damage or Hypoperfusion in Broca's Area	
	Present	Absent
Present	26	5
Absent	4	45

Source: Hillis et al. (2004b, p. 1483).

(e.g., Ogar et al., 2006; Baldo et al., 2011; Richardson et al., 2012; see also the section in Chapter 6 called "The island of Reil"). For present purposes, what matters is simply that much of this debate revolves around the sorts of methodological issues highlighted here.

Functional Neuroimaging

As mentioned in the introduction to this chapter, there are two main functional neuroimaging techniques—positron emission tomography (PET) and functional magnetic resonance imaging (fMRI)—with the latter being by far the most commonly used method for mapping the functional architecture of the human brain (see once again Figure 2.1). Both of these approaches are based on what Arbib (in press) calls "a sort of 'vampire theory' of the brain, as regions with more active processing . . . 'suck more blood' to support their increased metabolism." To put it less dramatically, the key physiological processes underlying both approaches are as follows. When the performance of a cognitive task engages a particular brain area, the most active neurons in that area rapidly consume the oxygen that is already available in the local capillaries, and during the next few seconds an overabundance of freshly oxygenated blood is automatically delivered. What PET and fMRI measure, albeit in different ways, are the regional changes in blood flow associated with neural activity. That's why both imaging techniques are sometimes called hemodynamic methods. Experts do not yet understand exactly why the amount of freshly oxygenated blood that is delivered to an activated area exceeds

the amount that is required, but the intimate relations between cognitive operations, neural activity, and blood flow have been known for over a century.

One of the most remarkable demonstrations of these links was made between 1926 and 1928 by Dr. John Fulton at the Peter Bent Brigham Hospital in Boston, Massachusetts (Fulton, 1928; see also Posner & Raichle, 1994, pp. 58–59). During that two-year period, Fulton worked closely with a young man referred to as Walter K., who suffered from severe headaches and visual disturbances due to a large collection of congenitally abnormal blood vessels—an arteriovenous malformation—overlying his occipital cortex. Amazingly enough, when blood coursed through those vessels intensely, it created a pulsating sound that the patient perceived as a kind of humming noise and that Fulton could also hear when he placed a stethoscope over the back of the patient's head. Through a series of well-designed experiments, Fulton discovered that the rushing sound correlated not only with Walter K.'s heartbeats, but also with his visual experiences. For instance, although the sound remained relatively soft when Walter K. sniffed tobacco or listened intently to the ticking of a wristwatch, it grew significantly louder when he suddenly began to use his eyes after lying in darkness for several minutes, and also when he effortfully focused on reading a newspaper. By carefully documenting these and many other observations about Walter K., Fulton was able to provide some of the first compelling evidence that regionally specific changes in blood flow reflect regionally specific changes in neural activity, which in turn reflect cognitively specific changes in mental life. Many years later, these tight relations between vascular, neural, and cognitive events served as the foundation for the development of the two most frequently used functional neuroimaging techniques—PET and fMRI.

The following overview of these techniques has four parts. The first part briefly describes the basic mechanics of PET and fMRI. The second part introduces the three-dimensional coordinate system that is often used as a kind of grid to specify the anatomical locations of significant activations across subjects. The third part focuses on the distinction between blocked and event-related designs. And the fourth part discusses some of the most widely employed experimental paradigms, illustrating each one with specific examples involving language.

Before delving into the details, a word of warning is in order. As Kriegeskorte (2010, p. 475) recently pointed out, functional neuroimaging is "dangerously seductive" because it "combines the prestige of serious science with the broad appeal of intuitive images." It is therefore important to emphasize here at the outset that the multicolored brain figures that one often sees in PET and fMRI papers, and that populate many of the pages of this book, should never be treated like photographs that somehow manage to capture the content of our mental lives in a transparent way. Rather, one should always bear in mind that such figures are the outcome of many stages of signal processing and statistical analysis, and that they depend on a number of assumptions that are still being debated in the professional community (e.g., Hanson & Bunzl, 2010).

Two Techniques

Positron Emission Tomography (PET)

Originally developed in the 1960s, PET measures regional cerebral blood flow—and, by inference, regional neural activity—by tracking the distribution of a radioactive isotope throughout the brain. In a typical experiment, the isotope is first created in a medical cyclotron and placed in water. Then this radioactive water is rapidly piped over to the imaging facility, where it is injected into the research subject's bloodstream and soon carried up into his or her brain. Several different types of isotopes can be used, but ^{15}O is the most common. Normal oxygen—the stable, nonradioactive kind that we breathe—is ^{16}O, since its nucleus has a balance of 8 protons and 8 neutrons. In contrast, ^{15}O contains 8 protons but only 7 neutrons. As it decays, it emits a proton, and this positively charged particle—a positron—travels just a few millimeters before it is attracted to the negative charge of an ambient electron. When these particles come together, they are annihilated, and two very powerful photons fly off in opposite directions at the speed of light (Figure 2.13A). These photons exit the head and are picked up by rings of detectors in the PET scanner (Figure 2.13B). Special computers are then able to reconstruct the location of the annihilation event inside the subject's brain. Where the number of such events is relatively large, there is greater blood flow, and where there is greater blood flow, there is greater neural activity.

Although a positron travels only 2–3 millimeters before colliding with an electron, the spatial resolution of PET is somewhat worse—about 10 millimeters. Still, that is good enough to localize patterns of activation at an anatomical scale that is relevant to a broad range of cognitive domains, including language. As for the temporal resolution of the technique, it is rather poor—about 30 seconds at best—because data must be averaged over at least that length of time in order to obtain a sufficient signal-to-noise ratio.

Finally, you may be wondering about the ethics of injecting a radioactive substance into a person's bloodstream. Virtually all of the isotope decays in about 10 minutes, and in a typical study involving several scans, a subject receives less than 10 percent of the annual amount of radioactivity permitted for professional radiologists such as x-ray technicians. Nevertheless, serious precautions are always taken to minimize the risk.

Functional Magnetic Resonance Imaging (fMRI)

Invented in 1991, fMRI is based on the discovery that the MRI signal is sensitive to the degree of oxygenation of blood in different parts of the brain. Specifically, the level of blood oxygenation constitutes what Bandettini (2012, p. A5) calls "an endogenous contrast agent," since it reduces the MRI signal when blood is deoxygenated and allows it to rise when blood is oxygenated. Hence, what fMRI measures is generally referred to as the **blood oxygenation level dependent (BOLD) signal** (Huettel et al., 2009). Dehaene (2009, p. 69) describes this phenomenon quite clearly as follows:

> Blood cells contain a high concentration of hemoglobin, the molecule responsible for carrying oxygen. Roughly speaking, if a hemoglobin molecule does not transport oxygen, it behaves like a small magnet and disrupts the local magnetic field, thus reducing the signal received by the fMRI machine. When a hemoglobin molecule does contain oxygen, it immediately becomes transparent in the magnetic field—a change that is seen by the machine as a small but measurable increase in the resonance signal.

When the neurons in a particular area increase their activity, they consume the oxygen that is immediately available. As a result, there is more deoxygenated than oxygenated blood in the area, and this is manifested as a slight decrease in the BOLD signal, lasting 1 or 2 seconds. Then, during the next 5 seconds or so, a surplus of freshly oxygenated blood is delivered to the area, and this is manifested as a gradual increase in the BOLD signal. The last phase of the cycle takes another 5 seconds or so and involves a gradual return to the baseline level, usually with a brief undershoot. This whole process, which is extended over approximately 12 seconds, is called the **hemodynamic response function** (Figure 2.14). The physiological changes that it reflects are not very large, but they can nevertheless be quite significant from a statistical perspective. Also, although the

---

Blood oxygenation level dependent (BOLD) signal Serving as the raw data of fMRI, this signal is reduced when blood is deoxygenated and allowed to rise when blood is oxygenated.

Hemodynamic response function Typically, the BOLD signal in a brain area that is sensitive to a particular stimulus initially dips for 1 or 2 seconds, then steadily rises for 5 seconds or so, then gradually drops back down over another 5 seconds or so. The precise shape of this curve can be modulated by several factors.

A

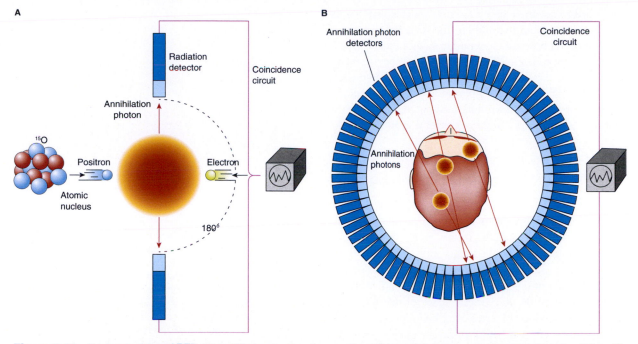

B

Figure 2.13 Basic principles of PET. (A) As ¹⁵O decays, it emits a positron. This particle travels only 2-3 mm before it collides with an electron, causing an annihilation event that sends photons off in opposite directions at the speed of light. The photons are picked up by radiation detectors, and the location of the annihilation event is reconstructed by a computer. (B) Where the number of such events is relatively large, there is greater blood flow and hence greater neural activity. (From Posner & Raichle, 1994, pp. 62-63.)

underlying cell biology of the BOLD signal is still unclear, there is some evidence that the signal is correlated more with the input than the output processing of neurons (for a review of recent findings see Goense et al., 2011).

For conventional scanners (1.5–3 T), the spatial resolution of fMRI is usually about 3 millimeters, although it is noteworthy that some approaches to data acquisition allow researchers to measure signal changes at a higher resolution of 1 or even 0.5 millimeters. Also, as the magnetic field gets progressively stronger (4 T and higher), the spatial resolution gets progressively better. With regard to the temporal resolution of fMRI, it too has steadily improved as the technology has advanced. Originally, it was only somewhat better than that of PET, but then the advent of event-related designs (see below) enabled researchers to analyze data at the temporal scale of the hemodynamic response function—roughly 10–12 seconds—and more recent innovations have led to ways of measuring task-related changes in the BOLD signal that are as rapid as 50–100 milliseconds (e.g., Menon et al., 1998; Bellgowan et al., 2003; Sigman et al., 2007).

Clearly, fMRI has many advantages over PET: It's cheaper, since it doesn't require a medical cyclotron; it's safer, since it doesn't involve radioactive isotopes; it has better spatial resolution; and it has better temporal resolution. Still, neuroimaging researchers have been forced

to confront a number of limitations of fMRI, two of which are as follows. First, the operation of the scanner is extremely noisy, analogous to the sound of a very loud pneumatic drill. And second, the BOLD signal tends to be distorted near air-filled cavities, which has made it difficult to acquire data from certain brain regions, most notably the anterior temporal lobes, which are near the sinuses. In recent years, however, clever strategies have been

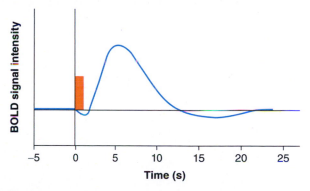

Figure 2.14 The hemodynamic response function. The colored rectangle at Time 0 represents the neural activity within a given voxel after a stimulus has been presented, and the blue line represents the subsequent changes in BOLD signal intensity over time—an initial dip followed by a gradual rise and fall, with a brief undershoot at the end. (From Huettel et al., 2004, p. 208.)

developed to circumvent or overcome these limitations, as well as many others. In addition, the statistical analysis of fMRI data has become increasingly sophisticated (Ashby, 2011; Poldrack et al., 2011). Hence, it is not surprising that fMRI has largely superseded PET as a research tool, and that, in a relatively short period of time, it has yielded a wealth of valuable information about the neural substrates of language and other cognitive domains.

Standardized Three-Dimensional Coordinates for Defining Stereotaxic Brain Space

In most functional neuroimaging studies, data are combined across subjects, and this is usually done by transforming the unique anatomical configuration of each subject's brain so that it fits a standard brain template. Statistically significant activations are then identified and reported within the common **stereotaxic space** of that template, which is itself defined in terms of a three-dimensional *x,y,z* coordinate system that has its origin at a midline structure called the anterior commissure (Figure 2.15):

- *x*-axis = the right–left dimension (right is positive and left is negative);
- *y*-axis = the anterior–posterior dimension (anterior is positive and posterior is negative);
- *z*-axis = the superior–inferior dimension (superior is positive and inferior is negative).

Two different atlases provide such three-dimensional grids for analyzing and presenting PET and fMRI results. The first one was created by Talairach and Tournoux (1988) on the basis of anatomical data from a single post-mortem brain, whereas the second one was created by the Montreal Neurological Institute (MNI) on the basis of MRI scans from 305 healthy volunteers (Collins et al., 1994). PET and fMRI studies conducted prior to 1994 were limited to using the so-called Talairach coordinates as a spatial frame of reference for reporting results, but studies conducted since the introduction of the alternative MNI system have had the option of using it instead, and an increasing number of them have done so. Although the two systems are by no means identical, they are similar insofar as they characterize particular anatomical sites in terms of fairly comparable *x,y,z* coordinates.

For example, a certain site in the posterior part of Broca's area—specifically, in the pars opercularis (roughly

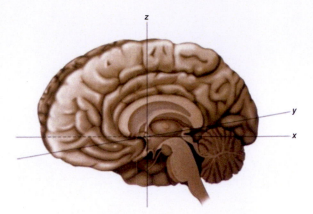

Figure 2.15   The three-dimensional coordinate system for mapping stereotaxic brain space. The origin of the frame of reference is at a midline structure called the anterior commissure. The *x*-axis represents the right–left dimension, with right being positive and left being negative. The *y*- axis represents the anterior–posterior dimension, with anterior being positive and posterior being negative. And the *z*-axis represents the superior–inferior dimension, with superior being positive and inferior being negative. (From Huettel et al., 2004, p. 273.)

BA44) of the left inferior gyrus—is located at [−55, 8, 15] in the Talairach system and at [−58, 11, 12] in the MNI system, according to an automatic converter that is available on the Internet. In both sets of coordinates, the number on the *x*-axis (−55/−58) is negative and large because Broca's area resides at a location that is left and far lateral to the anterior commissure, which, as mentioned above, is the origin of the reference system. The number on the *y*-axis (8/11) is positive and small because the relevant portion of Broca's area, namely a particular site within the pars opercularis, is at a location that is a bit anterior to the anterior commissure. And the number on the *z*-axis (15/12) is positive and small because the site at issue is a bit superior to the anterior commissure.

Anatomical sites that are defined in terms of Talairach or MNI coordinates constitute the centers of voxels, and in most of the functional neuroimaging studies that are reviewed in this book, the voxel size was 3–5 millimeters in each direction, or even larger. A growing number of fMRI investigations, however, have been using high-resolution techniques that employ voxel sizes of only 1 cubic millimeter, or even less (see Box 2.1).

The practice of co-registering and analyzing functional neuroimaging data from multiple subjects within a common stereotaxic brain space has many virtues, but it is not without shortcomings. In a recent paper, Fedorenko and Kanwisher (2009) highlighted what they regard as one of the most worrisome weaknesses of this approach—namely, that it has the potential to obscure individual differences in the neural organization of language, since

Stereotaxic space A way of mapping standard brain space using a three-dimensional *x,y,z* coordinate system.

Box 2.1   What's in a Voxel?

In functional neuroimaging studies, the primary unit of structural analysis is the voxel. And as indicated in the main text, what is measured within each of these three-dimensional elements is not neural activity per se, but rather its vascular surrogate: in the case of PET, changes in the concentration of a radioactive tracer; and in the case of fMRI, changes in the ratio of oxygenated and deoxygenated hemoglobin. Given that both PET and fMRI are sensitive to events occurring in the small blood vessels within voxels, it is important to recognize that, on average, less than 3 percent of the volume of a voxel is occupied by such vessels, with the rest of the space consisting mostly of neural tissue.

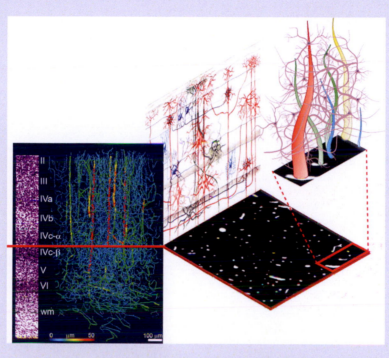

Figure 2B1.1   The neural and vascular contents of a voxel. (From Logothetis, 2008, p. 876.)

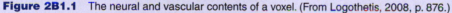

This is nicely illustrated in Figure 2B1.1, which was created by one of the world's foremost fMRI researchers, Nikos Logothetis (2008). The left panel depicts the vascular mesh in the visual cortex of a monkey, color-coded according to the diameter of the vessels. At the left of this panel is a Nissl-stained section of the same area, showing the density of neurons from cortical layers II through VI, with the white matter (wm) at the bottom. Although the network of blood vessels portrayed in the panel appears to be quite substantial, it actually takes up only a tiny amount of the overall volume of the area—less than 3 percent, as mentioned above. This is clearly revealed in the right panel, which represents a two-dimensional slice through layer IV about 800 × 800 micrometers (i.e., 0.8 × 0.8 millimeters) in size. The white spots are cross-sections of vessels, and it can be seen that they are in fact few and far between. The drawing at the top right shows a hypothetical distribution of vascular and neural elements above a small portion of the slice (red triangle), and the drawing in the background shows some common types of neurons (red = large pyramidal cells; dark blue = inhibitory basket cells; light blue = inhibitory chandelier cells; gray = stellate cells).

The upshot is this: A high-resolution voxel in an fMRI study may be a cubic millimeter in size, but while such a volume contains 20,000 to 30,000 neurons, it houses a much smaller set of blood vessels, and the latter are what constitute the anatomical foundation for functional neuroimaging. Thus, a close look at the contents of a voxel highlights the extent to which the data acquired in fMRI studies—and, to an even greater degree, in PET studies—are removed from the actual firing properties of individual neurons.

it effectively erases the substantial anatomical variability that exists between people's brains. As a different strategy, they advocate the single-subjects functional localization approach, which has proven to be beneficial in other branches of cognitive neuroscience, such as visual perception and social cognition. According to this approach, one plots each subject's unique functional data directly on his or her unique anatomical data, and the experimental procedure typically involves the following steps. First, one localizes a particular region of interest (ROI) in each subject—e.g., the fusiform face area (FFA), which responds more to faces than objects. Next, one carries out a more focused investigation to test a specific hypothesis about the other response properties of that ROI, again in each subject—e.g., whether the FFA is more sensitive to upright than inverted faces. Finally, if one wishes, one can conduct analyses across subjects that pool data from corresponding functional regions rather than from the same locations in Talairach or MNI space. Fedorenko and Kanwisher (2009) argue that if this approach were employed more often to study the functional neuroanatomy of language, it might lead to deeper insights (see also Fedorenko et al., 2010, 2012a, 2012b; Nieto-Castañón & Fedorenko, 2012; Glezer & Riesenhuber, 2013).

Blocked Versus Event-Related Designs

An important consideration in the design of functional neuroimaging studies is how to order the individual trials for each experimental condition. Suppose, for example, that you wanted to identify and compare the brain regions that respond to words for animals (e.g., *horse, wolf, rabbit*) and words for tools (e.g., *knife, pencil, scissors*) (for further information about this semantic distinction see Chapter 10). How should you sequence the trials containing animal words relative to those containing tool words?

To some extent, the answer is constrained by the imaging technique. If you were to use PET, you would be forced to employ a **block design** because of the poor temporal resolution of that technique. In such a design, trials belonging to the same experimental condition are grouped together in blocks, so that subjects must perform the same type of task for the same type of stimuli throughout a given block. For example, as shown in Figure 2.16A, you might set up your PET study so that it included the following three blocks, each lasting 1 minute: first, a block of trials in which subjects read words for animals (condition A); second, a block of rest in which subjects simply lie in the scanner without

> **Block design** Stimuli from the same condition are presented consecutively together.

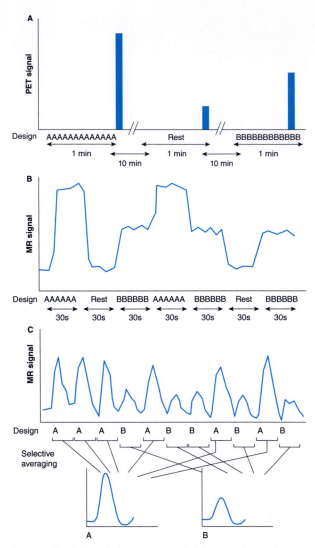

Figure 2.16   Blocked vs. event-related designs. (A) Block design for PET. (B) Block design for fMRI. (C) Event-related design for fMRI. See text for details. (From Purves et al., 2008, p. 76.)

performing any tasks (baseline condition); and third, a block of trials in which subjects read words for tools (condition B). The figure indicates that these blocks would be separated by 10-minute periods, the reason being that this would allow enough time for the radioactive isotope that subjects receive at the beginning of each block to decay. The figure also presents some hypothetical results for a particular site in the brain, with the magnitude of the PET signal at that site being plotted over the last trial in each block, thereby representing the amount of signal accumulated across the entire block. As can be seen, these imaginary results suggest that the neural activity at the given site is strongest when subjects read words for animals, somewhat weaker when they read words for tools, and even weaker when they rest.

If, on the other hand, you were to use fMRI, you would have more design options to choose from because of the better temporal resolution of this technique. One possibility would be to still employ a block design, but to make each block shorter—say, only 30 seconds—and to include more blocks for each condition, as shown in Figure 2.16B. Note that the hypothetical results depicted in this figure are for the same site as in Figure 2.16A, but here they reflect the magnitude of the BOLD response continuously over the course of each block. Once again, the imaginary neural activity shifts across the conditions in a step-wise manner, being strongest for animals words (condition A), somewhat weaker for tool words (condition B), and even weaker for rest.

An alternative possibility, however, would be to employ an **event-related design**. In this kind of approach, the trials belonging to different experimental conditions are interspersed, as shown in Figure 2.16C. Each trial evokes its own hemodynamic response function, and these individual signals are later extracted and averaged together according to condition. It can be seen in the hypothetical results that such an analysis would reveal essentially the same difference in neural activity described above—namely, a greater response to animal words (condition A) than to tool words (condition B) at the given site—except here the precise shape of the hemodynamic response function evoked by each lexical category would be apparent.

In the 1990s, fMRI studies were, for the most part, confined to block designs. But around the turn of the century, the basic principles of event-related designs were developed, and since then such designs have been progressively refined (Huettel, 2012). From 2000 to 2010, a growing number of studies explicitly indicated that they employed "event-related fMRI," and between 2010 and the present time event-related designs have become so popular that they are now virtually ubiquitous. Why do they have so much appeal? For one thing, they allow researchers to randomize stimuli; hence they reduce the probability that the results may be influenced by habituation, anticipation, or strategic processing, all of which are more likely in block designs. In addition, they provide much more experimental flexibility than block designs, since trials can be sorted in terms of a wide range of criteria, including not only the deliberately built-in conditions, but also uncontrollable factors like whether the subjects respond correctly or erroneously. Finally, they allow investigators to explore fine-grained aspects of the amplitudes and timecourses of hemodynamic response functions in different brain regions.

Event-related design Stimuli from one condition are randomly interspersed with stimuli from another condition.

Some Basic Experimental Paradigms

The vast majority of PET and fMRI studies address a specific question about language or some other cognitive domain by adopting one of several basic experimental paradigms. Some of these paradigms can be used with either blocked or event-related designs, but most are restricted to the latter. This section focuses on three commonly employed paradigms—subtraction, correlation, and multivariate pattern analysis. The first two—subtraction and correlation—are by far the most heavily represented paradigms in the myriad functional neuroimaging studies that are summarized in Parts III–VI of this book. And although the third paradigm—multivariate pattern analysis—is only represented by a few of the studies discussed in those chapters, it is rapidly becoming one of the most popular approaches to analyzing fMRI data. Some other paradigms—e.g., adaptation and resting state—are not included here but are briefly defined at the points where they become relevant later in the book, and additional ones—e.g., functional and effective connectivity—are not covered at all (for a review of the latter paradigms see Friston, 2011).

In the following survey, all of the focal paradigms are exemplified by referring to studies that tackle the very same linguistic issue, namely the auditory perception of intelligible versus unintelligible utterances. As we will see, the various sets of findings are similar in many respects, presumably because they probe from different perspectives the same underlying network for sentence comprehension. At the same time, however, the findings are inconsistent in several ways, and these non-overlapping results may reflect a number of factors, including not only the distinctive properties of the three paradigms, but also idiosyncratic aspects of the particular studies that are reviewed, such as the subjects, the stimuli, and the statistical analyses.

A caveat: Because our main concern is to clarify the logic of the paradigms themselves, we will concentrate primarily on how they work, and will not dwell very much on the precise interpretation of the experimental data. After all, the empirical details regarding the neural substrates of auditory sentence processing are elaborated much more fully in subsequent chapters (see especially Chapters 5, 7, and 15).

Subtraction

The **subtraction paradigm** was the first to be adopted for use in functional neuroimaging studies. It is

Subtraction paradigm A type of design in which the activity evoked during a control condition is subtracted from the activity evoked during an experimental condition.

compatible with both blocked and event-related designs, and it continues to be employed quite frequently by both PET and fMRI researchers. In abstract terms, this paradigm provides investigators with a general strategy for isolating the neural correlates of specific cognitive capacities. Traditionally, it involves designing a study that includes two key conditions—an "experimental" condition that requires the ability of interest, and a "baseline" or "control" condition that does not require it but is equivalent in all other respects. After the imaging data have been collected, the map of brain activity associated with the control condition is subtracted from the map of brain activity associated with the experimental condition, and whatever regions still show up as being significantly engaged in the experimental condition are treated as contributing uniquely to the ability of interest.

In order to enhance reliability, this basic method is sometimes supplemented by incorporating into the design multiple experimental conditions that require the ability of interest—e.g., conditions A and B—and multiple control conditions that do not—e.g., conditions C and D. The advantage of such a modification is that it allows the investigators to perform various kinds of so-called conjunction analyses that increase the likelihood of pinpointing the brain regions underlying the ability of interest (Price & Friston, 1997). For example, if each experimental condition is well-matched with a particular control condition—e.g., A with C, and B with D—separate subtractions between these corresponding conditions can be performed first, and then the outcomes of those independent analyses can be conjoined: $[(A - C) + (B - D)]$. The resulting map of brain activity is actually quite restricted, since it *includes* only the areas that are commonly engaged by both of the experimental conditions—i.e., the neural intersection of A and B—and it *excludes* all of the areas that are uniquely engaged by just one or the other of those conditions, as well as all of the areas that are engaged by either of the two control conditions. Thus, used skillfully, this advanced form of the subtraction paradigm can be a very powerful way to narrowly characterize the neural underpinnings of particular cognitive capacities.

To see how it works in practice, let's look at an fMRI study that Narain et al. (2003) conducted to disclose the brain regions that are linked with the auditory processing of intelligible versus unintelligible sentences (for a previous PET study that used comparable materials see Scott et al., 2000). Four conditions were constructed, two involving intelligible stimuli and two involving unintelligible stimuli, as shown in Figure 2.17 and described below:

- Intelligible conditions:
  A. *Speech (Sp):* Sentences that are completely normal.

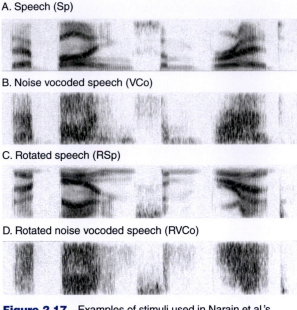

A. Speech (Sp)

B. Noise vocoded speech (VCo)

C. Rotated speech (RSp)

D. Rotated noise vocoded speech (RVCo)

Figure 2.17   Examples of stimuli used in Narain et al.'s (2003) fMRI study. Each panel shows a spectrogram of the sentence *They're buying some bread,* with time represented on the horizontal axis, frequency represented on the vertical axis, and intensity of acoustic energy represented by the darkness of the trace in each time/frequency region. See the text for details about each condition. (From Scott et al., 2000, p. 2402.)

  B. *Vocoded speech (VCo):* Sentences that have been artificially altered so that they have a rough sound quality, like a harsh robotic whisper, but can still be understood.

- Unintelligible conditions:
  C. *Rotated speech (RSp):* Sentences that have been spectrally rotated (i.e., inverted) so that they sound like an incomprehensible "alien" language but nevertheless retain some phonetic features, such as voiceless fricatives.
  D. *Rotated vocoded speech (RVCo):* Sentences that have first been vocoded and then spectrally rotated (i.e., inverted) so that they sound like intermittent fluctuating static.

Eleven subjects listened attentively to uniform blocks of stimuli from each of these conditions while undergoing fMRI scanning. In post-scan interviews all of them indicated that they could understand the stimuli in only two of the four conditions. To identify the brain regions that mediate the extraction of meaning from intelligible utterances, the researchers used the type of conjunction analysis described above—that is, $[(A - C) + (B - D)]$, which in the current context translates into $[(Sp - RSp) + (VCo - RVCo)]$. In the first stage of this analysis, they performed two separate subtractions, each of which involved contrasting the activation map evoked by a set of intelligible stimuli against the activation map evoked by a closely matched set of unintelligible stimuli. It is noteworthy that although the intelligible stimuli in the first subtraction consisted of normal sentences (Sp), the intelligible stimuli in the second subtraction consisted of noise-vocoded sentences that were harder to understand but still comprehensible (VCo). It is also noteworthy that in each subtraction the two conditions, intelligible and unintelligible, differed only in terms of spectral rotation and hence had equivalent acoustic complexity. In the second stage of the analysis, the researchers conjoined the activation maps that resulted from the two separate subtractions, thereby identifying their commonalities. By doing this, they were able to derive a highly constrained activation map that captured precisely those brain areas that responded to both types of intelligible stimuli, while ruling out all of the areas that responded to only one or the other of those types of stimuli, as well as all of the areas that responded to either type of unintelligible stimuli.

That final activation map is shown in Figure 2.18. Only three clusters of voxels passed the statistical threshold for significance, and all of them were in the left lateral temporal lobe—one in the posterior sector, and two in the anterior sector. The posterior region overlaps with Wernicke's area, damage to which is known to disrupt phonological and lexical aspects of spoken language comprehension (see Chapters 3, 5, and 15). And both of the anterior areas lie along portions of the superior temporal sulcus that other studies have recently implicated in syntactic and semantic aspects of spoken language comprehension (see Chapters 5 and 15). Based on these considerations, it seems reasonable to conclude that the three lateral temporal regions that survived Narain et al.'s (2003) conjunction analysis do in fact contribute to relatively high-level aspects of auditory sentence processing and are not critically involved in representing low-level acoustic and phonetic information. At the same time, however, it is important to bear in mind that because the analysis was quite restrictive, it may have eliminated a few other areas that also facilitate the perception of intelligible speech in one way or another. Evidence that this is probably the case comes from studies that have used other paradigms to explore the same issue, as described below.

Correlation

Like the subtraction paradigm, the **correlation paradigm** (also known as the parametric paradigm) is compatible with both blocked and event-related designs. Unlike the subtraction paradigm, however, it does not treat the ability of interest as an all-or-nothing mental phenomenon,

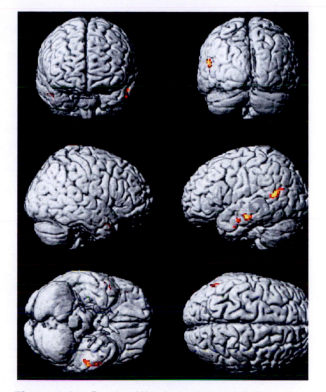

Figure 2.18 Results of Narain et al.'s (2003) fMRI study. Significant activations surviving the contrast [(Sp – RSp) + (VCo – RVCo)] are plotted on a template brain viewed from anterior (top left), posterior (top right), right lateral (middle left), left lateral (middle right), ventral (bottom left), and dorsal (bottom right) perspectives. (From Narain et al., 2003, p. 1365.)

but rather as a continuous cognitive dimension that can be manifested to varying degrees (Friston, 1997). From an intuitive point of view, what happens in a study employing this approach is that the subjects perform a series of tasks that recruit the ability of interest to different extents, and the investigators look for brain regions in which the magnitude of activity shifts in similarly incremental ways.

Before we discuss how this paradigm can be applied to the domain of language, let's take a quick look at its use in a rather amusing non-linguistic investigation called "Neural activity associated with monitoring the oscillating threat value of a tarantula" (Mobbs et al., 2010). The brave people who participated in this fMRI study were placed supine on the scanner bed, with one foot positioned at the end of a box containing five open-top compartments aligned at different degrees of proximity to the foot (top panel of Figure 2.19).

Correlation paradigm A type of design in which the subjects first perform a series of tasks that recruit a particular cognitive capacity to different degrees, and then the researchers search for brain regions that are correspondingly activated to different degrees.

Throughout the experimental procedure, these subjects believed they were observing, via a live camera feed, one of the researchers move a large tarantula from one box to another, either closer to or farther from their foot, even though in reality they were viewing pre-recorded clips of these movements. Parametric regression analyses yielded the following results: As the spider got progressively closer to the foot, brain activity progressively increased in several anxiety-related regions, including the dorsal anterior cingulate cortex and certain midbrain nuclei (Figure 2.19A); and as the spider got progressively farther from the foot, brain activity progressively increased in areas that have been linked with passively coping with relatively distant dangers, most notably the anterior orbitomedial prefrontal cortex (Figure 2.19B). Thus, by cleverly applying the correlation paradigm, this study was able to illuminate the neural circuitry underlying one of our most primitive forms of fear—arachnophobia.

Returning now to the realm of language, Davis and Johnsrude (2003) used the correlation paradigm to further elucidate the neural substrates of intelligibility, and they did so by acknowledging and exploiting the fact that there is not really a rigid distinction between intelligible and unintelligible utterances, but rather a graded continuum. In particular, they conducted an event-related fMRI study in which the subjects listened to the following types of stimuli:

- Undistorted condition:
  A. *Speech:* Sentences that are completely normal.

- Partially distorted conditions:
  B. *Vocoded speech:* Sentences altered in the same way as in Narain et al.'s (2003) study.
  C. *Segmented speech:* Sentences altered by dividing the speech stream into separate chunks and replacing some of them with signal-correlated noise, which retains many of the original acoustic features but lacks recognizable sounds.
  D. *Speech in noise:* Sentences placed in a background of continuous speech-spectrum noise.

- Completely distorted condition:
  E. *Signal-correlated noise:* Sentences altered in the same way as in the "segmented speech" condition, but with all of the chunks, rather than just some, being replaced with signal-correlated noise, thereby rendering the stimuli completely incomprehensible.

Crucially, for each of the three partially distorted conditions, there were three different *degrees* of distortion leading to three different *degrees* of intelligibility, as defined by the average number of words per sentence that a group of subjects in a separate pilot study could report:

- *High intelligibility:* Roughly 90 percent of the words reported correctly.
- *Medium intelligibility:* Roughly 65 percent of the words reported correctly.
- *Low intelligibility:* Roughly 20 percent of the words reported correctly.

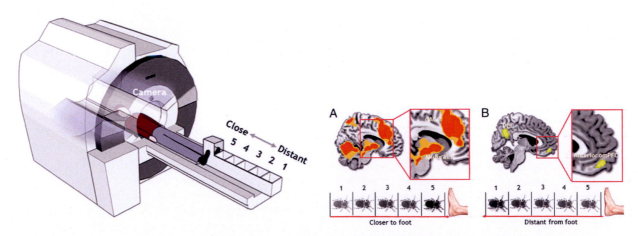

Figure 2.19　Set-up and results of Mobbs et al.'s (2010) fMRI study. (Left) While lying on the scanner bed, participants believed that, via a camera feed, they could watch the experimenter move a live tarantula between five boxes arrayed at different distances from their foot. (A) As the spider got progressively closer to the foot, brain activity progressively increased in several anxiety-related regions. (B) As the spider got progressively farther from the foot, brain activity progressively increased in several areas linked with danger management. dACC = dorsal anterior cingulate cortex; omPFC = orbitomedial prefrontal cortex; PCC = posterior cingulate cortex. (From Mobbs et al., 2010, pp. 20583-20584.)

During the scanning sessions, the subjects used button-presses to rate the intelligibility of each stimulus on a four-point scale, and their judgments fit well with the intelligibility measures obtained from the pilot study. To reveal meaningful patterns in the imaging data, the researchers conducted several analyses. First, they performed a simple subtraction that compared the completely distorted condition (E) with silence. Not surprisingly, they found significant bilateral activation in Heschl's gyrus and the immediately surrounding early auditory cortices (see the blue-to-pink spectrum in Figure 2.20A). Second, and much more interestingly, they carried out a correlation analysis that was designed to disclose any brain regions in which gradual increases in the strength of the BOLD signals reliably tracked gradual increases in the intelligibility of the stimuli. For this analysis, the stimuli included not only the undistorted condition (A) and the completely distorted condition (E), but also the three partially distorted conditions (B, C, and D), each of which was distorted to three different degrees. Significant effects—that is to say, neural sensitivity to *continuous variation* in the intelligibility of the stimuli—emerged in the following regions: (1) a large swath of cortical tissue along the length of the superior and middle temporal gyri in the left hemisphere, stretching anteriorly toward the temporal pole and posteriorly as far as the angular gyrus; (2) a similar but more anteriorly distributed cluster of voxels in the right hemisphere; and (3) a small part of Broca's area (see the red-to-yellow spectrum in Figure 2.20A). Finally, in a follow-up analysis the investigators discovered that a single "intelligibility sensitive" voxel in the left anterior temporal lobe (marked by the white arrow in Figure 2.20A) had the following response profile (shown in Figure 2.20B), which was representative of many other voxels in the same territory: It was activated quite strongly in the undistorted condition, quite weakly in the completely distorted condition, and to varying intensities across the three partially distorted conditions, depending on the *amount* but not the *type* of distortion. In other words, the voxel was sensitive to the different *extents* to which the partially distorted stimuli could be understood (roughly 90 percent, 65 percent, or 20 percent), but not to the different *ways* in which they had been distorted (vocoded, segmented, or embedded in background noise).

Davis and Johnsrude's (2003) study clearly suggests that the brain mechanisms underlying the comprehension of intelligible utterances are not limited to the areas identified by Narain et al.'s (2003) study. Rather, the complete network appears to encompass not only a broader range of regions in the left hemisphere, but also several regions in the right hemisphere (for further

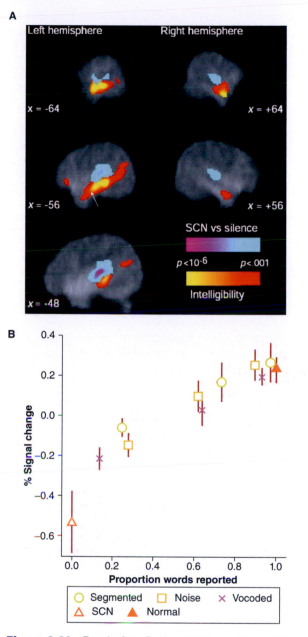

Figure 2.20 Results from Davis and Johnsrude's (2003) fMRI study. (A) Areas in which a basic subtraction analysis revealed significantly greater activity for signal-correlated noise (SCN) than silence (blue-to-pink spectrum), and in which a correlation analysis revealed gradual increases in activity as a function of gradual increases in intelligibility (red-to-yellow spectrum). (B) Signal strength across conditions for an "intelligibility sensitive" voxel in the anterior temporal lobe (marked by the white arrow in "A"). (From Davis & Johnsrude, 2003, p. 3427.)

information see Chapters 5, 7, and 15). For present purposes, the key point is that these additional anatomical details were brought to light in part because the researchers approached the issue from the perspective of the correlation paradigm, which can show how gradual changes in the extent to which a particular cognitive ability is tapped are directly reflected by gradual changes in the extent to which certain brain regions are engaged.

Multivariate Pattern Analysis

As mentioned above, the last paradigm that we will consider—**multivariate pattern analysis (MVPA)**—is a newcomer to the functional neuroimaging field, and for this reason it is not well-represented among the many fMRI studies reviewed in later chapters of this book. Nevertheless, it is worth introducing here because its popularity is rapidly increasing, due mainly to the widespread recognition that it has the potential to decode remarkably fine-grained patterns of brain activity with a degree of precision that far exceeds previous approaches to analyzing fMRI data (for a nontechnical discussion see Smith, 2013; for reviews and tutorials see Haynes & Rees, 2006; Mur et al., 2009; Schwartzkopf & Rees, 2011; Tong & Pratte, 2012; and for a historical perspective see Haxby, 2012).

In conventional approaches like the subtraction and correlation paradigms, every voxel is treated as an independent entity, and the statistical analyses extract separate measures of signal strength from all of them. When those analyses are applied to the whole brain, they typically focus on the mean response of each isolated voxel in each condition, and when they are applied to a specific region of interest (ROI), they often go one step further by spatially averaging the signals from all the voxels in that region for each condition. To be sure, these traditional forms of data analysis can provide valuable clues about the brain areas that contribute to certain tasks. At the same time, however, they have serious limitations. In the current context, the most relevant shortcoming is that they ignore the relationships between voxels and hence cannot detect any information that may be latent in the spatial distributions of activity across them. The purpose of MVPA is to identify such patterns and attempt to decipher their representational content by relating them to the unique cognitive requirements of the corresponding tasks.

The major differences between conventional approaches and MVPA are nicely illustrated in Figure 2.21, which shows how conflicting outcomes could potentially emerge in an experiment exploring whether the perception of similar syllables—specifically, /ra/ and /la/—is

> **Multivariate pattern analysis (MVPA)** An approach to analyzing fMRI data that is capable of showing how different spatially distributed patterns of activity across the same set of voxels may be related to different experimental conditions and hence to different mental representations or processes.

associated with distinctive levels and/or patterns of brain activity in a hypothetical superior temporal ROI consisting of just 9 voxels (Mur et al., 2009). As the diagram indicates, if the stimuli triggered orthogonal 4-voxel activation patterns in the ROI, a conventional analysis based on spatial signal averaging would completely miss the contrasting configurations and generate as output the same overall amounts of activity for the two speech sounds, incorrectly suggesting that the ROI does not discriminate between them. MVPA, however, would be able to expose the spatially intermingled yet separate patterns, raising the possibility that the ROI contains at least partially non-overlapping neural populations that represent the two syllables. (In an fMRI study employing MVPA, Raizada et al., 2010, did in fact find that in an early auditory ROI, the statistical separability of the activation patterns elicited by /ra/ and /la/ reliably predicted the behavioral ability of native English and Japanese speakers to tell the two syllables apart. For a related study involving vowels see Formisano et al., 2008, which is discussed in Chapter 5). In current practice, researchers draw upon a variety of sophisticated classification algorithms to find and decode the particular activation patterns that are linked with particular experimental and control conditions. We don't need to worry about the details of those algorithms here, however, because the essential point is simply that they allow researchers to go beyond what has been referred to, rather disparagingly, as mere "blobology," and address more focused questions about how specific types of brain states reflect specific types of mental states.

This is exemplified by a recent fMRI study that used MVPA to investigate with greater precision the neural substrates of the processing of intelligible versus unintelligible utterances. In this experiment, Abrams et al. (2013) presented 20 subjects with the following two types of stimuli, sequenced in alternating blocks:

- Intelligible condition:
  A. *Speech (Sp):* Excerpts of famous speeches from the 20th century (Martin Luther King, President Roosevelt, etc.).
- Unintelligible condition:
  B. *Rotated speech (RSp):* The same excerpts, only spectrally rotated (i.e., inverted), as in Narain et al.'s (2003) study.

The subjects were instructed to pay close attention to each sound excerpt and to push a button when it ended. After the imaging data had been collected, the researchers performed two analyses, one adopting the traditional subtraction paradigm, and the other employing MVPA. The former analysis was fairly straightforward—essentially (A – B), which in this case translated into (Sp – RSp). The latter analysis, however, was more complicated, since it involved a "searchlight" version of MVPA in which, for every voxel in the brain, a 3 × 3 × 3 neighborhood was created, centered at the given voxel, and within that 27-voxel space the activation patterns evoked by the two conditions were scrutinized by a special classification algorithm to determine whether they were fundamentally different. Finally, after conducting both analyses, the researchers compared the two sets of findings in order to explore how the outcomes of the alternative approaches converged and diverged.

The results are depicted in Figure 2.22. The areas that survived the subtraction analysis are highlighted in red and labeled GLM, which stands for General Linear Model—the technical name for the set of assumptions underlying the subtraction paradigm. These areas include the three left lateral temporal regions that emerged in the much more conservative subtraction study by Narain et al. (2003; see Figure 2.18) as well as most of the bilateral temporal regions that emerged in the correlation study by Davis and Johnsrude (2003; see Figure 2.20). Interestingly, as indicated by the green patches in Figure 2.22, the searchlight analysis revealed that, within the

extensive left lateral swath of tissue that responded significantly more to intelligible than unintelligible speech in the subtraction analysis, there were two patches in which the multi-voxel patterns of activity were significantly different for the two conditions. Even more intriguing, however, is that the searchlight analysis also picked out many other areas that discriminated between the two conditions, not only in the left hemisphere but also in the right. These areas are shown in blue, and they occupy portions of the temporal, parietal, and frontal lobes that, as the researchers observe, have been associated with various aspects of auditory sentence processing, albeit rather unevenly, across a number of previous functional neuroimaging studies and neuropsychological studies (see Chapters 7 and 15). Abrams et al. (2013, p. 1711) conclude that

results from the current study suggest that the use of new analytic tools, such as whole-brain MVPA, may help resolve some of the inconsistencies in this literature by bringing a new level of sensitivity to the data analysis and highlighting the role of fine-grain distributed neural representations.

(See also Evans et al., in press.)

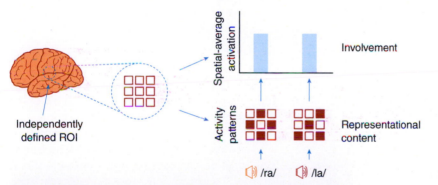

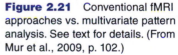

Figure 2.21 Conventional fMRI approaches vs. multivariate pattern analysis. See text for details. (From Mur et al., 2009, p. 102.)

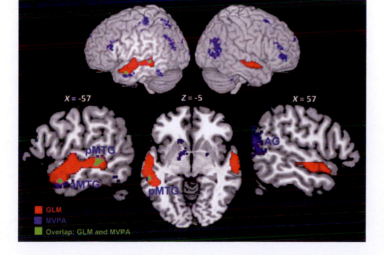

Figure 2.22 Results from Abrams et al.'s (2013) fMRI study. The images show significant responses to intelligible vs. unintelligible speech as revealed by a basic subtraction analysis (red) and a type of multivariate pattern analysis (blue), with only a few areas of overlap (green). GLM = General Linear Model; MVPA = multivariate pattern analysis. (From Abrams et al., 2013, p. 1709.)

Electrophysiology

We noted above that, strictly speaking, neither PET nor fMRI measure brain activity in any direct sense; instead, they track the metabolic consequences of brain activity. By contrast, electrophysiological techniques bring researchers much closer to the actual firing of neurons. In fact, one of these techniques involves directly stimulating specific parts of the exposed brain and observing the effects on cognition and behavior. The other main approach involves recording the electrical signals of neurons as they unfold on a millisecond timescale during mental processes. This is usually done in either of two ways: intracranially by means of electrodes that are placed directly in the brain so as to record the firing of either single cells or relatively small populations of cells; or extracranially by means of electrodes that are placed on the scalp so as to record, through the skull, the simultaneous firing of many thousands or even millions of cells. All of these methods are elaborated below, and several representative studies are briefly reviewed in order to illustrate how electrophysiology can provide unique insights about the neural substrates of language.

Stimulation

Direct electrical stimulation of the human brain was first performed in the late 19th century, but it did not become widely used for clinical and research purposes until the middle of the 20th century, when the famous Canadian neurosurgeon, Wilder Penfield, successfully employed this technique to map the functional organization of the exposed cortex in numerous patients with epilepsy prior to removing the putatively epileptogenic areas—i.e., the areas where seizures were thought to begin. Although seizures can be controlled with medication in most cases of epilepsy, this is not possible for some patients, and in such situations the surgical excision of the epileptogenic region often provides relief. At the same time, however, every effort must be made to avoid resecting tissue that is essential for language and other important abilities. The method that Penfield developed was to use a handheld electrode to stimulate tiny portions of the patient's brain while he or she was awake, and thereby identify sites where stimulation altered certain functions. Because the brain itself has no pain receptors, this kind of operation could be conducted while the patient was under local anesthesia, after the craniotomy had been completed.

Many of Penfield's classic findings are clearly summarized in a book that he co-authored with Lamar Roberts in 1959 called *Speech and Brain-Mechanisms*. In keeping with the work of earlier researchers, they reported that stimulation of some areas induced "positive" responses. For example, stimulation of the primary motor cortex evoked involuntary movements of specific body parts, and stimulation of the primary somatosensory cortex evoked vague feelings in specific body parts; moreover, in both cases the effects conformed fairly well to the topographic layout of the motor and somatosensory homunculi (see Figure 1.25 in Chapter 1). Similarly, stimulation of occipital regions induced elementary visual hallucinations such as colors, stars, and flickering lights, and stimulation of superior temporal regions induced elementary auditory hallucinations such as ringing, clicking, and buzzing.

These sorts of positive responses are obviously quite remarkable, but the kinds that were sometimes triggered by stimulating higher-order temporal regions are even more fascinating, since they involved vividly replaying particular experiences from the patient's past. Here is just one of many striking examples (Penfield & Roberts, 1959, p. 45):

> When an electrode, insulated except at the tip, was introduced . . . one centimeter into the cortex of the superior surface of the [anterior] temporal lobe and a gentle current was switched on, she exclaimed: "Oh, a familiar memory—in an office somewhere. I could see the desks. I was there and someone was calling to me—a man leaning on a desk with a pencil in his hand.

Some patients described such experiential responses as flashbacks, whereas others compared them to dreams. According to Penfield and Roberts, however, all of the patients who reported such effects agreed that they were much richer than ordinary recollections.

Although these types of responses have, not surprisingly, attracted considerable attention, they are relatively rare. It is far more common for direct electrical stimulation to have "negative" consequences, especially when it comes to speech. Thus, if the current is applied to a language-related region when the patient is talking, any of several different kinds of interference may occur. The forward flow of speech may suddenly slow down or stop altogether—a disturbance called **speech arrest**. The retrieval of an intended word may be blocked—a disturbance called **anomia**. Or the content of an intended word may be distorted semantically or phonologically—a disturbance called **paraphasia**. Penfield and Roberts not only documented all of these negative effects, but were

---

Speech arrest A sudden slowing or halting of speech production.

Anomia Inability to retrieve a word.

Paraphasia Distortion of the semantic or phonological content of a word.

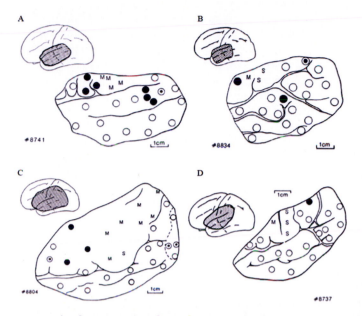

Figure 2.23 Results for four individual patients in Ojemann et al.'s (1989b) electrophysiological study using direct cortical stimulation. In each case, the window of the craniotomy is shown in the top left brain image, and the stimulation sites are represented by letters and circles in the expanded version of the window. Symbols: M = motor response; S = somatosensory response; open circle = no naming impairment; half-filled circle = naming impaired on only 1 trial (non-significant); filled circle = naming impaired on 2 or more trials (significant). (A and B) These two patients exhibit the typical pattern of two critical naming areas, one frontal and the other temporal or parietal. (C) This patient exhibits the unusual pattern of exclusively frontal naming sites. (D) This patient exhibits the unusual pattern of exclusively parietal naming sites. (From Ojemann et al., 1989b, pp. 413–414.)

among the first to explore how the precise nature of the linguistic errors caused by stimulation at specific sites could provide valuable information about the functions normally supported by those sites.

Following closely in Penfield's footsteps, a neurosurgeon at the University of Washington named George Ojemann went on to conduct what remain to this day some of the most influential studies of language using direct electrical stimulation. In a landmark investigation, he and his colleagues employed this method to map out the areas of so-called "eloquent" cortex in the left perisylvian territory of 117 patients with epilepsy (Ojemann et al., 1989b). The protocol was as follows. Line drawings of familiar objects were projected onto a screen at 4-second intervals, and the patient's task was to name each one, always beginning with the carrier phrase *This is a ____*. At the onset of some of the slides, the examiner stimulated one of several predetermined points on the exposed cortex. Each site was stimulated a total of three times, but all of the sites were stimulated once before any of them was stimulated a second time. The patient's naming responses were scored right after they were produced so that the examiner could receive immediate feedback. A given site was treated as being essential for naming if stimulation induced errors during at least two of the three trials.

A number of significant findings emerged from this seminal study, two of which are highlighted here. First, in the vast majority of cases, stimulation disrupted naming at just a few discrete sites, or mosaics of sites, roughly 1 cm² in extent. In 67 percent of the patients, two or more focal areas like this were identified, usually one in the frontal cortex and another in the temporal or parietal cortex, as shown in Figures 2.23A and 2.23B. However, among

the 90 patients who underwent stimulation mapping in both anterior and posterior perisylvian zones, 17 percent had only frontal naming sites (e.g., Figure 2.23C) and 15 percent had only temporal or parietal naming sites (e.g., Figure 2.23D). These individual differences are manifestations of the second key result, which is that the precise anatomical locations of the sites essential for naming varied greatly across patients. This diversity is captured by Figure 2.24. Close inspection of this diagram reveals that there was only one site where errors were evoked more than 50 percent of the time, this being the posterior part of Broca's area extending caudally into tongue-related motor cortex; and even at that site, errors were *not* evoked in 21 percent of patients. Overall, then, this study suggests that there is substantial variability across the population with regard to the exact cortical locations of language functions. And it is noteworthy that a similar conclusion was reached in a more recent study by Sanai et al. (2008) which used electrical stimulation to identify "eloquent" areas in the left perisylvian cortex of 250 patients suffering not from epilepsy but rather from brain tumors, specifically gliomas.

Although Ojemann et al.'s (1989b) investigation was restricted to object naming in English and did not systematically distinguish between different types of errors, other studies have used direct electrical stimulation to explore a wider range of linguistic abilities. Here are some examples:

- cortical separation of languages in the bilingual brain (Lucas et al., 2004);
- the roles of white matter tracts in phonological and semantic processing (Duffau, 2008);

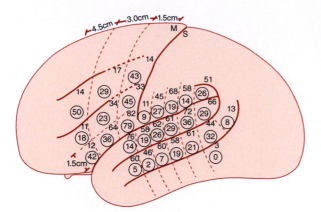

Figure 2.24   Group results for the 117 patients in Ojemann et al.'s (1989b) electrophysiological study using direct cortical stimulation. The cortex is divided into zones identified by dashed lines. In each zone, the upper number indicates how many patients were stimulated in that area, and the lower circled number indicates the percentage of patients for whom stimulation caused significant naming impairment. (From Ojemann et al., 1989b, p. 415.)

- dissociations between language production and comprehension (Boatman et al., 2000; see Figure 5.12 and the accompanying text in Chapter 5);
- dissociations between consonants and vowels (Boatman et al., 1995, 1997);
- dissociations between nouns and verbs (Corina et al., 2005);
- dissociations between various types of object naming errors (Corina et al., 2010; see Figure 6.11 and the accompanying text in Chapter 6);
- dissociations between object naming from pictures and object naming from spoken definitions (Hamberger et al., 2007).

It has been claimed that direct electrical stimulation is "the gold standard for brain mapping" (Mandonnet et al., 2010, p. 185; see also Desmurget et al., 2013). But it is crucial to bear in mind that despite its many virtues, this technique has several nontrivial limitations, especially when it is employed for research rather than clinical purposes (Borchers et al., 2012). Perhaps the most serious problem is that the physiological changes that are caused by passing a current through the cortex are still poorly understood. This problem is manifested in a variety of ways. For example, as mentioned above, stimulation usually has negative cognitive and behavioral effects, but sometimes it has positive effects, and experts are not yet able to predict which of these two contradictory outcomes will occur when certain sites are stimulated. In addition, the intensity of stimulation that is required to identify "eloquent" areas varies considerably not only across different patients, but also

across different regions within the same patient (Pouratian et al., 2004). Finally, studies that have combined direct electrical stimulation with other brain mapping methods have shown that the effects of stimulation are by no means restricted to the given site, but can propagate to remote regions in other gyri (Ishitobi et al., 2000; Matsumoto et al., 2004; Suh et al., 2006; Garell et al., 2013). Taken together, these concerns suggest that while direct electrical stimulation can definitely help to illuminate the neural circuitry underlying language and other mental capacities, the results of experiments that draw upon this technique should always be interpreted with caution.

Recording
Intracranial

In neurosurgical settings involving severely epileptic patients, it is possible to not only measure the effects of stimulating various brain areas, but also record the neural activity occurring in particular regions. In fact, this type of direct intracranial recording serves a vital clinical purpose, since it enables doctors to precisely localize the source of seizures. The standard procedure is to first implant electrodes in the tissue that is suspected to encompass the epileptogenic site, and then close the patient's head and record neural activity continuously for several days, so that when seizures occur spontaneously, their point of origin can be identified quite accurately, just as seismographs can reveal the source of an earthquake. Because such situations also provide rare opportunities to learn more about human functional neuroanatomy, researchers are sometimes allowed to conduct studies with the patient. These studies are usually designed to determine whether—and, if so, exactly how—the firing rates of neurons in the implanted tissue are modulated by carefully manipulated experimental variables. In some cases, neural activity is sampled at the level of single cells; in other cases, it is sampled at the level of cell assemblies that span several millimeters. These two types of data differ in many ways, but both of them carry important clues about the hidden workings of the human brain (see Engel et al., 2005, for a review of intracranial recording techniques and the kinds of results they can generate).

So far, very few studies have attempted to determine how the activity of single cells in particular parts of the brain may be related to the processing of specific aspects of language. But the handful of studies that have begun to address this challenging topic have yielded some very intriguing results. A nice example comes from an investigation by Creutzfeldt et al. (1989a) which found that individual neurons in the right superior temporal gyrus seem to be sensitive to certain features of auditorily perceived

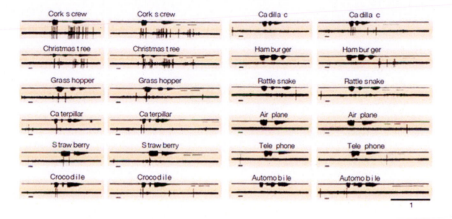

Figure 2.25   Results from Creutzfeldt et al.'s (1989a) single-cell recording study. The patient listened to a list of words twice, with the second presentation occurring 2 minutes after the first. After the second presentation of each word, the patient repeated it. Each panel in the figure shows, from top to bottom, the name of the word, the audio trace, and the recorded activity of a single cell in the right superior temporal gyrus. Note that the cell responds significantly more to both presentations of the words on the left than to both presentations of the words on the right. The horizontal lines below the audio trace after the second presentation of each word indicate the patient's repetition of the word. The short line to the left of the recorded activity indicates a 1000-Hz tone that preceded the word. (From Engel et al., 2005, p. 40; original version in Creutzfeldt et al., 1989a, p. 457.)

words, such as their phonemic, syllabic, or morphological structure. (In Chapters 5 and 7 we will encounter further evidence that speech perception recruits not only the left but also the right hemisphere.) For instance, as shown in Figure 2.25, when the patient listened to a list of multisyllabic words, the firing rate of one cell increased significantly in response to a restricted range of speech sounds. The most critical sounds appeared to be the velar consonants /k/ and /g/, especially in combination with either /r/ or /s/, as in the words *corkscrew*, *Christmas tree*, *grasshopper*, *caterpillar*, and *crocodile*. Interestingly, when the entire list of words was presented again after a two-minute interval, the cell's response to each word was similar to its response on the first occasion. The precise representational tuning properties of this cell remain unclear, however, because the researchers did not go on to investigate the issue more systematically (see Chan et al., in press, for a recent study that was methodologically more sophisticated).

A comparatively larger number of studies have recorded the **local field potentials**—i.e., the summed extracellular voltage fluctuations—of entire ensembles of cells while patients perform various linguistic tasks. One method for doing this is to employ depth electrodes that penetrate through many layers of cortex and white matter, sometimes targeting subcortical nuclei (e.g., Sahin et al., 2009; see Figures 13.3, 13.4, 13.5, 13.7 and the accompanying text in Chapter 13; see also Chan et al.,

2011). A more common strategy, however, is to use a high-density multi-electrode grid that is placed directly over the cortical surface to enable a type of data acquisition and analysis called **electrocorticography**.

An excellent illustration of this approach is a recent study by Flinker et al. (2011) that explored the spatially fine-grained cortical dynamics of speech perception in three epileptic patients, each of whom had a 64-contact 8 × 8 electrode array (4 mm inter-electrode spacing) placed over the posterior lateral surface of the left superior temporal gyrus (see also Chang et al., 2010). Each subject listened attentively to two types of stimuli: first, synthesized versions of the syllables /ba/, /da/, and /ga/, each approximately 150 ms in duration; and second, three kinds of words spoken by the same talker and controlled for phonotactic probabilities—specifically, 23 pseudowords (three phonemes in length), 23 real words (three phonemes in length), and four proper names (five phonemes in length). As shown in Figure 2.26, at some of the electrode sites high-frequency (>70 Hz) neural activity was recorded in response to both phonemes and words, starting within a time window of 200 ms; at other sites, however, such activity was found to be elicited much more robustly, and in some cases selectively, by words. In addition, many of the word-specific sites were like islands surrounded by sites only 4 mm away that were sensitive to both types of stimuli. From a methodological perspective, these findings

Local field potentials Extracellular voltage fluctuations that reflect the sum of events in the dendrites of a local population of neurons.

Electrocorticography A technique for acquiring and analyzing data from electrode grids placed directly over the cortex.

A

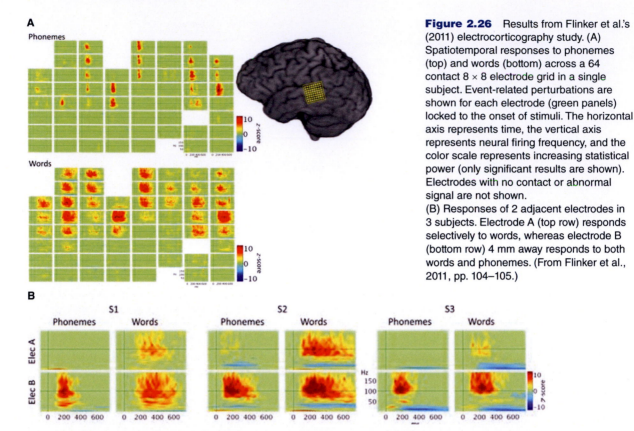

Figure 2.26   Results from Flinker et al.'s (2011) electrocorticography study. (A) Spatiotemporal responses to phonemes (top) and words (bottom) across a 64 contact 8 × 8 electrode grid in a single subject. Event-related perturbations are shown for each electrode (green panels) locked to the onset of stimuli. The horizontal axis represents time, the vertical axis represents neural firing frequency, and the color scale represents increasing statistical power (only significant results are shown). Electrodes with no contact or abnormal signal are not shown.
(B) Responses of 2 adjacent electrodes in 3 subjects. Electrode A (top row) responds selectively to words, whereas electrode B (bottom row) 4 mm away responds to both words and phonemes. (From Flinker et al., 2011, pp. 104–105.)

exemplify how electrocorticography can reveal remarkably detailed aspects of the functional neuroanatomy of language; and from a theoretical perspective, they converge with other data pointing to a hierarchical organization of receptive speech processing in the superior temporal cortex (for further information see Chapter 5).

Extracranial

Although the electrical potentials produced by relatively small cell assemblies are rather weak, those produced by large populations of simultaneously active neurons are strong enough to be conducted passively through the tissues of the brain, skull, and scalp. Hence it is possible to record widely distributed patterns of activity in a noninvasive manner by placing electrodes on the surface of the scalp and comparing the voltage fluctuations measured there with those measured at certain reference locations, like the mastoid bones behind the ears. The resulting plot of continuously changing voltages—one trace for each scalp electrode—is called the **electroencephalogram (EEG)**. Originally discovered in 1929, it is characterized by rhythmic undulations that vary in both amplitude and

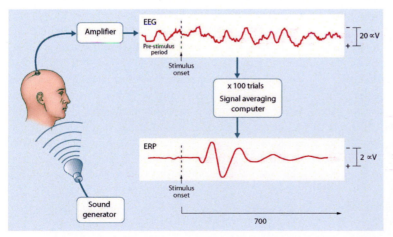

Figure 2.27   The large background oscillations of the EEG trace make it impossible to detect the evoked response to the sensory stimulus from a single trial. Averaging across tens or hundreds of trials, however, removes the background EEG, leaving the event-related potential (ERP). Note the difference in scale between the EEG and ERP waveforms. (From Gazzaniga et al., 2009, p. 149.)

Cortical surface

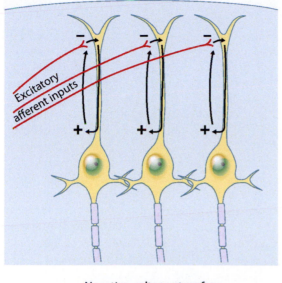

Negative voltage at surface

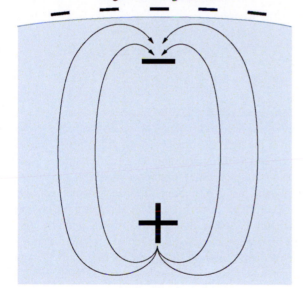

Figure 2.28 Dipole orientation as a source of ERP polarity. (Top) The long axes of these three neurons are perpendicular to the cortical surface. Each neuron is receiving an excitatory synaptic input at its dendrite, and the resulting postsynaptic potential causes the current to flow toward the cell body. This pattern produces an electrical field or "dipole" with the negative pole at the dendrite and the positive pole near the cell body. (Bottom) The electrical fields of the cells summate and are manifested as a predominantly negative voltage at the surface. (From Gazzaniga et al., 2009, p. 151.)

Electroencephalogram (EEG) A recording of the continuous electrical activity of the brain, derived from one or more electrodes on the scalp.

duration, depending on whether the subject is excited, relaxed, drowsy, or in a particular stage of sleep. Because the ongoing EEG profile reflects what Luck (2005, p. 4) calls "a mixed up conglomeration of hundreds of different neural sources of activity," it does not by itself provide much information about linguistic processes or other kinds of mental operations. Researchers can, however, probe the neural correlates of specific cognitive capacities by examining how the EEG traces recorded at different electrode sites are modulated during the performance of tasks in response to carefully controlled experimental stimuli. When this is done, the observed EEG effects are referred to as **event-related potentials (ERPs)**, as sketched in Figure 2.27 (Kappenman & Luck, 2012).

ERPs are multidimensional measures of brain activity, since they vary along four distinct parameters:

- *Latency:* The time point, in milliseconds poststimulus onset, when a particular deflection of the waveform either begins or reaches its peak.
- *Amplitude:* The strength of an effect, in terms of microvolts.
- *Polarity:* Whether a deflection is positive-going or negative-going.
- *Topography:* The scalp distribution of an effect, which involves the electrode positions at which it is observed.

With regard to polarity, most labs plot negative up and positive down (see Figure 2.27 once again), but some adopt the opposite convention, so one should always take note of which approach is being used in a given study. It is also important to realize that whether a waveform deviates positively or negatively is usually not of any cognitive significance in and of itself. This is because polarity depends largely on a host of functionally irrelevant factors, including the location of the reference electrodes and the orientation of the intracerebral sources of the scalp-recorded signals (Otten & Rugg, 2005). For instance, as indicated in Figure 2.28, if a population of cortical neurons happen to be oriented so that their dendrites point toward the surface, and if these neurons simultaneously receive a substantial amount of excitatory input, the resulting electrophysiological activity creates a set of current "dipoles," each of which has a negative end near the dendrites and a positive end near the cell body. The summation of these dipoles is then expressed at the scalp as a predominantly negative voltage. Clearly, however, this

Event-related potentials (ERPs) EEG patterns that are time-locked with the presentation of stimuli.

Box 2.2   Magnetoencephalography

Magnetoencephalography (MEG) is a noninvasive brain mapping technique closely related to the EEG/ERP approach (Ionnides, 2007). The electrical currents associated with neural activity generate tiny magnetic fields, and these fields can be recorded at the scalp and time-locked to the presentation of stimuli, yielding what are commonly called event-related fields (ERFs). In modern MEG systems, ERFs are detected by massive arrays of over 200 sensors known as "superconducting quantum interference devices" (SQUIDS). Compared to the EEG/ERP approach, the MEG/ERF approach has both advantages and disadvantages. On the positive side, it not only provides outstanding millisecond-level temporal resolution, but also affords relatively precise spatial resolution—good enough to allow neurosurgeons to identify the focus of seizures in epileptic patients (Tovar-Spinoza et al., 2008). This localizing capacity is possible because magnetic fields are not distorted as they pass through the brain, skull, and scalp, and moreover their strength falls off from their source in a systematic manner. On the negative side, although MEG is quite sensitive to neural activity in sulci, it is not very sensitive to neural activity in gyri. In addition, MEG systems are terribly expensive, and as a result there are not many labs around the world. The main reason for the high cost is that ERFs are extremely small signals—in the range of 50-100 femtoteslas, which is one-billionth the size of the earth's magnetic field—so the recording apparatus requires a special room to serve as a shield against all external magnetic fields (from the earth, sun, microwaves, everyday buildings, etc.). In addition, the SQUIDS must be encased in cylinders containing liquid helium. Due to these drawbacks, MEG has unfortunately not been used as much as the other methods to study the neural substrates of language. Still, the frequency of published studies employing this impressive technique has been rapidly increasing. For some representative papers see Cogan and Poeppel (2011), MacGregor et al. (2012), Brennan and Pylkkänen (2012), Moseley et al. (2013), and Almeida and Poeppel (in press).

outcome does not in any way reflect the computational operations being carried out by the neurons, since it is just a consequence of the more or less arbitrary orientation of the neurons vis-á-vis the scalp. On the other hand, because most ERP studies involve systematic comparisons between the waveforms elicited by an experimental condition and those elicited by a control condition, any differences that emerge along the dimension of polarity *do* have potential implications for cognitive processes. The key point, though, is that in such situations what matters is simply that polarity differences are present, and not whether they are realized as positive-going or negative-going effects. (As an aside, it is worth noting that sometimes the specific direction of an ERP effect does turn out to correlate with a specific experimental variable, but such outcomes are usually fortuitous. For instance, see Figure 5.10 and the accompanying text in Chapter 5.)

A few remarks are also in order regarding topography. Studies vary greatly with respect to the number of electrodes that are used, with arrays ranging in size from 16 to 32, 64, 128, 160, and 256. As the size of the array increases, so does the discriminability of ERP effects along the dimension of scalp distribution. In addition, the larger the array of channels, the easier it is to apply special forms of data analysis that allow researchers to infer, at least approximately, the underlying neural generators of ERP

effects (e.g., see Box 6.5 in Chapter 6). Even with relatively large electrode arrays, however, the spatial resolution of the ERP technique is always rather poor, especially compared to its outstanding temporal resolution. This is due to a fundamental limitation known as the "inverse problem." Basically, a given distribution of electrical activity recorded at the scalp could, in principle, have emerged from any of several different sets of neural generators in the brain. (See, however, Box 2.2 for a brief description of an alternative method that measures the magnetic counterpart of ERPs and that has better spatial resolution.)

To get a sense of how this method can shed light on language, let's briefly consider a classic ERP component—the N400. This component consists of a negativity—hence the "N"—that peaks about 400 ms post-stimulus onset—hence the "400"—with the greatest amplitude over centroparietal electrode sites. It was first reported by Kutas and Hillyard (1980) well over 30 years ago, and since then it has been the focus of over 1,000 articles (for reviews see Kutas & Federmeier, 2000, 2011; Hagoort, 2008; Lau et al., 2008). Very roughly, the N400 can be said to track the gradual build-up of semantic content during receptive sentence processing, such that its amplitude increases in proportion to the degree of difficulty of integrating the meaning of a word into the preceding context. This is shown in Figure 2.29, which is based on Kutas and

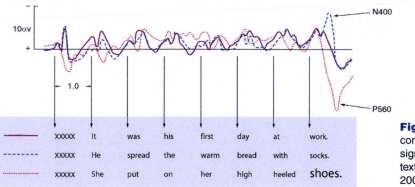

——	XXXXX	It	was	his	first	day	at	work.
- - - -	XXXXX	He	spread	the	warm	bread	with	socks.
········	XXXXX	She	put	on	her	high	heeled	shoes.

Figure 2.29 The N400 ERP component is an electrophysiological signature of semantic processing. See the text for details. (From Gazzaniga et al., 2009, p. 436.)

Hillyard's (1980) seminal study, and which depicts the waveforms evoked by three different types of sentences presented to subjects visually on a computer screen, one word at a time. In the first condition, all of the sentences were completely normal—e.g., *It was his first day at work.* In the second condition, all of the sentences ended with a word that was semantically anomalous in the given context—e.g., *He spread the warm bread with socks.* And in the third condition, all of the sentences ended with a word that was orthographically incongruous in the given context—e.g., *She put on her high heeled SHOES.* As indicated in the diagram, relative to the final word in the normal condition, the final word in the anomalous condition triggered a large N400. Interestingly, this effect appears to be a signature of effortful conceptual processing, as opposed to an index of general surprise, because it was not elicited by the final word in the condition involving orthographic violations; instead, the latter condition was associated with a P560, which differs from the N400 along the dimensions of both polarity and latency. The unique properties of the N400 are discussed in greater detail in Chapter 15, together with several other language-related ERP components.

Transcranial Magnetic Stimulation

As described above, the electrophysiological technique of directly stimulating specific parts of the brain has led to many interesting discoveries about the neural underpinnings of language. But because this method is extremely invasive and is restricted to individuals with a history of neurological dysfunction, its utility is very limited. In 1985 the state of play in research on brain stimulation changed dramatically when a new non-invasive way to "zap" the nervous systems of normal individuals was introduced by Barker et al. (1985). Referred to as transcranial magnetic stimulation (TMS), this brain mapping method allows investigators

to rapidly alter the organization of neural activity in particular cortical regions by placing a special kind of magnetic device on the overlying scalp. The parameters of the protocol can be adjusted so that one can either facilitate or suppress the operation of the target area. And as long as certain safety guidelines and precautions are followed, the technique is usually harmless, with only a very small possibility of seizures. In fact, it is now known that TMS can be used therapeutically to help offset several types of clinical disorders, including stroke-induced aphasia (e.g., Naeser et al., 2010, 2011; Barwood et al., 2011; Weiduschat et al., 2011). For these and other reasons, TMS has become increasingly popular since it first arrived on the scene, and it is now a mainstay of cognitive neuroscience, being used quite widely to study language and many other mental abilities (for recent overviews of the technique see O'Shea & Walsh, 2006; Hallett, 2007; Wassermann et al., 2008; Bolognini & Ro, 2010; Sandrini et al., 2011; see also the 2012 collection of articles called "Brain stimulation and language" in the journal *Aphasiology,* volume 26, issue 9).

How It Works

TMS is based on a fundamental principle of electromagnetic induction that is nicely summarized by O'Shea and Walsh (2006, p. R196) as follows:

> Michael Faraday showed that when an electrical current is passed through a wire, it generates a time-varying magnetic field. If a second wire is placed nearby, the magnetic field induces electrical current flow in that second wire. In TMS, the "first wire" is the stimulating coil and the "second wire" is a targeted region of the brain.

Several different coil designs are now on the market, but the most commonly used type has a figure-eight shape in which currents flow around two adjacent

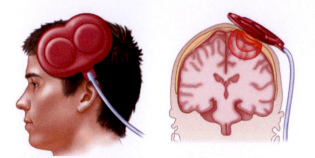

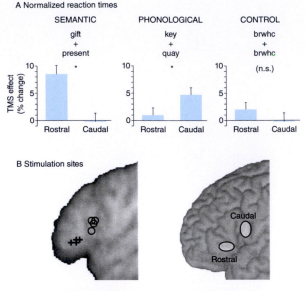

Figure 2.30 In TMS, a figure-8 coil is placed against the subject's scalp. The coil creates a magnetic field that is projected through the skull and into the target site in the underlying brain tissue, thereby altering the electrophysiological properties of the cells. (From Purves et al., 2008, p. 63.)

Figure 2.31 Results from Gough et al.'s (2005) TMS study. (A) The bar-plots represent the mean TMS effects (and standard errors) as percent change in reaction times from the non-TMS baseline during synonym judgments (left), rhyme judgments (middle), and visual judgments (right), with significant differences between stimulation sites indicated by an asterisk. (B) The left panel shows the locations of stimulation sites for 4 subjects plotted on their mean structural image, with rostral locations indicated by crosses and caudal locations indicated by circles. The right panel shows a 3D rendering of the stimulation sites, with ovals representing the 85% confidence intervals. Stimulation sites were on average 2.5 cm apart on the cortical surface. (From Devlin & Watkins, 2007, p. 617.)

circular components and summate at their point of intersection. The flux lines of the resulting magnetic field are oriented perpendicular to the plane of the coil, so that when the central part of the coil is placed at a predetermined position on the scalp, the magnetic field passes through the skull and temporarily changes the electrophysiological properties of the neurons in the underlying cortical region, as depicted in Figure 2.30.

The temporal resolution of TMS is in the order of milliseconds, since each pulse is quite brief, and the spatial resolution of the technique is in the order of millimeters, since each pulse is quite focal. For example, by shifting the coil between areas separated by 0.5–1.0 cm over the primary motor cortex, it is possible to evoke muscle twitches selectively in the face, fingers, hand, arm, trunk, and leg in a manner that conforms to the spatial layout of the motor homunculus (see Figure 1.25 in Chapter 1). In fact, researchers sometimes use the intensity threshold for triggering a finger twitch in a particular subject as a benchmark for calibrating the strength of pulses to be delivered to other regions involved in higher-level cognitive processes. Two different strategies are frequently used, either independently or in combination, to determine the most appropriate position of the coil in a given study. Functional localization involves moving the coil around a general territory until the ability of interest is either enhanced or disrupted, whereas anatomical localization involves using a neuronavigation system to guide the placement of the coil according to data acquired from structural and/or functional MRI scans,

or according to a set of standardized coordinates. Regardless of how accurately the coil position is identified, however, it must be acknowledged that, as with direct electrical stimulation, the effects of TMS can spread to remote brain regions, making it impossible to conclude with absolute certainty that any behavioral consequences are due to altered activity in just the target area (Sieber et al., 2009).

Whether the neurophysiological changes induced by TMS are facilitatory or inhibitory depends on a host of factors that have not yet been fully elucidated, but one critical parameter is the frequency of the pulses. For instance, O'Shea and Walsh (2006, p. R196) point out that "two single pulses separated by less than 5 milliseconds can produce intracortical inhibition, while two single pulses separated by a gap greater than 10 milliseconds and less than 30 milliseconds can produce intracortical facilitation." These and other types of short pulse sequences can be applied to subjects "online"—that is, during task performance. Other forms of TMS, however, are intended to be used "offline"—that is, prior to task performance. One widely used technique is to deliver repetitive trains of pulses to a target site continuously for several minutes before a task is performed. This reduces the excitability of the region for a period of time after the stimulation has stopped, so that the effects on subsequent task performance can be assessed. Usually the cognitive consequences of TMS are manifested as changes in reaction time, but sometimes they are manifested as changes in accuracy.

Applications to Language

TMS has been used to explore the neural substrates of numerous aspects of language, and several studies addressing topics as diverse as speech perception, verb meaning, and inflectional morphology are featured later in this book (for reviews covering the first major wave of TMS research in the language domain, see Devlin & Watkins, 2007, 2008, and for a captivating video of TMS-induced speech arrest, go to www.youtube.com/watch?v=XJtNPqCj-iA).

To gain some initial understanding and appreciation of how TMS can illuminate the functional architecture of language-related brain regions, consider the following investigation by Gough et al. (2005) that helped reveal the complementary roles of two different sectors of the left inferior frontal gyrus (LIFG)—rostral (i.e., pars orbitalis) and caudal (i.e., pars opercularis)—in making semantic and phonological judgments. The subjects in this experiment performed three tasks with visually presented pairs of letter strings:

- Synonym judgment—e.g., deciding whether *idea* and *notion* have the same meaning.
- Rhyme judgment—e.g., deciding whether *eye* and *fly* end with the same sound.
- Visual judgment—e.g., deciding whether *txbufr* and *txbufr* contain the same characters.

The procedure consisted of 15 pseudo-randomly organized blocks of 10 trials, with the trials in each block involving the same type of task. On 40 percent of the trials, three TMS pulses, separated by 100 ms and starting 100 ms post-stimulus onset, were delivered to either the rostral or the caudal sector of the LIFG.

Importantly, the procedure was constrained to ensure that there were an equal number of TMS trials for each task and that no more than two TMS trials occurred consecutively.

As indicated in Figure 2.31, a striking double dissociation emerged between the semantic and phonological tasks as a function of the site of stimulation. In particular, judgments about the meanings of word pairs were significantly delayed by rostral LIFG stimulation but not by caudal LIFG stimulation, relative to when no stimulation was administered. And conversely, judgments about the sounds of word pairs were significantly delayed by caudal LIFG stimulation but not by rostral LIFG stimulation, again relative to when no stimulation was administered. Finally, judgments about the appearances of letter strings were unaffected by stimulation at either site. Overall, then, Gough et al.'s (2005) study converges with other research in suggesting that the two target areas in the LIFG make different contributions to lexical processing (see also Katzev et al., 2013). From a methodological point of view, it is worth emphasizing that these areas are less than three centimeters apart, since this nicely exemplifies the potential of TMS to differentially modify the activity of brain regions that are anatomically quite close together.

Major Strengths and Weaknesses of the Different Methods

As mentioned in the Introduction, it is important to bear in mind that none of the brain mapping methods provides a perfectly clear window onto the functional–anatomical organization of the nervous system, since each one has its own unique merits and shortcomings. Table 2.5 brings together in a single convenient place a list of all the major methods, together with a comparative summary of their chief strengths and weaknesses. Even a cursory perusal of this "score-card" should be enough to convince most readers that the deepest insights about the neural substrates of language and other cognitive capacities will ultimately require not only careful experiments that capitalize on the distinctive virtues of specific techniques, but also integrative studies that attempt to synthesize the findings from many different approaches (Shallice & Cooper, 2011).

Table 2.5 Major Strengths and Weaknesses of the Different Brain Mapping Methods Covered in This Chapter

Method	Strengths	Weaknesses
Neuropsychology	a. Can reveal the componential architecture of cognitive systems b. Can reveal which neural structures are essential for certain abilities	a. Case studies may lack generalizability b. Group studies may lack sufficient uniformity across patients c. Deficit–lesion correspondences may be unreliable if the possibilities of functional–anatomical reorganization, hypoperfusion, and diaschisis are not taken into account
Functional neuroimaging: PET	a. Good spatial resolution (roughly 10 mm)	a. Requires radioactive isotopes b. Poor temporal resolution (30 s at best)
Functional neuroimaging: fMRI	a. Good spatial resolution (3 mm or less, depending on magnet strength and other factors) b. Temporal resolution can be at the scale of the hemodynamic response function (10-12 s) or better (as good as 50-100 ms). c. Widely available	a. Cannot be used with individuals who have metal in their bodies b. Noisy scanning environment c. BOLD signal tends to be distorted near air-filled cavities
Electrophysiology: Stimulation	a. Can reveal causal links between neural activity and cognitive processing b. Spatial resolution can be less than a centimeter c. Temporal resolution can be less than a second	a. Limited to neurosurgical settings involving individuals with a history of neurological dysfunction b. The neurophysiological changes induced by direct stimulation are still poorly understood c. The effects of stimulation can propagate to remote regions
Electrophysiology: Intracranial recording	a. Single-cell recording can reveal the unique response properties of particular neurons b. Electrocorticography can reveal correlations between cognitive processing and local field potentials at the sub-centimeter spatial scale and millisecond temporal scale	a. Limited to neurosurgical settings involving individuals with a history of neurological dysfunction
Electrophysiology: Extracranial recording (ERPs)	a. Excellent temporal resolution in the order of milliseconds b. Multidimensional data varying in latency, amplitude, polarity, and topography	a. Difficult to determine the underlying neural generators of the signals recorded at the scalp b. Difficult to detect the activity of cells oriented parallel to the scalp
Transcranial magnetic stimulation	a. Can reveal causal links between neural activity and cognitive processing b. Good spatial resolution (roughly 5 mm) c. Excellent temporal resolution (a few milliseconds) d. Can be used therapeutically to treat clinical syndromes	a. Small chance of seizures. b. Restricted to brain regions near the surface c. The effects of stimulation can propagate to remote regions

Summary and Key Points

Neuropsychology

- Two main goals:

  - Determine which components of the language faculty can be selectively disrupted.
  - Identify reliable links between specific linguistic deficits and specific lesion sites.

- The most valuable kinds of neuropsychological data are dissociations:

  - A *single dissociation* occurs when patient A performs significantly worse on task *X* than on task *Y*.
  - A *double dissociation* occurs when patient A performs significantly worse on task *X* than on task *Y*, and patient B performs significantly worse on task *Y* than on task *X*.

- In-depth case studies of individual patients are useful for documenting unusual types of dissociations, but large-scale group studies are essential for establishing reliable deficit–lesion correlations.
- The most common method for obtaining structural images of healthy and injured brains is *magnetic resonance imaging (MRI).*
- Language deficits are often caused by four types of brain damage:

  - stroke;
  - traumatic brain injury (closed head TBI or open head TBI);
  - neurodegenerative and infectious diseases;
  - tumors.

- There are two widely used techniques for analyzing deficit–lesion correlations in group studies:

  - In *lesion overlap and subtraction analysis,* the superimposed lesion sites of patients with a particular deficit are contrasted against the superimposed lesion sites of patients without the deficit, so that the brain image resulting from this subtraction reveals the areas of damage that are linked specifically with the deficit.
  - In *voxel-based lesion–symptom mapping*, for each voxel the behavioral performances of patients with damage at that locus are statistically compared with those of patients without damage at that locus, so that the results indicate the degree to which damage in particular regions disrupts the ability of interest.

- Several caveats should be kept in mind when studying deficit–lesion correlations:

  - To conclude that a given deficit is caused by damage to a given region, one must show not only that patients with the deficit tend to have lesions at that site, but also that patients with lesions at that site tend to have the deficit.
  - Patterns of impaired and preserved abilities may be influenced in part by functional–anatomical reorganization after lesion onset.
  - Some deficits may be due in part to *hypoperfusion* (i.e., areas that receive enough blood supply to survive but not enough to operate normally) and/or *diaschisis* (i.e., areas that are structurally intact but functionally abnormal because they no longer receive appropriate input from other areas that have been damaged).

Functional neuroimaging

- Functional neuroimaging methods are *hemodynamic* because they rely on the principle that when a cognitive task engages a particular brain area, that area rapidly receives a surplus of freshly oxygenated blood.
- Two main techniques:

  - *Positron emission tomography (PET)* tracks the distribution of a radioactive isotope through the blood vessels of the brain.
  - *Functional magnetic resonance imaging (fMRI)* measures the *blood oxygenation level dependent (BOLD)* signal, which is typically manifested as a *hemodynamic response function* lasting roughly 10–12 seconds.

- Significant areas of activation are often reported in terms of the common space of voxels of a standard brain template, with those voxels defined according to three-dimensional *x,y,z* coordinates.
- Two main designs:

  - In a *block design*, stimuli from the same condition are presented consecutively together. This type of design is possible for both PET and fMRI.
  - In an *event-related design*, stimuli from one condition are randomly interspersed with stimuli from another condition. This type of design is possible for fMRI but not PET.

- Three main experimental paradigms:

  - In the *subtraction paradigm,* the activity evoked during a control condition is subtracted from the activity evoked during an experimental condition.
  - In the *correlation paradigm*, the subjects first perform a series of tasks that recruit a particular cognitive capacity to different degrees, and then the researchers search for brain regions that are correspondingly activated to different degrees.
  - In *multivariate pattern analysis*, fMRI data are processed in a manner that can show how different spatially distributed patterns of activity across the same set of voxels are related to different experimental conditions and hence to different mental representations and/or operations.

(Continued)

(Continued)

Electrophysiology

- Direct electrical stimulation of the exposed cortex of neurosurgical patients can reveal language-related regions by temporarily interfering with naming and other abilities. For example, classic research by Ojemann et al. (1989b) suggests that most people have a small number of fairly focal "naming sites" that vary substantially in their precise anatomical positions within the left perisylvian territory.
- Intracranial recording techniques are sometimes used to measure neural activity at the level of single cells, but more often they are used to measure neural activity at the level of cell assemblies. A frequently used method is *electrocorticography*, which involves placing a high-density multi-electrode grid over the cortical surface, so that the *local field potentials* of cell assemblies can be measured with sub-centimeter spatial resolution and millisecond temporal resolution while the patient performs various linguistic tasks.
- Extracranial recording techniques usually involve placing an array of electrodes on the scalp, so that the *event-related potentials (ERPs)* evoked by different experimental conditions can be tracked along the dimensions of latency, amplitude, polarity, and topography.

Transcranial magnetic stimulation (TMS)

- TMS alters the organization of neural activity in a target cortical area by projecting a magnetic field through the overlying skull.
- The temporal resolution is in the order of milliseconds, since each pulse is quite brief, and the spatial resolution is in the order of millimeters, since each pulse is quite focal.
- The parameters of the protocol—including, most importantly, the frequency of the pulses—can be adjusted so that one can either facilitate or suppress the operation of the target region.

Recommended Reading

- Rapp, B. (Ed.) (2001). *The handbook of cognitive neuropsychology: What deficits reveal about the human mind.* Philadelphia, PA: Psychology Press. A splendid, albeit now rather dated, overview of cognitive neuropsychology, with chapters by leading researchers covering theoretical and methodological issues as well as experimental discoveries in a variety of domains, including language.
- Wassermann, E.M., Epstein, C.M., Ziemann, U., Walsh, V., Paus, T., & Lisanby, S.H. (Eds.) (2008). *The Oxford handbook of transcranial magnetic stimulation.* Oxford, UK: Oxford University Press. An excellent collection of chapters about TMS, with one chapter focusing specifically on language.
- Huettel, S.A., Song, A.W., & McCarthy, G. (2009). *Functional magnetic resonance imaging,* 2nd edition. Sunderland, MA: Sinauer. An outstanding textbook about fMRI.
- Luck, S.J., & Kappenman, E.S. (Eds.) (2012). *The Oxford handbook of event-related potential components.* Oxford, UK: Oxford University Press. An excellent collection of chapters about ERP components, with one chapter focusing specifically on language.

PART II

Aphasia

Classic Aphasia Syndromes

3

APHASIA

His signs flick off.
His names of birds
and his beautiful words—
eleemosynary, fir, cinerarium, reckless—
skip like pearls from a snapped necklace
scattering over linoleum.

His thinking won't
venture out of his mouth.
His grammar heads south.
Pathetic his subjunctives; just as pathetic
his mangling the emphatic enclitic
he once was the master of.

Still, all in all, he has
his inner weather of pure meaning,
though the wind is keening
through his Alps and his clouds hang low
and the forecast is "Rain mixed with snow,
heavy at times."

—Vijay Seshadri (2004)

Introduction

The first significant discoveries about the neural substrates of language came from research on **aphasia** over 150 years ago, and sophisticated clinical and experimental studies of aphasia continue to this day to provide important insights about how language is implemented in the brain. What exactly is aphasia? In simple terms, it is an impairment of the ability to produce, comprehend, or repeat language that results from an acquired brain injury, such as a stroke, tumor, head injury, or progressive degenerative disease. Regarding language production, some aphasic patients have great difficulty retrieving words for objects or actions; others have trouble expressing words in phonologically correct ways; and still others struggle with the grammatical structures of words, phrases, and sentences. Regarding language comprehension, aphasic patients may also manifest a variety of deficits, including impairments of phoneme perception, word recognition, and syntactic parsing. And regarding language repetition, many aphasic patients are impaired at reproducing sentences that are said to them, and some cannot even imitate single words accurately. Analogous disorders of production, comprehension, and repetition are found in aphasic patients who use sign language rather than spoken language (see Chapter 9). It is noteworthy, however, that the definition of aphasia given above rules out language disturbances that have congenital causes, such as genetically or environmentally induced perinatal brain disorders. It also excludes the following types of neurological conditions: hearing problems that arise from injury to the earliest stages of auditory processing; articulatory deficits that reflect damage to relatively low-level mechanisms for controlling the vocal apparatus; akinetic mutism, in which the patient may be completely immobile and silent; and confusional or psychotic states, in which the patient may generate abnormal language (A.R. Damasio, 1998). Aphasia, then, applies only to impairments that directly affect the linguistic system, and that are acquired as a

Aphasia An acquired language deficit due to brain injury.

consequence of brain injury after the individual has attained an appropriate level of linguistic competence. The National Aphasia Association estimates that 25–40 percent of stroke survivors develop aphasia. It also estimates that there are roughly one million persons in the United States with aphasia, and that roughly 100,000 new cases occur each year. Needless to say, the worldwide statistics are vastly greater.

This chapter provides an overview of some of the most common and well-studied forms of aphasia. It begins by setting the historical context for this area of research, and then it addresses the question of how aphasia syndromes should be defined and distinguished from each other. Next, eight classic aphasia syndromes are summarized, and for each one, emphasis is placed on the following features: production, comprehension, repetition, and lesion correlates. After reviewing the eight syndromes in detail, a flow chart is presented that can serve as a quick and easy, but also overly simplistic, guide for identifying each type of aphasia.

Historical Background

Links between language loss and brain damage initially appeared in the Hippocratic writings of the 5th century BC, but the scientific investigation of aphasia did not begin until the mid 19th century. In 1836, Marc Dax described an association between aphasia and disease of the left hemisphere in a paper called "Lesions of the left hemisphere coinciding with forgetfulness of the signs of thought" (Joynt & Benton, 1964). Unfortunately, however, he did not publish it, nor did he present it at a medical meeting. In fact, the paper would never have come to light if Marc's son, Gustav, had not drawn attention to it right after the French surgeon, anatomist, and anthropologist, Paul Broca (Figure 3.1), published a series of landmark studies between 1861 and 1865 showing, apparently for the first time, that the left hemisphere is dominant for language (for English translations of Broca's articles see Wilkins, 1964; Rottenberg & Hochberg, 1977; Berker et al., 1986; Grodzinsky & Amunts, 2006). Largely because Broca was the first to report such evidence in print, he, rather than Dax, has traditionally been credited with discovering that, as his famous dictum goes, "We speak with the left hemisphere." (For information about how the cerebral lateralization of language is partly related to handedness, see Box 3.1.)

Following quickly in Broca's footsteps, several other scientists in the late 1800s began to systematically explore the different forms that aphasia can take. Among the most influential figures was Carl Wernicke

Figure 3.1   Paul Broca (1824–1880).

(1874; Figure 3.2), who published a groundbreaking monograph when he was only 26 years old, documenting a new type of aphasia and correctly predicting the existence of several others (for an English translation see Eggert, 1977). Another important contributor was Ludwig Lichtheim (1885), who elaborated on Wernicke's ideas in significant ways. By the early 20th century, all of the major aphasia syndromes, and most of the major "hot button" points of theoretical debate, had already been identified. Nevertheless, clinical research on aphasia continued to develop during the first half of the 20th century, in part through the close examination of soldiers with head injuries in World Wars I and II. And in the second half of the 20th century, the study of aphasia advanced even further because of innovations in the neighboring disciplines of linguistics and psychology, and because of revolutions in the new fields of computational modeling and *in vivo* neuroimaging. Most valuable of all, perhaps, was the advent of high-resolution structural MRI, since it enabled significant improvements in the cerebral localization of the various aphasia syndromes. Still, apart from relatively recent findings involving the neural correlates of aphasia, researchers generally agree that the key discoveries in this area of inquiry occurred in the late 1800s and early 1900s. As Michael Alexander

Box 3.1   Handedness and Language Lateralization

Both Dax and Broca noticed that there were exceptions to the general rule of left cerebral dominance for language, and it did not escape their attention that these exceptions tended to be left-handers. Similar observations were reported later and led to the "classical doctrine of cerebral dominance," which maintained that language depends primarily on the hemisphere opposite the preferred hand. More recent research, however, has shown that the relationship between handedness and language lateralization is not nearly so straightforward.

Left-handers constitute about 11 percent of the population, but with regard to the brain organization of language, they are far more heterogeneous than right-handers. Whereas approximately 99 percent of right-handed aphasics have left-hemisphere lesions, only about 70 percent of left-handed aphasics have left-hemisphere lesions, with the remaining 30 percent having right-hemisphere lesions. Together with other findings, these patterns suggest that most left-handers are, like right-handers, left-hemisphere dominant for language, but that some are right-hemisphere dominant, and some may even have bilateral representation of language. Those left-handers with strongly bilateral language capacity may be more susceptible to aphasia, since damage to either hemisphere may induce the disorder, but at the same time they may be more likely to recover, since the unaffected hemisphere may be well-prepared to compensate.

What about the roughly 1 percent of right-handed aphasics with right-hemisphere lesions? They exhibit what is usually called "crossed aphasia," although the term "mirror image aphasia" is sometimes used. Such patients are generally regarded as having anomalous cerebral dominance for language.

For more information about handedness, cerebral asymmetries, and language lateralization, see Joanette (1990), Alexander & Annett (1996), Knecht et al. (2000a, 2000b), Coppens et al. (2002), Gonzalez & Goodale (2009), and Corballis et al. (2012).

Figure 3.2   Carl Wernicke (1848–1905).

(2002) wrote in a brief survey of aphasia similar to this one, "Much of this chapter—which reviews the basic clinical features of aphasia—could have been written 20, 50, or even 100 years ago." For more information about the history of aphasia research, see Caplan (1987), Goodglass (1993), Benson and Ardila (1996), Benton and Anderson (1998), and Hillis (2007a).

How Should Different Types of Aphasia be Classified?

Aphasia can be manifested in a tremendous variety of ways. In order to reduce this complexity, both clinicians and researchers have attempted to identify a relatively small number of aphasia **syndromes**, with a syndrome being defined (as noted in Chapter 2) as a set of symptoms that tend to co-occur statistically. Despite these efforts, however, there has never been a complete consensus about how the various kinds of aphasia should be categorized. On the contrary, ever since aphasia first began to receive serious scientific attention in the late 1800s, many diverse taxonomies have been offered (see Benson & Ardila, 1996, pp. 114–115, for a comparison of 15 competing classifications of aphasia syndromes).

Syndrome   A set of symptoms that tend to co-occur statistically.

The differences between these schemes reflect different perspectives regarding which criteria should be used to characterize the syndromes and how fine-grained those syndromes should be. For example, one of the most controversial issues in the 20th century was whether aphasia syndromes should be linguistically based, as suggested by Head (1926) and Wepman (1951), or anatomically based, as suggested by Geschwind (1965) and Luria (1970).

This chapter focuses on the classification system associated with the Boston school of aphasia, which thrived during the 1960s and 1970s under the leadership of Norman Geschwind, Harold Goodglass, and Edith Kaplan, and which trained some of world's foremost experts on aphasia. This system takes into account not only the contributions of 19th century investigators, but also the insights of modern clinicians. It captures all of the frequently encountered aphasia syndromes, as well as some less common ones, and although it relates directly to test scores obtained on the Boston Diagnostic Aphasia Examination (Goodglass & Kaplan, 1983), it can also be used in conjunction with other forms of laboratory and bedside assessment. The system distinguishes between the following eight classic syndromes: Broca's, Wernicke's, conduction, global, anomic, transcortical motor, transcortical sensory, and mixed transcortical.

Almost all of these syndromes map fairly straightforwardly onto a very simple localizationist model of the neural architecture of language that was originally proposed by Wernicke and Lichtheim in the 1880s, and later revived and further elaborated by Geschwind in the 1960s (Figure 3.3). According to this model, Broca's aphasia results from damage to the motor center (M) that subserves spoken language production; Wernicke's aphasia results from damage to the auditory center (A) that stores the "sound images" of words; conduction aphasia results from an interruption of the pathway that projects from the auditory center to the motor center; transcortical motor aphasia results from an interruption of the pathway that projects from the concept center (B) to the motor center; transcortical sensory aphasia results from an interruption of the pathway that projects from the auditory center to the concept center; mixed transcortical aphasia results from an interruption of both pathways connecting the auditory and motor centers with the concept center; and global aphasia results from damage to most or all of the whole system. These associations between particular aphasia syndromes and particular components of the model will become clearer as we explore the various syndromes in the main sections of this chapter. For

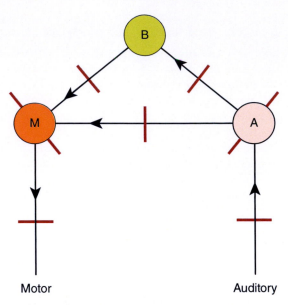

Figure 3.3   The Wernicke–Lichtheim–Geschwind "house" model of the neural architecture of language. The center for speech planning and production (Broca's area) is represented by "M." The center that stores information about word sounds (Wernicke's area) is represented by "A." The center that contains the meanings of words is represented by "B." Arrows indicate the direction of information flow. Lesion sites are represented by line segments transecting the centers and the connections between centers. (From Gazzaniga et al., 2009, p. 426.)

now, it is sufficient to note that the "house" model—as it is sometimes called because of its geometric similarity to the shape of a house—inspired a great deal of the earliest scientific research on the neural underpinnings of language. Nevertheless, it is very crude by today's standards, and in Parts III–VI of this book we will encounter a number of more advanced frameworks that are employed in contemporary theoretical and empirical research.

Before describing each of the classic aphasia syndromes in detail, it is important to consider some of the limitations that confront not only this particular classification system, but also all of the other syndrome-based approaches that have been proposed for categorizing different types of aphasia.

First, many of the criteria that are used to distinguish between the various syndromes involve entire modalities or channels of spoken language use—specifically, production, comprehension, and repetition. Such criteria are very general, however, especially when viewed from the perspective of linguistic theory, which emphasizes multiple levels of linguistic structure—phonological, morphological, syntactic, semantic, and pragmatic—that cut across the distinction between expressive and receptive processing (i.e., between production and comprehension). In addition, although the ability to repeat utterances verbatim is a major criterion for distinguishing between aphasia syndromes, this may reflect, at least to some extent, a Eurocentric bias, since word order and syntactic constituent structure play important roles in the grammatical systems of many Indo-European languages but not in those of many non-Indo-European languages. For example, normal speakers of some Australian Aboriginal languages, like Jiwarli and Warlpiri, rarely use the same word order when asked to repeat sentences, since they regard sentences with identical content words but different linear sequences as being essentially equivalent to each other (Hale, 1983, p. 5; Hale et al., 1995, p. 1431; Evans & Levinson, 2009, p. 441; for further information see the "syntax tutorial" in Chapter 14). Needless to say, however, employing repetition tasks to study aphasia can be valuable when dealing with speakers of languages like English, since most healthy individuals *do* reliably reproduce utterances verbatim when instructed to do so, thereby enabling researchers to interpret repetition errors by brain-damaged patients as indicative of some sort of impairment. Moreover, if repetition tasks are restricted to single words, they can be applied effectively not only to speakers of languages like English, but also to speakers of languages like Jiwarli and Warlpiri, since such tasks do not depend on how words are syntactically sequenced.

Second, each syndrome depends on specific symptoms being either present or absent, but the reality is that impairments of various aspects of language production, comprehension, and repetition are matters of degree rather than all-or-nothing phenomena. Take, for instance, Broca's aphasia, which is discussed in greater detail below. On the production side, the ability to generate syntactically well-formed sentences may be severely impaired in some patients but only moderately or mildly disrupted in others. Similarly, on the comprehension side, some patients may have significant trouble understanding complex utterances, whereas others may have far fewer interpretive difficulties.

Third, each syndrome is defined as a collection of symptoms that typically co-occur, but not every symptom must always be satisfied in order for the overall diagnosis to be given. For example, to continue with the syndrome of Broca's aphasia, although many patients with this disorder have apraxia of speech, not all of them do, and as discussed at length in Chapter 14, the specific manifestation of the sentence production impairment varies tremendously across patients.

Fourth, each syndrome typically involves a close connection between a set of behavioral symptoms and damage to a particular brain region or network of regions, but these deficit–lesion correlations are by no means straightforward. As an illustration, most patients with Broca's aphasia have lesions that include Broca's area—i.e., the posterior portion of the left inferior frontal gyrus. But in virtually all cases the damage extends beyond Broca's area, and in some cases it even spares that region (see Table 14.3 in Chapter 14).

Fifth, the syndromes are not necessarily stable over time, especially during the acute phase of recovery— that is, during roughly the first three months after lesion onset. For instance, a patient may initially exhibit symptoms compatible with global aphasia, but gradually shift to a behavioral profile more consistent with Broca's aphasia. Over the course of such transformations, two ostensibly distinct syndromes can blur into each other, making appropriate diagnostic decisions difficult.

These shortcomings of syndrome-based approaches to studying aphasia are not trivial. In fact, they have led some researchers to formulate compelling arguments to the effect that if one wants to use the performance of aphasic patients as a source of evidence about the detailed neural architecture of language, one should focus on specific symptoms rather than large-scale syndromes, since the former can be defined precisely, whereas the latter are too fuzzy and heterogeneous (Caramazza, 1984; Schwartz, 1984). At the same time, however, many researchers acknowledge that it would be foolhardy to throw the proverbial baby out with the bathwater. After all, the aphasia classification system described below has proven to be quite useful to clinicians for communicating effectively among themselves, for predicting the outcome of language examinations, and, in some cases, for determining the appropriateness of therapeutic interventions. Moreover, even though the deficit–lesion correlations of the classic aphasia syndromes are not perfect, they do have a fairly high degree of consistency, and any scientific theory of the neural underpinnings of language must be compatible with them.

Goodglass (1993, p. 218) has advanced the intriguing hypothesis that "the familiar syndromes of aphasia are the result of modal tendencies for the functional organization of language in adult human brains." According to this view, the relatively hard-wired neural networks that support auditory perception and motor control impose anatomical constraints on how language circuits can develop, and these constraints cause most brains to gravitate toward certain computational configurations for language, while still allowing for a fairly wide range of individual variation. Similar ideas have been discussed by Caplan

(1987, 2009). Although this line of thinking requires further development, it has the distinct virtue of being able to accommodate not only the common patterns of language breakdown that are captured by the classic aphasia syndromes, but also the deviations from these patterns that are sometimes observed.

The following summaries of the classic aphasia syndromes are intended to convey a sense of how each disorder appears in its prototypical form. It cannot be overemphasized, however, that these syndromes are by no means fixed behavioral and anatomical patterns; rather, they only reflect conspicuous similarities among patients who manifest a great deal of variation.

One final remark before proceeding. I have deliberately kept references to a minimum in the following summaries, because there is widespread agreement about most of the points that are made. Substantiation and additional details can be found in many of the references listed at the end of the chapter under "Recommended Reading." Also, many aspects of the aphasia syndromes described below are revisited in Parts III–VI of this book, where they are considered in the context other sources of evidence regarding the neurocognitive architecture of particular components of language.

Broca's Aphasia

As noted above, the founding father of aphasiology was Paul Broca. In 1861 he examined a 51-year-old man named Leborgne who had numerous medical problems and had been virtually incapable of speech for many years (Domanski, 2013). Leborgne was only able to produce a single syllable, *tan,* which he usually uttered twice in succession, regardless of the context. He could, however, vary the intonation of this sound, and he often combined it with expressive gestures. Moreover, Broca believed that Leborgne had well-preserved language comprehension. A few months later, Broca encountered another patient, Lelong, who manifested a production impairment much like Leborgne's, but who was able to utter five words instead of just one: *oui* ("yes"), *non* ("no"), *tois* ("a mispronunciation of "three"), *toujours* ("always"), and *Lelo* (a mispronunciation of his own name). At autopsy, Broca found that both patients had lesions on the surface of the left hemisphere, centered in the posterior inferior frontal gyrus. During the next four years, he reported several more patients with similar deficit–lesion correlations. The first major aphasia syndrome, which later came to be known eponymously as "Broca's aphasia," had been discovered.

Table 3.1   Prototypical Clinical Features of Broca's Aphasia

Production
Nonfluent, sometimes with apraxia of speech and/or dysarthria
Strong reliance on memorized formulaic expressions
Worse retrieval of verbs than nouns
Marked impairment of closed-class elements (e.g., determiners, auxiliary verbs, prepositions, suffixes)
Reduced syntactic complexity
Comprehension
Relatively preserved understanding of colloquial conversation
Poor comprehension of some types of syntactically complex grammatical constructions
Repetition
Disrupted, especially for multi-word sequences and closed-class items

It is now clear that Broca's two most famous patients, Leborgne and Lelong, exhibited extremely severe forms of the disorder. To be sure, all patients with Broca's aphasia have very debilitating language production deficits, but the majority of them are not as impaired as Leborgne and Lelong were. The prototypical features of this syndrome are summarized below (see Table 3.1).

Production

The spontaneous conversational speech of healthy adults is typically fluent—that is, it is produced in a continuous, flowing, effortless stream, with appropriately modulated rhythm and melody. In contrast, the verbal output of patients with Broca's aphasia is almost invariably **nonfluent**—that is, it is produced in a slow, hesitant, labored manner, with abnormal rhythm and melody. The average number of words generated per minute is greatly reduced, as is the average length of utterances. In addition, the motor programming of speech is often, but not always, impaired. When disturbances occur at the relatively high level of articulatory planning and coordination, patients manifest a disorder called **apraxia of speech**. For example, they may

Nonfluent   Speech that is slow, effortful, and halting.

Apraxia of speech   A speech production disorder that involves an impairment of articulatory planning mechanisms.

be able to produce the syllables "pa," "ta," and "ka" separately, but have difficulty combining them into the complex trisyllabic pseudoword "pataka." Speech production may also be compromised at the relatively lower level of sending specific motor commands to the muscles of the vocal apparatus. This gives rise to a disorder called **dysarthria**, which is characterized by disruptions of the speed, strength, range, timing, or accuracy of articulatory movements.

In their attempts to communicate effectively, Broca's aphasics often fall back on a few formulaic or idiomatic expressions that they can still produce in a fairly fluent manner; these are sometimes called "stereotypies." They may also retain the ability to recite overlearned sequences such as the days of the week, the months of the year, or number lines; in addition, they may be able to sing familiar songs. For the most part, however, their utterances are organized into small groupings of one to three words that are produced effortfully and laboriously. These expressions have minimal syntactic complexity, and they typically consist of content words with rather general meanings. Patients tend to be better at accessing nouns than verbs, but noun retrieval is usually impaired to some degree, and often to a great degree.

One of the most salient features of Broca's aphasia is that patients have considerable difficulty producing grammatical morphemes—not just free-standing items like articles (e.g., *the*), auxiliary verbs (e.g., *could*), prepositions (e.g., *in*), and conjunctions (e.g., *and*), but also affixes that are bound to stems (e.g., the regular past-tense suffix *-ed*). These kinds of morphemes have very schematic meanings, and their main role is to contribute to the grammatical structures of sentences. They are called **closed-class elements** because they constitute a relatively small, fixed inventory of vocabulary items that is not readily expanded; after all, we don't go around inventing new prepositions all the time. In contrast, nouns, verbs, and adjectives have comparatively richer meanings, perform different grammatical functions, and are called **open-class elements** because they make up a large set of vocabulary items that is always in flux; for example, new words are constantly entering our lexicon in the form of slang (e.g., *mosh*), pop culture terms (e.g., *twitter*), and specialized technical terms (e.g., *magnetoencephalography*). In the speech of patients with Broca's aphasia, one usually sees a striking dissociation between, on the one hand, markedly disrupted production of closed-class grammatical morphemes, and on the other, much less impaired production of open-class content words. Together with significantly reduced syntactic complexity, this aspect of the syndrome is called **agrammatism**. Although the general characterization of agrammatism provided here can serve as a very rough guide to the disorder, it is important to note that the disorder can be manifested in many different ways that depend, in part, on various grammatical properties of the patient's language, such as whether or not it is heavily inflected (Bates & Wulfeck, 1989; Menn & Obler, 1990a; Menn et al., 1995; see Chapter 14 for extensive discussion, including a "syntax tutorial").

The production deficit in Broca's aphasia is exemplified by the following speech sample, which was recorded from a patient who was asked to describe the Cookie Theft picture in the Boston Diagnostic Aphasia Examination (Obler & Gjerlow, 1999, p. 41; see Figure 3.4):

> kid … kk …. can … candy … cookie … candy … well I don't know but it's writ … easy does it … slam … fall … men … many no … girl … dishes … soap … soap … water … water … falling pah that's all … dish … that's all … cookies … can … candy … cookies cookies … he … down … that's all … girl … slipping water … water … and it hurts … much to do … her … clean up … dishes … up there … I think that's doing it … [The examiner asks: What is she doing with the dishes?] discharge no … I forgot … dirtying clothes [?] dish [?] water … [The examiner probes: What about it?] slippery water … scolded [?] … slipped

This excerpt illustrates many common characteristics of the nonfluent language production of Broca's aphasics. Overall, the patient's speech is sparse, effortful, slow, syntactically simplified, and rhythmically punctuated by many pauses and false starts. Some word-finding difficulties are evident (e.g., *discharge* instead of *washing dishes*). There are a few stereotypies (e.g., *that's all*), many more nouns than verbs and adjectives, and a paucity of closed-class grammatical morphemes.

Dysarthria   A speech production disorder that involves an impairment of motor control over the muscles constituting the vocal apparatus.

Closed-class elements   Grammatical morphemes like prepositions, conjunctions, and affixes; they form a small set that changes slowly over history.

Open-class elements   Content words like nouns, verbs, and adjectives; they form a large set that is easily expanded or contracted.

Agrammatism   A deficit involving reduced syntactic complexity and impaired production of closed-class elements.

Figure 3.4 Cookie theft picture (From *Boston Diagnostic Aphasia Examination*, Third Edition, by Harold Goodglass, Edith Kaplan, and Barbara Barresi, 2001, Austin, TX: PRO-ED. Copyright 2001 by PRO-ED, Inc. Reprinted with permission.)

Comprehension

In contrast to their prominent disorder of speech production, Broca's aphasics usually exhibit relatively intact understanding of colloquial conversation. More formal testing of their auditory comprehension, however, typically reveals abnormalities. For example, at the single-word level, most patients perform well when instructed to point to individual named objects, but encounter difficulties when asked to point to several different named objects in a specific sequence. Similarly, at the level of phrases and sentences, although most patients are able to understand syntactically simple expressions, they have trouble with more complex ones.

As an illustration, consider the following sentences, which exemplify a contrast between two types of relative clause, indicated in each case by brackets:

(1) The reporter [who attacked the senator] admitted the error.
(2) The reporter [who the senator attacked] admitted the error.

In both (1) and (2), the pronoun *who* in the relative clause stands for the noun-phrase *The reporter* in the main clause. This pronoun is associated with different semantic roles, however, in the two relative clauses. Specifically, in (1) it designates the actor of the verb *attacked*, whereas in (2) it designates the undergoer of that verb. The only cue to this fundamental difference in meaning, though, is the contrasting word order of the two relative clauses. Note that the word order of

the relative clause in (1) is similar to that of a simple transitive sentence, since the actor is expressed before the verb and the undergoer is expressed after it, whereas the word order of the relative clause in (2) is more unusual, since the undergoer precedes the actor, which in turn precedes the verb. Even neurologically normal individuals sometimes find sentences like (2) harder to understand than sentences like (1). This difference in difficulty, however, is often—not always, but often—significantly greater for Broca's aphasics, and many patients resort to guessing "who did what to whom" when they hear sentences like (2) (for an early study see Caramazza & Zurif, 1976; for further information see Chapter 15). The precise interpretation of such behavioral patterns is controversial, but there is general agreement that Broca's aphasics typically have trouble processing grammatical information not only during speech production, but also during auditory comprehension.

Repetition

In Broca's aphasia, repetition is usually better than spontaneous speech, but it is nevertheless abnormal. Some errors are phonetic or phonological in nature, involving mispronunciations, omissions, iterations, or substitutions of sound structure. Other errors occur at the lexical and grammatical levels of linguistic organization. For example, if asked to repeat a phase like *the beautiful purple butterfly*, a typical Broca's aphasic would omit the determiner and perhaps also one of the two adjectives, yielding an expression like *beautiful butterfly* or *purple butterfly*. Deficits are also observed when patients are instructed to repeat syntactically complex sentences like *Pry the tin lid off*. This sentence poses several challenges to a Broca's aphasic. It begins with a verb; it contains a compound noun; and it ends with a particle. Even more difficult to repeat are expressions that consist entirely of closed-class elements, such as *no ifs, ands, or buts*. Most Broca's aphasics are stymied by such expressions and can only repeat one or two of the words.

Lesion Correlates

According to most researchers, Broca's area encompasses the left posterior inferior frontal gyrus—specifically, the pars opercularis, which corresponds roughly to BA44, and the pars triangularis, which corresponds roughly to BA45. When damage encompasses this region as well as the ventral precentral gyrus, lateral striatum, and associated subcortical white matter, the patient may be virtually mute or may exhibit a form

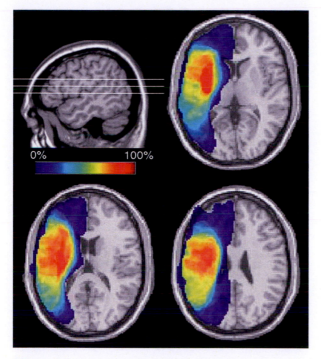

Figure 3.5 Lesion overlap of 36 stroke patients with chronic Broca's aphasia. (From Dronkers & Baldo, 2009, p. 344.)

of acute Broca's aphasia. However, the disorder often improves rapidly, so that minimal impairment is evident a year later. In contrast, chronic Broca's aphasia generally requires more widespread damage (Mohr et al., 1978). Lesion profiles are quite variable, but they often include not only the regions just mentioned, but also one or more of the following left-hemisphere structures: the dorsolateral prefrontal cortex (BAs 46 and 9) and underlying white matter; the supramarginal gyrus (BA40) and underlying white matter; the anterior superior temporal gyrus (anterior BA22) and underlying white matter; and much of the insula (Figure 3.5; see also Table 14.3 in Chapter 14). When Broca's aphasia includes apraxia of speech, the lesion usually includes the anterior superior portion of the left insula (Dronkers, 1996; Ogar et al., 2006; Baldo et al., 2011), although there are exceptions to this trend (Hillis et al., 2004b; Richardson et al., 2012), as already discussed in Chapter 2 (see also the section called "The Island of Reil" in Chapter 6). For a new analysis of the brains of Broca's original patients, see Box 3.2; and for an interesting case study of acute Broca's aphasia, see Box 3.3.

Box 3.2   New Analyses of the Brains of Broca's Original Patients

Showing great foresight, Broca did not dissect the brains of his two original patients, Leborgne and Lelong, but instead preserved them (except for Lelong's right hemisphere) in alcohol and then donated them to a Paris museum, in hopes that at some point in the future it would be possible for scientists to conduct more sophisticated neuroanatomical analyses of the brains than he himself was capable of performing. That time arrived just a few years ago, when Dronkers et al. (2007) took advantage of a unique opportunity to scan both brains using high-resolution volumetric MRI.

Representative images of Leborgne's brain are depicted in Figure 3B2.1. A photograph of the lateral surface of the left hemisphere is shown at the top, with colored lines indicating the major sulci. The lesion is clearly centered in the inferior frontal gyrus, most conspicuously in the middle third, but with additional softening in the posterior third. Some damage is also apparent in the middle frontal gyrus and the anterior superior temporal gyrus, and close inspection reveals deformed or necrotic tissue in the anterior inferior parietal lobe as well. The full extent of Leborgne's lesion, however, is only visible in the axial and coronal slices below the photograph. Notably,

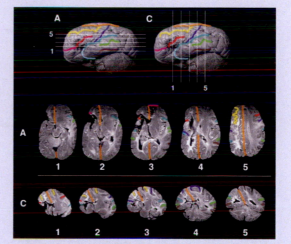

Figure 3B2.1 Photographs and MR images of the brain of Leborgne. (Top row) Photographs of the lateral surface of the brain, with colors indicating the major sulci, horizontal lines indicating the planes of axial slices (A), and vertical lines indicating the planes of coronal slices (C). (Middle row) Axial slices (A). (Bottom row) Coronal slices (C). Colors demarcate the following structures: interhemispheric/longitudinal fissure (orange); central sulcus/Rolandic fissure (dark blue); lateral/sylvian fissure (aqua); inferior frontal sulcus (red); superior frontal sulcus (yellow); frontomarginal sulcus (pink); superior temporal sulcus (light green); and inferior temporal sulcus (brown). (From Dronkers et al., 2007, p. 1437.)

the left hemisphere, as measured from the midline to the lateral surface, is nearly 50 percent smaller than the right hemisphere. The damage includes the following structures: the left inferior frontal gyrus (slices A2 and C1); the anterior superior temporal lobe (slices A2 and C1–2); the deep inferior parietal lobe (slices A4 and C4); the insula (slices A4 and C2–3); the claustrum, putamen, globus pallidus, head of caudate nucleus, and internal and external capsules (slices A2–3 and C2–3); and the entire length of the superior longitudinal fasciculus, which incorporates fibers of the arcuate fasciculus (slices A4 and C2–5).

Representative images of Lelong's brain are depicted in Figure 3B2.2. As in Figure 3B2.1, a photograph of the lateral surface of the left hemisphere is shown at the top, with colored lines indicating the major sulci. Dronkers et al. (2007) point out that the cortex is severely atrophied, which is consistent with Broca's indication that Lelong had suffered from dementia for at least eight years prior to his stroke. Evidence of the stroke itself can be seen in the posterior inferior frontal gyrus. It is worth mentioning that although the damage affected the pars opercularis (i.e., the posterior sector of Broca's

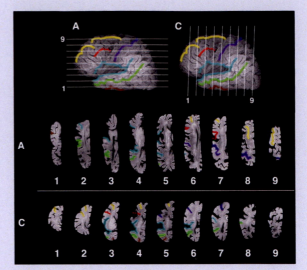

Figure 3B2.2 Photographs and MR images of the brain of Lelong. (Top row) Photographs of the lateral surface of the brain, with colors indicating the major sulci, horizontal lines indicating the planes of axial slices (A), and vertical lines indicating the planes of coronal slices (C). (Middle row) Axial slices (A). (Bottom row) Coronal slices (C). Colors as in Figure 3B2.1. (From Dronkers et al., 2007, p. 1439.)

area), it completely spared the pars triangularis (i.e., the anterior sector of Broca's area). The limited extent of the left inferior frontal damage can be seen in the axial and coronal slices (specifically, A6–7 and C4). Importantly, the anterior portion of the arcuate fasciculus is also lesioned (A7 and C4–5).

Dronkers et al.'s (2007) detailed analyses clearly show that the brains of Leborgne and Lelong had not only the surface lesions that Broca originally observed, but also deeper lesions affecting more medial structures. In fact, one of the most intriguing outcomes of this new neuroanatomical investigation is that the anterior segment of the arcuate fasciculus was damaged in both patients. This finding takes on special significance in light of recent research on how this white matter pathway contributes to language (e.g., Glasser & Rilling, 2008; Bonilha & Fridriksson, 2009). Dronkers et al. (2007) are undoubtedly correct in concluding that "Leborgne and Lelong can speak to us more eloquently now than they could over 140 years ago" (p. 1441).

Wernicke's Aphasia

After Paul Broca's pioneering work in the 1860s, the next major discovery in the history of aphasia research came from the young neuropsychiatrist and neuroanatomist Carl Wernicke. In his 1874 monograph, he described a new type of language disturbance that he called "sensory aphasia," but which later came to be known eponymously as "Wernicke's aphasia." The main symptoms included fluent but semantically incoherent and often phonologically distorted speech production, severely impaired auditory comprehension, defective repetition, and unawareness of errors. Wernicke found that this constellation of behavioral features was most reliably linked with lesions in the

posterior superior and/or middle temporal gyri of the left hemisphere. The prototypical characteristics of this classic aphasia syndrome are described in greater detail below (see Table 3.2).

Production

The spontaneous conversational speech of Wernicke's aphasics is **fluent**, sometimes even hyperfluent. In other words, patients tend to speak at either a normal rate or a faster than normal rate. When their output is excessive, the phenomenon is called "logorrhea" or

Fluent Speech that flows at a normal rate.

Box 3.3 A Rare Case of Acute, Selective, and Temporary Dysfunction of Broca's Area

A unique perspective on some of the language functions that are normally supported by Broca's area comes from a remarkable case study reported by Davis et al. (2008). The investigation focused on patient MJE, a man who suddenly developed severe language deficits the day after undergoing a surgical operation. Neurological and psycholinguistic examinations took place within hours after the symptoms appeared. Brain imaging revealed a very small (< 3 mm) infarct in the left posterior frontal lobe, surrounded by a much larger region of poor perfusion (i.e., low blood flow) that corresponded extremely well with the boundaries of Broca's area, as shown in Figure 3B3.1. Although MJE could understand simple commands, he could not repeat sentences, and his speech production was severely impaired. For example, he described the Cookie Theft picture as follows: "Kis-kitchen … in kitchen … picture. The laundry running over … kid on the thing." A formal battery of tests was administered 5 hours post-onset, and the results are shown in Figure 3B3.2. He was perfect at answering simple yes/no questions (e.g., *Do dogs fly?*), and also performed well in orally repeating and reading words, as long as his self-corrected articulatory errors were not penalized. His scores on the other tests, however, declined precipitously, starting with mild impairment in oral naming, and progressing through moderate impairment in oral spelling to increasingly severe impairment in understanding auditorily and orthographically presented active sentences (e.g., *The boy pushed the girl*) and passive sentences (e.g., *The girl was pushed by the boy*). His worst score was for answering complex yes/no questions (e.g., *Is a dog larger than an elephant?*).

The investigators suspected that because MJE's infarct was so tiny, his language deficits were most likely due to the reduced perfusion in Broca's area. He was therefore treated with intravenous saline to increase blood pressure and hence improve blood flow in Broca's area. The intervention was successful—indeed, dramatically so. The next day, new brain scans revealed that Broca's area was reperfused, and another administration of the test battery revealed that MJE's language capacity was fully restored, as shown in Figure 3B3.2. He even produced fluent, well-formed sentences when describing the Cookie Theft picture again.

Overall, this extraordinary case study provides compelling evidence that the following language functions depend on Broca's area: planning/programming speech; producing grammatical sentences; and comprehending grammatical sentences, especially ones with complex syntactic structures.

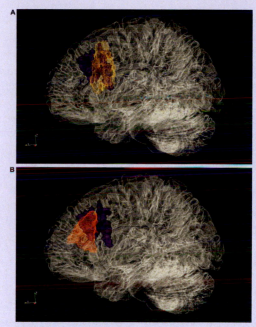

Figure 3B3.1 Three-dimensional reconstruction of the area of MJE's hypoperfusion at Day 1. (A) Overlap between MJE's area of hypoperfusion (shown in purple) and the area where any patient had cytoarchitecture of BA44 in the probabilistic map of Amunts et al. (1999, shown in yellow). (B) Overlap between MJE's area of hypoperfusion (shown in purple) and the area where any patient had cytoarchitecture of BA45 in the probabilistic map of Amunts et al. (1999, shown in orange). (From Davis et al., 2008, p. 54.)

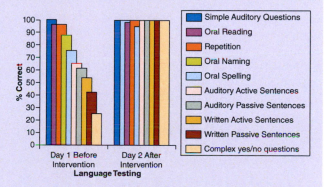

Figure 3B3.2 MJE's performance on psycholinguistic tests on Day 1 (5 hours post-onset of symptoms; pretreatment), and again on Day 2 (32 hours post-onset of symptoms; post-treatment). (From Davis et al., 2008, p. 55.)

Table 3.2   Prototypical Clinical Features of Wernicke's Aphasia

Production
Fluent, sometimes excessively so
Frequent phonemic paraphasias, which may be so severe as to constitute neologistic jargon
Morphological and syntactic substitution errors sometimes occur
Patients are often unaware of their deficits

Comprehension
Impaired for sentences, phrases, and in many cases even single words

Repetition
Disrupted, with errors involving word choice, phonological structure, and grammatical structure

"press of speech." In such cases, patients may continue to speak relentlessly until they are forcefully stopped by the examiner. Despite producing prodigious amounts of speech, however, Wernicke's aphasics are rarely able to communicate much in the way of meaningful information. There are several reasons for this. First, their utterances tend to be bizarre and incomprehensible, sometimes to such a degree that patients may be mistakenly diagnosed by an unskilled examiner as having a psychiatric rather than a neurological disorder. Second, they frequently produce **phonemic paraphasias**—that is, distortions of the phonological structures of words, like saying *paker* instead of *paper*. And third, although their sentences are often grammatically well-formed, they produce an above-average proportion of morphological and syntactic errors involving substitutions rather than omissions—a deficit called **paragrammatism**.

All of these aspects of Wernicke's aphasia are apparent in the following excerpt from a prototypical patient (Obler & Gjerlow, 1999, p. 43; the examiner's interpretations are in square brackets):

> Is this some of the work that we work as we did before? ... All right ... From when wine [why] I'm here. What's wrong with me because I ... was myself until the taenz took something about the time between me and my regular time in that time and they took the time in that time here and that's when the the time took around here and saw me and around in it it's started with me no time and then I bekan [began] work of nothing else that's the way the doctor find me that way ...

Although there are occasional pauses and word-finding problems, the patient's speech flows quite freely. It does not, however, make much sense. Moreover, it contains several phonemic paraphasias (e.g., *taenz*) and "paragrammatic" errors (e.g., *the doctor find me*).

In the most severe forms of Wernicke's aphasia, phonemic paraphasias can be so pervasive and disruptive that the patient's speech is reduced to a mostly indecipherable gibberish called "neologistic jargon aphasia" or simply "jargon aphasia." For example, patient JBN, who was studied in detail by Hillis et al. (1999a), routinely produced not only simple phonemic paraphasias like *plasses* for *glasses*, *kate* for *cake*, and *nisner* for *sister*, but also complex **neologisms** like *lawnerjot* for *leg*, *neckreckina* for *kangaroo*, and *yubersy* for *effort*. Systematic analyses suggested that JBN's errors may have been due to a disconnection between word-level and subword-level phonological structures (see Figure 3.6). According to this account, whenever she attempted to say a word, the high-level lexical form was correctly selected, but the projections from that form to the low-level phonemic representations that "flesh out" the word were disrupted, leading to either minor paraphasias or major neologisms. Jargon aphasia can be manifested in many ways, however, and different symptoms may require different explanations (Marshall, 2006).

Comprehension

Although incoherent speech production is a very salient symptom of Wernicke's aphasia, it is only one aspect of the full-blown syndrome. Patients also invariably exhibit impaired understanding of spoken language, which is why Wernicke himself originally called the syndrome "sensory aphasia." In the most severe cases, patients comprehend almost nothing that is said to them, failing to respond appropriately to verbal questions, commands, and even single words. In more moderate cases, however, patients may be able to

Phonemic paraphasia   A distortion of the phonological structure of a word.

Paragrammatism   A deficit involving substitution of closed-class elements or syntactic structures.

Neologism   A nonsense word that results from an extreme form of phonemic paraphasia.

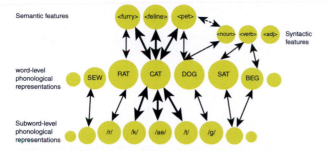

Figure 3.6 A lexical network showing semantic (top), syntactic (upper right), word-level phonological (middle), and subword-level phonological (bottom) representations. Arrows indicate information flow, and thick arrows indicate connections relevant to the target word, namely *cat*. If the bidirectional connections between word-level and subword-level phonological representations were weakened, phonemic paraphasias, neologisms, and semantic substitutions would occur during speech production, and lexical misidentifications would occur during speech perception. This is the deficit analysis that Hillis et al. (1999a) proposed to account for the pattern of errors observed in patient JBN. (Adapted from Goldrick & Rapp, 2002, p. 35.)

understand, with effort, a few words and statements. They may also give the impression of being able to follow the general topic of a conversation, but if the topic is suddenly changed, they usually cannot make the switch quickly enough to keep up, and hence need time to identify the new theme.

Formal testing can often help pinpoint the precise nature of the comprehension deficit in particular cases of Wernicke's aphasia. To return to the example of patient JBN, through careful examination Hillis et al. (1999a) found that, unlike many other Wernicke's aphasics, JBN retained the ability to discriminate between similar-sounding words. For instance, she accurately indicated that *bus* and *bun* are different. However, she performed quite poorly when given a word–picture verification task that involved the very same similar-sounding words. For instance, when shown a picture of a bus, she accepted *bun* as a correct description of it. This could not be attributed to a semantic deficit affecting her conceptual knowledge of buses and buns, because she completed the same task flawlessly when the words were presented as written rather than spoken input (although it should be noted that not all Wernicke's aphasics can read single words so well). Instead, Hillis et al. argued that JBN's behavior could best be explained by positing a disruption of the perceptual mechanisms that map phonemes onto lexical items (see Figure 3.6). This account can explain JBN's accurate word discrimination, since that ability could be supported by intact phoneme representations,

and it can also explain her poor word–picture verification, since that ability depends on the putatively impaired projections from subword-level to word-level phonological structures.

Interestingly, Hillis et al. took this line of reasoning a step further by suggesting that JBN's deficits in both production and comprehension might have a common source—specifically, a disturbance of *bidirectional* connections between the two levels of phonological representation that we have been discussing. On the output side, JBN's paraphasias and neologisms during speech production may have resulted from an inability to get from word-level to subword-level representations; and on the input side, her lexical misidentifications during auditory comprehension may have resulted from an inability to get from subword-level to word-level representations (see Figure 3.6). Hillis et al. provide substantial evidence in favor of this interpretation of JBN's performance. It must be borne in mind, however, that this is just one patient, and other cases of Wernicke's aphasia exhibit somewhat different behavioral patterns that have somewhat different underlying causes.

Repetition

Repetition of spoken language is typically abnormal in Wernicke's aphasia. Repetition errors are not restricted to word choice and grammatical structure, but may also involve phonemic paraphasias and neologisms.

Lesion Correlates

Wernicke's area is often defined as the posterior third of the left superior temporal gyrus; however, the precise boundaries of Wernicke's area have been controversial for over a century (Bogen & Bogen, 1976; see also the the supplementary discussion and figures in Rauschecker & Scott, 2009). In an 1881 paper Wernicke himself linked the aphasia syndrome that later came to bear his name with damage to much of the left superior temporal gyrus, but in a 1906 paper he noted that—as previously suggested by the Russian-Swiss neuropathologist Constantin von Monakow—the posterior portion of the left middle temporal gyrus is also frequently implicated (Eggert, 1977, pp. 271–272). Recent research supports the view that Wernicke's aphasia is typically associated with lesions affecting the posterior sectors of both the superior and middle temporal gyri (see Figure 3.7). It is also noteworthy that some patients with Wernicke's aphasia have even larger lesions that extend dorsally and caudally into the left inferior parietal lobule.

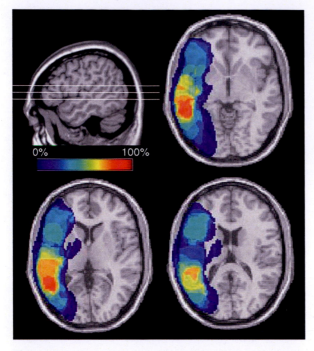

Figure 3.7 Lesion overlap of 11 stroke patients with chronic Wernicke's aphasia. (From Dronkers & Baldo, 2009, p. 345.)

Table 3.3 Prototypical Clinical Features of Conduction Aphasia

Production
More fluent than Broca's aphasics, but less fluent than Wernicke's aphasics
Frequent phonemic paraphasias
Recurrent attempts to correctly produce the sound structure of the desired expression
Comprehension
Relatively preserved
Difficulties may arise when confronted with long, complex sentences with high short-term memory demands
Repetition
Disrupted for multi-word sequences, and sometimes also for single words

Conduction Aphasia

Wernicke is known not only for discovering one of the most well-established aphasia syndromes, but also for correctly predicting the existence of another (Wernicke, 1874). His reasoning involved a careful consideration of how language would be deleteriously affected by damage to the connections between the left posterior language region (i.e., Wernicke's area) and the left anterior language region (i.e., Broca's area). He believed that speech production would be fluent, since Broca's area was still intact, and that speech perception would be normal as well, since Wernicke's area was also intact. However, he predicted that the expression of words would be disrupted—in particular, that patients would produce many phonemic paraphasias—because the disconnection between Wernicke's area and Broca's area would prevent the accurate delivery of the "sound images" of words from the posterior region to the anterior region where they were assumed to be translated into motor programs for articulation. Lichtheim (1885) subsequently elaborated on Wernicke's ideas by further predicting that patients with this type of disconnection would have severely impaired repetition of spoken utterances. These predictions were later confirmed, and the relevant syndrome is now commonly referred to as conduction aphasia. It occurs much less frequently than Broca's and Wernicke's aphasia, but is

still regarded as an independent syndrome. The prototypical features of this disorder are described in greater detail below (see Table 3.3).

Production

Language production is generally classified as fluent, but with the following qualifications. On the one hand, conduction aphasics are somewhat less fluent than Wernicke's aphasics, since they generate fewer words and have more pauses. But on the other hand, conduction aphasics are significantly more fluent than Broca's aphasics, since they can easily produce long sentences with complex grammatical structures. The hallmark feature of the spontaneous speech of conduction aphasics is that it contains abundant paraphasias, most often phonemic in nature. The patient may utter a few sentences quite fluently, but then suddenly reach a point where they cannot correctly produce the sound structure of the desired expression. Phonemic paraphasias are more likely to occur when the patient is trying to say a word or phrase that is semantically significant and/or phonologically complex. Unlike the majority of Wernicke's aphasics, however, conduction aphasics are acutely aware of their errors and make multiple attempts to repair them during ongoing speech—a phenomenon that is called *conduit d'approche* and that reveals preserved knowledge of how the target words should sound.

The production deficit in conduction aphasia is illustrated in the following excerpt from a patient who is trying to describe the Cookie Theft picture shown in Figure 3.4 (Goodglass & Wingfield, 1997, pp. 8–9):

Examiner:	Tell me about what's going on in this picture.
Patient:	Oh … he's on top o' the ss … ss … swirl … it's a … ss … sss … ss … sweel … sstool … stool. It's fallin' over. An' the girl, … the boy is … ss … 'ettin' his sister a …. He's. He'ss givin' her a ss … a … sss … sss … ssl … s … ss … sl cook … It's a soos … ss … ss … sss …
Examiner:	So he's giving his sister a cookie. What else is happening?
Patient:	Well he's he's fillin' out the ch ch ch … Oh, anyhow, his mother is … she's bissy, but the water's fallin' over … The water is fallin' over the … the … er … the er … It's going flink … ss …
Examiner:	Yes, it's falling over the sink.
Patient:	Sull … sit … flink … er …
Examiner:	Listen to me: sink.
Patient:	Stink … sink … sink … sink …
Examiner:	OK, what is she doing there?
Patient:	She's drawing the … she's drying the dishes.

For many of the errors, it is clear that patient's repeated attempts to produce the target word are based on an accurate representation of its unique phonological form. That form, however, cannot be organized properly for purposes of articulation.

Comprehension

Comprehension of spoken language is, for the most part, well-preserved in conduction aphasia. Most patients can effortlessly point to named objects and understand ordinary conversation in a normal manner. Difficulties do sometimes surface, however, especially when the patient is confronted with grammatically complex sentences that place high demands on auditory–verbal short-term memory.

Repetition

Despite having generally good comprehension, conduction aphasics are notably impaired at repetition. In fact, some scholars regard this as a major symptom of the disorder. Although the defect is most severe when the task is to repeat sentences, it is also apparent when the task is to repeat single words, at least for some patients. Errors are typically phonemic paraphasias, but complete word substitutions sometimes occur too. As in spontaneous speech, the patient usually makes multiple attempts to produce the target word correctly; however, it is common for patients to have more

trouble producing a word in a repetition task than in a more natural context. When all repetition attempts fail, the patient may shift to an appropriate paraphrase that is easily expressed. For example, when asked to say *rifle* an aphasic soldier said, "Riffe … riddil … oh hell, I mean a gun" (Benson & Ardila, 1996, p. 134).

Lesion Correlates

As mentioned above, conduction aphasia has traditionally been thought to arise from a disconnection between Wernicke's and Broca's areas. Support for this view comes from recent evidence that the white matter pathways of the arcuate fasciculus (see Figure 1.21 in Chapter 1) mediate a phonological circuit for mapping speech perception onto speech production, and that these pathways are frequently damaged in conduction aphasics who display pronounced repetition deficits (Berthier et al., 2012). At the same time, however, the disconnection account of the syndrome may be too simplistic to explain all of the cases in the literature (Bernal & Ardila, 2009). For instance, many conduction aphasics have lesions that are not restricted to subcortical white matter regions, but rather include the cortical tissue of the supramarginal gyrus and/or the posterior end of the supratemporal plane, deep within the sylvian fissure (see Figure 3.8; see also Figure 5.17 in Chapter 5). In addition, some studies have linked repetition deficits with hypoperfusion in precisely these cortical areas (Fridriksson et al., 2010).

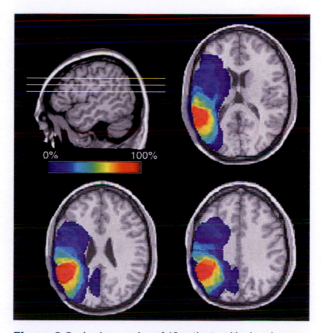

Figure 3.8 Lesion overlap of 13 patients with chronic conduction aphasia. (From Dronkers & Baldo, 2009, p. 346.)

Global Aphasia

Global aphasia is the easiest syndrome to describe because it is the most devastating. Virtually all linguistic communication is compromised (see Table 3.4). Spoken language production is extremely limited, and most patients are reduced to using a single stereotypic utterance (e.g., *yes, no, da*). Some patients can repeat their one utterance many times with richly modulated intonation, but while this enables them to express a wide range of emotions, it does not allow them to convey much else. Comprehension is also severely impaired. Some patients retain an understanding of a few highly familiar words and phrases, but cannot grasp anything beyond these simple expressions. Repetition is defective as well. The lesion typically encompasses the entire left perisylvian cortex and much of the underlying white matter (see Figure 3.9). Sometimes, however, the temporal component of the perisylvian region is preserved. When the damage affects predominantly the left inferior frontal lobe, the patient may manifest global aphasia during the acute phase of recovery, but later evolve into a Broca's aphasic.

Table 3.4   Prototypical Clinical Features of Global Aphasia

Production
Severely impaired
Comprehension
Severely impaired
Repetition
Severely impaired

Anomic Aphasia

All aphasic patients, regardless of their syndrome, experience word-finding difficulties—a deficit more technically known as **anomia**. Even neurologically healthy people sometimes encounter momentary blocks when they cannot retrieve the phonological form of a desired word, despite knowing exactly what it is they want to say. Such episodes are aptly called "tip-of-the-tongue states" and are often accompanied by a frustrating feeling of groping vainly in the dark for a word that seems to lie just beyond reach. For some brain-damaged patients, this is their primary, or even their only,

Anomia   A deficit involving impaired word retrieval, especially in naming tasks.

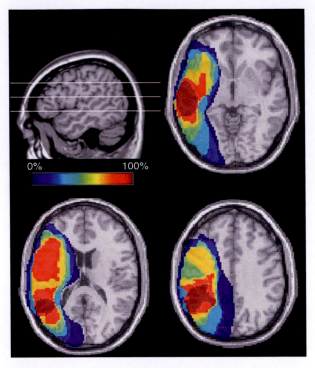

0%   100%

Figure 3.9   Lesion correlates of 7 patients with chronic global aphasia. (From Dronkers & Baldo, 2009, p. 346.)

language problem, and it is not just a rare annoyance but a chronic condition. Such patients are typically classified as having a special syndrome called anomic aphasia. The general characteristics of this disorder are described below (see Table 3.5).

Production

The spontaneous speech of anomic aphasics is considered to be fluent. Patients with this syndrome are capable of speaking at a relatively normal rate; however, somewhat similar to conduction aphasics, their

Table 3.5   Prototypical Clinical Features of Anomic Aphasia

Production
Fluent but with hesitations
Marked word-finding difficulties, sometimes worse for certain categories than others
Comprehension
Relatively preserved
Repetition
Relatively preserved

conversation is often rather choppy and hesitant because of frequent pauses when they cannot access a target word. Naming is by far the most severely impaired ability, and this deficit is revealed most dramatically when patients are directly confronted with either real objects or pictures of objects and asked to refer to them with the most appropriate words. Patients may be able to indicate that they recognize an object by, say, demonstrating or pantomiming how it is used, or by providing an adequate definition of it, but the name of the object escapes them. Sometimes they manage to retrieve the target word after a lengthy period of searching for it, or after another person, such as an examiner, gives them a cue, like the first phoneme or syllable. Often, however, the best that patients can do is produce a semantically related word, or perhaps a small portion of the phonological form of the correct word.

To take a specific case, patient RR was asked to orally name 160 pictures of objects (Kemmerer et al., 2005). Although he recognized 153 (96 percent) of them, he could only name 64 (44 percent). Of his 89 errors, 13 (15 percent) were complete omissions (basically saying "I don't know"), 21 (23 percent) were phonemic paraphasias, and 55 (62 percent) were semantic in nature. These semantic errors, which constituted the majority of his mistakes, were of two types. The first type involved oral descriptions that included semantic substitutions for the target word. Here are some examples: For a parakeet he said, "Bird, parrot, nope, little one, small thing." For a woodpecker he said, "Bird, makes a hell of a noise." For a sheep he said, "Lamb, but more than that." And for a rhinoceros he said, "Something like a lotomus." The second type involved oral descriptions that did not include semantic substitutions for the target word. Here are some examples: For a drill he said, "Everybody needs one, to take things out or put things in." For an umbrella he said, "If it's raining you've got to have one." For a buggy he said, "If you've got a baby you have one." And for a suitcase he said, "I've had a lot when traveling."

Severe word-finding difficulties often disrupt the narrative abilities of anomic aphasics, as shown by RR's description of the Cookie Theft picture shown in Figure 3.4:

The children are, they'd like to have some, uh, they'd like to have some, this, uh, thing. Uh, but they're going to fall down because the, uh, the … I take it you don't want me to run … The thing is falling apart, the falling apart, the, uh, uh, ssstool.

Uh, the same way the mother is forgetting of something and as a result of that the water sss … came out and is falling all over the place. Um, the um um … Do you mean everything or just the … I mean, uh … Okay, so there's a two, kids, the girl and boy, um … They have shoes and stockings, um … She has, uh … [sigh] Well, that's what normally do is girls do … And he had a, is a [cough] I can't think think um … She's at the process she was after lunch she was doing that, this was the, um … She, shoot, that and, uh, I have this … And this was the, uh, she'd normally she's got a, a little mm … ssskirt … And I, uh, have got, uh, I sh … Can't, uh, what they were doing there.

He was obviously able to describe many aspects of the scene, and the grammatical structures are, for the most part, correct, but the narrative is replete with gaps where he could not access certain content words, usually nouns for objects. As a result, minimal information is conveyed. However, his speech production was mostly well-articulated and contained only a few phonological errors.

It is not uncommon for anomia to affect certain categories of words more than others. For instance, as discussed in Chapter 2 (see Table 2.1 and the associated text), some patients are significantly more impaired at retrieving nouns than verbs, whereas others exhibit the opposite dissociation (Mätzig et al., 2009). Category-specific anomias can be even narrower than this, though. For instance, within the large domain of nouns for concrete entities, several subclasses can be distinguished according to both semantic and grammatical criteria, and word-finding deficits sometimes appear to either selectively or disproportionately affect certain subclasses relative to others. These subclasses include proper nouns for famous people and famous landmarks, as well as common nouns for animals, fruits/vegetables, and tools/utensils (Laine & Martin, 2006). As an illustration, we return to patient RR. Although he was clearly impaired at retrieving the phonological forms of common nouns for various kinds of objects (44 percent correct), he was much more impaired at retrieving the phonological forms of proper nouns for famous people (6 percent correct). For example, in response to a photograph of Liza Minnelli he said, "Judy Garland's daughter, I don't know her last name"; and in response to a photograph of Lee Iacocca he said, "Was at Ford and then he was Chrysler."

It is important to note that word-finding difficulties can result from a disturbance at any of several different levels of the naming process. Of course, if a patient's knowledge of the meaning of a target word is impaired, correct naming will be impossible, and performance on other tasks that depend on that knowledge, such as word–picture matching, will also be poor. If, however, the disturbance affects the mechanisms that map the meanings of words onto the corresponding high-level phonological forms, the patient may produce a large number of "definitional" responses during naming tasks, while performing within normal limits on all manner of comprehension tasks. Finally, if the impairment affects the projections from high-level to low-level phonological representations of words, the patient's naming errors may consist predominantly of phonemic paraphasias. All three of these different kinds of word-finding difficulties are sometimes considered to fall under the rubric of anomia, but the second type—that is, the type that involves a preponderance of "definitional" responses and that is exemplified by patient RR—is generally regarded as the prototypical manifestation of the classic syndrome of anomic aphasia.

Comprehension

Anomic aphasics usually have well-preserved comprehension at both the single-word level and the sentence level. The only exceptions are those patients whose word-finding deficits are due to semantic impairments.

Repetition

As a general rule, anomic aphasics also tend to have intact repetition. In fact, it is worth emphasizing that of the syndromes we have considered so far, anomia is the first one in which repetition is not typically impaired.

Lesion Correlates

Unlike the other classic aphasia syndromes, anomia is not reliably associated with damage to a specific brain region. However, this lack of a strong deficit–lesion correlation applies mainly to the general disorder of anomia. If one focuses instead on some of the more narrowly delineated category-specific anomias, there is growing evidence for links with certain areas of brain injury. For example, impaired noun retrieval is often associated with damage to the left temporal lobe, especially the temporal pole and the middle and inferior temporal gyri (e.g., Damasio et al., 2004), whereas impaired verb retrieval is often associated with damage to the left frontal lobe, especially Broca's area and the underlying white matter (e.g., Tranel et al., 2008).

Transcortical Aphasia Syndromes

The term "transcortical aphasia" was originally proposed by Lichtheim (1885) as an overarching label for a family of syndromes characterized by intact repetition but deficits involving the mappings between the forms and meanings of utterances. Three syndromes, all of which are rather rare, are traditionally distinguished: transcortical motor aphasia, which affects speech production; transcortical sensory aphasia, which affects speech comprehension; and mixed transcortical aphasia, which affects both production and comprehension. Note that, as just mentioned, repetition is preserved in all three of these disorders; in fact, this is a key feature that sets these syndromes apart from some of the previously described ones. These disorders are not, however, "transcortical" in any literal sense; the nomenclature has simply persisted because of its historical significance. The central features of all three syndromes are summarized below (see Table 3.6).

Transcortical Motor Aphasia

The spontaneous speech of patients with transcortical motor aphasia (TCMA) is invariably nonfluent. Although these individuals usually have normal articulation and are capable of generating grammatically well-formed sentences, they do not voluntarily initiate much verbal output. And when they do decide to talk, they typically use as few words as possible, sometimes beginning a sentence but not finishing it. Because of this breakdown of verbal initiative, TCMA is sometimes referred to as "dynamic aphasia" (Luria & Tsvetkova, 1967). In order to facilitate the initiation of speech and maintain its flow once it has started, some patients use nonlinguistic motor prompts such as nodding their head or moving their hands rhythmically. Fluency often increases when patients are instructed to recite a specific sequence of words, like the days of the week or the months of the year, but patients often have trouble producing the first few items in the list without the help of the examiner. When asked questions or given commands, patients sometimes reiterate part of what was said to them—a phenomenon called echolalia or, more precisely, incorporation echolalia. Similarly, patients sometimes perseverate in their own spontaneous speech, continuing to produce the same word or phrase again and again. Overall, the behavioral profile of TCMA

Echolalia   A deficit involving automatic repetition of what other people say.

Table 3.6 Prototypical Clinical Features of the Transcortical Aphasias

Feature	Transcortical Motor Aphasia (TCMA)	Transcortical Sensory Aphasia (TCSA)	Mixed Transcortical Aphasia (MTCA)
Production	Poor planning and initiation	Phonemic paraphasias	Combination of other two
Comprehension	Relatively preserved	Impaired	Impaired
Repetition	Good	Good	Good

points to an impairment of the ability to generate complex action plans for assembling semantically and grammatically novel utterances. Patients with this syndrome may manage to perform fairly well on some standardized aphasia tests, but will then appear to be completely flummoxed if asked to simply tell a story. For example, when instructed to describe the Cookie Theft picture shown in Figure 3.4, one patient responded with the following characteristically minimal description: "Well it's ... trouble with this ... I can't tell ... having trouble" (Goodglass, 1993, p. 149).

In contrast to their marked language production deficit, patients with TCMA are usually able to comprehend colloquial conversation. They may, however, have difficulty understanding relatively complicated narratives.

Even though patients with TCMA exhibit extreme hesitancy in the voluntary initiation of speech, they respond immediately and, for the most part, correctly when asked to repeat utterances, even when those utterances are full sentences rather than single words. In fact, this dramatic dissociation is generally considered to be the most striking feature of the syndrome.

This syndrome is classically linked with damage to the left dorsolateral prefrontal region. There is often some overlap with Broca's area, and always deep extension into the white matter. Variants of the syndrome have also been reported in patients with lesions affecting the dorsolateral caudate nucleus and adjacent paraventricular white matter. In addition, some of the symptoms of TCMA have been associated with damage to the left supplementary motor area (the medial portion of BA6), but such cases frequently manifest a severe form of mutism that may not qualify as a genuine aphasia (see the operational definition in the Introduction).

Transcortical Sensory Aphasia

The verbal output of patients with transcortical sensory aphasia (TCSA) is fluent but riddled with phonemic paraphasias, neologisms, and semantic substitutions. When these patients are able to generate coherent utterances, those utterances usually consist mainly of generic filler terms like *thing, one, does,* etc. The content of their speech therefore tends to be rather empty. Moreover, they frequently perseverate, and they are highly susceptible to echolalia, often parroting words and phrases produced by the examiner. They will even echo grammatically incorrect sentences, nonsense words, and foreign expressions. This behavior is more uncontrollable than in TCMA, reflecting the overall uninhibited nature of the verbal output in TCSA.

Comprehension is profoundly impaired in this syndrome. Although there are varying degrees of disruption, many patients fail virtually all tests that probe the understanding of spoken words, phrases, and sentences. For example, they typically cannot point to named objects, obey commands, answer yes/no questions, define words, or match words with pictures. This poor performance may be due to a disturbance of semantic knowledge per se, but an alternative possibility is that it arises from a disorder affecting the *interface* between word forms and the corresponding meanings.

Repetition is remarkably well-preserved in TCSA, ranging from good to excellent in quality, and extending from single words to lengthy sentences. Indeed, intact repetition is a central clinical feature of this syndrome, and is one of the major characteristics that distinguishes it from Wernicke's aphasia.

It is noteworthy that patients with TCSA are at risk of being misdiagnosed as psychotic, since their peculiar behavioral profile—generating a profusion of phonemic paraphasias and neologisms intermingled with real but semantically inappropriate words, understanding almost nothing that is said to them, yet accurately and involuntarily echoing other people's utterances—suggests a lack of contact with reality, at least at the verbal level, and hence may lead some health care professionals to suspect a variant of schizophrenia.

TCSA is most reliably linked with lesions near the junction of the left temporal, parietal, and occipital lobes. Involvement of the posterior middle and inferior temporal gyri (roughly the posterior portion of BA21 and the lateral portion of BA37) as well as the inferior angular gyrus (roughly the inferior portion of BA39) is commonly observed.

Mixed Transcortical Aphasia

Mixed transcortical aphasia (MTCA) is essentially a combination of TCMA and TCSA. Production is nonfluent, minimal, and characterized by echolalia and unfinished sentences like "I don't …" and "Not with the …." Comprehension is also severely impaired. Repetition, however, is still intact, and is actually the only spared linguistic capacity.

One of the most frequently cited cases of MTCA was a 22-year-old woman who acquired the disorder as a result of carbon monoxide poisoning (Geschwind et al., 1968). She produced almost no spontaneous speech and could not understand single words. However, she tended to repeat whatever questions were asked of her, she enjoyed singing familiar songs, and she would complete idiomatic expressions that her examiner began. For example, when he said "Ask me no questions," she replied "Tell me no lies." Her condition persisted with little change until she died nine years later. At autopsy, the investigators discovered that her brain had lesions affecting the following left-hemisphere regions: the temporal pole; the middle and inferior temporal gyri; the angular gyrus; the superior parietal lobule; the intraparietal sulcus; and the dorsolateral and ventrolateral prefrontal regions. In striking contrast, however, the phonological circuit that is putatively supported by Broca's area, Wernicke's area, and the interconnecting arcuate fasciculus was entirely spared, thereby enabling the patient to repeat utterances that she could not, unfortunately, associate with any meaning.

Flow Chart for Classifying the Aphasia Syndromes

The eight aphasia syndromes described above can be distinguished from each other according to three dichotomies: nonfluent vs. fluent; impaired vs. intact repetition; and impaired vs. intact comprehension (see Figure 3.10). Beginning with the first dichotomy, four syndromes are nonfluent (Broca's, global, TCMA, and MTCA), and four are fluent (Wernicke's, conduction, anomic, and TCSA). Turning to the second dichotomy, of the four nonfluent syndromes, two involve impaired repetition (Broca's and global) and two involve relatively preserved repetition (TCMA and MTCA); similarly, of the four fluent syndromes, two involve impaired repetition (Wernicke's and conduction) and two involve relatively preserved repetition (anomic and TCSA). Finally, the third dichotomy provides the last level of discrimination: Among the two nonfluent syndromes with impaired repetition, one involves

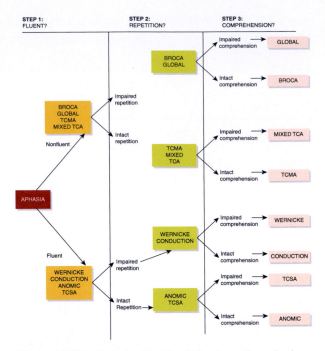

Figure 3.10 Flow chart for classifying the major aphasia syndromes. (From Kirshner et al., 1999, p. 52.)

impaired comprehension (global), whereas the other involves relatively preserved comprehension (Broca's); among the two nonfluent syndromes with relatively preserved repetition, one involves impaired comprehension (MTCA), whereas the other involves relatively preserved comprehension (TCMA); among the two fluent syndromes with impaired repetition, one involves impaired comprehension (Wernicke's), whereas the other involves relatively preserved comprehension (conduction); and among the two fluent syndromes with relatively preserved repetition, one involves impaired comprehension (TCSA), whereas the other involves relatively preserved comprehension (anomic).

The flow chart shown in Figure 3.10 gives clinicians a useful starting point for the differential diagnosis of aphasia, and it gives researchers an informative synopsis of the major behavioral features of the eight classic syndromes. The system is very simplistic, however, not only because it is based on dichotomies that do not allow for variable degrees of deficit, but also because some patients seem to fall between two categories, as noted above (see the section called "How Should Different Types of Aphasia be Classified?") Furthermore, there are many other factors that the scheme neglects (e.g., for information about aphasia in bilinguals and polyglots, see Box 3.4). Still, the classification system does capture in fairly clear terms the most frequently occurring and most carefully studied forms of aphasia.

Box 3.4   Aphasia in Bilinguals and Polyglots

For well over 100 years, researchers have been interested in what happens when bilinguals or polyglots (i.e., individuals who speak three or more languages) become aphasic. One early view was that the patient's original, native language would be impaired less than languages acquired later (Ribot's law), but a rival view maintained that the language used most frequently before the brain injury would show the best recovery (Pitres's law). It turns out that neither theory can account for all of the data that has accumulated during the past century.

Perhaps not surprisingly, most multilingual speakers who become aphasic exhibit fairly comparable degrees and types of impairment and recovery for all of their languages. A number of more complicated patterns have also been observed, however, as summarized in detail by Paradis (1989, 1998):

- *Selective:* One language is partially recovered, but the other(s) are never recovered.
- *Differential:* One language is recovered better than the other(s).
- *Successive:* At first, one language is partially recovered; then later—sometimes many months later—the other(s) are partially recovered.
- *Antagonistic:* Recovery of one language progresses while recovery of the other(s) regresses.
- *Alternating antagonism:* Availability shifts back and forth between one language and the other(s).
- *Blending or mixed:* Properties of multiple languages are mixed together—e.g., the patient speaks one language with the accent of another, or applies the inflectional affixes of one language to the stems of another.

As this brief survey suggests, it is very difficult to predict exactly how the various languages of a polyglot aphasic will be affected. Insights can be gained about particular patients, however, if they are carefully assessed for all of their languages in an equivalent manner (Lorenzen & Murray, 2008).

Summary and Key Points

- Aphasia is an acquired language disorder due to brain damage.
- Scientific research on aphasia began in the mid-to-late 1800s with pioneering discoveries by Paul Broca and Carl Wernicke.
- Different kinds of aphasia are often classified as belonging to different syndromes, where a "syndrome" is defined as a set of specific symptoms that tend to co-occur and that usually arise from damage to a particular brain region or network of regions.
- Many competing classification systems for aphasia have been proposed, but there has never been a complete consensus about which system is most appropriate.
- All syndrome-based approaches to categorizing different kinds of aphasia have several shortcomings: (1) They reflect patterns of impaired and preserved abilities that involve very general modalities or channels of language processing—namely, production, comprehension, and repetition; (2) specific symptoms are classified as being either present or absent, thereby ignoring different degrees of severity; (3) not all symptoms must be present in order for a patient to satisfy the diagnosis for a given syndrome; (4) the lesion correlates of particular syndromes are sometimes violated; and (5) syndromes can be unstable over time.
- Nevertheless, aphasia syndromes capture neuropsychological tendencies that are useful not only to clinicians who are interested in diagnosing and treating patients, but also to researchers who are interested in understanding the neurocognitive architecture of language. The following eight syndromes are commonly distinguished today.
  - *Broca's aphasia:* Nonfluent production, most notable for grammatical deficiencies; relatively preserved comprehension, except for syntactically complex sentences; impaired repetition. The lesion is typically centered in the left posterior inferior frontal lobe, but it often includes surrounding cortical areas, extends deep into the underlying white matter, and affects the anterior insula.

(Continued)

(Continued)

○ *Wernicke's aphasia:* Fluent production, but with conspicuous phonological deficiencies; impaired comprehension; impaired repetition. The lesion is usually found in the left posterior superior and/or middle temporal gyri and the underlying white matter.

○ *Conduction aphasia:* Fluent production, but with conspicuous phonological deficiencies; relatively preserved comprehension; impaired repetition. The lesion sometimes transects the segment of the arcuate fasciculus that connects Wernicke's and Broca's areas; it also commonly affects the left supramarginal gyrus and the most posterior portion of the dorsal plane of the superior temporal gyrus, deep inside the sylvian fissure.

○ *Global aphasia:* A severe language disorder affecting production, comprehension, and repetition, due to a large left perisylvian lesion.

○ *Anomic aphasia:* The deficit involves primarily or exclusively word-finding difficulties. Lesion sites vary, but some correlations have been documented between particular lesion sites and particular domains of word-finding difficulties.

○ *Transcortical motor aphasia (TCMA):* Nonfluent production, most notable for trouble initiating and maintaining spontaneous speech; relatively preserved comprehension; good repetition. The lesion most frequently affects the left dorsolateral prefrontal cortex and underlying white matter.

○ *Transcortical sensory aphasia (TCSA):* Fluent production, but with conspicuous phonological deficiencies; impaired comprehension; good repetition. The lesion usually affects the left posterior middle and inferior temporal gyri, and sometimes also the angular gyrus, with white matter extension.

○ *Mixed transcortical aphasia (MTCA):* Essentially the combination of TCMA and TCSA, with impaired production and comprehension but intact repetition. The lesion typically preserves Broca's area, Wernicke's area, and the interconnecting arcuate fasciculus, while affecting the surrounding frontal, parietal, and/or temporal regions of the left hemisphere.

Recommended Reading

- Goodglass, H. (1993). *Understanding aphasia.* San Diego, CA: Academic Press. A thoughtful, detailed consideration of all aspects of aphasia based on many decades of experience at the Boston University Aphasia Center.
- Benson, D.F., & Ardila, A. (1996). *Aphasia: A clinical perspective.* Oxford, UK: Oxford University Press. A fairly comprehensive book similar in coverage to Goodglass's, but with more emphasis on clinical issues.
- Alexander, M.P. (2002). Aphasia I: Clinical and antomical issues. In M.J. Farah & T.E. Feinberg (Eds.), *Patient-based approaches to cognitive neuroscience,* 2nd edition (pp. 181–198). Cambridge, MA: MIT Press. A well-referenced overview of the classic aphasia syndromes by one of the leading experts in the field.
- Whitworth, A., Webster, J., & Howard, D. (2005). *A cognitive neuropsychological approach to assessment and intervention in aphasia: A clinician's guide.* Hove, UK: Psychology Press. Provides both a theoretical framework and practical guidelines for working with people with aphasia.
- Dronkers, N.F., & Baldo, J. (2009). Language: aphasia. In L.R. Squire (Ed.), *Encyclopedia of neuroscience, Vol. 5* (pp. 343–348). Oxford, UK: Academic Press. An authoritative summary of the classic aphasia syndromes with some of the best neuroanatomical characterizations currently available.
- Ardila, A. (2010). A proposed reinterpretation and reclassification of aphasic syndromes. *Aphasiology, 24,* 363–394. One of the most recent efforts to organize the aphasia syndromes, developed by a major figure in the field, and accompanied by commentaries by three other authorities.
- Ackerman, D. (2011). *One hundred names for love: A stroke, a marriage, and the language of healing.* New York: W.W. Norton & Co. A profoundly humane, deeply insightful, and exquisitely written account of how the author's husband—Paul West, a renowned novelist—gradually recovered from severe aphasia.

Primary Progressive Aphasia Syndromes

Introduction

Aphasia can arise not only abruptly as a result of a sudden brain injury, but also gradually as a consequence of a neurodegenerative disease. During the past few decades, an increasing amount of research has focused on a closely related set of neurodegenerative conditions in which insidiously declining language abilities are the most salient clinical features and the principal cause of restrictions in daily life. These conditions fall under the rubric of what is called **primary progressive aphasia (PPA)**.

Three main PPA syndromes are currently recognized: progressive nonfluent/agrammatic aphasia; semantic dementia; and logopenic progressive aphasia (Gorno-Tempini et al., 2011). Each of these variants is defined in terms of a characteristic cluster of language deficits and a distinctive distribution of cortical atrophy. In addition, a growing number of studies have been investigating the causes of PPA at the levels of tissue abnormalities (i.e., histopathology) and genetic mutations. Reflecting on these advances, Marsel Mesulam, who is one of the leading experts in the field, remarked that "PPA offers a unique experiment of nature for exploring the molecular fingerprints that make the language network a primary disease target and for probing the cognitive architecture of human language as it undergoes a slow but relentless dissolution" (Mesulam, 2007, p. S11).

Demographically, although no studies have directly addressed the frequency of PPA, a rough estimate can be derived by considering that PPA is often in the clinical spectrum related to frontotemporal dementia (FTD). As noted by Murray Grossman (2010), who is another prominent authority on PPA, FTD has a prevalence in the range of 2.7–15.0 per 100,000, and roughly 20–40 percent of FTD cases have PPA, with an average age of onset in the late 50s and an average survival of roughly 7 years. (For additional epidemiological data on just semantic dementia, see Hodges et al., 2010.)

This chapter reviews some of the key findings about PPA. It begins by summarizing the history of research on this topic, and then it describes in detail the three main PPA syndromes. As with the classic aphasia syndromes covered in Chapter 3, each PPA syndrome is discussed in terms of the following features: production, comprehension, repetition, and lesion correlates. Unlike in Chapter 3, however, the discussion of the lesion correlates of each syndrome goes beyond findings about macroscopic areas of brain damage to encompass data on microscopic histopathological and genetic "biomarkers." In addition, the survey of each syndrome includes a brief description of associated neurological deficits. The chapter concludes by considering some of the unique ways in which PPA sheds light on the functional–anatomical organization of language in the brain.

Primary progressive aphasia (PPA) An acquired language deficit (*aphasia*) that is due to a neurodegenerative disease (*progressive*) and that is the most prominent aspect of the clinical picture (*primary*).

Historical Background

The earliest glimpses of PPA date back to the last decade of the 19th century. Working in Prague, the neurologist Arnold Pick (1892) described a man with progressive aphasia who eventually became mute. However, this patient also exhibited progressive amnesia, and moreover he appeared to have a social conduct disorder, since he once threatened his wife with a knife. Thus, his deficits were not restricted to the domain of language. The following year, though, the French neurologist Paul Sérieux (1893) described a woman with a slow deterioration of word comprehension, but without a concomitant loss of memory or intelligence. At autopsy, her brain showed cortical atrophy and neuronal loss in both temporal lobes (Dejerine & Sérieux, 1897). This patient is generally regarded as the first clearcut case of PPA in the history of neurology.

PPA did not surface again in the literature until the mid-1970s, when the British neuropsychologist Elizabeth Warrington (1975) reported three patients with progressive word-finding difficulties together with declining understanding of both words and pictures. In many respects, these patients were similar to the woman studied by Sérieux (1893). Warrington argued that they suffered from a selective deterioration of conceptual knowledge.

Then in the late 1970s, while working with Norman Geschwind in a newly established behavioral neurology unit at the Beth Israel Hospital in Boston, Mesulam unexpectedly encountered a handful of aphasic cases with atypical features. (This story is entertainingly told in a "25 year retrospective" article by Mesulam, 2007.) When asked about her problems, one patient said: "Syntax errors and no articles … Words in the my head and cut up… Writing syntax errors. Edit my work … computer." This patient's agrammatic speech was similar to that of a Broca's aphasic; however, a brain scan did not reveal a cerebrovascular lesion in Broca's area or, for that matter, anywhere in the left hemisphere. Her condition gradually worsened, though, as did that of other patients with analogous clinical profiles.

After these discoveries, it quickly became clear that progressive aphasia is manifested in at least two forms: fluent but with semantic disturbances, as in the cases observed by Sérieux and Warrington; and nonfluent/agrammatic, as in the cases observed by Mesulam. The official term "primary progressive aphasia" was not introduced, however, until the late 1980s, when Mesulam (1987) proposed it in a commentary on a pioneering neuropathological investigation by Kirshner et al. (1987). Shortly thereafter, in an effort to refine the definition of PPA, Mesulam (2001) suggested that in order for a patient to receive this diagnosis, slowly declining

Table 4.1 Inclusion and Exclusion Criteria for the Diagnosis of Primary Progressive Aphasia

Inclusion: Criteria 1–3 Must Be Answered Positively
1. Most prominent clinical feature is difficulty with language
2. These deficits are the principal cause of impaired daily living activities
3. Aphasia should be the most prominent deficit at symptom onset and for the initial phases of the disease

Exclusion: Criteria 1–4 Must Be Answered Negatively
1. Pattern of deficits is better accounted for by other nondegenerative nervous system or medical disorders
2. Cognitive disturbance is better accounted for by a psychiatric diagnosis
3. Prominent initial episodic memory, visual memory, and visuoperceptual impairments
4. Prominent initial behavioral disturbance

Source: Gorno-Tempini et al. (2011, p. 1008).

language abilities must be the dominant deficit for at least two years after the onset of symptoms. This two-year rule was admittedly somewhat arbitrary, especially in light of cases who have exclusively linguistic impairments for up to 14 years; but the criterion has been retained by the majority of researchers and clinicians, since it serves the purpose of distinguishing PPA from other neurodegenerative conditions in which aphasia develops in tandem with deficits in other domains such as episodic memory, visuospatial processing, executive functions, and social cognition (Neary et al., 1998; Kertesz et al., 2003; Mesulam & Weintraub, 2008; Grossman, 2010).

Currently accepted inclusion and exclusion criteria for the diagnosis of PPA are listed in Table 4.1. Increasing atrophy in the left perisylvian cortex is apparent in Figure 4.1, which shows MR scans taken from a PPA patient at two time periods—one year and four years post-symptom-onset. Greater cortical thinning in the left than the right temporal and parietal lobes can also be seen in Figure 4.2, which portrays a postmortem brain slice from a woman with PPA who eventually became mute.

During the past two decades, many of the most important advances in research on PPA have involved the identification and elucidation of distinct variants of the disorder. To be sure, opinions differ as to how boundaries should be drawn between subtypes of PPA, just as controversy has always surrounded the delineation of the more familiar aphasia syndromes reviewed in Chapter 3.

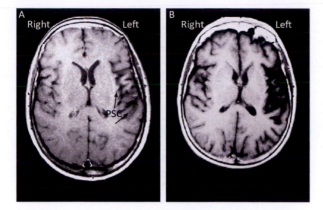

Figure 4.1 MR scans from a patient with PPA in whom symptoms first developed at the age of 61 years. The scan in panel A was obtained one year after the onset of symptoms, and the scan in panel B was obtained four years after the onset. The progression of atrophy in the left perisylvian cortex (PSC) indicates that the disease remained focal as it progressed. (From Mesulam, 2003, p. 1538.)

Nevertheless, the most prevalent view today is that there are three major variants of PPA: progressive nonfluent/agrammatic aphasia (PNFA); semantic dementia (SD); and logopenic progressive aphasia (LPA). Each of these syndromes is defined in terms of specific behavioral features: PNFA is characterized mainly by a degradation of morphology and syntax; SD is characterized mainly by a degradation of conceptual knowledge; and LPA is characterized mainly by a degradation of word retrieval and auditory–verbal short-term memory. In addition, each variant of PPA is linked with a unique anatomical distribution of cortical thinning (Figure 4.3; see also Figure 2.7 in Chapter 2): PNFA is associated with atrophy in the left posterior inferior frontal gyrus (i.e., Broca's area),

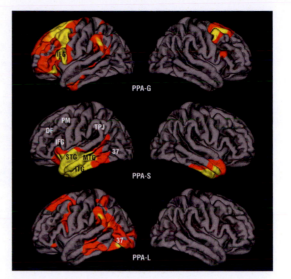

Figure 4.3 Distribution of cortical atrophy (i.e., thinning) in three variants of primary progressive aphasia: PPA-G, which is the agrammatic variant, referred to in the text as progressive nonfluent aphasia (PNFA); PPA-S, which is the semantic variant, referred to in the text as semantic dementia (SD); and PPA-L, which is the logopenic variant, referred to in the text as logopenic progressive aphasia (LPA). Red shading indicates a significance level of $p < .01$; yellow shading, $p < .001$. IFG indicates inferior frontal gyrus; DF, dorsolateral prefrontal cortex; PM, premotor cortex; STG, superior temporal gyrus; MTG, middle temporal gyrus; ITG, inferior temporal gyrus; TPJ, temporoparietal junction; 37, Brodmann area 37. (From Mesulam et al., 2009b, p. 1549.)

extending posteriorly, superiorly, and medially over time; SD is associated with atrophy in the anterior temporal lobes, bilaterally but often with greater involvement in the left hemisphere; and LPA is associated with atrophy in the left posterior superior temporal gyrus (i.e.,

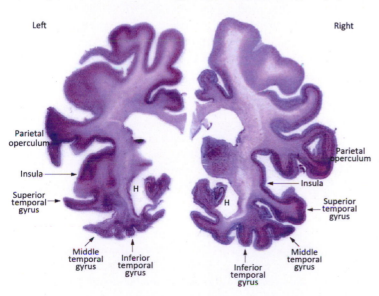

Figure 4.2 Postmortem specimen from a woman with PPA in whom the disease developed at the age of 44 years. The patient died 16 years after onset in a state of mutism and severe dementia. Even in the terminal stage of the disease, there is greater atrophy (thinning of the cortical band) in the parietal operculum, the insula, and superior, middle, and inferior temporal gyri of the left hemisphere, and the disease has spread to the hippocampus (H). (From Mesulam, 2003, p. 1540.)

Table 4.2 Major Features of Progressive Nonfluent/ Agrammatic Aphasia

Production
Nonfluent, hesitant, agrammatic, often with phonological disturbances and/or apraxia of speech

Comprehension
Mostly intact for single words and simple sentences; impaired for complex sentences

Repetition
Impaired

Distribution of Atrophy
Left posterior inferior frontal gyrus (i.e., Broca's area), extending posteriorly into insular, superior temporal, and inferior parietal cortices, superiorly into dorsolateral prefrontal cortex, and medially into orbital and anterior cingulate cortices; white matter pathways are also affected, especially the anterior arcuate fasciculus and anterior fronto-occipital fasciculus

Other Biomarkers
Tau pathology is common; ubiquitin pathology is less common; *PGRN* mutations may be involved

Associated Deficits
Working memory and executive dysfunction, especially in complex verbal and visual tasks

Figure 4.4 A beach scene, illustrating one means of eliciting spontaneous speech. (From Rohrer et al., 2008, p. 15.)

summarized in Table 4.2 and elaborated below (for a detailed review see Grossman, 2012).

Production

The spontaneous speech of patients with PNFA is markedly nonfluent; in fact, this is such a salient aspect of the syndrome that it is directly codified in the name of the disorder. Typically, the verbal output of PNFA patients is slow, effortful, and halting, with many phonological and articulatory mistakes as well as numerous grammatical errors, similar in some respects to the speech of Broca's aphasics (Thompson et al., 1997a; Mendez et al., 2003; Gorno-Tempini et al., 2004; Amici et al., 2007; Knibb et al., 2009; Ash et al., 2009, 2010; Wilson et al., 2010b). Some patients also have trouble initiating and maintaining speech, analogous to cases of transcortical motor aphasia (Cappa et al., 2006; Sajjadi et al., 2012b).

The production deficit in PNFA is illustrated by the following speech sample, which was recorded from a patient who was asked to describe the scene shown in Figure 4.4 (Rohrer et al., 2008, p. 13):

> The sea … er … er … er … um … a man in a soup … no suit … with a panner [pointing at paddle] falling out of the boat. Er … nice stand … no sand next to the sea and the boy making a nice h… h… house … houses. Another [long pause] m… m… m… man … a big men … no man … and little g… g… girl p… p… playing. The two skygurls [points to seagulls]. Water round castle …

Wernicke's area), expanding in several directions as the disease evolves. Although the first two variants of PPA—namely, PNFA and SD—have been recognized for over 20 years, the third variant—namely, LPA—was not identified as a separate syndrome until quite recently (Gorno-Tempini et al., 2004). All three syndromes are now distinguished by the majority of researchers and clinicians, but it is widely acknowledged that, like the classic aphasia syndromes covered in Chapter 3, each of them allows for a great deal of variability (Amici et al., 2006; Mesulam & Weintraub, 2008; Rohrer et al., 2008; Grossman, 2010; Gorno-Tempini et al., 2011; Harciarek & Kertesz, 2011; Sajjadi et al., 2012a).

Progressive Nonfluent/ Agrammatic Aphasia (PNFA)

As mentioned above, the hallmark of PNFA is a gradual deterioration of grammatical processing. However, this is only one part of a larger pattern of impaired and preserved language abilities. The specific behavioral and neuropathological features of this variant of PPA are

In addition to being hesitant and labored, this patient's output is distorted by speech sound errors. Some of these errors involve substitutions, insertions, and deletions that may reflect a disruption of the phonological system, but others involve mispronunciations and instances of groping that are characteristic of apraxia of speech—a deficit that, as noted in Chapters 3 and 6, compromises articulatory planning and often results from damage to either the left posterior inferior frontal gyrus (Hillis et al., 2004b) or the left anterior superior insula (Dronkers, 1996; Ogar et al., 2006; Baldo et al., 2011). Such speech sound errors, together with rhythm and melody impairments, are frequently observed in patients with PNFA (Gorno-Tempini et al., 2006; Josephs et al., 2006; Ogar et al., 2007; Knibb et al., 2009; Ash et al., 2010; Wilson et al., 2010b).

The speech sample above also illustrates what some investigators consider to be the central feature of PNFA: agrammatism (Grossman et al., 1996, 2005; Thompson et al., 1997a, 2013; Ash et al., 2009; Knibb et al., 2009; Mesulam et al., 2009; Wilson et al., 2010b; Sajjadi et al., 2012b; DeLeon et al., 2012). As the disease progresses, the mean length of patients' utterances becomes shorter, and the grammatical stuctures that they employ become simpler. Patients slowly lose their command of closed-class morphemes as well as their ability to generate complex sentences containing subordinate clauses and adjunct phrases. (Readers unfamiliar with these technical terms may wish to consult the "syntax tutorial" in Chapter 14.) In addition, several studies have shown that PNFA patients are significantly more impaired at producing verbs than nouns (Hillis et al., 2004a, 2006; Cotelli et al., 2006; Davis et al., 2010; Thompson et al., 2012). This may contribute to their expressive deficit in grammatical processing, since verbs play an important role in shaping the syntactic structures of sentences.

A final point—which is, unfortunately, rather discouraging—concerns the unremitting nature of the dissolution of language in PNFA. In the end-stages of the disease, most patients enter a state of global aphasia, with output ultimately becoming limited to single words, repeated syllables, or even just grunts.

Comprehension

In the early and middle stages of the disease, PNFA patients can usually follow ordinary conversational speech fairly well, but this ability gradually deteriorates. Single word comprehension is initially quite good; however, patients often have more trouble understanding verbs than nouns (Rhee et al., 2001; Cotelli et al., 2006; Hillis et al., 2006). As in Broca's aphasia, the most severe deficit in receptive language processing involves determining "who did what to whom" in syntactically complex sentences like *The reporter who the senator attacked admitted the error* (Grossman et al., 1996, 2005; Hodges & Patterson, 1996; Thompson

et al., 1997a; Grossman & Moore, 2005; Amici et al., 2007; Peelle et al., 2008; Wilson et al., 2010a).

This impairment of complex sentence comprehension may reflect a degradation of the neurocognitive mechanisms that are dedicated to rapidly, automatically, and unconsciously analyzing and integrating the grammatical features of words and phrases as they are heard. Evidence for this view comes from a study by Peelle et al. (2007) that employed a special online technique for measuring auditory sentence comprehension as it unfolds over time. On each trial, subjects listened to a short discourse via headphones, and their task was to push a button as soon as they heard a particular word. Crucially, in some trials a morphological or syntactic error occurred immediately before the target word. For example, in the following short discourse, the target word is COOK, but the word that precedes it is incorrect; specifically, it is the noun *wastage* instead of the adjective *wasteful* (Tyler, 1992, p. 5):

- Sally couldn't believe that John used so much butter. He was the most *wastage* COOK she had ever met.

Replicating previous studies, Peelle et al. (2007) found that when healthy adults performed this task, they were slower to detect target words that occurred right after errors, presumably because their processing resources were momentarily "captured" by those errors. However, a valuable new discovery was that when PNFA patients performed the task, their response times for detecting target words were not significantly influenced by the presence of errors. This suggests that the mental machinery that normally tracks the grammatical structures of sentences is no longer operating properly in PNFA patients.

Repetition

The ability to repeat words, phrases, and sentences is usually defective in this variant of PPA (Grossman et al., 1996; Mendez et al., 2003; Gorno-Tempini et al., 2004; Mesulam et al., 2009b). For example, in one study patients were administered the "Repeat and Point" task, in which participants are presented with 10 multisyllabic words and are asked, for each one, to first repeat it and then point to its referent in an array of six pictures (Hodges et al., 2008). Although PNFA patients were not impaired on the pointing aspect of the task, they performed significantly below normal on the repetition component.

Lesion Correlates and Other Biomarkers

PNFA is linked with a pattern of predominantly left-lateralized cortical thinning that usually begins in the

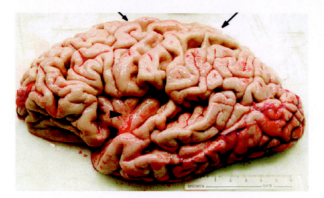

Figure 4.5 Brain of a patient who had progressive nonfluent/agrammatic aphasia (PNFA) associated with corticobasal degeneration. During life, this patient had hesitant, effortful speech with grammatical errors and some phonological errors, as well as impaired comprehension of syntactically complex sentences, consistent with PNFA. Inspection of this left-hemisphere specimen at autopsy revealed considerable atrophy in inferior frontal and anterior superior temporal regions, as well as superior parietal and frontal cortices. Arrowhead indicates insula revealed by marked atrophy in inferior frontal and superior temporal portions of the left hemisphere. Large arrow indicates atrophy of the superior parietal lobule; small arrow indicates superior frontal atrophy. Histopathological examination revealed tau-positive ballooned cells and other histopathological features consistent with corticobasal degeneration. (From Grossman, 2010, p. 92.)

posterior inferior frontal gyrus (i.e., Broca's area) and extends over time in several directions: posteriorly into the anterior insula, anterior superior temporal lobe, and anterior parietal cortex; superiorly into the dorsolateral prefrontal cortex; and medially into orbital and anterior cingulate regions (Gorno-Tempini et al., 2004; Schroeter et al., 2007; Peelle et al., 2008; Mesulam et al., 2009b; Rohrer et al., 2009b; Rogalski et al., 2011). This distribution of atrophy appears in MRI studies that employ voxel-based morphometry (Figure 4.3; see also Figure 2.7 in Chapter 2) as well as in studies of postmortem brains (Figure 4.5). Tissue loss in the inferior frontal and anterior insular regions correlates significantly with declining speech coordination and execution (Gorno-Tempini et al., 2006; Amici et al., 2007; Wilson et al., 2010b), whereas tissue loss in the inferior frontal, dorsolateral prefrontal, and supramarginal regions correlates significantly with declining sentence production and comprehension (Peelle et al., 2008; Mesulam et al., 2009b; Wilson et al., 2010a, 2010b; Sapolsky et al., 2010; Rogalski et al., 2011). It is also noteworthy that functional neuroimaging studies have revealed reduced blood flow and glucose metabolism in the left posterior inferior frontal gyrus and left anterior insula (Grossman et al., 1996; Nestor et al., 2003; Rabinovici et al., 2008).

Finally, white matter analyses indicate that the anterior arcuate fasciculus and anterior fronto-occipital fasciculus degenerate in PNFA (Rohrer et al., 2010; Whitwell et al., 2010; Galantucci et al., 2011; Grossman et al., 2013). Moreover, a recent study found that impaired verbal fluency in PNFA is closely related to abnormalities in a fiber tract that interconnects Broca's area (especially BA44) and the (pre)supplementary motor area, which resides on the dorsomedial surface of the superior frontal gyrus (Catani et al., 2013). This is especially interesting because, as described in greater detail in Chapter 6, the (pre)supplementary motor area has been implicated in the initiation of speech.

In recent years, tissue analyses have revealed that PNFA is often, but not always, linked with certain types of protein abnormalities in the brain (for a review see Grossman, 2010). The most common finding is **tau pathology**. Tau proteins reside in the axons of neurons. They play essential roles in forming the cytoskeleton of axons and in constructing the channels through which material is transported. Tau abnormalities are associated not only with PNFA, but also with several other neurodegenerative conditions, including **corticobasal degeneration**. In addition, but less frequently, PNFA is associated with **ubiquitin pathology**. Ubiquitin is yet another type of protein, but it has a much more diverse set of functions than tau. Basically, it contributes to various homeostatic systems such as cell-cycle regulation, DNA repair, and immunological operations. Ubiquitin dysfunctions have been implicated not just in PNFA, but in many other diseases as well, including cancer.

Further insights into the causes of PNFA have come from studies focusing on genetic mutations. For example, there are several reports of families in which the most affected members had PNFA in conjunction with a mutation of the **progranulin (PGRN) gene** on chromosome 17 (Snowden et al., 2006; Mesulam et al., 2007; Beck et al., 2008). Findings like these are very important because they show that a *PGRN* mutation is a significant risk factor for PNFA. At the same time, however, it is essential to realize that not everyone who has such a mutation develops the disease; in

Tau and ubiquitin pathologies Protein abnormalities that are found in the brains of PNFA patients and that are interpreted as signs of neurogeneration.

Corticobasal degeneration A progressive neurodegenerative disease that affects the cerebral cortex and the basal ganglia and that is characterized by movement dysfunctions similar to those seen in Parkinson's disease.

Progranulin (PGRN) gene A gene on chromosome 17 that is mutated in some patients with PNFA.

fact, only about one-third of carriers do (Pickering-Brown et al., 2008). In other individuals a *PGRN* mutation can, in concert with other causal factors, give rise to either a different variant of PPA, namely LPA (Rohrer et al., 2010), or any of several non-linguistic neuropsychological disorders, such as visual hallucinations or an episodic memory impairment (Le Ber et al., 2008). Caution is clearly warranted when interpreting the genetic data pertinent to PPA.

Associated Neurological Deficits

Throughout the early stages of the illness, core cognitive functions remain largely preserved. Patients are able to recall daily events and behave with sound judgment. Some patients even intensify their involvement in recreational activities that do not rely heavily on language, such as gardening, carpentry, sculpting, painting, and music (see Box 4.1). Even toward the beginning of the disease, however, PNFA is strongly associated with deficits involving working memory and executive function, especially in verbal tasks (Peelle et al., 2008) but also in some complex visual tasks (Grossman et al., 2008). In addition, as the disease advances, it is common for motor symptoms to develop, including diffuse slowing, reduced dexterity, mild rigidity, and repetitive movements, mostly affecting the right hand and the right side of the body (Kertesz et al., 2003; Kertesz & Munoz, 2004). This is consistent with the view that PNFA is frequently associated with corticobasal degeneration.

Box 4.1   Creativity in Art and Music: The Positive Side of PPA?

It has been suggested that degeneration of the left hemisphere, which is dominant for language and logical reasoning, can sometimes enhance the operation of the right hemisphere, which is more involved in non-verbal cognition and creativity (Miller et al., 1996). Interestingly, this may occur in some individuals with PNFA. A case in point is patient AA, an exceptional painter whose artistic, clinical, and neuropathological developments were carefully studied by Seeley et al. (2008).

In 1986, at the age of 46, AA left her job as a college chemistry teacher in order to take care of her son, who had been injured in a motor vehicle accident. The young man recovered quite well, but AA decided, instead of returning to her academic position, to pursue a newly acquired fascination with painting. Although she had dabbled in drawing and painting on a few occasions earlier in her life, she had never studied or practiced art in a serious way. Suddenly, however, she had an intense desire to paint, and she spent longer and longer periods of time in her studio, sharpening her skills and exploring various styles and themes. At age 54, six years before the first symptoms of PNFA emerged, she painted one of her greatest works, "Unravelling Boléro," which is essentially a visual translation of the musical score for "Boléro," written by the famous French composer Maurice Ravel. In an uncanny twist of fate, and unbeknownst to AA, Ravel was also stricken with an illness that some medically informed historians suspect may have been a variant of PPA. Moreover, AA created her painting at nearly the same age and pre-symptomatic disease stage that characterized Ravel when he created his score. Yet another intriguing coincidence is that both "Boléros" are exercises in compulsivity and perseveration. While maintaining a consistent staccato bass line, the musical piece repeats the same two melodic themes eight times over 340 bars, without a key change, but with slowly increasing volume and instrumentation, until it ultimately accelerates into a finale. To visually depict this auditory organization, the painting uses an upright rectangle to represent each musical bar, with height corresponding to volume, shape to timbre, and color to pitch (Figure 4B1.1).

In 2000, when she was 60, AA's language abilities started to decline in a manner consistent with PNFA. Her condition deteriorated precipitously over the next five years, and by the age of 65 she

Figure 4B1.1   "Unravelling Boléro," painted by AA in 1994, six years before the onset of symptoms consistent with PNFA. (From Seeley et al., 2008, p. 41.)

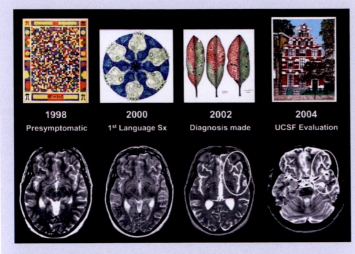

Figure 4B1.2 Serial MRI scans of AA's brain, showing emergent atrophy in the left posterior inferior frontal gyrus and anterior insula. Scans performed before her PPA diagnosis reveal no definite cortical atrophy, but scans performed after the diagnosis indicate worsening frontoinsular atrophy. Each MRI is paired with a representative painting from the same year: 1998, "pi," in which AA transformed the decimal expansion of pi into a visual matrix to capture the random nature of that expansion; 2000, a painting from the "ABC Book of Invertebrates," in which each letter of the alphabet was assigned an organism, which was painted in mandala format; 2002, "Arbutus leaves," which reflects a trend toward increasingly photographic reproductions of stimuli she encountered; and 2004, "Amsterdam," which was completed when she could barely speak, and which was one of many paintings from that period that focused on the facades of buildings and surrounding surfaces. (From Seeley et al., 2008, p. 44.)

was almost mute. Throughout this time, however, she continued to paint, and, remarkably enough, as her verbal skills progressively eroded, her artistic style gradually evolved away from transmodal and abstract concepts toward greater photographic realism, with increasing attention to the colors and structural details of natural objects, buildings, and scenes.

Because of an acoustic neuroma (a neurological disorder unrelated to PNFA), AA began undergoing brain scans in 1998, a few years before the onset of aphasia. It was therefore possible to document the complete course of cortical atrophy in this particular patient, from the preclinical period through the early, middle, and final stages of the disease. MRIs from 1998 to 2004 are shown in Figure 4B1.2 together with representative paintings from the year of each scan. These images capture the close temporal correspondence between AA's left frontoinsular degeneration and her transition from very abstract to very concrete artistic themes. Additional neuropathological findings are shown in Figure 4B1.3. Once again, left frontoinsular atrophy is apparent. In striking contrast, however, an above-normal volume of gray matter was discovered in the right intraparietal sulcus and superior parietal lobule—regions that have been implicated in high-level visuospatial and visuomotor functions as well as multisensory integration and attentional control. Seeley et al. (2008) acknowledge that it is not clear if this increase in gray matter reflects changes that occurred during the course of AA's illness. Nevertheless, as they point out, it is worth considering the possibility that "early degeneration within AA's left [inferior frontal cortex] disinhibited her right posterior cortices, causing her to experience a more vivid and connected perceptual world as her inner speech and other linguistic functions declined" (Seeley et al., 2008, p. 48).

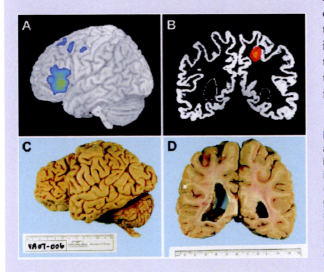

Figure 4B1.3 Neuropathological findings. (A, C) Severe atrophy of the left inferior frontal gyrus as demonstrated by voxel-based morphometry (A) and at autopsy (C). The interval between MRI acquisition and death was 3 years. (B, D) Voxel-based morphometry also revealed increased gray matter in AA vs. controls in the right intraparietal sulcus and superior parietal lobule (B), and this region was structurally normal (or better) at autopsy (D). The MRI slice in (B) corresponds to the autopsy slice in (D) to facilitate comparison. (From Seeley et al., 2008, p. 46.)

Semantic Dementia (SD)

The next PPA syndrome, SD, is quite different from PNFA. Grammatical and phonological aspects of language are largely spared, but semantic knowledge is slowly lost (Hodges & Patterson, 2007). The following anecdote relayed by Patterson et al. (2007, p. 976) gives a feeling for what this disorder is like:

> Mr. M, a patient with semantic dementia—a neurodegenerative disease that is characterized by the gradual deterioration of semantic memory—was being driven through the countryside to visit a friend and was able to remind his wife where to turn along the not-recently-travelled route. Then, pointing at the sheep in the field, he asked her 'What are those things?' Prior to the onset of symptoms in his late 40s, this man had normal semantic memory. What has gone wrong in his brain to produce this dramatic and selective erosion of conceptual knowledge?

The major behavioral and neuropathological features of SD are listed in Table 4.3 and reviewed below (for further information see Chapters 10–12).

Production

The spontaneous speech of SD patients is much more fluent than that of PNFA patients, but it is nevertheless abnormal. The most salient defect is that patients tend to avoid basic-level words like *dog* in favor of superordinate or generic terms like *animal* or *thing* (Snowden et al., 1989; Gorno-Tempini et al., 2004; Ash et al., 2009; Wilson et al., 2010b; Hoffman et al., in press). As a result, they rarely manage to convey much in the way of substantial information. For example, when asked to describe the picture shown in Figure 4.4, one patient gave the following account (Rohrer et al., 2008, p. 13):

> That's the father, playing with his son, that thing [points to ball] ... hitting the thing in the air. [Pointing to boy falling out of boat.] He's in the garden isn't he, playing that game again. I hope he doesn't fall down. Looks as if he's wobbling. [Pointing to sandcastle.] I'm not quite sure. That's the water there, coming right up to there, and that stays there and he's working, he's pressing that down, isn't he? He's working it. He's moving it down there because that's the equivalent of that, and that goes there ... both sides. I've seen something like that somewhere else.

This narrative is grammatically and phonologically well-formed, but it is lexically quite impoverished and falls far

Table 4.3 Major Features of Semantic Dementia (SD)

Production
Fluent but with semantic errors

Comprehension
Impaired

Repetition
Intact

Distribution of Atrophy
Anterior temporal lobes bilaterally but more severe in the left hemisphere and with posterior extension over time; white matter pathways are also affected, especially the inferior longitudinal fasciculus and the uncinate fasciculus

Other Biomarkers
Ubiquitin pathology in two-thirds of cases

Associated Deficits
Poor object recognition; abnormal social cognition and emotional regulation

short of what most people would consider to be an adequate linguistic portrayal of the scene. For instance, the ball is referred to as just a *thing*, and the boat is called a *garden*, which may reflect an error of either visual object recognition or spoken word selection. Furthermore, the description of the boy building a sandcastle is extremely vague, and it's not even clear if the patient really understands what's happening. Overall, the story has a grossly insufficient amount of conceptual content. However, this dearth of semantic specificity typifies the spontaneous speech of SD patients.

Against this background, it is not surprising that most SD patients perform quite poorly on confrontation naming tasks (Grossman et al., 2004; Jefferies & Lambon Ralph, 2006; Mesulam et al., 2009a). As the disease progresses, these naming difficulties become worse. This is exemplified by the responses of one patient, JL, who was evaluated at six-month intervals over a two-year period, with one of the tasks being to name pictures of several different kinds of birds (Table 4.4; Hodges et al., 1995). At the first assessment, JL correctly named many of the birds but also made a number of errors; for example, he used the word *duck* to designate an eagle, a peacock, and a penguin. At the second assessment, JL correctly named only two items and referred to almost all of the others with the basic-level term *bird*. At the third assessment, not only

Table 4.4 Picture-Naming Responses of One SD Patient Who Was Assessed Longitudinally (Hodges et al., 1995)

Item	September 1991	March 1992	September 1992	March 1993
Bird	+	+	+	Animal
Chicken	+	+	Bird	Animal
Duck	+	Bird	Bird	Dog
Swan	+	Bird	Bird	Animal
Eagle	Duck	Bird	Bird	Horse
Ostrich	Swan	Bird	Cat	Animal
Peacock	Duck	Bird	Cat	Vehicle
Penguin	Duck	Bird	Cat	Part of animal
Rooster	Chicken	Chicken	Bird	Dog

+ = correct response.

did he continue to refer to many of the items as simply *birds,* but for three items he went beyond the boundaries of the avian category and described them as *cats.* At the fourth and final assessment, JL used more words for non-avian animals, like *dog* and *horse,* to denote several birds, and he resorted to the superordinate term *animal* to denote several others; he even called the peacock a *vehicle,* apparently failing to recognize it as an animate entity. Stepping back from the details, what this longitudinal study reveals is a gradual loss of the semantic features that support the capacity to discriminate between various members of a particular conceptual category—in this case, the category of birds. The deterioration eventually reached the point where the patient could not even discriminate between birds and other species, or between animate and inanimate entities.

It is important to note, however, that the naming deficit in SD is sensitive to several factors. For instance, it is influenced by the familiarity of the stimulus, by the frequency of the target word, and by the age at which that word is usually acquired (Lambon Ralph et al., 1998). In addition, some classes of words are often harder to access than others, at least for some SD patients. Nouns sometimes pose a greater challenge than verbs (Hillis et al., 2004, 2006), and within the domain of nouns, words for living things are sometimes more difficult to retrieve than words for non-living things (Lambon Ralph et al., 2003; Zannino et al., 2006; Mesulam et al., 2009a).

Comprehension

The conceptual disorder in SD is displayed not only in expressive tasks, but also in receptive ones. For instance,

patients tend to perform poorly on single word comprehension tasks such as matching words with pictures, generating definitions of words (e.g., "What is a squirrel?"), judging the semantic relatedness of words (e.g., "Is a trench more like a ditch or a hedge?"), and drawing pictures of objects based on their names (Hodges et al., 1992; Lambon Ralph et al., 1999; Bozeat et al., 2003; Gorno-Tempini et al., 2004; Jefferies et al., 2009). Some of these patterns are nicely illustrated in a recent investigation of seven SD patients by Mesulam et al. (2009a). High error rates were observed on a word-to-picture matching task, but the majority of mistakes were not arbitrary, since most of the patients were more likely to match a word like *snake* with a categorically related object like a cat or a squirrel than with a perceptually related object like a tie or a belt. Only two patients had semantic impairments severe enough to blur large-scale inter-category boundaries, and they also appeared to be at a more advanced stage of the disease than the other patients. High error rates were observed on a word definition task as well, with moderately impaired patients making primarily intra-category confusions (e.g., *zebra* → "A small animal that would be a flying type of animal"), and more gravely impaired patients being more prone to inter-category confusions (e.g., *pumpkin* → "It's an animal also. It's relatively, well, I can't say if it is a small or a big animal"). Overall, Mesulam et al.'s (2009a) study provides an excellent demonstration of the gradual degradation of word meaning that characterizes SD.

This degradation does not, however, always affect all word classes equally. Paralleling the production data mentioned above, comprehension differences have been documented between word classes for at least some SD patients. Nouns are sometimes harder to understand than verbs (Hillis et al., 2006), and nouns for living things are sometimes harder to understand than nouns for non-living things (Lambon Ralph et al., 2003; Zannino et al., 2006; Mesulam et al., 2009a). There is also some evidence that words with concrete meanings are disrupted to a larger extent than words with abstract meanings (Breedin et al., 1994; Macoir, 2009; Papagno et al., 2009; Bonner et al., 2009), but this is by no means a consistent finding, and recent work suggests that the majority of SD patients are impaired to roughly the same degree for concrete and abstract words (Jefferies et al., 2009; Hoffman & Lambon Ralph, 2011; Hoffman et al., 2013; see Chapter 12 for further information).

It is notable that the semantic dysfunction in SD often encompasses various nonverbal ways of processing object concepts. For example, patients are frequently impaired at copying simple line drawings of objects after a 10-second delay (Figure 4.6; Patterson et al., 2007), at sorting objects according to similarity (Gorno-Tempini et al., 2004), at distinguishing between correctly and incorrectly colored objects (Adlam et al., 2006), and at recognizing objects from their sounds (Bozeat et al., 2000), smells (Luzzi et al., 2007), and tastes (Piwnica-Worms et al., 2010). These findings have led some researchers to conclude that SD is a neurodegenerative disease that targets amodal conceptual representations of objects (Lambon Ralph & Patterson, 2008; Lambon Ralph et al., 2010b). We return to this intriguing proposal in Chapters 10–12. It is also worth mentioning, however, that the very same findings have generated a controversy over whether SD does or does not satisfy the diagnostic criteria for PPA (Knibb & Hodges, 2005; Adlam et al., 2006; Mesulam et al., 2003, 2009a). This is not a trivial issue, because in some situations it is important to distinguish between patients who do and do not exhibit nonverbal object-recognition deficits during the first two years of the disease. In practice, though, most investigators tend to disregard the definitional debate, because even those patients who do not initially have such nonverbal deficits almost invariably develop them later on, and sometimes rather quickly.

Repetition

The ability to repeat words, phrases, and sentences is largely preserved in SD (Gorno-Tempini et al., 2004; Amici et al., 2006; Hodges et al., 2008; Mesulam et al. (2009a). For example, on the "Repeat and Point" task that was discussed earlier in connection with PNFA, individuals with SD tend to perform well on the repetition

Model   Delayed copy

Figure 4.6 Delayed-copy drawings produced by SD patients. The patients were shown a model picture which was then removed and, after a 10-second delay, they were asked to reproduce this picture from memory. (From Patterson et al., 2007, p. 979.)

component but consistently fail the comprehension (i.e., pointing) component (Hodges et al., 2008).

Lesion Correlates and Other Biomarkers

This variant of PPA is associated with anterior temporal lobe atrophy that is bilateral but frequently more pronounced in the left hemisphere (Figure 4.3; see also Figure 2.7 in Chapter 2 and Figure 10.11 in Chapter 10). The greatest tissue degeneration occurs in the polar, lateral, and ventral sectors of the anterior temporal cortex, as well as several white matter tracts, including the inferior longitudinal fasciculus and the uncinate fasciculus (Gorno-Tempini et al., 2004;

Schroeter et al., 2007; Mesulam et al., 2009b; Rohrer et al., 2009b, 2010; Sapolsky et al., 2010; Rogalski et al., 2011; Galantucci et al., 2011; Acosta-Cabronero et al., 2011). In addition, blood flow and glucose metabolism decrease in the anterior temporal lobes as the disease advances (Nestor et al., 2006; Desgranges et al., 2007; Rabinovici et al., 2008; Acosta-Cabronero et al., 2011). Importantly, the degree of atrophy and hypometabolism in one particular sector of the left anterior temporal lobe—specifically, the anterior sector of the fusiform gyrus—correlates most significantly with the degree of verbal semantic impairment (Binney et al., 2010; Mion et al., 2010; see Figure 10.17 in Chapter 10). Finally, if one zooms in to explore the tissue degeneration in SD at the level of neuronal structure, one finds that over two-thirds of the postmortem brains of SD patients have ubiquitin protein abnormalities (for a review see Grossman, 2010). Such abnormalities are much more common in SD than in PNFA.

Associated Neurological Deficits

In striking contrast to their profound disorder of semantic memory, SD patients often have relatively spared episodic memory, working memory, and nonverbal problem-solving, even at late stages of the disease (Scahill et al., 2005; Nestor et al., 2006). However, as the disease progresses, they frequently develop a disorder of social cognition and emotional regulation characterized by disinhibition, obsessive-compulsive tendencies, hypersexuality, and reduced empathy (Snowden et al., 2001; Liu et al., 2004; Rosen et al., 2006).

Logopenic Progressive Aphasia (LPA)

The third major PPA syndrome, LPA, has not been investigated in as much depth as the other two. Although it was initially reported in early descriptions of PPA (Mesulam, 1982; Mesulam, 2001; Kertesz et al., 2003), it did not begin to receive close attention until relatively recently, beginning with a landmark study by Gorno-Tempini et al. (2004) and continuing with a series of follow-up studies (for a review see Henry & Gorno-Tempini, 2010; see also Amici et al., 2006; Rosen et al., 2006; Gorno-Tempini et al., 2008; Rabinovici et al., 2008; Mesulam et al., 2009b; Rohrer et al., 2010; Sapolsky et al., 2010; Wilson et al., 2010b; Rogalski et al., 2011; Machulda et al., in press). The core deficits in LPA appear to involve word retrieval and auditory–verbal short-term memory, and these disturbances have consequences for all of the different

Table 4.5   Major Features of Logopenic Progressive Aphasia

Production
Profound word-finding difficulties, sometimes accompanied by phonemic paraphasias
Comprehension
Mostly intact for single words and simple sentences; impaired for complex sentences
Repetition
Usually normal for words but impaired for sentences; poor recall of sequences of digits, letters, and words
Distribution of Atrophy
Left posterior superior temporal gyrus (i.e., Wernicke's area), extending superiorly into the supramarginal gyrus, posteriorly into the angular gyrus, and inferiorly into the posterior middle temporal gyrus; more anterior left-hemisphere areas may also be affected as the disease develops; white matter pathways associated with all of these cortical areas may be implicated as well
Other Biomarkers
About 50 percent of cases have pathology suggesting a form of Alzheimer's disease; ubiquitin pathology is also frequent
Associated Deficits
Ideomotor apraxia; calculation difficulties

forms of language use that we have been considering—production, comprehension, and repetition. The main features of this variant of PPA are listed in Table 4.5 and discussed in greater detail below.

Production

The language output in LPA is semantically and, for the most part, grammatically correct but often rather slow, with frequent and prolonged word-finding pauses as well as intermittent self-repairs and rephrasings. According to Mesulam and Weintraub (2008), the salient anomic symptoms can be manifested in either of two ways. On the one hand, some LPA patients experience word-finding difficulties most frequently when they are speaking spontaneously and without reference to directly perceptible stimuli—for example, when telling an examiner about their occupation. Mesulam and Weintraub refer to this as "intrinsic" anomia because the route to the lexicon starts with internal thoughts and feelings. On the other hand, some LPA patients experience word-finding difficulties most frequently when they are attempting to name an object or action, or when they are asked to describe a scene. Mesulam and Weintraub refer to this as "extrinsic" anomia because the route to the lexicon starts with external stimuli. This second manifestation of anomia is illustrated in the following passage, which was recorded from a patient describing the picture in Figure 4.4 (Rohrer et al., 2008, p. 13):

> A beach scene … playing on the beach. A pier … and a building on the pier and a row of beach … things. [Long pause] In the middle ground, a father and child playing with a large ball on the…. On the left … er … a rower has overbalanced next to the beach really … and is falling out over the … side of the er … rowing boat. In the foreground is a youngster building some … sandcastles.

The narrative is well-constructed in terms of both form and content, but it is relatively simple, and, most conspicuous of all, it is punctuated by many lengthy pauses during which the patient cannot retrieve the desired words. Although the two types of anomia—intrinsic and extrinsic—dissociate from each other in some LPA patients, they are similar insofar as they both compromise the capacity to access lexical–phonological representations. As the disease progresses, patients become increasingly anomic and hence increasingly nonfluent. Most of the time, their word-finding errors consist of either tip-of-the-tongue states or the production of semantically superordinate words. Once in a while, though, LPA patients commit phonological paraphasias—for example, substituting *tamp* for *lamp* (Weintraub et al., 1990; Kertesz et al., 2003; Gorno-Tempini et al., 2008; Wilson et al., 2010b). Full-blown neologistic jargon aphasia can also occur (e.g., Rohrer et al., 2009a), but it seems to be quite rare, which raises some interesting questions in light of the fact that, as indicated below, the atrophy in LPA is typically centered in Wernicke's area.

Comprehension

LPA patients usually have relatively preserved comprehension of single words and simple sentences well into the middle and late stages of the disease. However, their ability to determine "who's doing what to whom" in syntactically complex sentences gradually deteriorates, even to a greater extent than in PNFA (Gorno-Tempini et al., 2004, 2008). The nature of the impairment that underlies this difficulty in decoding complex sentences is not currently understood, but it will undoubtedly become clearer as research on LPA continues to develop.

Repetition

So far, the investigation of repetition in LPA has yielded somewhat mixed results. Several studies have found that repetition is generally normal for words but impaired for sentences (Gorno-Tempini et al., 2004, 2008; Rohrer et al., 2010), yet at least one study has found that repetition can be well-preserved for both words and sentences (Mesulam et al., 2009b). Despite these inconsistencies, however, there is independent evidence that auditory–verbal short-term memory is severely disrupted in LPA. In particular, patients tend to perform quite poorly on tasks that load heavily on the phonological loop, such as recalling sequences of digits, letters, and words in both forward and backward linear order (Gorno-Tempini et al., 2008; Rohrer et al., 2010).

Lesion Correlates and Other Biomarkers

Unlike both PNFA and SD, LPA is linked with atrophy in the posterior regions of the left hemisphere language system. The neurodegeneration usually affects the posterior superior temporal gyrus (i.e., Wernicke's area) with extension superiorly into the supramarginal gyrus, posteriorly into the angular gyrus, and inferiorly into the posterior middle temporal gyrus (Figure 4.3; see also Figure 2.7 in Chapter 2; Gorno-Tempini et al., 2004, 2008; Mesulam et al., 2009b; Sapolsky et al., 2010). Reductions in blood flow and glucose metabolism have also been reported in these brain regions (Gorno-Tempini et al., 2008; Rabinovici et al., 2008; Madhavan et al., 2013). As the disease evolves, other regions in the left temporal, parietal, and frontal lobes may be affected, including not only various cortical areas but also the white matter axonal pathways that connect them (Mesulam et al., 2009b; Rohrer et al., 2010, 2013).

The language disturbances in LPA are analogous to those seen in Alzheimer's disease (AD), so it is not surprising that about half of LPA patients have associated AD pathology (Grossman, 2010; Leyton et al., 2011). Many other LPA patients, however, have ubiquitin pathology tied to *PGRN* mutations (Grossman, 2010). An important direction for future research will be to study these pathologically defined subgroups of LPA more carefully to determine whether they also differ neuropsychologically and neuroanatomically (e.g., Rohrer et al., 2010, 2013).

Associated Neurological Deficits

Individuals with LPA sometimes exhibit ideomotor apraxia (i.e., difficulty imitating hand gestures and pantomiming tool use) and acalculia (i.e., deficits in performing mathematical calculations). But they usually do not develop either the sorts of executive dysfunctions that often emerge during the course of PNFA, or the sorts of behavioral abnormalities that often emerge during the course of SD (Gorno-Tempini et al., 2004; Amici et al., 2006; Rosen et al., 2006; Rohrer et al., 2010).

PPA as a Window on the Neurobiology of Language

The three major PPA syndromes described above are molecularly based degenerative diseases that target specific neural networks within the language-dominant left hemisphere, thereby leading to the slow but relentless deterioration of particular aspects of verbal communication. They present not only a formidable challenge to clinicians who aspire to alleviate patients' deficits, but also a valuable source of data for researchers who aim to understand the functional–anatomical organization of language in the brain. In this concluding section, we first discuss various similarities and differences between the major PPA syndromes and the classic aphasia syndromes, and then we turn to some ways in which the PPA syndromes can be construed as signatures of distinct patterns of regional vulnerability within the language system.

As one would expect, aphasias that emerge gradually from progressive diseases share many features with aphasias that emerge abruptly from cerebrovascular accidents. For instance, PNFA is remarkably similar to Broca's aphasia insofar as both disorders have the following properties: effortful, nonfluent, agrammatic production; phonological disturbances and/or apraxia of speech; impaired comprehension of syntactically complex sentences; poor repetition; and dysfunction of the left posterior inferior frontal gyrus and surrounding regions. Likewise, LPA has several features in common with the three classic aphasia syndromes that are associated with posterior lesions. As in Wernicke's aphasia, LPA involves phonological paraphasias, impaired sentence comprehension, poor repetition, and dysfunction of the posterior superior and middle temporal gyri. As in conduction aphasia, LPA involves phonological paraphasias, poor repetition, and dysfunction of the supramarginal gyrus and underlying white matter. And as in transcortical sensory aphasia, LPA involves impaired sentence comprehension together with dysfunction of the angular gyrus and the posterior middle temporal gyrus.

At the same time, however, the PPA syndromes differ from the classic aphasia syndromes in nontrivial ways. For example, despite the fact that the atrophy in LPA is centered in Wernicke's area, LPA patients do not typically produce phonological paraphasias as often as Wernicke's aphasics, and neologistic jargon aphasia is only rarely observed in the former condition but is frequently seen in the latter. These discrepancies may be due to the fact that whereas tissue destruction is abrupt and complete in stroke-induced Wernicke's aphasia, it is slow and incomplete in LPA, allowing for the possibility that some neurons may survive and continue to operate, albeit in a "noisy" manner, even in the most atrophied areas. Another point of interest is that the kind of disorder found in SD almost never occurs in the classic aphasia syndromes. This is probably because of differences between pathophysiological processes and vascular anatomy. In particular, although the anterior temporal lobes appear to be selectively vulnerable to the progressive disease that underlies SD, they are rarely affected by cerebrovascular accidents.

The three major PPA syndromes are closely related but nevertheless distinct language disorders that are associated with circumscribed patterns of brain atrophy and that follow an insidious trajectory of decline. As noted by Rohrer et al. (2008, p. 30), "The progressive aphasias are more than the sum of their neurolinguistic parts: they are diseases of neural networks, distributed both in space (functionally connected brain regions) and time (evolution of deficits)." Importantly, the notion that each syndrome involves a set of functionally connected brain regions receives support from a study showing that in PNFA and SD the affected neural networks are tightly integrated constellations of cortical areas that exhibit, in the healthy brain, synchronous baseline activity and correlated gray matter volume (Seeley et al., 2009; see also Zhou et al., 2012). Thus, the diseases that give rise to these two variants of PPA are by no means random, but instead appear to target specific functional–anatomical components of the brain's language system. Moreover, these diseases—as well as the one that produces LPA—are manifested as molecular pathologies that originate from, in some cases, genetic mutations. To be sure, "molecular neurolinguistics" is still very much in its infancy, and it is essential to bear in mind that each PPA syndrome can result from diverse protein abnormalities (Grossman, 2010). But there is great hope that further research on PPA will eventually reveal reliable correspondences between linguistic, neurobiological, and molecular levels of analysis, and that these discoveries will not only open the way to effective treatments, but also help illuminate the architecture of language in the brain.

Summary and Key Points

- Primary progressive aphasia (PPA) is an acquired language deficit (*aphasia*) that is due to a neurodegenerative disease (*progressive*) and that is the most prominent aspect of the clinical picture (*primary*).
- The first clear-cut case of PPA was reported in 1897, but rigorous and intense scientific research on PPA did not begin until the 1980s. Since then, however, the literature has been growing rapidly, and PPA is now recognized as a molecularly based disorder with significant implications not only for clinical practice, but also for theoretical and experimental work on the neural substrates of language.
- PPA is often considered to be part of the spectrum of disorders related to frontotemporal dementia (FTD), with an average age of onset in the late 50s and an average survival of roughly 7 years.
- The diagnostic criteria for PPA stipulate that language difficulties must be the principal cause of limitations in daily living for at least two years. In some patients, the most salient symptoms may in fact be restricted to the domain of language for over ten years. But in others, cognitive problems in domains beyond language may emerge after only a few years. What all patients have in common is an insidious deterioration of language abilities.
- Although the classification of different subtypes of PPA is controversial, most investigators accept the following breakdown into three major variants or syndromes:

  - *Progressive nonfluent/agrammatic aphasia (PNFA):* Nonfluent production characterized by effortful, hesitant speech, phonological and/or articulatory errors, and agrammatism; initially intact but gradually worsening comprehension of single words and simple sentences; impaired comprehension of complex sentences; impaired repetition. Atrophy is centered in the posterior inferior frontal gyrus (i.e., Broca's area), but spreads posteriorly, superiorly, and medially as the disease advances. Tau pathology is common; ubiquitin pathology is less common; *PRGN* mutations are frequently involved.
  - *Semantic dementia (SD):* Fluent production but with frequent semantic errors; impaired comprehension; intact repetition. Atrophy is centered in the anterior temporal lobes bilaterally but with greater coverage in the left hemisphere and progressive extension posteriorly. Ubiquitin pathology is present in about two-thirds of cases.
  - *Logopenic progressive aphasia (LPA):* Fluent production characterized by word-finding difficulties and occasional phonological paraphasias; mostly intact comprehension of single words and simple sentences, but gravely impaired comprehension of complex sentences; usually intact repetition of words, but impaired repetition of sentences. Atrophy is centered in the left posterior superior temporal gyrus (i.e., Wernicke's area), but spreads in all directions over time. Roughly 50 percent of cases have a pathology related to Alzheimer's disease; ubiquitin pathology is also common.

- PPA provides a unique window on the neurobiology of language because each of the major syndromes constitutes a distinctive clinical profile of deficits that is associated with a distinctive neuroanatomical profile of atrophy. Moreover, these patterns are linked with molecular abnormalities that, in some cases, can be traced to genetic mutations.

Recommended Reading

- Rohrer, J.D., Knight, W.D., Warren, J.E., Fox, N.C., Rossor, M.N., & Warren, J.D. (2008). Word-finding difficulty: A clinical analysis of the progressive aphasias. *Brain, 131,* 8–38. An in-depth review of all aspects of PPA, with instructive comparisons between the progressive aphasia syndromes and the classic aphasia syndromes.
- Grossman, M. (2010). Primary progressive aphasia: Clinicopathological correlations. *Nature Reviews Neurology, 6,* 88–97. A well-informed and well-illustrated survey of the pathological bases of the major PPA syndromes, written by one of the leading authorities in the field.
- Wilson, S.M., Henry, M.L., Besbris, M., Ogarm J.M., Dronkers, N.F., Jarrold, W., Miller, B.L., & Gorno-Tempini, M.L. (2010). Connected speech production in three variants of primary progressive aphasia. *Brain, 133,* 2069–2088. A meticulous investigation of the expressive deficits in all three variants of PPA, with detailed quantitative measurements along several motor speech and linguistic dimensions, as well as corresponding neuroanatomical analyses of the degree to which the patients' scores on those dimensions correlated with atrophy in certain brain regions.
- Harciarek, M., & Kertesz, A. (2011). Primary progressive aphasias and their contribution to contemporary knowledge about the brain-language relationship. *Neuropsychology Review, 21,* 271–287. An excellent overview all aspects of PPA syndromes.

PART III

The Perception and Production of Speech

Speech Perception

5

Introduction

Many of our cognitive capacities seem to be quite simple because, from a subjective point of view, they're effortless, reliable, fast, unconscious, and require no explicit instruction. Some familiar examples include our ability to recognize faces, our ability to reach for a cup of coffee and bring it to our lips, and our ability to recall what we had for lunch yesterday. The apparent simplicity of these various capacities is, however, deceptive. As is now known, all of them pose fantastically complex computational problems, and our brains contain dedicated, special-purpose information-processing machinery to solve each one. Moreover, the reason they strike us as being so simple is precisely because they are supported by such well-adapted neural networks.

Speech perception is another fascinating case of a deceptively simple cognitive capacity. Someone speaks, the sounds enter our ears, and we understand immediately.

But in order for such seemingly effortless comprehension to occur, numerous computational operations must be carried out beneath the surface of conscious awareness (Moore et al., 2010). Some of the operations that distinguish speech perception from other kinds of auditory processing are as follows.

First, analog acoustic patterns must be converted to digital codes at multiple levels of language-specific structure, including distinctive features, phonemes, syllables, and words (Box 5.1). After all, the sentences *John appeared to Mary to be brave* and *John appealed to Mary to be brave* differ by only one distinctive feature at one phoneme position in one word, but that is nevertheless sufficient to lead to radically different interpretations (Jackendoff & Pinker, 2005, p. 215). It is also worth noting that while the subtle contrast between /r/ and /l/ is easily noticed by native speakers of English, it is very difficult to detect, even with close attention, for speakers of languages that do not make such a phonological distinction, like Japanese.

Box 5.1 Some Basic Properties of Speech Sounds

The sounds of human speech are complex acoustic patterns, precisely sculpted by a set of independently adjustable articulatory organs. Vocalization begins when air is exhaled from the lungs through the trachea (windpipe) into the larynx (voice-box, visible on the outside as the Adam's apple). The larynx consists of the glottis (an opening) and the vocal folds (two flaps of retractable muscular tissue). During whispered "voiceless" speech, the vocal folds are spread apart, allowing the air stream to pass through in a turbulent manner that is perceived as hissing. But during normal "voiced" speech, the vocal folds are stretched over the glottis and the air pressure from the lungs causes them to vibrate rapidly in a manner that is perceived as a buzz. The difference can be heard by comparing the sound *sssss*, which lacks voicing, with the sound *zzzzz*, which has it. The rate or frequency of vocal fold vibration is the basis of auditory pitch, which is

(Continued)

(Continued)

a major parameter of prosody (see Chapter 7). It is important to realize, however, that although voicing creates a sound with a dominant frequency, that sound is not a pure tone but instead has many "harmonics." For example, a typical male voice has vibrations not only at 100 hertz (cycles per second), but also at 200, 300, 400, and so on, all the way up to 4,000 and beyond. Crucially, the richness of this sound source constitutes the raw acoustic material that the rest of the vocal tract sculpts into particular vowels and consonants.

Above the larynx, the vocal tract contains several chambers: the pharynx (throat); the nasal cavity; the oral cavity; and the opening between the lips. Each chamber has a certain range of resonances that are determined by its shape and length. As a result, each one operates like a bandpass filter or "window" that enables some sound frequencies to flow through unhindered while blocking the transmission of others. The specific configurations of the chambers, and hence their specific resonant properties, are modified during speech production by moving the following articulators: the velum (soft palate), which opens or closes the nasal cavity; the tongue body, tongue tip, and tongue root; and the lips.

Interestingly, the anatomical location of the larynx descended over the course of human evolution, and this greatly expanded the variety of discriminable speech sounds that people could produce, because it allowed the tongue to move both vertically and horizontally. In contrast, the standard mammalian tongue lies flat in a long oral cavity, and therefore it cannot create vowels like the /i/ in *beet* or the /u/ in *boot* (Fitch, 2000).

This brings us to an essential point: a speech sound is not the outcome of a single gesture of a single organ, but rather the outcome of a combination of gestures of several organs, each of which sculpts the acoustic pattern in distinctive ways. In fact, that is why phonologists have traditionally characterized phonemes as bundles of so-called distinctive features. For instance, vowels are often defined along the following dimensions: front vs. central vs. back; high vs. mid vs. low; nasal vs. non-nasal; rounded vs. unrounded; and tense vs. lax. Comparative research has revealed that the average number of vowels in a language is just under 6, and that the smallest vowel inventory is 2 (Yimas, Papua New Guinea) and the largest is 14 (German) (Maddieson, 2005c). Consonants are also differentiated according to a wealth of distinctive features, most of which have to do with the voicing, place, and manner of articulation. Although the average number of consonants in a language is 22, the smallest repertoire on record is 6 (Rotokas, Papua New Guinea) and the largest is 122 (!Xóõ, Botswana; incidentally, the huge size of this language's consonant inventory is due in part to the addition of an array of click sounds) (Maddieson, 2005a).

Of course, phonemes rarely occur in isolation; instead, they are usually grouped into hierarchically organized syllables, which in turn are often grouped into hierarchically organized multisyllabic words. Many of the phonological rules that constrain these assemblages are language-specific in nature. To take a few examples, *thile, plast,* and *flutch* are possible (but not real) English words, whereas *ptak, vlit,* and *nyip* are not. The latter expressions are, however, possible words in other languages.

Finally, it is noteworthy that one of the many factors that make speech perception computationally difficult is coarticulation. A general principle of motor control is that when multiple actions are executed sequentially by the same set of body parts, the gestures are gracefully smoothed together and partially overlapped in order to reduce the forces that are necessary and increase the efficiency of the whole performance. In the speech domain, this is manifested as phonemes being pronounced in ways that are influenced by those that come before and after. Thus, even though /n/ and /d/ are normally articulated at the alveolar ridge, they are articulated at the teeth in *month* and *width* in anticipation of the subsequent *th* sound. Similarly, the /s/ in *horseshoe* becomes a *sh* sound, and the two instances of /k/ in *Cape Cod* are produced at different tongue positions to facilitate the formation of the different vowels. (These examples come from Pinker, 1994, p. 182.) In these ways, coarticulation warps and blends the sound signatures of phonemes. But even though this poses a nontrivial challenge for the listener, it is a significant advantage for the speaker, since it allows consonants and vowels to be signaled simultaneously, thereby increasing the speed of communication.

Second, although the categorization of speech signals must be exquisitely sensitive to fine-grained cues, it must also be flexible enough to accommodate the tremendous acoustic variability that exists across talkers. For example, a word like *goat* must be recognized as such, and distinguished from similar-sounding words like *coat, boat,* and *moat,* regardless of whether it is spoken by a man or a woman, by an adult or a child, or by Bill, Susan, or anyone else whose voice is as unique as their face.

Third, the boundaries between words must be identified even though there are rarely corresponding gaps in the acoustic waveform. Indeed, our phenomenological impression of hearing little silences between words when we listen to people talk is actually a remarkable illusion that reflects the extraordinary efficiency of the unconscious mechanisms that segment the incoming speech stream into discrete pieces that map neatly onto lexical items stored in long-term memory. To appreciate this, one need only listen for a few seconds to two people conversing in a foreign language, because one's inability to recognize any of the words will immediately cause the seamless nature of the speech stream to stand out in sharp relief.

Fourth, all of the computational operations mentioned above, in addition to many others, must be executed with breathtaking speed in order for comprehension to unfold at a normal pace, and in fact the rate of receptive phoneme processing has been shown to be almost unbelievably fast: 10–15 phonemes per second in casual speech, 20–30 in fast speech, and as many as 40–50 in artificially accelerated speech (Liberman et al., 1967; Cole & Jakimik, 1980).

Finally, speech input must ultimately be routed not only to the grammatical and semantic systems that analyze the forms and meanings of utterances, but also to the motor system that subserves articulation. This is because we depend critically on high-fidelity auditory–motor transformations when we learn how to say new words that we hear, especially during the early phase of language acquisition. Such transformations also contribute to the overt repetition of familiar words, and they are involved in covert auditory–verbal short-term memory as well, like when you silently repeat to yourself a piece of important information, such as a phone number, so as not to forget it. Some researchers even argue that the motor system plays a functional role in ordinary, passive speech perception by constantly "resonating" to the speaker's articulatory movements. As we will see, however, this is currently a very controversial topic.

This chapter provides a synopsis of one of the most influential contemporary theories concerning the neural substrates of speech perception, namely the Dual Stream Model, which was developed by two cognitive neuroscientists—Gregory Hickok at the University of California, Irvine, and David Poeppel at New York University (Figure 5.1; Hickok & Poeppel, 2000, 2004, 2007; Poeppel et al., 2008; Hickok, 2009a, 2009b; Hickok et al., 2011b; for a similar approach see Scott & Johnsrude, 2003; and for a closely related computational model see Ueno et al., 2011). In some ways, this framework can be construed as an elaborate extension of the traditional Wernicke–Lichtheim–Geschwind "house" model of the architecture of linguistic processing, which we encountered in Chapter 3 (see Figure 3.3). In that model, the center that stores the sound-based representations of words has separate links with two other components: one pathway projects to the center that contains the meanings of words, and a different pathway projects to the center for speech planning and production. Similarly, in the Dual Stream Model, after the initial cortical stages of speech perception have been completed in superior temporal regions, further processing splits into two separate computational channels: the "ventral stream" funnels into other temporal regions that contribute to comprehension, while the "dorsal stream" funnels into temporoparietal and frontal areas that underlie auditory–motor transformations. This theory is, without a doubt, far more sophisticated than the antiquated "house" model, but it shares with the older approach the basic idea that speech perception serves two complementary purposes: mapping sound onto meaning, and mapping sound onto action. In the following sections, the major elements of the Dual Stream Model are described in detail and evaluated in the context of relevant empirical findings from studies employing various experimental techniques.

Early Cortical Stages of Speech Perception

The long sequence of processing operations that leads from vibrating air molecules at the eardrum to a conceptual representation of the speaker's message includes a number of steps in the auditory periphery that are not incorporated into the Dual Stream Model (Box 5.2). Instead, the theory picks up the story at the level of the primary auditory cortex in Heschl's gyrus (Da Costa et al., 2011), together with neighboring cortical fields on the dorsal plane of the superior temporal gyrus (STG; see the green components in Figure 5.1; see also

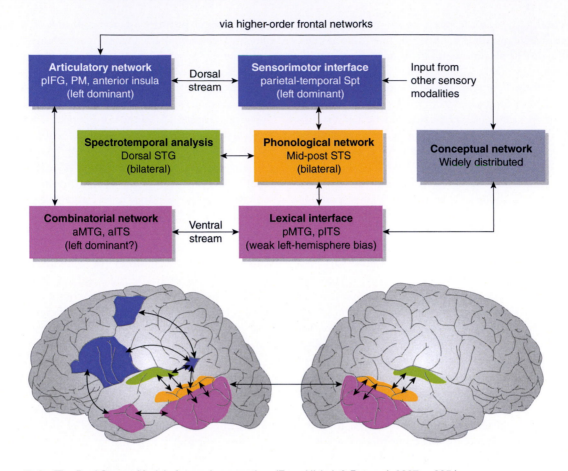

Figure 5.1 The Dual Stream Model of speech perception. (From Hickok & Poeppel, 2007, p. 395.)

the discussion of hearing in Chapter 1). These areas conduct **spectrotemporal analyses** of auditory signals received from the thalamus—that is, they extract information about which sound frequencies are modulated at which rates, for speech as well as nonspeech stimuli. They then project to other sectors of both the STG and the superior temporal sulcus (STS) that are believed to represent a "phonological network" (see the orange components in Figure 5.1). According to the Dual Stream Model, these early cortical stages of speech perception are organized both hierarchically and bilaterally.

Hierarchical Organization

As noted above, speech patterns are complex auditory stimuli that consist of multiple levels of language-specific structure. Consider, for example, the word *cat*. At the level of segmental structure, it is composed of

three phonemes—/k/, /æ/, and /t/—each of which is made up of a matrix of distinctive features that have both acoustic (e.g., [±sononant]) and articulatory (e.g., [±coronal]) interpretations. At the level of syllabic structure, it is a monosyllabic unit with a consonant–vowel–consonant (CVC) organization divisible into two parts: the onset, which consists of the consonant /k/; and the rime (i.e., the part of a syllable that remains the same in rhymes), which consists of a nucleus, namely the vowel /æ/, plus a coda, namely the consonant /t/. Finally, at the level of morphophonological structure, the entire assembly of auditory information constitutes a word. Exactly how these hierarchical levels of phonological information are computed during speech perception is far from understood, but the relevant neural mechanisms may involve several layers of pattern detectors that integrate increasingly complex sets of features.

Support for this view comes from animal models—in particular, from research on how rhesus and macaque monkeys perceive the vocal communicative calls that

Spectrotemporal analysis The computation of which sound frequencies are modulated at which rates.

Box 5.2   From Cochlea to Cortex

Auditory information undergoes many transformations before it reaches the cerebral cortex (Figure 5B2.1). The physical aspects of sound are initially encoded as electrical signals in the spiral ganglion, which is part of the cochlea in the inner ear. The traveling wave of sound moves across approximately 16,000 sensory receptors called hair cells, which are topographically arrayed along the length of the spiral ganglion in a frequency-specific manner, with cells toward the base being more sensitive to low-frequency sounds, and cells toward the apex being more sensitive to high-frequency sounds. Neural signals are then propagated along the cochlear nerve to the brainstem, where they pass through three levels of nuclei—the superior olivary nucleus, the lateral lemniscus, and the inferior colliculus. From there, signals are transmitted to the medial geniculate body of the thalamus, and ultimately to the primary auditory cortex in Heschl's gyrus (also known as the transverse superior temporal gyrus). Electrophysiological studies have shown that this ascending pathway preserves with exquisite fidelity the elementary acoustic features of human "soundscapes," including the spectral and temporal properties of speech. Information processing is not only bottom-up, however, since the ascending pathway is paralleled by a descending pathway that reaches all the way to the spiral ganglion, thereby allowing cognitive states, such as selective attention, to modulate the early stages of auditory perception in a top-down manner. In recent years, an especially interesting line of research has been investigating how the physiology of the auditory brainstem is neither passive nor hardwired, but can be modified in significant ways by experience, such as the development of musical skills or the acquisition of a tone language like Thai as opposed to a non-tone language like English (see Chapter 7 for more information about tone languages). This work therefore constitutes a valuable warning against "cortical chauvinism" when it comes to studying the neural substrates of speech perception. For a review see Chandrasekaran and Kraus (2010).

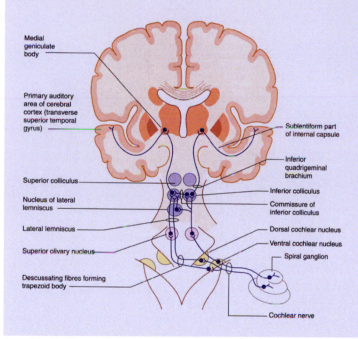

Figure 5B2.1 Illustration of the human auditory system showing pathways and subcortical nuclei in the ascending and descending pathways. (From Baars & Gage, 2010, p. 203.)

are characteristic of their species (for reviews see Petkov et al., 2009; Rauschecker & Scott, 2009; Romanski & Averbeck, 2009; Ghazanfar, 2010). A good example is the tonal scream. As shown in Figure 5.2, the neural circuitry for recognizing this type of sound is thought to consist of a hierarchical network in which lower-order cells that are tuned to specific frequency-modulated (FM) sweeps in specific time windows project to higher-order cells that combine these inputs in successive layers of integration. More precisely, at the lowest level of the network, there are cells that detect each FM component in the upward sweep in the first time window (roughly the first 200 ms), as well as cells that detect each FM component in the downward sweep in the second time window (roughly the second 200 ms). At the middle level, there are cells—labeled T1 and T2 in the diagram—that combine the inputs from each array at the lower level, thereby serving as detectors for particular harmonic patterns in each temporal window. And at the highest level, there are cells that combine the inputs from the middle level, thereby serving as detectors for complex auditory stimuli that have all the spectrotemporal features of tonal screams. (Note that the connection from the T1 cell to the cell at the highest level passes through a delay function, symbolized as $\Delta t1$, which holds up the signal long

enough so that the inputs from both T1 and T2 arrive at the top cell simultaneously.)

This overall scheme is only hypothetical, and it is idealized in many ways, but empirical data from single-cell recording studies suggest that such hierarchically organized levels of processing may be implemented in the brains of monkeys as feedforward synaptic pathways projecting from middle to anterior cortical fields along the STG. A similar type of neural architecture, only scaled up to accommodate the complexity of the phonological systems of human languages, may underlie the early cortical processing of speech sounds in our brains. There is some evidence that, as in monkeys, this hierarchy extends anteriorly along the STG (Leaver &

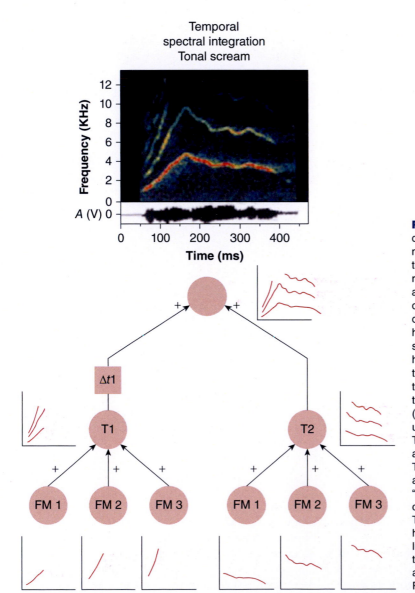

Figure 5.2 Communication calls consist of elementary features such as frequency-modulated (FM) sweeps. Harmonic calls, like the vocal scream from the rhesus monkey repertoire depicted here by its spectrogram and time signal amplitude (*A*, measured as output voltage of a sound meter), consist of fundamental frequencies and higher harmonics. The neural circuitry for processing such calls is thought to consist of small hierarchical networks. At the lowest level, there are neurons serving as FM detectors tuned to the rate and direction of FM sweeps; these detectors extract each FM component (shown in cartoon spectrograms) in the upward and downward sweeps of the scream. The output of these FM detectors is combined at the next level: The target neurons T1 and T2 possess a high threshold and fire only if all inputs are activated. At the final level, a "tonal scream detector" is created by again combining output from neurons T1 and T2. Temporal integration is accomplished by having the output of T1 pass through a delay line with a latency $\Delta t1$ sufficient to hold up the input to the top neuron long enough that all inputs arrive at the same time. (From Rauscheker & Scott, 2009, p. 720.)

Rauschecker, 2010; Chevillet et al., 2011; DeWitt &
Rauschecker, 2012). But there is also quite a bit of evidence that it extends ventrally from the STG into the
STS, and the Dual Stream Model emphasizes this latter pathway, as shown in Figure 5.1 and discussed in
greater detail below. In addition, a central claim of the
Dual Stream Model is that the phonological processing
hierarchy does not reside exclusively in the left hemisphere but is instead bilaterally organized.

Bilateral Organization

Both Hemispheres Contribute to Speech Perception

Evidence that the early cortical stages of speech perception are bilaterally organized comes from many
sources. In what follows, we first consider a number
of fMRI studies which show that both left and right
superior temporal regions are typically activated by
speech stimuli. Then we discuss several neuropsychological studies which indicate that either hemisphere
by itself is capable of perceiving speech, and that an
extremely severe impairment of speech perception usually requires bilateral damage to the STG/STS.

In one of the first and most often cited fMRI
studies of speech perception, Binder et al. (2000) presented participants with five types of auditory stimuli:
unstructured noise; FM tones; words (e.g., *desk, fork,
stream*); pronounceable pseudowords, which were created by rearranging the phoneme order of the word
stimuli (e.g., *sked, korf, reemst*); and reversed words,
which were temporally reversed versions of the word
stimuli (Figure 5.3A). The stimuli were grouped into
blocks, each lasting 12 seconds, and the task was simply
to press a buttton whenever a block began or ended.
The following patterns of activation were found in
both hemispheres with only minor leftward asymmetry, especially for words (Figure 5.3B). An auditory
area on the dorsal plane of the STG responded more
to tones than noise; a region further downstream in
the mid-lateral STG responded not only more to tones
than noise, but also more to speech than tones; and
finally, a region even further downstream in the middle sector of the STS responded more to speech than
tones. These results support the hypothesis that the
early cortical stages of speech perception are organized
both hierarchically and bilaterally, with areas located
on the dorsal surface of the STG conducting elementary spectrotemporal analyses, and areas located in
the lateral STG and middle STS detecting the kinds
of complex feature combinations that characterize
human speech. It is worth adding that evidence for

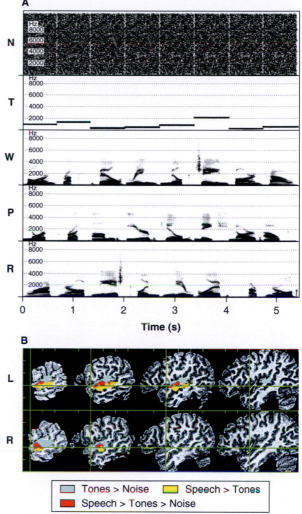

Figure 5.3 Stimuli and results of Binder et al.'s (2000) fMRI
study of the perception of speech and nonspeech sounds.
(A) Example narrow-band spectrograms of the five types of
stimuli: N = noise; T = tones; W = words; P = pseudowords; R
= reversed words. (B) Hierarchical contrasts between noise,
tones, and the three types of speech stimuli. Tones activate
the dorsal STG relative to noise (blue), whereas speech
activates more ventral regions in the STS (yellow). (From
Binder et al., 2000, p. 515.)

the sequential engagement of these areas, at least in
the left hemisphere, comes from electrophysiological
studies that employed direct intracranial recording
(e.g., Canolty et al., 2007; Flinker et al., 2011; Chan
et al., in press; see Figure 2.26 and the accompanying
text in Chapter 2).

A limitation of Binder et al.'s (2000) fMRI study,
however, is that essentially indistinguishable patterns of activation were found in the STS for words,
pseudowords, and reversed words. Some possible

explanations for these outcomes are as follows. First, and most straightforwardly, pseudowords may have recruited the same regions as real words because the former stimuli shared phonemic and syllabic features with the latter stimuli. Second, Binder et al. (2000) propose that the simplest reason why reversed words engaged the same regions as both real words and pseudowords is that all three types of stimuli were basically equivalent in terms of acoustic complexity. Both of these accounts are plausible, and numerous fMRI studies have gone on to investigate the hierarchical and bilateral nature of speech perception in greater detail.

In a prominent article about the Dual Stream Model, Hickok and Poeppel (2007) point out that many fMRI studies converge on the view that portions of the lateral STG and middle STS, not only in the left hemisphere but also in the right, contribute more to the perceptual analysis of phonological than non-phonological information. Figure 5.4A shows the peak activations from seven different studies, all of which appeared between 2001 and 2006, that demonstrate this preference of the lateral STG and middle STS for speech stimuli relative to various non-speech controls, in both hemispheres (Vouloumanos et al., 2001; Jancke et al., 2002; Joanisse & Gati, 2003; Dehaene-Lambertz et al., 2005; Liebenthal et al., 2005; Rimol et al., 2005; Benson et al., 2006).

Focusing on the main results of a separate study that was conducted around the same time, Figure 5.4B highlights the areas within the STS, bilaterally, that Okada and Hickok (2006a) found to be sensitive to an important variable that reliably reflects the structure of phonological networks—namely, **phonological neighborhood density**. Some words are nodes in large constellations of similar-sounding words—for example, *cat* belongs to a huge neighborhood that includes *cab, cad, calf, cash, cap, can, cot, kit, cut, coat, bat, mat, rat, scat, pat, sat,* and *vat.* Other words, however, have very few phonological associates—for example, there are not many words that sound much like *spinach* or *obtuse.* Psycholinguistic research has shown that during speech perception, words from high-density neighborhoods temporarily activate a greater range of phonological competitors than words from low-density neighborhoods (e.g., Luce & Pisoni, 1998; Vitevich & Luce, 1999; Vitevich, 2003; Vitevich & Rodríguez, 2005). And this is precisely the distinction that Okada and Hickok's (2006a) fMRI study isolated in the brain.

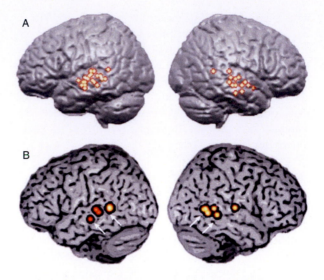

Figure 5.4 Phonological networks in the STS. (A) Distribution of activation in seven studies of speech perception using sublexical (i.e., pseudoword) stimuli contrasted with nonspeech controls. (B) Highlighted areas represent sites of activation in an fMRI study contrasting high-neighborhood-density words (those with many similar-sounding neighbors) with low-neighborhood-density words (those with few similar-sounding neighbors). The middle to posterior portions of the STS in both hemispheres (arrows) showed greater activation for high-density than low-density words (colored blobs), presumably reflecting the partial activation of larger neural networks when high-density words are processed. Neighborhood density is a property of lexical phonological networks; thus, modulation of neural activity by density manipulation probably highlights such networks in the brain. (From Hickok & Poeppel, 2007, p. 399.)

Specifically, they found that in both hemispheres high-density words engaged the STS more extensively and robustly than low-density words, which suggests that the STS plays a key role in representing the pool of phonological competitors that are automatically activated in a bottom-up fashion during the process of auditory word recognition. (For additional data regarding the neural correlates of lexical competition during speech perception, see Prabhakaran et al., 2006; Righi et al., 2010; Zhuang et al., in press).

More recently, a host of other fMRI studies have explored even more carefully how superior temporal regions in both hemispheres mediate speech perception (e.g., Formisano et al., 2008; Myers & Blumstein, 2008; Obleser et al., 2010; Okada et al., 2010; Vaden et al., 2010; Woods et al., 2011; for meta-analyses see Turkeltaub & Coslett, 2010, and DeWitt & Rauschecker, 2012). We will restrict our attention, however, to just one of them. Formisano et al. (2008) took a giant leap forward by showing that it is

Phonological neighborhood density   The size of a given word's network of similar-sounding words.

possible to determine not only which of three vowels a person is hearing, but also which of three speakers is producing it, simply by observing the complex patterns of neural activity that these auditory stimuli elicit in the superior temporal regions of the person's brain. This remarkable feat of "mind reading" was achieved in the following way. Subjects were scanned while listening to three vowels—/u/, /i/, and /a/—each of which was uttered several times by three speakers—sp1, sp2, and sp3 (Figure 5.5). Drawing principally on a form of multivariate pattern analysis (see Chapter 2), the researchers analyzed the data in three main steps.

First, in the "discrimination" analysis, they initially trained a classification algorithm to differentiate between the cortical responses (50 trials) evoked by either two vowels (/u/ vs. /i/, /u/ vs. /a/, /i/ vs. /a/) or two speakers (sp1 vs. sp2, sp1 vs. sp3, sp2 vs. sp3). Then they demonstrated that the algorithm could also categorize, with a high degree of accuracy, the remainder of the cortical responses (10 trials). Next, they created "discriminative maps" to depict the brain regions that carry the greatest functional load in distinguishing between the various vowels and the various speakers (Figure 5.6A–C). The areas most important for vowel discrimination were distributed across several sectors of the lateral STG and middle STS in both hemispheres, but with greater STS involvement on the right side. Although the areas most important for speaker discrimination were partly interspersed with those most important for vowel discrimination, they were sparser and more right-hemisphere dominant—a finding that converges with other evidence that voice recognition depends more on the right than the left hemisphere (for a review see Belin, 2006; see also Figure 7.1 in Chapter 7).

Second, in the "generalization" analysis, the researchers showed that the classification algorithm could learn to correctly interpret neural activity patterns triggered by completely novel stimuli (i.e., stimuli not used during training). For example, if the algorithm was initially trained to discriminate between the cortical responses to two vowels produced by one speaker, it could later discriminate between the cortical responses to the same two vowels produced by a different speaker. Likewise, if the algorithm was initially trained to discriminate between the cortical responses to two speakers producing one vowel, it could later discriminate between the cortical responses to the same two speakers producing a different vowel. Notably, the areas associated with the capacity to track vowel distinctions irrespective of speaker variation were embedded within those that were previously linked with vowel discrimination

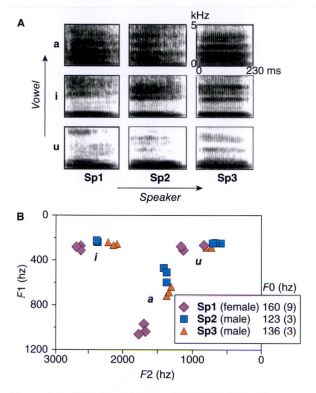

Figure 5.5 Experimental design and stimuli of Formisano et al.'s (2008) fMRI study of speech perception. (A) Example of spectrograms of the stimuli from the nine conditions (three vowels × three speakers). (B) Representation of the vowels based on the first two formants (F1, F2). The insert indicates the mean value and standard deviation of the fundamental frequency (F0) for each speaker. (From Formisano et al., 2008, p. 971.)

(see the regions outlined in white in Figure 5.6B), and the areas associated with the capacity to track speaker distinctions irrespective of vowel variation were embedded within those that were previously linked with speaker discrimination (see the regions outlined in white in Figure 5.6C).

Third, in the "neural fingerprint" analysis, the researchers found that by focusing on the combined activation levels of just the 15 most discriminative voxels for each separate dimension (i.e., for the vowel dimension and the speaker dimension), they could reveal relatively speaker-invariant representations of vowels (Figure 5.6D) and relatively vowel-invariant representations of speakers (Figure 5.6E). For example, the three circles aligned horizontally along the top row of Figure 5.6D show the activation patterns associated with the perception of the vowel /a/ as produced by sp1, sp2, and sp3, with the 15 polar axes in each circle indicating the signal strengths of the 15 voxels. The shapes formed by the activation patterns plotted in these three circles are remarkably similar,

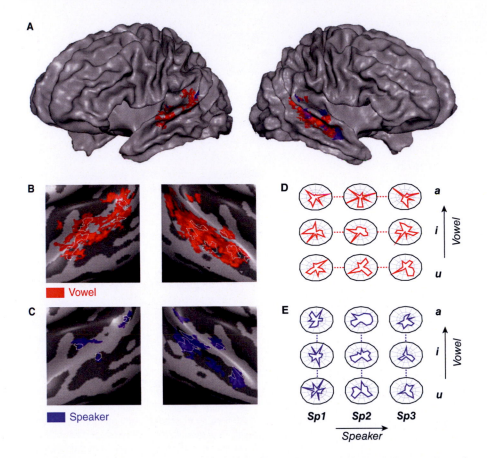

Figure 5.6 Cortical discriminative maps and activation fingerprints for decoding vowels and speakers in Formisano et al.'s (2008) fMRI study of speech perception. (A–C) Group discriminative maps visualized on the folded (A) or inflated (B, C) representation of the cortex (light gray, gyri; dark gray, sulci). Outlined regions in B and C indicate cortical regions that were also included in the group maps obtained with the generalization analysis. (D and E) Activation fingerprints created from the 15 most discriminative voxels for decoding vowels (D) and speakers (E) (single-subject data, subject 1). Each axis of the polar plot forming a fingerprint displays the activation level in a voxel. Note the similarity among the fingerprints of the same vowel (horizontal direction in D) or speaker (vertical direction in E). (From Formisano et al., 2008, p. 972.)

and the common elements constitute what Formisano et al. (2008) call the "neural fingerprint" of the vowel /a/. Note that the middle row of circles for /i/ and the bottom row of circles for /u/ capture equally idiosyncratic neural fingerprints. The same principle also applies to the abstract representations of speakers portrayed in Figure 5.6E. For instance, the three circles aligned vertically along the left column show the activation patterns associated with the perception of sp1 producing each of the three vowels. Once again, it is clear that the shapes have a very close family resemblance, while at the same time appearing quite different from those linked with sp2 and sp3.

Taken together, these findings help to unveil what Formisano et al. (2008, p. 970) call "the detailed cortical layout and computational properties of the neural populations at the basis of human speech

recognition and speaker identification." It is worth emphasizing the value of their discovery that the most informative voxels for vowel discrimination were not clustered together in a single cortical area, but were instead widely distributed across several anatomically segregated patches of the STG and STS in both hemispheres. This outcome is significant because it suggests that detecting phonemes is a highly interactive process that culminates in a distinctive pattern of firing rates—a "neural fingerprint"—across several different groups of cells scattered over the STG and STS bilaterally. This intriguing possibility will no doubt be investigated in greater depth in the near future.

The fMRI studies reviewed above clearly indicate that listening to speech engages the superior temporal regions of both hemispheres. However, it is important to recall that one of the main shortcomings of fMRI as a brain mapping technique is that it does not easily allow one to determine whether the areas that are activated by a particular task are actually necessary for that task. For this reason, we must acknowledge that, despite their many virtues, the studies summarized above do not tell us whether the superior temporal regions of both hemispheres play causal roles in speech perception. To address this issue, we turn now to neuropsychology.

If it were the case that speech perception relied almost entirely on the superior temporal regions of just the left hemisphere, one would expect that unilateral damage to those regions would result in a profound impairment of speech perception. To be sure, such lesions do disrupt speech perception, but the deficits are not always severe; on the contrary, they are sometimes only moderate (e.g., Miceli et al., 1980; Baker et al., 1981; Gainotti et al., 1982). Might that be due, however, to a compensatory process in which the right hemisphere gradually becomes relatively proficient at perceiving speech after the left-lateralized areas that putatively specialize in that capacity have been compromised? This interpretation predicts that if patients with left superior temporal damage were tested during the acute epoch of recovery—i.e., shortly after lesion onset, before substantial brain reorganization can occur—they would tend to be severely impaired on tasks that probe speech perception. Contrary to this prediction, however, several studies have shown that, like chronic patients, acute patients often manifest only moderate deficits in speech perception (Breese & Hillis, 2004; Rogalsky et al., 2008a).

Further neuropsychological support for the view that both the left and the right hemisphere are independently capable of perceiving speech comes from a recent study by Hickok et al. (2008) that employed the **Wada procedure** (Wada & Rasmussen, 1960). This is a technique for temporarily anesthetizing—or, more figuratively, "putting to sleep"—each hemisphere in turn with injections of sodium amobarbitol, a fast-acting sedative. It is named after Juhn Wada, the Japanese-Canadian neurologist who first proposed its use for exploring the cerebral lateralization of cognitive functions in presurgical epileptic patients. (See Paul Broks's 2003 essay called "The seahorse and the almond" for a dramatic and entertaining account of this method for isolating and interrogating each side of the brain.) In Hickok et al.'s (2008) study, a series of 20 patients

were given a task in which, on every trial, they first listened to a word (e.g., *bear*) and then had to point to the matching picture on a card that contained the target picture (e.g., a bear), a phonemic distractor (e.g., a pear), a semantic distractor (e.g., moose), and an unrelated picture (e.g., grapes). As shown in Figure 5.7, although the proportion of phonemically based errors was greater during left than right-hemisphere anesthesia, it was still quite low (5–12 percent). These findings indicate than even when the entire left hemisphere is briefly incapacitated, the right hemisphere can still perceive speech fairly well. Hence, the study bolsters the hypothesis that, as maintained by the Dual Stream Model, the early cortical stages of speech perception are bilaterally organized.

Yet another source of evidence for this hypothesis comes from research on a rare neurological disorder called **word deafness** (for reviews see Buchman et al., 1986; Poeppel, 2001; Stefanatos et al., 2005; Bauer & McDonald, 2006; Stefanatos, 2008). In this disorder, basic aspects of hearing are largely preserved—e.g., pure tone thresholds are within normal limits—but speech perception is profoundly disrupted, in some

Word deafness A disorder in which speech perception is impaired, despite intact hearing and sometimes even intact recognition of nonspeech sounds.

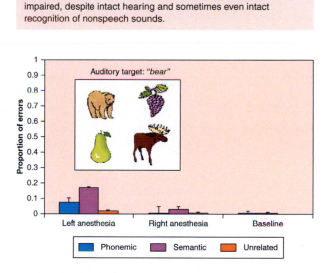

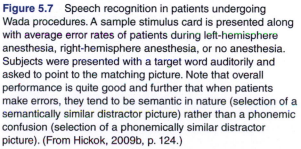

Figure 5.7 Speech recognition in patients undergoing Wada procedures. A sample stimulus card is presented along with average error rates of patients during left-hemisphere anesthesia, right-hemisphere anesthesia, or no anesthesia. Subjects were presented with a target word auditorily and asked to point to the matching picture. Note that overall performance is quite good and further that when patients make errors, they tend to be semantic in nature (selection of a semantically similar distractor picture) rather than a phonemic confusion (selection of a phonemically similar distractor picture). (From Hickok, 2009b, p. 124.)

Wada procedure A way to temporarily shut down an entire hemisphere by injecting sodium amobarbitol into either the left or the right carotid artery.

Table 5.1 Subjective Descriptions of How Speech Is Phenomenologically Perceived by Patients with Word Deafness

Description	Reference
"a noise"	Coslett et al. (1984); Buchman et al. (1986)
"a hurr or buzzing"	Mendez & Geehan (1988)
"like wind in the trees"	Ziegler (1952)
"like the rustling of leaves"	Luria (1966)
"like jabbering or a foreign language"	Denes & Semenza (1975); Auerbach et al. (1982); Buchman et al. (1986); Mendez & Geehan (1988)
Speech simply does not "register"	Saffran et al. (1976)
"words just run together"	Klein & Harper (1956)
"words come too quickly"	Albert & Bear (1974)

Based on Stefanatos et al. (2005).

Reports of patients with severe disturbances are toward the top, and reports of patients with subtler disturbances are toward the bottom.

cases much more than the recognition of non-linguistic environmental sounds. The subjective descriptions provided by patients with word deafness suggest that there is a continuum of severity, since some patients report that spoken language sounds like a noise or a buzz to them, whereas others say that they can identify utterances as speech but the words occur too quickly to be understood (Table 5.1). What is most relevant in the current context is that the majority of cases (approximately 72 percent) have fairly symmetric bilateral lesions that affect the middle and posterior portions of the STG and/or the underlying white matter, while often sparing Heschl's gyrus. Thus, damage to the higher-order auditory systems of both hemispheres is usually required to cause the disorder, consistent once again with the Dual Stream Model.

In summary, fMRI data and neuropsychological data converge on the view that the superior temporal regions of both hemispheres contribute to speech perception. It is worth noting, though, that, as Hickok and Poeppel (2007, p. 398) point out, and as has traditionally been assumed, there may be "a mild leftward bias." Some fMRI studies reveal greater left than right STG/STS involvement for words compared to control stimuli (e.g., see the meta-analysis by DeWitt & Rauschecker, 2012). Some Wernicke's aphasics with unilateral left posterior STG/STS lesions are not just moderately impaired, but are instead severely impaired, at mapping subword-level phonological representations onto word-level phonological representations during speech perception tasks (e.g., see the description of

Hillis et al.'s [1999] case JBN in Chapter 3). And some patients with word deafness have damage to the STG in just the left hemisphere (e.g., Stefanatos et al., 2005; Slevc et al., 2011). Nevertheless, as indicated above, there are good reasons to believe that superior temporal regions in the right hemisphere also play a role in speech perception. In the next subsection, we take a brief tour of a growing literature which suggests that the higher-order auditory areas of the two hemispheres may have the following functional asymmetry: Areas on the left may be dominant for integrating signals on the time scale of rapidly varying phonemes, whereas areas on the right may be dominant for integrating signals on the time scale of longer-duration syllables.

The Two Hemispheres Have Partially Different Temporal Windows for Speech Perception

The phonological structures of words are organized at multiple levels of granularity, and because these different levels have different durations in running speech, listeners must process them in different temporal windows (Rosen, 1992). For example, some types of phonological information, such as the contrast in voice-onset time between /k/ and /g/, or the contrast in linear order between *pets* and *pest*, occur very quickly, on the time scale of roughly 20–80 ms. But other types of phonological information, such as cues for syllabic stress, occur more slowly, on the time scale of roughly 150–300 ms.

Based on considerations like these, Poeppel (2003) developed a proposal that has become a key ingredient of the Dual Stream Model—namely, the "asymmetric sampling in time" hypothesis (see also Poeppel et al., 2008; Ghitza, 2011). According to this theory, the primary auditory cortices in the two hemispheres first create fairly symmetric high-fidelity representations of auditory signals, and then the higher-order auditory cortices in the two hemispheres effectively carve those representations into somewhat asymmetrically sized "chunks" by filtering them through partially different temporal windows. As shown in Figure 5.8, the left hemisphere may be better equipped than the right to handle rapid auditory variation in the range of around 20–80 ms, which is ideal for detecting fine-grained distinctions at the phonemic level; conversely, the right hemisphere may be more sensitive than the left to longer-duration auditory patterns in the range of around 150–300 ms, which is optimal for extracting information at the syllabic level.

This hypothesis has only recently begun to receive close attention from an experimental perspective, so its validity is still very much an open question (for critiques see Rosen et al., 2011, and McGettigan & Scott, 2012). Nevertheless, a number of brain mapping studies have generated results that either support it or lead to interesting refinements of it (Liégeois-Chauvel et al., 1999; Zaehle et al., 2004; Boemio et al., 2005; Hesling et al., 2005b; Schonwiesner et al., 2005; Giraud et al., 2007; Luo & Poeppel, 2007, 2012;

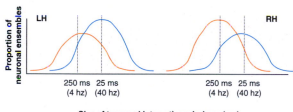

Figure 5.8   The "asymmetric sampling in time" hypothesis. Neuronal ensembles in the auditory cortices of the left hemisphere (LH) tend to have a temporal integration window centered around 25 ms, with an associated electrophysiological oscillatory frequency of around 40 Hz. In contrast, neuronal ensembles in the auditory cortices of the right hemisphere (RH) tend to have a temporal integration window centered around 250 ms, with an associated electrophysiological oscillatory frequency of around 4 Hz. The relatively short LH sampling rate may be optimal for registering rapid phonemic contrasts, whereas the relatively long RH sampling rate may be optimal for registering more protracted syllabic information. (From Giraud et al., 2007, p. 1128.)

Britton et al., 2009; Millman et al., 2011). Below we discuss just two studies, one that bears on the proposal about the left hemisphere, and another that focuses on the proposal about the right hemisphere.

In an influential fMRI investigation, Liebenthal et al. (2005) compared discrimination of familiar phonemic sounds with discrimination of equally complex but unfamiliar nonphonemic sounds (Figure 5.9A). The stimuli for the phonemic discrimination task consisted of a synthetically created continuum of eight CV syllables, with /ba/ at one end, /da/ at the other end, and six intervening syllables that varied in stepwise fashion. The stimuli for the nonphonemic discrimination task were derived from the original continuum of eight CV syllables by systematically altering those sounds. In particular, prior to forming the new continuum, the first and third formants of each endpoint or "anchor" sound were manipulated in order to disrupt their phonemic value. These formants normally rise from lower to higher frequencies, reflecting the transition from consonant to vowel production, but they were inverted so as to shift from higher to lower frequencies. As a consequence, the stimuli did not correspond to any sounds that are naturally produced by the human vocal tract. Participants were scanned while performing a task that required them to determine, on each trial, whether a given sound X was identical to the first or second sound in a previously presented pair, with pairs consisting of tokens 2&4, 4&6, and 6&8 of either the phonemic continuum or the nonphonemic continuum.

As expected, the behavioral results revealed **categorical perception** of the phonemic continuum but not of the nonphonemic continuum (Figure 5.9B). On the one hand, for the phonemic continuum, discrimination of tokens 4&6 was quite good because those two tokens straddle the mid-point of the sharp boundary between the /ba/ and /da/ categories, whereas discrimination of tokens 2&4 and 6&8 was relatively poor because both tokens in the former pair fall squarely within the /ba/ category and both tokens in the latter pair fall squarely within the /da/ category. On the other hand, for the nonphonemic continuum, discrimination performance was not significantly different across the three pairs of tokens, suggesting that no category boundary was detected.

Categorical perception   The tendency to subjectively perceive two speech sounds that belong to the same category (e.g., two instances of /b/) as being more similar to each other than two speech sounds that belong to different categories (e.g., an instance of /b/ and an instance of /d/), even when the objectively defined acoustic differences between them are the same.

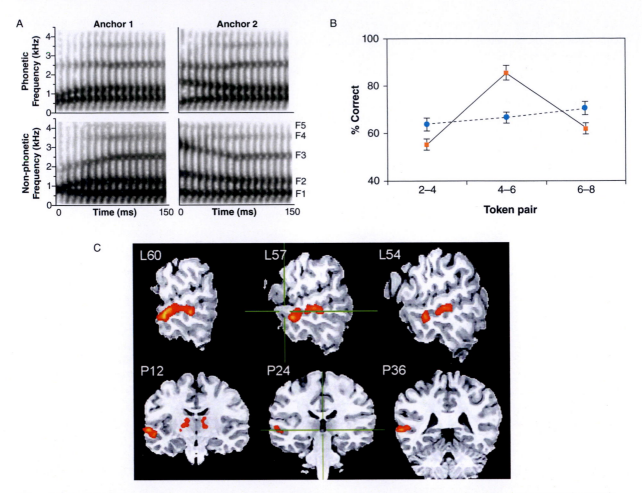

Figure 5.9 Stimuli and results of Liebenthal et al.'s (2005) fMRI study of the perception of phonemic and nonphonemic sounds. (A) Spectrograms of the anchor points /ba/ (upper left) and /da/ (upper right) of the phonemic continuum and of their nonphonemic analogs (lower panel). The horizontal stripes represent the formants (F1, F2, F3, F4, F5), which are peaks of acoustic energy at the vocal tract resonance frequencies. The spectral transition segments of F1 and F3 of the phonemic anchor points were manipulated to create the nonphonemic anchor points. (B) Discrimination accuracy for the phonemic (solid line) and nonphonemic (dashed line) stimuli. (C) Areas showing stronger activation during discrimination in the phonemic relative to the nonphonemic condition, overlaid on an anatomical image of one subject. Sagittal sections are shown in the top row together with *x*-coordinates, and coronal sections are shown in the bottom row together with *y*-coordinates. (From Liebenthal et al., 2005, pp. 1622, 1624, and 1626.)

Importantly, this perceptual contrast between the two continua of stimuli was clearly reflected in the fMRI results (Figure 5.9C). Although all of the sounds, regardless of which continuum they belonged to, engaged areas in the dorsal STG bilaterally and to equal degrees, the phonemic stimuli engaged the middle STS in the left hemisphere to a significantly greater extent than the nonphonemic stimuli. Indeed, no areas were activated significantly more by the non-phonemic stimuli than by the phonemic stimuli. In addition, a follow-up interhemispheric comparison confirmed that the volume and intensity of STS activation associated with the contrast between phonemic and nonphonemic stimuli was strongly left-lateralized.

How do these findings bear on the "asymmetric sampling in time" hypothesis? The discovery that discriminating between sounds along the phonemic /ba/–/da/ continuum engaged the left STS more than the right STS fits perfectly with the predictions of the hypothesis, since the relevant acoustic cues were rapidly changing formant transitions, and the theory maintains that such signals are routed mainly to higher-order auditory areas in the left hemisphere. However, the fact that this leftward bias involving the STS was of greater magnitude for the phonemic than the nonphonemic sounds appears to be somewhat at odds with the theory, since the latter sounds also varied in terms of rapidly changing formant transitions.

Two points are worth making here. First, it is possible that the nonphonemic sounds did engage the left STS to a greater degree than the right STS, but not as much as the phonemic sounds; unfortunately the researchers did not indicate whether this was the case. Second, even if it was the case, one would still need to account for the discrepancy between the two conditions in the magnitude of the left STS responses. The most obvious explanation hinges on the fact that, not surprisingly, the phonemic stimuli were perceived categorically as familiar sounds, whereas the nonphonemic stimuli were perceived continuously as unfamiliar sounds. Liebenthal et al. (2005, p. 1628) emphasize this behavioral result and advocate the view that "what underlies the left dominance for speech consonants in the temporal lobes is their categorical perception."

Overall, then, this study suggests that the aspect of the "asymmetric sampling in time" hypothesis that focuses on the left hemisphere may need to be refined along the following lines. The left hemisphere seems to have a preference not just for processing short auditory signals in the 20–80 ms range, but for processing them in a categorical manner (for other pertinent studies see Näätänen et al., 1997; Möttönen et al., 2006; Desai et al., 2008; Liebenthal et al., 2010; see also the meta-analysis by Turkeltaub & Coslett, 2010). As an interesting side note, there is also growing evidence that during ordinary face-to-face linguistic communication, the posterior portion of the left STS is part of a network of brain structures that contribute to speech perception by taking into account not only auditory information about the sounds that the speaker produces, but also visual information about the lip and tongue movements that the speaker makes (Box 5.3).

Box 5.3 The Neural Substrates of Auditory–Visual Integration During Speech Perception: A Combined fMRI and TMS Study of the McGurk Effect

Named after one of its discoverers, the "McGurk effect" is an astonishing illusion which demonstrates that during normal face-to-face speech perception, the brain automatically fuses the simultaneously occurring auditory and visual signals (McGurk & MacDonald, 1976). In a typical experimental scenario, participants are presented with an audio recording of the syllable /ba/ together with a video recording of a face or mouth producing the syllable /ga/, and what they end up consciously perceiving is, remarkably enough, neither one nor the other but instead an amalgamation of both—the syllable /da/. This striking effect presumably arises because the best way that the brain can integrate the two competing sensory signals about the place of articulation of the initial consonant is by adopting an intermediate interpretation, specifically that the syllable must be the alveolar /da/, since it lies mid-way between the labial /ba/, which is auditorily signaled, and the velar /ga/, which is visually signaled.

To determine whether the left posterior STS is causally involved in creating the McGurk effect, Beauchamp et al. (2010) conducted a study that involved both fMRI and TMS. The study had two stages. First, fMRI was used to measure participants' brain activity in the following conditions: listening to spoken words while fixating on crosshairs, and watching faces produce words without any accompanying auditory stimuli. A conjunction analysis revealed, in each individual participant, a region in the left posterior STS that responded to both auditory and visual speech (Figure 5B3.1A). Second, single-pulse TMS was used to stimulate the center of the STS region, as well as a control site dorsal and posterior to that region, in the following conditions: perception of McGurk stimuli with a male voice and face (Experiment 1), and perception of McGurk stimuli with a female voice and face (Experiment 2). Similar results were obtained in both conditions. TMS delivered to the STS significantly reduced the likelihood of fusing the competing auditory and visual signals of the McGurk stimuli, but TMS delivered to the control site did not alter the perception of those stimuli (Figure 5B3.1B, C). What did participants actually experience when TMS disrupted the McGurk effect? Most of the time, their reports suggested that the auditory input dominated over the visual input (e.g., TMS delivered with auditory /ba/ and visual /ga/ yielded the auditory-dominant percept /ba/ instead of either the visual-dominant percept /ga/ or the McGurk percept /da/). On a few trials, however, participants said they heard something between the auditory and McGurk percepts (e.g., between /ba/ and /da/). Another important

(Continued)

(Continued)

discovery was that TMS only disrupted the McGurk effect when it was delivered to the STS during a narrow time window—in particular, during a 200 ms period extending from 100 ms before to 100 ms after the onset of the auditory–visual stimuli (Figure 5B3.1D). Thus, TMS interfered with a multisensory computation that is closely time-locked to stimulus presentation.

In summary, by bringing together the complementary virtues of fMRI and TMS, Beauchamp et al. (2010) were able to shed new light on a classic illusion—the McGurk effect. In so doing, they provided compelling evidence that the left posterior STS plays a critical role in auditory–visual integration during speech perception.

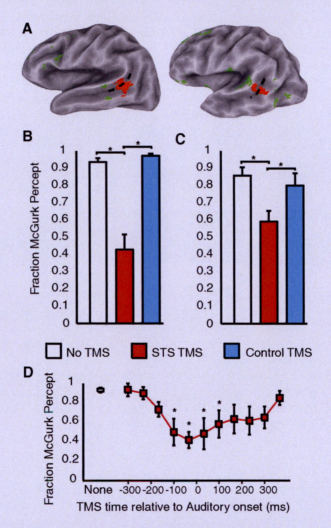

Figure 5B3.1   fMRI-guided TMS of congruent and incongruent auditory–visual speech. (A) Colored regions in the partially inflated left hemisphere of two individual participants show cortical areas active during the perception of both unimodal auditory speech and unimodal visual speech. Orange indicates active cortex in the STS; green indicates active cortex in other areas; the dashed line indicates the fundus of the posterior STS. (B, C) During presentation of the McGurk stimuli in Experiment 1 (B) and Experiment 2 (C), participants were likely to experience the McGurk effect when there was no TMS (white bars) and when TMS was delivered to the control site (blue bars); however, participants were significantly less likely to experience the McGurk effect when TMS was delivered to the STS (red bars). (D) The effectiveness of TMS of the STS depended on the time at which it was delivered. TMS delivered near the onset of the auditory–visual stimuli reduced the likelihood of the McGurk effect, but TMS at other times did not. (From Beauchamp et al., 2010, p. 2416.)

Turning now to the aspect of the "asymmetric sampling in time" hypothesis that focuses on the right hemisphere, an especially relevant study was conducted by Abrams et al. (2008) using one of the most time-sensitive brain mapping techniques available—namely, electrophysiology. These investigators recorded the temporal patterns of left and right cortical activity in 12 healthy children between the ages of 9 and 13 while they listened passively to the sentence *The young boy left home* produced in three modes of speech: "clear," in which the sentence was spoken with enhanced diction to improve intelligibility; "conversational," in which the sentence was spoken in a natural, informal manner; and "compressed," in which the sentence in the "conversational" condition was doubled in rate so as to last 750 ms instead of 1,500 ms. Waveforms representing the amplitude of the three stimuli are shown in Figure 5.10A, together with broadband traces that isolate the relatively slow time scale of syllabic variation, sometimes called the **speech envelope** (Rosen, 1992). Previous work has shown that although cortical event-related potentials (ERPs) often synchronize or phase-lock with perceived speech sounds, they tend to lag behind those sounds by 50–150 ms (Sharma & Dorman, 2000). For this reason, when Abrams et al. (2008) analyzed their data, they shifted the speech envelope in each sentence condition forward in time, so as to facilitate comparison between those envelopes and the cortical responses to them.

What they found was that, relative to three electrodes over the left temporal lobe, three matched electrodes over the right temporal lobe more reliably tracked the time-course of the speech envelope in all three conditions and also showed larger responses to magnitude. Figure 5.10B plots some of the findings for just the "clear" condition; analogous results emerged for the other conditions. On the left side of the figure, it can be seen that the red lines (representing the three right-hemisphere electrodes, T4, T6, and Tp8) conform to the contours of the speech envelope with greater accuracy than the blue lines (representing the three left-hemisphere electrodes, T3, T5, and Tp7). And on the right side of the figure, it is apparent that the ERPs recorded from the right-hemisphere electrodes correlated better with the speech envelope than those recorded from the left-hemisphere electrodes; moreover, those correlations were strongest when the neural responses were assumed to lag behind the

stimuli by about 85 ms (see Figure 5.10C for a more detailed depiction of this result). (As a brief digression, it is worth highlighting the rather fortuitous nature of the finding that at the electrode sites that were selected for analysis, the waveforms shown in Figure 5.10B just happened to "follow" the slow intensity changes of the speech envelope in such a way that greater positivities indexed greater intensities, especially in the right hemisphere. As noted in Chapter 2, ERP polarities usually don't correspond so well to stimulus parameters.)

Taken together, the results of Abrams et al.'s (2008) study suggest that the right hemisphere is dominant for processing speech on the relatively slow time scale of syllabic patterns. Accordingly, the study supports the part of the "asymmetric sampling in time" hypothesis that concentrates on the specific functional nature of the right-hemisphere contribution to speech perception. Further research is needed, however, to determine whether the key cortical structure for syllable perception is the right STS.

Summary

The early cortical stages of speech perception depend on pathways that begin in Heschl's gyrus and project into the STG and STS. Auditory processing along these pathways is hierarchically organized, with lower levels conducting elementary spectrotemporal analyses and higher levels extracting increasingly complex phonological patterns. These computational stages are also bilaterally organized, with the two hemispheres arguably making somewhat different functional contributions. The left hemisphere may be dominant for detecting (and categorizing) rapidly changing phonemic features in the 20–80 ms range, whereas the right hemisphere may be dominant for dealing with longer-duration syllabic information in the 150–300 ms range.

A Double Dissociation Between Comprehension and Repetition: Initial Evidence for Separate Streams of Speech Processing

Scientific theories often have peculiar pedigrees. In the case of the Dual Stream Model, one of Hickok and Poeppel's (2000, 2004, 2007) key insights was inspired in part by suspecting that the architecture of the auditory system may be similar in some respects to that of the visual system. As indicated in Chapter 1, the early cortical stages of visual processing take place in the occipital lobes, but then there is a major split

---

Speech envelope   The slow temporal variation of acoustic energy in speech that reflects syllabic patterns.

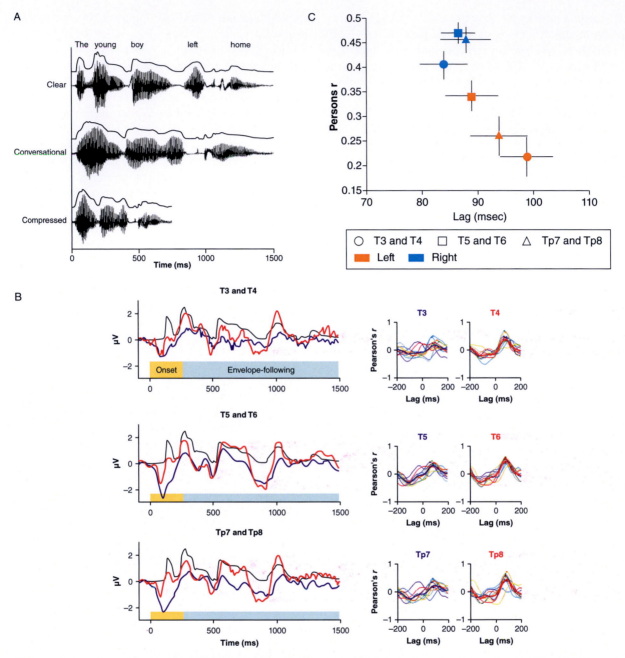

Figure 5.10 Stimuli and results of Abrams et al.'s (2008) electrophysiological study of speech perception. (A) Speech waveforms for the sentence *The young boy left home* in clear (top), conversational (middle), and compressed (bottom) speech modes. The broadband speech envelope for these stimuli is plotted immediately above each speech waveform. (B) Left column: Grand average cortical responses from three matched electrode pairs and broadband speech envelope for the clear stimulus condition. The black lines represent the broadband speech envelope for the clear speech condition, the red lines represent cortical activity measured at right-hemisphere electrodes, and the blue lines represent cortical activity measured at left-hemisphere electrodes. 95 ms of the prestimulus period is plotted. The speech envelope was shifted forward in time 85 ms to enable comparison to cortical responses; this time shift is for display purposes only. Right column: Cross-correlograms between clear speech envelope and individual subjects' cortical responses for each electrode pair. A small dot appears at the point chosen for subsequent stimulus-to-response correlation analyses. Thick blue and red lines represent averages. (C) Average cross-correlogram peaks. Values represent the average peak lag and *r* value, collapsed across stimulus conditions, for each stimulus envelope-cortical response correlation at the three electrode pairs. Right-hemisphere electrodes are blue, and left-hemisphere electrodes are orange. (From Abrams et al., 2008, pp. 3960–3961 and supplemental material.)

into two distinct computational channels. One stream funnels into the ventral temporal cortices and is sometimes called the "what" pathway because it represents information about shape, color, and apparent texture that is essential for recognizing the objects that we see. The other stream runs dorsally through the superior parietal cortices to the premotor cortices and is sometimes called the "how" pathway because it subserves the visual–motor transformations that are necessary for coordinating our bodily interactions with objects, allowing us to, for example, reach out and grasp an apple, a pen, or a book. Although the details of this "duplex" theory of vision are still being worked out, the general framework is supported by a wealth of evidence (for a recent review see Goodale, 2008; for an in-depth discussion see Milner & Goodale, 2006; and for a non-technical introduction see Goodale & Milner, 2004). Among the most compelling findings is a double dissociation showing that each of the two visual streams can be selectively impaired independently of the other. On the one hand, damage to the "what" pathway can disrupt the ability to perceive and identify visually presented objects while preserving the ability to act on them appropriately. For instance, the famous patient DF cannot say whether a pencil that an examiner holds up in front of her is oriented vertically or horizontally, but she can nevertheless reach out and grasp it perfectly. On the other hand, damage to the "how" pathway can disrupt the ability to act appropriately on visually presented objects while preserving the ability to recognize them. Thus, when patients with so-called optic ataxia attempt to reach out and grasp objects, they often aim in the wrong direction and use incorrect hand configurations, but despite these errors of visual–motor coordination, they can recognize objects without significant difficulty.

When Hickok and Poeppel began developing the Dual Stream Model, they were aware of these striking discoveries about the neuropsychology of vision, and they realized that a similar double dissociation had been reported in the realm of speech processing long ago. The key observation in the old aphasia literature was that, as indicated in Chapter 3, focal brain damage can selectively impair either comprehension (i.e., knowing "what" is being said, which pertains to conceptual content) or repetition (i.e., knowing "how" it is being said, which pertains to vocal action). For example, patients with transcortical sensory aphasia are severely deficient at understanding the meanings of words and sentences, but they can still repeat the very same words and sentences. Conversely, patients with conduction aphasia perform quite well on most comprehension tasks,

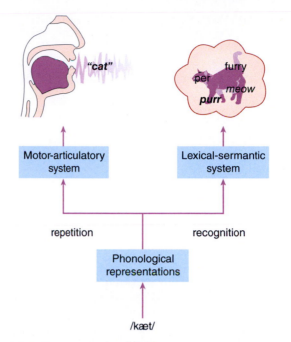

Figure 5.11 Distinct mappings from phonological representations to the semantic system and the motor system. (From Hickok, 2009a, p. 768.)

but they are profoundly impaired at repetition. This double dissociation between comprehension and repetition has been confirmed by recent lesion studies (see especially Kümmerer et al., 2013), and it suggests that after the early cortical stages of speech perception have been completed, further processing bifurcates into two separate streams: One route links phonological representations with the lexical-semantic system, whereas the other route links phonological representations with the motor–articulatory system (Figure 5.11). Hence the name of the theory: the Dual Stream Model.

Hickok and Poeppel also noticed that in the late 1970s and early 1980s, double dissociations were reported between, on the one hand, auditory comprehension tasks like word–picture matching, and on the other hand, what could be called auditory "monitoring" tasks like phoneme discrimination and identification. For example, in one study Miceli et al. (1980) administered both comprehension and discrimination tasks to 69 Italian aphasic patients. The comprehension task involved matching words with pictures, where each array of pictures contained six items: the target, a semantically related distractor, a phonologically related distractor, and three unrelated distractors. The discrimination task involved making same–different judgments about pairs of syllables drawn from the following set: "prin," "trin," "krin," "brin," "drin," and "grin." Not surprisingly, some patients performed brilliantly on

Table 5.2 Relation Between a Word Comprehension
Task and a Phoneme Discrimination Task Administered to 69
Aphasic Patients

Word Comprehension	Phoneme Discrimination	
	Normal	Impaired
Normal	23	19
Impaired	9	15

Data from Table 3 in Miceli et al. (1980). (Adapted from Hickok &
Poeppel, 2004, p. 75.)

Note the double dissociation: 19 patients had normal word
comprehension but pathological phoneme discrimination, and 9
patients had the opposite performance profile.

both tasks, and others performed poorly on both tasks.
Much more interesting, however, was the emergence of
a robust double dissociation. Overall, 19 patients were
normal on the comprehension task but impaired on the
discrimination task, whereas 9 patients exhibited the
opposite profile, being impaired on the comprehension
task but normal on the discrimination task (Table 5.2).
Moreover, an earlier study by Basso et al. (1977) showed
that the ability to understand spoken words also doubly
dissociates from the ability to identify phonemes along
a /ta/–/da/ continuum. For other relevant studies see
Blumstein et al. (1977) and Caplan et al. (1995).

As Hickok and Poeppel point out, perhaps the most
remarkable aspect of these neuropsychological findings
is that performance on auditory monitoring tasks like
phoneme discrimination and identification can be compromised while performance on auditory comprehension
tasks like word–picture matching is left intact. For example, some patients cannot distinguish between *cat* and *cot*
or indicate whether *cat* contains the vowel /æ/, but can
nevertheless match *cat* with a picture of a cat instead of
with a picture of a cot. What this suggests is that monitoring tasks probably recruit a different processing pathway
than comprehension tasks. Below we discuss Hickok and
Poeppel's proposal, which is that monitoring tasks actually
recruit some of the same neural mechanisms as repetition
tasks. First, however, let's take a closer look at the pathway
that flows toward the most important endpoint of receptive speech processing—comprehension.

The Ventral "What" Stream: From Sound to Meaning

The ventral stream can be broadly construed as an auditory "what" system that is designed to not only map
the sound structures of words onto the corresponding

semantic representations, but also contribute to forming
the integrated meanings of complex utterances like phrases
and sentences. According to Hickok and Poeppel (2007),
this pathway has two main functional–anatomical components (see the pink components in Figure 5.1). First,
the "lexical interface" has reciprocal connections with the
phonological network and is thought to be implemented
in the posterior middle and inferior portions of the temporal lobes bilaterally, but with a left-hemisphere bias.
Second, the "combinatorial network" has reciprocal connections with the lexical interface and is believed to reside
in the anterior middle and inferior portions of the temporal lobes, predominantly in the left hemisphere. Before
describing each of these components in greater detail, it is
important to note at the outset that the ventral stream has
not been investigated in as much depth as the other elements of the Dual Stream Model, and for this reason it is
the least developed part of the theory.

The Lexical Interface

In all of their major presentations of the Dual Stream
Model, Hickok and Poeppel (2000, 2004, 2007) have
consistently portrayed the lexical interface as functioning like a relay station for getting from the phonological
structures of words to their semantic structures during
spoken language comprehension. As indicated above, the
phonological structures of words are believed to depend
on the middle STS bilaterally. The semantic structures
of words, however, are thought to be widely distributed
across a variety of cortical regions (see the gray component in Figure 5.1). This hypothesis about the neural
substrates of conceptual knowledge is discussed at length
in Part V of this book. In the current context, what matters is simply that the lexical interface is not assumed
to actually store the meanings words, but is instead
proposed to serve as an intermediary for mapping phonological structures onto semantic structures.

How might this mapping process work? The computational details are not understood, but some
interesting possibilities come from the closely related
literature on language production, since it deals with
what is essentially the reverse process of mapping
semantic structures onto phonological structures. In
that literature, there is a debate over whether the mapping process involves just one stage or two (Caramazza,
1997; Levelt et al., 1999; see the section in Chapter 6
called "The Lemma Dilemma"). On the one-stage
view, the meaning of a word (e.g., the concept of a
cat) projects to a composite word-level phonological
representation (e.g., /kæt/), and this in turn projects to a
set of more specific and isolated subword-level phonological

representations that effectively "spell out" the syllabic and phonemic content of the word (e.g., /k/, /æ/, and /t/). On the two-stage view, another level called the **lemma** intervenes between the meaning and the word-level phonological representation; it is basically an abstract word node that operates not only as a bridge between semantics and phonology, but also as a pointer to syntactic features (e.g., *cat* is a type of noun). The nature of lemmas, and the controversy over whether they are neurocognitively real, is addressed in Chapter 6. The motivation for briefly raising these issues here is that there is a genuine question as to whether they also apply to language comprehension. In a discussion of this topic, Hickok and Poeppel (2004, p. 81) point out that although there is not yet enough data to resolve these matters concerning the computational architecture of the lexical interface, it is still reasonable to posit some sort of relay mechanism:

> For present purposes, these distinctions, should they exist, would constitute subdivisions of our 'auditory-conceptual interface' system. Thus, we are taking an agnostic stand on the computational details of this interface system. Our claim is simply that there exists a cortical network which performs a mapping between (or binds) acoustic-phonetic representations on the one hand, and conceptual-semantic representations on the other.

What kinds of evidence support the proposal that the lexical interface is subserved by the posterior middle temporal gyrus (pMTG) and the posterior inferior temporal gyrus (pITG) in both hemispheres, albeit with a leftward bias? As Hickok and Poeppel (2007) observe, this view is consistent with a number of functional neuroimaging studies that have focused on semantic processing (e.g., Rissman et al., 2003; Rodd et al., 2005; Humphries et al., 2006; Saur et al., 2008; see also the meta-analysis by Binder et al., 2009). A more valuable source of data, however, comes from aphasia. As noted in Chapter 3, the subgroup of Wernicke's aphasics with the worst comprehension deficits tend to have lesions that encompass the left pMTG (Dronkers et al., 1995; Robson et al., 2012). In addition, damage to the pMTG and pITG in the left hemisphere can give rise to transcortical sensory aphasia, a syndrome in which the understanding of spoken words, phrases, and sentences is severely impaired (Kertesz et al., 1982). For both types of disorders, the interpretation

Lemma An abstract word node that not only intervenes between semantics and phonology, but also points to syntactic features like grammatical category.

from the perspective of the Dual Stream Model is that the impairment may not necessarily affect word meanings per se, but may instead affect the neural mechanisms that map the phonological structures of words onto the corresponding semantic structures.

Further evidence for this idea comes from an important study by Boatman et al. (2000). Working with a group of six neurosurgical patients in whom electrode arrays had been implanted over the left lateral cortex, these researchers investigated how direct electrical interference at various sites influenced performance on the following seven tasks:

- syllable discrimination;
- word and sentence repetition;
- auditory comprehension as assessed by the Token Test, which includes commands like *Move the green square*;
- spontaneous speech as assessed by responses to questions about the patients' families and interests;
- oral reading of words;
- oral reading of paragraphs;
- oral object naming.

Immediately before each trial of each task, an electrical current was generated between two adjacent electrodes, and the effects of this stimulation lasted roughly 5 seconds. Across the six patients, a total of 81 electrode pairs were tested (mean = 14; range = 6–18 per patient; see Figure 5.12A). Remarkably, a pattern of disturbances very similar to transcortical sensory aphasia was elicited by stimulation at 29 of the 81 electrode pairs (mean = 5; range = 3–8 per patient; see Figure 5.12B). Most of the critical electrode pairs were in the pMTG, but some were located more superiorly, inferiorly, or anteriorly. Although stimulation at these sites did not affect syllable discrimination or word/sentence repetition, it did interfere significantly with auditory comprehension; in fact, all six patients "reported hearing but not understanding the examiner" (Boatman et al., 2000, p. 1637). Spontaneous speech and oral reading of words/paragraphs were fluent but riddled with both phonemic paraphasias (e.g., saying *orly* instead of *nearly*) and semantic substitutions (e.g., saying *stick* instead of *pencil*). Stimulation at 19 of the 29 critical sites also impaired oral object naming, but, interestingly enough, stimulation at the other 10 sites left naming intact (see Figure 5.12C). This latter finding is important in the context of the other findings, because it suggests that semantic knowledge was not affected. According to the researchers, these results "confirm that a one-way disruption can occur between otherwise intact left-hemisphere phonology and lexical-semantic processing in patients who have impaired auditory comprehension, with spared repetition and fluent speech" (Boatman et al., 2000, p. 1641). From the point of view of the Dual Stream Model, this study supports the hypothesis that the ventral stream contains a lexical interface that serves as a conduit between sound and meaning during the comprehension of spoken words. It is noteworthy, however, that the relevant electrode sites varied considerably across the six patients and extended beyond the pMTG to encompass not only more anterior areas of the MTG, but also some portions of the STG. This raises the possibility that the lexical interface may have a somewhat idiosyncratic localization in different individuals.

On the other hand, neuropsychological evidence that the lexical interface depends largely on the left pMTG comes from a different study in which 64 chronic stroke patients with widely distributed left-hemisphere lesion sites were given 11 subtests of a comprehension battery called the Curtiss–Yamada Comprehensive Language Evaluation—Receptive (CYCLE-R; Dronkers et al., 2004; for additional details about this study see Chapter 15). All of the subtests involved sentence–picture matching, but the sentence types ranged from being very simple and easy to understand (e.g., *The clown has a balloon*) to being very complex and hard to understand (e.g., *The girl is kissing the boy that the clown is hugging*). The relationships between the patients' behavioral performances and their lesion sites were analyzed with voxel-based lesion–symptom mapping

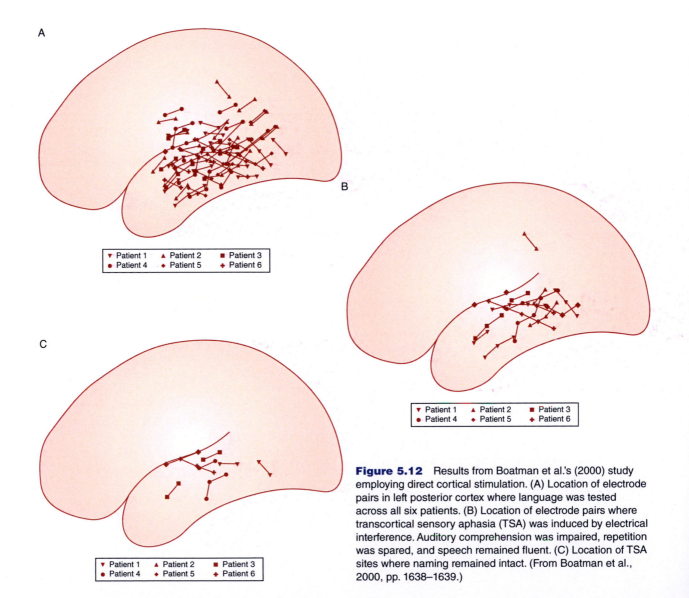

Figure 5.12 Results from Boatman et al.'s (2000) study employing direct cortical stimulation. (A) Location of electrode pairs in left posterior cortex where language was tested across all six patients. (B) Location of electrode pairs where transcortical sensory aphasia (TSA) was induced by electrical interference. Auditory comprehension was impaired, repetition was spared, and speech remained fluent. (C) Location of TSA sites where naming remained intact. (From Boatman et al., 2000, pp. 1638–1639.)

(see Chapter 2). Among the many significant findings was that the deepest, most pervasive deficits were strongly associated with damage to the left pMTG. More specifically, although patients with damage to this region performed within normal limits on the simplest sentence type (i.e., possession, which is exemplified above), they scored below normal, and in many cases far below normal, on all of the other sentence types (see Figure 15.3 in Chapter 15). Moreover, they also failed three comprehension tasks drawn from the Western Aphasia Battery: Yes/No Questions, Single Word Comprehension, and Sequential Commands (Kertesz, 1982). Taken together, these results led the researchers to conclude that the left pMTG probably plays a key role in understanding words. They acknowledge, however, that their data are not sufficient to ascertain the precise functional contribution of this cortical region to word comprehension: "Whether it is specifically the conceptual-semantic side, the phonological form side, or the actual linking between form and concept is unclear" (Dronkers et al., 2004, p. 167). Such caution is definitely warranted here. At the same time, though, it is worth highlighting the fact that the last possibility mentioned by the researchers—namely, that the left pMTG may serve as a bridge between the sounds and meanings of words—converges quite well with the study by Boatman et al. (2000) summarized above. And, needless to say, it is also the account that accords best with the Dual Stream Model, since executing sound–meaning mappings is the main operation that the theory ascribes to the lexical interface. Nevertheless, this issue remains controversial, since other researchers have argued that the left pMTG plays a more direct role in semantic representation (e.g., Hart & Gordon, 1990; Binder et al., 2009; Wei et al., 2012; Hoffman et al., 2012b; Fairhall & Caramazza, 2013).

Finally, what about the notion that, to use Hickok and Poeppel's (2007, p. 398) own words, "there is some degree of bilateral capability in lexical and semantic access"? This assumption has not been explored in depth. It receives some support, however, from studies demonstrating that the isolated right hemisphere of split-brain patients—i.e., patients whose corpus collosum has been surgically severed—can understand some words (Zaidel, 1985; for a historical perspective on this line of work see Wolman, 2012).

The Combinatorial Network

According to the theory, the lexical interface not only maps the phonological structures of words onto the corresponding semantic structures, but also projects forward to lateral portions of the anterior temporal lobe (ATL), especially in the left hemisphere. This higher-order region is thought to implement a combinatorial network that plays an important role in constructing the integrated meanings of phrases and sentences, drawing upon both semantic and grammatical information. This proposal has not been elaborated in much detail; however, as discussed in Chapter 2, the general idea has received some preliminary support from fMRI studies which indicate that the left lateral ATL responds significantly more to intelligible than unintelligible multi-word utterances (see Figures 2.18, 2.20, and 2.22, together with the accompanying text). Additional evidence comes from PET and fMRI studies which show that listening to semantically coherent, syntactically well-formed sentences engages the left lateral ATL, among other areas, more than listening to word lists and several other types of auditory stimuli (e.g., Mazoyer et al., 1993; Stowe et al., 1999; Friederici et al., 2000; Vandenberghe et al., 2002; Humphries et al., 2001, 2005, 2006; see also the MEG studies by Bemis & Pylkkänen, 2011, 2013). A few of these studies also suggest that the left lateral ATL may be functionally partitioned, with one sector being more sensitive to compositional semantics than to syntactic structure, and another sector having the opposite response preferences (Vandenberghe et al., 2002; Humphries et al., 2006). A limitation of the latter studies, however, is that they used anomalous sentences as stimuli, which may have triggered atypical neurocognitive processes.

To avoid this problem, Rogalsky and Hickok (2009) conducted an fMRI study in which they very cleverly manipulated the attention of the participants instead of the naturalness of the stimuli. First, they identified their main region of interest (ROI) in the left ATL by determining which voxels in this territory were engaged significantly more when the participants listened passively to sentences than when they listened passively to noun lists. Then, to further investigate the question of whether this ROI contains separate sectors that are differentially modulated by the semantic and syntactic aspects of sentences, they administered two main tasks. In one task, the participants listened to sentences and pressed a button whenever they detected a semantic anomaly (e.g., *The infant was spilling some carpet on the milk*); in the other task, the participants listened to sentences and pressed a button whenever they detected a syntactic anomaly (e.g., *The plumber with the glasses were installing the sink*). Crucially, only 20 percent of the trials in each task consisted of anomalous sentences, and the normal sentences in the two tasks were identical. Furthermore, when the researchers analyzed their data, they discarded the anomalous sentences and concentrated on just the two sets of identical normal sentences. By adopting this strategy, they could be confident that if the two sets of sentences turned out to elicit different patterns of activity in the ATL ROI, those differences could not be attributed to any differences between the sentences themselves, but must instead reflect the top-down "enhancement" effects of the participants' attentional focus on either the semantic or the syntactic aspects of the sentences in the two tasks.

Four main findings emerged (Figure 5.13). First, almost the entire ATL ROI responded more strongly during the two selective attention tasks than during the two passive listening tasks that were initially used to define the ROI. Second, almost the entire ATL ROI was equally sensitive to semantic attention and syntactic attention. Third, at a slightly relaxed statistical threshold, a small cluster of voxels appeared that was more sensitive to semantic attention than syntactic attention. And fourth, even at the relaxed statistical threshold, no voxels responded more to syntactic attention than semantic attention. Overall, then, Rogalsky and Hickok's (2009) fMRI study suggests that the left lateral ATL implements a combinatorial network in which the semantic and syntactic features of sentences are processed in a highly interactive, as opposed to a strictly segregated, manner. (This topic is discussed in greater detail in Chapter 15; see especially Figure 15.14 and the associated text.)

Summary

According to the Dual Stream Model, the ventral pathway is the main computational channel underlying the comprehension of spoken language. It has two functional–anatomical components. First, the lexical interface maps the phonological structures of words onto the corresponding semantic structures. This component is implemented primarily in the pMTG and pITG, bilaterally but with a leftward bias. Second, the combinatorial network plays a central role in constructing integrated message-level representations of the meanings of phrases and sentences. This component is housed in the lateral ATL, predominantly in the left hemisphere.

Although this characterization of the ventral pathway is supported by several sources of evidence, it is still very schematic and tentative, and a great deal of work remains to be done to flesh out this part of the overall theory. Among the various modifications that may need to be made in the future, two are as follows. First, there are now good reasons to suppose that the ATL contributes not only to the transient formation of the message-level representations of multi-word expressions, but also to the long-term storage of single word meanings. In particular, the ATL may serve as a semantic hub that binds together and organizes the diverse, anatomically distributed features that constitute the main content of individual lexical concepts (e.g., the visual, functional, and manipulative aspects of the type of object denoted by the word *spoon*). We first encountered this idea in Chapter 4, specifically in connection with the variant of primary progressive aphasia

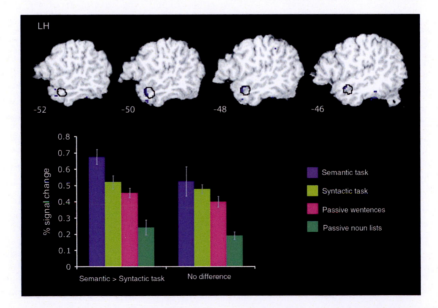

Figure 5.13   Results from Rogalsky and Hickok's (2009) fMRI study of sentence processing. (Top) Regions outlined in black correspond to the ATL ROI identified by the sentences > noun list contrast. Blue patches inside the outlined regions indicate voxels that were more active during the perception of correct sentences in the semantic task than during the perception of the very same correct sentences in the syntactic task. (Bottom) The bar graphs represent the mean peak amplitudes for, on the left, the voxels in the ATL ROI that had a semantic vs. syntactic task preference (shown in blue in the top part of the figure) and, on the right, the voxels in the ATL ROI that did not have a preference for either task. (From Rogalsky & Hickok, 2009, p. 792.)

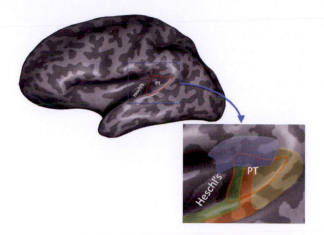

Figure 5.14 Location and cytoarchitectonic organization of the planum temporale (PT). The location of the PT on the posterior supratemporal plane is indicated in red outline on an inflated representation of the brain which shows structures buried in sulci and fissures. The inset shows a close-up of the PT region. Colors indicate approximate locations of different cytoarchitectonic fields as delineated by Galaburda and Sanides (1980). Note that there are four different fields within the PT suggesting functional differentiation, and that these fields extend beyond the PT. Area Spt falls within the yellow region. (From Hickok, 2009b, p. 129.)

known as semantic dementia, and we will discuss the idea more fully in several of the chapters to come (see especially Chapters 10–12). For now, the main point is simply that it may be worthwhile to incorporate this notion of a semantic hub into subsequent portrayals of the ventral stream. For instance, one could hypothesize that the semantic hub in the ATL is the first main stage of conceptual processing after the lexical interface in the pMTG (Chan et al., 2011), and that it feeds into the combinatorial network that also resides in the ATL.

Second, future efforts to elaborate the treatment of how phrases and sentences are processed will need to accommodate recent evidence that the ventral stream does not operate alone, but rather in conjunction with the dorsal stream, especially when it comes to computing certain aspects of morphology and syntax (see especially Rolheiser et al., 2011, and Wilson et al., 2011; see also Chapters 13 and 15).

The Dorsal "How" Stream: From Sound to Action

From the perspective of the Dual Stream Model, the dorsal pathway can be thought of as an auditory "how" system that is designed to map perceptual representations of vocal sounds onto motor representations of how the very same sounds would be produced (Hickok

et al., 2011b). Like the ventral stream, the dorsal stream has two main functional–anatomical components (see the blue components in Figure 5.1). First, the "sensorimotor interface" has reciprocal connections with the phonological network (as well as with the lower-order system for spectrotemporal analysis) and is believed to reside in a cortical area deep inside the posterior end of the sylvian fissure, predominantly in the left hemisphere. Second, the "articulatory network" has reciprocal connections with the sensorimotor interface and depends on a variety of motor-related regions in the posterior frontal lobe, predominantly in the left hemisphere. This whole neural circuit contributes significantly to language acquisition because, as Hickok and Poeppel (2007, p. 399) point out,

> Learning to speak is essentially a motor leaning task. The primary input to this is sensory, speech in particular. So, there must be a neural mechanism that both codes and maintains instances of speech sounds, and can use these sensory traces to guide the tuning of speech gestures so that the sounds are accurately reproduced.

Besides enabling the precise imitation of speech patterns, the dorsal stream also provides a foundation for the phonological loop, which is sometimes referred to more technically as auditory–verbal short-term memory—i.e., the type of memory in which phonological material is kept "alive" in a conscious, active state by means of covert repetition. Finally, there is growing evidence that the dorsal stream facilitates speech perception, especially when we attend closely to the phonological details of the utterances that we hear. All of these points are elaborated below.

The Sensorimotor Interface

The most posterior portion of the supratemporal plane, caudal to Heschl's gyrus, is called the **planum temporale (PT)**. Cytoarchitectonic studies have shown that this region straddles at least four distinct cortical fields (Figure 5.14; Galaburda & Sanides, 1980; Sweet et al., 2005). Given this anatomical complexity, it is not surprising that the PT has been associated with a wide range of functions (e.g., Griffiths & Warren, 2002; Warren et al., 2005; Zheng, 2009; Tremblay et al., 2013). What is most relevant to the

Planum temporale (PT) A cortical region at the posterior end of the supratemporal plane deep inside the sylvian fissure.

Dual Stream Model, however, is that a particular region within the left PT—a region that Hickok and Poeppel (2004, 2007) refer to as "area Spt" for "sylvian parietal-temporal"—appears to operate as a device for coordinating, or translating between, the sound-based phonological network in the lateral temporal lobe and the motor-based articulatory network in the posterior frontal lobe. In other words, area Spt may function as a sensorimotor integration system that uses primarily auditory information to help guide the movements of the vocal tract, just as certain cortical areas in the intra-parietal sulcus are believed to function as sensorimotor integration systems that use primarily visual information to help guide the movements of the arms, hands, and eyes (Milner & Goodale, 2006). As a concrete illustration, the basic idea is that when you produce a word like *strawberry,* your articulatory programming is influenced in part by a stored auditory representation of how that word should sound, and area Spt is critically involved in mediating that influence, specifically by serving as a bridge that connects the "sound image" of the word in the middle STS with the "motor image" of the word in the posterior frontal lobe. Now, how exactly area Spt accomplishes this mediating function is a complex topic, and we will not delve into those computational details until Chapter 6. Here, we will just treat area Spt at a relatively abstract level and focus on the general hypothesis that it serves as a sensorimotor interface for the vocal tract. In what follows, we consider several sources of evidence for this view.

If the hypothesis is correct, one would expect area Spt to be engaged not only during speech perception, but also during speech production, even when the production is covert so there is no auditory feedback. A number of fMRI studies have generated results that are consistent with this prediction (e.g., Buchsbaum et al., 2001; Hickok et al., 2003; Buchsbaum et al., 2005b, 2005c; Okada & Hickok, 2006b; Hickok et al., 2009b). For example, Hickok et al. (2003) report a study in which each trial of the "speech" condition had the following sequential structure: (1) Participants heard a 3-second-long meaningless sentence in which the real nouns and verbs had been replaced with pseudowords; (2) participants covertly rehearsed the sentence for 15 seconds; (3) participants heard another 3-second-long meaningless sentence; and (4) participants rested for 15 seconds. The response profile of area Spt across the four phases of the trials conformed perfectly with the theoretical predictions: It was activated not only during the two auditory stimulation phases, but also during the covert rehearsal phase; in addition, its activation level dropped to baseline during the rest phase (Figure 5.15). Interestingly,

more anterior portions of the dorsal STG were activated during the two auditory stimulation phases but not during the rehearsal phase, which supports the notion that although these cortices are involved in speech perception, they are not part of the sensorimotor interface for the vocal tract (Figure 5.15).

As a novel extension of this study, the researchers investigated whether area Spt contributes to the sensorimotor coordination of not just speech, but also other vocal sounds/actions. To do this, they included a "music" condition in which each trial had a sequential structure similar to the "speech" condition: (1) Participants heard a 3-second-long unfamiliar melody; (2) participants covertly hummed the melody for 15 seconds; (3) participants heard another 3-second-long unfamiliar melody; and (4) participants rested for 15 seconds. The results for the "music" condition were remarkably parallel to those for the "speech" condition, both in area Spt and in more anterior portions of the dorsal STG (Figure 5.15). Overall, these findings suggest that in performing its function as a sensorimotor interface, area Spt deals not only with phonological material, but also with other sorts of sounds that are vocally "do-able."

A subsequent fMRI study by Pa and Hickok (2008), however, demonstrated that even though area Spt traffics in both speech and non-speech sounds/actions, its purview seems to be restricted to the sensorimotor regulation of the vocal tract. This experiment was similar to the one described above in two ways. First, each trial had four phases: auditory stimulation, covert rehearsal, auditory stimulation, and rest. Second, there was a "music" condition in which the stimuli were unfamiliar melodies and the covert rehearsal phase required the participants to silently hum the tunes. The study was unique, however, insofar as all of the participants were skilled pianists, and a "play" condition was included in which the stimuli were, once again, unfamiliar melodies, but the covert rehearsal phase required the participants to imagine playing the tunes on a keyboard. Thus, the only difference between the two conditions in this study was that the "music" condition involved silent reproduction of sounds by means of covert vocal tract movements, whereas the "play" condition involved silent reproduction of sounds by means of covert hand movements. As in the previous study, the "music" condition led to increased activation in area Spt during both the auditory stimulation and the covert rehearsal phases, but not during the rest phase (Figure 5.16A, C). The new finding was that the "play" condition led to increased activation not in

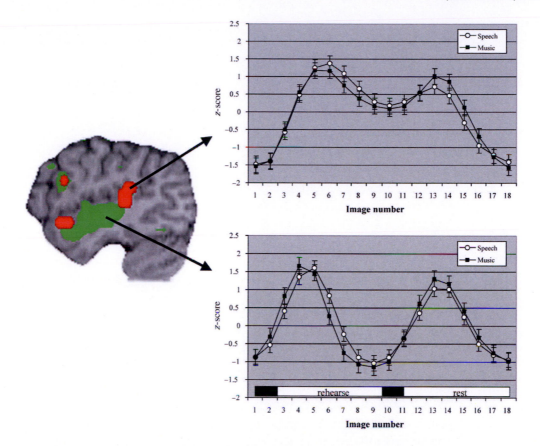

Figure 5.15   Results from Hickok et al.'s (2003) fMRI study of speech and music processing. A trial is composed of 3 seconds of auditory stimulation followed by 15 seconds of covert rehearsal (speech or humming) of the heard stimulus followed by 3 seconds of auditory stimulation followed by 15 seconds of rest. The brain image on the left shows the activation map on a single left hemisphere slice in a representative subject (red = "auditory + rehearsal" responses; green = "auditory" responses). The time-course data on the right are averaged over all subjects. The top panel shows "auditory + rehearsal" activation in area Spt, and the bottom panel shows "auditory" activation in the middle STG. Note that in the top panel the two humps represent sensory responses, the shallow valley between the humps represents the covert rehearsal process, and the baseline values at the onset and offset of the trial represent resting activation levels. In the bottom panel the response curves between the two humps are reduced to the baseline level, suggesting that the middle STG does not contribute to the rehearsal process. (From Hickok et al., 2003, p. 678.)

area Spt, but rather in the anterior intraparietal sulcus, during both the auditory stimulation and the covert rehearsal phases, but not during the rest phase (Figure 5.16B, D). This outcome converges with other evidence that the anterior intraparietal sulcus operates as a sensorimotor interface for the perceptual guidance of hand actions, including piano-playing (Meister et al., 2004; Makuuchi et al., 2005; Bangert et al., 2006; Milner & Goodale, 2006). For present purposes, the main upshot of the study is that area Spt appears to coordinate mappings between sounds and actions only for a particular motor effector system—the vocal tract.

Further evidence that area Spt plays an essential role in mediating between the perception and production of speech comes from aphasia. As noted in Chapter 3, damage to the left supramarginal gyrus and the inferiorly adjacent tissue deep inside the sylvian fissure—including, importantly, area Spt—frequently brings about conduction aphasia, a syndrome in which language comprehension is, for the most part, intact, but language production is distorted by phonemic paraphasias and repetition is severely compromised (see also the earlier section in this chapter called "A Double Dissociation Between Comprehension and Repetition"). From the perspective of the Dual Stream Model, this type of aphasia can be regarded as essentially a disorder of the sensorimotor interface. Comprehension is fairly well-preserved because the lesion spares the ventral stream. Phonemic paraphasias are rampant during spontaneous speech—and are especially likely for long, complex, and low-frequency words—because the motor programming of words can

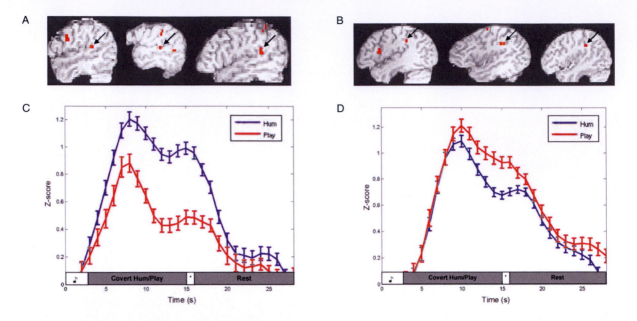

Figure 5.16 Results from Pa and Hickok's (2008) fMRI study of music processing. (A) Representative activation maps from three subjects in area Spt during covert humming. (B) Representative activation maps from three subjects in the anterior intraparietal sulcus during covert piano playing. (C) The averaged time-course of the top four activated voxels from all subjects in area Spt during the covert humming phase. (D) The averaged time-course of the top four activated voxels from all subjects in the anterior intraparietal sulcus during the covert piano playing phase. (From Pa & Hickok, 2008, p. 365.)

no longer be guided by the sound-based representations that specify the auditory "targets" of production. And repetition is profoundly impaired because it depends on precisely the mechanism that is damaged the most, namely the neural relay station that translates what one hears into how to say it.

Support for this view comes from an impressive study by Buchsbaum et al. (2011) that had several parts. In one part of the investigation, the researchers overlaid the lesion sites of 14 patients with chronic conduction aphasia and found that, as expected, the most commonly damaged region, affected in 12 (85 percent) of the cases, was the left temporoparietal territory, including area Spt (see the left panel of Figure 5.17). In another part of the investigation, the researchers combined the imaging data from 105 healthy subjects who participated in five different fMRI studies of phonological working memory, all of which were designed like the ones by Hickok et al. (2003) and Pa and Hickok (2008) described above. A conjunction analysis revealed that during both the auditory stimulation (encoding) and covert rehearsal phases of the tasks, nearly 50 percent of the subjects exhibited significant activation in area Spt, as well as in several other parietal and frontal regions (see the middle panel of Figure 5.17). Fifty percent may seem rather low, but Buchsbaum et al. (2011) point out

that this is due mainly to individual differences in the neuroanatomy of the planum temporale and consequent difficulties in aligning area Spt across subjects. Finally, and most importantly, when the researchers superimposed the lesion data and the fMRI data, they found that the region of maximal overlap—i.e., 85 percent lesion overlap plus significant activation during both encoding and rehearsal—was located squarely in area Spt (see the right panel of Figure 5.17). These findings clearly bolster the hypothesis that conduction aphasia can be characterized, to a large extent, as an impairment of the sensorimotor interface component of the Dual Stream Model. It is also noteworthy that, as observed in Chapter 4, a similar but milder set of symptoms is often found in logopenic progressive aphasia, a neurodegenerative disease that is associated with gradual atrophy of the left posterior perisylvian cortex, including area Spt (see Figure 2.7 in Chapter 2 and Figure 4.3 in Chapter 4).

The Articulatory Network

Figure 5.1 indicates that the sensorimotor interface is connected not only with the phonological network, but also with the articulatory network, which depends on a number of regions in the left posterior frontal lobe, including Broca's area, premotor and primary

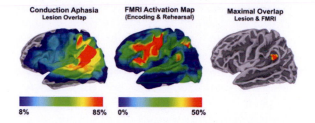

Conduction Aphasia
Lesion Overlap

FMRI Activation Map
(Encoding & Rehearsal)

Maximal Overlap
Lesion & FMRI

8%   85%   0%   50%

Figure 5.17 Results of Buchsbaum et al.'s (2011) comparison of lesion data from 14 conduction aphasics and fMRI data from 105 healthy subjects. (Left) Among the conduction aphasics, 12/14 (85%) had lesions in the left temporoparietal region, including area Spt. (Middle) For the healthy subjects, nearly 50% exhibited significant activation in area Spt (as well as in other parietal and frontal regions) during both the encoding and covert rehearsal phases of phonological working memory tasks. (Right) The region of maximal overlap between the lesion and fMRI maps was squarely in area Spt. (From Buchsbaum et al., 2011, p. 125.)

motor cortices for controlling the vocal apparatus, and the anterior insula. In what follows, we will not discuss the detailed functional neuroanatomy of overt speech production, since that topic is covered in Chapter 6. Instead, we will concentrate on how the articulatory network contributes to two capacities that are important in the context of the Dual Stream Model—auditory–verbal short-term memory, and certain forms of speech perception.

Auditory–verbal short-term memory (STM), also known as the phonological loop, is the neurocognitive resource that allows one to keep phonological information "in mind," which is to say, in an activated state. It is usually experienced as "that little voice in your head" (Buchsbaum, 2013), and it was heavily engaged during the covert rehearsal phases of the tasks that were used in the fMRI studies reported by Hickok et al. (2003), Pa and Hickok (2008), and Buchsbaum et al. (2011). Auditory–verbal STM is often tested in laboratory settings by means of a **digit span task**, which determines the longest string of arbitrary digits that a person can repeat correctly. Most people can retain up to about seven items (Miller, 1956), which may be partly why telephone numbers typically have that many digits. A more real-world example, however, of the kind of situation that strains the upper

limits of auditory–verbal STM is when you are forced to hold online a complicated set of driving directions that someone has just told you, like "Go up this street to the stoplight, turn left and go another four blocks, then turn right and look for the green house on right." To some extent, such situations require a mixture of auditory–verbal STM and long-term memory encoding, but what is most salient when you find yourself in that kind of predicament is the urgent need to continually rehearse the instructions, if not out loud, then silently to yourself. When the rehearsal is overt, it is essentially repetition, but when it is covert, it falls under the rubric of auditory–verbal STM.

What are the neural substrates of auditory–verbal STM? This has been a controversial issue for many years. However, research and theorizing within the framework of the Dual Stream Model point to an approach like the one depicted in Figure 5.18. Basically, the perception of an utterance activates phonological representations in the STS bilaterally; these phonological representations are kept "alive" by means of corresponding subvocal articulatory processes in the left frontal lobe; and this reverberatory cycle is mediated by the sensorimotor interface in area Spt (for relevant data and discussion see, e.g., Baldo & Dronkers, 2006; Buchsbaum & D'Esposito, 2008; Leff et al., 2009; Koenigs et al., 2011; Baldo et al., 2012; Herman et al., 2013; for a broader perspective see Fuster, 2009; and for connections with sentence comprehension see Chapter 15). In short, auditory–verbal STM recruits the entire dorsal stream, although it is driven, so to speak, primarily by the frontal articulatory network, since that component functions as the executive controller that continually refreshes, via the sensorimotor interface, the sound-based representations in the phonological network. Not surprisingly, in the fMRI studies by Hickok et al. (2003), Pa and Hickok (2008), and Buchsbaum et al. (2011) that were summarized above in the context of the sensorimotor interface, elements of the frontal articulatory network were activated during the covert rehearsal phase of each trial, when participants were required to silently reproduce to themselves the auditory sequence they had just heard (see Figures 5.15–5.17; see also Buchsbaum et al., 2001, 2005b, 2005c; Okada & Hickok, 2006b).

An even more interesting feature of the articulatory network is that its scope of operation does not seem to be restricted to overt and covert speech production, but appears to embrace some aspects of speech perception as well. This is consistent with a growing body of data suggesting that the motor system is not just in the

Auditory–verbal short-term memory (STM) A memory system that allows a person to keep phonological information in an active state for a relatively short period of time.

Digit span task A task that measures a person's auditory–verbal short-term memory capacity by determining the longest string of arbitrary digits that they can repeat correctly.

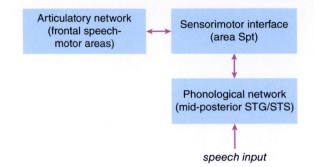

Figure 5.18   A sketch of the auditory–verbal short-term memory system, also known as the phonological loop. The perception of an utterance activates sound-based representations in the phonological network; these representations are kept "alive" by means of corresponding subvocal motor processes in the articulatory network; and this reverberatory cycle is mediated by the sensorimotor interface. The whole architecture is neurally implemented by the dorsal stream. (Adapted from Hickok, 2009b, p. 133.)

business of programming and executing actions, but is also involved in perceiving and recognizing them (for reviews see Rizzolatti & Sinigaglia, 2010, and Fogassi & Ferrari, 2011). The precise nature of the functional contribution of the articulatory network to speech perception is, however, a contentious topic, as described below.

Earlier in this chapter (see the section called "A Double Dissociation Between Comprehension and Repetition"), we noted that some brain-damaged patients manage to perform well on auditory comprehension tasks like word–picture matching—e.g., correctly matching the word *cat* with a picture of a cat instead of with a picture of a cot—despite being impaired on auditory monitoring tasks like phoneme discrimination and identification—e.g., having difficulty determining whether *cat* and *cot* are different words, or whether *cat* contains the vowel /æ/. Importantly, the patients who exhibit this type of dissociation tend to have either Broca's aphasia or conduction aphasia, and their lesions tend to be either left frontal or left frontoparietal (Basso et al., 1977; Blumstein et al., 1977; Miceli et al., 1980; Caplan et al., 1995). These neuropsychological findings therefore constitute evidence that monitoring tasks—i.e., tasks that demand explicit attention to the phonological structure of perceived utterances—rely on the integrity of the dorsal stream. According to Hickok and Poeppel (2000, 2004, 2007), there are at least two computational reasons for this. First, such tasks require auditory–verbal STM in order to keep the relevant phonological representations online

long enough to make the necessary discrimination or identification. Second, such tasks involve segmenting syllables into their constituent phonemes, and this kind of perceptual analysis might be facilitated by consulting the motor counterparts of the auditory inputs—an operation that draws upon the articulatory network.

Additional evidence that the dorsal stream—and, in particular, the articulatory network—is employed in auditory monitoring tasks comes from numerous TMS studies that have targeted Broca's area (Sehm et al., 2013), the premotor cortex (Meister et al., 2007; Sato et al., 2009; Krieger-Redwood et al., in press), and the primary motor cortex (Möttönen & Watkins, 2009; D'Ausilio et al., 2009, 2011a, 2011b; Murakami et al., 2011; Bartoli et al., in press). For instance, D'Ausilio et al. (2009) conducted an experiment in which they first identified the areas for controlling the lips and tongue in the left primary motor cortex of each participant. (As shown in Figure 1.25 in Chapter 1, the lip area is superior to the tongue area in the ventral portion of the motor homunculus.) The localization procedure was based on the coordinates of the peak activations that were observed during movements of these articulators in a previous fMRI study, which is discussed below (Pulvermüller et al., 2006). The researchers then administered the following task to the participants. On each trial, one of four speech sounds was presented through headphones—two produced with the lips (/bæ/ or /pæ/), and two produced with the tongue (/dæ/ or /tæ/). The participants were asked to identify each sound by pressing one of four buttons. To avoid ceiling effects, the sounds were embedded in 500 ms of white noise, leading to correct responses in ~75 percent of cases. The crucial manipulation was that on 60 of the 80 trials, two TMS pulses were delivered to either the lip area or the tongue area. These pulses occurred 100 ms and 150 ms after noise onset, with the second one occurring 50 ms prior to consonant presentation (Figure 5.19A, B). Because the pulses were assumed to enhance activity in the underlying cortical areas, it was predicted that stimulation of the lip area would improve discrimination between the labial sounds /bæ/ and /pæ/, whereas stimulation of the tongue area would improve discrimination between the dental sounds /dæ/ and /tæ/. These predictions were confirmed, as shown in Figure 5.19C, which portrays for each condition the magnitude of the reaction time (RT) difference between the trials with TMS and the trials without TMS. More precisely, the *y*-axis in the graph shows the following ratio: {[RTs (with TMS) ÷ RTs (without TMS)] ×100}.

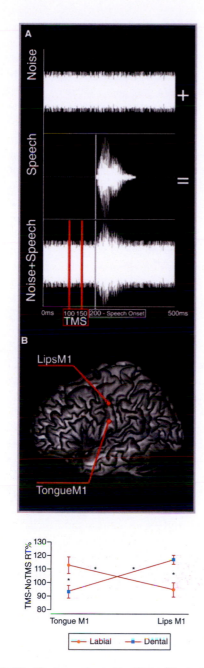

Thus, if TMS induces faster RTs than no TMS, the resulting value will be smaller than 100. And this is exactly what was found for the key analyses. Consider first the lip area: Relative to the trials without TMS, the trials with TMS led to faster RTs (i.e., values less than 100) for recognizing lip-produced sounds, but led to slower RTs (i.e., values greater than 100) for recognizing tongue-produced sounds. Turning to the tongue area, the opposite effects occurred: Relative to the trials without TMS, the trials with TMS led to faster RTs (i.e., values less than 100) for recognizing tongue-produced sounds, but led to slower RTs (i.e., values greater than 100) for recognizing lip-produced sounds. Overall, then, stimulation of a given motor representation—lips or tongue—facilitated the ability to identify speech sounds produced with the concordant articulator, but inhibited the ability to identify speech sounds produced with the discordant articulator. This study therefore supports the view that the articulatory network actively contributes to tasks that involve paying close attention to the phonological makeup of perceived speech.

A variety of other studies suggest that elements of the articulatory network are also engaged when people listen passively to utterances—that is, when they don't explicitly monitor the sound structure of the input. Although this frontal activation is more robust during the multisensory audiovisual perception of talking faces than during the purely auditory perception of speech (Skipper et al., 2005), it does occur in the latter circumstances, even when participants are not given any particular task other than to listen carefully to the stimuli (TMS studies: Fadiga et al., 2002; Watkins et al., 2003; Möttönen et al., 2013; fMRI studies: Wilson et al., 2004, 2006; Pulvermüller et al., 2006; Londei et al., 2010; MEG studies: Pulvermüller et al., 2003). For instance, in the fMRI study that set the stage for the TMS study by D'Ausilio et al. (2009) described above, Pulvermüller et al. (2006) measured the motor activity in participants' brains while they performed three tasks: (1) lip and tongue movements; (2) silent production of lip-related (/pa/) and tongue-related (/ta/) sounds; and (3) passive perception of lip-related (/pa/) and tongue-related (/ta/) sounds. The researchers found that parts of the motor area that was engaged during lip movements were also engaged during both the production and the perception of lip-related (/pa/) sounds, and parts of the motor area that was engaged during tongue movements were also engaged during both the production and the perception of tongue-related (/ta/) sounds (Figure 5.20). These findings,

Figure 5.19 Design and results of D'Ausilio et al.'s (2009) TMS study of speech perception. (A) Noise and speech recordings were mixed into a single trace. TMS (vertical red lines) was applied in double pulses 100 and 150 ms after noise onset. Speech sounds started 200 ms afer noise onset (gray vertical line). (B) Mean coordinates of the areas in the left primary motor cortex for the lips (Lips M1) and tongue (Tongue M1) where TMS was delivered. (C) Effect of TMS on reaction times (RTs) shows a double dissociation between stimulation site (Lips M1 vs. Tongue M1) and discrimination performance (labial vs. dental speech sounds). The y-axis represents the amount of RT change induced by the TMS stimulation (see text for details). Aserisks indicate significance ($p < 0.05$). (From D'Ausilio et al., 2009, p. 382.)

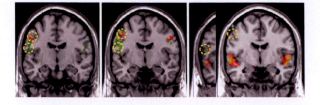

Figure 5.20   Results from Pulvermüller et al.'s (2006) fMRI study of speech production and perception. Frontal slices show differential activation during lip and tongue movements (left), silent articulation of syllables containing /p/ and /t/ (center), and listening to syllables containing /p/ and /t/ (right). Note the relatively superior activations for lip-related actions and perceptions (red) and the relatively inferior activations for tongue-related actions and perceptions (green). (From Pulvermüller et al., 2006, p. 7867.) Copyright (2006) National Academy of Sciences, U.S.A.

as well as the results of the other studies cited above, provide some neurobiological evidence for psycholinguistic theories that ascribe a functional role to motor representations even during passive speech perception (e.g., Galantucci et al., 2006; Skipper et al., 2006; Schwartz et al., 2012a). Yet the true meaning of these discoveries remains unclear.

One problem is that, as observed by Scott et al. (2009), the majority of the studies referred to above have not demonstrated in a compelling way that the motor responses to speech sounds are significantly different from those to other kinds of sounds. For example, Watkins et al. (2003) reported that the motor activations triggered by speech sounds were only somewhat greater than those triggered by nonverbal sounds, such as car engines and breaking glass (but see Osnes et al., 2011). Additional concerns have been voiced by one of the principal architects of

the Dual Stream Model, Gregory Hickok, together with his collaborators (Hickok, 2009b; Hickok et al., 2009a; Lotto et al., 2009; Venezia & Hickok, 2009). Most of these concerns revolve around the central point that while the articulatory network might *modulate* the passive perception of speech in various ways, it is probably not a necessary resource for comprehension. Drawing upon a bevy of findings, many of which we have already encountered in this chapter, Hickok et al. (2009a, p. 330) defend this position as follows:

> Evidence for this claim comes from the fact that even large left frontal lesions that reduce speech production to nil or to stereotyped output do not produce considerable impairments in speech recognition (Naeser et al., 1989; [see also Hickok et al., 2011a]); that deactivating the entire left hemisphere in Wada procedures produces mutism yet results in only a 7.5% error rate in discriminating minimal phonemic pairs (hearing *bear* and pointing to a matching picture among phonemic distractors [Hickok et al., 2008; see Figure 5.7]); that the failure to develop speech production does not preclude normal receptive speech development (Lenneberg, 1962; Christen et al., 2000); and that infants as young as 1-month-old exhibit sophisticated speech perception ability including categorical perception well before they acquire the ability to speak (Eimas et al., 1971).

Given these and other considerations, it seems likely that understanding the real role of motor activations during passive speech perception will require a lot more theoretical and empirical work in the years to come (Box 5.4).

Box 5.4   Might Articulatory Activation During Speech Perception Facilitate Turn-Taking?

Reversing the title of a famous Elvis Presley song, Scott et al. (2009) suggest that "a little more conversation, a little less action" is needed in research on the function of motor activity during speech perception. In particular, they propose that the motor "resonance" that many brain mapping studies have observed when participants listen to speech could potentially reflect a neurocognitive adaptation for efficient dialogue, since it might allow listeners to use their own articulatory networks to track the rhythm and rate of talkers and thereby facilitate smooth and well-coordinated turn-taking (Figure 5B4.1). Although this intriguing hypothesis has not yet been directly tested, it is consistent with a number of relevant findings. For example, during conversational interactions, people involuntarily align not only their conceptual and syntactic structures (Garrod & Pickering, 2004; Pickering & Garrod, 2007), but also their breathing and pronunciation (McFarland, 2001; Pardo, 2006). In addition, turn-taking transitions are typically quite rapid, not just among English speakers but worldwide, as shown by a recent study which found that in ten languages from five continents, the average amount of time from the end of one speaker's turn to the beginning of the other's was about half a second (Stivers et al., 2009; see also de Ruiter et al., 2006). Based partly on such discoveries, Scott et al. (2009, pp. 300–301) argue that "the motor system is not only crucial to organizing the act of speaking, it is also essential in facilitating the conversational dance of turn-taking and coordinating the other factors, such as interactional synchrony and convergence, that make conversation possible." To motivate this idea even more, they refer to a model of turn-taking that relies heavily on the notion of entrained oscillations, claiming specifically that the listener locks onto the talker's speech rate at the syllabic level and uses it as a timing device to accurately synchronize the onset of their own speech production with the end of the talker's turn (Wilson & Wilson, 2005). Scott et al. (2009) suggest that the computation of these entrained oscillations may depend on the motor system (see also Giraud et al., 2007). More generally, they summarize their proposal by saying that the "sound-to-action pathway is highly refined in human language to allow us to talk smoothly in turn with one another" (Scott et al., 2009, p. 301). This provocative idea will no doubt be explored in detail in the near future.

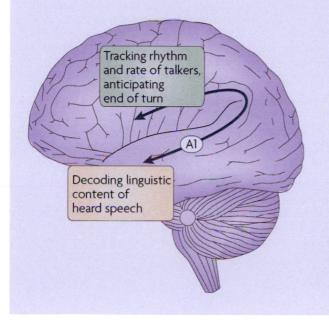

Figure 5B4.1 Candidate roles for auditory streams of processing during conversation. The arrows originating from the primary auditory cortex (A1) illustrate a functional division in how sounds are processed. As in Hickok and Poeppel's model, it is proposed that the conceptual content of heard speech is decoded primarily in the lateral anterior temporal lobe. In a novel twist, however, it is proposed that the dorsal pathway contributes to speech perception by tracking the rhythm and rate of talkers, thereby facilitating smooth turn-taking. (From Scott et al., 2009, p. 300.)

Summary

Within the framework of the Dual Stream Model, the dorsal pathway is the processing route that allows speech perception to be mapped onto speech production. Auditory representations in the dorsal STG and middle STS are first transmitted to area Spt, which resides in the depths of the posterior-most part of the left sylvian fissure. Area Spt then carries out a kind of sensorimotor transformation of this input before sending the signals forward to the articulatory network in the left posterior frontal lobe. This neural circuit, which includes both feedforward and feedback projections, contributes to several aspects of the human capacity for language: It underpins the acquisition of auditorily-anchored speech-motor patterns; it subserves auditory–verbal STM; and it facilitates the perceptual processing of speech, especially in situations when the listener must pay close attention to the phonological structure of utterances.

Summary and Key Points

- The early cortical stages of speech perception rely on a pathway that begins in Heschl's gyrus and projects into the STG and STS. This pathway is organized both *hierarchically* and *bilaterally*.

    - It is *hierarchically* organized because the initial stage of processing, in the dorsal STG, involves analyzing the elementary spectrotemporal properties of speech sounds, whereas the later stages, in the lateral STG and middle STS, involve detecting increasingly complex language-specific phonological patterns, such as phonemes and syllables.
    - It is *bilaterally* organized because both hemispheres are recruited, albeit in somewhat different ways since they appear to have partially different temporal windows for speech perception. According to the "asymmetric sampling in time" hypothesis, the pathway in the left hemisphere is dominant for processing rapid auditory variation in the 20–80 ms range, which is ideal for registering and classifying fine-grained distinctions at the phonemic level; conversely, the pathway in the right hemisphere is dominant for processing longer-duration auditory patterns in the 150–300 ms range, which is ideal for tracking speech input at the syllabic level.

- According to the Dual Stream Model, after the early cortical stages of speech perception have been completed, further processing proceeds along two separate pathways: One channel, which is called the ventral stream, leads into brain regions that are involved in comprehending utterances; the other channel, which is called the dorsal stream, leads into brain regions that are involved in converting the auditory representations of words into matching articulatory codes.
- Initial evidence for separate streams comes from neuropsychology, since brain-damaged patients exhibit double dissociations between, on the one hand, the ability to comprehend utterances and, on the other hand, the ability to repeat utterances or closely monitor their phonological makeup.
- The *ventral stream* can be thought of as the "what" pathway, since it allows the listener to understand the conceptual content of utterances. It has the following two functional–anatomical components.

    - The *lexical interface* is a relay station that maps the sound structures of words onto the corresponding semantic structures. It depends on the pMTG and pITG in both hemispheres, but with a leftward bias.
    - The *combinatorial network* is a system for integrating the semantic and grammatical aspects of phrases and sentences. It depends on the lateral ATL, predominantly in the left hemisphere.

- The *dorsal stream* can be thought of as the "how" pathway, since it allows the listener to link speech perception with speech production. It has the following two functional–anatomical components.

    - The *sensorimotor interface* is a relay station that maps the sound structures of words onto the corresponding motor representations. It depends on area Spt in the left hemisphere.
    - The *articulatory network* underlies the production of utterances. It depends on a variety of regions in the left posterior frontal lobe.
    - The dorsal stream supports not only the overt imitation and repetition of heard utterances, but also covert auditory–verbal STM and some aspects of speech perception, most notably those aspects that require selective attention to specific phonological structures.

Recommended Reading

- Hickok, G., & Poeppel, D. (2007). The cortical organization of speech processing. *Nature Reviews Neuroscience, 8,* 393–402. A comprehensive presentation of the Dual Stream Model for cognitive neuroscientists and professionals in related fields.
- Hickok, G. (2009). The functional neuroanatomy of language. *Physics of Life Reviews, 6,* 121–143. An overview of the Dual Stream Model for a general academic audience.
- Poeppel, D., Idsardi, W.J., & van Wassenhove, V. (2008). Speech perception at the interface of neurobiology and linguistics. *Philosophical Transactions of the Royal Society, B, Biological Sciences, 363,* 1071–1086. A technical discussion of how developing a thorough understanding of speech perception will require combining insights from neurobiology and linguistics.
- DeWitt, I., & Rauschecker, J.P. (2012). Phoneme and word recognition in the auditory ventral stream. *Proceedings of the National Academy of Sciences, 109,* E505-E514. A valuable meta-analysis of over 100 functional neuroimaging studies of speech perception, showing that phonemes and words are recognized along a hierarchical pathway in the ventral stream.

Speech Production

6

Introduction

The ability to produce spoken words comes so naturally to us that we often take it for granted, but it is surely one of the most remarkable and distinctive traits of the human species. In ordinary conversational settings, English speakers generate about two to three words per second, which is roughly equivalent to three to six syllables consisting of ten to twelve phonemes (Levelt, 1989). These words are retrieved from a mental lexicon that contains, for the average literate adult, between 50,000 and 100,000 entries, and articulating them requires the accurate coordination of up to 80 muscles (Bhatnagar, 2002). Yet errors are only rarely made, occurring just once or twice every 1,000 words (Garnham et al., 1981; Hotopf, 1983). The fact that speech production has such a low susceptibility to interference is undoubtedly due in part to its biological basis, but it may also reflect the prodigious amount of experience that most people have with talking. After all, we are loquacious animals, and there aren't many skills that we exercise as much as uttering words.

This chapter is about the neural substrates of speech production. It is organized in three main sections that track the time course of generating words, beginning with the formulation of communicative intentions in the realm of thoughts and feelings, and ending with the transmission of precise motor commands to the muscles constituting the respiratory, laryngeal, and supralaryngeal components of the vocal apparatus. The first section focuses on the processes that underlie the conceptually driven selection of words and the encoding of their phonological and phonetic forms. In order to provide a coherent theoretical context for this material, emphasis is placed on one of the most prominent frameworks, namely the Lemma Model, which was developed by Willem (Pim) J. M. Levelt and his collaborators at the Max Planck Institute for Psycholinguistics in Nijmegen, The Netherlands. The second section concentrates on the processes that underlie speech motor control and the learning of new articulatory patterns. As a strategy for making sense of this complex domain, we will approach it from the perspective of one of the most advanced theories, specifically the Directions into Velocities of Articulators (DIVA) Model, which was created by Frank Guenther and his colleagues at Boston University. Finally, the third section addresses some of the features of the peripheral motor system that are essential for speech production.

Before commencing, it is worth noting that the three-part organization of this chapter is by no means arbitrary, but instead reflects genuine divisions within the broad field of research on speech production. One scientific community concentrates almost exclusively on lexical representation and processing, another focuses primarily on articulation, and a third deals mainly with the peripheral motor system. For the most part, these three communities study different empirical phenomena, argue about different theoretical issues, publish their findings in different journals, and attend different conferences. Such academic specialization has definitely accelerated progress in each separate subfield, but it has also inhibited the development of large-scale, unified frameworks that bring all of the major insights together in a single model. The growing need for such integration will become clearer as we work our way through the chapter.

The Lemma Model of Lexical Selection and Form Encoding

Although his PhD thesis in 1965 was about the visual phenomenon known as binocular rivalry, W. J. M. Levelt soon switched to the field of psycholinguistics, which at that time was just starting to take off, driven by both the cognitive revolution in psychology and the Chomskyan revolution in linguistics. Levelt quickly became a major force to reckon with, and in 1980 he co-founded with Wolfgang Klein what remains to this day the world's foremost research center devoted solely to the study of language—the Max Planck Institute for Psycholinguistics (Box 6.1). Altogether, Levelt has published 18 books and over 230 articles on various issues involving the representation and processing of language in the mind/brain. He is most widely recognized, however, as the chief proponent of a theory of word production called the Lemma Model (Figure 6.1; Levelt, 1989, 1999a, 1999b, 2001; Levelt et al., 1999; Indefrey & Levelt, 2000, 2004).

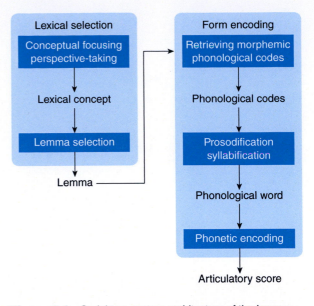

Figure 6.1   Serial two-system architecture of the Lemma Model: Two stages of lexical selection followed by three stages of form encoding. (From Levelt, 2001, p. 13465.) Copyright (2001) National Academy of Sciences, U.S.A.

Box 6.1   "Close to Scientific Paradise"

The Max Planck Institute for Psycholinguistics (www.mpi.nl; henceforth MPI) is situated on the campus of the Radboud University in the lovely old city of Nijmegen, which lies in the eastern part of the Netherlands near the German border. Since its inception in 1980, the guiding mission of the MPI has been to undertake basic research into the psychological, social, and biological foundations of language. Largely because it was the first institution to bring together linguists, psychologists, and neuroscientists to collaborate on numerous cutting-edge research projects, the MPI has played an instrumental role in shaping the agenda for the rest of the world. As Levelt remarked in an interview conducted in January, 2010, the month when the MPI officially turned 30 years old, "There is one important rule about scientific innovation: If one well-developed tradition meets another well-developed tradition, the sparks of innovation are likely to fly. Scientific innovation thrives by multidisciplinarity." He went on to say that "The ever available opportunity to start new things, to innovate your research, is the luxury of the MPI. There is no other institute like this, it's just fantastic."

Historically, the primary organizational units of the MPI have been research groups, each of which concentrates on a broadly characterized domain of inquiry, such as language production, language comprehension, language acquisition, language and cognition, or the neurobiology of language. Although the various groups pursue their projects in a semi-autonomous fashion, they regularly interact, and this vibrant atmosphere leads to intellectual synergies and cross-fertilizations that are often far richer than those that sometimes occur in other institutions or departments. To encourage the mixing of ideas even more, the MPI hosts visiting scholars, trains PhD students, and holds conferences and workshops on all sorts of language-related topics. An especially exciting development is that the MPI recently strengthened its connections with the Centre for Cognitive Neuroimaging in the Donders Institute for Brain, Cognition and Behaviour, which also resides in Nijmegen. This state of affairs will surely facilitate advances in the cognitive neuroscience of language in the years to come.

In sum, the MPI is, without a doubt, one the premier centers for research on how language is represented and processed in the mind/brain. Wolfgang Klein, who co-founded the institute with Levelt, captured the essence of the place when he said that it "comes close to scientific paradise."

This framework provides a kind of "blueprint of the speaker" (Levelt, 1999b). It posits a complex series of computational operations that begins with an intention of what to say and proceeds within milliseconds through semantic, morphosyntactic, phonological, and phonetic stages of processing. It can be thought of in much simpler terms, however, as assuming an architecture that consists of two main subsystems: one for "lexical selection," that is, identifying the most appropriate word in the mental lexicon; and another for "form encoding," that is, preparing the word's articulatory shape. Although the theory is partly inspired by, and can readily account for, data involving spontaneous speech errors (Box 6.2), it is based primarily on data involving reaction times, especially in carefully controlled laboratory settings where speakers' word production latencies can be precisely measured. The major components and principles of the theory have been instantiated in a computer model called WEAVER++ (for Word-form Encoding by Activation

and VERification; see Roelofs, 1992, 1997b, 2003, 2004a, 2004b, 2005, 2008; Levelt et al., 1999). Given that science thrives on debate, it is not surprising that the Lemma Model is quite controversial (for reviews of several competing approaches from a neuropsychological perspective, see Laine & Martin, 2006, and Rapp & Goldrick, 2006). Nevertheless, it is without question one of the most well-supported frameworks of its kind.

In what follows, Levelt's theory is presented in three subsections. The first one summarizes the architecture of the model. More specifically, it describes the types of mental representations and computational operations that are found at each processing stage. The second subsection discusses neurobiological evidence for the framework. Drawing upon a variety of studies employing diverse brain mapping techniques, it surveys some of the key findings about the cortical regions that may subserve the different processing stages. Finally, the third subsection briefly considers a few of the challenges that confront the theory.

Box 6.2   "Where Wings Take Dream"

During a campaign speech given in LaCrosse, Wisconsin, on October 18, 2000, former president George W. Bush said, with all the gravitas he could muster, "We want to promote families in America. Families is where our nation finds hope, where wings take dream." This slip of the tongue was by no means an isolated incident; on the contrary, Bush made so many speech errors during his years in office that several books of so-called Bushisms have been compiled and widely sold. Speech errors are not just a source of amusement, however; they are also a source of insight into the hidden workings of the language production system. For instance, in the case of *where wings take dream,* if we assume that the intended utterance was *where dreams take wing,* then the fact that the two noun stems were exchanged while the plural *-s* suffix remained in its proper position suggests that the placement of the noun stems and the placement of the suffix occurred during separate stages of grammatical encoding (for further details see Chapter 14).

The scientific study of speech errors began in the late 1800s, but such data were not used extensively to help constrain psycholinguistic theories of language production until the 1970s, when researchers like MacKay (1970), Fromkin (1971, 1973), Garrett (1975), and Shattuck-Hufnagel (1979) published influential investigations. Here are some of the types of phonological errors discussed by Fromkin (1973):

- Phoneme anticipation: *a reading list* spoken as *a leading list.*
- Anticipatory phoneme addition: *an early period* spoken as *a pearly period.*
- Phoneme shift: *black boxes* spoken as *back bloxes.*
- Phoneme perseveration: *beef noodle* spoken as *beef needle.*
- Rhyme exchange: *heap of junk* spoken as *hunk of jeep.*
- Consonant cluster exchange: *squeaky floor* spoken as *fleaky squoor.*

The fact that all of these kinds of slips involve either single phonemes or coherent groups of phonemes, such as consonant clusters and rhymes, constitutes evidence that the mind/brain treats these structures as discrete units—or, more precisely, as elements of the hierarchical organization of words—during the planning of speech. The errors therefore support theories that postulate such structures. For a review of linguistic, psycholinguistic, and computational perspectives on speech errors, see Dell (1995).

The Architecture of the Model

Conceptual Focusing and Perspective-Taking

The first step in word production is to map the idea one wishes to express onto a **lexical concept**—that is, a unit that integrates the multifarious semantic features that constitute the meaning of a particular word (Figure 6.1). This process essentially involves transforming mental states into linguistic representations, and for this reason it is sometimes called "thinking for speaking" (Slobin, 1996, 2003). Several factors influence the selection of lexical concepts, including cross-linguistic variation, point of view, and subjective construal, all of which are elaborated below.

In recent years, the branch of linguistics known as semantic typology has generated substantial evidence that the approximately 6,000 languages of the world differ tremendously in their inventories of lexical concepts (for a nontechnical introduction see Evans, 2010; for other reviews see Malt & Wolff, 2010, and Malt & Majid, 2013). Although this may come as a surprise, many languages don't have counterparts for what English speakers would consider to be fairly basic, commonplace words. For instance, some languages lack color terms like *blue* or *green,* others lack body part terms like *hand* or *leg,* and still others lack logical terms like *if* or *or* (Evans & Levinson, 2009). Equally if not more striking, however, is the discovery that many languages make semantic distinctions that carve the world of experience much more finely that

English speakers are accustomed to doing. Imagine, if you will, a Christmas scene in which a group of people are exchanging gifts. Greg is giving Sylvia a ring, Jane is giving Steve a pen, and Bill is giving Jessica a shirt. An English speaker wouldn't think twice about using the verb *give* to refer to all three events. But a speaker of Chipewyan—a language of Alberta, Canada—would use a different verb to describe each event: one for giving a ring (or any other round object); another for giving a pen (or any other stick-like object); and a third for giving a shirt (or any other flexible object). This is because there is no single, general verb of giving in Chepewyan; instead, there are at least ten different verbs that are sensitive to the animacy/shape/consistency features of the object being transferred, and speakers must attend to those features in order to select the most appropriate lexical concept to represent a specific act of giving (Rice, 1998). Similarly, although an English speaker wouldn't hesitate to use the same verb, *carry,* to describe carrying something in both arms, on one's head, on one's shoulders, in one's hand, or in one's mouth, a speaker of Tzeltal—a language of Chiapas, Mexico—would use a different verb for each situation (Table 6.1; Brown, 2001). And when it comes to communicating about such seemingly simple notions as standing, lying, and sitting, Tzeltal speakers routinely take into account a range of spatial contrasts that go far beyond what most English speakers typically notice (Table 6.2; Brown, 2006). What these examples of crosslinguistic diversity imply is that translating thoughts into words is not nearly as straightforward as it sometimes appears to be, since it requires molding the thoughts to fit the idiosyncratic meanings of the words that happen to be available in one's language. As Levelt (1989, p. 71) put it, "messages must be *tuned* to the target language."

> **Lexical concept**   A unit that integrates the multifarious semantic features that constitute the meaning of a particular word.

Table 6.1   The Many Ways of Carrying in Tzeltal

	Ways of carrying things	Verbs for carrying
Carry/hold (no generic term)	in both arms	*pet*
	weight on head/back	*kuch*
	weight across shoulders	*k'ech*
	in hand, supported from top	*lik*
	vertically extended from hand	*tuch'*
	in mouth	*lut*
	etc.	etc.

Source: Brown (2001, p. 529).

Table 6.2 The Many Ways of Standing, Lying Down, and Sitting in Tzeltal

Forms of 'standing', canonically upright	
tek'el	'standing', of human or animal standing on its hind legs; also of any long, thin inanimate object vertically erect supported underneath
tekel	'standing' of trees on their own roots
kotol	'standing' of 4-legged animals or 2-legged birds, or human on hands and knees; also chillies and harps*
chotol	'standing' of furniture with 4 or 3 legs, or stationary wheeled vehicle
luchul	'standing' on legs, perched up high
tz'apal	'standing' of stick-shaped object vertically erect with base buried in support
xik'il	'leaning vertically', i.e. standing but leaning slightly against vertical support, of either humans or inanimate objects
ta'al	'leaning at a strong angle', i.e. at approximately 45-degree angle against a vertical support, of either humans or long thin objects
t'uchul	'vertically standing' of inanimate object taller than wide, providing its own support on its base
telel	"vertically erect' of solid oblong object
waxal	'standing' of inanimate container or solid object, taller than wide
pachal	'standing' (right side up) of bowl-shaped container
Forms of 'lying down', body stretched out horizontally	
chawal	'lying face up'
echel	'lying on back, face up'
jawal	'lying face up, arms outspread'
pakal	'lying face down', of animate or inanimate object with 'face' downwards
metzel	'lying down on body-part side'
mochol	'lying down, curled up on side'
tz'eel	'lying on its side', of human, animal, or inanimate
lechel	'lying flat', of inanimate 2D flat thing
Forms of 'sitting' (at rest, top half of body in semi-vertical position)	
nakal	'sitting' on butt (bottom), of humans, animals
jukul	'squatting, resting on haunches' (of human or animal, or inanimate blob resting on base which is wider than its top)
jot'ol	'squatting' on haunches
xok'ol	'sitting with knees drawn up to body'
tinil	'crouching, with head hanging"
kujul	'kneeling'
wutzui	'sitting' of objects or people
chepel	'sitting' of things in a bag supported underneath

* Chillies 'stand' like animals despite not having any 'legs'; they are also 'eaten' with the verb for eating meat *(ti')*. This illustrates the cultural embeddedness of the shape and position assessments underlying the use of these spatial terms.

Source: Brown (2006, p. 249).

Another factor that affects the selection of lexical concepts during spoken word production is perspective-taking. Regardless of what language one speaks, there are always multiple ways in which any given situation could be described, and speakers must constantly make decisions about which ways are most suitable on particular occasions. For example, two of the many ways in which the scene in Figure 6.2 could be described are as follows (Levelt et al., 1999). One could say *I see a chair with a ball to the left of it,* or one could say *I see a chair with a ball to the right of it.* Thus, the converse terms *left* and *right* could both be used to refer to the same scene, but they reflect different perspectives on it. The term *left* portrays the scene in such a way that the speaker's own viewpoint is used as a frame of reference for locating the ball relative to the chair; this is sometimes called "deictic" perspective-taking. Alternatively, the term *right* portrays the scene in such a way that the inherent front/back/left/right axes of the chair are used as a frame of reference for locating the ball relative to it; this is sometimes called "intrinsic" perspective-taking.

More generally, it is important to recognize that a key characteristic of all human languages is that they allow speakers to choose words that express certain subjective conceptualizations of situations. Michael Tomasello (1999, pp. 8–9), a developmental psychologist and primatologist with a very pragmatic view of language, makes this point as follows:

> For example, in different communicative situations one and the same object may be construed as a dog, an animal, a pet, or a pest; one and the same event may be construed as running, moving, fleeing, or surviving; one and the same place may be construed as the coast, the shore, the beach, or the sand—all depending on the communicative goals of the speaker.

When speakers make such choices, they often take into account the knowledge and attitudes of the interlocutor (Clark, 1996). Perspective-taking therefore embraces social competence and, more specifically, the capacity to imagine what other people are thinking. This ability, which is highly evolved in humans, is sometimes called "mentalizing" or the exercise of a "theory of mind" (for a review see Epley & Waytz, 2009).

Turning now to more technical, theory-dependent matters, within the framework of the Lemma Model, lexical concepts are assumed to be represented in a non-decomposed format—that is, as unitary nodes

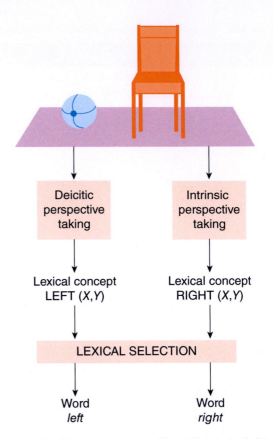

Figure 6.2   Illustration of perspective taking. Is the ball to the left of the chair or to the right of the chair? (From Levelt et al., 1999, p. 9.)

that lack complex internal structure (see the nodes in the upper stratum of Figure 6.3; see also Roelofs, 1997a). This is a controversial issue (Bierwisch & Schreuder, 1992; Caramazza, 1997), but the basic idea can be fleshed out by imagining an experiment in which a person is asked to name a series of pictured objects, one of which is a horse. The visual properties of the horse—including, most critically, its shape features—are initially processed along a perceptual hierarchy that is a much more intricate version of the one that was used in Chapter 1 to demonstrate how neurons can capture complex patterns of sensory information (see the "table detection network" in Figure 1.7). At each successive layer of this hierarchy, features are progressively integrated by means of "conjunctive" units, leading eventually to the visual recognition of the object as a horse, and after that to the activation of an even higher-order unit that, according to the Lemma Model, constitutes the language-specific lexical concept encoded by the word *horse.* Crucially, the very same node would also be engaged if the task were to name a horse not on the basis of its shape, but rather on the basis of its characteristic neighing sound; in that case, however, the node's activation would be triggered by a series of hierarchical processing operations along a perceptual pathway in the auditory modality. What this example demonstrates is that the essential meaning of the word *horse,* which is captured by the high-level lexical concept node, can be reached through different channels of perceptual input, thereby allowing one to name a horse regardless of whether one sees it or hears it. The key point is this: in the Lemma Model, a lexical concept does not explicitly represent all of the diverse bits of information (visual, auditory, etc.) that make up the concrete content of a word's meaning, but it does have rich connections with all of those far-flung features, connections that serve to bind the features together as a multifaceted semantic representation. We will return to these ideas in Chapters 10–12.

A final point is that in most circumstances involving word production, several lexical concepts are co-activated in parallel (i.e., simultaneously), with one—the target—ultimately being activated to a higher degree than the others (Levelt et al., 1991). For example, in the horse-naming situation described above, if we assume that the person does in fact produce the word *horse,* the lexical concept encoded by that word is activated to the highest degree. But several related lexical concepts, such as those encoded by the words *animal* and *goat,* are also likely to be activated, albeit to lesser degrees, as illustrated by the nodes in the upper left part of Figure 6.3.

Lemma Selection

Once a lexical concept has been selected, it activates the corresponding **lemma** at the next level of representation in the framework (see Figure 6.1 as well as the nodes in the lower stratum of Figure 6.3). As noted in Chapter 5, a lemma is an abstract word node—analogous to an arbitrary number (e.g., lexical entry #2,478)—that not only intervenes between semantics and phonology, but also points to various morphosyntactic features like grammatical category (noun, verb, etc.), nominal gender/class (masculine, feminine, etc.), verbal transitivity (intransitive, transitive, etc.), and so on (see Chapter 14 for further details). For instance, although English nouns like *horse* and *goat* are not specified for gender, comparable nouns in many other languages do have such specifications (Corbett, 1991), and these features must be retrieved together with the lemmas (Figure 6.3). In fact, some gender-marking languages require the speaker to indicate the gender of a noun on the preceding adjective, so the faster the gender can be accessed, the faster the preceding adjective can be formulated. Thus, if one were to say *I saw a big horse* in German, it would be *Ich sah ein grosses Pferd,* with the neuter gender of *Pferd* ("horse") indicated by the *-es* suffix on the preceding adjective; in contrast, if one were to say *I saw a big goat* in German, it would be *Ich sah ein grosse Ziege,* with the feminine gender of *Ziege* ("goat") indicated by the *-e* suffix on the preceding adjective.

We observed above that during the conceptual preparation phase of word production, the target lexical concept is activated the most, but related lexical concepts are also activated to lesser degrees. The theory assumes that these activation patterns propagate to the lemma level, so that the lemma that matches the target lexical concept is activated the most, but the lemmas that match the various related lexical concepts are also activated to lesser degrees (Figure 6.3). The correct lemma is selected according to what are essentially probabilistic principles (see Roelofs, 1992, and Levelt et al., 1999, for the mathematical equations implemented in the WEAVER++ model). The central claim is that during any minimal time unit of processing, the likelihood of a given lemma being selected is its degree of activation divided by the total activation of all the lemmas that happen to be engaged. This approach leads to interesting predictions about the

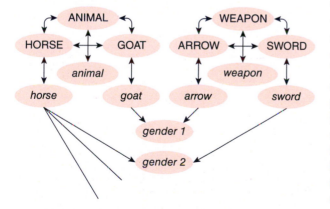

Figure 6.3 Fragment of the WEAVER++ lexical selection network. The upper stratum shows lexical concept nodes. The lower stratum shows lemma and gender nodes. (From Levelt, 2001, p. 13465.) Copyright (2001) National Academy of Sciences, U.S.A.

Lemma An abstract word node that not only intervenes between semantics and phonology, but also points to morphosyntactic features like grammatical category.

latency of lemma selection, and these predictions have received some empirical support from reaction-time experiments.

Interlude: Crossing the Rift

At this juncture, it is worthwhile to step back from the details for a moment and take notice of where we are in the context of the entire framework. As shown in Figure 6.1, the first two stages of spoken word production—namely, conceptual preparation and lemma selection—collectively constitute an integrated subsystem called "lexical selection." The next three stages—namely, retrieving morphemic phonological codes, prosodification/syllabification, and phonetic encoding—collectively constitute another integrated subsystem called "form encoding." Levelt (2001, p. 13465) points out that these two subsystems

> perform radically different functions. The function of lexical selection is to rapidly focus on a single lexical item, given the speaker's intentional state. This selection is subject to competition. The function of form encoding is to generate an articulatory score for just the selected item in its context. Competition is hardly an issue here.

Levelt et al. (1999) refer to the gap between these two processing subsystems as a "major rift" (p. 2) and state that crossing it "is not an entirely trivial matter" (p. 4). After all, everyone occasionally experiences "tip-of-the-tongue" states in which the sound structure of a desired word is partly or wholly unavailable, even though its meaning and morphosyntactic features are easily accessed (e.g., Vigliocco et al., 1997). And as noted in Chapters 3 and 4 and discussed in further detail below, the rift between the two subsystems is magnified much more for brain-damaged patients with anomia, since they suffer from chronic blocking when attempting to retrieve the phonological forms of words. With these considerations in mind, we turn now to the organization of the form encoding subsystem, as characterized by the Lemma Model.

Retrieving Morphemic Phonological Codes

The first stage of form encoding involves retrieving the morphemic phonological code of the target word (Figure 6.1). This stage consists of two subprocesses: accessing the morphemic representation, and "spelling out" its segmental phonemic content. So, to continue with the example of naming a picture of

a horse, selection of the target lemma *horse* would trigger activation of the corresponding morpheme <horse> together with its linear sound structure as stored in the mental lexicon. Suppose, however, that the picture to be named showed not just one horse but two. In that case, the target lemma would again be *horse,* but marked for plural number. The specification of plural number would then trigger activation of the corresponding suffix morpheme <ɪz> together with its phonemic makeup (Figure 6.4). (The morphemic phonological code of the English plural suffix is actually more abstract than this, but the technicalities are not relevant here; for a clear discussion see Pinker, 1999.)

Three points are important to note about this stage of the model. First, a fundamental assumption is that only the selected lemma spreads activation across the "rift" between the lexical selection subsystem and the form encoding subsystem; other lemmas that happen to be engaged to some extent during the process of lemma selection do not activate the corresponding morphemic phonological codes. This view is quite controversial (see *Language and Cognitive Processes,* 2013, Volume 28, Issue 5, which is devoted to the topic of lexical competition in language production). It has

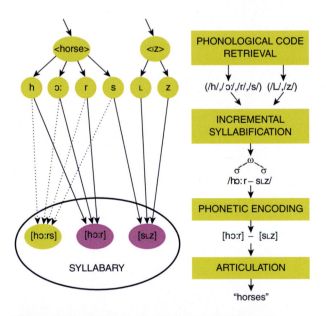

Figure 6.4 Form encoding of the word *horses.* (Left) Fragment of the WEAVER++ form encoding network. The upper stratum shows nodes representing morphemic phonological codes and their phonemic "spellouts." The lower stratum shows nodes representing syllabic articulatory scores. (Right) Corresponding form-processing stages. Symbols: ω = phonological word; σ = syllable. (From Levelt, 2001, p. 13465.) Copyright (2001) National Academy of Sciences, U.S.A.

received some support, however, from experimental psycholinguistic studies (Levelt et al., 1991), and it is also consistent with speech error data (Levelt, 1999a). For instance, slips of the tongue very rarely involve phonological blends of semantically related words like *horse* and *goat*. The main exception appears to be synonym blends. Such errors—e.g., *clear* as a mixture of *close* and *near*—are not uncommon and can be accommodated by the theory.

Second, the retrieval of morphemic phonological codes is strongly influenced by word frequency. As originally discovered by Oldfield and Wingfield (1965), naming an object with a high-frequency word (e.g., *dog*) takes less time than naming an object with a low-frequency word (e.g., *broom*). This phenomenon is called the **word-frequency effect**. Wingfield (1968) subsequently showed that it does not occur at the level of lexical concepts, since it does not emerge when the task is to judge whether a given noun correctly describes a pictured object. And Jescheniak and Levelt (1994) later demonstrated that it does not occur at the level of lemmas either, but rather at the level of accessing phonological forms. To do this, they compared subjects' response times for retrieving **homophones**—i.e., words that have different lexical concepts and different lemmas but share the same phonological representation, like the high-frequency adjective *more* and the low-frequency noun *moor* (Figure 6.5). If the word-frequency effect resided at the lemma level, the response time for producing *more* would be significantly faster than the response time for producing *moor*. However, if the effect resided at the level of phonological form, the response times for producing the two words would be the same because, somewhat paradoxically, low-frequency *moor* would inherit the fast accessing speed of its high-frequency twin *more* by virtue of sharing the same phonological form. Remarkably enough, Jescheniak and Levelt (1994) obtained the latter results.

The actual experiment was designed as follows. Dutch subjects with good mastery of English performed a translation task in which they orally produced, as quickly as possible, the Dutch equivalents of printed English words. The target words were of three types:

Figure 6.5   Illustration of the homonyms *more* and *moor*. (From Levelt, 1999b, p. 102.)

- low-frequency Dutch homophones (analogous to *moor*);
- low-frequency Dutch non-homophones that were matched with the low-frequency homophones (analogous to *marsh*, which has the same frequency as *moor*);
- high-frequency Dutch non-homophones that were matched with the high-frequency twins of the low-frequency homophones (analogous to *much*, which has the same frequency as *more*).

The results are shown in Figure 6.6, which presents the average response times for the three conditions, corrected by subtracting out the independently determined latencies for visually recognizing the printed English words. It is clear that the low-frequency homophones (analogous to *moor*) were produced just as quickly as the high-frequency controls (analogous to *much*) and substantially faster than the low-frequency controls (analogous to *marsh*). This outcome suggests that, as mentioned above, low-frequency homophones inherit the fast accessing speed of their high-frequency partners, and this in turn supports the hypothesis that the word-frequency effect occurs during phonological form retrieval. As Levelt (1999b, p. 102) put it, "the word-frequency effect arises precisely in the speaker's effort to 'cross the rift' from the semantic/syntactic subsystem to the phonological/articulatory subsystem." It is noteworthy, however, that at least part of the effect may actually be due to age-of-acquisition, since several studies have shown that it is easier to access words that were acquired early in life (e.g., Carroll & White, 1973; Morrison et al., 1992; Snodgrass & Yuditsky, 1996; see also Kuperman et al., 2012).

The third and final point about morphemic phonological codes is that they are retrieved incrementally, beginning with the initial segment and proceeding to the last one. Evidence for this assumption comes from several experiments (Meyer, 1990, 1991; Wheeldon & Levelt, 1995; Van Turennout et al., 1997; Wheeldon & Morgan, 2002; Schiller et al., 2006). For instance, the participants in one study were faster in naming a banana when they knew beforehand that the target word began with *ba*, but not when they knew beforehand

---

Word-frequency effect   The phonological forms of high-frequency words are retrieved faster than those of low-frequency words.

Homophones   Different words that sound the same, like *more* and *moor*.

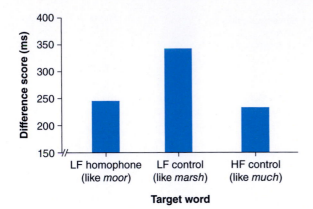

Figure 6.6 The homophone effect. Based on a task requiring the rapid translation of printed English words into their spoken Dutch equivalents, response times (corrected for visual word recognition) are shown for low-frequency Dutch homophones (analogous to *moor* as opposed to *more*) as well as for Dutch non-homophone controls matched to either the low-frequency homophone (analogous to *marsh,* which has the same frequency as *moor*) or to the high-frequency twin (analogous to *much,* which has the same frequency as *more*). The data indicate that the low-frequency homophone inherits the fast accessing speed of its high-frequency twin. (From Levelt et al., 1999, p. 18.)

that it ended with *na* (Meyer, 1990, 1991). Similarly, when the participants in another study were asked to monitor for pre-specified segments while generating the Dutch translations of English words, their detection times were faster for earlier than later segments (Wheeldon & Levelt, 1995). To take one interesting case, when translating the English word *hitchhiker* into the Dutch word *lifter*—which has the structure $C_1VC_2C_3VC_4$, where C stands for "consonant" and V stands for "vowel"—participants were faster when monitoring for C_1 than C_2, faster when monitoring for C_2 than C_3, and faster when monitoring for C_3 than C_4; moreover, all of these differences in detection time were statistically significant except the last one. Such findings strongly support the view that during the process of phonological encoding, segments are retrieved in a rightward incremental manner.

Prosodification and Syllabification

Morphemic phonological codes serve as input to the next stage of processing—prosodification, which in English consists largely of syllabification (although metrical structure is also important, as discussed in Chapter 7). Basically, the ordered phonemic segments of the target word are bundled into syllables that conform to universal as well as language-specific

rules, yielding as output a "phonological word" (Figure 6.1). An essential aspect of this process is that it too takes place in an incremental manner that is context-sensitive (Meyer, 1990, 1991; Cholin et al., 2004). This is illustrated by the fact that there are many situations in which syllable boundaries diverge from morpheme boundaries. For instance, the word *horses* is bimorphemic and bisyllabic, yet, as shown in Figure 6.4, the final segment of the first morpheme—specifically, /s/—is not treated as the final segment of the first syllable, but is instead treated as the initial segment of the second syllable. Syllabification can also transcend word boundaries, as exemplified by the utterance *He'll escort us,* in which the last two words are usually syllabified in casual speech as *e-scor-tus* (Levelt et al., 1999). The key point is that an item's syllabification is not necessarily stored in long-term memory in the mental lexicon, but is computed "on the fly" during real-time language production.

Phonetic Encoding and Articulation

Fully syllabified phonological representations are projected to the level of phonetic encoding, which is the last stage of spoken word production that is explicitly incorporated into the Lemma Model (Figure 6.1). An important assumption about this stage of processing is that it draws heavily upon a "mental syllabary," which is an inventory of highly practiced syllabic gestures (e.g., Levelt, 1992; Levelt & Wheeldon, 1994; Levelt et al., 1999; Cholin et al., 2006). Levelt (2001, p. 13468) describes this component of the model as follows:

> Assume you talk, from your 2nd to your 21st birthday, on average 30 minutes a day. If you speak at an average rate of 4 syllables per second, you will have produced 5.10^7 syllable tokens at reaching adulthood. If your language counts 500 different syllables, each of them will, on average, have been produced some 10^5 times. This is a classic case of "overlearning." Articulatory syllables are among the most exercised motor patterns we produce.

Now, although some languages, such as Mandarin Chinese, allow even less than 500 different syllables, others, like English and Dutch, allow well over 10,000. Statistical analyses indicate, however, that speakers of the latter languages do most of their talking (about 80 percent) with no more than 500 different high-frequency syllables, and it is likely that those syllables are stored in a precompiled, internally coherent form so that they don't need to be recomputed time and again.

In the case of generating the word *horses*, the phonetic encoding mechanism takes as input a phonological representation that specifies the syllable boundaries of the item, and it matches each unit in that representation with the corresponding node in the syllabary (Figure 6.4). In addition, it determines how the string of syllabic routines can be smoothly concatenated. Ultimately, the activated syllable nodes and the instructions for combining them constitute what is called an "articulatory score." This is then sent to the motor system that controls the speaker's vocal apparatus, so that the whole action program can be executed.

Self-Monitoring

Before going on to see what has been learned so far about the neural correlates of the various components of the Lemma Model, we need to address one other aspect of the theory—"self-monitoring," which underlies our capacity to detect and correct our own speech errors. Although dysfluencies, inappropriate word choices, and other mistakes occur relatively rarely, we all make them every so often, and when we do, we are sometimes able to pause and fix the problem. The Lemma Model maintains that self-monitoring is mediated by two feedback loops, one "external" and the other "internal" (Wheeldon & Levelt, 1995; Levelt et al., 1999; Roelofs, 2003, 2004a, 2004b, 2005; Schiller et al., 2006; for a broader review see Postma, 2000; see also the discussion of feedback loops in the summary of the DIVA Model below). To get a sense of how these loops operate, consider the following examples of speech errors, both of which involve the word *yellow* (Levelt et al., 1999, p. 33):

(1) *entrance to yellow . . . er, to gray*
(2) *we can go straight to the ye- . . . to the orange dot*

In the first example, the speaker produced the whole word *yellow* before pausing to repair the error. It is therefore possible, even likely, that the speaker noticed the mistake by hearing it. This kind of error detection is believed to depend on an "external" feedback loop that monitors the auditory signals of self-produced speech. Such an account is less plausible for the second example, however, because the speaker produced only the first syllable of *yellow* before pausing to repair the error. In this case, it is reasonable to suppose that the problem was identified at, or perhaps just before, the onset of articulation. This type of error detection is thought to rely on an "internal" feedback loop that monitors the covert process of generating phonological words.

Neurobiological Evidence for the Model

A Meta-Analysis of 82 Brain Mapping Experiments Involving Word Production

Despite the sheer complexity of the Lemma Model's functional architecture, with its two distinct stages of lexical selection and its three distinct stages of form encoding, an impressive amount of headway has been made in attempting to graft all of the components onto the brain. In one of the most ambitious efforts, Indefrey and Levelt (2004) conducted a meta-analysis of localization data from 82 word production studies, the vast majority of which used either PET or fMRI. They also explored the time course of the activation of different cortical regions by drawing upon chronometric data from several studies that used magnetoencephalography (MEG). (More recently, Indefrey [2011] reported a follow-up meta-analysis of studies published since 2004. The results largely confirmed those of the initial meta-analysis.)

Indefrey and Levelt's (2004) meta-analysis included brain mapping experiments that employed any of the following four types of spoken word production tasks:

- picture naming (e.g., saying *horse* in response to a picture of a horse);
- associative word generation (e.g., producing words belonging to a category like "animals," "tools," "jobs," etc.);
- word reading (i.e., accessing the phonological forms of printed words like *horse*);
- pseudoword reading (i.e., computing the phonological forms of pronounceable pseudowords like *blicket*).

The investigators point out that these tasks differ with respect to the "lead-in" processes that must be executed before the core processes of the word production system can be engaged (Table 6.3). Specifically, picture naming requires visual object recognition; associative word generation requires recognition of the visually or auditorily presented stimulus as well as strategic memory search; word reading requires visual word recognition; and pseudoword reading requires grapheme recognition and conversion of graphemic to phonological representations (see Chapter 8). Indefrey and Levelt (2004) also argue that many of the tasks differ with respect to which of the core stages of word production they recruit (Table 6.3). Both picture naming and associative word generation engage all of the stages. However, word reading does not necessarily engage either conceptual preparation or lemma selection in a semantically driven way, so the first stage that is definitely engaged is phonological code retrieval. Moreover, because pseudowords cannot be matched with stored entries in the mental lexicon, the first stage that is triggered during pseudoword reading is syllabification. Finally, the last stage of processing, namely phonetic encoding, is assumed to be eliminated whenever word production tasks are performed covertly (i.e., silently). As described below, when Indefrey and Levelt (2004) conducted their meta-analysis, they exploited these factors in order to isolate the neural correlates of the various stages of word production postulated by the Lemma Model.

Because the two tasks of picture naming and associative word generation have different lead-in processes but share all of the core processes of word production, one of Indefrey and Levelt's (2004) first aims was to identify and plot not only the brain regions that are uniquely activated by each of these tasks, but also, and more importantly, the brain regions that are jointly activated by both of them. The results are depicted in Figure 6.7. Overall, they found that a total of 15 areas are reliably activated in common by both tasks. Eleven of these areas are in the left hemisphere (the last two are not shown in the figure):

- mid superior temporal gyrus/sulcus (mid STG/STS);
- posterior superior temporal gyrus/sulcus (posterior STG/STS, i.e., Wernicke's area);
- mid middle temporal gyrus (mid MTG);
- posterior middle temporal gyrus (posterior MTG);
- posterior fusiform gyrus;
- posterior inferior frontal gyrus (posterior IFG, i.e., Broca's area);
- ventral precentral gyrus (premotor and primary motor cortex);
- supplementary motor area (SMA);
- thalamus;
- anterior insula;
- medial cerebellum.

The other four areas are in the right hemisphere (the last two are not shown in the figure):

- mid superior temporal gyrus/sulcus (mid STG/STS);
- supplementary motor area (SMA);
- lateral cerebellum;
- medial cerebellum.

Table 6.3 Core Processing Stages in Word Production Together with Specifications Regarding the Involvement of Core and Lead-in Processes in Four Word Production Tasks

Tasks	(Silent) Picture Naming	(Silent) Associative Word Generation	(Silent) Word Reading	(Silent) Pseudoword Reading
Lead-in processes	Visual object recognition	Visual or auditory word recognition, strategic memory search	Visual word recognition	Visual grapheme recognition, conversion of graphemic to phonological code
Core processes: Conceptual focusing & perspective-taking	+	+	?	–
Lemma selection	+	+	?	–
Phonological code retrieval	+	+	+	–
Syllabification	+	+	+	+
Phonetic encoding	(+)	(+)	(+)	(+)

Adapted from Indefrey & Levelt, (2000, p. 849).

+ = involvement of the component process in the task. (+) = process is assumed to be engaged during overt but not covert (i.e., silent) word production.

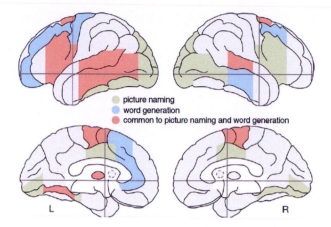

Figure 6.7 Reliable regions for picture naming and associative word generation. Regions shared by both tasks are assumed to be involved in the core processes of language production (see Table 6.3). Additional regions shared by both tasks but not depicted in the figure were the right medial and lateral cerebellum, the left medial cerebellum, and the left anterior insula. (From Indefrey & Levelt, 2004, p. 122.)

Indefrey and Levelt (2004) propose that, taken together, these 15 areas can be regarded as constituting the central word production network of the human brain. As they observe, many of the regions have also been implicated in speech perception. These include, most notably, the mid-to-posterior STG/STS in both hemispheres, as well as the left mid-to-posterior MTG, the left posterior IFG, and the left ventral precentral gyrus. This high degree of neuroanatomical overlap for the expressive and receptive modalities of speech processing suggests that they share at least some levels of representation. A few of the commonalities were addressed in the review of Hickok and Poeppel's (2000, 2004, 2007) Dual Stream Model of speech perception in Chapter 5. We will briefly touch on these commonalties again in the following discussion, and we will refer to others as well, but we will refrain from exploring in detail the precise nature of the shared resources for producing and perceiving speech, since this topic is fraught with complications and would take us too far afield.

Conceptual Focusing and Perspective-Taking

The next step in Indefrey and Levelt's (2004) meta-analysis was to investigate how the different brain areas that collectively constitute the word production network shown in Figure 6.7 relate to the different processing stages that are posited by the Lemma Model. Regarding the first stage—i.e., the stage that involves selecting a lexical concept that adequately represents the thought to be expressed—it is unfortunate that,

as yet, very few studies have tried to discern its neural correlates (for some attempts based on semantic interference paradigms, see Abel et al., 2009; de Zubicaray & McMahon, 2009; Hocking et al., 2010; Aristei et al., 2011; for a different approach see Menenti et al., 2012). In addition, although picture naming and associative word generation are the only two tasks among the four shown in Table 6.3 that clearly recruit the core process of conceptual preparation, they enlist this process in rather dissimilar ways, leading to uncertainty as to whether the conjunction analysis depicted in Figure 6.7 adequately captures the process. For these reasons, not much can be said with confidence about the neural correlates of conceptual preparation. Nevertheless, a few relevant findings have been made in recent years, and they warrant some consideration here.

One development has to do with the neural substrates of lexical concepts per se. There are good reasons to suppose that the multifarious semantic features that constitute the actual content of word meanings are widely distributed across the cerebral cortex (see Chapters 10–12). However, if one adopts the assumption of the Lemma Model that lexical concepts are unitary nodes that bind together the far-flung features of particular word meanings, then it is noteworthy that, according to a growing body of literature, such nodes may reside in the anterior temporal lobes (ATLs) of both hemispheres, but with a mild leftward bias (for reviews see Patterson et al., 2007; Lambon Ralph & Patterson, 2008; Visser et al., 2009). We addressed this topic briefly in the review of semantic dementia in Chapter 4, and we will explore it in greater depth in Chapters 10–12. For present purposes, what matters is simply that data from diverse approaches—neuropsychology, functional neuroimaging, and TMS—converge on the notion that when a speaker selects lexical concepts for various kinds of entities and events, those representations may be housed in the ATLs. This idea was recently incorporated into the Lemma Model by Roelofs (2008). If it is true, though, why didn't the ATLs show up in Figure 6.7 as being reliably activated during picture naming and associative word generation tasks? The answer is not entirely clear, but one possibility is that, as observed by Patterson et al. (2007), the ATLs are "shy" to fMRI because their proximity to the air-filled sinuses substantially diminishes the signal-to-noise ratio of BOLD effects (for further information see Chapter 10).

Another important advance involves the competitive nature of the process of selecting lexical concepts. As mentioned earlier, "thinking for speaking" often requires that a single lexical concept be chosen from a pool of several co-activated representations. For example, one may need to decide, either consciously or unconsciously, whether to refer to an object in a picture as an *animal*, a *horse*, a *stallion*, a *mare*, or something even more specific, such as an *Appaloosa*. An increasing number of studies suggest that in such situations the left posterior IFG (i.e., Broca's area) plays a critical role in resolving conflicts among alternative items (for reviews see Thompson-Schill, 2005, and Badre & Wagner, 2007; see also Thompson-Schill et al., 1998; Fletcher et al., 2000; Badre et al., 2005; Moss et al., 2005; Grindrod et al., 2008; Snyder et al., 2011). Schnur et al. (2009) provided especially compelling evidence for this proposal in a study that combined fMRI and the lesion method. The main task was picture naming, and lexical competition was systematically manipulated as follows. In the "blocked" condition successive trials depicted semantically related objects (truck, car, bike, etc.), thereby leading to a high degree of competition and interference. In contrast, in the "mixed" condition successive trials depicted semantically unrelated objects (truck, foot, dog, etc.), thereby leading to a low degree of competition and interference. Using fMRI, the researchers found that activity in the left IFG was significantly greater when subjects named objects in the blocked condition than when they named the same objects in the mixed condition. Moreover, the researchers ensured that this effect was due to semantic competition rather than phonological competition. Then, in a neuropsychological experiment with 12 patients, they showed that the patients who evinced the greatest "blocking growth"—i.e., the greatest increase in interference in

the blocked condition—also had the largest amount of damage in the left IFG (Figure 6.8). This study strongly supports the hypothesis that the left IFG is essential for resolving conflicts among competing lexical items during picture naming. In addition, the results are consistent with, and help to explain, the types of word production deficits that are frequently manifested by patients with Broca's aphasia, transcortical motor aphasia, and progressive nonfluent aphasia (see Chapters 3 and 4). A limitation of the study, however, is that, from the perspective of the Lemma Model, it is not clear whether the left IFG supports conflict resolution for lexical concepts, lemmas, or both kinds of linguistic structures.

A third line of research that deserves to be mentioned in this context involves the neural underpinnings of perspective-taking. When perspective-taking is restricted to the spatial domain, as illustrated by the distinction between *left* and *right* in Figure 6.2, it depends primarily on mechanisms for language-specific spatial representation in the left inferior parietal lobule (for reviews see Kemmerer, 2006b, 2010a). But when perspective-taking is treated more broadly as covering the sorts of social factors that influence speakers' word choices, it most likely depends on a widely distributed network of frontal, temporal, and parietal regions that collectively underlie "mentalizing" or the "theory of mind" (for reviews see Saxe, 2006; Frith & Frith, 2006, 2010; Mitchell, 2009). Research on this complex network has been developing quite rapidly, but it

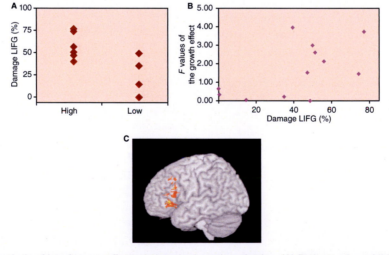

Figure 6.8   Lesion analysis of interference effects on impaired word production. (A) Patients who exhibited a large growth of interference across cycles of blocked naming (*high*) had a greater extent of damage to the left IFG than did patients with a small growth effect (*low*). (B) The correlation ($r = 0.56$) between the magnitude of the growth effect (individual *F* values describing the linear increase in semantic blocking across cycles) and the extent of damage to the left IFG. (C) Results of a voxel-based comparison of the lesion locations of patients with a large or small growth effect. The subtraction overlay analysis reveals the number of lesioned voxels in one group that overlap in a location not shared by the other group, across the whole brain. Voxels colored yellow were damaged in 7 of 7 patients with a large growth effect and 0 of the 5 patients with a small growth effect; voxels colored orange were damaged in at least 6 of the patients with a large growth effect and in no more than 1 of the patients with a small growth effect. (From Schnur et al., 2009, p. 325.) Copyright (2008) National Academy of Sciences, U.S.A.

has been carried out almost entirely within the burgeoning field of social neuroscience and has not yet interfaced in a direct or systematic way with parallel research on conceptual preparation during word production. The bridge between the neural substrates of social cognition and the neural substrates of "thinking for speaking" is therefore a topic that is ripe for investigation.

Lemma Selection

According to Indefrey and Levelt (2000, 2004), both picture naming and associative word generation involve semantically driven lemma selection, but word reading does not necessarily engage this process, and pseudo-word reading most certainly doesn't engage it (Table 6.3). Thus, by contrasting studies that employed either of the first two tasks with studies that employed either of the second two tasks, it should be possible to identify, at least in an approximate way, the neural correlates of lemma selection. When Indefrey and Levelt (2004) performed this analysis, they found that just one region was reliably activated—specifically, the left mid MTG. Moreover, when they took into account the available chronometric data, they discovered that in picture-naming tasks this region is activated during a time window between 150 and 225 ms post-stimulus onset (Figure 6.9).

It is notable that the left mid MTG lies just anterior to the left posterior MTG, which is the area that Hickok and

Poeppel (2000, 2004, 2007) proposed as the neural basis of the "lexical interface" component of the ventral pathway in their Dual Stream Model of speech perception. As indicated in Chapter 5, the main function of that processing component is to map the phonological structures of words onto the corresponding semantic structures during comprehension. And as indicated earlier in this chapter, one of the key purposes of lemmas in Levelt et al.'s (1999) framework is to enable the opposite kind of mapping, from the semantic structures of words to the corresponding phonological structures during production. Picking up on these parallels, Indefrey and Levelt (2004) explicitly adopt the view that the lemma level of representation is likely to be shared by the cortical networks for word production and word perception, and they cite psycholinguistic as well as neurolinguistic evidence to support this hypothesis. It is important to realize, however, that some data cannot easily be accommodated by the assumption that the very same lemmas are utilized bidirectionally in both the output and input processing of speech. For example, in Chapter 5 we reviewed a study by Boatman et al. (2000) which demonstrated that direct cortical stimulation at some sites in the left mid/posterior MTG does not affect picture naming (suggesting preservation of the output mapping from semantics to phonology) but nevertheless impairs word comprehension (suggesting disruption of the input mapping from phonology to semantics) (see Figure 5.12 and the accompanying text). Thus, much work remains to be done to determine exactly how the left mid/posterior MTG contributes to lexical processing during both the production and the perception of speech.

Independently of Indefrey and Levelt's (2004) meta-analysis of functional neuroimaging studies, a great deal of neuropsychological research has explored the brain structures that are involved in accessing lexical items during word production. For instance, studies with large groups of either acute (DeLeon et al., 2007) or chronic (Baldo et al., 2013) stroke patients have found that defective lexical retrieval is most frequently linked with dysfunction in the left mid-to-posterior MTG. Other lesion studies have also shown that disturbances affecting lexical retrieval are often associated with damage to regions of the left temporal lobe that are close to, but mostly outside, the mid MTG.

Along these lines, an influential set of studies was conducted by Hanna Damasio, Daniel Tranel, and their colleagues at the University of Iowa. By administering picture-naming tasks to large cohorts of patients, they discovered that accessing nouns for different categories of concrete entities may hinge on lemma-like units that mediate between semantics and phonology and that are distributed in an orderly manner extending from the temporal pole (TP) along the inferotemporal (IT)

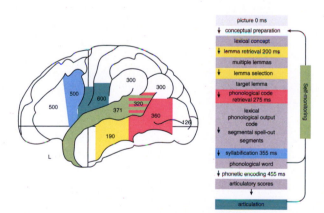

Figure 6.9   A meta-analysis of 82 neuroimaging studies of spoken word production. (Left) Schematic representation of localization and chronometric results. The numbers indicate the time windows (in milliseconds) during which the regions are activated in picture naming. Further regions involved in phonetic encoding and articulation include the right ventral motor and somatosensory cortices, the left and right SMA, the left and right cerebellum, the left and right thalamus, and the right midbrain. A further region involved in self-monitoring is the right mid superior temporal gyrus. (Right column) Time course of picture naming as estimated from chronometric data. (From Indefrey & Levelt, 2004, p. 126.)

cortices (Damasio et al., 1996, 2004; Tranel, 2006, 2009). More specifically, their results support the following generalizations, among others (Figure 6.10):

- Impaired access to proper nouns for unique persons (e.g., *Barack Obama*) is typically associated with left TP lesions (for further information see Box 6.3, and for qualifications see Gesierich et al., 2012).
- Impaired access to common nouns for animals (e.g., *horse*) is typically associated with damage to the anterior sector of the left IT region.
- Impaired access to common nouns for tools (e.g., *hammer*) is typically associated with damage to the posterior sector of the left IT region, an area called IT+.

Crucially, the patients who exhibited these kinds of lexical retrieval deficits appeared to have intact object recognition and conceptual knowledge, since they could provide accurate verbal descriptions of the entities they couldn't name. For example, one patient who was unable to name a skunk was nevertheless able to describe it as follows: "Oh, that animal makes a terrible smell if you get too close to it; it's black and white and gets squashed on the road by cars sometimes." (See, however, footnote 29 of Caramazza & Shelton, 1998, for a critique.) Furthermore, functional neuroimaging data from related PET studies revealed that the same temporal areas mentioned above are activated in healthy subjects in the same category-specific ways when concrete entities are named from either pictures (Damasio et al., 1996, 2004; Grabowski et al., 2001) or characteristic sounds (Tranel et al., 2003a, 2005).

All of the studies considered so far have focused on the neural substrates of noun retrieval, but a number of other studies have investigated the neural substrates of verb retrieval. Drawing upon several different brain mapping methods, these studies suggest that the cortical regions that underlie semantically driven lexical selection during various kinds of verb production tasks are to some extent distinct from those that have been linked with access to nouns (for reviews see Mätzig et al., 2009; Vigliocco et al., 2011; see also Kemmerer et al., 2012). In particular, the regions that have been most strongly linked with verb retrieval include the left IFG and, to a lesser extent, the left inferior parietal lobule and mid/posterior MTG. Some of

Box 6.3 Happy Faces Are Named Faster than Neutral Faces

As everyone knows, not being able to quickly recall the names of familiar people when we see them can be a source of awkwardness and embarrassment. Given the tremendous social significance of proper name retrieval, it is not surprising that this ability has been studied intensively in cognitive neuroscience (for a review see Álvarez et al., 2009). One recent discovery that is especially striking was made by Gallegos and Tranel (2005).

They were interested in whether the presence of an emotional expression facilitates the recognition and naming of familiar faces. A few previous studies had suggested that this might be possible, and other work had shown that, for faces as well as other kinds of stimuli, emotional signals tend to "boost" neural processing in early visual areas of the brain. But the specific question of whether people name emotional faces faster than neutral faces had not been directly addressed. To explore this issue, Gallegos and Tranel first chose 57 famous individuals—actors, sports figures, and politicians—all of whose faces were readily visualized by normal subjects in response to the persons' names. Then they obtained from the Internet two images of each person's face, one happy and one neutral, but similar in terms of age, hairstyle, orientation, etc. (see Figure 6B3.1 for examples). Using these stimuli, they administered a naming task to the following three groups of participants: 30 normal subjects; 8 neurological patients with left anterior temporal lobectomies (henceforth LTL patients); and 10 neurological patients with right anterior temporal lobectomies (henceforth RTL patients). All of the patients' lobectomies had been performed to alleviate otherwise intractable epilepsy. With regard to naming accuracy, there was no effect of emotional expression, but both groups of patients achieved significantly lower scores than the normal subjects, which is consistent with previous research. In analyzing the reaction time data, Gallegos and Tranel only considered famous faces that the patients named accurately in both the happy and neutral conditions. For example, in order for a patient's reaction time data for Brad Pitt to be included, the patient must have named both the happy picture of him and the neutral picture of him correctly. In support of the hypothesis that motivated the study, a highly significant effect of emotional expression emerged, with happy faces being named much faster than neutral faces. Moreover, this facilitation effect produced by positive faces held for all three groups of participants (Figure 6B3.2).

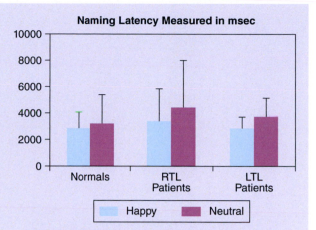

Naming Latency Measured in msec

Figure 6B3.2   Reaction time for naming famous faces, as a function of group (normals; right temporal lobectomy, RTL; left temporal lobectomy, LTL) and expression (happy, neutral). The error bars denote standard deviations. For all three groups, happy faces were named significantly faster than neutral faces. (From Gallegos & Tranel, 2005, p. 344.)

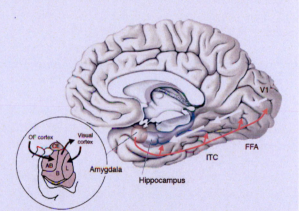

Figure 6B3.3   Anatomical connections of the amygdala with visual cortices. Nuclei of the amygdala are shown in the lower left: The lateral nucleus (L) receives input from high-level visual cortices in the temporal lobe, whereas sectors of the basal nucleus (B) in turn project to all temporal visual cortices, including the inferotemporal cortex (ITC), the fusiform face area (FFA), and the primary visual cortex (V1). (From Vuilleumier, 2005, p. 588.)

What neural mechanism might underlie this peculiar phenomenon? Although the study was not designed to tackle this deeper question, Gallegos and Tranel propose an explanation based on independent evidence that the amygdala, which is well-established as playing a key role in emotional processing (Adolphs, 2010a, 2010b), can

Figure 6B3.1   Examples of famous face pairs. (From Gallegos & Tranel, 2005, p. 342).

(Continued)

(Continued)

modulate early visual areas in a top-down manner (Figure 6B3.3). Specifically, they develop the following account:

> It could be the case that the presence of an emotional expression on a familiar face triggers amygdala activation, which in turn could yield enhanced processing in early visual cortex via feedback connections. The enhanced processing could, in turn, support the facilitation effect we observed, namely, quicker face naming (for example, by activating various conceptual features associated with a particular famous face, which could in turn increase the efficiency and effectiveness of lexical retrieval connected to that face).
>
> (p. 345)

It remains to be seen whether this sort of explanation is on the right track (see also Calvo & Beltrán, 2013). But the behavioral results stand by themselves, and they might even have meaningful practical implications for helping patients compensate for their acquired deficits in naming familiar faces.

the strongest evidence for the view that noun retrieval and verb retrieval have partially segregated neural underpinnings comes from studies which show that these abilities can be impaired independently of each other (see Table 2.1 and the associated text in Chapter 2). For example, some patients can access a certain phonological form when it is used as a noun but not when it is used as a verb, and other patients manifest the opposite performance profile (for a review see Shapiro & Caramazza, 2009). Thus, when asked to name a picture of a comb, a patient might say "I don't know what that's called, but you comb your hair with it." Alternatively, a patient might be able to produce the sentence "This person guides" but not the sentence "These are guides" (see Table 13.1, Figure 13.8, and the associated text in Chapter 13). In many cases, however, it can be difficult to determine whether allegedly noun-specific or verb-specific disorders arise at the level of lexical concepts, lemmas, morphosyntactic processes, or phonological codes (e.g., Laiacona & Caramazza, 2004).

Retrieving Morphemic Phonological Codes

According to the Lemma Model, successfully bridging the gap between the lexical selection subsystem and the form encoding subsystem entails selecting and spelling out a single morphemic phonological representation. Where do these word-level phonological representations reside in the brain? To answer this question, Indefrey and Levelt (2004) performed the following contrast, based on the logic of the componential task analysis shown in Table 6.3. They grouped together all of the studies that employed any of the three tasks that clearly involve phonological code retrieval—picture

naming, associative word generation, and word reading—and subtracted from them all of the studies that employed the one task that clearly doesn't involve phonological code retrieval—pseudoword reading. This contrast revealed common activation in several regions: the left posterior STG/STS (Wernicke's area); the left posterior MTG; the left anterior insula; and the right SMA. In addition, a separate analysis of chronometric data suggested that when subjects name pictures, these areas are engaged during a time window between 200 and 400 ms post-stimulus onset (Figure 6.9). We will discuss the anterior insula and the SMA further below in the context of the DIVA Model. Here we will concentrate on how the left posterior STG/STS and MTG may contribute to the process of accessing the segmental phonemic content of words during speech production.

It is interesting that this cortical territory intersects with one of the major functional–anatomical components of Hickok and Poeppel's (2000, 2004, 2007) Dual Stream Model of speech perception, namely the "phonological network," which is believed to depend on the mid-to-posterior STG/STS bilaterally (see Chapter 5). This convergence provides some support for the hypothesis, originally put forth by Carl Wernicke, that the same sound-based phonological codes are used in both perceiving and producing words, and that these codes are housed in the posterior superior temporal region. However, the question of whether we operate with a single phonological lexicon, or with separate but anatomically adjacent ones for input and output processing, has been highly contentious throughout the history of neurolinguistics, and answering it once and for all will require new insights from future research (for an informative review that emphasizes neuropsychological data, see Hillis, 2001; and for a

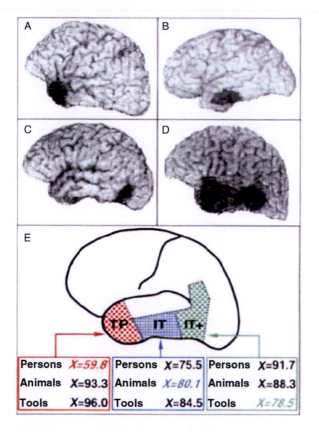

Figure 6.10 Lesion sites linked with impaired retrieval of words for persons, animals, and tools. (A–D) 3D reconstructed brains of individual patients with defects in accessing words for (A) persons only (lesion in the left temporal pole, TP); (B) animals only (lesion in the anterior sector of the left inferotemporal cortex, IT); (C) tools only (lesion in the posterior sector of the left inferotemporal cortex extending into the lateral occipital cortex); and (D) all three categories (lesion in all three regions involved separately in the first three cases). (E) For each word category, the naming scores of three groups of patients were calculated, with lesions in: TP only red, n = 6); IT (blue, with outer borders overlapping in some instances into either TP or IT+, n = 11); IT+ only (green, n = 6). For persons, the TP group had the lowest score, followed by the IT group and the IT+ group. For animals, the IT group had the lowest score, followed by the IT+ group and the TP group. For tools, the IT+ group had the lowest score, followed by the IT group and the TP group. These differences were statistically significant. (From Damasio et al., 1996, p. 501.)

discussion from the perspective of computational modeling, see Roelofs, 2003).

If morphemic phonological codes are retrieved from the left posterior superior temporal region during speech production, one would expect activity in this region to be modulated by word frequency, since the Lemma Model assumes that frequency effects occur at this particular stage of processing. This prediction has been confirmed by several fMRI studies. For instance, using a

picture-naming paradigm in which word frequency was systematically manipulated, Graves et al. (2007) found that as the frequency of target words decreased, not only did behavioral response times increase, but neural activity in the left posterior STG increased as well, suggesting greater retrieval effort. Moreover, this cortical modulation seemed to be due solely to word frequency, since it could not be attributed to either concept familiarity, which is related to semantic processing, or word length, which is related to articulatory load (for a follow-up study see Graves et al., 2008; and for another relevant investigation see Wilson et al., 2009b).

Data from disorders of word production provide further support for the view that phonological code retrieval depends on the left posterior STG/STS and MTG. Damage to this territory often brings about Wernicke's aphasia, in which phonological paraphasias and neologisms are among the most salient symptoms (see Chapter 3). Such symptoms are also associated, although to a lesser degree, with logopenic progressive aphasia, which has been linked with gradual atrophy in these brain areas (see Chapter 4). Another valuable source of information involves the types of naming errors that tend to be committed by neurosurgical patients undergoing direct cortical stimulation. Of special significance in this regard is a recent study by Corina et al. (2010) in which 36 patients were asked to name various kinds of common objects while different sites in their left cerebral cortices were stimulated with an electrode. Errors were treated as belonging to one of six categories:

- semantic paraphasias (e.g., saying *lion* in response to a tiger);
- circumlocutions (e.g., saying *sit down* in response to a chair);
- phonological paraphasias (e.g., saying *ragon* in response to a wagon);
- neologisms (e.g., saying *herp* in response to a fish);
- performance errors (e.g., distorting the target word-form by slurring, stuttering, or articulating imprecisely);
- no-response errors (i.e., the lack of any utterance).

In addition, two kinds of results were calculated for each cortical region of interest:

- error ratio (i.e., the ratio of a specific error type to the total number of errors in a specific region);
- patient ratio (i.e., the number of patients with one or more target errors over the total number of patients that incurred stimulation in that region).

Overall, phonological paraphasias and neologisms were among the least frequent types of errors, constituting just 7.4 percent and 4.0 percent of all errors, respectively. Nevertheless, according to both the error ratios and the patient ratios, these sorts of errors (as well as circumlocutions) tended to emerge during stimulation in the vicinity of the left mid-to-posterior STG/STS and MTG (Figure 6.11). In fact, Corina et al. (2010, p. 110) remarked that "phonological paraphasias, neologisms, and circumlocutions were primarily confined to regions bordering the posterior STS." These findings are clearly congruent with the other findings mentioned above, all of which point to an important role of the left posterior STG/STS and MTG in accessing and spelling out the segmental phonemic content of words during speech production. Still, it is worth noting that, according to recent neuropsychological research, frontoparietal regions also contribute to phonological retrieval during object-naming tasks (Schwartz et al., 2012b).

A final issue that warrants attention is that the region identified by Indefrey and Levelt (2004) as subserving phonological code retrieval appears to encompass area Spt ("sylvian parietal-temporal"), which lies deep within the left posterior sylvian fissure. However, according to Hickok

and Poeppel's (2000, 2004, 2007) Dual Stream Model of speech processing, this area does not really contribute to lexical–phonological access per se; instead, it is believed to implement the "sensorimotor interface," which operates as a relay station that connects the phonological network in the posterior STG/STS with the articulatory network in the posterior frontal lobe. As discussed in Chapter 5, a considerable amount of evidence derived from both fMRI studies and research on conduction aphasia supports this hypothesis regarding area Spt. Hence, in the context of a task like picture naming, it may be best to think of area Spt as a kind of translational device that takes as input the sound-based representation of the target word in the posterior STG/STS, and generates as output a call for the frontal cortex to activate the appropriate vocal action schema.

Prosodification and Syllabification

Indefrey and Levelt (2004) did not address the question of how various aspects of prosodification, such as the determination of metrical structure, are implemented in the brain, but they did investigate the neural correlates of the closely related syllabification stage of word production.

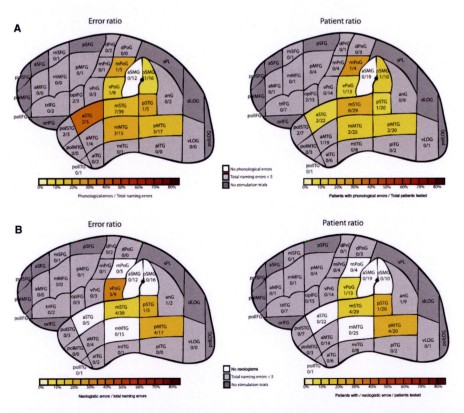

Figure 6.11   Cortical regions where direct electrical stimulation induces (A) phonological paraphasias or (B) neologisms during picture naming. Regions indicate errors ratios (left) or patient ratios (right). (From Corina et al., 2010, pp. 106–107.)

As shown in Table 6.3, syllabification is assumed to be engaged by all four types of tasks—picture naming, associative word generation, word reading, and pseudoword reading—regardless of whether the tasks are performed overtly or covertly. In contrast, the subsequent stage of phonetic encoding is assumed to be engaged by all four types of tasks only when they are performed overtly. Based on these assumptions, Indefrey and Levelt (2004) attempted to isolate the neural correlates of syllabification by searching their database for brain regions that were commonly activated across not only all word production experiments with overt responses and silent control conditions, but also all word production experiments with covert responses. The only region that survived this intersection analysis was the left posterior IFG (i.e., Broca's area), and a separate analysis of chronometric data revealed that when subjects name pictures, this region is activated within a time window of 400–600 ms post-stimulus onset (Figure 6.9). These findings are compatible with the results of more recent fMRI studies that have explored the neural substrates of syllabification processes in the context of polysyllabic word production (e.g., Bohland & Guenther, 2006; Papoutsi et al., 2009; for other pertinent studies see Shuster & Lemieux, 2005; Sörös et al., 2006, 2011; Riecker et al., 2008).

Phonetic Encoding and Articulation

Owing to several methodological complications, the brain regions that underlie phonetic encoding and articulation were the most difficult for Indefrey and Levelt (2004) to identify. Nevertheless, they attempted to overcome these complications by adopting a number of reasonable assumptions, such as that the relevant regions would be reported as least twice as often in studies that employed overt tasks as in studies that employed covert tasks. Ultimately, they found the following regions to be plausibly (but not definitively) linked with phonetic encoding and articulation (Figure 6.9):

- left and right ventral primary motor and primary somatosensory cortices;
- right SMA;
- right dorsal primary motor cortex;
- left and right cerebellum;
- left and right thalamus;
- right midbrain.

Other studies utilizing diverse techniques have independently associated many of these areas, as well as others (such as the left SMA and the left anterior insula), with various aspects of the planning and execution of speech gestures during word production. We will refrain,

however, from discussing the specific functional roles of these areas until the next main section of this chapter, which is devoted to elaborating the DIVA Model of speech motor control. Still, it is interesting to note here that most—not all, but most—of the brain regions that have been implicated in speech articulation have also been found to be active during the oral production of sounds that lack phonemic content, such as coughs, sighs, snorts, laughs, kisses, tongue clicks, whistles, and cries (Chang et al., 2009). This is consistent with the idea that the neural substrates of speech articulation evolved from the mechanisms that support vocal communication in non-human primates.

Self-Monitoring

Although Indefrey and Levelt's (2004) meta-analysis was not designed to uncover the neural correlates of self-monitoring, they still made an effort to address this final issue. To recapitulate, the Lemma Model postulates two feedback loops—an external loop that takes as input the acoustic speech signal of the speaker's own voice, and an internal loop that takes as input the output of syllabification. Indefrey and Levelt (2004) assumed that the brain regions subserving the external loop could be isolated by conjoining the following two types of neuroimaging results: first, the activation patterns from studies that employed overt word production tasks (note that such tasks involve hearing one's own voice); and second, the activation patterns from studies that employed auditory word perception tasks (to obtain the necessary data they pooled together a number of pertinent studies). They found that the most likely candidate for the neural basis of the external loop is the posterior two-thirds of the bilateral superior temporal region, which encompasses both low-level and high-level auditory areas. Additional evidence for this view is presented below in the context of the DIVA Model.

The neural basis of the internal loop is much harder to pin down because, by definition, it operates in a completely subvocal manner. Indefrey and Levelt (2004) point out, however, that the range of realistic possibilities can be significantly reduced if one assumes that, like the external loop, the internal loop enters the pathway used for speech perception. If this is correct, then the key brain structures must include either all or part of the posterior two-thirds of the bilateral superior temporal cortices, depending on whether the loop enters the speech perception pathway at an early stage or a late one. This hypothesis has not yet been explored in detail, but it receives indirect support from a growing body of literature on the neural substrates of imagined voices. A number of studies indicate that several bilateral superior temporal areas are activated not only when healthy subjects voluntarily generate images of their own voices (such as during verbally mediated thought), but also when schizophrenic subjects and so-called nonclinical hallucinators involuntarily hear voices in their "mind's ear"—voices that seem to be beyond their subjective control, but that actually derive from their own internal speech processes (e.g., McGuire et al., 1996; Shergill et al., 2000; Aleman et al., 2005; Allen et al., 2007; Linden et al., 2011).

Some Challenges Facing the Model

Despite the fact that the Lemma Model is theoretically coherent, instantiated in a computer simulation, and capable of accommodating a great deal of psychological and neurobiological data, it has been criticized by many different researchers for many different reasons. Some of these concerns are elaborated in the nearly two dozen commentaries that accompany Levelt et al.'s (1999) comprehensive presentation of their framework in *Behavioral and Brain Sciences,* and others are discussed in numerous articles scattered throughout the literature. Since it is obviously beyond the scope of this chapter to explore these issues in depth, we will restrict our attention to two of the most prominent challenges confronting the Lemma Model.

The Lemma Dilemma

One of the central tenets of the theory is that lemmas operate as a bridge between the semantic and phonological structures of words, and also serve as pointers to morphosyntactic features. It has been argued, however, most notably by Alfonso Caramazza and his colleagues, that this kind of architecture cannot easily account for several classes of neuropsychological findings (Caramazza, 1997; Caramazza & Miozzo, 1998). Here we will focus on just one rather striking set of observations. Specifically, when some patients perform various word production tasks, they make semantic substitution errors in spoken output but not in written output, whereas other patients exhibit the opposite dissociation (e.g., Caramazza & Hillis, 1990, 1991; Rapp & Caramazza, 1998a, 2002; Rapp et al., 1997; Hillis et al., 1999b, 2002a, 2003; Kemmerer et al., 2005). For example, in response to a picture of a clam, patient RGB said *octopus* but wrote *clam* (Caramazza & Hillis, 1990); conversely, in response to a picture of a turtle, patient RCM said *turtle* but wrote *snake* (Hillis et al., 1999b).

To be sure, the Lemma Model was not designed to address written word production; however, given that lemmas are assumed to be amodal lexical nodes, it is reasonable to assume that they would project not only to phonological representations but also to orthographic

ones, as shown in Figure 6.12A. The question then arises as to how the neuropsychological dissociations described above could be explained within such a framework. Might RGB and RCM have deficits at the level of lemmas? This interpretation fails because it predicts that both spoken and written word production would be impaired. As an alternative approach, suppose the patients were still able to access amodal lemmas, but were no longer able to access modality-specific lexical representations—phonological codes for RGB, and orthographic codes for RCM. This type of deficit analysis also fails because it cannot account for the fact that the errors in the impaired output modality are semantic in nature. After all, the theory assumes that just one lemma is activated and that it is the semantically appropriate one, as revealed by correct naming in the preserved output modality, so it is unclear why semantic errors are made in the affected channel of word production.

Now, advocates of the Lemma Model could try to accommodate the data by postulating separate components for modality-specific phonological and orthographic lemmas, and arguing that difficulties with just spoken or just written word production arise from dysfunctions involving just one pathway (Roelofs et al., 1998). But this would be tantamount to abandoning one of the key

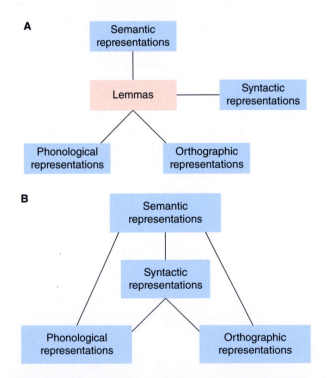

Figure 6.12 Schematic of (A) the Lemma Model of spoken and written word production, and (B) the Independent Network Model of spoken and written word production. (From Rapp & Goldrick, 2006, p. 45.)

claims of the theory, namely that lemmas are modality-neutral (Caramazza & Miozzo, 1998). A simpler solution, first proposed by Caramazza (1997), would be to give up the notion of lemmas completely, and posit instead direct connections between semantic, phonological, and orthographic representations, as well as an independent network for morphosyntactic features, as shown in Figure 6.12B. This type of architecture can handle the neuropsychological data, as well as many other sorts of findings. It remains controversial, however, whether a framework that dispenses with a separate level for lemmas has greater overall explanatory power than one that includes such a level.

Discrete Versus Interactive Processing

Another aspect of the Lemma Model that has been challenged involves its assumptions about activation dynamics. The theory claims that processing is **discrete**. What this means is that processing proceeds in a strictly unidirectional fashion, from higher to lower levels, without any feedback. It also means that, from the lemma stratum on down, the computations at a given level are completed before activation propagates to the subsequent level. Thus, only the selected lemma engages the corresponding phonological code; competing lemmas that are also activated, but to lesser degrees, do not engage the corresponding phonological codes.

In recent years, these assumptions have come under attack, mostly because of analyses of both spontaneous and experimentally induced speech errors produced by both healthy subjects and brain-damaged patients (for a review see Rapp & Goldrick, 2006). These analyses suggest that mixed errors—i.e., words that are both semantically and phonologically related to the target, like saying *skirt* instead of *shirt,* or *calf* instead of *cat*—occur more often than would be expected in an architecture like the Lemma Model. There is also evidence that the speech production system is biased to produce errors that are real words instead of pseudo-words, and this too has been argued to go against what the Lemma Model would predict.

These findings have led some researchers to favor an alternative kind of framework in which processing is **interactive**. In this type of architecture, activation propagates back and forth between levels, in both feedforward and

feedback directions. Moreover, activation cascades rapidly from multiple units at one level to multiple units at the subsequent level before the computations at the first level have been completed. Several different kinds of frameworks have been instantiated in computer models that vary along such parameters as the degree of interactivity and the degree of cascading activation (Figure 6.13). In addition, a number of attempts have been made to determine how well certain types of "lesions" to certain types of computer models can simulate the sorts of speech errors that are most frequently made by healthy subjects and different categories of aphasic patients (e.g., N. Martin et al., 1994, 1996; Dell et al., 1997, 2004; Rapp & Goldrick, 2000; Goldrick & Rapp, 2002; see also Ruml et al., 2000; Ruml & Caramazza, 2000; Dell et al., 2000). What is especially relevant in the current context is that some lively debates have taken place between advocates of discrete architectures like the Lemma Model and advocates of more interactive architectures like those shown in Figure 6.13

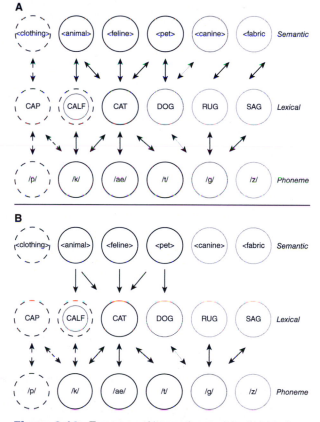

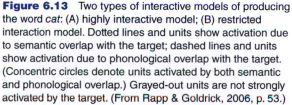

Figure 6.13   Two types of interactive models of producing the word *cat*: (A) highly interactive model; (B) restricted interaction model. Dotted lines and units show activation due to semantic overlap with the target; dashed lines and units show activation due to phonological overlap with the target. (Concentric circles denote units activated by both semantic and phonological overlap.) Grayed-out units are not strongly activated by the target. (From Rapp & Goldrick, 2006, p. 53.)

Discrete processing   Processing is strictly feedforward, and the computations at a given level are completed before activation propagates to the next level.

Interactive processing   Processing flows both forward and backward, and the computations at a given level need not be completed before activation propagates to the next level.

(see the exchanges between Roelofs, 2004a, 2004b, and Rapp & Goldrick, 2000, 2004). Most of the key issues have not yet been fully resolved, but one thing is clear: Computer simulations of spoken word production can be extremely valuable sources of insight when it comes to evaluating the virtues and shortcomings of competing theoretical approaches.

The DIVA Model of Speech Motor Control

One of the most impressive illustrations of how computer simulations can illuminate the nature of language processing is the DIVA (Directions Into Velocities of Articulators) Model of speech motor control. In short, this is a mathematically and neurobiologically grounded computational framework that was originally designed to promote better understanding of the brain circuits that subserve the acquisition and deployment of speech motor skills. To some extent, the DIVA Model begins where the Lemma Model leaves off—with phonetic encoding and articulation. It also provides a more sophisticated treatment of some of the feedback mechanisms that are involved in self-monitoring. The framework was created by Frank Guenther, a researcher at Boston University with an extraordinary ability to integrate speech science, computer science, and brain science. Although the DIVA Model was first presented in the mid 1990s (Guenther, 1994, 1995), it has undergone many refinements and has been used to generate and test numerous predictions about the kinds of neural activation patterns that are associated with speech production (for a recent review see Guenther & Vladusich, 2012; see also Bohland & Guenther, 2006; Guenther et al., 2006; Ghosh et al., 2008; Tourville et al., 2008; Peeva et al., 2010; Golfinopolous et al., 2010, 2011). As we will see, the framework also provides a useful context for understanding a variety of disorders of spoken language production. Several competing accounts of speech motor control are currently available (for a recent collection see Maassen & van Lieshout, 2010), but the DIVA Model is unquestionably one of the most advanced.

The following review of Guenther's theory begins with a bird's eye view of how the DIVA Model learns to talk. After that general introduction, we will delve into the mechanical minutiae of the various computational components of the framework. First, we will explore the feedforward control subsystem, which is thought to be sufficient for producing well-learned speech sounds under normal circumstances. Then we will discuss the feedback control subsystem, which has both auditory and somatosensory elements.

This subsystem not only guides the development of speech motor skills, but also influences production in unusual situations, such as when you are holding a pencil between your teeth, or—to foreshadow a few of the experiments that we will encounter—when a fiendish scientist suddenly distorts the sound of your voice or inflates a tiny balloon inside your mouth. At the end of the section, we will consider some of the challenges that confront the model.

How Do You Say "Good Doggie"?

The organization of the DIVA Model is schematized in Figure 6.14, and its putative neural correlates are portrayed in Figure 6.15. Because these diagrams are, to say the least, rather "busy," it is easy to be intimidated by the framework. But the basic design of the model is actually quite logical and can be appreciated without too much difficulty, as long as one is willing to invest a reasonable amount of time and energy. The network feeds into a computer-simulated vocal tract—essentially a modified speech synthesizer—that generates acoustic signals, so this gives DIVA a real voice, albeit a rather robotic one. And to make the model even friendlier, Guenther has given it a cartoon-like face and body, thereby allowing one to both see and hear it talk (Figure 6.16). A variety of demos are available on the Internet (see Guenther's website), and after some of them, the little character flicks its eye and waves its arms, showing that even complex computer models can have playful personalities.

The mechanics of the DIVA Model are elaborated in detail further below. Here at the outset, our goal is simply to get a sense of the big picture. Perhaps the best way to do this is to work through a concrete example while maintaining a relatively general level of description. Among the demos that can be viewed on Guenther's website, there is a set of simulations that indicate how the network learns to say *good doggie* after initially being exposed to the proper pronunciation of this utterance. The model's first attempt is quite garbled, but over the course of multiple subsequent efforts, its output progressively improves and eventually becomes fairly accurate (Figure 6.17; Guenther et al., 2006). How does the model do this?

First, the utterance that is presented to the model is used to specify an **auditory target representation**—that is, a representation of how the model's own production should sound. Then a speech sound representation in the model's high-level motor system is committed to controlling the generation of that kind of utterance. Every

Auditory target representation A representation of how an utterance is expected to sound.

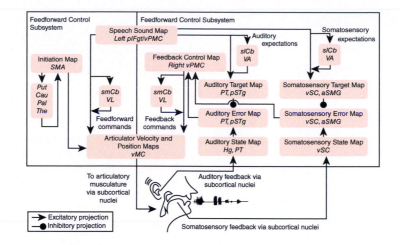

Figure 6.14 Schematic of the DIVA Model of speech motor control. Each box corresponds to a set of neurons (or map), and arrows between the boxes correspond to synaptic projections that transform one type of neural representation into another. The model is divided into two basic subsystems: the Feedforward Control Subsystem on the left, and the Feedback Control Subsystem on the right. The neural substrates underlying this integrated control scheme include the premotor and primary motor cortices, auditory cortices, somatosensory cortices, the cerebellum, and the basal ganglia. pIFg = posterior inferior frontal gyrus; vPMC = ventral premotor cortex; SMA = supplementary motor area; Put = putamen; Cau = caudate; Pal = pallidum; Tha = thalamus; smCb = superior medial cerebellum; VL = ventral lateral nucleus of the thalamus; vMC = ventral motor cortex; sICb = superior lateral cerebellum; VA = ventral anterior nucleus of the cerebellum; PT = planum temporale; pSTg = posterior superior temporal gyrus; Hg = Heschl's gyrus; vSC = ventral somatosensory cortex; aSMg = anterior supramarginal gyrus. (From Golfinopoulos et al., 2010, p. 863.)

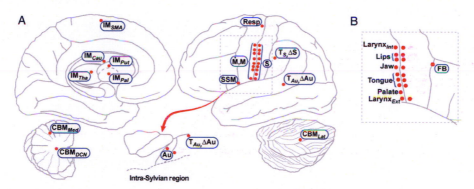

Figure 6.15 Neuroanatomical mapping of the DIVA Model. (A) The locations of DIVA Model component sites (red dots) are plotted on a schematic of the left hemisphere. Medial regions are shown on the left, lateral regions on the right. (B) A schematic of the right hemisphere lateral inferior frontoparietal region. The corresponding left hemisphere region is outlined by the dashed box in A. The right hemisphere plot in B demonstrates the location of the Feedback Control Map (FB) and the location of motor and somatosensory representations of the articulators. IM_{SMA} = Supplementary Motor Area Initiation Map; IM_{Cau} = Caudate Initiation Map; IM_{Put} = Putamen Initiation Map; IM_{Pal} = Pallidum Initiation Map; IM_{Tha} = Thalamus Initiation Map; CBM_{Med} = medial cerebellum; CBM_{DCN} = deep cerebellar nuclei; CBM_{Lat} = lateral cerebellum; Au = Auditory State Map; T_{Au} = Auditory Target Map; ΔAu = Auditory Error Map; Resp = respiratory motor cells; M,M = Articulatory Velocity and Position Maps; SSM = Speech Sound Map; S = Somatosensory State Map; T_S = Somatosensory Target Map; ΔS = Somatosensory Error Map. (From Golfinopoulos et al., 2010, p. 870.)

time the model attempts to say *good doggie*, this speech sound representation sends output along two pathways. One pathway transmits motor instructions to the model's articulatory component, which in turn feeds into the computerized speech synthesizer. The other pathway projects to the model's auditory component and activates

the auditory target representation as a way of predicting how the utterance should sound. It's as if the model is telling itself, "If all goes well, what I produce should sound like this." Next, the acoustic signals produced by the speech synthesizer are detected and processed, and this auditory input pattern is compared with the auditory

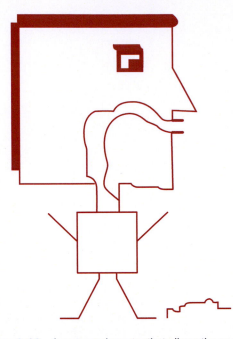

Figure 6.16 A cartoon character that allows the operation of the DIVA Model to be visualized. (Courtesy of Frank Guenther, Boston University.)

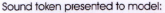

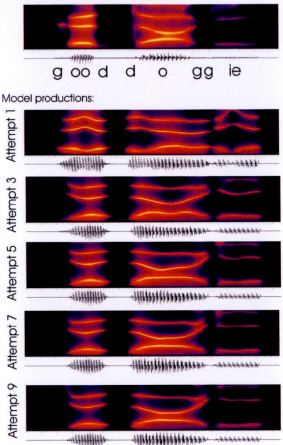

Figure 6.17 Spectrograms showing the first three formants of the utterance *good doggie* as produced by an adult male speaker (top panel) and by the DIVA Model (bottom panels). The model first learns an acoustic target for the utterance based on the sample it is presented (top panel). Then the model attempts to produce the sound, at first primarily under feedback control (Attempt 1), then with progressively improved feedforward commands supplementing the feedback control (Attempts 3, 5, 7, and 9). By the ninth attempt the feedforward control signals are accurate enough for the model to closely imitate the formant trajectories from the sample utterance. (From Guenther et al., 2006, p. 289.)

target representation to determine how well the utterance was executed. Finally, errors are registered and used to make long-term corrective adjustments to the motor instructions that are sent to the articulatory component. After numerous iterations of this cycle of speech production and corrective auditory feedback, the model ultimately hones in on a motor program that regularly gives rise to the desired sound pattern. At this point, the model is able to say *good doggie* in a remarkably fluent manner. Incidentally, the transformation from auditory errors to corrective motor commands is the source of the model's name, since that transformation embodies a mapping from Directions in sensory space Into Velocities of Articulators—hence, DIVA.

Two additional points are worth making about the network's acquired capacity to say *good doggie*. First, after this capacity has developed by virtue of the corrective auditory feedback mechanism, the model is able to generate the phrase by relying entirely on its motor system, which is to say, without depending any more on auditory feedback. Nevertheless, this feedback mechanism still continues to operate in the background, so that in the unlikely event that the acoustic signals generated by the model are distorted by externally imposed perturbations, those deviations from what was expected can rapidly be perceived and used to transmit corrective information to the motor system in an online manner. Second, over the course of multiple successful productions of *good doggie*,

the model gradually acquires a **somatosensory target representation**. This is analogous to the auditory target representation, but is in the somatosensory modality. Basically, it specifies the tactile and proprioceptive (i.e., body-part positional) sensations that are expected to be felt in the vocal tract whenever the phrase is produced. Once this representation is in place, it serves as a kind of

Somatosensory target representation   A representation of how an utterance is expected to feel, in terms of tactile and proprioceptive (i.e., body-part positional) sensations.

template against which incoming somatosensory signals are compared. In this way, if errors occur, they can be detected right away and used to get the motor system back on track.

Now that we have surveyed the operations of the DIVA Model from a relatively distant perspective, we are ready to zoom in on its inner workings, as depicted in Figures 6.14 and 6.15. To begin with a fundamental point, this model is strongly inspired by the brain. The framework consists of many interconnected modules that are referred to as maps. Every map contains a group of computational units, each of which corresponds to a population of neurons; and every pointed or rounded pathway represents a bundle of excitatory or inhibitory projections that correspond to axons in a fiber tract. In addition, the activation dynamics and learning algorithms of the model are based on well-established neurobiological principles. Architecturally, the model contains two large subsystems, one for feedforward control and another for feedback control, with the latter subsystem breaking down further into separate auditory and somatosensory feedback loops. The feedforward control subsystem is housed primarily in the frontal lobes, with some routes through subcortical structures; the auditory feedback mechanism is housed primarily in the temporal lobes, again with some routes through subcortical structures; and the somatosensory feedback mechanism is housed primarily in the parietal lobes, once more with some routes through subcortical structures. In what follows, we will discuss each part of the network in turn.

Feedforward Control

As noted above, the feedforward control subsystem is thought to be sufficient for producing well-learned speech sounds under normal circumstances. This view is supported by evidence that speech motor control is quite resistant to the removal of auditory and/or somatosensory feedback (Gammon et al., 1971; Cowie & Douglas-Cowie, 1983; Goehl & Kaufman, 1984). For example, Gammon et al. (1971) found that articulation was only moderately altered when healthy subjects generated phonetically complex speech in the following conditions: (1) extensive white noise masking; (2) extensive anaesthetization of the oral cavity; and (3) both masking and anaesthetization.

According to the DIVA Model, articulation starts with activation of the appropriate unit in the **Speech Sound Map**. Every unit in this module represents a particular speech sound, which could be a phoneme, a syllable, or even a "chunked" syllable sequence, although the prototypical speech sound is assumed to be a syllable, in accord with the Lemma Model's notion of a mental syllabary (Levelt & Wheeldon, 1994). Also consistent with the Lemma Model is the neural localization of the Speech Sound Map in the left posterior IFG (BA44, i.e., part of Broca's area) and the caudally adjacent ventral premotor cortex (Indefrey & Levelt, 2004; see also Eckers et al., 2013). Damage to these structures can cause apraxia of speech, which is a high-level disorder of articulatory planning and coordination (Hillis et al., 2004b; Richardson et al., 2012). When asked to say *cushion,* one patient with this disorder said, "Oh, uh, uh, chookun, uh, uh, uh, dook, I know what it's called, it's c-u, uh, no it's chookun, no …" (Ogar et al., 2005; Table 6.4). This deficit is frequently found in patients with Broca's aphasia (see Chapter 3) and in patients

> **Speech Sound Map**   A repository of acquired speech sound representations (mostly syllables) that serve as the starting point for articulation, and that reside in the left posterior IFG and ventral premotor cortex.

Table 6.4 Tasks from the Motor Speech Evaluation (Wertz et al., 1984) that Elicit the Lowest Scores in Patients with Apraxia of Speech (Ogar et al., 2006)

Task	Example
Alternating diadochokinesis	The examinee repeats between the three-syllable utterance *pataka* as rapidly and smoothly as possible (For fMRI studies of this task see Lotze et al., 2000; Sörös et al., 2006, 2011)
Multiple repetitions of multisyllabic words	The examinee repeats three polysyllabic words (*artillery, impossibility,* and *catastrophe*) five times each. Words include consonant clusters and require rapid movement between multiple places of articulation during productions of each word
Repetition of sentences	The examinee repeats sentences composed of frequent and infrequent word choices (e.g., *In the summer they sell vegetables; Arthur was an oozy, oily sneak*)
Reading the Grandfather passage	The examinee reads a brief, phonetically balanced paragraph that contains most of the sounds produced by English speakers

with progressive nonfluent aphasia (see Chapter 4). Furthermore, blockage of speech motor plans, experienced as an inability to "get the words out," can be induced by direct electrocortical stimulation of the left posterior IFG (Penfield & Rasmussen, 1949; Ojemann et al., 1989b; Corina et al., 2010) as well as by applying repetitive TMS to the same region (Stewart et al., 2001).

In order for a unit in the Speech Sound Map to be assigned to a specific speech sound, it must initially be labelled for this function by auditory input from a phonological representation, probably stored in the mid-to-posterior STG/STS. This input pathway is not shown in Figure 6.14, largely because it is omitted from current implementations of the DIVA Model for the sake of simplicity. Despite this gap, it is important to bear in mind that the pathway plays a pivotal role in the development of the Speech Sound Map, which is to say, in the imitative learning of speech sounds. Moreover, by virtue of this pathway, the Speech Sound Map is predicted to be engaged during both the production and the perception of acquired speech sounds—a view that is well-supported (e.g., Eckers et al., 2013; see also the discussion of the "articulatory network" component of the Dual Stream Model in Chapter 5).

Units in the Speech Sound Map send excitatory feed-forward projections to the **Articulator Velocity and Position Maps**, which contain pools of units for all the parts of the vocal tract—larynx, lips, jaw, tongue, and palate. Together, the Articulator Velocity and Position Maps represent what is referred to by the Lemma Model as the "articulatory score" of an utterance (Levelt, 2001). This can be thought of as the time series of vocal tract gestures that are necessary to produce the utterance. The maps reside in the ventral primary motor cortex bilaterally, in agreement with the Lemma Model (Indefrey & Levelt, 2004). As shown in Figure 6.15, the units in these maps are organized in a somatotopic manner (for a review see Conant et al., in press; see also Brown et al., 2009; Grabski et al., 2012; Bouchard et al., 2013). Damage to these cortical regions, and/or to their white matter projections to subcortical nuclei, can give rise to **spastic dysarthria**, which is characterized by reductions of the speed, strength, range, and accuracy

of articulatory movements (Duffy, 2005). This impairment of the capacity to voluntarily "steer" the vocal tract muscles can be severe when the damage is bilateral, but it is relatively mild when the damage is restricted to either the left or right hemisphere (Ackermann & Ziegler, 2010). A related finding is that speech arrest, which involves a slowing and distortion of speech due to an inability to control one's oral and facial muscles, can be induced by direct electrocortical stimulation of either the left or right ventral primary motor cortex (Penfield & Rasmussen, 1949; Ojemann et al., 1989b) as well as by applying repetitive TMS to either of these areas (Stewart et al., 2001).

Like the Speech Sound Map, the Articulator Velocity and Position Maps are predicted to be engaged not only during speech production, but also during speech perception, and data consistent with this hypothesis come from several brain mapping studies (again, see the discussion of the "articulatory network" component of the Dual Stream Model in Chapter 5). In the DIVA Model, the activation patterns in these maps serve as the final output of the whole network, and they are fed directly into the computer-simulated vocal tract that generates acoustic signals, thereby giving the model its voice. Amazingly enough, Guenther and his colleagues recently found that a similar artificial speech synthesizer could be driven by the readout from an electrode implanted in the ventral primary motor cortex of a profoundly paralyzed individual, allowing this person to produce simple vowels through a brain–computer interface (Box 6.4). This extraordinary discovery is an excellent example of how neurocomputational simulations of language processing can have significant clinical implications.

The projections from the Speech Sound Map to the Articulator Velocity and Position Maps include a branching route that passes through the superior medial cerebellum and part of the thalamus. Interestingly, these regions also emerged in Indefrey and Levelt's (2004) investigation of the brain structures that are linked with articulation. Although the role of the cerebellum in language processing is not well understood (Murdoch, 2010), the superior medial region may contribute to speech motor control by facilitating the precise timing of feedforward commands. This idea is motivated by evidence that damage to that region can engender **ataxic dysarthria**, which involves slurred,

Articulator Velocity and Position Maps Vocal tract representations (including the larynx, lips, jaw, tongue, and palate) that specify the "articulatory score" of utterances, and that reside in the ventral primary motor cortex bilaterally.

Spastic dysarthria A disorder of speech motor control that involves reductions of the speed, strength, range, and accuracy of articulatory movements, and that is manifested in its most severe form following bilateral damage to the ventral primary motor cortex, or to the underlying white matter projections from those cortical areas to subcortical nuclei.

Ataxic dysarthria A disorder of speech motor control that involves problems with the precise timing and coordination of articulatory movements, and that has been linked with damage to the superior medial cerebellum.

Box 6.4   A Brain–Machine Interface Restores Rudimentary Speech in a Patient with Locked-In Syndrome

One of the most devastating neurological conditions that can befall a person is "locked-in" syndrome. First studied by Fred Plum, an immensely influential neurologist who himself succumbed to primary progressive aphasia in 2010, this syndrome occurs when part of the brain stem, such as the pons, is damaged in its anterior aspect, right in front of the area where damage causes coma or persistent vegetative state. Such a precisely positioned lesion leaves consciousness and cognition intact but destroys the motor pathways that innervate the skeletal muscles, thereby preventing all bodily action with just one exception—vertical eye movement. This isolated channel of motor output allows locked-in patients to communicate, albeit quite tediously, via eye blinks. In fact, Jean-Dominique Bauby, the former editor of the popular French magazine *Elle* who acquired locked-in syndrome after suffering a massive stroke, managed to use eye blinks to laboriously dictate, letter by letter, an entire memoir, *Le Scaphandre et le Papillon* (translated into English as *The Diving Bell and the Butterfly*) (Bauby, 1997), which was later made into an award-winning film.

In a recent breakthrough, Guenther et al. (2009) took the initial steps toward providing locked-in patients with a much more efficient and naturalistic means of communication. They implanted an electrode in the ventral precentral gyrus, near the boundary between the premotor and primary motor cortex for the articulators, of a 26-year-old man with locked-in syndrome, and then routed the neural signals detected by this electrode along a processing pathway that went first to a transmitter mounted outside the man's skull but under his scalp, then to a receiver external to the scalp, then to two highly sophisticated computer systems for sorting and decoding the signals, and finally to an artificial speech synthesizer that could generate immediate auditory feedback (Figure 6B4.1). Over the course of a 90-minute training session with this brain–machine

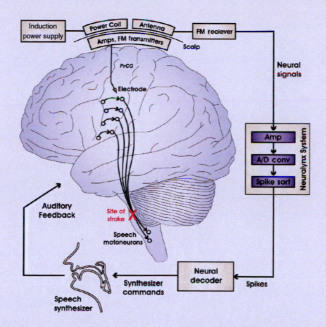

Figure 6B4.1   Schematic of the brain–machine interface for real-time synthetic speech production. Black circles and curved arrows represent neurons and axonal projections, respectively, in the neural circuitry for speech motor output. The patient's stroke-induced lesion in the motor pathways (red X) disconnects motor plans represented in the cerebral cortex from the speech motoneurons, thus disabling speech output while sparing somatic, auditory, and visual sensation as well as speech motor planning centers in the cerebral cortex. Signals collected from an electrode implanted in the patient's speech motor cortex are amplified and sent wirelessly across the scalp as FM radio signals. The signals are then routed to an electrophysiology recording system for further amplification, analog-to-digital conversion, and spike sorting. The sorted spikes are sent to a neural decoder which translates them into commands for a speech synthesizer. Audio signals from the synthesizer are fed back to the patient in real time. (From Guenther et al., 2009, p. 2.)

(Continued)

(Continued)

interface, the patient was able to quickly and significantly improve his performance on a simple vowel production task, shifting from an average success rate of 45 percent in the first block to 70 percent in the last block. These results are extremely encouraging, since they suggest that it may eventually be possible to decode and synthesize entire words that this otherwise mute man intends to produce. Guenther et al.'s pioneering study, which was partly inspired by insights about speech motor control derived from the DIVA Model, clearly marks an important milestone in the development of neural prosthetics to enhance the communicative abilities of profoundly paralyzed individuals (see also Brown, 2008).

poorly coordinated speech (Ackermann et al., 1992; Duffy, 2005).

The last major component of the feedforward control subsystem is the **Initiation Map**. Each unit in the Speech Sound Map is associated with a matching unit in the Initiation Map, and like the units in the Speech Sound Map, the units in the Initiation Map project to the units in the Articulator Velocity and Position Maps. As described above, the function of the Speech Sound Map is to set up specific motor commands in

---

Initiation Map   A module that sends a "go" signal to prepared speech motor commands, and that resides in the SMA bilaterally, with modulatory influences from the basal ganglia.

---

the Articulator Velocity and Position Maps. The job of the Initiation Map is to "release" those commands at the right time. In other words, the Initiation Map provides the "go" signal that causes a fully prepared speech motor pattern to be put into action. The Initiation Map is believed to reside in the supplementary motor area (SMA, i.e., medial BA6), although the rostrally adjacent pre-supplementary motor area, not indicated in Figure 6.14 or Figure 6.15, is probably involved as well (see Bohland et al., 2010).

It is well known that these regions are essential for all kinds of voluntary behaviors (for reviews see Nachev et al., 2008, and Haggard, 2009). In the domain of speech, the SMA has been shown to be more active

---

Box 6.5   What the Brain Does Before the Tongue Slips

Speech errors in which the initial consonants of two words are exchanged are sometimes called spoonerisms, in commemoration of Reverend W.A. Spooner, who was notorious for saying things like "You have hissed all my mystery lectures." What happens in the brain when such errors are made? To address this question, Möller et al. (2007) conducted an ERP study that utilized the "spoonerisms of laboratory induced predisposition" (SLIP) technique (Motley & Baars, 1976). As indicated in Figure 6B5.1, subjects were shown word pairs on a computer screen and were instructed to read them silently for a subsequent memory test; 1,000 ms after some pairs, however, subjects were cued to say them out loud. Each of the key trials involved a series of "inductor" pairs like *duck bill, dart board,* and *dust bin,* followed by a "target" pair like *barn door,* which, because of its reversal of initial phonemes relative to the inductor pairs, could potentially induce either the complete spoonerism *darn bore* or a partial spoonerism like *darn door* or *barn bore.* In contrast, none of the control trials involved a close relation between the initial phonemes of the inductor and target pairs.

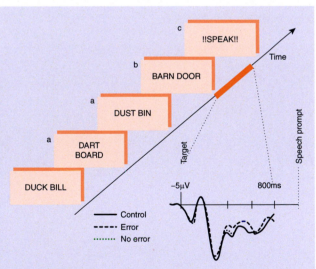

Figure 6B5.1   In critical trials, several inductor word pairs (a) were followed by a target word pair (b), after which a prompt (c) required subjects to overtly vocalize the immediately preceding word pair. Group average brain potentials recorded from a central midline electrode site (Cz) during the interval between target pairs and speech prompts are shown for target pairs that elicited errors, target pairs that did not elicit errors, and control pairs. Only error trials are associated with a more negative ERP between 350 and 600 ms. (From Möller et al., 2007, p. 1174.)

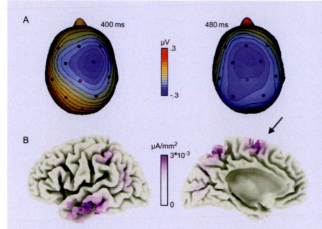

Figure 6B5.2 (A) Voltage maps of the (error minus correct) difference waves showing a clear medial frontocentral maximum. (B) Source model for the difference potential projected onto a 3D standard brain at 400 ms. The arrow points to the left SMA as the most likely generator. (From Möller et al., 2007, p. 1175.)

Full or partial spoonerisms were in fact produced on nearly 10 percent of the key trials that were expected to elicit them. When the researchers analyzed the brain potentials that were recorded during the period between the target pairs and the speech prompts—that is, while subjects were silently preparing to articulate the words—they found that on the key trials that elicited errors, but not on either the key trials that didn't elicit errors or the control trials, an increased negativity occurred at the central midline electrode site (Cz) 350–600 ms after the onset of the target pairs (Figure 6B5.1). Further analyses using source localization methods suggested that the neural generator of this effect was most likely in or near the left SMA (Figure 6B5.2).

How should we interpret these findings about the neural activity that occurs right before people produce spoonerisms? When subjects say *darn bore* instead of *barn door*, it is reasonable to suppose that two competing speech motor programs are competing with each other, and that the wrong one ultimately wins out (Baars, 1980). From the perspective of the DIVA Model, these processes can be understood more precisely as follows. The two programs are neurally fleshed out in the Articulator Velocity and Position Maps, and the incorrect one is accidentally released for execution by the Initiation Map, which is believed to reside in the SMA bilaterally. Thus, Guenther's neurocomputational framework converges quite nicely with Möller et al.'s (2007) ERP data, and in doing so it helps explain what the brain does before the tongue slips.

Box 6.6 When the Will Is Gone

The world-renowned neurologist Antonio Damasio provides the following account of a patient with akinetic mutism (Damasio, 1994, pp. 72–73):

The stroke suffered by this patient, whom I will call Mrs. T, produced extensive damage to the dorsal and medial regions of the frontal lobe in both hemispheres. She suddenly became motionless and speechless, and she would lie in bed with her eyes open but with a blank facial expression; I have often used the term "neutral" to convey the equanimity—or absence—of such an expression.

Her body was no more animated than her face. She might make a normal movement with arm and hand, to pull her bed covers for instance, but in general, her limbs were in repose. When asked about her situation, she usually would remain silent, although after much coaxing she might say her name, or the names of her husband and children, or the name of the town where she lived. But she would not tell you about her medical history, past or present, and she could not describe the events leading to her admission to the hospital. There was no way of knowing, then, whether she had no recollection of those events or whether she had a recollection but was unwilling or unable to talk about it. She never became upset with my insistent questioning, never showed a flicker or worry about herself or anything else. Months later, as she gradually emerged from this state of mutism and akinesia (lack of movement), and began to answer questions, she would clarify the mystery of her state of mind. Contrary to what one might have thought, her mind had not been imprisoned in the jail of her immobility. Instead it appeared that there had not been mind at all, no real thinking or reasoning. The passivity in her face and body was the appropriate reflection of her lack of mental animation. At this later date she was certain about not having felt anguished by the absence of communication. Nothing had forced her not to speak her mind. Rather, as she recalled, "I really had nothing to say."

when utterances are actually produced than when they are merely prepared for production (Indefrey & Levelt, 2004; Alario et al., 2006; Bohland & Guenther, 2006). It has also been linked with spoonerisms—like saying *darn bore* instead of *barn door*—which may occur when two competing speech plans are activated simultaneously and the incorrect one is inadvertently released instead of the correct one (Box 6.5). Furthermore, direct electrocortical stimulation of the SMA induces either speech arrest or involuntary vocalizations of simple consonant–vowel sequences such as *da-da-da* or *ta-ta-ta* (Brickner, 1940; Erickson & Woolsey, 1951; Penfield & Welch, 1951; Woolsey et al., 1979; Dinner & Lüders, 1995). Even more interesting, however, is that bilateral damage to the SMA and to surrounding regions along the medial wall of the prefrontal cortex sometimes brings about a peculiar disorder called **akinetic mutism**, in which spontaneous speech and movement are substantially reduced, while externally cued behaviors, including the repetition of utterances, are preserved (Laplane et al., 1977; Jonas, 1981; Krainik et al., 2003; Ure et al., 1998). By all appearances, this disturbing condition of silent passivity suggests the loss of what is commonly called the capacity for free will (Box 6.6). Fortunately for those who are affected, the impairment is typically transient (Rostomily et al., 1991; Chainay et al., 2009). It is worth adding that damage to the SMA in just the left hemisphere can cause a reduction of self-initiated verbal behavior that may be a variant of transcortical motor aphasia (Freedman et al., 1984; Robinson et al., 2013; see Chapter 3).

According to Guenther, the Initiation Map in the SMA is modulated by a circuit through the basal ganglia and thalamus. The basal ganglia form a tightly interconnected set of subcortical nuclei that contribute to the acquisition and online selection of adaptive (i.e., rewarding) vs. maladaptive (i.e., non-rewarding) cognitive and behavioral routines (see Chapter 1). Because they are part of a reciprocal loop with the SMA, the basal ganglia are believed to exert a powerful influence over which actions, including speech plans, are initiated in certain contexts. Among the many sources of evidence for this view is the fact that patients with Parkinson's disease, in whom the output from the basal ganglia to the SMA is diminished, have difficulty executing voluntary movements and also exhibit hypokinetic dysarthria, which is characterized by reduced speech

volume, speech freezing, and a tendency for syllables to run together (Duffy, 2005).

In summary, the feedforward control subsystem of the DIVA Model underlies the production of well-learned speech sounds under normal circumstances. Phonemes, syllables, and "chunked" syllable sequences are represented by single units in the Speech Sound Map, which is hypothesized to reside in the left posterior IFG and ventral premotor cortex. Activation of a particular unit in the Speech Sound Map sets up the corresponding vocal tract motor commands in the Articulator Velocity and Position Maps, which are hypothesized to reside in the ventral primary motor cortex bilaterally. Finally, these motor commands are released for execution by a "go" signal from the Initiation Map, which is hypothesized to reside in the SMA bilaterally, with modulatory influences from the basal ganglia.

A Quick Look at the Roles of Forward and Inverse Models in Motor Control

As a prelude to exploring the feedback control subsystem of the DIVA Model, it is worthwhile to familiarize ourselves with how so-called forward and inverse models contribute to motor control. This is because Guenther's framework draws heavily on these notions, which are well-established in computational neuroscience and engineering (e.g., Wolpert & Kawato, 1998; Wolpert & Flanagan, 2001) and which are well-suited to explain a variety of disorders involving motor cognition and behavior (e.g., Blakemore et al., 2002). Basically, a **forward model** indicates how certain motor commands should give rise to certain sensory consequences, whereas an **inverse model** indicates how certain sensory consequences can be achieved by executing certain motor commands.

Let's consider forward models first. Suppose you need to pick up a very large rock. You kneel down, grasp the rock firmly around its sides, channel all the strength you can muster into your arms and hands, and lift. Suddenly the rock rises up much faster than you expected, and your body along with it, because—surprise!—it turns out not to be a real rock at all, but rather a fake one made of styrofoam. When you were preparing to lift the rock, your brain was not only setting all its motor parameters for acting on a heavy object, but was also using those motor specifications to predict how your body would feel and how the rock would move when the action was executed. These

---

Akinetic mutism A neurological condition that frequently follows from damage to the SMA, and that involves a virtually complete loss of voluntary speech and movement.

Forward model A specification of how certain motor commands should give rise to certain sensory consequences.

Inverse model A specification of how certain sensory consequences can be achieved by executing certain motor commands.

predictions constituted your forward model, and in this particular instance, they turned out to be wrong, since the actual sensory feedback differed dramatically from what was anticipated. Such prediction errors are valuable, however, because your brain can use them to update forward models not only during online behavior (shortly after discovering that your lift was too fast, you no doubt slowed down), but also over the long term (when you lift large rocks again in the future, you may approach them with some suspicion).

What about inverse models? They are essentially the opposite of forward models, since their function is to estimate in advance the motor commands that are required to achieve particular sensory effects. Inverse models are, however, generally harder to construct than forward models. For example, think about how difficult it is to consistently hit the bullseye when throwing darts, or to sink three-point shots when playing basketball. The feedback that one receives is in visual coordinates, so correct and incorrect outcomes in this frame of reference must be converted to correct and incorrect behavioral instructions in terms of, most importantly, arm and hand movements. This is obviously not a straightforward learning process, although some people are able to fine-tune these skills to a remarkable degree.

Returning to the domain of speech processing, forward and inverse models play central roles not only in Guenther's framework, but also in many other approaches (Wilson & Iacoboni, 2006; Christoffels et al., 2007; Dhanjal et al., 2008; Rauscheker & Scott, 2009; Tian & Poeppel, 2010; Zheng et al., 2010; Price et al., 2011; Hickok, 2012; Perkell, 2012). In the specific context of Guenther's framework, they are incorporated roughly as follows (Figure 6.14). Forward models indicate how certain speech acts should have certain auditory and somatosensory consequences, and they are implemented as projections that extend from the Speech Sound Map to the auditory and somatosensory components. Inverse models indicate how certain speech sounds and feelings in the vocal tract can be achieved by certain articulatory commands, and they are implemented as projections that extend from the auditory and somatosensory components to the Articulator Velocity and Position Maps, via an intermediary mechanism for feedback control. These aspects of the framework are elaborated below. We will focus first on the auditory feedback circuit, and then shift to the somatosensory feedback circuit. (Warning: Don't be misled by the similar terminology of "forward models" and "feedforward control subsystem." The former are *not*, strictly speaking, part of the latter. Rather, forward models project *from* the feedforward control subsystem *to* the feedback control subsystem.)

Auditory Feedback Control

According to the DIVA Model, every time a speaker produces an utterance, the Speech Sound Map sends excitatory input not only to the Articulator Velocity and Position Maps, but also to a component of the feedback control subsystem called the **Auditory Target Map**. In agreement with the concept of a forward model, the latter pathway transmits a prediction about the kind of auditory feedback that should arise when the speaker hears himself or herself generate the utterance. This prediction is instantiated as the activation of an auditory target representation in the map (Niziolek et al., 2013). Because any linguistic expression, like *good doggie*, can be produced in a wide range of different but equally acceptable ways, auditory target representations are not specified as rigidly defined "points," but rather as loosely defined "regions," in auditory space; more precisely, they are specified as temporally extended trajectories through regions of auditory space, since they typically consist of sequences of sounds. The Auditory Target Map is believed to reside in the posterior STG and planum temporale bilaterally, and it is worth recalling that Hickok and Poeppel's (2000, 2004, 2007) Dual Stream Model of speech perception localizes the "phonological network" in the posterior STG/STS bilaterally. In addition, Guenther argues that the pathway leading from the Speech Sound Map to the Auditory Target Map includes a branching route that passes through portions of the cerebellum.

When an utterance is actually produced, the self-generated acoustic patterns are initially represented at the cortical level in the **Auditory State Map**, which is housed in the primary auditory cortex (Heschl's gyrus) and the planum temporale bilaterally. This feedback is then compared with the auditory target representation that was activated in the Auditory Target Map just milliseconds before, in order to determine whether the goal was successfully met. How does this comparison process work? It relies on yet another component called the **Auditory Error Map**, which is hypothesized to reside in the posterior STG and planum temporale bilaterally. As shown in Figure 6.14, both the Auditory Target

Auditory Target Map   A module that subserves auditory target representations (i.e., acoustic expectations) during speech production, and that resides in the posterior STG and planum temporale bilaterally.

Auditory State Map   A module that represents speech-related auditory input (including self-generated utterances), and that resides in Heschl's gyrus and the planum temporale bilaterally.

Auditory Error Map   A module that computes discrepancies between the anticipated and the actual sounds of self-generated utterances, and that resides in the posterior STG and planum temporale bilaterally.

Map and the Auditory State Map project to the Auditory Error Map, but the input from the Auditory Target Map is inhibitory, whereas the input from the Auditory State Map is excitatory. These different kinds of signals have the following effects. As a way of telling the Auditory Error Map exactly what would constitute a successfully produced utterance in the given situation, the Auditory Target Map *turns off* just those units in the Auditory Error Map that correspond to its own activated target representation. And as a way of telling the Auditory Error Map exactly what the generated utterance actually sounds like, the Auditory State Map *turns on* just those units in the Auditory Error Map that correspond to its own state representation. If the utterance was produced correctly, these two streams of top-down inhibitory and bottom-up excitatory input end up focusing on the very same units in the Auditory Error Map and hence cancel each other out, with the result being that the output of the map is zero activation. If, however, the utterance was produced somewhat incorrectly, the two streams end up focusing on somewhat different units in the Auditory Error Map, with the units inhibited top-down indicating features that *should have been present but were not,* and the units activated bottom-up indicating features that *were present but should not have been.*

Incidentally, this characterization of the neural substrates of the auditory feedback mechanism fits nicely with the Lemma Model's assumption that the "external" self-monitoring loop, which involves hearing one's own voice, depends on the posterior two-thirds of the bilateral superior temporal region (Indefrey & Levelt, 2004). It also predicts that neural responses to the sound of one's own voice should, at least in normal speaking conditions, be reduced relative to neural responses to the sound of other people's voices, and this has been confirmed by many studies (Creutzfeldt et al., 1989a, 1989b; Numminen & Curio, 1999; Numminen et al., 1999; Curio et al., 2000; Christoffels et al., 2007; Flinker et al., 2010; Jones et al., 2013; see also Eliades & Wang, 2008). Furthermore, it is notable that the planum temporale, which is thought to be part of the neural basis of the Auditory Error Map, includes area Spt (sylvian parietal-temporal), which supports the left-lateralized "sensorimotor interface" component of the Dual Stream Model of speech perception (see Chapter 5; see also Zheng, 2009).

How are the prediction error signals that are computed by the Auditory Error Map actually used to improve speech motor control? Consistent with the

> **Feedback Control Map**   A module that adjusts or updates articulatory commands in light of sensory feedback, and that resides in the right ventral premotor cortex.

concept of an inverse model, they are conveyed to an action programming module that is devoted to adjusting articulatory commands in light of sensory feedback. This component, which is a relatively new addition to the DIVA Model, is called the **Feedback Control Map**, and it is believed to reside in the right ventral premotor cortex. In the final stage of processing, the Feedback Control Map transmits updated motor instructions to the Articulator Velocity and Position Maps, both directly and through an indirect pathway that includes the superior medial cerebellum and part of the thalamus.

To test these ideas about the nature of auditory feedback control, Guenther and his colleagues conducted the following fMRI study (Tourville et al., 2008). While in the scanner, subjects read aloud visually presented one-syllable words (*bet, head,* etc.). During one of every four trials (randomly dispersed), the first formant frequency (F1) of the speaker's auditory feedback was shifted upward or downward by 30 percent—a perturbation that may seem large, but that is not very noticeable to the subject. About 4 seconds after the onset of the target word, two whole-brain scans were collected, each of which was 2 seconds in duration, and both of which were timed to occur during the peak period of the hemodynamic response function triggered by the subject's production of the word (Figure 6.18; as pointed out in Chapter 2, hemodynamic response functions take 4–6 seconds to peak).

Behaviorally, even though the auditory perturbations were not very salient, subjects compensated for them exactly as the investigators expected, based on previous research (Figure 6.19; Houde & Jordan, 1998; Bauer et al., 2006; Jones & Munhall, 2005; Purcell & Munhall, 2006; see also Cai et al., 2011). When the F1 of the vowel

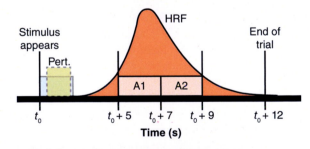

Figure 6.18   Timeline of a single trial in the fMRI study by Tourville et al. (2008). At the onset of each trial, the visual stimulus appeared and remained onscreen for 2 s (blue rectangle). On perturbed trials, auditory feedback was shifted during the subject's response (green). About 3 s after stimulus offset, two whole-brain volumes were acquired (A1 and A2). Data acquisition was timed to cover the peak of the hemodynamic response to speech; the putative hemodynamic response function (HRF) is schematized in orange. The next trial started 3 s after data acquisition was complete, resulting in a total trial length of 12 s. (From Guenther & Vladusich, 2012, p. 414.)

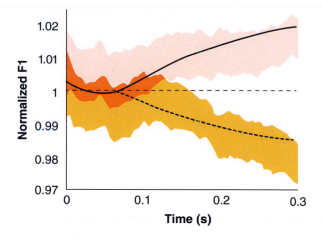

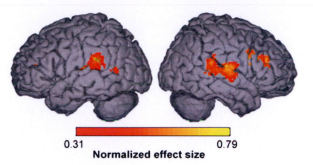

0.31 ━━━━━━━━ **0.79**
Normalized effect size

Figure 6.19 Comparison of the first formant frequency (F1) trajectories produced by human subjects (shaded regions) and the DIVA Model (lines) when F1 is unexpectedly perturbed during production of a syllable. Utterances were perturbed by shifting F1 upward or downward by 30% throughout the syllable. Traces are shown for 300 ms starting from the onset of the perturbation at the beginning of vocalization. Shaded areas denote the 95% confidence intervals for normalized F1 values during upward (lower region) and downward (higher region) perturbations in the experimental study. Lines indicate values obtained from a DIVA Model simulation of the auditory perturbation experiment. Both the human subjects and the model show compensation for the perturbation starting approximately 75-100 ms after perturbation onset. (From Guenther & Vladusich, 2012, p. 415.)

Figure 6.20 Neural responses in the *shift–no shift* contrast in the fMRI study by Tourville et al. (2008). Activation of the posterior perisylvian region occurred bilaterally. This activation included the planum temporale, which is not visible in the figure. In the right hemisphere, greater responses were found in the ventral premotor cortex and inferior frontal gyrus. (From Guenther & Vladusich, 2012, p. 415.)

Sakai, 2003; Fu et al., 2006; Toyomura et al., 2007; see also Levy & Wagner, 2011).

As a final observation, it is worth mentioning that stuttering has been hypothesized to reflect, in part, an overreliance on auditory feedback during speech production, and this idea recently received new support from a series of computer simulations using the DIVA Model (Civier et al., 2010; Box 6.7).

Somatosensory Feedback Control

The DIVA Model's somatosensory feedback circuit operates alongside the auditory one and has essentially the same kind of functional organization. When an utterance is produced, the Speech Sound Map activates (directly as well as indirectly via portions of the cerebellum) a somatosensory target representation in the **Somatosensory Target Map**, which is believed to reside in certain sectors of the inferior parietal lobule bilaterally—specifically, the ventral somatosensory cortex and the anterior supramarginal gyrus. In line with the notion of a forward model, this target representation specifies the range of tactile and proprioceptive sensations that are expected to be felt in the vocal tract if the utterance is produced correctly. For example, when the consonant /t/ is produced, the tongue tip should be felt as touching the alveolar ridge, and when the vowel /i/ is produced, the tongue body should be felt as occupying a high front position without touching

was artificially shifted upward, subjects adjusted their speech by moving it back down, and when it was artificially shifted downward, subjects adjusted their speech by moving it back up. Even more interesting, however, is that a computer simulation of essentially the same experimental protocol using the DIVA Model led to comparable results (Figure 6.19).

Turning to the brain, a contrast between the shift condition and the no-shift condition revealed activations in many of the regions that were predicted to be engaged (Figure 6.20; see also Hashimoto & Sakai, 2003; Fu et al., 2006; van de Ven, 2009; Zheng et al., 2010). Most importantly, significant increases were found in the posterior STG and planum temporale bilaterally. These changes may reflect the operation of the Auditory Error Map, since that component should respond more strongly when it detects discrepancies between anticipated and actual acoustic patterns. Also noteworthy is the engagement of the right ventral premotor cortex, since it may subserve the Auditory Feedback Map that functions as a hub for transforming prediction errors into corrective commands to the Articulator Velocity and Position Maps (for supporting data see Hashimoto &

Somatosensory Target Map A module that subserves somatosensory target representations (i.e., tactile and proprioceptive expectations) during speech production, and that resides in the ventral somatosensory cortex and anterior supramarginal gyrus bilaterally.

Box 6.7   Using the DIVA Model to Simulate Stuttering

Civier et al. (2010) point out that in a classic book called *The Nature of Stuttering*, Charles Van Riper (1982, p. 383) describes a man who stopped stuttering "after an incident in which he became completely deafened. The cessation of stuttering occurred within three hours of the trauma and shortly after he began to speak." This remarkable anecdote dovetails nicely with the view that stuttering may be due, at least in part, to overreliance on auditory feedback (Max et al., 2004). This approach maintains that for persons who stutter (PWS), the primary disorder involves a delay in the propagation of motor commands through the feedforward control subsystem (for recent evidence see Chang et al., 2011). Because the intended speech output is slowed down, the auditory feedback control subsystem does not receive the expected acoustic input. It therefore sends a "reset" signal to the feedforward control subsystem, which attempts to repair the problem by effectively restarting the current syllable. The whole cycle can occur multiple times, giving rise to the repetitions that are characteristic of PWS. Interestingly, neuroimaging studies of speech production in PWS have reliably found increased activity in the right ventral premotor cortex, which is the hypothesized locus of the Feedback Control Map in the DIVA Model (Brown et al., 2005). In addition, Civier et al. (2010) demonstrated that a "neurally impaired" version of the DIVA Model can simulate several prominent aspects of stuttering. Basically, when the model was biased away from feedforward control and toward feedback control, it mimicked both the types of errors that are produced by PWS and the ways in which they are repaired. Moreover, like PWS, the model's fluency improved not only when it was given more time to generate its output, but also when background noise was introduced to prevent the detection of errors. Although the hypothesis that stuttering reflects overreliance on auditory feedback has some non-trivial limitations (Namasivayam et al., 2009), it is clearly bolstered by these findings.

the palate or teeth. Somatosensory feedback is initially represented at the cortical level in the **Somatosensory State Map**, which is housed in the ventral somatosensory cortex. The determination of whether an utterance was in fact produced correctly is made by the **Somatosensory Error Map**, which is thought to depend on the ventral somatosensory cortex and the anterior supramarginal gyrus. The units in this map that correspond to the target representation are inhibited in a top-down manner by the Somatosensory Target Map, while the units that correspond to the actual feedback are excited in a bottom-up manner by the Auditory State Map. If the utterance was produced correctly, the very same units are both inhibited from above and excited from below, leading to a final output of zero activation. But if errors were made, they are revealed by (1) the units that end up being fully suppressed by the inhibitory input from the Auditory Target Map, and (2) the units that end up being fully engaged by the excitatory input from the Auditory State Map. Consistent with the notion of an inverse model, these prediction error signals are then propagated to the Feedback

Control Map, which participates in both the auditory and somatosensory feedback circuits. From there, corrective commands are sent to the Articulator Velocity and Position Maps, just as described above in the context of the auditory feedback circuit.

Before going on to look at some experimental data, it is worth highlighting the fact that by postulating parallel circuits for both auditory and somatosensory feedback control, the DIVA Model goes considerably beyond the Lemma Model, since the latter framework only incorporates a loop for auditory self-monitoring. In addition, whereas the feedback component of the Lemma Model is mostly limited to repairing relatively large errors—i.e., ones that require interrupting the flow of speech—the feedback subsystem in the DIVA Model is also capable of repairing relatively small errors—i.e., ones that do not require interrupting the flow of speech.

Guenther and his colleagues tested their conception of the somatosensory feedback circuit by conducting the following fMRI study (Golfinopoulos et al., 2011). While in the scanner, subjects read aloud visually presented two-syllable pseudowords (*abi, agi,* etc.). During one of every seven trials (randomly dispersed), a small, stiff balloon lying between the molars was rapidly inflated to a diameter of 1–1.5 cm while the vowel of the first syllable was being uttered. Previous work had shown that subjects immediately compensate for this blockage of upward jaw movement by raising their tongue higher. The aim of the fMRI study was to investigate the neural underpinnings

Somatosensory State Map   A module that represents tactile and proprioceptive input during speech production, and that resides in the ventral somatosensory cortex bilaterally.

Somatosensory Error Map   A module that computes discrepancies between the anticipated and the actual tactile and proprioceptive sensations associated with speech production, and that resides in the ventral somatosensory cortex and anterior supramarginal gyrus bilaterally.

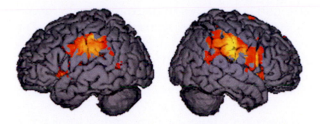

Figure 6.21 Neural responses in the *perturbed–unperturbed* contrast in an fMRI experiment investigating the effects of unexpected jaw perturbation when pseudowords are read aloud. Activation occurred in the ventral somatosensory cortex and anterior supramarginal gyrus bilaterally. The right ventral premotor cortex was also engaged. (From Guenther & Vladusich, 2012, p. 417.)

of this process. As in the study of the auditory feedback circuit, after each pseudoword was presented, two whole-brain scans were collected during the peak period of the hemodynamic response function. Relative to the unperturbed condition, the perturbed condition was associated with significantly greater activation in several key areas (Figure 6.21). First, the supramarginal gyrus was engaged bilaterally, a finding that may reflect the recruitment of the Somatosensory Error Map, as predicted by the theory. In addition, activation was observed in the right ventral premotor cortex, which is the hypothesized location of the Feedback Control Map. These results not only provide further support for the DIVA Model, but add substantially to other studies that point to an important role of the somatosensory system in speech motor control (Tremblay et al., 2003; Nasir & Ostroy, 2006, 2008, 2009; Lametti et al., 2012).

In light of these considerations, it is rather surprising that the inferior parietal cortex did not show up in Indefrey and Levelt's (2004) meta-analysis of functional neuroimaging studies of spoken word production (see Figure 6.9). After all, our discussion of the DIVA Model suggests that this brain region contributes to self-monitoring processes, especially when they involve corrective feedback from tactile and proprioceptive signals originating in the vocal tract. An initial step toward reconciling the data does come, however, from the more recent meta-analysis reported by Indefrey (2011), since it supports the view that the inferior parietal cortex plays an important role in generating words.

Some Challenges Facing the Model

The DIVA Model is, without a doubt, one of the most sophisticated neurocomputational approaches to speech motor control currently available. It is not, however, without limitations, and Guenther and his colleagues will surely

continue to refine it as new theoretical, empirical, and technological developments unfold in the future. Below we briefly consider two issues that may require more attention.

The Island of Reil

Deep inside the sylvian fissure there lies a large expanse of cortical tissue that is now called the **insula**, but which was once referred to rather poetically as the "island of Reil" (Figure 6.22). Throughout most of the history of human neurobiology, virtually nothing was known about this hidden region of the brain. In recent years, however, it has received intense scrutiny, and in early 2010 a PubMed search for "insula AND imaging" yielded 30,415 references (Craig, 2010)! Although the insula has been associated with a wide range of functions, most of them seem to involve, in one way or another, interoception—that is, the representation of the internal physiological condition of the body, including heart rate, temperature, pain, visceral sensations, and so forth (for reviews see Craig, 2002, 2009; but see also Damasio et al., 2013). In the domain of language, however, the insula is best known as possibly playing a role in speech motor control (for a review see Ackermann & Riecker, 2010).

Insula A large cortical region stretched along the floor of the sylvian fissure.

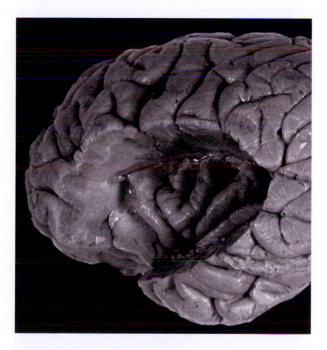

Figure 6.22 The exposed left insular cortex of a human brain. (From the Digital Anatomist: http://www9.biostr.washington.edu/da.html.)

The first major breakthrough was made by Dronkers (1996). As noted in Chapter 2, she found that each of 25 chronic stroke patients with apraxia of speech (AOS) had damage in a particular portion of the left anterior insula—specifically, the superior tip of the precentral gyrus—whereas none of 19 patients without AOS had damage there (Figure 6.23; see also Table 6.4). This discovery was interpreted as constituting strong evidence that the left anterior insula is necessary for at least some aspect(s) of the planning of complex articulatory movements during speech production, and several subsequent neuropsychological studies provided further support (Nagao et al., 1999; Ogar et al., 2006; Baldo et al., 2011).

Other neuropsychological studies, however, have generated results that are at odds with this view. For instance, as noted, once again, in Chapter 2, Hillis et al. (2004b) examined 80 acute stroke patients, 40 with and 40 without left anterior insula damage, and did not find a close connection between AOS and lesions in that brain region; instead, AOS was most reliably linked with damage in Broca's area (see Tables 2.3 and 2.4 in Chapter 2). Similar results were also reported by Richardson

et al. (2012) in a study involving chronic stroke patients. In addition, AOS does not frequently appear after the surgical removal of the left anterior insula in patients suffering from brain tumors that infiltrate or encroach on that territory (Zentner et al., 1996; Duffau et al., 2001). And finally, in those cases where damage to the left anterior insula does give rise to AOS, it is conceivable that the deficit is not really due to the cortical lesion per se, but rather to the severing of the arcuate fasciculus, which occupies the white matter immediately beneath the cortical tissue (Figure 6.24; Bonilha & Fridriksson, 2009).

Unlike the rather mixed picture painted by the neuropsychological data, functional neuroimaging studies more consistently support the idea that the left anterior insula is an important node within the distributed neural network that subserves speech motor control (Eickhoff et al., 2009). For instance, this region is engaged in the following conditions that place high demands on articulatory orchestration: production of randomly changing utterances relative to repetition of the same utterance (Nota & Honda, 2003); repetition of pseudowords relative to repetition of real words (Shuster, 2009); and repetition of pseudowords with novel non-native syllables relative to repetition of pseudowords with familiar native syllables (Moser et al., 2009). In addition, both Bohland and Guenther (2006) and Riecker et al. (2008)

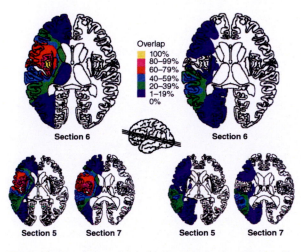

Overlap
100%
80–99%
60–79%
40–59%
20–39%
1–19%
0%

Section 6   Section 6

Section 5   Section 7   Section 5   Section 7

Figure 6.23 Comparison of lesion overlap in patients with and without chronic apraxia of speech. (A) Overlapping the lesions of 25 patients with apraxia of speech yields a common area of infarction (yellow) on section 6 of the reconstruction program (top of figure). This region represents an area of 100% overlap, that is, all 25 patients with this articulatory planning disorder have lesions that include this one area of the insula. In the bottom row are shown the neighboring sections either below (section 5) or above (section 7) the critical slice. (B) Overlapping the lesions of 19 patients without apraxia of speech shows infarctions over much of the left hemisphere as in the previous group. However, a comparison of section 6 in the two groups reveals that not one of these 19 patients without apraxia of speech has a lesion in the same region of the insula as those who do exhibit the disorder. (From Dronkers, 1996, p. 159.)

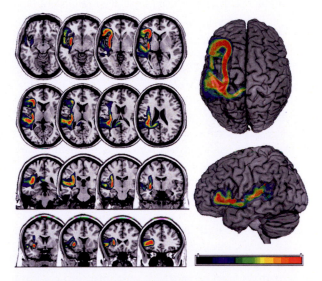

Figure 6.24 Results of a DTI study showing the anatomical location of reconstructed white matter pathways of the arcuate fasciculus travelling from the posterior superior temporal gyrus (BA22) to the posterior inferior frontal gyrus (BA44 and BA45). The scale bar represents the degree of overlap of fiber tracts among the subjects. Pathways are overlaid onto multiple slices as well as a transparent 3D reconstruction of a normal brain template. Note that the pathways course directly beneath the left anterior insula. (From Bonilha & Fridriksson, 2009, p. 2.)

showed that increases in the complexity of consonant cluster production correlate with increases in the strength of anterior insula activation. A caveat, however, is that the activation reported by Bohland and Guenther (2006) extended through the transition zone from the left anterior insula to the adjacent ventromedial portion of Broca's area. They suggest that this stretch of cortex "may be a substrate for the integration of the lower level aspects of the speech motor plan with more abstract representations of speech sounds used in sequence planning" (Bohland & Guenther, 2006, p. 835). Later in the same passage, however, they point out that, "alternatively, this region may be a portion of the speech sound map itself" (Bohland & Guenther, 2006, p. 835).

It is not yet clear exactly how the left anterior insula contributes to speech motor control, but the weight of evidence seems to favor the general hypothesis that it does play some sort of role (for an evolutionary perspective see Jezzini et al., 2012). One intriguing proposal—an idea that takes into account the literature implicating this brain region in interoception—is that the left anterior insula may facilitate speech fluency by monitoring the kind of voluntary respiratory activities that are needed in order to talk at a normal rate and volume without running out of breath (Ackermann & Riecker, 2010). This conjecture, along with many others, will undoubtedly be tested in the years to come. And as this field of research continues to advance, it may become increasingly worthwhile for the insula to be incorporated into the architecture of the DIVA Model.

Are the Auditory and Somatosensory Feedback Circuits Integrated in the Planum Temporale?

Another issue that warrants closer attention involves the functional–anatomical relation between the auditory and somatosensory feedback circuits. According to the DIVA Model, these circuits converge in the Feedback Control Map, which is thought to depend on the right ventral premotor cortex, but otherwise they are assumed to be segregated. However, an fMRI study conducted by Dhanjal et al. (2008) suggests that the two modalities of feedback may be integrated at an earlier stage of processing, specifically in the planum temporale.

The participants in this study performed the following four tasks: (1) propositional speech (defining simple, high-frequency nouns like *car*); (2) non-propositional speech (counting upward from 1 at a rate of one number per second); (3) silent jaw movements; and (4) silent tongue movements. As expected, relative to a baseline rest condition, the two overt speech tasks engaged the planum temporale, a region that the DIVA Model treats as a critical part of the auditory feedback circuit. Somewhat surprisingly, however, these two tasks did not engage the anterior inferior parietal cortex, a region that the DIVA Model treats as a critical part of the somatosensory feedback circuit. In addition, relative to the baseline rest condition, the two non-speech tasks engaged not only the anterior inferior parietal cortex, in accord with the predictions, but also the planum temporale, which was not anticipated, since the tasks did not involve either vocal content or auditory feedback.

These results have several implications. First, they indicate that the planum temporale is sensitive to both the auditory and somatosensory consequences of movements of the articulators. Other evidence that the planum temporale is capable of integrating information perceived through hearing and touch/proprioception comes from previous studies with both humans (Foxe et al., 2002; Schurmann et al., 2006) and monkeys (Leinonen et al., 1980; Schroeder et al., 2001; Fu et al., 2003; Kayser et al., 2005). In the domain of language, Dhanjal et al. (2008) propose that during self-initiated speech, the anatomical convergence of auditory and somatosensory feedback in the planum temporale may serve the function of facilitating the precise temporal coordination of rapid articulatory gestures. Another implication of the fMRI study has to do with the lack of significant neural responses in the anterior inferior parietal cortex in the two speech conditions. According to Dhanjal et al. (2008), this may reflect a learning process. In particular, they suggest that as speech skills are acquired and refined, somatosensory feedback is shifted from the anterior inferior parietal cortex to the planum temporale, where it can be more accurately synchronized and integrated with auditory feedback. (Incidentally, such an account may also help explain why the parietal region was not found to be reliably activated in Indefrey & Levelt's [2004] meta-analysis of imaging studies of speech production.) Overall, this study sheds new light on the perceptual systems that influence speech production, and in doing so it raises interesting questions about the DIVA Model's assumptions regarding the relation between auditory and somatosensory feedback circuits.

Peripheral Mechanisms of Speech Production

As shown in Figure 6.14, the final output of the DIVA Model is a set a motor commands that project from the Articulator Velocity and Position Maps to the vocal apparatus via subcortical nuclei. When we talk, these pathways implement the rapid coordination of up to 80 different muscles, most of which belong to the following three systems: control of respiration; control of laryngeal activity; and control of supralaryngeal movements involving the lips, jaw, velum, and tongue. Needless to say, the peripheral mechanisms of speech production are quite complex. Because this topic is covered in detail elsewhere (e.g., Smith, 1992; Jürgens, 2002; Bhatnagar, 2002; Wilson-Pauwels et al., 2002), only a very brief description is given here in this final section of the chapter.

Motor commands to the vocal apparatus are routed first from the ventral motor cortex to a set of subcortical nuclei, and then from those nuclei to the appropriate muscle groups. Most of the relevant subcortical nuclei are located in the brainstem and contain **cranial nerves (CNs)** that provide motor and sensory innervation for the head and neck (Figures 6.25–6.26 and Table 6.5). However, some of the relevant subcortical nuclei, particularly those involved in respiration and some aspects of laryngeal control, are located in the spinal cord. Here we will restrict our attention to the CNs, of which there are a total of twelve. Cell bodies of the olfactory nerve (CN I) reside in the olfactory bulb (not shown in Figure 6.25); cell bodies of the optic nerve (CN II) reside in the optic tract; cell bodies of the oculomotor nerve (CN III) reside in the midbrain; cell bodies of the trochlear nerve (CN IV) and trigeminal nerve (CN V) reside in the pons; and cell bodies of the abducens nerve (CN VI), facial nerve (CN VII), vestibulocochlear nerve (CN VIII), glossopharyngeal nerve (CN IX), vagus nerve (CN X), accessory nerve (CN XI), and hypoglossal nerve (CN XII) reside in the medulla.

Cranial nerves (CNs)   A set of brainstem nuclei that provide motor and sensory innervation for the head and neck.

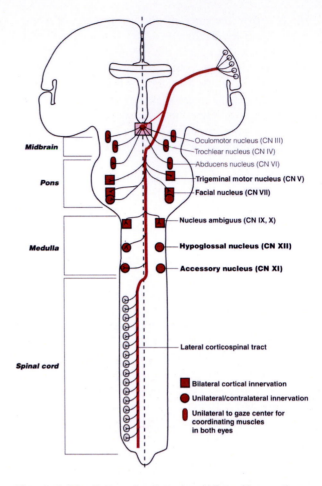

Figure 6.26   Pattern of unilateral and bilateral innervation of cranial nerves. (From Bhatnagar, 2002, p. 284.)

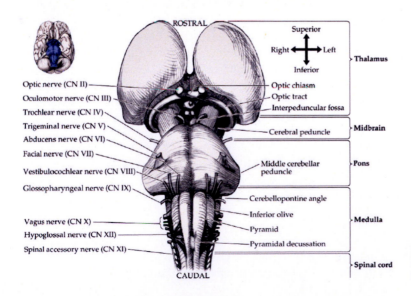

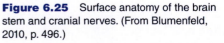

Figure 6.25   Surface anatomy of the brain stem and cranial nerves. (From Blumenfeld, 2010, p. 496.)

Table 6.5   Cranial Nerve Functions

Number	Name	Function
I	Olfactory	Sensory: Smell
II	Optic	Sensory: Vision
III	Oculomotor	Motor: Controls muscles for moving eyeball, pupil, and upper lid
IV	Trochlear	Motor: Controls oblique muscle of eye
V	Trigeminal	Motor: Jaw movement Sensory: Tactile and proprioceptive sensations from skin and muscles in face, mouth, teeth, and anterior two-thirds of tongue
VI	Abducens	Motor: Eye movement
VII	Facial	Motor: Controls muscles for facial expression, including lip movement; regulates secretions of salivary glands Sensory: Taste for anterior two-thirds of tongue
VIII	Vestibulocochlear	Sensory: Balance and hearing
IX	Glossopharyngeal	Motor: Swallowing; elevation of pharynx and larynx Sensory: General sensation from palate and posterior third of tongue; taste for posterior third of tongue
X	Vagus	Motor: Controls muscles of larynx, pharynx, soft palate; innervates glands, muscles in heart, blood vessels, trachea, bronchi, esophagus, stomach, intestine Sensory: General sensation from pharynx, larynx, thorax, abdomen, heart
XI	Accessory	Motor: Turning of head and shrugging of shoulders
XII	Hypoglossal	Motor: Tongue movement

The axonal projections from the motor cortex to the CNs constitute what is called the **corticobulbar pathway**. The neurons in the motor cortex are sometimes called **upper motor neurons (UMNs)**, and those constituting the cranial nerves are sometimes called **lower motor neurons (LMNs)**. As noted above in the summary of the Articulator Velocity and Position Maps, damage to UMNs in the ventral motor cortex can cause spastic dysarthria, but the disorder is only severe if the lesions are bilateral. This is because each side of the trigeminal, facial, glossopharyngeal, and vagal nerves—which together regulate the movements of the jaw, lips, larynx, pharynx,

Corticobulbar pathway   Projections from neurons in the motor cortex to the cranial nerves.

Upper motor neurons (UMNs)   Another term for neurons in the motor cortex.

Lower motor neurons (LMNs)   Another term for cranial nerves.

Flaccid dysarthria   A disorder of speech motor control that involves breathy voice, monotonous pitch and loudness, hypernasality, and impaired consonant production, and that results from damage to the cell bodies and/or axons of the cranial nerves that regulate the muscles of the vocal apparatus.

and palate—receives input from both sides of the motor cortex, so the effects of a unilateral cortical lesion can usually be compensated for by the intact contralateral hemisphere. However, each side of the hypoglossal nerve—which regulates tongue movement—receives input from just the contralateral motor cortex, so unilateral damage to tongue-related UMNs can impair movement of the contralateral side of the tongue, causing mild to moderate problems with speech motor control (Figure 6.26).

Lesions in the brainstem that damage the bodies and/or the muscle-directed axons of the LMNs critical for speech production can bring about a different kind of disorder called **flaccid dysarthria**. Because the pertinent muscles no longer receive their normal innervation, they become weak and gradually degenerate. The speech of patients with this condition is characterized by breathy voice, monotonous pitch and loudness, hypernasality, and impaired consonant production (Duffy, 2005).

Many of the CNs have sensory functions, and some of them contribute to the somatosensory feedback circuit of the DIVA Model by providing tactile and proprioceptive input from the peripheral organs of the vocal apparatus (Table 6.5). These sensory pathways have the following organization. First-order cells innervate the relevant sensory organs (lips, tongue, larynx, etc.). These cells transmit signals to second-order cells in the brainstem, which then relay information up to third-order cells in the thalamus, which finally project to cells in the ventral somatosensory cortex. (For an illustration of the peripheral auditory system, see Box 5.2 in Chapter 5.)

Summary and Key Points

The Lemma Model of Lexical Selection and Form Encoding

- According to this theory, the architecture that supports word production consists of two main subsystems: one for lexical selection, that is, identifying the most appropriate word in the mental lexicon; and another for form encoding, that is, preparing the word's articulatory shape.
- The lexical selection subsystem handles the first two stages of processing, which are as follows.

  - *Conceptual focusing and perspective-taking* involve converting the thought one wishes to express into the most appropriate lexical concept, that is, into a semantic structure that constitutes the meaning of a particular word. The neural correlates of this initial stage of processing are not yet understood. However, the lexical concepts encoded by concrete nouns may reside in the ATLs, the resolution of conflicts between co-activated lexical concepts may depend on the left IFG, and socially oriented perspective-taking may recruit a distributed network of frontal, temporal, and parietal regions that collectively underlie "mentalizing" or the "theory of mind."
  - *Lemma selection* involves mapping the selected lexical concept onto the corresponding lemma, that is, onto an abstract word node that not only intervenes between semantics and phonology but also points to pertinent morphosyntactic features. When the target word is a concrete noun, this second stage of processing may be subserved by the left mid MTG during a time window between 150 and 225 ms post-stimulus onset. Neighboring areas in the left temporal pole and inferotemporal cortex may also contribute to lemma selection in category-specific ways. Also, when the target word is an action verb, the critical brain regions may be the left IFG and, to a lesser extent, the left inferior parietal lobule and mid/posterior MTG.

- The form encoding subsystem handles the last three stages of processing, which are as follows.

  - *Retrieving morphemic phonological codes* involves selecting and spelling out the segmental phonological representation of the target word. This stage may depend on the left posterior STG/STS as well as the left posterior MTG, and it may take place during a time window between 200 and 400 ms post-stimulus onset. Importantly, the speed of lexical–phonological retrieval is modulated by word frequency.
  - *Prosodification and syllabification* involve determining the metrical and syllabic structure of the target word. The syllabification process is incremental and context-sensitive, taking place "on the fly." It may be executed by the left posterior IFG during a time window between 400 and 600 ms post-stimulus onset.
  - *Phonetic encoding and articulation* involve activating precompiled units in the "syllabary" and generating an "articulatory score" to drive the vocal apparatus. The syllabary depends on the left posterior IFG, and the articulatory score is subserved in part by the left and right ventral primary motor and primary somatosensory cortices, the SMA, and the cerebellum.

- The ability to detect and correct our own speech errors is facilitated by a self-monitoring system that consists of the following two feedback loops.

  - The "external" feedback loop monitors the auditory signals of self-produced speech. It may be implemented in the posterior two-thirds of the superior temporal region bilaterally.
  - The "internal" feedback loop monitors the covert process of generating phonological words. Its neural substrates may overlap those of the external feedback loop.

- The Lemma Model faces several challenges, two of which are as follows.

  - Based on data from brain-damaged patients who make semantic errors that are restricted to either oral output or written output, some neuropsychologists have questioned the plausibility of a representational level for amodal lemmas.
  - The theory assumes that processing is discrete, that is, strictly feedforward and such that the computations at a given level are completed before activation propagates to the next level. But there is evidence supporting the alternative view that some processing is interactive, that is, flowing bidirectionally and such that the computations at a given level need not be completed before activation propagates to the next level.

The DIVA Model of Speech Motor Control

- To some extent, the DIVA Model begins where the Lemma Model leaves off—with phonetic encoding and articulation. It provides a more sophisticated treatment of these processes, and it attributes a more important role to feedback mechanisms.
- According to this theory, the architecture that supports speech motor control consists of two main subsystems: one for feedforward control, that is, activating motor commands for articulatory gestures and transmitting them to the vocal apparatus via subcortical nuclei; and another for feedback control, that is, using auditory and somatosensory input from self-produced speech to recognize errors and send corrective instructions to the articulatory component.
- The feedforward control subsystem is organized as follows.

  - The Speech Sound Map is a repository of acquired speech sound representations (mostly syllabic units) that serve as the starting point for articulation, and that reside in the left posterior IFG and ventral premotor cortex.
  - The Articulatory Velocity and Position Maps contain vocal tract representations (of the larynx, lips, jaw, tongue, and palate) that specify the "articulatory score" of utterances, and that reside in the ventral primary motor cortex bilaterally.
  - The Initiation Map is a module that sends a "go" signal to prepared speech motor commands, and that resides in the SMA bilaterally, with modulatory influences from the basal ganglia.
  - During speech production, activation of a particular unit in the Speech Sound Map engages the corresponding vocal tract motor commands in the Articulatory Velocity and Position Maps, and those commands are released by a "go" signal from the Initiation Map.

- The auditory feedback circuit is organized as follows.

  - The Auditory Target Map is a module that subserves auditory target representations (i.e., acoustic expectations) during speech production, and that resides in the posterior STG and planum temporale bilaterally.
  - The Auditory State Map is a module that represents speech-related auditory input (including self-generated utterances), and that resides in Heschl's gyrus and the planum temporale bilaterally.
  - The Auditory Error Map is a module that computes discrepancies between the anticipated and the actual sounds of self-generated utterances, and that resides in the posterior STG and planum temporale bilaterally.
  - The Feedback Control Map is a module that adjusts or updates articulatory commands in light of sensory feedback, and that resides in the right ventral premotor cortex.
  - During speech production, the Speech Sound Map not only sends feedforward instructions to the Articulatory Velocity and Position Maps, but also sends an anticipatory message to the Auditory Target Map, indicating how the utterance should ideally sound. The acoustic signals of the actual utterance are represented in the Auditory State Map, and those signals are matched against the target representation by the Auditory Error Map. If the utterance was produced correctly, the error map does not generate any output, but if it was produced incorrectly, the error map alerts the Feedback Control Map, which then sends corrective motor commands to the Articulatory Velocity and Position Maps.

- The somatosensory feedback circuit is organized along the same lines as the auditory one.

  - The Somatosensory Target Map is a module that subserves somatosensory target representations (i.e., tactile and proprioceptive expectations) during speech production, and that resides in the ventral somatosensory cortex and anterior supramarginal gyrus bilaterally.
  - The Somatosensory State Map is a module that represents tactile and proprioceptive input during speech production, and that resides in the ventral somatosensory cortex bilaterally.
  - The Somatosensory Error Map is a module that computes discrepancies between the anticipated and the actual tactile and proprioceptive sensations accociated with speech production, and that resides in the ventral somatosensory cortex and anterior supramarginal gyrus bilaterally.
  - The Feedback Control Map is the same as described above.
  - During speech production, the Speech Sound Map not only sends feedforward instructions to the Articulatory Velocity and Position Maps, but also sends an anticipatory message to the Somatosensory Target Map, indicating how the utterance should ideally feel in the vocal tract. The tactile and proprioceptive signals of the actual utterance are represented in the Somatosensory State Map, and those signals are matched against the target representation by the Somatosensory Error Map. If the utterance was produced correctly, the error map does not generate any output, but if it was produced incorrectly, the error map alerts the Feedback Control Map, which then sends corrective motor commands to the Articulatory Velocity and Position Maps.

- Among the limitations of the DIVA Model are the following two issues.

  - Based on a combination of neuropsychological and neuroimaging studies, it seems likely that the left anterior insula contributes to speech motor control, but this brain region is not explicitly taken into account by the theory.

(Continued)

(Continued)

    o The framework assumes that the auditory and somatosensory feedback circuits do not converge until the Feedback Control Map, but there are reasons to suppose that the two types of sensory input are integrated at an earlier stage of processing, specifically in the planum temporale.

Peripheral Mechanisms of Speech Production

- Vocal tract representations in the primary motor cortex project to brainstem nuclei via the corticobulbar pathway.
- These brainstem nuclei contain 12 sets of cranial nerves that innervate the head and neck.
- The cells in the primary motor cortex are sometimes called upper motor neurons, and those constituting the cranial nerves are sometimes called lower motor neurons.
- The cranial nerves not only transmit outgoing motor signals to the organs constituting the vocal apparatus, but also carry incoming sensory signals from the very same organs.

Recommended Reading

The Lemma Model of Lexical Selection and Form Encoding

- Levelt, W.J.M., Roelofs, A., & Meyer, A.S. (1999). A theory of lexical access in speech production. *Behavioral and Brain Sciences, 22,* 1–75. A comprehensive presentation of the Lemma Model, together with commentaries by 23 experts in the field and a response by Levelt, Roelofs, and Meyer.
- Levelt, W.J.M. (2001). Spoken word production: A theory of lexical access. *Proceedings of the National Academy of Sciences, 98,* 13464–13471. A concise summary of the theory for non-specialists.
- Indefrey, P., & Levelt, W.J.M. (2004). The spatial and temporal signatures of word production components. *Cognition, 92,* 101–144. A meta-analysis and in-depth discussion of 82 studies investigating the neural correlates of different aspects of spoken word production, interpreted from the perspective of the Lemma Model.
- Indefrey, P. (2011). The spatial and temporal signatures of word production components: A critical update. *Frontiers in Psychology,* Vol. 2, Article 255. An important follow-up to the previous paper.
- Rapp, B., & Goldrick, M. (2006). Speaking words: Contributions of cognitive neuropsychological research. *Cognitive Neuropsychology, 23,* 39–73. A survey of major neuropsychological insights about spoken word production, some of which putatively challenge the assumptions of the Lemma Model.

The DIVA Model of Speech Motor Control

- Guenther, F.H., & Vladusich, T. (2012). A neural theory of speech acquisition and production. *Journal of Neurolinguistics, 25,* 408–422. An accessible synopsis of the architecture and operation of the model, together with summaries of some important supporting studies.
- Bohland, J.W., & Guenther, F.H. (2006). An fMRI investigation of syllable sequence production. *NeuroImage, 32,* 821–841. A detailed exploration of the neural substrates of speech motor control, partly inspired by the model.
- Tourville, J.A., Reilly, K., & Guenther, F.H. (2008). Neural mechanisms underlying auditory feedback control of speech. *NeuroImage, 39,* 1429–1443. An fMRI study testing the model's predictions about the neural substrates of the auditory feedback circuit.
- Ackermann, H., & Ziegler, W. (2010). Brain mechanisms underlying speech motor control. In W.J. Hardcastle, J. Laver, & F.E. Gibbon (Eds.), *The handbook of phonetics,* 2nd edition (pp. 202–250). Malden, MA: Wiley-Blackwell. An excellent overview of the neural substrates of speech motor control from a different perspective.

Peripheral Mechanisms of Speech Production

- Wilson-Pauwels, L., Akesson, E.J., Stewart, P.A., & Spacey, S.D. (2002). *Cranial nerves in health and disease,* 2nd edition. London: B.C. Decker. A beautifully illustrated and clearly written survey of the cranial nerves that emphasizes problem-based learning and that includes a CD featuring high-resolution graphics as well as animations of cellular processes.

Prosody

7

Introduction

"I don't mind what he said, but I don't like the way he said it." Most people are familiar with this kind of complaint. Such annoyances stem from the fact that the information conveyed by utterances isn't restricted to the meanings of the words and their combinations, but extends to the emotions that are signaled by the speaker's tone of voice. Prosody is an umbrella term that encompasses a number of ways in which vocal tone can be modulated, including fluctuations in pitch, variations in loudness, and changes in the length of syllables, words, phrases, and breath groups. Together, these and other acoustic parameters are frequently used by speakers to express a broad spectrum of feelings (happiness, sadness, anger, fear, etc.) and attitudes (sympathy, politeness, dominance, sarcasm, etc.).

Besides carrying valuable information about a speaker's emotions, prosody is also employed to express several kinds of linguistic distinctions. For example, in the vast majority of languages, yes/no questions are marked by rising intonation at the end of the sentence (Dryer, 2005b). In addition, some lexical contrasts in English and many other languages depend entirely on the placement of stress, as shown by the fact that when the word *content* receives stress on its first syllable it functions as a noun referring to "stuff," but when it receives stress on its second syllable it functions as an adjective meaning "satisfied." Moreover, as we will see later in this chapter, tone languages, which comprise about half the languages in the world, use prosody even more extensively to encode lexical contrasts, but with pitch variation rather than stress assignment as the relevant acoustic parameter (Yip, 2003; Maddieson, 2005b).

Research on the neural substrates of prosody dates back to the late 1870s, when John Hughlings Jackson (1835–1911), a British neurologist who made many seminal discoveries about the relation between language and the brain, noted that even densely aphasic patients with large left-hemisphere lesions could nevertheless convey a great deal of information by continuously repeating a meaningless expression while modulating the prosodic contour of the utterance in various ways. These observations led him to challenge the prevailing view (attributable to Broca and Wernicke) that language was a fully left-lateralized capacity, and to argue that the right hemisphere plays an essential role in regulating the melody of speech (Jackson, 1878 & 1879). More recent studies have generated a substantial amount of evidence to support the hypothesis that prosody relies heavily on the right hemisphere, but they have also shown that the left hemisphere makes important contributions as well. In fact, during the past few decades, much of the research in this field of inquiry has focused on cerebral lateralization—that is, on the question of which types of prosodic processing are handled predominantly by the right hemisphere, and which types are handled predominantly by the left.

Several sophisticated proposals have been developed, but most of them can be classified as belonging to one of two general theoretical perspectives (for reviews see Baum & Pell, 1999; Sidtis & Van Lancker Sidtis, 2003; Zatorre & Gandour, 2008). The first approach maintains that the key factor involves acoustic features, such that prosodic elements characterized mainly by long duration and/or pitch variation tend to be right-lateralized, whereas those characterized mainly by short duration and/or temporal variation tend to be left-lateralized. (Note that the "asymmetric sampling in time" hypothesis, which we encountered in the context of the Dual Stream Model of speech perception in Chapter 5, is a variant of this perspective.) The second approach maintains that the key factor involves functional features, such that prosodic elements that express emotional states tend to be right-lateralized, whereas those that express linguistic contrasts tend to be left-lateralized.

To be sure, both of these perspectives can account for an impressive array of data, and in some (but by no means all) respects they are not really at odds with each other. At the same time, however, both perspectives suffer from several shortcomings, and neither one can be said to constitute a comprehensive theory of the neural underpinnings of prosody. One important limitation of both approaches is that they assume, rather simplistically, that the cerebral lateralization of different aspects of prosody hinges on a single factor. Given that prosodic processing is a fairly complex capacity, it is probably more realistic to suppose that multiple factors are relevant, including the nature of the task, structural aspects of one's native language, and so on (e.g., Pell, 2006a; Wildgruber et al., 2006, 2009; Zatorre & Gandour, 2008). Another important limitation of both approaches is that they focus primarily on the cortex and pay little attention to subcortical structures. Many studies suggest, however, that subcortical structures, especially the amygdala and basal ganglia, play significant roles in prosodic processing (e.g., Scott et al., 1997; Pell & Leonard, 2003; Van Lancker Sidtis et al., 2006; Wiethoff et al., 2009).

This chapter summarizes some of the most influential findings about the implementation of prosody in the brain. It is organized in two main parts, the first of which concentrates on the perception and production of emotional prosody (i.e., the use of intonation to convey feelings), and the second of which concentrates on the perception and production of linguistic prosody (i.e., the use of intonation to make lexical and phrasal distinctions). In both sections, the discussion of perception is longer and more elaborate than the discussion of production, but this simply reflects an inherent imbalance in the literature. Although advances have been made in elucidating all aspects of prosodic processing, the fact of the matter is that, during the past few decades, the greatest progress has involved unraveling the neural systems that enable us to *comprehend* the feelings and attitudes, as well as the linguistic distinctions, expressed by different vocal modulations.

Before proceeding, it is important to acknowledge a nontrivial shortcoming of this chapter, compared to the previous two chapters. Whereas the discussion of basic speech perception in Chapter 5 is guided by the Dual Stream Model, and the discussion of basic speech production in Chapter 6 is guided by both the Lemma Model and the DIVA Model, the discussion of prosody in this chapter is not guided by any particular neuro-cognitive framework. This is because a detailed model of the cortical and subcortical circuitry underlying prosodic processing has not yet been developed. Now, we will soon see that in several corners of this field, the literature has matured to a point where it is possible to get at least a rough sense of not only which brain structures contribute to prosodic processing, but also how they do so. What is still missing, however, is a broad synthesis of what has been learned so far, one that integrates linguistic, psycholinguistic, and neurolinguistic levels of description in a single, unified theory, much like the models in the previous chapters.

Emotional Prosody

Perception

Because intonation patterns are almost always imbued with emotional colorings, they provide listeners with valuable clues about how speakers are feeling. The ability to accurately distinguish between different types of affective prosody varies across individuals and correlates positively with "emotional intelligence" (Trimmer & Cuddy, 2008; see also Kreifelts et al., 2010). However, most healthy adults can judge fairly well from a person's tone of voice whether that person is excited or calm, angry or afraid, happy or sad, sincere or sarcastic, seductive or dismissive (van Bezooijen et al., 1983; Scherer et al., 1991). And this is often possible even when the speaker uses a language that is foreign to the listener, which suggests that the recognition of emotional intonation contours draws upon universal principles (Pell et al., 2009).

How do our brains allow us to make such discriminations and thereby gain insight into other people's affective states through the vocal auditory modality? This is perhaps the most intensively investigated topic in the literature on the neural substrates of prosody, and although many questions remain open, a great deal has been learned (for reviews see Schirmer & Kotz, 2006; Kotz et al., 2006; Pell, 2006b; Wildgruber et al., 2006, 2009; Kotz & Paulmann, 2011; see also the meta-analyses reported by Witteman et al., 2011, 2012). Considerable support has emerged for the traditional view that the right hemisphere is dominant for perceiving emotional prosody, but there is also growing evidence that the left hemisphere mediates at least some aspects of this capacity. Moreover, it is gradually becoming clear which structures in each hemisphere are most critical.

The following survey focuses on five major brain regions and their likely roles in the perception of emotional prosody. Here's a brief preview: First, the right mid to anterior superior temporal cortex constructs coherent auditory representations of affective intonation contours. Second, the amygdala may detect the personal relevance of these contours (e.g., registering the potential threat of an angry voice), so that high-order brain regions can devote more resources to interpreting them. Third, the right ventral frontoparietal cortex appears to be involved in simulating the feelings expressed by affective intonation contours, as a way of understanding them better. Fourth, the basal ganglia may facilitate this simulation process, while also analyzing the temporal profiles of the stimuli and triggering appropriate cognitive/behavioral responses to them. Finally, the bilateral orbitofrontal and inferior frontal cortices are essential for explicitly judging the meanings of emotionally tinged tones of voice (e.g., figuring out whether a speaker is really angry or just mildly irritated).

The Right Mid to Anterior Superior Temporal Cortex: Auditory Integration

Among the many functional neuroimaging studies that have investigated emotional prosody, one of the most consistent findings is significantly greater right-than left-hemisphere activity in the mid to anterior superior temporal gyrus (STG) and superior temporal sulcus (STS) when subjects listen to affectively charged intonation patterns, relative to various control conditions. To take a representative example, Beaucousin et al. (2007) conducted an fMRI study in which subjects listened to sentences with emotional semantic content, such as the following: *I finished my entire exam in June; I finally realized that I would never see her again; I found my car with a scratch, which is unacceptable* (note that the sentences used in the experiment were in French). For each sentence, the task was to classify it as expressing happiness, sadness, or anger. The crucial manipulation was that all of the sentences were produced in two ways—by actors who used appropriate emotional prosody, and by a text-to-speech software program called Kali that builds expressions out of naturally spoken syllables but lacks emotional prosody. To isolate the neural correlates of emotional prosody, the researchers subtracted the activation patterns associated with the Kali condition

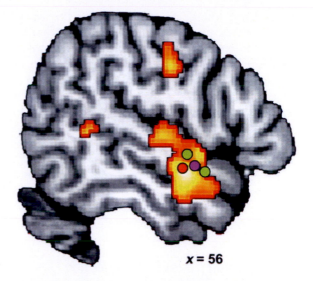

Figure 7.1   Results from Beaucousin et al.'s (2007) fMRI study. The right mid to anterior superior temporal cortex is engaged more during the perception of emotional prosody than during the perception of neutral prosody. The cluster of activity encompasses the human voice-sensitive area, indicated by colored circles (green, Belin et al., 2000; purple, Belin & Zatorre, 2003; red, von Kriegstein et al., 2003). (From Beaucousin et al., 2007, p. 345.)

from those associated with the actor condition. This contrast revealed that the most strongly engaged region was the right mid to anterior STG/STS (Figure 7.1).

This region is quite interesting for several reasons. First, it is known to receive input from early auditory areas (Romanski & Averbeck, 2009). Second, as indicated by the colored circles in Figure 7.1, it is especially sensitive to the perception of human voices (for a review see Belin, 2006). Third, relative to neutral intonation contours, the region's responses to angry, fearful, happy, and alluring intonation contours correlate significantly with a number of acoustic parameters (stimulus duration, mean intensity, mean pitch, and pitch variability), and while these responses can be explained by all of the parameters taken together, they cannot be explained by any one of them taken individually (Wiethoff et al., 2008). This suggests that the region may serve to integrate the multifarious acoustic parameters that jointly give rise to emotional prosody. Fourth, the region is significantly engaged by the emotional prosody of utterances even when subjects concentrate on unrelated aspects of the stimuli, such as the semantic content (Ethofer et al., 2006), whether the sounds are presented to the left or right ear (Grandjean et al., 2005), or whether the speaker is male or female (Sander et al., 2005). This supports the idea that the region processes the affective features of intonation contours in a more or less automatic, pre-attentive, stimulus-driven manner. Importantly, all of the fMRI results mentioned above involve significantly greater effects in the right than the left mid to anterior STG/STS. Overall, then, this region in the right hemisphere appears to contribute to the perception of emotional prosody by automatically integrating the diverse acoustic cues that collectively signal different kinds of affective states.

The Amygdala: Relevance Detection

The amygdala is believed to play a pivotal role in rapidly registering the subjective value or relevance of stimuli, and it has been implicated in the processing of emotionally or socially salient information, such as threatening facial expressions or body postures (Sander et al., 2003; Adolphs, 2010a, 2010b; see Chapter 1). Hence one might expect this subcortical structure to contribute to the perception of emotional prosody, especially during the early stages of processing. So far, however, the studies that have addressed this issue have yielded mixed results.

On the one hand, a number of functional neuroimaging experiments have revealed significant amygdala activity—either bilaterally or predominantly right-lateralized—when participants hear emotionally charged intonation patterns, relative to baseline conditions such as neutral prosody (e.g., Morris et al., 1999; Sander et al., 2005; Wildgruber et al., 2005; Bach et al., 2008; Ethofer et al., 2008; Schirmer et al., 2008b; Wiethoff et al., 2009; Leitman et al., 2010; Frühholz et al., 2012; see also Fecteau et al., 2007; Kuraoka & Nakamura, 2007). And in accord with those findings, a neuropsychological study by Scott et al. (1997) showed that the recognition of angry and fearful prosody was impaired in a patient with bilateral amygdala lesions. On the other hand, some functional neuroimaging studies have not reported significant amygdala activity during the perception of affective prosody (e.g., Grandjean et al., 2005), and moreover several neuropsychological studies involving groups of patients with amygdala damage have not found deficits in this domain (Anderson & Phelps, 1998; Adolphs & Tranel, 1999; Bach et al., 2013).

How can these discrepant results be explained? It could be that the sensitivity of the amygdala to emotional prosody is not a straightforward all-or-nothing phenomenon, but is instead modulated by various factors. Support for this nuanced approach comes from several sources, including studies showing that the responsiveness of the amygdala to different tones of voice depends on the following factors: how much the listener cares about other people (Schirmer et al., 2008b); how neurotic the listener happens to be (Brück et al., 2011); the degree to which the prosodic pattern is expected (Ethofer et al., 2008; Wiethoff et al., 2009); and the salience of the acoustic cues for certain emotions (Leitman et al., 2010).

Here's a hypothetical but concrete example. Suppose that all of a sudden, out of the blue, someone you're conversing with says something in a distinctly angry manner. Your amygdala will most likely register this surprising, potentially threatening change and rapidly alert higher-level "evaluative" brain regions, such as the bilateral orbitofrontal and inferior frontal cortices, which are discussed in detail below. Now, if you're usually pretty good at regulating your feelings, these higher-level regions will probably dampen the amygdala's response in a top-down manner, as a form of affective control that allows you to "keep your cool," so to speak. But if instead you tend to be rather neurotic, you may have more trouble managing your emotional reaction to the aversive speech signals, and this difficulty may be manifested in part by stronger and more persistent amygdala activation.

Much more work needs to be done on how the amygdala contributes to the perception of emotional prosody. But the data currently available seem to support the hypothesis that this subcortical structure is involved in the early detection of affective intonation contours that are subjectively relevant, contextually novel, and acoustically salient.

The Right Ventral Frontoparietal Cortex: Emotion Simulation

Switching back to the cortical level, another sector of the right hemisphere that seems to be essential for representing the affective import of intonation contours is the ventral frontoparietal region. Although some evidence for this view comes from fMRI studies (e.g., Buchanan et al., 2000), the most compelling findings derive from neuropsychological studies (e.g., Starkstein et al., 1994; Adolphs et al., 2002; Ross & Monnot, 2008).

For instance, Adolphs et al. (2002) analyzed behavioral as well as lesion data for 66 patients with stable, widely distributed lesions, all of whom performed the following task. The stimuli consisted of four semantically neutral sentences—*Men play football*, *There are trees in the forest*, *This is my pencil*, and *People read books*—each of which was produced with five clearly distinguishable types of emotional prosody—happy, sad, angry, afraid, and surprised—leading to a total of 20 sentences. The subjects listened to all of the sentences five times in random order, and on each trial they rated on a scale from 0 ("not at all") to 5 ("very much") the degree to which the speaker's tone of voice expressed one of the five kinds of emotion listed above.

To determine whether the patients' behavioral performances co-varied with their lesion sites, the investigators first rank-ordered the accuracy scores from best to worst. Then they used a median-split to divide the patients into two subgroups of equal size—one with high performance (the top 50 percent) and the other with low performance (the bottom 50 percent). And finally they subtracted the lesion sites associated with the high-performance subgroup from those associated with the low-performance subgroup. They found that difficulty recognizing different types of emotional prosody was linked most reliably and specifically with damage to the following areas: the right anterior STG, which we discussed above; the bilateral orbitofrontal and inferior frontal cortices, which we will discuss further below; and the right ventral frontoparietal cortex, which is our main focus here (Figure 7.2).

Interestingly, 46 of the patients in this study also participated in a previous study about recognizing emotions from facial expressions (Adolphs et al., 2000), and a comparison of data across the two studies revealed that damage to the right ventral frontoparietal cortex tends to impair the ability to recognize various kinds of emotions from both prosodic contours and facial expressions (Figure 7.3). Further evidence that this region is essential for appreciating emotional prosody as well as emotional faces comes from more recent studies which have shown that when rTMS is applied to the region in healthy subjects, performance is significantly reduced for both types of emotion perception (prosody: Van Rijn et al., 2005, Banissy et al., 2010; faces: Pitcher et al., 2008).

What role does the right ventral frontoparietal cortex play in recognizing emotions from prosodic and facial patterns? The answer to this question is

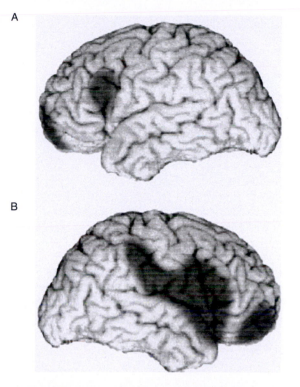

Figure 7.2 Lesion sites associated with impaired recognition of emotional prosody. The key regions are as follows: the right mid to anterior superior temporal cortex; the right ventral frontoparietal cortex; and the bilateral orbitofrontal and inferior frontal cortices. The data are based on a study involving 66 brain-damaged patients. (A) Left hemisphere; (B) right hemisphere. (From Adolphs et al., 2002, p. 41.)

not entirely clear, but the interpretation favored by Adolphs et al. (2000, 2002) converges with the general view, popular among advocates of so-called "embodied cognition," that we understand other people's emotional states in large part by covertly and unconsciously simulating them in our own brains (e.g., Wicker et al., 2003; Goldman & Sripada, 2005; Harrison et al., 2006; Niedenthal, 2007; Oberman et al., 2007). When it comes to recognizing how someone feels based on the tone of their voice or the configuration of their face, the basic idea is that this simulation or mirroring process involves drawing upon predominantly right-lateralized sensorimotor circuits to reconstruct the bodily states, including the visceral changes, that partly constitute the emotions that are perceived—emotions such as joy, sorrow, anger, fear, and so on (Damasio, 1999). In other words, the claim is that the right ventral frontoparietal cortex may contribute to recognizing the emotions expressed by prosodic and facial patterns by mimicking the very same emotions, albeit

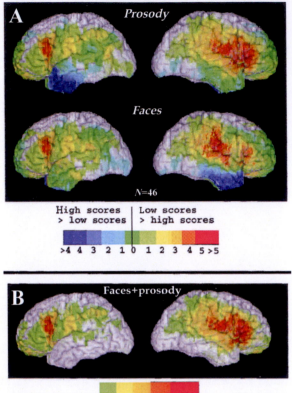

Figure 7.3 Lesion sites associated with impaired recognition of emotions from prosodic and facial expressions. (A) Data from prosodic and facial stimuli shown separately. Colors represent, at each voxel, the difference between the number of lesions from patients in the low-performing subgroup (bottom 50%, N = 23) and the number of lesions from patients in the high-performing subgroup (top 50%, N = 23). Warm colors indicate areas where damage is associated more with low than high scores, and cool colors indicate areas where damage is associated more with high than low scores. (B) Lesion sites linked with compromised recognition of emotion from both prosodic and facial expressions (N = 13). Colors represent the number of lesions in the overlap at each voxel. (From Adolphs et al., 2002, p. 40.)

typically beneath the surface of awareness. Further research is needed, however, to explore this proposal in greater detail.

The Basal Ganglia: Emotion Simulation, Sequence Decoding, and/or Response Triggering

The basal ganglia have also been linked with emotional prosody perception. Although some of the evidence for this connection comes from functional neuroimaging studies (e.g., Morris et al., 1999;

Kotz et al., 2003; Bach et al., 2008; Wittforth et al., 2010), perhaps the strongest support derives from investigations of patients with basal ganglia disturbances. Impaired categorization of different tones of voice has been found not only in patients with infarcts affecting the basal ganglia (e.g., Cancelliere & Kertesz, 1990; Starkstein et al., 1994; Karow et al., 2001), but also in patients with neurodegenerative diseases affecting the basal ganglia, especially Parkinson's disease (e.g., Blonder et al., 1989; Pell, 1996; Breitenstein et al., 2001; Pell & Leonard, 2003; Monetta et al., 2008). Importantly, as with patients who have suffered damage to the right ventral frontoparietal cortex, patients with basal ganglia dysfunction not only have trouble recognizing emotions conveyed by prosodic patterns, but also perform poorly at recognizing emotions conveyed by facial expressions (e.g., Blonder et al., 1989; Breitenstein et al., 1998; Yip et al., 2003). Moreover, there are even some hints that these patients are impaired at understanding words with emotional meanings (e.g., Karow et al., 2001; Castner et al., 2007; Hillier et al., 2007). Hence they appear to have a fairly broad impairment in perceiving emotion (Paulmann & Pell, 2010). It is worth noting that some studies suggest that the basal ganglia may be more critical for identifying negative than positive emotions (e.g., Sprengelmeyer et al., 2003; Dujardin et al., 2004; Dara et al., 2008; Paulmann et al., 2009a). But the evidence for such valence specificity is far from conclusive, and a number of studies point to a more general involvement of the basal ganglia in comprehending a wide range of emotions, including happiness (e.g., Morris et al., 1996; Breiter et al., 1997; Paulmann & Pell, 2010).

Given the findings described above, it is now commonly assumed that the basal ganglia are necessary for accurately understanding affective intonation contours and facial expressions. It is by no means clear, however, exactly how these subcortical structures contribute to these perceptual processes. Nevertheless, several intriguing hypotheses have been offered, some of which are as follows.

- First, the basal ganglia may work in concert with the right ventral frontoparietal cortex to simulate the types of emotions that are signaled by prosodic and facial patterns (Adolphs et al., 2002).
- Second, in light of evidence that the basal ganglia are highly sensitive to the temporal structure of perceived events, it has been proposed that they facilitate the identification of emotionally

meaningful patterns in dynamic sequences of vocal and facial stimuli (Pell & Leonard, 2003; Paulmann & Pell, 2010; Kotz & Schwartze, 2010; Paulmann et al., 2011).

- Third, because the basal ganglia are known to trigger adaptive, well-learned cognitive and behavioral routines in response to stimuli, it is conceivable that they react to emotional prosodic and facial patterns by promoting the appropriate routines, such as withdrawal when anger is detected and approach when happiness is encountered (Panksepp, 1998).

These three hypotheses are not mutually exclusive, and all of them warrant further investigation.

The Bilateral Orbitofrontal and Inferior Frontal Cortices: Cognitive Evaluation

Finally, a variety of studies suggest that the explicit judgment or appraisal of affectively tinged tones of voice relies on two large sectors of the prefrontal cortex in both hemispheres—specifically, the orbitofrontal region (approximately BA10 & BA11) and the inferior frontal region (approximately BA47, BA45, & BA44). We will consider each of these regions in turn.

Regarding the bilateral orbitofrontal cortices, we noted above that Adolphs et al. (2002) found them to be among the areas most frequently damaged in patients with poor recognition of emotional prosody (Figure 7.2). Those findings were subsequently corroborated by Hornak et al. (2003), who discovered similar deficits in patients with surgically created focal lesions in the unilateral right, unilateral left, or bilateral orbitofrontal areas (see also Hornak et al., 1996). The same patients also had abnormal social behavior, which is consistent with other research linking the orbitofrontal cortices with many relatively high-level aspects of emotion and personality (Zald & Andreotti, 2010; Grabenhorst & Rolls, 2011).

More recently, Paulmann et al. (2009b) extended this line of investigation by combining behavioral and electrophysiological approaches. First, they found that at a purely behavioral level, a group of patients with orbitofrontal lesions were impaired at explicitly judging whether the intonation patterns of sentences conveyed anger, disgust, fear, happiness, or no strong emotion at all. Next, they found that at an electrophysiological level, the patients nevertheless exhibited normal online discrimination of affective vs. neutral prosody during the first

few hundred milliseconds of processing. This dissociation highlights the fact that understanding the communicative significance of a speaker's tone of voice does not occur in one fell swoop, but unfolds over several stages. For patients with orbitofrontal lesions, it appears that the early bottom-up stage of perceptual integration is completely normal, whereas the late top-down stage of cognitive evaluation is severely impaired.

Several fMRI studies support the view that the orbitofrontal cortices are involved in the explicit appraisal of emotional intonation contours. For example, Wildgruber et al. (2004) conducted a study in which subjects listened to multiple instances of the German sentence *Der Schal ist in der Truhe* (*The scarf is in the chest*). Prior to the experiment, the investigators systematically manipulated the acoustic structure of this sentence in two ways: In five versions of the sentence, the linguistic prosody varied so that the focus (i.e., the emphatic stress) ranged between *Schal* and *Truhe*; in another five versions of the sentence, the emotional prosody varied so that the degree of perceived excitement ranged between high and low (Figure 7.4A). During the experiment, there were two conditions in which subjects made different discriminations between sentence pairs: In the "focus position" condition, they decided which sentence was better suited to respond to the question *Where is the scarf?*; and in the "expressiveness" condition, they decided which sentence was produced in a more excited manner. When the investigators subtracted the activation patterns evoked by the focus position condition from those evoked by the expressiveness condition, they found that the orbitofrontal region was significantly engaged in both hemispheres (Figure 7.4B). They interpreted this result as evidence that "the evaluation of emotional tone is bound to bilateral orbitofrontal regions" (Wildgruber et al., 2004, p. 1388). (The opposite subtraction is discussed further below in the section on linguistic prosody.)

It is noteworthy that the sensitivity of the orbitofrontal cortices to the emotional prosody of perceived utterances seems to depend on how closely people attend to those utterances. This was shown by Sander et al. (2005), who conducted an fMRI study in which subjects listened to meaningless utterances pronounced with either angry or neutral intonation. Different stimuli were presented to both ears simultaneously, and the task was to make male/female judgments about the speakers of the utterances heard on either just the right side or just the left side. The orbitofrontal region, especially in the right hemisphere, was activated more

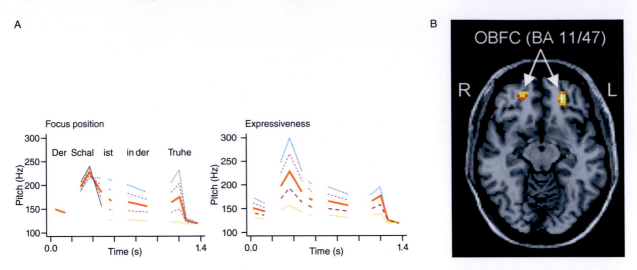

Figure 7.4   Stimuli and results from the fMRI study by Wildgruber et al. (2004). (A) Subjects heard multiple versions of the German sentence *Der Schal ist in der Truhe (The scarf is in the chest)*. In five versions (indicated by the different types of lines), the focus position ranged between *Schal* and *Truhe*. In another five versions (indicated again by the different types of lines), the expressiveness ranged from highly excited to unexcited. (B) Subtraction of the condition involving "focus position" judgments from the condition involving "expressiveness" judgments revealed activity in the ventromedial prefrontal (orbital) cortices bilaterally. (From Wildgruber et al., 2004, p. 1386.)

strongly by the angry voices than the neutral voices, but only when the angry voices were presented on the to-be-attended side (Figure 7.5A). This finding converges with other studies which suggest that the response of the orbitofrontal region to emotional stimuli is not automatic, but is instead modulated by top-down cognitive factors such as expectations, goals, and task demands (e.g., Armony & Dolan, 2002; Winston et al., 2003).

In a follow-up analysis, Sander et al. (2005) explored this issue in greater detail and discovered that when the subjects in their experiment attended to angry voices, a particularly potent factor that influenced each individual subject's degree of orbitofrontal activity was that subject's dispositional proneness to anxiety. Specifically, the subjects who exhibited the greatest signal strength in the right orbitofrontal cortex also obtained the highest scores on a standardized behavioral inhibition scale (Figure 7.5B). In discussing this correlation, the researchers wrote that

> it is plausible that angry voices might convey aversive or negative social signals, possibly of punishment, and that these signals were more extensively processed [by the anxiety-prone subjects] when they were heard in the to-be-attended ear and required a response, relative to when they could be ignored, leading to a greater engagement of orbitofrontal cortex ...
>
> (Sander et al., 2005, p. 855)

Shifting to the bilateral inferior frontal cortices, a number of studies suggest that they also contribute to fairly high-level evaluative processes during the perception of emotional prosody. As indicated above, Adolphs et al. (2002) reported that the patients in their neuropsychological study who manifested an impaired ability to recognize various types of affective intonation contours tended to have lesions that included either the right or left inferior frontal cortex (Figure 7.2). Additional evidence that these regions play essential roles in the receptive processing of emotional prosody comes from a recent rTMS study by Hoekert et al. (2010). This experiment had two conditions: In the semantics condition, participants listened to sentences spoken in a neutral tone of voice and judged as quickly as possible whether each sentence expressed angry, fearful, or neutral content; in the prosody condition, participants listened to sentences with neutral content and judged as quickly as possible whether each sentence was spoken in an angry, fearful, or neutral tone of voice. During one third of the trials, a train of 12 TMS pulses at 5 Hz was delivered to the right inferior frontal cortex (approximately BA45); during another third of the trials, a similar train of TMS pulses was delivered to the homologous area in the left hemisphere (i.e., part of Broca's area); and during the last third of the trials, sham rTMS, which the participants could not distinguish from real rTMS, was administered as a control over the right-hemisphere

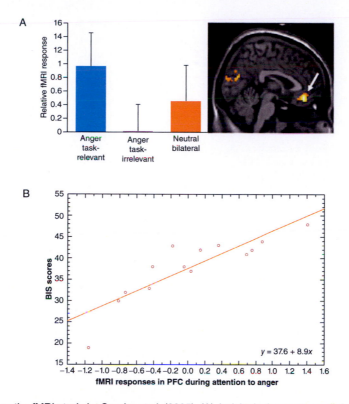

Figure 7.5 Results from the fMRI study by Sander et al. (2005). (A) Activity in the ventromedial prefrontal (orbital) cortex was greater when angry voices were heard in the ear that was being attended (task-relevant) than when they were heard in the ear that was not being attended (task-irrelevant). (B) The effect of attention on the orbitofrontal response to angry voices correlated with scores on a behavioral inhibition scale that measures proneness to anxiety. (From Sander et al., 2005, pp. 852 & 854.)

region. Although the participants' reaction times in the semantics condition were not significantly affected by rTMS, their reaction times in the prosody condition were significantly longer when either the right or the left inferior frontal region was stimulated, compared to when sham stimulation was used instead. These findings are valuable because they suggest that both the right and the left inferior frontal regions are critically involved in the explicit appraisal of different kinds of emotional intonation.

A few fMRI studies have generated results that bolster this idea. For example, in the study by Sander et al. (2005) that we considered earlier, the bilateral inferior frontal cortices had a response profile very much like that of the bilateral orbitofrontal cortices: greater engagement by angry than neutral voices, but only when the angry voices were attended. And in a study by Ethofer et al. (2006), the bilateral inferior frontal cortices were activated more when subjects evaluated the emotional intonation contours of auditorily perceived adjectives than when they evaluated the emotional semantic contents of the same adjectives (Figure 7.6).

It is important to acknowledge, however, that some fMRI studies have found activity in just the right inferior frontal cortex (George et al., 1996; Buchanan et al., 2000; Wildgruber et al., 2005), or in just the left inferior frontal cortex (Bach et al., 2008), when participants perceive emotional prosody, relative to various baseline conditions. These inconsistencies raise questions about the specific functional contributions of the right and left inferior frontal regions to the processing of affective intonation patterns. There are no simple answers, but recent work suggests that the right-hemisphere region may be recruited mainly when attention is focused on the emotional significance of prosodic contours, whereas the left-hemisphere region may be recruited mainly when attention is focused on the relation between the vocal and verbal aspects of utterances (for a review see Schirmer & Kotz, 2006; see also Kotz et al., 2013). The latter type of situation is nicely illustrated by sarcastic remarks, such as when someone says *Great job!* in a derisive tone of voice that conflicts with the meaning of the phrase. To fully understand the intent

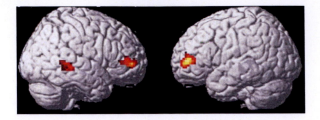

Figure 7.6   Results of the fMRI study by Ethofer et al. (2006). Evaluating the emotional intonation contours of auditorily perceived adjectives engages the lateral orbitofrontal cortices of both hemispheres significantly more than evaluating the emotional semantic contents of the same adjectives. (From Ethofer et al., 2006, p. 584.)

of such expressions, the listener must process the prosodic and semantic features in parallel, register their incompatibility, and infer that the speaker's goal was actually to convey the opposite of the literal meaning of the message. Evidence for the idea that the left inferior frontal cortex mediates the integration of (in)congruent vocal and verbal information comes from several studies (Schirmer et al., 2004; Mitchell, 2006; Wittforth et al., 2010), and it is notable that sex differences have been discovered in this domain (Box 7.1).

Summary

A comprehensive, well-supported, neurocognitive theory of the perception of emotional prosody has not yet emerged. The available data suggest, however, that this capacity is subserved by a network of anatomically distributed cortical and subcortical structures in both hemispheres. One plausible yet still conjectural scenario is roughly as follows.

During an early pre-attentive stage of processing, the right mid to anterior superior temporal cortex automatically integrates the multifarious acoustic cues (e.g., changes in pitch, intensity, length, voice quality, etc.) that collectively signal different shades of emotion. The amygdala also comes into play quite rapidly, especially when the perceived prosodic patterns are subjectively relevant, contextually novel, and acoustically salient. During later stages of processing, several other brain regions are recruited in a fairly complex interactive manner to both recognize and evaluate the affective significance of particular intonation contours. By evoking representations of the body states that are associated with certain feelings, the right ventral frontoparietal region carries out covert simulations of the types of emotions that are conveyed by different tones of voice, and this

mirroring process may be facilitated by the basal ganglia (although it must be acknowledged that the basal ganglia may perform other operations as well). In addition, the bilateral orbitofrontal and inferior frontal cortices guide various top-down executive processes such as explicitly attending to and categorizing perceived prosodic patterns, and judging how well those patterns match the semantic content of what is said.

Overall, this scenario is consistent with a wide range of findings, but it is still very sketchy. As more empirical and theoretical work is conducted in the coming years, it will surely be possible to flesh out in greater detail the neural mechanisms underlying the perception of emotional prosody. (For recent research on the white matter fiber tracts that interconnect many of the regions discussed above, see Ethofer et al., 2012, 2013.)

Production

Substantially more neuroscientific research has addressed the perception than the production of emotional prosody, in part because the former is more amenable than the latter to investigation with fMRI, ERP, and TMS approaches. Nevertheless, scholars have gradually been elucidating the brain systems that allow us to inflect our voices in ways that express a broad spectrum of feelings and attitudes. Because most of the key results come from studies of patients with impaired production of emotional prosody, the following brief review focuses on neuropsychological data. (See Pichon & Kell, 2013, for a rare fMRI study of normal emotional prosody generation.)

In the previous section, we observed that many aspects of the receptive processing of emotional prosody seem to rely on the right hemisphere. On the production side, there is also evidence that the right hemisphere may be especially important. It is not uncommon for damage to the right hemisphere to induce a generalized blunting of affect that is partly manifested by a tendency to speak in a rather flat manner—if not in a monotone, then with a significantly reduced amount of melodic and rhythmic variation. For example, in one of the first experiments to explore this issue, Tucker et al. (1977) asked 16 individuals—eight patients with right-hemisphere lesions, and eight healthy comparison participants—to produce certain semantically neutral sentences with specific kinds of emotional prosody. Then they asked three normal listeners to identify

Box 7.1   Sex Differences in the Perception of Emotional Prosody

For the most part, there are few reliable sex differences involving the brain organization for language (Wallentin, 2009). However, in keeping with age-old stereotypes and most people's everyday intuitions, there is substantial evidence that, on average, women tend to be more attuned to other people's feelings than men (Baron-Cohen, 2003), and this turns out to have interesting implications for the perception of emotional prosody. Annett Schirmer and her colleagues have investigated this topic in some detail and have found that women are generally more sensitive to affective voices than men. For example, compared to men, women display greater activity in Broca's area and also exhibit a larger N400 effect (i.e., an electrophysiological index of anomaly detection; see Chapter 15) when they listen to words with mismatching meanings and prosodic patterns, like the word *loved* spoken in an angry tone of voice, relative to when they listen to words with matching meanings and prosodic patterns, like the word *loved* spoken in a happy tone of voice (Schirmer & Kotz, 2003; Schirmer et al., 2004; Figure 7B1.1). Male readers will be pleased to learn, however, that these sex differences are only present when the task is to focus on the emotional valence of either just the word meanings or just the prosodic patterns; they disappear when the task is to explicitly judge whether the emotional valences of word meanings and prosodic patterns match (Schirmer et al., 2005). Thus,

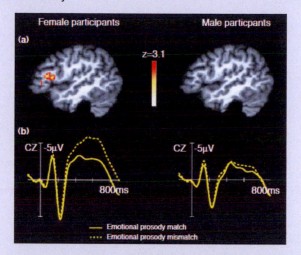

Figure 7B1.1   Sex differences in vocal emotional processing. (A) fMRI contrast and (B) ERPs for emotional words (e.g., *loved*) spoken with congruous (e.g., happy, solid line) compared with incongruous (e.g., angry, dotted line) emotional prosody when emotional prosody is task-irrelevant. The fMRI contrast reveals activity in the left inferior frontal gyrus in women but not in men. The ERPs reveal an N400 effect in women but not in men. These results suggest that listeners integrate vocal and verbal emotional information approximately 400 ms following word onset and that this integration is mediated by Broca's area. Moreover, women seem to use emotional prosody more automatically for language processing than men. (From Schirmer & Kotz, 2006, p. 27.)

the results suggest that the female advantage seems to involve rapidly and involuntarily—that is to say, pre-attentively—registering the degree of congruity between *what* people say and *how* they say it. As Schirmer and Kotz (2006, p. 27) put it, "men and women differ in how automatically they access and integrate emotional-prosodic information into language processing." Not surprisingly, women's superiority in this domain has recently been linked with estrogen, one the major female hormones (Schirmer et al., 2008a).

the emotions that were expressed. On average, the listeners were better able to recognize the emotions that were prosodically conveyed by the normal subjects than those that were prosodically conveyed by the brain-damaged patients.

During the past few decades, Elliott Ross and his colleagues have been among the strongest proponents of the view that the right hemisphere is essential for producing affective intonation contours (e.g., Ross, 1981, 2000; Ross et al., 1988, 1997; Ross & Monnot, 2008). To take a representative study, Ross and Monnot (2008) recently reported that, relative to a group of 43 healthy comparison participants, 12

of 21 patients with right-hemisphere damage performed poorly at spontaneously generating emotional prosody when asked to talk about personal life events that made them feel happy, frightened, angry, or sad. The lesion sites of the 12 impaired patients were widely distributed across frontal, parietal, temporal, occipital, and subcortical sectors of the right hemisphere; however, the greatest lesion overlap involved the posterior inferior frontal gyrus, the ventral precentral gyrus, and the anterior insula (Figure 7.7). These findings suggest that the right-hemisphere homologue of Broca's area, together with some of the surrounding tissue, may be critical for the efficient and appropriate expression of affective prosodic patterns.

Further research is needed, however, to test this hypothesis more rigorously, ideally by conducting more elaborate neuropsychological studies that employ more carefully controlled tasks and more sophisticated voxel-based lesion analyses, along the lines of Adolphs et al.'s (2002) investigation of the recognition of emotional prosody. It would also be worthwhile for future studies to consider the possible influence of time post-stroke. This is because all of the patients in Ross and Monnot's (2008) study were examined within three to eight weeks post-stroke, but other studies suggest that when patients with right-hemisphere cortical lesions are tested during the chronic epoch of recovery (>3 months post-stroke), they are less likely to exhibit impaired production of emotional prosody (Brådvik et al., 1990, 1991; Baum & Pell, 1997).

Does the production of emotional prosody also depend on the left hemisphere? The data currently available are equivocal. On the one hand, left-sided lesions do sometimes disrupt the capacity to express particular feelings by appropriately modulating one's tone of voice. This was demonstrated in an early study by Cancelliere and Kertesz (1990), and the point was recently reinforced by Ross and Monnot's study (2008). Specifically, the latter researchers showed that the spontaneous generation of affective intonation patterns was defective not only in 12 of 21 patients with right-hemisphere damage, but also in 8 of 18 patients with left-hemisphere damage. On the other hand, it is not clear if the problems

with emotional prosody production that are sometimes observed in patients with left-hemisphere damage really reflect intonational impairments per se, since they may instead be at least partly reducible to verbal-articulatory deficits. Ross and Monnot (2008) found, for instance, that on a separate task involving the repetition of emotional prosodic patterns carried by sentences (*I'm going to the other movie*), monosyllables (*ba ba ba ba ba*), and asyllabic vocalizations (*aaaaaahhhh*), the patients with left-hemisphere lesions progressively improved as the verbal-articulatory demands declined, whereas the patients with right-hemisphere lesions did not. These results suggest that the right hemisphere may play a more important role than the left in the generation of affective intonation contours. However, this issue requires further investigation.

Finally, we turn to subcortical structures. The key point here is that the basal ganglia have been implicated not only in the perception but also in the production of emotional prosody (e.g., Blonder et al., 1989; Cancelliere & Kertesz, 1990). Patients with basal ganglia disturbances often generate intonationally flat speech, and in many cases this is thought to reflect a mood disorder characterized by apathy—i.e., reduced motivation and difficulty initiating action (e.g., Bhatia & Marsden, 1994; Masterman & Cummings, 1997).

A detailed case study by Van Lancker Sidtis et al. (2006) provides an instructive illustration of the condition. The patient was a 36-year-old woman who suffered a deep midline infarction that affected the putamen and globus pallidus bilaterally. Although

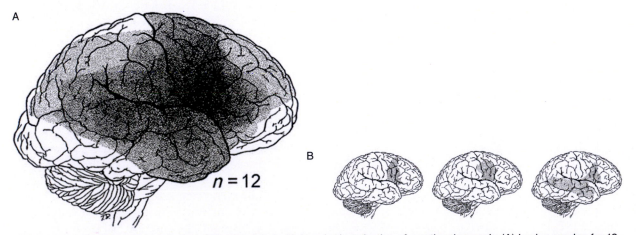

Figure 7.7 Right-hemisphere lesion sites associated with impaired production of emotional prosody. (A) Lesion overlap for 12 patients. (B) Lesion sites for three individual patients. The damage included the anterior insula (not shown in the figure) for two of these three patients. (From Ross & Monnot, 2008, pp. 60–61.)

limb weakness resolved within four months, a general lack of interest in doing anything, together with a predominantly unhappy mood, persisted. Her fiancé noted that this was revealed most clearly by her speech, which he described as "sounding different … monotone." An examination of telephone conversations that had been recorded before the patient's injury confirmed that she had previously displayed a much more dynamic range of expression in her spontaneous speech. Her prosodic deficit was investigated in greater detail by administering two tasks: In the elicitation task, she was asked to produce certain semantically neutral sentences with happy, angry, sad, or surprised intonation; and in the imitation task, she was asked to copy the examiner's renditions of the same sentences with the same prosodic contours. Recordings of the patient's utterances were then presented to 22 listeners. These individuals subjectively rated the utterances as "good," "questionable," or "poor" expressions of the intended emotions, and they also tried to objectively identify which utterances were meant to be produced in a happy, angry, sad, or surprised manner. Among the utterances produced in the elicitation task, only 18.5 percent were subjectively rated as "good," and only 42.9 percent were objectively identified correctly; however, among the utterances produced in the imitation task, 75 percent were subjectively rated as "good," and 73.0 percent were objectively identified correctly (Figure 7.8). These findings

suggest that the patient was, as the authors put it, vocally "competent" to produce affective intonation patterns, but her ability to do so in a spontaneous fashion was defective (Van Lancker Sidtis et al., 2006, p. 141). Overall, this case study supports the view that the basal ganglia are essential for the normal generation of emotional prosody.

Linguistic Prosody

Perception

As noted in the Introduction, speakers manipulate the acoustic parameters of pitch, length, and loudness not only to express specific feelings and attitudes, but also to convey various types of purely linguistic distinctions. In the neurolinguistics literature, three major domains of linguistic prosody are often treated separately: syntactic, lexical, and tonal.

In the syntactic domain, intonation is often used to distinguish between declarative and interrogative sentences, and in some situations it is the only cue for this function. For example, the two sentences in (1) are segmentally identical, but the first one would have either level or falling pitch on the final word, since it is an assertion, whereas the second one would have rising pitch on the final word, since it is a question:

(1) a. *Sam is going to the party too.*
    b. *Sam is going to the party too?*

Prosody is also employed to signal intonational phrase boundaries that correspond to syntactic junctures, and once again, sometimes it is the only cue for this function. As an illustration, the two sentences in (2) are segmentally identical, but the first one would be produced with a single pause after *said,* whereas the second one would be produced with two pauses, one after *boy* and another after *girl.* These pauses are overtly marked by commas in the printed versions of the sentences, but in ordinary spoken language they are only manifested by relatively subtle acoustic features. And yet they carry heavy communicative loads, since they are the main, if not the sole, cues that allow the listener to determine which person is supposedly cute, the girl or the boy:

(2) a. *The boy said, "The girl is cute."*
    b. *The boy, said the girl, is cute.*

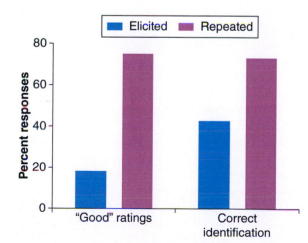

Figure 7.8 Listeners' ratings of elicited and repeated utterances produced by a patient with bilateral basal ganglia damage. The listeners' tasks were subjective evaluation of "goodness" of emotion type, and objective identification of emotion type. (From Van Lancker Sidtis et al., 2006, p. 141.)

In the lexical domain, syllabic stress is frequently employed to serve several functions. It can indicate whether a word operates as a noun or a verb, as shown in (3a); it can indicate whether a word operates as an adjective or part of a compound noun, as shown in (3b); and it can indicate whether a word is given special emphasis in its context, as shown in (3c):

(3) a. *object* vs. *object*;
    b. *green **house*** vs. ***green**house*;
    c. *I like the **big** dog, not the little one.*

Lastly, in the tonal domain, many languages use pitch variation in a highly systematic manner to signal differences in word meaning. For instance, as shown in (4), in Mandarin Chinese the syllable *ma* can have four different meanings depending on its tone:

(4) a. *ma* (high level tone) = "mother";
    b. *ma* (rising tone) = "numb," "numbness," "hemp," or "cannabis";
    c. *ma* (falling–rising tone) = "horse";
    d. *ma* (falling tone) = "scold."

What are the neural underpinnings of the perception of linguistic prosody? Less research has been devoted to addressing this question than to exploring the brain systems that subserve the perception of emotional prosody. Still, a considerable amount of work has been done, and many important insights have been made, especially regarding the vexing issue of lateralization. The following review summarizes some of the key findings that have emerged in each of the three domains of linguistic prosody. As we will see, the data regarding the syntactic domain are complex and somewhat equivocal, but the weight of evidence suggests that the pertinent brain systems are bilateral, albeit with perhaps a moderate right-hemisphere bias for the receptive processing of prosodically conveyed declarative/interrogative distinctions, and perhaps a moderate left-hemisphere bias for the receptive processing of phonological phrase boundaries that mark syntactic junctures. In contrast, the data regarding the lexical and tonal domains are more straightforward and point to strong left-hemisphere dominance. After working through the three domains, we will consider some possible explanations for the observed patterns of lateralization.

The Syntactic Domain

Evidence that the perception of sentence-level linguistic prosody may be bilateral comes from an fMRI study by Meyer et al. (2003; see also Meyer et al., 2004, and

Hesling et al., 2005a). In this experiment, German participants underwent brain scanning while listening to three types of utterances: normal speech, in which all of the content words were real, as in *Die besorgte Mutter sucht das weinende Kind* (*The anxious mother searches for the crying child*); pseudo speech, in which all of the content words were replaced with nonwords, as in *Das mumpfige Folofel hongert das apoldige Trekon* (*The mumpfy folofel hongers the apoldish trekon*); and degraded speech, in which all of the segmental, lexical, and syntactic cues were filtered out, but the prosodic contours were preserved. The major foci of activity elicited by these conditions are depicted in Figure 7.9. For present purposes, the most interesting result was that all three types of stimuli engaged the mid to anterior superior temporal cortex in both hemispheres. This activity was weakest in the degraded speech condition, most likely because that condition lacked all linguistic features except prosody. However, the fact that the activity was evoked not only in the first two conditions but also in the third suggests that the mid to anterior superior temporal cortex, bilaterally, may subserve, among other computations, the analysis of precisely those acoustic features that were common across all three conditions—namely, slowly changing sentence-level intonation contours.

It is worth mentioning that another intriguing result was that the pseudo speech condition and the degraded speech condition, but not the normal speech condition, engaged several frontal areas—specifically, the posterior inferior frontal cortex bilaterally, and the inferior precentral sulcus in the right hemisphere. Based on some of the points that were made above in the discussion of the possible roles of the bilateral inferior frontal cortices in understanding emotional prosody, it would not be unreasonable to suppose that in the current study these areas underlie various kinds of top-down effortful processing associated with the difficulty of interpreting utterances in which some of the normal linguistic cues have been removed. In particular, the right frontal regions may be recruited when subjects direct their attention toward intonation patterns, whereas the left frontal regions may be more involved when subjects attempt to relate those intonation patterns to other levels of linguistic representation, such as the syntactic information that is still present in the pseudo speech condition (for additional fMRI data consistent with this account, see Plante et al., 2002; Meyer et al., 2004; Hesling et al., 2005a).

A number of neuropsychological studies have also addressed the question of whether there are hemispheric

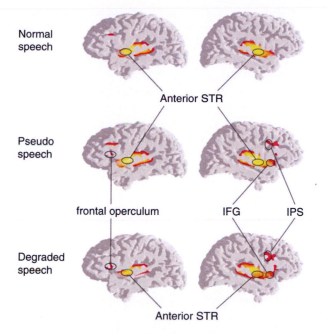

Figure 7.9 Results of the fMRI study by Meyer et al. (2003). All three types of stimuli engaged the anterior superior temporal region (STR) bilaterally. In addition, the pseudo speech stimuli and the degraded speech stimuli, but not the normal speech stimuli, engaged the posterior inferior frontal cortices (IFG, frontal operculum) in both hemispheres as well as the inferior precentral sulcus (IPS) in the right hemisphere. (From Meyer et al., 2003, p. 289.)

asymmetries in the perception of sentence-level linguistic prosody. For instance, several studies have investigated how patients with either left- or right-hemisphere lesions perform, relative to healthy comparison subjects, on tasks that require them to use prosodic information to identify declarative and interrogative utterances. Some of these studies, however, have yielded seemingly conflicting results. On the one hand, there is evidence that the ability to recognize prosodically conveyed declarative/interrogative distinctions in natural utterances is more likely to be severely impaired by left- than right-hemisphere damage (Heilman et al., 1984; Bryan, 1989; Perkins et al., 1996; Walker et al., 2002). On the other hand, there is also evidence that this ability can be significantly compromised by right-sided lesions (Weintraub et al., 1981; Borod et al., 1990; Brådvik et al., 1991).

To shed more light on how each hemisphere might contribute to the comprehension of declarative and interrogative intonation patterns, a few neuropsychological investigations have asked patients to categorize not only natural utterances, but also utterances that, like the degraded speech condition in Meyer et al.'s

(2003) fMRI study, have been filtered so as to obscure the segmental, lexical, and syntactic details while retaining the overarching prosodic contours (Heilman et al., 1984; Bryan, 1989; Perkins et al., 1996; Pell & Baum, 1997). Among the most important generalizations to have emerged from these studies are the following: Patients with left-hemisphere lesions tend to be worse at identifying declarative and interrogative intonation patterns in natural utterances than in filtered utterances; conversely, patients with right-hemisphere lesions tend to have greater difficulty recognizing the two types of intonation patterns in filtered utterances than in natural utterances. These findings suggest that the left hemisphere may be dominant when the linguistic processing load is increased by the presence of segmental, lexical, and syntactic information, whereas the right hemisphere may be dominant when the linguistic processing load is reduced by the absence of such information. Crucially, the latter situation is when the slow melodic modulations that signal declarative and interrogative speech acts stand out in sharp relief, which raises the possibility that these modulations may be processed primarily, but not exclusively, in the right hemisphere (see also Sammler et al., 2010).

Shifting now to the perception of syntactically relevant intonational phrase boundaries, evidence that this capacity may be implemented bilaterally comes from an fMRI study by Ischebeck et al. (2008). As in Meyer et al.'s (2003) study, the participants were native speakers of German. They were presented with both natural and hummed versions of sentences that were equated for overall length as well as the number of syllables. The key experimental manipulation was that one half of the stimuli contained just one intonational phrase boundary (indicated by #), as in (5a), whereas the other half contained two, as in (5b):

(5) a. *Peter verspricht Anna zu arbeiten # und das Büro zu putzen.*
(*Peter promises Anna to work and to clean the office.*)
b. *Peter verspricht # Anna zu entlasten # und das Büro zu putzen.*
(*Peter promises to support Anna and to clean the office.*)

To isolate the neural correlates of the perception of intonational phrase boundaries in naturally spoken sentences, the researchers subtracted the activation patterns associated with the natural sentences containing just one intonational phrase boundary from

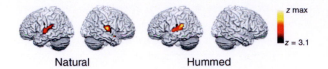

Natural   Hummed

Figure 7.10 Results of the fMRI study by Ischebeck et al. (2008). When natural sentences with just one intonational phrase boundary were subtracted from natural sentences with two intonational phrase boundaries, activity was found in the middle sector of the superior temporal cortex bilaterally. When the same type of contrast was performed with hummed sentences, activity was found in same region in the left hemisphere. (From Ischebeck et al., 2008, p. 546.)

those associated with the natural sentences containing two. This contrast revealed significant engagement of the middle sector of the superior temporal cortex in both hemispheres (Figure 7.10). When the same type of contrast was performed with the hummed versions of the sentences, essentially the same region was activated in the left hemisphere, but not in the right hemisphere. Although it is not clear why the effect for the hummed sentences was left-lateralized, the fact that the effect for the natural sentences was bilateral suggests that the mid superior temporal cortex in both hemispheres usually contributes to the detection of syntactically relevant intonational phrase boundaries.

Interestingly, these superior temporal regions may be the neural generators of an ERP component that is referred to as the **closure positive shift (CPS)**, since it appears to be elicited by the endpoints of intonational phrases. The CPS was first described by Steinhauer et al. (1999), but it was subsequently investigated in greater depth by Steinhauer & Friederici (2001) and Pannekamp et al. (2005) (for a review see Bögels et al., 2011). For example, Pannekamp et al. (2005) demonstrated that when subjects listen to either natural or hummed sentences that contain either one or two intonational phrase boundaries, as in (5), those boundaries reliably trigger a positive deflection in the waveform (Figure 7.11). Analogous deflections were also observed when the stimuli were utterances in which the content words were replaced with non-words, and when the stimuli were utterances in which all of the words were replaced with nonwords. Taken together, these findings suggest that the CPS is a robust electrophysiological index of the perceived closure of intonational phrases.

Closure positive shift (CPS) An ERP component that is evoked by the endpoints of intonational phrases.

Returning to the topic of lateralization, it is important to ask whether neuropsychological data can illuminate the issue of whether the perception of intonational phrase boundaries is genuinely bilateral, or whether it depends primarily on just one of the two hemispheres. Several studies have explored how patients with either left- or right-hemisphere lesions perform, relative to healthy comparison subjects, on tasks that require them to use prosodic cues to detect intonational phrase boundaries that correspond to syntactic junctures, as in the examples shown in (2). The results, however, are rather mixed; and moreover, they are mixed in a way that resembles some of the investigations involving the recognition of prosodically conveyed declarative/interrogative distinctions. On the one hand, a few studies have reported that the recognition of syntactically relevant intonational phrase boundaries is more likely to be disrupted in patients with left- than right-hemisphere lesions (Perkins et al., 1996; Walker et al., 2002). On the other hand, it is also clear that this ability can be impaired to a non-trivial degree by right-sided lesions (Baum et al., 1997; Walker et al., 2001; Aasland & Baum, 2003; Baum & Dwivedi, 2003). Some researchers have argued that a careful inspection of the available data favors the view that the pertinent perceptual processes are mediated more by the left than the right hemisphere (e.g., Baum & Dwivedi, 2003). Whether this is really the case, however, remains uncertain. In short, further experiments using neuropsychological as well as other brain mapping techniques are needed in order to elucidate the precise functional contributions of the left and right hemispheres to the receptive processing of syntactically relevant intonational phrase boundaries.

The Lexical Domain

When we turn to the perception of linguistic prosody in the lexical domain, we find that the question of lateralization receives a much less ambiguous answer, since there is convergent evidence from both fMRI and neuropsychology pointing to strong left-hemisphere dominance. From the perspective of fMRI, one of the most valuable discoveries to date emerged from the study by Wildgruber et al. (2004) that we first encountered in our discussion of the roles of the frontal lobes in the perception of emotional prosody. As indicated in Figure 7.4A and the accompanying text, the participants in this experiment were German speakers who listened to multiple versions of the sentence *Der Schal ist in der Truhe* (*The scarf is in the chest*) that varied continuously along two acoustic dimensions—the placement of emphatic stress, and the degree of

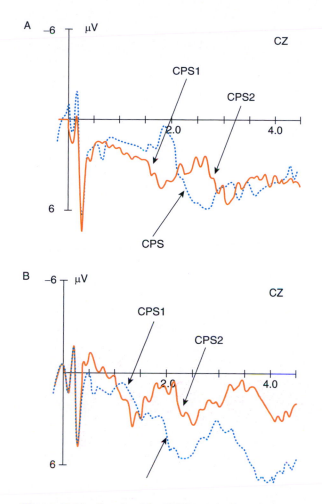

Figure 7.11 Results of the ERP study by Pannekamp et al. (2005). (A) Grand average ERPs elicited by natural sentences. Recordings from the CZ electrode, which is at the vertex (top center) of the head, show that natural sentences with just one intonational phrase boundary (dotted line) evoked a single "closure positive shift" (CPS) starting around 2,000 ms, whereas natural sentences with two intonational phrase boundaries (solid line) evoked two such shifts, one starting around 1,500 ms and another around 2,700 ms. (B) Grand average ERPs elicited by hummed sentences. Again at CZ, hummed sentences with just one intonational phrase boundary (dotted line) evoked a single CPS starting around 2,500 ms, whereas hummed sentences with two boundaries (solid line) evoked two CPSs, the first starting around 1,000 ms and the second around 2,000 ms. (From Pannekamp et al., 2005, pp. 410 & 413.)

expressed excitement. To reiterate, the subjects' task in the "focus position" condition was to determine which of two sentences was better suited to respond to the question *Where is the scarf?*, and their task in the "expressiveness" condition was to determine which of two sentences was produced in a more excited manner. Earlier we considered the subtraction of the focus position condition from the expressiveness condition,

since our topic was emotional prosody; here what matters is the opposite contrast—namely, the subtraction of the expressiveness condition from the focus position condition—since our topic is linguistic prosody. The results are depicted in Figure 7.12. A single "hot spot" appeared, and it was centered squarely in Broca's area (left BA44/45). This finding suggests not only that the explicit discrimination of emphatic stress placement relies more on the left than the right hemisphere, but that it may be subserved by what has traditionally been regarded as one of the major computational hubs for language processing. In keeping with previous theoretical proposals (Schirmer & Kotz, 2006), it is conceivable that during speech perception, Broca's area facilitates the integration of prosodic information—in this case, emphatic stress—with other levels of linguistic representation, such as the forms, meanings, and grammatical categories of words.

Further evidence for left-lateralization comes from a variety of neuropsychological studies. In general, what these studies demonstrate is that left-hemisphere damage is far more likely than right-hemisphere damage to disrupt the perception of not only emphatic stress (Bryan, 1989; Baum, 1998; Geigenberger & Ziegler, 2001) but also lexical/metrical stress (Blumstein & Goodglass, 1972; Baum et al., 1982; Emmorey, 1987; Baum, 1998; Walker et al., 2002). For example, Walker et al. (2002) asked 24 individuals—eight patients with left-sided lesions, eight patients with right-sided lesions, and eight healthy comparison participants—to determine the meanings and grammatical assignments (noun vs. verb) of two-syllable words that could only be disambiguated by detecting stress cues, as in (3a). Although the patients with right-sided lesions did not perform significantly worse than the healthy participants, the patients with left-sided lesions were severely impaired on the task. These results, among many others, strongly support the view that the discrimination

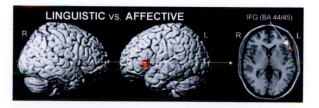

Figure 7.12 Results of the fMRI study by Wildgruber et al. (2004). Note that the stimuli are shown in Figure 7.4. Subtraction of the condition involving affective "expressiveness" judgments from the condition involving linguistic "focus position" judgments revealed activity in Broca's area. (From Wildgruber et al., 2004, p. 1386.)

of linguistic accentuation in the lexical domain depends predominantly on left-lateralized neural mechanisms.

The Tonal Domain

Although the literature on the neural substrates of linguistic tonal perception is still relatively small, it is already full of fascinating findings. One of the most intriguing and important discoveries to date is that the same auditory signals—in this case, pitch patterns— are processed in radically different ways depending on whether they are treated as non-linguistic or linguistic information (for reviews see Wong, 2002; Zatorre & Gandour, 2008; Wong et al., 2009). A large body of data based on diverse brain mapping techniques indicates that non-linguistic pitch judgments rely more on the right than the left hemisphere. At the same time, however, there is increasing evidence that linguistic pitch judgments—more precisely, judgments about the kinds of tones that serve to distinguish between words in languages like Mandarin Chinese, as in (4)—involve the opposite asymmetry, relying more on the left than the right hemisphere.

Support for the notion that linguistic tonal perception depends predominantly on the left hemisphere comes from several sources. Neuropsychological studies have shown that native speakers of tone languages frequently lose their ability to identify lexically distinctive tones following left- but not right-hemisphere lesions (Gandour & Dardaranandad, 1983; Yiu & Fok, 1995; Kadyamusuma et al., 2011; see also Gandour, 1998). In addition, a number of functional neuroimaging studies have shown that a network of left perisylvian temporal, parietal, and frontal areas are typically recruited during linguistically relevant tonal processing (e.g., Gandour et al., 1998, 2000, 2003, 2004; Hsieh et al., 2001; Klein et al., 2001; Li et al., 2003; Wong et al., 2004; Xu et al., 2006).

For example, Wong et al. (2004) used PET to measure brain activity in both Chinese- and English-speaking subjects while they discriminated tones embedded in both Chinese words (where the tones were linguistically relevant to the Chinese speakers but not the English speakers) and English words (where the tones were not linguistically relevant to either group of subjects). When the discrimination task for tones embedded in Chinese words was contrasted with a baseline condition involving passive listening to the same stimuli, the Chinese speakers exhibited increased activity in the left anterior insula, whereas the English speakers exhibited increased activity in the right anterior insula (Figure 7.13A). And when

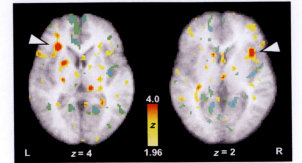

Figure 7.13   Results of the PET study by Wong et al. (2004). (A) PET activations for the discrimination of pitch patterns embedded in Mandarin Chinese words, minus the passive perception of the same stimuli. (B) PET activations for the discrimination of pitch patterns embedded in English words, minus the passive perception of the same stimuli. (From Wong et al., 2004, p. 9156.)

the discrimination task for tones embedded in English words was contrasted with a baseline condition involving passive listening to the same stimuli, both groups of subjects exhibited increased activity in the right anterior insula (Figure 7.13B). These results provide strong evidence that the neural underpinnings of pitch perception are shaped by linguistic experience. In short, when lexically associated tones are treated as linguistic information, they engage left-lateralized cortical regions, but when they are not treated as linguistic information, they engage right-lateralized cortical regions.

Although Wong et al.'s (2004) PET study has many virtues, it leaves open an important question—namely, whether the greater left-hemisphere activity that the Chinese speakers displayed during the discrimination of Chinese tones reflects the linguistic processing of pitch patterns per se, or instead the linguistic processing of meaningful words. To address this issue, Xu et al.

(2006) conducted an fMRI study that was cleverly designed to isolate the neural bases of prelexical tone processing. Native speakers of both Chinese and Thai (another tone language) discriminated tonal contours in the following two types of stimuli: Chinese words, in which Chinese tones were superimposed on Chinese syllables (C^C), yielding sounds that were identifiable as real lexical items in Chinese; and "tonal chimeras," in which Thai tones were superimposed on Chinese syllables (C^T), yielding sounds that were not identifiable as real words in either language. (Readers familiar with ancient Greek mythology will recall that a chimera is a monstrous creature with three heads—a lion's head in front, a goat's head rising out of the spine, and a snake's head at the end of the tail.) To determine which brain regions were most responsive to native vs. non-native tones, the researchers performed a $C^C > C^T$ contrast for the Chinese subjects and a $C^T > C^C$ contrast for the Thai

subjects. Overlapping activation for both contrasts was found in the left planum temporale, which is known to contribute to speech perception (Figure 7.14A-C; see Chapter 5). More precisely, the following double dissociation between language experience and pitch processing was manifested in this cortical area: significantly greater responsiveness to Chinese tones than Thai tones for the Chinese subjects; and conversely, significantly greater responsiveness to Thai tones than Chinese tones for the Thai subjects (Figure 7.14D). Because the tonal chimeras were meaningless sounds for both groups of subjects, these cross-over effects in the left planum temporale are independent of lexical-semantic processing. Presumably, they reflect a relatively early prelexical stage of linguistic tonal perception.

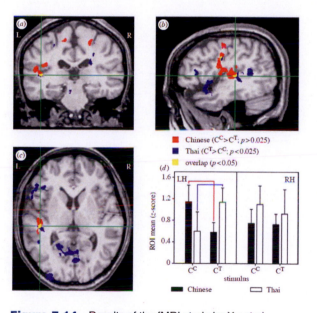

Figure 7.14 Results of the fMRI study by Xu et al. (2006). A common focus of activation, associated with the discrimination of both Chinese and Thai tones, is indicated by the overlap (yellow) between Chinese and Thai groups in the functional activation maps. Green cross-hair lines mark the stereotactic center coordinates for the overlapping region in the left planum temporale, shown in (A) coronal, (B) sagittal, and (C) axial sections. A double dissociation, shown in (D), between tonal processing and language experience reveals that for the Thai group, Thai tones elicit stronger activity than Chinese tones, whereas for the Chinese group, Chinese tones elicit stronger activity than Thai tones. C^C: Chinese tones superimposed on Chinese syllables, i.e., Chinese words; C^T: Thai tones superimposed on Chinese syllables, i.e., tonal chimeras; ROI: region of interest. (From Xu et al., 2006, p. 178.)

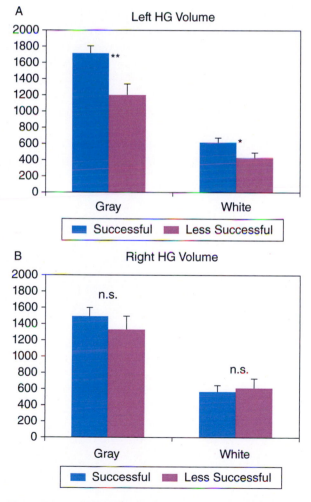

Figure 7.15 Gray and white matter volume of Heschl's gyrus (HG) in the left (A) and right (B) hemispheres of subjects who were either very successful (blue bars) or less successful (purple bars) at learning an artificial tone language. (From Wong et al., 2008, p. 831.)

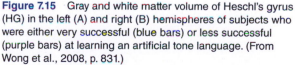

Box 7.2 Correlations Between the Geographic Distributions of Tone Languages and Genes for Brain Development

Tone languages are attested worldwide, but they are more prevalent in some places than others. On the one hand, they are fairly common in sub-Saharan Africa, the Far East, Central America, the Carribean, and the Amazon basin; on the other hand, they are relatively rare in North Africa, Europe, central and western Asia, Australia, and North America. At first sight, these geographic patterns seem to be more or less arbitrary. It turns out, however, that they correlate very significantly with the population frequencies of two genes that are involved in brain development, *ASPM* and *Microcephalin* (Dediu & Ladd, 2007).

Each of these genes has two alleles (i.e., variant structural realizations), one "original" and the other "derived," where "derived" means that it emerged more recently in evolutionary time (about 5.8 thousand years ago for the derived version of *ASPM*, and about 37 thousand years ago for the derived version of *Microcephalin*). Dan Dediu and D. Robert Ladd, both whom work in the Psychology and Language Sciences program at the University of Edinburgh, noticed that, according to previous data, the population frequencies of the original alleles are greatest in those geographic regions where tone languages are common, whereas the population frequencies of the derived alleles are greatest in those geographic regions where non-tone languages are common. To explore these relationships more carefully, they performed a number of statistical analyses on a large database comprising 26 linguistic features and 983 genes collected for 49 world populations. What they found was that, in general, linguistic features and genes are not well-correlated, but when it comes to the linguistic feature of tone and the *ASPM* and *Microcephalin* genes, there are very strong relationships—indeed, stronger than 98.5 percent of all of the 25,558 relationships that were considered. As the previous data suggested, populations that speak tone languages tend to have the original alleles of the genes, whereas populations that speak non-tone languages tend to have the derived alleles.

Given these findings, the following three-way correspondence is quite striking: first, tone languages are the norm in sub-Saharan Africa; second, tone languages are associated with the phylogenetically original alleles of *ASPM* and *Microcephalin;* and third, sub-Saharan Africa is where modern *Homo sapiens* evolved roughly 150-180 thousand years ago. Taken together, these points raise the intriguing possibility that the oldest human languages may have been tone languages.

How, though, do the genes actually influence pitch processing? The answer to this question is far from clear, but some progress was recently made by Wong et al. (2012), who found that in a group of Americans who did not speak a tone language, the amount or "load" of the derived allele of one of the genes—specifically, *ASPM*—correlated not only with purely behavioral measures of lexical tone perception, but also with neural responses to lexical tones in primary and secondary auditory cortices.

Striking evidence that linguistic tonal perception is facilitated by even earlier stages of auditory processing comes from two other lines of research. First, Wong et al. (2008) invented an artificial tone language consisting of 18 words—six syllables with three tones each—and tried to teach 17 native English speakers to recognize the sounds. The participants, none of whom had ever studied a tone language, varied considerably in their degree of success at learning this task. Amazingly enough, the researchers discovered that, compared to the least successful subjects, the most successful ones had significantly greater gray and white matter volume in the left primary auditory region—i.e., in Heschl's gyrus, which lies anterior to the planum temporale on the supratemporal plane (Figure 7.15; see the section on hearing in Chapter 1). These results suggest that the primary auditory cortex, particularly in the left hemisphere, may play a special role in encoding the basic acoustic cues that are relevant to the perception of linguistic pitch contours. In addition, the results may be related to recent data linking the geographical distribution of tone languages with the population frequency of certain alleles of two genes involved in brain growth (Box 7.2).

Second, a number of subcortical electrophysiological studies have provided compelling evidence that the receptive processing of linguistic pitch contours is enhanced as early as the brainstem, well before the auditory signals reach Heschl's gyrus (for a review see Krishnan & Gandour, 2009). These investigations have focused on the **frequency-following response (FFR)**, an electrophysiological component that reflects a process whereby neurons in the inferior colliculus phase-lock with the acoustic cycles of the stimulus waveform (see Box 5.2 in Chapter 5). A key finding is that, compared to native English speakers, native Chinese speakers exhibit FFRs that more accurately track perceived pitch contours. Thus, long-term exposure to a tone language may sharpen the tuning characteristics of neurons deep in the "basement" of the brain—specifically, in auditory brainstem nuclei that were once believed to be completely hardwired and hence impervious to experience-dependent plasticity. In the coming years, much more will undoubtedly be learned about the brainstem contributions to linguistic tonal perception.

Summary

Linguistic prosody is manifested in three major domains: syntactic, lexical, and tonal. A substantial amount of data regarding the neural substrates of the perception of linguistic prosody has accumulated in recent years; however, a richly elaborated, explanatorily coherent theory has not yet been developed. Nevertheless, some important insights about one of the central issues—cerebral lateralization—have been gained. In the syntactic domain, the receptive processing of prosodic information appears to be mediated bilaterally, but perhaps with some rightward asymmetry for declarative/interrogative distinctions and some leftward asymmetry for intonational phrase boundaries that mark syntactic junctures. In the lexical domain, stress cues seem to be detected and analyzed predominantly by the left hemisphere. And in the tonal domain, although the perception of non-linguistic pitch contours takes place mainly in the right hemisphere, the perception of linguistic pitch contours takes place mainly in the left hemisphere.

It is not yet possible to provide rigorous, detailed explanations for all of these findings, but it is noteworthy that they can be loosely accommodated by a combination of the two general theoretical perspectives described in the Introduction. First, acoustic considerations, and especially the timing dimension, can account for some of the data. Prosodic elements that are realized over relatively long periods of time—like the slowly rising vocal inflection that characterizes

yes/no questions—depend more on the right than the left hemisphere, whereas prosodic elements that are realized over relatively short periods of time—like intonational phrase boundaries, contrastive stress patterns, and tonal features—depend more on the left than the right hemisphere. Second, functional considerations must also be invoked in order to account for some of the data. In particular, the left-hemisphere dominance for most aspects of language seems to be the main reason why tonal features are lateralized to the left when treated as linguistic information but lateralized to the right when treated as non-linguistic information. Thus, both acoustic and functional factors are apparently necessary to accommodate the array of findings reviewed above. Further research will undoubtedly shed more light on not only inter-hemispheric but also intra-hemispheric aspects of the receptive processing of linguistic prosody in the brain. On a final note, it can also be anticipated that new studies will improve our understanding of a topic that was not discussed above but that nevertheless warrants greater attention, namely the likely contribution of the basal ganglia to the perception of linguistic prosody (Blonder et al., 1989; Gandour & Dechongkit, 1992).

Production

As with the production of emotional prosody, the production of linguistic prosody has been investigated from a neuroscientific perspective primarily by documenting the patterns of impaired and preserved capacities that are typically associated with damage to particular brain regions. So far, most of the research in this field has revolved around the same general issue emphasized above—cerebral lateralization. Careful distinctions are usually made, however, between the three major domains of linguistic prosody—syntactic, lexical, and tonal.

In the syntactic domain, the ability to generate intonation patterns that appropriately distinguish between statements and questions appears to depend on the cooperative interaction of both hemispheres. Evidence for such bilateral implementation comes from studies showing that deficits in producing sentence-level prosodic contours arise from both right-sided lesions (Weintraub et al., 1981; Cooper et al., 1984; Shapiro & Danley, 1985; Behrens, 1989) and left-sided lesions (Danley & Shapiro, 1982; Danley et al., 1983; Cooper et al., 1984). As an illustration of the effects of right-sided lesions, Behrens (1989) administered a story completion task to eight patients and seven healthy comparison participants and found that out of 24 trials

---

Frequency-following response (FFR) An electrophysiological component that indexes a process whereby neurons in the inferior colliculus phase-lock with the acoustic cycles of the stimulus waveform.

in which utterances with specific intonation patterns were required, the patients produced the correct patterns on average only 14 times, according to a panel of listeners. Regarding the effects of left-sided lesions, all of the relevant studies cited above revealed impairments involving the control of both pitch and timing during sentence production. It is noteworthy, however, that the types of expressive prosodic disturbances in the syntactic domain that frequently follow from right- or left-hemisphere damage are sometimes relatively mild. For example, Baum and Pell (1997) demonstrated that seven patients with right-sided lesions and four patients with left-sided lesions (the latter four all meeting criteria for Broca's aphasia) performed comparably to ten healthy control subjects in utilizing intonational cues to signal distinctions between declarative and interrogative utterances. To be sure, the two groups of patients were not completely normal on the production tasks, since they differed from the control subjects in manipulating some of the pertinent prosodic parameters. Their deficits, however, were far from severe, and this led Baum and Pell (1997) to suggest that the generation of sentence-level linguistic prosody may not be regulated entirely by cortical structures, but may instead be influenced by subcortical structures such as the basal ganglia. Support for this proposal has in fact come from investigations of patients with Parkinson's disease (Blonder et al., 1989).

In the lexical domain, the available data suggest that the programming of syllabic stress is mediated primarily by the left hemisphere, but that the right hemisphere may also contribute in certain situations, particularly when the assignment of stress must be determined in the context of a whole sentence. Evidence for left-hemisphere dominance in generating syllabic stress comes from several studies which indicate that this capacity is disrupted significantly more often by left-than right-sided lesions (Emmorey, 1987; Behrens, 1988; Ouellette & Baum, 1994). And evidence for a special context-sensitive contribution from the right hemisphere comes from an important neuropsychological investigation by Balan and Gandour (1999). These researchers asked 32 individuals—eight patients with left-hemisphere lesions and nonfluent aphasia, eight patients with left-hemisphere lesions and fluent aphasia, eight patients with right-hemisphere lesions, and eight healthy comparison participants—to produce the names of pictured objects in the context of three carrier sentences that varied in length from short (*Take the _____*) to medium (*Take the _____ to Sue*) to long (*Take the _____ to Sue today*). The target expressions were segmentally identical phrases that differed only in

stress placement, as in (3b), such as **blackboard** vs. *black board*. Relative to the normal control subjects, both groups of left-hemisphere-damaged aphasic patients were impaired at producing the target expressions with the appropriate stress patterns, and moreover the fluent aphasics displayed a moderate effect of sentence length, performing worse on the medium than the short sentences. The most interesting result, however, was that the patients with right-sided lesions also had considerable difficulty with stress assignment in all three sentence contexts. Although they did not perform as poorly as the two groups of aphasic patients, their scores were nevertheless significantly below normal. This outcome contrasts sharply with the previous studies mentioned above, which linked stress production disorders with left- rather than right-sided lesions (Emmorey, 1987; Behrens, 1988; Ouellette & Baum, 1994). As Balan and Gandour (1999) point out, however, those studies evaluated stress production in single word situations. What the results of their own study suggest is that the right hemisphere may become relevant to stress production when the overall temporal period of speech planning is relatively large. Such an interpretation is clearly consistent with some of the general ideas about hemispheric asymmetries discussed above. It should also be mentioned, though, that, as with the expression of sentence-level prosodic contours, the expression of syllabic stress has been associated not only with the cerebral cortex, but also with the basal ganglia (Blonder et al., 1989).

In the tonal domain, deficits in generating conventional word-specific pitch contours are almost invariably linked with left- rather than right-sided lesions, thereby pointing to a powerful left-hemisphere lateralization of the pertinent neural mechanisms (e.g., Packard, 1986; Ryalls & Reinvang, 1986; Gandour et al., 1994, 1996, 1997; Yiu & Fok, 1995; Liang & Heuven, 2004; for reviews see Wong, 2002, and Gandour, 1998, 2006; for exceptions see Kadyamusuma et al., 2011). In general, the severity of a given patient's impairment in tone production tends to correlate with the severity of that patient's other aphasic symptoms. However, one of the most remarkable and theoretically significant discoveries in this area of research is that it is possible for tonal disturbances to dissociate from other types of phonological disturbances. For example, in a detailed case study of a conduction aphasic who was a native speaker of Thai, Gandour et al. (1994) found that during the patient's "sequences of phonemic approximations" to target words, information about tones was not only accessed faster than information about consonants and vowels, but was also more stable. Conversely, in a detailed case study of a Broca's aphasic who was a native speaker of Mandarin Chinese, Liang and Heuven (2004) found that tone production was more gravely impaired that vowel production. Taken together, these results suggest that tonal and segmental aspects of speech planning may rely on partially separate neural mechanisms that can be compromised independently of each other. There is even some evidence that within the tonal domain, some tones can be disrupted more than others. For instance, the Chinese Broca's aphasic studied by Liang and Heuven (2004) was impaired at producing the rising, falling–rising, and falling tones, but was nevertheless still able to correctly produce the high level tone (see (4)). Gandour (2006) proposed that this may reflect the greater difficulty of producing tones that involve dynamic pitch changes, but further research is needed to explore this hypothesis. Finally, patients with Parkinson's disease who speak tone languages exhibit reduced tonal spaces, which is due in part to an overall reduction in their pitch range for speech (Wong & Diehl, 1999). This suggests that, as with the syntactic and lexical domains, tone production relies to some extent on the basal ganglia.

Summary and Key Points

- Two types of prosody are usually distinguished:

  - Emotional prosody encompasses all the ways in which intonation can be modulated to convey feelings (happiness, sadness, anger, fear, etc.) and attitudes (sympathy, politeness, dominance, sarcasm, etc.).
  - Linguistic prosody encompasses all the ways in which intonation can be modulated to signal linguistic distinctions in three different domains: syntactic, lexical, and tonal.

- A comprehensive model of the neural substrates of prosody has not yet been developed. However, during the past few decades, the principal terms of debate have been strongly influenced by two general theoretical perspectives regarding one of the central issues, namely cerebral lateralization:

  - One approach assumes that the key factor involves acoustic features, such that prosodic elements characterized mainly by long duration and/or pitch variation tend to be right-lateralized, whereas those characterized mainly by short duration and/or temporal variation tend to be left-lateralized.
  - The other approach assumes that the key factor involves functional features, such that prosodic elements that express emotional states tend to be right-lateralized, whereas those that express linguistic contrasts tend to be left-lateralized.
  - Recent studies have shown that although each approach has some justification, neither one by itself can account for all of the available data.

- The *perception of emotional prosody* has been investigated more intensively that any other topic in this area of inquiry. It is most likely subserved by a network of anatomically distributed cortical and subcortical structures in both hemispheres. More specifically, the following five hypotheses have been supported:

  - The right mid to anterior superior temporal cortex underlies the integration of the various acoustic cues that conjointly signal different emotions.
  - The amygdala facilitates the detection of prosodic patterns that are subjectively relevant, contextually novel, and acoustically salient.
  - The right ventral frontoparietal cortex subserves covert simulations of the different types of emotions that are conveyed by different tones of voice.
  - The basal ganglia may also contribute to emotion simulation. In addition, or alternatively, these structures may help decode emotionally meaningful patterns in dynamic sequences of vocal stimuli, or trigger appropriate cognitive and behavioral responses to such stimuli.
  - The bilateral orbitofrontal and inferior frontal cortices guide top-down executive processes such as explicitly attending to and categorizing perceived prosodic patterns, and judging how well those patterns match the semantic content of what is said.

- The *production of emotional prosody* has not been studied so carefully, but it has nevertheless been linked with several brain structures:

(Continued)

(Continued)

- The right hemisphere is necessary for generating affective intonation contours, with the most critical regions being the posterior inferior frontal gyrus (i.e., the right-hemisphere homologue of Broca's area), the ventral precentral gyrus, and the anterior insula.
- The left hemisphere has also been implicated in this capacity, but its involvement in the production of emotional prosody per se, as opposed to the associated verbal-articulatory processes, remains controversial.
- The basal ganglia provide essential subcortical support for the expression of vocal affect.

- The *perception of linguistic prosody* exhibits different patterns of lateralization in different domains:

  - In the syntactic domain, the receptive processing of prosodic information appears to be mediated bilaterally, but with a moderate right-hemisphere bias for the slowly changing vocal modulations that signal declarative/interrogative distinctions, and a moderate left-hemisphere bias for the more rapidly occurring intonational phrase boundaries that mark syntactic junctures.
  - In the lexical domain, stress cues are detected and analyzed predominantly by the left hemisphere.
  - In the tonal domain, although the perception of non-linguistic pitch contours takes place mainly in the right hemisphere, the perception of linguistic pitch contours takes place mainly in the left hemisphere.
  - Finally, the basal ganglia may contribute to the perception of some aspects of linguistic prosody.

- The *production of linguistic prosody* also exhibits different patterns of lateralization in different domains, and these patterns closely parallel those for perception:

  - In the syntactic domain, the production of vocal modulations that convey declarative/interrogative distinctions appears to rely on both hemispheres.
  - In the lexical domain, the assignment of stress is controlled predominantly by the left hemisphere.
  - In the tonal domain, the programming of pitch contours is likewise controlled predominantly by the left hemisphere.
  - And once again, the basal ganglia may contribute to the production of some aspects of linguistic prosody.

Recommended Reading

- Baum, S.R., & Pell, M.D. (1999). The neural bases of prosody: Insights from lesion studies and neuroimaging. *Aphasiology, 13,* 581–608. A somewhat old, but still quite informative, summary of primarily neuropsychological studies of the perception and production of emotional and linguistic prosody.
- Wildgruber, D., Ackermann, H., Kriefelts, B., & Ethofer, T. (2006). Cerebral processing of linguistic and emotional prosody: fMRI studies. *Progress in Brain Research, 156,* 249–268. An integrative review of some of the most influential fMRI studies of the perception of emotional and linguistic prosody.
- Zatorre, R.J., & Gandour, J.T. (2008). Neural specializations for speech and pitch: Moving beyond the dichotomies. *Philosophical Transactions of the Royal Society, B, Biological Sciences, 363,* 1087–1104. A technical discussion of the theoretical and empirical issues surrounding research on the cerebral lateralization of linguistic and non-linguistic tonal perception.
- Kotz, S.A., & Paulmann, S. (2011). Emotion, language, and the brain. *Language and Linguistics Compass, 5,* 108–125. A very useful and accessible overview of the neural substrates of emotional prosody, integrating data from neuropsychological, functional neuroimaging, and electrophysiological studies.

PART IV

Other Modalities of Language Use

Reading and Writing

8

Introduction

The vocal channel of linguistic communication is the one that people use most often, but there are obviously other modalities of language use, and they are the focus of the two chapters in this part of the book. In particular, the current chapter addresses the neural substrates of reading and writing, and the next one addresses the neural substrates of sign language.

Even though our species, *Homo sapiens,* arose roughly 150–180 thousand years ago, writing—which is to say, the practice of rendering linguistic messages as graphic markings—did not emerge until roughly 5,400 years ago. Around that time, ancient scribes in Mesopotamia invented the very first forms of writing, which were highly pictorial in nature. Egyptian hieroglyphs, for example, consisted largely of schematic drawings of animals, tools, body parts, and other objects. These signs had the advantage of being easy to interpret, but they suffered from two serious shortcomings: They were time-consuming to produce, and they were unable to capture abstract concepts like freedom, victory, or religion. Due to these limitations, the original pictorial approach gradually gave way to more efficient systems that employed simplified, conventionalized symbols to represent speech sounds rather than meanings. Still, the shapes of some of these symbols were borrowed from hieroglyphs, and as a result many of the letters that we routinely use today in our Roman alphabet derive from drawings that date back thousands of years. For example, as shown in Figure 8.1, the capital letter A is an inverted ox head—the end point of a long period of cultural evolution that began with cave paintings and progressed through multiple stages of stylization and rotation (Dehaene, 2009).

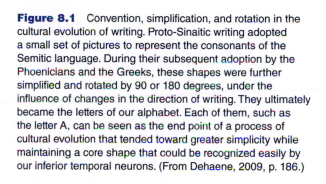

Lascaux   Proto-Sinaitic   Phoenician   Greek/Latin

Figure 8.1 Convention, simplification, and rotation in the cultural evolution of writing. Proto-Sinaitic writing adopted a small set of pictures to represent the consonants of the Semitic language. During their subsequent adoption by the Phoenicians and the Greeks, these shapes were further simplified and rotated by 90 or 180 degrees, under the influence of changes in the direction of writing. They ultimately became the letters of our alphabet. Each of them, such as the letter A, can be seen as the end point of a process of cultural evolution that tended toward greater simplicity while maintaining a core shape that could be recognized easily by our inferior temporal neurons. (From Dehaene, 2009, p. 186.)

In alphabetic writing systems, letters usually represent phonemes or groups of related phonemes, but in other kinds of writing systems, individual symbols encode phonetic features (as in Korean Hangul), syllables (as in Japanese Kana), or whole words (as in Japanese Kanji or Chinese) (see Figure 8.2; see also Daniels & Bright, 1996, and Coulmas, 2003). Despite this diversity, however, all writing systems share a number of interesting properties, three of which are as follows. First, although different systems impose different orientations on the script, once an orientation has been selected, it is used consistently. English, for example, is always written left-to-right, whereas Arabic is always written right-to-left. Second, printed symbols tend to be composed of about three strokes, give or take a couple, where a "stroke" is defined as a line or curve that can be traced without ever lifting or stopping the pen (Changizi & Shimojo, 2005). Thus, the capital letters in the Roman alphabet are produced with either one stroke (C, I, J, O, S, U), two strokes (D, G, L, P, Q, T, V, X), three strokes (A, B, F H, K, N, R, Y, Z), or four strokes (E, M, W), but never more. Finally, disregarding rotational considerations, the shapes of the symbols that appear most often in the world's writing systems correspond to the shapes of the most frequently occurring features in natural scenes (Changizi et al., 2006). For instance, the most common shapes in writing systems are L and T, and the very same shapes recur with astonishing regularity when ordinary objects touch each other or partially hide each other. This suggests that the reason why L and T shapes are favored in writing systems is because they are especially salient stimuli for the human brain (Dehaene, 2009). And this in turn leads to the question at the heart of this chapter: What is the neurotopography of the cortical circuits that underlie reading and writing?

Figure 8.2 In spite of their obvious diversity, all writing systems share numerous visual features—highly contrasted contours, an average number of about three strokes per character, and a reduced set of shapes that constantly recur, even in unrelated cultures. (From Dehaene, 2009, p. 175.)

The first section concentrates on the following aspects of reading: how letter strings are initially processed along a hierarchically organized pathway in the ventral occipitotemporal cortex; how the invariant perceptual properties of printed words are recognized in a region called the Visual Word Form Area (VWFA); and how subsequent processing streams project from the VWFA to two higher-level networks—one devoted to accessing the phonological forms of words, and the other devoted to accessing their meanings. The second section then turns to writing and considers how the mind/brain goes in the opposite direction, starting with phonological and semantic structures and ending up with a richly specified hand-action program for producing a particular sequence of letters on a page or screen. In both sections of the chapter, several types of research are covered, but most of the data come from functional neuroimaging studies with normal subjects and neuropsychological studies with brain-damaged patients. Although all of these studies focused on English, French, and other languages with similar writing systems, it is noteworthy that a growing body of research has been investigating the neural substrates of languages with quite different kinds of writing systems (e.g., see the debate between Tan et al., 2005, and Bi et al., 2009; see also Nakamura et al., 2012; Wu et al., 2012).

Reading

As you read this sentence, you are able to recognize all of the printed words quite easily. The apparent simplicity of this process, however, is an illusion. To begin with, even though your conscious experience is one of seeing the entire text before you and of scanning the lines in a fairly smooth and continuous manner, in reality your eyes are making four or five jerky movements, technically referred to as **saccades,** every second. Each time your gaze lands on a particular spot, the amount of detail that you perceive is optimal at the center of fixation but drops off rather precipitously toward the periphery. The small circular space of maximal visual acuity is called the **fovea.** As a result of these inherent constraints on visual processing, you can only identify one or two short words with each fixation, as shown in Figure 8.3. One of the world's leading experts on the neural substrates of reading, Stanislas Dehaene, expressed this point as follows in his book *Reading*

Saccade An eye movement from one location in a scene to another location.

Fovea The small circular space of maximal visual acuity at the center of fixation.

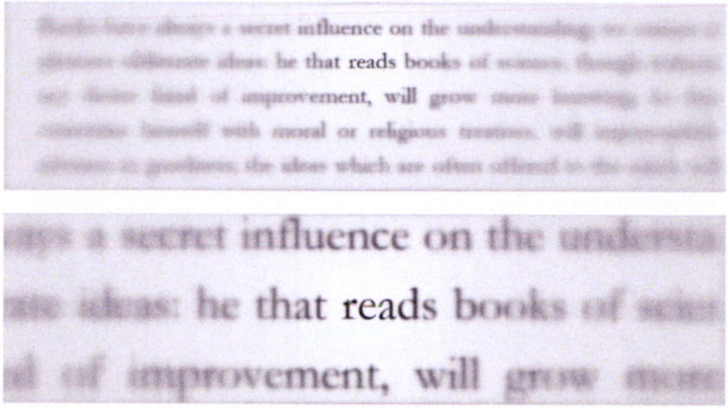

Figure 8.3 The retina stringently filters what we read. In this simulation, a page from Samuel Johnson's *The Adventurer* (1754) was filtered using an algorithm that copies the decreasing acuity of human vision away from the center of the retina. Regardless of size, only letters close to fixation can be identified. This is why we constantly explore pages with jerky eye movements when we read. When our gaze stops, we can only identify one or two words. (From Dehaene, 2009, p. 14.)

in the Brain: The Science and Evolution of a Human Invention: "Reading is nothing but the word-by-word mental restitution of a text through a series of snapshots" (Dehaene, 2009, p. 17).

The complexity of reading, however, is by no means limited to the mechanics of saccadic eye movements, for the most daunting computational challenges arise during the fraction of a second when a string of letters enters the fovea. The essence of the problem is this: In order to recognize a printed word, it is necessary to extract precisely those features that invariantly characterize that word across all of its possible manifestations, including changes in ^position^, size, CASE, and font. To accomplish this feat, large differences in visual form must be ignored (e.g., between "a" and "A"), small ones must be noticed (e.g., between "e" and "c"), and alternative linear orders must be registered (e.g., between "dog" and "god"). The fact that skilled readers can effortlessly and accurately satisfy all of these requirements in a time window of just a few hundred milliseconds is truly remarkable. Even the smartest artificial intelligence devices are still no match for ordinary people when it comes to deciphering convoluted sequences of squiggly letters. As Alison Gopnik (2010) observed in her review of Dehaene's book,

Every time you complete a word recognition security test on a Web site, you are paying unconscious homage to the sophistication and subtlety of the reading brain. The most advanced spambots can't even recognize letters as well as we can, let alone recover the meaning that lurks behind them.

Hierarchical Coding of Letter Strings in the Ventral Occipitotemporal Cortex

So how, exactly, does the reading brain manage to convert mere marks on a page into full-fledged words that can be plugged into the major cortical circuits for language? Not surprisingly, it uses an assembly line composed of multiple stages of neural representation, organized in such a way that increasingly complex combinations of visual features can be integrated at each successive stage. We have already seen several perceptual systems like this in previous chapters—e.g., the cartoon "table detector network" sketched in Figure 1.7 in Chapter 1, and the somewhat more realistic "tonal scream detector network" portrayed in Figure 5.2 in Chapter 5. In the domain of reading, one of the most influential frameworks is the **Local Combination Detector (LCD) Model** proposed by Dehaene et al. (2005; see also Grainger et al., 2008, for an overview of other models of letter perception). Inspired by research on invariant object recognition in the primate visual system, as well as by numerous studies of the neural substrates of reading, this theory maintains that the perception of printed words relies on a hierarchy of convergent feature detectors that extends from very early to very late stages of visual processing. The functional–anatomical architecture of this putative hierarchy is illustrated in Figure 8.4 and described below.

- The lowest level is the lateral geniculate nucleus (LGN) of the thalamus, which receives input directly from the retina. At this initial stage, each cell has a very small **receptive field**, which is the part of the visual field that it can "see," or, more precisely, the part that it is sensitive to. As a consequence, these cells can only represent the presence or absence of very simple stimuli— essentially tiny points like the dot of an "i"—at very specific locations in retinotopically defined space, where the frame of reference is anchored at the center of fixation.
- The second level is V1, which is the primary visual cortex at the very back of the brain. At this stage, the cells have slightly larger receptive fields

Local Combination Detector (LCD) Model A neurally based framework for characterizing reading that posits multiple levels of feature detectors, hierarchically organized in such a way that increasingly larger fragments of printed words are represented at each successive level.

Receptive field The preference of a neuron for particular visual properties in a particular location of the visual field.

Putative area	Coded units	RF size and structure	Examples of preferred stimuli

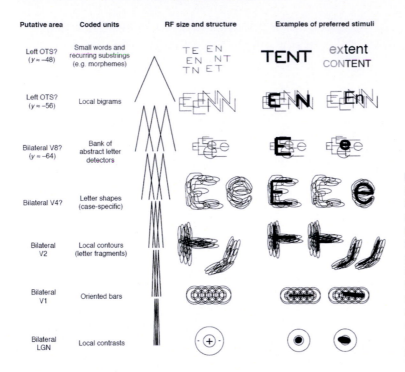

Figure 8.4 The Local Combination Detector (LCD) Model of visual word recognition. At each level of the hierarchy (beginning at the bottom and moving upwards), neurons are assumed to pool activity from subsets of neurons at the immediately lower level, thus leading to progressive increases in the size of receptive fields, the complexity of integrated features, and the invariance of orthographic properties. RF = receptive field; LGN = lateral geniculate nucleus of the thalamus; V1, V2, V4, V8 = cortical areas involved in visual perception; OTS = occipitotemporal sulcus. (From Dehaene et al., 2005, p. 337.)

that allow them to represent oriented lines or bars at certain positions, specifically by integrating the inputs from groups of LGN cells which themselves have adjacent or partially overlapping receptive fields.

- The third level is V2, which is the second visual cortical area in the occipital lobe. At this stage, the cells still have tiny receptive fields, but they are somewhat broader than those at the previous level. Hence, V2 cells can conjoin the kinds of features that are detected by V1 cells and thereby capture local contours corresponding to letter fragments, like the descending curvy part of a "g."
- The fourth level may be V4, which is a ventral occipital region. As described in Chapter 10, this area is essential for color processing (see Figure 10.2 and the associated text), but there is substantial evidence that it also contributes to shape processing. In fact, the coding of alphabetic stimuli starts to get more interesting at this stage, because it is now possible to recognize entire letter shapes (see also Box 8.1). The degree of representational abstraction is still quite minimal, however, since letter shapes can only be captured in a case- and font-specific manner that distinguishes between, say, "E" and "e," but doesn't register their commonality.
- The fifth level may be V8, which is a more anterior ventral occipital region that is centered at [y = −64] in stereotaxic space (see Figure 2.15 in Chapter 2

for an illustration of this coordinate system). This is the stage at which truly abstract letter identities are represented in a way that transcends the superficial differences between upper and lower case and between various fonts. Here, the cells fulfill their functions as invariant letter detectors by generalizing over the activation patterns at the previous level of processing (i.e., V4). But because the receptive fields of these cells are not yet very big, they have only a moderate tolerance for changes in the size and location of stimuli.

- The sixth level may be a sector of the left occipitotemporal sulcus (OTS) that is centered at [y = −56]. This area is about a centimeter anterior to V8, and, importantly, it is the first stage that is presumably left-lateralized, since all of the earlier ones are assumed to be bilateral. (Later on, however, we will encounter recent evidence that some of the earlier stages may also be left-hemisphere dominant.) According to the LCD Model, the cells at this level have receptive fields that are large enough to encompass two-letter sequences—i.e., bigrams—at particular locations in the visual field. One neuron, for instance, might respond optimally to the combination "E left of N." Such a cell would fire significantly above its baseline rate whenever the person saw words like "**ENTER**," "**RENT**," or "**HEN**."

- Finally, the highest level shown in Figure 8.4 may be a region in the left OTS that is centered at [$y = -48$], nearly a centimeter anterior to the previous level. At this stage, the cells have even wider receptive fields that allow them to include within their "spotlight" relatively long strings of up to four letters—i.e., quadrigrams like "TENT." By

pooling the activity of populations of cells at the immediately earlier stage, these quadrigram detectors can recognize small words or morphemes. The perception of longer words, however, may require even higher-order cells that are sensitive to complex patterns of activity at this level as well as at earlier levels.

Box 8.1   Reading Printed Letters Activates the Motor Region for Writing the Same Letters

Although recognizing letters seems to be a purely visual affair, there is growing evidence that motor skills for handwriting are also involved (for a review see Velay & Longcamp, 2013). The first hint came from an fMRI study which showed that the mere sight of real vs. unreal letters activates not only the ventral occipitotemporal cortex, but also the same dorsal premotor region (PMd) that is engaged during handwriting (Longcamp et al., 2003). This captivating discovery raised the possibility that when we see letters, our brains automatically recall the motor memories of how we manipulate a pen or a pencil to produce them. Subsequent studies both reinforced and refined this idea, as demonstrated by the following findings. Although letter perception ignites the left PMd in right-handers, it ignites the right PMd in left-handers (Longcamp et al., 2005a; see Figure 8B1.1). These activations lead to increased muscle excitation in the dominant hand (Papathanasiou et al., 2004). And the activations are not only more robust for handwritten than typed stimuli, but also more robust for self-handwritten than other-handwritten stimuli (Longcamp et al., 2006; Wamain et al., 2012; see also Knoblich et al., 2002).

All of these results clearly support the notion that letter perception triggers motor simulation, but they do not directly address what some scholars regard as the key question: Does the simulation process actually facilitate perception, or is it just a functionally irrelevant association? Evidence that reading does in fact benefit from accessing hand gestures comes from several studies. For example, when the multiple strokes constituting Roman letters or Chinese ideograms are flashed to subjects sequentially, recognition is fastest when the order of presentation matches the order in which the strokes are typically written (Flores d'Arcais, 1994; Parkinson & Khurana, 2007; Parkinson et al., 2010). Moreover, when similar stimuli are used in an fMRI setting, the PMd is maximally sensitive to the sight of motorically correct sequences of strokes (Nakamura et al., 2012). It is also noteworthy that young children (ages 3-5) learn to recognize Roman letters, and adults learn to recognize novel graphic shapes, more efficiently when they are trained via handwriting than via typing (Longcamp et al., 2005b, 2008).

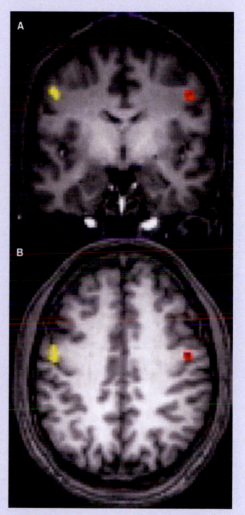

Figure 8B1.1   During letter perception, the left premotor cortex is activated in right-handers (yellow), whereas the homologous right premotor cortex is activated in left-handers (red). Clusters are shown on a coronal slice (A) and an axial slice (B). (From Longcamp et al., 2005a, p. 1806.)

(Continued)

(Continued)

In addition, motor skills for handwriting have been shown to enhance the identification of letters that have mirror image twins, like "d" vs. "b" and "p" vs. "q" (Longcamp et al., 2006). Finally, although there are very few neuropsychological studies on this topic, one remarkable investigation found that a right-handed woman with a focal lesion in the left PMd was significantly impaired not only at writing letters and words, but also at recognizing them (Anderson et al., 1990).

In summary, there is mounting support for the view that recognizing letters, especially handwritten ones, is a multimodal process mediated by both the occipitotemporal cortex (reading by eye) and the PMd (reading by hand). Although much remains to be explored (e.g., see the controversy between Tan et al., 2005, and Bi et al., 2009), this field of research is making significant headway.

Stepping back from the details of the LCD Model, the basic idea is this: When we read, letter strings are rapidly routed through a hierarchically organized assembly line that extends from the retina to the LGN in the thalamus, from there to the primary visual cortex at the back of the brain, and then forward through several way-stations along the ventral occipitotemporal stream. At each successive level, a larger amount of the visual field is covered, and a greater degree of representational synthesis and abstraction is achieved, so that the content of the coded information progresses from mere points and lines to letter fragments, case- and font-specific letter shapes, case- and font-invariant letter identities, bigrams, and quadrigrams, ultimately culminating in the recognition of real words. Although we have focused on the bottom-up flow of processing through this pipeline, it is important to realize that there is also a great deal of top-down flow, and that this can facilitate the resolution of ambiguities by drawing upon background knowledge, expectations, and aspects of the context.

To test the major claims of the LCD Model, Vinckier et al. (2007) conducted an fMRI study in which 12 French-speaking subjects were presented with six sets of stimuli, each consisting of 320 strings of six upper-case characters, with increasing structural similarity to real words. As shown in Figure 8.5, the different categories were as follows: (1) strings of "false font" characters made up of the same visual features as real letters (see the example in Figure 8.5); (2) strings of infrequent letters (e.g., JZWYWK); (3) strings of frequent letters (e.g., QOADTQ); (4) strings of frequent bigrams

	False Fonts	Infrequent Letters	Frequent Letters	Frequent Bigrams	Frequent Quadrigrams	Words
Strings	0	0	0	0	0	high
Quadrigrams	0	low	low	low	high	high
Bigrams	0	low	low	high	high	high
Letters	0	low	high	high	high	high
Features	high	high	high	high	high	high
	ꓶꓱꓰꓷ�…ꓵꓘ	JZWYWK	QOADTQ	QUMBSS	AVONIL	MOUTON

Figure 8.5 Types of stimuli employed in Vinckier et al.'s (2007) fMRI study of reading: (1) strings of false font units made up of the same visual features as real letters; (2) strings of infrequent letters; (3) strings of frequent letters; (4) strings of frequent bigrams; (5) strings of frequent quadrigrams; and (6) real words. Dark orange cells, high-frequency components; light orange cells, low-frequency components; blue cells, zero-frequency components. (From Vinckier et al., 2007, p. 144.)

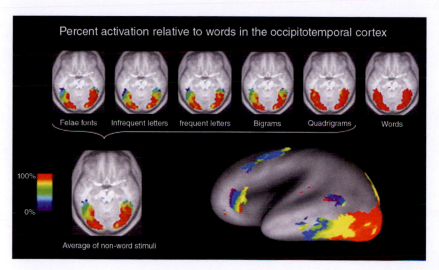

Percent activation relative to words in the occipitotemporal cortex

Felae fonts   Infrequent letters   frequent letters   Bigrams   Quadrigrams   Words

100%

0%

Average of non-word stimuli

Figure 8.6   Results from Vinckier et al.'s (2007) fMRI study of reading. The experiment revealed a spatial gradient of cortical responses to different types of orthographic stimuli. (Top) More anterior sectors of the ventral occipitotemporal cortex are activated by increasingly closer approximations to real words. (Bottom left) The gradient image averaged over non-word stimuli shows a progressive drop of signal toward more anterior regions, indexing an increasing sensitivity to stimulus structure, most clearly manifested in the left hemisphere. (Bottom right) Inferolateral view of the same averaged gradient image, overlaid on an inflated left hemisphere. (From Vinckier et al., 2007, p. 147.)

(e.g., QUMBSS); (5) strings of frequent quadrigrams (e.g., AVONIL); and (6) real words (e.g., MOUTON). Each item was displayed for only 100 ms, and the task was to push a button whenever a string of six hash marks (######) appeared. Based on the LCD Model, the key prediction was that, relative to rest, the six types of increasingly word-like stimuli would engage increasingly anterior sectors of the ventral occipitotemporal cortex, especially in the left hemisphere.

For the most part, the results confirmed the prediction. As shown in Figure 8.6, a spatial gradient of stimulus selectivity did in fact emerge in the ventral occipitotemporal cortex, indicating that as one moves along the posterior-to-anterior axis (i.e., the y-axis in stereotaxic space), the voxels become more preferential for closer approximations to real words. In addition, this continuum was found to be more prominent in the left than the right hemisphere.

To further investigate the internal organization of this anteriorly directed processing stream, the researchers compared the average BOLD signals in six small regions of interest (ROIs) arrayed along the extent of the left ventral occipitotemporal cortex (see the red circles in Figure 8.7, each of which represents a sphere containing 33 voxels). Interestingly, three of these ROIs were centered at the y-coordinates where, according to the LCD Model, three successive levels of word representation putatively reside—specifically, abstract letter identities [$y = -64$], bigrams [$y = -56$], and quadrigrams [$y = -48$]. As revealed by the red-framed graphs in Figure 8.7, the activation levels in the six ROIs tended to track the scale of stimulus similarity to real words. More precisely, as the ROIs became more anterior, the signals elicited by less word-like

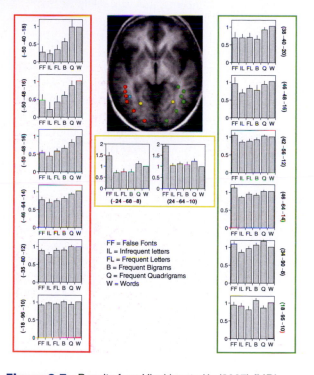

FF = False Fonts
IL = Infrequent letters
FL = Frequent Letters
B = Frequent Bigrams
Q = Frequent Quadrigrams
W = Words

Figure 8.7   Results from Vinckier et al.'s (2007) fMRI study of reading. The bar graphs show percent activation relative to real words in occipitotemporal regions of interest. At the left-hemisphere sites (red), activation levels tracked the scale of stimulus similarity to real words, with the amplitude of this effect increasing steadily toward more anterior regions. However, at the homologous right-hemisphere sites (green), such a pattern was not observed. The bilateral lingual cortex (yellow) showed larger activations for false fonts than for the different types of stimuli containing real letters, which did not differ. Finally, the blue cross indicates the peak of the Visual Word Form Area (VWFA) as identified by Cohen et al. (2002) at coordinates [−42, −57, −15]. (From Vinckier et al., 2007, p. 148.)

stimuli gradually dropped off, whereas those elicited by more word-like stimuli remained relatively strong. The only exception to this pattern was the false font condition; it is possible, however, that the subjects needed to pay extra attention to those stimuli in order to distinguish them from the target stimuli (i.e., strings of hash marks) in the behavioral task.

It is noteworthy that the researchers also compared the average BOLD signals in six ROIs in the right hemisphere but failed to find any evidence for the type of hierarchy manifested in the left hemisphere (see the circles and graphs coded green in Figure 8.7). In addition, when the researchers focused on two ROIs in the left and right lingual gyri, they discovered larger activations for the false font condition than for any other condition (see the circles and graphs coded yellow in Figure 8.7). These findings about the lingual gyri, though, are not relevant to our concerns and can safely be ignored. (Incidentally, the lingual gyri got their name because they happen to be shaped like the tongue. They are not, however, functionally involved in language.)

In sum, the main take-home message from Vinckier et al.'s (2007) fMRI study is this: Just as the LCD Model maintains, the perception of letter strings appears to depend on a multilevel hierarchy of ventral occipitotemporal regions, with increasingly complex combinations of features being captured at increasingly anterior levels of processing, and with greater lateralization toward the left hemisphere. In fact, near the top of this hierarchy, in the left hemisphere, there lies a patch of cortex that responds so robustly and preferentially to printed words that it is commonly referred to as the Visual Word Form Area (VWFA). The center of this region is marked by the blue cross in Figure 8.7, and its unique functional properties are described in greater detail below.

The Visual Word Form Area (VWFA)

Normal Response Properties

Ever since it was discovered in 2000 (Cohen et al., 2000), the VWFA has been the focus of intense investigation, and a great deal has been learned about its normal operation (for reviews see McCandliss et al., 2003; Cohen & Dehaene, 2004; Dehaene & Cohen, 2011; Wandell, 2011; for historical and critical perspectives see Price, 2012, and Price & Devlin, 2003, 2011). Some of the most significant findings are as follows:

- It responds to printed words regardless of their location—e.g., right or left of visual fixation (Cohen et al., 2000; Dehaene et al., 2004; for qualifications see Rauschecker et al., 2012).

- It detects the identity of printed words regardless of their case—e.g., "RAGE" or "rage" (Dehaene et al., 2001, 2004).

- It detects the identity of printed words regardless of their font—e.g., "table" or "table"—and is also sensitive to handwritten stimuli (Qiao et al., 2010; Nakamura et al., 2012).

- It detects the identity of printed words regardless of whether they are perceived consciously or unconsciously (Dehaene et al., 2001, 2004; Qiao et al., 2010; Nakamura et al., 2012).

- It has greater sensitivity to real than unreal printed words (Glezer et al., 2009; but see also Binder et al., 2006, and Devlin et al., 2006).

- It responds more to printed than spoken words (Dehaene et al., 2002; Cohen et al., 2004; Tsapkini & Rapp, 2010) but is also activated during some attention-demanding speech perception tasks such as rhyme judgment (Yoncheva et al., 2010).

- It responds equally to different types of familiar scripts—e.g., alphabetic as in English, syllabic as in Japanese Kana, or morphosyllabic as in Japanese Kanji and Chinese (Bolger et al., 2005; Liu et al., 2008; Nakamura et al., 2012)—but it responds more to familiar than unfamiliar scripts (Baker et al., 2007).

- It responds more to printed words than other categories of visually presented objects (Baker et al., 2007; Ben-Shachar et al., 2007; Szwed et al., 2011; Hamamé et al., 2013; Glezer & Riesenhuber, 2013).

Because the last point listed above addresses a key issue—namely, whether the VWFA is specialized for recognizing printed words—it deserves to be discussed in greater depth. As discussed more fully in Chapter 10, there is substantial evidence that the ventral occipitotemporal cortex has some degree of functional–anatomical parcellation according to object category, with partially segregated areas being maximally sensitive to faces (e.g., Kanwisher & Yovel, 2006), non-facial body parts (e.g., Peelen & Downing, 2007), animals (e.g., Chao et al., 1999, 2002), tools (e.g., Chao et al., 1999, 2002), and places (e.g., Epstein & Kanwisher, 1998; Epstein et al., 2001). The issue here is whether the VWFA constitutes yet another member of this menagerie, one that is tuned to the category of printed words. Some researchers have claimed that this is not really the case, since several studies have shown that line drawings of common objects activate the VWFA just as much as printed words (e.g., Price & Devlin, 2003; Wright et al., 2008; Kherif et al.,

2011). Other researchers, however, have argued that the results of those studies are by no means conclusive, because various physical parameters of the two classes of stimuli were not adequately matched. When great care is taken to equate the low-level visual features of words and objects as much as possible, it turns out that the VWFA does in fact favor the former type of stimuli.

This was demonstrated in an especially compelling way by Szwed et al. (2011). Their fMRI study employed the four types of stimuli depicted in Figure 8.8 (a few other types of stimuli were also used, but they are not considered here). The main experimental stimuli consisted of printed French words and line drawings of objects, all of which were systematically degraded by removing certain fragments of the contours while preserving the highly informative vertices (i.e., the junctions between two or more lines, and the transitions of straight lines into curved lines, like in the letter "J"). For both words and objects, 55 percent of the contour was always retained. Moreover, the two classes of items were matched for the following variables: total contour length; average number of vertices; overall height, width, and luminance; and recognizability. Each set of experimental stimuli was paired with a corresponding set of control stimuli, the latter being created by randomly scrambling line fragments while keeping constant the horizontal and vertical boundaries of the composite images. During the brain scanning session, each item was presented very briefly, for only 200 ms, so as to minimize top-down processing effects. Items of the same type were grouped into short blocks, and the task was simply to push a button whenever the exact same item occurred twice in a row.

The researchers first contrasted each experimental condition against its corresponding control condition, and then they contrasted the resulting activation map for words against the one for objects. As shown in Figure 8.8, this analytic approach revealed that when low-level visual features were factored out, significantly greater responses to words than objects emerged not only in the VWFA, but also in more posterior left-hemisphere occipitotemporal areas. These findings suggest that the tuning of cortical neurons to alphabetic stimuli may begin at relatively early stages of the visual processing hierarchy and carry forward all the way to the VWFA.

A caveat, however, is that even though these neurons appear to be *engaged* more strongly by words than objects, this does not entail that they are *dedicated*, completely and exclusively, to reading. To put it somewhat differently, even though these neurons seem to prefer printed letter strings as stimuli, this does not prevent them from also participating, albeit to a lesser degree, in the networks that underlie the representation of other kinds of stimuli. In fact, this is probably why the superior sensitivity of the VWFA to words than objects could only be exposed by conducting an fMRI study in which both types of stimuli were carefully matched along a number of relevant dimensions.

Effects of Damage

If the identification of printed words depends critically on the VWFA, that ability should be impaired by damage either to the VWFA itself or to earlier stages of the processing hierarchy that leads up to it. Support for this prediction comes from a number of neuropsychological studies, some of which are summarized below (see also Mani et al., 2008, for a closely related electrophysiological study involving direct intracranial stimulation).

The technical term for an acquired disturbance of printed word recognition is **alexia**, and the first detailed case study was reported back in 1892 by the

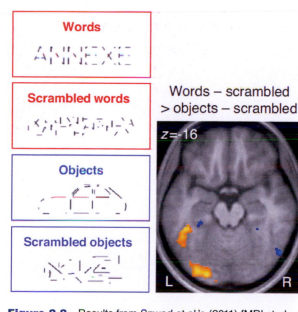

Figure 8.8   Results from Szwed et al.'s (2011) fMRI study of reading. When words were matched to pictures in terms of number of strokes, using scrambled stimuli as a control, a clear superiority for words over pictures was found in the left occipitotemporal sulcus (VWFA) as well as in a more posterior left occipital area. (From Dehaene & Cohen, 2011, p. 255.)

Alexia   A reading disorder with two subcategories: One subcategory includes patients who cannot even recognize single letters, let alone complete words.   The other subcategory includes patients who cannot read whole words with just one quick glance, but must instead decipher each sequential letter in a slow and deliberate manner and then put all the pieces together.

eminent French neurologist Joseph-Jules Déjerine. His patient, Oscar C, was a retired salesman who suffered a stroke that rendered him incapable of recognizing not only printed words, but also the individual letters that make them up. When presented with such stimuli, he had no trouble seeing their shapes, and he could copy them quite accurately if asked to do so, but he could no longer name them or derive any kind of meaning from them. Importantly, his deficit may have been a form of what is now called "pure alexia," since it seemed to be *restricted* to the domain of written letters and words. Thus, he could still identify faces, recognize objects, navigate through various environments, and appreciate art. Moreover, apart from his reading impairment, his other linguistic skills were fully intact. He even retained the ability to write, although when he tried to make sense of his own written expressions, he was flummoxed! Déjerine characterized this puzzling aspect of Mr. C's profile as follows:

> Spontaneously, the patient writes as well as he speaks. When I compare the numerous specimens of writing that I asked of him, there are no mistakes, no spelling errors, no letter switching . . . . Writing under dictation can still be done easily and fluently, but the patient finds it impossible to read what he has just written down . . . . He gets impatient with these phenomena, writes several letters one after the other and says: 'I can still write those letters, so why can't I read them?'
> (English translation from Dehaene, 2009, p. 56)

Since Déjerine's classic paper was published, many other cases of alexia have been documented (see Montant & Behrmann, 2000, for a survey; and see Sacks, 2010, for a very accessible and entertaining discussion aimed at a general audience). This research suggests that there are at least two different subcategories of the disorder. One subcategory includes patients like Oscar C whose deficits are so severe that they cannot even recognize single letters, let alone complete words. These patients may also be unable to match upper- and lower-case versions of the same letter, such as "A" and "a." Hence, in the context of the LCD Model shown in Figure 8.4, it is likely that their damage affects, at the very least, one or more of the stages of the visual processing hierarchy that precede the level at which abstract letter identities are detected (see Wilson et al., 2013, for two interesting cases of this type of alexia, resulting from posterior cortical atrophy).

The other subcategory includes patients who can still identify letters but cannot read whole words with

just one quick glance; instead, they can only do so by first deciphering each sequential letter in a slow and deliberate manner, and then putting all the pieces together. Whereas normal literate people don't require any more time to recognize five-letter words than four- or three-letter words, patients with this type of alexia display "letter-by-letter reading" such that their reading times increase linearly as a function of word length. This behavioral pattern suggests that the damage may only affect the later stages of the hierarchy posited by the LCD Model—i.e., the stages that follow the detection of abstract letter identities and involve the rapid, efficient recognition of bigrams, quadrigrams, and complete words.

In keeping with this idea, recent studies have shown that alexic patients who manifest laborious letter-by-letter reading, and who therefore fall into the second subcategory described above, tend to have left-hemisphere lesions in or near the VWFA (e.g., Leff et al., 2001; Cohen et al., 2003; Gaillard et al., 2006; Pflugshaupt et al., 2009). This is illustrated in Figure 8.9, which

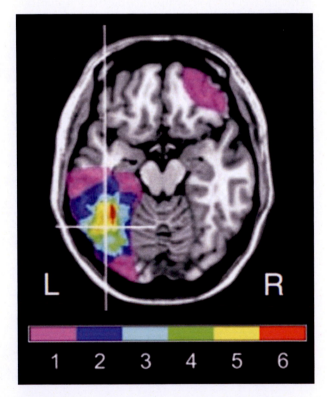

Figure 8.9 Overlay of lesion sites of six patients with pure alexia and letter-by-letter reading. The color bar indicates the number of patients contributing to the overlap at each voxel. The white crosshairs show the coordinate assigned to the center of the VWFA in healthy adults, based on the meta-analysis of functional neuroimaging studies reported by Jobard et al. (2003). (From Pflugshaupt et al., 2009, p. 1912.)

presents an overlay plot of the lesions of six patients with the pertinent form of alexia (Pflugshaupt et al., 2009). It can clearly be seen that five of the six patients had damage at the very center of the VWFA, with that center being defined in terms of a meta-analysis of functional neuroimaging studies of reading (Jobard et al., 2003). It is also apparent that all six patients had damage at a site that was located just a few millimeters anterior to the center of the VWFA, and that may well have overlapped with the anterior segment of that area.

Additional data come from a remarkable case study of a 46-year-old man who underwent neurosurgery to alleviate epileptic seizures that had plagued him since he was 12 (Gaillard et al., 2006; see also Epelbaum et al., 2008). The resected tissue was in the left occipitotemporal region, immediately posterior to the typical location of the VWFA. Both pre- and post-operative fMRI scans were conducted to evaluate the patient's neural responses to different kinds of objects, and while there were not many differences between the two scanning sessions with regard to the activation patterns elicited by faces, houses, and tools, significant differences did emerge for printed words (Figure 8.10). Specifically, prior to surgery, printed words engaged the VWFA just anterior to the area targeted for resection, but after surgery, such stimuli no longer triggered any activity in that region. Moreover, behavioral tests revealed that although the patient's ability to recognize objects other than words appeared to be unaffected by the surgery, his ability to identify words was gravely impaired (Figure 8.11). When an assessment was carried out 15 days post-surgery, he exhibited very effortful letter-by-letter reading, with reaction times increasing in direct proportion to word length. Whereas before the operation it only took him about 600 ms to read words ranging from three to eight letters in length, after the operation he needed about 1,000 ms to read words containing just three letters, and his reaction times for longer words increased by roughly 100 ms for each additional letter. Not surprisingly, the accuracy of his reading also declined precipitously as a function of word length. Comparable deficits, though not quite as severe, were observed during another assessment conducted six months later, implying that, unfortunately, the alexia induced by the surgery was a long-lasting condition. Overall, it seems likely that this particular patient's selective reading disorder resulted from a highly focal lesion that deprived the VWFA from receiving its normal input from earlier stages of the visual processing hierarchy for perceiving alphabetic stimuli.

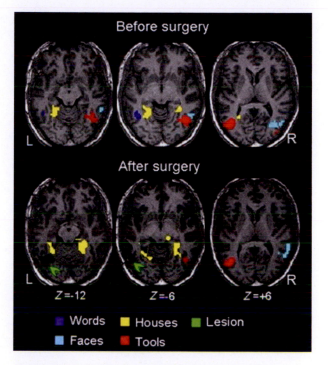

Figure 8.10   Occipitotemporal activations before and after surgery, for each stimulus type relative to the others. Following surgery (green arrow), the patient had pure alexia, and the activations induced by printed words in the VWFA disappeared. All the other clusters remained present. (From Gaillard et al., 2006, p. 194.)

The research reviewed above suggests that the VWFA is not only preferentially involved in visual word processing, but causally necessary for that function. Other neuropsychological studies, however, have revealed some complications. For example, in an experiment that included 53 acute stroke patients with damage or dysfunction of the VWFA, Hillis et al. (2005) found that only 31 (58 percent) had defective written word comprehension. To account for these results, they proposed that although the right-hemisphere homologue of the VWFA does not usually contribute as much to visual word processing as the VWFA itself, it can sometimes compensate for disturbances of the VWFA (for additional data see Cohen et al., 2004). Another concern is that while many patients with lesions in and/or around the VWFA appear at first sight to manifest "pure" alexia, rigorous testing often discloses at least mild abnormalities in the visual perception of certain types of non-lexical stimuli, such as faces (Behrmann & Plaut, in press), numerals (Starrfelt & Behrmann, 2011), and other objects that, like printed words, require high-resolution spatial discrimination (e.g., Behrmann et al., 1998; Starrfelt & Gerlach, 2007; Starrfelt et al., 2009;

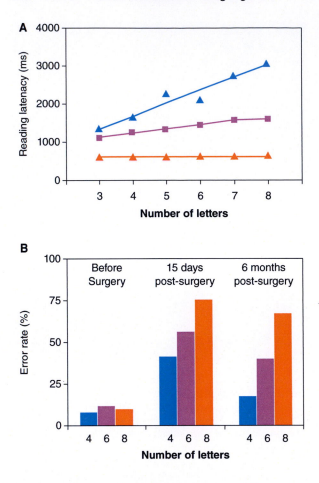

Figure 8.11 Reading performance before and after surgery. (A) Word-reading latencies. Before surgery, latencies were short and showed no influence of word length (orange triangles). Two weeks after surgery, responses were slow, showing a pattern of letter-by-letter reading (blue triangles). Six months later, despite some improvement, the same pattern persisted (purple squares). (B) Error rate for briefly flashed words. Before surgery, errors were few. After surgery, both early and late, the patient made numerous errors, with a clear influence of word length. (From Gallaird et al., 2006, p. 193.)

Roberts et al., 2013). These findings support the idea that, as mentioned earlier, even though the primary function of the VWFA does appear to be the recognition of printed words, this is probably not its only role. In the next subsection, we will see why this idea makes sense from an evolutionary perspective.

Developmental Origins: The Neuronal Recycling Hypothesis

At the very outset of this chapter, we noted that although *Homo sapiens* emerged between 150,000 and 180,000 years ago, writing was not invented until 5,400 years ago. A logical consequence of this huge discrepancy is that none of our brain structures or circuits could have evolved specifically for the purpose of reading. Why, then, has a single, well-demarcated cortical region, namely the VWFA, been found to contribute more to the recognition of printed words than to any other category of objects?

To resolve this apparent paradox, Dehaene and his colleagues have formulated the **Neuronal Recycling Hypothesis** (Dehaene & Cohen, 2007, 2011; Dehaene, 2009). At a fairly general level of description, this proposal consists of three closely related claims (quoted directly from Dehaene and Cohen, 2007, pp. 384–385):

- Human brain organization is subject to strong anatomical and connectional constraints inherited from evolution. Organized neural maps are present early on in infancy and bias subsequent learning.
- Cultural acquisitions (e.g., reading) must find their "neuronal niche," a set of circuits that are sufficiently close to the required function and sufficiently plastic as to reorient a significant fraction of their neural resources to this novel use.
- As cortical territories dedicated to evolutionarily older functions are invaded by novel cultural objects, their prior organization is never entirely erased. Thus, prior neural constraints exert a powerful influence on cultural acquisition and adult organization.

The following discussion demonstrates that when the Neuronal Recycling Hypothesis is applied to the domain of reading, it provides a useful framework for understanding several interesting aspects of the VWFA, including its reliable anatomical placement, its response properties in illiterate people, and its activation even when congenitally blind people read words that are perceived through non-visual modalities.

The VWFA has a remarkably consistent location across individuals. It always resides in the lateral portion of the left ventral occipitotemporal cortex (the approximate coordinates being [−42, −57, −15], with a standard

Neuronal Recycling Hypothesis The idea that culturally acquired abilities like reading invade evolutionarily older brain circuits and inherit many of their structural and functional constraints. According to this view, the VWFA is ideally suited to represent the spelling patterns of printed words because it is apparently designed to register complex combinations of spatially fine-grained shapes.

deviation of about 5 mm), regardless of the nature of the subject's writing system. In the context of the Neuronal Recycling Hypothesis, the reliability of this anatomical placement may reflect a number of interacting factors, each of which influences a particular aspect of the localization (see especially Dehaene, 2009, pp. 164–169; see also Hasson et al., 2002; Plaut & Behrmann, 2011). First of all, why does the VWFA fall within the ventral occipitotemporal cortex, as opposed to some other part of the brain? This is no doubt the easiest question to answer, since it is well established that the ventral occipitotemporal cortex subserves the visual recognition of objects based largely on their shape features, and printed words are identified entirely according to shape. Next question: Why does the VWFA occupy the lateral instead of the medial sector of the ventral occipitotemporal cortex? This question is somewhat more challenging, but the answer is probably related to recent evidence that the ventral occipitotemporal cortex is, to some extent, retinotopically organized in the following way: Relatively small, fine-grained stimuli that demand foveal processing, like faces and, crucially, printed words, tend to be routed more toward the lateral than the medial sector of this cortical territory; conversely, relatively large, coarse-grained stimuli that impose peripheral processing, like buildings and landscapes, tend to be routed more toward the medial than the lateral sector. Finally, why is the VWFA lateralized primarily to the left rather than the right hemisphere? One reason could be that, according to long-standing assumptions, the left hemisphere is dominant for analytic, feature-based shape processing, whereas the right hemisphere is dominant for holistic, configural shape processing. But surely another reason is that the left hemisphere plays a greater role in language than the right, and the perception of printed words must be integrated with that language circuitry as quickly and efficiently as possible. Taken together, then, all of these considerations support the view that a variety of innate cortical biases conspire to make the precise location of the VWFA the ideal "sweet spot" for reading.

To investigate the response properties of the VWFA *before* it has been invaded and recycled for the purpose of reading, Dehaene et al. (2010) conducted an fMRI study that involved 63 Portuguese and Brazilian adults with the following breakdown in terms of literacy: 31 learned to read during childhood and hence were called "literates"; 22 learned to read after reaching adulthood and hence were called "ex-illiterates"; and 10 never learned to read and hence were called "illiterates." A preliminary assessment of these subjects' reading skills indicated that they fell into six groups with the following order of descending ability:

- Brazilian literates with high socioeconomic status (LB1);
- Portuguese literates (LP);
- Brazilian literates with low socioeconomic status (LB2);
- Brazilian ex-illiterates (EXB);
- Portuguese ex-illiterates (EXP);
- Brazilian illiterates (ILB).

In the first part of the fMRI study, the researchers showed the subjects written sentences and found that the degree of activation in the VWFA increased in proportion to reading performance, which was measured as the number of words read per minute (Figure 8.12A). Of course, the illiterates could not read any of the words, so it was not surprising that their VWFA did not respond very much to the stimuli. For the other subjects, however, as their reading performance rose, so did their VWFA activation, even among the ex-illiterates. Essentially the same linear relationship between literacy and VWFA activation also emerged in a separate condition in which the stimuli were letter strings instead of sentences (Figure 8.12B-C). The most illuminating results of the study, though, were discovered when the researchers examined, for each group of subjects, the extent to which the VWFA was engaged by different types of non-orthographic stimuli—specifically, faces, houses, tools, false fonts, and checkers. For faces, tools, and checkers, as the reading ability of the subjects increased, the magnitude of activation in the VWFA decreased (Figure 8.12C). Most notably, the literates tended to have the weakest VWFA responses to these types of stimuli, whereas the illiterates tended to have the strongest responses.

These results are consistent with the Neuronal Recycling Hypothesis, since they clearly show that for people who have not yet learned to read, the VWFA is heavily involved in the representation of several kinds of non-orthographic stimuli, especially those that require high-resolution foveal processing. As one gradually becomes literate, however, complex orthographic representations begin to develop in the VWFA, and their growth engenders a competition for cortical space. Ultimately, it seems that this competition causes many—certainly not all, but many—of the non-orthographic representations to get "crowded out," which is to say, relocated to other cortical regions. This raises the intriguing possibility that the cost of literacy may be a slight reduction in some other forms of visual perception, such as face processing. But whether this is really the case remains to be seen.

To be sure, the results of Dehaene et al.'s (2010) study of how the VWFA is affected by literacy are quite impressive and informative. But equally if not more

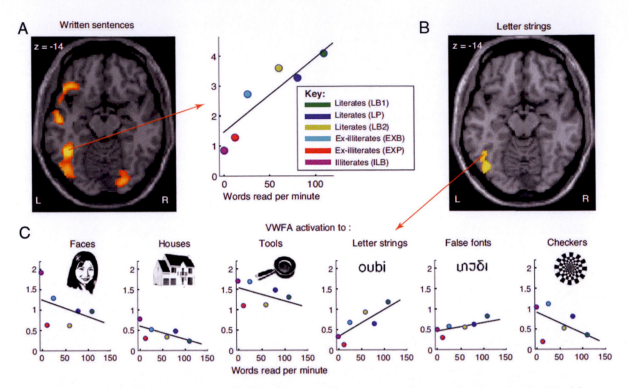

Figure 8.12 Results from Dehaene et al.'s (2010) fMRI study of reading. In this experiment, schooled and unschooled adult subjects of varying degrees of literacy were scanned. (A) When subjects were presented with written sentences, the activation in the VWFA increased in proportion to reading performance (words read per minute). The VWFA, in particular, showed little activation in illiterates, but its activation increased sharply with literacy, even in unschooled subjects who learned to read as adults (ex-illiterates). (B) The VWFA activation increase with literacy was replicated in a distinct block with passive presentation of letter strings. In this case, no other brain region was modulated by literacy, making it difficult to explain the VWFA activation as a top-down effect from higher-level regions. (C) The VWFA was also activated by passive presentation of faces, tools, and checkers, particularly in illiterates. In agreement with the Neuronal Recycling Hypothesis, this activation decreased as reading performance increased, suggesting a competition between the nascent orthographic code and prior visual responses. (From Dehaene & Cohen, 2011, p. 258.)

striking results come from another recent study that explored the response properties of the VWFA in eight congenitally blind subjects who achieved reading expertise not through the visual modality but rather through the tactile modality, specifically by using Braille (Reich et al., 2011, 2012). The main experimental conditions involved real versus unreal Braille words. Given that the subjects distinguished between these two types of stimuli via touch rather than sight, one might expect the critical brain region(s) to be in the parietal cortex rather than the occipitotemporal cortex. But that's not the way things turned out. In their first analysis, the researchers focused exclusively on the VWFA, as originally defined for sighted people, and found that in the blind subjects it had a highly significant preference for real versus unreal Braille words (Figure 8.13A). Then, to determine whether any other areas were also engaged, perhaps even more so, by real versus unreal Braille words, the researchers carried out a whole-brain analysis. What they found was substantial activation along the entire length of the left ventral

occipitotemporal cortex, extending all the way back to V1 (Figure 8.13B–C). Amazingly enough, however, the peak voxel was still located very close to the central coordinates of the VWFA for sighted people.

How can these findings be explained, and what do they imply about the origin and functional characteristics of the VWFA? The inherent biases that predispose the VWFA to being recruited for reading have traditionally been thought to be visual in nature, but the results of the current study obviously challenge that view, since they show that the involvement of the VWFA in reading does not require any visual experience whatsoever. According to Reich et al. (2011, 2012), a plausible alternative approach is the "metamodal theory," which maintains that many brain regions are innately characterized not so much by their primary input sense as by the kind of representation or computation that they typically support (Pascual-Leone & Hamilton, 2001; see also Mahon & Caramazza, 2011). With regard to the VWFA, it may be that the major function of this particular area is to register complex combinations of spatially fine-grained shapes. Crucially, however, it may perform this operation regardless of whether those shapes derive from the visual modality, as in the case of printed words, or the tactile modality, as in the case of the Braille words (see also Striem-Amit et al., 2012). For present purposes, the key point is simply that the VWFA is task-oriented rather than input-oriented: It cares more about fulfilling its high-level role in recognizing shape-based word forms than about the sensory source of the stimuli.

From Print to Sound and Meaning

A Cognitive Model

Up to this point, we have focused almost entirely on the perceptual processing of letter strings. But of course the goal of reading is not just to recognize the forms of printed words, but to map them onto the corresponding phonological and semantic structures so they can be pronounced and understood. During the past 30 years or so, there has been a great deal of debate over the precise organization of the pathways that project from orthographic representations to other components of the linguistic system (for reviews see Rapp et al., 2001; Hillis, 2002; Coltheart, 2006; Patterson & Lambon Ralph, 2006; see also Ziegler & Goswami, 2005; Perry et al., 2007). One type of cognitively oriented approach, however, about which there is now considerable (but probably not unanimous) agreement, is depicted in Figure 8.14.

Although the LCD Model discussed earlier posits many different stages of written word processing, the top half of the central stream shown in Figure 8.14 is much simpler. Beginning with the presentation of a printed stimulus, the first process is "visual feature analysis." It encompasses the first four stages of the

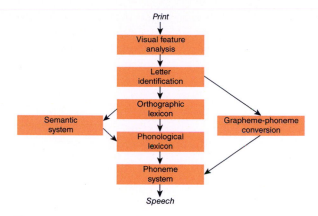

Figure 8.14 A cognitive model of reading aloud. See the main text for details.

LCD Model, and it leads to the activation of abstract (i.e., case- and font-invariant) letter representations in a component called "letter identification." The activation of these units is then followed by lexical access, which involves retrieving the unique representation of the stimulus word in the "orthographic lexicon."

Branching off to the right of this visual processing stream, the first route that leads to the sounds of printed words extends from letter identification to "grapheme–phoneme conversion" and from there to the "phoneme system." (Note that graphemes are the same as abstract letter representations.) Basically, this pathway allows us to pronounce printed words by using rules that capture rough mappings between particular graphemes or grapheme clusters and particular phonemes or phoneme clusters. This is the route that we usually pursue when we read aloud rare words like *splendiferous* or completely made-up pseudowords like *blicket*. But is it also employed when we encounter extremely common words like *rose*? A number of

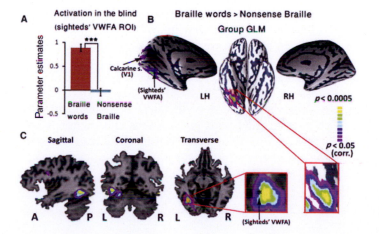

Figure 8.13 Results from Reich et al.'s (2011, 2012) fMRI study of reading. In this experiment, congenitally blind subjects were scanned while reading real and unreal Braille words. (A) Using as a region of interest (ROI) the VWFA as defined in sighted subjects, the researchers found that in congenitally blind subjects this area responded significantly more to real than unreal Braille words. (B, C) A whole-brain analysis revealed that, relative to unreal Braille words, real ones activated a much larger extent of the left occipitotemporal cortex, but the peak was still located near the center of the VWFA of sighted subjects. These results are shown on an inflated brain in (B) and on sagittal, coronal, and transverse brain sections in (C). (From Reich et al., 2012, p. 350.)

psycholinguistic studies suggest that such words are in fact phonemically recoded in a more or less automatic manner, even when we read them for the purpose of comprehension rather than pronunciation (e.g., Van Orden, 1987; Perfetti et al., 1988; Lukatela & Turvey, 1994a, 1994b; Savill et al., 2011; see also the intracranial recording studies by Perrone-Bertolotti et al., 2012, and Chan et al., in press). For example, in an experiment in which subjects were given a list of written words and had to decide, for each one, whether it referred to a kind of flower, Van Orden (1987) found that incorrect "yes" responses were more frequent for homophones of category exemplars (e.g., *rows*, which sounds like *rose*) than for control words (e.g., *robs*, which doesn't sound like *rose*). But while such results support the automaticity of grapheme–phoneme conversion, they also highlight the fact that for homophonous word pairs like *rose* and *rows*, *maid* and *made*, *raise* and *raze*, *board* and *bored*, or *muscles* and *mussels*, some other reading route must be used to distinguish between the two meanings.

As shown in Figure 8.14, this route starts in the orthographic lexicon, which represents the printed forms of whole words, and projects to the "semantic system," which represents the corresponding concepts. The diagram also indicates that the sound structures of whole words are represented in the "phonological lexicon," and that they can be accessed during reading either from the semantic system or via a pathway that leads directly from the orthographic lexicon to the phonological lexicon. Both of these channels are probably recruited when we read aloud all types of words, but they are especially important for words with irregular mappings between print and sound, such as *yacht*, *colonel*, and *choir*. Although some languages, like Italian, have very transparent writing systems that are characterized by highly reliable relationships between printed symbols and speech sounds, many others, like English, have more opaque systems that are riddled with exceptions to the standard rules. In addition to the highly irregular English words just mentioned, consider the pronunciation differences between the following pairs of similarly spelled words: *has* and *was*, *tough* and *dough*, *header* and *reader*, and *friend* and *fiend*.

Evidence from Acquired Dyslexia

Perhaps the strongest evidence for the multiple reading routes shown in Figure 8.14 comes from various neuropsychological dissociations that have been observed in brain-damaged patients who manifest certain types of reading impairments known as "acquired dyslexias."

These disorders have been investigated in great detail, but because their many nuances are beyond the scope of the current discussion, we will restrict our attention to some of the most salient findings (for reviews from different perspectives see Coltheart, 2006, and Patterson & Lambon Ralph, 2006). We will also hold off on considering the lesion correlates of the disorders until the next subsection. Here our focus is on the behavioral patterns and their implications for the model in Figure 8.14. (A brief aside: These disorders are sometimes referred to as particular types of "alexia," but we will use the term "dyslexia" instead, since it seems to be preferred in the relevant literature. It is important to bear in mind, however, that the dyslexias described here are acquired in adulthood as the result of brain injury, and hence are distinct from those that afflict some children as the result of congenital abnormalities.)

First, when patients with **phonological dyslexia** are given oral reading tasks, they perform fairly well, though often below ceiling, on most real words, regardless of whether the print-to-sound mappings are regular or irregular; however, they make many mistakes when confronted with pseudowords like *mifpum*. Now, some of these patients also have trouble with purely phonological tasks such as repetition, rhyme judgment, and phoneme identification, and the following proposal has been offered to account for their disproportionate difficulty in reading aloud pseudowords. Basically, the claim is that they suffer from a mild to moderate phonological impairment, and this interferes significantly more with their oral reading of pseudowords than real words because the former not only have less familiar articulatory patterns, but also lack the top-down benefits of associated semantic representations (Farah et al., 1996; Harm & Seidenberg, 2001; Patterson et al., 2006; Crisp & Lambon Ralph, 2006). Importantly, however, not all patients with phonological dyslexia exhibit speech processing deficits independent of reading, and for these cases an alternative line of explanation seems to be called for. Specifically, it is reasonable to suppose that their differential difficulty in reading aloud pseudowords relative to real words is due to a selective disruption of the grapheme–phoneme conversion pathway (Beauvois & Dérouesné, 1979; Bisiacchi et al., 1989; Caccappolo-van Vliet et al., 2004a, 2004b; Tree & Kay, 2006).

Second, patients with **surface dyslexia** are able to read aloud both pseudowords and regular words, but they tend to break down when presented with

> **Phonological dyslexia** A disorder of reading aloud in which patients perform significantly worse on pseudowords than real words.

irregular words, often committing over-regularization errors like pronouncing *yacht* as "yatched," and usually having the greatest difficulty with low-frequency items. This performance profile suggests that the grapheme–phoneme conversion pathway is still intact and is sufficient to support the oral reading of both pseudowords and regular words; however, at least one of the higher-level pathways has been affected, and this interferes with the oral reading of irregular words. Surface dyslexia is commonly found in patients with semantic dementia, whose knowledge of the meanings of words gradually deteriorates (see Chapters 4 and 10–12). And for this reason, some researchers have argued that in order to read aloud irregular words—especially those that are low-frequency—it is necessary to access their meanings (e.g., Patterson & Hodges, 1992; Fushimi et al., 2003; Patterson et al., 2006). On the other hand, Coltheart (2006) maintains that such a view cannot easily be reconciled with evidence that not all brain-damaged patients with semantic impairments display surface dyslexia (Schwartz et al., 1980; Cipolotti & Warrington, 1995; Lambon Ralph et al., 1995; Gerhand, 2001; Blazely et al., 2005). Also, Coltheart et al. (2001) demonstrated that a computer implementation of the processing framework shown in Figure 8.14 could be made to simulate surface dyslexia by keeping the semantic system fully functional but degrading the operation of the orthographic lexicon. At present, the nature of surface dyslexia is still controversial, and further work is needed to resolve all of the open questions. We will return to this challenging issue in the next section.

Finally, patients with **deep dyslexia** are not only impaired at reading aloud pseudowords, but are also prone to making mistakes when reading aloud both regular and irregular words. Interestingly, their errors with real words are often semantic in nature, like saying "dog" when presented with the printed word *cat*, and moreover they tend to perform worse with abstract than concrete words. The difficulty that these patients have with pseudowords is probably due to a defective grapheme–phoneme conversion pathway, but their peculiar behavior with real words is harder to understand. Several theories have been formulated, but to review them all here would take us too far afield (for a broad survey see Coltheart et al., 1980; see also Plaut & Shallice, 1993; Weekes

et al., 1997; Jefferies et al., 2007; Shallice & Cooper, 2011). Suffice it to say that the two most common approaches are roughly as follows. One view maintains that the semantic route has been compromised in such a way that similar lexically encoded concepts are likely to blur together. In contrast, the other view maintains that the patients' unusual errors reflect greater reliance on a right- than a left-hemisphere reading system.

The major behavioral properties of the three types of acquired dyslexia are summarized in Table 8.1. Overall, these disorders—especially the first two—illustrate how the cognitive system that underlies our capacity to map print onto sound and meaning can be fractionated in various ways as the result of brain injury. And this leads naturally to the next topic, which involves the neural substrates of that system.

Neural Substrates

The cortical architecture that allows us to link orthographic representations with phonological and semantic representations has been intensively investigated for several decades, but its precise configuration remains poorly understood. Nevertheless, there is mounting evidence that, as shown in Figure 8.15, after the visual form of a written word has been adequately processed in the ventral occipitotemporal stream (illustrated by the blue and red patches), access to its pronunciation is enabled by a complex perisylvian network (illustrated by the orange patches), and access to its meaning is enabled by an equally complex but more inferior temporal-parietal-frontal network (illustrated by the green patches).

Needless to say, the extremely "bushy" diagram in Figure 8.15 is far more complicated than the comparatively simple box-and-arrow diagram in Figure 8.14, and for this reason we will not attempt to draw any direct connections between them. To a large extent, the color-coded networks shown in Figure 8.15 are based on an influential meta-analysis of 35 PET and fMRI studies of reading (Jobard et al., 2003). Over 10 years have passed, however, since that meta-analysis was published, and in the meantime many other imaging experiments have been conducted in an effort to further elucidate the functional neuroanatomy of reading (for a recent historical survey see Price, 2012, and for additional updates see Price, 2013). To be sure, most of these studies support the general organization of Figure 8.15, but some of them suggest that modifications and refinements are needed. This is, however, entirely in keeping with the progressive, self-correcting nature of science; and furthermore, it is becoming increasingly clear that the neural substrates of reading are significantly modulated by numerous factors,

Surface dyslexia A disorder of reading aloud in which patients perform significantly worse on irregular words, especially low-frequency ones, than on regular words and pseudowords.

Deep dyslexia A disorder of reading aloud in which patients are impaired on pseudowords as well as real words, with errors on the latter often being semantic in nature and worse for abstract items.

Table 8.1   Oral Reading Performance of Patients with Acquired Dyslexia

	Regular Words	Irregular Words	Pseudowords
Phonological dyslexia	Variably preserved	Variably preserved	Impaired
Surface dyslexia	Variably preserved	Impaired Over-regularization errors Low-frequency items worse	Preserved
Deep dyslexia	Impaired Semantic errors Abstract items worse	Impaired Semantic errors Abstract items worse	Impaired

including skill level, which varies greatly across individuals, and lexical properties such as the length, frequency, imageability, and spelling-sound consistency of printed words (e.g., Seghier et al., 2008; Levy et al., 2009; Graves et al., 2010; Boukrina & Graves, 2013).

In the following discussion, we will look more closely at the different ways in which the orange- and green-coded networks in Figure 8.15 contribute to the act of reading. We will sidestep the myriad complexities of the imaging literature, however, and concentrate instead on the lesion correlates of phonological dyslexia and surface dyslexia. This approach will not only help us understand the two networks, but also give us deeper insight into the nature of these disorders.

In a valuable group study, Rapcsak et al. (2009) examined 31 patients who suffered left-hemisphere strokes and discovered that 21 of them had behavioral patterns consistent with phonological dyslexia. On the one hand, they performed equally well at reading aloud regular and irregular words, achieving mean scores of 74 percent and 72 percent, respectively; but on the other hand, they performed significantly worse on pseudowords, achieving a mean score of only 35 percent (Figure 8.16). For present

purposes, the key findings emerged when the researchers compared the lesion sites of these patients with the regions that were associated more with phonological processing than with either semantic or syntactic processing in a large meta-analysis of functional neuroimaging experiments involving normal subjects (Vigneau et al., 2006). In short, many correspondences were observed throughout the orange-coded perisylvian network depicted in Figure 8.15 (for similar results see Henry et al., 2012). For example, the meta-analysis revealed several "hot spots" for phonological processing in Broca's area and the inferior half of the precentral gyrus (Figure 8.17A), and one of the patients with phonological dyslexia had a frontal lesion that included the very same territory (Figure 8.17D) (see Fiez et al., 2006, for further evidence that damage to Broca's area, and particularly to BA44, often gives rise to phonological dyslexia; see also Woollams & Patterson, 2012). The meta-analysis also pointed to a phonological "hot spot" in the part of the posterior superior temporal gyrus that overlaps Wernicke's area (Figure 8.17B), and another patient with phonological dyslexia had damage there (Figure 8.17E). Finally, an additional "hot spot" for phonological processing was located in

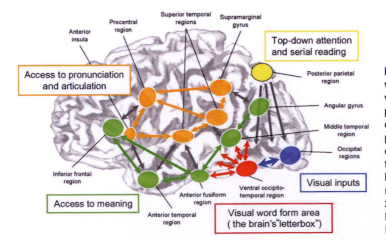

Figure 8.15   After the visual form of a printed word has been adequately processed in the ventral occipitotemporal stream (blue and red patches), access to its phonological structure is enabled by a complex perisylvian network (orange patches), and access to its semantic structure is enabled by an equally complex but more inferior temporal-parietal-frontal network. This diagram is based loosely on a meta-analysis of 35 functional neuroimaging studies of reading (Jobard et al., 2003). The precise configurations of the networks, however, are still being elucidated. (From Dehaene, 2009, p. 63.)

the inferior portion of the supramarginal gyrus (Figure 8.17C), and the lesion site of yet another patient with phonological dyslexia was centered in exactly that area (Figure 8.17F).

Given these results, as well as the material about speech perception and production covered in Chapters 5 and 6, it should come as no surprise that the phonological dyslexics in Rapcsak et al.'s (2009) study also manifested more general speech processing deficits. The researchers therefore argued that the patients' reading problems were best explained by the first account of phonological dyslexia described above. In particular, their higher error rates in reading aloud pseudowords than real words most likely reflected the greater challenge of producing unfamiliar, meaningless articulatory patterns after the phonological system had been disrupted to some degree. Importantly, the researchers noted that because the patients' lesion sites were distributed across the entire perisylvian network, it appears that damage to any anatomical sector of the phonological system can give rise to this kind of reading disorder. At the same time, however, they acknowledged that different perisylvian areas probably play somewhat different roles in phonological processing, and that, as a consequence, focal lesions to these areas might induce somewhat different forms of the disorder—forms that might be identified in future investigations.

We have just seen that those phonological dyslexics who manifest more general speech processing deficits

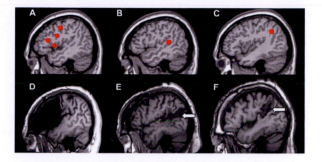

Figure 8.17 Anatomical results from Rapcsak et al.'s (2009) neuropsychological study of phonological dyslexia/dysgraphia. There is a close spatial overlap between the cortical regions that show activation in functional neuroimaging studies of phonological processing in normal individuals (A–C, derived from Vigneau et al., 2006) and the lesions that produce phonological dyslexia/dysgraphia (D–F). (From Rapcsak et al., 2009, p. 586.)

tend to have damage in the orange-coded perisylvian network in Figure 8.15. But what about the other class of phonological dyslexics—namely, those who lack such additional deficits and whose disproportionate difficulty in reading aloud pseudowords is, as mentioned above, probably due to a relatively selective disturbance of the grapheme–phoneme conversion pathway? Where are their lesions? The available data are rather limited, but two sets of findings are illuminating. First, this kind of phonological dyslexia has been reported in a few patients with left inferior occipitotemporal lesions, and although their general speech processing abilities were not formally assessed, it is safe to assume that they were intact (Rapcsak et al., 1987; Friedman et al., 1993). Second, three of the most convincing cases of this type of reading disorder had Alzheimer's disease (Caccappolo-van Vliet et al., 2004a, 2004b), which is interesting because that pathology typically affects the temporoparietal regions *bordering* the perisylvian network before it affects the core components of that network (Braak & Braak, 1996; Thompson et al., 2003).

Building on Figure 8.15, these findings can be integrated with some other ideas and discoveries to support the following hypothesis about how our brains allow us to convert letter strings into phoneme strings so that we can read aloud novel expressions like *wapkesh*. The putative pathway begins in an occipital area—probably V8—which, according to the LCD Model discussed earlier, houses abstract letter detectors, i.e., graphemes (see Figure 8.4). Note that this level of the LCD Model corresponds to the box labeled "letter identification" in Figure 8.14, and that the relevant brain area resides below the blue patch in Figure 8.15. The pathway proceeds from there to an "extrasylvian" parietal area—specifically, the

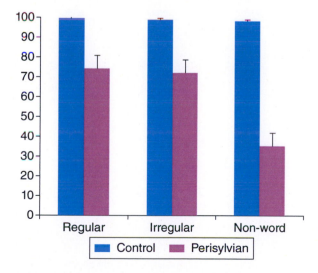

Figure 8.16 Behavioral results from Rapcsak et al.'s (2009) neuropsychological study of phonological dyslexia/dysgraphia. The graph shows the percentage correct of control subjects and patients with perisylvian lesions on an oral reading task involving regular words, irregular words, and non-words. (From Rapcsak et al., 2009, p. 579.)

superior portion of the supramarginal gyrus—which, according to several fMRI studies, contributes to the transcoding of letters into sounds (e.g., Booth et al., 2002; Joseph et al., 2003; Levy et al., 2008, 2009). And finally, from that parietal area the pathway enters the perisylvian network for speech processing through multiple routes. This hypothesis is consistent with a growing body of theory and data, and it can explain how some cases of phonological dyslexia may reflect an impairment of the neural mechanisms that underlie grapheme–phoneme conversion. But it is still quite speculative, and further work is needed to determine if it is on the right track.

Shifting now to surface dyslexia, as already indicated, it is most often exhibited by patients with semantic dementia (SD), whose conceptual knowledge slowly erodes because of tissue loss in the anterior temporal lobes. With regard to Figure 8.15, the regions that are hit hardest by this disease are the green-colored temporal areas that lie anterior to the VWFA (see Figure 2.7 in Chapter 2 and Figure 4.3 in Chapter 4). After a printed word has been recognized in the VWFA, these areas, among others, are believed to provide access to its meaning. In the current context, though, the key point is this: Research with SD patients has raised the possibility that this process of semantic retrieval is particularly important for reading

aloud low-frequency words with irregular mappings between spelling and pronunciation.

For instance, Patterson et al. (2006) investigated the oral reading abilities of 14 SD patients—seven with relatively mild semantic impairments and seven with relatively severe semantic impairments. The stimuli consisted of 168 single-syllable words, with 42 items in each of four conditions: high-frequency regular (e.g., *nine*); low-frequency regular (e.g., *sag*); high-frequency irregular (e.g., *none*); and low-frequency irregular (e.g., *sew*). As shown in Figure 8.18A, the patients were influenced by both frequency and regularity, performing significantly worse on low- than high-frequency items and significantly worse on irregular than regular items. There was also a powerful interaction between the two factors, such that the low-frequency irregular items were by far the most difficult, giving rise to abundant over-regularization errors—e.g., pronouncing the vowel in *sew* like the one in *stew* (see also Wilson et al., 2009a). This type of reading disorder constitutes surface dyslexia, and, interestingly, Figure 8.18A reveals that it was manifested more strongly by the patients with severe semantic deficits than by those with mild ones. This correlation is demonstrated even more clearly in Figure 8.18B, which plots the relationship between, first, the patients' proportion correct on all of the irregular words in the oral reading task, and second, their "composite semantic

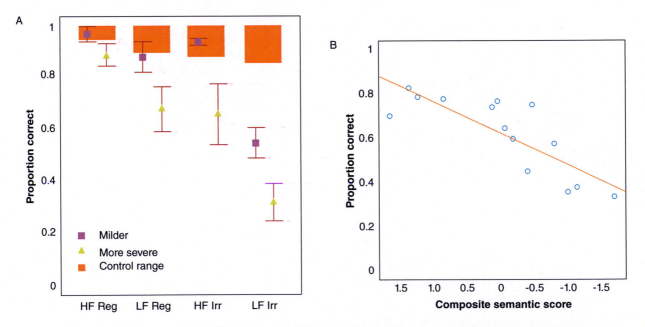

Figure 8.18   Behavioral results from Patterson et al.'s (2006) neuropsychological study of semantic dementia (SD). (A) Proportion correct of mild SD patients, more severe SD patients, and control subjects on an oral reading task involving high- and low-frequency regular and irregular words. (B) Scatterplot showing the correlation for SD patients between their proportion correct in orally reading irregular words and their composite semantic scores, which reflect their overall degree of conceptual impairment. (From Patterson et al., 2006, pp. 172 & 176.)

score," which reflects their performance on a battery of tasks that probe conceptual knowledge, including word meaning. It is quite apparent that as the patients' ability to read aloud irregular words declined, so did their ability to retrieve and process concepts.

According to Patterson et al. (2006), these findings support the following hypothesis about the neural substrates of reading (see also Woollams et al., 2007). Because regular words are, by definition, characterized by fairly consistent, rule-governed correspondences between orthography and phonology, they can be read aloud without necessarily being routed through the semantic system in the anterior temporal lobes. But because irregular words have idiosyncratic and atypical print-to-sound mappings, the SD data suggest that they do in fact require the stabilizing support of semantic access in order to be pronounced properly, especially if their mappings have not been overlearned by virtue of high familiarity.

This view certainly seems reasonable, but we would be remiss if we did not return, if only briefly, to two critical points made earlier. First, there are a few reports of brain-damaged patients who, despite exhibiting semantic deficits, do not have surface dyslexia (Schwartz et al., 1980; Cipolotti & Warrington, 1995; Lambon Ralph et al., 1995; Gerhand, 2001; Blazely et al., 2005). And second, a computer implementation of the processing model shown in Figure 8.14 demonstrated that surface dyslexia could be simulated by leaving the semantic system intact and selectively disrupting just the orthographic lexicon (Coltheart et al., 2001, 2010). If we assume that the orthographic lexicon resides in the VWFA, then these two findings, taken together, lead to the following possibility. When SD patients manifest surface dyslexia, their reading disorder may not always derive from their semantic impairment, but may instead emerge from the posterior extension of their atrophy all the way back to the VWFA (see, for example, Figure 4.3 in Chapter 4 and Figure 10.11 in Chapter 10). Together with related ideas, this proposal has generated some spirited debate, but we will refrain from delving into the details of those arguments here, since it is time to bring our discussion of reading to a close (for more information see Coltheart, 2006; Patterson et al., 2006; Coltheart et al., 2010; Woollams et al., 2007, 2010).

Summary

The act of reading hinges on the rapid, efficient operation of numerous, widespread brain regions that are enlisted not only to support the perceptual processing of printed stimuli, but also to provide bridges that connect visually recognized letters and words with other components of the linguistic system. Although the intricacies of this complex neural architecture have not yet been elucidated, the general outline is gradually coming into view.

According to the LCD Model, the sight of a written word triggers a cascade of transformations that extends from the retina to the thalamus, from there to the primary visual cortex, and from there through a series of occipitotemporal way-stations that extract increasingly rich and informative combinations of orthographic features. From a representational perspective, this visual processing hierarchy starts with mere points and lines, but it leads progressively to case- and font-specific letter shapes, case- and font-invariant letter identities, bigrams, quadrigrams, and even longer alphabetic strings. Many of the stages of this hierarchy are bilateral, but there is growing evidence that the left hemisphere begins to dominate fairly quickly.

The hierarchy culminates in the VWFA, which is an occipitotemporal area with the following properties: it detects the identities of printed words regardless of their location, case, or font, and regardless of whether they are perceived consciously or unconsciously; it is more sensitive to real than unreal words; it is engaged equally by different types of familiar scripts (English, Arabic, Chinese, etc.), but it responds more strongly to familiar than unfamiliar scripts; and perhaps most important of all, it prefers printed words to other kinds of visual objects. Damage to the VWFA often engenders a form of alexia in which words can no longer be recognized with just one quick glance, but must instead be processed in a slow and effortful letter-by-letter fashion. Some patients with this type of reading disorder may appear superficially to have otherwise intact visual perception, but careful testing usually reveals at least minor deficiencies in the processing of certain kinds of non-lexical stimuli—specifically, those that, like printed words, require high-resolution spatial discrimination, such as faces and numerals. This is consistent with the Neuronal Recycling Hypothesis, which claims that the reason the VWFA becomes relatively specialized for recognizing printed words when we learn to read is because it is inherently well-suited to handling complex combinations of spatially fine-grained shapes.

The mapping of print onto sound and meaning is enabled by multiple pathways—some sublexical, others lexical—but their precise neural underpinnings remain unclear. Still, several generalizations can be made. Access to the proper pronunciations of printed words seems to depend mainly on the perisylvian network for speech processing, whereas access to the concepts encoded by printed words seems to depend mainly on a more inferior network comprising various temporal, parietal, and frontal regions. Evidence for these proposals comes from functional neuroimaging studies with healthy subjects as well as neuropsychological studies with brain-damaged patients, but in our review we concentrated on the latter, focusing primarily on two types of acquired dyslexia. First, patients with phonological dyslexia are significantly worse at reading aloud pseudowords than real words. Some of them have lesions within the perisylvian network itself and exhibit general phonological deficits that may be the basis of their disproportionate difficulty in orally reading pseudowords. Others, however, have "extrasylvian" parietal or occipitotemporal lesions and do not manifest general phonological deficits; for them, the inability to orally read pseudowords may reflect a selective disturbance of the sublexical pathway for grapheme–phoneme conversion. Second, patients with surface dyslexia can read aloud pseudowords and also real words with regular print-to-sound mappings, but they are deficient at reading aloud real words with irregular print-to-sound mappings, especially those that are low-frequency. Their lesions tend to affect the anterior and ventral temporal lobes, and they usually have semantic impairments. These findings have led some researchers to infer that when we read aloud relatively uncommon irregular words, we cannot pronounce them correctly unless we first retrieve their meanings. Other researchers disagree, however, primarily because a few patients have been found who have semantic impairments but not surface dyslexia.

Writing

Having discussed in some detail the receptive side of printed language processing—i.e., reading—we turn now to the expressive side—i.e., writing. Throughout this section, we will use the term "writing" rather liberally to cover both handwriting and typing, these being the two most common ways of creating orthographic expressions. The ability to write not only requires certain manual skills, but also depends crucially on knowledge of spelling conventions. Until well into the 20th century, the vast majority of people in the world did not need to acquire this special capacity in order to lead rich and fulfilling lives. Since then, however, knowing how to write has become an increasingly important asset, and nowadays it is a fundamental prerequisite for participating in a variety of routine activities, some of which are rather serious, like taking lecture notes, composing professional documents, and filling out checks, and others of which are simply fun, like sending e-mail, texting, and surfing the Internet.

In cognitive neuroscience, writing has not received nearly as much attention as reading. Nevertheless, a number of valuable discoveries have been made about the different ways in which the ability to write can be

impaired by brain damage, and about the organization of the relevant cortical circuitry. The following review is structured in a manner similar to the last main part of the previous section on reading. It begins by presenting a model of the types of mental representations and processes that are widely believed to underlie writing. Then it shows how that model can account for several patterns of dissociation displayed by patients with certain kinds of writing disorders. And finally it addresses the neural substrates of the model's multiple components.

For many years, one of the most interesting and controversial issues in this area of inquiry has involved the degree to which the neural substrates of writing overlap with those of reading (for reviews see Hillis, 2001; Tainturier & Rapp, 2001; Hillis & Rapp, 2004; Purcell et al., 2011b). As we will see, there is growing evidence that some brain regions do in fact contribute to both "directions" of orthographic processing. Not surprisingly, however, there also appear to be some regions that are only necessary for one or the other.

From Sound and Meaning to Print

A Cognitive Model

Several different frameworks for characterizing written word production have been offered during the past few decades (e.g., Roeltgen & Heilman, 1985; Van Galen, 1991; Rapp & Caramazza, 1997; Tainturier & Rapp, 2001; Rapcsak & Beeson, 2002; Hillis & Rapp, 2004; Purcell et al., 2011b). The model that we will adopt is depicted in Figure 8.19. As with the model of reading

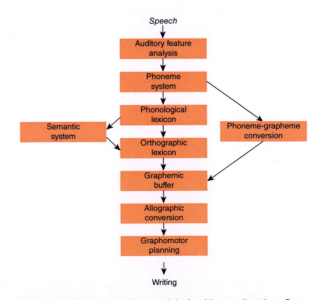

Figure 8.19 A cognitive model of writing to dictation. See the main text for details.

depicted in Figure 8.14, this box-and-arrow architecture posits multiple levels and pathways about which there is currently widespread (but probably not universal) agreement.

Writing is often motivated by the desire to record in print what people say, like when you quickly jot down what someone has just told you over the phone. In such situations, the speech input is processed along a pathway that leads from "auditory feature analysis" through the "phoneme system" to the "phonological lexicon," where the sound structures of perceived words are recognized (for details see Chapter 5). From there, the spelling patterns of the very same words are accessed in the "orthographic lexicon." As indicated above in the context of reading, these spelling patterns are couched in terms of sequences of graphemes (i.e., abstract letter identities that are unspecified for size, case, and style). For example, the word *banana* can be thought of as having the spelling "BANANA." This immediately raises the question of whether reading and writing share the same orthographic lexicon or make use of different ones. But while this is obviously an issue of considerable theoretical significance, we will defer dealing with it until we get to the discussion of neural substrates.

The model in Figure 8.19 assumes that when writing is prompted by speech input, the abstract spelling patterns of words can be retrieved from the orthographic lexicon in either or both of two ways: One route goes straight from the phonological lexicon to the orthographic lexicon, and the other passes through the semantic system. The latter route is also used when writing begins not with speech input, but rather with inner thoughts and feelings, like when you craft a letter to a friend. Notably, the idea that the spelling patterns of words can be accessed directly from their meanings, without any mediation by the associated phonological forms, has been controversial (e.g., Head, 1926; Geschwind, 1969; Perfetti, 1997; Van Orden et al., 1997). However, many brain-damaged patients have been described who can name stimuli by writing down the correct words but cannot name them by saying the correct words, and this dissociation strongly supports the existence of a pathway that leads directly from the semantic system to the orthographic lexicon, bypassing the phonological lexicon (e.g., Bub & Kertesz, 1982b; Caramazza & Hillis, 1990; Rapp et al., 1997; Kemmerer et al., 2005). Interestingly, the opposite dissociation, which involves impaired written naming but intact spoken naming, has also been reported, and this provides additional evidence that during language production the orthographic and phonological forms of words are accessed from the semantic system along separate channels (e.g., Hillis et al., 1999b; 2002a, 2003;

Caño et al., 2010; see also Figure 2.3 and the accompanying text in Chapter 2, as well as Figure 6.12 and the accompanying text in Chapter 6).

After the spelling pattern of a target word has been selected in the orthographic lexicon, the next processing stage is called the "graphemic buffer." It is basically a limited capacity working memory system that temporarily maintains in an activated state the identities and positions of the appropriate graphemes while the word is being written.

As shown in Figure 8.19, the graphemic buffer receives input not only from the orthographic lexicon, but also from the "phoneme–grapheme conversion" mechanism, which itself receives input from the phoneme system. This conversion device operates in essentially the opposite way as the grapheme–phoneme conversion device in Figure 8.14. In short, it uses a set of rules to map particular phonemes or phoneme clusters onto the corresponding graphemes or grapheme clusters, so that a person can write down novel expressions that they hear, like *feshkap*. This transcoding system may also facilitate the written production of auditorily perceived familiar words, especially if those words have regular mappings between sound and print, like *desk*. If they have irregular mappings instead, like *women*, their proper spelling must be retrieved from, and guided by, the orthographic lexicon. According to some researchers, irregular words with relatively low frequency, like *debut*, must also be routed through the semantic system in order to be spelled correctly. The evidence for this proposal is presented further below, but it is worth noting here, as a quick preview, that the line of argumentation is not only similar to the one we elaborated earlier with regard to reading aloud the same types of words, but is also vulnerable to analogous criticisms.

The model shown in Figure 8.19 posits two final stages of written word production. The first one is called "allographic conversion," which involves translating the abstract letter identities held in the graphemic buffer into concrete forms (upper or lower case, separate or cursive letters, etc.). The representations generated at this stage then serve as input to "graphomotor planning," which provides even more precise instructions to the motor system that controls the hand, such as specifications for the size, direction, and sequence of strokes. Incidentally, when writing is executed with a keyboard instead of a pen or pencil, a distinct processing component devoted to graphomotor planning for the purpose of typing may take information directly from the graphemic buffer and use it to assemble a set of commands for consecutive button presses. So far, however, the mental operations that underlie typing have not been investigated as much as those that underlie handwriting.

Evidence from Acquired Dysgraphia

The model described above provides a useful framework for explaining several types of writing impairments that are collectively called "acquired dysgraphias." These impairments seem to parallel, in fairly straightforward ways, the forms of acquired dyslexia discussed earlier. But although they have received quite a bit of attention in the neuropsychological literature, we will only summarize their main behavioral properties here (for further information see Shallice, 1988; Hillis, 2001; Tainturier & Rapp, 2001; Miceli & Capasso, 2006; note also that these conditions are sometimes referred to as particular types of "agraphia").

First, when patients with **phonological dysgraphia** are given "writing to dictation" tasks (i.e., tasks that require them to print auditorily perceived linguistic stimuli), they perform significantly worse with pseudowords than with either regular words or irregular words (e.g., Shallice, 1981; Roeltgen et al., 1983; Baxter & Warrington, 1985). This disorder is clearly the twin of phonological dyslexia, and the two impairments usually occur together. Because such patients tend to have more general speech processing deficits, their pseudoword reading and writing impairments may both be byproducts of reduced phonological capacity (Rapcsak et al., 2009). It is essential to realize, however, that double dissociations—not a lot, but a few—have been documented between phonological dyslexia and phonological dysgraphia. For example, case RG, described by Beauvois and Dérouesné (1981), was very poor at reading aloud pseudowords but could still spell them with 99 percent accuracy; and conversely, case MH, described by Bub and Kertesz (1982b), could read aloud pseudowords with 90 percent accuracy but was profoundly impaired at spelling them, even though he could repeat them perfectly. Despite the fact that such double dissociations are relatively rare, they support the existence, as well as the independence, of the two sublexical conversion pathways posited by the models in Figures 8.14 and 8.19, since they suggest that each one can be selectively disrupted.

Second, during writing to dictation tasks, patients with **surface dysgraphia** perform quite well with pseudowords, and they also have little trouble with most regular words, but they make many mistakes with irregular words, especially low-frequency ones, and their errors are usually over-regularizations, like spelling *yacht* as YOT

or *subtle* as SUTTEL (e.g., Beauvois & Dérouesné, 1981; Hatfield & Patterson, 1983; Roeltgen & Heilman, 1984; Goodman & Caramazza, 1986; Baxter & Warrington, 1987). Obviously, this disorder is very similar to surface dyslexia. The phoneme–grapheme conversion mechanism still functions more or less normally, and it can apparently support the writing of not only pseudowords but also regular words. The disproportionate difficulty with irregular words, on the other hand, presumably stems from an impairment affecting one or more of the central lexical components. Like surface dyslexia, surface dysgraphia is commonly found in patients with SD, and this has led some researchers to argue that, as with the reading disorder, the writing disorder can be interpreted as evidence for the following hypothesis: In order to fully access the atypical and only weakly memorized spelling patterns of relatively infrequent irregular words, the meanings of those words must also be activated—meanings that gradually disintegrate in patients with SD (Graham et al., 2000; Patterson et al., 2006). As before, however, this hypothesis faces several challenges. Most importantly, some brain-damaged patients can accurately spell irregular words without knowing their meanings (Patterson, 1986; Roeltgen et al., 1986). In addition, there are numerous reports of the exact opposite dissociation—for instance, case JG was impaired at spelling many irregular words that he could nevertheless define (Goodman & Caramazza, 1986). These findings raise the possibility that surface dysgraphia may be due not so much to semantic problems as to a disturbance involving the orthographic lexicon. We will return to this idea later on, when we address the neural substrates of writing more directly.

Third, mirroring deep dyslexia and usually co-occurring with it, **deep dysgraphia** is characterized by an inability to write pseudowords, together with a tendency to commit semantic errors when attempting to write both regular and irregular words, like spelling DOG in response to the spoken word *cat* (e.g., Bub & Kertesz, 1982a; Nolan & Caramazza, 1983; Shallice, 1988; Miceli et al., 1997; Jefferies et al., 2007). As in deep dyslexia, the semantic errors tend to be more pronounced for abstract than concrete words. But while the difficulty with pseudowords most likely reflects an impairment at some point along the phoneme–grapheme conversion pathway, the semantic errors with real words are not entirely understood and may have different causes in different patients. Some of the accounts that have been offered to explain

---

Phonological dysgraphia   A disorder of writing to dictation in which patients perform significantly worse on pseudowords than real words.

Surface dysgraphia   A disorder of writing to dictation in which patients perform significantly worse on irregular words, especially low-frequency ones, than on regular words and pseudowords.

Deep dysgraphia   A disorder of writing to dictation in which patients are impaired on pseudowords as well as real words, with errors on the latter often being semantic in nature and worse for abstract items.

deep dyslexia may also apply to some cases of deep dysgraphia. Other cases, however, may require alternative explanations. Unfortunately, to review all of the proposals that have been developed in this complex literature would be too much of a digression.

The primary behavioral features of the three types of acquired dysgraphia described above are summarized in Table 8.2. The fact that the contents of this table are virtually identical to the contents of Table 8.1, with the only differences involving the terms "dyslexia" and "dysgraphia," clearly underscores the striking parallelisms between the corresponding kinds of reading and writing disorders. Before going on to look more closely at the neural substrates of writing, however, we will briefly consider one other form of impairment.

As indicated earlier, the graphemic buffer is a short-term memory component that holds on to a string of abstract letter identities while the word (or pseudoword) is being written. During this stage of processing, noise or interference between letters can sometimes lead even normal individuals to make mistakes—so-called "slips of the pen"—that involve transpositions (e.g., HOS*R*E for HORSE), substitutions (e.g., HO*P*SE for HORSE), omissions (e.g., HOSE for HORSE), and additions (e.g., HOR*E*SE for HORSE). Interestingly, there is abundant evidence that the graphemic buffer can be selectively disrupted by brain damage (for a list of over 20 case studies, see Table 1 in Miceli & Capasso, 2006; see also Shallice & Cooper, 2011). Among the most representative patients is LB, whose deficit was investigated in great detail by Alfonso Caramazza and his colleagues (Caramazza et al., 1987; Caramazza & Miceli, 1990). Not only was LB highly susceptible to committing the kinds of "slips of the pen" just mentioned, but he tended to make such mistakes in the middle of words, and he was more likely to mis-spell long words than short ones. In addition, his error patterns for real words and pseudowords were quite comparable, and they were manifested in both handwriting and oral spelling as well as across a wide range of tasks, including writing/spelling to dictation, delayed copying, and naming. Overall, LB's performance profile points to a critical role for the grapheme buffer in the cognitive model of writing depicted in Figure 8.19.

Neural Substrates

Now that we have seen how the model can accommodate the various dissociations that are found in the major types of writing disorders, we can begin to explore how its key components are physically implemented in the brain. To that end, the following discussion revolves chiefly around the results of a recent meta-analysis of functional neuroimaging studies of written word production. This meta-analysis was conducted by Purcell et al. (2011b), and it focused on 11 PET and fMRI studies that collectively reported 17 experimental contrasts based on a total of 146 subjects (see also Planton et al., in press). The major results are shown in Figure 8.20, with red patches marking regions putatively associated with "central" components—these being the orthographic lexicon, the graphemic buffer, and the phoneme–grapheme conversion pathway—and blue patches marking regions putatively associated with "peripheral" components—these being allographic conversion and graphomotor planning. As the color labels in the figure indicate, the latter, blue-coded results were obtained by contrasting two independent analyses. In particular, the analysis that isolated central components was subtracted from the one that isolated [central + peripheral] components, so that the outcome reflected just peripheral components. In order to both leverage our interpretation of the imaging results and gain deeper insight into the nature of writing disorders, we will also consider several neuropsychological studies that have documented correlations between specific kinds of acquired dysgraphia and specific sites of brain damage.

Table 8.2 Writing to Dictation Performance of Patients with Acquired Dysgraphia

	Regular Words	Irregular Words	Pseudowords
Phonological dysgraphia	Variably preserved	Variably preserved	Impaired
Surface dysgraphia	Variably preserved	Impaired Over-regularization errors Low-frequency items worse	Preserved
Deep dysgraphia	Impaired Semantic errors Abstract items worse	Impaired Semantic errors Abstract items worse	Impaired

Perhaps the most intriguing result of Purcell et al.'s (2011b) meta-analysis is that the set of regions that turned out to be reliably linked with the central processes of written word production included a portion of the left ventral occipitotemporal cortex. This area, which is among those marked in red, can be seen in Figure 8.20 not only on the lateral view of the brain, but also on the horizontal section at $z = -16$. The theoretical significance of this finding derives from the fact that the area identified here as contributing to writing has also been identified by many other studies as contributing to reading. Indeed, the meta-analysis revealed that one of the activation peaks in this area lies at the coordinates $[-44, -56, -12]$, and the heart of the VWFA is often placed at the nearly identical coordinates $[-42, -57, -15]$ (Cohen et al., 2002). To fully appreciate this remarkable degree of similarity, it is worth taking a moment to compare the location of the red patch at $z = -16$ in Figure 8.20 with the location of the VWFA in some of the previous figures—for example, the blue cross in Figure 8.7 and the anterior "hot spot" in Figure 8.8. In keeping with these close correspondences, four recent fMRI studies that examined both spelling and reading in the same subjects found overlapping activation for the two tasks in the left ventral occipitotemporal cortex (Cho et al., 2009; Rapp & Dufor, 2011; Rapp & Lipka, 2011; Purcell et al., 2011a). Given this impressive convergence of imaging data, it seems quite reasonable to infer that the region of interest contains a single orthographic lexicon that is employed for both the production and the recognition of printed words.

Does this interpretation receive additional support from neuropsychological studies? Earlier we observed that some patients with alexia retain the ability to write, and at first sight this dissociation seems to challenge the notion of a shared orthographic lexicon. In principle, however, such cases of impaired reading and preserved writing *can* be reconciled with the idea that there is just one storehouse for the spelling patterns of words. It is only necessary to assume that *access* to those patterns is no longer possible from visual input, but is still possible from the phonological and semantic systems.

Importantly, several other neuropsychological findings actually strengthen the hypothesis that both reading and writing rely on a single orthographic lexicon in the left ventral occipitotemporal cortex. First, damage to this region often disrupts both capacities (Rapcsak & Beeson, 2004; Philipose et al., 2007; Tsapkini & Rapp, 2010). Second, some patients with impairments of both capacities exhibit a high degree of consistency in the specific words for which they make errors, even when effects of length and frequency are partialed out (Coltheart & Funnell, 1987; Behrmann & Bub, 1992). And third, when such patients receive treatment in only one modality—either just in reading or just in writing—the benefits sometimes carry over to the other modality in item-specific ways (Hillis, 1993).

Before returning to the meta-analysis, it is worth dwelling a bit on the discovery that when damage to the left ventral occipitotemporal cortex does disrupt writing, the impairment often takes the form of surface dysgraphia—i.e., relatively good performance on pseudowords and regular words, but poor performance on irregular words, especially low-frequency ones like *chamois*. This deficit–lesion correlation has been documented

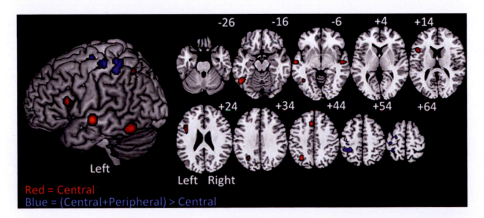

Figure 8.20   Results from Purcell et al.'s (2011b) meta-analysis of functional neuroimaging studies of writing. Red patches mark regions putatively associated with central components (the orthographic lexicon, the graphemic buffer, and the phoneme–grapheme conversion pathway). Blue patches mark regions putatively associated with peripheral components (allographic conversion and graphomotor planning). To identify the latter sites, the analysis that isolated central components was subtracted from the one that isolated [central + peripheral] components, so that the outcome reflected just peripheral components. (From Purcell et al., 2011b, p. 10.)

in a sizeable group study (Rapcsak & Beeson, 2004) and also in a detailed case study (Tsapkini & Rapp, 2010). In the current context, though, the main reason it matters is because it has implications for the controversial hypothesis described earlier regarding the underlying nature of surface dysgraphia.

Here's the background: We already noted that this particular type of writing disorder is commonly found in patients with SD. For example, the group of 14 SD patients studied by Patterson et al. (2006) displayed not only surface dyslexia, as indicated in Figure 8.18, but also surface dysgraphia, as indicated in Figure 8.21. More precisely, Figure 8.21A shows that these patients made far more spelling errors on irregular than regular items, with significant effects of both word frequency and dementia severity; and Figure 8.21B shows that when dementia severity was measured specifically in terms of the degree of semantic deterioration, it correlated quite strongly with the proportion of spelling errors on irregular items.

Now, according to Patterson et al. (2006), these results support the hypothesis that retrieving the atypical spelling patterns of infrequent irregular words depends on prior activation of the meanings of those words—a process that becomes increasingly difficult for SD patients. But an alternative account of the SD data—one that is comparable to the counter-explanation offered earlier for the very similar reading results in Figure 8.18—has the following logic. As the disease progresses, the temporal lobe atrophy extends posteriorly until it most likely encroaches upon the VWFA (again, see Figure 4.3 in Chapter 4 and Figure 10.11 in Chapter 10). The VWFA, as discussed above, appears to subserve a single

orthographic lexicon that is engaged during both reading and writing, especially when the words have atypical spelling patterns. Hence, the real cause of the worsening symptoms of surface dysgraphia in SD patients may not be the deterioration of the semantic system, but rather the gradual loss of the orthographic lexicon. Not only is this account internally coherent, but it also fits nicely with independent evidence that focal lesions restricted to the left ventral occipitotemporal cortex, including the VWFA, sometimes induce surface dysgraphia, as well as reading problems, without any noticeable semantic deficits (Tsapkini & Rapp, 2010). Still, it must be acknowledged that the true nature of the spelling deficit in SD remains mysterious, and that further research is needed to resolve this issue.

Shifting back to Purcell et al.'s (2011b) meta-analysis, there are three other red patches in Figure 8.20 that mark regions putatively associated with the central processes of written word production: one in the inferior frontal gyrus straddling the boundary between BA44 and BA45; one in the mid sector of the superior temporal gyrus extending into the superior temporal sulcus; and one in the supramarginal gyrus extending into the intraparietal sulcus. All three of these regions probably contribute in various ways to the rule-governed transformations that mediate the conversion of sound sequences into letter sequences, as when one first hears a pseudoword like *dabrick* and then spells it. Evidence for this interpretation comes from several neuropsychological studies which have shown that patients with phonological dysgraphia, who are disproportionately impaired at writing pseudowords, tend to have lesions affecting one or more of these

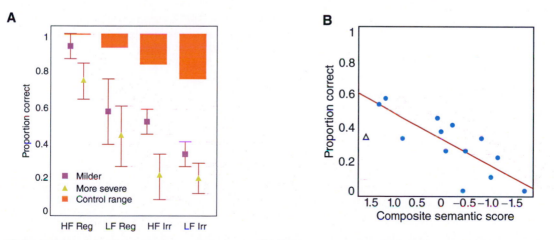

Figure 8.21 Behavioral results from Patterson et al.'s (2006) neuropsychological study of semantic dementia (SD). (A) Proportion correct of mild SD patients, more severe SD patients, and control subjects on a writing-to-dictation task involving high- and low-frequency regular and irregular words. (B) Scatterplot showing the correlation for SD patients between their proportion correct in writing irregular words and their composite semantic scores, which reflect their overall degree of conceptual impairment. (From Patterson et al., 2006, pp. 172 & 176.)

brain areas (e.g., Henry et al., 2007, 2012; Philipose et al., 2007; Rapcsak et al., 2009). As mentioned earlier, these patients often exhibit not only phonological dysgraphia but also phonological dyslexia. This was the case, for example, for the three patients in Figure 8.17 whose lesions overlapped with certain nodes of the perisylvian phonological network. In such situations, it is likely that the parallel deficits in mapping phonology onto orthography and orthography onto phonology reflect more general speech processing impairments. It is also worth recalling, however, that phonological dysgraphia and phonological dyslexia sometimes dissociate from each other, which suggests that the phoneme–grapheme and grapheme–phoneme conversion pathways are, at least to some extent, separate.

With respect to the graphemic buffer component of the model in Figure 8.19, Purcell et al. (2011b) point out that it may be subserved in part by the inferior frontal area highlighted in Figure 8.20. Consistent with this view, a recent study involving 69 acute stroke patients revealed that, compared to patients without graphemic buffer deficits, those with such deficits had significant tissue dysfunction in the left inferior frontal cortex and underlying white matter, as well as in neighboring precentral areas (Cloutman et al., 2009).

Finally, the blue patches in Figure 8.20 mark regions putatively associated with the peripheral processes of written word production—namely, allographic conversion and graphomotor planning. These patches are all clustered in dorsolateral frontoparietal areas that have been implicated, to varying degrees, in the programming of manual movements. In this context, the most anterior blue patch, which is located in the dorsal premotor cortex (PMd) at the junction of the posterior middle and superior frontal gyri, warrants special attention, since it appears to play a uniquely important role in relatively low-level aspects of writing (see also Box 8.1). This was demonstrated in a compelling way by Roux et al. (2009), who used direct cortical stimulation to chart the functional properties of this anatomical territory in 12 patients who were undergoing neurosurgery for tumor resection. As indicated by the blue dots in Figure 8.22, for six of these patients, stimulation at specific sites in and around the area corresponding to the most anterior blue patch in Figure 8.20 disrupted handwriting by distorting, slowing down, or arresting word production; however, such stimulation did not impair other manual movements or spoken word production. Interestingly, one of these patients was left-handed, and for him the critical site was in the homologous area of the right hemisphere. It is also noteworthy that for five of the other six patients, stimulation at different sites, most of which were more inferior,

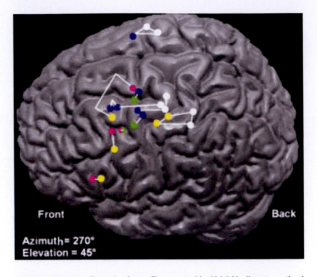

Figure 8.22 Results from Roux et al.'s (2009) direct cortical stimulation study of writing. The image shows an oblique view of a standard brain with the stimulation sites positioned according to MNI coordinates. Each patient corresponds to a group of dots linked together with white lines. Blue dots: sites where stimulation disrupted handwriting but did not impair other manual movements or spoken word production. Yellow dots: sites where stimulation disrupted handwriting as well as oral naming. Purple dots: sites where stimulation disrupted handwriting, oral naming, and reading aloud. White dots: sites where stimulation caused hand contractions. Green dots: sites where stimulation caused eye movements. Note that the patient who received right-hemisphere stimulation was left-handed. (From Roux et al., 2009, p. 541.)

impaired handwriting together with oral language tasks—either just naming, as shown by the yellow dots, or both naming and reading aloud, as shown by the purple dots. (Incidentally, the white and green dots indicate sites where stimulation caused hand contractions and eye movements, respectively.) Overall, these findings strongly support the idea that the most anterior blue patch in Figure 8.20 is essential for the peripheral processes of written word production. It remains unclear, however, whether that area is more involved in allographic conversion or graphomotor planning.

Summary

Although writing has not been investigated as much as reading from the perspective of cognitive neuroscience, progress is definitely being made in understanding how our brains allow us to produce printed words. When the task is to write down novel expressions like *roshtap*, processing proceeds along a phoneme–grapheme conversion pathway that translates the perceived sound sequences into the corresponding letter sequences. A disturbance at any stage of this pathway can induce phonological dysgraphia, a disorder characterized by significantly worse writing of pseudowords than real words. On the other hand, when the task is to write down real words, processing can move along any of several routes, depending on the nature of the stimuli. If the words have regular spelling patterns, like *shelf* or *drink*, it would certainly be possible to use the phoneme–grapheme conversion pathway, but it would also be possible to use a more central route that includes the phonological and orthographic lexicons as well as the semantic system. If, however, the words have irregular spelling patterns, like *depot* or *indict*, the only way to succeed is by following the central lexical route. Damage to this route can induce surface dysgraphia, a disorder characterized by significantly worse writing of irregular words, especially infrequent ones, than of regular words and pseudowords. There is some debate, however, over which specific component of the central route is critically impaired in this disorder—the semantic system or the orthographic lexicon. Regardless of whether one is writing a real word

or a pseudoword, once the intended letter string has been activated, it is temporarily held in a short-term memory system called the graphemic buffer. While it is maintained there, the particular forms of the letters (upper or lower case, separate or cursive, etc.) are determined during a process called allographic conversion, and the appropriate hand movements are programmed during a process called graphomotor planning.

As for the underlying brain structures, there is growing evidence that the VWFA in the left ventral occipitotemporal cortex contains a single orthographic lexicon that is engaged during both reading and writing. In addition, the neural mechanisms that enable phoneme–grapheme conversion seem to be distributed across several frontal, temporal, and parietal areas. The graphemic buffer seems to rely strongly on the left inferior frontal cortex, including part of Broca's area. And finally, the peripheral processes of allographic conversion and graphomotor planning appear to depend on hand-related dorsolateral frontoparietal regions.

Summary and Key Points

- When we read, letter strings are processed along the ventral occipitotemporal stream. According to the Local Combination Detector (LCD) Model, this pathway contains multiple levels of feature detectors, hierarchically organized in such a way that increasingly larger fragments of printed words are represented at each successive level.
- The pathway culminates in the Visual Word Form Area (VWFA).

    o This region normally responds to printed words in the following ways:

    - invariant to location;
    - invariant to case;
    - invariant to font;
    - sensitive to both consciously and unconsciously perceived words;
    - more sensitive to real words than pseudowords;
    - more sensitive to printed words than spoken words;
    - equally sensitive to different types of familiar scripts, but more sensitive to familiar than unfamiliar scripts;
    - more sensitive to printed words than other categories of objects.

    o Damage to the VWFA, or to its inputs, can cause alexia, a reading disorder with two subcategories:

    - One subcategory includes patients who cannot even recognize single letters, let alone complete words.
    - The other subcategory includes patients who cannot read whole words with just one quick glance, but must instead decipher each sequential letter in a slow and deliberate manner and then put all the pieces together.

    o Because reading and writing are cultural inventions that arose only 5,400 years ago, the VWFA could not have evolved specifically for the purpose of recognizing printed words. The Neuronal Recycling Hypothesis maintains that culturally acquired abilities invade evolutionarily older brain circuits and inherit many of their structural and functional constraints. From this perspective, the VWFA is the ideal site for representing the spelling patterns of printed words because it is apparently designed to integrate complex combinations of spatially fine-grained shapes.

- After the orthographic structures of printed words have been adequately processed, the corresponding phonological and semantic structures are accessed.

(Continued)

(Continued)

○ According to a widely adopted cognitive model of reading, the mapping of print onto sound and meaning can be accomplished in several ways, depending on the nature of the items:

▪ Pseudowords like *blicket* can only be read aloud by using a grapheme–phoneme conversion pathway.
▪ Words with regular spelling patterns like *leg* can be read aloud by using either the grapheme–phoneme conversion pathway or a central route that includes the orthographic and phonological lexicons as well as the semantic system.
▪ Words with irregular spelling patterns like *yacht* can only be read aloud by using the central route, but it is controversial whether the proper pronunciation of these words requires prior activation of their meaning.

○ Three types of acquired dyslexia have been distinguished:

▪ Phonological dyslexia is a disorder of reading aloud in which patients perform significantly worse on pseudowords than real words.
▪ Surface dyslexia is a disorder of reading aloud in which patients perform significantly worse on irregular words, especially low-frequency ones, than on regular words and pseudowords.
▪ Deep dyslexia is a disorder of reading aloud in which patients are impaired on pseudowords as well as real words, with errors on the latter often being semantic in nature and worse for abstract items.

○ The neural substrates of mapping print onto sound and meaning are quite complicated and still poorly understood. However, two major networks are as follows:

▪ Access to the pronunciations of printed words is enabled by a complex perisylvian network.
▪ Access to the meanings of printed words is enabled by an equally complex but more inferior temporal-parietal-frontal network.

• When we write, we begin by activating the phonological and semantic structures of words, and we end by producing the appropriate letter strings, either with a pen or a keyboard.

○ According to a widely adopted cognitive model of writing, the mapping of sound and meaning onto print can be accomplished in several ways, depending on the nature of the items, and with obvious similarities to reading:

▪ Pseudowords like *blicket* can only be written by using a phoneme–grapheme conversion pathway.
▪ Words with regular spelling patterns like *leg* can be written by using either the phoneme–grapheme conversion pathway or a central route that includes the phonological and orthographic lexicons as well as the semantic system.
▪ Words with irregular spelling patterns like *yacht* can only be written by using the central route, but it is controversial whether the proper spelling of these words requires prior activation of their meaning.
▪ Once the intended letter string has been activated, it is held in the graphemic buffer.
▪ The last two stages of written word production are allographic conversion, which involves transforming abstract graphemes into concrete letter shapes, and graphomotor planning, which involves programming the appropriate hand movements.

○ Three types of acquired dysgraphia have been distinguished, paralleling the three types of acquired dyslexia:

▪ Phonological dysgraphia is a writing disorder in which patients perform significantly worse on pseudowords than real words.
▪ Surface dysgraphia is a writing disorder in which patients perform significantly worse on irregular words, especially low-frequency ones, than on regular words and pseudowords.
▪ Deep dysgraphia is a writing disorder in which patients are impaired on pseudowords as well as real words, with errors on the latter often being semantic in nature and worse for abstract items.

○ Regarding the neural substrates of writing, some of the main findings are as follows:

▪ The learned spelling patterns of words are stored in the VWFA, which contains a single orthographic lexicon that contributes to both reading and writing.
▪ Phoneme–grapheme conversion seems to rely on several frontal, temporal, and parietal areas.
▪ The graphemic buffer is implemented largely in the inferior frontal cortex, including part of Broca's area.
▪ Allographic conversion and graphomotor planning depend on hand-related dorsolateral frontoparietal regions.

Recommended Reading

- Dehaene, S. (2009). *Reading in the brain: The science and evolution of a human invention.* New York: Viking. A very clear and entertaining overview of the cognitive neuroscience of reading, written for a general audience by one of the leading figures in the field.
- Wolf, M. (2008). *Proust and the squid: The story and science of the reading brain.* New York: Harper Perennial. Another popular book that brings together the archaeology, psychology, linguistics, and neuroscience of reading.
- Dehaene, S., & Cohen, L. (2011). The unique role of the visual word form area in reading. *Trends in Cognitive Sciences, 15,* 254–262. A useful survey of findings about VWFA.
- Price, C.J., & Devlin, J.T. (2011). The interactive account of ventral occipitotemporal contributions to reading. *Trends in Cognitive Sciences, 15,* 246–253. A critical perspective on the VWFA.
- Purcell, J.J., Turkeltaub, P.E., Eden, G.F., & Rapp, B. (2011). Examining the central and peripheral processes of written word production through meta-analysis. *Frontiers in Psychology, 2,* Article 239. An outstanding investigation of the neural substrates of writing, focusing on functional neuroimaging data but also taking into account neuropsychological data.

Sign Language

9

Introduction

Sign languages are the primary communication systems of the deaf, but up until the 1960s they were widely regarded as just crude visual–gestural codes consisting mostly of simplistic pantomimes and fingerspelling. The initial step toward overturning this misconception took place in 1965, when William Stokoe and his colleagues published a seminal analysis of American Sign Language (ASL) which began to show, for the first time, that sign languages are in fact full-fledged languages, with the same degree of structural complexity and expressive power as spoken languages (Stokoe et al., 1965). This landmark study served as a springboard for further research, and during the 50 years since it appeared many valuable discoveries have been made about how sign languages work (for recent surveys see Sandler & Lillo-Martin, 2006; Brentari, 2010; Pfau et al., 2012).

Over 120 different sign languages have been identified so far, and, like spoken languages, they qualify as independent because they are mutually unintelligible. For example, signers of American Sign Language, Indian Sign Language, and Madagascar Sign Language cannot understand each other any more than speakers of English, Tamil, and Malagasy can. Nevertheless, as we will see, sign languages do tend to have more in common with each other than spoken languages, largely because the visual–gestural medium is conducive to similar strategies of spatial representation.

One of the most fascinating and informative advances in this field of inquiry involves the origins of sign languages. Although no one has ever witnessed a new spoken language being created out of thin air, scientists have been able to track the gradual emergence of several new sign languages under different social conditions (Senghas et al., 2004; Sandler et al., 2005; Meir et al., 2010; Padden et al., 2010; see also Goldin-Meadow, 2003). In the case of Nicaraguan Sign Language, 50 deaf children who had not acquired any type of conventional language, spoken or signed, were brought together from different places for educational purposes, and while they interacted with each other outside the classroom—in the schoolyard, in the streets, and on the buses—they spontaneously invented a rudimentary sign language of their own. This "first stage" system was then passed on to later generations of deaf students, who elaborated and refined it by adding more lexical and grammatical structure. In another remarkable case, namely that of Al-Sayyid Bedouin Sign Language, a sophisticated visual–gestural communication system arose in a small village in southern Israel with a high incidence of genetically based deafness, and over the course of a single generation it developed a preference for subject–object–verb (SOV) order, in contrast to the dominant subject–verb–object (SVO) order of the main spoken language in the area, namely Arabic. These and other cases of emerging sign languages have much to teach us, but the most important lesson is probably this: people are biologically and culturally driven to communicate with each other through language no matter what, so if they find themselves in a situation where there isn't a good model to emulate—that is, no immediately available language—they will create one from scratch, even if that means doing so in the visual–gestural modality.

Because spoken and signed languages employ different input and output channels, it is obvious that they must recruit different sensory and motor networks in the brain—specifically, auditory and vocal networks for the peripheral aspects of spoken language processing, and visual and manual networks for the peripheral aspects of sign language processing. (As shown below, the production of sign language also requires precise motor control of the torso, head, and face.) A much more interesting and theoretically important issue, however, is whether the two types of languages also seek out different neural circuits for the central aspects of processing—i.e., those that involve lexical and grammatical structure—or if instead they gravitate toward the same circuits. During the past few decades, cognitive neuroscientists have explored this issue from many different perspectives, and it has become increasingly clear that the central aspects of both types of languages are subserved, for the most part, by the same cortical regions and fiber tracts in the left hemisphere. Why only "for the most part"? Because it appears that for some lexical and grammatical functions, there are genuine anatomical differences between the two types of languages, differences that are manifested not only in the left hemisphere, but also in the right.

The main purpose of this chapter is to describe these complex but exciting findings about the neural underpinnings of sign language (see also Poizner et al., 1987; Hickok et al., 1998a; Corina & McBurney, 2001; Emmorey, 2002; Campbell et al., 2007; MacSweeney et al., 2008; Corina & Spotswood, 2012). The first section sets the stage by explaining in greater detail how sign languages constitute full-blown languages. The second section demonstrates that, like spoken languages, sign languages depend predominantly on the left hemisphere. The third section looks more closely at how sign languages are represented and processed within the left hemisphere. And the last section shows that the right hemisphere also contributes to certain aspects of sign languages.

Structural Aspects of Sign Language

Like spoken languages, sign languages have multiple levels of structure. Even though individual signs are completely devoid of sound, their forms can still be characterized in terms of a special kind of phonology, and their combinatorial properties can still be characterized in terms of grammatical rules involving both morphology and syntax. These structural aspects of sign language are briefly described below.

Phonology

In spoken languages meaningful words are built out of meaningless phonemes that fall into categories like consonants and vowels. Similarly, in sign languages meaningful signs are built out of formational elements that do not themselves have any semantic content (Liddell & Johnson, 1989; Sandler, 1989; Brentari, 1998; Brentari

& Eccarius, 2010; Jantunen & Takkinen, 2010). There are three major parameters in sign language phonology: handshape, location, and movement. (Another one is orientation, but it is not discussed here.) Because many distinctions can be made along each parameter, sign languages usually contain at least a few minimal pairs of signs that differ in just one feature, analogous to minimal pairs of words such as *pat* and *bat*. Some examples from Israeli Sign Language (ISL) are shown in Figure 9.1 (Meir et al.,

A

MOTHER   NOON

B

HEALTH   CURIOSITY

C

ESCAPE   BETRAY

Figure 9.1 Minimal pairs of signs in Israeli Sign Language (ISL), phonologically distinguished by (A) handshape features, (B) location features, and (C) movement features. (From Meir et al., 2007, p. 538.)

CRY   AEROPLANE

Figure 9.2   Examples of iconic signs in British Sign Language (BSL). (From Perniss et al., 2010, p. 4.)

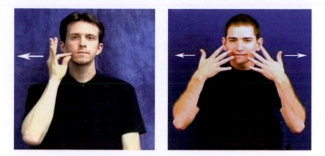

Figure 9.3   The signs for CAT in (A) American Sign Language (ASL) and (B) British Sign Language (BSL) are both iconic, but in different ways. (From Perniss et al., 2010, p. 5.)

2007). First, the signs MOTHER and NOON vary only in handshape, since they have the same specifications for both location and movement (Figure 9.1A). Second, the signs HEALTH and CURIOSITY differ in location, being produced at the chest and nose, respectively; however, they share features for both handshape and movement (Figure 9.1B). Third, the signs ESCAPE and BETRAY contrast in movement, with the former involving a straight trajectory and the latter an arc trajectory, but they are identical with regard to both handshape and location (Figure 9.1C).

All of the signs in Figure 9.1 have arbitrary mappings between form and meaning. But because the visual–gestural medium in which sign languages are transmitted is inherently multidimensional and continuous, it should come as no surprise that some signs are **iconic** (for recent discussions see Perniss et al., 2010, and Wilbur, 2010). In these signs, the form of the expression physically resembles, to some extent, the kind of entity or event that it designates. This is nicely illustrated by the examples from British Sign Language (BSL) in Figure 9.2. The sign CRY is made with two extended index fingers, which move like tears in an alternating pattern downward from an eye on the signer's face. And the sign AIRPLANE is made by configuring the extended thumb and pinky in a manner that mimics a plane's wings, and moving the hand high across the signing space so as to mimic the plane's flight.

It is important to note, however, that different sign languages often represent the same referent iconically in different ways. Thus, whereas the ASL sign LION depicts the animal's mane, the BSL sign LION depicts its pouncing paws. And even when two

iconic signs focus on the same part of an object, they may portray it differently. This point is exemplified by Figure 9.3, which shows that whereas the ASL sign CAT is formed by using the pinched index finger and thumb of one hand to trace a single whisker beside one cheek, the BSL sign CAT is formed by spreading the fingers of both hands to trace all of the whiskers beside both cheeks.

No description of sign languages would be complete without mentioning a special set of mostly iconic expressions called **classifiers**. They use fairly direct, non-arbitrary mappings between form and meaning to specify a great deal of spatial/topographic information about the shapes, sizes, positions, and paths of their real-world referents. The proper analysis of classifiers is a matter of debate (for a variety of opinions see Emmorey, 2003). Typically, however, they have two parts: (1) a handshape that encodes, more or less iconically, a certain class of objects (people, vehicles, etc.) or geometric properties of objects (flat, narrow, etc.); and (2) a location and/or movement that encodes, again more or less iconically, the location/movement of the designated entity (on, upward, etc.).

The distinction between purely lexical signs and classifiers can easily be appreciated by comparing Figures 9.4A and 9.4B. Both of these examples are drawn from BSL, and both of them are translated into English as "The pen is on the paper," but they encode this locative relationship in different ways. In Figure 9.4A, the relationship is conveyed in the last frame by means of the lexical sign ON, which is analogous to the corresponding English preposition (although, technically speaking, it is actually a verb). In Figure 9.4B, however, it is conveyed in the last frame by means of a classifier construction with the following characteristics. The signer uses his right hand

Iconic signs   Signs in which the form of the expression physically resembles, to some extent, the entity or event that it designates.

Classifiers   A special set of mostly iconic signs that represent a great deal of spatial/topographic information about objects and their locations/movements.

to refer to the pen with an extended index finger, a handshape that embraces all objects that are long and thin. At the same time, he uses his left hand to refer to the paper by keeping the fingers flat and close together, a handshape that embraces all objects construed as two-dimensional. Finally, he indicates that the pen is horizontally supported by the paper by placing the index finger of his right hand on the flat fingers of his left hand. Classifier constructions like this are used quite frequently, presumably because they mirror the spatial/topographic layout of scenes in a gradient manner that is very transparent.

Morphology

As described more fully in Chapter 13, morphology involves the internal grammatical structure of words. In spoken languages, three main types of morphology are distinguished. The first is compounding, in which two roots are joined together to form a complex stem with an idiosyncratic meaning (e.g., *sweet* + *heart* = *sweetheart*; *wheel* + *chair* = *wheelchair*). The second is derivation, in which a root or stem is modified, usually through affixation, to yield a complex word that often belongs to a different grammatical category (e.g., *quick* + *-ly* = *quickly*; *happy* + *-ness* = *happiness*). And the third is inflection, in which a root or stem is modified, usually through affixation, to create a complex word that

fits properly into the syntactic structure of the sentence by virtue of being marked for features like number and tense (e.g., *dog* + *-s* = *dogs*; *bark* + *-ed* = *barked*).

All three types of morphology are well attested in sign languages. Although these aspects of grammar are sometimes encoded sequentially, they are most often conveyed by simultaneously incorporating different symbolic elements into the visual–gestural flow of expression. Moreover, iconicity is frequently exploited to enhance clarity. Here we will restrict our attention to just two forms of inflection, both involving verbs.

Verb agreement, which is perhaps the prototypical example of morphology in sign languages, uses space to organize grammatical information in a systematic, motivated manner (Mathur & Rathmann, 2010). At the most basic level, correspondences are established between regions in space and referents in discourse, such that the location of the signer's body is equated with "first person," the location of the addressee's body is equated with "second person," and other locations in front of the signer's torso are equated with "third person." These correspondences provide a spatial foundation for encoding the grammatical relations of subject and object, since the initial location of a verb denotes the subject and the final location denotes the object, while the handshape that is either maintained or changed during the movement denotes the type of event. Figure 9.5 illustrates these points by focusing on agreement for the ISL verb SHOW. The left panel depicts the expression I-SHOW-YOU, which has a trajectory from the signer toward the addressee; the center panel depicts the expression YOU-SHOW-ME, which has a trajectory from the addressee toward the signer; and the right panel depicts the expression HE/SHE-SHOWS-YOU, which has a trajectory from a specific location in front of the signer's torso toward the addressee. Note that although the direction of the movement changes across the three expressions, the two-handed configuration of the sign stays the same. This is because that configuration constitutes the root of the verb SHOW.

A

PAPER   PEN   ON

B

PAPER   PEN   LONG THIN OBJECT (pen) ON FLAT OBJECT (paper)

Figure 9.4 Comparison of (A) prepositional and (B) classifier constructions for "the pen is on the paper" in British Sign Language (BSL). (From Atkinson et al., 2005, p. 243.)

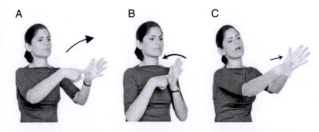

A   B   C

Figure 9.5 Inflection for verb agreement in sign language. Different inflections of the verb SHOW in Israeli Sign Language (ISL) are shown. (A) I-SHOW-YOU. (B) YOU-SHOW-ME. (C) HE/SHE-SHOWS-YOU. (From Sandler, 2009, p. 246.)

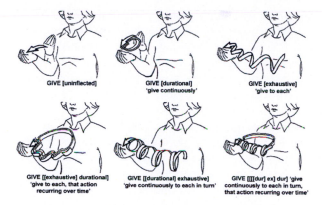

Figure 9.6   Inflection for verb aspect in sign language. Different inflections of the sign GIVE in American Sign Language (ASL) are shown. Increasingly complex inflections are conveyed by increasingly complex movements. (From Perniss et al., 2010, p. 5; originally from Poizner et al., 1987.)

Another good example of sign language morphology involves inflection for various qualitative and temporal aspects of events. The degree of complexity that can be achieved by this system is captured in Figure 9.6, which shows how the ASL verb GIVE, depicted in its bare form in the upper left panel, can be modified by different inflectional morphemes to convey different manifestations of giving. Specifically, adding the "durational" morpheme means "give continuously," adding the "exhaustive" morpheme means "give to each," and adding layered combinations of both morphemes gives rise to more intricate interpretations like "give continuously to each in turn." Although the English translations of these multifaceted concepts can be rather cumbersome, the inflected ASL signs are much clearer, due to their high degree of iconicity.

Syntax

As discussed at length in Chapter 14, syntax consists of the rules, principles, and patterns that determine how words can be strung together in certain ways so that their separate meanings can be integrated into composite messages. Spoken languages draw upon several syntactic devices to fulfill this function, including word order, case marking, and closed-class items. Analogues of these devices have been found in sign languages, so it is safe to say that these languages are just as capable as spoken languages of generating a potentially infinite number of distinct, complex expressions (e.g., Neidle et al., 2000; Sandler & Lillo-Martin, 2006; de Quadros & Lillo-Martin, 2010; Pfau et al., 2012).

We will not examine sign language syntax in any depth, but will instead concentrate on a single example

that reveals how efficiently space is exploited. In particular, the ASL sentence portrayed in Figure 9.7 shows how the morphological mechanisms for verb agreement that we considered above can be applied in the realm of syntax to indicate the roles of all the participants associated with two consecutive verbs. The English translation of the sentence at issue is *Mother forced him to give her the box,* and it is noteworthy that *her* is not co-referential with *Mother* but instead designates a different participant. As shown in the leftmost panel of the figure, the first element of the ASL sentence is the noun MOTHER/INDEX$_i$, which is produced near the signer's head in what is, from the addressee's perspective, the left side of space. Here INDEX$_i$ means that this location stands for this participant, which now has the role of subject. The second element is the verb $_i$FORCE$_j$, which is expressed as a unique change of handshape together with a lateral movement from the left to the right side of space, again from the addressee's perspective. Importantly, this verb is marked for agreement such that the subject, notated "i," is the participant at the initial location, namely MOTHER, and the object, notated "j," is the participant at the final location, interpreted simply as HIM. The third element is the verb $_j$GIVE$_k$, which is expressed as a unique change of handshape (see also Figure 9.6) together with a right-to-left movement that terminates farther forward from the signer than the original left-sided location, i.e., the one linked with MOTHER. This verb is also marked for agreement, but now the indexations are different such that the subject, notated "j," is the participant linked with the right side of space, namely HIM, and the object is a new participant, notated "k," that is interpreted simply as HER. The last element is the noun BOX, which is expressed as a distinctive two-handed sign in front of the signer's torso. It obviously refers to the entity that was given. Overall, the main point of this example is that syntax is highly spatialized in sign languages, with the visual–gestural medium serving as a kind of scaffolding for the specification of complex grammatical relationships between separate signs.

Nonmanual Signs

Finally, it is important to realize that the articulatory action in sign languages is not restricted to the arms and hands, but encompasses a number of other body parts (Pfau & Quer, 2010). The tilt of the torso and/or head can convey discourse information about topic-comment relationships, and facial expressions can convey a variety of lexical and grammatical signals. For instance, facial expressions involving the lips, tongue, and cheeks often constitute nonmanual signs for adjectives and adverbs, as

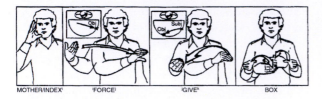

MOTHER/INDEX'   'FORCE'   'GIVE'   BOX

Figure 9.7   Syntactic structure in sign language. A complete sentence in American Sign Language (ASL) is shown, "Mother forced him to give her the box." The grammatical relations of subject and object are conveyed by the spatial relations between signs. Different stages of the sentence are seen from both above and in front of the signer. (From Hickok et al., 1998a, p. 131.)

shown in Figure 9.8A–C, and facial expressions involving the eyebrows, eyelids, and cheeks often constitute nonmanual syntactic cues, as shown in Figure 9.8D-F. All of these nonmanual signs are fully conventionalized elements of the linguistic system and are formally distinguished from emotional facial expressions. Moreover, while some of them are similar across a wide range of sign languages (especially those for yes/no and WH questions), most of them are unique to particular sign languages.

Summary

Even though sign languages are transmitted in the visual–gestural modality rather than the auditory–vocal modality, they have just as much communicative potential as spoken languages. This is because, like spoken languages, they are sophisticated coding systems with multiple levels of structure. At the phonological level,

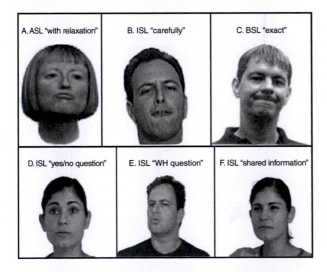

A. ASL "with relaxation"   B. ISL "carefully"   C. BSL "exact"

D. ISL "yes/no question"   E. ISL "WH question"   F. ISL "shared information"

Figure 9.8   Nonmanual expressions in sign language. (A–C) Examples of adjectives and adverbs in American Sign Language (ASL), Israeli Sign Language (ISL), and British Sign Language (BSL). (D–F) Examples of syntactic markers in ISL. (From Sandler, 2005, p. 334.)

individual signs are specified along the parameters of handshape, location, and movement. At the morphological level, complex signs can be created out of simpler ones by applying rule-governed processes of compounding, derivation, and inflection. And at the syntactic level, discrete signs can be combined with each other, again in rule-governed ways, to convey an unlimited number of complete propositions. In addition, the expressive capacity of sign languages is greatly augmented by the availability of nonmanual signs that are articulated by the torso, head, lips, tongue, cheeks, eyebrows, and eyelids, usually in synchrony with manual signs. Finally, due to the intrinsically analogue nature of the visual–gestural medium, sign languages tend to exploit spatial iconicity at every level of organization, thereby maximizing the naturalness of form-meaning relationships.

Left-Hemisphere Dominance

Turning now to the neural substrates of sign language, it is useful to begin by noting that, as with spoken language, there is substantial evidence for left-hemisphere dominance. Moreover, the left-hemisphere mechanisms that underlie sign language are at least partially segregated from those that support non-linguistic visuospatial cognition and symbolic gesture.

Wada Testing

Some of the most compelling evidence for left lateralization comes from the Wada procedure. As indicated in Chapter 5, this technique involves temporarily shutting down an entire hemisphere by injecting sodium amobarbitol, a fast-acting sedative, into either the left or right carotid artery (Wada & Rasmussen, 1960). It is typically used to infer the lateralization of various cognitive functions, such as language and memory, in epileptic patients prior to the surgical removal of seizure-generating structures. And that is why, back in the mid-1980s, at a time when solid data about the cortical organization of sign language was still scarce, Damasio et al. (1986) administered the Wada procedure to a 27-year-old, right-handed, epileptic woman who had normal hearing but was fluent in both English and ASL and actually worked as an interpreter for deaf people. What the researchers found was that when this woman's left hemisphere was briefly incapacitated by the drug, she exhibited aphasia not only in English, but also in ASL. In fact, her error rate for naming objects was even higher in ASL than in English, and during the recovery period it took longer for her ASL skills than her English skills to become fully restored. For medical reasons, it was not possible to perform the procedure on her right hemisphere. But after her right anterior temporal lobe was resected, there were no noticeable effects on her language abilities in either English or ASL, as measured by detailed assessments conducted at both 3-month and 12-month intervals post-surgery. Taken together, these findings support the view that, like spoken language, sign language depends mainly on the left hemisphere (for similar Wada testing results see Wolff et al., 1994, and Corina et al., 1999).

Dissociations Between Sign Language and Visuospatial Cognition

Given that sign language is transmitted in a visuospatial medium, it is natural to ask whether sign language abilities rely on the same neural resources as visuospatial abilities. This question has been addressed by several lesion studies, and the data indicate that the two types of abilities can be impaired independently of each other, which suggests that their neural underpinnings are at least somewhat distinct.

In a major investigation, Hickok et al. (1996a) evaluated 23 right-handed deaf ASL signers who had unilateral lesions due to stroke ($n = 18$), haematoma ($n = 3$), aneurism rupture ($n = 1$), or tumor ($n = 1$).

Among these patients, 13 were left-hemisphere-damaged (LHD) and 10 were right-hemisphere-damaged (RHD). Using an ASL-adapted version of the Boston Diagnostic Aphasia Examination (BDAE; Goodglass & Kaplan, 1983), the researchers evaluated several aspects of the patients' sign language competence, including production, comprehension, and repetition. As shown in Figure 9.9, the LHD patients performed significantly worse than the RHD patients on all of the measures. Moreover, follow-up analyses revealed that these behavioral differences did not correlate with demographic differences in age at the onset of deafness, age of first exposure to ASL, or age at the time of testing.

To determine whether sign language deficits might simply be a by-product of more general visuospatial deficits, the researchers also gave the same 23 patients a battery of standardized tests of gross visuospatial functions. What emerged was a robust double dissociation. The LHD patients tended to have impaired sign language but normal visuospatial cognition, whereas the RHD patients tended to have normal sign language but impaired visuospatial cognition. Some of these findings are illustrated in Figure 9.10, which presents examples of the performances of eight patients. The four LHD patients in the left column were quite deficient at processing visuospatial

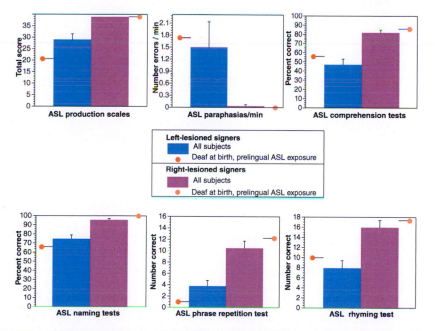

Figure 9.9 Performances of left-hemisphere-damaged (LHD, $n = 13$) and right-hemisphere-damaged (RHD, $n = 10$) deaf signers on six measures of ASL ability. Graphs provide means and standard error bars. Circles indicate the level of performance of the subset of patients who were prelingually deaf native signers (LHD, $n = 4$; RHD, $n = 3$). Production, comprehension, naming, and repetition tests are ASL-adapted versions of tests in the Boston Diagnostic Aphasia Examination (BDAE). Paraphasias/min indicate the number of sign errors per minute in a sign sample elicited according to a BDAE protocol. The rhyming test requires subjects to choose from an array of four pictured objects the two whose signs are most similiar in terms of sign-phonological features. (From Hickok & Bellugi, 2001, p. 36; data originally from Hickok et al., 1996a.)

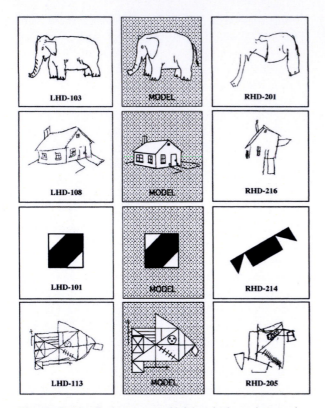

Figure 9.10 Performances of left-hemisphere-damaged (LHD) and right-hemisphere-damaged (RHD) deaf signers on non-linguistic visuospatial tasks. The RHD patients, but not the LHD patients, displayed many impairments. *Top two rows:* figure copy tests. *Third row:* block design from model test. *Bottom row:* Rey Osterrieth figure copy test. (From Hickok & Bellugi, 2001, p. 38; data originally from Hickok et al., 1996a.)

information for the purpose of communicating in sign language, but they were still fairly proficient at processing such information for the purpose of copying drawings and block designs. Conversely, the four RHD patients in the right column displayed precisely the opposite pattern of impaired and preserved abilities.

It is apparent from Figure 9.10 that the RHD patients' visuospatial impairments affected mainly their capacity to perceive and reproduce the holistic shapes of the "models" portrayed in the central column. This is consistent with a sizeable literature indicating that the right hemisphere is dominant for processing the global, large-scale configurations of stimuli. It is noteworthy, however, that the left hemisphere is known to play a greater role than the right in processing the local, small-scale visuospatial features of stimuli. This is important because it raises a question as to whether the types of sign language disturbances that follow from left-hemisphere lesions might be related to problems in processing local rather than global visuospatial information.

To explore this issue, Hickok et al. (1998c) administered numerous subtests of the ASL-adapted BDAE to 12 LHD signers and 8 RHD signers, and also asked them to "copy exactly" a set of complex, hierarchically organized figures with both global and local features. In keeping with the original experiment by Hickok et al. (1996a), the LHD patients, but not the RHD patients, were significantly impaired on the language measures. And in keeping with the earlier work on hemispheric asymmetries in visuospatial cognition, the LHD patients were less sensitive to local than global properties of the hierarchical images, whereas the RHD patients manifested the opposite performance profile. The most theoretically relevant result, however, was that the LHD patients' language scores did *not* correlate with their local visuospatial processing scores. This dissociation supports the view that the primary factor driving the cortical organization of sign language in the left hemisphere is not the superficial nature of the visuospatial signals that are transmitted, but rather the deeper nature of the phonological, morphological, syntactic, and semantic representations that those signals convey (see also Hickok et al., 1996b).

Dissociations Between Sign Language and Symbolic Gesture

Another issue that has been receiving increasing attention involves the relationship between sign language and symbolic gesture, particularly pantomime. As described above, many signs are iconic, so it is reasonable to ask whether the brain structures that underlie the production of such signs are shared with or segregated from those that underlie the production of perceptually and motorically similar pantomimes. This question has been addressed from both neuropsychological and functional neuroimaging perspectives, and the results suggest that the two types of manual expression have at least partly separate neural substrates.

In a detailed case study, Marshall et al. (2004) reported a 56-year-old deaf BSL signer, "Charles," who suffered a left temporoparietal stroke that severely disrupted his ability to produce signs, including iconic ones, but left intact his ability to produce analogous pantomimes (for a similar patient see Corina et al., 1992). This dissociation was observed across several tasks involving objects for which Charles could still comprehend the correct signs. For example, even though he was still familiar with the iconic sign TOOTHBRUSH, which looks a lot like moving a toothbrush over one's teeth, he failed to retrieve it when an examiner asked him to name a picture of a toothbrush. Nevertheless, when the examiner showed him the same picture in a subsequent testing session and asked him to gesture how the object is used, he produced an elaborate, and accurate, pantomime. First, he demonstrated how he would squeeze toothpaste from a tube onto the head of a toothbrush, then he pretended to rub the brush back and forth over his teeth (the component of the pantomime that is almost identical to the sign he couldn't access in the naming condition), and finally he showed how he would rinse his mouth with water. The fact that Charles's linguistic sign production was significantly worse than his non-linguistic gesture production, even when the output forms were superficially similar, is powerful evidence that the two routes for mapping meanings onto manual expressions are underpinned by different neural pathways.

Further evidence for this view comes from an interesting PET study by Emmorey et al. (2011a). In this experiment, 10 deaf native ASL signers and 14 hearing non-signers were shown pictures of objects. For both groups of subjects there were two conditions: (1) a pantomime condition in which the task was to "show me how you would use the pictured object" (for an example see Figure 9.11A); and (2) a baseline condition in which the task was to use either a "yes" gesture (thumb up) or a "no" gesture (palm down horizontal hand wave) to indicate whether the pictured object could be held in the hand. For just the deaf subjects, however, there was also a third condition: (3) a verb condition in which the task was to produce an ASL verb that was semantically associated with the pictured object. Half of the target verbs were so-called "handling verbs" that are highly iconic in pantomime-like

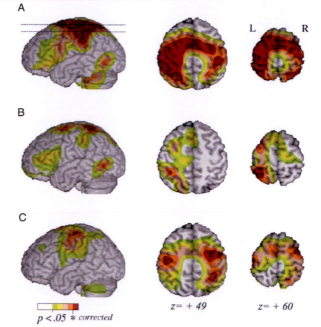

Figure 9.12 Results from Emmorey et al.'s (2011) PET study of pantomime production and sign production. (A) Contrast between pantomime and baseline conditions for deaf signers. (B) Contrast between pantomime and baseline conditions for hearing non-signers. (C) Contrast between the two groups for same task comparison. Note that for (A–C) the planes of the horizontal sections on the right are marked by the dotted lines on the left lateral brain image in (A). (From Emmorey et al., 2011a, p. 892.)

ways (for an example see Figure 9.11B), and the other half were so-called "general verbs" that are not iconic. Importantly, the pictured objects that were used to elicit handling verbs from the deaf subjects were also used to elicit pantomimes from the hearing subjects.

Figure 9.12 shows the results for the contrast between the pantomime condition and the baseline condition, broken down by group. For the deaf subjects, significant activation was found bilaterally, but with some leftward asymmetry, in superior frontoparietal regions. A similar activation profile was also observed in the hearing subjects, but it was not as strong or extensive as in the deaf subjects. According to the researchers, these group differences in the magnitude and distribution of activation may reflect the fact that, compared to the hearing subjects, the deaf subjects produced pantomimes that were longer, crisper, richer, and more often two-handed. For example, although both groups responded to a picture of a teapot by producing a pouring gesture with one hand, most of the deaf subjects also produced a gesture representing a teacup with the other hand.

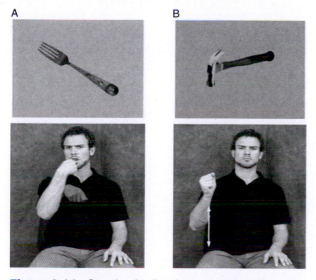

Figure 9.11 Sample stimuli and responses from Emmorey et al.'s (2011) PET study of (A) pantomime production (eating with a fork) and (B) sign production (TO-HAMMER). (From Emmorey, 2011a, p. 881.)

Figure 9.13 shows the results, relative to baseline, for just the items that were used to elicit handling verbs from the deaf subjects and analogous pantomimes from the hearing subjects. As expected, the manual expressions that the two groups generated were similar in form, but they derived from different neural sources. For the deaf subjects, the production of handling verbs was associated with activation in the left inferior/middle frontal cortex, including part of Broca's area. But for the hearing subjects, the production of overtly similar pantomimic gestures was associated with activation in superior frontoparietal regions, much like in the previous contrast. Although Figure 9.13 does not include data regarding the deaf subjects' production of general verbs, it is noteworthy that

the activation profile for those verbs was almost identical to the profile for handling verbs—a finding that replicates previous studies of verb production not only in sign language (e.g., Corina et al., 2003), but also in spoken language (e.g., Tranel et al., 2005). Overall, the results of Emmorey et al.'s (2011a) PET study support the idea that the neural substrates of linguistic sign production are distinct from those of non-linguistic gesture production, even when the physical forms of the expressions are virtually the same (see also Emmorey et al., 2004).

Summary

Several sources of data indicate that sign language depends predominantly on the left hemisphere of the brain, just like spoken language. Moreover, whereas the peripheral sensory and motor aspects of sign language are necessarily supported by modality-specific neural systems for the perception and execution of arm/hand actions, the central lexical and grammatical aspects of sign language seem to be supported by supramodal neural systems that are dedicated to those particular types of representations. Evidence for this view comes from studies showing that sign language dissociates from both visuospatial cognition and symbolic gesture. Thus, the leftward asymmetry of sign language is determined not so much by the purely physical properties of the signals that are used, but more by the fact that those signals are fundamentally linguistic in nature.

Functional–Anatomical Organization Within the Left Hemisphere

The studies that we have reviewed so far demonstrate that sign language relies on left-hemisphere structures that support lexical and grammatical representations independently of other types of information. Now let's take a closer look at some of the ways in which sign language is organized within the left hemisphere.

Different Sign Language Aphasias Associated with Anterior and Posterior Lesions

As discussed in Chapters 3 and 4, one of the most well-established findings in aphasiology is that, for individuals with normal hearing, anterior and posterior lesions tend to induce systematically different types of spoken language disorders. On the one hand, anterior lesions often cause production to become nonfluent (i.e., slow and effortful) and agrammatic (i.e., syntactically reduced with

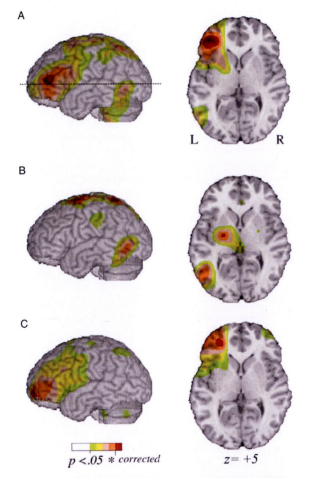

A

B

C

$p < .05$ * *corrected* $z = +5$

Figure 9.13 Results from Emmorey et al.'s (2011) PET study of pantomime production and sign production. (A) Contrast between handling verbs and baseline condition for deaf signers. (B) Same contrast but for hearing non-signers, who did not produce handling verbs but instead produced superficially similar pantomimes. (C) Contrast between the two groups for same task comparison. Note that for (A–C) the plane of the horizontal section on the right is marked by the dotted line on the left lateral brain image in (A). (From Emmorey et al., 2011a, p. 893.)

omission/substitution of closed-class items); however, such lesions usually spare most aspects of comprehension, especially in ordinary conversational settings. On the other hand, posterior lesions generally impair comprehension, sometimes severely, while leaving production quite fluent and grammatically well-formed but very vulnerable to phonemic paraphasias.

Do the same contrasting lesion–deficit patterns show up in brain-damaged users of sign language? Back in the 1980s, when research on the neural correlates of sign language initially began to take off, this was among the first questions to be addressed. And an indisputably positive answer was returned by Howard Poizner, Edward Klima, and Ursula Bellugi, who conducted a pioneering series of neuropsychological case studies at the Salk Institute and the University of California, San Diego (Poizner et al., 1987; for reviews of prior work, which was quite limited, see Poizner & Battison, 1980; Kimura, 1981; Poizner et al. 1987, pp. 37–41). Here we will focus on just two of the patients who they studied in depth, Gail D. and Karen L.

A

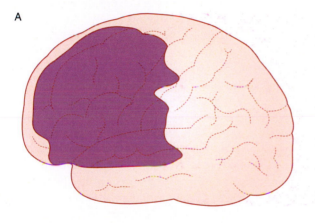

B

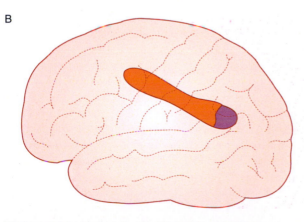

Figure 9.14 Lesion sites for (A) Gail D. and (B) Karen L., based on CT scans. (From Poizner et al., 1987, pp. 63 & 81.)

At the time of the investigations, Gail D. was a 38-year-old congenitally deaf woman. Although both of her parents had normal hearing, she had two older sibling who were also congenitally deaf. She learned ASL at a very young age, originally at home and later in school. After finishing high school, she married a deaf classmate, gained employment as a postal worker and a photograph retoucher, and had three children, all of whom were deaf. In addition, she became active in the local association for the deaf and had many deaf friends. At the age of 37, however, she suddenly suffered a terrible stroke. A CT scan revealed that the lesion affected Broca's area and much of the surrounding frontal lobe as well as the anterior half of the superior temporal gyrus (Figure 9.14A). This left Gail D. with a form of sign language aphasia that closely resembled the type of spoken language aphasia that usually follows from left anterior brain damage: nonfluent agrammatic production in the context of largely intact comprehension.

Gail D.'s profoundly impaired production is exemplified by her attempt to describe an episode from her childhood (Poizner et al., 1987, p. 120):

Examiner:	What else happened?
Gail D.:	CAR . . . DRIVE . . . BROTHER . . . DRIVE . . . I . . . S-T-A-D [fingerspelled]. [Attempts to gesture "stand up."]
Examiner:	You stood up?
Gail D.:	YES . . . I . . . DRIVE . . . [Attempts to gesture "wave goodbye."]
Examiner:	Wave goodbye?
Gail D.:	YES . . . BROTHER . . . DRIVE . . . DUNNO . . . [Attempts to gesture "wave goodbye."]
Examiner:	Your brother was driving?
Gail D.:	YES . . . BACK . . . DRIVE . . . BROTHER . . . MAN . . . MAMA . . . STAY . . . BROTHER . . . DRIVE.
Examiner:	Were you in the car?
Gail D.:	YES.
Examiner:	Or outside?
Gail D.:	NO.
Examiner:	In the car.
Gail D.:	YES.
Examiner:	You were standing up with your mother?
Gail D.:	NO . . . BROTHER . . . DRIVE . . . [Points in back.] . . . DEAF BROTHER . . . I . . .
Examiner:	Your brother didn't know you were in the car?

Gail D.:   YES.
Examiner: Your brother was driving and saw you in the back seat?
Gail D.:   YES, YES. [Laughs.]
Examiner: Oh, I see.

Although her pre-stroke signing had been rich and effortless, her post-stroke signing was clearly impoverished and laborious. In the narrative above, her output was extremely sparse, consisting almost entirely of isolated, unadorned open-class items that were slowly strung together without any hierarchical organization or any of the spatialized morphological and syntactic devices of ASL. This paucity of content and structure was not, however, due to a reluctance to communicate, since Gail D. tried to supplement her starkly abbreviated signing by adding fingerspelled words and non-linguistic gestures. Moreover, she constantly monitored the examiner's responses and had no difficulty indicating whether they were correct or not—a bit of behavior that, together with much experimental evidence, demonstrates that Gail D.'s comprehension was, for the most part, preserved.

One might suspect that Gail D.'s production deficit was basically motoric in nature, but several sources of data point to a more central linguistic impairment. For one thing, although she usually had significant trouble signing fluently, there were occasions when she could make the appropriate signs smoothly and rapidly. What's even more compelling, however, is that she could sometimes perform certain movements when they functioned as sublexical components of signs, but not when they functioned as inflectional components of phrases. For example, a path movement toward the signer's own body is part of the sign ACCEPT, and Gail D. was able to execute that movement properly when producing the sign. As noted earlier, however, the very same movement also serves as an inflectional marker for "first person" (see Figure 9.5), and Gail D. was never observed using it for that purpose. Thus, her large anterior lesion appears to have brought about a fundamentally linguistic disorder that was remarkably similar to agrammatic Broca's aphasia, since it was characterized by morphologically and syntactically minimal production, but with few sublexical phonological errors and relatively intact comprehension.

Another patient who Poizner et al. (1987) studied carefully was Karen L. When she was only six months old, she became deaf as the result of scarlet fever. She learned ASL in school and later married a deaf man and worked at various jobs ranging from manufacturing to house-cleaning to child care. She also attended a church with a deaf congregation and had several deaf friends. At the age of 67, however, she was the victim of a stroke

that, according to a CT scan, caused a mostly subcortical slit-like lesion that extended through the white matter beneath the precentral and postcentral cortices back to the supramarginal and angular gyri (Figure 9.14B). Interestingly, this led to a profile of impaired and preserved sign language abilities that was, in some respects, the opposite of Gail D.'s: very poor comprehension, and production that was fluent and grammatical but riddled with sublexical phonological errors—the equivalent of phonemic paraphasias in spoken language.

Karen L.'s comprehension deficit was manifested not only in casual conversational situations, but also in more formal testing sessions. Although she had only mild difficulty understanding individual signs, she was often unable to decipher more complex expressions like commands and questions (e.g., "Will a cork sink in water?"). With regard to production, Karen L. made full and accurate use of the grammatical apparatus of ASL, in striking contrast to Gail D. However, she sometimes groped for signs, and, as just noted, she committed abundant sublexical phonological errors, some examples of which are shown in Figure 9.15. These errors affected all of the phonological parameters of ASL—handshape, location, and movement—but the most severely disrupted dimension was handshape. For instance, when signing CAREFUL, which has a "K" handshape, Karen L. used a "W" handshape instead. The specifications for location and movement were both correct, though. Due largely to contextual constraints, the resulting form was still recognizable as the intended sign CAREFUL, but as Poizner et al. (1987, p. 83) point out, it was "like saying *tareful* instead of *careful* in English." Such mistakes qualified as genuine aphasic errors rather than mere motoric glitches, because they tended to occur in the midst of a free-flowing stream of otherwise normal—which is to say, quite dexterous and intricate—signing.

The fact that Karen L.'s lesion affected the supramarginal gyrus is noteworthy for several reasons. Like her, hearing individuals who have damage to that region (and/or to the underlying white matter) are prone to producing phonemic paraphasias. In fact, this lesion–deficit pattern is frequently found in conduction aphasia (see Chapter 3). In the next subsection, however, we will see that the supramarginal gyrus plays an even greater role in the manual production of signs than in the oral production of words. Another intriguing aspect of Karen L.'s neuropsychological profile has to do with her comprehension impairment. Hearing individuals with comparable deficits usually have damage to the temporal lobe rather than the parietal lobe. And yet we will see below that, in keeping with Karen L.'s pattern, functional neuroimaging studies support a special role for the supramarginal gyrus in the receptive processing of sign language.

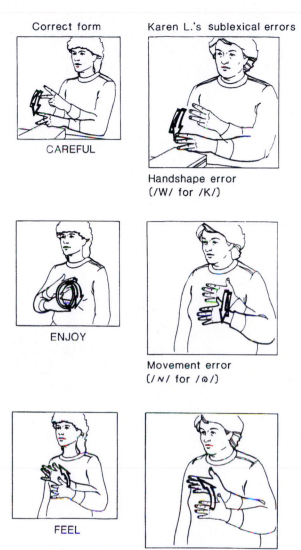

Figure 9.15 Sublexical errors typical of Karen L.'s signing. Note selection errors within major formational parameters of ASL. These are the equivalent of phonemic paraphasias in spoken language. (From Poizner et al., 1987, p. 84.)

The Production of Signs

In recent years, there has been increasing evidence that in the domain of language production some left-hemisphere areas are modality-neutral, since they contribute to the generation of both manual signs and spoken words, whereas others are modality-specific, since they are implicated in just one or the other channel of expression (Pettito et al., 2000; Braun et al., 2001; Corina et al., 2003; Horwitz et al., 2003; Emmorey et al., 2003, 2007; Kassubek et al., 2004; San José-Robertson et al., 2004). This was demonstrated in a particularly impressive way by

Emmorey et al. (2007), who re-analyzed previously collected PET data from 29 deaf ASL signers and 64 hearing English speakers. For all of the subjects, the main experimental task was to overtly name objects from various semantic categories (animals, tools, etc.), and the baseline task was to overtly indicate with signed or spoken "yes"/"no" responses whether unfamiliar faces were presented in an upright or inverted orientation. The researchers first subtracted the baseline task from the experimental task for each group of subjects in order to create two activation maps that uniquely reflected object naming in each language, and then they compared those maps in order to identify conjunctions as well as disjunctions.

Figure 9.16A shows three brain regions in which significant overlapping activation was found during object naming, relative to facial orientation judgment, in both ASL and English. One region extended from the mesial occipital cortex (visible in the rightmost axial image) to the lateral occipitoparietal cortex (visible in the left lateral image). According to Emmorey et al. (2007), this activation was probably distinct from purely linguistic processes, being attributable instead to the greater demands on visual attention in the experimental task than the baseline task. Another region was BA45, the anterior part of Broca's area. We observed in Chapter 6 that this region may facilitate lexical selection by carrying out certain cognitive control functions, such as choosing one among many possible concepts, and corresponding lemmas, for an object (see Figure 6.8 and the accompanying text). The key point here, however, is that the region appears

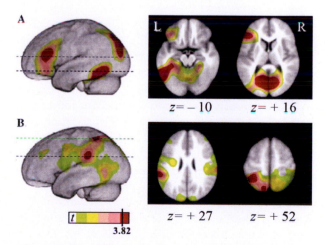

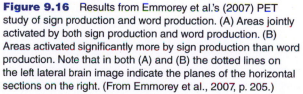

Figure 9.16 Results from Emmorey et al.'s (2007) PET study of sign production and word production. (A) Areas jointly activated by both sign production and word production. (B) Areas activated significantly more by sign production than word production. Note that in both (A) and (B) the dotted lines on the left lateral brain image indicate the planes of the horizontal sections on the right. (From Emmorey et al., 2007, p. 205.)

to perform this operation regardless of the modality of linguistic output. (Broca's area may also mediate syllabification during spoken language production; however, it is unlikely to serve this function during sign language production because most signs are monosyllabic.) Finally, the third region was in the middle/inferior temporal cortex. As discussed in Chapter 6, this territory has been associated with the lemma stage of lexical retrieval—i.e., the stage that supposedly intervenes between semantic access and phonological encoding (see Figures 6.9–6.10 and the accompanying text). What the PET data suggest is that this stage may have similar neural underpinnings for oral word production and manual sign production.

Figure 9.16B shows two brain regions that were significantly engaged during object naming, relative to facial orientation judgment, in ASL but not in English. One of these regions was in the superior parietal cortex, and Emmorey et al. (2007) suggest that its activation may reflect proprioceptive feedback from the relevant arm/hand articulators. After all, signers rarely watch their own signing behavior, so they may rely on feeling rather than seeing the continually changing positions and configurations of their body parts. The other region was the supramarginal gyrus. It has been linked with the planning of arm/hand actions, and, as indicated above, it was damaged in Karen L., who committed abundant sublexical phonological errors involving handshape, location, and movement. In this connection, it is also noteworthy that Corina et al. (1999) conducted a direct intracranial stimulation study with a deaf ASL signer and found that stimulating the supramarginal gyrus induced sublexical phonological errors similar to those displayed by Karen L. For example, as shown in Figure 9.17, when the patient attempted to produce the sign SCISSORS, which is iconic insofar as the index and middle fingers mimic the movement of scissor blades, he began with the correct "V" handshape but made no movement, then he bent his fingers, switched abruptly to a "Y" handshape, executed a wrist-twisting movement, switched back to the appropriate "V" handshape, and finally bent his fingers again rather than "scissoring" them as required. Taken together, all of these findings—i.e., the PET data, neuropsychological data, and direct stimulation data—suggest that the supramarginal gyrus may help to integrate the different phonological components of ASL signs. And because these components consist of the spatial and temporal features of arm/hand actions, they are unique to the visual–gestural modality of sign language.

The Perception of Signs

When non-signers observe signing, they see a rapidly shifting series of uninterpretable arm and hand movements. But when signers observe such behavior, they see

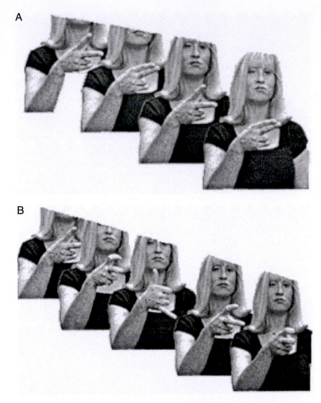

Figure 9.17 Transient disruption of sign language phonology by direct electrical stimulation of the left supramarginal gyrus. (A) Correct articulation of the ASL sign SCISSORS. (B) Incorrect articulation of that sign caused by stimulation. (From Corina et al., 1999, p. 575.)

a coherent stream of meaningful linguistic expressions. During the past few decades, cognitive neuroscientists have begun to identify the brain regions that underlie the automatic recognition of signs (e.g., Neville et al., 1998; Nishimura et al., 1999; Petitto et al., 2000; MacSweeney et al., 2002a, 2004; Capek et al., 2008, 2010; Emmorey et al., 2011b). Many of these regions overlap substantially with those that have been implicated in auditory speech perception (see Chapter 5); others, however, appear to be more involved in perceiving signs than words. Some of the most striking anatomical differences that have emerged between the two modalities of receptive language processing have to do with hemispheric asymmetries. While it is quite clear that the left hemisphere is essential for understanding both sign language and spoken language, a few fMRI studies suggest that the right hemisphere is engaged more extensively during the comprehension of sign language than spoken language (Neville et al., 1998; Bavelier et al., 1998a; Newman et al., 2002; Capek et al., 2004). We will not tackle this intriguing topic until the next section, however, since our main focus here is on how the left hemisphere contributes to the perception of signs.

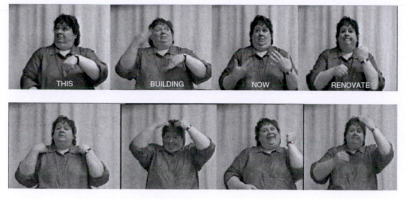

THIS   BUILDING   NOW   RENOVATE

Figure 9.18 Examples of stimuli used in MacSweeney et al.'s (2004) fMRI study of sign language comprehension. (Top row) Still images from a sentence in British Sign Language (BSL) meaning "This building is being renovated." (Bottom row) Still images from a sequence of TicTac gestures. (From MacSweeney et al., 2004, p. 1608.)

One of the cleverest and most revealing investigations of the neural substrates of sign perception was carried out by MacSweeney et al. (2004). The main aim of their fMRI study was to answer the following question: "What is the cortical circuitry recruited for the perception of a signed language when compared with a non-linguistic visual input similar in terms of its perceptual and articulatory characteristics?" (MacSweeney et al., 2004, pp. 1605–1606). To address this issue, they compared the perception of simple sentences in BSL with the perception of gesture sequences in TicTac, the manual signaling code that, until the turn of the 21st century, was commonly used by bookmakers at racecourses to communicate the betting odds of horses. TicTac is like sign language insofar as the meaningful units consist of movements and configurations of the arms and hands in relation to the torso and head—e.g., the gesture for "9-to-4 odds" involves both hands touching the top of the head. TicTac differs from sign language, however, because it lacks genuine phonological, morphological, and syntactic structure.

Three groups of subjects participated in the experiment: nine congenitally deaf native signers of BSL; nine hearing native signers of BSL; and eight hearing non-signers. In one condition, the subjects were shown blocks of five BSL sentences, and for each block their task was to indicate with a button-press which sentence did not make sense (see the top row of Figure 9.18). For this condition, the hearing non-signers were instructed to guess which sentence was anomalous. In another condition, the subjects were shown blocks of five TicTac "sentences," and for each block they were told that even though they didn't understand the code, they should guess which "sentence" did not make sense and indicate their choice with a button-press (see the bottom row of Figure 9.18). Unbeknownst to them, all of the "sentences" were equally meaningless, since only individual TicTac gestures have content. Finally, the last condition was a baseline in which the subjects watched the signer at rest, paid attention to five 1,000-ms occasions

when a small square appeared on her chin, and indicated with a button-press when that square changed from black to gray.

The left-hemisphere activation patterns for the deaf and hearing signers are presented separately in Figure 9.19, and the imaging results for the hearing non-signers are described further below. Both groups of native signers recruited numerous anterior and posterior cortical regions during both the BSL condition

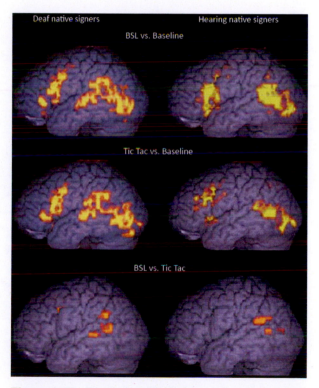

Deaf native signers   Hearing native signers

BSL vs. Baseline

Tic Tac vs. Baseline

BSL vs. Tic Tac

Figure 9.19 Results from MacSweeney et al.'s (2004) fMRI study of sign language comprehension. Each of the three rows shows a different labeled contrast between conditions for deaf native signers (left column) and hearing native signers (right column). (Adapted from MacSweeney et al., 2004, pp. 1611 & 1613.)

and the TicTac condition, relative to the baseline condition. For both groups, however, the BSL condition evoked greater activity than the TicTac condition in one particular region: the posterior superior temporal gyrus/sulcus, which is part of Wernicke's area. The fact that this region responded significantly more to familiar linguistic signs than to unfamiliar nonlinguistic gestures is extremely interesting because the very same area is well-established as playing a crucial role in auditory speech perception (see Chapter 5). Indeed, these convergent results invite the inference that the relevant region is innately predisposed to process phonological information irrespective of the sensory modality through which it is perceived (for additional data see Petitto et al., 2000; MacSweeney et al., 2002a; Emmorey et al., 2011b).

But even though the deaf and hearing signers had very similar activation profiles, some nontrivial differences were found. The most important differences can be seen in the two images at the bottom of Figure 9.19,

which depict for each group the BSL condition versus the TicTac condition. First of all, the deaf signers had more extensive activation than the hearing signers in the region just mentioned—i.e., the posterior superior temporal gyrus/sulcus. In addition, the deaf signers, but not the hearing signers, recruited the supramarginal gyrus—an area that has already turned up several times in our survey of the neural correlates of sign language. Finally, the deaf signers, but not the hearing signers, also engaged a frontal region immediately superior to BA44, which is the posterior part of Broca's area. Since the deaf and hearing signers were all native users of BSL with comparable skill levels, it seems likely that these group differences in activation profiles reflect some of the alternative ways in which deaf and hearing brains become organized for sign language. Most importantly, the discovery that several superior temporal areas traditionally considered to be "auditory" were activated more in the deaf than the hearing signers supports the notion that, in the absence of auditory input, these

---

Box 9.1   The Plasticity of Left-Hemisphere "Auditory" Areas in Congenitally Deaf Brains Reflects Sign Language Rather than Sensory Deprivation

There is now abundant evidence that when congenitally deaf individuals acquire a sign language, superior temporal regions that would normally process linguistic information from auditory input become reconfigured to process it from visual input. A long-standing challenge, however, has been to distinguish between those aspects of cross-modal plasticity that are due specifically to sign language and those that are due more generally to sensory deprivation.

Recently, an important breakthrough was made by Cardin et al. (2013), who conducted an fMRI study with three different groups of seven subjects: (1) "Deaf Signers" (DS) = congenitally deaf individuals who were native users of BSL but never learned to speak or speechread English; (2) "Deaf Oral"

(DO) = congenitally deaf individuals who did not know any sign language but had learned to both speak and speechread English; and (3) "Hearing Oral" (HO) = hearing individuals who did not know any sign language but were native users of English. For all of these subjects, the experimental condition involved viewing a series of BSL signs and pressing a button whenever a sign had the same handshape or location as a cue presented at the beginning of the block, and the baseline condition involved viewing the signer at rest. When the researchers analyzed the imaging data, they first subtracted the baseline condition from the experimental condition for each group, and then they performed the following comparisons between groups. To identify the cross-modal plasticity that was influenced by sign language, they conjoined

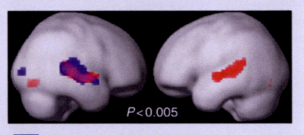

$P < 0.005$

■ Effect of auditory deprivation
■ Overlap
■ Effect of sign language

Figure 9B1.1   Results from Cardin et al.'s (2013) fMRI study of sign language comprehension. (From Cardin et al., 2013, p. 2.)

the results of the [DS > DO] and [DS > HO] contrasts and found activation in the superior temporal gyrus/sulcus of both hemispheres (Figure 9B1.1). And to identify the cross-modal plasticity that was influenced by auditory deprivation, they conjoined the results of the [DS > HO] and [DO > HO] contrasts and found activation in the superior temporal gyrus/sulcus of just the right hemisphere (Figure 9B1.1). Interestingly, this cluster of voxels exceeded and mostly subsumed the one associated with sign language (Figure 9B1.1).

What this study implies is that for congenitally deaf individuals who have acquired a sign language, reorganizational processes have led the *left* superior temporal cortex to be sensitive almost exclusively to signed stimuli and the *right* superior temporal cortex to be sensitive to both signed stimuli and other kinds of visual stimuli. Thus, both regions have adapted to a different modality of input, but the one in the left hemisphere has not only retained but sharpened its specialization for linguistic content, whereas the one in the right hemisphere has become relatively neutral with respect to representational content.

areas are capable of substantial functional plasticity (see also Box 9.1 and many of the references cited above).

Lastly, what about the imaging results for the hearing non-signers? Compared to the baseline condition, both BSL and TicTac engaged large swaths of the left hemisphere, much like in the signers. But the two experimental conditions did not differentially activate any of the classic language areas, which is not at all surprising, since the subjects could not decipher either type of stimuli.

Summary

Within the left hemisphere, the functional–anatomical organization of sign language is, for the most part, similar to that of spoken language. From the perspective of neuropsychology, detailed case studies indicate that, as with spoken language, anterior lesions often give rise to agrammatic production in the context of largely preserved comprehension, whereas posterior lesions often give rise to poor comprehension in the context of production that is fluent and syntactically well-formed but punctuated by sublexical phonological errors. And from the perspective of functional neuroimaging, PET and fMRI studies indicate that, as with spoken language, the normal production of signs engages Broca's area together with the middle/inferior temporal cortex, whereas the normal perception of signs recruits the posterior superior temporal gyrus/sulcus, which is part of Wernicke's area.

Despite these striking parallels between the left-lateralized neural configurations of the two types of languages, some interesting differences have also been detected. For one thing, unlike spoken word production, manual sign production activates the superior parietal cortex, presumably as a reflection of proprioceptive feedback from the arms and hands. In addition, sign language seems to depend on the supramarginal gyrus more than spoken language, and it is possible that this inferior parietal region plays a key role in integrating the different phonological components of signs—i.e., their specifications for handshape, location, and movement—not only during production, but also during comprehension.

Right-Hemisphere Contributions

In previous chapters we have seen that although spoken language depends primarily on the left hemisphere, it also enlists the right hemisphere for some functions—e.g., for certain aspects of speech perception (see Chapter 5) and for certain aspects of prosodic processing (see Chapter 7). With regard to sign language, recent research similarly suggests that although the left hemisphere is dominant, the right hemisphere also participates is some aspects of processing. In the case of sign language, however, the precise nature of the right-hemisphere contributions is only beginning to emerge. The following discussion focuses on two domains of sign language processing where this issue has been especially prominent: sentence comprehension in general, and classifier constructions in particular.

Activation During Sentence Comprehension: A Mysterious and Controversial Phenomenon

The possibility of significant right-hemisphere involvement in sign language first came to the attention of the cognitive neuroscience community when Neville et al. (1998) used fMRI to identify and compare the cortical bases of sentence comprehension in two groups of subjects: twelve congenitally deaf signers whose native language was ASL, and eight hearing non-signers whose native language was English. (The study also included nine hearing subjects who were native users of both ASL and English, but we will not discuss that group.) For the deaf subjects, the experimental task was to first observe a series of ASL sentences and then answer a series of yes/no questions about them, and the baseline task was to first observe a series of nonsense sentences composed of ASL-like gestures and then answer a series of yes/no questions about them. Similar tasks were administered to the hearing subjects, but the materials involved written stimuli. As predicted, for both groups the subtraction of the baseline condition from the experimental condition revealed activation in classic left-hemisphere language areas. Unexpectedly, however, the same analysis also indicated that whereas the hearing subjects only engaged a small part of the right hemisphere, the deaf subjects engaged a much greater proportion of the right hemisphere, including the entire extent of the superior temporal sulcus, the angular gyrus, the homologue of Broca's area, and some adjacent frontal regions (see Figure 9.20).

What do these remarkable findings imply about the neural organization of sign language? Neville et al. (1998) suggested that the greater right-hemisphere involvement in understanding signed than written sentences may reflect the unique visuospatial processing

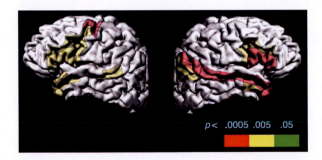

Figure 9.20   Results from Neville et al.'s (1998) fMRI study of sentence comprehension in ASL. When ASL sentences were contrasted against nonsense sentences comprising strings of ASL-like gestures, activations were found, at different levels of significance (color bar), not only in classic left-hemisphere language areas, but also in a wide range of right-hemisphere areas. Activations are shown in specific regions of interest that were predetermined for purposes of data analysis. Not shown are the results of a similar contrast involving written stimuli that did not reveal nearly as much right-hemisphere involvement. (From Capek et al., 2004, p. 114.)

requirements of ASL grammar (see also Bavelier et al., 1998a, 1998b; Paulesu & Mehler, 1998; Newman et al., 2002). But this interpretation has been challenged for several reasons.

One concern has to do with the neuropsychological data reviewed earlier. In particular, if the right hemisphere were really essential for sign language comprehension, damage to it would presumably give rise to comprehension deficits more often than is usually found (see again Figure 9.9; Hickok et al., 1996a, 1996b, 1998a, 1998b, 2002; Atkinson et al., 2005). In addition, the account favored by Neville et al. (1998) seems to be at odds with the discovery of significant double dissociations between sign language abilities and visuospatial cognitive abilities (see again Figure 9.10; Hickok et al., 1996a, 1996b, 1998c).

Another concern has to do with a confound in the design of Neville et al.'s (1998) study. The tasks that the two groups of subjects performed differed not only in the form of linguistic input, but also in the presence/absence of a dynamic visual display of a person communicating. Hence it is conceivable that the greater right-hemisphere recruitment during the sign language condition than the written language condition was actually due to the sight of a moving human being in the former condition but not in the latter condition. This account is consistent with independent evidence that the visual perception of human movement engages some of the same right-hemisphere regions that showed up in Neville et al.'s (1998) investigation (see Figure 11.1 in Chapter 11; see also Campbell et al., 2001; Santi et al., 2003; Grossman, 2006). Moreover, in a follow-up fMRI study MacSwinney et al. (2002a) found extensive right-hemisphere activation not only when congenitally deaf signers comprehended BSL sentences, but also when hearing subjects comprehended English sentences that were presented in audiovisual format rather than written format. Thus, "when like was compared with like, using face-to-face sentence-length utterances in both languages, the neural systems engaged were very similar" (Campbell et al., 2007, p. 12; see also Söderfeldt et al., 1994).

But this is hardly the end of the story. In MacSweeney et al.'s (2002a) fMRI study, the baseline condition for the deaf subjects involved detecting infrequent color changes in a small square superimposed on the signer's chin (just like in the TicTac study described earlier), and the baseline condition for the hearing subjects involved detecting infrequent pitch changes of a tone while simultaneously viewing a still speaker. These visual/auditory discriminations were very low-level, however, so after they had been subtracted out of the imaging analysis, it was not really a straightforward matter to determine the source(s) of the remaining right-hemisphere activations associated with the main sentence comprehension tasks. Some of the activated areas may have reflected the visual perception of human movement, as MacSweeney et al. (2002a) claimed, but others may have reflected aspects of linguistic processing, and these functional–anatomical relationships may even have differed somewhat between the deaf and hearing groups of subjects.

To overcome this limitation of MacSweeney et al.'s (2002a) investigation, Capek et al. (2004) conducted yet another fMRI study of face-to-face sentence comprehension, only they modeled their experimental design quite closely on the one originally employed by Neville et al. (1998) (see also Sakai et al., 2005, for a different approach). Specifically, they contrasted audiovisually presented English sentences against a relatively high-level baseline condition involving audiovisually presented nonsense sentences composed of strings of pseudowords. As shown in Figure 9.21, left-hemisphere activation was observed in all of the classic language areas, but right-hemisphere activation was restricted to the mid and anterior sectors of the superior temporal gyrus. Importantly, because the subjects saw a "talking head" in both the experimental condition and the baseline condition, the right superior temporal activation was probably not due to the visual perception of speech-related facial movements.

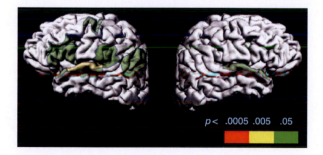

$p<$ .0005 .005 .05

Figure 9.21 Results from Capek et al.'s (2004) fMRI study of sentence comprehension in English. When audiovisual English sentences were contrasted against audiovisual nonsense sentences comprising strings of pseudowords, activations were found, at different levels of significance (color bar), primarily in classic left-hemisphere language areas and only minimally in the right hemisphere. Activations are shown in specific regions of interest that were predetermined for purposes of data analysis, exactly as in Neville et al's (1998) study of ASL (see Figure 9.20). (From Capek et al., 2004, p. 114.)

Instead, it may have indexed sentence-level prosodic processing, as discussed in Chapter 7 (see Figure 7.9 and the accompanying text). In the current context, however, the most critical point is this: Even when signed stimuli are compared with audiovisual stimuli (as opposed to merely written stimuli) and appropriate control conditions are used, the right hemisphere still appears to be engaged more extensively during the comprehension of ASL sentences (Figure 9.20) than English sentences (Figure 9.21).

This outcome is certainly very interesting, but it leaves us with a perplexing situation. After all, as mentioned above, it is hard to reconcile the fMRI evidence that the right hemisphere contributes substantially to sign language comprehension with the neuropsychological evidence that it is not absolutely necessary for such comprehension. Needless to say, much more theoretical and empirical work will be required to resolve these issues (for a thoughtful discussion see Corina et al., 2013). At the same time, however, there is one domain in which considerable progress has been made in elucidating how the right hemisphere facilitates the processing of sign language, and that is the domain of classifier constructions.

Involvement in Classifier Constructions

In our overview of the structural aspects of sign language, we noted that classifiers constitute a special set of mostly iconic signs that represent a great deal of spatial/topographic information about objects and their locations/movements (see Figure 9.4 and the accompanying text). Because these signs typically use the coding dimensions of handshape, location, and movement in analogue ways to denote the geometric and dynamic properties of scenes, it is reasonable to suppose that they might recruit the spatial processing resources of not only the left hemisphere but also the right. So far, this hypothesis has only been tested in a few studies, but the balance of evidence is largely positive (Emmorey et al., 2002, 2005, 2013; MacSweeney et al., 2002b; Atkinson et al., 2005; Hickok et al. 2009c). Although bilateral contributions to classifiers have been documented for both production and comprehension, we will focus on some representative studies involving production.

In a particularly valuable neuropsychological investigation, Hickok et al. (2009c) examined 21 unilaterally brain-damaged ASL signers, 13 LHD and 8 RHD. All of them were deaf except one, and all of them had been highly proficient users of ASL prior to their injury. Each patient was shown an amusing wordless book, *The Paint Story,* which consisted of black-and-white drawings portraying the shenanigans of two young children who, instead of painting a picture together, put paint on each other's faces and then dumped paint over each other's heads before finally being scolded by their mother. The task for each patient was to describe, one page at a time, everything that happened in the story. The researchers had deliberately designed the story, however, to elicit both lexical signs and classifiers, so when they analyzed the narratives that the two groups of patients produced, they concentrated primarily on those types of expressions.

The main results are shown in Figure 9.22. To begin with, Figure 9.22A presents the raw counts

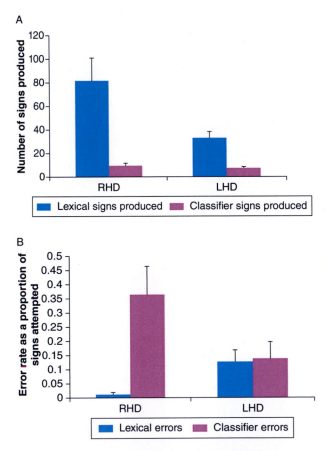

Figure 9.22   Results from Hickok et al.'s (2009) study of the production of lexical signs and classifiers by left-hemisphere-damaged (LHD) and right-hemisphere-damaged (RHD) deaf signers. (A) Number of signs elicited, regardless of whether they were expressed correctly or incorrectly. (B) Error rate as a proportion of signs attempted. (From Hickok et al., 2009, p. 386.)

for each type of expression, regardless of whether the signs were produced correctly or incorrectly. Consistent with normal ASL narratives (Morford & MacFarlane, 2003), both groups produced significantly more lexical signs than classifiers. But while the two groups did not differ significantly in the number of classifiers that they produced, the RHD patients produced significantly more lexical signs than the LHD group. This dissociation converges with the other neuropsychological studies discussed earlier, since it indicates that when the most commonly occurring types of signs are considered—namely, lexical signs—lesions to the left hemisphere lead to more severe deficits than lesions to the right hemisphere. Turning now to the error data, Figure 9.22B shows some intriguing patterns. Collapsing across groups, more errors were committed for classifiers than lexical signs. However, this effect was carried entirely by the RHD patients, since they had, on average, a 36 percent error rate for classifiers but only a 1 percent error rate for lexical signs, whereas the LHD patients had almost identical average error rates for the two types of expressions—14 percent for classifiers and 13 percent for lexical signs.

Hickok et al. (2009c) interpreted their findings as follows. Although the left hemisphere participates equally in the production of lexical signs and classifiers, it strongly dominates the right hemisphere in the production of the former expressions. By contrast, although the right hemisphere plays only a negligible role in the production of lexical signs, it plays a major role in the production of classifiers; indeed, its contribution to classifiers may even be greater than that of the left hemisphere. Despite these captivating implications, however, the study was limited in two ways: The specific relationships between behavioral profiles and lesion profiles were not explored, and different kinds of classifiers were not analyzed separately.

Fortunately, Emmorey et al. (2013) recently reported a PET study that did provide detailed functional–anatomical data for several types of classifiers, thereby yielding deeper insight into the neural substrates of these unique constructions. In this experiment, 11 congenitally deaf native ASL users were administered the following four conditions, all of which required the production of certain signs:

- *Locative classifier condition* (Figure 9.23A): The task was to generate the appropriate locative classifiers for 50 line drawings of spatial arrays, of which 25 items showed a clock in different positions relative to a table, and 25 items showed a mirror in different positions relative to a table. For each set of 25 items, the handshapes denoting the two objects remained the same, as did the location in signing space of the handshape denoting the reference object (i.e., the table); what changed was the location in signing space of the handshape denoting the figure object (i.e., the clock or mirror). Note that whereas English locative prepositions like *above* and *below* encode static spatial relationships in a highly categorical manner, ASL locative classifiers encode such relationships in a much more gradient fashion and hence convey much more fine-grained distinctions.

- *Motion classifier condition* (Figure 9.23B). The task was to generate the appropriate motion classifiers for 50 line drawings of spatial arrays, of which 25 items showed a ball moving along different trajectories relative to a table, and 25 items showed a toy car moving along different trajectories relative to a table. As in the previous condition, for each set of 25 items, the handshapes denoting the two objects remained the same, as did the location in signing space of the handshape denoting the reference object (i.e., the table); what changed in this condition, however, was the dynamic path through signing space of the handshape denoting the figure object (i.e., the ball or toy car). Note that because ASL motion classifiers fully exploit the analogue properties of the multidimensional visual–gestural medium in which signs are expressed, they represent paths with far greater fidelity than English phrases like *roll off* or *roll under*.

- *Object type classifier condition* (Figure 9.23C). The task was to generate the appropriate object type classifiers for 50 line drawings of objects. Each item showed a different object at a particular orientation on a table. As in the locative and motion classifier conditions, the handshape denoting the reference object (i.e., the table) remained in front of the torso; what changed was the handshape for the type of target object, and sometimes also the orientation of that handshape in the sector of signing space immediately above the handshape for the table. The following object type classifiers were elicited: flat object (B handshape); flat round object (curved L handshape); upright standing object (A-bar

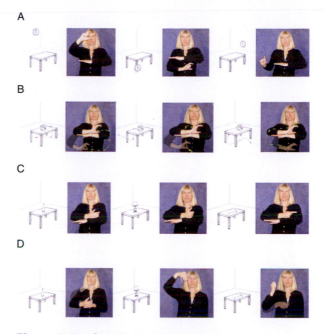

Figure 9.23 Sample stimuli and responses from Emmorey et al.'s (2013) PET study of classifier vs. lexical sign production. (A) Locative classifier constructions. (B) Motion classifier constructions. (C) Object type classifier constructions. (D) Lexical signs. (From Emmorey et al., 2013, pp. 518–519.)

handshape); cylindrical object (C handshape); long thin object (1 handshape); spherical object (curved 5 handshape); airplane (ILY handshape); and vehicle (3 handshape).

- *Lexical sign condition* (Figure 9.23D): The task was to generate the appropriate lexical signs for 50 line drawings of objects. This condition employed the same stimuli as the object type classifier condition, but the task was to produce the lexical signs for the target entities, rather than the object type classifiers. This condition served as a baseline for all three classifier conditions.

When the researchers analyzed the imaging data, they found that, compared to the lexical sign condition, the locative classifier condition and the motion classifier condition led to almost identical patterns of activation. Specifically, as shown in Figure 9.24A, both kinds of classifiers significantly engaged the superior parietal lobule, as well as the adjacent posterior portion of the superior frontal cortex, in both hemispheres. It is well-established that these regions are critically involved in spatial attention, visuomotor transformation, and the on-line control of reaching movements,

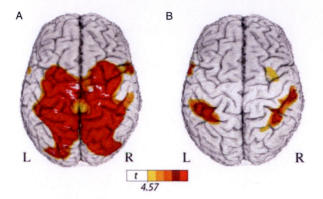

Figure 9.24 Results from Emmorey et al.'s (2013) PET study of classifier vs. lexical sign production. (A) Areas activated significantly more by both location and motion classifiers than lexical signs. (B) areas activated significantly more by object type classifiers than lexical signs. (From Emmorey et al., 2013, pp. 526–527.)

and Emmorey et al. (2013) point out that all of these capacities are needed to produce locative and motion classifiers. For example, to indicate the various positions of the clock in Figure 9.23A or the various paths of the ball in Figure 9.23B, one must first attend to the locations/trajectories of the entities, then map those visual representations onto a body-centered coordinate system, and finally execute arm movements that iconically convey the appropriate static or dynamic spatial information. Given that the overarching topic of this section concerns the right-hemisphere contributions to sign language, it is worth highlighting the fact that the right superior parietal lobule has been heavily implicated in the processing of coordinate (i.e., precise or metric) spatial relationships, as opposed to categorical (i.e., rough or schematic) ones (Laeng et al., 2003; Postma & Laeng, 2006). This is important because it supports the possibility that the right parietal recruitment for locative and motion classifiers may reflect the spatially gradient nature of the form and content of those signs.

When the researchers contrasted the object type classifier condition against the lexical sign condition, they again observed bilateral superior parietal activation, only not as extensive as in the contrasts for the other two classifier conditions (Figure 9.24B). It seems likely that in this case the parietal involvement was due to the need to iconically represent, in the object type classifier condition but not in the lexical sign condition, the particular orientation of each target entity relative to the reference entity (i.e., the table). For example, in Figure 9.23C the signer uses handshape orientation to indicate that the bottle and

the lamp are both standing upright, whereas the hammer is lying lengthwise, vis-á-vis the table. As with locative and motion classifiers, it is quite conceivable that the gradient nature of this orientation coding for object type classifiers depends in part on the right parietal cortex.

Summary

Although the left hemisphere is clearly dominant for sign language, the right hemisphere is also known to contribute. The exact manner in which it is involved, however, has been controversial. Most of the debate has centered on the role(s) of the right hemisphere in comprehending signed sentences. The essence of the problem is that different fMRI studies have revealed different degrees of right-hemisphere recruitment during the comprehension of ASL/BSL sentences, relative to different baseline conditions and also relative to different types of spoken/written sentence processing. Despite the variability of the data, however, it seems safe to say that when the proper controls are employed, the right hemisphere does in fact respond more strongly and extensively to the linguistic properties of signed than spoken/written sentences. This still leaves us, though, with some difficult questions. If the right hemisphere contributes substantially to sign language comprehension, why don't lesions to that side of the brain disrupt that capacity more often? Also, which aspects of signed sentences does the right hemisphere putatively support?

The answers to these questions remain uncertain, but some progress in addressing both of them has recently been made by focusing specifically on classifier constructions, which iconically encode a great deal of spatial information about the shapes, locations, and movements of objects. Neuropsychological studies as well as functional neuroimaging studies indicate that while lexical signs depend almost exclusively on the left hemisphere, classifiers are implemented in both hemispheres, with special reliance on the superior parietal lobules. It is likely that these bilateral cortical territories underlie the attentional, visuomotor, and spatial mapping operations that are necessary to produce topographically appropriate classifiers. And, most importantly for present purposes, the right-sided superior parietal region may be essential for computing correspondences between, on the one hand, the gradient spatial relationships in the scene to be described, and on the other hand, the gradient spatial relationships in the classifier that describes it.

Summary and Key Points

- Sign languages are complex coding systems with multiple levels of organization; hence they have the same communicative potential as spoken languages. As a group, they are characterized by the following structural properties:

  - *Phonology:* Signs are specified along the parameters of handshape, location, and movement.
  - *Morphology:* The internal complexity of signs can be increased through rule-governed processes of compounding, derivation, and inflection.
  - *Syntax:* Signs can be combined in principled ways to generate an unlimited number of multifaceted messages.
  - *Nonmanuals:* Some signs are articulated not by the arms/hands, but rather by the torso, head, lips, tongue, cheeks, eyebrows, and eyelids.
  - *Iconicity:* Although the majority of signs have arbitrary form-meaning relationships, many are iconic insofar as the form of the expression physically resembles, to some extent, the entity or event that it designates.

- The left hemisphere is dominant for sign language, just like it is for spoken language:

  - Support for this asymmetry comes from Wada testing, neuropsychological studies with brain-damaged patients, and functional neuroimaging studies with healthy subjects.
  - The ability to use sign language dissociates not only from the ability to perform visuospatial cognitive tasks, but also from the ability to produce symbolic gestures, particularly pantomimes.
  - These findings suggest that the neural implementation of sign language is driven mainly by the lexical and grammatical aspects of the signals that are transmitted, as opposed to their purely physical features.

- The left-lateralized organization of sign language is similar in many respects to that of spoken language:

  - Neuropsychological studies indicate that anterior lesions often cause production to become nonfluent and agrammatic, while mostly sparing comprehension. In contrast, posterior lesions often impair comprehension and lead to production that is fluent and syntactically well-formed but susceptible to sublexical phonological errors.
  - Functional neuroimaging studies indicate that the normal production of signs engages Broca's area and the middle/inferior temporal cortex. In contrast, the normal perception of signs engages the posterior superior temporal gyrus/sulcus, which is part of Wernicke's area.

- The left-lateralized organization of sign language also differs in some ways from that of spoken language:

  - Unlike spoken word production, manual sign production activates the superior parietal cortex, perhaps as a reflection of proprioceptive feedback from the arms/hands.
  - Furthermore, sign language relies on the supramarginal gyrus more than spoken language. This region may play a key role in integrating the different phonological components of signs—i.e., their specifications for handshape, location, and movement—during both production and comprehension.

- Despite the fact that the left hemisphere is dominant for sign language, the right hemisphere is also involved:

  - Although the data are mixed, the right hemisphere seems to respond more strongly and extensively to the linguistic properties of signed than spoken/written sentences.
  - The right superior parietal lobule, in particular, contributes to the processing of classifier constructions, perhaps by capturing the gradient spatial relationships that are specified by these constructions.

Recommended Reading

- Campbell, R., MacSweeney, M., & Waters, D. (2007). Sign language and wthe brain: A review. *Journal of Deaf Studies and Deaf Education, 13,* 3–20. A very accessible survey of research on the neural substrates of sign language, covering findings from neuropsychology, functional neuroimaging, and electrophysiology.
- MacSweeney, M., Capek, C.M., Campbell, R., & Woll, B. (2008). The signing brain: The neurobiology of sign language. *Trends in Cognitive Sciences, 12,* 432–440. Another review of research on the neural substrates of sign language, shorter and more focused than the previous one.
- Corina, D.P., Lawyer, L.A., & Cates, D. (2013). Cross-linguistic differences in the neural representation of human language: Evidence from users of signed languages. *Frontiers in Psychology, 3,* Article 587. A thoughtful discussion of similarities and differences between signed and spoken languages, from a neuroscientific perspective.

PART V

The Meanings of Words

Object Nouns

10

Introduction

The vocabulary of the average adult English speaker contains roughly 10,000 names for things—that is, nouns that denote different kinds of concrete objects (Landau & Jackendoff, 1993). There are words for animals like *squirrel, racoon, hawk, turtle, snake, octopus,* etc.; words for fruits and vegetables like *apple, pear, cherry, tomato, zucchini, carrot,* etc.; words for tools and utensils like *fork, knife, pencil, needle, broom, umbrella,* etc.; words for vehicles like *bicycle, car, bus, train, plane, boat,* etc.; words for musical instruments like *flute, clarinet, piano, guitar, violin, drum,* etc.; words for body parts like *eye, nose, elbow, finger, chest, thigh,* etc.; and so forth. How are the meanings of all these words represented in our brains? Some people might be tempted to suppose that the cortical implementation of lexical knowledge includes, for every word, a nice, neat, neurally discrete dictionary definition that spells out all the relevant semantic information in an abstract symbolic code that might be called "mentalese." Recent research suggests, however, that the real story is not only much more complicated than that, but also much more interesting.

The purpose of this chapter is to describe some of the advances that have been made in the branch of cognitive neuroscience that focuses on the representation and organization of the kinds of object concepts that are typically expressed by nouns. Here at the outset, it is important to note that this area of inquiry is fraught with controversy (for reviews of several competing positions see Gainotti, 2006; Patterson et al., 2007; Taylor et al., 2007; Martin, 2007, 2009; Mahon & Caramazza, 2008, 2009; Kemmerer, 2010b; Binder & Desai, 2011; Kiefer & Pulvermüller, 2012; Meteyard et al., 2012; Jefferies, 2013). Because it would require

a whole separate book to do proper justice to all of the key theoretical and empirical issues that are at stake, we will restrict our attention to a few of the most salient themes. The first section focuses on the provocative proposal that the modality-specific aspects of object concepts—e.g., how the things we call *apples* typically look, taste, and smell, and how we typically interact with them—depend on the same modality-specific neural systems that subserve high-level perception and action. The second section then turns to the closely related hypothesis that the anatomically distributed sensory and motor features of object concepts are bound together and organized by an integrative system that resides in the anterior temporal lobes. Finally, the third section addresses the question of how the brain groups object concepts into higher-order categories or domains such as those mentioned above (i.e., animals, fruits/vegetables, tools/utensils, etc.).

Before delving into the details, a few points about technical terminology and cross-linguistic differences are in order. Most of the time, in this chapter as well as in Chapters 11 and 12, the words "semantic" and "conceptual" are used interchangeably. However, it is important to note that, as indicated toward the beginning of the discussion of the Lemma Model in Chapter 6, languages around the world vary greatly in how they lexically "carve up" what are essentially the same domains of meaning (Evans, 2011; Malt & Majid, 2013). The greatest diversity occurs for relational domains like motion events and spatial locations, since distinctions in those domains are the least likely to be "given by the world" (Gentner & Boroditsky, 2001). Substantial cross-linguistic differences have also been reported, however, for numerous classes of objects (e.g., Senft, 2000; Aikhenvald, 2003). For example, in a study that used as stimuli a set of 60 photographs of common household containers, Malt et al. (1999, 2003) found that although English, Spanish, and Chinese speakers grouped the objects in comparable ways according to physical and functional features, they grouped them in orthogonal, cross-cutting ways according to names, as illustrated by results like the following. Of the 60 objects, 16 were preferentially called *bottle* in English, but there was not a matching lexical category in either Spanish or Chinese. Instead, the 16 objects fell into 7 smaller Spanish categories, and 13 of them were subsumed within a larger Chinese category that also included all 19 of the objects called *jar* plus 8 of the 15 objects called *container* (Table 10.1). Such discoveries are significant because they demonstrate that languages impose different "semantic maps" on the same "conceptual spaces." This idea has had a major influence on developmental psychologists who investigate the acquisition of language during childhood (Bowerman, 2011) and on cognitive scientists who

who investigate the relation between language and thought (Gentner & Goldin-Meadow, 2003; Malt & Wolff, 2010). It has not, however, had much impact on cognitive neuroscientists who investigate the implementation of word meanings in the brain, and for this reason, cross-linguistic variation will not figure prominently in what follows. Nevertheless, I encourage readers to keep this topic in mind, since it arguably warrants greater attention from a neuroscientific perspective (e.g., Boutonnet et al., 2013).

Perceptual and Motor Features of Object Concepts

Theoretical Background

From roughly the 1970s through the 1990s, the dominant theory of conceptual knowledge was the **Amodal Symbolic Model**. It emerged from earlier developments in logic, formal linguistics, and computer science, and its central claim was that concepts, including word meanings, consist entirely of abstract symbols that are represented and processed in an autonomous semantic system that is completely separate from the modality-specific systems for perception and action (e.g., Fodor, 1975; Smith, 1978; Pylyshyn, 1984). For example, according to this view, the concept encoded by the word *banana* is made up solely of amodal features like [fruit], [long], [curved], [yellow], [peel], etc., and understanding the word only requires accessing those features, not retrieving memories of how bananas are typically sensed and used.

Prior to the advent of the Amodal Symbolic Model, however, and in fact going all the way back to ancient philosophers such as Epicurus (341–270 BC), the favored theory regarding concepts was quite different. Basically, it was that concepts are rooted in modality-specific representations. This traditional approach was resurrected in the 1990s and has been attracting increasing interest ever since. It is often called the **Grounded Cognition Model**, but other names have also been employed (e.g., the Embodied Cognition

Table 10.1 English, Spanish, and Chinese Names for 60 Common Household Containers

English, Spanish, and Chinese linguistic categories for 60 stimuli					
English	N	Spanish	N	Chinese	N
Jar	19	Frasco	28	Ping2	40
Bottle	16	Envase	6	Guan4	10
Container	15	Bidón	6	Tong3	5
Can	5	Aerosol	3	He2	4
Jug	3	Botella	3	Guan3	1
Tube	1	Pote	2		
Box	1	Lata	2		
		Tarro	2		
		Mamadera	2		
		Gotero	1		
		Caja	1		
		Talquera	1		
		Taper	1		
		Roceador	1		
		Pomo	1		

Source: Malt et al. (2003, p. 25).

Numbers after the Chinese words indicate lexical tones.

Amodal Symbolic Model   The view that concepts consist entirely of abstract symbols that are represented and processed in a semantic system that is completely separate from modality-specific systems for perception and action.

Grounded Cognition Model   The view that concepts are anchored in modality-specific systems, such that understanding word meanings involves activating high-level perceptual and motor representations.

Model or the Simulation Model). The key idea is that semantic knowledge does not reside in an abstract realm that is totally segregated from perception and action, but instead overlaps with those capacities to some degree (Barsalou, 1999, 2008; Pecher & Zwaan, 2005; Gibbs, 2006; Semin & Smith, 2008; Shapiro, 2010). To return to the *banana* example mentioned above, understanding this object noun is assumed to involve activating modality-specific records in long-term memory that capture generalizations about how bananas look, how they taste, how they feel in one's hands, how they are manipulated, etc. (Figure 10.1). In other words, the theory maintains that conceptual processing amounts to recapitulating modality-specific states, albeit in a manner that draws mainly on high-level rather than low-level components of the perceptual and motor systems.

Of course, there are situations when conceptual processing is so deep and rich that it leads to vivid mental imagery (Kosslyn et al., 2006). This may occur, for instance, when you read a well-crafted novel or listen to a talented story-teller. According to most researchers, however, such explicit, detailed imagery is not really an essential part of the comprehension process; instead, it tends to occur afterward as a kind of embellishment that plays an elaborative rather than a constitutive role with respect to understanding the meanings of words (Machery, 2007; Mahon & Caramazza, 2008; Hauk & Tschentscher, 2013; for an alternative view see Barsalou et al., 2008; Simmons et al., 2008). What matters from the perspective of the Grounded Cognition Model is that modality-specific activations need not be manifested as full-fledged, conscious, sensory and motor

images in order to support conceptual processing. On the contrary, during ordinary language comprehension, such activations usually take place beneath the surface of awareness in an implicit and more or less automatic manner (Ansorge et al., 2010; Hauk et al., 2008a, 2008b; Moseley et al., 2013; Trumpp et al., in press). For example, when you read the word *banana*, you probably don't experience the distinctive flavor of that type of fruit. This lack of conscious gustatory imagery does not, however, imply that gustatory representations appropriate to the concept of a banana play no role in the comprehension process. In fact, there is growing evidence that they *are* activated, as we will see when we discuss this topic at greater length below.

Attentive readers will have noticed that the geometric layout of visual elements, auditory elements, tactile elements, etc., in Figure 10.1 reflects the anatomical distribution of the corresponding modality-specific systems in the brain (for comparison see Figure 1.24 in Chapter 1). This is not an accident, since the Grounded Cognition Model maintains that the neural correlates of conceptual knowledge encompass the high-level components of precisely those systems. What this implies is that the meaning of an object noun like *banana* does not reside in any single place in the brain; instead, different fragments of this complex concept are scattered across different cortical regions according to the sensory or motor content of the type of information that is represented. Thus, visual-semantic information about how bananas typically look may be stored in the same ventral temporal areas that are engaged when bananas are visually recognized; gustatory-semantic information about how bananas typically taste may be stored in the same orbitofrontal and insular areas that are engaged when bananas are gustatorily recognized; spatiomotor- and action-semantic information about how bananas are typically handled may be stored in the same parietal and frontal areas that are engaged when bananas are grasped and manipulated in customary ways; etc.

It is noteworthy that in the history of brain research, this kind of scheme was first introduced in the late 19th century by none other than Carl Wernicke (for an insightful discussion see Gage & Hickok, 2005). It was also explored by several other neurologists during that period, including William Henry Broadbent (1878), Heinrich Lissauer (1890/1988), and even Sigmund Freud (1891/1953). Roughly 100 years later, in the 1980s, the modern era of investigating the cortical organization of conceptual knowledge was ushered in by Elizabeth Warrington, who immediately began using a similar framework to interpret the performance of brain-damaged patients who exhibited strikingly

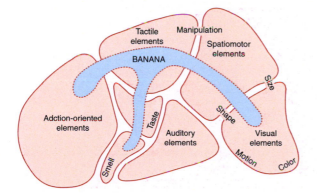

Figure 10.1 An illustration of the idea that, as maintained by the Grounded Cognition Model, concepts are anchored in modality-specific systems for perception and action. (Based on a figure from Thompson-Schill et al., 2006, which was itself based on a figure from Allport, 1985.)

selective impairments of particular semantic domains (Warrington & McCarthy, 1983, 1987; Warrington & Shallice, 1984; see the section called "Domains of Object Concepts" below). And around the same time, Antonio Damasio proposed a large-scale theory of brain function that was based on some of the same principles and that significantly influenced later work on the Grounded Cognition Model (Box 10.1; Damasio, 1989b; see also Damasio & Damasio, 1994; Simmons & Barsalou, 2003; Meyer & Damasio, 2009). Since the early 1990s, this overall approach has motivated an increasing number of studies that have employed diverse brain mapping techniques to test various predictions about the extent to which conceptual processing recruits modality-specific systems for perception and action. In what follows, we consider some of the major findings of these studies, with special reference to several kinds of semantic features that enter into the meanings of concrete object nouns. We begin by discussing three types of visual features—color, shape, and motion—and then go on to discuss three types of nonvisual features—motor, auditory, and gustatory/olfactory.

Color Features

Many kinds of objects have typical or "canonical" colors. This applies to numerous categories of artifacts whose colors are determined by social convention (e.g., yellow taxis) and even more strongly to various categories of animals (e.g., white swans) and plant life (e.g., orange carrots) whose colors are genetically programmed. Such object–color associations constitute an important part of a person's semantic knowledge of the relevant nouns.

Turning to the brain, although color perception is mediated by a multitude of neural mechanisms that begin in the retina, two main cortical regions are particularly important. First, *passive color sensation,* which occurs when one simply gazes at a garden of flowers, depends on area V4, a patch of cortex that resides in the lingual gyrus of the occipital lobe (Figure 10.2). Functional neuroimaging studies have shown that this area is engaged significantly more when people view colored stimuli than when they view grayscale equivalents (e.g., Zeki et al., 1991; Kleinschmidt et al., 1996; Hadjikhani et al., 1998). In addition, neuropsychological studies have shown that damage to this area causes

---

Box 10.1   What Is a Violin?

Antonio Damasio (1989a) illustrates his version of the Grounded Cognition Model by describing how the concept of a violin might be implemented in the brain:

The presentation of a line drawing of a violin, or presentation of the word 'violin' (aurally or orthographically), generates a set of time-locked activations of sensory and motor representations. The activations are generally pertinent to manipulable man-made objects, more specifically pertinent to musical instruments of the string variety, and even more narrowly so to the class of violins. In the visual realm the perceiver is likely to evoke representations of shape, motion, color, and texture which will vary from individual to individual according to the personal experience with violins that each has enjoyed. For those who have held violins in their own hands, or even played a violin, numerous somatosensory representations will also be evoked related to tactile impressions of wood and strings, or relative to the pressure the instrument will have exerted in the perceiver's body. But that is hardly all. Auditory representations of the range of sounds produced by the instrument may also be generated; motor programs according to which the appropriate posture and motions applicable to a violin can be organized may also be evoked and readied for appropriate display; finally, a range of somatic states appropriate to one's experience with violins, e.g., like or dislike, pleasurable or painful sensation, and so on, will also be activated. In short, a wide array of representations will be generated that together define the meaning of the entity, momentarily …. The mechanism that permits co-activation of representations depends on devices I have called convergence zones, which are ensembles of neurons that 'know about' the simultaneous occurrence of patterns of activity during the perceived or recalled experience of entities and events. The probability of simultaneous activation of representations prompted by a stimulus thus depends on the operation of convergence zones which, so to speak, embody a binding code for those representations …

(p. 27)

achromatopsia, which is an impairment of the capacity to consciously see color (e.g., Zeki, 1990; Bouvier & Engel, 2006; see also Sacks, 1995). Second, *active color perception,* which occurs when one deliberately, attentively compares the shades of different flowers, recruits a region in the middle sector of the fusiform gyrus (which corresponds roughly to ventral BA20), further downstream from V4. The fusiform gyrus is part of the ventral temporal cortex, which itself comprises much of the so-called "what" pathway—i.e., the branch of the visual processing hierarchy that deals with the shape, color, and texture properties of objects (see Chapter 1). The region of the fusiform gyrus that is especially responsive during color discrimination is sometimes referred to as V4α (i.e., V4-alpha) in order to highlight its close connection with V4 (Figure 10.2; e.g., Lueck et al., 1989; Zeki & Bartels, 1999; Murphey et al., 2008; see also Conway & Tsao, 2009). It has been found to be quite sensitive to a common clinical test of active color perception known as the

Farnsworth–Munsell 100 Hue Test (Beauchamp et al., 1999, 2000). In this test, subjects must determine whether five circularly arrayed wedges form a clockwise sequence of incrementally changing hues; in a baseline measure, subjects must make similar judgments only for grayscale equivalents (Figure 10.3).

Are either of the two main color perception areas—V4 and/or V4α—engaged when a person retrieves semantic knowledge about the color features of entities encoded by nouns like *taxi, swan,* and *carrot*? To address this question, Simmons et al. (2007) conducted an fMRI study that had two parts. In one part of the study, they localized the subjects' color perception areas by administering the Farnsworth–Munsell 100 Hue Test and subtracting the activation pattern evoked by grayscale wheels from the activation pattern evoked by color wheels. In the other part of the study, they asked the subjects to perform a conceptual property verification task that had three conditions (Table 10.2). In each trial of the color property condition, subjects were shown an object noun (e.g., *eggplant*) followed by a color adjective (e.g., *purple*) and had to indicate whether the color usually applies to the object. In each trial of the motor property condition, they were shown an object noun (e.g., *football*) followed by an action verb (e.g., *throw*) and had to indicate whether the action usually applies to the object. Finally, in each trial of the concept-only condition, they were shown an object noun (e.g., *lightbulb*) that was not followed by a property word, and made no response. This last condition was included solely for technical reasons, specifically to allow the researchers to separate the BOLD signals elicited by object words from those elicited by property words in the first two conditions (for further details see Simmons et al., 2007). Trials from all three conditions were mixed together and presented randomly to the subjects. After

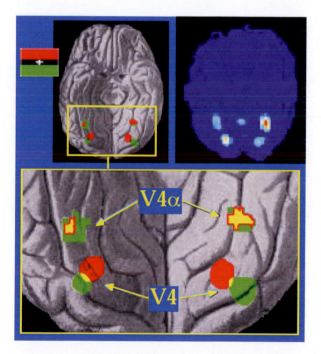

Figure 10.2 Two main color-sensitive areas in the human brain: V4, which is retinotopically organized, and V4α, which is not. Colors indicate activity elicited by chromatic vs. achromatic stimuli projected in the upper (red) or lower (green) visual field (yellow indicates overlap). (From Zeki & Bartels, 1999, p. 1375.)

Achromatopsia An impaired ability to consciously see color, due to damage to V4.

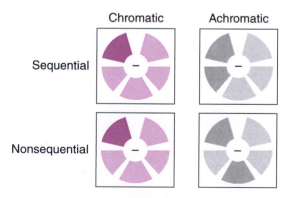

Figure 10.3 Oversimplified mock-up of sample stimuli from the Farnsworth–Munsell 100 Hue Test, as adapted for use in fMRI settings. See text for details. (From Simmons et al., 2007, p. 2804.)

both parts of the study were completed, the researchers analyzed the fMRI data with an eye toward answering the following question: Were any of the voxels that were activated more for color wheels than grayscale wheels in the first part of the study also activated more for color property judgments than motor property judgments in the second part of the study? As shown in Figure 10.4, these dual criteria were in fact satisfied by a large cluster of voxels in the left mid-fusiform gyrus, most likely overlapping V4α.

This finding is consistent with the Grounded Cognition Model, since it supports the view that semantic knowledge is anchored in the brain's modality-specific systems. An advocate of the Amodal Symbolic Model could argue, however, that the fusiform activity observed during the color property judgments may not reflect the unconscious, implicit retrieval of conceptual color features per se, but may instead reflect the conscious, explicit generation of color imagery, a process that may occur after the relevant color knowledge has been accessed from a purely abstract semantic system located elsewhere in the brain. Simmons et al. (2007) concede that their data are, in principle, compatible with this alternative interpretation, but at the same time they point out that such a view does not sit well with one of the core assumptions of the Amodal Symbolic Model, namely that abstract representations should be sufficient to perform all semantic tasks. In particular, they note that

> it would seem extremely odd for a proponent of amodal accounts to argue that the task cannot be performed using the amodal representations that are central to amodal theories, but instead must be performed using additional, ancillary, effortful processes .... If property information is amodal, then why would one need to 'imagine' the property? Yet subjects do activate modality-specific cortex when accessing property knowledge.
>
> (pp. 2807–2808)

To further support their position, Simmons et al. (2007) invoke some relevant neuropsychological data. Specifically, they note that damage to the left fusiform gyrus can cause **color agnosia**, a disorder that impairs knowledge of precisely the sorts of canonical object–color associations that their own color property verification task probed (Miceli et al., 2001). This certainly bolsters the idea that the fusiform activity observed in the fMRI study reflects the retrieval of genuinely conceptual color features, as opposed to mere color imagery. No one would deny, however, that these issues are quite complicated and that resolving them once and for all will require a great deal of further research (for related studies see Kellenbach et al., 2001; Goldberg et al., 2006b; Hsu et al., 2011, 2012; Wang et al., 2013b).

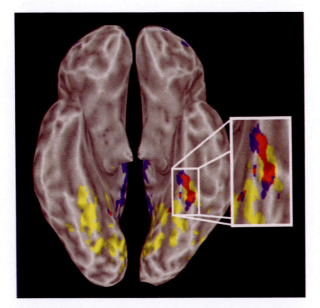

Figure 10.4 Results from Simmons et al.'s (2007) fMRI study of the color features of object concepts. Yellow = greater activity for color wheels than grayscale wheels in the Farnsworth–Munsell 100 Hue Test. Purple = greater activity for color property judgments than motor property judgments in the semantic task. Red = overlapping activity for the previous contrasts. (From Martin, 2009, p. 1034.)

Table 10.2 Experimental Conditions in Simmons et al.'s (2007) fMRI Study of the Color Features of Object Nouns (See Text for Details)

Condition	Concept Word	Property Word
Color property verification	Eggplant	Purple
Motor property verification	Football	Throw
Concept-only trial	Lightbulb	–

Source: Simmons et al. (2007, p. 2804).

Shape Features

On average, the most critical visual-semantic component of object nouns is shape (Vinson & Vigliocco, 2008; Gainotti et al., 2009, 2013; Hoffman & Lambon

Color agnosia An impaired ability to retrieve knowledge about the typical colors of objects, due to damage to the ventral temporal cortex, especially the fusiform gyrus.

Ralph, 2013). Landau and Jackendoff (1993, p. 218) make this point as follows:

> For a large proportion of object categories, shape is among the most important criteria for identification, and in particular for judgments of what a thing should be called. Categories of things with the same shape, including natural kind objects and artifacts, often share the same name.

Based on numerous studies using diverse brain mapping techniques, it is now well-established that, like color properties, the shape properties of visually perceived objects are represented in the ventral occipitotemporal cortex. In recent years, one of the most intensively investigated questions has been the following. Across this large expanse of cortex, are the shape properties of different categories of objects evenly distributed, or are they clustered together in patches (Reddy & Kanwisher, 2006; Op de Beeck et al., 2008, Bell et al., 2011)? While there is some evidence for evenly distributed coding (e.g., Haxby et al., 2004), there is even greater evidence that certain areas are preferentially responsive to certain categories of objects, particularly faces (e.g., Kanwisher & Yovel, 2006), non-facial body parts (e.g., Peelen & Downing, 2007), animals (e.g., Chao et al., 1999, 2002), tools (e.g., Chao et al., 1999, 2002), places (e.g., Epstein & Kanwisher, 1998; Epstein et al., 2001), and printed words (e.g., Dehaene & Cohen, 2011; see Chapter 8).

The following discussion focuses on several fMRI studies that point to separate cortical representations of the shapes of animals and tools, where the category of tools is restricted to man-made objects that are manipulated in conventional ways to serve specific functions. In one set of experiments, Chao et al. (1999) evaluated the perceptual processing of animals and tools by using passive viewing tasks and match-to-sample tasks, and in another set of experiments, they evaluated the conceptual processing of animals and tools by using silent picture-naming tasks and property verification tasks, the latter requiring subjects to answer yes/no questions like "Forest animal?" and "Kitchen tool?" in response to printed words for animals and tools. Across all of the tasks, perceptual as well as conceptual, significantly greater bilateral activation for animals was consistently found in a lateral portion of the mid-fusiform gyrus, whereas significantly greater bilateral activation for tools was consistently found in a medial portion of the mid-fusiform gyrus (see the left panel of Figure 10.5). As the authors point out, it is especially interesting that these adjacent but nevertheless distinct regions of the fusiform gyrus were activated not only by pictures, but

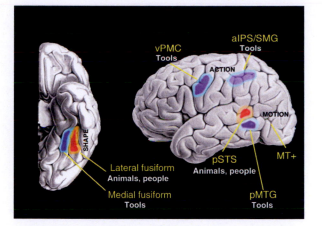

Figure 10.5 Cortically distributed representations of the shape, motion, and motor features of object concepts. See text for details. (Modified from a figure kindly provided by Alex Martin.)

also by words. Such results clearly fit the predictions of the Grounded Cognition Model.

The same question arises here, however, as arose for Simmons et al.'s (2007) investigation of color features. Specifically, one might suppose that the activations evoked by words were merely a reflection of the subjects' deliberate efforts to conjure up explicit visual images of the shapes of the lexically encoded animals and tools. Evidence against this interpretation, and in favor of the hypothesis that the lexically driven category-related fusiform activations are indicative of genuine semantic processing, comes from an fMRI study by Wheatley et al. (2005). This study took advantage of the neurophysiological phenomenon known as "repetition suppression." In short, if a given population of neurons codes for a specific type of information, its response will decrease when that information is repeated, as a reflection of greater processing efficiency (for a review see Grill-Spector et al., 2006). In Wheatley et al.'s study, subjects read rapidly presented word pairs (each word shown for only 150 ms with a 100-ms inter-stimulus interval) that were either unrelated (e.g., *celery giraffe*), related (e.g., *horse goat*), or identical (e.g., *camel camel*). The investigators found that as the degree of semantic relatedness between the two words progressively increased for a particular category—in this case, animals—the neural activation evoked by the second word progressively decreased in the lateral portion of the mid-fusiform gyrus, this being the same area that Chao et al. (1999) linked with the animal category. Given the processing time constraints imposed by the task, it seems unlikely that these repetition suppression effects could be due to explicit, conscious images that the subjects intentionally generated after understanding the words. Rather, as Wheatley et al. (2005, p. 1877) put it,

> it may be that the visual image of an object is automatically retrieved as an unconscious and obligatory by-product of normal word reading. In this case, automatic, implicit generation of an object image would be the mechanism by which we access an important property underlying the meanings of words denoting concrete entities.

(For related data and arguments see Gold et al., 2006; Hauk et al., 2008a.)

The convergent results of the studies by Chao et al. (1999) and Wheatley et al. (2005) suggest that the shape features of the meanings of object nouns are captured by populations of neurons in the ventral temporal cortex that not only overlap partially with those that subserve visual perception of the very same features, but are also segregated according to semantic category. Further evidence for these ideas comes from other fMRI studies (e.g., Kan et al., 2003; Devlin et al., 2005; Mechelli et al., 2006; Noppeney et al., 2006; Mahon et al., 2007, 2009; Chouinard & Goodale, 2010; Peelen et al., 2013; Tyler et al., 2013b). Moreover, neuropsychological studies have shown that, as predicted by the Grounded Cognition Model, damage to the mid-fusiform gyrus, especially in the left hemisphere, frequently impairs the understanding of concrete object nouns (for a review see Gainotti, 2006, and for a recent study see Capitani et al., 2009). For reasons described below, however, such lesions tend to affect semantic knowledge about living things, such as animals and fruits/vegetables, more severely than semantic knowledge about nonliving things, such as tools (see the section called "Domains of Object Concepts").

Motion Features

Yet another visual-semantic component of many object nouns involves the characteristic motion patterns of the designated entities. To take a few simple examples, part of the meaning of *rabbit* is the typical hopping movement of this kind of animal, and part of the meaning of *scissors* is the idiosyncratic cutting movement of this kind of tool. How are these semantic representations of motion implemented in the brain?

It is well-established that an area called MT+, which is most commonly located in the vicinity of the anterior occipital and lateral occipital sulci, is critically involved in the passive perception of moving visual stimuli (Malikovic et al., 2007; see the right panel of Figure 10.5). Damage

to this area can cause **akinetopsia**, that is, acquired motion blindness, a neurological disorder that is just as striking as achromatopsia for its specificity (e.g., Zeki, 1991; Zihl et al., 1991). Although MT+ does not itself appear to distinguish systematically between different types of object-associated motion, it projects to higher-level posterolateral temporal areas that clearly do (see the right panel of Figure 10.5). One processing stream extends from MT+ into a sector of the posterior superior temporal sulcus (pSTS) that responds preferentially to the sight of biological (e.g., animal) motion patterns (for a review see Saygin, 2012). Another processing stream extends from MT+ into a sector of the posterior middle temporal gyrus (pMTG) that responds preferentially to the sight of nonbiological (e.g., tool) motion patterns (for a review see Beauchamp & Martin, 2007). (As an aside, it is worth recalling that the pSTS and pMTG, especially in the left hemisphere, have also been associated with certain aspects of the perception and production of speech, as discussed in Chapters 5 and 6. These speech-related functions may be interdigitated, in ways that are not yet understood, with the visual motion processing functions described here. Additional cognitive operations may be carried out in this cortical territory too, as shown by Hein & Knight, 2008.)

Do these two parallel motion processing pathways contribute not only to the high-level visual perception, but also to the long-term semantic representation, of category-specific object-associated motion patterns? The Grounded Cognition Model predicts that they should, and supporting evidence comes from the same fMRI study by Chao et al. (1999) that was discussed above in the context of shape properties. The most relevant findings are as follows. The pSTS (independently linked with the sight of biological motion patterns) was engaged not only when subjects performed perceptual tasks with animal pictures, but also when they performed conceptual tasks with animal nouns, and the pMTG (independently linked with the sight of nonbiological motion patterns) was engaged not only when subjects performed perceptual tasks with tool pictures, but also when they performed conceptual tasks with tool nouns. These results are consistent with the hypothesis that understanding words like *rabbit* and *scissors* involves, as one part of the comprehension process, implicitly reactivating visual generalizations about the typical motion patterns of the designated objects. It is notable, however, that, according to several large-scale neuropsychological studies, damage to the pSTS/pMTG

Akinetopsia An impaired ability to consciously see motion, due to damage to MT+.

territory in the left hemisphere is more likely to impair the recognition and naming of tools than animals (Damasio et al., 1996; Tranel et al., 1997a; Campanella et al., 2010). This discrepancy—which, interestingly, is the opposite of the one involving shape features in the mid-fusiform gyrus—suggests that the relevant brain regions may be somewhat more important for the semantic processing of tools than animals (see also Binder et al.'s 2009 meta-analysis of fMRI studies). We will return to this topic later (see the section called "Domains of Object Concepts").

Motor Features

Sit back for a moment and think about the kinds of tools that are designated by the words *hammer*, *screwdriver*, and *knife*. As discussed above, visual representations of how these objects typically appear no doubt come to mind. But memories of how they are typically handled may occur to you as well. After all, the three kinds of tools are operated in quite different ways, with hammers being swung, screwdrivers being twisted, and knives being moved in a sawing manner. These motor representations are arguably important aspects of the meanings of the words, and the Grounded Cognition Model predicts that they reside in some of the same high-level components of the motor system that subserve the actual use of tools.

Tool use reliably recruits a complex network of motor-related brain structures that includes two cortical regions which are strongly left-lateralized in most right-handed individuals: first, the anterior intraparietal sulcus (aIPS), together with the inferiorly adjacent supramarginal gyrus (SMG); and second, the ventral premotor cortex (vPMC) (see the right panel of Figure 10.5). The precise ways in which these regions contribute to tool use have been carefully investigated for many years but are still not fully understood (for reviews see Johnson-Frey, 2004; Lewis, 2006; Goldenberg, 2009). Nevertheless, some well-supported assumptions are as follows. The cortical territory encompassing the aIPS and SMG (especially the latter) stores long-term gestural representations that indicate, at a fairly schematic and invariant level of abstraction, how certain tools should be grasped and manipulated in order to achieve certain goals. A classic source of evidence for this view is that damage to the aIPS/SMG can give rise to **ideational apraxia**, a disorder in which patients no longer understand the proper use of tools—for instance, they might try to use a comb to brush their teeth. During normal tool use, after an appropriate gestural representation has been selected in the aIPS/SMG, it is sent forward to the vPMC, which then transforms the

rough plan into a more specific motor program for physical action. That program may include settings for various parameters such as hand configuration, grip force, movement direction, movement speed, etc. Interestingly, both of these cortical regions—the aIPS/SMG and the vPMC—are engaged not only when one actually uses a tool in the conventional way, but also when one pantomimes such an action, imagines performing it, or sees or hears someone else perform it (Lewis, 2006; for an example of aIPS/SMG activation during imagined piano playing, see Figure 5.16 in Chapter 5). This leads naturally to the question of whether the same regions also underlie the motor features of the meanings of tool nouns. A growing body of literature suggests that the answer is "yes." What follows are some relevant findings from a variety of studies employing methods as diverse as fMRI, neuropsychology, electrophysiology, and rTMS.

First, let's look at some results pertaining to both regions—the aIPS/SMG as well as the vPMC. Naming tools activates both regions more than naming animals (Chao & Martin, 2000; Chouinard & Goodale, 2010). Similarly, naming manipulable artifacts—i.e., tools like a hairbrush or a key—activates both regions more than naming non-manipulable artifacts—i.e., non-tools like an airplane or a balcony (Saccuman et al., 2006). In the same vein, damage to these regions impairs the naming of manipulable artifacts more than the naming of non-manipulable artifacts (Arévalo et al., 2007). And at an even more fine-grained level of conceptual analysis, both regions respond more to words for manipulable artifacts that must be handled in specific ways to fulfill their functions, like *cup*, than to words for manipulable artifacts that don't have such requirements, like *clock* (Rueschemeyer et al., 2010b). Finally, with respect to the time-course of activation, both regions are engaged within 150 ms when subjects perform semantic tasks such as verifying that certain tool nouns are linked with certain hand actions (Hoenig et al., 2008). And the fact that this ignition speed is extremely quick supports the view that the regions are automatically activated as an inherent part of the comprehension process, as opposed to being deliberately engaged through an optional process of post-comprehension motor imagery.

Now let's turn to some results regarding just the aIPS/SMG. This region is activated more strongly when subjects judge word pairs as denoting objects that are manipulated in similar ways—e.g., *piano* and

Ideational apraxia   An impaired ability to understand the proper use of tools, due to damage to the left aIPS/IPL.

keyboard—than when they judge word pairs as denoting objects that have similar functions—e.g., *match* and *lighter* (Boronat et al., 2005; see also Noppeney et al., 2006). In addition, patients with lesions affecting the aIPS/SMG, as well as normal subjects receiving rTMS to it, have more difficulty with the former type of judgment—i.e., the one focusing on manipulation—than with the latter type of judgment—i.e., the one focusing on function (Buxbaum & Saffran, 2002; Ishibashi et al., 2011). Furthermore, using the "body–object interaction" index (Tillotson et al., 2008), which measures the ease with which a human body can interact with an object denoted by a noun, Hargreaves et al. (2012) found that words with high ratings, like *belt*, engaged the aIPS/SMG more than words with low ratings, like *sun*. And along similar lines, Pobric et al. (2010b) demonstrated that applying rTMS to the very same site delayed naming responses for high vs. low manipulability objects, whereas applying rTMS to the occipital pole (a control site) did not interfere with naming responses for either class of objects (see also Mahon et al., 2007, for closely related fMRI and neuropsychological data).

Last of all, here are a few results involving just the vPMC. Its degree of activity when subjects name tools varies with the amount of motor experience that those subjects have had with those tools (Kan et al., 2006). In addition, patients with progressive nonfluent aphasia—a neurodegenerative disease that affects the vPMC (see Chapter 4)—are more impaired at naming tools than animals (Reilly et al., 2011).

Taken together, this array of findings provides substantial evidence for the hypothesis that the motor-semantic aspects of tool nouns rely on some of the same motor-related cortical regions that subserve the actual use of the designated objects, most notably the aIPS/SMG and the vPMC. In short, the basic idea is that processing the meanings of words like *hammer*, *screwdriver*, and *knife* involves covertly simulating the kinds of actions that are usually performed with those sorts of tools. This is, of course, entirely in keeping with the Grounded Cognition Model.

It should be acknowledged, however, that there are still many open questions surrounding this general topic. For instance, a number of neuropsychological studies have shown that some apraxic patients cannot use tools correctly (as measured by pantomime and imitation tasks) but can nevertheless name the very same tools and retrieve other types of semantic information about them, such as their functions (e.g., Rapcsak et al., 1995; Rumiati et al., 2001; Rosci et al., 2003; Negri et al., 2007; Garcea et al., 2013). This seems to imply that even though tool nouns normally trigger motor simulations

in parietal and frontal regions, those simulations are not always necessary to understand the words. But then what do such simulations ordinarily contribute to the comprehension process? And how can the dissociation between impaired tool use and intact tool naming be reconciled with all the other data described above? These are just a few of the vexing issues that must be confronted by future research (for thoughtful discussions see Mahon and Caramazza, 2005, 2008; Mahon, in press).

Auditory Features

Moving on, it is clear that some concrete nouns refer to objects that are characterized in part by how they typically sound. For instance, in the animal domain, dogs and cats make distinctive vocal sounds, and in the tool domain, the conventional use of hammers and saws generates certain mechanical sounds. These examples illustrate how auditory features are nontrivial components of the concepts encoded by words for many kinds of objects.

The higher-order perception of non-linguistic environmental sounds shares much of the cortical territory associated with the higher-order perception of speech, including the pSTG, pSTS, and pMTG in both hemispheres (Saygin et al., 2003; Lewis et al., 2004; Dick et al., 2007; Leech & Saygin, 2011). Despite this substantial overlap, however, the following differences have been documented: fMRI studies have shown that the perception of speech tends to be somewhat more left-lateralized than the perception of non-linguistic environmental sounds (Dick et al., 2007), and neuropsychological studies have shown that the two auditory realms can dissociate from each other in rare cases of brain damage; in particular, the perception of speech can be selectively compromised in pure word deafness (see Chapter 5), and the perception of non-linguistic environmental sounds can be selectively compromised in **auditory agnosia** (e.g., Saygin et al., 2010a).

To explore the neural correlates of the auditory-semantic features of object nouns, Kiefer et al. (2008) conducted two studies, one involving fMRI and the other involving electrophysiology. In both studies, subjects performed the same task, which was to make lexical decisions (i.e., yes/no decisions as to whether letter strings are real words) for 100 words and 100 pronounceable pseudowords. Crucially, the 100 words consisted of two subsets that, according to a previous norming study, differed significantly with regard to the relevance of auditory features, but did not differ

Auditory agnosia An impaired ability to recognize non-linguistic environmental sounds, but with intact speech perception.

significantly with regard to the relevance of visual, motor, or emotional features, or with regard to nuisance factors such as word frequency and word length. Thus, the words were carefully selected so that the key parameter of variation was the semantic dimension of auditory content, with some words being rated quite positively (e.g., *telephone*) and others being rated quite negatively (e.g., *cup*). Two other aspects of the experimental design are noteworthy. First, the lexical decision task is generally assumed to not require deliberate, effortful processing of the meanings of words; hence whatever semantic access does occur is, for the most part, automatic and implicit (Chumbley & Balota, 1984; Binder et al., 2003). Second, in the fMRI study, the subjects not only performed the lexical

decision task, but also listened to sounds produced by animals and tools; these stimuli were included in order to localize the cortical regions that subserve high-level non-linguistic auditory perception.

So what did Kiefer et al. (2008) discover? Beginning with the fMRI study, when they subtracted the activation patterns elicited by words without auditory-semantic features from the activation patterns elicited by words with auditory-semantic features, they found a large cluster of voxels in the left pSTG, pSTS, and pMTG (see also Kiefer et al., 2012). Moreover, when they compared this cluster with the much larger one that was associated with hearing sounds produced by animals and tools, they found significant overlap (Figure 10.6A).

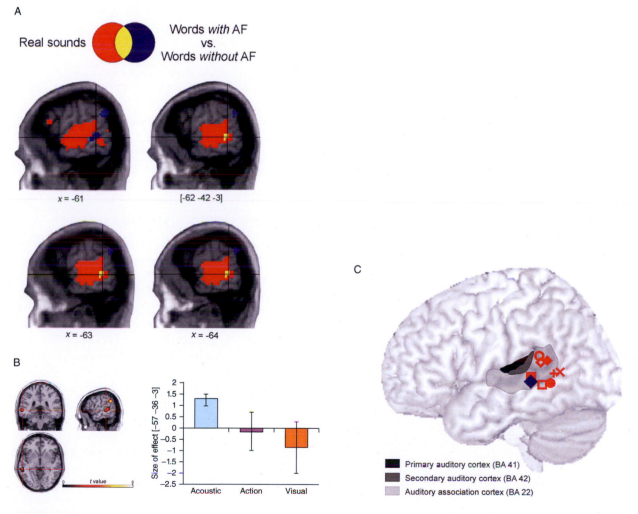

Figure 10.6   Results from Kiefer et al.'s (2008) fMRI study of the auditory features of object concepts. (A) Overlapping activity for the perceptual and conceptual processing of acoustic information (AF = auditory features). (B) Linear correspondence between, on the one hand, increasing activity in the left pSTG, pSTS, and pMTG, and on the other hand, increasing ratings for the auditory features, but not the visual or motor features, of word meanings. (C) The findings from this study (blue diamond) in relation to those from other studies (red symbols; see text for details). (From Kiefer et al., 2008, pp. 12227, 12229.)

Interestingly, as the ratings for the auditory-semantic features of words gradually increased, so did the BOLD signals in this cortical region (Figure 10.6B). In addition, previous fMRI studies have linked the same general territory with a variety of high-level auditory processes, including the following (Figure 10.6C):

- explicitly verifying the auditory-semantic features of object nouns (Kellenbach et al., 2001; Goldberg et al., 2006b);
- voluntarily recalling certain sounds (Wheeler et al., 2000);
- imagining music (Zatorre et al., 1996; Kraemer et al., 2005);
- recognizing familiar environmental sounds (Lewis et al., 2004);
- hearing human voices (Belin et al., 2000; Specht & Reul, 2003).

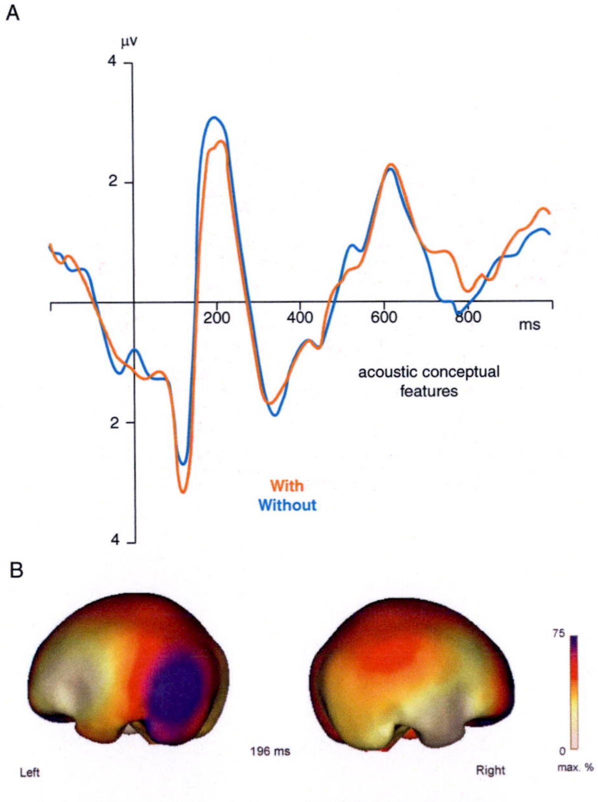

Figure 10.7 Results from Kiefer et al.'s (2008) ERP study of the auditory features of object concepts. (A) ERPs, collapsed across central electrode sites, showing divergence between words with and without auditory features during a time window of 150-200 ms. (B) Source analyses of the scalp ERPs, indicating that the strongest cortical currents were in and close to the left pSTG, pSTS, and pMTG. (From Kiefer et al., 2008, p. 12228.)

Turning now to the ERP study, when the researchers overlaid the waveforms elicited by the two main types of words, they found that the traces diverged significantly during a time window of 150–200 ms at all of the central (i.e., midline) electrode sites (Figure 10.7A). In addition, source analyses revealed that the neural generators for these effects were most likely in and close to the left pSTG, pSTS, and pMTG (Figure 10.7B).

Overall, these results provide compelling evidence for the Grounded Cognition Model. As Kiefer et al. (2008, p. 12229) put it,

the implicitness of the conceptual task, the selective modulation of left pSTG/pMTG activity by acoustic feature relevance, the early onset of this activity at 150 msec, and its anatomical overlap with perceptual sound processing show that the left pSTG/pMTG represents auditory conceptual features in a modality-specific manner.

What's more, it has recently been demonstrated that damage to the left pSTG/pMTG induces greater processing deficits for words with auditory-semantic features than for words without them (Bonner & Grossman, 2012; Trumpp et al., 2013). This additional finding is important because it confirms the causal involvement of the auditory association cortex in the comprehension of lexically encoded sound concepts.

Gustatory and Olfactory Features

Two other nonvisual aspects of the meanings of object nouns are gustatory and olfactory features—or, more colloquially, how the designated entities typically taste and smell. These are obviously important ingredients of the meanings of words for fruits, vegetables, and other kinds of food. Just think, for example, of the flavors and odors conveyed by the words *peach, lemon, garlic, onion*, and, last but not least, *chocolate*. The neural substrates of these sorts of modality-specific semantic features have not yet received much attention, but a few studies have yielded results that are consistent with the Grounded Cognition Model.

The sensory capacities of taste and smell are often grouped together because they both begin with chemical stimulation. This commonality is also reflected at higher levels of processing, since both kinds of perception are known to depend on the orbitofrontal cortex bilaterally (e.g., De Araujo et al., 2003; Small & Prescott, 2005; Small et al., 2007). This region contributes not only to the recognition of flavors and odors, but also to the computation of reward value, which is experienced as different degrees of pleasantness or unpleasantness. In addition, the region responds strongly to the mere sight of appetizing foods (Simmons et al., 2005, in press), and, as described below, its activity even increases when words for various foods are processed.

Two influential fMRI studies that explored this topic were reported by Goldberg et al. (2006a,b). In one of the studies (Goldberg et al., 2006a), participants were scanned while performing a complex task involving semantic similarity judgments among object nouns belonging to four categories: birds, body parts, clothing, and fruits. On each trial, they first covertly generated the most similar item they could think of in relation to a target item (e.g., "What is the most similar

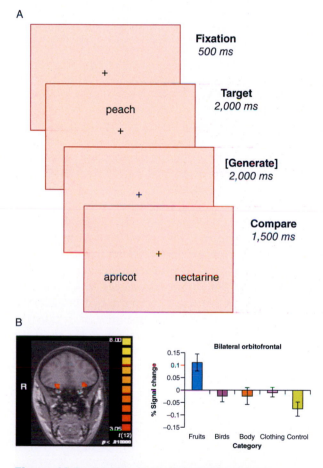

A

Fixation
500 ms

peach

Target
2,000 ms

[Generate]
2,000 ms

Compare
1,500 ms

apricot   nectarine

B

Bilateral orbitofrontal

% Signal change

0.15
0.1
0.05
0
-0.05
-0.1
-0.15

Fruits   Birds   Body   Clothing   Control
Category

Figure 10.8   Design and results of Goldberg et al.'s (2006a) fMRI study of object concepts. (A) A sample trial for the fruit category. In response to the word *peach,* subjects first covertly generated the most similar item they could think of, and then they decided which of two words, *apricot* and *nectarine,* was most similar to the item they generated. (B) Significantly greater bilateral orbitofrontal activity during the conceptual processing of fruits than of birds, body parts, and clothing. (From Goldberg et al., 2006a, pp. 216, 219.)

item to *peach?*"), and then they chose one of two alternatives (e.g., *apricot* or *nectarine*) as being most similar to the item they generated (Figure 10.8A). The investigators found that, relative to the categories of birds, body parts, and clothing, the category of fruits induced significant activity in the orbitofrontal cortex bilaterally (Figure 10.8B). In the other study (Goldberg et al., 2006b), participants were scanned while performing a conceptual property verification task in which words for different kinds of objects—including foods as well as non-foods—were presented, and after each one a property term appeared that had to be judged as being either true or false of the given type of object. The property terms probed semantic knowledge in four perceptual modalities: color, sound, touch, and taste. The investigators found that, relative to the conditions involving color, sound, and touch properties, the condition involving taste properties induced significant activity in, once again, the orbitofrontal cortex, only this time predominantly in the left hemisphere.

These results are in keeping with the idea that the gustatory/olfactory features of food concepts depend on high-level components of the gustatory/olfactory system in the brain (see also Gonzalez et al., 2006; Hwang et al., 2009; Barrós-Loscertales et al., 2012; Carota et al., 2012). The data must be interpreted with caution, however, because the tasks, especially in the first study, involve a fair bit of effortful thought, leaving open the possibility that the orbitofrontal activity is a reflection of voluntary explicit imagery instead of involuntary implicit semantic retrieval.

Summary

The research reviewed above supports the hypothesis that, as proposed by the Grounded Cognition Model, the meanings of object nouns are anchored in modality-specific brain systems, such that comprehension involves accessing high-level perceptual and motor representations that capture generalizations about what it's usually like to sense and interact with the designated entities. According to this theory, object concepts are not compact representations that reside in an autonomous semantic module; instead, they consist of multiple fragments of information that are widely distributed across the cerebral cortex in a manner dictated by their content. Thus, color features may be stored in the same part of the ventral temporal cortex that underlies high-level color perception; shape features may be stored in the same part of the ventral temporal cortex that underlies high-level shape perception; motion features may be stored in the same part of the lateral temporal cortex that underlies high-level motion perception; motor features may be stored in the same parts of the parietal and frontal cortices that underlie high-level motor programming; auditory features may be stored in the same part of the superior/middle temporal cortex that underlies high-level auditory perception; and olfactory/gustatory features may be stored in the same part of the orbitofrontal cortex that underlies high-level olfactory/gustatory perception. This account of conceptual knowledge assumes that whenever an object noun with complex multimodal features is understood—e.g., an animal word like *squirrel* or a tool word like *spoon*—a correspondingly complex network of multimodal cortical areas is rapidly and, for the most part, unconsciously engaged. Indeed, the theory maintains that it is precisely this evocation of perceptual and motor representations that constitutes the bedrock of comprehension.

This field of research is quite controversial, however, and a number of difficult questions have only recently begun to be addressed. How much do the modality-specific conceptual features of object nouns actually overlap with the representations that are employed in perception and action? How much do they vary across individuals as a function of different degrees of experience with the designated entities? To what extent can their activation be influenced by top-down attentional control? And to what extent can their activation be modulated by linguistic and situational contexts? These and other issues will undoubtedly be investigated in greater depth in the years to come.

Two additional issues that are especially interesting have been the focus of a closely related line of research since the mid 1990s. They are as follows: How are the anatomically distributed modality-specific features of object concepts bound together, and how are they organized in such a way that it is possible to determine which entities fall within the scope of a given concept and which ones fall outside that scope? We turn now to a detailed discussion of these topics.

A Semantic Hub for Object Concepts

A growing body of data suggests that the neural substrates of object concepts include not only high-level components of modality-specific systems for perception and action, but also certain sectors of the anterior temporal lobes (ATLs) bilaterally. According to a theory of semantic knowledge called the **Hub and Spoke Model**, the ATLs are integrative regions that have bidirectional connections with each of the anatomically distributed modality-specific systems, as well as with the systems that subserve the phonological and orthographic

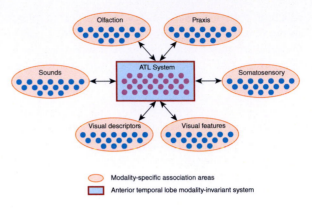

Figure 10.9 The Hub and Spoke Model. (From Lambon Ralph et al., 2010b, p. 2718.)

representations of words (Figure 10.9; e.g., Rogers et al., 2004; Patterson et al., 2007; Lambon Ralph & Patterson, 2008; McClelland et al., 2009; see also Simmons & Barsalou, 2003). Because the ATLs are assumed to contain modality-invariant representations, this approach brings together aspects of both the Amodal Symbolic Model and the Grounded Cognition Model to form a single unified framework. It is also noteworthy that the modality-invariant representations posited by this approach are similar in some respects to the undecomposed "lexical concept" nodes posited by the Lemma Model of speech production (Roelofs, 2008; see Chapter 6).

There are a number of purely computational reasons to suppose that some sort of integrative device is necessary to bind and organize the multifarious semantic features of object nouns (Lambon Ralph et al., 2010b). For one thing, features that belong to different modalities are not always experienced simultaneously, so a mechanism is needed to ensure that cross-modal features are ultimately correlated with each other in long-term memory. To take a simple example, the word *duck* designates a kind of bird with certain visual and auditory properties, but the sight of ducks is not always accompanied by the sound of their quacking. A second point is that features vary greatly in their typicality for a given concept, so a mechanism is needed to distinguish between entities that are central members, peripheral members, and nonmembers of the category specified by the concept. For instance, the word *chair* is perhaps most often associated with the kind of four-legged,

Hub and Spoke Model The view that concepts are based not only on modality-specific brain systems for perception and action, but also on modality-invariant integrative mechanisms in the anterior temporal lobes (ATLs). This theory combines aspects of the Grounded Cognition Model and the Amodal Symbolic Model.

straight-backed, wooden artifact customarily used for sitting at a dining table, but chairs can have any number of legs (even zero, as in beanbag chairs), they need not have backs (just think of some modern ergonomic designs), and they can be made of many different types of material (wood, metal, plastic, etc.) (Figure 10.10; Box 10.2). Yet another consideration is that some objects may be perceptually very similar to each other but nevertheless belong to different categories, so a mechanism is needed to overcome the superficially misleading modality-specific commonalities and register the deeper conceptually discriminative features. As an illustration, some of the animals that belong to the category referred to as *donkeys* look very much like some of the animals that belong to the category referred to as *horses*, yet they are demonstrably different species.

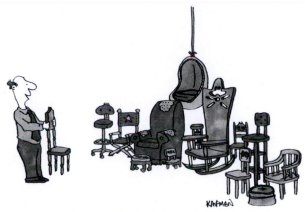

"Attention, everyone! I'd like to introduce the newest member of our family."

Figure 10.10   Cartoon by Jeff Kaufman. (The New Yorker Collection/The Cartoon Bank.)

Box 10.2   The Concept of a Nest in the Brain of a Mouse

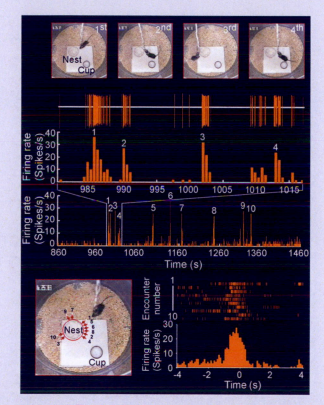

Figure 10B2.1   A nest-responsive cell. The top of the figure shows four snapshots of the mouse approaching its nest from four different angles during a 35-s period. Below the snapshots, three rows of recordings show that the cell fired robustly during each of the four encounters (first two rows) as well as during six other encounters over a longer period of time (third row). The bottom of the figure shows, on the left, the positions and angles of all ten encounters and, on the right, the "peri-event" recordings, with the time "zero" set to the point at which the tip of the animal's nose was 1 cm away from the edge of the nest before crossing. (From Lin et al., 2007, p. 6067.) Copyright (2007) National Academy of Sciences, U.S.A.

(Continued)

(Continued)

Nonhuman animals don't talk, but that's no reason to think that they lack sophisticated object concepts. This was demonstrated in a compelling way by Lin et al. (2007), who showed that certain neurons in the anterior temporal lobes (ATLs) of mice respond selectively to the perception of nests, regardless of their location, environment, shape, style, color, odor, or construction materials.

For example, Figure 10B2.1 illustrates how one particular cell increased its firing rate transiently, but drastically, whenever the animal encountered its home nest, independently of the position and angle of approach. Subsequent experiments revealed several other remarkable characteristics of this cell. It discharged robustly not only when the nest was moved to different locations in the same environment, but also when the nest was moved to completely different environments. In addition, it responded equivalently to circular, triangular, and square nests, as well as to nests made of tin can caps, plastic bottle caps, porcelain caps, and cotton. However, the cell did not fire significantly when the mouse encountered non-nest-like objects such as food items, floor pads, corner fences, novel toys, or even five cotton balls that were placed together haphazardly. Moreover, although the cell discharged above its baseline frequency when the mouse encountered a nest that was twice the normal diameter, it no longer did so when the mouse encountered a "giant" nest that was four times the normal diameter. To directly investigate whether the cell was tuned to the fundamental functional features of nests—i.e., to the features of "serving as a refuge for the animal to stay in a cozy and safe manner in a given environment" (Lin et al., 2007, p. 6070)—the researchers compared its responses to, first, a plastic bottle cap that was oriented in the "open," nest-like position, and second, the very same object only flipped over in the "closed," non-nest-like position. The cell fired significantly in the first condition but not in the second one, suggesting that it is sensitive specifically to the defining functional properties of nests.

These findings show that the functionality-based conceptualization of nests is implemented at the level of single cells in the ATLs of mice. Nest-specific responses were only observed in a tiny percentage of the cells that were studied, which supports the view that the development of such tuning characteristics is a highly specialized capacity that enables the animal to discriminate efficiently between objects that do and do not satisfy the criteria of "nesthood." If mice could talk, perhaps they would argue about the fine nuances of nests the way we humans debate the subtle contrasts between chairs.

All of these factors have been taken into account in the construction of several sophisticated computer simulations of both the development and breakdown of object concepts (McClelland & Rogers, 2003; Rogers & McClelland, 2004; Rogers et al., 2004). These simulations adopt an architecture in which information represented in distinct modality-specific systems is fed into a central modality-invariant system, as sketched in Figure 10.9. Setting aside the technical details of how the simulations actually work, what matters is that they are able to mimic many basic aspects of human semantic cognition. Most significantly, the modality-invariant hub is able to solve the problems described above. It can bind features in different modalities that are encountered in separate episodes (like the shapes and sounds of ducks); it can capture the complex statistical variation among features that gives rise to typicality effects (like the bewildering diversity of chairs); and it can extract relatively subtle features that differentiate otherwise similar concepts (like the contrasts between donkeys and horses). It is important to realize, however, that the hub does not actually represent much conceptual content. Instead, most of the content of object nouns resides in the modality-specific systems for perception and action, and the function of the hub is to identify and organize combinatorial patterns of features within and across those systems.

As mentioned above, the Hub and Spoke Model maintains that the integrative system—i.e., the semantic hub—resides in the ATLs bilaterally. These regions occupy the apex of complex processing hierarchies in both hemispheres. They receive convergent input from, and send divergent output back to, a broad range of other brain areas that subserve different perceptual and motor functions (Binney et al., 2012). Hence, they appear to be well-suited to serve the various feature binding and systematizing functions that the theory ascribes to the hub. Empirical support for this proposal comes from numerous studies. The discussion below focuses on evidence from the following sources: neuropsychological investigations of patients with semantic dementia, and fMRI and rTMS investigations of healthy individuals. (For some other important studies not explicitly considered below, see de Zubicaray et al., 2011; Walker et al., 2011; Chan et al., 2011; Peelen & Caramazza, 2012).

Evidence from Semantic Dementia

As described in some detail in Chapter 4, semantic dementia (SD) is a neurodegenerative disease—one particular variant of primary progressive aphasia—in which conceptual knowledge gradually deteriorates (for a review see Hodges & Patterson, 2007). Patients with SD tend to have trouble with essentially all verbal and nonverbal tasks that require them to retrieve and process object concepts. Thus, they perform poorly when asked to name pictures, match words with pictures, verify whether words refer to pictures, sort words according to similarity, sort objects according to similarity, demonstrate the proper use of objects, or recognize objects based on visual, auditory, somatosensory, or gustatory/olfactory features (for qualifications see Mesulam et al., 2013). Despite these impairments, however, patients usually perform well on independent tests of basic perception, autobiographical

memory, working memory, problem-solving, and attention, at least until late in the course of the disease. The anatomical specificity of the atrophy observed in SD is striking (see Figure 2.7 in Chapter 2, Figure 4.3 in Chapter 4, and Figures 10.11 and 10.17D below). Without exception, it targets the ATLs bilaterally, although often with a left > right asymmetry. As the disease progresses, there is increasing tissue loss and hypometabolism in these structures, especially in the ventral and lateral parts, as well as gradual extension into neighboring brain regions. From the perspective of the Hub and Spoke Model, the amodal hub is disrupted first, and then the visual spoke begins to malfunction as the atrophy spreads into more posterior parts of the inferior and middle temporal gyri (Hoffman et al., 2012a).

A representative case of SD is patient EK, whose cortical atrophy and conceptual disturbances were tracked longitudinally during a three-year period by Bright et al. (2008). When these researchers first encountered EK in 2001, she was a 60-year-old right-handed woman who worked part-time as a cook and cleaner and who had been experiencing gradually worsening word-finding problems over the

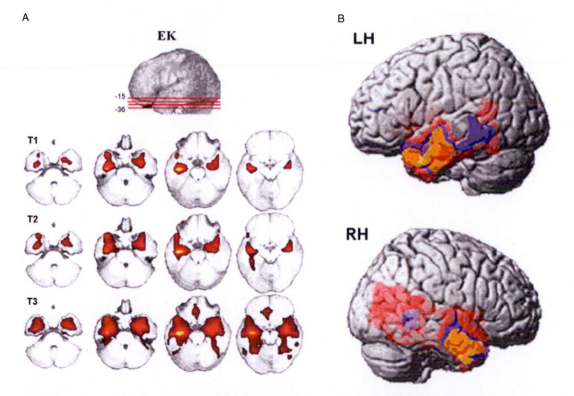

Figure 10.11 Lesion profiles derived from three annually acquired scans of patient EK. (A) Four inferior axial slices (planes indicated in top image) showing the extent of atrophy at each time period (T1, T2, and T3). (B) Full lesion extents portrayed on rendered brains (yellow = T1; blue = T2; pink = T3). (From Bright et al., 2008, p. 2182.)

course of approximately five years. EK's pattern and degree of tissue loss, as well as her behavioral performances on a battery of standarized semantic tasks, were assessed annually on three occasions (T1, T2, and T3), beginning in 2002.

The neuroimaging results for EK are shown in Figure 10.11. Across the three time periods, the distribution of tissue loss was similar in the left and right hemispheres, but somewhat more severe in the left. At T1, the atrophy appeared to be restricted to the ATLs, affecting especially the temporal pole and, on the ventral surface, the anterior fusiform gyrus and anterior parahippocampal gyrus. At T2, there was further development of the atrophy observed at T1, together with some extension posteriorly into the inferior and middle temporal gyri (more pronounced in the left hemisphere). Finally, by T3, although EK's tissue loss was still most severe in the ATLs, it had spread even further into other parts of the temporal lobes.

The four semantic tasks that were administered to EK at each time period were as follows. The first task, object naming, involved orally naming a set of pictures of common objects (control mean = 98 percent). The second task, word–picture matching, involved hearing a spoken word and matching it with the correct picture in a four-item array consisting of the target (e.g., a horse), a within-domain distractor (e.g., a lion), and two cross-domain distractors (e.g., an apple and a car) (control mean = 100 percent). The third task, category fluency, involved hearing a category label (e.g., *animals*) and producing the names of as many members of the category as possible within one minute (control mean = 17.1). The fourth task, property verification, involved giving yes/no responses to questions about the features of common objects, with some features being shared by many types of objects in the domain (e.g., "Does a camel have legs?") and others being distinctive for a particular type of object

(e.g., "Does a camel have a hump?") (control mean = 97 percent).

As shown in Figure 10.12, EK's performance on all four tasks declined over time, paralleling the progression of her cortical atrophy. At T1, when her tissue loss was apparently confined to the ATLs, she already manifested significant semantic deficits. On the object naming task, her score was only 20 percent, and there were roughly equal proportions of superordinate errors (17 percent; e.g., saying *animal* instead of *horse*) and coordinate errors (19 percent; e.g., saying *dog* instead of *cat*), with the majority of other errors consisting of "don't know" responses. Although she achieved a score of 89 percent on the word–picture matching task, this was still below normal. Moreover, she was quite impaired on both the category fluency task (only 7 items) and the property verification task (72 percent). On the latter test, she had much greater difficulty making judgments about distinctive than common features of objects—a pattern that is frequently exhibited by SD patients. At T2, when her tissue loss had extended into the MTG, her performances on all four tasks were worse. And at T3, when the atrophy had spread even further, although her performance on the word–picture matching task remained stable, her performance on the category fluency task declined, and she was unable or unwilling to complete the object naming and property verification tasks. For instance, on the property verification task, she refused to answer the first question, "Does an apple have a handle?", stating that an apple is "something you put food into." Overall, then, the parallel courses of EK's cortical atrophy and conceptual disturbances not only exemplify the insidious nature of the neurocognitive deterioration in SD, but also support the view that, as maintained by the Hub and Spoke Model, the ATLs play critical roles in the processing of object concepts.

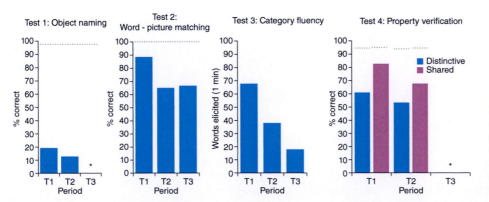

Figure 10.12 Scores obtained by patient EK on a subset of the tasks administered by Bright et al. (2008) during three annual examinations. (From Bright et al., 2008, p. 2183.)

Additional evidence for this theory comes from a clever study by Lambon Ralph et al. (2010b) that directly tested the prediction that when the ATL hub is damaged, "performance will become dominated by modality-specific surface similarities and be less reflective of higher-order semantic structure" (p. 2719). Control participants and six SD patients were given a matching-to-sample task that was specially constructed for this study. On each trial, the subjects were presented with a word and an array of nine pictures, and their task was to indicate which pictures showed objects that belonged to the category specified by the word. The subjects were told that there was always more than one target in the array, and in fact the experiment was set up so that the number of targets varied between two and three. A crucial aspect of the design was that the targets and distracters were chosen in such a way as to allow the researchers to pit surface similarities against category membership. Besides having typical targets (e.g., a standard cat), there were also atypical targets (e.g., a hairless cat), and besides having completely unrelated distractors (e.g., a train) and partially related distractors (e.g., an otter), there were also pseudo-typical distractors (e.g., a chihuahua) that were superficially similar to the typical targets but did not really belong to the

category. Given this kind of design, the researchers expected the SD patients to commit two major types of error: undergeneralizations, in which they failed to pick atypical targets; and overgeneralizations, in which they incorrectly picked pseudo-typical targets. As shown in Figure 10.13, both of these predictions were robustly confirmed.

According to Lambon Ralph et al. (2010b), these results reinforce the claim that the ATLs implement an integrative semantic system of the kind posited by the Hub and Spoke Model. Moreover, further support comes from a follow-up study that employed a comparable methodology but used words instead of pictures in the choice arrays (Mayberry et al., 2011; see also Woollams, 2012, for a closely related investigation). To clarify how the ATL hub might operate, and how it might break down in SD, Lambon Ralph et al. (2010b) focus on a specific example—namely, the concept of a "cat." In Figure 10.14A, an assortment of animals are spatially organized in terms of approximate visual similarity. This may reflect the way they are represented in the shape-sensitive lateral portion of the mid-fusiform gyrus, as discussed above in the context of the grounded cognition model. However, to identify all of the cats in this modality-specific representational space, one must

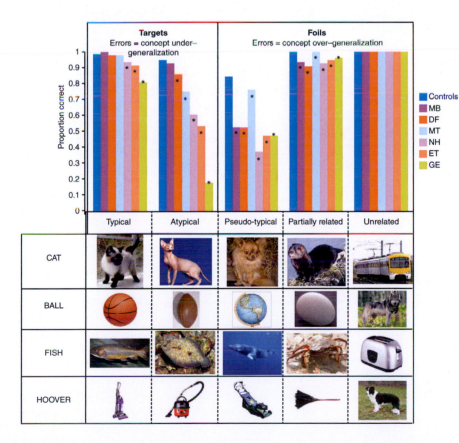

Figure 10.13 Design and results of Lambon Ralph et al.'s (2010b) study of SD. See text for details. (From Lambon Ralph et al., 2010b, p. 2719.)

draw a convoluted boundary that includes the typical items as well as the atypical items, and that excludes the unrelated items as well as the superficially related items. Establishing such a category boundary is assumed to be one of the main functions of the ATL hub, and when the hub is damaged, as happens in SD, the precise configuration of the boundary becomes blurry, as shown in Figure 10.14B. In such a situation, it is still possible to recognize typical members of the category, but atypical members are likely to be incorrectly excluded (undergeneralization), and superficially related items

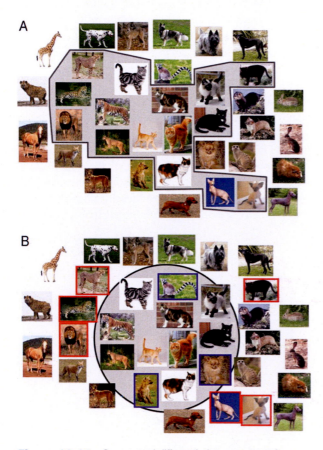

Figure 10.14   Conceptual differentiation versus surface similarity structure. These animal pictures are arranged (approximately) according to visual similarity. As a result, the boundary of the concept "cat" has to have a complex shape if the structurally different exemplars of cats are to be included and if the visually similar non-cats are to be excluded. (A) Such complex boundaries can be coded within a fully functional, multidimensional, amodal semantic space like the one postulated to reside in the ATLs. When this space breaks down in the context of brain damage, however, only simple boundaries can be coded (B). As a result, some items are falsely excluded from the "cat" concept (undergeneralizations, marked in red), and some are incorrectly drawn within the "cat" concept boundary (overgeneralizations, marked in blue). (From Lambon Ralph et al., 2010b, p. 2721.)

are likely to be incorrectly included (overgeneralization), as Lambon Ralph et al. (2010b) demonstrated in their experiment.

Evidence from fMRI and TMS

Many researchers believe that findings from SD, like those reviewed above, provide strong evidence that the ATLs are essential nodes in the neural architecture of object concepts. Such findings are limited, however, in at least two ways. First, because SD is a progressive neurodegenerative disease, it is hard to rule out the possibility that even in early-stage patients, for whom the atrophy is often thought to be confined to the ATLs, the observed semantic deficits might actually be due to subthreshold damage (i.e., damage that escapes detection by current brain imaging technology) in areas outside the ATLs. And second, because SD affects many different sectors of the ATLs, it is not feasible to infer from neuropsychological studies of SD patients whether certain sectors of the ATLs contribute more to conceptual knowledge than others. To overcome these limitations, research within the framework of the Hub and Spoke Model has drawn upon other methods, especially fMRI and rTMS.

Historically, using fMRI to explore the ATLs has been problematic because of a well-known weakness of this particular form of brain imaging. In short, BOLD signals are broken up near air-filled cavities due to discrepancies in the magnetic susceptibility of air, bone, and water. Thus, because the ATLs are very close to the air-filled sinuses, they are, as Patterson et al. (2007) put it, "shy" to fMRI (see also Visser et al., 2009). Fortunately, advances in the world of fMRI now make it possible to correct for such signal loss. By employing such corrections, Visser et al. (2010) were able to reveal significant semantically driven activity in the ATLs using an experimental protocol that had previously been shown to engage the ATLs only with PET imaging, which does not have the same weakness as fMRI (Devlin et al., 2000).

The protocol had the following design. On each trial of the semantic condition, subjects first read three words denoting objects in a particular domain, and then they decided whether a fourth word (in uppercase font) denoted an object in the same domain or in a different domain (e.g., a sequence like *taxi–boat–bicycle–AIRPLANE* would elicit a "yes" response, whereas a sequence like *taxi–boat–bicycle–SPOON* would elicit a "no" response). On each trial of the baseline condition, subjects first saw three strings of a particular letter, and then they decided whether a fourth string

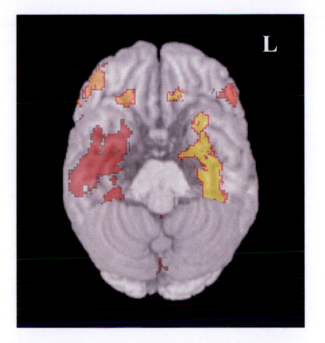

Figure 10.15 Results from Visser et al.'s (2010) fMRI study of object concepts. Activity patterns are portrayed on the ventral surface of a rendered brain (L = left). See text for details. (From Visser et al., p. 1692.)

(in upper-case font) showed the same letter or a different one (e.g., a sequence like *rrrr–rrr–rrrrr–RRR* would elicit a "yes" response, whereas a sequence like *rrrr–rrr–rrrrr–DDD* would elicit a "no" response). When

Visser et al. (2010) contrasted the semantic condition against the baseline condition, they found significant activity in the ATLs (Figure 10.15). The activity was stronger in the left than the right hemisphere and was predominantly ventral, centered in the anterior fusiform gyrus with some extension both rostrally and medially. This study therefore suggests that these portions of the ATLs may be especially important for object concepts.

Analogous results were obtained by Binney et al. (2010), who also corrected for signal loss in an fMRI investigation that focused on the contribution of the ATLs to semantic processing. In their study, the semantic condition involved making synonym judgments. On each trial of this task, participants decided which of three choice words (e.g., *scoundrel*, *polka*, and *gasket*) was most similar in meaning to a probe word (e.g., *rogue*). All of the words were carefully matched for both imageability and frequency. The baseline task had a comparable format but involved numbers, so that on each trial participants decided which of three choice numbers was closest in value to a probe number. When Binney et al. (2010) contrasted the semantic condition against the baseline condition, they found significant activity in some of the same sectors of the ATLs that turned up in Visser et al.'s (2010) study, most notably the anterior fusiform gyrus, together with the anterior part of the inferior temporal gyrus (Figure 10.16A, B). The ATL activity in this study, however, was more strongly left-lateralized than in Visser et al.'s (2010)

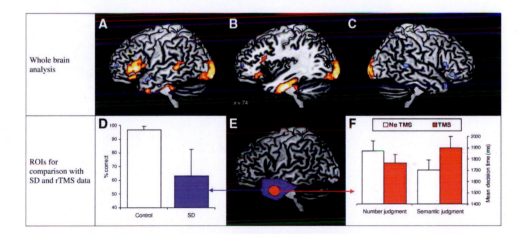

Figure 10.16 Brain activation maps versus SD and rTMS behavioral data from Binney et al. (2010). Brain activation maps show left hemisphere (A, B) and right hemisphere (C) activation in the whole-brain analysis of the contrast between a semantic task (synonym judgments) and a baseline task (number judgments). Activations shown in the red/yellow color scale survived a stricter statistical threshold than those shown in the blue/green color scale. (D) Mean accuracy of SD patients performing the semantic task compared to a healthy age-matched control group. (E) "Region of interest" (ROI) derived from a map of hypometabolism in SD patients (blue) and another ROI centered on the mean coordinates of TMS stimulation (red). (F) Decision times for the semantic task and the baseline task both prior to and following rTMS over the left ATL. (From Binney et al., 2010, p. 2731.)

study, perhaps because the semantic task in this study drew more heavily on lexical relations that are likely to be left-hemisphere dominant.

A unique virtue of Binney et al.'s (2010) study is that the semantic and baseline tasks that were employed in the fMRI experiment had previously been employed not only in a neuropsychological experiment with SD patients (Jefferies et al., 2009), but also in two rTMS experiments with healthy subjects (Pobric et al., 2007; Lambon Ralph et al., 2009). It was therefore possible to look for convergent results across the three methods.

Regarding SD, Jefferies et al. (2009) demonstrated that patients with this disease are, on average, gravely impaired on the synonym judgment task (Figure 10.16D). Binney et al. (2010) followed up on those findings by seeking to determine whether any of the specific ATL regions that were activated in their fMRI experiment fell within the large ATL territory that is typically affected in SD. To do this, they carried out a "region of interest" analysis using the map of tissue loss in SD reported by Galton et al. (2001). They discovered that two particular cortical areas—the left anterior fusiform gyrus and the left anterior inferior temporal gyrus—not only exhibited the most significant activity when healthy subjects performed the synonym judgment task, but also exhibited the most significant amount of atrophy in

SD patients (Figure 10.17). Clearly, the fMRI data dovetail remarkably well with the SD data.

Regarding rTMS, it is not possible to stimulate the anterior fusiform gyrus because it lies on the ventral surface of the temporal cortex and is hence too far from the scalp. It is possible, however, to stimulate the inferolateral ATL region that comprises the anterior parts of the inferior and middle temporal gyri, so that region was targeted in two studies that were designed to determine whether temporarily disrupting the region's functionality in healthy subjects would delay their responses on the synonym judgment task (Pobric et al., 2007; Lambon Ralph et al., 2009). The predictions were confirmed. Participants' reaction times were slower on the synonym judgment task, but not on the number judgment task, when rTMS was applied to the target region in the left hemisphere, compared to when no rTMS was applied there (Figure 10.16F). Thus, like the SD results, these rTMS results are quite compatible with the fMRI results reported by Binney et al. (2010).

What about the homologous inferolateral ATL region in the right hemisphere? Would rTMS at that site have similar effects? Although the region did not cross the statistical threshold for significant activation in Binney et al.'s (2010) fMRI study, it does tend to be dysfunctional in SD, and this well-established fact supports the possibility that it cooperates with its

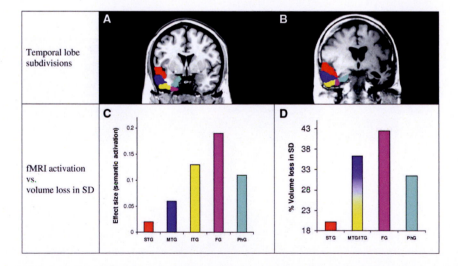

Figure 10.17   Additional data from Binney et al. (2010) showing the temporal lobe distribution of semantic activation in healthy individuals versus volume loss in SD patients. (A) Temporal lobe regions of interest (ROIs) used to assess the distribution of semantic activation in the anterior temporal lobe. (B) Example MR scan of an SD patient overlaid with representations of the temporal lobe ROIs used in a previous volumetric study of SD (Galton et al., 2001). (C) Semantic activation (synonym judgments versus number judgments) within each of the temporal lobe subdivisions marked in A. (D) Distribution of temporal lobe volume loss observed in a group of SD patients. STG = superior temporal gyrus; MTG = middle temporal gyrus; ITG = inferior temporal gyrus; FG = fusiform gyrus; PhG =parahippocampal gyrus. (From Binney et al., 2010, p. 2733.)

left-hemisphere twin in implementing the semantic hub. To test this hypothesis, Lambon Ralph et al. (2009) applied rTMS not only to the target region in the left hemisphere, but also to the target region in the right hemisphere, while subjects performed both the synonym judgment task and the number judgment task. The outcome was essentially the same regardless of which hemisphere was stimulated. In particular, interfering with the operation of either the left or the right hemisphere region significantly increased reaction times on the lexical task but not the number task (Figure 10.18). These findings are valuable because they bolster one of the key claims of the Hub and Spoke Model—namely, that object concepts depend on the ATLs *bilaterally* (see also Pobric et al., 2010a; Lambon Ralph et al., 2010a, 2012).

An important caveat, however, is that the rTMS protocols that Pobric et al. (2007) and Lambon Ralph et al. (2009) used involved stimulating the target sites continuously for 10 minutes prior to task performance. Such stimulation has been shown to produce behavioral effects that last for several minutes after the rTMS train has concluded (e.g., Kosslyn et al., 1999; Hilgetag et al., 2001). The question arises, however, as to whether those behavioral effects are due to neurophysiological changes that occur near the site of stimulation, remote from that site, or some combination of both (see Chapter 2).

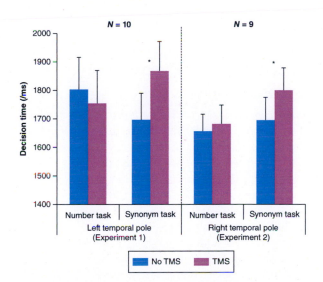

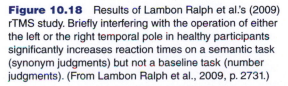

Figure 10.18   Results of Lambon Ralph et al.'s (2009) rTMS study. Briefly interfering with the operation of either the left or the right temporal pole in healthy participants significantly increases reaction times on a semantic task (synonym judgments) but not a baseline task (number judgments). (From Lambon Ralph et al., 2009, p. 2731.)

Summary

According to the Hub and Spoke Model, objects concepts of the kind typically encoded by concrete nouns are subserved not only by modality-specific brain systems for perception and action (the spokes), but also by an amodal integrative system that resides in the ATLs bilaterally (the hub). The latter system is believed to have several functions: It binds together the anatomically distributed modality-specific features that constitute the main content of object concepts, and it organizes those features in such a way that it is possible to distinguish between entities that fall within the scope of a given concept and entities that fall outside that scope. Evidence that the semantic hub is underpinned by the ATLs bilaterally comes from numerous sources. SD patients exhibit a progressive dissolution of object concepts that is closely linked with gradual atrophy of the ATLs. Studies using PET and distortion-corrected fMRI show that the ATLs are activated when healthy individuals process object concepts. And studies using rTMS show that temporarily disrupting the ATLs in healthy individuals reduces their capacity to process object concepts. Furthermore, studies using both distortion-corrected fMRI and rTMS suggest that the semantic hub may not depend equally on all aspects of the ATLs, but may instead rely especially on two particular sectors—the anterior fusiform gyrus, and the inferolateral cortex that encompasses the anterior parts of the inferior and middle temporal gyri.

Despite these theoretical and empirical advances, many questions remain unanswered. Are there hemispheric asymmetries in the functions of the ATLs, perhaps with the left-sided structure contributing more to linguistically than non-linguistically encoded concepts and the right-sided one having the opposite profile (Mion et al., 2010)? Do the two supposedly key regions within the ATLs—namely, the anterior fusiform region and the inferolateral region—carry out different kinds of semantic operations? What about other studies which suggest that more medial parts of the ATLs play important roles in integrative crossmodal conceptual processing (Bright et al., 2007; Taylor et al., 2006, 2009; Quiroga, 2012; Tyler et al., 2013b)? How can the findings that we have discussed be reconciled with independent data suggesting that the ATLs are associated more strongly with social concepts than with other semantic domains (for a review see Olson et al., 2013; see also Wong & Gallate, 2012)? Finally, how do the hub-like conceptual functions of the ATLs relate to the apparently similar hub-like conceptual functions of the left angular gyrus (Bonner et al., 2013; Seghier,

2013)? All of these questions, and more, will need to be addressed in future research.

Domains of Object Concepts

The types of object concepts that tend to be encoded by concrete nouns do not exist in isolation from each other, but instead are usually grouped together to form multilayered taxonomic hierarchies. For example, my furry friend Zlatik (Figure 10.19) belongs to the category of golden retrievers, golden retrievers belong to the category of dogs, dogs belong to the category of animals, animals belong to the category of living things, and living things belong to the category of physical objects. A great deal of research has explored how such categories or domains of object concepts are implemented in the brain. The modern era of this line of inquiry began in the mid-1980s with a series of groundbreaking neuropsychological studies by Elizabeth Warrington, Tim Shallice, and Rosaleen McCarthy (Warrington & McCarthy, 1983, 1987; Warrington & Shallice, 1984; see also Goodglass et al., 1966, 1986). They described several patients with semantic disorders that affected certain categories of object concepts more than others. Since those seminal papers were published, many other patients with remarkably selective semantic disorders have been documented, and a large literature, mostly reflecting the single-case

study approach, has blossomed around the general topic of so-called category-specific deficits.

The most common dissociation involves impaired knowledge of living things (especially animals and fruits/vegetables) in the context of relatively preserved knowledge of nonliving things (especially tools and other artifacts), but the opposite dissociation has also been reported. For example, in 2003 a detailed review of the clinical literature focused on 42 patients with category-specific deficits involving living things and 34 patients with category-specific deficits involving nonliving things (Capitani et al., 2003). It is important to bear in mind that the performance of some patients is strongly influenced by variables such as the visual complexity of pictures, the familiarity of concepts, or the frequency of words; however, many studies have been conducted in which these sorts of factors were carefully controlled, and double dissociations between conceptual categories have been reported using the same materials (e.g., Hillis & Caramazza, 1991). Thus, category-specific deficits are indubitably real phenomena. Not only are they fascinating in their own right, but they also have important implications for theories about the neural architecture of conceptual knowledge (for a recent review see Mahon & Caramazza, 2009). In the following discussion, we first take a close look at three major domains of selective semantic impairment—specifically, animal concepts, fruit/vegetable concepts, and tool concepts—and then we address the question of how such narrowly circumscribed disorders can be explained.

Three Major Domains of Selective Semantic Impairment

Animal Concepts

As mentioned above, the most frequently observed type of category-specific deficit involves the very large realm of concepts for living things. This realm can be decomposed, however, into two smaller domains, one for living things that are animate—what we ordinarily call animals—and the other for living things that are inanimate—especially plants such as fruits and vegetables. In the literature on category-specific deficits, one of the most intriguing findings is that some patients manifest semantic disorders that selectively or disproportionately affect one or the other of these two domains (for in-depth discussion see Capitani et al., 2009; Capitani & Laiacona, 2011; Gainotti, 2010, 2011; see also Box 10.3). This section focuses on patients with impairments that primarily affect animal concepts, and the next section focuses on patients with impairments that primarily affect fruit/vegetable concepts.

Figure 10.19 Zlatik, a golden retriever, together with the author.

Box 10.3   The Influences of Gender and Culture on Concepts for Animals and Fruits/Vegetables

People obviously differ in their familiarity with specific kinds of animals and fruits/vegetables, so it is important to ask whether these differences are large enough to significantly modulate the patterns of category-specific semantic disorders that have been documented in the neuropsychological literature. Two factors that warrant close attention are gender and culture.

Regarding gender, in a review of single-case studies, Gainotti (2010) found that 9/11 (80 percent) of patients with a prevalent impairment of animal concepts were women, and 20/21 (95 percent) of patients with a prevalent impairment of fruit/vegetable concepts were men. These striking gender differences cannot explain all of the data because neuroanatomical differences involving lesion site are also relevant; however, they are clearly too large to ignore. One possibility is that differential gender-related vulnerabilities to category-specific deficits are partly due to differential gender-related social roles, with men being more familiar with animals because they are more likely to hunt, and women being more familiar with fruits/vegetables because they are more likely to cook (Gainotti, 2010). As an extension of this approach, it is not inconceivable that the male advantage for animal knowledge and the female advantage for plant knowledge reflect somewhat different innate predispositions that evolved during the tens of thousands of years when our ancestors are believed to have maintained a sexual division of labor such that men contributed more to hunting and women contributed more to gathering (Laiacona et al., 2006).

Regarding culture, it is essential, but also rather unsettling, to realize that the vast majority of people living in post-industrial societies today suffer, often unwittingly, from a peculiar condition that Scott Atran and Douglas Medin (2008) diagnosed as "nature-deficit syndrome" in their book *The Native Mind and the Cultural Construction of Nature*. This syndrome consists of woefully impoverished understanding and appreciation of the flora and fauna that populate the natural world. In striking contrast, the level of folk-biological knowledge exhibited by modern, and presumably also ancestral, hunter-gatherer and small-scale agricultural societies is extremely rich. We're talking here about the difference between being able to name, say, 50 types of plants versus 500 types. What does this discrepancy imply about category-specific semantic disorders involving animals and fruits/vegetables? For one thing, it alerts us to the fact that most if not all of the disorders reported so far have been observed in patients who were already afflicted with a fairly generalized form of nature-deficit syndrome. In addition, it makes one wonder how such disorders would be manifested in members of traditional societies—that is, in people who ordinarily possess the high degree of folk-biological expertise that was almost certainly the norm for *Homo sapiens* until relatively recently. Would the disorders be significantly more debilitating, since they would wipe out significantly larger databases of knowledge? Would they fractionate into even more fine-grained disorders, reflecting even more elaborate neural groupings of object concepts? Would the gender-based differences described above still appear? These are only a few of the many questions that arise when the factor of culture is taken into account.

The vast majority of patients with semantic disorders restricted mainly to the animal domain have lesions in mid-to-anterior ventral and medial temporal regions, especially in the left hemisphere but sometimes also in the right (Gainotti, 2010, 2011). For some of these patients, the brain injury was due to stroke, but for many others it was due to **herpes simplex encephalitis (HSE)**, a viral infection that rapidly destroys portions of the temporal lobes bilaterally. In patients with HSE, the tissue loss typically includes the ATLs, which are also affected in patients with SD. These two populations, however, display a striking behavioral difference: Patients with HSE often have significantly worse knowledge of living things (particularly animals) than nonliving things, whereas patients with SD usually have impaired knowledge of both conceptual domains and only exhibit a slight trend toward worse understanding of the former than the latter (Lambon Ralph et al., 2003, 2007; Noppeney et al., 2007; but see also Libon et al., 2013). Although the cause of this discrepancy is not entirely clear, computational modeling suggests that it is partly due to differences in the underlying neuropathology. In short, the rapid necrosis in HSE may "distort" conceptual representations in a way that gives rise to category-specific deficits, whereas the

Herpes simplex encephalitis (HSE)   A viral infection that rapidly destroys portions of the temporal lobes bilaterally, including the medial sectors of the ATLs.   Some patients have worse knowledge of animals than of other conceptual domains.

gradual atrophy in SD may "dim" conceptual representations in a way that leads to across-the-board deficits (Lambon Ralph et al., 2007).

The selective impairment of animal concepts is exemplified by KC, a patient with HSE whose category-specific deficit was meticulously studied by Blundo et al. (2006). At the time of the investigation, KC was a 25-year-old, unemployed, right-handed woman with 11 years of education. Three years earlier, she had been hospitalized for fever and confusion, and an MRI conducted the day after admission revealed damage to the anterior ventral and medial temporal lobes bilaterally but with greater extension in the left hemisphere. Other symptoms confirmed a diagnosis of HSE, and treatment was initiated immediately. Six weeks later, she was discharged from the hospital, complaining only of memory problems and trouble concentrating. When Blundo et al. (2006) began to study her, they found that although she performed within normal limits on a battery of standardized verbal and nonverbal tasks, she had great difficulty with the animal items on the Boston Naming Test. This led to

a series of carefully designed experiments that gradually exposed, step by step, a severe semantic disorder that was clearly confined to the domain of animals.

The scores obtained by KC and by a group of healthy comparison subjects on a subset of the tasks are shown in Table 10.3. KC's category-specific deficit first emerged on the picture-naming task, which required her to provide the appropriate terms for 260 black-and-white line drawings of concrete entities. She successfully named 93 percent of the fruits/vegetables and 92 percent of the artifacts, but only 49 percent of the animals. When she could not name a particular animal, she tended to say, "I know it's an animal, but I don't know which one." Her errors could not be attributed to familiarity effects, since many of the animals that she could not name are quite common— e.g., a cat and a pig. She generated semantically related naming responses for only four items: (1) She called the ant a fly; (2) she called the eagle a parrot; (3) she called the fox a wolf; and (4) she called the pig a hippopotamus (note that they both have roundish shapes).

Table 10.3 Scores Obtained by Patient KC and by a Group of Healthy Comparison Subjects on a Subset of the Tasks Administered by Blundo et al. (2006)

Task	N	KC	Comparison Subjects
Picture naming:			
Animals	54	26 (49%)	50.4 (93%)
Fruits/vegetables	27	25 (93%)	25.2 (93%)
Artifacts	179	164 (92%)	172.8 (97%)
Oral definition:			
Animals	51	17 (33%)	51 (100%)
Non-animals	51	51 (100%)	51 (100%)
Drawing from memory:			
Animals	51	17 (33%)	51 (100%)
Non-animals	51	51 (100%)	51 (100%)
Decision test for visual features:			
Animals	38	19 (50%)	38 (100%)
Non-animals	38	38 (100%)	38 (100%)
Animal color recognition:			
Verbal presentation	47	23 (49%)	47 (100%)
Visual presentation (black-and-white)	47	33 (70%)	47 (100%)
Visual presentation (color)	47	35 (74%)	47 (100%)

Animal sound recognition:			
Verbal identification	8	2 (25%)	8.0 (100%)
Auditory mimicry identification	8	1 (13%)	6.2 (78%)
Verbal discrimination	8	2 (25%)	8.0 (100%)
Auditory mimicry discrimination	8	1 (13%)	7.1 (89%)
Naming to definition:			
Animals	20	0 (0%)	19.0 (95%)
Non-animals	20	16 (80%)	19.8 (99%)
Semantic judgments about animals:			
Habitat (verbal presentation)	51	33 (65%)	50.7 (99%)
Habitat (visual presentation)	51	31 (61%)	50.7 (99%)
Ferocity (verbal presentation)	51	42 (82%)	50.9 (99%)
Ferocity (visual presentation)	51	45 (88%)	50.9 (99%)
Edibility (verbal presentation)	51	38 (75%)	50.7 (99%)
Edibility (visual presentation)	51	36 (71%)	50.7 (99%)

On the next task, oral definition, the researchers probed KC's conceptual knowledge further by asking her the following questions about each of 102 objects (51 animals and 51 non-animals): "What is a(n) XXX—animal, fruit/vegetable, or artifact? Please describe it, including information about its size and structure." KC was able to indicate the superordinate category of all 102 objects, and her definitions of the 51 non-animals were rated by three independent judges as being quite good. For example, her definition of a bus was as follows: "It is a very large vehicle, there are places to let the people sit, there is the driver and a machine to stamp the tickets." In contrast, she only gave adequate definitions of 17 animals. Her definition of a mouse is representative of the kinds of errors she was prone to making: "It has four legs and a beautiful tail, it's one meter high and one meter long." On the subsequent task, drawing from memory, KC was asked to draw recognizable pictures of the same 102 objects that were used in the oral definition task. Once again, she performed well on the 51 non-animals, but she could only produce accurate depictions of the same 17 animals that she managed to describe accurately in the oral definition task (Figure 10.20). To explore KC's conceptual knowledge of the visual properties of objects in a more controlled manner, the researchers gave her the decision test for visual features. For each of 76 items (38 animals and 38 non-animals), she was asked a yes/no question about whether a certain type of object has a certain type of visual attribute—e.g., "Does a fly have wings?", "Does a bear have fins?", "Does a potato have seeds?", "Does a saw have a blade?" She answered all of the questions about non-animals flawlessly, but gave correct answers to only half of the questions about animals.

Several other results shed even more light on the precise nature of KC's category-specific deficit. Besides being impaired at retrieving conceptual knowledge about the shapes of animals, she was also impaired at retrieving conceptual knowledge about their colors and sounds. With respect to color features, she had great difficulty judging these attributes, regardless of whether she was probed with verbal questions, black-and-white drawings, or correctly vs. incorrectly colored drawings. And with respect to sound features, she had comparable difficulties across a variety of presentation formats. Finally, it is crucial to note that KC's selective semantic disorder for the animal domain encompassed associative/functional features. One task that revealed this aspect of her deficit was naming to definition. For each of 40 items (20 animals and 20 non-animals), the examiner gave her a definition consisting of primarily associative/functional features and asked her to provide the corresponding name—e.g., "It is an animal, it is a bug that stings, it sucks nectar from flowers, and it produces honey" (answer = bee); "It is an artifact, it is

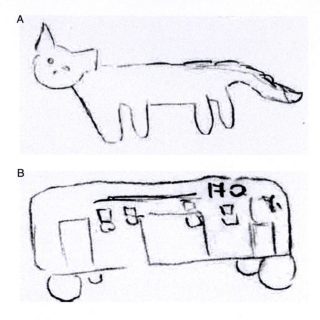

Figure 10.20 Drawings made by patient KC. (A) KC's drawing of a mouse looks more like a cat. (B) In contrast, KC's drawing of a bus contains many accurate details. (From Blundo et al., 2006, p. 1254.)

a wind musical instrument, it produces a melody, and it is used for military signals" (answer = trumpet). She produced the right response for 80 percent of the non-animals but for none of the animals. She simply said "I don't know" for 17 of the 20 animals, and her other errors were as follows: camel → horse; squirrel → snake; rabbit → pig. Another task that led to similar results was semantic judgments about animals. For each of 51 animals, KC was asked about its habitat, ferocity, and edibility. She performed poorly on all three features, regardless of whether the animals were presented verbally as names or visually as pictures.

Overall, the case of KC is an excellent illustration of how the conceptual domain of animals can be selectively and severely disrupted. Her category-specific deficit was displayed for different kinds of stimuli (verbal and nonverbal), for different kinds of responses (again, verbal and nonverbal), and for different kinds of semantic features (shape, color, sound, and associative/functional). In this particular patient, as in many others, the impairment was due to lesions in the anterior ventral and medial temporal lobes bilaterally, which suggests that normal knowledge of animals depends critically on these brain structures, or on some subset of them.

Fruit/Vegetable Concepts

As mentioned above, while some patients have semantic disorders that are restricted mainly to the domain of

animate living things, others have semantic disorders that are restricted mainly to the domain of inanimate living things, especially fruits and vegetables. Similarities as well as differences have been found in the lesion sites of these two kinds of patients (Gainotti, 2010, 2011). The chief similarity is that both kinds of patients often have damage to mid-to-anterior ventral and medial temporal regions. The chief differences involve both laterality and intra-hemispheric localization. Regarding laterality, patients with a predominant impairment of animal concepts are more likely to have bilateral than unilateral lesions, whereas those with a predominant impairment of fruit/vegetable concepts are more likely to have unilateral left-hemisphere lesions. Regarding intra-hemispheric localization, the former patients almost always have damage to very anterior temporal areas, whereas the latter ones more often have damage to relatively more posterior areas, including the mid-fusiform gyrus.

A representative case of selectively impaired conceptual knowledge of fruits and vegetables is patient RS, who was studied in depth by Samson and Pillon (2003). At the time of the investigation, RS was a 64-year-old, right-handed man who had worked as a civil engineer in an international company until he suffered a stroke in the territory of the left posterior cerebral artery. The damage included ventral and medial temporal areas (fusiform, parahippocampal, and hippocampal gyri), some medial occipital areas, and part of the thalamus. Standardized neuropsychological tests revealed primarily language deficits involving reading and oral word retrieval. The authors remarked that

> RS was aware of his word-finding problems and appeared to be particularly dismayed by difficulty in handling fruits, vegetables, and food items. He reported, for instance, that he never knew what he would find on his plate when ordering a meal in a restaurant.
>
> (p. 381)

This aspect of his disorder then became the principal focus of an intensive investigation.

RS's scores on a variety of semantic tasks are shown in Figure 10.21. As indicated on the left side of the figure, he was quite good at naming pictures of nonliving things, but quite bad at naming pictures of living things; moreover, within the realm of living things, he was worse on fruits/vegetables than animals, despite the fact that items in the former category are, on average, more familiar and less visually complex than those in the latter category. A similar pattern emerged when he was asked to name objects in response to verbal descriptions, only here the dissociation between fruits/vegetables and animals was even more pronounced. And when RS went on to perform several semantic tasks that did not require oral naming responses—specifically, word–picture matching, description from a word, description from a picture, and attribute verification—it became increasingly clear that his conceptual impairment was in fact confined to the domain of fruits and vegetables, since his scores for that category were consistently far below those for the categories of animals and nonliving things, whereas his scores for the latter two categories tended not to differ significantly from each other. Thus, the case of RS demonstrates how a category-specific deficit for fruit/vegetable concepts can develop as the result of a left posterior cerebral artery infarct.

Tool Concepts

Shifting to the semantic realm of nonliving things, a number of neuropsychological studies have shown that it can be selectively or disproportionately impaired, relative to the parallel semantic realm of living things. Most of these studies have focused on patients who display defective conceptual knowledge of tools. Compared to patients with a predominant impairment of animal concepts and/or fruit/vegetable concepts, patients with a predominant impairment of tool concepts tend to have lesions that spare the

ventral and medial temporal lobes and instead affect the posterior lateral temporal region (pMTG), inferior parietal region (aIPS/SMG), and/or inferior frontal region (vPMC), almost always in the left hemisphere (Tranel et al., 1997a; Gainotti, 2006; Mahon et al., 2007; Campanella et al., 2010).

To illustrate this type of category-specific deficit, we turn to one of the first carefully studied patients who manifested it, namely YOT, who was described in a classic paper by Warrington and McCarthy (1987). When this investigation was conducted, YOT was a 50-year-old, right-handed woman who had suffered a stroke that damaged the left temporoparietal region of her brain. Although she was alert and cooperative, her ability to produce and comprehend propositional speech was virtually absent, and her ability to process written language was also disrupted. Nevertheless, she did have a partially preserved capacity to understand single words, whether spoken or printed, and the researchers capitalized on this in their experiments.

The nature of YOT's semantic disorder was probed with a variety of tasks, three of which were as follows. First, she was given a task in which, for each item, she had to match a spoken word produced by the examiner with the correct picture in a five-choice array. Three categories of objects were used—animals, fruits/vegetables, and artifacts—and each array of pictures showed objects belonging to the same category. In addition, the same task was administered in two different sessions in

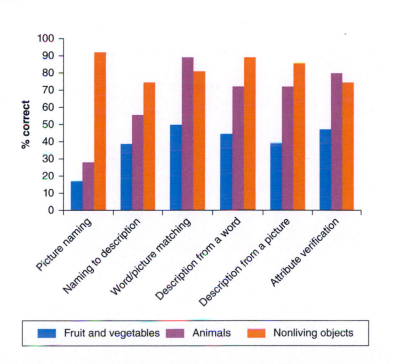

Fruit and vegetables   Animals   Nonliving objects

Figure 10.21 Scores obtained by patient RS on a subset of the tasks administered by Samson & Pillon et al. (2003). (From Samson & Pillon, 2003, p. 390.)

which the "response–stimulus interval" (RSI, i.e., the amount of time between the patient's response to one item and the examiner's presentation of the next item) varied between 2 seconds and 5 seconds. As shown in Table 10.4A, when the RSI was only 2 seconds long, YOT performed significantly worse on artifacts (63 percent) than on animals (85 percent) and fruits/vegetables (93 percent); however, when the RSI was increased to 5 seconds, her category-specific deficit for artifacts disappeared (90 percent). The investigators interpreted this as evidence that YOT "has difficulty in accessing semantic information rather than in the absolute loss or degradation of the semantic representation per se" (Warrington & McCarthy, 1987, p. 1280).

Next, YOT was given another task that involved spoken-word/picture matching, except this time the categories were fruits/vegetables and two subclasses of artifacts—large non-manipulable ones (i.e., non-tools) and small manipulable ones (i.e., tools). As shown in Table 10.4B, she performed fairly well on the fruits and vegetables (83 percent), which is consistent with the previous results. Somewhat surprisingly, however, she displayed a striking dissociation between the two subclasses of artifacts, with significantly better performance on the large non-manipulable ones (78 percent) than on the small manipulable ones (58 percent). These findings led the researchers to suppose that YOT's difficulty in retrieving conceptual knowledge might not apply to the entire domain of artifacts, but might instead apply more narrowly to just the subclass of tools.

To explore this possibility in greater detail, they gave YOT a task in which, for each item, she had to match a spoken word produced by the examiner with the corresponding written word in a six-choice array. A wide range of fine-grained semantic classes were used, including animals, fruits/vegetables, buildings, vehicles, kitchen utensils, office supplies, furniture, and body parts. Moreover, each array of written words designated objects belonging to the same class. It is also noteworthy that the task was administered on two different occasions separated by a day. As shown in Table 10.4C, YOT's average performance across the two testing sessions was relatively good for the two classes of living things (animals [88 percent] and fruits/vegetables [83 percent]), but it declined somewhat for the two classes of large outdoor artifacts (buildings [77 percent] and vehicles [66 percent]), and it declined much more for the three classes of small indoor artifacts (kitchen utensils [47 percent], office supplies [39 percent], and furniture [22 percent]). These findings support the hypothesis that YOT's knowledge retrieval deficit was significantly worse for tool-like than non-tool-like objects. In this context, it may initially seem rather puzzling that her lowest score was for the semantic class of body parts (19 percent). However, the patterning of body parts with tool-like objects has also been documented in several other neuropsychological studies (Capitani et al., 2003), and it may reflect the fact that, like tools, body parts are defined to some extent according to the semantic dimensions of function, action, and spatial relationships (Kemmerer & Tranel, 2008).

In summary, the case of YOT exemplifies a type of disorder in which the semantic representations of tools (and of closely related objects like body parts) are much harder to access than other kinds of concepts. Like many similar patients, YOT's lesion was in the left

Table 10.4   Scores Obtained by Patient YOT on a Subset of the Tasks Administered by Warrington and McCarthy (1987)

(A) Spoken-Word/Picture Matching

RSI	Animals	Fruits/Vegetables	Artifacts
2 s	85	93	63
5 s	93	93	90

(B) Spoken-Word/Picture Matching

Fruits/Vegetables	Large Non-manipulable Artifacts (i.e., Non-tools)	Small Manipulable Artifacts (i.e., Tools)
83	78	58

(C) Spoken-Word/Written-Word Matching

Category	1st Session	2nd Session	Mean
Animals	83	94	88
Fruits/vegetables	83	83	83
Buildings	72	83	77
Vehicles	61	72	66
Kitchen utensils	44	50	47
Office supplies	50	27	39
Furniture	33	11	22
Body parts	17	22	19

temporoparietal region, which suggests that this cortical territory may play an especially important role in subserving the meanings of tool nouns.

Explanatory Approaches

Ever since category-specific deficits became the focus of rigorous investigation in the mid-1980s, researchers have been trying to account for them in terms of a theory of brain organization that is consistent not only with all of the relevant neuropsychological data, but also with other sources of evidence about the neural substrates of object concepts. Several different explanatory approaches have been pursued, but as yet none of them has proven to be completely satisfactory (for a review see Mahon & Caramazza, 2009). The following discussion highlights some of the central issues in this area of inquiry, viewing them from the perspective of the Grounded Cognition Model and the more general Hub and Spoke Model.

As indicated earlier, both of these theories assume that most of the features constituting object concepts are neurally implemented in widely distributed modality-specific systems for perception and action. What distinguishes them is that the Hub and Spoke Model also assumes that these features are bound together and organized by an integrative system that resides in the ventral and inferolateral sectors of the ATLs bilaterally. Now, because this system—i.e., the semantic hub—is believed to be domain-general, its disruption would not be expected to give rise to category-specific deficits. This prediction has been largely confirmed by the following findings: First, SD patients almost always exhibit pervasive semantic impairments that affect concepts for living and nonliving things more or less equally (Lambon Ralph et al., 2003, 2007; Noppeney et al., 2007); and second, when rTMS is applied to the inferolateral sector of the ATLs in healthy individuals, similar, but much milder, across-the-board semantic impairments are temporarily induced (Pobric et al., 2010b). For these and other reasons, many researchers suspect that the proper explanation for category-specific deficits is likely to be found in the various spokes that radiate out from the hub—i.e., in the modality-specific systems for perception and action.

For many years, the most prominent proposal has been the **Differential Weighting Hypothesis**, which was originally formulated by Elizabeth Warrington and her colleagues (Warrington & Shallice, 1984; Warrington & McCarthy, 1987). The basic idea is that different domains of object concepts are characterized by different mixtures and "weightings" of modality-specific features,

and this causes them to gravitate, over the course of cognitive development, toward different networks of brain regions. As a consequence, the disruption of a particular region that is functionally more important for one conceptual domain than for others may be sufficient to generate a category-specific deficit.

An attempt to illustrate the major aspects of the Differential Weighting Hypothesis is provided in Figure 10.22, which comes from Crutch and Warrington (2003). As the diagram indicates, different domains of object concepts, including those considered above (i.e., animals, fruits/vegetables, and tools), are thought to vary with respect to how much they depend on certain sensory and motor channels of information. Empirical support for these assumptions comes from numerous experiments in which normal subjects have rated the relative importance of certain types of features for certain types of concepts (e.g., Tranel et al., 1997b; Vigliocco et al., 2004; Vinson & Vigliocco, 2008; Gainotti et al., 2009, 2013; Hoffman & Lambon Ralph, 2013).

Visual properties enter into most kinds of long-term object representations, but shape features are especially critical for animal concepts, in part because many animals have very similar forms (e.g., donkeys, horses, and cows) and hence require fine-grained shape analysis in order to be identified. Because such detailed shape analysis is known to rely on the mid-to-anterior portions of the ventral and medial temporal lobes, it is understandable that damage to those regions can lead to a category-specific deficit for animal concepts.

Turning to fruit/vegetable concepts, although they too depend on shape features, color features are also very important (e.g., lemons vs. limes, raspberries vs. blackberries), and of course gustatory and olfactory features are quite significant as well (note that the lack of a connection between the olfactory channel and the fruit/vegetable domain in Figure 10.22 was just an oversight on the part of Crutch and Warrington, 2003). Based on these factors, it is not surprising that the vast majority of patients with selectively or disproportionately impaired knowledge of the fruit/vegetable domain have ventral temporal lesions.

> **Differential Weighting Hypothesis**   Different domains of object concepts are characterized by different mixtures and "weightings" of modality-specific features, and this causes them to gravitate, over the course of cognitive development, toward different networks of brain regions.   As a consequence, disrupting a particular region that is functionally more important for one conceptual domain than for others may be sufficient to generate a category-specific deficit.

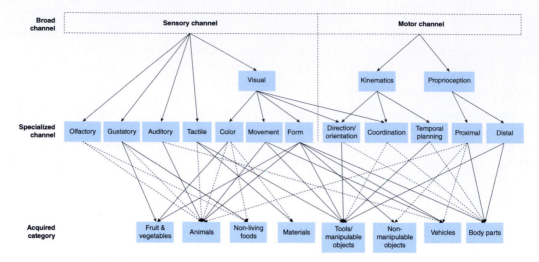

Figure 10.22 An illustration of some of the major aspects of the Differential Weighting Hypothesis. (From Crutch & Warrington, 2003, p. 369.)

Finally, regarding tool concepts, visual motion patterns are major features (e.g., the characteristic oscillations of a hammer), as are the motor programs that specify how such objects should be manipulated in order to carry out their appropriate functions. It therefore makes sense that semantic disorders involving the tool domain are almost always associated with damage to the left pMTG, aIPS/SMG, and/or vPMC (see also Figure 10.5).

The Differential Weighting Hypothesis clearly has many virtues, but it also suffers from several shortcomings. First, if the proposal were true, one would expect that patients with a deficit for a particular conceptual domain would have markedly worse knowledge of features that are weighted heavily for that domain than of features that are not. A number of case studies,

however, have found this prediction to be invalid. Consider, for example, patient KC, who, as discussed above, was shown by Blundo et al. (2006) to have a category-specific deficit for animal concepts. According to the hypothesis, because animal concepts are assumed to depend more on visual shape features than on nonvisual associative/functional features, KC's knowledge of the former should be more disrupted than her knowledge of the latter. But this turned out to be false, since she was in fact equally impaired on both kinds of features. Moreover, several other patients with deficits primarily for living things have been shown to have equally defective knowledge of perceptual and nonperceptual features of the affected concepts (Figure 10.23). Hence their semantic problems cannot be reduced completely to visual disturbances.

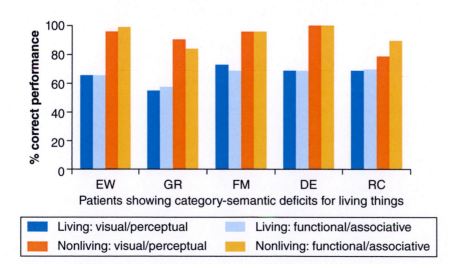

Figure 10.23 Many patients with category-specific deficits for living things have impairments for all types of knowledge—visual/perceptual as well as functional/associative—about the affected concepts. Data for EW from Caramazza & Shelton (1998); data for GR and FM from Laiacona et al. (1993); data for DB from Lambon Ralph et al., 1998; and data for RC from Moss et al. (1998). (From Mahon & Caramazza, 2009, p. 53.)

Second, if a sensory or motor channel is deemed to be especially important for a particular conceptual category, it should probably be impaired in patients with a deficit for that category. But this prediction is also incorrect. An exemplary case is patient RC, who was shown by Samson and Pillon (2003) to have a category-specific deficit for fruit/vegetable concepts. Based on the assumption that color information plays a major role in those concepts, one would anticipate that RS's color knowledge would be disrupted, but in fact it was spared.

Finally, inverting the previous idea yields yet another interesting prediction of the Differential Weighting Hypothesis. If a sensory or motor channel is deemed to be especially important for a particular conceptual category, damage to it should probably lead to a deficit for that category. Once again, however, the data suggest otherwise. For example, as indicated earlier, some apraxic patients who can no longer use tools correctly can nevertheless still name them correctly. This dissociation entails that even though manipulation knowledge may be weighted heavily for tool concepts, it does not always need to be retrieved in order to process those concepts.

Another approach to explaining category-specific deficits is the **Distributed Domain-Specific Hypothesis**, advocated by Alfonso Caramazza and Bradford Z. Mahon (Caramazza & Mahon, 2003, 2006; Mahon & Caramazza, 2003, 2008, 2009, 2011; Mahon, in press). This hypothesis makes the following two claims. First, the major factor driving the neural architecture of object concepts is domain, with the greatest constraints being innately programmed to apply to the three domains with the most evolutionarily relevant histories for human beings, these being the same ones discussed above: animals, which can be predators or prey; fruits/vegetables, which can be used for food and medicine; and tools, which can be used to transform the environment. Second, the factor of domain shapes the neural architecture of object concepts at two separate levels of representation: at the level of widely distributed modality-specific systems for perception and action, along the lines shown in Figure 10.5; and at a more abstract level

that is restricted exclusively to conceptual knowledge and that, unlike the semantic hub in the Hub and Spoke Model, is partitioned according to category, thereby allowing for the possibility of category-specific deficits.

Interestingly, there is some impressive neuropsychological support for the proposal that the neural networks for acquiring certain domains of object concepts have genetic foundations derived from natural selection. The key data come from a very unusual patient whose case name is Adam (Farah & Rabinowitz, 2003). He suffered bilateral occipital and occipitotemporal lesions at approximately one day of age, and when his knowledge of object concepts was investigated at the age of 16, he exhibited a striking dissociation, with significantly impaired understanding of living things (animals as well as fruits/vegetables), but normal understanding of nonliving things (especially tools). Moreover, his deficit was manifested for both perceptual and nonperceptual features of living things, indicating that it could not be reduced to, say, just a visual problem (Figure 10.24). As the researchers pointed out, these findings imply that

> prior to any experience with living and nonliving things, we are destined to represent our knowledge of living and nonliving things with distinct neural substrates. This in turn implies that the distinction between living and nonliving things, and the anatomical localization of knowledge of living things, are specified in the human genome.
>
> (p. 408)

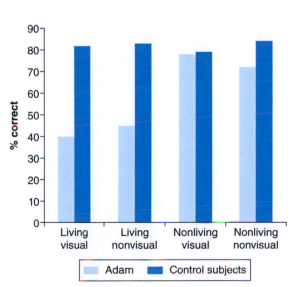

Distributed Domain-Specific Hypothesis The major factor driving the neural architecture of object concepts is domain, with the three most evolutionarily relevant domains—animals, fruits/ vegetables, and tools—being innately programmed. The factor of domain shapes the neural architecture of object concepts not only at the level of cortically distributed modality-specific systems for perception and action, but also at a more abstract level that is exclusively conceptual and that, unlike the semantic hub in the Hub and Spoke Model, is differentiated by category, thereby allowing for the possibility of category-specific deficits.

Figure 10.24 Scores obtained by Adam and control subjects on a subset of the tasks administered by Farah and Rabinowitz (2003). (From Farah & Rabinowitz, 2003, p. 404.)

It is also noteworthy that, unlike the Differential Weighting Hypothesis, the Distributed Domain-Specific Hypothesis is formulated in such a manner that it can explain why many patients with category-specific deficits—such as KC, Adam, and the patients in Figure 10.23—have impaired knowledge of perceptual as well as nonperceptual features of concepts in the affected domain(s). Basically, the reason is that the disorders are assumed to occur at a purely semantic level of representation that is more abstract than the level of modality-specific systems, and that is also partitioned in category-specific ways. This account is internally coherent, in part because it takes category-specific deficits more or less at face value—that is, as reflections of genuinely category-specific assortments of object concepts in the brain. Despite its strengths, however, it also has limitations. Perhaps the most serious one is that, apart from the neuropsychological data that the hypothesis is meant to explain, there is not much evidence for a level of representation that has the proposed properties—namely, both abstractness and category-based divisions. It is important to recognize that if such a level did exist, it would constitute a third representational system, in addition to the two posited by the Hub and Spoke Model. Are the neural substrates of object concepts really that complex? It is still too soon to tell. As mentioned above, a completely adequate theory of the nature of category-specific deficits is not yet within our grasp.

Summary

Whereas patients with SD almost invariably display comprehensive impairments for all kinds of object concepts, patients with other types and sites of brain damage sometimes exhibit impairments that selectively or disproportionately affect certain domains of object concepts. In such cases, the ability to produce and comprehend words is most severely disrupted for just those concrete nouns that happen to encode the affected concepts. Category-specific deficits have been reported for three major conceptual domains: animals, fruits/vegetables, and tools. Patients with a prevalent impairment of animal concepts tend to have bilateral damage to the ventral and medial sectors of the mid-to-anterior temporal lobes. Patients with a prevalent impairment of fruit/vegetable concepts tend to have unilateral left-hemisphere damage to relatively more posterior areas, including the mid-fusiform gyrus. And patients with a prevalent impairment of tool concepts tend to have unilateral left-hemisphere damage to the posterior lateral temporal region (pMTG), inferior parietal region (aIPS/SMG), and/or inferior frontal region (vPMC).

Two attempts to explain these findings, and to integrate them with other data about the neural substrates of object concepts, are as follows. First, the Differential Weighting Hypothesis holds that different conceptual domains have different patterns of regionalization in the brain because they depend on different combinations and rankings of modality-specific sensory and motor features. According to this account, a particular type of category-specific deficit could result from a lesion that primarily affected the type of modality-specific information that is weighted most heavily for the given category. Second, the Distributed Domain-Specific Hypothesis maintains that different conceptual domains are innately programmed to have segregated neural implementations not only at the level of modality-specific systems for perception and action, but also at a more abstract level of pure semantic structure. According to this account, a particular type of category-specific deficit would most likely result from damage to the corresponding category-specific component(s) of the system that is restricted exclusively to representing conceptual knowledge. While both of these explanatory approaches have many strengths, they also suffer from several shortcomings, and further research is needed in order to fully accommodate all of the available data.

Summary and Key Points

- According to the Amodal Symbolic Model, concepts consist of abstract symbols that are represented and processed in a semantic system completely separate from modality-specific systems for perception and action. This framework is popular in some branches of cognitive psychology, but it has not been well-supported by neuroscience.
- According to the Grounded Cognition Model, concepts are anchored in modality-specific systems, such that understanding word meanings involves activating high-level perceptual and motor representations. Research guided by this framework supports the following proposals about the neural substrates of the meanings of object nouns:

- ○ Color features may be stored in the same part of the ventral temporal cortex that underlies high-level color perception, especially area V4α.
- ○ Shape features may be stored in the same part of the ventral temporal cortex that underlies high-level shape perception. More specifically, the shape features of animal concepts may depend mainly on the lateral portion of the mid-fusiform gyrus, whereas the shape features of tool concepts may depend mainly on the medial portion of the mid-fusiform gyrus.
- ○ Motion features may be stored in the same part of the posterolateral temporal cortex that underlies high-level motion perception. More specifically, the motion features of animal concepts may depend mainly on the pSTS, whereas the motion features of tool concepts may depend mainly on the pMTG.
- ○ Motor features may be stored in the same parts of the parietal and frontal cortices that underlie high-level motor programming, especially the aIPS/SMG and the vPMC.
- ○ Auditory features may be stored in the same part of the posterior superior/middle temporal cortex that underlies high-level auditory perception.
- ○ Olfactory and gustatory features may be stored in the same part of the orbitofrontal cortex that underlies high-level olfactory and gustatory perception.

- The Hub and Spoke Model combines aspects of the Grounded Cognition Model and the Amodal Symbolic Model. It maintains that concepts are based not only on modality-specific brain systems for perception and action, but also on a modality-invariant integrative device—the semantic hub—in the anterior temporal lobes (ATLs).
- The semantic hub has several functions:

  - ○ It binds together the anatomically distributed modality-specific features that constitute the main content of object concepts.
  - ○ It organizes those features in such a way that it is possible to distinguish between objects that fall within the scope of a given concept and objects that fall outside that scope.

- Evidence that the semantic hub is underpinned by the ATLs bilaterally comes from several sources:

  - ○ SD patients exhibit a progressive dissolution of object concepts that is closely linked with gradual atrophy of the ATLs.
  - ○ Studies using fMRI show that the ATLs are activated when healthy individuals process object concepts.
  - ○ Studies using rTMS show that temporarily disrupting the ATLs in healthy individuals reduces their capacity to process object concepts.
  - ○ Studies using both fMRI and rTMS suggest that the semantic hub may not depend equally on all aspects of the ATLs, but may instead rely especially on two particular sectors—the anterior fusiform gyrus, and the inferolateral cortex that encompasses the anterior parts of the inferior and middle temporal gyri.

- Brain damage can selectively or disproportionately impair certain domains of object concepts. Such category-specific deficits tend to be linked with distinctive lesion sites:

  - ○ Category-specific deficits for animal concepts often result from bilateral damage to the ventral and medial sectors of the mid-to-anterior temporal lobes.
  - ○ Category-specific deficits for fruit/vegetable concepts often result from unilateral left-hemisphere damage to relatively more posterior areas, including the mid-fusiform gyrus.
  - ○ Category-specific deficits for tool concepts often result from unilateral left-hemisphere damage to the posterior lateral temporal region (pMTG), inferior parietal region (aIPS/SMG), and/or inferior frontal region (vPMC).

- Two approaches to explaining category-specific deficits are as follows:

  - ○ According to the Differential Weighting Hypothesis, different domains of object concepts are characterized by different mixtures and "weightings" of modality-specific features, and this causes them to gravitate, over the course of cognitive development, toward different networks of brain regions. Thus, disrupting a particular region that is functionally more important for one conceptual domain than for others may be sufficient to generate a category-specific deficit.
  - ○ According to the Distributed Domain-Specific Hypothesis, different conceptual domains are innately programmed to have segregated neural implementations not only at the level of modality-specific systems for perception and action, but also at a more abstract level of pure semantic structure. Thus, a particular type of category-specific deficit would most likely result from damage to the corresponding category-specific component of the system that is restricted exclusively to representing conceptual knowledge.
  - ○ Neither approach provides a completely satisfactory account of the available data.

Recommended Reading

- Martin, A. (2007). The representation of object concepts in the brain. *Annual Review of Psychology, 58,* 25–45. A survey of fMRI data regarding the neural substrates of object concepts, from the perspective of the Grounded Cognition Model.
- Kiefer, M., & Pulvermüller, F. (2012). Conceptual representations in mind and brain: Theoretical developments, current evidence and future directions. *Cortex, 48,* 805–825. A broad discussion of research on semantic knowledge, based largely on the Grounded Cognition Model.
- Lambon Ralph, M.A. (2014). Neurocognitive insights on conceptual knowledge and its breakdown. *Philosophical Transactions of the Royal Society, B, Biological Sciences, 369,* 20120392. A general overview of the Hub and Spoke Model for a wide audience.
- Gainotti, G. (2006). Anatomical, functional, and cognitive determinants of semantic memory disorders. *Neuroscience and Biobehavioral Reviews, 30,* 577–594. A survey of neuropsychological data regarding category-specific deficits, with emphasis on the Differential Weighting Hypothesis.
- Mahon, B.Z., & Caramazza, A. (2009). Concepts and categories: A cognitive neuropsychological perspective. *Annual Review of Psychology, 60,* 27–51. A detailed discussion of the theoretical implications of category-specific deficits, with careful consideration of the Differential Weighting Hypothesis, the Distributed Domain-Specific Hypothesis, and other approaches.

Action Verbs

Introduction

In a beguiling collection of poetic vignettes called *Einstein's Dreams*, the physicist and novelist Alan Lightman (1993) describes a series of possible worlds that Albert Einstein might have imagined when he was creating his theory of relativity in 1905. According to one of these stories, there is a place, sought after by lovers and parents clinging to their children, where time stands still:

> Raindrops hang motionless in the air. Pendulums of clocks float mid-swing. Dogs raise their muzzles in silent howls. Pedestrians are frozen on the dusty streets, their legs cocked as if held by strings. The aromas of dates, mangoes, coriander, cumin are suspended in space.
>
> As a traveler approaches this place from any direction, he moves more and more slowly. His heartbeats grow farther apart, his breathing slackens, his temperature drops, his thoughts diminish, until he reaches the dead center and stops. For this is the center of time.
>
> (pp. 53–54)

This imaginary world is, of course, radically different from the real world that we inhabit, because in our world time flows relentlessly forward, and all of our actions unfold in its medium. To accommodate the pivotal role that bodily movement plays in human life, languages all around the globe provide their speakers with a special inventory of words—namely, verbs—that are devoted to encoding many different kinds of events (Croft, 2012). And as Healy and Miller (1970, p. 372) observed, "To use a theatrical metaphor, the main verb of a sentence defines the plot; the subject merely indicates one of the actors." In English there are well over 3,000 verbs that fall into roughly 50 classes and 200 subclasses, most of which cover a broad array of semantic fields in the enormous conceptual realm of action (Levin, 1993): There are verbs of body-internal motion, like *fidget, twitch, squirm, wiggle, sway, rock*; verbs of assuming a position, like *crouch, kneel, stoop, lean, slump, sprawl*; verbs of gesturing with specific body parts, like *nod, shrug, point, wave, squint, wink*; verbs of ingesting, like *chew, chomp, munch, nibble, gobble, devour*; verbs of exerting a force, like *press, push, shove, pull, tug, yank*; and so forth.

This chapter focuses on how the kinds of action concepts typically encoded by verbs are represented and organized in the brain. Although this topic has not received as much attention as the neural substrates of object concepts, it has been attracting increasing interest in recent years, and the relevant literature has been rapidly growing (for reviews see Pulvermüller, 2005, 2008; Chatterjee, 2008; Kemmerer & Gonzalez Castillo, 2010; Rueschemeyer & Bekkering, 2012). The following survey is broken down into three main sections that parallel those of the previous chapter with regard to both the headings and, except for the third section, the guiding theoretical frameworks. Picking up on the "embodiment" theme of the Grounded Cognition Model, the first section deals with the hypothesis that the modality-specific aspects of action concepts—in particular, the semantic features that involve visual motion patterns and motor specifications—depend on the same modality-specific neural systems that underlie high-level visual perception and action preparation. Then, continuing with the central ideas of the Hub and Spoke Model, the second section concentrates on the question of whether the various components of action concepts are bound together and structured by an integrative device in the anterior temporal lobes. Finally, the third section considers some of the factors that may influence how the brain groups action concepts together to form semantically coherent classes like those mentioned above.

Before commencing, it is worthwhile to briefly acknowledge a few points about cross-linguistic variation, just as we did at the outset of the previous chapter. Although there appear to be some universal properties of verb meaning (Van Valin, 2006), there is also a great deal of diversity (e.g., Levinson & Wilkins, 2006; Majid et al., 2008; Malt et al., 2008). This is nicely illustrated by the semantic field of "manner of motion." In English this multidimensional psychological space is intricately partitioned into discrete categories by well over 100 verbs that fall into specialized subclasses such as the following: rapid motion (e.g., *dash, rush, scramble, sprint*), leisurely motion (e.g., *amble, drift, stroll, mosey*), furtive motion (e.g., *creep, sneak, tiptoe, sidle*), smooth motion (e.g., *glide, slide, slink, slip*), awkward motion (e.g., *limp, lurch, stagger, stumble*), manners of walking (e.g., *strut, sashay, trudge, plod*), manners of jumping (e.g., *bound, hop, leap, spring*), and many others (Levin, 1993; Slobin, 2000). Such highly specialized verbs are not just dictionary entries, but are actively employed by speakers in a variety of contexts, including oral narrative, spontaneous conversation, creative writing, naming videoclips of motion events, and speeded fluency, which involves listing as many motion verbs as possible in one minute (Slobin, 2003). At the other end of the continuum, however, there are languages (e.g., Spanish, French, Turkish, and Hebrew) that make far fewer distinctions in this semantic field. For example, *creep, glide, slide, slip,* and *slither* are all translated into Spanish as *escabullirse,* and *bound, hop, jump, leap,* and *spring* are all translated into French as *bondir.* Additional cross-linguistic diversity can be found for several other domains of action concepts, especially if one casts a wide net and takes into account languages that routinely employ constructions that don't exist in English, such as serial verbs (Aikhenvald & Dixon, 2006) and coverbs (Wilson, 1999; McGregor, 2002; Schultze-Berndt, 2006). Unfortunately, however, such variation has not yet had much influence on the cognitive neuroscience of action concepts, and for this reason we will not discuss it further here, but will simply treat it as a topic worthy of greater attention down the line.

Perceptual and Motor Features of Action Concepts

As indicated in Chapter 10, the Grounded Cognition Model maintains that concepts are anchored in modality-specific systems for perception and action, such

that understanding word meanings involves activating high-level sensory and motor representations in a lexically driven fashion (see Figure 10.1). This theoretical framework has been used to investigate the neural substrates of not only object concepts, but also action concepts. As with object concepts, action concepts are assumed to not have a single locus in the brain, but to consist instead of long-term records of sensory and motor patterns that are stored in different cortical areas depending on their content. Consider, for example, a relatively simple verb like *hop,* as in *The boy hopped off the schoolbus.* According to the Grounded Cognition Model, the visual-semantic records that specify how hopping events usually appear may be stored in the same posterolateral temporal areas that contribute to the recognition of such movements, and the motor-semantic records that specify how hopping events are usually performed may be stored in the same parietal and frontal areas that contribute to the preparation of such movements. When the verb *hop* is understood, these anatomically scattered fragments of information are assumed to be activated simultaneously, so that the most common sensory and motor elements of the designated type of action are momentarily reconstructed. The theory claims that this simulation process normally operates in a fairly automatic, implicit manner, but on some occasions it may induce conscious imagery. Such imagery cannot easily be said, however, to actually constitute comprehension; instead, it appears to occur afterward as a way of fleshing out the given concept once it has been accessed. As shown below, a number of experimental studies have begun to test these proposals about the implementation of action concepts in the brain. Many of the findings are supportive, but others are more challenging and hence generate new questions for future research.

Visual Features

In the discussion of the motion features of object concepts in Chapter 10, we noted that the perceptual processing of visual motion patterns extends from area MT+ into several higher-order regions of the posterolateral temporal cortex (PLTC). The posterior superior temporal sulcus (pSTS) responds preferentially to the movements of living creatures, especially people, whereas the posterior middle temporal gyrus (pMTG) is somewhat more sensitive to the movements of inanimate entities, such as tools that are wielded by people (see Figure 10.5 and Figure 11.1; for reviews see Beauchamp & Martin, 2007; Grosbras et al., 2012; Saygin, 2012; see also van Kemenade representative studies involving verbs see Kable et al., 2002, 2005; Noppeney et al., 2005; Tranel et al., 2005; Kemmerer et al., 2008; Pirog Revill et al., 2008; Pulvermüller et al., 2009b; Lin et al., 2011; and for studies comparing action with non-action sentences see Wallentin et al., 2005, 2011; Chen et al., 2008; Deen & McCarthy, 2010; Saygin et al., 2010b; Humphreys et al., 2013).

To take a specific example, Kemmerer et al. (2008) used fMRI to investigate the neural substrates of the following five classes of verbs, as defined by Levin (1993): running verbs (e.g., *run, jog, sprint*), hitting verbs (e.g., *hit, poke, jab*), cutting verbs (e.g., *cut, slice, hack*), speaking verbs (e.g., *yell, shout, sing*), and change of state verbs (e.g., *shatter, smash, snap*). The main task involved making fine-grained discriminations among triads of verbs within each class—for instance, determining that *limp* is more like *trudge* than *stroll*—and the baseline task involved making similarity judgments about strings of meaningless characters in a peculiar font called Wingdings. Relative to the baseline condition, the five verb classes elicited widely distributed patterns of brain activity that differed from each other in many theoretically interesting ways. For present purposes, however, what is most relevant is that all of them recruited the left PLTC, as depicted in Figure 11.2. Comparable results were obtained in the other studies cited above, and in the context of the Grounded Cognition Model such findings could be interpreted as reflecting the automatic, implicit evocation of the distinctive types of visual motion patterns encoded by particular verbs.

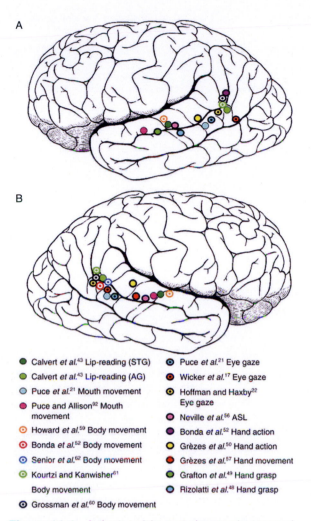

Figure 11.1 Activation of the posterior superior temporal sulcus (pSTS) region in (A) the left hemisphere and (B) the right hemisphere during the observation of biological motion. See the original source for the references cited in the color key. (From Allison et al., 2000, p. 269.)

et al., 2012; Gilaie-Dotan et al., 2013). Because the meanings of many action verbs specify how certain kinds of human movements typically appear, the Grounded Cognition Model predicts that those visual-semantic features should depend on the PLTC, especially the pSTS. Evidence for this view comes from functional neuroimaging studies involving healthy subjects as well as neuropsychological studies involving brain-damaged patients.

A number of PET and fMRI studies have shown that the PLTC is significantly engaged, more strongly in the left than the right hemisphere, when people process the meanings of action verbs, relative to when they perform various baseline tasks (for a review see Gennari, 2012; for a meta-analysis see Watson et al., 2013; for

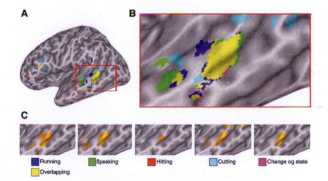
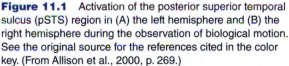

Figure 11.2 Results of Kemmerer et al.'s (2008) fMRI study of verb processing. Relative to a baseline condition, semantic similarity judgments involving five classes of verbs—running, speaking, hitting, cutting, and change of state—engaged the left posterolateral temporal cortex (PLTC). (A) Activations rendered on an inflated brain. (B) Enlargement of the box in (A). (C) Activations for each separate verb class. Yellow patches signify areas of overlapping activation for two or more verb classes. (From Kemmerer et al., 2008, p. 29.)

Table 11.1   Scores Obtained by Two Chronic Stroke Patients on Six Tasks Probing Conceptual Knowledge of Actions in Various Verbal and Nonverbal Ways

Task	Case 1808		Case 1172	
	% Correct	z Score	% Correct	z Score
Naming	57	–5.6	33	–10.4
Word–picture matching	78	–3.1	72	–4.4
Word attribute	77	–4.9	79	–4.4
Word comparison	64	–3.0	59	–3.7
Picture attribute	78	–2.9	82	–2.0
Picture comparison	21	–7.5	25	–7.1
Average	62.5	–4.5	58.3	–5.3

Adapted from Kemmerer et al. (2012, p. 831).

Case 1808 had a lesion in the left PLTC and underlying white matter (see Figure 11.3), whereas case 1172 had a lesion in the left inferior frontoparietal territory (see Figure 11.13).

z scores of –2.0 or lower are considered to be significantly below normal.

While such an interpretation is certainly plausible, an alternative possibility is that the left PLTC activity is merely the neural signature of post-comprehension visual imagery. On this view, the participants in Kemmerer et al.'s (2008) study may have performed each trial in two stages: First, they rapidly retrieved the meanings of the three verbs from some brain region(s) outside the left PLTC, and then they deliberately generated explicit, conscious "mental movies" of the designated types of actions in the left PLTC in order to help them make the required discriminations. From this perspective, the left PLTC would serve an optional rather than a necessary function in verb comprehension.

Evidence against this account comes from several neuropsychological studies which suggest that the left PLTC plays a causal role in understanding the kinds of action concepts that are typically encoded by verbs (Aggujaro et al., 2006; Tranel et al., 2003b, 2008; Kemmerer et al., 2012). In one of the largest investigations of this topic to date, Kemmerer et al. (2012) administered the following battery of six standardized tasks to 226 brain-damaged patients with widely distributed lesions in the left and right hemispheres:

- *Naming* (N = 100 items): For each item, the participant is shown a photograph of an action, and the task is to orally name each one with a specific verb.
- *Word–picture matching* (N = 69 items): For each item, the participant is shown a printed verb together with two photographs of actions, and the task is to determine which action the verb describes.
- *Word attribute* (N = 62 items): For each item, the participant is shown two printed verbs, and the task is to indicate which one designates a type of action that satisfies a certain value for a single attribute (e.g., which one would be more tiring).
- *Word comparison* (N = 44 items): For each item, the participant is shown three printed verbs, and the task is to determine which one is most different in meaning from the other two.
- *Picture attribute* (N = 72 items): This task is analogous to the word attribute task, but the stimuli are photographs of actions instead of verbs.
- *Picture comparison* (N = 24 items): This task is analogous to the word comparison task, but the stimuli are photographs of actions instead of verbs.

Of the 226 patients who were studied, 61 failed one or more of the six tasks. Among the few patients who failed the entire battery was a man identified as case 1808. Not only did he average only 62.5 percent correct (Table 11.1), but his lesion was highly focal, being confined to the left PLTC and underlying white matter (Figure 11.3). In addition, the same region was implicated in a series of group analyses that explored lesion–deficit relationships in the 147 patients for whom brain scans were available. On a task-by-task basis, brain maps were created that indicated, at each voxel, the likelihood of a lesion being significantly associated with impaired

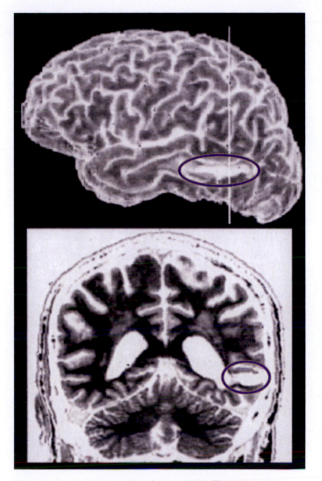

Figure 11.3 Lesion site of case 1808. The damage, highlighted in purple, is restricted to the posterior portion of the left middle temporal gyrus and underlying white matter. The vertical line in the upper panel indicates the plane of the coronal section shown below, where the left hemisphere is depicted on the right side. (Adapted from Tranel et al., 2003b, p. 421.)

vs. unimpaired performance. (More technically, the statistical analyses calculated, at each voxel, the difference between the following two values: first, the number of patients with a lesion at that voxel and a deficit (N_{LD}) among all the patients with a deficit (N_D); and second, the number of patients with a lesion at that voxel and no deficit (N_{LnD}) among all the patients with no deficit (N_{nD}).) As shown by the yellow circles in Figure 11.4, these analyses yielded significant results in, among other regions, the left PLTC and underlying white matter for five of the six tasks—specifically, naming, word attribute, word comparison, picture attribute, and picture comparison. Overall, these findings from both the single case of 1808 and the larger group of patients constitute

strong evidence that the left PLTC plays an essential role in representing action concepts. Moreover, they are consistent with the hypothesis that this cortical region subserves specifically the visual motion features of those concepts.

This last claim, however, regarding a putative link between the left PLTC and the visual motion features of action concepts, has been challenged by two fMRI studies by Marina Bedny and her colleagues. In the first study, Bedny et al. (2008) measured subjects' brain activity while they made semantic similarity judgments about auditorily presented word pairs. The words consisted of three categories of verbs—high motion (e.g., *to kick*), medium motion (e.g., *to bleed*), and low motion (e.g., *to think*)—as well as three corresponding categories of nouns—high motion (e.g., *the tiger*), medium motion (e.g., *the drill*), and low motion (e.g., *the rock*)—with the different degrees of motion for each category deriving from an independent rating experiment. The researchers found that, relative to a baseline condition involving the perception of backward speech, the BOLD signals in the left PLTC were equally high for the three categories of verbs and equally low for the three categories of nouns. They interpreted these results as evidence that, contrary to the assumptions of the Grounded Cognition Model, the left PLTC may not represent specifically the visual motion features of action concepts, but may instead represent more abstract kinds of semantic and/or grammatical features that tend to be associated more strongly with verbs than nouns. Among the possibilities are generalized event participant roles like agent, experiencer, instrument, patient, etc., as discussed further below (see the section "Domains of Action Concepts").

In the second study, Bedny et al. (2012) followed up on their first study by administering the same task to both sighted and congenitally blind subjects. Remarkably enough, they obtained very similar results for the two groups of subjects. Multiple analyses indicated that the left PLTC responded significantly more to verbs than nouns, regardless of the amount of motion conveyed by the words, and, even more strikingly, regardless of whether the subjects were sighted or blind. According to Bedny et al. (2012), the data bolster the view that the left PLTC represents abstract rather than visual aspects of action concepts.

Problems still remain, however, because the results of Bedny et al.'s studies must somehow be reconciled with the results of two other lines of investigation. First of all, contradicting Bedny et al.'s findings and

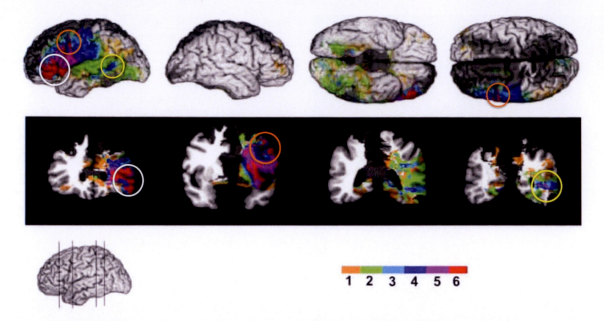

Figure 11.4 Results of Kemmerer et al.'s (2012) neuropsychological study of action concepts. The color bar indicates the number of tasks, ranging from one to six, for which significant lesion–deficit associations were found in the given area. Dark gray shading indicates regions where there was insufficient data to obtain reliable results. (Upper tier) From left to right, left lateral, right lateral, ventral, and dorsal views of the cortex. (Lower tier) Four coronal sections along the planes indicated by the vertical lines on the brain shown below. Yellow circles highlight significant effects in the posterolateral temporal cortex (PLTC) and underlying white matter. Orange circles highlight significant effects in putatively arm/hand-related motor areas. White circles highlight significant effects in the inferior frontal gyrus. (Adapted from Kemmerer et al., 2012, p. 836.)

supporting instead the Grounded Cognition Model, several other fMRI studies have reported that the left PLTC does in fact respond significantly more to motion-related than non-motion-related verbal descriptions (Tettamanti et al., 2005; Deen & McCarthy, 2010; Saygin et al., 2010b; Lin et al., 2011; Wallentin et al., 2011). The explanation for these empirical discrepancies is not clear, but it is noteworthy that Bedny et al.'s studies used single words as stimuli, whereas the other studies (except for Lin et al., 2011) used sentences, paragraphs, and stories. For example, Wallentin et al. (2011) asked a group of Danish-speaking subjects to simply listen to Hans Christian Andersen's famous fairy tale *The Ugly Duckling,* and as shown in Figure 11.5, they found that the left PLTC was significantly engaged when all the clauses describing motion events were contrasted against all the clauses describing non-motion events. Importantly, the researchers controlled for a host of nuisance factors, including sound intensities, word frequencies, word co-occurrences, emotional content, and even physiological noise associated with cardiac pulsation and respiration.

The second challenge is how to square Bedny et al.'s fMRI findings from both sighted and blind subjects with Kemmerer et al.'s (2012) neuropsychological findings from brain-damaged patients. As mentioned above, the results from patient 1808 indicate that, at least in some cases, focal damage to the left PLTC and underlying white matter is sufficient to severely disrupt conceptual knowledge of actions, and the results from the group-level lesion–deficit analyses corroborate the view that this brain region plays an integral role in representing such knowledge. Moreover, the six tasks that Kemmerer et al. (2012) employed probe concrete rather than abstract aspects of action concepts, which suggests that the patients who failed those tasks have impaired knowledge of the former semantic features, most likely including visual motion patterns.

Taking all of these considerations into account, a highly speculative proposal is that the left PLTC may be innately predisposed to represent several different components of verb meaning, including visual motion patterns as well as more abstract types of information (for data consistent with this view see Peelen et al., 2012). Even though this region does not receive normal visual input in congenitally blind individuals, it may nevertheless serve as the default region for storing long-term records of whatever conceptual knowledge can be acquired through other senses about the idiosyncratic motion patterns encoded by verbs. Time will tell.

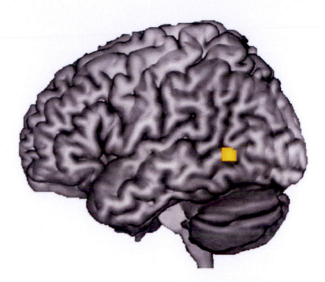

Figure 11.5 Results of Wallentin et al.'s (2011) fMRI study of the comprehension of motion vs. non-motion clauses in *The Ugly Duckling.* (From Wallentin et al., 2011, p. 222.)

Motor Features

The motor cortex resides in the frontal lobes and has a heterogeneous architecture that includes the primary motor cortex and perhaps as many as ten premotor areas—two ventral, two dorsal, and six medial—creating a complex mosaic that Graziano (2009, p. 65) calls "the premotor zoo." The primary motor cortex is traditionally thought of as containing a somatotopically organized map of the body's muscles, with the tongue and lips represented close to the sylvian fissure, the hand and arm represented at lateral and dorsolateral sites, and the leg and foot represented at the vertex and in the interhemispheric sulcus. It is important to realize, however, that the famous motor homunculus depicted in Figure 11.6 only captures the general trend. In fact, representations of adjacent body parts overlap a great deal in the primary motor cortex (see the classic paper by Penfield & Boldrey, 1937; for a more contemporary view see Meier et al., 2008). In addition, recent studies with monkeys suggest that the primary motor cortex as well as many premotor areas are topographically parcellated not only according to the layout of the body, but also in terms of different categories of ethologically important behaviors that require the coordination of multiple joints—e.g., licking/chewing behaviors, defensive behaviors, reach-to-grasp behaviors, central-space manipulation behaviors, and climbing/leaping behaviors (Figure 11.7; for a review see Graziano & Aflalo, 2007; see also Stepniewska et al., 2011).

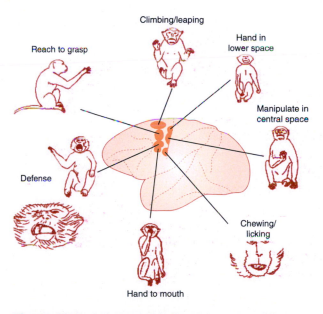

Figure 11.6 The motor homunculus of the human brain as portrayed by Penfield and Rasmussen (1950). A coronal section through the motor cortex is shown. (From Graziano, 2009, p. 33.)

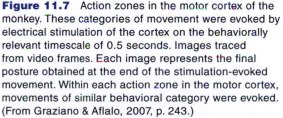

Figure 11.7 Action zones in the motor cortex of the monkey. These categories of movement were evoked by electrical stimulation of the cortex on the behaviorally relevant timescale of 0.5 seconds. Images traced from video frames. Each image represents the final posture obtained at the end of the stimulation-evoked movement. Within each action zone in the motor cortex, movements of similar behavioral category were evoked. (From Graziano & Aflalo, 2007, p. 243.)

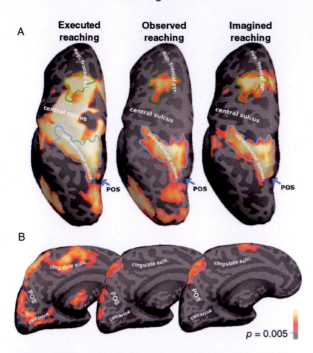

A Executed reaching   Observed reaching   Imagined reaching

B

p = 0.005

Figure 11.8 Overlapping activations in left frontal and parietal cortices during the execution, observation, and imagination of reaching. (A) Left hemisphere, dorsal view. (B) Medial view. (From Filimon et al., 2007, p. 1323.)

In recent years, some of the most exciting and controversial research in cognitive neuroscience has revolved around evidence that certain motor-related frontal and parietal areas in the human brain are engaged not only when actions are executed by the self, but also when they are seen or heard being performed by someone else (for reviews see Rizzolatti & Sinigaglia, 2010; Fogassi & Ferrari, 2011; Cook et al., in press). For example, whenever you passively watch someone perform an ordinary action like reaching for a cup of coffee, motor areas in your own brain are engaged, as if you were the one doing the reaching (Figure 11.8). These findings, and others like them, have led many researchers to suspect that understanding other people's actions may depend, at least to some degree, on unconsciously mirroring them. (See also the section in Chapter 5 about the role of the articulatory network in speech perception, as well as Box 8.1 in Chapter 8.)

Partly because of this line of work, there has been increasing interest in the provocative notion that when people understand linguistic descriptions of bodily actions, motor regions in their frontal and parietal lobes may be recruited (for reviews see Pulvermüller, 2005, 2008, 2013; Kemmerer & Gonzalez Castillo, 2010; Fernandino & Iacoboni, 2010). One influential proposal, originally formulated by Friedemann

Pulvermüller at Freie Universität Berlin, is the **Semantic Somatotopy Hypothesis**. It maintains that the motor features of action verbs are represented, in part, in somatotopically mapped frontal areas such that (1) verbs for face-related actions, like *lick,* depend on some of the same ventral areas that control those kinds of actions, (2) verbs for arm/hand-related actions, like *pick,* depend on some of the same lateral and dorsolateral areas that control those kinds of actions, and (3) verbs for leg/foot-related actions, like *kick,* depend on some of the same dorsal and dorsomedial areas that control those kinds of actions (Figure 11.9). This hypothesis, which is clearly a manifestation of the Grounded Cognition Model, also assumes that relatively subtle kinematic contrasts among verbs in the same class—contrasts that may be specified in terms of parameters for the direction, speed, and force of movement—are captured by neuronal populations in adjacent or even overlapping frontal areas. For instance, the fine-grained motor distinctions between *pat, pinch,* and *poke* may rely on intertwined neuronal populations in lateral motor areas that contribute to the execution of those types of arm/hand-related actions.

In accord with the Semantic Somatotopy Hypothesis, a number of fMRI studies have found that, compared to various control stimuli, action verbs and sentences do in fact tend to engage the left frontal lobe in a manner that corresponds, at least in general outline, to the familiar homuncular organization of the motor strip (Figure 11.10; see also the similar figure in Carota et al., 2012; and for notable exceptions see Postle et al., 2008, and Watson et al., 2013). Importantly, some of these studies included functional localizer scans to verify that the motor areas that are ignited when subjects process body-part-related action verbs and sentences are also ignited when they execute congruent body-part-related movements (Hauk et al., 2004; Raposo et al., 2009; Desai et al., 2010; Moody & Gennari, 2010).

It is noteworthy, however, that all of the data plotted in Figure 11.10 come from strongly right-handed individuals whose dominant hand is controlled mainly by the left hemisphere. Why does this matter? Given that nearly 90 percent of the people in the world are right-handed, it leaves open the possibility that the multiple

Semantic Somatotopy Hypothesis The motor features of action verbs are represented, in part, in somatotopically mapped frontal areas—e.g., *lick* depends on ventral areas for lip/tongue movements, *pick* depends on lateral and dorsolateral areas for arm/hand movements, and *kick* depends on dorsal and dorsomedial areas for leg/foot movements.

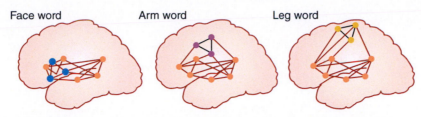

Figure 11.9 Schematic depiction of the Semantic Somatotopy Hypothesis. Spoken verb forms are indicated by orange perisylvian circuits. The motor features of verbs for face-related actions, like *lick,* are indicated by the blue nodes in the inferior frontal region. The motor features of verbs for arm/hand-related actions, like *pick,* are indicated by the purple nodes in the lateral frontal region. And the motor features of verbs for leg/foot-related actions, like *kick,* are indicated by the yellow nodes in the dorsal frontal region. (From Pulvermüller et al., 2009a, p. 2028.)

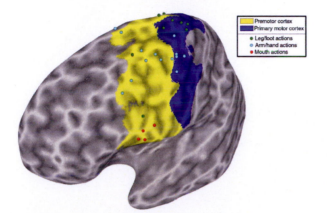

Figure 11.10 Activation peaks in left primary motor and premotor cortices reported by some of the fMRI studies that have investigated the neural substrates of the motor features of verbs and sentences encoding mouth-related actions (red circles), arm/hand-related actions (light blue circles), and leg/foot-related actions (green circles). Activations are plotted on an inflated brain with boundaries for the primary motor cortex (dark blue) and premotor cortex (yellow) based on Mayka et al.'s (2006) Human Motor Area Template. The activation peaks are drawn from the following sources: Hauk et al. (2004) [with corrections reported by Kemmerer & Gonzalez Castillo (2010)]; Tettamanti et al. (2005); Aziz-Zadeh et al. (2006); Rueschemeyer et al. (2007); Kemmerer et al. (2008); Beilock et al. (2008); Boulenger et al. (2009); Raposo et al. (2009); Desai et al. (2010); Pulvermüller et al. (2009b); and Willems et al. (2010a). (From Kemmerer et al., 2012, p. 843.)

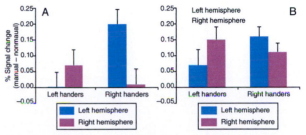

Figure 11.11 Results of Willems et al.'s (2010a) fMRI study of action verbs. Percent signal change in the premotor cortex (BA6) is presented as a function of handedness and hemisphere during lexical decisions for manual vs. nonmanual action verbs. Results are shown separately for (A) a 4-mm subject-specific spherical region of interest around the BA6 voxel maximally activated for manual action verbs, and (B) all BA6 voxels responsive to manual action verbs. Error bars represent standard errors of the mean. (From Willems et al., 2010a, p. 71.)

"hot spots" for arm/hand-related action concepts in Figure 11.10 might not really reflect motor simulations of how the subjects themselves usually execute such actions, but might instead reflect motor simulations of how they usually see other people execute them.

This issue can be resolved by investigating strongly left-handed individuals whose dominant hand is controlled mainly by the right hemisphere. When they process manual action verbs like *throw,* do they recruit mainly right-sided arm/hand areas to simulate the way they themselves usually execute the designated types of

actions, or do they recruit mainly left-sided arm/hand areas to simulate the way they almost always see other people execute those actions? To address this question, Willems et al. (2010a) scanned the brain activity of both righties and lefties while they performed a lexical decision task that included manual action verbs, non-manual action verbs, and pronounceable pseudowords. As indicated in Chapter 10, a lexical decision task only requires participants to judge whether letter strings are real words or pseudowords, so when real words are presented, whatever semantic retrieval takes place is relatively automatic (Chumbley & Balota, 1984; Binder et al., 2003). Replicating previous studies, the researchers found that in righties manual action verbs (compared to non-manual action verbs) engaged mainly left-sided motor areas for controlling the arm and hand. The fascinating new discovery was that, as shown in Figure 11.11, lefties displayed exactly the opposite hemispheric asymmetry. These results support the view that when people process verbs, they automatically simulate the way they

Box 11.1 Hockey Players Do It Better

Do people with specialized motor skills perform better than novices at understanding sentences that describe the corresponding kinds of actions? And if so, does this enhanced comprehension draw directly on some of the same neural networks that underlie the acquired motor expertise?

To address these questions, Beilock et al. (2008) conducted an experiment with three groups of subjects: advanced ice-hockey players; fans with extensive viewing experience but no playing experience; and novices with neither viewing nor playing experience. All of these subjects passively listened to sentences describing everyday actions (e.g., *The individual pushed the cart*) and sentences describing hockey actions (e.g., *The hockey player finished the shot*) while undergoing fMRI. Immediately afterward, they were given a task that evaluated the speed and accuracy of their comprehension of the very same sentences. For each item, they initially heard a sentence and then saw a picture of a person performing an action; the task was to indicate as quickly as possible, with a "yes" or "no" button-press, whether the pictured person, but not necessarily the pictured action, matched the one mentioned in the sentence (Figure 11B1.1). There were three categories of items: those in which both the person and the action matched ("yes" decision); those in which the person but not the action matched ("yes" decision); and those in which neither the person nor the action matched ("no" decision). The researchers focused on the first two categories of items. They assumed that even though the

Figure 11B1.1 Examples of stimuli used in the sentence comprehension task. (From Beilock et al., 2008, pp. 13269.) Copyright (2008) National Academy of Sciences, U.S.A.

task did not require judgments about whether the actions in the sentences and pictures matched, if subjects understood the nature of those actions, this would speed up their decisions for the first category of items relative to the second category. This index of comprehension was called the "action-match effect."

All of the subjects displayed a significant action-match effect for the everyday sentences, but only the experts and fans did so for the hockey sentences. This suggests that experience either playing or viewing hockey facilitates the comprehension of linguistic descriptions of hockey maneuvers. Turning to the brain, the researchers investigated whether the subjects' action-match effects for hockey sentences were related to their neural responses to the same sentences in the passive listening condition. Two regions emerged as being critically important. First, comprehension efficiency correlated *positively* with recruitment of the left dorsal premotor cortex, which is believed to support the selection of well-learned plans for action, regardless of which body parts are involved (see Figure 11B1.2A). This region was strongly engaged in both the experts and the fans, but not in the novices; moreover, the right dorsal premotor cortex was also activated in just the fans, perhaps reflecting more effortful action selection. Second, comprehension efficiency correlated *negatively* with bilateral engagement of the dorsal primary sensory-motor cortex, which is believed to support the specific step-by-step movements necessary to execute a task (see Figure 11B1.2B). The novices presumably engaged this region because they lacked sophisticated motor programs for hockey maneuvers.

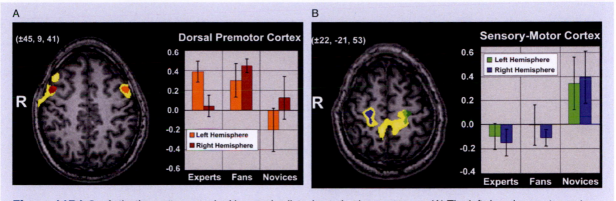

Figure 11B1.2   Activation patterns evoked by passive listening to hockey sentences. (A) The left dorsal premotor cortex was engaged in experts and fans but not novices. This effect correlated positively with comprehension efficiency. The right dorsal premotor cortex was also engaged in just fans. (B) The dorsal primary sensory-motor cortex was engaged bilaterally in novices but not experts or fans. This effect correlated negatively with comprehension efficiency. (From Beilock et al., 2008, pp. 13271–13272.) Copyright (2008) National Academy of Sciences, U.S.A.

These findings suggest that sports experience changes the brain in a way that causally influences language understanding. As Beilock et al. (2008, p. 13272) put it,

experience alters the extent to which premotor and primary sensory-motor cortex are called on during language listening, which, in turn, produces differences in comprehension. As such, experience-dependent activation of motor areas when listening to action-based language is not an epiphenomenal byproduct of comprehension, but is an integral component of effective understanding.

(For a follow-up study see Lyons et al., 2010; and for related work see Locatelli et al., 2012.)

themselves usually perform the designated types of actions, as opposed to the way they usually see others perform them (for a somewhat different perspective see Hauk & Pulvermüller, 2011). More generally, Willems et al.'s (2010a) study suggests that people who use their bodies in systematically different ways exhibit systematically different neural responses to linguistic descriptions of action (see also Box 11.1).

If somatotopically mapped frontal regions represent the motor features of action verbs, they should not simply be engaged when verbs are processed, but should be engaged quite rapidly. To test this prediction, Pulvermüller and colleagues conducted several ERP experiments that used source localization techniques to identify the underlying neural generators of the scalp-recorded signals elicited by verbs encoding different body-part-related categories of actions. They found that within the time window of 200–250 ms, verbs for face-related actions engaged ventral motor areas, verbs for arm/hand-related actions engaged lateral motor areas, and verbs for leg/foot-related actions engaged dorsal motor areas (Pulvermüller et al., 2001;

Hauk & Pulvermüller, 2004; see also Shtyrov et al., 2004; Pulvermüller et al., 2005b; Hauk et al., 2008b; Boulenger et al., 2008; Aravena et al., 2010; van Elk et al., 2010). In keeping with these results, a number of purely behavioral studies also suggest that the motor aspects of verb meaning are retrieved extremely fast (e.g., Borreggine & Kaschak, 2006; Boulenger et al., 2006; Zwaan & Taylor, 2006; Scorolli & Borghi, 2007; Nazir et al., 2008; Taylor & Zwaan, 2008). Overall, these findings provide additional evidence that the somatotopically mapped motor responses triggered by action verbs reflect the automatic comprehension process itself, as opposed to deliberate post-comprehension imagery. It must be acknowledged, however, that this issue remains controversial (e.g., Papeo et al., 2009; Willems et al., 2010b; Tomasino & Rumiati, 2013).

Another important prediction that follows from the Semantic Somatotopy Hypothesis is that altering the functional operations of body-part-related motor areas should affect the semantic processing of the corresponding types of action verbs. This prediction has been directly tested in several TMS studies. Although

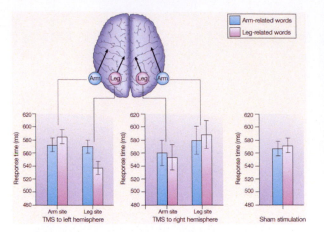

Figure 11.12 Results of Pulvermüller et al.'s (2005a) TMS study of action verbs. TMS was applied to arm and leg loci over the left and right hemispheres and compared with sham stimulation while subjects made lexical decisions about arm-related and leg-related action verbs. Significant effects on response time were found only in the left hemisphere. TMS at the arm site induced faster responses for arm-related than leg-related verbs, whereas TMS at the leg site had the opposite effect. (From Pulvermüller, 2005, p. 581.)

the results of these studies are not entirely consistent, for the most part they confirm the prediction (for discussion see Kemmerer & Gonzalez Castillo, 2010). For example, in an influential study by Pulvermüller et al. (2005a), subjects performed a lexical decision task while, 150 ms before the onset of each letter string, either a single weak TMS pulse or a sham TMS pulse was delivered to either an arm/hand or a leg/foot site in the left or right hemisphere. Stimulation of the left leg/foot region led to significantly faster responses to verbs encoding leg/foot-related actions than to verbs encoding arm/hand-related actions, whereas stimulation of the left arm/hand region had the opposite effect (Figure 11.12). No differences were found, however, when TMS was delivered to the right hemisphere (or when sham TMS was used), which is not surprising since all of the subjects were strongly right-handed. In short, this study suggests that brief stimulation of body-part-related motor areas facilitates the automatic retrieval of concordant body-part-related motor features of verbs. Of course, as we have seen in previous chapters, TMS can also be applied repetitively to disrupt rather than facilitate cortical computations. Adopting this kind of approach, Gerfo et al. (2008) showed that rTMS to a left arm/hand site significantly slowed down subjects' responses when they changed the inflectional form of arm/hand-related action verbs, relative to when they changed the inflectional form of non-action

verbs (the inflectional transformations involved shifting between the first-person and second-person forms of Italian verbs). The results of these studies support the idea that somatotopically mapped motor areas are causally involved, as opposed to just incidentally involved, in automatically accessing the motor features of action concepts (see also Repetto et al., 2013).

Finally, we turn to several neuropsychological studies that have addressed this topic by investigating patients with damage to frontal motor areas. In general agreement with the Grounded Cognition Model, there is growing evidence that patients with a movement disorder called **amyotrophic lateral sclerosis (ALS)**—also known as motor neuron disease or Lou Gehrig's disease—have significantly worse conceptual knowledge of actions than objects, due to degeneration of frontal motor areas for controlling muscle groups throughout the body (Bak & Hodges, 2004; Hillis et al., 2004a, 2006; Grossman et al., 2008). In addition, results consistent with the more specific Semantic Somatotopy Hypothesis come from the following two studies.

First, in an experiment involving 21 left-hemisphere-damaged aphasic patients, Arévalo et al. (2007) found a significant relationship between impaired retrieval of "manipulation" verbs and damage to arm/hand-related motor areas not only in the frontal lobe, but also in the parietal lobe. And second, as mentioned above, Kemmerer et al. (2012) reported an experiment in which 226 patients were administered a battery of six standardized tasks that probed conceptual knowledge of actions in a variety of verbal and nonverbal ways. Although the tasks did not employ a well-controlled set of verbs encoding arm/hand-related actions, all of the tasks did have a preponderance (roughly 70 percent) of arm/hand-related stimuli. And as shown by the orange circles in Figure 11.4, the group-level lesion–deficit analyses revealed that arm/hand-related motor areas in the left lateral frontal lobe were among the regions most reliably linked with impairment across all six tasks. The lesion of one particular patient who failed all six tasks—namely, case 1172—is portrayed in Figure 11.13, and his scores are shown in Table 11.1. The lesion clearly affected the midlateral and dorsolateral sectors of the precentral gyrus, including the cortex as well as the underlying white matter—territory that is well-established as being crucial for the control of arm/hand actions (see especially the fourth and fifth

Amyotrophic lateral sclerosis (ALS) A movement disorder due to degeneration of frontal motor areas, among other structures. Patients often have significantly worse conceptual knowledge of actions than objects.

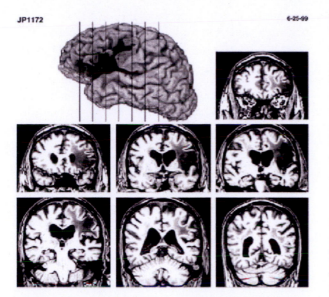

Figure 11.13 Lesion site of case 1172. The damage is centered in the heart of Broca's area but extends superiorly into the middle part of the premotor cortex, a region known to be important for hand actions. As shown in the coronal sections, the damage included some of the white matter underneath the inferior frontal, middle frontal, precentral, postcentral, and supramarginal gyri. (From Kemmerer & Tranel, 2003, p. 426.)

coronal sections, ordered from front to back). At the same time, however, it is apparent that the lesion also affected Broca's area, so it remains possible that the patient's severe verb deficit was due to that damage rather than to the damage involving specifically arm/hand-related tissue.

It is also important to acknowledge that other neuropsychological studies have yielded results that are rather hard to explain in terms of the Grounded Cognition Model and its specific instantiation, the Semantic Somatotopy Hypothesis. For instance, Arévalo et al. (2012) conducted an experiment in which 27 left-hemisphere-damaged patients were given a task that required judging, on every trial, whether a given word correctly described a picture of an action. The actions involved face-related movements, arm/hand-related movements, and leg/foot-related movements. Many of the patients had lesions that included frontal motor areas, but contrary to the predictions of the theory, significant correlations were not found between impaired performance on specific body-part-related action categories and damage to the corresponding body-part-related motor areas (see also Maieron et al., 2013).

In another notable study, Papeo et al. (2010) investigated the ability of 12 left-hemisphere-damaged patients to not only imitate pantomimes of certain actions, but

also produce and comprehend the verbs that designate them. Challenging the theory once again, double dissociations were observed between the imitation and verb processing tasks. Of greatest relevance in the current context are a few patients who could no longer imitate actions accurately, but could nevertheless understand the associated verbs without major difficulty. These results suggest that motor simulations may not always be necessary to appreciate linguistic descriptions of actions (for further discussion see Papeo & Hochmann, 2012; see also the discussion in Chapter 10 of the motor-semantic features of nouns that encode tools).

Such a view has been explored to some extent by Lawrence Taylor and Rolf Zwaan, two cognitive scientists who advocate what they call the **Fault Tolerant Theory of Conceptual Representation** (Taylor and Zwaan, 2009, 2012; for related ideas see Mahon & Caramazza, 2008). Like the Grounded Cognition Model, this approach assumes that possessing rich modality-specific memories of certain types of actions will undoubtedly enhance one's ability to understand utterances about those actions. However, this approach also maintains that lacking such experiential traces, or being unable to run appropriate visual and/or motor simulations because of brain damage, will not completely preclude comprehension, but will instead reduce the depth and richness of comprehension to various degrees. Taylor and Zwaan (2009, p. 55) provide the following example to illustrate what they have in mind:

> If a person had never witnessed an athlete performing a high-jump and had never high-jumped himself, but did understand that high-jumpers compete to jump over the highest bar, then they could understand the sentence *The athlete attempted to win the gold medal by high-jumping over the bar*. However, if the remainder of the discourse required experiential knowledge to comprehend, then a person without visual or motor experience would fail to construct an adequate situation model. If a second sentence read, *His form was slightly off on his last attempt and he injured his neck on the landing*, a person who had never witnessed or performed a high-jump would have difficulty understanding how this is a reasonable outcome, as the Fosbury flop is not an incredibly intuitive way to jump over horizontal bars.

Fault Tolerant Theory of Conceptual Representation   The view that as a person's capacity to mentally simulate certain types of actions decreases, their ability to understand linguistic descriptions of those actions does not suddenly disappear, but degrades gracefully.

Figure 11.14   The Fosbury flop, performed by the high-jumper Nicole Forrester. (From http://en.wikipedia.org/wiki/Nicole_Forrester, licensed under Creative Commons.)

If, like the hypothetical person described by Taylor and Zwaan, you aren't familiar with high-jumping and, in particular, with the Fosbury flop, you need only consult Figure 11.14 to fully grasp the import of their example (see also, once again, Box 11.1). It only takes a moment of reflection to realize that, as proposed by the Fault Tolerant Theory of Conceptual Representation, language comprehension is not really an all-or-nothing affair, but is instead a graded one. It will take a lot longer, however, to figure out whether—and, if so, exactly how—this fundamental insight can be used to develop a fully satisfactory account of the various discrepancies in the experimental literature described above.

Summary

According to the Grounded Cognition Model, the meanings of action verbs are anchored in modality-specific brain systems, such that comprehension involves accessing long-term records of sensory and motor patterns in a fairly automatic, unconscious manner. The visual motion features of action verbs are

thought to depend on some of the same brain regions that normally subserve high-level motion perception, most notably the left PLTC. And the motor features of action verbs are thought to depend on some of the same brain regions that normally subserve movement preparation, most notably the left premotor and primary motor cortices. More specifically, the Semantic Somatotopy Hypothesis holds that the motor features of action verbs are represented in the frontal lobes in a way that conforms, at least roughly, to the layout of the motor homunculus. By and large, these proposals have been supported by numerous studies using diverse brain mapping techniques. However, not all of the available data are easily explained, and a great deal of additional work will be needed to resolve the many open questions. A relatively new approach is the Fault Tolerant Theory of Conceptual Representation, which is based on the notion that understanding action verbs is not an absolute, all-or-nothing phenomenon, but is instead a multifaceted process that is sensitive to the vagaries of experience and that admits varying degrees of precision, especially regarding the content of modality-specific simulations.

A Semantic Hub for Action Concepts

In Chapter 10, a substantial amount of space was devoted to discussing a theory of conceptual knowledge called the Hub and Spoke Model (see Figure 10.9). To recapitulate, this framework incorporates and transcends the Grounded Cognition Model, since it maintains that concepts are based not only on modality-specific brain systems for perception and action, but also on a modality-invariant brain system that resides in the anterior temporal lobes (ATLs) bilaterally. This amodal device, which is referred to as the semantic hub, serves two main functions: First, it binds together the cortically distributed sensory and motor features of concepts; and second, it organizes those representations so that the boundaries of concepts are delimited more or less precisely, thereby allowing individuals to efficiently judge category membership. As indicated in Chapter 10, when it comes to object concepts, this theory has been gaining increasing support from a variety of sources, including neuropsychological investigations of patients with semantic dementia (SD), and fMRI and rTMS investigations of healthy subjects. So far, however, comparatively less effort has been invested in exploring how well the theory applies to action concepts. Nevertheless, evidence that these kinds of concepts also depend critically on the ATLs has been slowly accumulating. As shown below, most of the pertinent data come from patients with SD.

It will be recalled from Chapters 4 and 10 that SD is a neurodegenerative disease in which conceptual knowledge progressively erodes as a result of gradual atrophy of the ATLs and neighboring structures. The following brief review demonstrates that, as with the meanings of object nouns, the meanings of action verbs deteriorate significantly in the vast majority of cases. Moreover, these deficits are manifested across a wide range of tasks, including lexical decision, picture naming, picture description, semi-structured interviews, word–picture matching, semantic similarity judgments with words, semantic similarity judgments with pictures, and novel word learning.

It is useful to begin with an experiment by Pulvermüller et al. (2009a) that builds directly on some of the research summarized in the previous section. Eleven SD patients and ten healthy control subjects were given a lexical decision task that consisted of 210 real words and 210 pronounceable pseudowords. The real words belonged to the following six classes, with 35 words in each one:

- words involving abstract concepts;
- words involving colors;
- words involving shapes;
- words involving face-related actions;
- words involving arm/hand-related actions;
- words involving leg/foot-related actions.

It was not possible to match all six classes of words for various "nuisance" factors, but it was nevertheless possible to do so for certain subsets of classes. In particular, the two classes of words emphasizing object properties (i.e., color and shape) were matched for length, frequency, imageability, and concreteness, and the three classes of words emphasizing movement properties (i.e., face-related, arm/hand-related, and leg/foot-related actions) were matched along the same dimensions. Because a few of the SD patients were not comfortable expressing their lexicality judgments with button presses, all of the patients responded verbally to each stimulus by saying "yes" or "no," or if they preferred, "word" or "no word." The data were then analyzed in terms of accuracy. As depicted in Figure 11.15, across all six classes of words, the SD patients obtained significantly lower d' values than the healthy control subjects. (Note: d', pronounced "dee prime," is a signal detection measure that reflects a subject's propensity to give a particular response when presented with

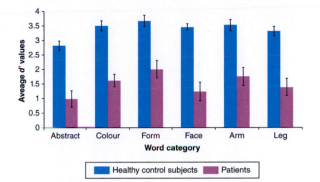

Figure 11.15   Results of Pulvermüller et al.'s (2009a) neuropsychological study with SD patients. SD patients performed significantly worse than healthy control subjects on a lexical decision task involving three classes of nouns and three classes of verbs. See text for details. (From Pulvermüller et al., 2009a, p. 2035.)

a stimulus weighed against their propensity to give the same response in the absence of the stimulus. Hence, it can be used as a sensitivity index that takes into account both the hit rate and the false-alarm rate.) The fact that the patients were impaired at recognizing not only the two object-related word classes but also the three action-related ones suggests that the ATLs play essential roles in supporting the meanings of both nouns and verbs. (The patients' poor performance on words for abstract concepts is discussed in Chapter 12).

To account for their findings involving verbs, Pulvermüller et al. (2009a) present a diagram (Figure 11.16) that nicely illustrates how the Semantic Somatotopy Hypothesis can be combined with the Hub and Spoke Model. As discussed above, the idiosyncratic motor patterns encoded by verbs for certain types of body-part-related actions are assumed to be represented in the corresponding body-part-related regions of the left frontal lobe. In the new framework, however, these features are also assumed to be interconnected with integrative semantic specifications in the ATLs. Although the diagram ignores the visual motion components of verb meaning that may depend on the left PLTC, those features could easily be incorporated (compare Figure 11.16 with Figure 10.9 in Chapter 10). In such a scenario, the somatotopically mapped motor components and the visual motion components would constitute some of the modality-specific "spokes" for verb meaning, and they would be integrated and systematically organized in the amodal "hub"—i.e., the neurocognitive system that degenerates in SD.

Additional evidence for this kind of scheme comes from several studies that have compared the noun and verb production abilities of SD patients. For example,

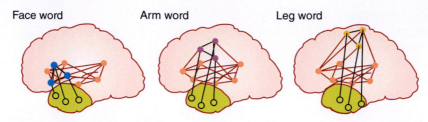

Figure 11.16 Schematic depiction of the combination of the Semantic Somatotopy Hypothesis and the Hub and Spoke Model. Relative to the illustration in Figure 11.9, what has been added are nodes for each type of word in the anterior temporal lobe. (From Pulvermüller et al., 2009a, p. 2038.)

Cotelli et al. (2006) asked six SD patients to orally name 60 pictures of objects and 60 pictures of actions, with the two sets of target words being matched for length and frequency. The patients were equally impaired on both tasks: object naming = 40 percent; action naming = 38 percent. Similar results were obtained in a separate study by Hillis et al. (2006) that involved a larger group of patients and a wider range of production tasks. Specifically, these researchers asked 16 SD patients to name, in both spoken and written forms, 30 pictures of objects and 30 pictures of actions, with the two sets of target words again being matched for length and frequency. As in Cotelli et al.'s (2006) study, the patients were impaired across the board: oral object naming = 53 percent; written object naming = 40 percent; oral action naming = 63 percent; written action naming = 42 percent (for additional data see Méligne et al., 2011). It is also noteworthy that, as demonstrated by a few other studies, the profound difficulties that SD patients experience in producing both nouns and verbs are not restricted to the confrontation picture-naming paradigm, but extend to more naturalistic discourse contexts like describing the Cookie Theft picture (Bird et al., 2000; see Figure 3.4 in Chapter 3) and talking about memorable events that took place during specific periods in their lives (Meteyard & Patterson, 2009).

Shifting from production to comprehension, the Hub and Spoke Model predicts that SD patients should perform poorly on tasks that directly probe knowledge of the sorts of action concepts that are typically encoded by verbs. This prediction has received support from a small but growing body of literature. For example, when given a detailed description of a particular kind of event, SD patients are impaired at judging which of four choice verbs best matches it (Yi et al., 2007). Likewise, when given a single pivot verb (e.g., *grind*), SD patients are impaired at judging which of two choice verbs (e.g., *crush* or *sip*) is most similar to it (Patterson et al., 2001; Bak & Hodges, 2003; Hillis et al., 2006; Bonner et al., 2009). Importantly, SD patients also tend to fail the latter type of semantic similarity judgment task when the stimuli are action pictures instead of action verbs (Bak & Hodges, 2003; Hillis et al., 2006). Taken together, these findings point to a major disturbance of action concepts in SD.

As one would expect, this disturbance interferes with the ability of SD patients to learn new verbs. Consider, for instance, the verb *lour*. This is a real but very low-frequency word that means "to look angry or sullen as if in disapproval." In a cleverly designed experiment, Murray et al. (2007) first identified a group of 11 SD patients who were unfamiliar with this word, and then exposed them to it without warning in the context of a narrated story from a children's picture book. The story revolved around the adventures of an energetic but disobedient girl named Louise. In the final scene, an illustration depicted an older man in a chair leaning forward and frowning at the girl, and the accompanying text was as follows: "Louise sees her father lour at her." Shortly after the narrative, the patients were given a task that required them to decide, on every trial, which of three words—a common verb of facial expression, a pseudoword, or *louring*—best described a picture of a person with a particular facial expression. Relative to a group of healthy control subjects, the patients were significantly impaired. Not only were they unable to link the novel word with pictorial representations of its meaning, but they also made many errors involving the common verbs and the pseudowords. These results provide further evidence that in SD the gradual atrophy of the ATLs disrupts action concepts to roughly the same degree as object concepts.

In summary, the Hub and Spoke Model maintains that, like object concepts, action concepts contain not only modality-specific semantic components that reside in relatively high-level sensory and motor areas (the "spokes"), but also modality-invariant semantic components that reside in the ATLs bilaterally (the "hub"). Evidence that action concepts do in fact depend on the ATLs has been accruing. However, this field of investigation is still very much in its infancy, and future work will need to address a number of issues, including the following. As yet, almost all of the relevant findings come from neuropsychological studies with SD patients, so it will be important to determine whether other approaches—e.g., fMRI and rTMS studies with healthy subjects—yield convergent or divergent results regarding the possible involvement of the ATLs in action concepts. In addition, research on the representational and computational nature of the ATL hub has concentrated almost entirely on object concepts, so the precise ways in which this system contributes to action concepts will need to be explored carefully.

Domains of Action Concepts

During the past few decades, a great deal of research in linguistics has focused on identifying the optimal principles for grouping verbs into coherent classes (e.g., Pinker, 1989; Levin, 1993; Fellbaum, 1998; Levin & Rappaport Hovav, 2005; Rappaport Hovav et al., 2009; Croft, 2012). Most of this research has taken into account both semantic and syntactic factors, because a verb is not just a word for a particular kind of event, but is also, as Pinker (2007, p. 31) put it, "the chassis of the sentence. It is a framework with receptacles for the other parts—the subject, the object, and various oblique objects and subordinate clauses—to be bolted onto." Moreover, the meaning of a verb tends to correlate quite closely with the range of syntactic constructions that it can occur in. Based on such correlations between semantics and syntax, Levin (1993) was able to sort over 3,000 English verbs into roughly 50 classes and 200 subclasses. Some of these classes are mentioned in the introductory section of this chapter, and ten others are listed below:

- Verbs of putting: *put, immerse, install, lodge, mount, perch, set, stash*, etc.
- Verbs of removing: *remove, erase, flush, pluck, skim, wipe, sweep, strip*, etc.
- Verbs of sending: *send, deliver, hand, pass, shift, ship, smuggle, sneak*, etc.
- Verbs of change of possession: *give, lend, offer, sell, buy, borrow, steal, receive*, etc.
- Verbs of throwing: *throw, flick, fling, hurl, lob, pitch, toss, bat*, etc.
- Verbs of contact by impact: *jab, prod, poke, prick, tap, slap, spank, whack*, etc.
- Verbs of attaching: *attach, clamp, harness, lock, nail, pin, tape, zip*, etc.
- Verbs of image creation: *draw, doodle, scribble, scrawl, inscribe, paint, trace, write*, etc.
- Verbs of searching: *search, hunt, prowl, rummage, root, forage, scrounge, snoop*, etc.
- Verbs of killing: *kill, murder, slaughter, butcher, slay, assassinate, execute, dispatch*, etc.

So far, very little research on the neural substrates of action concepts has taken advantage of the various insights from linguistics regarding the organization of verbs into myriad semantically and syntactically defined classes (e.g., Kemmerer, 2000, 2003, 2006a, 2014; Kemmerer & Wright, 2002; Kemmerer et al., 2008). In recent years, however, some headway has been made in understanding how two large-scale domains of action concepts—those typically encoded by transitive verbs, and those typically encoded by intransitive verbs—are implemented in the brain. The following discussion therefore focuses on this fundamental distinction.

Transitive and Intransitive Verbs

Transitivity is one of the most basic aspects of the linguistic representation of action. Although it can be conceptualized in different ways (LaPolla et al., 2011), the central idea in fairly straightforward. Transitive verbs designate events that involve two core participants, an "actor" and an "undergoer," with the actor being syntactically expressed as a subject noun-phrase and the undergoer being syntactically expressed as an object noun-phrase. The terms "actor" and "undergoer" come from a theory called Role and Reference Grammar and are defined roughly as follows: The actor of an event is the individual that performs, instigates, or controls it, whereas the undergoer is the one that is affected by it in some way (Van Valin & LaPolla, 1997; see also the notions of proto-agent and proto-patient described by Dowty, 1991, and Ackerman & Moore, 2001). For example, *kiss* is a transitive verb because it specifies both a kisser and a kissee, with these two participants being syntactically realized as subject and object, respectively, as in *The housewife kissed the mailman*. Note that even though a person's lips play a key role in kissing, and even though comprehending the verb *kiss* may engage the lip region of the motor homunculus, these body parts do not qualify as core participants of the action. That's because, from a grammatical perspective, what matters is not how a kiss is mediated, but rather that there is both an initiator and a receiver of the action. More precisely, the prototypical transitive action scenario can be characterized as follows: "The event originates in a volitional actor, extends beyond the actor's personal sphere, and terminates in a distinct undergoer achieving an intended effect on it" (Shibatani, 2006, p. 257). In contrast to transitive verbs, intransitive verbs designate events that involve just one core participant, syntactically expressed as a subject noun-phrase. Usually this participant is a volitional actor, as in *The mailman bolted*, but sometimes it is a passive undergoer, as in *The mailman blushed*. It all depends on the nature of the verb (for a cross-linguistic perspective see Donohue & Wichmann, 2008).

Transitivity itself also depends, ultimately, on the lexical specifications of particular verbs, not the real-world properties of the designated events. For example, the general notion of "eating" is associated with the verbs *eat, devour,* and *dine,* but these three verbs exhibit different types of transitivity. The first verb, *eat,* is, technically speaking, ambitransitive, since it can be either transitive, as in *Bill ate the lasagna,* or intransitive, as in *Bill ate.* The second verb, *devour,* is strictly transitive, since one can say *Bill devoured the lasagna* but not **Bill devoured* (the asterisk indicates ungrammaticality). And the third verb, *dine,* is strictly intransitive, since one can say *Bill dined* but not **Bill dined the lasagna.* Despite these and other complications, there is still a strong overall tendency for two-participant verbs to be syntactically transitive and one-participant verbs to be syntactically intransitive (Næss, 2007; Dixon, 2010b). And as described below, a small but growing body of neuroscientific literature suggests that, on average, transitive verbs and sentences recruit certain temporal and parietal regions, as well as Broca's area, significantly more than intransitive verbs and sentences (especially when the latter have actor subjects).

Involvement of Temporal and Parietal Regions

A few recent fMRI studies have generated evidence that transitive verbs and sentences depend more than intransitive verbs and sentences on certain temporal and parietal regions. The first study was conducted by a major figure in this field of inquiry, Cynthia Thompson, together with her colleagues at Northwestern University (Thompson et al., 2007). The subjects performed a lexical decision task that included 40 transitive verbs, 40 intransitive verbs, 80 nouns, and 50 pronounceable pseudowords. All of the items were matched for length and frequency, and the two sets of verbs were also matched in terms of imageability. For present purposes, the key finding was that a direct contrast between the transitive and intransitive verbs revealed significant bilateral activation in the inferior parietal lobule—more precisely, in the angular gyrus and posterior supramarginal gyrus (BAs 39 and 40; Figure 11.17; see also Meltzer-Asscher et al., 2013).

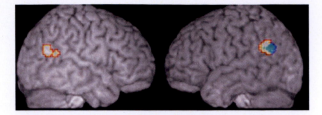

Figure 11.17   Results of Thompson et al.'s (2007) fMRI study of verb processing. During a lexical decision task, greater activation was found for transitive than intransitive verbs in the inferior parietal lobule bilaterally. The differences between the yellow and blue patches are not relevant here. (From Thompson et al., 2007, p. 1760.)

Two aspects of these results warrant special emphasis. First, the inferior parietal "hot spot" was present even though the task—lexical decision—did not require the subjects to attend to the semantic or syntactic properties of the verbs. This suggests that the transitivity features of verbs are accessed automatically during language comprehension. Second, in the left hemisphere the "hot spot" was very close—just posterior and superior—to the PLTC territory that numerous studies have linked with the sorts of visual motion patterns that are typically encoded by action verbs, as discussed earlier. This suggests that transitive verbs may rely more than intransitive verbs on some kind of event processing that derives, at least partly, from the visual modality. We return to this idea below, after first reviewing additional data.

Following up on Thompson et al.'s (2007) results, den Ouden et al. (2009) conducted a study that focused on the effortful production, rather than the automatic comprehension, of action verbs. The researchers first selected 20 verbs—10 transitive and 10 intransitive (all with actor subjects)—on the basis of their imageability and "filmability." Then they created, for each verb, both a static picture and a dynamic video (Figure 11.18). The experiment consisted of three runs, and in each run all 20 pictures and all 20 videos were presented in random order, with each stimulus being shown for two seconds. The task was to overtly name each action with the most appropriate verb, and the subjects performed quite well, achieving over 95 percent accuracy. The dynamic videos elicited more widespread activation than the static pictures, which is not surprising. Of greater theoretical importance is that there were consistent effects of transitivity across the two modes of stimulus presentation. Specifically, relative to the naming of intransitive actions in both modes, the naming of transitive actions in both modes was associated with significantly stronger activation

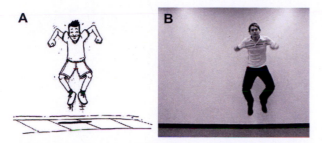

Figure 11.18 Stimuli for (A) picture-naming and (B) video-naming tasks. (From den Ouden et al., 2009, p. 200.)

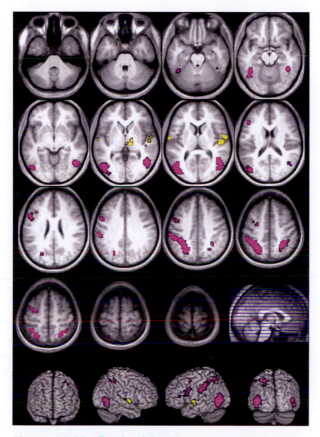

Figure 11.19 Results of den Ouden et al.'s (2009) fMRI study of verb processing. During both picture-naming and video-naming tasks, greater activation was found for transitive than intransitive verbs in several frontal, parietal, and temporal regions. Pink = transitive vs. intransitive conditions. Yellow = intransitive vs. transitive conditions. (From den Ouden et al., 2009, p. 203.)

in a number of frontal, parietal, and temporal regions (Figure 11.19). The frontal regions are discussed in the next subsection; here our main concern involves the parietal and temporal regions.

One prominent cluster of voxels, much larger in the left than the right hemisphere, included the anterior supramarginal gyrus, intraparietal sulcus, and superior parietal lobule. Most of this cortical tissue is believed to contribute to the spatial and somatomotor aspects of object-directed actions like reaching and grasping, regardless of whether those actions are executed, observed, or imagined (see Figure 11.8; see also Figure 5.16 in Chapter 5, as well as Buccino et al., 2001; Milner & Goodale, 2006; Shmuelof & Zohary, 2007). Since the two transitive conditions—static and dynamic—involved seeing and naming object-directed actions, it is understandable that these parietal areas were engaged.

Another prominent cluster of voxels, only slightly larger in the left than the right hemisphere, had its activation peak in a posterior part of the PLTC (BA37), but included both the inferior angular gyrus (BA39, overlapping the area observed by Thompson et al., 2007) and the anterolateral occipital cortex (BA19). As suggested above, it is conceivable that these areas are recruited more by transitive than intransitive verbs because the former rely more than the latter on some sort of visually related event processing. One very tentative hypothesis is roughly as follows. Perhaps the PLTC and angular gyrus are essential for representing the energy flow and causal relations between the two core participants, actor and undergoer, in the kinds of events that are typically encoded by transitive verbs. If so, then representing this sort of information about agency would be particularly important when both participants are animate entities capable of willful behavior. In this connection, it is notable that both participants were in fact people in five of the ten transitive action scenarios in the experiment; hence these scenarios may have required the subjects to devote extra effort to recognizing and distinguishing between the actor and the undergoer (the relevant verbs were *kiss, pinch, tickle, hug,* and *push*).

Additional leverage for this hypothesis comes from an fMRI study by Grewe et al. (2007) in which the subjects made acceptability judgments about four types of transitive German sentences that varied along two dimensions: animacy and word order. Regarding animacy, both the actor (indicated by nominative case) and the undergoer (indicated by accusative case) were animate in two of the sentence types (1a and 1b), whereas only the actor was animate in the other two sentence types (2a and 2b). Regarding word order, the actor was syntactically expressed before the undergoer (a natural sequence) in two of the sentence types (1a and 2a), whereas the undergoer was syntactically expressed before the actor (an unnatural sequence) in the other two sentence types (1b and 2b).

(1) Both participants are animate:

  a   Natural order

   i   Sentence: *Wahrscheinlich hat [der Mann]*_{NOM} *[den Direktor]*_{ACC} *gepflegt.*

   ii   Transliteration: Probably has the man the director taken care of.

   iii Gloss: "The man probably took care of the director."

  b   Unnatural order

   i   Sentence: *Wahrscheinlich hat [den Direktor]*_{ACC} *[der Mann]*_{NOM} *gepflegt.*

   ii   Transliteration: Probably has the director the man taken care of.

   iii Gloss: "The man probably took care of the director."

(2) Only the actor is animate:

  a   Natural order

   i   Sentence: *Wahrscheinlich hat [der Mann]*_{NOM} *[den Garten]*_{ACC} *gepflegt.*

   ii   Transliteration: Probably has the man the garden taken care of.

   iii Gloss: "The man probably took care of the garden."

  b   Unnatural order

   i   Sentence: *Wahrscheinlich hat [den Garten]*_{ACC} *[der Mann]*_{NOM} *gepflegt.*

   ii   Transliteration: Probably has the garden the man taken care of.

   iii Gloss: "The man probably took care of the garden."

In the current context, the most relevant discovery involved the effect of variation along the animacy dimension. When the investigators contrasted the two sentence types in which both participants were animate (1a and 1b) against the two sentence types in which only the actor was animate (2a and 2b), they found significant activation in a posterior part of the left PLTC that extended into the angular gyrus (Figure 11.20). These results are similar to those obtained by Thompson et al. (2007) and den Ouden et al. (2009), and the overall outcome is in keeping with the conjecture outlined above. As mentioned earlier, this proposal really has two parts. First, the pertinent temporoparietal region may play a critical role in representing the sorts of actor–undergoer relationships that are typically encoded by transitive verbs; and second, it may be recruited most heavily during the processing of transitive sentences in which each participant is animate and hence capable, at least in principle, of deliberately exerting force on the other. For example, independently of the syntactic specifications of the sentences in (1a) and (1b), either the man

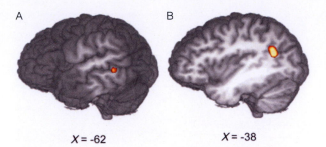

X = -62   *X* = -38

Figure 11.20   Results of Grewe et al.'s (2007) fMRI study of sentence processing. Greater activation in the left pMTG (A) and left pSTS/angular gyrus (B) was found for transitive sentences with two animate participants (actor and undergoer) than for transitive sentences with just one animate participant (actor). (From Grewe et al., 2007, p. 347.)

or the director could potentially be the actor. Because of this confusability (sometimes referred to as semantic reversibility), it is especially important to ensure that the actor role is linked with the proper participant, and that extra effort may be neurally manifested, in part, as greater activation in the temporoparietal region.

As a brief digression, it is interesting to note that these ideas converge nicely with non-linguistic studies which have shown that essentially the same general temporoparietal region is associated with the following functions: the perception of mechanistic "billiard-ball" causality (Blakemore et al., 2001), and the ability to take alternative social and spatial perspectives on the same situation (for reviews see Hein & Knight, 2008; Perner & Leekam, 2008). Perspective-taking is one aspect of the human "mentalizing" or "theory-of-mind" capacity that, according to several scholars, interacts closely with the linguistic representation of action, particularly at the level of information packaging in the clause (e.g., Foley, 2007; MacWhinney, 2008). Thus, it may not be an accident that adjacent or even interleaving sectors of the left PLTC and angular gyrus are engaged during biological motion perception, sentence comprehension, and theory-of-mind tasks (Figure 11.21; see also Redcay, 2008).

Returning to the main line of argumentation, the hypothesis that we have been considering predicts that damage to the left PLTC and/or angular gyrus should disrupt the comprehension of actor–undergoer relationships in transitive sentences in which both participants are animate. Several recent neuropsychological studies have in fact generated results that are consistent with this prediction (Thothathiri et al., 2012b; Newhart et al., 2012), but we will refrain from discussing them until Chapter 15 (see Figure 15.18 and the accompanying text).

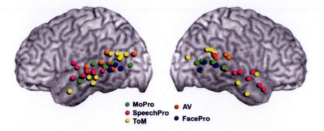

Figure 11.21 Activation of the territory surrounding the superior temporal sulcus in a variety of conditions involving motion processing (MoPro), speech processing (SpeechPro), theory of mind (ToM), audiovisual integration (AV), and face processing (FacePro). (From Hein & Knight, 2008, p. 2130.)

Involvement of Broca's Area

It is well-established that Broca's area (i.e., BAs 44 and 45) is essential for many forms of linguistic computation. When it comes to semantic processing, however, there is growing evidence that this region may contribute more to the meanings of action verbs than object nouns. Consider, for example, the traditional confrontation naming paradigm. Although the functional neuroimaging literature on this topic is full of inconsistencies and complications (for a review see Crepaldi et al., 2011), several studies have revealed greater engagement of Broca's area during action naming than object naming (e.g., Tranel et al., 2005; Berlingeri et al., 2008). And in keeping with these findings, a plethora of neuropsychological studies have demonstrated that damage to Broca's area is implicated more in defective action naming than in defective object naming (for a review see Mätzig et al., 2009; see also, e.g., Bak et al., 2001; Tranel et al., 2001; Hillis et al., 2002a, 2002b, 2004a, 2006; Cotelli et al., 2006; Kemmerer et al., 2012). Moreover, if one turns from naming tasks to comprehension tasks, one finds further support for the view that Broca's area plays a vital role in processing the kinds of action concepts that are typically encoded by verbs. For instance, as shown by the white circles in Figure 11.4, Kemmerer et al. (2012) found that in a very large group of brain-damaged patients, lesions in Broca's area were linked with impaired vs. unimpaired performance on all six of the tasks that probed knowledge of action concepts.

Broca's area does not, however, treat all verbs the same way. Rather, it appears to be more involved in processing transitive than intransitive verbs (especially when the latter have actor subjects). Some evidence for this comes from the fMRI study by den Ouden et al. (2009) that was discussed above. As indicated in Figure 11.19, Broca's area was engaged significantly more when the research participants retrieved transitive verbs than when they retrieved intransitive verbs (see also Raettig et al., 2010). Additional evidence comes from a host of neuropsychological studies with aphasic patients who exhibit agrammatism—i.e., a sentence production disorder that involves omission/substitution of closed-class elements and reduced syntactic complexity (see Chapters 3 and 14). These patients often—not always, but often—have lesions that encompass Broca's area (Vanier & Caplan, 1990), and they tend to have great difficulty retrieving verbs. For present purposes, what matters most is that the degree to which a given verb is difficult for an agrammatic patient to access depends in part on its transitivity, with transitive verbs usually being significantly harder than intransitive verbs (Thompson et al., 1997b; Caplan & Hanna, 1998; Kemmerer & Tranel, 2000; Kiss, 2000; Kim & Thompson, 2000, 2004; Luzzatti et al., 2002; Cho-Reyes & Thompson, 2012; for unusual cases of the opposite pattern see Jonkers & Bastiaanse, 1996, 1997, 1998; Kemmerer & Tranel, 2000).

How can these findings be explained? The correct account is not yet clear, but three possibilities, which are not mutually exclusive, are as follows. One approach is based primarily on syntactic factors. Broca's area has been implicated in syntactic processing (see Chapters 14 and 15), so its greater involvement in transitive than intransitive verbs may reflect the greater syntactic complexity of the former than the latter. Another approach revolves around the notion of competition for selection. As mentioned in Chapter 6, research on the "conceptual focusing" stage of the Lemma Model of speech production suggests that Broca's area is heavily recruited in situations when the speaker must resolve conflicts between multiple lexical items that compete with each other for selection (see Figure 6.8 and the accompanying text). It is not known if transitive verbs tend to interfere with each other more than intransitive verbs, but if they do, they would presumably place greater demands on Broca's area. The third approach deals directly with the conceptualization of action. It hinges on an apparent connection between, on the one hand, recent evidence regarding the contribution of Broca's area to high-level motor cognition, and on the other hand, the fundamental semantic properties that distinguish transitive from intransitive verbs. Although this last approach is not really that complicated, it does require some space to be properly developed. For this reason, it is elaborated over the course of the next few paragraphs (for a more detailed discussion see Kemmerer, 2012).

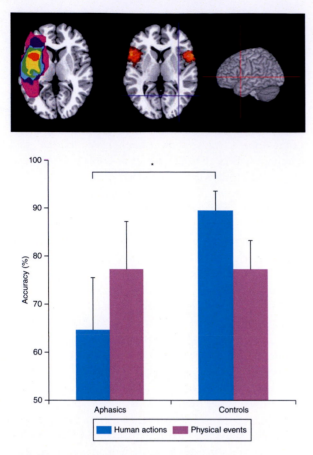

Figure 11.22 Results of Fazio et al.'s (2010) neuropsychological study of the spatiotemporal representation of human actions and physical events. Top panel: (Left) Overlay of the six patients' lesions, with a different color for each patient. (Middle) Probablistic extension of Broca's area as identified by Amunts et al. (1999). (Right) 3D rendering of a standard brain with the maximal overlap of lesions marked with a red cross. Note that the overlap corresponds perfectly with BA44. Bottom panel: Mean accuracies of the aphasic patients and control subjects on the tasks involving human actions and physical events. The patients differed significantly from the controls only on the task involving human actions. (From Fazio et al., 2010, pp. 1983 & 1985.)

There is increasing evidence that Broca's area (especially BA44) plays a critical role in processing the spatiotemporal organization of object-directed bodily actions, regardless of whether they are performed, perceived, imagined, or linguistically represented (for reviews see Binkofski & Buccino, 2004; Fadiga et al., 2009). In the non-linguistic realm, evidence that Broca's area has this function comes from numerous studies employing many different brain mapping methods, but the results of two "companion" neuropsychological and rTMS investigations are particularly compelling. The

neuropsychological investigation was conducted by Fazio et al. (2009) with six aphasic patients whose lesions overlapped maximally in Broca's area (see the top panel of Figure 11.22). These patients were given an action comprehension task that had almost no linguistic requirements. On each trial, they first watched a video clip of either an object-directed human action (e.g., a man reaching for and grasping a bottle) or a nonhuman physical event (e.g., a train entering a station). Then they were shown four randomly ordered photographs that were snapshots of different stages of the video clip that they had just seen. The task was to re-order the sequence of photographs so that they were lined up in a way that reflected the natural unfolding of the action or event. The striking discovery was that, compared to a group of healthy control subjects, the patients were significantly impaired in the human action condition, but not in the nonhuman event condition (see the bottom panel of Figure 11.22). Furthermore, in a parallel rTMS study, Clerget et al. (2009) demonstrated that temporarily disrupting the operation of Broca's area when healthy subjects performed a variant of the same task led to significantly slower response times in the human action condition than in the nonhuman event condition. Taken together, these two studies bolster the view that Broca's area is necessary for appreciating the logical goal-oriented structure of object-directed bodily movements.

Such findings suggest that, in the linguistic realm, Broca's area may contribute to the processing of transitive expressions by computing the linear rankings of the core participants and their corresponding syntactic positions (e.g., Bornkessel & Schlesewsky, 2006; Dominey et al., 2006; Fiebach & Schubotz, 2006; van Schie et al., 2006; Kemmerer & Gonzalez Castillo, 2010). This idea can be unpacked as follows. An inherent aspect of object-directed actions is that they always unfold in both space and time, starting with an intention inside the actor and progressing outward toward the undergoer. This natural linearization of action in the real world is captured by the most common type of linearization of action in language. Imagine, for example, a situation in which—as in one of the video clips used by Fazio et al. (2009) and Clerget et al. (2009)—a man reaches out and grasps a bottle. In languages worldwide, there is an overwhelming tendency for such an action to be described by a transitive sentence in which the noun-phrase encoding the actor occurs before the noun-phrase encoding the undergoer, as in *The man grasped the bottle* (see the analysis and map of 1,228 languages provided by Dryer, 2005a). In fact, this word order pattern—i.e., the powerful tendency for subjects (actors) to precede objects (undergoers)—is one of the most solidly grounded universals of human languages, since relatively few languages have been found that violate it. Thus, it can safely be assumed that, with respect to linear sequencing, the default linguistic description of a simple transitive action ordinarily matches, in an isomorphic or iconic manner, the real-world unfolding of that action.

Now, to come back to the main theme, this whole line of thinking may help explain why Broca's area is more involved in processing transitive than intransitive expressions. The basic argument is as follows. First, Broca's area is essential for understanding the spatiotemporal organization of volitional goal-oriented actions that are directed at particular objects. Second, these kinds of actions are almost always represented linguistically by transitive rather than intransitive expressions. Therefore, one would expect Broca's area to contribute more to the former than the latter kinds of expressions, and to also rank the actor higher than the undergoer. This argument is clearly consistent with the data discussed above, and it also fits with evidence that when the default actor > undergoer linearization is reversed—as in the example sentences (1b) and (2b) presented earlier in connection with Grewe et al.'s (2007) study—activity in Broca's area increases, presumably because the linguistic sequence of participants no longer corresponds to the real-world unfolding of the action (Grewe et al., 2007; Meyer et al., 2012a, 2012b; see also Figure 15.19 and the accompanying text in Chapter 15). Despite the strengths of the argument, however, it remains quite speculative, and whether or not it is on the right track remains to be seen (for related ideas see Box 11.2).

Box 11.2 Do Action Concepts Have a Default Directionality?

In our everyday lives, we continually see people perform actions that, from our egocentric vantage point, unfold in all kinds of different directions. But when we *think* about actions, we usually conceptualize them as unfolding along a horizontal vector with the actor on the left and the undergoer on the right (for a review see Chatterjee, 2010).

The first evidence for this came from several detailed investigations of a single aphasic patient, WH, who regularly used a spatial strategy when producing and comprehending sentences. For example, when describing pictures he consistently treated the participant on the left as the actor. Thus, in reference to the upper left picture in Figure 11B2.1, he would correctly state that the square was shooting the circle, but in reference to the upper right picture, he would incorrectly state that the circle was kicking the square (Maher et al., 1995). Similarly, when matching sentences with pictures he routinely attributed the actor role to the left-most participant in each picture. Thus, when given a choice between the upper left and lower left pictures in Figure 11B2.1, he would correctly pick the upper left one as a match for the sentence *The square is shooting the circle*, but when given a choice between the upper right and lower right pictures, he would incorrectly pick the upper right one as a match for the sentence *The circle is kicking the square* (Chatterjee et al., 1995a). To account for these findings, the researchers speculated that "the dissolution of this patient's linguistic abilities by brain damage might have released a

Figure 11B2.1 Examples of visual stimuli used in experiments with case WH. (From Chatterjee et al., 1995a, p. 130.)

primitive prelinguistic representation making explicit an underlying spatial schema that we all might be harboring" (Chatterjee, 2010, p. 101; for related data and discussion see Rinaldi & Pizzamiglio, 2006).

Subsequent experiments with healthy subjects supported this conjecture by generating the following findings (Chatterjee et al., 1995b, 1999; see also Cohn & Paczynski, 2013). When people are asked to draw an

(Continued)

(Continued)

action in which a circle pushes a square, they tend to place the circle to the left of the square. When people are asked to draw actions that have horizontal trajectories, like a staggering drunk, they tend to depict them as moving left-to-right rather than right-to-left. And when people are asked to match sentences with pictures, they are faster if the pictures show the actor on the left and the energy flow moving left-to-right.

Interestingly, more recent work has shown that the predilection to conceptualize actions as having a default directionality is not a *sui generis* phenomenon, but is instead strongly influenced by the directionality of orthographic systems. English and Italian are written and read left-to-right, and speakers of these languages are inclined to think of actions as proceeding left-to-right; conversely, Arabic is written and read right-to-left, and speakers of this language are inclined to think of actions as proceeding right-to-left (Maass & Russo, 2003; Altmann et al., 2006). Still, it remains unknown whether imaginary action vectors are usually thought of as moving left-to-right, right-to-left, or in some other direction by people who live in cultural and linguistic communities in which the egocentrically anchored left/right frame of reference does not play a prominent role. One such community consists of the Australian Aborigines who live in Hopevale, North Queensland, and speak Guugu Yimithirr, a language in which cardinal directions like north, south, east, and west are vastly more important than the bodily based left/right axis (Levinson, 2003). Might these people tend to think of actions as moving, say, from south to north?

Summary

Action verbs fall into two large domains: transitive verbs, which designate events with two core participants (e.g., *The girl* **petted** *the cat*); and intransitive verbs, which designate events with only one core participant (e.g., *The cat* **purred**). Research suggests that transitive verbs and sentences depend more than intransitive verbs and sentences on certain temporal and parietal regions, especially the junction of the PLTC and angular gyrus. These regions may carry out some sort of high-level visually derived event processing that is more important for transitive than intransitive expressions. One possibility is that they represent force-dynamic information about the energy flow and causal relations between the two core participants in transitive expressions. Research also suggests that transitive verbs and sentences depend more than intransitive verbs and sentences on Broca's area. This difference could be the neural signature of the greater syntactic complexity of transitive expressions, but it could also reflect the fact that, according to numerous studies, Broca's area is essential for processing the hierarchical spatiotemporal organization of precisely the types of object-directed actions that are usually encoded by transitive, as opposed to intransitive, expressions. These are obviously rather complicated issues, however, and a great deal of future work will be needed to resolve them.

Summary and Key Points

- As indicated in Chapter 10, the Grounded Cognition Model maintains that concepts are anchored in modality-specific systems, such that understanding word meanings involves activating high-level perceptual and motor representations. Research guided by this framework supports the following proposals about the neural substrates of the meanings of action verbs:

  - Motion features may be stored in the same sectors of the posterolateral temporal cortex (PLTC) that underlie high-level motion perception.
  - Motor features may be stored in the same sectors of the parietal and frontal cortices that underlie high-level motor programming.

- The claim about motor features is further developed by the Semantic Somatotopy Hypothesis, which holds that these aspects of action verbs are represented, in part, in somatotopically mapped frontal areas—e.g., *lick* depends on ventral areas for lip/tongue movements, *pick* depends on lateral and dorsolateral areas for arm/hand movements, and *kick* depends on dorsal and dorsomedial areas for leg/foot movements.

- Although there is substantial evidence for the Semantic Somatotopy Hypothesis, some studies suggest that motor simulations may not always be necessary to appreciate the basic meanings of action verbs. These findings, together with other considerations, have led to the Fault Tolerant Theory of Conceptual Representation, which states that as a person's capacity to mentally simulate actions decreases, their ability to comprehend linguistic descriptions of those actions does not suddenly disappear, but degrades gracefully.
- As indicated in Chapter 10, the Hub and Spoke Model assumes that concepts are based not only on modality-specific brain systems for perception and action, but also on a modality-invariant integrative device—the semantic hub—in the anterior temporal lobes. Evidence that this device plays a crucial role in representing the meanings of action verbs comes from semantic dementia.
- There are two major domains of action verbs—transitive and intransitive. Findings from fMRI studies and neuropsychological studies suggest that transitive expressions depend more than intransitive expressions on certain temporal and parietal regions, as well as on Broca's area. Some tentative semantically based accounts are as follows:

  ○ The temporal and parietal regions—more specifically, the junction of the PLTC and angular gyrus—may represent visually derived information about the energy flow and causal relations between the two core participants in transitive expressions.
  ○ Broca's area may represent motor-related information about the hierarchical spatiotemporal organization of the kinds of object-directed actions that are typically encoded by transitive expressions.

Recommended Reading

- Chatterjee, A. (2008). The neural organization of spatial thought and language. *Seminars in Speech and Language, 29,* 226–238. An accessible discussion of the inherently relational nature of verb meanings, written by one of the leading researchers in the field.
- Kemmerer, D., Rudrauf, D., Manzel, K., & Tranel, D. (2012). Behavioral patterns and lesion sites associated with impaired processing of lexical and conceptual knowledge of actions. *Cortex, 48,* 826–848. A neuropsychological study that focuses on 226 brain-damaged patients, all of whom were given a set of six tasks that probe knowledge of action concepts in a wide variety of ways.
- Watson, C.E., Cardillo, E.R., Ianni, G.R., & Chatterjee, A. (2013). Action concepts in the brain: An activation-likelihood estimation meta-analysis. *Journal of Cognitive Neuroscience, 25,* 1191–1205. A valuable meta-analysis of functional neuroimaging studies of action concepts assessed both verbally and non-verbally.
- Papeo, L., Negri, G.A.L., Zadini, A., & Rumiati, R.I. (2010). Action performance and action-word understanding: Evidence of double dissociations in left-damaged patients. *Cognitive Neuropsychology, 27,* 428–461. A neuropsychological study that reveals some of the limitations of the Grounded Cognition Model.

Abstract Words

Introduction

By focusing on the meanings of object nouns and action verbs, the two previous chapters remained within conceptual realms that are solidly grounded in the physical world. This chapter, however, expands into the more nebulous world of words for various kinds of abstract concepts. This is a very large and heterogeneous semantic universe, as indicated by the fact that well over 90 percent of the words in this book are fairly abstract in content. Consider, for example, some of the words that have already been used in this paragraph, like *focusing, two, previous, however, more, various, indicated, fact, consider, some, already, the, this, of*, and *are*. Although we produce and understand abstract words like these all the time, their meanings are obviously much harder to imagine and characterize than those of more concrete words like *horse, shovel, walk,* and *bite*. Moreover, as we all know, definitional difficulties become even more challenging when we turn to loftier notions like *democracy, freedom, truth, love, beauty, infinity, eternity, life,* and *death*. Indeed, the mystery of how people acquire and mentally represent abstract concepts has preoccupied philosophers and scientists for many centuries, and significant breakthroughs are only now beginning to be made.

The aim of this chapter is to review some of the major theoretical and empirical developments that have taken place in the branch of cognitive neuroscience that investigates abstract concepts. From an experimental perspective, this area of inquiry is still in its infancy, and much less has been learned about the neural bases of abstract concepts than about the neural bases of object concepts and action concepts. However, the pace of research has been accelerating in recent years, and an increasing amount of exciting, high-quality work is being done. The first section of the following survey discusses the major cognitive and neural distinctions

between concrete and abstract concepts. It begins by summarizing several prominent theoretical models, and then it covers an assortment of findings from PET, fMRI, aphasia, and rTMS. The second section parallels the corresponding sections of Chapters 10 and 11 by invoking once again the hypothesis that the anterior temporal lobes (ATLs) house a semantic hub that binds and organizes the disparate conceptual features of words. As we will see, evidence that the ATLs do in fact contribute to abstract concepts comes from many sources. Finally, the third section parallels the corresponding sections of Chapters 10 and 11 by exploring the neural underpinnings of two specific domains of abstract concepts—in particular, emotions and numbers.

Cognitive and Neural Distinctions Between Concrete and Abstract Concepts

Theoretical Background

In what ways do the meanings of abstract words differ from those of concrete words? Over the course of the past few decades, several different theoretical accounts have been offered. The following overview begins by briefly describing a classic theory called the Dual Coding Model, and then it turns to an alternative approach known as the Context Availability Model (see also Box 12.1).

Originally formulated over 40 years ago by the Canadian psychologist Allan Paivio (1971, 1986, 1991, 2007), the **Dual Coding Model** maintains that

> **Dual Coding Model** Word meanings are based on both modality-specific representations (nonverbal codes) and lexical associations (verbal codes). Concrete concepts draw equally on both systems, whereas abstract concepts rely primarily on the verbal system.

Box 12.1   Do Abstract Concepts Have Metaphorical Foundations?

An alternative approach to analyzing abstract concepts originated in one of the classic texts of cognitive linguistics, namely Lakoff and Johnson's (1980) *Metaphors We Live By*. As the title of this book suggests, the basic idea is that abstract concepts derive much of their structure and content from concrete concepts by means of systematic metaphorical mappings. Consider, for example, the following metaphors, all of which are implicit in many everyday expressions:

- LOVE IS A JOURNEY: Look *how far we've come*. We're *at a crossroads*. We'll just have to *go our separate ways*. We can't *turn back now*. It's been a *long, bumpy road*. This relationship is a *dead-end street*. We're just *spinning our wheels*. We've gotten *off the track*.
- HAPPY IS UP and SAD IS DOWN: I'm feeling *up*. That *boosted* my spirits. My spirits *rose*. You're in *high* spirits. Thinking about her always gives me a *lift*. I'm feeling *down*. He's really *low* these days. I *fell* into a depression. My spirits *sank*.
- ARGUMENT IS WAR: Your claims are *indefensible*. He *attacked every weak point* in my argument. His criticisms were *right on target*. I *demolished* his argument. If you use that *strategy*, he'll *wipe you out*. He *shot down* all of my arguments.
- LINGUISTIC EXPRESSIONS ARE CONTAINERS and COMMUNICATION IS SENDING: It's difficult to *put* my ideas *into* words. The idea is *buried in* terribly dense paragraphs. Your words seem *hollow*. It's hard to *get* that idea *across to* him. I *gave* you that idea. Your reasons *came through* to us. His words *carry* little meaning.
- TIME IS SPACE: She left *at* 6:30. She swam *in* the morning. His appointment is *on* Monday. He likes to run *between* 4:00 and 5:00. She worked *through* the evening. He lectured *over* three hours. She had dinner *around* 7:00.

These are only a few of the large number of metaphors that have been claimed to underlie abstract concepts. So far, relatively little experimental research has explored the psychological status of such metaphors, but some studies support the view that they do in fact help us think (for reviews see Pecher et al., 2011, and Santiago et al., 2011). Still, it is important to recognize the limits of figurative cognition. For instance, as Pinker (2007, p. 250) observed in connection with the LOVE IS A JOURNEY metaphor,

> When reasoning about a relationship, it's fine to mull over the metaphorical counterpart to a common destination, the rate at which one reaches it, and the bumps along the way. But someone would be seriously deranged if he started to wonder whether he had time to pack or where the next gas station was.

In a similar vein, a neuropsychological investigation of the TIME IS SPACE metaphor demonstrated that some brain-damaged patients could understand the temporal meanings of English prepositions (*at* 6:30, *in* the morning, *on* Monday, etc.) even though they could not understand the corresponding spatial meanings of the very same prepositions (*at* the corner, *in* the room, *on* the floor, etc.; Kemmerer, 2005). This dissociation suggests that even though the TIME IS SPACE metaphor may have influenced the historical development of English and other languages, it does not appear to play a necessary role in the linguistic processing of contemporary adults (see also Kranjec & Chatterjee, 2010).

To be sure, metaphors reflect advanced forms of analogical cognition that go a long way toward explaining why we're so smart relative to other species (Gentner, 2003). By themselves, however, they cannot fully account for our ability to represent and appreciate abstract concepts.

word meanings are represented in two separate but interconnected cognitive systems—one that consists of nonverbal codes called "imagens," and another that consists of verbal codes called "logogens." These technical terms will not be used here, however. The basic

architecture is shown in Figure 12.1, which illustrates how the theory characterizes the concept expressed by the word *telephone*. (These days, of course, people use wireless smartphones, but I trust that most readers can remember back when phones were comparatively

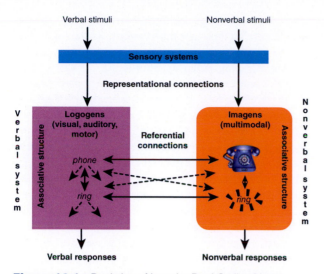

Figure 12.1 Depiction of how the Dual Coding Model characterizes the concept of a telephone. The verbal system (left) contains "logogens" for the phonological and orthographic forms of the word *phone* and for the phonological and orthographic forms of associated words like *ring*. The nonverbal system (right) contains "imagens" for the modality-specific aspects of concepts, such as the visual, auditory, tactile, and motor features of telephones. Also shown are pathways that connect these representations to the perceptual world and to response systems, so that words and telephones "out there" can be recognized and responded to in appropriate ways. Furthermore, there are connecting pathways between the different modalities of verbal and nonverbal representations, so that telephones as seen, heard, or felt can be named, and conversely, their names can evoke images in any modality. (From Paivio, 2007, pp. 142–143.)

dumb devices with cords, like the one in Paivio's drawing.) As in the Grounded Cognition Model, the nonverbal system implements the modality-specific features of concepts, such as how telephones typically look, sound, feel, etc. The verbal system, on the other hand, is a purely linguistic storehouse of word forms. It includes, for example, the phonological form of the word *telephone* and the auditory/motor instantiation of that form during both overt and covert (i.e., subvocal) speech processing. A key aspect of the verbal system is that, rather than representing word forms in complete isolation from each other, it captures complex networks of frequency-based associations among them. Thus, as indicated in Figure 12.1, *telephone* is linked with many other lexical items that tend to co-occur with it, like *ring, number, directory, call, conversation,* etc.

In the current context, the inherently associative nature of the verbal system is very important because it lies at the heart of the Dual Coding Model's account of the major difference between the meanings of concrete and abstract words. According to the theory,

conceptual knowledge is not limited to nonverbal information; instead, it embraces verbal word associations as well. Concrete concepts are thought to have more or less equal amounts of nonverbal and verbal content. For instance, the meaning of *telephone* includes not only the various modality-specific semantic features mentioned above, but also the web of associative links with other lexical items. Abstract concepts, on the other hand, are believed to depend more immediately, and in some cases more substantially, on verbal than nonverbal content. For instance, as Paivio (2007, p. 46) points out, "*religion* might activate *church* first as a verbal associate and then as an image of a church." To take another example, because of their statistical tendency to co-occur in the same discourse contexts, abstract words like *corporation, business, management, money, stock, profit,* etc., have strong associative links with each other in the verbal system, and far from being semantically irrelevant, these reciprocal links are assumed to actually constitute, to a large extent, the meanings of the words. In short: "The main theoretical claim is that imagery and verbal processes contribute jointly to the comprehension of concrete language, whereas verbal processes predominate in the case of abstract language" (Paivio, 2007, p. 105).

Because the Dual Coding Model maintains that concrete words engage both systems to roughly equal degrees, whereas abstract words rely primarily on the verbal system, it predicts that concrete words should have distinct processing advantages over abstract words. This prediction has been borne out by a variety of findings that are usually referred to as **concreteness effects**. For example, when people perform a lexical decision task that requires them to distinguish between real words and pseudowords, they tend to respond faster to concrete words like *table* than to abstract words like *special* (e.g., James, 1975; Rubin, 1980; Kroll & Merves, 1986; for an important qualification see Kousta et al., 2011, which is discussed later). And when people are asked to remember certain words, they tend to be more accurate for concrete than abstract items (e.g., Ter Doest & Semin, 2005; Romani et al., 2007). Researchers who explore these sorts of phenomena often derive their stimuli from large databases that provide standardized normative ratings for lexical variables like the directness with which words refer to concrete entities, and the ease and speed with

Concreteness effects Concrete words have certain processing advantages over abstract words, like being recognized faster and remembered better.

which words elicit mental images in various modalities (Paivio et al., 1968; Coltheart, 1981; Clark & Paivio, 2004; Schock et al., 2012).

It is noteworthy that Gabriella Vigliocco and her colleagues at the University College London have recently developed an interesting extension of the Dual Coding Model (Andrews et al., 2009; Vigliocco et al., 2009; see also Kousta et al., 2011, and Vigliocco et al., 2013). This approach posits two main systems: first, an "experiential" system that stores long-term modality-specific representations; and second, a "distributional" system that registers the statistical co-occurrence patterns of words across discourses. This approach also assumes that concrete and abstract concepts incorporate different proportions of experiential and distributional information. Compared to abstract concepts, concrete concepts have relatively more experientially based modality-specific content than distributionally based encyclopedic content; and compared to concrete concepts, abstract concepts have relatively more distributionally based encyclopedic content than experientially based modality-specific content. Although this new approach has much in common with the classic Dual Coding Model, one salient feature that sets it apart and makes it especially compelling is that it brings together under a single rubric a substantial amount of psycholinguistic and computational data, the latter reflecting many sophisticated analyses of the 100-million word British National Corpus of contemporary written and spoken English. (For similar lines of theoretical and experimental work, see Barsalou et al., 2008; Simmons et al., 2008; Santos et al., 2011; Scorolli et al., 2011; Recchia & Jones, 2012; Connell & Lynott, 2012.)

Perhaps the most prominent alternative to the Dual Coding Model is the **Context Availability Model**. It maintains that the meanings of concrete and abstract words do not differ in terms of the qualitative nature of the underlying representations, since all semantic knowledge is assumed to be amodal in format. Rather, the two types of words differ in terms of how hard it is to identify the most appropriate interpretation (for a review see Schwanenflugel, 1991). For concrete words presented in isolation, this is a relatively quick and easy process, since their meanings are constrained by their physical referents. For abstract words presented in isolation, however, the process is slower and more difficult,

> **Context Availability Model** All word meanings are amodal in format, but they differ with regard to how hard they are to pin down. Concrete concepts tend to be fairly stable and insensitive to context, whereas abstract concepts tend to be more variable and sensitive to context.

since their meanings are more variable and context-dependent. To illustrate this contrast, Saffran and Sholl (1999, p. 245) point out that "a *rose* is always a rose, but the meaning of an abstract word like *phase* varies with the context in which it is used (compare *phase of the moon* with *phase of infant development*)." Similarly, Hoffman et al. (2010, p. 15451) observe that, whereas *spinach* always designates a specific type of vegetable and is only used in food-related contexts, *chance* has a more malleable meaning that generally involves luck or uncertainty but is easily modulated by context—for instance, it can denote "a situation governed by luck (*It's down to chance*), an opportunity that may arise in the future (*I'll do it when I get a chance*), or a risky option (*Take a chance*)." Hence, when *spinach* and *chance* are encountered by themselves—i.e., without a linguistic context that might bias their interpretation, as is often the case in experimental studies—the latter is somewhat harder to understand than the former, since it has several different shades of meaning, all of which are rather amorphous.

Support for the Context Availability Model comes from many sources. For example, large-scale corpus analyses have confirmed that, relative to concrete words, abstract words not only tend to appear in a wider range of linguistic contexts involving diverse topics, but also tend to have a larger number of distinct senses (Hoffman et al., 2011). In addition, several experimental studies have shown that when a conceptually constraining context is provided in the form of one or more prior sentences, thereby creating a rich semantic scaffolding for interpretation, abstract words are no longer disproportionally difficult to process, but instead are recognized and understood just as efficiently as concrete words (e.g., Schwanenflugel & Shoben, 1983; Schwanenflugel et al., 1988; Schwanenflugel & Stowe, 1989).

Nevertheless, Paivio and his colleagues have documented significant concreteness effects for linguistic stimuli beyond the single word level. For example, Sadoski et al. (2000) measured people's capacity to comprehend and recall entire texts, and found that their performance was significantly better for concrete than abstract material. Thus, the debate between the two theories continues.

Multiple brain mapping methods have been used to explore the neural correlates of the distinction between concrete and abstract words, and most of the studies that have been conducted so far have been theoretically framed in terms of the two models discussed above. The following review focuses first on data from PET and fMRI, and then shifts to data from neuropsychology and rTMS. A number of informative electrophysiological studies have also been reported, but they are not addressed here (Holcomb et al., 1999; Kounios & Holcomb, 1994; West & Holcomb, 2000; van Schie et al., 2005; Barber et al., 2013). In addition, several interesting neuropsychological studies have provided some support for a rather different theoretical approach, but again, they are not addressed here (Crutch, 2006; Crutch & Warrington, 2005, 2007, 2010; but see also Hamilton & Coslett, 2008).

Evidence from PET and fMRI

Several different research teams have begun to employ functional neuroimaging techniques to investigate the concrete/abstract distinction. Overall, the results of these studies are quite diverse, most likely because of differences involving the stimuli, tasks, and analyses (for an insightful discussion see Binder, 2007). Nevertheless, there are also many points of convergence, as revealed by two recent meta-analyses that had similar outcomes (Binder et al., 2009; Wang et al., 2010). Here we will restrict our attention to the meta-analysis reported by Wang et al. (2010). These researchers combined data from 303 participants across 19 PET and fMRI studies that explored the concrete/abstract distinction in various ways. The main findings are shown in Figure 12.2.

For the *concrete > abstract* contrast, significant effects were found in three main regions. One was the left ventral temporal cortex, especially the fusiform gyrus. As indicated in Chapter 10, this region has been strongly linked with the shape and color features of object concepts. Hence, its greater response to concrete than abstract words most likely reflects the retrieval of these visual-semantic features. This finding is clearly more compatible with the Dual Coding Model (which posits modality-specific conceptual knowledge) than the Context Availability Model (which posits only amodal conceptual knowledge). A qualification, however, is that the degree to which the fusiform gyrus is engaged by concrete vs. abstract words depends to some extent on how deeply the meanings of those words are processed (Sabsevitz et al., 2005).

Another region was the bilateral posterior cingulate gyrus. This activation can be seen on the sagittal slices at $x = -10$, -3, 4, and 11. The cingulate gyrus lies above the corpus collosum on the medial surface of each hemisphere (see Chapter 1). Its most posterior segment, which encompasses a region called the retrosplenial cortex, has been associated with numerous functions, including visual imagery, spatial attention, navigation, and episodic memory (i.e., recalling specific experiences in one's life). This region's contribution to

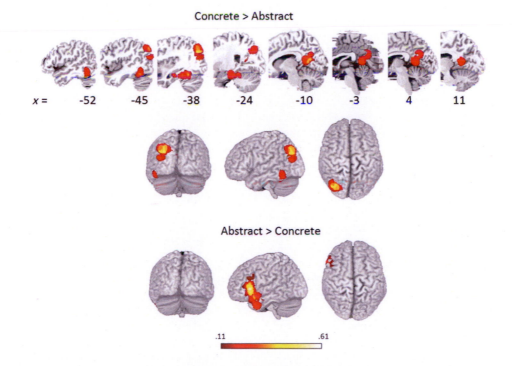

Figure 12.2 Results from Wang et al.'s meta-analysis of PET and fMRI studies of the concrete/abstract distinction. See text for details. (From Wang et al., 2010, p. 1462.)

the conceptual processing of concrete words remains uncertain, but one highly speculative possibility is that it facilitates the situational placement of particular types of objects in particular types of environments, as when a person reacts to the word *toaster* by imagining, from an egocentric perspective, an object of that kind in the setting of a kitchen (for further discussion see Binder et al., 2009, and Vann et al., 2009; see also Yeh & Barsalou, 2006). If this interpretation is on the right track, the greater response of the posterior cingulate to concrete than abstract words can probably be regarded as more compatible with the Dual Coding Model than the Context Availability Model, since it would reflect the enactment of situated perceptual simulations rather than the retrieval of amodal semantic structures.

The last region was the left inferior parietal lobule, particularly the angular gyrus. Despite the fact that this territory was not discussed in Chapter 10, it has been implicated in conceptual processing, especially for concrete words. For instance, Binder et al.'s (2009) meta-analysis of 120 PET and fMRI studies revealed that the most dense concentration of activation foci was in the left angular gyrus. The precise manner in which this cortical region aids conceptual processing is not known, but in light of its anatomical position at the intersection of the temporal, parietal, and occipital lobes, it may subserve a variety of high-level integrative operations (Binder et al., 2009; Seghier et al., 2010; Seghier, 2013; Bonner et al., 2013). At this stage of research, the greater response of the left angular gyrus to concrete than abstract words seems to be consistent with both the Dual Coding Model and the Context Availability Model.

For the *abstract > concrete* contrast, significant effects were found in two main regions. One was the middle/superior sector of the left anterior temporal lobe (ATL). The contribution of this territory to the conceptual processing of abstract words is not clear, but two possibilities with different theoretical implications are as follows. Given that the region is thought to be heavily involved in high-level speech perception and sentence comprehension (see Chapters 5 and 15; see also the fMRI studies of intelligibility in Chapter 2), one possibility is that it plays a role in verbal word associations. Such an interpretation fits better with the Dual Coding Model than the Context Availability Model, since the former but not the latter assumes that verbal word associations are more critical to the meanings of abstract than concrete words. On the other hand, given that the same region—particularly the anterior sector of the middle temporal gyrus—is part of the semantic hub postulated by the Hub and Spoke

Model (see Chapters 10 and 11), an alternative possibility is that it implements amodal semantic structures. Such an interpretation fits better with the Context Availability Model than the Dual Coding Model, since the former but not the latter admits amodal representations and assumes that they are engaged more by abstract than concrete words when the stimuli are presented individually—i.e., without disambiguating information—as they were in 16 of the 19 studies that Wang et al. (2010) included in their meta-analysis. We will return to this issue later (see the section called "A Semantic Hub for Abstract Concepts").

The other region was the left inferior frontal gyrus (IFG; see also Wang et al., 2013a). It encompasses Broca's area and has been linked with many linguistic functions. Two of those functions may be especially relevant to the processing of abstract vs. concrete words; however, as with the left middle/superior ATL, each interpretive possibility reflects a different theoretical perspective. First, the left IFG is believed to subserve the articulatory component of auditory–verbal short-term memory (see Chapters 5 and 15). Hence, from the point of view of the Dual Coding Model, this region may help to maintain in an activated state the verbal word associations that are more integral to the meanings of abstract than concrete words. Second, the left IFG has also been implicated in the strategic control of semantic processing (see Figure 6.8 and the accompanying text in Chapter 6). Hence, from the point of view of the Context Availability Model, it may help to regulate the selection of specific word senses—an operation that is more important for abstract than concrete words, particularly when the stimuli are presented by themselves, which, as noted above, they were in the vast majority of studies that Wang et al. (2010) included in their meta-analysis. As shown in the next subsection, recent evidence from both neuropsychology and rTMS supports the interpretation based on the Context Availability Model rather than the one based on the Dual Coding Model.

Evidence from Neuropsychology and rTMS

To determine which theoretical approach—the Dual Coding Model or the Context Availability Model—provides the best characterization of the role that the left IFG plays in processing abstract vs. concrete words, Hoffman et al. (2010) conducted a study in which they evaluated people's ability to understand these two types of words in two separate conditions: first, in the absence of any context; and second, in presence of a specific context. The Dual Coding Model does not predict that this experimental manipulation should differentially affect the comprehension of the two types of words. The Context Availability Model, on the other hand, predicts that abstract words should be easier to understand when relevant contextual information is given that facilitates the selection of certain meanings.

The two experimental conditions were as follows. In the first condition, subjects performed a semantic similarity judgment task in which, on each trial, a probe word was presented together with three choice words, one of which was closely related in meaning to the probe, and two of which were not. The task was to determine which choice word was most semantically similar to the probe. Some of the trials included concrete words, and others included abstract words, as shown below:

Concrete trial	Abstract trial
frog	*advantage*
jewel toad pickle	*tendency benefit condition*

In the second condition, subjects performed the very same task again, only this time each trial was preceded by two sentences that jointly composed a cue which was either relevant or irrelevant to the probe word, as illustrated in Table 12.1. Both of these experimental conditions were employed in two separate studies—one with a group of brain-damaged patients, and the other with a group of healthy subjects who underwent rTMS.

The first study involved six brain-damaged patients with stroke-induced left-hemisphere lesions that varied considerably in their focus and extent but overlapped maximally in the IFG—more precisely, in BA45 (Figure 12.3A). In light of the PET and fMRI results reviewed above—results that point to a greater contribution of the left IFG to abstract than concrete words—one would expect these patients to exhibit, on average, worse comprehension of abstract than concrete words. However, the Context Availability Model, but not the Dual Coding Model, makes the following additional predictions. First, the patients' comprehension of abstract words should significantly improve when relevant contextual cues are provided, because such cues should reduce the need for the kind of regulatory semantic processing that the left IFG is thought to subserve—processing that, in the case of semantically variable abstract words, helps select the most appropriate interpretation for the task at hand. Second, such a benefit should be minimal for concrete words, since their meanings tend to be more stable and tangible than those of abstract words.

The results were consistent with the predictions (Figure 12.4). Overall, the patients' accuracy was much worse for abstract than concrete words. However, their accuracy for abstract words was significantly boosted when relevant contextual cues were given (blue bars), compared to when no cues were given (purple bars). Although the same kind of effect also occurred for concrete words, it was fairly small and did not reach statistical significance, in keeping with the expectations. It is also noteworthy that the presence of irrelevant cues influenced the patients' comprehension of abstract and concrete words in different ways (orange bars). Relative to the no-cue condition, irrelevant cues had only a minor negative impact on the understanding of abstract words, but had a major negative impact on the understanding of concrete words. This may have happened because, compared to abstract words, concrete words have more rigid meanings and hence are less able to accommodate competing information.

The second study was designed to test, in a more direct and carefully controlled manner, the hypothesis that left BA45—the site of greatest lesion density among the patients in the first study—is essential for the type of strategic semantic processing that, according to the Context Availability Model, is required more by abstract than concrete words. Thirteen healthy adults performed modified versions of the tasks that had been given to the patients. One important change was that only relevant contextual material was provided in the cue condition. Another change was that the subjects also performed a task that consisted of making similarity judgments about numbers. This was included to control for general task difficulty, and, based on reaction times, some of the trials were classified as "easy" (analogous to the concrete words in the no-cue condition) whereas others were classified as "hard" (analogous to the abstract words in the no-cue condition). The main goal of the study was to determine whether the

Table 12.1 Sample Probe Words and Contextual Cues from Hoffman et al. (2010)

Probe Word	Contextually Relevant Cue	Contextually Irrelevant Cue
Frog (concrete)	I saw something in the pond. It was a frog.	It was a windy day. We flew our kite.
Advantage (abstract)	Sue got the job. Her skills were an advantage.	He is late to work. This is out of the ordinary.

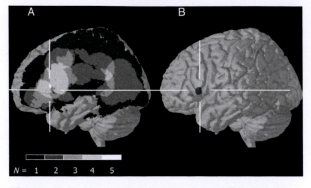

Figure 12.3 Neuroanatomical data from Hoffman et al.'s (2010) combined neuropsychological and rTMS investigation of the concrete/abstract distinction. (A) Lesion overlap for 5 of the 6 patients, showing maximal overlap in left BA45. No scan was available for the 6th patient, but a radiologist's report of an earlier CT scan indicated a left prefrontal lesion. (B) Site stimulated in the rTMS experiment, centered in left BA45 ([–54, 24, 3]). (From Hoffman et al., 2010, p. 15452.)

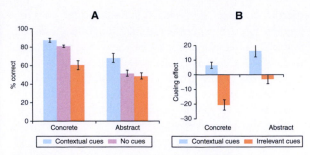

Figure 12.4 Results of Hoffman et al.'s (2010) neuropsychological experiment. (A) Proportion of correct responses in each condition. (B) Effects of contextual (i.e., relevant) cues and of irrelevant cues, calculated by subtracting accuracy in the no-cue condition from accuracy in each cue condition. Note that the orange bars in (A) stand for the condition with irrelevant cues, just like in (B). (From Hoffman et al., 2010, p. 15454.)

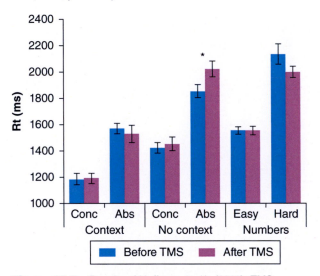

Figure 12.5 Results of Hoffman et al.'s (2010) rTMS experiment. Reaction times are shown before and after rTMS in each condition. Conc = concrete words; Abs = abstract words. (From Hoffman et al., 2010, p. 15454.)

application of rTMS to left BA45 (Figure 12.3B) would significantly affect the comprehension of abstract vs. concrete words. The specific protocol involved delivering a train of TMS pulses to the target site for a period of 10 minutes prior to the administration of the tasks. As mentioned in Chapter 10 (see also Chapter 2), such stimulation has been shown to produce behavioral effects that last for several minutes after the rTMS train has concluded (e.g., Kosslyn et al., 1999; Hilgetag et al., 2001; see also Pobric et al., 2007, 2009; Lambon Ralph et al., 2009).

Now, completely independent of rTMS, one would expect that, on average, reaction times would be slower for abstract than concrete words, due to the inherently greater processing difficulty of the former. From a theoretical perspective, however, the key point is that the Context Availability Model predicts that in the no-cue condition, rTMS should lengthen reaction times for abstract words even more, but should not necessarily affect reaction times for concrete words. This is because the repetitive stimulation of left BA45 should disrupt its capacity to guide the selection of the most appropriate word meanings—a process that is required more by abstract than concrete words, especially when conceptually constraining contextual cues are absent. When such cues are present, however, they might be sufficient to overcome, or compensate for, the deleterious effects of rTMS, in which case reaction times for abstract words would not increase significantly. The Dual Coding Model, on the other hand, leads to different expectations. In particular, it predicts that rTMS should lengthen reaction times for abstract but not concrete words in both the no-cue condition

and the cue condition, because in both conditions abstract but not concrete words require that verbal word associations be kept in an activated state.

The results favored the Context Availability Model over the Dual Coding Model (Figure 12.5). Overall, the subjects' reaction times were slower for abstract than concrete words. Of greater theoretical importance, however, is that for abstract but not concrete words, an interaction was found between the variables of rTMS and contextual cues. Specifically, reaction times for abstract words were significantly longer after than before rTMS, but only when those words had to be understood without the benefit of semantically relevant contextual cues. In contrast, reaction times for concrete words were not influenced in these ways.

Moreover, the fact that abstract but not concrete words were affected by rTMS in the no-cue condition could not be attributed to the inherently greater processing difficulty of abstract words, because the "hard" number judgment task was unaffected by rTMS.

Taken together, the findings from this study converge with those from the neuropsychological study to support the following hypothesis: Left BA45 contributes to the comprehension of abstract words by helping to resolve competitions between the various subtly different interpretations that are often possible for these words, most notably when they are encountered without disambiguating contexts (see also Rodd et al., 2005; Bedny et al., 2007; Zempleni et al., 2007).

Summary

Concrete words like *apple* tend to be processed more efficiently than abstract words like *rule,* especially when they are encountered individually. Two traditional accounts of these so-called concreteness effects are as follows. According to the Dual Coding Model, concrete words are relatively easy to understand because their meanings draw more or less equally on two representational systems: nonverbal codes that consist of modality-specific perceptual and motor features, and verbal codes that consist of frequency-based word associations. In contrast, abstract words are relatively hard to understand because their meanings depend much more on verbal than nonverbal codes. According to the Context Availability Model, on the other hand, the representational format of all word meanings is amodal, and the processing advantage that concrete words often have over abstract words is due to the fact that the meanings of the former are usually fairly stable and insensitive to context, whereas the meanings of the latter are usually more variable and sensitive to context.

Wang et al.'s (2010) meta-analysis of 19 PET and fMRI studies of the concrete/abstract distinction yielded several general conclusions that are important for both empirical and theoretical reasons. Compared to abstract words, concrete words tend to activate three major brain areas: the left fusiform gyrus (associated with visual shape and color representations), the bilateral posterior cingulate gyrus (associated with visual imagery, spatial attention, navigation, and episodic memory), and the left angular gyrus (associated with various integrative functions). In contrast, compared to concrete words, abstract words tend to activate just two major brain areas: the left middle/superior ATL (associated with high-level spoken language comprehension and amodal semantic structures), and the left IFG (associated with

auditory–verbal short-term memory and the strategic control of semantic processing). The neuroimaging data regarding concrete words can be handled better by the Dual Coding Model than the Context Availability Model, but the neuroimaging data regarding abstract words can be handled equally well by both theories.

To shed more light on why the left IFG contributes more to abstract than concrete words, and to help adjudicate between the two alternative theories, Hoffman et al. (2010) conducted a combined neuropsychological and rTMS investigation. Their results favor the view that the left IFG facilitates the comprehension of abstract words by helping to identify the most appropriate interpretation for the task at hand—an operation that (1) is most valuable when abstract words are encountered without disambiguating contexts, (2) is a specific manifestation of the strategic control of semantic processing, and (3) is more in keeping with the Context Availability Model than the Dual Coding Model.

Still, it remains unclear why the left middle/superior ATL plays a greater role in understanding abstract than concrete words. As mentioned above, this region has been linked with two functions that may be relevant: first, high-level spoken language comprehension, which could potentially be related to the sorts of verbal word associations that, according to the Dual Coding Model, are more critical to the meanings of abstract than concrete words; and second, amodal semantic structures, which could potentially be related to the wider range of interpretations that, according to the Context Availability Model, are more characteristic of abstract than concrete words. The next section explores these possibilities in greater detail.

A Semantic Hub for Abstract Concepts

In the two previous chapters, we discussed in some detail the theoretical framework known as the Hub and Spoke Model. A key component of this approach is the idea that the ATLs in both hemispheres contain a modality-invariant integrative device called the semantic hub which serves to bind and organize the various conceptual features that constitute the meanings of words. Chapter 10 reviewed evidence that the ATLs are essential for representing the sorts of object concepts that are typically encoded by concrete nouns, and Chapter 11 reviewed evidence that these regions are also essential for representing the sorts of action concepts that are typically encoded by concrete verbs. Here, we will consider several neuropsychological and rTMS studies which suggest that—in accord with the neuroimaging data analyzed by Wang et al. (2010)—the semantic functions of the ATLs encompass abstract concepts as well, regardless of whether they are encoded by nouns or verbs (see also Figure 11.15 and the accompanying text in Chapter 11).

Evidence from Semantic Dementia

As indicated in Chapters 4, 10, and 11, semantic dementia (SD) is a neurodegenerative disease—one variant of primary progressive aphasia—in which conceptual knowledge gradually deteriorates as a consequence of worsening atrophy of the ATLs and neighboring temporal lobe structures. Up to now, most of the research on SD has focused on describing, explaining, and attempting to ameliorate the relentless degradation of concrete concepts. However, a growing literature has begun to chart the fate of abstract concepts in this population. So far, the results that have emerged are very mixed, but also very interesting.

On the one hand, a number of studies have described SD patients who exhibit so-called "reverse concreteness effects"—i.e., better knowledge of abstract than concrete words. These patients are puzzling for several reasons. Not only does their behavior violate the well-documented superiority of concrete over abstract words for normal individuals, but it also seems to contradict the neuroimaging findings reviewed above. This is because those findings suggest that the left ATL is recruited more by abstract than concrete words, leading to the expectation that damage to that region should cause a greater impairment of abstract than concrete words. On the other hand, several recent studies suggest that reverse concreteness effects are not really a typical feature of SD, since they only show up in a relatively small proportion of patients. These new results are clearly more consistent with the normal concreteness effect as well as the neuroimaging and neuropathological data. In addition, some intriguing proposals have been offered to explain why a minority of SD patients do display reverse concreteness effects. All of these issues are elaborated more fully below.

The most captivating reports of reverse concreteness effects come from detailed case studies. Such effects have been observed not only in SD patients (Warrington, 1975; Breedin et al., 1994; Cipolotti & Warrington, 1995; Macoir, 2009; Papagno et al., 2009), but also in patients with herpes simplex encephalitis (HSE)—a virus that, as noted in Chapter 10, invades the ATLs bilaterally (Warrington & Shallice, 1984; Sirigu et al., 1991). Table 12.2 shows how both types of patients sometimes manifest significantly better

Table 12.2 Definitions of Concrete and Abstract Words Produced by Three SD Patients (AB, DRN, and DM) and Two Patients with Herpes Simplex Encephalitis (SBY and FB), All of Whom Exhibited Reverse Concreteness Effects

AB (Warrington, 1975)	
Cabbage	Eat it.
Geese	An animal, but I've forgotten precisely.
Supplication	Making a serious request for help.
Pact	Friendly agreement.
DRN (Cipolotti & Warrington, 1995)	
Leopard	Some sort of animal … it's small like an insect … I think it flies.
Giraffe	I don't know … it's a sort of foreign term … something to do with furniture.
Vigorous	Very forceful.
Free	Not restricted by anything.
DM (Breedin et al., 1994)	
Ink	Something that covers.
Cheese	Something sweet to eat.
Try	Try is to endeavor to accomplish something.
Opinion	Your concept or perspective.
SBY (Warrington & Shallice, 1984)	
Cabbage	Used for eating, material that's usually made from an animal.
Ink	Food—you put on top of food you are eating—a liquid.
Malice	To show bad will against somebody.
Caution	To be careful how you do something.
FB (Sirigu et al., 1991)	
Duck	A small animal with four legs.
Thimble	We often say sewing thimble.
Society	A large group of people who live in the same manner and share the same principles.
Culture	A way to learn life's customs, it varies from country to country.

Adapted from Saffran & Sholl (1999, p. 246).

knowledge of abstract than concrete words (see also the stroke patient described by Marshall et al., 1996).

Reverse concreteness effects are illustrated in greater depth by Macoir's (2009) meticulous investigation

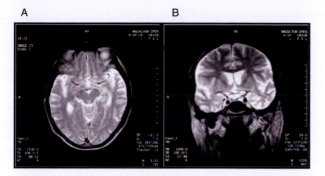

Figure 12.6   MRI of case SC. The two panels show (A) axial and (B) coronal T2-weighted images in which the left hemisphere is on the right side. The atrophy is most prevalent in the anterior inferolateral and polar regions, and is also worse in the left than the right hemisphere. (From Macoir, 2009, p. 521.)

of a single SD patient referred to as case SC. When this study began, SC was a 54-year-old right-handed Frenchman who had earned a PhD and was employed as a psychology professor. During the previous four years, he had experienced increasing difficulty retrieving words and understanding other people's speech. He also had trouble recognizing objects and using them appropriately. For example, at one point he took his car to a mechanic because "a button got very hot when pushed," but it turned out to be the cigarette lighter! Administration of a battery of standardized neuropsychological tests indicated that SC suffered from a significant impairment of conceptual knowledge in the context of otherwise intact perception, motor control, and executive functions. In addition, an MRI revealed atrophy in the polar and inferolateral sectors of the ATLs, more advanced in the left than the right hemisphere (Figure 12.6). Taken together, these behavioral and anatomical findings led to a diagnosis of SD.

From the very outset, it was apparent that SC found it much easier to talk about abstract than concrete topics. This is clearly demonstrated by the following two examples of his spontaneous speech. (These passages, as well as all of the examples of stimuli described below, are translated from French.)

> I progressively discover that my personal thoughts develop my well-being. I do not wish to prove that these thoughts are absolute. On the other hand, I wish to try them out daily to check if they can maintain this well-being. What emerges gradually is the awareness of the symptom. What happens is that I am not able any more to increase my personal well-being. When I wake up in the morning, my anxiety emerges immediately. The probability that I will make mistakes is huge. I constantly live in danger.

> When there is a lot of snow on the roof of my house and my driveway, I remove the snow. I go on the roof of my house with my legs. I cannot tell you how I go up there. Also, I cannot tell you what I use to remove the snow. Also, for my driveway, I use another object that I cannot name. To defrost also, I do it but I do not remember the word for it.

The primary purpose of Macoir's study was to carefully examine this striking dissociation between relatively preserved abstract knowledge and relatively impaired concrete knowledge. To that end, he tracked the development of SC's dementia longitudinally by administering the same set of tasks on three different occasions over the course of 21 months (T1 = January 1999, T2 = October 1999, and T3 = September 2000). A total of 14 tasks were used, but here we will restrict our attention to just three.

In one experiment, SC was given an "odd one out" task in which, on each trial, a probe word was presented together with two choice words, and the requirement was to determine which choice word was semantically more different from the probe word. There were 80 items, 40 of which involved abstract words (e.g., probe = *authorization;* choices = *permission* or *instruction*), 20 of which involved concrete words for living things (e.g., probe = *rabbit;* choices = *hare* or *beaver*), and 20 of which involved concrete words for nonliving things (e.g., probe = *couch;* choices = *sofa* or *stool*). The results are shown in Table 12.3. In the abstract condition, SC was only mildly impaired at T1 (72.5 percent) and T2 (70 percent), but declined much further at T3 (40 percent). In the two concrete conditions, however, he started out with very low scores at T1 (mean = 40 percent) and continued to deteriorate across T2 (mean = 30 percent) and T3 (mean = 12.5 percent). Although the differences between the two concrete conditions were never significant, the differences between those conditions and the abstract condition were significant at each of the three time periods.

In another experiment, SC was given a matching task in which, on each trial, a word was presented together with four pictures, and the requirement was to identify the picture that corresponded best to the word. Once again, there were 80 items—40 involving abstract concepts, 20 involving concrete living things, and 20 involving concrete nonliving things. To illustrate the abstract condition, Macoir described the picture set associated with *chance:* The correct picture showed a person finding money; a related distractor showed a person banging his leg on a desk; an unrelated distractor showed a person placing a flashlight in a backpack; and another unrelated distractor showed a person walking

Table 12.3 Case SC's Performance on an "Odd One Out" Task

	T1	T2	T3	Controls
Abstract items (40)	29 (72.5%)*	28 (70%)*	16 (40%)***	36.2 (34–39)
Concrete items (40):	16 (40%)***	12 (30%)***	5 (12.5%)***	37.2 (35–39)
Living (20)	6 (30%)***	6 (30%)***	3 (15%)***	18 (17–20)
Nonliving (20)	10 (50%)***	6 (30%)***	2 (10%)***	19 (18–20)

Source: Macoir (2009, p. 522).

Columns show the number and percentage correct for SC at three time periods, as well as the average number correct and the range for control subjects.

*Significant difference of $p < .05$ between SC and the control subjects.

***Significant difference of $p < .001$.

Table 12.4 Case SC's Performance on a Word--Picture Matching Task (Format as Table 12.3)

	T1	T2	T3	Controls
Abstract items (40)	35 (87.5%)	36 (90%)	26 (65%)***	37.4 (36–39)
Concrete items (40):	24 (60%)***	25 (62.5%)***	17 (42.5%)***	39.4 (39–40)
Living (20)	13 (65%)***	15 (75%)***	9 (45%)***	19.6 (10–20)
Nonliving (20)	11 (55%)***	10 (50%)***	8 (40%)***	20 (20)

Source: Macoir (2009, p. 523).

on a tight-rope. To illustrate the concrete condition involving living things, Macoir described the picture set associated with *snake:* The correct picture showed a snake; a semantically related distractor showed a turtle; a semantically and visually related distractor showed an alligator; and a visually related distractor showed a belt. Although Macoir did not provide an example of the concrete condition involving nonliving things, those items had pictures sets similar to the ones for the other concrete condition. The results are shown in Table 12.4. In the abstract condition, SC achieved remarkably high scores at both T1 (87.5 percent) and T2 (90 percent), but was very impaired at T3 (65 percent). By contrast, in the two concrete conditions, he performed quite poorly at T1 (mean = 60 percent) and T2 (62.5 percent), and was even worse at T3 (42.5 percent). The differences between the two concrete conditions were never significant, but the differences between those conditions and the abstract condition were significant at T1 and T2, and nearly so at T3.

In yet another experiment, SC was given a word definition task in which, on each trial, a word was presented and the requirement was to generate the "most complete" definition possible. The stimuli consisted of 47 abstract words (24 high-frequency and

23 low-frequency), 15 concrete words for living things (8 high-frequency and 7 low-frequency), and 28 concrete words for nonliving things (15 high-frequency and 13 low-frequency). Each of SC's definitions was rated on a scale of 1 (bad) to 7 (good) by three different groups of ten graduate students in psychology, and definitions that elicited a mean rating of lower than 5 were classified as incorrect. The results are shown in Table 12.5. Irrespective of word frequency, the proportion of correct definitions was consistently higher for abstract than concrete items across all three time periods. Moreover, as in the previous experiments, while the abstract condition dissociated from the two concrete conditions, the two concrete conditions did not dissociate from each other. Nevertheless, when frequency was taken into account, it became clear that SC's better performance for abstract than concrete items was limited to high-frequency words. Columns show the number and percentage of SC's word definitions with a mean rating of 5 or higher.

The results of these three experiments with SC provide an excellent illustration of how reverse concreteness effects usually appear. As mentioned above, similar effects have been documented in several other case studies of individual patients with either SD or HSE. And

Table 12.5   Case SC's Performance on a Word Definition Task

	T1		T2		T3	
	High-freq.	**Low-freq.**	**High-freq.**	**Low-freq.**	**High-freq.**	**Low-freq.**
Abstract	16/24 (67%)	7/23 (30%)	11/24 (46%)	3/20 (15%)	8/24 (33%)	2/10 (20%)
Concrete	4/23 (17%)	4/20 (20%)	2/23 (9%)	0/17 (0%)	5/22 (23%)	0/15 (0%)
Living	1/8 (12.5%)	1/7 (14%)	0/8 (0%)	0/6 (0%)	0/8 (0%)	0/6 (0%)
Nonliving	3/15 (20%)	3/13 (23%)	2/15 (13%)	0/11 (0%)	5/14 (36%)	0/9 (0%)

Source: Macoir (2009, p. 523).

Columns show the number and percentage of SC's word definitions with a mean rating of 5 or higher.

more recently, such effects have been reported in a few group studies of SD patients (Yi et al., 2007; Bonner et al., 2009). However, given that, by definition, reverse concreteness effects violate the normal processing advantage of concrete over abstract words, it is important to determine whether they are common or rare occurrences, especially among SD patients, since their disease targets the ATLs, whose contribution to abstract concepts is the overarching topic of this discussion.

Although it has been suggested that reverse concreteness effects may be a typical feature of SD (Grossman & Ash, 2004), several experimental investigations have challenged this view (Jefferies et al., 2009; Hoffman & Lambon Ralph, 2011; Hoffman et al., 2013). For instance, in a highly detailed study, Hoffman and Lambon Ralph (2011) administered seven tasks to seven SD patients who spanned the full range of severity observed in the disorder. Each task probed knowledge of both concrete and abstract concepts, and a total of 436 data points were obtained for each patient. The specific tasks were as follows (for examples see Figure 12.7):

- *Synonym judgment (N = 64):* Originally devised by Jefferies et al. (2009), this task requires the subject to decide, on each trial, which of three choice words is most similar in meaning to a probe word. Most of the items involve nouns (Figure 12.7C).
- *Description-to-noun matching (N = 40):* Originally devised by Yi et al. (2007), this task requires the subject to decide, on each trial, which of four choice words best matches a brief description. All of the items involve nouns (Figure 12.7A).
- *Description-to-verb matching (N = 40):* Originally devised by Yi et al. (2007), this task has the same format as the previous one, except all of the items involve verbs (Figure 12.7B).
- *Verb similarity (N = 40):* Originally devised by Bonner et al. (2009), this task requires the subject to decide, on each trial, which of two choice words

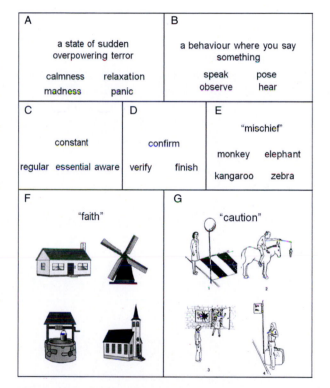

Figure 12.7   Tasks employed in Hoffman and Lambon Ralph's (2011) study of SD patients. (A) Description-to-noun matching. (B) Description-to-verb matching. (C) Synonym judgment. (D) Verb similarity. (E) Mischievous monkey test with words. (F) Mischievous monkey test with pictures. (G) Shallice and McGill word–picture matching. (From Hoffman et al., 2011, p. 2105.)

is more similar in meaning to a probe word. All of the items involve verbs (Figure 12.7D).

- *Shallice & McGill word–picture matching (N = 60):* Originally devised by Shallice & McGill but as yet unpublished, this task has been used in several studies of concreteness effects (e.g., Warrington & Shallice, 1984; Breedin et al., 1994). It requires the subject to decide, on each trial, which of four pictures corresponds best to a word (Figure 12.7G).

- *Mischievous monkey test (MMT) with pictures (N = 96):* This new task is analogous to the previous one, but the concrete and abstract items are controlled better for difficulty and involve identical picture sets (Figure 12.7F).
- *Mischievous monkey test (MMT) with words (N = 96):* This new task parallels the previous one, but it is entirely verbal (Figure 12.7E).

The researchers found that, overall, the patients performed better on the concrete than the abstract conditions of the tasks—a pattern than clearly conforms to the normal trend (Figure 12.8). This superiority of concrete over abstract conditions was manifested at the level of numerical scores for all but two of the tasks (namely, the two description-to-word tasks), and it was statistically significant, or nearly so, for three of them (namely, synonym judgment, Shallice & McGill, and MMT with pictures). Moreover, the significant dissociations were due primarily to the performances of the four mildest patients, and no reverse concreteness effects emerged in any of the patients' mean percentage correct scores across all of the tasks (Table 12.6). Hence, the upshot of this study is that reverse concreteness effects do not appear to occur frequently enough to be considered a reliable part of the general symptom complex of SD. Instead, for the majority of patients, as their semantic

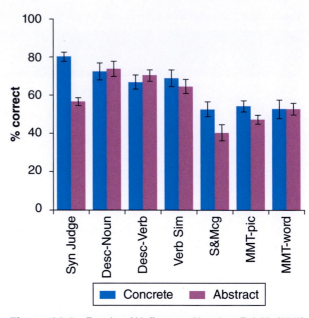

Figure 12.8   Results of Hoffman and Lambon Ralph's (2011) study of SD patients. The conditions correspond to the tasks shown in Figure 12.7. (From Hoffman et al., 2011, p. 2106.)

knowledge gradually deteriorates, abstract concepts tend to be affected somewhat more than concrete concepts. As Hoffman and Lambon Ralph (2011, p. 2109) point out, "the performance of SD patients simply

Table 12.6   Performances of Individual SD Patients on Tasks

	Condition	Max.	DF	MT	MB	PL	NH	PW	ET
Synonym judgment	Concrete	32	32*	29*	29*	29*	18	22	20
	Abstract	32	23	19	20	21	13	16	14
Description–noun	Concrete	20	19	19	12	19	10	14	8
	Abstract	20	19	20	13	17	12	9	13
Description–verb	Concrete	20	14	16	12	17	12	11	11
	Abstract	20	17	17	15	16	12	9	12
Verb similarity	Concrete	20	19	15	9	17	11	13	12
	Abstract	20	15	14	11	18	11	11	10
Shallice & McGill	Concrete	30	29*	18*	15	19	10	10	9
	Abstract	30	17	10	15	12	11	9	10
MMT with pictures	Concrete	48	35	34	30	23	20	23	16
	Abstract	48	36	27	26	25	18	17	9
MMT with words	Concrete	48	40	36	30	19	20	—	11
	Abstract	48	40	32	28	22	18	—	16
All tasks	Concrete	Mean %:	88*	78*	62	72	48	57*	43
	Abstract	Mean %:	77	67	60	66	47	43	43

Source: Hoffman & Lambon Ralph (2011, p. 2106).

*Significantly better performance on concrete vs. abstract conditions (*p* < .05).

Table 12.7 Occupations of Patients Exhibiting Large Reverse Concreteness Effects

Study	Case	Occupation	Etiology	More Severely Damaged Hemisphere
Warrington (1975)	AB	High-level civil servant	SD	Unknown
Cipolotti & Warrington (1995)	DRN	Biological scientist	SD	Left
Breedin et al. (1994)	DM	Professional with master's degree	SD	Left
Macoir (2009)	SC	Psychology professor	SD	Left
Papagno et al. (2009)	MC	Teacher	SD	Left
Warrington & Shallice (1984)	SBY	Naval officer (engineer)	HSE	Symmetric
Sirigu et al. (1991)	FB	Engineering student and semi-professional musician	HSE	Symmetric

Source: Hoffman & Lambon Ralph (2011, p. 2109).

reflects an exaggeration of the normal pattern." This turns out to be perfectly compatible with Wang et al.'s (2010) neuroimaging data, since SD often affects the middle/superior sector of the left ATL, and the neuroimaging data suggest that this region plays a greater role in processing abstract than concrete words. (But see Loiselle et al., 2012, for a recent neuropsychological study that raises some new questions.)

From a theoretical perspective, both Hoffman and Lambon Ralph's (2011) SD data and Wang et al.'s (2010) neuroimaging data can be accommodated by each of the three frameworks mentioned earlier. According to the Dual Coding Model, the left middle/superior ATL may contribute more to abstract than concrete concepts because it has been implicated in high-level spoken language comprehension, which in turn may be related to verbal word associations, these being more critical for abstract than concrete concepts. According to the Context Availability Model, the basic reason why the left middle/superior ATL is more involved in processing abstract than concrete words is that it may store amodal semantic representations; and, crucially, such representations may be engaged more by abstract than concrete words when the stimuli are encountered individually, since the former words have a wider range of potential interpretations. Finally, the Hub and Spoke Model yields an explanation that is more or less along the same lines as the one provided by the Context Availability Model. To be sure, none of these approaches provides a rigorous, in-depth account of why the left middle/superior ATL is recruited to a greater degree by abstract than concrete words. But all of them do offer some general insights about this issue, and thereby serve as springboards for further research.

Still, an important question remains unanswered: Why do some SD patients—apparently a small minority of them—display reverse concreteness effects? Two intriguing possibilities have been proposed. The first one has to do with the functional–anatomical parcellation of the ATLs and the distribution of atrophy in SD (for relevant discussion see Wong & Gallate, 2012). Let's assume that, as suggested by Wang et al.'s (2010) neuroimaging data, abstract words depend more than concrete words on the middle/superior sector of the left ATL. If the atrophy in a given patient affected that sector significantly *less* than the ventral sector (which, as shown in Chapter 10, has been heavily implicated in concrete object concepts), reverse concreteness effects might arise. Interestingly, this account may apply to case SC because, as indicated above, his tissue loss seems to have been much greater in the ventral than the middle/superior sector of the left ATL.

The second possibility hinges on individual differences in the sophistication of abstract conceptual knowledge prior to the onset of brain injury. If some patients had above-normal familiarity with abstract concepts before their disease emerged, they might be predisposed to exhibit less impairment of those concepts. Some support for this account comes from the fact that, as shown in Table 12.7, most of the SD and HSE patients who have manifested dramatic reverse concreteness effects have been well-educated professionals who probably had unusually large and deeply entrenched abstract vocabularies before their first symptoms appeared. Once again, this account applies well to case SC, since he was a psychology professor. A limitation of the account, however, is that there are undeniable exceptions. For instance, one of the SD patients studied by Jefferies et al. (2009) had a PhD but did not display reverse concreteness effects.

Further work is obviously needed to determine the merits and shortcomings of both of the explanatory approaches described here, and to explore other possibilities as well.

Evidence from rTMS

Owing to its capacity to transiently disrupt the operations of precisely targeted brain regions, rTMS provides a unique opportunity to gather additional data about whether the left middle/superior ATL plays a greater role in understanding abstract than concrete words. Pobric et al. (2009) took advantage of this opportunity by conducting an experiment with 12 healthy subjects. These subjects were given a semantic similarity judgment task in which, on each trial, they had to decide which of three choice words was most similar in meaning to a probe word. This task was very much like the one that Hoffman et al. (2010) used to study the contribution of the left IFG to abstract word comprehension, except that here there were three sets of trials instead of just two. Specifically, 48 trials included words with high imageability, 48 trials included words with medium imageability, and 48 trials included words with low imageability. As in Hoffman et al.'s (2010) experiment, the subjects were also given a control task that had the same format as the main task but required judgments about numbers rather than words. Because the researchers wanted to investigate the potential involvement of not only the left but also the right ATL in abstract word processing, they marked two sites for rTMS in each subject. These sites were selected by first identifying the tip of the temporal pole in each hemisphere, and then measuring 10 mm posterior along the middle temporal gyrus. (Interestingly, the MNI coordinates for the left-hemisphere site were [−53, 4, −32], and those for the left anterolateral temporal "hot spot" revealed by Wang et al.'s (2010) meta-analysis of *abstract > concrete* contrasts in the neuroimaging literature were [−52, 8, −32].) Analogous once again to Hoffman et al.'s (2010) experiment, the subjects performed the tasks both before and after the delivery of 10 minutes of rTMS. The stimulation was applied to the left-hemisphere site in one testing session, and to the right-hemisphere site in another testing session.

The results were informative not only in terms of reaction times, but also in terms of accuracies. Reaction times were significantly longer after than before rTMS for the lexical task but not the number task, and these effects were present at both left- and right-hemisphere

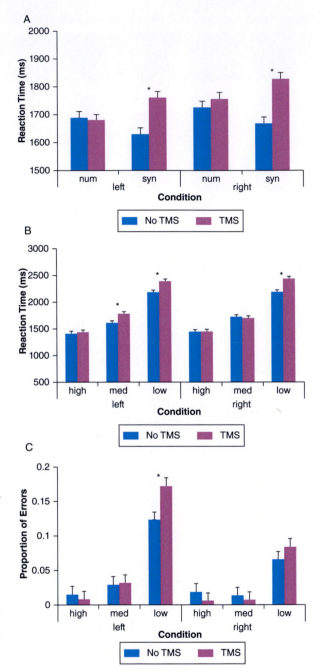

Figure 12.9   Results of Pobric et al.'s (2009) rTMS study of the concrete/abstract distinction. (A) The effect of left or right stimulation on number (num) and synonym (syn) judgment times. (B) The rTMS effect for high, medium, or low imageability trials in the synonym judgment task. (C) The proportion of errors induced by rTMS for each imageability condition in the synonym judgment task. (From Pobric et al., 2009, pp. 1107–8.)

sites (Figure 12.9A). Moreover, and of greater theoretical importance, as the imageability of the items in the lexical task decreased, the impact of rTMS on reaction times increased, with greater effects at the left- than the right-hemisphere site (Figure 12.9B). Turning to accuracies, both left and right rTMS led to a greater error rate in the lexical task, but only for low image-ability items (Figure 12.9C).

These rTMS findings bolster the view that the left lateral ATL—in particular, the most anterior portion of the left middle temporal gyrus—is more critical to the processing of abstract than concrete concepts. The study also provides new evidence that the homologous region in the right hemisphere plays a similar, albeit somewhat weaker, semantic role. Overall, the results converge with the neuroimaging and neuropsychological findings reviewed above, and are consistent with all of the theoretical frameworks that we have considered, but perhaps especially with the Hub and Spoke Model, since it places special emphasis on the notion that conceptual knowledge is underpinned by the ATLs bilaterally.

Summary

Findings from neuropsychological studies with SD patients and rTMS studies with healthy subjects support the hypothesis—derived from Wang et al.'s (2010) meta-analysis of neuroimaging studies—that the middle/superior sector of the left ATL contributes more to the processing of abstract than concrete concepts. With regard to SD, progressive tissue loss in the ATLs leads to the gradual degradation of both types of concepts; however, over the course of this cognitive decline, and especially during the early stages, the majority of patients conform to the normal pattern of worse performance on abstract than concrete items. Although some patients exhibit dramatic reversals of this performance profile, they appear to be atypical. They might have less atrophy in the left middle/superior ATL than in the left ventral ATL, or they might have had above-average capacities for abstract thought prior to the onset of their symptoms. Further research is needed to explore the viability of these and other possible accounts. With regard to rTMS, temporarily disrupting the left anterior middle temporal gyrus in healthy subjects impairs their semantic processing of abstract but not concrete words. Similar but less robust effects also occur when the homologous right-hemisphere region is stimulated. These results suggest that abstract concepts rely not only on the middle sector of the left ATL, but also, to a lesser degree, on its right-hemisphere twin. Taken together, the data from SD and rTMS can be accommodated by the Dual Coding Model, the Context Availability Model, and the Hub and Spoke Model. The last theoretical approach, however, may have the greatest explanatory adequacy, since

it maintains that both left and right ATLs contribute to the semantic structures of words.

Domains of Abstract Concepts

Most of the research reviewed so far is consistent with the widely held view that the meanings of abstract words are rather far removed from the physical realm of bodily experience. But what about the spokes of the Hub and Spoke Model (see Figure 10.9 in Chapter 10) and the corresponding sensory and motor components of the Grounded Cognition Model (see Figure 10.1 in Chapter 10)? Are these modality-specific representational systems completely irrelevant to abstract concepts? Although the results of the studies summarized above suggest that the answer may be "yes," it is important to realize that all of those studies treated the vast sphere of abstract concepts as homogeneous, without semantically important subdivisions. Because of this limitation, it is possible that when the spotlight is focused more narrowly on specific, well-defined domains of abstract concepts, neuroscientific evidence for embodied grounding will begin to emerge. As shown below, this kind of scenario has in fact been gradually developing for two particular domains of abstract concepts—namely, emotions and numbers.

Emotions

In the literature on conceptual knowledge, the meanings of emotion words like *fear*, *anger*, *happiness*, and *sadness* are usually considered to be abstract. There is growing evidence, however, that when the meanings of such words are processed deeply, they take the form of complex conceptualizations that are neurally implemented as widely distributed activation patterns which draw not only on systems for verbal associations and amodal representations, but also on systems for perception, action, and introspection (i.e., the sense of one's own mental and physical states). One especially interesting study that generated results along these lines was recently reported by Wilson-Mendenhall et al. (2011). Before discussing it, however, we will first look at some equally interesting new work which suggests that, on average, abstract words have more affective connotations than concrete words.

As noted in the first main section of this chapter ("Cognitive and Neural Distinctions Between Concrete and Abstract Concepts"), psycholinguists often organize words according to ratings along the following two dimensions: concreteness, which is the directness with which words refer to concrete entities; and imageability,

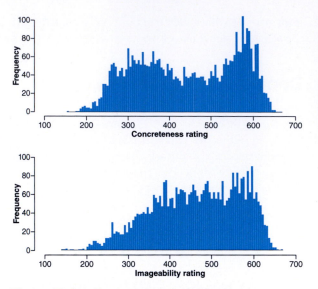

Figure 12.10 Frequency plots for concreteness and imageability ratings for 4,274 words from the MRC Psycholinguistic Database. (From Kousta et al., 2011, p. 17. Reprinted with permission.)

which is the ease and speed with which words elicit mental images in various modalities. These two scales are sometimes thought to be more or less interchangeable, but Kousta et al. (2011) demonstrated that they are in fact partially distinct. Specifically, when these researchers analyzed both kinds of ratings for a set of 4,274 words, they found that while the words tended to cluster into two major classes along the dimension of concreteness—one class for concrete concepts and another for abstract concepts—they varied in a fairly continuous, linear fashion along the dimension of imageability (Figure 12.10).

After showing that the dimensions of concreteness and imageability are partially distinct, Kousta et al. (2011) conducted several experiments that generated valuable new insights about the mental representation of abstract concepts. First, a group of healthy subjects performed a lexical decision task in which the real words included 80 items with the following properties: they differed in terms of concreteness, with 40 being rated relatively high and 40 being rated relatively low; however, the two subsets of 40 words were precisely matched in terms of not only imageability, but also context availability, familiarity, frequency, age of acquisition, number of letters, number of phonemes, number of syllables, number of orthographic neighbors, mean neighbor frequency, and several other variables (Table 12.8). The results revealed that, contrary to the predictions of the traditional view, abstract words were recognized *faster* than concrete words.

Table 12.8 Eighty Words Differing in Concreteness but Matched for Imageability, Context Availability, Familiarity, Frequency, Age of Acquisition, Number of Letters, Number of Phonemes, Number of Syllables, Number of Orthographic Neighbors, Mean Neighbor Frequency, and Several Other Nuisance Variables

Concrete	Abstract
Office	Horror
Cancer	Beauty
Ounce	Grief
Relic	Demon
Trunk	Spree
Lamp	Hell
Estate	Luxury
Duke	Fury
Cousin	Angel
Rector	Frenzy
Leek	Oath
Gig	Woe
Ether	Havoc
Guest	Crime
Prong	Wealth
Creature	Concert
Oak	Joy
Date	Love
Stomach	Romance
Author	Thrill
Block	Panic
Asbestos	Paradise
Jersey	Danger
Channel	Protest
Column	Temper
Material	Fashion
Sound	Minute
Stick	Ghost
Plate	Space
Voice	Dream
Monsoon	Slumber
Belt	Joke
Freight	Expanse
Starch	Burden
Disease	Number
Weapon	Dozen
Manure	Plunge
Garment	Bargain
Lobby	Quest
Bureau	Triumph

Source: Kousta et al. (2011, p. 31).

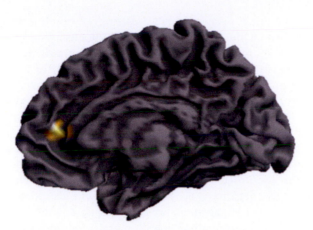

Figure 12.11   Results of Vigliocco et al.'s (2014) fMRI study of the concrete/abstract distinction. The affect-related rostral (pregenual) portion of the left anterior cingulate cortex is engaged significantly more during lexical decisions for abstract than concrete words when the two sets of words are matched for imageability. (From Vigliocco et al., 2014, p.1771.)

To explain this rather surprising outcome, the investigators carefully analyzed a much larger collection of nearly 500 words for which many different kinds of ratings were readily available. What they found was quite remarkable: Abstract words tend to be more emotionally loaded than concrete words, and this turned out to be the key factor that influenced subjects' reaction times in the initial lexical decision experiment (see also Newcombe et al., 2012; Vigliocco et al., 2013; Vinson et al., in press).

Finally, to explore the neural underpinnings of these phenomena, Vigliocco et al. (2014) carried out another lexical decision experiment with another group of healthy subjects, only this time the subjects performed the task while their brain activity was being scanned with fMRI. The real words consisted of 60 concrete nouns and 60 abstract nouns that were carefully matched in terms of imageability as well as 13 other variables. In accord with Kousta et al.'s (2011) study, however, the abstract words were significantly more "valenced" and "arousing" than the concrete words. And when the neural responses elicited by the abstract words were contrasted against those elicited by the concrete words, significant activation was observed in just one region—the rostral (pregenual) portion of the anterior cingulate cortex, which is well-established as playing a central role in emotional processing (Figure 12.11; for reviews see Etkin et al., 2011; Grabenhorst & Rolls, 2011). In addition, it is interesting to note that as the affective connotations of all 120 words increased, the signal strength in this region also increased.

These findings cannot easily be accounted for by either the Dual Coding Model or the Context Availability Model. Instead, Vigliocco et al. (2014) argue that they support an alternative hypothesis—namely, that the distinction between concrete and abstract concepts arises in part because the former have a statistical preponderance of sensory and motor features, whereas the latter have a statistical preponderance of affective features (see also Andrews et al., 2009; Vigliocco et al., 2009; Newcombe et al., 2012). In light of these considerations, it is natural to wonder about the neural substrates of words that directly denote emotions, so let's turn now to that topic.

As mentioned above, Wilson-Mendenhall et al. (2011) recently reported a study that was deliberately designed to explore the neural circuitry subserving emotion concepts. Because they were strongly motivated by the Grounded Cognition Model, one of their main goals was to test the hypothesis that when people think deeply about the meanings of emotion words, they simulate certain high-level aspects of affective processing by recruiting some the same brain regions that underlie the construal and regulation of feelings. In addition, these researchers wanted to test a closely related idea, which is that emotion concepts are not always activated in exactly the same way, but rather take different forms depending on the circumstances. As they point out in a discussion of the meaning of *fear*, this idea is based on the tremendous range of affective situations that may fall within the boundaries of a single emotion concept (Wilson-Mendenhall et al., 2011, p. 1108):

Fear can look and feel quite differently in different instances. When you fear a flying cockroach, you might grab a magazine and swat it; when you fear disappointing a loved one, you might think of ways to make them feel good about you; when you fear a mysterious noise late at night, you might freeze and listen; when you fear giving a presentation, you might ruminate about audience reactions or overprepare; when you fear getting a flu shot, you might cringe anticipating the pain; when you fear hurting a friend's feelings, you might tell a white lie. Sometimes you will approach in fear, and sometimes you will avoid. Sometimes your heart rate will go up, and sometimes it will go down. Whatever the situation demands.

We are dealing, then, with not one but two theoretical proposals. First, the authors claim that the comprehension of emotion words relies in part on neural networks that contribute to emotion in general. And second, they claim that this comprehension process also relies on other neural networks that represent various aspects (e.g., sensory, motor, social) of the different kinds of background situations in which emotions occur.

To test these proposals, Wilson-Mendenhall et al. (2011) conducted an fMRI study that concentrated on just four abstract concepts, two of which involved emotions—*fear* and *anger*—and two of which did not—*observe* and *plan*. On each critical trial, the subjects first heard a description of a situation and were encouraged to imagine being there; then they heard one of the four concept words and were asked to judge how easy it was to have that experience in the situation. Crucially, the situations were of two general types: Half of them were associated with physical danger brought about by the protagonist's own carelessness (e.g., becoming lost during a spontaneous run in the woods), and half of them were associated with social evaluation in unfair circumstances (e.g., being unprepared for a work presentation because others on the team did not contribute). A final methodological point is that, in order to distinguish between the neural responses to situations and the neural responses to concept words, the researchers randomly mixed into the protocol "catch trials" in which a situation was presented without a subsequent concept word. (For a similar design, see the discussion in Chapter 10 of Simmons et al.'s [2007] fMRI study of the color features of object concepts). From a theoretical perspective, the major predictions were as follows. First, the two concept words of greatest interest—namely, the emotion terms, *fear* and *anger*—should consistently engage some of the neural circuitry implicated in emotion in general. And second, those words should also engage a variety of other brain regions involved in perception, action, language, and social cognition, but in a manner partly contingent on the preceding situations.

Both of these predictions were robustly confirmed. During the deep semantic processing of the two emotion terms, activation was reliably found in several brain areas that have been independently linked with certain aspects of affective construal and regulation (Lindquist et al., 2012). These areas included the anterior cingulate cortex (specifically, a sector dorsal to the one identified by Vigliocco et al., 2014) as well as the lateral and medial portions of the orbitofrontal cortex (note that this territory is discussed in Chapter 7 in the context of emotional prosody). Importantly, these areas were recruited by both words, regardless of whether the preceding situations involved physical danger or social evaluation. At the same time, though, each emotion word also ignited several other mostly non-emotion-related regions, some of which

were situation-specific. For present purposes, it is sufficient to illustrate these findings by focusing on just *fear*. In response to the physical danger situations, *fear* was processed in terms of the possibility of bodily harm, and accordingly there was engagement of areas implicated in visceral sensation (insular cortex), place recognition (parahippocampal cortex), auditory perception (superior temporal cortex), and motor programming (inferior parietal cortex). In response to the social evaluation situations, on the other hand, *fear* was processed in terms of the possibility of being judged negatively by other people, and accordingly there was engagement of areas implicated in social knowledge (temporal poles), moral judgment (ventromedial prefrontal cortex), and cognitive control (dorsolateral prefrontal cortex).

What were the results for the other two abstract words—namely, *observe* and *plan*? Although both them, and especially *plan*, activated some emotion-related regions, they did so to a lesser degree than *fear* and *anger*. In addition, and not surprisingly, they tended to engage regions associated with visual, motor, and executive processes.

In summary, Wilson-Mendenhall et al.'s (2011) fMRI study appears to support the view that even though emotion concepts are, technically speaking, abstract, they are not completely divorced from the brain's bodily-based representational systems for perception, action, and affect, but are instead fundamentally anchored in them. Hence, this investigation seems to provide some leverage for the notion that abstract concepts may not be beyond the explanatory scope of the Grounded Cognition Model (see also Box 12.2; Havas et al., 2007, 2010; Foroni & Semin, 2009; Gendron et al., 2012). Still, caution is definitely warranted. For instance, the interpretation of Wilson-Mendenhall et al.'s (2011) fMRI study may need to be qualified by the following caveat.

As indicated above, on each of the critical trials, the subjects first immersed themselves in the verbally described situation and then vividly imagined the degree to which the subsequently given concept word could be experienced in that situation. Although this experimental approach had the benefit of ensuring that the meanings of the two emotion terms, *fear* and *anger*, were processed deeply, it came at the cost of making it impossible to distinguish between, on the one hand, the neural circuitry mediating the rapid, automatic comprehension of those words, and on the other hand, the neural circuitry mediating the slow, effortful evocation of conscious, explicit images derived from them. In Chapters 10 and 11,

Box 12.2   Good and Bad in Right- and Left-Handers

Idioms like *my right-hand man* and *two left feet* attest to the cultural convention of associating good things with the right side of space and bad things with the left. Even the Latin root for *right* (*dexter*) has positive connotations (cf. *dextrous*), whereas the Latin root for *left* (*sinister*) has negative ones. In a recent series of experiments, Daniel Casasanto and his colleagues have shown that these asymmetric space–valence associations are psychologically real, but, interestingly enough, only for right-handers. Left-handers, it turns out, exhibit the opposite pattern (for a review see Casasanto, 2011).

When asked to judge which of two products is better, which of two job applicants is more qualified, or which of two alien creatures looks more trustworthy, right-handers display subtle and unconscious, but nevertheless statistically significant, preferences for the stimuli presented on their right side; left-handers, however, are more likely to pick the ones on their left side (Casasanto, 2009). These differential tendencies are manifested even when the judgments are made orally, as opposed to manually, and they can be discerned in children as young as five (Casasanto & Henetz, 2012). Body-specific space–valence associations can also be seen in the spontaneous co-speech gestures of righties and lefties. During the final debates of the 2004 and 2008 U.S. presidential elections, the two right-handed candidates (Kerry and Bush) made more right- than left-handed gestures when discussing positive ideas and made more left- than right-handed gestures when discussing negative ideas, whereas the two left-handed candidates (Obama and McCain) displayed the opposite patterns (Figure 12B2.1; Casasanto & Jasmin, 2010).

The link between "good" and the side of hand dominance may arise because people tend to like things that they can interact with easily (Ping et al., 2009). Support for this hypothesis comes from two experiments in which space–valence associations were explored in subjects who either had or had not undergone a recent reversal of hand dominance (Casasanto & Chrysikou, 2011). The first experiment focused on a group of stroke patients who had lost the use of either their right or left arm/hand, and who had been right-handed prior to their brain injury. The patients whose left side was affected, and who therefore continued to be right-handed, performed like normal right-handers insofar as they tended to link good things with the right side of space. But the patients whose right side was affected, and who therefore became left-handed, performed like normal left-handers insofar as they tended to link good things with the left side of space. Similar causal connections between motor fluency and space–valence associations were found in the second experiment, which focused on a group of healthy, right-handed university students. Each subject was asked to carry out a difficult manual task for 12 minutes while wearing a bulky ski glove on either their left hand, which did not interfere with their natural right-handedness, or their right hand, which forced them to temporarily become left-handers. Their space–valence associations were tested afterward, and while the subjects who had worn the glove on their left hand exhibited the expected right-is-good bias, those who had worn it on their right hand manifested the opposite left-is-good bias. Thus, as Casasanto (2011, p. 381) points out, "even a few minutes of acting more fluently with the left hand can change right-handers' implicit associations between space and emotional valence, causing a reversal of their usual judgments."

Of course, the meanings of abstract evaluative terms like *good* and *bad* cannot be reduced completely to mere habits of motor control. These studies show, however, that such concepts are colored, in subtle but predictable ways, by how we use our bodies to interact with the world.

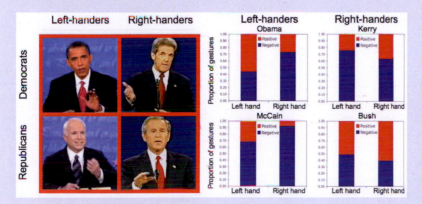

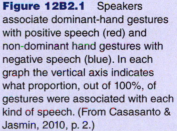

Figure 12B2.1 Speakers associate dominant-hand gestures with positive speech (red) and non-dominant hand gestures with negative speech (blue). In each graph the vertical axis indicates what proportion, out of 100%, of gestures were associated with each kind of speech. (From Casasanto & Jasmin, 2010, p. 2.)

we noted that this sort of distinction is relevant to evaluating how well the Grounded Cognition Model can account for data involving concrete concepts for objects and actions, and here we see that it is also relevant to evaluating how well the theory can account for data involving abstract concepts for emotions. Another way to express the basic problem is like this: The experiment leaves open the possibility that the emotion-related brain regions linked with *fear* and *anger* were not really activated during the initial comprehension of those words, but were instead activated a bit later, during the deliberate generation of post-comprehension affective imagery (see also Mahon & Caramazza, 2008; Tomasino & Rumiati, 2013). According to this logic, it would be necessary to use a method that taps into implicit semantic access—like the lexical decision paradigm employed by Vigliocco et al. (2014)—to verify that the brain regions at issue do in fact contribute to the types of emotion concepts encoded by *fear* and *anger*.

We would be remiss, however, if we did not acknowledge that not everyone agrees with this line of thinking. Indeed, Lawrence Barsalou and Kyle Simmons were among the co-authors of Wilson-Mendenhall et al.'s (2011) paper, and they have developed a version of the Grounded Cognition Model which maintains that it is not really plausible to suppose that a clear division can be drawn between automatically accessing the meanings of words and voluntarily pondering them (Barsalou et al., 2008; Simmons et al., 2008; Santos et al., 2011). According to this approach, when it comes to word comprehension, explicitly generated images are no less "conceptual" in nature than implicitly activated representations. As we have seen so many times before, despite the fact that significant progress is being made, many issues remain contentious, and there is still a long way to go.

Numbers

Another interesting domain of abstract concepts that has begun to receive close attention in cognitive neuroscience is numbers. From a semantic perspective, numbers are surely among the most abstract kinds of concepts, for they are essentially pure magnitudes or quantities that exist independently of the various types of symbols that we use to refer to them. For example, the number expressed by the English word *two* can also be expressed by the Arabic numeral *2*, the Roman numeral *II*, two fingers, two dots, two drum beats, and so on and so forth. Many different brain mapping techniques have been used to investigate the neural substrates of numerical representations and calculations,

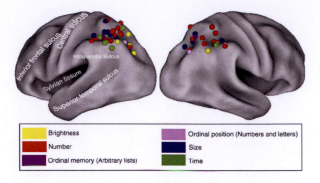

Figure 12.12 The major magnitude representation system in the human brain resides in the intraparietal sulcus bilaterally. (From Cantlon et al., 2009, p. 88.)

and, as described below, there is some evidence that, despite being highly abstract, these sorts of concepts are at least partly grounded in bodily experience.

First of all, it is noteworthy that, unlike other kinds of abstract concepts, number concepts do not appear to depend on the ATLs. We have already encountered one study that supports this view—namely, Pobric et al.'s (2009) demonstration that although the application of rTMS to the ATLs interferes with semantic similarity judgments for abstract (low-imageability) words, it does not disrupt analogous judgments about Arabic numerals (see also Pobric et al., 2007, and Lambon Ralph et al., 2009). Additional evidence comes from the fact that patients with SD almost invariably have spared numerical knowledge, including preserved abilities to compare the magnitudes of numbers, order them serially, and read and write both number words and numerals (e.g., Cappelletti et al., 2001; Halpern et al., 2004a; Jefferies et al., 2005). Some SD patients even become rather obsessed with numbers, displaying compulsive counting, clock-watching, and financial thriftiness (Snowden et al., 1996).

It is widely believed that the reason SD patients have intact numerical cognition is because the disease does not affect the central magnitude representation system in the brain, which is housed primarily in the intraparietal sulcus (IPS) and adjacent inferior parietal lobule (IPL) bilaterally. Many functional neuroimaging studies have implicated this region in magnitude processing in general, since it responds not only when people think about numbers, but also when they evaluate other quantitative stimulus parameters such as brightness, size, and time (Figure 12.12; for a review see Cantlon et al., 2009). With specific regard to numbers, some studies suggest that the IPS/IPL represents them in terms of a "supramodal" coding scheme that transcends different notational formats (e.g., words like

Table 12.9 Body-Part-Based Number Words in Mamvu, Orthographically Simplified

Expression	Number Concept	Literal Meaning
Reli	1	
Jue	2	
Jeno	3	
Jeto	4	
Jimbu	5	
Eli qode reli	6	"The hand seizes one"
Eli qode jue	7	"The hand seizes two"
Jeto jeto	8	"Four four"
Eli qobo reli	9	"The hand spares one"
Eli bosi	10	"All hands"
Qaru qode reli	11	"The foot seizes one"
Qaru qode jue	12	"The foot seizes two"
Mudo ngburu reli	20	"One whole person"
Mudo ngburu reli, ijuni qa reli	21	"One whole person, above there is one"
Mudo ngburu reli, mudo-na-qiqa eli bosi	30	"One whole person, another person, all hands"
Mudo ngburu jue	40	"Two whole persons"
Mudo ngburu jimbu	100	"Five whole persons"

Source: Heine (1997, p. 20).

four and numerals like *4*); however, other studies suggest that the IPS/IPL also contains notation-sensitive coding schemes (for reviews see Nieder & Dehaene, 2009; Cohen Kadosh & Walsh, 2009).

This brings us to the topic of how number concepts might be anchored in the sensorimotor systems of our brains, because it turns out that the most basic notational devices for symbolizing numbers are actually things that we carry around with us everywhere we go—namely, our own body parts, especially our hands. Children spontaneously use their fingers when learning to count, and the best predictor of the mathematical skills of six-year-olds is their ability to identify, in the absence of visual feedback, which of their fingers an experimenter touches (Noel, 2005). In addition, Heine (1997) points out that in diverse languages all over the world, number words often derive historically from body-part words. An excellent example is Mamvu, a language spoken in northeastern Africa that, as shown in Table 12.9, employs a mathematical system grounded in terms for not only the hands, but also the feet.

Based on these considerations, one would expect number representations to be closely linked with body-part representations—particularly finger representations—in the IPS/IPL, and in fact there is substantial evidence for such functional–anatomical connections. Damage to this region, especially in the left hemisphere, sometimes gives rise to both **acalculia**—i.e., impaired numerical cognition—and **finger agnosia**—i.e., impaired recognition, differentiation, and naming of fingers, one's own as well as others' (e.g., Gerstmann, 1940; Cipolotti et al., 1991; Benton, 1992; Mayer et al., 1999). Moreover, both types of deficits can be transiently induced by stimulating certain sites in the left IPS/IPL either directly with

Acalculia   Impaired numerical knowledge, including problems with counting, comparing the magnitudes of numbers, and carrying out mathematical calculations like addition, subtraction, multiplication, and division.

Finger agnosia   Impaired recognition, differentiation, and naming of fingers, one's own as well as others'.

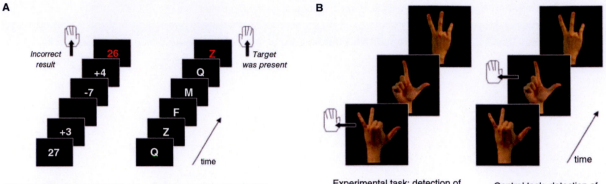

Figure 12.13 Experimental paradigm in Rusconi et al.'s (2009) fMRI study of (A) number and (B) finger representations. See text for details. (From Rusconi et al., 2009, p. 656.)

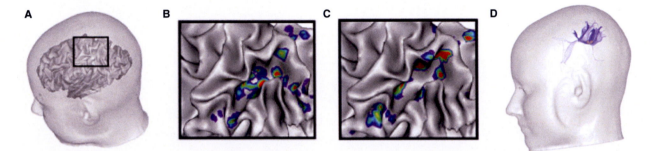

Figure 12.14 Results of Rusconi et al.'s (2009) combined fMRI and DTI study of number and finger representations. Activation clusters in B (number) and C (finger) are shown on the warped surface of the left parietal cortex of a single subject (box shown in A), with warm colors indicating greater signal strength. (D) White matter fibers connecting activated areas shown in B and C. (From Rusconi et al., 2009, pp. 659 & 661.)

intracranial electrodes (Morris et al., 1984; Roux et al., 2003) or indirectly with rTMS (Rusconi et al., 2005).

To investigate more precisely the relations between number and finger representations in the left IPS/IPL, Rusconi et al. (2009) conducted a very sophisticated study that included both an analysis of activation patterns measured with fMRI and an analysis of fiber pathways measured with diffusion tensor imaging (DTI) (see also Rusconi et al., 2010). In the fMRI part of the study, there were several experimental and baseline conditions, the most relevant of which were as follows (Figure 12.13). First, numerical knowledge was probed by asking subjects to add and subtract sequentially presented numbers and then indicate whether a final number in red font was the correct result. The baseline task involved viewing a sequence of letters and then indicating whether a final letter in red font had been in the sequence. Second, finger knowledge was probed by presenting subjects with a sequence of hand postures and asking them to identify those in which the ring finger was extended. The baseline task involved

viewing a sequence of hand postures and reporting those in which the palm was visible. To achieve maximal neuroanatomical precision, the researchers used a brain scanning procedure with high spatial resolution and analyzed the data as a series of single cases. When they subtracted the two baseline conditions from the two experimental conditions, they found that the activation patterns for number and finger representations in the left IPS/IPL were extremely close to each other (Figure 12.14A-C). Next, in the DTI part of the study, the researchers went on to demonstrate that, in each subject, the parietal areas associated with number and finger representations were directly connected by white matter pathways (Figure 12.14D).

These results invite the inference that even though number concepts are highly abstract, they may nevertheless be anchored, at least to some degree, in bodily experience. It is reasonable to suppose that the finger-counting strategies that emerge spontaneously in childhood provide a sensorimotor foundation, implemented partly in the parietal lobe, for the subsequent development of other types of symbolic representations of numbers, such as words and numerals. In adulthood, finger representations may still be accessed in an automatic manner when relatively small numbers are processed (e.g., Rusconi et al., 2005; Andres et al., 2007; Sato et al., 2007; Fischer, 2008; Badets et al., 2010). It seems rather unlikely, however, that a mathematical notion as abstract as *infinity* could be grasped with our hands alone.

Summary

So far, very little research has explored the neural substrates of particular domains of abstract concepts. But for two domains that have begun to receive some attention—specifically, emotions and numbers—evidence has been accumulating which suggests that, in each case, distinct brain systems are involved which serve to relate the given types of abstractions to relevant aspects of more concrete mental life.

Regarding the emotion domain, recent work has led to two important discoveries. First, as a general rule, compared to concrete words, abstract words are more likely to have affective connotations and to engage brain areas linked with affective processing, especially the anterior cingulate cortex. Second, when people think carefully about the meanings of explicitly emotional words, significant activity is found not only in the anterior cingulate cortex, but also in several other

affect-related regions, such as the orbitofrontal cortex. Furthermore, these kinds of words recruit a variety of additional areas that presumably represent diverse aspects of the kinds of scenarios in which the designated emotions frequently occur. Thus, understanding emotion words seems to involve a situated simulation of the type of experience that is linguistically expressed.

Turning to the number domain, an increasing amount of data suggests that the meanings of words like *eight*, and of corresponding numerals like *8*, are represented primarily in the left IPS/IPL. Interestingly, the pertinent cortical areas lie immediately adjacent to, and are tightly interconnected with, areas implicated in finger representations. This arrangement may provide a critical part of the neural platform that enables children to use finger-counting strategies to bootstrap into the complex world of abstract mathematical ideas.

Overall, the evidence reviewed here concerning the conceptual domains of emotions and numbers suggests that they depend to some extent on modality-specific systems for perception, action, and introspection, and hence are not completely outside the purview of the Grounded Cognition Model and the spokes of the Hub and Spoke Model. It goes without saying, however, that much more research is necessary to determine whether these theoretical frameworks can accommodate the many other domains of abstract concepts that have yet to be investigated from a neuroscientific perspective.

Summary and Key Points

- Two traditional accounts of the cognitive differences between concrete and abstract words have strongly influenced neuroscientific research on this topic:
  - According to the Dual Coding Model, all word meanings are based on both modality-specific representations (nonverbal codes) and lexical associations (verbal codes), but they differ with regard to the relative preponderances of the two types of information. Concrete concepts draw more or less equally on both systems, whereas abstract concepts rely primarily on the verbal system.
  - According to the Context Availability Model, all word meanings are amodal in format, but they differ with regard to how hard they are to pin down. Concrete concepts are fairly stable and insensitive to context, whereas abstract concepts are more variable and sensitive to context.

- A meta-analysis of 19 functional neuroimaging studies of the concrete/abstract distinction revealed that, relative to abstract words, concrete words tend to activate three main regions:
  - The left fusiform gyrus (associated with visual shape and color representations).
  - The bilateral posterior cingulate gyrus (associated with visual imagery, spatial attention, navigation, and episodic memory).
  - The left angular gyrus (associated with various integrative functions).
  - These findings, especially the first two, are more compatible with the Dual Coding Model than the Context Availability Model.

(Continued)

(Continued)

- The same meta-analysis also revealed that, relative to concrete words, abstract words tend to activate two main regions:

  o The left inferior frontal gyrus (IFG, associated with auditory–verbal short-term memory and the strategic control of semantic processing).
  o The left middle/superior sector of the anterior temporal lobe (ATL, associated with high-level spoken language comprehension and amodal semantic structures).
  o These findings can be handled equally well by the Dual Coding Model and the Context Availability Model.

- To clarify the role that the left IFG plays in abstract word processing, a group of researchers conducted a study that combined neuropsychological and rTMS techniques. The results favored the view that the left IFG facilitates the comprehension of abstract words by helping to resolve competitions between the various subtly different interpretations that are often possible for these words. This account is more consistent with the Context Availability Model than the Dual Coding Model.
- To clarify the role that the left middle/superior ATL plays in abstract word processing, investigators have drawn, once again, on both neuropsychological and rTMS techniques:

  o Data from neuropsychology indicate that the majority of SD patients have more impaired knowledge of abstract than concrete concepts. Some of them, however, display the opposite performance profile (i.e., reverse concreteness effects). These rare cases may have greater atrophy in the ventral than the middle/superior portion of the left ATL, or they may have had exceptionally good knowledge of abstract concepts prior to the onset of the disease.
  o Data from rTMS indicate that healthy subjects have greater difficulty understanding abstract than concrete words, and hence perform in a manner similar to mild SD patients, when their middle ATLs are temporarily disrupted. Although these effects are greatest when the left hemisphere is stimulated, they also emerge when the right hemisphere is stimulated.
  o These convergent findings from neuropsychology and rTMS reinforce the view that the left middle/superior ATL contributes more to the processing of abstract than concrete concepts. The findings are equally compatible, however, with the Dual Coding Model and the Context Availability Model. They are also compatible—indeed, they may be *most* compatible—with the Hub and Spoke Model, since it assumes that the ATLs in both hemispheres contain mechanisms that bind and organize the multifarious features of word meanings.

- Studies that have focused on two specific domains of abstract concepts—emotions and numbers—suggest that they are not completely removed from the physical realm of bodily experience, but are instead grounded partly in modality-specific representational systems:

  o In general, compared to concrete words, abstract words are more emotionally loaded and more likely to engage the affect-related anterior cingulate cortex. Words for specific types of emotions, like *fear* and *anger,* tend to activate not just the anterior cingulate cortex, but also other affect-related regions, such as the orbitofrontal cortex. Moreover, they tend to activate additional areas that represent the kinds of sensory, motor, and social situations in which the relevant emotions are experienced.
  o The meanings of number words and numerals, like *six* and *6,* rely on areas in the left IPS/IPL that are adjacent to, and connected with, areas that represent fingers. This supports the view that mathematical knowledge is anchored, to some extent, in finger-counting strategies.

Recommended Reading

- Wang, J., Conder, J.A., Blitzer, D.N., & Shinkareva, S.V. (2010). Neural representation of abstract and concrete concepts: A meta-analysis of neuroimaging studies. *Human Brain Mapping, 31,* 1459–1468. A meta-analysis of data from 303 participants across 19 PET and fMRI studies that investigated the concrete/abstract distinction in various ways.
- Hoffman, P., & Lambon Ralph, M.A. (2011). Reverse concreteness effects are not a typical feature of semantic dementia: Evidence for the Hub-and-Spoke Model of conceptual representation. *Cerebral Cortex, 21,* 2103–2112. An in-depth examination of the status of abstract concepts in SD patients.
- Vigliocco, G., Kousta, S.T., Della Rosa, P.A., Vinson, D.P., Tettamanti, M., Devlin, J.T., & Cappa, S.F. (2014). The neural representation of abstract words: The role of emotion. *Cerebral Cortex, 24,* 1767–1777. A compelling demonstration that abstract concepts tend to be more affectively loaded than concrete concepts.
- Santiago, J., Román, A., & Ouellet, M. (2011). Flexible foundations of abstract thought: A review and a theory. In T.W. Schubert & A. Maass (Eds.), *Spatial dimensions of social thought* (pp. 39–108). Berlin: Mouton de Gruyter. An illuminating discussion of several competing theories about the nature of abstract concepts.

PART VI

Morphology, Syntax, and Discourse

Morphology

Introduction

It is often said that what makes human languages special, compared to the communication systems of other species, is that they have boundless expressive power, allowing their speakers to convey a potentially infinite number of thoughts. This power has two main sources. First, every language has an inventory of basic, undecomposable symbols that reflect historically shaped, culturally shared conventions for conceptual coordination. Some familiar examples include the various English words for objects, actions, and abstract notions that we considered in Chapters 10, 11, and 12. From a cognitive perspective, these units are stored in the mental dictionary. Second, every language also has a set of rules that specify how the simplest lexical items can be combined to create increasingly complex expressions with increasingly complex meanings. From a cognitive perspective, these rules are stored in the mental grammar. Traditionally, grammar is divided into syntax—the structure of phrases, clauses, and sentences—and morphology—the structure of words. The neural substrates of syntax are addressed in Chapters 14 and 15. Here our focus is restricted to the neural substrates of morphology.

The term *morphology* entered the technical vocabulary of linguistics around 1860, having been imported from biology, where it was first used around 1820 to refer to the structure of organisms (Dixon, 2010a, p. 138). The roughly 6,000 languages of the world differ tremendously in the extent to which they employ morphological processes (Haspelmath & Sims, 2010). At one extreme, there are highly analytic languages that use almost no such processes, so that virtually every word is a single **morpheme**—that is,

an isolated, minimal pairing of form of meaning. One of the most commonly spoken languages on the planet, Mandarin Chinese, operates this way. At the other extreme, there are highly synthetic languages that use morphological processes quite extensively, so that intricate ideas are frequently encoded as long words composed of many parts. A good example is Greenlandic Eskimo, in which the single word *angya-ghlla-ng-yug-tuq* means roughly "He wants to acquire a big boat" and is translated literally, morpheme by morpheme, as "boat-AUGMENTATIVE-acquire-DESIDERATIVE-3SINGULAR" (Comrie, 1989, p. 45; see also Box 13.1). Not suprisingly, most languages fall somewhere between these two extremes of morphological complexity. For instance, Romance languages such as Spanish and Italian lie toward the middle of the continuum, with verbs coming in myriad forms marked for several grammatical features, most notably person (first, second, or third), number (singular or plural), tense (present, past, or future), and mood (indicative, subjunctive, or conditional). Such systems may strike many monolingual English speakers as being very complex, rather than just moderately complex, but that is only because English morphology turns out to be fairly rudimentary, occupying a place on the continuum that's somewhat closer to Mandarin Chinese than to Spanish and Italian.

English draws upon three main types of morphological processes. First, **compounding** involves joining two roots together to form a complex word that usually has an idiosyncratic meaning and a unique stress pattern. For example, the compound *blackbird* refers to a particular species of bird, and it receives stress on

---

Morpheme An isolated, minimal pairing of form and meaning.

Compounding Two roots are joined together to form a complex word that usually has an idiosyncratic meaning and a unique stress pattern.

Box 13.1 How to Build a Noun in Tabasaran

One interesting way in which languages vary with respect to morphological complexity involves case systems. These are sets of inflections, usually suffixes, that indicate the function of a noun in a clause. For example, anyone who learned a little Latin in high school will remember that for every noun there is a menu of endings to choose from, each of which signals one of five cases. A simple illustration is the word for friend, *amicus,* which takes different forms to express different grammatical roles: *amicus* (nominative); *amicum* (accusative); *amici* (genitive); *amico* (dative); and, once again, *amico* (ablative).

Languages with five case categories, like Latin, are relatively common, but many languages have larger systems with six-to-seven categories, eight-to-nine categories, or even ten or more categories (Iggesen, 2005). The current world record for the richest case system probably goes to Tabasaran and the nearby Tsez, two closely related languages spoken in the Caucasus mountains of southern Russia, both of which are reputed to have somewhere between 14 and 18 categories (Comrie & Polinsky, 1998). These categories specify not only "core" syntactic functions like subject vs. object, but also a variety of "non-core" relational distinctions involving multifarious semantic factors, such as the location and movement of other entities vis-á-vis the entity encoded by the inflected noun (Figure 13B1.1). Because the different case suffixes can be combined in complex ways to express unique meanings, Tabasaran nouns have been estimated to take up to 53 forms.

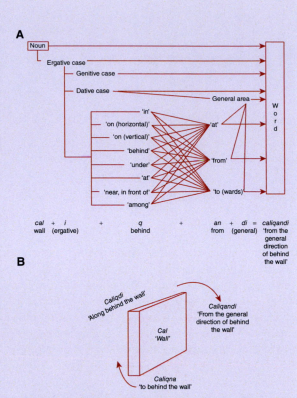

Figure 13B1.1 Case morphology in Tabasaran. (A) A flow chart showing how to assemble a complex noun by adding case suffixes with syntactic and spatial functions. (B) Location, direction, and motion expressed by complex nouns. (From Harrison, 2007, p. 225.)

the first syllable, whereas the phrase *black bird* refers to any bird that happens to be black, and it receives stress on the second syllable (see Chapter 7 for a discussion of the relevant prosodic factors). Some other instances of compound words are *boathouse, penknife, girlfriend, boy-king, sky-blue,* and *razor-sharp.*

Second, **derivation** involves modifying a root or stem, usually through affixation, to create a complex word that often belongs to a different grammatical category and has a different meaning. For example, *establish* is a verb that designates a kind of event, but when the suffix *-ment* is attached to it, the result is *establishment,* which is a noun that designates a kind of entity. Some other manifestations of derivation are as follows: *pure + ify = purify; beauty + ful = beautiful;*

good + ness = goodness; slow + ly = slowly; central + ize = centralize; produce + tion = production.

Third, **inflection** involves modifying a root or stem, usually through affixation, to create a complex word that fits properly into the syntactic structure of the sentence. Importantly, there is no change in grammatical category and only a minimal change in meaning. To take a few straightforward examples, the plural suffix *-s* can be attached to the root noun *hawk* to create the complex noun *hawks,* and the past-tense suffix *-ed* can be attached to the root verb *walk* to create the complex verb *walked.*

Research on the neural substrates of morphological processes has been progressing quite rapidly in recent years, driven in part by a great deal of lively interplay

Derivation A root or stem is modified, usually through affixation, to form a complex word that often has a different grammatical category and a different meaning.

Inflection A root or stem is modified, usually through affixation, to create a complex word that fits properly into the syntactic structure of the sentence. There is no change in grammatical category and only a minimal change in meaning.

between empirical and theoretical issues (for reviews see Pinker & Ullman, 2002a; Marslen-Wilson & Tyler, 2007; Shapiro & Caramazza, 2009; Bornkessel-Schlesewsky & Schlesewsky, 2009a; Bozic & Marslen-Wilson, 2010; see also Pinker, 1999). Before summarizing some of the major discoveries and debates, however, it is worth highlighting two ways in which this field of inquiry has been somewhat limited. First, although some neuropsychological, electrophysiological, and neuroimaging studies have involved speakers of morphologically rich languages (e.g., Menn & Obler, 1990a; Rodríguez-Fornells et al., 2002; Lehtonen et al., 2006; Finocchiaro et al., 2010), the vast majority of studies have been conducted with speakers of English—a language that, as mentioned above, is morphologically more impoverished than most other languages in the world. Second, although a fair bit of work has been done on both compounding and derivation (e.g., Semenza & Mondini, 2006; Bozic et al., 2007; Marangolo & Piras, 2010; Lehtonen et al., 2011; Bozic et al., 2013), the bulk of experimental research has concentrated on inflection.

Because of these limitations, the following survey is restricted primarily, but not exclusively, to English data regarding the neural underpinnings of inflectional morphology. There are three main sections. The first one focuses on two linguistically distinct aspects of inflection—morphosyntax and morphophonology—and presents evidence that they are associated with spatiotemporally distinct patterns of neural activity during speech production. The next section then looks more closely at morphosyntax by considering several studies which suggest that noun and verb inflection (e.g., *hawks* and *walked*) depend on partially segregated brain mechanisms. Finally, the third section elaborates the nature of morphophonology by discussing a long-lasting controversy over whether regular and irregular inflection (e.g., *walked* and *ran*) are handled by separate processes or by the same fundamental process.

Morphosyntactic and Morphophonological Aspects of Inflection

Linguists often distinguish between two aspects of inflection. One aspect, which is generally called **morphosyntax**, involves the content and distributional agreement (i.e., between-word consistency) of the various grammatical features that are expressed, such as number and tense.

For example, in the sentence *Those annoying dogs barked all night long,* the demonstrative *Those* and the noun *dogs* are concordantly marked for plural number, meaning that more than one dog is being referred to, and the verb *barked* is marked for past tense, meaning that the episode took place before the time of the utterance. It is important to realize, however, that grammatical features are not always semantically meaningful. Sometimes they are more or less arbitrary, as in the gender systems of many languages (Corbett, 1991). For example, in German *das Messer* ("knife") is neuter, *die Gabel* ("fork") is feminine, and *der Löffel* ("spoon") is masculine (see also Figure 6.3 in Chapter 6 and the accompanying text).

The other aspect of inflection, which is generally called **morphophonology**, involves the form that inflections take when they are encoded as sound patterns. There are several subtypes of morphophonology. For instance, although plural number is usually encoded by the regular noun suffix -*s*, as in *dogs,* there are a handful of irregular nouns for which the same information is encoded by an internal sound change, as in *man–men, mouse–mice,* and *goose–geese*. Similarly, although past tense is usually encoded by the regular verb suffix -*ed*, as in *barked,* there are about 150 irregular verbs for which the same information is encoded, once again, by an internal sound change, as in *think–thought, hold–held,* and *rise–rose*. Finally, it is noteworthy that sometimes grammatical features are not encoded by either an overt suffix or an internal sound change, but rather by "a silent bit of nothing," as Pinker (1999, p. 31) puts it. This is called zero or null morphology, and it is cross-linguistically quite common. In English, for example, singular nouns take the zero suffix, which is symbolized by -*ø*, as in *I only have one car-ø*. Verbs also take this suffix in certain situations, such as when they are used in the present tense together with a subject noun that is first person, second person, or third person plural, as in *I, you, they run-ø*. In cases like these, the lack of an explicit suffix is itself morphologically informative, since it contrasts with the presence of an explicit suffix that would signify something else.

What sorts of cortical computations take place when the morphosyntactic and morphophonological aspects of inflection are processed during speech production? Although we are not even close to understanding the actual computations that the brain carries out, recent research suggests that these two aspects of inflection are correlated with fine-grained spatiotemporal patterns of activity in the left inferior frontal gyrus (IFG),

Morphosyntax The content and distributional agreement (i.e., between-word consistency) of the various features that are expressed by inflection, such as number and tense.

Morphophonology The encoding of inflectional features in sound patterns that may be regular (e.g., dogs, barked), irregular (e.g., mice, held), or null (e.g., one car-ø, they *run-ø*).

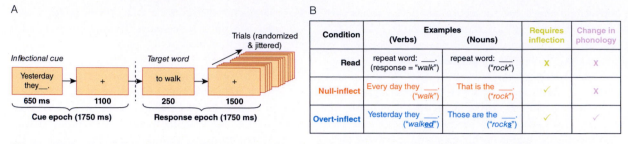

Figure 13.1   Experimental design for Sahin et al.'s (2006, 2009) fMRI and electrophysiological studies. (A) Structure of trials. (B) Experimental conditions, example trials, and required psycholinguistic processes. (From Sahin et al., 2009, p. 446.)

including Broca's area (i.e., BAs 44 and 45). That the left IFG may be a critical site for these operations is not surprising, since it is well-known that inflectional disorders are a frequent consequence of damage to this territory (and to adjacent regions), as seen in many cases of Broca's aphasia (see Chapter 3) and virtually all cases of progressive nonfluent aphasia (see Chapter 4). During the past few years, however, sophisticated brain mapping techniques, combined with clever experimental paradigms, have allowed investigators to gain much deeper insights into not only which neuronal populations in the left IFG are linked with which aspects of inflection, but also when they are engaged during the generation of complex words.

To convey a sense of what these exciting new developments are like, the following discussion focuses on two closely related studies that were conducted by Ned Sahin, Steven Pinker, and their colleagues. The first study used fMRI to show that partially segregated sectors of the left IFG contribute to morphosyntactic and morphophonological aspects of inflection (Sahin et al., 2006). And the second study used direct intracranial electrophysiology to show that these two aspects of inflection are also computed sequentially within the left IFG (Sahin et al., 2009).

Sahin et al.'s (2006) fMRI study

In the first study, 18 healthy adults performed a cued covert word production task while undergoing fMRI. Each trial consisted of a cue epoch and a response epoch, each of which lasted 1,750 ms (Figure 13.1A). During the cue epoch, a short context frame appeared (e.g., *Yesterday they* _____), and during the response epoch, a target word appeared (e.g., *to walk*). The task was to silently produce the form of the word that was most appropriate for the context (e.g., *walked*), and then press a button with the left hand. Word generation was performed covertly so as to minimize head movement and avoid auditory feedback, and post-trial button-presses

were included to keep subjects alert and to warn the experimenter of potentially waning attention.

The experiment was designed so that three different types of context frames co-occurred with both verbs and nouns (Figure 13.1B). First, in the "Read" condition, the frame for both verbs and nouns was *Repeat word: _____.* This condition served as a baseline, because the frame does not call for any kind of inflectional processing whatsoever. Thus, the correct response to *walk* was simply *walk,* and the correct response to *rock* was simply *rock.*

Second, in the "Null-Inflect" condition, the frame for verbs was *Every day they _____,* and the frame for nouns was *That is the _____.* This condition probed morphosyntactic processing in the absence of explicit morphophonological processing, because each frame requires that the target word be inflected with the zero suffix *-ø.* For example, given the verb frame, the correct response to *walk* was *walk-ø,* since this is the form that satisfies the contextually specified set of grammatical features (third person, plural, present tense). Likewise, given the noun frame, the correct response to *rock* was *rock-ø,* since this is the form that fits the singular context. Crucially, while these words are morphosyntactically different from the ones produced in the Read condition, they are superficially the same.

Third, in the "Overt-Inflect" condition, the frame for verbs was *Yesterday they _____,* which calls for a past-tense form, and the frame for nouns was *Those are the _____,* which calls for a plural form. This condition tapped into both morphosyntactic and morphophonological processing, because each frame requires that the target word be explicitly modified to signal certain grammatical features. Thus, given the verb frame, the correct response to *walk* was *walked,* and given the noun frame, the correct response to *rock* was *rocks.* Irregular verbs (e.g., *think–thought*) and nouns (e.g., *man–men*) were also included in the experiment.

Because our primary interest involves the neural correlates of the general distinction between morphosyntactic and morphophonological aspects of inflection, we will concentrate on the fMRI results that emerged

A Labeled gyri and Brodmann areas

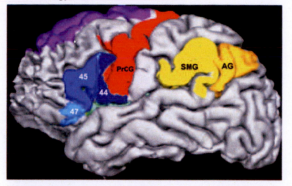

B Labeled regions on inflated brain

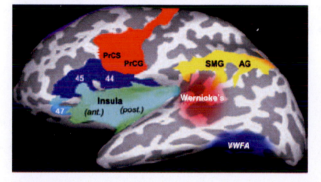

C Overt-Inflect > Read: Isolates both morphosyntactic and morphophonological processing

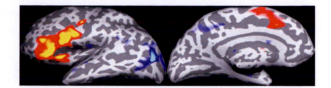

D Null-Inflect > Read: Isolates morphosyntactic processing

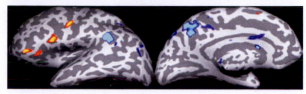

E Overt-Inflect > Null-Inflect: Isolates morphophonological processing

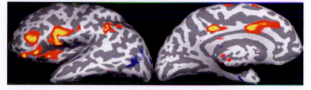

Figure 13.2 Cortical regions implicated in Sahin et al.'s (2006) fMRI study. (A, B) Labeled gyri and Brodmann areas on a normal brain (A) and an artificially inflated brain (B). PrCG = precentral gyrus; SMG = supramarginal gyrus; AG = angular gyrus; VWFA = Visual Word Form Area. (C) The contrast Overt-Inflect > Read, which isolates both morphosyntactic and morphophonological processing. (D) The contrast Null-Inflect > Read, which isolates morphosyntactic processing. (E) The contrast Overt-Inflect > Null-Inflect, which isolates morphophonological processing. (From Sahin et al., 2006, pp. 550–551.)

from several key contrasts between the three experimental conditions, averaging over nouns and verbs as well as regular and irregular forms. (In later sections of this chapter, we will consider some of the analyses that took into account the noun–verb distinction at the level of morphosyntax and the regular–irregular distinction at the level of morphophonology.) To clarify the anatomical locations of the major activation patterns, some familiar gyri and Brodmann areas are labeled on normal and inflated brain images in Figure 13.2A and Figure 13.2B. The central findings were as follows.

The first contrast involved subtracting the Read condition from the Overt-Inflect condition. The intent was to disclose the cortical areas that contribute to both morphosyntactic and morphophonological aspects of inflection, eliminating other regions that mediate processes shared by the two conditions, such as reading and understanding the stimuli. As shown in Figure 13.2C, the contrast revealed significant metabolic activity in most of the left IFG, including BAs 47, 45, and 44, the latter two constituting Broca's area. Significant effects were also observed in the anterior insula, in portions of the precentral

gyrus and sulcus, and in the supplementary motor area (SMA), which is located on the medial surface of the frontal lobe. Overall, these findings are consistent with numerous neuropsychological studies which indicate that deficits in producing inflected words often result from damage to left anterior brain regions, especially the IFG (e.g., Goodglass & Berko, 1960; Menn & Obler, 1990a; Wilson et al., 2010b; Meteyard et al., 2013).

In the second contrast, the investigators subtracted the Read condition from the Null-Inflect condition in an effort to isolate the neural substrates of just the morphosyntactic aspect of inflection. This contrast is especially intriguing because, as emphasized above, even though the words that the subjects generated in the two conditions were superficially the same, they differed at the level of morphosyntax, since the zero suffix -ø was used in the Null-Inflect condition to encode the contextually required grammatical features for both verbs and nouns. As shown in Figure 13.2D, the contrast indicated that this sort of purely morphosyntactic processing was linked with a relatively small subset of the left inferior frontal regions that were identified by the first contrast. Three specific areas were identified: a superior portion of BA47, an anterior portion of BA44, and a patch of cortex at the junction of the precentral and middle frontal gyri. Now, because individual differences in gyral/sulcal patterns are distorted during stereotactic normalization—i.e., during the process of mapping each subject's brain onto a standard brain template (see Chapter 2)—it is likely that the three narrowly circumscribed areas pinpointed by the contrast are not a completely accurate reflection of the neural infrastructure of morphosyntax. It is reasonable to suppose, however, that they are close approximations.

Finally, the researchers contrasted the Overt-Inflect condition against the Null-Inflect condition so as to isolate the brain areas implicated in just the morphophonological aspect of inflection—i.e., the aspect that is manifested in the production of, say, the -ed in *faded* and the -s in *horses*. As shown in Figure 13.2E, this subtraction yielded significant effects in a relatively large subset of the regions revealed by the first contrast. Importantly, this subset of regions did not overlap very much with the subset that turned up in the second contrast. Most conspicuously, more of Broca's area was engaged, and the anterior insula and SMA responded too. These findings converge with a substantial literature linking these left frontal regions with various aspects of language production, such as syllabification, high-level articulatory programming, and the initiation of speech (see Chapter 6).

In summary, Sahin et al.'s (2006) fMRI study used a carefully designed experimental task to investigate the neural substrates of inflectional morphology. In accord with previous research, the results suggest that this type of linguistic computation relies to a large extent on a network of left frontal regions, and that different aspects of the process—morphosyntax and morphophonology—recruit different components of the network. But while this study helps to illuminate the specific brain structures that underlie inflection, it remains silent regarding the time-course of their activation. To address this question, a follow-up study was conducted using direct intracranial electrophysiology.

Sahin et al.'s (2009) Intracranial Electrophysiological Study

In this study, three individuals (ages 38 to 51, with above-average language and intelligence) performed a version of the same task that was used in the fMRI study, only this time depth electrodes were used to record the local field potentials from populations of neurons in Broca's area and other regions. The

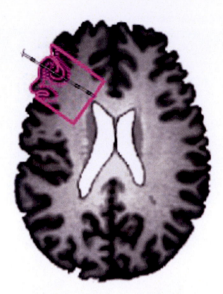

Figure 13.3   Anatomical location of Probe A in Patient A in Sahin et al.'s (2009) electrophysiological study, based on MRI scans. The black segments of the probe are contact points for recording electrophysiological activity, and several of these segments occupied portions of the pars triangularis (roughly BA45) of the left inferior frontal gyrus. (From Sahin et al., 2009, supporting online material, p. 7.)

electrodes had been implanted in the patients' brains as part of a clinical evaluation for epilepsy, and the placement of some of them in the left IFG provided a rare opportunity to explore the fine-grained spatiotemporal response properties of this cortical tissue during on-line language processing.

To simplify matters somewhat, the following discussion focuses mainly on the data acquired from a single depth probe (Probe A) in a single patient (Patient A). The trajectory of this probe is shown in Figure 13.3, which is based on an MRI scan. As can be seen, the probe passed through several folds of cortex in the left IFG, all of which were assumed to lie within BA45, which corresponds roughly to the pars triangularis. The probe was 1.0 mm in diameter and had six contact points that were separated by 5.0 mm, center to center. In the figure, the contacts are visible as the segments of the probe that are outlined in black. Each contact allowed recordings to be made of the electrophysiological activity in the surrounding gray matter structures. Close inspection of the figure indicates that, if one counts from the deepest contact up to the most superficial one, contact 3 was in the fundus (bottom) of the pars triangularis, contact 4 was in the medial (inner) wall of the pars triangularis, facing the fundus, and contact 5 was in the lateral (outer) wall of the pars triangularis. It is worth noting that recordings were made from

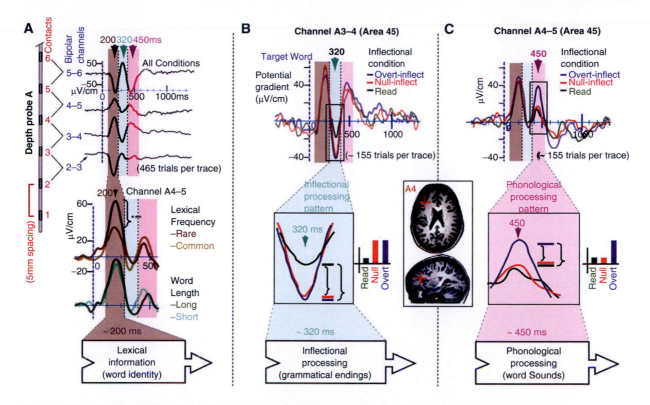

Figure 13.4 Main results for Sahin et al.'s (2009) electrophysiological study, based on recordings from Probe A in Patient A, as shown in Figure 13.3. (A) Top: Neural activity recorded from several channels in Broca's area shows three components (200, 320, and 450 ms) evoked by all task conditions, with time-point 0 corresponding to the visual presentation of the target word, as shown in Figure 13.1. Bottom: The 200-ms component is sensitive to word frequency but not length, suggesting that it indexes lexical identification, not simply perception. (B) The pattern for the 320-ms component suggests that it indexes morphosyntactic processing, referred to the figure as simply inflectional processing. (C) The pattern for the 450-ms component suggests that it indexes morphophonological processing, referred to in the figure as simply phonological processing. (From Sahin et al., 2009, p. 446.)

successive pairs of contacts, each subtracted from the next—e.g., 2–3, 3–4, 4–5, and 5–6. Such "bipolar" recordings were obtained to reduce noise.

The primary results, which average across nouns and verbs, are portrayed in Figure 13.4. The first thing to note—and this point cannot be overemphasized—is that in each panel of the figure, the timescale is arranged so that 0 marks the onset of the target word that the subject was instructed to reproduce in a form that fit the preceding context (see Figure 13.1). Across all of the experimental conditions, the investigators observed an electrophysiological waveform characterized by three distinctive peaks that were temporally distributed over just a few hundred milliseconds and spatially distributed over just a few millimeters (see the top half of Figure 13.4A). Moreover, further analyses suggested that the three main components of this waveform may index lexical (200 ms), morphosyntactic (320 ms), and morphophonological (450 ms) aspects of word processing. Let's look more closely at each one in turn.

As just mentioned, the 200-ms component seems to be related to lexical representation. More precisely, it may reflect rapid access to the unique identity of each target word—a process that is required by all of the experimental conditions. Because lexical retrieval during speech production is generally associated with the temporal lobe rather than Broca's area (see Chapter 6), Sahin et al. (2009, p. 448) suggest that the 200-ms component "may index delivery of word identity information into Broca's area for subsequent processing …." Evidence supporting this interpretation comes from the following findings. As shown in the bottom half of Figure 13.4A, the 200-ms component was highly sensitive to target word frequency, since it had significantly greater amplitude for rare than common items; however, it was not sensitive to target word length, since it had the same profile for short items (2 to 4 characters) and long items (6 to 11 characters). Frequency effects are generally assumed to reflect the identities of words, whereas length effects are generally assumed to reflect the complexity of phonological processing—a point we return to below.

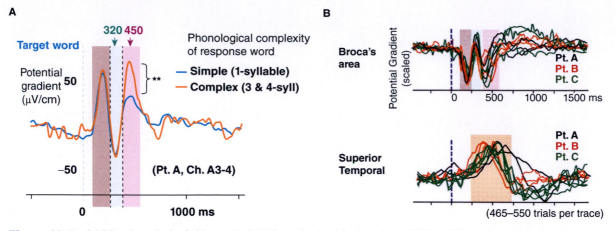

Figure 13.5   Additional results for Sahin et al.'s (2009) electrophysiological study. (A) The 450-ms component has greater amplitude for multisyllabic than monosyllabic words, confirming its involvement in morphophonological processing. (B) The three-component pattern was exhibited by all three patients (Pt.) and was observed in Broca's area but not in the superior temporal gyrus. (From Sahin et al., 2009, p. 448.)

Although the 200-ms component was not affected by the distinction between the Read condition and the two inflectional conditions (i.e., Null- and Overt-Inflect), the 320-ms component was greatly influenced by this distinction. As Figure 13.4B clearly shows, the 320-ms component had a significantly larger amplitude for both of the inflectional conditions than for the Read condition, but its profile for the two inflectional conditions was the same; in fact, the red and blue waveforms that represent those two conditions overlap almost perfectly. This response pattern invites the inference that the 320-ms component is the electrophysiological signature of morphosyntactic processing, since that is the kind of computation which is shared by the two inflectional conditions.

Finally, the properties of the 450-ms component are depicted in Figure 13.4C. This component was far more sensitive to the Overt-Inflect condition than to the Null-Inflect and Read conditions, and its profile for the latter two conditions was quite similar. It is therefore reasonable to suppose that the 450-ms component indexes the sort of neurocognitive operation that is unique to the Overt-Inflect condition, namely morphophonological processing. Further evidence for this hypothesis comes from another interesting result. As shown in Figure 13.5A, the 450-ms component was influenced by target word length, exhibiting significantly greater amplitude for complex (3 and 4-syllable) than simple (1-syllable) items. This reinforces the idea that the component probably reflects the preparation of sound patterns for articulation.

Before stepping back from the details, it is worthwhile to make a few more points. First, although the three-component waveform was observed in Broca's area, it was not observed in the superior temporal cortex, where additional recordings were obtained (see Figure 13.5B). This supports the regional specificity of the findings. Second, all of the major effects were manifested not only by Patient A, but also by the other two patients who were studied. This supports the inter-individual validity of the findings. And third, with regard to Patient A, the 320-ms and 450-ms components were separated not just in time but also in space, since the former component was recorded most reliably from Channel A3–4 in a relatively medial portion of Broca's area, whereas the latter component was recorded most reliably from Channel A4–5 in a relatively lateral portion of Broca's area. Further evidence that these two components were generated by partially distinct neuronal populations comes from the fact that they had opposite polarities, with the 320-ms component being negative and the 450-ms one being positive (see Figure 13.4B, C). (As discussed in Chapter 2, whether an electrophysiological component is positive or negative depends on the shape of the electrical field being recorded. In this particular study, that field was intracranial but still extracellular.)

Overall, then, the upshot of this study is basically as follows. By directly recording the local field potentials from neuronal populations in Broca's area while subjects generated contextually constrained, morphologically inflected words, Sahin et al. (2009) discovered that different kinds of linguistic information appear to be sequentially computed in this brain region. As the authors put it, "the location, behavioral correlates, and timing of the components of neuronal activity in

Broca's area suggest that they embody, respectively, lexical identification (200 ms), grammatical inflection (320 ms), and phonological processing (450 ms) ..." (Sahin et al., 2009, p. 449).

Summary

There are two distinct aspects of inflection. Morphosyntax has to do with the content and distributional agreement (i.e., between-word consistency) of the various features that are expressed, such as plural number for nouns and past tense for verbs, whereas morphophonology has to do with the encoding of those features in sound patterns, such as the -s and -ed suffixes. In an fMRI study, Sahin et al. (2006) demonstrated that these two aspects of inflection engage different sectors of Broca's area during the planning of word production. Then in a subsequent study involving intracranial electrophysiology, Sahin et al. (2009) demonstrated that the two aspects of inflection also seem to be handled sequentially in Broca's area. After a target word is visually presented, the lexical identity of the word is first delivered to Broca's area at a latency of about 200 ms, then the appropriate morphosyntactic features are processed at a latency of about 320 ms, and finally the appropriate morphophonological form is processed at a latency of about 450 ms. Thus, the two aspects of inflection seem to be separated in the brain both spatially and temporally. As shown in the next two sections, however, the neural substrates of inflection are much more complex and widespread than this, encompassing many brain regions beyond Broca's area.

Noun and Verb Inflection: A Closer Look at Morphosyntax

Toward the beginning of the previous section, we noted that nouns and verbs are usually inflected for different sorts of grammatical features at the level of morphosyntax. In fact, the following cross-linguistic contrasts have been well-documented: Nouns tend to be inflected for object-related features like number, gender, possession, definiteness, and case, whereas verbs tend to be inflected for action-related features like tense, aspect, mood, negation, and transitivity (Croft, 1991). This leads naturally to the question that is the main focus of this section. Do the different kinds of morphosyntactic processes associated with nouns and verbs depend on shared or segregated neural systems in the brain? As we will see, recent findings don't really favor one of these alternative possibilities

over the other, but instead suggest that both of them have some degree of truth, since the relevant neural systems appear to be partly shared and partly segregated.

Here's a quick preview of the main points that we will cover. First, there is growing evidence that noun and verb inflection share a common pathway in Broca's area—a pathway that may underlie a relatively late, category-neutral phase of morphosyntactic processing. Second, there is also growing evidence that noun and verb inflection can be differentially impaired by damage to separate regions of the brain—regions that may underlie a relatively early, category-specific phase of morphosyntactic processing. And third, although the regions that contribute more to the morphosyntactic processing of nouns than verbs are not yet clear, those that contribute more to the morphosyntactic processing of verbs than nouns seem to include the left middle frontal gyrus. All of these points are elaborated in greater detail below. Most of the discussion concentrates on inflectional processing during language production. The section concludes, however, with a brief consideration of inflectional processing during language comprehension.

A Common Pathway in Broca's Area

A good place to start is with the two studies by Sahin et al. (2006, 2009) that we reviewed in the previous section, since both of them included both nouns and verbs. Beginning with the fMRI study, the strictest way to address the question posed above—i.e., the question as to whether the different kinds of morphosyntactic processes associated with nouns and verbs depend on shared or segregated neural systems—would be to focus once again on the contrast that isolates morphosyntactic processing—namely, Null-Inflect > Read. This time, however, the proper procedure would be to first carry out the contrast separately for nouns and verbs, and then determine whether there are statistically significant similarities and differences between the two resulting maps of metabolic activity. Unfortunately, Sahin et al. (2006) did not report these kinds of analyses. They did, however, provide the next best thing: separate results for nouns and verbs in the contrast that uncovers both morphosyntactic and morphophonological processing—namely, Overt-Inflect > Read.

As shown in Figure 13.6, the explicit inflection of nouns engaged a few left parietal and temporal regions that were not engaged by the explicit inflection

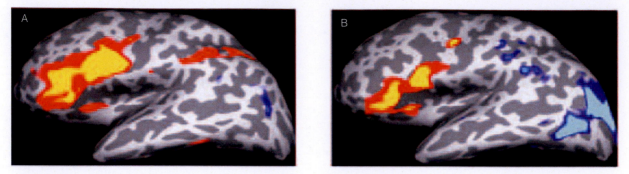

Figure 13.6 Separate results for (A) nouns and (B) verbs in Sahin et al.'s (2006) fMRI study. In each panel, yellow/red patches indicate areas activated significantly more when the Overt-Inflect condition was contrasted with the Read condition, and blue patches indicate areas activated significantly more when the opposite subtraction was performed. For anatomical reference points, see the labeled regions in Figure 13.2B. (From Sahin et al., 2006, p. 554.)

of verbs. It is not entirely clear how these noun-specific posterior activations should be interpreted, but one possibility is that they have something to do with the semantic aspects of plural marking for nouns. First, the activity in the intraparietal sulcus may reflect the meaning of the plural suffix -*s*, which specifies reference to more than one instance of the designated kind of entity. Support for this account comes from independent evidence that the intraparietal sulcus is critically involved in all forms of numerical cognition (for reviews see Nieder & Dehaene, 2009; Cohen Kadosh & Walsh, 2009; see also Chapter 12 as well as Domahs et al., 2012). Second, the activity in the ventral temporal cortex may reflect access to one of the "core" semantic properties of nouns in general—namely, that they refer schematically to "things," which are defined technically as phenomena construed as individuals in various physical and abstract conceptual domains (for a similar finding and interpretation see Shapiro et al., 2006; and for an overview of pertinent linguistic theory see Langacker, 2008).

Of greater interest from a morphosyntactic perspective is the extensive left frontal activity depicted in both panels of Figure 13.6. One notable aspect of this finding is that noun inflection appears to have engaged the superior part of Broca's area more strongly than verb inflection. This could potentially reflect noun-specific morphosyntactic processing (a possibility that we return to below), but an important qualification is that it may have been due largely to the presence of a few very low-frequency irregular nouns (e.g., *nucleus–nuclei*), because when the investigators removed those items from a follow-up analysis, they found that the differences between nouns and verbs in the left frontal lobe were greatly reduced.

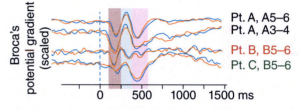

Figure 13.7 Separate results for nouns and verbs in Sahin et al.'s (2009) electrophysiological study. Noun (blue) and verb (orange) inflection (Null and Overt conditions combined; see Figure 13.1) involved nearly identical patterns of neural activity across patients (Pt.) and across recording sites in Broca's area. The vertically oriented brown, blue, and pink bars correspond to the three time windows shown in the top half of Figure 13.4A. (From Sahin et al., 2009, p. 448.)

Setting this issue aside, perhaps the most significant aspect of Figure 13.6 is that the explicit inflectional processing of both nouns and verbs induced overlapping activity in the inferior part of Broca's area as well as the anterior insula. The fact that both types of words recruited a portion of Broca's area has major theoretical implications, for it suggests that, in Sahin et al.'s (2006, p. 556) words, "there may be a common circuit supporting inflectional morphology across different grammatical categories."

Further evidence for this hypothesis comes from Sahin et al.'s (2009) subsequent electrophysiological study. All of the data from this study that we considered in the previous section derived from analyses that averaged across nouns and verbs. The researchers also reported, however, the results of separate analyses of the two word classes, specifically reflecting the combination of the Null- and Overt-Inflect conditions. As Figure 13.7 shows, noun and verb inflection elicited virtually identical patterns of electrophysiological activity in the parts of Broca's area where local field potentials were recorded. Moreover, these striking similarities were exhibited not only by Patient A, but also by the other two patients. Such robust parallels between nouns and verbs bolster the idea that, as Sahin et al. (2009, p. 448) put it, "words from different lexical classes feed a common process for inflection."

So, pulling together the data from fMRI and electrophysiology, we find convergent support for the view that, even though nouns and verbs are associated with different sorts of morphosyntactic features, the processing of those features relies, at least to some extent, on shared neural resources in Broca's area. (Additional support comes from an rTMS study by Cappelletti et al., 2008.) In a review paper, Shapiro and Caramazza (2009, p. 783) express essentially the same point as follows:

> We propose that the left inferior frontal gyrus represents a common pathway for the production of words bearing functional morphemes [like inflectional suffixes] that specify grammatical information relevant to one category or another. In other words, this area … may be important for the conversion of morphological elements into phonological segments.

That last observation is especially interesting, since it implies that Broca's area—perhaps especially the inferior portion of Broca's area—may subserve a relatively late phase of morphosyntactic processing, one that interfaces directly with morphophonological processing.

Might there also be an earlier, higher-order phase of morphosyntactic processing that is mediated by other cortical regions? Yes, this is conceivable, and in fact Shapiro and Caramazza (2009, p. 783) pursue precisely this line of thinking in their next statement: "The process of selecting syntactically appropriate functional morphemes [like inflectional suffixes] may be handled by different upstream regions …." What's more, at this relatively high level of morphosyntactic processing, the regions that subserve the mental manipulation of grammatical features for nouns may be anatomically segregated from those that subserve the mental manipulation of grammatical features for verbs. Support for this possibility comes from some remarkable neuropsychological studies which, as described in the next subsection, show that these two category-specific kinds of inflectional computation can be differentially impaired by focal brain injury.

A Neuropsychological Double Dissociation

The key studies were conducted, not surprisingly, by Shapiro, Caramazza, and their colleagues (Shapiro et al., 2000; Shapiro & Caramazza, 2003a). These researchers reported two brain-damaged patients who displayed essentially opposite patterns of performance on tasks that were carefully designed to evaluate the morphosyntactic processing of both nouns and verbs during language production. The following summary focuses first on the patients' demographic and neurological characteristics, and then it turns to the methods, results, and implications of the studies.

One of the patients was JR, a 55-year-old right-handed man who had worked as a professor of mathematics and philosophy. In 1995 he suffered a stroke that damaged all of Broca's area, the lower two-thirds of the sensorimotor cortex, and the white matter underlying these structures, as shown in Figure 13.8. In addition, the left supramarginal and angular gyri were affected, although this is not indicated in the figure. The experiments described below were conducted 2–3 years after the injury, and at that time JR had a clinical classification of predominantly anomic aphasia. The other patient was RC, a 65-year-old right-handed man who had worked as the manager of a school bus transportation company. In 1994 he suffered a stroke that damaged all of Broca's area together with the posterior middle frontal gyrus, the anterior superior temporal gyrus, parts of the anterior insula, parts of the basal ganglia, and the white matter in the vicinity of these regions (Figure 13.8). At the time of the experiments, 4–5 years post-onset, RC fit the criteria for Broca's aphasia.

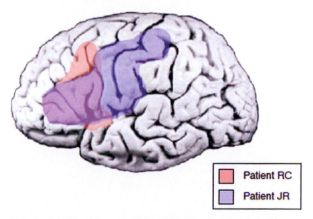

| | Patient RC |
| | Patient JR |

Figure 13.8 Lesion sites for patients JR and RC. Note that, although this is not shown in the figure, JR's lesion reportedly extended into the left supramarginal and angular gyri. (From Shapiro & Caramazza, 2003b, p. 204.)

To assess JR's and RC's capacity to select and produce the grammatically appropriate inflections for both nouns and verbs, the researchers administered two tasks, both of which required the patients to complete sentence frames with the correct forms of words, just as in Sahin et al.'s (2006, 2009) studies. In the first task, the target words were real noun–verb homonyms (e.g., *a guide, to guide*). This ensured that the phonological structures of the stems were equivalent across the noun and verb conditions. As shown below, two sentence frames called for singular and plural forms of nouns (1a and 1b), and two sentence frames called for third person plural and third person singular forms of verbs (2a and 2b):

(1) Inflection of real nouns
    a.   "These are *guides*; this is a _____" (*guide-ø*)
    b.   "This is a *guide*; these are _____" (*guides*)

(2) Inflection of real verbs
    a.   "This person *guides*; these people _____" (*guide-ø*)
    b.   "These people *guide*; this person _____" (*guides*)

In the second task, the target words were meaningless pseudowords (e.g., *a fleeve; to fleeve*). This ensured that semantic factors could not influence the patients' responses. As illustrated in (3) and (4), the sentence frames were identical to those employed in the first task:

(3) Inflection of pseudo-nouns
    a.   "These are *fleeves*; this is a _____" (*fleeve-ø*)
    b.   "This is a *fleeve*; these are _____" (*fleeves*)

(4) Inflection of pseudo-verbs
    a.   "This person *fleeves*; these people _____" (*fleeve-ø*)
    b.   "These people *fleeve*; this person _____" (*fleeves*)

Although both tasks were given to both patients, JR received slightly more than twice as many trials of the real-word conditions as RC.

The results are shown in Table 13.1. Looking first at the data for JR, what stands out most prominently is that he had significantly greater difficulty inflecting nouns than verbs. This dissociation was manifested in the two real-word conditions, but it was magnified even more in the two pseudoword conditions, no doubt because they were more challenging due to the unfamiliarity of the stems. Across the board, JR's

Table 13.1 Performances of Patients JR and RC on Sentence Completion Tasks

	JR		RC	
	N	%	N	%
Real words:				
Nouns	550	81.0	220	72.7
Verbs	550	93.0	220	29.5
Pseudowords:				
Nouns	96	54.1	96	50.0
Verbs	96	81.3	96	28.1

Source: Shapiro & Caramazza (2003a, p. 1194).

worse performance for nouns than verbs arose from a tendency to omit the overt *-s* suffix from contextually stipulated plural forms, as in (1b) and (3b). It is essential to note, however, that these errors could not have reflected a purely phonological deficit, since JR was able to produce the phonologically identical suffix much more reliably when it served to mark the third person singular forms of verbs, as in (2b) and (4b). Moreover, separate experiments demonstrated that JR did not have a basic repetition disorder. The data therefore suggest that JR was disproportionately impaired at processing the morphosyntactic features of nouns relative to verbs.

Shifting to RC, it is clear from Table 13.1 that his dissociation was the opposite of JR's, since he had significantly greater difficulty inflecting verbs than nouns. This pattern was quite robust for both the real-word conditions and the pseudoword conditions. Although RC committed several types of errors for verbs, the most frequent type involved repeating the cued word without transforming it properly to express the required grammatical features. Remarkably enough, he made such errors more than twice as often for verbs as for nouns, even though the required word forms were homonyms. For instance, he had far more trouble saying *This person guides* than saying *These are guides*. Thus, the data suggest that RC was disproportionately impaired at processing the morphosyntactic features of verbs relative to nouns. Patients with similar dissociations have been reported by Tsapkini et al. (2002) and Laiacona and Caramazza (2004).

In their discussion of the complementary deficits exhibited by JR and RC, Shapiro and Caramazza (2003a, p. 1194) emphasize that in both cases the disrupted capacities are not only category-related, but also "seem to be grammatical, and not directly involved in retrieving stored information about word form or meaning; otherwise it is not clear how we might account for the observed deficits with pseudowords, which presumably have no memorized features." In fact, the neuropsychological double dissociation suggests that certain high-level grammatical aspects of noun and verb inflection—like the contextually constrained determination of number features for nouns and person/number/tense features for verbs—may be handled by separate, category-specific brain regions during a relatively early phase of morphosyntactic computation, before the two streams of processing meet in Broca's area, or, more narrowly, in the inferior portion of Broca's area. Where might those separate, category-specific regions reside? That is the question we turn to next.

Neural Correlates of Noun-Specific and Verb-Specific Morphosyntactic Processing

At this stage of research, it is by no means clear which brain structures implement noun-specific morphosyntactic circuitry and which ones implement verb-specific morphosyntactic circuitry. As described below, however, more progress has been made on the latter front than on the former.

Beginning with the neural correlates of noun-specific processing, some initial hints come from the lesion data for JR, since he was significantly more impaired for noun than verb inflection. Given that JR's lesion extended more posteriorly than RC's, one possibility is that noun-specific circuitry depends on the left inferior parietal lobule. In accord with this proposal, we indicated above that the left parietal cortex was recruited more by noun than verb inflection in Sahin et al.'s (2006) fMRI study (see Figure 13.6). We also pointed out, however, that this region is more likely to mediate the semantic than the strictly morphosyntactic aspects of the singular/plural distinction for nouns. An alternative possibility is that the morphosyntactic aspects of noun inflection depend on the superior portion of Broca's area. Although this hypothesis is quite speculative, it is consistent with several findings. For one thing, the relevant region was damaged in both JR and RC, and, as predicted by the hypothesis, both patients were impaired to roughly the same degree for noun inflection. (As shown in Table 13.1, their behavioral differences were manifested mainly for verb inflection, since JR performed better, and RC

performed worse, for verb than noun inflection.) In addition, the hypothesis is supported by at least two independent fMRI studies: First, as mentioned above, Sahin et al. (2006) found that the superior portion of Broca's area responded more to noun than verb inflection (see Figure 13.6, but note the caveat regarding that discovery); and second, Miceli et al. (2002) found that this region is also sensitive to the grammatical gender of Italian nouns. Despite these convergent results, however, further research is obviously needed to explore the neural substrates of noun-specific morphosyntactic processing in greater detail.

What about the locus of verb-specific circuitry? In recent years, there has been increasing evidence that the left middle frontal gyrus (MFG), which lies just above and in front of Broca's area, plays a special role in the morphosyntactic processing of verbs. The data are equivocal, however, as to whether the posterior or anterior sector of the left MFG is more critical for this function. Let's look at each sector in turn.

Support for the importance of the *posterior* portion of the left MFG comes from case RC, since he was disproportionately impaired for verb inflection, and his lesion, but not JR's, extended into this cortical territory. In addition, several fMRI studies suggest that, relative to noun inflection, verb inflection recruits the left posterior MFG, especially the part of BA9 located immediately superior to BA44. For instance, Shapiro et al. (2006) obtained results along these lines in a study that used real-word and pseudoword tasks analogous to those used by Shapiro and Caramazza (2003a; see the examples in (1)–(4) above; see also Shapiro et al., 2012). When the verb conditions were contrasted against the noun conditions, one of the only activated areas was the left posterior MFG (Figure 13.9). Essentially the same region was also engaged significantly more by verb than noun inflection in an fMRI study by Willms et al. (2011). However, these researchers went two steps farther than Shapiro et al. (2006): first, they employed tasks that required English–Spanish bilingual speakers to inflect words in both languages; and second, they used multi-voxel pattern analysis (see Chapter 2) to show that within the posterior MFG the specific activation patterns elicited by the verb conditions, relative to the noun conditions, were virtually identical across the two languages. Finally, Kielar et al. (2011) recently found that both the overt and covert production of tense and agreement morphology for English verbs recruited the left posterior MFG, together with the caudally adjacent precentral gyrus. Overall, then, there appears

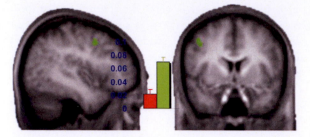

Figure 13.9   Greater left posterior middle frontal activity elicited by verb inflection (green) than noun inflection (red) in Shapiro et al.'s (2006) fMRI study. (From Shapiro et al., 2006, p. 1646.) Copyright (2006) National Academy of Sciences, U.S.A.

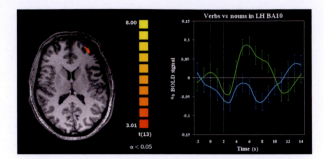

Figure 13.10   Greater left anterior middle frontal activity elicited by verb inflection (green) than noun inflection (blue) in Finocchiaro et al.'s (2010) fMRI study. (From Finocchiaro et al., 2010, p. 558.)

to be a fair amount of neuropsychological and fMRI data implicating the posterior sector of the left MFG in verb-specific morphosyntactic processing. (It isn't clear why this pattern wasn't also supported by Sahin et al.'s [2006] fMRI study.)

At the same time, however, it is noteworthy that a recent fMRI study by Finocchiaro et al. (2010) generated results which suggest that the *anterior* portion of the left MFG also contributes to verb-specific morphosyntactic processing. The subjects in this experiment performed tasks that required them to inflect Italian target words in ways that conformed to certain phrasal contexts. Some of the expressions involved nouns (e.g., *uno starnuto* "a sneeze"; *molti starnuti* "many sneezes"), and others involved verbs (e.g., *io taglio* "I cut"; *tu tagli* "you cut"). When the verb conditions were contrasted against the noun conditions, one of the only activated areas was the left anterior MFG, at the intersection of BAs 10, 46, and 47, immediately anterior to BA45 (Figure 13.10). Surprisingly, the posterior portion of the left MFG was not engaged.

So, what we have here is a situation in which some fMRI results (and neuropsychological results) point to the left *posterior* MFG as playing a special role in verb inflection, whereas other fMRI results point to the left *anterior* MFG as being more important for this function. Given these inconsistencies, it makes sense to ask whether other brain mapping methods have been used to address the same issues. In fact, a few rTMS studies have yielded two key findings that are directly relevant. First, Cappelletti et al. (2008) showed that, relative to sham stimulation, the application of rTMS to the *posterior* portion of the left MFG did not interfere significantly with either verb or noun inflection (see also Shapiro & Caramazza, 2009). Second, both Cappelletti et al. (2008) and Shapiro et al. (2001) showed that, relative to sham stimulation,

the application of rTMS to the *anterior* portion of the left MFG did interfere significantly more with verb inflection than noun inflection (see also Finocchiaro et al., 2008). Taken together, these rTMS findings are at odds with the fMRI studies by Shapiro et al. (2006), Willms et al. (2011), and Kielar et al. (2011), and also with the neuropsychological data for patient RC; however, they are congruent with the fMRI study by Finocchiaro et al. (2010).

What, then, can we conclude about the specific sector of the left MFG that is most critical for verb inflection? At this point, nothing, because the discrepancies in the available data will need to be resolved through further experimentation and argumentation. It is worth emphasizing, however, that this is simply how science normally works, especially in the hurly-burly of the early exploration of exciting topics, when the first few rounds of results draw a great deal of attention but are hard to reconcile. It is also important to realize that the uncertainties surrounding the precise localization of verb inflection in the left MFG do not detract from the value of the more general discovery that *some* portion of the left MFG most likely contributes more to the morphosyntactic processing of verbs than nouns.

What About Comprehension?

Up to this point, we have focused entirely on the morphosyntactic processing of nouns and verbs during language production. This is partly because the literature on that topic is larger and richer than the literature on the morphosyntactic processing of nouns and verbs during language comprehension. Nevertheless, the latter literature does contain a number of valuable studies, many of which generated convergent results. Most notably, several PET and fMRI investigations suggest that when words are perceived, inflected verbs tend to activate the left middle temporal and inferior frontal gyri more strongly than inflected nouns, even when the items are compared with the corresponding stems (e.g., Perani et al., 1999; Tyler et al., 2004; Longe et al., 2007; Palti et al., 2007; for another relevant study see Cooke et al., 2006).

This pattern is nicely illustrated by an fMRI study conducted by Longe et al. (2007). The subjects in this experiment were presented with printed words, one at a time and interspersed with baseline stimuli (these being XXX's matched in length to the words). The words were of four types: uninflected nouns and verbs matched for familiarity and imageability (e.g., nouns: *joy, chore, myth*; verbs: *soothe, drown, assist*), and the same nouns and verbs inflected with the *-s* suffix (e.g., nouns: *joys, chores, myths*; verbs: *soothes, drowns, assists*). For the nouns this suffix only marked plural number, but for the verbs it marked a combination of three distinct grammatical features—specifically, third person, singular, and present tense. On each trial, the subjects decided as quickly as possible whether the given word was pleasant or unpleasant. Because this task directed the subjects' attention to the meanings of the words, the morphological structures of the words were presumably processed in an automatic manner. Behaviorally, the subjects' reaction times were slightly slower for inflected than uninflected words; however, these differences did not vary as a function of grammatical category (Figure 13.11). With regard to the imaging results, the most important outcome was a significant interaction between morphological status (inflected vs. uninflected words) and grammatical category (nouns vs. verbs). In particular, inflected verbs compared to their stems engaged two left-hemisphere sites—the middle temporal gyrus (MTG) and the IFG—more strongly than inflected nouns compared to their stems (Figure 13.12).

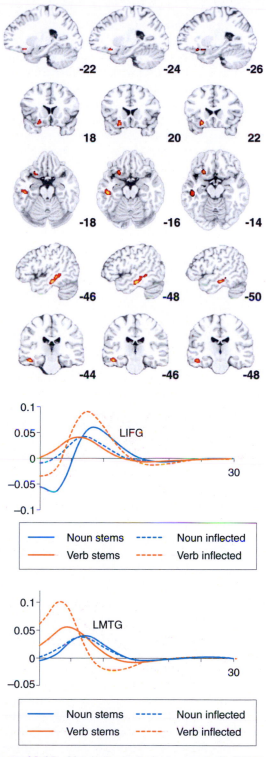

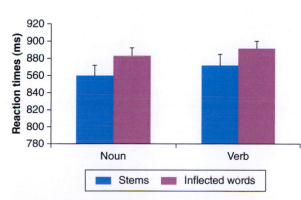

Figure 13.11 Reaction time results for Longe et al.'s (2007) fMRI study. (From Longe et al., 2007, p. 1815.)

Figure 13.12 Metabolic results for Longe et al.'s (2007) fMRI study. In a semantic judgment task, inflected verbs compared to their stems engaged two regions—the left inferior frontal gyrus (LIFG) and the left middle temporal gyrus (LMTG)—more strongly than inflected nouns compared to their stems. (From Longe et al., 2007, p. 1817.)

According to Longe et al. (2007), the greater temporal and frontal activation for inflected verbs than inflected nouns, relative to the corresponding stems, was most likely due to the fact that the -s suffix carried more grammatical weight for the former words than for the latter ones. The researchers also point out that similar patterns of activation have emerged in other studies that probed the neural underpinnings of receptive morphological processing (in addition to the references cited above, see Stamatakis et al., 2005; Tyler et al., 2005b). These findings suggest that the left MTG and IFG may operate as an integrated network during language comprehension, perhaps being coordinated via the arcuate fasciculus (for further discussion of this network see Chapter 15). This intriguing proposal is elaborated more fully in the last part of the next section.

Summary

Several sources of evidence indicate that when words are inflected during language production, the morphosyntactic processes associated with nouns and verbs are subserved by neural systems that are partly shared and partly segregated. Broca's area—or, more narrowly, perhaps the inferior portion of Broca's area—seems to implement a common pathway for these two types of words. This pathway may underlie a relatively late, category-neutral phase of morphosyntactic processing, just before the transition to morphophonological processing. The selection of appropriate grammatical features, such as number features for nouns and person/number/tense features for verbs, may take place during an earlier, higher-order phase of morphosyntactic processing. At this stage, the computational operations for nouns and verbs appear to rely on distinct cortical regions, since the ability to inflect the two types of words can be differentially impaired by brain damage. While it is not yet clear which regions implement noun-specific circuitry, one plausible candidate requiring greater research attention is the superior portion of Broca's area. Regarding the regions that implement verb-specific circuitry, there is growing evidence that the left MFG plays a special role, but it is controversial whether the posterior or anterior sector is more critical. Turning to the comprehension of inflected words, less research has been conducted, but a number of studies support the view that inflected verbs tend to recruit the left MTG and IFG more strongly than inflected nouns. This may occur because the former items tend to carry more grammatical weight than the latter items, but further work is needed to test this hypothesis.

Regular and Irregular Inflection: A Closer Look at Morphophonology

Theoretical Background

As noted earlier, there are two major ways in which grammatical features like number and tense are morphophonologically realized as sound patterns: regular and irregular inflection. To recapitulate, regular inflection involves the predictable attachment of a suffix to a stem, as in *hawk–hawks* and *walk–walked*, whereas irregular inflection involves the idiosyncratic modification of the internal sound structure of a stem, as in *goose–geese* and *run–ran*. Although this distinction may seem rather trivial, it has been the focus of a lively, high-profile debate that has persisted from the mid-1980s up to the present, encompassing all of the key disciplines in the mind/brain sciences, including linguistics, psychology, neuroscience, and artificial intelligence. What, you may wonder, is so important about the regular/irregular distinction? Well, just as the common fruit fly, *Drosophila*, has come to serve as a "model organism" for addressing many basic issues in developmental biology, so the regular/irregular distinction—especially as it pertains to the production of English past-tense verb forms—has come to serve as an ideal test case for tackling some of the central issues in the mind/brain sciences. In particular, it has been used extensively to evaluate competing theories about the nature and scope of two fundamentally different types of cognitive operations in language processing—rule-based computation and associatively based memory (for overviews see Chapter 4 of Bornkessel-Schlesewsky & Schlesewsky, 2009a, and pp. 315–324 of Shallice & Cooper, 2011; for a more detailed but less technical discussion see Pinker, 1999).

Some theories attempt to collapse the regular/irregular distinction by arguing that both types of morphophonology are cognitively processed in essentially the same manner. These **Single System Models** fall into two main groups. One group claims that a mechanism suitable for processing regulars—namely, rules—can embrace irregulars too (Chomsky & Halle, 1968/1991; Halle & Mohanan, 1985).

Single System Models   Theories that attempt to collapse the regular/irregular distinction by arguing that both types of morphophonology are cognitively processed in the same way. Some of these theories claim that both types are handled by means of rules, whereas others claim that both types are handled by means of associative memory.

According to this view, regular past-tense verb forms are computed by applying the simple, broad-range rule "add -*ed*," as in *fold–folded*, while irregular past-tense verb forms are computed by applying a battery of more complex, narrow-range rules that capture minor patterns: *keep–kept, sleep–slept, feel–felt*, and *dream–dreamt*; *wear–wore, bear–bore, tear–tore*, and *swear–swore*; *sting–stung, sling–slung, fling–flung*, and *cling–clung*; etc. The last pattern is captured, for example, by the rule "change /i/ to /ə/ when the coda is a velar-nasal consonant." This approach, however, has several shortcomings. One problem is that it doesn't fully explain the "family resemblance" quality of similar-sounding irregular items (Bybee and Slobin, 1982). For instance, the rule mentioned above ignores the fact that the relevant verbs share various aspects of their onsets—specifically, consonant clusters like *st, sl, fl, cl*, and so on, which are statistical tendencies that are inherently hard to express as all-or-nothing rules. Another problem is that the narrow-range rules that supposedly accommodate irregular patterns have numerous exceptions. The rule mentioned above is again a case in point, since the past-tense form of *bring* is not *brung* but *brought* (at least in standard English), and the past-tense forms of *sing, spring*, and *ring* are not *sung, sprung*, and *rung* but *sang, sprang*, and *rang*. (See, however, Albright & Hayes, 2003, for a more theoretically sophisticated and explanatorily coherent approach based on multiple probabilistic rules with different levels of confidence.)

Pursuing the opposite strategy, other Single System Models try to collapse the regular/irregular distinction by showing that a mechanism suitable for processing irregulars—namely, associative memory—can embrace regulars too (e.g., Rumelhart & McClelland, 1986; MacWhinney & Leinbach, 1991; Hare et al., 1995; Joanisse & Seidenberg, 1999; McClelland & Patterson, 2002a). Advocates of this approach draw heavily on connectionist computer simulations that are very good at extracting and generalizing the sorts of statistical tendencies that characterize the input–output mappings of similar-sounding irregular items. As described more fully in Box 13.2, such simulations capture irregular patterns not by means of explicit rules, but rather by means of variable connection strengths between arrays of input and output nodes that represent the phonological features of stems and past-tense forms, respectively. What makes this approach controversial is that its advocates claim that the same kind of pattern-association mechanism can also handle regular inflection. To be sure, connectionist models that implement this type of mechanism can learn to produce the correct past-tense forms of many regular verbs. But they still make numerous errors, and critics have argued that the reason they fall short of normal human performance is because they depend crucially on memorized patterns of phonologically defined input–output mappings, whereas regular inflection is not constrained by such patterns, operating instead on abstract symbols for stems and suffixes. More precisely, connectionist models have great difficulty accommodating a variety of situations in which regular inflection applies by default, regardless of the familiarity or phonology of the stems (Pinker & Prince, 1988; Pinker, 1999):

- Rare words: *acclimatize–acclimatized*.
- Strange-sounding novel words: *ploamph–ploamphed*.
- Foreign borrowings: *deride–derided (*derode)*.
- Onomatopoeia: *The engine pinged (*pung)*.
- Quotations: *While checking for sexist writing, I found three "man"s (*"men") on page 1*.
- Derived words in which an irregular form is grammatically "trapped": *In the 9th inning, Boggs flied out (*flew out) to center field*.

In contrast to both kinds of Single System Models, the **Dual System Model** (not to be confused with the Dual Stream Model of speech perception summarized in Chapter 5) does not try to collapse the regular/irregular distinction, but instead treats it as a reflection of the traditional division between lexicon and grammar. This approach has been elaborated and defended most prominently by Steven Pinker at Harvard University, together with his colleagues, especially Michael Ullman at Georgetown University (e.g., Pinker & Prince, 1988; Pinker, 1991, 1999; Pinker & Ullman, 2002a; Ullman et al., 1997, 2005). The central assumptions of the theory are sketched in Figure 13.13. Let's begin at the top of the diagram by supposing that a verb (e.g., *walk* or *hold*) must be produced in the proper past-tense form. Information about the verb stem is accessed, most likely in the left MTG (as discussed in Chapter 6), and the morphosyntactic specification of "past tense" is computed, most likely in the left MFG (as discussed in the previous section). These lexical and morphosyntactic inputs are then fed into two neurocognitive systems simultaneously—the lexical system and the grammatical system—in

Dual System Model Irregulars are retrieved from an associatively organized lexical system, whereas regulars are computed through a suffixation process in a rule-based grammatical system.

Box 13.2 Connectionist Computer Simulations of the Regular/Irregular Distinction

The mid-1980s were heady times in artificial intelligence, for that was when connectionism, also known as parallel distributed processing, suddenly ignited, swept across the field like a forest fire, and began to encroach upon many branches of psychology, linguistics, neuroscience, and philosophy (Rumelhart et al., 1986; McClelland et al., 1986; Clark, 1989; Bechtel & Abrahamsen, 1991). The general aim of this movement was, and continues to be, to simulate cognitive processes in terms of networks of massively interconnected simple units that vaguely resemble neurons, and to thereby gain deeper insight into how the brain creates the mind.

One of the first and most famous connectionist networks was designed to compute both regular and irregular past-tense forms of verbs by using the very same pattern-association machinery (Rumelhart & McClelland, 1986). The basic architecture of this network is shown in Figure 13B2.1. Verb stems are entered in the input layer, which contains 460 units, each of which can be either on or off, and each of which represents a tiny stretch of sound, like a high vowel between two stop consonants. The beginning and end of a verb are symbolized by "[" and "]" brackets, respectively, and a whole verb is represented by turning on all the units for the sounds that it contains. Thus, similar-sounding verbs, like *shrink* and *drink*, share lots of units. The past-tense forms of verbs are represented in a separate layer of 460 output units that have the same representational properties as the input units. Every input unit projects to every output unit through an artificial "axon" with a "synaptic weight" that can

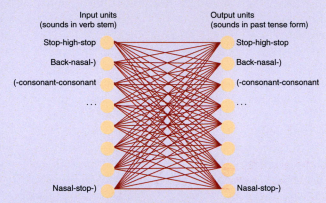

Figure 13B2.1 Simplified architecture of Rumelhart & McClelland's (1986) connectionist network for past-tense verb generation. (From Pinker, 1999, p. 105. Reprinted from: McClelland, James L., David E. Rumelhart, and PDP Research Group, *Parallel Distributed Processing, Volume 2: Explorations in the Microstructure of Cognition: Psychological and Biological Models,* figure from pages 216-271, © 1986 Massachusetts Institute of Technology, by permission of The MIT Press.)

vary from strongly excitatory to strongly inhibitory. Overall, then, there are $460 \times 460 = 211,600$ connections, making the model a gigantic pattern-associator. Learning takes place by means of an algorithm that adjusts the strength of every input–output connection by a tiny amount, up or down, after every trial, so that on the next trial the model will be slightly more likely to map a given verb stem onto the correct past-tense form.

The network was trained on a set of 420 verbs, each of which was presented 200 times, for a total of 84,000 trials. Remarkably enough, when the training was complete, the network could successfully convert most of the verb stems into the appropriate past-tense forms. For instance, it could convert *look* to *looked*, *seem* to *seemed*, *make* to *made*, *sing* to *sang*, and even *go* to *went*. Even more impressive, though, is that the network managed to perform reasonably well with 86 new verbs that had not been on the training list. To take a few examples, it correctly applied the *-ed* suffix to about three-quarters of the novel regular items, and it committed plausible overregularization errors for most of the novel irregular items (e.g., *catched* and *digged*).

Nevertheless, the model was completely flummoxed by a number of novel regular verbs like *jump* and *warm,* and it generated strange blends for several others, turning *squat* into *squakt*, *tour* into *toureder*, and *mail* into *membled.* These sorts of errors reflect the fact that the network does not make any use whatsoever of symbols for linguistic structures like "stem" and "suffix," but instead relies entirely on probabilistic correlations between phonological fragments of input and output forms. Many of the limitations of this particular network have been overcome by more sophisticated networks (e.g., MacWhinney & Leinbach, 1991; Hare et al., 1995; Joanisse & Seidenberg, 1999). However, as mentioned in the main text, some of the problems may be insurmountable by connectionist computer simulations which assume that all of the work traditionally ascribed to distinct representations for words and rules can be done by mere associations between sound patterns. Opinions about these issues remain sharply divided—see the debate between (Pinker & Ullman, 2002a, 2002b, and McClelland & Patterson, 2002a, 2002b; see also Albright & Hayes, 2003).

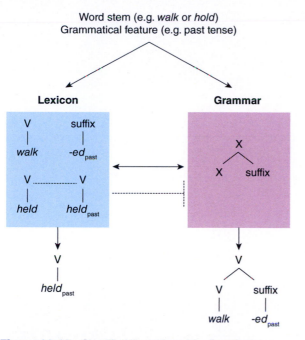

children go through a developmental period in which they are susceptible to overregularization errors (e.g., *holded*). Basically, they haven't had enough exposure to the correct irregular forms to build strong memory traces for them, so the regular suffixation process is not blocked (Marcus et al., 1992; Pinker, 1995).

What sorts of predictions do these competing approaches make about the neural underpinnings of the regular/irregular distinction? Because the two groups of Single Mechanism Models assume that both types of inflection are computed in essentially the same way—either entirely by rules or entirely by associative memory—they predict largely overlapping brain regions. These regions may include, but go considerably beyond, the portions of Broca's area identified by Sahin et al. (2006, 2009) as contributing to morphophonological processing. What matters most is that, according to Single Mechanism Models, regular and irregular inflection should rely on mostly shared neural resources. In contrast, because the Dual System Model assumes that the two types of inflection are computed in different ways, it predicts substantially separate brain regions. Although Broca's area may be recruited by both regulars and irregulars, it, perhaps together with neighboring regions, may play a greater role in processing regulars than irregulars, since damage to those structures is often linked with impairments of combinatorial grammatical operations, as seen in Broca's aphasia and progressive nonfluent aphasia (see Chapters 3, 4, and 14). Conversely, temporal and temporoparietal cortices may play a greater role in processing irregulars than regulars, since damage to those structures frequently gives rise to impairments of lexical–phonological operations, as seen in Wernicke's aphasia, conduction aphasia, anomia, and logopenic progressive aphasia (see Chapters 3, 4, and 6).

The next two subsections discuss how the different predictions of the competing theories fare in light of recent results from, first, neuropsychological studies, and second, functional neuroimaging studies. As we will see, the weight of evidence seems to favor the Dual System Model over the various Single System Models, but there are still a number of nontrivial complications that raise new questions for future work. The last subsection then shifts from the expressive to the receptive processing of regularly and irregularly inflected words. It describes several sources of evidence which suggest that, as expected by the Dual System Model, when a regularly inflected word is perceived, the stem and suffix are rapidly segmented to facilitate comprehension.

Figure 13.13 Simplified illustration of the Dual System Model of regular and irregular morphophonology. When a word must be inflected, the lexical and grammatical systems are accessed in parallel. If an inflected form of a verb (V) exists in the lexical system, as with irregulars (e.g., *held*), it is retrieved, and an inhibitory signal is sent to the grammatical system, blocking the suffixation process so that an overregularization error (e.g., *holded*) is not committed. If no inflected form is found in the lexical system, the grammatical system concatenates the appropriate suffix with the stem, generating a regular form (e.g., *walked*). (From Pinker & Ullman, 2002, p. 457.)

order to determine the correct morphophonological output. The lexical system contains entries not only for stems like *walk* and *hold* (which serve as inputs in the current example), but also for suffixes like *-ed* and irregular forms like *held* that are tagged with the appropriate morphosyntactic information, in this case "past tense." Stems are linked with the corresponding irregular forms (e.g., *hold–held*), and families of similar-sounding irregular items are captured by a pattern-association mechanism analogous to what is exploited in connectionist computer simulations. If an irregular form that satisfies the given input criteria is found in the lexical system (e.g., *held*), it is selected, and at the same time an inhibitory signal is sent to the grammatical system, effectively shutting it down. If, on the other hand, an irregular match is not found in the lexical system, the grammatical system automatically generates a regular form (e.g., *walked*) by means of a rule-governed process that concatenates the verb stem with the necessary suffix. Interestingly, this theory provides a straightforward explanation for why most

The Perspective from Neuropsychology

Many neuropsychological studies have explored disorders that disproportionately affect the capacity to produce either regularly or irregularly inflected words (e.g., Badecker & Caramazza, 1991; Ullman et al., 1997; Penke et al., 1999; Bird et al., 2003; Miozzo, 2003; Druks, 2006; Faroqi-Shah, 2007; Miozzo et al., 2010; Meteyard et al., 2013). So far, however, the most sophisticated investigation was arguably conducted by Ullman et al. (2005; see also the commentaries by MacWhinney, 2005, and Embick & Marantz, 2005, as well as the reply by Ullman & Walenski, 2005). In their paper, these researchers not only provide a detailed integrative review of previous studies on this topic, but also present behavioral and lesion data for 20 new patients—specifically, eleven nonfluent aphasics with damage to left inferior frontal regions, and nine fluent aphasics with damage to left temporal or temporoparietal regions. The following synopsis focuses on the methods, outcomes, and implications of two of the tasks that were performed by some of these patients.

The first task was completed by two nonfluent aphasics and six fluent aphasics. It was carefully designed to evaluate their ability to generate regular and irregular past-tense forms of verbs. Each trial consisted of two sentences—a "verb presentation sentence" and a "past tense sentence"—such as "*Every day I **look** at Susan. Just like every day, yesterday I _____ at Susan.*" The task was to fill in the blank by orally producing the appropriate form of the target verb, in this case *looked*. One condition involved 20 regular verbs (e.g., *look–looked*), and another condition involved 20 irregular verbs (e.g., *dig–dug*). These two sets of verbs were well-controlled for frequency and several other factors. (There were also two conditions that involved novel regular and irregular verbs, but they are not discussed here.) All of the items were presented to the patients in random order.

Figure 13.14 shows the lesion sites and behavioral results for two of the most interesting patients—FCL, an agrammatic Broca's aphasic with left inferior frontal damage, and JLU, an anomic fluent aphasic with left temporoparietal damage. It is apparent that these patients displayed a robust double dissociation between regular and irregular inflection, in accord with the predictions of the Dual System Model. On the one hand, FCL was significantly more impaired at generating regular (20 percent correct) than irregular (69 percent correct) past-tense forms of verbs. He failed 16/20 items in the regular condition, and his errors were distributed as follows: eight involved *-ing* suffixation (e.g., *chopping* instead of *chopped*); six involved stem repetition (e.g.,

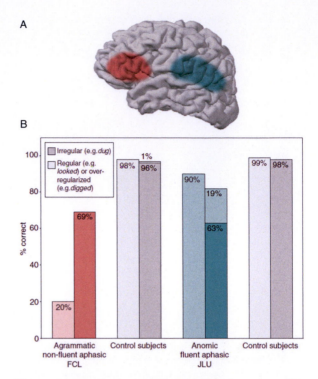

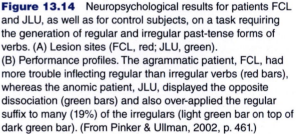

Figure 13.14   Neuropsychological results for patients FCL and JLU, as well as for control subjects, on a task requiring the generation of regular and irregular past-tense forms of verbs. (A) Lesion sites (FCL, red; JLU, green). (B) Performance profiles. The agrammatic patient, FCL, had more trouble inflecting regular than irregular verbs (red bars), whereas the anomic patient, JLU, displayed the opposite dissociation (green bars) and also over-applied the regular suffix to many (19%) of the irregulars (light green bar on top of dark green bar). (From Pinker & Ullman, 2002, p. 461.)

drop instead of *dropped*); one involved word substitution (*ran* instead of *rushed*); and one involved no response at all. Ullman et al. (2005, p. 203) argue that the data are best explained in terms of "an impairment of *-ed* suffixation and a relative sparing of stored irregular past-tense forms." On the other hand, JLU manifested the opposite performance profile, being significantly worse at inflecting irregular (63 percent correct) than regular (90 percent correct) verbs. He failed 6/20 items in the irregular condition, and his errors were distributed as follows: three involved overregularization (e.g., *maked* instead of *made;* note that these errors comprised 19 percent of the 20 irregular items); two involved inaccurate irregularization (*dung* instead of *dug*, and *thank* instead of *thought*); and one involved a false start. According to Ullman et al. (2005, p. 206), these findings suggest "an impairment of memory-based ... irregulars" in the face of "a relative sparing of the use of *-ed* suffixation."

Box 13.3   Do the Basal Ganglia Contribute to Regular Inflection?

The basal ganglia interact closely with the frontal lobes and are thought to be necessary for initiating, suppressing, and shifting between motor procedures, especially those that are habitual and hence implicitly rule-governed (see Chapter 1). Because the Dual System Model of morphophonology assumes that the regular past-tense forms of verbs are generated by concatenating a suffix with a stem in a rule-governed procedural manner, some advocates of this approach have wondered whether the process is mediated not only by the left IFG and surrounding cortical regions, but also by the basal ganglia. This question has received some research attention, but so far the results are rather mixed.

On the one hand, Ullman et al. (1997) presented data suggesting that the basal ganglia do participate in the neural circuitry subserving regular inflection. First of all, they studied 28 patients with Parkinson's disease (PD) who suffered from various degrees of hypokinesia—i.e., reduced motor activity—due to disturbances affecting the basal ganglia and the outflow from those nuclei to the frontal lobes. The researchers found that the five most severely hypokinetic patients performed significantly worse at generating regular than irregular past-tense forms of verbs, and they interpreted the results as evidence for weakened triggering of grammatical rules. In addition, Ullman et al. (1997) studied 17 patients with Huntington's disease (HD) who suffered from various degrees of hyperkinesia—i.e., excessive motor activity—due to a different type of basal ganglia dysfunction. They discovered that the patients with the greatest motor impairments not only made significantly more overregularization errors (e.g., *digged* instead of *dug*), but also produced some very unusual multiply suffixed forms (e.g., *walkeded*). The researchers interpreted these errors as evidence for overactive rule use. Bringing together all of their findings, Ullman et al. (1997) proposed that grammatical rules should be viewed as cognitive skills that, by analogy to over-learned motor behaviors, rely on a procedural system underpinned in part by the basal ganglia (for similar ideas see Lieberman, 2002).

On the other hand, Longworth et al. (2005a) presented data suggesting that the basal ganglia do *not* participate in the neural circuitry subserving regular inflection. Like Ullman et al. (1997), they studied sizeable groups of PD and HD patients; moreover, they also studied a group of patients with basal ganglia damage due to cerebrovascular accidents. Although all of the patient groups manifested mild deficits in generating the past-tense forms of verbs, none of them performed significantly worse with regular than irregular morphophonology, contrary to Ullman et al.'s (1997) investigation (see also Almor et al., 2002). Interestingly, these results emerged even though Longworth et al. (2005a) employed some of the same experimental methods as Ullman et al. (1997).

Given this state of affairs, all we can say is that the available data regarding the potential involvement of the basal ganglia in regular inflection are inconsistent. As with so many other controversial topics in the cognitive neuroscience of language, further research is needed to explore the issues in greater depth.

As for the remaining patients who performed the first task, the basic results are as follows. The other nonfluent aphasic had a lesion centered in Broca's area and the underlying white matter, with superior and posterior extension into premotor, primary motor, and somatosensory areas as well as into portions of the white matter in the anterior temporal lobe. Like FCL, he achieved only 20 percent correct in the regular condition, but unlike FCL, he did not perform significantly better in the irregular condition, since his score was only 25 percent correct. Although these findings seem to point to fairly equal deficits for the two types of morphophonological processing, it is noteworthy that his reaction times in the regular condition were on average nearly four times longer than in the irregular condition (6.5 seconds vs.

1.75 seconds). Ullman et al. (2005) suggest that this may reflect a somewhat more severe disruption of grammatical than lexical operations (see also Box 13.3). With regard to the other five fluent aphasics, all of them had left temporal or temporoparietal lesions, and as a group they had significantly greater difficulty with irregular than regular inflection (means = 73 percent vs. 85 percent correct, respectively). These results are consistent with the Dual System Model, since they "underscore a role for left posterior structures in lexical memory, and strengthen the hypothesis that structures in this region are not particularly important for -*ed* suffixation" (Ullman et al., 2005, p. 209).

The second task was completed by nine nonfluent aphasics and five fluent aphasics. This task simply required the patients to read aloud, in random order,

17 regular and 17 irregular past-tense forms of verbs. For present purposes, however, we will restrict our attention to the results for nine regulars (*slipped*, *tried*, *tied*, *died*, *sighed*, *weighed*, *learned*, *seemed*, and *stayed*) and nine irregulars (*swore*, *fled*, *clung*, *slid*, *bought*, *swept*, *kept*, *held*, and *drove*) that were closely matched on the following variables: the frequencies of both the stem and past-tense forms; the number of consonants in the initial and final consonant clusters; and the consistency of orthography-to-phonology mappings (note that "inconsistent" words have many neighbors with different mappings—e.g., some of the "enemies" of *pint* are *lint*, *mint*, *dint*, etc.).

As illustrated in Figure 13.15, the two groups of patients once again exhibited a striking double dissociation, in keeping with the Dual System Model. The nonfluent aphasics had significantly more trouble reading regular (30 percent correct) than irregular (50 percent correct) past-tense forms of verbs. These patients' errors were quite revealing: They produced far more uninflected forms for regulars than irregulars; they never produced any overregularizations for irregulars; and their phonological distortion rate was not reliably different for regulars and irregulars. Overall, the data support the hypothesis that the dissociation manifested by these patients reflects a rule-computing dysfunction that leads to the omission of *-ed* suffixes. In contrast, the fluent aphasics had significantly more trouble reading irregular (44 percent correct) than regular (64 percent correct) past-tense forms of verbs. Interestingly, unlike the nonfluent aphasics, they produced far more phonological distortions for irregulars than regulars (e.g., saying *cug* or *lig* instead of *dug*). Ullman et al. (2005, p. 217) argue that

> the data are consistent with the claim that the left posterior structures damaged in the present cases of fluent aphasia underlie lexical memory, in particular phonological forms, and do not play an important grammatical role either in affixation or in the syntactic computation of tense.

Although the results reported by Ullman et al. (2005) provide impressive neuropsychological evidence for the Dual System Model, it is important to acknowledge that other studies have yielded different outcomes. For example, Shapiro and Caramazza's (2003a) patient RC, who we discussed above in the context of verb-specific morphosyntactic processing, had a left inferior frontal lesion (see Figure 13.8); however, contrary to the specific neuroanatomical predictions of the Dual System Model, he was significantly better at generating

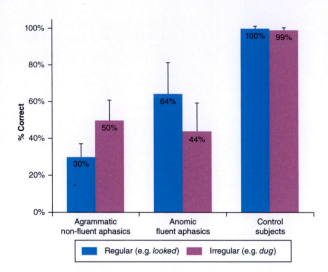

Figure 13.15 Neuropsychological results for agrammatic patients, anomic patients, and control subjects on a task requiring the oral reading of regular and irregular past-tense forms of verbs. (From Ullman et al., 2005, p. 210.)

regular (60 percent correct) than irregular (29 percent correct) past-tense forms of verbs. A similar advantage for regulars over irregulars was also displayed by two nonfluent aphasics who were bilingual speakers of Spanish and Catalan (Balaguer et al., 2004). More generally, in a recent meta-analysis Faroqi-Shah (2007) analyzed data from 75 patients across 25 different studies of the regular/irregular distinction. She found that over half the datasets failed to show a significant difference between the two types of inflection, and when valid differences did arise, they often failed to fit the specific neuroanatomical predictions of the Dual System Model. As she put it, "there seems to be no evident correlation between any pattern of performance and specific frontal and temporal lesion sites" (Faroqi-Shah, 2007, p. 10).

Now, it is certainly possible that some of the studies in Faroqi-Shah's (2007) meta-analysis did not control properly for various "nuisance" factors. At the same time, however, it is also possible that the neural circuits underlying regular and irregular morphophonology are more intricate than the Dual System Model assumes, and that they interact in complicated ways with the circuits underlying morphosyntax as well as semantics, making it difficult to decipher the overall architecture with the lesion method (see Meteyard et al., 2013, for a thoughtful discussion in the context of novel experimental data). Stepping back from the details, perhaps the most meaningful generalization to draw from the extant neuropsychological data is this: The simple fact that compelling double dissociations between precisely matched regulars and irregulars have been documented in at least some studies (e.g., Ullman et al., 2005) is easier to explain in terms of the Dual System Model than in terms of the various Single System Models.

The Perspective from Functional Neuroimaging

Motivated partly by the theoretical need to adjudicate between the competing conceptual frameworks and partly by the empirical need to better understand the brain regions that underlie the generation of regularly and irregularly inflected words, many researchers have approached the issues from the perspective of functional neuroimaging (e.g., Jaeger et al., 1996; Beretta et al., 2003; Sach et al., 2004; Joanisse & Seidenberg, 2005; Balaguer et al., 2006; Desai et al., 2006; Sahin et al., 2006). On the theoretical front, the vast majority of these PET and fMRI studies have bolstered the Dual System Model by disclosing substantially separate networks of brain regions for the two kinds of morphophonology. On the empirical front, however, these studies have not shed much light on the actual makeup of those networks, because the specific metabolic results have been extremely heterogeneous. As Shallice and Cooper (2011, p. 322) put it, "The imaging findings are at worst contradictory and at best open to multiple interpretations, although on balance they are less tortuously explained by the dual process account [i.e., the Dual System Model]." Given the messiness of the hemodynamic data, I will not even attempt to formulate some useful take-home messages here, but will instead just refer interested readers to other reviews (see especially Bornkessel-Schlesewsky & Schlesewsky, 2009a, pp. 50–56, and Shallice & Cooper, 2011, pp. 315–324).

Why is this literature so inconsistent? The answer is not clear, but one possibility is that functional neuroimaging techniques may be unusually sensitive to both salient and subtle differences across experiments that probe inflectional processing—differences that involve such variables as the following: the frequency, complexity, and orthographic-to-phonological consistency of the stimuli; the timing of the stimuli and the responses; the task; the baseline conditions; the data analyses; and various aspects of the subjects, including their sex (Jaeger et al., 1998). Furthermore, Sahin et al. (2006, p. 557) point out that "the regular-irregular distinction maps only imperfectly onto the computation-memory distinction," and they conclude their own discussion of the puzzling discrepancies in the functional

neuroimaging literature with the following statement: "Future studies may need more subtle manipulations, involving carefully selected subsets of words, rather than an across-the-board regular-irregular dichotomy, to systematically map the effect of irregularity on the interplay between memory and computation." (For an instructive step in this direction, see the recent fMRI study by Oh et al., 2011.)

What About Comprehension?

The two main theoretical frameworks that we have been considering—the Dual System Model and the various Single System Models—were originally designed to account for the production of regularly and irregularly inflected words. Some researchers believe, however, that the basic architectural assumptions of these alternative approaches can be extended to cover comprehension as well. From this vantage point, the Dual System Model predicts that during the receptive processing of inflected words, irregular forms like *ran* are recognized as holistic lexical items stored in the mental dictionary, whereas regular forms like *walked* are automatically decomposed into distinct morphemes—a stem and a suffix—by a rule-governed process. In contrast, according to the group of Single System Models that posit a unified associative memory for all inflected forms, both irregulars and regulars are predicted to be recognized as stored words. (The other group of Single System Models, which maintain that all inflected forms are handled by rules, has not been discussed in the literature on comprehension and hence is not treated here.) These issues have been the focus of several decades of psycholinguistic research, and the lion's share of the results favor the Dual System Model (for a review see Marslen-Wilson, 2007). The neural correlates of the relevant cognitive processes, however, have only recently begun to receive close attention. The following survey highlights some especially influential work on this topic by William Marslen-Wilson, Lorraine Tyler, and their colleagues at Cambridge University (for a review see Marslen-Wilson & Tyler, 2007).

Many of the studies by this team capitalized on a well-established phenomenon called **auditory priming**. The essence of this phenomenon is that an auditorily presented "target" word is normally recognized as a real word significantly faster when it is immediately

Auditory priming   An auditorily presented "target" word is normally recognized as a real word significantly faster when it is preceded by a related "prime" word than when it is preceded by an unrelated "prime" word.

Table 13.2 Examples of Stimuli Employed in Marslen-Wilson & Tyler's (1997) Auditory Priming Study

Condition	Related Prime	Unrelated (Control) Prime	Target Word
Semantic	*swan*	*hay*	*goose*
Regular past	*walked*	*locked*	*walk*
Irregular past	*ran*	*shows*	*run*

Adapted from Marslen-Wilson & Tyler (1997, p. 593).

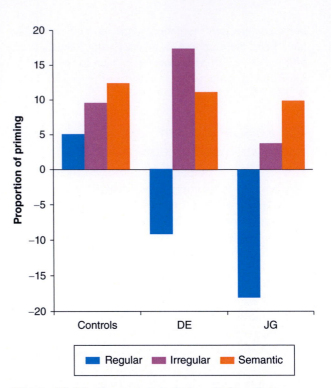

Figure 13.16 Neuropsychological results for patient DE, patient JG, and control subjects in an auditory priming experiment. Effects are expressed as response proportions (mean priming effect for each condition as a proportion of mean control reaction time for that condition) to normalize for differences in base reaction time between subjects. Note that a positive value means that the reaction time to the primed stimulus was faster than to the unprimed stimulus, and a negative value means the opposite. Thus, unlike control subjects, patients DE and JG failed to exhibit positive priming effects in the regular inflection condition, but like control subjects, they did exhibit such effects in the irregular inflection condition and in the semantic condition. (From Tyler & Marslen-Wilson, 1997, p. 592.)

preceded by a related "prime" word than when it is immediately preceded by an unrelated "prime" word. Although this facilitation effect is very weak when the prime and target words are only related through phonology (e.g., *clamp–clam*), it is quite strong when they are related through semantics (e.g., *swan–goose*), regular inflection (e.g., *walked–walk*), or irregular inflection (e.g., *ran–run*). Presumably, the reason the effect occurs is because the lexical information that is shared by the two related items is first activated by the prime word, so when the target word is subsequently encountered, that information is still partially activated, thereby speeding up the recognition process.

By conducting several cleverly designed auditory priming experiments with brain-damaged patients, Marlsen-Wilson, Tyler, and their colleagues have been able to shed valuable light on the neural substrates of regular and irregular morphophonological processing during language comprehension (Marslen-Wilson & Tyler, 1997, 1998; Tyler et al., 2002a, 2002b, 2005a; Longworth et al., 2005b). For example, in one of their studies, they investigated the sensitivity of two agrammatic Broca's aphasics and six healthy control subjects to all three of the critical types of prime–target relationships mentioned above—semantic, regular inflection, and irregular inflection (Marslen-Wilson & Tyler, 1997, 1998; see Table 13.2 for examples of the stimuli). As shown in Figure 13.16, the control subjects exhibited significant priming effects in all three conditions, consistent with previously acquired data from other healthy individuals. The two patients also exhibited significant priming effects in the semantic condition, but both of them manifested a dramatic dissociation between the two inflection conditions, with positive priming in the irregular condition but not in the regular condition.

This pattern of results suggests that, in keeping with the Dual System Model, irregularly inflected verbs like *ran* are stored as "whole forms" in the normal brain,

but regularly inflected verbs like *walked* are not. After all, if the latter verbs were stored that way, they would have been recognized by the patients as single units and would have positively primed their stems in the same way that the irregularly inflected verbs did. The fact that such effects were not found supports the alternative view that during normal receptive language processing, regularly inflected verbs are automatically subjected to a kind of morphophonological parsing which segments the surface form into its components—a stem and a suffix—so that they can separately guide further processing. According to Marslen-Wilson and Tyler (1997, 1998), it is precisely this decompositional operation that appears to be defective in the two agrammatic patients.

Both of those patients had large left-hemisphere lesions that encompassed Broca's area and extended posteriorly into temporoparietal areas. To gain additional insight into the neural underpinnings of the decompositional operation that applies to regularly but not irregularly inflected verbs, Tyler et al. (2005a) ran a similar auditory priming experiment with a sample of 22 other patients who had predominantly left-hemisphere lesions, and then looked for correlations between, on the one hand, the patients' behavioral performances, and on the other hand, voxel-by-voxel structural variations in their MRIs. The investigators found that reduced priming effects in the regular inflection condition, but not in the irregular inflection condition, correlated most significantly with damage to Broca's area; moreover, at lower statistical thresholds there was posterior extension into temporoparietal areas, as well as deep extension into the underlying white matter, including the arcuate fasciculus (Figure 13.17). When these results are brought together with the data reviewed above regarding the production of regularly inflected verbs, it seems quite likely that Broca's area plays an essential role in both the expressive and the receptive processing of regular morphophonology. On the receptive side, it also seems possible that when regularly inflected verbs are heard, they are rapidly broken down into a stem and a suffix by a left-lateralized temporo-frontal network that overlaps substantially with the one referred to as the dorsal stream in Hickok and Poeppel's Dual Stream Model of speech perception (see Chapter 5).

To explore this idea in greater detail, Tyler et al. (2005b) conducted an fMRI study in which, on each trial, the subjects were required to determine whether two auditorily presented stimuli were the same or different (see also Wright et al., 2011). There were several conditions, but for present purposes the most relevant ones involved, once again, our familiar friends—regular verbs (e.g., same: *played–played*; different: *stayed–stay*) and irregular verbs (e.g., same: *bought–bought*; different: *taught–teach*). When the regulars were subtracted from the irregulars, no brain regions were found to be significantly engaged. But when the irregulars were subtracted from the regulars, activity emerged not only in the superior/middle temporal gyri bilaterally, but also in Broca's area and the left anterior cingulate cortex (Figure 13.18). Follow-up analyses suggested that the anterior cingulate cortex contributes to the receptive processing of regularly inflected verbs by helping to regulate the interaction between temporal regions and Broca's area. In a discussion of this study, Marslen-Wilson and Tyler (2007, pp. 830–831) emphasize how nicely the outcomes converge with the other results reviewed

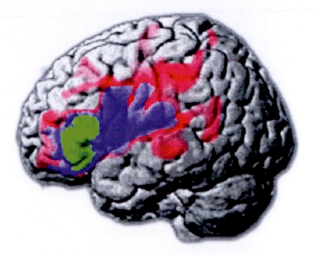

Figure 13.17 Lesion sites correlated with reduced auditory priming effects for regularly inflected verbs at three different voxel-level thresholds: $p < 0.001$ (green), $p < 0.01$ (blue), and $p < 0.05$ (red). The statistical peak is in the left inferior frontal gyrus (BA47), and the cluster extends superiorly into BA45. At lower thresholds, the cluster extends from Broca's area to Wernicke's area and includes the arcuate fasciculus. (From Tyler et al., 2005a, p. 8377.) Copyright (2005) National Academy of Sciences, U.S.A.

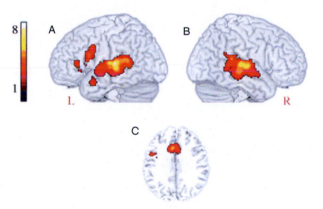

Figure 13.18 Results from Tyler et al.'s (2005b) fMRI study of same-different judgments for regular and irregular verbs. The subtraction of irregulars from regulars revealed significant activity in the superior/middle temporal gyri bilaterally (A, B), in Broca's area (A), and in the left anterior cingulate cortex (C). (From Marslen-Wilson & Tyler, 2007, p. 832.)

above, all of which favor the Dual System Model: "In summary, this experiment is consistent with our basic hypotheses for an underlying grammatically driven neurocognitive system, instantiated in a left-lateralized network linking temporal and inferior frontal areas, which prioritizes the identification and interpretation of inflectional morphemes."

Before concluding this final section, it is worth noting that a sizeable ERP literature has built up around the regular/irregular distinction. In large part because of space limitations, this literature is not considered here. A useful review is provided, however, by Bornkessel-Schlesewsky and Schlesewsky (2009a, pp. 57–66). As they point out, many of the ERP findings are consistent with the Dual System Model, but there are also a number of complications that can only be resolved through further research.

Summary

Morphosyntactic specifications like "past tense" are morphophonologically realized in two different ways: regular inflection, which involves fairly systematic suffixation, as in *walk–walked*; and irregular inflection, which involves fairly idiosyncratic modification, as in *run–ran*. The major competing theoretical accounts of these alternative inflectional patterns are as follows: Single System Models maintain that the two types of inflection are handled in the same manner—either entirely by rules or entirely by associative memory; in contrast, the Dual System Model maintains that the two types of inflection are handled in different manners—regulars by suffixation rules, and irregulars by associative memory. The available neurolinguistic data regarding the generation of regularly and irregularly inflected words are by no means consistent, especially in the functional neuroimaging literature. However, the weight of evidence, most notably in the neuropsychological literature, seems to favor the Dual System Model over the various Single System Models. In particular, Ullman et al. (2005) reported striking double dissociations between regular and irregular items that

were extremely well-matched for several "nuisance" variables. Disproportionate difficulty producing regulars was most strongly linked with damage to Broca's area and adjacent frontal regions, whereas disproportionate difficulty producing irregulars was most strongly linked with damage to left temporal and temporoparietal regions. These discoveries support the hypothesis that the generation of regular past-tense forms of verbs depends on a rule-governed suffixation process subserved largely by Broca's area, whereas the generation of irregular past-tense forms of verbs depends on a memory look-up process subserved largely by more posterior cortical structures.

With respect to comprehension, neuropsychological studies as well as functional neuroimaging studies suggest that, in accord with the Dual System Model, when the past-tense forms of verbs are heard, regulars and irregulars are processed differently. On the one hand, regulars are rapidly segmented into their morphophonological components—a stem and a suffix—by a neural network that connects superior/middle temporal regions with Broca's area via the arcuate fasciculus. On the other hand, irregulars are mapped directly onto "whole form" lexical representations stored in superior/middle temporal regions.

In closing, it is important to note that the research summarized above by no means exhausts the literature on the neural underpinnings of the regular/irregular distinction. On the contrary, many studies have been set aside for the sake of simplicity, and some of them have yielded results that support alternative theoretical frameworks (e.g., Stockall & Marantz, 2006). This area of investigation will no doubt continue to develop in new directions in the future.

Summary and Key Points

- There are two aspects of inflection:
  - Morphosyntax involves the content and distributional agreement (i.e., between-word consistency) of the various features that are expressed by inflection, like number and tense.
  - Morphophonology involves the encoding of inflectional features in sound patterns that may be regular (e.g., *dogs*, *barked*), irregular (e.g., *mice*, *held*), or null (e.g., *one car-ø*; *they run-ø*).
- Recent studies suggest that during spoken language production, these two aspects of inflection are correlated with distinct spatiotemporal patterns of activity in Broca's area:
  - An fMRI study showed that the two aspects of inflection engage separate parts of Broca's area.
  - A closely related electrophysiological study showed that the two aspects of inflection are handled sequentially:
  - 200-ms latency: delivery of word identity to Broca's area.
  - 320-ms latency: morphosyntactic processing.
  - 450-ms latency: morphophonological processing.
  - However, other studies indicate that the neural substrates of inflection are much more complex than this.

- A substantial amount of research on the neural substrates of morphosyntax has focused on the noun/verb distinction:

  - There is increasing evidence that noun and verb inflection share a common pathway in Broca's area, or, perhaps more narrowly, in the inferior portion of Broca's area. This pathway may underlie a relatively late, category-neutral phase of morphosyntactic processing.
  - There is also increasing evidence that noun and verb inflection can be differentially impaired by damage to separate regions of the brain. These regions may underlie a relatively early, category-specific phase of morphosyntactic processing.
  - The regions that implement noun-specific circuitry for selecting features like singular vs. plural number are not yet known, but they may include the superior portion of Broca's area.
  - The regions that implement verb-specific circuitry for selecting features like present vs. past tense most likely include the left MFG, but it is not clear whether the posterior or anterior sector is more critical.
  - Regarding comprehension, several studies suggest that the perception of inflected verbs engages the left MTG and IFG more strongly than the perception of inflected nouns, even when the items are compared with the corresponding stems.

- A substantial amount of research on the neural substrates of morphophonology has focused on the regular/irregular distinction, especially as manifested by the past-tense forms of English verbs:

  - The major competing theories are as follows:
    - Single System Models maintain that the two types of morphophonology are handled in the same manner—either entirely by rules or entirely by associative memory. These approaches predict substantially shared neural substrates.
    - The Dual System Model maintains that the two types of morphophonology are handled in different manners—regulars by rules, and irregulars by associative memory. This approach predicts substantially separate neural substrates.
  - The weight of neuropsychological evidence supports the Dual System Model, since compelling double dissociations have been documented between regular and irregular verbs. Disproportionate difficulty producing regulars was most strongly linked with damage to Broca's area and adjacent frontal regions, whereas disproportionate difficulty producing irregulars was most strongly linked with damage to left temporal and temporoparietal regions.
  - The functional neuroimaging literature on this topic is less informative, since it contains many inconsistencies.
  - Regarding comprehension, several sources of evidence suggest that, in accord with the Dual System Model, when the past-tense forms of verbs are heard, regulars and irregulars are processed differently. Regulars are rapidly segmented into their morphophonological components—a stem and a suffix—by a neural network that connects superior/middle temporal regions with Broca's area via the arcuate fasciculus. In contrast, irregulars are mapped directly onto "whole form" lexical representations stored in superior/middle temporal regions.

Recommended Reading

- Shapiro, K.A., & Caramazza, A. (2009). Morphological processes in language production. In M.S. Gazzaniga (Ed.), *The cognitive neurosciences*, 4th edition (pp. 777–788). Cambridge, MA: MIT Press. An informative review of recent research on the production of inflected words, covering data from a variety of brain mapping methods.
- Marslen-Wilson, W.D, & Tyler, L.K. (2007). Morphology, language and the brain: The decompositional substrate for language comprehension. *Philosophical Transactions of the Royal Society, B. Biological Sciences, 362,* 823–836. An excellent summary of recent research on the comprehension of inflected words, emphasizing the authors' own studies but situating them in the context of a broader range of work.
- The following debate, while somewhat old, reveals the different perspectives of researchers who advocate either the Dual System Model (Pinker & Ullman) or the Single System Model (McClelland & Patterson) regarding the regular/irregular distinction:
- Pinker, S., & Ullman, M. (2002). The past and future of the past tense. *Trends in Cognitive Sciences, 6,* 456–463.
- McClelland, J.L., & Patterson, K. (2002). "Words *or* Rules" cannot exploit the regularity in exceptions. *Trends in Cognitive Sciences, 6,* 464–465.
- McClelland, J.L., & Patterson, K. (2002). Rules or connections in past-tense inflections: What does the evidence rule out? *Trends in Cognitive Sciences, 6,* 465–472.
- Pinker, S., & Ullman, M. (2002). Combination and structure, not gradedness, is the issue. *Trends in Cognitive Sciences, 6,* 472–474.

Sentence Production

Introduction

Up to this point, we have dealt almost exclusively with the neural substrates of language at the level of single words. By restricting the scope of our inquiry in this manner, we have gained considerable insight into the complex networks of brain regions that allow us to represent and process the phonological, orthographic, semantic, and morphological structures of individual words. One could argue, however, that we have not yet gotten much purchase on the biological bases of naturalistic language use because, to put it bluntly, people don't go around all day communicating with each other in single-word utterances. On the contrary, they routinely combine words in systematic ways to formulate novel propositions of every imaginable kind, from idle gossip, driving directions, and pasta recipes to medical diagnoses, legal judgments, and religious exhortations.

The engine that drives and regulates the generation of multi-word utterances is syntax—a set of rules, principles, and patterns that determine how words can be strung together in sequences so that their separate meanings can be integrated into composite, distinctive messages. To take a straightforward example from Pinker (1994, p. 84): "We know the difference between the forgettable *Dog bites man* and the newsworthy *Man bites dog* because of the order in which *dog*, *man*, and *bites* are combined. That is, we use a code to translate between orders of words and combinations of thoughts."

Many, perhaps even most, syntactic rules are functionally motivated in one way or another, but as anyone who has studied a foreign language knows, there are always cases of apparent, and often real, arbitrariness. It is therefore rather remarkable that native speakers are, for the most part, very diligent about obeying all sorts of seemingly nonsensical syntactic rules, even when flouting those rules would not significantly reduce the comprehensibility of their utterances. In English, for instance, it would be fine to ask someone *What does Jessica like wine with?*, the answer being *She likes wine with cheese,* but it would be grammatically unacceptable to ask someone **What does Jessica like wine and?*, the answer being *She likes wine and cheese* (Ross, 1967; note that an asterisk indicates ungrammaticality). Similarly, it would be fine to convert *Jessica tapped Bob's arm* to *Jessica tapped Bob on the arm,* but it would be grammatically unacceptable to convert *Jessica broke Bob's arm* to **Jessica broke Bob on the arm* (Fillmore, 1967; Kemmerer, 2003). For native English speakers, these intuitions about well-formed versus ill-formed expressions are the conscious reflexes of unconscious syntactic rules that were acquired effortlessly during childhood, but that, amazingly enough, professional linguists still have trouble characterizing precisely. Our mental grammars consist of countless rules like these, and somehow, whenever we participate in ordinary conversation, they are deployed rapidly and efficiently beneath the surface of awareness, so that we can concentrate on the content of the messages we wish to convey, instead of worrying about the minute details of how the individual words should be combined.

The purpose of this chapter is to review some of the most important discoveries that have been made about the neural substrates of syntactic encoding during sentence production. The first section sets the stage by providing a brief survey of a number of fundamental aspects of syntax. This material is relevant not only to the issues discussed in the rest of the current chapter, but also to those discussed in the next chapter, which focuses on sentence comprehension. The second section presents a rudimentary theory of normal syntactic encoding that accords with the Lemma Model of speech production outlined in Chapter 6. The third section addresses a variety of disorders of sentence production, starting with the controversial syndrome of agrammatism, then shifting to several more narrowly defined deficits displayed by stroke patients, and ending with the kinds of impairments exhibited by patients with primary progressive aphasia, especially the nonfluent type. Taken together, these neuropsychological findings suggest that syntactic encoding depends on a complex, widely distributed network of mostly left-lateralized brain regions, with one of the most important regions being Broca's area. Finally, the fourth section summarizes a few functional neuroimaging studies which support the hypothesis that Broca's area is indeed a major component of the network that underlies the concatenation of words into phrases and clauses.

Syntax: A Short Tutorial

In the 1960s, Noam Chomsky became the dominant figure in the branch of modern linguistics that deals with syntax, and from the 1970s all the way through the 1990s, a series of reactions to his influential approach spawned a plethora of competing frameworks. This is clearly revealed by the *Concise Encyclopedia of Syntactic Theories* (Brown & Miller, 1996), which has separate chapters on, among other topics, the following theories, to name but a few: Autolexical Syntax, Categorial Grammar, Cognitive Grammar, Construction Grammar, Dependency Grammar, Functional Grammar, Generalized Phrase Structure Grammar, Head-Driven Phrase Structure Grammar, Lexical Functional Grammar, Relational Grammar, Role and Reference Grammar, Word Grammar, and three versions of Chomskyan Generative Grammar— Transformational Grammar, Principles and Parameters Theory, and the Minimalist Program.

This profusion of highly specialized frameworks has recently led to a backlash. For example, R.M.W. Dixon's Basic Linguistic Theory

> has its origins in the pioneering work of Sanskrit and Greek grammarians between 3,000 and 2,000 years ago [and] is continually enhanced through descriptions of new languages, each revision making it able to characterize a little more fully the essential nature of language as a cultural trait of human beings.
>
> (Dixon, 2010a, p. 3;
> see also Dixon, 2010b, 2012)

An even more extreme position, however, is advocated by Martin Haspelmath, whose Framework-Free Grammatical Theory is based on the notion that "all languages have different categories, and languages should be described in their own terms" (Haspelmath, 2010, p. 341).

The following survey of some fundamental aspects of syntax does not presuppose any particular theory, either explicitly or implicitly. It does, however, lean toward the approaches propounded by Dixon and Haspelmath, since they are among the approaches that are most sensitive to cross-linguistic diversity—an issue that has been gaining significance as fieldworkers have learned more about the roughly 6,000 languages in the world (see especially Evans & Levinson, 2009; see also Kemmerer, 2014).

Devices for Indicating Participant Roles

One of the main purposes of syntactic rules is to provide speakers and hearers with shared conventions for indicating "who did what to whom." As Pinker (1994) pointed out in the passage quoted above, English relies primarily on word order for this function. In a simple transitive clause, the actor is typically expressed before the verb, and the undergoer is typically expressed after it, giving rise to the radically different interpretations of *Dog bites man* and *Man bites dog*. But while word order is a cross-linguistically common strategy for distinguishing between participant roles, it is by no means the only one.

For instance, many languages use **case marking** instead—a device that lies at the intersection of syntax and morphology. This is illustrated by Kayardild, an Australian Aboriginal language documented by Evans (1995). In this language, one could describe a man chasing a turtle by using the same type of actor–verb– undergoer word order that we would use in English: *Dangkaa durrwaaja bangaya*. But one could also describe the same situation by using any of the other five possible word orders, because the final *-a* suffix after *dangka* ("man") is a case marker that identifies him as the actor, and the *-ya* suffix after *banga* ("turtle") is a case marker that identifies it as the undergoer. Evans (2010, p. 65) remarked that "When I was first learning Kayardild, and did not understand something, my teachers used to just repeat it, working through the permutations, hoping one of them would hit the spot for me."

Case marking   A grammatical device for indicating "who did what to whom" in which different nominal suffixes encode different participant roles.

A third way to signal participant roles is by placing special markers not on the nouns, but rather on the verb. This method is adopted by another Australian Aboriginal language called Ilgar. In this language, one could scramble the words *arrkbi* ("man"), *ayan* ("sees"), and *wurduwajba* ("woman") in any of the six possible sequences to express either that the man sees the woman or that the woman sees the man. The interpretation would depend on which of two prefixes is attached to the verb: *iny-* ("he acting upon her") or *ying-* ("she acting upon him"). Thus, *arrkbi inyayan wurduwajba* means "The man sees the woman," regardless of how the words are ordered, and *wurduwajba yingayan arrkbi* means "The woman sees the man," again regardless of how the words are ordered (Evans, 2010, pp. 65–66).

Yet another device that is sometimes used to flag participant roles is tone (see Chapter 7 for a fuller discussion of tone). Although this strategy is not widespread, it has been observed in a number of Nilotic languages spoken in East Africa (Bennett, 1974). In Teso, for example, when the word for "river" has the role of actor, it is produced with low tone on just the first vowel (*ecilet*), but when it has the role of undergoer, it is produced with low tone across all of the vowels (*ecílét*).

Hierarchical Structure

A central aspect of syntax is that words can be grouped together to form increasingly complex assemblages that encode increasingly complex meanings. In many languages, this process of building hierarchically organized expressions is regulated by **phrase structure rules** that, according to Pinker and Bloom (1990, p. 713), "force concatenation in the string to correspond to semantic connectedness in the underlying proposition . . ., distinguishing, for example, *Large trees grow dark berries* from *Dark trees grow large berries*." In these two example sentences, linear adjacency is clearly what determines which adjective—*large* or *dark*—modifies which noun—*trees* or *berries*. It is essential to realize, however, that contiguity is only one way of indicating that certain words belong to the same larger unit.

A large class of languages achieve the same goal by adopting a different coding device, namely **agreement rules**. In Classical Latin, for instance, links between

adjectives and nouns are signaled by concordant case markers, so that speakers need not position the relevant words right next to each other, but can instead exploit linear order for purely pragmatic purposes, as in the following sentence from Virgil (Matthews, 1981, p. 255; quoted by Evans & Levinson, 2009, p. 441):

ultima	Cumaei	venit	iam	carminis	aetas
last (NOM)	Cumae (GEN)	come (3.SG.PAST)	now	song (GEN)	age (NOM)

"The last age of the Cumaean song has now arrived"

Here the words *ultima* and *aetas* are not contiguous; on the contrary, they lie at opposite ends of the sentence. Nevertheless, they are symbolized as belonging to the same larger unit by virtue of being inflected for the same case, specifically nominative (NOM). Similarly, the words *Cumaei* and *carminis* are not adjacent, but they are flagged as being related to each other through concordant inflection for genitive case (GEN). By identifying these distinct patterns of agreement, a hearer can discern the semantic structure of the message (for further discussion see Austin & Bresnan, 1996).

Argument Structure

Argument structure involves the interaction between, on the one hand, the various participant roles, like actor and undergoer, that enter into the meanings of verbs, and on the other hand, the expression of those roles in various grammatical relations, like subject and object (for a review see Levin & Rappaport Hovav, 2005). In Chapter 11, we noted that there is a strong tendency for semantically one-participant verbs to be syntactically intransitive (e.g., *Karen squinted*) and for semantically two-participant verbs to be syntactically transitive (e.g., *Karen rubbed her eyes*) (Næss, 2007; Dixon, 2010b). We also noted, however, that there are some verbs for which these mappings between semantics and syntax are not so simple. For instance, *eat, dine,* and *devour* all designate events in which an agent consumes food, but *eat* can be either intransitive or transitive (*Bill ate* or *Bill ate the lasagna*), *dine* can only be intransitive (*Bill dined* vs. **Bill dined the lasagna*), and *devour* can only be transitive (**Bill devoured* vs. *Bill devoured the lasagna*). Developing a proper account of such phenomena

Phrase structure rules   Syntactic rules that specify how adjacent words can be grouped together to form hierarchically organized units.

Agreement rules   Syntactic rules that specify how words that are concordantly marked for certain features (e.g., case, number, gender) can be grouped together to form hierarchically organized units.

Argument structure   The interaction between, on the one hand, the various participant roles, like actor and undergoer, that enter into the meanings of verbs, and on the other hand, the expression of those roles in various grammatical relations, like subject and object.

Table 14.1   Examples of English Argument Structure Constructions

Construction	Form	Meaning	Example
1. Transitive	Subject Verb Object	*X* acts on *Y*	Bill kicked the ball.
2. Caused motion	Subject Verb Object Oblique	*X* causes *Y* to move along path *Z*	Bill kicked the ball into the lake.
3. Conative	Subject Verb Oblique$_{at}$	*X* attempts to contact *Y*	Bill kicked at the ball.
4. Ditransitive	Subject Verb Object$_1$ Object$_2$	*X* causes *Y* to receive *Z*	Bill kicked Bob the ball.
5. Resultative	Subject Verb Object Complement	*X* causes *Y* to become *Z*	Bill kicked Bob black and blue.
6. Possessor ascension	Subject Verb Object Oblique$_{in/on}$	*X* contacts *Y* in/on body-part *Z*	Bill kicked Bob in the knee.
7. Contact *against*	Subject Verb Object Oblique$_{against}$	*X* causes *Y* to contact *Z*	Bill kicked his foot against the chair.
8. *X's* way	Subject Verb *X's* way Oblique	*X* makes progress by performing action	Bill kicked his way through the crowd.
9. Habitual	Subject Verb	*X* performs action habitually	That horse kicks.

is one of the many challenges of contemporary research on argument structure.

Another important point is that many verbs can be used in a surprisingly wide range of syntactic argument structure frames. For instance, even though *kick* is usually regarded as a prototypical transitive verb, it occurs in at least nine distinct active-voice constructions (Goldberg, 1995):

(1) Bill kicked the ball.
(2) Bill kicked the ball into the lake.
(3) Bill kicked at the ball.
(4) Bill kicked Bob the ball.
(5) Bill kicked Bob black and blue.
(6) Bill kicked Bob in the knee.
(7) Bill kicked his foot against the chair.
(8) Bill kicked his way through the crowd.
(9) That horse kicks.

These sentences describe very different kinds of events: (1) simple volitional bodily action directed at an object; (2) causing an object to change location; (3) attempting to contact an object; (4) transferring possession of an object; (5) causing an object to change state; (6) inducing a feeling in a person by contacting part of their body; (7) causing part of one's own body to contact an object; (8) making progress along a path by moving in some manner; and (9) having a tendency to perform an action.

According to recent "constructionist" approaches to syntax (e.g., Goldberg, 1995, 2006; Hoffman &

Trousdale, 2013), argument structure constructions are in fact clausal patterns that directly encode certain schematic meanings, and the interpretation of a sentence depends to a large extent on a division of labor between the meaning of the construction and the meaning of the verb. For instance, the *X's way* construction consists of a particular syntactic structure—roughly "Subject Verb *X's way* Oblique"—that is paired with a particular semantic structure—roughly "X makes progress along a path by V-ing." Thus, in a sentence like *Bill kicked his way through the crowd,* the general concept of "motion of the subject referent along a path" comes from the *X's way* construction itself, and the more specific notion of "forceful leg action" comes from *kick.* Table 14.1 shows how each of the sentences with *kick* listed in (1)–(9) instantiates a construction that designates an idealized event type. It is worth noting, however, that although these issues have been attracting a great deal of attention in linguistics, they have not yet had much impact on neurolinguistics (Kemmerer, 2006a).

Although there are many cross-linguistic similarities involving argument structure, there is also a great deal of diversity (Bowerman & Brown, 2008). To take a single example, most languages have multiple causative constructions, and there is usually if not always a semantic difference between them involving any of several distinct parameters. One such parameter involves animacy. For instance, in Nivkh, which is spoken in Outer Manchuria, a causer must be animate, so that one cannot say something like *The mist made us stay in the village*, but must instead resort to an alternative construction like *We stayed in the village because of the mist* (Dixon, 2000).

Closed-Class Elements

As mentioned in Chapter 3, a distinction must be made between open-class and closed-class elements. Open-class elements consist primarily of nouns, verbs, adjectives, and adverbs that collectively constitute a large inventory of vocabulary items that is always changing, as some words fall into disuse while new ones are coined. These elements provide most of the semantic content of utterances, and for this reason they are sometimes called content words. In contrast, closed-class elements consist of several small classes of morphemes that are fairly stable over time, have fairly abstract meanings, and play important grammatical roles. Many closed-class elements are affixes that are always bound to stems, like case markers, agreement markers, and the regular past-tense suffix *-ed* that we discussed at length in Chapter 13. Many others, however, are free-standing items that are often called function words or, more simply, functors. Some English examples include articles like *a* and *the*; demonstratives like *this* and *that*; auxiliary and modal verbs like *do*, *can*, *could*, *may*, *might*, *must*, *ought*, *should*, *would*, and *will*; prepositions like *in*, *on*, *over*, *under*, *across*, *through*, *for*, *of*, *until*, *during*, and *since*; and conjunctions like *and*, *or*, *but*, *because*, *therefore*, *moreover*, and *however*.

A well-established cross-linguistic generalization is that, apart from the intriguing exception of demonstratives (Diessel, 2006), virtually all closed-class elements can be shown to have derived historically from more concrete open-class elements through a process called **grammaticalization** (Narrog & Heine, 2011). Although some grammaticalization "paths" are unique to particular languages, others are quite common. For instance, in English the past perfective use of *have*, as in *I have broken my finger*, can be traced to the possessive use of *have*, as in *I have a broken finger*, and the same channel of grammaticalization has been documented in many other languages (Heine & Kuteva, 2002).

Complex Sentences

Yet another aspect of syntax that warrants brief consideration has to do with complex sentences—that is,

sentences that consist of more than one clause. This is a very intricate domain, but only a few basic issues are pertinent to the neurolinguistic material covered later in this chapter and in the subsequent chapter. The most fundamental distinction is between **coordination** and **subordination**. Coordination refers to complex sentences that contain multiple clauses that have equal syntactic status and are related either through juxtaposition, as in Julius Caesar's famous line *Veni vidi vici* ("I came, I saw, I conquered"), or through some sort of linking device such as a conjunction, as in *Allison didn't see the robber, **but** he saw her*. Subordination refers to complex sentences that contain two clauses that are syntactically asymmetrical insofar as one is embedded within the other. There are three different kinds of subordination. First, an adverbial clause provides ancillary situational details, such as the spatial, temporal, or causal context for the event described in the main clause, as in *Allison was shocked **when the robber suddenly emerged*** and *She ran away quickly **because he looked very dangerous***. Second, a complement clause is an argument of, and hence essential to, the verb in the main clause, as in *Everyone knew **that a robber had been prowling around*** and ***That such a thing could happen** upset me*. Third, a relative clause functions as a modifier of a noun phrase, as in *A policeman caught the robber **that frightened Allison*** and *All of the people **who he harmed** can now rest easy*. Most if not all languages have syntactic rules for coordination as well as all three kinds of subordination, but there is a great deal of variation in the exact nature of those rules (Shopen, 2007).

Syntactic Encoding: A Rudimentary Model

Much less is known about syntactic processing during sentence production than during sentence comprehension. Needless to say, this is not because formulating sentences is any less important than interpreting them. Rather, the research imbalance seems to reflect the fact that, with regard to experimental design, it is much harder to control the relevant input

---

Grammaticalization   The historical process whereby concrete open-class elements give rise to abstract closed-class elements.

Coordination   The combination of multiple clauses that have equal syntactic status and that are related either through juxtaposition or through some sort of linking device such as a conjunction.

Subordination   The combination of two clauses that are syntactically asymmetrical insofar as one is embedded within the other.   There are three subtypes: adverbial clauses, complement clauses, and relative clauses.

variables when investigating sentence production than when investigating sentence comprehension. Despite these limitations, however, our understanding of the processes involved in syntactic encoding has gradually increased over the course of the past 40 years or so. A few of the major findings are summarized below in the context of a basic theoretical framework that fits well with the Lemma Model of speech production (for more detailed reviews see Bock & Levelt, 1994; Ferreira & Engelhardt, 2006; Ferreira & Slevc, 2007; Jaeger & Norcliffe, 2009; Ferreira, 2010; for alternative modeling approaches see Chang et al., 2006; Fitz, 2009; Takac et al., 2012; Chang & Fitz, in press).

If asked to describe the photograph shown in Figure 14.1, an average English speaker would be able to initiate an utterance like *The boy is petting the dog* after about one second, and would be able to complete it within another two or three seconds. From the perspective of the Lemma Model, during this short period of time the speaker passes through a number of computational stages, as depicted in Figure 14.2 (see also Figure 6.1 in Chapter 6). The process begins with "conceptual preparation" in the "rhetorical/semantic/syntactic system." At this stage, the speaker draws upon several sources of information, including the addressee's presumed state of mind and various situational and discourse factors, to create a "preverbal message" that consists of a set of interrelated lexical concepts—i.e., concepts that correspond to English words. It is at this stage that the speaker decides to map the two objects in the picture onto the lexical concepts specified by *boy* and *dog*, to map the action onto the lexical concept specified by *pet*, and to focus attention on the agent—i.e., the boy. At the next stage, which is called "syntactic encoding" (also known as "grammatical encoding"), the lexical concepts that make up the preverbal message are mapped onto the appropriate abstract word nodes—technically referred to as lemmas—which are then configured into a hierarchically organized, linearly sequenced string that conforms to the syntactic rules of English and captures the intended composite meaning. This is the stage that we are most concerned about here. It yields as output a "surface structure" that feeds incrementally into the "phonological/phonetic system," where the sound structures of words are retrieved and ultimately articulated, along the lines discussed in Chapter 6.

How exactly does syntactic encoding operate? As mentioned above, very little is known about the inner workings of this component of speech

Figure 14.1   A boy petting a dog.

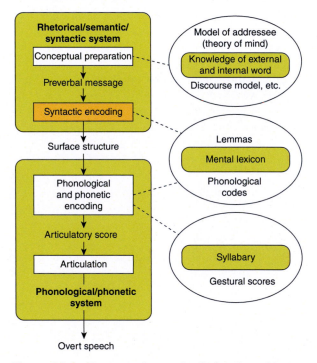

Figure 14.2   How syntactic encoding fits into the architecture of the Lemma Model. (From Indefrey et al., 2001, p. 5934.)

production. During the past few years, the pace of research in this field has been accelerating, and new ways of thinking about the nature of syntactic encoding have begun to emerge. Historically, however, the dominant view has been that it consists of two successive levels of planning, both of which are sketched in Figure 14.3. This approach derives from a relatively old but still influential series of papers by Merrill Garrett, a psycholinguist at the University of Arizona (Garrett, 1975, 1976, 1980, 1982, 1988).

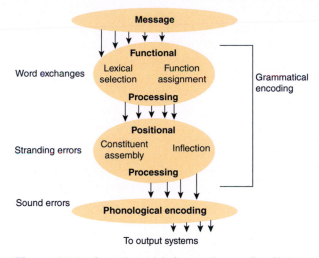

Figure 14.3 Garrett's model of syntactic encoding. Note that at the level of positional processing, inflection takes place together with the insertion of functors in the proper slots. (From Ferreira & Engelhardt, 2006, p. 63.)

The first level of syntactic encoding is called **functional processing**, and it is where the lemmas of open-class elements are accessed together with their associated grammatical features, such as syntactic category (noun, verb, etc.), nominal gender/class (masculine, feminine, etc.), verbal transitivity (intransitive, transitive, etc.), and so forth. The lemmas are not explicitly sequenced at this stage, but the core aspects of argument structure are computed, which is to say that linkages are established between, on the one hand, participant roles like actor and undergoer, and on the other hand, grammatical relations like subject and object. These linkages are referred to as function assignment in Figure 14.3. For example, it is at this level that a speaker formulating the utterance *The boy is petting the dog* determines that the lemma for *boy*, whose corresponding concept has the actor role in the preverbal message, will be the subject of the sentence, and that the lemma for *dog*, whose corresponding concept has the undergoer role in the preverbal message, will be the object of the sentence. Note that if, at the earlier stage of conceptual preparation, the speaker had made the rhetorical decision to focus attention not on the boy but rather on the dog, this might have led, at the level of functional processing, to the selection of a passive-voice instead of an active-voice construction, as in *The dog is*

being petted by the boy, in which the lemma for *dog* serves as the subject. The essential point is simply that bindings between participant roles and grammatical relations take place at the level of functional processing, before the relevant lemmas have been linearized and before their phonological forms have been retrieved. It is also worth mentioning that some other functional aspects of syntax may be computed at this level, such as modificational relationships between adjectives and nouns.

The second level of syntactic encoding is called **positional processing**, and it is where serial order is imposed on the utterance. In languages that use phrase structure rules to guide the assembly of multi-word constituents, this is the level at which they come into play. For instance, in formulating the sentence *The boy is petting the dog*, the subject–verb–object pattern of English dictates the sequencing of the major phrasal units—specifically, that *The boy* precedes *is petting*, which in turn precedes *the dog*—and other rules dictate the internal linear structures of those units—specifically, that articles precede nouns in noun phrases (NPs), and that auxiliary verbs precede main verbs in verb phrases (VPs). In addition, this is the level at which the grammatically relevant features of closed-class elements are inserted in the appropriate syntactic and morphological slots. Although the pertinent oval in Figure 14.3 only mentions inflection on the right-hand side, Garrett's model stipulates that free-standing functors are also accessed during this part of positional processing. Thus, in the sentence *The boy is petting the dog*, the slots for the two articles in the NPs specify that these items are "definite" (phonologically expressed as *the*) as opposed to "indefinite" (phonologically expressed as *a*); the slot for the auxiliary verb specifies that this item is *be* inflected for both present tense and singular number (phonologically expressed as *is*); and the slot for the main verb specifies that it is inflected for progressive aspect (phonologically expressed as *-ing*). It is noteworthy that in languages that rely heavily on case and/or agreement, attaching the right inflections to the right words is a crucial part of positional processing; in fact, this aspect of positional processing overlaps a great deal with the notion of morphosyntactic processing discussed in Chapter 13.

What is the evidence for this two-stage model of syntactic encoding? When Garrett originally developed the theory, he drew primarily on data from spontaneous

Functional processing The first stage of syntactic encoding, when the lemmas of open-class elements are retrieved together with their grammatical features (e.g., noun vs. verb, transitive vs. intransitive), and when participant roles like actor and undergoer are linked with grammatical relations like subject and object.

Positional processing The second stage of syntactic encoding, when the words that compose the utterance are linearly sequenced, and when the grammatically relevant features of closed-class elements are inserted in the proper places.

speech errors, and that kind of data still provides the strongest support for the basic architecture of the framework (for a brief overview of speech errors see Box 6.2 in Chapter 6). Two types of errors are especially relevant here. First, speakers sometimes make **word exchanges**, like saying *The dog is petting the boy* instead of the intended *The boy is petting the dog* (Ferreira & Engelhardt, 2006). Such errors usually involve words that belong to the same grammatical category but serve different grammatical functions in the sentence, as in the example just given, where the intended subject noun *boy* is swapped with the intended object noun *dog*. Word exchanges are generally believed to involve lemmas and semantic-syntactic linking patterns at the level of functional processing, as indicated in Figure 14.3. Second, speakers also sometimes commit **stranding errors**, like saying *I went to get my park trucked* instead of the intended *I went to get my truck parked* (Garrett, 1980). In this type of mistake, open-class elements are misordered while closed-class elements are retained in their proper places. Such errors not only constitute evidence for an independent stage at which serial order is established, but also suggest that the grammatical features of closed-class elements are incorporated into the phrasal frames that are generated at that stage. In short, stranding errors are generally assumed to occur at the level of positional processing, as indicated in Figure 14.3. Additional evidence for the two-stage model of syntactic encoding comes from research on lexical and syntactic priming and on the computation of subject–verb agreement, but we need not delve into those details here (for a deeper discussion of evidence both for and against the two-stage model, see Ferreira & Engelhardt, 2006).

Insights from Neuropsychology

The infrastructure of syntactic encoding has been explored in considerable detail from the perspective of cognitive neuropsychology. This is largely because scientific interest in sentence production deficits increased dramatically in the early 1980s and has remained quite strong ever since. The most fertile period of research, however, arguably extended from the mid-1980s

through the mid-1990s, for that was when a tremendous amount of attention was devoted to unraveling the many empirical and theoretical complexities surrounding what can now, in retrospect, be regarded as one of the most hotly debated neurological syndromes in history—namely, agrammatism.

This section begins by reviewing not only the major clinical characteristics of agrammatism, but also the major reasons why this disorder has generated so much controversy. The heterogeneous lesion correlates of agrammatism are described as well. We then move on to discuss in greater depth—and, for the most part, independently of the contentious notion of agrammatism—some of the most distinctive and theoretically significant types of sentence production deficits that have been documented in patients with vascular aphasia—i.e., aphasia resulting from vascular pathologies such as stroke. Using Garrett's model of syntactic encoding as a point of reference, deficits that putatively involve the functional level are considered first, followed by deficits that putatively involve the positional level. As we will see, some of these neuropsychological findings provide tantalizing clues about how the model might be further refined. Finally, the last part of the section looks at a few recent studies that have focused on sentence production deficits in primary progressive aphasia, especially the nonfluent variety. These studies are important not only because they illuminate the behavioral aspects of the patients' impairments, but also because they suggest that Broca's area plays a vital role in the widely distributed left-hemisphere network for syntactic encoding.

Agrammatism: A Complex Syndrome Steeped in Controversy

In his book *Understanding Aphasia*, Harold Goodglass (1993) notes that the earliest description of agrammatism is attributed by Tissot et al. (1973) to an 1819 work by Deleuze, whose French-speaking patient "used exclusively the infinitive of verbs and used no pronouns. For example, she said, *Souhaiter bonjour, rester, mari venir* ('Wish [infinitive] good day, stay [infinitive], husband come [infinitive]'). She produced absolutely no conjugated verbs." Roughly a century later, this kind of expressive language disturbance, generally involving reduced syntactic complexity and impaired production of closed-class elements, was labeled **agrammatism** by the eminent aphasiologist

---

Word exchanges   Speech errors that involve swapping open-class elements that belong to the same grammatical category but serve different grammatical functions in the sentence. Such errors provide evidence for the functional level of syntactic encoding.

Stranding errors   Speech errors that involve misordering open-class elements while keeping closed-class elements in their proper places. Such errors provide evidence for the positional level of syntactic encoding.

Agrammatism   A deficit involving reduced syntactic complexity and impaired production of closed-class elements.

Arnold Pick (1913). And now, roughly another century later, the disorder is still commonly referred to by that name (for a landmark set of papers see Kean, 1985; for a very lucid and informative review see Berndt, 2001; and for a survey of more recent perspectives see Bastiaanse & Thompson, 2012).

Agrammatism has been observed in connection with several different classical aphasia syndromes, but it is most often manifested by Broca's aphasics; indeed, the core symptoms of agrammatism constitute some of the central features of Broca's aphasia. This is demonstrated by the following speech sample from a fairly prototypical agrammatic Broca's aphasic, who is narrating the fairytale "Cinderella" after having just seen a wordless picture book illustrating the plot of the story (Berndt, 2001, p. 382):

> one time long ago [4 sec] Cinderella [5 sec] mother and one two sisters [9 sec] uh one two sisters and [4 sec] pants shoes [5 sec] and uh two sisters [9 sec] "what's wrong?" "you stay home you stay home Cinderella" [2 sec] one two sisters at a ball [3 sec] a magic wand a nice lady [2 sec] fairy godmother "what's wrong?" [3 sec] at the ball no money [2 sec] so one two three four five six men magic wand [4 sec] rats now men oh [8 sec] magic wand ok nice [3 sec] glass slippers [2 sec] twelve o'clock no money now rich [3 sec] ok castle uh prince [3 sec] and too short too big [6 sec] and many girls uh [8 sec] Cinderella is [4 sec] I like you [3 sec] dance oh [2 sec] quarter to twelve [4 sec] go home go home hey come on prince come on [4 sec] twelve o'clock hurry up go home uh one she fell off [4 sec] prince is sad [2 sec] "what's wrong?" [3 sec] tomorrow I go [3 sec] prince and a shoe [3 sec] "oh good to see you" [3 sec] sit down [2 sec] then ah too small too small [2 sec] "you try it" [5 sec] fit [4 sec] prince is [3 sec] a lady [3 sec] prince and [8 sec] Cinderella [2 sec] happy after

This speech sample exemplifies how agrammatism often appears in English-speaking Broca's aphasics. However, to get a deeper and more well-rounded sense of the constellation of symptoms that constitute prototypical agrammatism, it is worthwhile to adopt a broader cross-linguistic point of view. Such a perspective is provided by the monumental three-volume collection called *Agrammatic Aphasia: A Cross-Language Narrative Sourcebook,* edited by Lise Menn and Lorraine K. Obler and published in 1990 (for a more accessible synopsis of the main results see Menn et al., 1995, and for additional data see Bates & Wulfeck, 1989). Based on the collaboration of clinician–linguist teams in 14 countries, this collection includes detailed descriptive reports of 26 agrammatic patients who speak languages as typologically diverse as English, Polish, Finnish, Hebrew, Hindi, Japanese, and Chinese. The most salient findings, which Menn and Obler (1990b) itemize and discuss in the concluding chapter, are as follows (Table 14.2):

- *Paucity of main verbs.* Agrammatic patients tend to omit lexical verbs significantly more than lexical nouns. According to some researchers, this is consistent with their general proclivity for syntactic simplification (described next), since the argument structures associated with verbs are highly relevant to the grammatical organization of clauses.

- *Syntactic simplification.* Agrammatic patients tend to use a markedly reduced range of syntactic structures, and the few structures that they do use tend to be produced haltingly with frequent and often inappropriate pauses. Subordinate clauses are either absent or poorly constructed, and main clauses exhibit simplification of both NPs and VPs. At the level of the NP, there is rarely any modification by adjectives or adpositional phrases (i.e., prepositional or postpositional phrases). And at the level of the VP, event-related grammatical-semantic features like mood are often unexpressed, regardless of whether they are normally encoded by free-standing auxiliary verbs or bound morphemes.

- *Omission of free-standing closed-class elements (i.e., functors).* Functors are frequently omitted, especially those that require syntactic computation because they carry information relevant to the internal structure of phrases and clauses. Examples include auxiliary verbs (e.g., *should*), infinitive markers (e.g., *to*), genitive markers (e.g., *of*), personal pronouns (e.g., *him*), articles (e.g., *the*), and—in languages where they happen to be free-standing elements, like Japanese—case markers.

- *Substitution of bound closed-class elements (i.e., inflections).* Inflections, particularly on nouns and verbs, are far more likely to be substituted than omitted. However, this fact cannot be fully grasped or appreciated by considering just English, because English has a very impoverished inflectional system. Instead, it is necessary to cast a wider net by taking into account inflectionally richer languages. Compare, for instance, English and Italian. As noted by Miceli et al. (1989), if one were to omit the inflection from the English verb *walking*, the result would still be a legitimate word, namely *walk*, but if one were to omit the inflection from the Italian verb *portare* ("to carry"), the result would be an illegitimate nonword,

400 Part VI | Morphology, Syntax, and Discourse

namely *port. Now, the key point is that, as Miceli et al. (1989, p. 450) emphasize, "there are no reports of Italian patients who systematically omit bound morphemes and produce uninflected nonwords." Rather, Italian-speaking agrammatic patients tend to produce incorrect inflections. Moreover, the data from Menn and Obler's (1990a) cross-linguistic project indicate that agrammatic speakers of other heavily inflected languages, like Finnish and Hindi, fit the Italian pattern quite well. Indeed, the more complex the inflectional possibilities are, the more likely the substitution errors will be. Somewhat surprisingly, there does not appear to be a reliable directional hierarchy for these errors, since the same patient may substitute a singular for a plural form on one occasion and a plural for a singular form on another occasion. However, many patients do seem to gravitate toward forms with relatively low degrees of semantic and syntactic specificity. And this leads to the intriguing notion, underscored by Menn and Obler (1990b), that when English-speaking agrammatic patients incorrectly produce "bare" nouns and verbs, they may not really be omitting inflectional endings, but instead substituting less-marked forms for more-marked ones.

- *Reliance on canonical word order.* Agrammatic patients tend to favor the canonical sequencing of subject, verb, and object in the given language. For example, German-speaking patients avoid constructions that require the noncanonical verb–final word order, and Swedish- and Icelandic-speaking patients usually maintain the canonical subject–verb–object order even in adverb-initial clauses where that order is ungrammatical. It is also noteworthy that in languages that have fairly flexible word order, like Finnish and Polish, patients often adopt a favorite word order and stick with it.

In their attempt to make sense of this cluster of symptoms, Menn and Obler (1990b) suggest that while the paucity of main verbs may reflect, at least in some cases, a disturbance at the functional level of processing in Garrett's model of syntactic encoding, the other symptoms are more likely to reflect impairments involving the positional level. Syntactic simplification may be due to "difficulty maintaining a normal-sized positional frame in a workspace during lexical form retrieval, and/or in computing expansions of the basic frame and syntactically-governed word orders" (Menn & Obler, 1990b, p. 1385). Similarly, problems with closed-class elements, both free-standing and bound, may be due to the "blurring," "fading," or, in

Table 14.2 Main Symptoms of Agrammatism

1	Paucity of main verbs
2	Syntactic simplification
3	Omission of free-standing closed-class elements (i.e., functors)
4	Substitution of bound closed-class elements (i.e., inflections)
5	Reliance on canonical word order

severe cases, complete loss of morphosyntactic markers. According to this account, free-standing functor slots that are labeled with blurred, faded, or lost specifications usually go empty—hence the prevalence of omissions—whereas bound slots with such degraded specifications usually lead to near-miss errors—hence the prevalence of substitutions. Finally, the reliance on canonical word order probably reflects a kind of "stay out of trouble" strategy on the part of agrammatic patients (for a strategy-oriented "adaptation" theory of agrammatism see Kolk et al., 1985).

Given this fairly straightforward characterization of the symptomology of prototypical agrammatism, one could be forgiven for wondering why the syndrome has stirred up so much controversy. The principal concern, which has been elaborated most clearly and defended most forcefully by Alfonso Caramazza and his colleagues, is this: Despite the seemingly coherent picture painted above, the specific manifestations of agrammatism vary so greatly across individual cases that it is extremely difficult, if not ultimately impossible, to formulate a firm, unambiguous definition of the disorder that indicates exactly which linguistic structures and/or operations are consistently affected (Caramazza & Berndt, 1985; Badecker & Caramazza, 1985, 1986; Miceli et al., 1989; for a broader perspective see Caramazza, 1984, 1986; Caramazza & McCloskey, 1988; McCloskey & Caramazza, 1988; Caramazza & Badecker, 1989, 1991).

The most serious challenge to the empirical integrity and theoretical utility of the clinical concept of agrammatism is that all of the different symptoms dissociate from each other. For instance, not all patients who exhibit what are traditionally regarded as the two central features of agrammatism—namely, syntactic simplification and problems producing closed-class elements—also display defective verb retrieval; and conversely, not all patients who have trouble accessing verbs also generate agrammatic speech (e.g., Breedin & Martin, 1996; Berndt et al., 1997a, 1997b; Caramazza & Hillis, 1991). In addition, the two

Box 14.1   Similar Symptoms, Different Causes

Some of the hazards inherent in using the general notion of agrammatism to classify patients are nicely illustrated by Rapp and Caramazza's (1998b) comparison of two cases: ML, an English-speaking patient investigated in depth by Caramazza and Hillis (1989); and FS, an Italian-speaking patient investigated in depth by Miceli and Caramazza (1988). In their spontaneous and elicited discourse, both patients produced abundant errors involving free-standing as well as bound closed-class elements, thereby satisfying some of the core criteria for agrammatism (see the top half of Table 14B1.1). However, on a follow-up task that required each patient to simply repeat function words, prefixed words, and suffixed words, ML performed flawlessly across the board, whereas FS was severely impaired across the board (see the bottom half of Table 14B1.1). These findings suggest that the patients' superficially similar sentence production deficits may have fundamentally different causes. On the one hand, ML may have what Rapp and Caramazza (1998b, p. 216) characterize as "an impairment at the level of the sentence planning mechanisms that specify the morphemes and function words to be selected from the output lexicons for production." On the other hand, FS is likely to have an impairment that directly affects closed-class items. More generally, the lesson to be learned from this comparison of two cases is that agrammatism is *not* a unitary disorder. Just because a group of patients exhibit similar problems producing sentences does *not* mean that they have similar cognitive dysfunctions. More careful testing is always necessary to get a detailed and, ideally, accurate sense of each patient's underlying impairment. And, needless to say, these concerns have serious implications for treatment, since patients stand the greatest chance of improvement when their impairments are correctly targeted for intervention.

Table 14B1.1   Performance Profiles of ML and FS

	ML	FS
Error Rates in Spontaneous and Elicited Speech Samples		
Omission of function words	62% (108/173)	22% (54/242)
Substitution of function words	2% (4/173)	20% (48/242)
Inflection/derivation errors	15% (5/33)	27% (75/275)
Accuracies in Single Word Repetition Tasks		
Function words	100%	31%
Prefixed words	100%	48%
Suffixed words	100%	33%

aspects of agrammatism just described as being central to the disorder do not always occur together; on the contrary, they doubly dissociate, since some patients have impoverished and/or aberrant syntactic structure but preserved production of closed-class elements, while others have impaired production of closed-class elements in the context of otherwise normal syntactic complexity (e.g., Tissot et al., 1973; Berndt, 1987; Nespoulous et al., 1988; Saffran et al., 1989; Nadeau & Gonzalez Rothi, 1992; Webster et al., 2007). Finally, even the two main types of closed-class elements—free-standing and bound—can be impaired independently of each other, as shown in several group studies (e.g., Miceli et al., 1989; Saffran et al., 1989; Rochon et al.,

2000). Based on these sorts of considerations, some of which are discussed more fully below, Caramazza and his colleagues conclude that there are "no grounds on which to support the claim that 'agrammatism' constitutes a 'natural kind' category representing those patients with deficit to a single, well-defined component of the language processing system (or even common and equivalent deficits to multiple components)" (Miceli et al., 1989, p. 474; see also Box 14.1).

When one looks at the available lesion data regarding agrammatism, one is again confronted with a remarkable degree of variability. So far, no large-scale group studies have used sophisticated voxel-based techniques to investigate the fine-grained distribution of lesion sites linked with agrammatic sentence production. However, Vanier and Caplan (1990) did analyze the CT-scan correlates of agrammatism in 20 of the 26 patients who participated in Menn and Obler's (1990a) cross-linguistic project, and their results are still quite informative. Here at the outset, it is worth mentioning that 18/20 patients in that sample had lesions that included subcortical nuclei and/or white matter pathways. For example, 9/20 patients had some degree of involvement of the caudate nucleus in the basal ganglia, and 18/20 patients had moderate to severe damage to the arcuate fasciculus. For present purposes, however, we will not dwell on the subcortical components of the patients' lesions, but will instead concentrate on the cortical components—in particular, those cortical components that included the perisylvian territory, as shown in Table 14.3.

Several important points can be made about these results. The first and most obvious point, which can be gleaned from just a brief glance at the data, is that the cortical lesions in this population of patients differed substantially in spatial extent. At one extreme, some of the patients had very large lesions. For instance, both Case 1 (Heck) and Case 2 (Tanaka) suffered massive strokes that destroyed virtually all of the perisylvian territory; in fact, it is rather remarkable that they did

Table 14.3 Involvement of the lateral portions of perisylvian cortical areas in the lesions of 20 agrammatic patients. Degree of involvement is indicated by the number of + signs

Case	Language	IFG-tri	IFG-op	Insula	Precentral	Postcentral	SMG	AG	STG	MTG
1 Heck	Dutch	+++	+++	+++	+++	+++	+++	+++	+++	+++
2 Tanaka	Japanese	+	+++	+++	+++	+++	+++	+++	++	+
3 Barn	Dutch	+	+++	+++	+++	+++	+++	+	+++	
4 Franklin	English	+++	+++	+++	+++	+++	+++		++	+++
5 Peltonen	Finnish	+++	+++	+++	+++	+++		+	+++	
6 Aaltonen	Finnish	+++	+++	+++	+++	+++	+++			
7 Saitoo	Japanese	+++	+++	+++	+++	+++	+++			
8 Sharma	Hindi	+++	+++	+++	+++	+++				
9 Radomska	Polish	+++	+++	+++	+++				++	
10 Chen	Chinese	++	++	+++	++	++				
11 Hayasi*	Japanese	+++	(+)	++						
12 Clermont	French		+++	+++	+++	+++	+++			
13 Auvergne	French		+++	+++	+++	+++	+			
14 Meyer	German		+++	+++	+++					
15 Eastman	English			+++	++	++	+++	(+)	+	++
16 Togga	Icelandic			+++	+++	+++	+++		++	
17 Rossi	Italian			++	(+)	+(+)	+++	+++	+++	+++
18 Braun	German			+++		++	+++			
19 Verdi	Italian	(+)	(+)	+++					+	
20 Kiddi	Icelandic			++						

Adapted from Vanier & Caplan (1990, p. 110).

IFG-tri = pars triangularis of the inferior frontal gyrus; IFG-op = pars opercularis of the inferior frontal gyrus; SMG = supramarginal gyrus; AG = angular gyrus; SP = superior parietal lobule; STG = superior temporal gyrus; MTG = middle temporal gyrus.

* Right hemisphere.

not exhibit global aphasia. At the other extreme, some of the patients had very small lesions. For instance, both Case 19 (Verdi) and Case 20 (Kiddi) had injuries confined for the most part to the insula. Another significant point pertains to Broca's area. Many of the patients' lesions—specifically, those of Cases 1–10—encompassed both the anterior sector (pars triangularis, BA45) and the posterior sector (pars opercularis, BA44) of Broca's area. However, the lesions of several other patients—specifically, those of Cases 12–14—included the posterior but not the anterior sector of Broca's area, and the lesions of an even larger number of patients—specifically, those of Cases 15–20—either completely spared or only minimally affected both sectors. This last finding is especially valuable because it demonstrates that damage to Broca's area is not a necessary prerequisite for agrammatism. Yet another point is that agrammatism is frequently associated with damage to the supramarginal, angular, superior temporal, and/or middle temporal gyri. And finally, it appears that the only area of 100 percent lesion overlap in this population of patients was the insula.

While it seems unlikely that the insula itself supports syntactic encoding, it is worth mentioning that a recent study involving 50 left-hemisphere-damaged patients with various types of aphasia found that injury to the anterior insula was predictive of low scores on two measures of conversational speech in structured interviews: mean length of utterance (MLU), which is related to grammatical complexity; and the number of words spoken, which indicates the overall amount of language produced (Borovsky et al., 2007). Given that anterior insula damage has also been independently associated with apraxia of speech (e.g., Dronkers, 1996; Ogar et al., 2006; Baldo et al., 2011; see Figure 6.23 and the accompanying text in Chapter 6), these results suggest that there may be close neurocognitive connections between syntactic encoding on the one hand, and complex articulatory coordination on the other. Because both of these linguistic capacities may be thought of as forms of motor planning, albeit at different levels of abstraction, perhaps they are different aspects of the same overarching ability—fluency.

At the same time, however, it is important to bear in mind the following caveat. As emphasized by Hillis et al. (2004b), due to its unique anatomical position, the insula is one of the brain regions most likely to be affected by strokes that involve occlusion of the middle cerebral artery (MCA) (e.g., Caviness et al., 2002; Payabvash et al., 2011). And because the insula is usually not affected in isolation, but rather in combination with various other areas supplied by the MCA, it can be quite difficult for investigators to distinguish between deficits that are due to infarction of the insula and deficits that are due to infarction of other areas. In the current context, these considerations imply that we should be very cautious about interpreting the correlations described above between impairments of sentence production and damage to the insula.

In much of the foregoing discussion, we have highlighted the behavioral and neuropathological heterogeneity of agrammatism. In the next section, we continue to discuss sentence production deficits, but independently (at least for the most part) of the contentious clinical concept of agrammatism. Instead, we focus on patients whose impairments have discernible theoretical implications because they seem to affect fairly specific computational operations at either the functional or the positional level in Garrett's model of syntactic encoding.

Sentence Production Deficits in Vascular Aphasia

Deficits Involving the Functional Level

As noted above in connection with Figure 14.3, the functional level of syntactic encoding includes two main types of operations. First, a crucial aspect of lexical retrieval is activating the argument structure properties associated with the lemmas of verbs, such as the fact that the verb *pet* is transitive, requiring the syntactic realization of two participant roles—actor and undergoer. Second, function assignment involves mapping the participant roles of verbs onto the appropriate grammatical relations. For example, if a speaker intends to produce an active-voice sentence in which the main verb is *pet*, the actor of that verb must be assigned the grammatical relation of subject and the undergoer must be assigned the grammatical relation of object. Remarkably enough, the neuropsychological literature contains some hints that these two types of operations can be selectively impaired, giving rise to different kinds of sentence production problems.

Evidence that the sentence production problems manifested by some stroke patients may be due, at least in part, to impaired retrieval of the argument structure properties of verbs comes from an influential investigation by Berndt et al. (1997a, 1997b; see also Thompson et al., 1997b, and Webster et al., 2004, 2007). This study focused on 10 patients, four of whom—LR, EA, FM, and ML—not only displayed disproportionately worse production of verbs than nouns across a variety of single-word tasks, but also generated errors which suggested that their deficits were at a relatively high level of lexical access, prior to the stage of phonological code retrieval. To explore the sentence production abilities of all 10 patients, the researchers elicited samples of narrative speech by first presenting each patient with a wordless picture book illustrating the plot of "Cinderella," and then removing the book and asking the patient to tell the story. Subsequently, the researchers used standardized procedures (Saffran et al., 1989) to analyze the lexical, morphological, and syntactic characteristics of the utterances constituting each patient's narrative. The results revealed that although impaired access to verbs did not correlate significantly with defective generation of closed-class elements, it did correlate significantly with a tendency to produce utterances that were syntactically so oversimplified that they often did not even form complete sentences.

To determine whether the relationship between impaired verb retrieval and impaired sentence formulation was, at least in some cases, causal rather than merely correlational, the researchers went on to conduct an experiment in which all 10 patients were asked to describe 30 scenes for which certain target sentences could reliably be elicited from healthy control subjects. In one condition that was designed to elicit active-voice sentences (e.g., *The woman is tickling the man*), the patients were instructed to describe each scene by mentioning the actor first; and in another condition that was designed to elicit passive-voice sentences (e.g., *The man is being tickled by the woman*), the patients were instructed to describe each scene by mentioning the undergoer first. Because the participant to be mentioned first was always named by the examiner, it was expected that the patients would produce those nouns fairly accurately, and this prediction was confirmed. In addition, it was expected that the four verb-impaired patients would frequently falter when attempting to produce the verbs in the target sentences, and this prediction was confirmed as well. Moreover, those patients were equally impaired at retrieving verbs in the active and passive conditions.

The most interesting result was as follows. As shown in Figure 14.4, two of the four verb-impaired

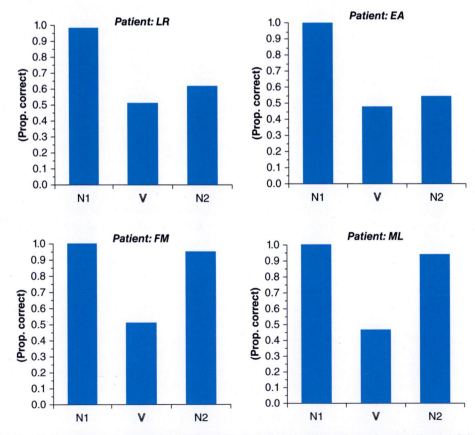

Figure 14.4 Results from Berndt et al.'s (1997a) neuropsychological study of the effects of verb retrieval deficits on sentence production. Each panel shows the proportion of trials of a constrained sentence production task in which the given patient correctly generated the first noun (N1), the verb (V), and the second noun (N). (From Berndt et al., 1997a, p. 123.)

patients—LR and EA—had significant difficulty producing not only the verbs in the target sentences, but also the second nouns. This problem involving the second nouns could in principle reflect a more general deficit in accessing nouns; however, such an account is hard to reconcile with the independent data described earlier, indicating that both patients were significantly better at generating nouns than verbs in several single-word tasks. An alternative possibility with a strong theoretical motivation is that the patients' poor performance in producing the second nouns may have been a consequence of a deficit in activating specifically the argument structure properties associated with the lemmas of verbs. For example, suppose the patients had trouble retrieving the lemma for the verb *tickle*. If that disturbance included difficulty accessing the knowledge that *tickle* is syntactically transitive, this might prevent the patients from expressing both the actor and the undergoer in sentences.

To test this hypothesis, the researchers conducted a follow-up experiment in which they administered the very same sentence production tasks to the verb-impaired patients, only this time they explicitly told the patients what the verb should be on each trial. As predicted by the hypothesis, this manipulation greatly increased LR's and EA's success at producing not only the verbs in the target sentences, but also the second nouns. In discussing these results, Berndt et al. (1997a, p. 131) conclude that

> providing these patients with a verb seemed not only to improve their ability to produce the verb, but also to enhance other aspects of sentence production. For this to be the case, verb production difficulties for these patients are likely to emanate from a failure of functional level selection of the abstract lemma representation . . .

Unfortunately, the researchers did not include any details about their patients' lesion sites. Hence a limitation of this study is that it does not shed any light on the neurological correlates of the unique type of deficit exhibited by LR and EA—namely, impaired retrieval of the argument structure properties of verbs. In Chapter 11 we noted that the left temporoparietal region seems to play an essential role in representing the two core participants—actor and undergoer—specified by transitive verbs, and one might suppose that those findings are relevant here. While that might be the case, it is important to bear in mind that those findings pertain primarily to the

semantic aspects of transitivity—i.e., those aspects that enter into the "preverbal message" shown in Figure 14.2). In contrast, according to Berndt et al. (1997a), it is likely that LR and EA have trouble mainly with the syntactic aspects of transitivity—i.e., those aspects that are somewhat idiosyncratic across verbs (recall the differences between *eat*, *dine*, and *devour*), that are associated with the lemmas of verbs, and that are accessed at the functional level of syntactic encoding. The bottom line, then, is that further research is needed to investigate the neural substrates of the interaction between the semantic and syntactic aspects of argument structure processing during sentence production.

Next, we turn to another type of sentence production problem that is manifested by some stroke patients and that appears to involve the functional level. This disorder, however, does not affect the operation of accessing the argument structure properties of verbs, but instead seems to affect the operation of function assignment—i.e., the process of mapping participant roles like actor and undergoer onto grammatical relations like subject and object. The basic finding is that some patients are especially prone to making "reversal" mapping errors in which the linkages between participant roles and grammatical relations are switched, much like the sorts of "word exchange" errors that normal people sometimes make (see the overview of Garrett's model above).

Although most of these patients do not commit such errors very often in their spontaneous speech, they are quite likely to do so when asked to perform certain experimental tasks that are deliberately designed to expose such deficits (e.g., Saffran et al., 1980b; Caramazza & Berndt, 1985; Schwartz et al., 1985; Martin & Blossom-Stach, 1986; Berndt, 1987; Caramazza & Miceli, 1991). For example, when asked to describe a picture of a girl kissing a boy, a patient might say *Boy kiss girl*. Now, the interpretation of an error like this is complicated, because it is possible that it doesn't really reflect an impairment of function assignment, but instead reflects a failed attempt to produce a passive sentence. This kind of concern is greatly reduced, however, for a few patients who have been found to frequently commit reversal mapping errors despite having only mildly impaired production of closed-class elements.

Consider, for instance, the utterances shown in (1), which are the attempts of four patients to describe a picture of a girl running toward a man whose arms are stretched out to greet her (Schwartz et al., 1985, p. 122).

(1) a. PN: The boy running the girl.
b. VS: The father is running, no . . . The girl is running father.
c. SK: The man's running . . . no . . . The little girl's running in her arms . . . her father.
d. PW: The man is running the girl.

In this situation, both of the participants in the event to be described are animate and hence capable, in principle, of being the actor. As one might expect, some patients make reversal mapping errors significantly more often when asked to describe these kinds of events than when asked to describe events in which only one of the participants is animate (see Caramazza & Miceli, 1991, for a detailed case study as well as an insightful discussion of the theoretical questions raised by such performance profiles). However, there are several reports of patients who often make reversal mapping errors even when trying to describe the latter kinds of events. For instance, the utterances shown in (2) are the attempts of four patients to describe a picture of a boy being hit on the head by a ball (Schwartz et al., 1985, p. 122).

(2) a. DE: The boy hits the ball.
b. PW: The boy . . . or a man is bumping the ball.
c. ME: Boy is hitting . . . bask'ball.
d. AT: A teenager hit the ball on the head.

Overall, these results support the view that the operation of function assignment is a distinct aspect of syntactic encoding that is vulnerable to fairly selective impairment by brain injury. As with the operation of argument structure retrieval, however, its specific neural underpinnings are largely unknown.

Deficits Involving the Positional Level

Like the functional level of syntactic encoding, the positional level includes two main types of operations. First, under the guidance of phrase structure rules (at least in languages that have them), words are strung together to form complex syntactic constituents. Second, the grammatically relevant features of both free-standing and bound closed-class elements are inserted in the appropriate syntactic and morphological slots (Figure 14.3). As indicated above in connection with the behavioral heterogeneity of patients classified as agrammatic, one of the most striking discoveries is that the two symptoms

that are traditionally regarded as being central to this clinical syndrome—namely, syntactic simplification and impaired production of closed-class elements—appear to dissociate from each other in some cases. These types of deficits are discussed below, with an emphasis on how they may reflect separate disturbances of the two main types of operations carried out at the positional level of syntactic encoding.

A number of patients have been documented who are impaired at generating syntactically complex expressions, but who are nevertheless capable of supplying the correct closed-class items (Tissot et al., 1973; Berndt, 1987; Saffran et al., 1980a, 1989; Webster et al., 2007). For instance, Saffran et al. (1989) systematically analyzed the sentence production abilities of 10 nonfluent aphasics and found that five of them displayed abnormal simplification of sentence structure but normal use of grammatical morphemes, suggesting a relatively selective deficit of constituent assembly. The attempt of one of these patients, CJ, to narrate the story of "Cinderella" is as follows (Berndt, 2001, p. 385):

in [6 sec] toytown [5 sec] mother and two [2 sec] daughters lived in [2 sec] the house . . . and a step-daughter Cinderella [3 sec] the girls and her mother [7 sec] said Cinderella [3 sec] light the light uh Cinderella wash the dishes Cinderella [9 sec] the uh woman and two daughters met uh a knight . . . he had [3 sec] uh invitation to the ball [8 sec] March 15th . . . uh he rode away [4 sec] merrily . . . he tried to find a better dress [3 sec] Cinderella worked [3 sec] uh worked at spinning yarn or rat poisoning . . . they went away for the ball and [5 sec] Cinderella stayed home . . . suddenly she heard a noise . . . she turned and the fairy godmother arrived . . . she said godmother said I will dress you up uh a pumpkin is magically a carriage . . . the mice has [4 sec] the horses . . . she hurried [8 sec] hurried to fill the clothes and she uh godmother said remember [3 sec] you're [3 sec] going to the ball . . .

Conversely, some patients have been reported who can still formulate sentences of normal complexity, but who are deficient at providing the appropriate closed-class items (Miceli et al., 1983; Kolk et al., 1985; Nespoulous et al., 1988; Nadeau & Gonzalez Rothi, 1992; Webster et al., 2007). For instance, the case described by Nadeau and Gonzalez Rothi (1992) had an average sentence length of 9.8 words, and 64 percent of his sentences contained embedded clauses. However, he omitted 43 percent of articles, 40 percent of complementizers, 43 percent of purely grammatical prepositions, 27 percent of semantically determined prepositions, 23 percent of conjunctions, 22 percent of auxiliary verbs, and 20 percent of pronouns; moreover, he made numerous errors involving inflections for both nouns and verbs. This performance profile seems to reflect a syntactic encoding impairment that affects primarily the production of closed-class elements. It is important to note, however, that the patient's ability to build syntactic constituents was not completely normal, since he often committed errors which suggested that he was intermingling incompatible constructions. And as pointed out by Berndt (2001), most of the other patients in the studies cited above also manifested at least mild problems with sentence structure that seem to be at least partly separate from their problems with closed-class items. In light of these considerations, we must exercise caution and not overinterpret the theoretical implications of the data. According to Berndt (2001, p. 386), "the postulation of a double dissociation between structural and morphological impairments does not appear tenable without additional supporting cases."

In a more positive vein, however, several studies that have focused on patients with impaired production of closed-class elements have convincingly shown that the two main subtypes of these elements—free-standing functors and bound inflections—can be differentially disrupted (Miceli et al., 1989; Saffran et al., 1989). These opposing patterns are nicely illustrated by the following contrast between two patients described by Saffran et al. (1989). On the one hand, ME correctly produced articles before nouns only 2 percent of the time, but correctly produced verb inflections 80 percent of the time. On the other hand, FM correctly produced articles before nouns 70 percent of the time, but correctly produced verb inflections only 9 percent of the time. The fact that functors and inflections can be disproportionately impaired has been taken by some researchers as evidence for a further subdivision within the positional level of processing in Garrett's model of syntactic encoding. Most prominently, Lapointe (1985) and Lapointe and Dell (1989) have argued that the two subtypes of closed-class elements are computed by somewhat different mechanisms during the construction of sentence frames. Basically, they proposed that inflections are generated, for the most part, together with phrasal fragments, whereas functors are generated, for the most part, by separate operations.

It is noteworthy, however, that even more fine-grained processing distinctions may need to be posited within each closed-class domain. For example, some functors are selected primarily on the basis of semantic criteria, whereas others are selected primarily on the basis of syntactic criteria. Thus, in the sentence *She ran*

up the stairs, the preposition *up* denotes a particular direction of motion, whereas in the sentence *She called up her friend*, the particle *up* is just an obligatory element in the verb–particle expression *call up*. Interestingly, these two instances of *up* have different grammatical behavior. Although it would be fine to say *Up the stairs she ran*, it would be very weird to say ** Up her friend she called*, and although one could never get away with ** She ran the stairs up*, there is clearly nothing wrong with *She called her friend up*. Given such contrasts, one might expect that semantically determined prepositions and syntactically determined particles could be impaired to different degrees by brain injury, and in fact double dissociations have been reported between these two kinds of functors (e.g., Friederici, 1982; Friederici et al., 1982; Kohen et al., 2011). These sorts of findings highlight the remarkable complexity of sentence production and remind us that even though theoretical models like Garrett's are extremely useful, they only capture the general outline of the cognitive system they purport to explain.

Finally, as with the various deficits involving operations at the functional level of syntactic encoding, those involving operations at the positional level have not yet been reliably linked with well-defined lesion sites. (See Chapter 13, however, for relevant data regarding the lesion sites of patients with impaired computation of the morphosyntactic features of inflections for nouns and verbs.) An important goal of future research will be to investigate these issues more carefully, drawing upon recent advances in the voxel-based analysis of deficit–lesion relationships.

Sentence Production Deficits in Primary Progressive Aphasia

In recent years, an increasing number of studies have explored both the behavioral properties and the neuropathological correlates of sentence production deficits in patients with primary progressive aphasia (PPA). As described in detail in Chapter 4, there are three main variants of PPA. First, in progressive nonfluent aphasia (PNFA), the most salient symptom is an impairment of grammar (sometimes in conjunction with apraxia of speech), and this is associated with atrophy that is typically centered in the left ventrolateral prefrontal cortex, including Broca's area. Second, in semantic dementia (SD), the most salient symptom is an impairment of conceptual knowledge, and this is associated with atrophy that is typically centered in the anterior temporal lobes of both hemispheres, although usually with some leftward asymmetry. And third, in logopenic

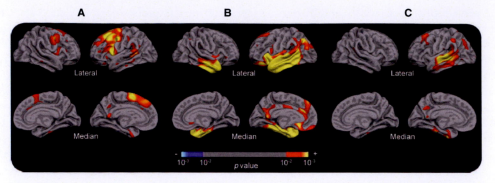

Figure 14.5 Patterns of cortical atrophy in the PNFA group (A), the SD group (B), and the LPA group (C) in Sapolsky et al.'s (2010) study of the neuroanatomical correlates of symptom severity in PPA. (From Sapolsky et al., 2010, p. 364.)

progressive aphasia (LPA), the most salient symptom is intermittent word-finding difficulty (sometimes in conjunction with phonemic paraphasias), and this is associated with atrophy that is typically centered in the left posterior superior/middle temporal gyri.

Given these deficit–lesion relationships, one would certainly expect PNFA to be the variant of PPA most germane to questions concerning the neural substrates of syntactic encoding during sentence production. And in keeping with this assumption, several studies have shown that patients with PNFA do in fact have more severe grammatical disturbances than patients with either SD or LPA; moreover, the magnitude of these disturbances correlates significantly with the degree of cortical thinning in the left ventrolateral prefrontal region (see especially Mesulam et al., 2009b, Sapolsky et al., 2010, and Wilson et al., 2010b; see also Grossman et al., 1996; Gorno-Tempini et al., 2004; Ash et al., 2009; Knibb et al., 2009; Thompson et al., 1997a, 2012, 2013). These findings are nicely illustrated by the two investigations summarized below.

In a study that included 9 PNFA patients, 8 SD patients, and 6 LPA patients, Sapolsky et al. (2010) evaluated each patient's linguistic capacity using a new instrument called the Progressive Aphasia Severity Scale (PASS). This clinical tool provides guidelines for rating a given patient's fluency, grammar, and single word comprehension on separate 5-point scales that range from normal (0) to mildly (1.0), moderately (2.0), or severely (3.0) impaired. After obtaining PASS scores for all of the patients in their study, the researchers investigated the relationships between those scores and the patients' patterns of regional cortical atrophy, which are depicted in Figure 14.5.

Two of the outcomes are especially relevant here. First, when the researchers conducted a region of interest (ROI) analysis that focused specifically on the pars opercularis of the left inferior frontal lobe (i.e., BA44,

the posterior sector of Broca's area), they found that the degree of cortical thinning in this region correlated significantly with the severity of impairment on both the fluency and grammar measures of the PASS (Figure 14.6A, B). Second, when the researchers conducted a more exploratory whole-brain analysis, they found that worse scores on the grammar measure were strongly linked with greater cortical thinning not only in the pars opercularis, but also in the posterior middle frontal gyrus and lateral precentral gyrus (Figure 14.6C). Although both of these analyses included all 23 patients, it should come as no surprise that the significant effects were driven almost entirely by the PNFA patients.

In another study, this one carried out by Wilson et al. (2010b), the subjects consisted of 14 PNFA patients, 25 SD patients, and 11 LPA patients, as well as 10 patients with a non-aphasic syndrome called the behavioral variant of frontotemporal dementia (bvFTD), and 10 healthy individuals matched in age with the brain-damaged patients. The patterns of regional cortical atrophy for the three PPA groups are depicted in Figure 14.7A. To get a well-rounded sense of each subject's expressive language skills, the researchers asked all of them to describe the "picnic picture" in the Western Aphasia Battery (Kertesz, 1982), which is shown in Figure 14.7B. The subjects' descriptions were then carefully analyzed along a number of dimensions, including speech rate, speech sound errors, lexical content, and several aspects of syntactic structure and complexity. Here we will focus on the lexical and syntactic dimensions.

Regarding lexical content, it is noteworthy that, according to a group-level analysis, the PNFA patients, but not the SD, LPA, or bvFTD patients, produced fewer free-standing closed-class elements than the control subjects; however, follow-up analyses revealed that this effect was carried by only five of the 14 PNFA patients. The researchers also found that, compared to the control subjects, the PNFA patients produced

A

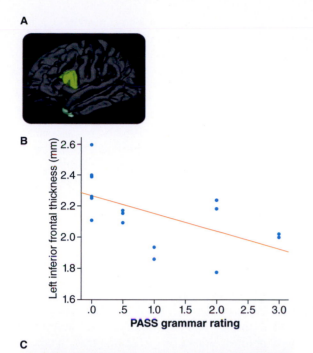

B

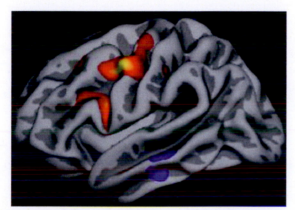

C

Figure 14.6 Correlations between the grammatical measure of the Progressive Aphasia Severity Scale (PASS) and areas of cortical thinning in the three variants of PPA. (A, B) A region of interest analysis focusing specifically on the left pars opercularis (BA44, green) revealed that greater grammatical impairment correlated significantly with greater cortical thinning in this area. (C) An exploratory whole-brain analysis revealed that greater grammatical impairment correlated significantly with atrophy not only in the left pars opercularis, but also in the region where the left posterior middle frontal gyrus meets the precentral gyrus. (From Sapolsky et al., 2010, p. 363 and supplemental figure.)

significantly fewer verbs; however, once again, follow-up analyses revealed that the effect was due to just three patients who tended to produce isolated nouns or NPs.

Turning to the various syntactic dimensions, the main results are shown in Figure 14.8A–F. First, although mean length of utterance (MLU)—a simple measure

A

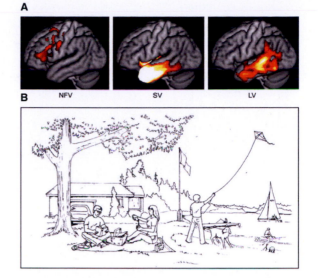

NFV   SV   LV

B

Figure 14.7 (A) Patterns of cortical atrophy in the nonfluent variant (NFV), the semantic variant (SV), and the logopenic variant (LV) in Wilson et al.'s (2010b) study of sentence production in PPA. (B) The "picnic picture" from the Western Aphasia Battery. (From Wilson et al., 2010b, p. 2073.)

of syntactic complexity—was significantly reduced in all three variants of PPA, it was lowest for the PNFA patients (Figure 14.8A). Second, and more interestingly, relative to all of the other groups, the PNFA patients—in particular, six of those individuals—tended to generate utterances that were not full-fledged sentences, like *dog on the ground . . . sailboat in the water* (Figure 14.8B). Third, the PNFA patients committed the largest proportion of syntactic errors, some of which involved omitting articles (e.g., *the man is reading book*), omitting auxiliaries (e.g., *the man flying a kite*), omitting inflections (e.g., *the family is have a picnic*), and garbling grammatical constructions (e.g., *a thongs off the man* [i.e., the man has taken off his thongs/sandals]) (Figure 14.8C). Fourth, to obtain a summary measure of syntactic competence, the researchers conducted a principal components analysis that combined both of the two previous measures—specifically, non-sentence utterances and syntactic errors. As predicted, the PNFA patients had the lowest scores on this summary measure (Figure 14.8D). Fifth, compared to all of the other groups, the PNFA patients produced the fewest embedded clauses, which is indicative of significantly reduced syntactic complexity (Figure 14.8E). And sixth, all three PPA groups committed more semantic errors than either the bvFTD group or the control group, but there were no significant differences between the three PPA groups (Figure 14.8F).

Finally, the researchers explored the neural correlates of some of the syntactic variables just described.

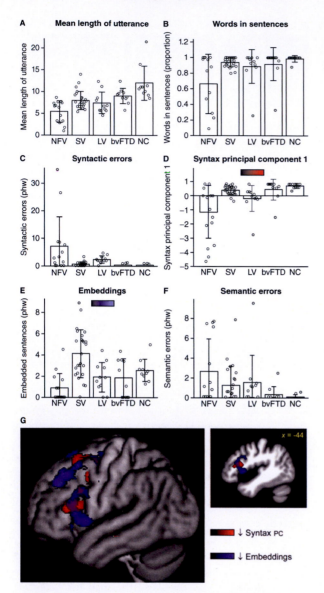

A Mean length of utterance

B Words in sentences

C Syntactic errors

D Syntax principal component 1

E Embeddings

F Semantic errors

G

x = -44

↓ Syntax PC

↓ Embeddings

Figure 14.8 Results from Wilson et al.'s (2010b) study of sentence production in PPA. See the main text for details. (From Wilson et al., 2010b, p. 2081.)

As illustrated in Figure 14.8G, lower scores on the summary syntactic measure correlated significantly with lower tissue volume in the left posterior inferior frontal gyrus as well as in a more superior left frontal area. In addition, lower scores on the measure of embeddings correlated significantly with lower tissue volume in more extensive portions of essentially the same regions identified by the first analysis.

These deficit–lesion correlations are remarkably similar to those reported by Sapolsky et al. (2010), and both sets of results strongly implicate Broca's area (especially the pars opercularis) in syntactic encoding. It should be emphasized, however, that neither study speaks directly to

the issue of whether this brain region contributes equally to the functional and positional levels of processing in Garrett's model of syntactic encoding. Hence, this remains an open question requiring further investigation (see Box 14.2). Nevertheless, the PPA data—as well as the PET and fMRI data presented in the next main section—do provide powerful evidence for the view that, in ways that still need to be deciphered, Broca's area is a central computational hub in the widely distributed neural system that supports one of the major purposes of language—namely, to allow speakers to express unique thoughts and feelings by formulating complex multi-word utterances according to largely unconscious combinatorial rules and principles (see also Box 15.1 in Chapter 15).

Summary

Neuropsychological insights about the infrastructure of syntactic encoding come from several sources. First, patients diagnosed as agrammatic tend to display five main symptoms: a paucity of main verbs; syntactic simplification; omission of free-standing closed-class elements (i.e., functors); substitution of bound closed-class elements (i.e., inflections); and reliance on canonical word order. However, all of these symptoms have been found to dissociate from each other, and agrammatic patients also have very heterogeneous lesion sites. This variability has a negative side, since it implies that agrammatism is not a unitary disorder, but it also has a positive side, since it helps us recognize and appreciate the astonishing complexity of syntactic encoding, not only in terms of the many cognitive processes that are vulnerable to damage, but also in terms of the many brain regions that appear to be involved.

Second, some patients with vascular aphasia have deficits with discernible theoretical significance, since they seem to affect fairly specific computational operations that have counterparts in Garrett's model of normal syntactic encoding. Thus, there is some evidence that the two main operations at the functional level of processing—namely, retrieving the argument structure properties associated with the lemmas of verbs, and mapping participant roles onto grammatical relations—can be impaired independently of each other; and there are also some hints that the two main operations at the positional level of processing—namely, assembling syntactic constituents, and inserting closed-class items in the appropriate slots—can be disrupted to different degrees.

Finally, the growing literature on PPA is especially relevant to issues regarding the neural substrates of syntactic encoding. This is because patients with the nonfluent variant have significantly worse sentence

Box 14.2   Selection for Position: A Possible Contribution of Broca's Area to Syntactic Encoding

Some intriguing evidence that Broca's area may contribute to positional processing during syntactic encoding comes from a clever neuropsychological study by Thothathiri et al. (2010) that focused on four stroke patients with left ventrolateral prefrontal lesions: CBD, TB, UT, and MD. On each trial of the main task, the patients were shown two pictures of objects aligned horizontally on a computer screen, and were asked to name both of them using a simple *The X and the Y* phrase, with *X* denoting the object on the left and *Y* denoting the one on the right. For example, the correct response to the stimulus shown in Figure 14B2.1A would be *The eye and the pencil*. There were two sessions, each with 200 trials, and randomly distributed among those trials were 40 three-trial sets, or "triads," that were crucial for the experiment. One half of the triads were "consistent" because one of the two objects in the array repeatedly occurred in the same position on all three trials (e.g., *eye–pencil, eye–toaster, eye–camel*), whereas the other half of the triads were "inconsistent" because one of the two objects in the array repeatedly occurred in the same position on the first two trials, but then occurred in the other position on the third trial (e.g., *glove–duck, glove–carrot, whistle–glove*).

As expected, the reaction times of healthy control subjects were longer, to a marginally significant degree ($p < .077$), for the inconsistent triads than for the consistent ones, pointing to what the researchers call a "positional interference effect." Of greater interest, however, were the results for the four patients. Most importantly, two of them—CBD and TB—displayed significantly exaggerated positional interference effects, relative to controls. In addition, compared to the other two patients, CBD and TB had the following notable behavioral characteristics: They made more omission errors throughout the task; their error rates were especially high when the sequence of nouns in the target phrase went counter to the prevailing order in English, with an initial inanimate noun and a final animate noun (e.g., *chair–dog*), instead of the other way around; and they generated lower proportions of well-formed sentences on a separate task that involved narrating the "Cinderella" story. Furthermore, neuroanatomical analyses revealed that both CBD's and TB's lesions, but neither UT's nor MD's lesions, affected a narrow swath of tissue along the junction of BA44 and BA6, with some dorsal extension into BA9 (Figure 14B2.1B).

What are the implications of these findings? They suggest that the cortical region at the border of BA44 and BA6 is essential for a process that the researchers call "selection for position." Consider, for example, the following triad in the main task: *cup–chain, cup–book,* and *sock–cup*. During the planning of the third response, both nouns are presumably activated, but there is an unusually high degree of competition for the initial position, because even though *sock* is the correct description of object on the left, *cup* receives positional priming from the two preceding trials. In such situations, BA44/BA6 may provide the kind of cognitive control that is necessary to bias the choice of the initial noun in accordance with the task demands. But if that mechanism is impaired, as it appears to be in CBD and TB, resolving the sorts of competitions that are induced by positional interference may require more time, and may even fail completely in some cases. In the real world of linguistic communication, it is not hard to see how such a disturbance could have deleterious effects for many aspects of positional processing during syntactic encoding.

A

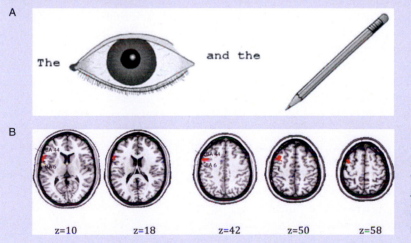

B

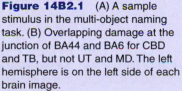

z=10   z=18   z=42   z=50   z=58

Figure 14B2.1   (A) A sample stimulus in the multi-object naming task. (B) Overlapping damage at the junction of BA44 and BA6 for CBD and TB, but not UT and MD. The left hemisphere is on the left side of each brain image.

production deficits than patients with either the semantic variant or the logopenic variant, and those deficits correlate strongly with atrophy in the left ventrolateral prefrontal cortex, especially the posterior sector of Broca's area. These findings fit well with the hemodynamic data described below, and they bolster the hypothesis that, even though many different left perisylvian regions contribute to syntactic encoding (as shown by the broadly distributed lesion sites of agrammatic patients), Broca's area seems to have the privileged status of being a major computational hub in the network.

Insights from PET and fMRI

The daunting challenge of experimentally controlling all the different variables that influence sentence production has impeded the use of hemodynamic methods to investigate this topic. In fact, so far only a handful of PET and fMRI studies have sought to isolate the cortical mechanisms that underlie syntactic encoding. The good news, however, is that these studies have yielded largely convergent results that point to a pivotal role for Broca's area. Some of the most significant studies are summarized below.

Indefrey et al.'s (2001, 2004) PET Studies

In order to distinguish syntactic encoding from the other stages of sentence production, Indefrey et al. (2001, 2004) devised a clever paradigm called restrictive scene description. The beauty of this design is that it allows investigators to elicit utterances that require systematically different degrees of syntactic encoding, but that remain fairly constant in terms of conceptual and phonological complexity. In the specific version of the paradigm that Indefrey et al. (2001, 2004) employed, the stimuli consisted of dynamic scenes in which colored geometric shapes interacted in various ways. In response to each scene, the subjects, all of whom were native speakers of German, were asked to produce three utterances in separate conditions: (1) a grammatically well-formed sentence; (2) two NPs with local grammatical structure, together with an uninflected verb; and (3) a list of words without any grammatical structure.

An example is shown in Figure 14.9. This particular scene involved a red square launching a blue ellipse. In the "sentence" condition, the target utterance was *Das rote Viereck stösst die blaue Ellipse weg.* This utterance has a hierarchically organized syntactic structure in which the initial subject NP encodes the actor and the final object NP encodes the undergoer, and in which

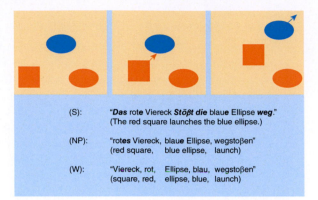

Figure 14.9 Example of an animated stimulus in Indefrey et al.'s (2001, 2004) PET studies of syntactic encoding. In this scene the red square launches the blue ellipse. Arrows are added to indicate the movement direction of the objects on the computer screen. Stimuli of the same kind were used in all three conditions. Examples of the three response types are given below (S, sentence condition; NP, noun phrase condition; W, single word condition). The response types differed in the degree of syntactic encoding and the corresponding application of grammatical markers (printed in bold) in German. See the main text for details. (From Indefrey et al., 2004, p. 314.)

each NP includes a modifying adjective. In addition, the utterance contains several closed-class grammatical markers, which are highlighted in bold: The article and adjective in the subject NP are marked for nominative case and neuter gender (agreeing with the inherent gender of *Viereck* "square"); the verb is inflected for present tense; the article and adjective in the object NP are marked for accusative case and feminine gender (agreeing with the inherent gender of *Ellipse* "ellipse"); and the particle *weg* is placed at the end of the sentence, in accord with a special rule for the syntactic treatment of so-called separable prefix verbs like *wegstossen*. Thus, formulating the utterance requires syntactic encoding at both functional and positional levels of processing.

In the "NP" condition, the target utterance was somewhat simpler: *rotes Viereck, blaue Ellipse, wegstossen.* With regard to syntactic encoding, both levels of processing are still required, but to lesser degrees. At the functional level, the modificational relationship between the adjective and the noun in each NP must be specified; and at the positional level, the local linearization and gender agreement in each NP must be computed.

Finally, in the "word-list" condition, the target utterance was *Viereck, rot, Ellipse, blau, wegstossen.* This sequence clearly has no real grammatical structure whatsoever.

To explore the neural correlates of syntactic encoding, Indefrey et al. (2001) conducted a PET study using the paradigm described above, and a few years later Indefrey et al. (2004) conducted another PET study in an effort to replicate the results of the first one. In both experiments, the subjects were given a training session one week before the brain imaging session. During that training session, they received precise instructions about how to describe each scene in each condition, and they practiced the tasks in several blocks of trials. When the brain imaging session took place, two different stimulus presentation rates were used (eight scenes per minute and six scenes per minute) in order to control for the extra nongrammatical (lexical, phonological, and articulatory) processing load imposed by the additional grammatical markers that the subjects produced in the sentence and NP conditions, relative to the word-list condition. As discussed in greater detail below, this was an important part of the experimental design of each study, because it allowed the researchers to determine whether any brain regions that responded significantly more to the sentence and NP conditions than to the word-list condition were really indexing syntactic encoding, as opposed to nongrammatical factors.

Not surprisingly, the two studies generated very similar results. In each study, when the researchers subtracted the blood flow data associated with the condition requiring the least amount of syntactic encoding—i.e., the word-list condition—from the blood flow data associated with the condition requiring the greatest amount of syntactic encoding—i.e., the sentence condition—they found a single "hot spot" that included the posterior sector of Broca's area. These results are depicted in Figure 14.10. The top panel shows the results of the second study, and the bottom panel shows the results of the first one. In each panel, the yellow patches serve as anatomical landmarks, since they demarcate the boundaries of BA44 with a probability of 50 percent, based on the guidelines provided by Amunts et al. (1999). In the top panel, activations are shown in blue and green, with green indicating overlap with BA44. Here, 37 percent of the activated voxels fell within the 50 percent probability area for BA44, and most of the other activated voxels were medial and dorsal to that area. In the bottom panel, activations are shown in red and orange, with orange indicating overlap with BA44. Here, 29 percent of the activated voxels fell within the 50 percent probability area for BA44, and most of the other voxels were posterior to that area, specifically in the ventral premotor cortex (BA6). Although the activation focus shifted by a few millimeters across the two studies, this could easily have occurred because of inter-subject variability in the unique anatomical configuration of

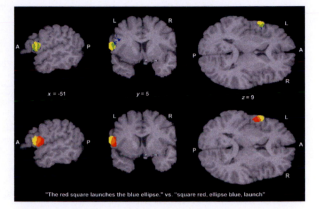

Figure 14.10   Results of Indefrey et al.'s (2001, 2004) PET studies of syntactic encoding. Each row shows the cortical activation that was observed when the sentence condition was contrasted against the word condition. Yellow patches indicate the boundaries of BA44 with a probability of 50%. (Top row) Results from the 2004 study, with activations shown in blue and green, the latter indicated overlap with BA44. (Bottom row) Results from the 2001 study, with activations shown in red and orange, the latter indicated overlap with BA44. (From Indefrey et al., 2004, p. 314.)

the left inferior frontal cortex. The main generalization is that in both studies the sentence condition engaged the posterior sector of Broca's area, together with some of the surrounding cortex, significantly more than the word-list condition.

What about the NP condition, which demanded an intermediate amount of syntactic encoding? To address this question, in each study the researchers defined as a region of interest the activated volume shown in the appropriate panel of Figure 14.10, and compared the mean blood flow within that region across all three experimental conditions. In the first study, a graded response pattern was observed, such that the sentence condition engaged the region significantly more than the NP condition, which in turn engaged it significantly more than the word-list condition. In the second study, there was a trend in the same direction, but the statistical analysis revealed a less continuous pattern, such that the sentence and NP conditions engaged the region to the same degree, and both of them engaged it significantly more than the word-list condition (see the left side of Figure 14.11). Given this discrepancy between the two sets of findings, a strong interpretation is not warranted. While it is tempting to suppose that the magnitude of left inferior frontal activity increases in proportion to the degree of syntactic encoding, it must be acknowledged that the evidence for this view comes more from the first study than from the second. In addition, it remains unclear whether functional and

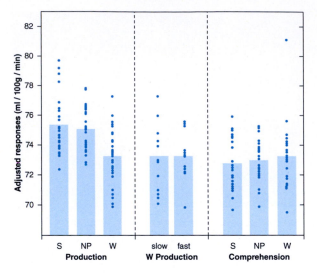

Figure 14.11 Mean regional cerebral blood flow in the activated volume shown in the top row of Figure 14.10, across all of the experimental conditions. S = sentence condition; NP = NP condition; W = word-list condition; slow = slow stimulus presentation rate; fast = fast stimulus presentation rate. (From Indefrey et al., 2004, p. 316.)

positional levels of processing have largely overlapping or partially segregated neural substrates. Although the results of these two PET studies suggest that the two levels of syntactic encoding may be tightly intertwined in the brain, further neuroimaging research is needed to investigate this topic more carefully.

Another important issue involves the theoretical possibility that the hemodynamic effects that we have been discussing might not reflect syntactic encoding per se, but might instead reflect the greater nongrammatical processing load imposed by the sentence and NP conditions than by the word-list condition. As mentioned above, the reason why the researchers included two different stimulus presentation rates in their experimental design was so they could address this issue directly. The logic of their approach was basically as follows. For the sake of argument, let's imagine that the greater left inferior frontal activity that was evoked by the sentence and NP conditions than by the word-list condition did not really have anything to do with syntactic encoding, but was instead due to the fact that the subjects simply produced more syllables in first two conditions than in the third one. If that were the case, one would expect the same brain region to be engaged significantly more by the fast presentation rate of the word-list condition than by the slow presentation rate of that condition, since there would be greater overall speech output in former situation than in the latter, yet syntactic encoding would be absent in both. When

the researchers conducted this analysis, however, they found that the mean blood flow was essentially the same across the two presentation rates of the word-list condition. The results from the second study are shown in the middle of Figure 14.11, and the results from the first study are comparable. These findings support the view that it really is syntactic encoding, as opposed to nongrammatical factors like speech rate, that is indexed by the greater left inferior frontal responses in the sentence and NP conditions than in the word-list condition.

Finally, it is noteworthy that in the second study the researchers took one step further by investigating whether the posterior sector of Broca's area contributes to syntactic processing not only during sentence production, but also during sentence comprehension. To address this issue, they expanded their experimental protocol by including three additional conditions in which the subjects viewed the same types of dynamic scenes that they viewed in the production part of the study, but instead of having to generate sentences, NPs, and word-lists, their task was instead to indicate with button-presses whether the corresponding kinds of auditorily presented utterances matched or mismatched the scenes. The researchers created the mismatching utterances by reversing the participant roles, using adjectives that denoted the wrong colors, and using verbs that denoted the wrong actions. To analyze the data, they defined as a region of interest the activated volume shown in the top panel of Figure 14.10—i.e., the left inferior frontal territory that was engaged significantly more by the sentence condition than the word-list condition in the production part of the study— and compared the mean blood flow within that region across all three conditions in the comprehension part of the study. As shown on the right side of Figure 14.11, there were no significant activation differences between the sentence, NP, and word-list conditions.

Nevertheless, Indefrey et al. (2004) argue that this negative result does not necessarily imply that Broca's area is irrelevant to syntactic processing during sentence comprehension. They point out, for instance, that the lack of significant effects may have been due to one or both of two factors. First, the sentence and NP conditions involved utterances that were syntactically rather simple, and other studies have shown that Broca's area is in fact engaged by sentences that are syntactically more complex (e.g., see the review by Kaan & Swaab, 2002, which is cited by Indefrey et al., 2004; see also the fMRI studies by Menenti et al., 2011, and Segaert et al., 2012, which, as discussed in Box 15.1 in Chapter 15, showed that Broca's area

Table 14.4 Sample Stimuli and Expected Responses Illustrating the Three Experimental Conditions in Haller et al.'s (2005) fMRI Study of Syntactic Encoding

Condition	Stimulus	Expected Response
Sentence generation	*Werfen Ball Kind* ("throw ball child")	***Das** Kind wirft **den** Ball* ("The child throws the ball")
Word reading	*Werfen Ball Kind* ("throw ball child")	*Werfen Ball Kind* ("throw ball child")
Sentence reading	***Das** Kind wirft **den** Ball* ("The child throws the ball")	***Das** Kind wirft **den** Ball* ("The child throws the ball")

Source: Haller et al. (2005, p. 809).

Closed-class elements are highlighted in bold.

distinguishes between syntactically identical and syntactically different sentences during both speaking and listening). Second, the subjects could have performed over half the judgments by relying on semantic instead of syntactic information, and other studies have shown that Broca's area is in fact more responsive to more syntactically demanding tasks (again, see the review by Kaan & Swaab, 2002). To be sure, these are interesting and important considerations. It is essential to realize, however, that the question of whether—and if so, exactly how—Broca's area contributes to syntactic processing during sentence comprehension is one of the most controversial issues in the cognitive neuroscience of language (for a critical perspective see Rogalsky & Hickok, 2011). We will return to this much debated topic in Chapter 15 and discuss it at greater length.

Haller et al.'s (2005) fMRI Study

To further illuminate the neural underpinnings of syntactic encoding during sentence production, Haller et al. (2005) conducted an fMRI study that was similar to Indefrey et al.'s (2001, 2004) two PET studies insofar as the subjects were all native speakers of German, but was different from those studies insofar as the experimental paradigm did not involve restrictive scene description. Instead, an alternative approach was taken that involved the following three conditions (Table 14.4).

First, in the "sentence generation" condition, the stimulus on each trial consisted of three visually presented content words—two object nouns and an action verb—in a pseudo-random sequence that did not conform to the order in which they would normally occur in an active-voice sentence—e.g., *Werfen Ball Kind* ("throw ball child"). The task was to formulate and overtly produce an active-voice sentence by assigning the participant roles (which could always be inferred) to the appropriate grammatical relations,

re-arranging the words to form a subject–verb–object sequence, inflecting the verb for present tense, and inserting the properly case- and gender-marked articles before the nouns—e.g., ***Das Kind wirft den Ball*** ("The child throws the ball"). Performing all of these cognitive operations clearly required both functional and positional levels of syntactic encoding.

Second, in the "word reading" condition, which served as a control, the stimuli were exactly the same as in the sentence generation condition, but the task was simply to read aloud each set of words, just as they appeared. This task obviously did not require any syntactic encoding at all.

Third, in the "sentence reading" condition, which served as another control, the stimuli were visually presented sentences of the type that were targeted in the sentence generation condition, and the task was to read them aloud. Since the stimuli were already grammatically structured, there was no need for the sort of creative, internally driven syntactic encoding that was demanded by the sentence generation condition. And yet the spoken output in this condition was equivalent to that in the sentence generation condition with respect to the number, identity, and linearization of the words that the subjects produced.

When the researchers analyzed the fMRI data, they first contrasted the two control conditions—word reading and sentence reading—against each other to see if there were any significant differences. None emerged. Then they carried out two contrasts that were intended to disclose the key brain regions underlying syntactic encoding—sentence generation minus word reading, and sentence generation minus sentence reading. The results are portrayed in Figure 14.12. As can be seen, both contrasts revealed very similar activation patterns predominantly in the left hemisphere. Most importantly, in both cases the strongest activation, in terms of cluster size as well as signal strength, occurred in Broca's

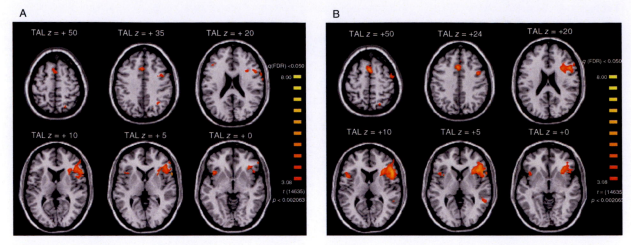

Figure 14.12 Results from Haller et al.'s (2005) fMRI study of syntactic encoding. (A) Significant activations for the comparison of the sentence generation condition minus the word reading condition. (B) Significant activations for the comparison of the sentence generation condition minus the sentence reading condition. The left hemisphere is on the right side of each brain image. (From Haller et al., 2005, pp. 810-811.)

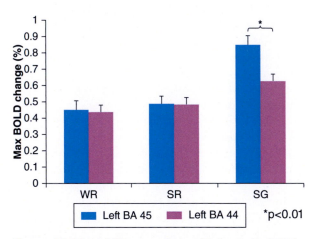

Figure 14.13 Additional results from Haller et al.'s (2005) fMRI study of syntactic encoding. The maximum BOLD signal changes (%) are shown for the word reading (WR), sentence reading (SR), and sentence generation (SG) conditions in left BA44 (gray columns) and left BA45 (black columns). (From Haller et al., 2005, p. 812.)

area—not just the posterior sector (BA44), but also the anterior one (BA45). To investigate these effects more carefully, the researchers conducted separate region of interest analyses for BA44 and BA45. As shown in Figure 14.13, although the signal changes in both areas were statistically equivalent across the two control conditions, they were significantly greater in the sentence generation condition; moreover, in that condition the changes were more pronounced in BA45 than in BA44.

These results differ only slightly from those reported by Indefrey et al. (2001, 2004), and they provide further support for the view that syntactic encoding relies heavily on Broca's area. This fMRI study goes beyond the previous PET studies, however, because it suggests that a few other cortical regions may also contribute to syntactic encoding. In particular, Figure 14.12 indicates that in both contrasts additional activations were present in the left supplementary motor area (medial BA6), the left superior parietal lobule (BA7), and the right insula. It is by no means clear what distinct roles these areas might play in syntactic encoding. However, it would not be unreasonable to suppose that they are among the nodes of an even larger and more widely distributed neural network—a network that has so far eluded complete detection with functional neuroimaging techniques, but that may nevertheless mediate the many facets of syntactic encoding through complex interactive processing.

Summary

Owing for the most part to serious methodological challenges, as yet only a few hemodynamic studies have explored the neural substrates of syntactic encoding during sentence production. Still, the available data provide some valuable insights into how this critical aspect of language is implemented in the brain. The main generalization is that syntactic encoding seems to rely heavily on Broca's area—a finding that fits quite well with the data reviewed earlier involving progressive nonfluent aphasia. The two pioneering PET studies by Indefrey et al. (2001, 2004) support this conclusion, and so does the subsequent fMRI study by Haller et al. (2005). Unfortunately, however, none of these studies was designed to tease apart the two different levels of syntactic encoding—namely, the functional level and the positional level.

Summary and Key Points

- Syntax has many facets, some of which are as follows:
  - devices for indicating participant roles, such as word order, case marking, verbal affixes, and even tone;
  - rules for signaling the hierarchical structure of multi-word expressions, such as phrase structure rules and agreement rules;
  - argument structure, which involves the interaction between, on the one hand, the various participant roles, like actor and undergoer, that enter into the meanings of verbs, and on the other hand, the realization of those roles in various grammatical relations, like subject and object;
  - closed-class elements, which can be either free-standing words or bound affixes;
  - complex sentences, which can involve either coordination or various kinds of subordination.

- The most influential model of syntactic encoding during sentence production was originally developed by Merrill Garrett and posits two separate levels of processing:
  - the functional level, where two types of operations occur: retrieving the argument structure properties associated with the lemmas of verbs, and mapping participant roles onto grammatical relations;
  - the positional level, where two types of operations occur: assembling syntactic constituents, and inserting closed-class items in the appropriate slots.

- The neuropsychological literature on sentence production is rather extensive. From the mid-1980s through the mid-1990s, a great deal of scientific attention was devoted to agrammatism. The prototypical manifestation of this disorder includes the following symptoms:
  - paucity of main verbs;
  - syntactic simplification;
  - omission of free-standing closed-class elements (i.e., functors);
  - substitution of bound closed-class elements (i.e., inflections);
  - Reliance on canonical word order.

- However, it has been argued that agrammatism does not really constitute a "natural kind," because all of the symptoms dissociate from each other. Furthermore, just as the specific behavioral profiles of agrammatic patients vary greatly, so do the specific lesion sites, since they range across the entire left perisylvian zone.
- Still, some brain-damaged patients have sentence production deficits with discernible theoretical implications, since they appear to affect certain processing operations in Garrett's model of syntactic encoding. In particular, at the functional level of processing, the two main operations (summarized above) can be differentially impaired; and at the positional level of processing, the two main operations (summarized above) can be differentially impaired.
- Recent research on primary progressive aphasia has shown that patients with the nonfluent variant are not only more impaired at sentence production than patients with the other two variants, but also have atrophy centered in the left ventrolateral prefrontal cortex, including Broca's area. These findings are important because they highlight the vital role that Broca's area seems to play in syntactic encoding.
- Due largely to methodological challenges, so far only a few studies have used hemodynamic techniques, like PET and fMRI, to investigate the neural substrates of syntactic encoding. However, those studies have yielded results which suggest that Broca's area plays a pivotal role, in keeping with the neuropsychological data from progressive nonfluent aphasia.

Recommended Reading

- Menn, L., O'Connor, M., Obler, L.K., & Holland, A. (1995). *Nonfluent aphasia in a multilingual world*. Amsterdam: John Benjamins. An accessible survey of the similarities and differences among agrammatic aphasic speakers of various languages, based partly on the three-volume collection edited by Menn and Obler (1990a).
- Berndt, R.S. (2001). Sentence production. In B. Rapp (Ed.), *The handbook of cognitive neuropsychology: What deficits reveal about the human mind* (pp. 375–396). Philadelphia: Psychology Press. An outstanding overview and critical analysis of the various types of sentence production deficits manifested by vascular aphasic patients, with an eye toward understanding how those deficits relate to theoretical models of normal syntactic encoding.
- Thompson, C.K., & Faroqi-Shah, Y. (2002). Models of sentence production. In A.E. Hillis (Ed.), *The handbook of adult language disorders: Integrating cognitive neuropsychology, neurology, and rehabilitation* (pp. 311–330). New York: Psychology Press. An instructive summary of Garrett's model of syntactic encoding, with some discussion of relevant data from vascular aphasic patients.
- Wilson, S.M., Henry, M.L., Besbris, M., Ogarm J.M., Dronkers, N.F., Jarrold, W., Miller, B.L., & Gorno-Tempini, M.L. (2010). Connected speech production in three variants of primary progressive aphasia. *Brain, 133,* 2069–2088. An excellent study of the sentence production abilities of patients with primary progressive aphasia, demonstrating that patients with the nonfluent variant have syntactic encoding disturbances that correlate with atrophy in Broca's area.

Sentence Comprehension

15

Introduction

In a delightfully entertaining essay on the intricate interactions between language and cognition, Douglas Hofstadter (2001), the director of the Fluid Analogies Research Group at Indiana University, describes communication as follows:

> The usual goal of communication is, of course, to set up "the same thought" in the receiver's brain as is currently taking place in the sender's brain. The mode by which such replication is attempted is essentially a drastic compression of the complex symbolic dance occurring in the sender's brain into a temporal chain of sounds or a string of visual signs, which are then absorbed by the receiver's brain, where, by something like the reverse process of said compression—a process that I will here term "just adding water"—a new symbolic dance is launched in the second brain. The human brain at one end drains the water out to produce "powdered food for thought," and the one at the other end adds the water back to produce full-fledged food for thought.
>
> (pp. 524–525)

In the previous chapter, we focused on how the sender's brain "drains the water out" during the process of converting thoughts into sentences. In this chapter, we focus instead on how the receiver's brain "adds the water back" during the reverse process of converting sentences into thoughts.

Although it is amusing to suppose that sentence comprehension may be as simple as pouring hot water into a bowl of instant oatmeal, the reality is that it depends on a host of complex mental operations, most of which are executed automatically and unconsciously, but some of which require deliberate cognitive control

(for reviews from different perspectives see Pickering & van Gompel, 2006; MacDonald & Seidenberg, 2006; Tanenhaus, 2007; Jackendoff, 2007; Crocker et al., 2010; Traxler, 2011; MacDonald, 2013; Sanz et al., 2013). To get an initial sense of what's involved, let's consider once again the pair of sentences that we originally examined in Chapter 3 in the context of Broca's aphasia:

(1) The reporter [who attacked the senator] admitted the error.
(2) The reporter [who the senator attacked] admitted the error.

These two sentences use the very same words to describe equally plausible yet partially different scenarios. Numerous psycholinguistic and neurolinguistic studies have shown, however, that most people think the second sentence is harder to understand than the first (e.g., Hakes et al., 1976; Holmes & O'Regan, 1981; Ford, 1983; King & Kutas, 1995; Just et al., 1996a, 1996b). Why is this the case? (Readers unfamiliar with the technical linguistic details discussed below may wish to consult the syntax tutorial at the beginning of Chapter 14.)

Since we are concerned more with spoken than written sentence comprehension, let's suppose that someone heard rather than read the sentences in (1) and (2). For both utterances, as each word is encountered, its phonological, semantic, and syntactic properties must be accessed as quickly as possible. In addition, based largely on their syntactic category specifications (noun, verb, etc.), the words must be incrementally grouped into hierarchically organized constituents that express coherent fragments of the overall message. Note that a crucial part of this process is the need to properly analyze the relative clause that modifies

The reporter (i.e., the constituent enclosed in brackets). In fact, this must be the major source of the differential comprehension difficulty of the two sentences, since they only vary with respect to the structure of the relative clause. In (1) this constituent is called a subject-relative because the initial pronoun *who* corresponds to the subject of the embedded verb. Thus, the entire expression *who attacked the senator* has the canonical word order of a transitive clause, with the actor expressed before the verb and the undergoer expressed after it. In contrast, in (2) the constituent is called an object-relative because the initial pronoun *who* corresponds to the object of the embedded verb. Thus, the entire expression *who the senator attacked* has a noncanonical syntactic–semantic organization, since the undergoer argument occurs first, then the actor argument, and finally the verb.

Now, there are several reasons why the object-relative construction in (2) is harder to understand than the subject-relative construction in (1) (Gibson, 1998). As a general rule, the processing of noncanonical syntactic–semantic linking patterns is computationally more costly than the processing of canonical ones because, by definition, the former patterns deviate from the norm and hence violate the system's expectations. For the sentence in (2), if the listener is not able to determine who attacked whom on the first pass, he or she may need to rapidly replay—"in the mind's ear," so to speak—the phonological forms of all the words, assuming these forms have been retained in auditory–verbal short-term memory. In addition, he or she may need to use top-down executive or supervisory processes, referred to above as cognitive control, to ensure that the noncanonical linking pattern is ultimately selected instead of the canonical one. This would be consciously experienced as the need to concentrate more intensely than usual on figuring out exactly who attacked whom. Furthermore, whereas in (1) the NP *The reporter* designates the actor of both the embedded verb *attacked* and the main verb *admitted*, in (2) it designates the undergoer of the embedded verb and the actor of the main verb. This requirement to assign different participant roles to the same NP—a requirement that entails a rather tricky perspective shift—may increase even more the need for strategic cognitive control. Pulling together all of these considerations about the differential comprehension difficulty of the sentences in (1) and (2), the basic point I would like to make is simply that understanding multi-word utterances is much more complicated than "just adding water."

This chapter provides a survey of recent research on the neural correlates of sentence comprehension, with special emphasis on the kinds of operations mentioned above: accessing lexical properties, grouping words into hierarchically organized constituents, determining syntactic–semantic linking patterns, holding linguistic information in short-term memory, and using top-down strategies to facilitate the understanding of especially complex sentences. As with many of the other topics discussed in this book, however, the literature on how sentence comprehension is subserved by the brain is vast (for other surveys see Friederici, 2002, 2011; Kaan & Swaab, 2002; Caplan, 2006, 2009; Kutas et al., 2006; Friederici & Weissenborn, 2007; Kuperberg, 2007; Bornkessel-Schlesewsky & Schlesewsky, 2009a, 2009b; Swaab et al., 2012; Osterhout et al., 2012). For this reason, the coverage here is restricted to some of the most salient advances of the past few decades.

The first main section describes several recent studies which suggest that sentence comprehension is accomplished by massively interactive processing within a large-scale neural network that consists of a variety of strongly left-lateralized, tightly interconnected cortical regions. It is important to note that this section concentrates primarily on the anatomical organization of the network. The next section, however, addresses a wide range of challenging functional issues by discussing, from both theoretical and empirical perspectives, how each component of the network might contribute to sentence comprehension. Although some of the hypotheses presented in this section are fairly well-supported, others are much more speculative and controversial, reflecting the need for further research in this domain of neurolinguistics. Finally, the last section shifts from "where" to "when" questions by reviewing the major electrophysiological response patterns that have been associated with certain aspects of receptive sentence processing.

A Large-Scale Neural Network for Sentence Comprehension: Anatomical Organization

Historically, from the late 1800s up to the mid 1970s, virtually all aspects of sentence comprehension were thought to rely primarily on the left posterior superior/middle temporal region of the brain, owing to the fact that the most profound disturbances of this linguistic capacity were observed in patients with Wernicke's aphasia, whose lesions were found to be centered there (see Chapter 3). From the mid 1970s up to the present time, however, it has become increasingly clear that, as mentioned above, sentence comprehension is subserved by a much more extensive network of mostly

Table 15.1   CYCLE-R Subtests Used for Assessing Auditory Sentence Comprehension in Stroke Patients

Subtest	Pictures	Example
Possession (3)	3	The clown has a balloon
Simple declarative (2)	3	The boy is jumping
Active voice (4)	4	The girl is pushing the boy
Double embedding (4)	4	The clown that is big has the balloon that is red
Agentless passive (4)	4	The boy is being chased
Agentive passive (5)	4	The boy is being chased by the girl
Subject–subject (S–S)-relative (7)	4	The boy who is pulling the girl is mad
Object–subject (O–S)-relative (8)	4	The girl is chasing the clown who is big
Object-cleft (8)	4	It's the clown that the girl chases
Negative passive (9)	3	The girl is not being led by the boy
Object–object (O–O)-relative (9)	4	The girl is kissing the boy that the clown is hugging

Adapted from Dronkers et al. (2004, p. 153).

The number in parentheses after each subtest indicates the age by which English-speaking children are able to understand the sentence type.

left-hemisphere regions. Although a number of tricky problems have yet to be resolved, evidence for this modern view comes from many different sources, some of which are considered below. In the first part of this section, we delve into the anatomical organization of the network for sentence comprehension by concentrating on two parallel lesion and connectivity studies conducted by Dronkers et al. (2004) and Turken and Dronkers (2011). Then in the second part we bring into the picture additional evidence from a few other investigations.

Lesion and Connectivity Studies by Dronkers et al. (2004) and Turken and Dronkers (2011)

Dronkers et al.'s (2004) Lesion Study

The influential lesion study reported by Dronkers et al. (2004) provides an excellent entry to the large literature on the neural circuitry underlying sentence comprehension. This is because it was among the first investigations to combine sophisticated behavioral and neuroanatomical techniques in order to relate auditory sentence comprehension deficits to well-defined lesion sites in a sizable group of chronic stroke patients. (Note that we first encountered this study in Chapter 5; see the section on the "lexical interface" component of the Dual Stream Model of speech perception.)

Of the 72 patients who participated in the study, 64 had left-hemisphere lesions and 8 had right-hemisphere lesions. Although none of the right-hemisphere-damaged patients had significant language impairments, 46 (72 percent) of the left-hemisphere-damaged patients were aphasic, with the following breakdown across classic syndromes, based on the Western Aphasia Battery (Kertesz, 1982): 16 Broca's, 6 Wernicke's, 8 conduction, 1 global, 12 anomic, and 3 unclassifiable.

Each patient's ability to understand spoken sentences was assessed by administering 11 subtests of the Curtiss–Yamada Language Evaluation—Receptive (CYCLE-R). On each trial, the patient was presented with a sentence together with an array of three or four line drawings, and the task was to pick the picture that best matched the meaning of the sentence. The distractor pictures involved mismatching actions, mismatching people or objects, mismatching properties of people or objects, and mismatching actor/undergoer roles of people or objects. (A limitation of the study is that the patients' errors were not analyzed according to these different kinds of distractor pictures.) Each of the 11 subtests included five instances of a particular type of sentence, for a total of 55 items. As indicated in Table 15.1, the sentence types ranged from being very simple and easy to understand (e.g., *The clown has a balloon*) to being very complex and hard to understand (e.g., *The girl is kissing the boy that the clown is hugging*). The child-oriented content of many of the sentences reflects

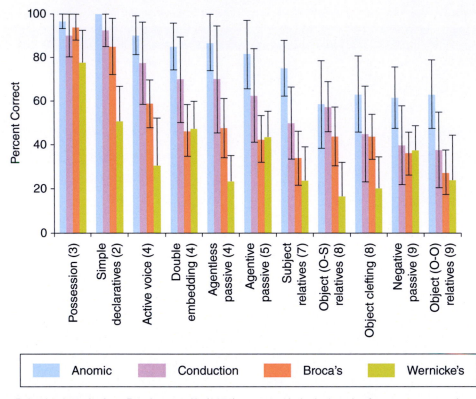

Figure 15.1   Behavioral results from Dronkers et al.'s (2004) neuropsychological study of sentence comprehension. Percent correct scores (and 95% confidence intervals) on each of the 11 subtests are shown for patients with different aphasia types. (From Dronkers et al., 2004, p. 157.)

the fact that the CYCLE-R was originally designed to chart the developmental course of sentence comprehension. And in this context it is worth noting that, as shown in Table 15.1, although the simplest sentence types tend to be acquired by the age of 2–4, the most complex ones are usually not acquired until the age of 8–9.

Not surprisingly, the right-hemisphere-damaged patients and the non-aphasic left-hemisphere-damaged patients performed well on all—or, in a few cases, almost all—of the subtests. The aphasic left-hemisphere-damaged patients, on the other hand, displayed different degrees of impairment, as illustrated in Figure 15.1. The anomic aphasics exhibited the mildest deficits, declining below an average of 80 percent correct on just the five most challenging subtests, and not dropping as low as 50 percent correct on any of them. In comparison, the conduction aphasics manifested more pronounced problems, with average scores below 80 percent correct on all but the two simplest subtests, and means below 50 percent correct on four subtests. Like the conduction aphasics, the Broca's aphasics dropped below the 80 percent mark on all but the two simplest subtests, but they clearly had worse

deficits than the conduction aphasics because they sunk below the 50 percent mark on eight subtests. Overall, the Wernicke's aphasics had the most severely compromised sentence comprehension abilities. In fact, the only subtest on which they approached passable performance (with an average of 78 percent correct) was the simplest one in the entire battery, namely Possession. Moreover, their mean scores on almost all of the other subtests were lower than those of the other three aphasic groups. Finally, it should be noted that the single global aphasic performed similarly to the Wernicke's aphasics, and the three patients whose aphasia type could not be classified performed fairly well on all but the last few subtests.

In order to identify the specific areas of brain damage that were associated with impaired performance on the CYCLE-R, Dronkers et al. (2004) employed the method known as voxel-based lesion–symptom mapping (VLSM). In short, for all 64 left-hemisphere-damaged patients, data regarding their lesion sites and their composite CYCLE-R scores were entered into the following statistical analyses. At every voxel that contained *at least* eight patients with lesions and eight patients without lesions, *t*-tests were used to compare the behavioral scores of the two groups and thereby determine whether the performance of the lesioned group was significantly worse than that of the non-lesioned group. These analyses revealed that sentence comprehension deficits were reliably linked with damage to the five regions of the left hemisphere depicted in Figure 15.2 and described below:

- the posterior middle temporal gyrus (pMTG), including the posterior portion of BA21 and the superior portion of BA37;
- the anterior superior temporal gyrus (aSTG), especially anterior BA22;
- the left temporoparietal region, especially the portion of the posterior superior temporal sulcus (pSTS) that extends into the angular gyrus (roughly BA39);
- most of left BA47;
- part of left BA46.

In a series of follow-up analyses, the researchers first used their neuroanatomical findings to create six groups of patients. One group consisted of those patients whose lesions spared all five VLSM-defined brain regions, and each of the other five groups consisted of those patients whose lesions encompassed

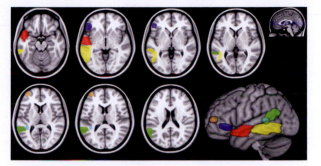

Figure 15.2   Five main lesion sites identified by Dronkers et al. (2004) as giving rise to significant sentence comprehension deficits. The planes of the horizontal slices are marked on a mid-sagittal view of the brain template on the upper right side. Yellow = pMTG; red = aSTG; green = pSTS/BA39; blue = BA47; orange = part of BA46. (From Turken & Dronkers, 2011, p. 4.)

the bulk of a given VLSM-defined region. (Note that some patients' lesions included more than one of these regions, so the groups were not completely independent of each other in terms of membership.) Then the researchers calculated the mean percent correct scores of all six groups on all 11 subtests in the CYCLE-R. The results are plotted in Figure 15.3. This graph indicates

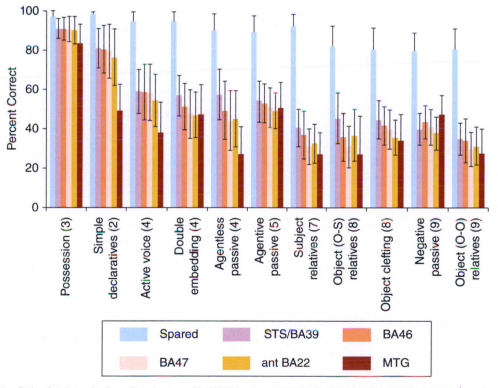

Figure 15.3   Behavioral results from Dronkers et al.'s (2004) neuropsychological study of sentence comprehension. Percent correct scores (and 95% confidence intervals) on each of the 11 subtests are shown for patients with different lesion sites. (From Dronkers et al., 2004, p. 163.)

that the patients whose lesions spared all of the VLSM-defined regions performed quite well on all but the four most challenging subtests, and their mean scores on those subtests were still at or above the 80 percent mark—not significantly lower than the mean scores of healthy control subjects. In striking contrast, the patients whose lesions included the pMTG (n = 12) only managed to pass the Possession subtest, and their mean scores plummeted below 50 percent correct for all of the other subtests, indicating profoundly impaired sentence processing abilities. Not surprisingly, many of the patients in this group were Wernicke's aphasics. As for the patients whose lesions included one or more of the other four brain regions (n = 27), they passed both Possession and Simple Declaratives but failed the remaining subtests, indicating moderate to severe disorders. Nevertheless, it is noteworthy that, for the most part, they tended to outperform the pMTG-damaged patients on most of the tasks in the battery.

These results provide powerful evidence that although all five VLSM-defined regions appear to play critical roles in auditory sentence comprehension, the pMTG may be the most important. To investigate this possibility in greater detail, Dronkers et al. (2004) looked at how the six neuroanatomically determined groups of patients performed on the Single Word Comprehension task in the Western Aphasia Battery. On each trial of this task, the patients heard a word and had to point to the best-matching picture in an array. Interestingly, the researchers found that the pMTG-damaged group had significantly worse scores than all of the other groups. This suggests that lesions affecting the pMTG are likely to disrupt the earliest stage of sentence comprehension—i.e., the stage at which the stored semantic and syntactic properties of words are accessed (see also Ogar et al., 2011). We will develop this idea more fully in the second main section of this chapter, which is devoted to discussing the functional contributions that each cortical component of the network might make to the complex process of understanding multi-word utterances.

Turken and Dronkers' (2011) Connectivity Study

The lesion study reported by Dronkers et al. (2004) provides compelling evidence that auditory sentence comprehension depends on the coordinated activity of a widely distributed set of left-lateralized brain regions. As shown above, damage to any of the areas constituting this large-scale circuit can significantly impair a person's ability to extract the meanings of complex sentences. This sensitivity of the entire system to local disturbances suggests that its components normally communicate with each other rapidly and efficiently. To explore this topic in greater depth, Turken and Dronkers (2011) set out to delineate the connectional architecture of the whole network by applying two MRI techniques, one structural and the other functional, to two separate groups of healthy subjects.

The first technique was diffusion tensor imaging (DTI), which reveals the structural organization of white matter in the living brain, thereby allowing long-distance fiber tracts to be traced (see Chapter 1). Using this approach, the investigators were able to discern, or make reasonable inferences about, the pathways that interconnect the five regions isolated by Dronkers et al.'s (2004) VLSM analyses. The second technique was **resting-state functional MRI (rs-fMRI)**, which reveals correlated fluctuations of spontaneous activity across different brain areas over relatively long periods of time, thereby allowing networks of physiologically integrated areas to be identified. Using this approach, the investigators were able to generate, for each of their five regions of interest, a map depicting all of the other areas with which the given region had correlated BOLD signals while the subjects were simply lying in the scanner without performing any tasks.

Together, these two types of connectivity analyses yielded two complementary perspectives, one structural and the other functional, on the architecture of the sentence comprehension network disclosed by Dronkers et al. (2004). The main generalizations are captured in Table 15.2. First of all, for each region of interest, both types of analyses generated similar results, but the patterns of functional connectivity were consistently somewhat richer than the patterns of structural connectivity. While this may seem incongruous, it is not really all that surprising, since functional couplings between different brain areas are sometimes mediated by indirect rather than direct pathways. Second, even though Dronkers et al. (2004) did not find sentence comprehension deficits to be significantly related to lesions in Broca's area (BAs 44 & 45), Turken and Dronkers (2011) discovered that this region is nonetheless strongly interconnected with virtually all the nodes in the network.

Resting-state functional MRI (rs-fMRI) A form of fMRI in which the subjects simply lie quietly in the scanner without performing any tasks, and the researchers measure how the spontaneous fluctuations of the BOLD signals in one brain area correlate with those in certain other areas over a long period of time. This approach can disclose the intrinsic functional networks of the brain.

Table 15.2   Patterns of Structural and Functional Connectivity Among the Regions Identified by Dronkers et al. (2004) as Being Essential for Sentence Comprehension

Region of Interest	Structural Connectivity	Functional Connectivity
pMTG	aSTG	aSTG
	pSTS/BA39	pSTS/BA39
	BA47	BA47
	(Broca's area)	BA46
		(Broca's area)
aSTG	pMTG	pMTG
	pSTS/BA39	pSTS/BA39
	(Broca's area)	BA47
		(Broca's area)
pSTS/BA39	pMTG	pMTG
	(Broca's area)	aSTG
		BA47
		(Broca's area)
BA47	pMTG	pMTG
	(Broca's area)	pSTS/BA39
		(Broca's area)
BA46	—	—

Based on Turken & Dronkers (2011).

Broca's area is in parentheses because it was not actually implicated in Dronkers et al.'s (2004) lesion study, even though other work supports its inclusion in the large-scale network for sentence comprehension.

And this fits with many other studies—some of which are discussed later in this chapter—which suggest that Broca's area does make important contributions to sentence comprehension and hence should be treated as part of the underlying circuit. Third, the various regions clearly have different degrees of interconnectivity with each other. The pMTG stands out prominently as being the most well-connected. The aSTG, pSTS/BA39, and BA47 are less well-connected but still obviously "major players" in the network. As for BA46, significant results did not emerge, but this is most likely because the part of BA46 that the researchers focused on was quite small.

What do these patterns of structural and functional connectivity actually look like in the brain? As an illustration, Figure 15.4 shows the results for the most

densely interconnected area—the pMTG. The connectivity profiles of the entire region are portrayed in the left panel of the figure. Let's begin with the white matter pathways depicted on the bottom. Scrutinizing all of these intertwined fiber tracts may bring to mind the bewildering spaghetti junctions of highway on- and off-ramps that motorists must navigate when they drive through large American cities like Atlanta (Figure 15.5). Anxious readers should take heart, however, for these anatomical complexities are not really as daunting as they initially appear to be. The key point is that, according to this analysis, the pMTG is structurally interconnected with the other components of the sentence comprehension network via five white matter pathways: the **middle longitudinal fasciculus** (green) links the pMTG with the aSTG; the **inferior occipito-frontal fasciculus** (purple) links the pMTG with BA47; the **long segment of the arcuate fasciculus** (dark blue) links the pMTG with Broca's area; the **short segment of the arcuate fasciculus** (light blue) links the pMTG with the pSTS/BA39; and the **tapetum** (white) links the pMTG in the left hemisphere with its twin in the right hemisphere.

Still focusing on the entirety of the pMTG, let's consider next the functional connectivity results, which are shown in the middle of the left panel in Figure 15.4. When the investigators searched for cortical areas in which the spontaneous fluctuations of resting-state activity correlated strongly with those in the pMTG, they found significant effects in all of the regions mentioned above, as well as in several others, including BA46.

The extensive, and mostly convergent, structural and functional connectivity profiles that emerged for the pMTG dovetail with other data indicating that this region is among the most highly connected cortical "hubs" in the human brain (Buckner et al., 2009). Borrowing a vivid term from Mesulam (1990, 1998), Turken and Dronkers (2011) suggest that this region may even constitute a "neural epicenter"—i.e., a region that makes key contributions to several broadly

Middle longitudinal fasciculus   A fiber tract that interconnects the pMTG and aSTG.

Inferior occipito-frontal fasciculus   A fiber tract that interconnects the pMTG and BA47.

Long segment of the arcuate fasciculus   A fiber tract that interconnects the pMTG and Broca's area.

Short segment of the arcuate fasciculus   A fiber tract that interconnects the pMTG and the pSTS/BA39.

Tapetum   A fiber tract that interconnects the pMTG in the left hemisphere with its twin in the right hemisphere.

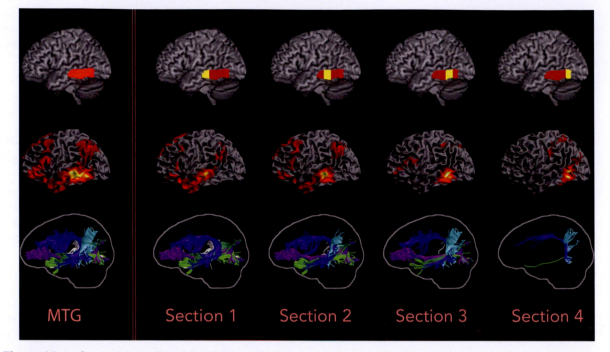

Figure 15.4 Connectivity profiles of the pMTG, divided into four parts of equal length along its anterior–posterior extent. (Left panel) The entire region of interest is shown on top, highlighted in red. The overall functional connectivity profile of this region is shown in the middle, with yellow voxels (within the region itself) indicating the highest correlated activity and red voxels indicating lower but still significantly correlated activity. The overall structural connectivity profile is shown on the bottom and is derived from one subject chosen as an exemplar. Green = middle longitudinal fasciculus; purple = inferior occipito-frontal fasciculus; dark blue = long segment of the arcuate fasciculus; light blue = short segment of the arcuate fasciculus; white = tapetum. (Right panel) The top row shows four sections of the pMTG, highlighted in yellow. The middle row shows the functional connectivity profiles of the sections demarcated in the top row. The bottom row shows the structural connectivity profiles of the sections demarcated in the top row. (From Turken & Dronkers, 2011, p. 12.)

Figure 15.5 Spaghetti junction in Atlanta, Georgia (produced by the U.S. Geological Survey).

distributed neurocognitive capacities. With specific regard to sentence comprehension, the discovery that the pMTG normally interacts with all of the other areas in the network described by Dronkers et al. (2004)—as well as with Broca's area—is especially valuable because it helps explain why damage to this region usually has such devastating effects.

The images shown in the right panel of Figure 15.4 are refinements of those shown in the left panel, for they indicate how the structural and functional connectivity profiles of the pMTG progressively change as one moves along the anterior–posterior axis of the area. It is apparent from these findings that the anterior half of the pMTG has richer structural and functional connections than the posterior half. And a close inspection of the images reveals that the connectivity profiles of the second subdivision (among the four shown) seem to be the most intricate, implying that a lesion affecting this particular sector would probably have the most deleterious consequences for sentence comprehension.

Now, having examined much of the connectional architecture of the large-scale network for sentence comprehension, it's time to step back from the details and ponder their broader ramifications. The most significant point is that, as Turken and Dronkers (2011, p. 11) put it, "a complex process such as understanding spoken sentences is not mediated by a single region or pathway alone, but requires the integrated functioning of a widely distributed constellation of regions interacting via multiple routes. . . ." For example, the results of both the lesion study and the connectivity study suggest that the pMTG plays an especially important role in auditory sentence comprehension, but the findings of both studies also indicate that this region does not operate alone; instead, it operates in conjunction with many other regions, each of which performs unique functions, so that the ultimate goal of extracting the meanings of multi-word utterances ends up being achieved by synergies among the various nodes of the whole network. In the second main section of this chapter, we will discuss in depth the possible functions of each component of the network. Here, however, the central message is pitched at the level of the entire system, and it is simply this: The ability to understand sentences is subserved by numerous cortical regions tied together by numerous white matter pathways. This complex circuit spans three major lobes of the left hemisphere—temporal, parietal, and frontal—and the long-distance fiber tracts that undergird it constitute what Turken and Dronkers (2011, p. 16) call the "structural backbone" of language comprehension.

Convergent Results from Other Studies

So far we have been exploring the anatomical organization of the sentence comprehension network entirely from the point of view of the parallel lesion and connectivity studies conducted by Dronkers et al. (2004) and Turken and Dronkers (2011). It is essential to realize, however, that these two studies are by no means the only ones that point to the kind of neurocognitive system described above. On the contrary, during the past few decades a growing number of other studies have yielded similar results, with one of the only major differences being that—in contrast to Dronkers et al.'s (2004) lesion study, but in accord with Turken and Dronkers's (2011) connectivity study—many of these investigations suggest that Broca's area is an important part of the network, together with the five regions shown in Figure 15.2. To get a rough sense of what this larger literature is like, we will first look at a meta-analysis of 36 PET and fMRI studies of receptive sentence processing, and then we will briefly discuss a particularly interesting fMRI study that focused on the neural correlates of constituent structure.

To characterize the distribution and clustering of activation peaks evoked during sentence comprehension,

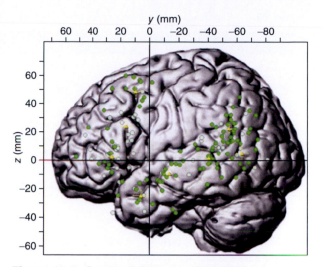

Figure 15.6   Results of Vigneau et al.'s (2006) meta-analysis of 36 PET and fMRI studies of sentence comprehension. Circles represent activation peaks (n = 161). Dark green circles derive from studies that investigated sentence comprehension in general, whereas light green circles derive from studies that attempted to isolate syntactic processing. Yellow triangles and lines indicate the centers and standard errors of clusters of peaks determined by an algorithm for spatial classification. (From Vigneau et al., 2006, p. 1421.)

Vigneau et al. (2006) conducted a meta-analysis of 36 PET and fMRI studies published between 1992 and 2004. These studies used a wide range of tasks to explore the neural substrates of sentence comprehension, including the following: processing sentences vs. word lists; processing sentences with high vs. low syntactic complexity; processing sentences with high vs. low semantic imageability; making plausibility judgments about sentences; and making emotional judgments about sentences. Collectively, the 36 studies reported a total of 65 contrasts between experimental conditions, resulting in 102 activation peaks in the left temporal lobe and 59 activation peaks in the left frontal lobe. All of these peaks are shown in Figure 15.6, with dark green circles representing peaks derived from studies that investigated sentence comprehension in general, light green circles representing peaks derived from studies that attempted to isolate syntactic processing, and yellow triangles representing the "centers of gravity" of major clusters of peaks, as computed by a special algorithm for spatial classification.

If one compares Figure 15.6 with Figure 15.2, one can easily see that there's a fair degree of consistency between, on the one hand, the set of areas that, according to functional neuroimaging studies, tend to be *engaged* during sentence comprehension, and on the other hand, the set of areas that, according to

Table 15.3 Experimental Conditions in Pallier et al.'s (2011) fMRI Study of Constituent Structure

Condition	Constituent Size	Example
c12	12 words	I believe that you should accept the proposal of your new associate
c06	6 words	The mouse that eats our cheese two clients examine this nice couch
c04	4 words	Mayor of the city he hates this color they read their names
c03	3 words	Solving a problem repair the ceiling he keeps reading will buy some
c02	2 words	Looking ahead important task who dies his dog few holes they write
c01	1 word	Thing very tree where of watching copy tensed they states heart plus

Source: Pallier et al. (2011, p. 2523).

lesion–deficit analyses, tend to be *necessary* for sentence comprehension. In fact, as indicated by the yellow triangles in Figure 15.6, Vigneau et al.'s (2006) meta-analysis revealed several clusters of peaks that appear to be centered in, or very near, some of the key regions identified by Dronkers et al. (2004). In particular, there are two clusters in the pMTG, two near the aSTG, one near the pSTS/BA39, and one near BA47, centered at the boundary between this area and BA45. It is also noteworthy that the meta-analysis revealed two additional clusters in regions beyond those identified by Dronkers et al. (2004): one in the vicinity of the lateral premotor cortex, centered at the boundary between the posterior middle frontal gyrus and the precentral gyrus; and another in the superior part of Broca's area, centered at the boundary between BA44 and BA45. The latter cluster is especially interesting because most of the peaks composing it seem to be associated primarily with the syntactic aspects of sentence processing (symbolized by light green circles). We will return to this topic later on, when we discuss the possible contributions of Broca's area to sentence comprehension.

More recently, Pallier et al. (2011) conducted a very clever fMRI experiment that was designed to determine which brain regions are sensitive to the size of linguistic constituents during receptive sentence processing. Previous electrophysiological studies with macaque monkeys had shown that when the animals were presented with certain learned sequences of stimuli, different neurons not only increased but sustained their firing rates at different times, suggesting that "cumulative codes" were being created. Inspired by those findings, Pallier et al. (2011) proposed that increasingly complex cell assemblies might be needed to represent increasingly complex linguistic constituents. For example, a phrase consisting of three elements, like *Mary's father's car*, might require a larger cell assembly than a phrase consisting of only two elements, like *Mary's car*,

and these neural differences might be discernible in the BOLD signals measured by fMRI.

To test their hypothesis, the researchers presented French-speaking subjects with word sequences that always contained 12 items, but that varied parametrically with respect to the size of the linguistic constituents that could be constructed (Table 15.3). Thus, in condition "c01" the words could not be combined into larger units of any size (e.g., *thing very tree where of watching copy tensed they states heart plus*); in condition "c02" the words could be combined into constituents of size 2 (e.g., *looking ahead important task who dies his dog few holes they write*); in condition "c03" the words could be combined into constituents of size 3 (e.g., *solving a problem repair the ceiling he keeps reading will buy some*); and so on. Note that although the examples given here and in Table 15.3 are in English, the actual stimuli were in French.

Based on the electrophysiological data described above, the researchers assumed that if certain brain regions are sensitive to constituent structure, neural activity in those regions should increase by a fixed amount every time a new item is incorporated into a preceding constituent, and should return to baseline whenever a new item cannot be incorporated into a preceding constituent. As shown in Figure 15.7A, these assumptions predict that the BOLD responses to linguistic sequences should increase systematically as a function of constituent size. And remarkably enough, when the researchers looked for such effects in their imaging data, they found them in virtually all the areas identified by Dronkers et al. (2004). These results are portrayed in Figure 15.7B. Specifically, significant constituent size effects were detected in several left temporal areas extending from the pole to the pSTS/BA39, as well as in BAs 47 and 45. In short, these findings suggest that almost the entire network for sentence comprehension, including

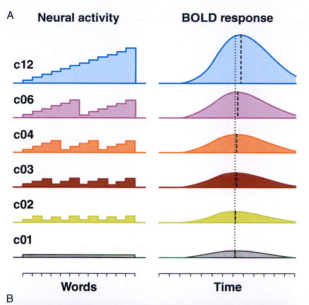

A

Neural activity   **BOLD response**

c12

c06

c04

c03

c02

c01

Words   **Time**

B

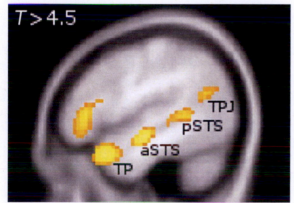

$T > 4.5$

TPJ

pSTS

aSTS

TP

Figure 15.7 Theory and data from Pallier et al.'s (2011) fMRI study of constituent structure. (A) A model assumes that in brain regions that are sensitive to the size of syntactic constituents, neural activity as indexed by the blood oxygen-level dependent (BOLD) response increases by one unit each time a new word is incorporated into a phrase. (B) Precisely such results were observed in a network of left-lateralized cortical areas. (From Pallier et al., 2011, pp. 2523–2524.)

part of Broca's area, is typically recruited during the computation of phrasal and clausal organization. Presumably, this multi-regional recruitment takes place in a coordinated fashion, with different cortical components contributing to the analysis and retention of constituent structure in somewhat different ways, as discussed further below (see also other aspects of the study by Pallier et al., 2011).

Summary

Sentence comprehension involves many different kinds of computational operations and processing resources,

and recent research has shown that they are not subserved by a single "center" in the brain, but instead depend on a large-scale network of anatomically distributed yet highly interactive cortical areas, primarily in the left hemisphere. In a frequently cited neuropsychological study, Dronkers et al. (2004) identified five major components of this network: the pMTG; the aSTG; the pSTS/BA39; most of BA47; and part of BA46. Then in a follow-up connectivity study, Turken and Dronkers (2011) demonstrated that most of these regions, together with Broca's area, are not only tied together structurally by means of long-distance fiber tracts, but are also functionally linked by means of closely correlated resting-state physiological activity. A number of other investigations have generated convergent results regarding the cortical components of the sentence comprehension network, with many of them supporting the inclusion of Broca's area.

A Large-Scale Neural Network for Sentence Comprehension: Functional Considerations

In the previous section we maintained, for the most part, a bird's-eye view of the complex neural circuit that underlies auditory sentence processing. In this section we will zoom in on each individual component of the network and consider some of the specific ways in which it might contribute to sentence comprehension. Before delving into the details, however, let's take a quick look at some of the key ideas.

- Beginning with the pMTG, as mentioned above, Dronkers et al. (2004) suggest that it may be essential for retrieving both the semantic and syntactic features of auditorily perceived words—features that are obviously of direct relevance to receptive sentence processing. In connection with this proposal, it is useful to recall that, according to Hickok and Poeppel's (2000, 2004, 2007) Dual Stream Model of speech perception, the pMTG implements a "lexical interface" that serves as a kind of relay station which takes as input the phonological forms of words and yields as output pointers to their meanings and grammatical properties (see Chapter 5). The first subsection below summarizes several studies that support and expand on these views, thereby bolstering the more general hypothesis that the pMTG is critically involved in the earliest stage of sentence comprehension.

- Turning next to the aSTG, Dronkers et al. (2004) propose that it plays a central role in grouping words into hierarchically organized phrases and clauses, based largely on the information retrieved by the pMTG. As described in the second subsection below, this notion is consistent with a number of recent investigations, and it also relates to the claim of the Dual Stream Model that the immediately inferior region—namely, the anterior lateral temporal cortex—houses a "combinatorial network" that integrates the syntactic and semantic aspects of sentences to yield composite message-level representations (see Chapter 5). We will see, however, that even though these ideas have received substantial support, they cannot easily accommodate certain neuropsychological findings which suggest that the relevant brain regions may not be absolutely necessary for sentence comprehension.

- With regard to the pSTS/BA39, Dronkers et al. (2004) argue that it retains the phonological forms of words in auditory–verbal short-term memory (STM), especially when long and/or complex sentences must be matched with appropriate pictures. This account fits nicely with the characterization of the "phonological loop" in the Dual Stream Model (see Chapter 5), and, as indicated in the third subsection below, it has been supported by several recent studies. However, a number of other studies suggest that sentence processing may not really require that the phonological forms of words be kept active. And there is also growing evidence that, to some extent independent of auditory–verbal short-term memory, the pSTS/BA39 may directly implement some of the syntactic–semantic mapping operations that determine "who's doing what to whom" in sentences, particularly when (1) both the actor and the undergoer are animate, so that the described action is "semantically reversible," and (2) the word order is noncanonical, as in passive sentences and object-relative clauses.

- Finally, Dronkers et al. (2004) propose that the two prefrontal areas that they identified—namely, BAs 47 and 46—may facilitate sentence comprehension by providing what we referred to earlier as top-down cognitive control. This is certainly a reasonable idea; however, as already mentioned, a neighboring prefrontal region—namely, Broca's area—has also been associated with sentence comprehension in a variety of studies, and there is a great deal of controversy regarding its precise contributions. The fourth subsection below elaborates and evaluates two different families of approaches—those that emphasize certain types of sequential and hierarchical processing, and those that emphasize other sorts of mental resources, such as auditory–verbal STM and cognitive control.

Now, having previewed the main ideas regarding the functional architecture of the sentence comprehension network, we are ready to explore them in depth. Before doing so, however, I must make the following important qualification—one that I already alluded to in the points just mentioned, but that deserves to made explicit here. Virtually all of these ideas have only just begun to be developed theoretically and tested experimentally, and hence none of them should be treated as an established fact. On the contrary, they should be treated as educated guesses—or, more formally, well-motivated hypotheses—that are useful for guiding further research and that may or may not turn out, in the fullness of time, to be on the right track. With that caveat in mind, let's proceed.

Possible Contributions of the pMTG

A number of researchers, including Dronkers et al. (2004), have suggested that the pMTG might play a pivotal role in what is effectively the earliest stage of auditory sentence processing, this being the stage at which the stored semantic and syntactic properties of incoming words are retrieved from the mental lexicon. In Chapter 5 we observed that, according to Hickok and Poeppel's (2000, 2004, 2007) Dual Stream Model of speech perception, after the phonological forms of spoken words have been recognized in the pSTG/pSTS, further processing splits into two separate channels. One of them is the ventral stream, which is devoted to figuring out what the perceived utterances mean; and the other is the dorsal stream, which is devoted to figuring out how those utterances could be reproduced (see Figure 5.1 in Chapter 5). For present purposes, what matters most is that the first stop along the ventral pathway is the "lexical interface," which is implemented in part by the pMTG, and which operates as an intermediary device that matches the phonological codes of perceived words with the corresponding semantic and syntactic structures. For example, if you heard someone say *The cat sat on the mat,* the lexical interface in the pMTG would receive as input the fully analyzed sound structures of all the words, and would generate as output pointers to their meanings as well as their inherent grammatical specifications (i.e., their specifications for category, transitivity, etc.). Might this process of mapping phonological representations onto semantic and syntactic ones be accomplished by lemma-like units that perform the reverse transformation during speech production (see Chapter 6)? Perhaps, but this remains a rather speculative proposal. Turning to a less theoretical question, what do we know about the neural substrates of the semantic and syntactic representations that the lexical interface calls up? As we saw in Chapters 10 and 11, there is mounting evidence that the multifarious semantic features expressed by words like *cat, sat,* and *mat* rely on complex webs of modality-specific cortical areas (including but extending well beyond the pMTG), and that the anterior temporal lobes serve as "hubs" that integrate and systematize those features. Much less is known, however, about the localization of the syntactic properties of words. Still, several studies suggest that they depend, at least to some degree, on the same general region that implements the lexical interface—the pMTG. A few of these studies are summarized below.

Snijders et al.'s (2009) Investigation

In a study reported by Snijders et al. (2009), the critical stimuli involved Dutch noun-verb homonyms, a good example being *bewijzen,* which functions equally often as a noun meaning "proof/evidence" and as a verb meaning "prove/provide evidence." The researchers assumed that when words like this are encountered, they trigger the activation of two different syntactic frames, one noun-based and the other verb-based (Figure 15.8); however, when words that function exclusively as either nouns or verbs are encountered, they trigger the activation of just one syntactic frame. Now, if these assumptions are correct, they have interesting implications with regard to the neural substrates of the grammatical properties of words. Specifically, whatever those neural substrates are, they should be engaged significantly more during the perception of category-ambiguous than category-unambiguous words, because the former have a larger number of associated syntactic frames than the latter.

Snijders et al. (2009) suspected that the pMTG might display precisely this type of response pattern, and to test their prediction they conducted an fMRI experiment that had a total of eight conditions, all of which are illustrated in Table 15.4. In the first four conditions, the subjects were presented with semantically coherent, grammatically well-formed sentences. Conditions 1 and 2 were identical except for the following manipulation: In condition 1 the sentences contained category-ambiguous words like *bewijzen* that were resolved as nouns, whereas in condition 2 those items were replaced with category-unambiguous words that functioned exclusively as nouns. Similarly, conditions 3 and 4 were identical except for the following manipulation: In condition 3 the sentences contained category-ambiguous words like *bewijzen* that were resolved as verbs, whereas in condition 4 those

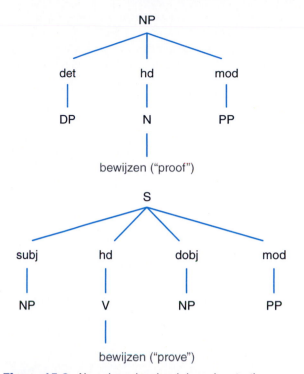

Figure 15.8 Noun-based and verb-based syntactic frames associated with the category-ambiguous Dutch word *bewijzen.* (Based on Snijders et al., 2009, p. 1494.)

items were replaced with category-unambiguous words that functioned exclusively as verbs. In the last four conditions, the subjects were presented with scrambled sequences of words. Conditions 5 and 6 were identical except for the following manipulation: In condition 5 the sequences contained category-ambiguous words like *bewijzen* that were never resolved, whereas in condition 6 those items were replaced with category-unambiguous words that functioned exclusively as nouns. Similarly, conditions 7 and 8 were identical except for the following manipulation: In condition 7 the sequences contained category-ambiguous words like *bewijzen* that were never resolved, whereas in condition 8 those items were replaced with category-unambiguous words that functioned exclusively as verbs.

Three other aspects of the experimental design are worth noting before turning to the most relevant results. First, the stimuli were carefully distributed over four lists that were given to different subjects, so that no subject encountered the same critical word more than once. Second, each list contained a sizeable number of "filler" sentences and scrambled word sequences that were intended to prevent the subjects from detecting the key variables. And third, to ensure that the subjects paid close attention to all the stimuli, they were

Table 15.4 Experimental Conditions in Snijders et al.'s (2009) fMRI Study of Word-Category Ambiguity

1. SAn: Sentence Ambiguous (Noun Context)

Zodra jullie bewijzen$_{(n/v)}$ leveren kunnen we beginnen

As-soon-as you evidence$_{(n/v)}$ provide can we start

(As soon as you provide evidence$_{(n/v)}$ we can start)

2. SUn: Sentence Unambiguous (Noun Context)

Zodra jullie kopij$_{(n)}$ leveren kunnen we beginnen

As-soon-as you copy$_{(n)}$ provide can we start

(As soon as you provide copy$_{(n)}$ we can start)

3. SAv: Sentence Ambiguous (Verb Context)

Zodra jullie bewijzen$_{(n/v)}$ dat hij erbij betrokken is arresteren we hem

As-soon-as you prove$_{(n/v)}$ that he in-it involved is arrest we him

(As soon as you prove$_{(n/v)}$ that he is involved we will arrest him)

4. SUv: Sentence Unambiguous (Verb Context)

Zodra jullie beweren$_{(v)}$ dat hij erbij betrokken is arresteren we hem

As-soon-as you claim$_{(v)}$ that he in-it involved is arrest we him

(As soon as you claim$_{(v)}$ that he is involved we will arrest him)

5. WAn: Words Ambiguous (Derived from SAn)

Genoemd tegen bewijzen$_{(n/v)}$ uit helaas gezeten jullie

Named against proof/prove$_{(n/v)}$ from alas seated you

6. WUn: Words Unambiguous (Derived from SUn)

Genoemd tegen kopij$_{(n)}$ uit helaas gezeten jullie

Named against copy$_{(n)}$ from alas seated you

7. WAv: Words Ambiguous (Derived from SAv)

In nogal bewijzen$_{(n/v)}$ meestal maar dit in struikelen hem verschil opeens

In quite proof/prove$_{(n/v)}$ mostly but this in stumble him difference suddenly

8. WUv: Words Unambiguous (Derived from SUv)

In nogal beweren$_{(v)}$ meestal maar dit in struikelen hem verschil opeens

In quite claim$_{(v)}$ mostly but this in stumble him difference suddenly

Source: Snijders et al. (2009, p. 1495).

instructed to spot consonant strings (e.g., *cdsnl*) that were placed at random positions in the filler sentences.

The investigators expected that in the sentence conditions as well as the scrambled sequence conditions, the category-ambiguous words would impose a larger load on the mental lexicon than the category-unambiguous words, since the former items trigger the activation of two syntactic frames whereas the latter items trigger the activation of only one. Moreover, the investigators expected that this cognitive distinction would be reflected by the BOLD signals evoked in the pMTG, since they hypothesized that this region subserves not only the stimulus-driven retrieval but also the long-term storage of the grammatical properties of words. All of these predictions were confirmed, as shown in Figure 15.9.

At the most general level of analysis, when all of the ambiguous conditions (i.e., conditions 1, 3, 5, & 7) were compared with all of the unambiguous conditions (i.e., conditions 2, 4, 6, & 8), the only region in the left hemisphere that exhibited a robust response was the pMTG (Figure 15.9A). Interestingly, further analyses revealed that this effect of ambiguity was larger for the sentence conditions (i.e., conditions 1 & 3 vs. 2 & 4) than for the scrambled sequence conditions (i.e., conditions 5 & 7 vs. 6 & 8) (Figure 15.9B). According to Snijders et al. (2009, p. 1500), this difference may have arisen because sentence processing requires the sustained activation of lexically associated syntactic frames: "During sentence comprehension, the lexical information has to be available for longer time intervals than during the processing of random word sequences."

In connection with this idea, it is also notable that for the sentence conditions but not the scrambled sequence conditions, the ambiguity effect was manifested not only in the pMTG but also in the posterior part of Broca's area at the boundary between BA44 and the precentral gyrus (Figure 15.9C). This suggests that the resolution of syntactic ambiguities during online sentence processing requires dynamic interplay between these temporal and frontal regions, perhaps mediated by the arcuate fasciculus. As Snijders et al. (2009) point out, it is reasonable to suppose that competing syntactic frames are represented by the pMTG, and that selection of the contextually appropriate one is executed by the inferior frontal cortex.

Tyler et al.'s (2011) and Papoutsi et al.'s (2011) Investigations

Further support for this notion comes from some closely related studies by Tyler et al. (2011) and Papoutsi et al. (2011). In these studies the expressions of interest were ambiguous phrases like *bullying teenagers*. This particular example is preferentially interpreted as meaning that the teenagers are the ones doing the bullying, as in *The newspaper reported that bullying teenagers are a problem for the local school*, but it can also mean that the teenagers are the ones being bullied, as in *The newspaper reported that bullying teenagers is bad for their self-esteem*. In each case, the correct interpretation is signaled by the grammatical number, singular or plural, of the verb that immediately follows the phrase, and when that syntactic cue indicates that the correct interpretation is not the preferred one but rather the alternative one, listeners must rapidly revise their analysis of the expression. The purpose of the experimental investigations was to explore the neural substrates of these syntactic processes by combining the methods of fMRI, DTI, and lesion analysis.

First of all, the researchers conducted an fMRI experiment in which a group of healthy subjects heard 42 sentences containing ambiguous phrases like *bullying teenagers*. In the "dominant" condition the phrases were followed by verbs that supported the preferred interpretation, and in the "subordinate" condition they were followed by verbs that supported the dispreferred interpretation. (Note that the researchers determined which interpretations were dominant/preferred and subordinate/dispreferred in a separate rating study.) The subjects also heard 42 sentences containing structurally similar but unambiguous phrases (e.g., *The teacher knew that rehearsing plays is necessary for a good performance*) as well as 126 "filler" sentences that were deliberately designed to have different syntactic structures so as to prevent the subjects from noticing the key manipulations. Even though the subjects simply listened to the randomly presented stimuli without making any overt responses, when the researchers contrasted the brain activity elicited by the relatively challenging "subordinate" condition against the brain activity elicited by the relatively straightforward "dominant" condition, they found significantly stronger activity in the pMTG as well as in the inferior frontal gyrus, specifically BAs 45 and 47 (Figure 15.10A). Moreover, when they used a sophisticated technique to decipher the psychophysical interactions between these regions, they discovered that the direction of influence was primarily "top-down" from the frontal region to the temporal one.

These results are remarkably similar to those reported by Snijders et al. (2009), and they suggest that the dynamic interplay between the middle temporal and inferior frontal components of the sentence comprehension network may underlie our capacity to recognize, and quickly recover from, misinterpreted

A

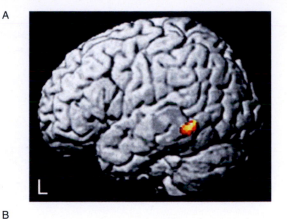

B

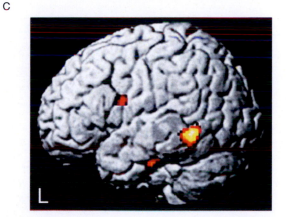

Figure 15.9 Results from Snijders et al.'s (2009) fMRI study of word-category ambiguity. (A) Greater activation was found in the pMTG for all of the ambiguous conditions than for all of the unambiguous conditions. (B) The ambiguity effect in the pMTG was larger for sentences than word lists. (C) The greater ambiguity effect for sentences than word lists was observed not only in the pMTG, but also in the posterior part of Broca's area at the boundary between BA44 and the precentral gyrus. (From Snijders et al., 2009, p. 1495.)

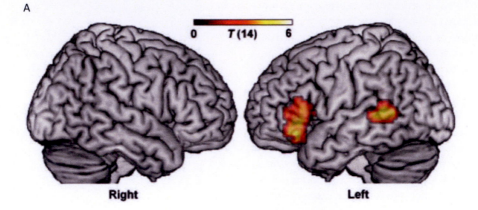

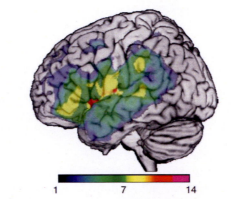

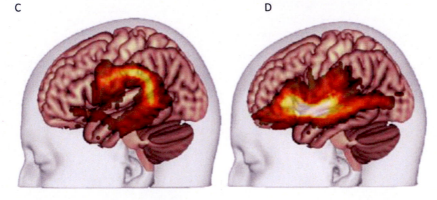

Figure 15.10   Results from Tyler et al.'s (2011) and Papoutsi et al.'s (2011) investigations of sentence processing. (A) Greater activation was found in the left pMTG and the inferior frontal gyrus for sentences with dispreferred ("subordinate") than preferred ("dominant") interpretations of structurally ambiguous phrases. (B) The lesion sites of 14 stroke patients were widely distributed across the left perisylvian territory, with only a moderate amount of overlap. (C) The arcuate fasciculus. (D) The extreme capsule. (From Tyler et al., 2011, p. 424, and Papoutsi et al., 2011, pp. 657, 661.)

phrasal ambiguities. For instance, it is conceivable that when an expression like *bullying teenagers* is first encountered, the pMTG rapidly retrieves two competing syntactic representations, but assigns greater weight to the one that is consistent with the "dominant" interpretation—i.e., the interpretation that treats the teenagers as the agents rather than the recipients of the bullying. If, however, the subsequent words in the utterance turn out to be incompatible with that analysis, the inferior frontal cortex may intervene to suppress the initially favored analysis and select instead the alternative one.

To explore this topic further, the researchers conducted several more experiments, only this time with 14 stroke patients whose lesions were widely distributed across the left perisylvian territory (Figure 15.10B). (Note that only a few of these experiments are summarized here.) Behaviorally, the patients varied greatly in their sensitivity to the kind of syntactic ambiguity described above. This was determined by administering a task in which, on each trial, they first heard a sentence fragment that ended with a phrase like *bullying teenagers*, and then had to decide whether a particular verb was an acceptable or unacceptable continuation of the sentence. All of the verbs were in fact possible continuations, but some of them supported the preferred interpretation, whereas others supported the dispreferred one. As a group, the patients frequently judged the unexpected verbs as being unacceptable, and in this respect their performance resembled that of healthy control subjects. However, unlike the control subjects, some of the patients also judged a substantial number of the expected verbs as being unacceptable. These error patterns therefore exposed deficits in their ability to parse the syntactic structures of ambiguous phrases, even when the default interpretations were the correct ones.

Importantly, the researchers were able to capitalize on the variability in the patients' behavioral scores by looking for correlations with the variability in their lesion sites. Through a complex series of procedures, they discovered that, indeed, as the behavioral scores decreased, the amount of damage at the following sites increased: first, the gray matter in both of the regions identified by the fMRI study, specifically the pMTG and BA47/45; and second, the white matter in two of the fiber tracts that interconnect those regions, specifically the arcuate fasciculus and **extreme capsule**, the latter running adjacent to the inferior occipito-frontal fasciculus (Figure 15.10C, D; Makris & Pandya, 2009; Rolheiser et al., 2011; Griffiths et al., 2013). Together with the fMRI results described above, these findings help illuminate the interactive nature of the large-scale neural network for sentence comprehension. In particular, they suggest that successful syntactic processing depends not just on the co-activation of the middle temporal and inferior frontal components of the network, but also on their functional coupling, which is mediated by the white matter pathways that allow them to communicate with each other.

Extreme capsule   A fiber tract that interconnects the pMTG and BA47.

Summary

In accord with the notion of a lexical interface posited by the Dual Stream Model of speech perception, there is growing support for the hypothesis that during auditory sentence processing the pMTG operates like a relay station that takes as input the phonological forms of words and produces as output pointers to the corresponding semantic and syntactic codes. But while the semantic properties of words most likely depend on widely distributed brain regions, the syntactic properties of words may be stored, at least to some extent, directly within the pMTG. In addition, these grammatical specifications may interact closely with higher-order cognitive mechanisms in the inferior frontal cortex, especially in situations involving syntactic ambiguity. The studies by Snijders et al. (2009) and by Tyler et al. (2011) and Papoutsi et al. (2011) are clearly consistent with this general approach, as are several other investigations (e.g., Keller et al., 2001; January et al., 2009; Rodd et al., 2010; Tyler et al., 2013a).

At the same time, however, it must be acknowledged, if only in passing, that the pMTG may contribute to sentence comprehension in other ways too. Most notably, some researchers suspect that this region directly represents not only syntactic but also semantic information. As indicated in Chapters 10 and 11, even though the multifarious semantic features of object nouns and action verbs seem to be scattered across a broad range of cortical areas, the pMTG appears to be one of the major substrates. Further support for this view comes from a meta-analysis of 120 functional neuroimaging studies which found that the pMTG is a critical component of the semantic system of the human brain (Binder et al., 2009). And additional leverage comes from several other studies that have employed diverse methods (e.g., Hart & Gordon, 1990; Wei et al., 2012; Hoffman et al., 2012b; Visser et al., 2012; Fairhall & Caramazza, 2013). All of these considerations fit nicely with the notion that, as discussed earlier, the pMTG is a massively interconnected "neural epicenter" that probably performs many different kinds of operations. As a consequence of such complexity, however, it is safe to say that much more work will be needed to determine the precise roles that the pMTG plays in sentence comprehension.

Possible Contributions of the aSTG and Some Adjacent Regions

Numerous functional neuroimaging studies have shown that when sentences are compared with various

Table 15.5 Experimental Conditions in Obleser et al.'s (2011) fMRI Study of Syntactic Complexity

A. Low Complexity
Heute hat der Opa dem Jungen den Lutscher geschenkt
Today has the grandfather$_{NOM}$ the boy$_{DAT}$ the lollipop$_{ACC}$ given
(Today the grandfather gave the lollipop to the boy)

B. Middle Complexity
Heute hat dem Jungen der Opa den Lutscher geschenkt
Today has the boy$_{DAT}$ the grandfather$_{NOM}$ the lollipop$_{ACC}$ given
(Today the grandfather gave the lollipop to the boy)

C. High Complexity
Heute hat dem Jungen den Lutscher der Opa geschenkt
Today has the boy$_{DAT}$ the lollipop$_{ACC}$ the grandfather$_{NOM}$ given
(Today the grandfather gave the lollipop to the boy)

Based on Obleser et al. (2011) and Friederici et al. (2006b).

baseline conditions, there is significant activation in the aSTG as well as in several adjacent regions—specifically, the anterior superior temporal sulcus (aSTS), the anterior middle temporal gyrus (aMTG), and neighboring parts of the temporal pole (BA38) (e.g., Mazoyer et al., 1993; Tzourio et al., 1998; Stowe et al., 1999; Vandenberghe et al., 2002; Humphries et al., 2001, 2005, 2006; see also the MEG studies by Bemis & Pylkkänen, 2011, 2013). When sentences are presented auditorily, some of the activation in the aSTG may reflect prosodic processing (e.g., Humphries et al., 2001; see Chapter 7). But the fact that the aSTG also responds strongly to visually presented sentences suggests that it contributes to other aspects of comprehension too.

In reviewing the literature on this topic, we will focus on two main hypotheses. First, several researchers, including Dronkers et al. (2004), have proposed that the aSTG plays an important role in analyzing the syntactic structures of sentences; for example, it may facilitate the grouping of words into hierarchically organized phrases and clauses, based in part on the lexically encoded grammatical specifications that, as indicated above, may reside in the pMTG. Second, according to Hickok and Poeppel's (2000, 2004, 2007) Dual Stream Model of speech perception, the region immediately inferior to the aSTG—namely, the aSTS and aMTG—implements a "combinatorial network" that is critically involved in constructing the integrated,

composite meanings of multi-word utterances, taking into account both syntactic and semantic information (see Figure 5.13 and the associated text in Chapter 5). The following discussion considers the evidence for each of these ideas in turn.

Syntactic Analysis

The notion that the aSTG contributes to the basic syntactic analysis of sentences has been supported by a number of fMRI studies. In one line of investigation, several studies have shown that the degree to which the aSTG is engaged correlates positively with the degree to which the perceived utterances are syntactically complex (Obleser et al., 2011; Brennan et al., 2012; but see Stowe, 2005, for counter-arguments).

For instance, in an experiment reported by Obleser et al. (2011), the key stimuli consisted of 48 triplets of auditorily presented German sentences. As shown in Table 15.5, the three sentences constituting each triplet used the very same words to describe a "transfer" event in which one person, marked by nominative case, caused another person, marked by dative case, to receive an object, marked by accusative case. The sentences differed, however, in the conventionality, and hence also in the complexity, of the syntactic arrangement of the words. At the lowest level of complexity (A), the sequence of case-marked NPs was *nominative > dative > accusative;* at the middle level (B), it was *dative > nominative > accusative;* and at the highest level (C), it was *dative > accusative > nominative* (for evidence that these sequences do in fact differ in complexity, see Friederici et al., 2006b). The stimuli were distributed over multiple lists that were given to different subjects, so that each subject heard only one sentence from each triplet, mixed together with a variety of experimentally irrelevant "filler" sentences. In addition, to ensure that the subjects listened carefully to all of the items, the researchers included a few randomly placed trials in which a sentence was suddenly presented visually, and the task was to indicate with a button-press whether it was identical to the sentence that had just been presented auditorily.

The imaging results are presented in Figure 15.11, and they clearly show that as the syntactic complexity of the sentences increased, so did the amount of activation near the boundary between the aSTG and BA38. Similar complexity effects were also observed in two other regions—specifically, BA44 and the pSTS—but we will refrain from discussing those findings until later. For present purposes, the main point is that Obleser et al.'s (2011) study gives some teeth to the

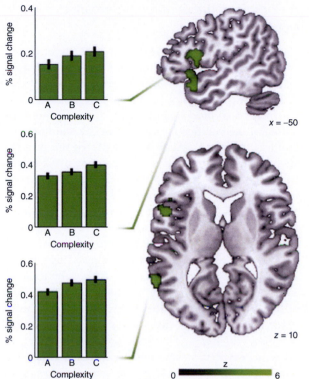

Figure 15.11 Results of Obleser et al.'s (2011) fMRI study of syntactic complexity. Significant effects are shown for BA44 (top bar chart), the aSTG (middle bar chart), and the pSTS (bottom bar chart). (From Obleser et al., 2011, p. 2313.)

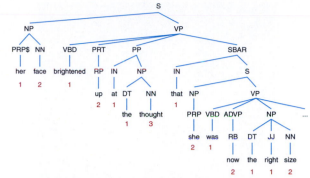

Figure 15.12 A sentence fragment from *Alice in Wonderland,* with aspects of the syntactic structure shown. The numbers beneath the words indicate "node counts," which reflect the number of phrases that become closed at each word. For details see Brennan et al. (2012). (From Brennan et al., 2012, p. 165.)

hypothesis that the aSTG contributes to the syntactic aspects of auditory sentence processing.

This hypothesis is strengthened even more by an fMRI study by Brennan et al. (2012) in which the subjects simply listened to a 30-minute segment of Lewis Carroll's famous story *Alice in Wonderland* and then completed a multiple-choice questionnaire to confirm that they had understood the plot. While the subjects were enjoying the story, the researchers were carefully tracking the brain regions in which the magnitude of the BOLD signals correlated significantly with either of two types of word-by-word processing difficulty: first, the frequency of each open-class word; and second, the number of syntactic structure-building operations that were required to incorporate each word into the preceding context, based on an automated parser created by Bikel (2002; see Figure 15.12; see also Hawkins, 1994, 2011).

The results were quite striking. Whereas the frequency metric correlated with the hemodynamic responses in a variety of frontal, temporal, and parietal regions, the syntax metric correlated with the hemodynamic responses in only one area—namely, a portion of

the aSTG that extended into BA38 (Figure 15.13). It is worth noting that the syntax metric used in Brennan et al.'s (2012) study is similar in some respects to the one used in Pallier et al.'s (2011) study of constituent structure, which we discussed earlier (see Figure 15.7 and the accompanying text). But while Pallier et al.'s (2011) study implicated virtually the entire sentence comprehension network in the processing of constituent structure, Brennan et al.'s (2012) study suggests that the aSTG, together with the adjacent sector of BA38, may be especially important for assembling hierarchical syntactic representations.

Additional evidence for this idea comes from a few fMRI studies that have investigated how the brain reacts to violations of phrase structure. For example, Friederici et al. (2003) reported an experiment in which the subjects listened to three types of German sentences: (1) correct sentences like *Das Hemd wurde gebügelt* ("The shirt was ironed") and *Der Rock wurde am Freitag gebügelt* ("The skirt was on Friday ironed"); (2) syntactically incorrect sentences like *Die Bluse wurde am gebügelt* ("The blouse was on ironed"); and (3) semantically incorrect sentences like *Das Gewitter wurde gebügelt* ("The thunderstorm was ironed"). Relative to the correct sentences, the ones with syntactic violations, but not the ones with semantic violations, elicited significant activation in the aSTG, as well as in BA44 and the basal ganglia (see also Friederici et al., 2010, for similar results based on similar materials).

In another study that explored the neural responses to phrase structure violations, Herrmann et al. (2012) presented the subjects with the following types of two-word German utterances: (1) correct pronoun–verb combinations like *er kniet*

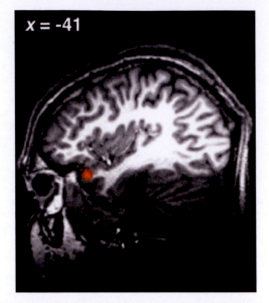

Figure 15.13 Results of Brennan et al.'s (2012) fMRI study of syntactic complexity. Increases in the number of syntactic structure-building operations necessary to incorporate each word into the preceding context correlated significantly with increases in activation in just one region—namely, a portion of the aSTG that extended in BA38. (From Brennan et al., 2012, p. 171.)

("he kneels"); (2) correct preposition–noun combinations like *im Knie* ("in the knee"); (3) syntactically incorrect pronoun–noun combinations like *er Knie* ("he knee"); and (4) syntactically incorrect preposition–verb combinations like *im kniet* ("in the kneels"). In comparison with the correct utterances, the incorrect ones engaged the aSTG, as well as BA44.

The outcomes of both of these studies suggest that during spoken language processing, when a word is encountered whose grammatical specifications are incompatible with the syntactic structure that has already been built up, the neural mechanisms that subserve syntactic integration are recruited intensively in an effort to cope with the problem. These mechanisms seem to reside, at least partially, in the aSTG, and moreover they appear to operate in concert with higher-order mechanisms in BA44, especially when the computations are unusually challenging. Incidentally, the collaboration between the anterior superior temporal cortex and the inferior frontal cortex is likely to be enabled by a white matter fiber tract called the **uncinate fasciculus** (Friederici et al., 2006a; see Figure 1.22 in Chapter 1).

Uncinate fasciculus A fiber tract that interconnects the anterior temporal cortex and the inferior frontal cortex.

A Combinatorial Syntactic–Semantic Network

Shifting now to the aSTS and aMTG, as noted above, the Dual Stream Model of speech perception maintains that this territory subserves a "combinatorial network" that uses both syntactic and semantic information to bind together the various elements of sentences into unified messages (Hickok and Poeppel, 2000, 2004, 2007). We first encountered this provocative hypothesis in Chapter 5, and here we will briefly consider it again (see also the fMRI studies of intelligibility summarized in Chapter 2).

One fruitful approach to investigating this topic has involved experimental designs in which genuine sentences are compared with mere word lists. For instance, in an fMRI study that followed up on earlier work by Vandenberghe et al. (2002), Humphries et al. (2006) systematically manipulated the variables of both syntax and semantics to create four conditions (two other conditions that involved pseudowords are not discussed here). The first condition consisted of 40 sentences that were syntactically well-formed and semantically congruent (e.g., *the man on a vacation lost a bag and a wallet*). The second condition consisted of 40 word lists that lacked syntactic structure but were semantically congruent (e.g., *on vacation lost then a and bag wallet man then a*). The third condition consisted of 40 sentences that were syntactically well-formed but semantically random (e.g., *the freeway on a pie watched a house and a window*). And the fourth condition consisted of 40 word lists that lacked syntactic structure and were semantically random (e.g., *a ball the a the spilled librarian in sign through fire*).

As shown in Figure 15.14, when the researchers analyzed the hemodynamic data, they found the following effects. By contrasting the two sentence conditions against the two word list conditions, a main effect of syntactic structure was observed in several anterior temporal areas, including a portion of the aSTG, a large swath of the aSTS, and some clusters of voxels in the aMTG. In addition, by contrasting the two semantically congruent conditions against the two semantically random conditions, a main effect of semantic structure was observed in a number of temporal and parietal areas, with the temporal activations encompassing a few patches of the aSTS and aMTG just posterior to those that responded to syntactic structure. And last but not least, by identifying areas in which both of the previous contrasts yielded overlapping activation, an interaction between syntax and semantics was observed in two regions: first, the angular gyrus (which is a finding we will return to in the

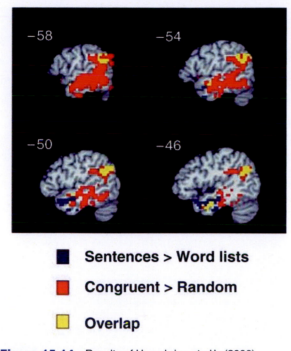

Sentences > Word lists

Congruent > Random

Overlap

Figure 15.14   Results of Humphries et al.'s (2006) fMRI investigation. Activation maps showing the effect of syntactic structure (sentences > word lists) in blue, the effect of semantic structure (congruent > random) in red, and the overlap of both contrasts in yellow. (From Humphries et al., 2006, p. 673.)

subsection about the pSTS/BA39); and second, several parts of the aSTS and aMTG.

When considered collectively, these results fit quite nicely with the notion that the aSTS/aMTG contains a "combinatorial network" of the kind posited by the Dual Stream Model. Under normal circumstances, such a device is thought to rely mainly on grammatical cues like linear order and closed-class morphemes to join together the separate meanings of nouns, verbs, and adjectives in rule-governed ways, thereby assembling the overall meanings of multi-word utterances. And what the results of Humphries et al.'s (2006) study suggest is that this system may be implemented in the anterior temporal lobe (ATL) in an intricate manner, with some neuronal populations handling primarily syntactic information, others handling primarily semantic information, and still others handling both types of information (see also Crinion et al., 2006; Brennan & Pylkkänen, 2012).

Some Challenging Data from Neuropsychology

Now, because we have been considering how certain sectors of the ATL might contribute to sentence comprehension, it is worthwhile to ask whether sentence comprehension is significantly impaired by one of the major neurodegenerative diseases that affects the ATL—namely, semantic dementia (SD). Remarkably enough, the data available so far indicate that even though patients with SD slowly lose their grasp of most word meanings (see Chapters 4, 10, 11, and 12), they usually retain their appreciation of most grammatical rules, at least until late in the course of the illness (Hodges et al., 1992, 1994; Breedin & Saffran, 1999; Rochon et al., 2004; Ogar et al., 2011).

To take a rather striking example of this dissociation, Breedin and Saffran (1999) described an SD patient who could no longer distinguish between pigs and cows in single word comprehension tasks, but could nevertheless perform accurately when instructed to "point to the cow" after being presented with, first, a picture of a pig chasing a cow, and second, the passive sentence *The cow is being chased by the pig*. Apparently, the patient was able to identify the cow in the picture by relying entirely on grammatical information about "who's doing what to whom" in the sentence. And the fact that the sentence was in the passive voice suggests that the patient retained an appreciation of noncanonical syntactic–semantic linking patterns.

Further evidence that grammatical knowledge is more or less preserved in SD (at least until late in the disease) comes from a valuable experiment by Ogar et al. (2011) in which 10 SD patients and 10 Wernicke's aphasics were administered the CYCLE-R—i.e., the sentence comprehension test that Dronkers et al. (2004) employed in the study summarized earlier (see Table 15.1). The SD patients, all of whom were in the middle stage of the disease (mean = 3.7 years post-onset), displayed the typical pattern of predominantly anterior temporal atrophy; and the Wernicke's aphasics, all of whom were chronic (mean = 2 years post-onset), displayed the typical pattern of left posterior superior/middle temporal lesions (Figure 15.15). The key behavioral results were as follows. Whereas the Wernicke's aphasics were, not surprisingly, profoundly impaired on the sentence comprehension test (mean = 40 percent correct), the SD patients performed extremely well (mean = 95 percent correct).

Fitting into this intriguing neuropsychological story is another important discovery that also challenges the idea that the ATL is indispensable for sentence comprehension. In a recent investigation, Kho et al. (2008) assessed the sentence comprehension abilities of 32 patients with temporal lobe epilepsy both before and after the surgical removal of either the left (*n* = 16) or the right (*n* = 16) ATL. No significant deficits in

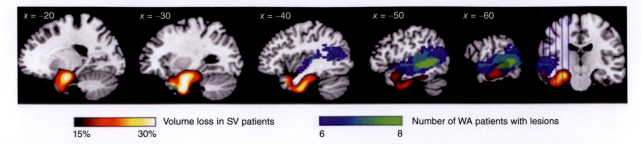

Figure 15.15 Results of Ogar et al.'s (2011) neuropsychological study of sentence comprehension. Patients with the semantic variant (SV) of primary progressive aphasia displayed predominantly anterior temporal atrophy (red-to-yellow colors), whereas patients with Wernicke's aphasia (WA) displayed predominantly posterior temporal lesions (blue-to-green colors). The planes of the five sagittal slices are shown in the coronal section on the right. (From Ogar et al., 2011, p. 31.)

syntactic processing were found, despite the fact that the resected tissue in the left-hemisphere group of patients included portions of the ATL that were implicated not only in the lesion study by Dronkers et al. (2004), but also in the various fMRI studies discussed above.

Summary

We appear, then, to be left with a puzzle. On the one hand, the study by Dronkers et al. (2004) as well as a growing body of fMRI data suggest that the ATL—more precisely, the territory comprising the aSTG, aSTS, aMTG, and neighboring parts of BA38—is an essential component of the large-scale neural network for sentence comprehension. As we have seen, although the specific functional contributions of these cortical areas are not entirely clear, they may involve grouping words into hierarchically organized constituents (aSTG/BA38) and integrating their syntactic and semantic specifications (aSTS/aMTG/BA38). On the other hand, a number of additional findings suggest that the ATL may not be absolutely necessary for understanding sentences. After all, neither the progressive atrophy of the ATL in SD patients nor the surgical resection of this region in epilepsy patients significantly compromises their ability to decipher the meanings of sentences.

Resolving this dilemma will no doubt require a substantial amount of further research. But one possibility is that some of the specific computational operations that are often targeted in sentence comprehension tasks recruit not only the ATL, but also, and perhaps even more so, other components of the widely distributed circuit for receptive sentence processing. In fact, in the next subsection we will encounter some evidence for the idea that the important operation of mapping grammatical relations onto participant roles—i.e., of determining "who's doing what to whom"—relies more on the pSTS/BA39 than the ATL.

Possible Contributions of the pSTS/BA39 and Some Adjacent Regions

In the foregoing discussion, two of the fMRI studies that we considered found significant effects not only in certain sectors of the ATL, but also in the pSTS/BA39. To reiterate: Obleser et al. (2011) discovered that as the sequence of case-marked NPs in German sentences became increasingly complex and difficult to decipher, the amount of activity in the pSTS/BA39 steadily rose (see Table 15.5, Figure 15.11, and the associated text; see also Friederici et al., 2009). And Humphries et al. (2006) made the following observations: First, a large proportion of the temporoparietal cortex was highly sensitive to the semantic coherence of utterances; and second, the angular gyrus (roughly BA39) responded strongly to both the semantic and syntactic aspects of utterances (see Figure 15.14 and the associated text). How exactly should these findings be explained, not to mention the many other activation peaks in the vicinity of the pSTS/BA39 that were revealed by Vigneau et al.'s (2006) meta-analysis of sentence processing studies (see Figure 15.6 and the associated text)?

During the past few years, several thoughtful proposals have been made about how the pSTS/BA39 might contribute to sentence comprehension. Here we will concentrate on two specific hypotheses, both of which have received increasing support. First, Dronkers et al. (2004) suggested that the pSTS/BA39 might subserve the storage component of **auditory–verbal short-term memory (STM)**, this being an essential resource for keeping the sound-based

Auditory–verbal short-term memory (STM) A memory system that allows a person to keep phonological representations in an active state for a relatively short period of time.

representations of perceived utterances "in mind," which is to say, in an activated state. As we will see, evidence for this view has been rapidly accumulating, although some dorsally adjacent temporoparietal areas have also been implicated. Second, as mentioned at the end of the previous subsection, there is also mounting evidence for the idea that the pSTS/BA39 is critically involved in identifying the actor and undergoer in sentences, especially when (1) both participants are animate, so that the described action is "semantically reversible," and (2) the grammatical organization is noncanonical, as in passive sentences and object-relative clauses.

Before looking at these two proposals more closely, it is important to note that they are related to each other in complicated ways that are not yet fully understood. In particular, there is a long history of controversy about the precise nature of the relationship between auditory–verbal STM and sentence comprehension (for an overview see Martin, 2006; for a more technical discussion see Caplan & Waters, 1999, and the associated commentaries). We will not delve into all of the intricacies of this debate, but we will touch upon some of the major issues, including the following. One set of studies suggests that the way in which the pSTS/BA39 helps listeners figure out "who's doing what to whom" in hard-to-understand sentences is by replaying the phonological forms of the words so that *other* brain regions can have a second chance to determine the proper linkages between NPs and participant roles. But a different set of studies suggests that the comprehension of even long and complex sentences may not necessarily require auditory–verbal STM, and that the pSTS/BA39 may contribute *directly* to participant role assignment. All of these points are elaborated below, and a strategy for reconciling the seemingly discrepant findings is offered.

Associations Between Auditory–Verbal STM and Sentence Comprehension

Auditory–verbal STM—also known as "phonological/verbal working memory" or the "phonological loop"—has been called a "cornerstone of human cognition" (Koenigs et al., 2011, p. 3612) and "a fundamental factor in the evolution of complex language and culture" (Aboitiz, 2012, p. 4). This is because it aids linguistically mediated thought by allowing us to briefly maintain verbatim records of all kinds of utterances, as long as they don't exceed the capacity of the system, which is, on average, about seven "chunks" of information, such as words or digits (Miller, 1956). In Chapter 5 we saw that, from the perspective of Hickok and Poeppel's (2000, 2004, 2007) Dual Stream Model of speech perception, auditory–verbal STM has the following architecture: First, the storage component retains the sound-based forms of utterances and probably depends on the pSTS; second, the rehearsal component frequently refreshes the material in the storage component and probably depends on articulatory mechanisms in the frontal lobe; and third, these two components interact via the "sensorimotor interface," which is an intermediary device lodged in the posterior tip of the planum temporale, deep within the sylvian fissure (see Figure 5.18 and the associated text in Chapter 5). Here we are concerned mainly with the storage component and its involvement in sentence processing.

Although some studies suggest that this component relies on the supramarginal gyrus (for a review see Buchsbaum & D'Esposito, 2008), the balance of evidence seems to favor the claim of the Dual Stream Model that the most critical structure is instead the pSTS, perhaps together with the dorsally adjacent pSTG and portions of the angular gyrus. For instance, Richardson et al. (2011) recently demonstrated that, relative to all other regions in the brain, the amount of gray matter in the pSTS correlates most strongly with **digit span**, which is the longest string of arbitrary digits that a person can repeat correctly. Thus, people who have a digit span of eight—i.e., who can repeat correctly a sequence like 5, 2, 9, 1, 2, 7, 6, 4—tend to have more neuronal machinery in their pSTS than people who have a digit span of only five—i.e., who can only recall a sequence like 1, 7, 3, 5, 2. Similarly, several recent lesion studies with large groups of patients have generated mostly convergent results that relate significant reductions of digit span to damage centered in the pSTS and pSTG, extending only somewhat into the inferior parietal lobule—i.e., the supramarginal gyrus (roughly BA40) and angular gyrus (roughly BA39) (Leff et al., 2009; Koenigs et al., 2011; Baldo et al., 2012). Because one of these studies—specifically, the one by Leff et al. (2009)—showed that pSTS/pSTG lesions are associated with deficits involving not only auditory–verbal STM but also sentence comprehension, it warrants special attention here.

Digit span   The longest string of arbitrary digits that a person can repeat correctly.

In this impressive investigation, Leff et al. (2009) first used an advanced technique to analyze the lesions in 210 stroke patients. This technique employed an automated algorithm that could determine, on a case-by-case basis, the probability that each high-resolution (1 cubic millimeter) voxel contained normal gray matter, normal white matter, lesioned brain matter, or non-brain matter. Then the researchers explored the relationships between the anatomical data and the patients' scores on a carefully selected set of linguistic tasks. The task of greatest interest was digit span, since it is well-established as being a reliable measure of auditory–verbal STM capacity. But because the digit span task also depends on several other mental abilities, such as the perception and production of speech as well as various executive processes, a number of additional tasks were administered to control for those variables. These secondary tasks included auditory word and pseudoword repetition, picture naming, and verbal fluency (e.g., retrieving the names of as many animals as possible in one minute). Finally, an important part of the experiment was that the researchers also administered two sentence comprehension tasks. Both of them involved sentence–picture matching; however, one of them used written sentences that were available for inspection throughout each trial, whereas the other used auditory sentences that were inherently ephemeral and hence had high STM demands.

The key findings are depicted in Figure 15.16. The top panel of Figure 15.16A indicates that when significant reductions of digit span were taken as the sole behavioral factor, they correlated with damage in a wide range of left perisylvian cortical and subcortical structures. The bottom panel of Figure 15.16A indicates, however, that when the patients' scores on all of the secondary tasks were also taken into account, thereby controlling for cognitive processes that are necessary to perform the digit span task but don't contribute directly to auditory–verbal STM capacity, significant reductions of digit span still correlated with damage in one narrowly circumscribed region—namely, a cluster of voxels stretching from the lateral edge of the pSTS up along the surface of the pSTG to the most inferior portion of the planum temporale. This finding constitutes powerful evidence that the storage component of auditory–verbal STM depends primarily on the pSTS/pSTG.

The results of two additional analyses are presented in Figure 15.16B. These graphs indicate that as the amount of gray matter in the cluster of pSTS/pSTG voxels progressively declined, so did the patients'

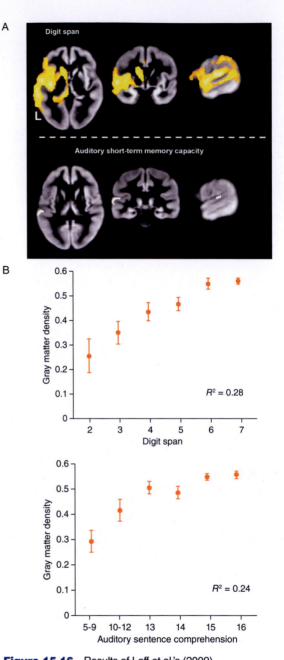

Figure 15.16 Results of Leff et al.'s (2009) neuropsychological study of auditory–verbal STM. (A) The top panel shows that when significant reductions of digit span were taken as the sole behavioral factor, they correlated with damage in a wide range of left perisylvian and subcortical structures. The bottom panel shows, however, that when the scores on all of the control tasks were also taken into account, significant reductions of digit span still correlated with damage in one narrowly circumscribed region—namely, a cluster of voxels stretching from the pSTS up along the pSTG and into the planum temporale. (B) Means (and standard error bars) of gray matter density in the region of interest—i.e., in the cluster of voxels depicted in the bottom panel of (A)—plotted against scores of digit span (top panel) and spoken sentence comprehension (bottom panel). (From Leff et al., 2009, pp. 3407–3408.)

scores on not only the digit span task (top panel) but also the auditory sentence comprehension task (bottom panel). It is crucial to note, however, that a significant correlation did *not* emerge between the gray matter density in the region of interest and the patients' scores on the written sentence comprehension task. This is important because it implies that the decrements in auditory sentence comprehension associated with pSTS/pSTG damage were not due to impairments of syntactic or semantic processing per se, but were instead most likely due to deficits in STM capacity, as reflected by the corresponding reductions of digit span. Based on these considerations, Leff et al. (2009, p. 3409) concluded that their study "supports the hypothesis that auditory short-term memory is likely to have a necessary role in normal propositional speech comprehension, insofar as speech comprehension requires multiple auditory lexical representations to be concurrently active."

Although Leff et al.'s (2009) study has many virtues, one limitation is that it did not address the following question: In connection with the status of the pSTS/pSTG, did auditory–verbal STM capacity interact with the comprehension of *different types* of auditorily presented sentences? Fortunately, a few other studies have tackled this issue by systematically manipulating two linguistic factors, both of which we have already encountered.

The first factor is "semantic reversibility." Sentences that contain two animate NPs, such as *The boy chased the girl*, are semantically reversible because each participant is, in principle, capable of acting on the other; hence determining which one is the actor and which one is the undergoer requires attending to the appropriate syntactic cues. In contrast, sentences that contain only one animate NP, such as *The boy chased the ball*, are semantically nonreversible because the causal direction of action can only go one way; hence the assignment of actor and undergoer roles does not necessarily require syntactic processing, but can instead be achieved by relying entirely on the meanings of the individual words, plus real-world knowledge of how those meanings could plausibly be integrated.

The second factor is "syntactic canonicity." Sentences with a canonical syntactic organization preserve the typical linear arrangement of participant roles, which in English—and in the vast majority of other languages, too—involves the actor preceding the undergoer, as in the semantically reversible and nonreversible active-voice examples given above: *The boy chased the girl* and *The boy chased the ball*. In contrast, sentences with a noncanonical word order

Table 15.6 Experimental Conditions in Richardson et al.'s (2009) fMRI Study of the Comprehension of Semantically Reversible and Nonreversible Sentences

Sentence Type	Number	Example
Reversible		
Active	8	The old dog bites the fox
Passive	8	The rat is sniffed by the gray squirrel
Subject-cleft	8	It is the dancer that hugs the clown
Object-cleft	8	It is the cook that the woman loves
Locative	4	The circle is in the gold star
Dative	4	Give the happy boy to the girl
Total	40	
Nonreversible		
Active	8	The rich queen spends the money
Passive	8	The giant safe is locked by the guard
Subject-cleft	8	It is the drunk that starts the fight
Object-cleft	8	It is the dress that the model hates
Locative	4	The marble temple is in the field
Dative	4	Put the salt on the plain meal
Total	40	

Source: Richardson et al. (2009, p. 1287).

deviate from the typical pattern by placing the undergoer NP before the actor NP, as in the semantically reversible and nonreversible passive-voice sentences *The girl was chased by the boy* and *The ball was chased by the boy*.

Returning to our main thread, a highly relevant fMRI study by Richardson et al. (2009) found that a cortical region very close to the one described by Leff et al. (2009) exhibited the following response properties: not only was it significantly modulated by the semantic reversibility of perceived sentences, but it was also sensitive to a separate task requiring auditory–verbal STM (see also Meyer et al., 2012a).

This study was rather distinctive insofar as it involved an unusually large number of subjects—47 in all, ranging in age from 7 to 73 years. These subjects were presented with 80 sentences, 40 of which were semantically reversible and 40 of which were not. The sentences in each set instantiated a wide range of canonical and noncanonical constructions, including active, passive, subject-cleft, object-cleft, locative, and dative (Table 15.6). In addition, the sentences in each set were split into two groups, one of which was presented auditorily and the other of which was presented visually.

When the researchers contrasted the auditory and visual sentences in the semantically reversible set against the auditory and visual sentences in the semantically nonreversible set, thereby isolating the linguistic factor of reversibility, they found that just one brain area was significantly engaged—namely, an area at the left temporoparietal boundary, bridging the pSTG and the neighboring parietal cortex, and hence directly above the pSTS (Figure 15.17A; for a similar experimental contrast that implicated the pSTS/BA39, see Figure 11.20 in Chapter 11 and the associated discussion of Grewe et al.'s [2007] fMRI study). This area was activated more for children than adults, and also more for visual than auditory sentences (Figure 15.17B). In the current context, however, what is most relevant and intriguing is that the very same region also responded significantly during a phonological repetition task that involved saying "1" and "3" alternately, again and again.

Given this remarkable overlap, as well as other evidence relating the activated area to auditory–verbal STM, Richardson et al. (2009, p. 1295) drew the following conclusion: "Our results suggest that semantically reversible sentences increase the demands on a brain region associated with phonological working memory." In other words, the implication seems to be that the activated temporoparietal area facilitates the mapping of NPs onto participant roles in semantically reversible (and hence potentially confusing) sentences not so much by carrying out the actual syntactic–semantic linking operations, but rather by replaying the phonological records of the sentences so that *other* brain regions can execute those operations properly.

Taking this line of inquiry one step further, Newhart et al. (2012) recently demonstrated that both of the linguistic factors described above—semantic reversibility as well as syntactic canonicity—interact closely with auditory–verbal STM in the angular gyrus (roughly BA39), just posterior to the region

A

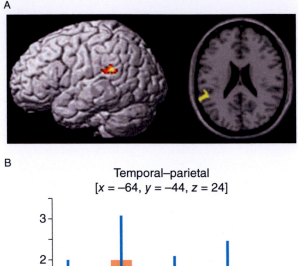

B

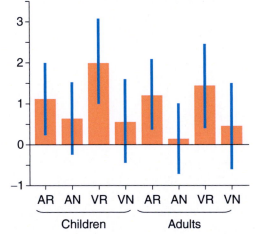

Figure 15.17 Results of Richardson et al.'s (2009) fMRI study of sentence comprehension. (A) Greater activation in a left temporoparietal region for reversible than nonreversible sentences. (B) Activation profiles at the peak coordinates in (A) as a function of age group, processing modality, and sentence type. AR = auditory reversible sentences; AN = auditory nonreversible sentences; VR = visual reversible sentences; VN = visual nonreversible sentences. (From Richardson et al., 2009, pp. 1292–1293.)

that was engaged in the studies by Leff et al. (2009) and Richardson et al. (2009). This particular investigation involved 53 brain-damaged patients whose linguistic abilities were evaluated within 24 hours after the onset of left-hemisphere stroke. Sentence comprehension was assessed by administering semantically reversible and nonreversible versions of two types of canonical sentences—actives and subject-clefts—and two types of noncanonical sentences—passives and object-clefts (the same constructions were also used in Richardson et al.'s 2009 fMRI study, and examples are provided in Table 15.6). The patients simultaneously heard and saw each item on a computer screen, and responded by performing two tasks in separate sessions: first, sentence–picture matching; and second, enactment, which involved selecting the correct paper objects and moving them in ways that indicated the correct actor and undergoer roles (for other studies comparing these two tasks see Caplan et al., 2006b, 2007a, 2007b). In addition, auditory–verbal STM was assessed by means of the digit span task.

Of the 53 patients who were examined, 14 manifested "asyntactic comprehension," which the researchers defined as follows: performance at or below chance for reversible passives on at least one of the two tasks (matching and/or enactment); ≥10 percentage points lower accuracy on passives than actives and on object-clefts than subject-clefts; and ≥10 percentage points lower accuracy on reversible than non-reversible sentences. Analyses that were designed to relate this behavioral profile to regions of hypoperfusion (i.e., reduced blood flow) did not find significant associations with any part of Broca's area (i.e., either BA44 or BA45), but did find significant associations with the angular gyrus (i.e., BA39). Moreover, follow-up analyses that went the opposite direction—from brain to behavior instead of from behavior to brain—revealed that while hypoperfusion in BA45 reliably predicted impaired comprehension of just reversible passives, hypoperfusion in BA39 reliably predicted impaired comprehension of both reversible passives and reversible object-clefts. As for auditory–verbal STM, the researchers found that significant reductions of digit span correlated with hypoperfusion in several regions: BA39, which may contribute to the storage component; and BAs 44, 45, and 6, which most likely subserve the rehearsal component (see the next subsection on Broca's area).

Thus, like the other studies summarized above, this study supports the view that the cortical tissue in the vicinity of the pSTS/BA39 may enhance the processing of hard-to-understand sentences by keeping the sound-based representations of those sentences active in "the mind's ear," thereby allowing more time to figure out exactly "who's doing what to whom."

Dissociations Between Auditory–Verbal STM and Sentence Comprehension

As mentioned earlier, however, the precise nature of the relationship between auditory–verbal STM and sentence comprehension is far from straightforward. Indeed, this is a highly contentious topic that has vexed the psycholinguistic and neurolinguistic research communities for several decades (for a historical review see Martin, 2006). It is not feasible

to delve into the large literature on this topic here, but it is nevertheless worth considering some of the key aspects of the debate.

Dating all the way back to Clark and Clark's (1977) highly esteemed textbook *Psychology and language*, it has traditionally been assumed that auditory–verbal STM does in fact facilitate sentence processing by keeping the phonological forms of words active until syntactic parsing and semantic interpretation have been completed. For instance, in an influential article Vallar and Baddeley (1984, p. 126) stated that

> the phonological short-term store is useful for the comprehension of long sentences with a complex syntactic structure, containing too much information to be processed during presentation. Under these conditions the phonological short-term store holds the sentence while the subject processes it.

And in the same vein Caramazza et al. (1983, p. 160) wrote that "comprehension of these [long] sentences is dependent on the normal functioning of phonological working memory."

Beginning in the mid 1980s, however, papers began to appear that described individual brain-damaged patients who had severely reduced auditory–verbal STM capacities, with digit spans of only two or three items, but who could still understand a variety of long and syntactically complex sentences (Butterworth et al., 1986; McCarthy & Warrington, 1987; Waters et al., 1991; Hanten & Martin, 2000; Friedmann & Gvion, 2003; Gvion & Friedmann, 2012; Caplan et al., 2013). To take a representative case, even though the patient described by Butterworth et al. (1986) had a profound auditory–verbal STM impairment and could not "hear words in her head," she had no trouble understanding convoluted utterances like *The bus is preceded by the train which the triangle is below.* Moreover, she could easily detect grammatical violations that hinged on the relationships between distantly separated words, as in *Airline pilots should never forget that the safety of their passengers is their paramount concern,* *OUGHT (should) they?*

Such findings have been treated by some scholars as seriously challenging the view that in order for syntactic computations to be successful, it is necessary for auditory–verbal STM to retain a record of the phonological forms of words (e.g., Caplan & Waters, 1999). However, other scholars have argued that many of the pertinent studies are flawed and that the traditional view, or some version of it, is still supported by independent evidence (e.g., Papagno et al., 2007; Romero Lauro et al., 2010). Given that the issues at stake in this controversy are both very complicated and very relevant to the nature of sentence comprehension, it is safe to say that they will continue to receive intense scrutiny for a long time to come, and with increasing ties to neurobiological data.

Since our overarching concern here involves the possible contributions of the pSTS/BA39 to sentence comprehension, it is appropriate to round out the discussion by briefly reviewing a recent neuropsychological study by Thothathiri et al. (2012b) which found that, in striking contrast to the study by Newhart et al. (2012), impairments of participant role assignment are strongly associated with damage to BA39 *independently of auditory–verbal STM capacity*. This investigation focused on 79 patients, all of whom had aphasia due to left-hemisphere stroke. The breakdown across classic aphasia syndromes was as follows: 21 Broca's, 15 conduction, 34 anomic, 1 transcortical motor, and 8 "recovered." Each patient performed a sentence–picture matching task that included two types of semantically reversible, syntactically canonical sentences—actives (e.g., *The girl washes the boy*) and subject-relatives (e.g., *The dog that followed the hunter was alert*)—and two types of semantically reversible, syntactically noncanonical sentences—passives (e.g., *The man is served by the woman*) and object-relatives (e.g., *The girl that the boy washed was talkative*). The sentences were presented auditorily, and the researchers ensured that the patients understood the meanings of all the nouns, so that no comprehension errors could be attributed to impairments involving object concepts. In addition, each patient's auditory–verbal STM was evaluated with two tasks. One of them measured "rhyme probe span," which was the maximum list length for which the patient could correctly judge whether a probe word rhymed with one of the words in the list (e.g., list: *some–black–more*; probe: *plum*; response: *yes*). The other task was "nonword repetition," which required the patient to repeat 60 nonwords that ranged from one to three syllables (e.g., *fos, tayson, dunapour*).

The main results were as follows. Using voxel-based lesion–symptom mapping (VLSM), which is the same technique that Dronkers et al. (2004) employed, the researchers found that (1) poor comprehension of canonical sentences was significantly linked with a large cluster of 3,009 voxels in the left temporoparietal cortex, and (2) poor comprehension of noncanonical sentences was significantly linked with an even larger cluster of 10,439 voxels in the same general territory.

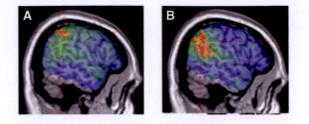

Figure 15.18 Results of Thothathiri et al.'s (2012b) neuropsychological study of sentence comprehension. Significant effects are shown in orange-to-yellow colors. (A) Links between poor comprehension of canonical sentences and damage to part of the left temporoparietal cortex, viewed from the right side. (B) Links between poor comprehension of noncanonical sentences and damage to an even larger part of the left temporoparietal cortex, viewed from the right side. (From Thothathiri et al., 2012b, p. 217.)

These results are shown in Figure 15.18, which portrays the relevant cortical areas from the perspective of the right, rather than the left, side of the head. Interestingly, a series of subsequent region-of-interest analyses indicated that worse performance on noncanonical than canonical sentences was significantly linked with damage to just one region—BA39. In the current context, though, what's even more important is that these close ties between impaired participant role assignment and lesions in BA39 remained valid when the patients' scores on the two auditory–verbal STM tasks were also taken into account. As Thothathiri et al. (2012b) point out, these results do not argue against a major contribution of BA39 to auditory–verbal STM, but they do constitute powerful evidence that this region "plays some other additional role in sentence comprehension."

What might that be? The answer is not yet clear, but Thothathiri et al. (2012b) offer a provocative proposal that capitalizes on the idea that mapping grammatical relations like subject and object onto participant roles like actor and undergoer may involve transiently binding information about "what" entities are with information about "where" they belong in action scenarios. As described in Box 11.2 in Chapter 11, there is some evidence that people tend to think of actions as having, by default, a horizontal directionality of energy flow, with the actor on the left and the undergoer on the right. And given that the inferior parietal lobule has been strongly associated with the processing of spatial relations (Kemmerer, 2010a), it is conceivable that, as Thothathiri et al. (2012b, p. 220) put it, "a nonlinguistic spatial representation might underlie our understanding of thematic relations [i.e., participant roles] in language . . .." Time will tell.

Summary

Together with the pSTG, the pSTS/BA39 appears to underlie the storage component of auditory–verbal STM. A number of studies have shown that the structural density and integrity of this cortical territory are associated not only with digit span, which is a reliable measure of auditory–verbal STM capacity, but also with sentence comprehension, especially when the utterances are hard to understand because they are semantically reversible and/or syntactically noncanonical. In light of these findings, it is possible that, in conjunction with the pSTG, the pSTS/BA39 facilitates the determination of "who's doing what to whom" in complicated sentences by covertly reactivating the phonological forms of the words, thereby giving *other* areas a second pass at establishing the proper syntactic–semantic relationships.

At the same time, however, there is also evidence for double dissociations between auditory–verbal STM and sentence comprehension. Some patients have severe auditory–verbal STM deficits but can nevertheless understand long and complex sentences fairly well; and conversely, some patients manifest significant sentence comprehension deficits that are statistically independent of their auditory–verbal STM capacities. These findings suggest that, beyond its contribution to phonological working memory, the temporoparietal cortex may *directly* subserve at least some of the processing operations that are essential for mapping grammatical relations like subject and object onto participant roles like actor and undergoer.

Given the patterns in the data described above, one possibility is that the region that extends from the pSTS up into the pSTG may be more involved in auditory–verbal STM, whereas the region that extends from the pSTS back into BA39 may be more involved in linking NPs with participant roles. Further research will no doubt shed more light on these challenging issues.

Possible Contributions of Broca's Area and Some Adjacent Regions

Last but certainly not least, this subsection tackles one of the most controversial questions in the cognitive neuroscience of language: What role does Broca's area play in sentence comprehension? Historically, most of the debate surrounding this question has focused squarely on Broca's area itself, which, as we know, is usually regarded as encompassing BA44 (roughly the pars opercularis) and BA45 (roughly the pars triangularis). In the following discussion, we too will devote most of our attention to this region, but we will also consider, now and then, a few adjacent regions, especially BA47 (roughly the pars orbitalis) and the ventral portion of BA6 (premotor cortex). Warning: The road ahead gets a bit bumpy in places, so brace yourself.

Is Broca's Area Necessary for Sentence Comprehension?

Perhaps the best way to begin is by taking a step back and asking whether Broca's area plays *any* essential role in sentence comprehension. Answering this question is by no means a simple matter, because the available data are quite mixed. On balance, however, the weight of evidence from both the neuropsychological literature and the functional neuroimaging literature seems to favor the view that Broca's area probably makes important contributions to at least some aspects of sentence comprehension.

Starting with the perspective from neuropsychology, it is, of course, noteworthy that the large group study by Dronkers et al. (2004) did not find any significant associations at all between sentence comprehension deficits and damage to Broca's area. In addition, the somewhat larger group study by Thothathiri et al. (2012b) revealed only a marginal correlation ($p < .06$) between the severity of sentence comprehension impairment and the extent of damage to BA44 (see also the study by Caramazza et al., 2005, which is discussed below). On the other hand, a number of other investigations have discovered more robust associations between defective syntactic processing and dysfunction in Broca's area. Here are some examples. First, as described in the subsection focusing on the pMTG, Papoutsi et al. (2011) and Tyler et al. (2011) found that among 14 chronic stroke patients whose lesions were widely distributed across the left perisylvian territory, the degree of difficulty in parsing syntactically ambiguous utterances was strongly related to the extent of damage to BA47/45 (see Figure 15.10B and the accompanying text). Second, as described in the subsection focusing on the pSTS/BA39, Newhart et al. (2012) found that among 53 patients with acute left-hemisphere strokes, hypoperfusion in BA45 was reliably linked with poor understanding of reversible passives, but not, interesting enough, with poor understanding of reversible object-clefts (see also Box 3.3 in Chapter 3). Third, in a study involving a group of 21 patients who had tumors in various sectors of the left frontal lobe, Kinno et al. (2009) discovered that significantly worse comprehension of reversible passives than reversible actives was associated specifically with damage to Broca's area. Finally, the growing literature on progressive nonfluent aphasia (PNFA) has generated increasing evidence that patients with this disorder manifest gradually worsening sentence processing abilities that are closely tied to the degree of atrophy in Broca's area and some neighboring regions (Peelle et al., 2008; Wilson et al., 2010a, 2011; Rogalski et al., 2011; Thompson et al., 2013; see also Chapter 4).

Shifting now to the perspective from functional neuroimaging, a similar mixture of results can be seen regarding the relation between Broca's area and sentence comprehension. On the negative side, it is well-established that Broca's area is usually not engaged when genuine sentences, which contain both semantic and syntactic information, are compared with mere word lists, which contain only semantic information (Stowe et al., 1999; Friederici et al., 2000; Kuperberg et al., 2000; Vandenberghe et al., 2002; Humphries et al., 2005, 2006). This lack of a response to basic syntactic structure in Broca's area is exemplified by Humphries et al.'s (2006) fMRI study, which we discussed in the subsection on the aSTG (see Figure 15.14 and the accompanying text). On the positive side, however, a plethora of separate studies have shown that Broca's area does tend to be significantly activated in several kinds of situations that involve sentence comprehension. At a fairly general level, this is illustrated by the many activation peaks in Broca's area that were identified by Vigneau et al.'s (2006) meta-analysis of PET and fMRI studies (see Figure 15.6 and the accompanying text). And at a more specific level, we have already encountered three different types of effects. First, Broca's area is engaged more by syntactically ambiguous than unambiguous sentences, as shown by Snijders et al. (2009), Papoutsi et al. (2011), and Tyler et al. (2011) (see Figure 15.9C and Figure 15.10A, together with the accompanying discussions; see also Rodd et al., 2010). Second, Broca's area is engaged more by syntactically complex than simple sentences, as shown by Obleser et al. (2011) (see Figure 15.11 and the associated text; see also the meta-analysis of 14 studies by Kaan & Swaab, 2002). And third, Broca's area is engaged more by syntactic than semantic violations, as shown by Friederici et al. (2003) and Herrmann et al. (2012) (but note that there are many exceptions to this trend, as pointed out by Kaan & Swaab, 2002).

It appears, then, that the question posed above—"Is Broca's area necessary for sentence comprehension?"—does not allow a simple, unqualified "yes" or "no" answer, but does admit a tentative "yes, but . . ." response that must ultimately be fleshed out in

a carefully nuanced manner. In other words, just as there seems to be enough data to confidently implicate Broca's area in sentence production, but not enough data to decipher its precise contribution to that ability (see Chapter 14), so there seems to be plenty of evidence that Broca's area is involved in sentence comprehension, but not enough information to determine exactly how it supports that ability (for details about the recruitment of Broca's area during both sentence production and sentence comprehension, see Box 15.1). And yet, whereas the literature on the role of Broca's area in sentence production has not been growing very fast (again, see Chapter 14), the literature on the role of Broca's area in sentence comprehension has been advancing quite rapidly. In fact, at least half-a-dozen distinct hypotheses have been developed during the past few decades, and countless experimental papers have been published. Rogalsky and Hickok (2011) recently did the field a great service by summarizing and assessing the most prominent hypotheses, and the following review is based partly on their insights. For ease of exposition, this review groups the hypotheses into two large families—those that emphasize sequential and hierarchical processing, and those that emphasize auditory–verbal STM and cognitive control.

Hypotheses that Emphasize Sequential and Hierarchical Processing

Two of the most fundamental properties of spoken sentences are, first, that they always unfold in time, and second, that they usually consist of nested assemblies of expressions. These two aspects of syntactic structure—sequential and hierarchical—are clearly manifested in the pair of sentences that we considered at the very outset of this chapter:

(1) The reporter [who attacked the senator] admitted the error.
(2) The reporter [who the senator attacked] admitted the error.

The inherently sequential nature of each sentence is thumpingly obvious, but it is far from trivial that the opposite linearizations of the verb *attacked* and the NP *the senator* in the two relative clauses signal opposite interpretations of "who's doing what to whom." With regard to the hierarchical organization of each sentence, it is highlighted, at least in part, by the explicitly bracketed boundaries of the center-embedded relative clauses, which serve to modify the preceding NP *The*

Box 15.1 Shared Syntax for Producing and Comprehending Sentences in Broca's Area

One of the most hotly debated questions in the cognitive neuroscience of language is whether Broca's area processes syntactic information during both the encoding and the decoding of sentences. Some remarkably convergent evidence supporting this possibility comes from two recent studies.

In the first study, Segaert et al. (2012) used fMRI to scan the brain activity of healthy subjects while they performed a task that involved randomly shifting back and forth between producing and comprehending spoken sentences that described photographs showing various kinds of scenes, including, most importantly, transitive events in which one person acted on another. Production trials were distinguished from comprehension trials by colored versus grayscale stimuli. For the production trials, subjects were instructed to name the participant colored green before the participant colored red, and for the comprehension trials, subjects were instructed to determine whether the sentence correctly represented the scene. Crucially, across consecutive trials the syntactic structure and processing modality of the sentences could be repeated (for syntax, active–active or passive–passive; for modality, production–production or comprehension–comprehension), or it could be novel (for syntax, active–passive or passive–active; for modality, production–comprehension or comprehension–production). This manipulation was central to the experimental design because when the researchers analyzed the fMRI data, they took advantage of a neurophysiological phenomenon called "adaptation" or "repetition suppression." Basically, if a given neuronal population codes for a specific type of information, its response will decrease when that information is repeated (Grill-Spector et al., 2006). Using this approach, the researchers were able to search for brain areas exhibiting adaptation effects of syntactic repetition independent of processing modality—that is, areas in which the BOLD signals for consecutive sentences with repeated syntax were significantly reduced relative to the BOLD signals for consecutive sentences with different syntax, regardless of whether the sentences were produced or com-

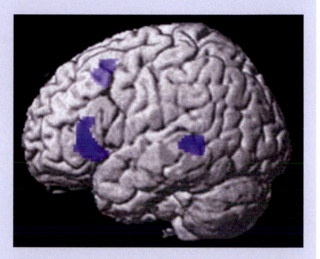

Figure 15B1.1 Results of Segaert et al.'s (2012) fMRI study. (From Segaert et al., 2012, p. 1667.)

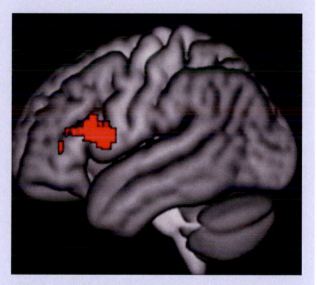

Figure 15B1.2 Results of Wilson et al.'s (2011) neuropsychological study. (From Wilson et al., 2011, p. 400.)

prehended. Precisely such effects were observed in three regions: Broca's area (BA45 extending into BA47); the lateral premotor cortex at the boundary between the posterior middle frontal gyrus and the precentral gyrus; and the pMTG (Figure 15B1.1). The upshot is that these regions seem to constitute a common workspace for syntactic computations during both expressive and receptive sentence processing.

(Continued)

(Continued)

In the second study, Wilson et al. (2011) used voxel-based morphometry to investigate the degree to which gray matter atrophy in Broca's area correlated with the sentence production and comprehension abilities of 27 patients with primary progressive aphasia (PPA; 11 = nonfluent; 10 = semantic; 6 = logopenic; see Chapter 4). Syntactic processing during sentence production was assessed by carefully evaluating the grammatical properties of each patient's spontaneous and elicited speech, and syntactic processing during sentence comprehension was assessed by means of an auditory sentence–picture matching task that contained 84 items varying in difficulty. A highly significant brain–behavior relationship emerged, such that as the tissue volume in Broca's area declined across the patients, so did their scores on both the production and comprehension measures (Figure 15B1.2). Not surprisingly, most of the patients who exhibited the greatest atrophy in Broca's area and the worst syntactic processing deficits fit the criteria for the nonfluent variant of PPA (see also Figure 14.8 in Chapter 14). Interestingly, a separate DTI investigation revealed that syntactic deficits for both encoding and decoding were also linked with atrophy in the arcuate fasciculus. For our purposes, though, the main point is that Wilson et al.'s (2011) neuropsychological study dovetails beautifully with Segaert et al.'s (2012) fMRI study, since both sets of results bolster the view that Broca's area plays an essential role in syntactic processing not only when we formulate sentences, but also when we understand them (see also Humphreys & Gennari, 2014).

reporter. Other aspects of hierarchical structure include the three determiner–noun combinations that form the NPs *The reporter, the senator,* and *the error,* as well as the verb–NP combination that forms the higher-order constituent *admitted the error* (see also the phrase structure geometry shown in Figure 15.12, and note too that, as discussed in the syntax tutorial in Chapter 14, some languages use agreement rules together with, or instead of, phrase structure rules to specify hierarchical structure). The point of these examples is simply that in order to understand spoken sentences, listeners must accurately represent both the linear arrangements of the words and their multi-layered groupings into increasingly complex expressions.

Turning to the brain, there is growing evidence that Broca's area, perhaps in conjunction with the ventral premotor cortex, is involved in extracting the hierarchical structure that is latent in many different kinds of sequential events, including not only spoken sentences, but also goal-directed bodily actions, musical pieces, and visuospatial arrays (e.g., Fiebach & Schubotz, 2006; Koechlin & Jubault, 2006; Bahlmann et al., 2009b; Fadiga et al., 2009; Tettamanti et al., 2009). Here we will focus on three different hypotheses about how Broca's area may perform such operations specifically for spoken sentences. As we will see, although all of these hypotheses are concerned with the sequential and hierarchical aspects of receptive syntactic processing, they vary a great deal in their theoretical assumptions and claims, as well as in their explanatory power.

One of the oldest accounts has been propounded in various forms by Yosef Grodzinsky and his colleagues

ever since the mid 1980s (e.g., Grodzinsky, 1986, 1989, 1990, 2000, Drai & Grodzinsky, 2006a, 2006b, Grodzinsky & Santi, 2008). This approach is firmly committed to the Chomskyan tradition in syntactic theory, and especially to the notion of so-called "movement," which can be unpacked in a somewhat simplistic manner as follows. First, transitive verbs uniformly assign the participant roles of actor and undergoer to the grammatical positions of subject and object, respectively. Second, in noncanonical constructions, such as passives, object-relatives, and object-clefts, the undergoer NP "moves" from the direct object position to an earlier position that precedes the actor NP. Third, the undergoer NP leaves behind a syntactic "**trace**" to which the participant role is assigned. And fourth, during comprehension, the undergoer NP receives its participant role through a "chain" that connects it with its trace. Traces are sometimes represented by "*t*" symbols, and chains by co-indexation markers, as shown below:

(3) a. Active: The boy is pushing the girl.
    b. Passive: The girl$_i$ is being pushed t_i by the boy.
(4) a. Subject-relative: The boy who is pushing the girl is tall.

Trace Posited by Chomskyan theories, this is a phonologically empty syntactic category that occupies the original position of a "moved" NP and that receives from the verb the participant role that would have been assigned directly to that NP. The NP ultimately gets the participant role by being linked with its trace via a "chain."

b. Object-relative: The girl$_i$ who the boy is pushing t_i is tall.

(5) a. Subject-cleft: It is the boy who is pushing the girl.
b. Object-cleft: It is the girl$_i$ who the boy is pushing t_i.

Now, the essence of Grodzinsky's hypothesis is that Broca's area subserves the processing of syntactic movement, including the associated phenomena of traces and chains. Although he has argued that this view is compatible with fMRI data, the lion's share of the evidence that he has invoked comes from aphasia. In particular, he maintains that damage to Broca's area disrupts the computation of movement, and that this has the following consequences. First, patients can no longer represent traces and therefore can no longer determine the participant roles of moved NPs in the normal fashion. And second, they regularly employ a compensatory strategy of granting the role of actor to these disenfranchised NPs, because in most cases they are the first referential NPs in the clause. For example, with regard to the sentences in (3)–(5), the key predictions, which Grodzinsky believes to be well-supported by the neuropsychological literature, are as follows. Patients tend to perform well on the canonical (a) sentences because the interpretation of those sentences does not depend on the processing of traces. In contrast, they tend to perform at chance on the noncanonical (b) sentences because the actor role is assigned to two NPs—the correct one by means of intact operations, and the incorrect one by means of the compensatory strategy—thereby forcing patients to guess.

This hypothesis has many virtues, but it also has many shortcomings. For one thing, its heavy reliance on the theoretical notion of movement can easily be construed as problematic. This is partly because the only approach to syntactic analysis that makes extensive use of that idea is the Chomskyan framework that Grodzinsky endorses. The other approaches that are mentioned at the beginning of the syntax tutorial in Chapter 14—and there are no less than 10 of them—either do not posit movement at all, or apply it much less. Thus, movement appears to be the minority view in syntactic theory. Furthermore, any psycholinguistic findings that might be regarded as supporting the cognitive reality of movement could in principle be handled equally well by approaches that reject it, because traces are completely confounded with the lexical properties of the putatively moved elements.

Apart from these largely theoretical issues, however, a more serious limitation of Grodzinsky's hypothesis is

that it does not appear to be as consistent with the neuropsychological literature as he thinks it is. The results of the group studies by Dronkers et al. (2004) and Thothathiri et al. (2012b) pose formidable challenges, and although the results of the group study by Newhart et al. (2012) provide some support for the theory's prediction about reversible passives, they go against the theory's prediction about reversible object-clefts. In addition, several scholars have pointed out that the proposal is at odds with data indicating that patients with agrammatic Broca's aphasia exhibit tremendous variability not only in their ability to produce spoken sentences (see Chapter 14), but also in their ability to comprehend them (Berndt et al., 1996; Caramazza et al., 2001, 2005). For instance, Caramazza et al. (2005) conducted a study in which 38 Italian agrammatic patients with verified damage to Broca's area performed a sentence–picture matching task involving reversible active and passive sentences. Contrary to Grodzinsky's hypothesis, analyses at the level of individual patients revealed that only 6/38 cases (15.8 percent) obtained scores that were above chance for actives and within the chance range for passives; moreover, analyses at the level of the entire group revealed that the scores for passives were not aggregated around the expected mean of 50 percent correct (i.e., chance), but were instead skewed toward greater-than-chance values. To be sure, Grodzinsky has made several attempts to address these criticisms (e.g., Drai & Grodzinsky, 2006a, 2006b). But many researchers remain skeptical of his account (e.g., Caplan et al., 2006a; De Bleser et al., 2006; Willems & Hagoort, 2009).

Another hypothesis about the role of Broca's area in sentence comprehension has been advocated by Angela Friederici and her colleagues at the Max Planck Institute for Human Cognitive and Brain Sciences in Leipzig, Germany (e.g., Friederici, 2002, 2009, 2011, 2012; Friederici et al., 2003, 2006a, 2006b). Based on data from both fMRI and DTI, this proposal maintains that different sectors of Broca's area operate in concert with certain other regions to subserve different kinds of processing. First, a ventral and medial sector called the **frontal operculum (FO)** is thought to work in tandem with the aSTG to build local phrase structures, like an NP consisting of a determiner and a noun. Second, BA44 is thought to work in tandem with the aSTG as well as with the

Frontal operculum (FO) The most ventral and medial portion of the inferior frontal gyrus.

pSTG and pSTS/BA39 to build complex, hierarchically structured sequences, like a sentence containing a relative clause. This circuit is also assumed to handle linkages between NPs and participant roles. Finally, BAs 45 and 47 are thought to work in tandem with various temporal regions to handle mostly semantic aspects of sentence comprehension.

As with Grodzinsky's approach, Friederici's model has both strengths and weaknesses. On the one hand, it is backed up by a substantial amount of imaging data. But on the other hand, it has trouble explaining a number of findings. As Rogalsky and Hickok (2011) observed, one of the most conspicuous problems is as follows. By definition, sentences consist of hierarchically organized groupings of words. Hence, the hypothesis predicts that the processing of any full-fledged sentences should engage both the FO and BA44 significantly more than the processing of unstructured word lists. And yet, as mentioned above, many studies have shown that these regions usually do *not* respond more to simple sentences than to word lists (Stowe et al., 1999; Friederici et al., 2000; Kuperberg et al., 2000; Vandenberghe et al., 2002; Humphries et al., 2005, 2006; again, for an illustration see Figure 15.14 and the accompanying text). It is important to note, however, that this problem may not be quite as bad as it initially appears, because a somewhat revised version of Friederici's proposal may be able to accommodate the imaging data more efficiently. In particular, as suggested earlier in this chapter, the mechanisms that underlie the fairly automatic, bottom-up process of hierarchical phrase structure analysis may depend primarily on the aSTG, and Broca's area may be recruited mainly when those computations are especially demanding, such as when the word order is complex (e.g., Obleser et al., 2011; see Figure 15.11 and the accompanying text) or when a syntactic violation is encountered (e.g., Friederici et al., 2003).

This idea brings us to a third hypothesis about the role of Broca's area in sentence comprehension. This approach, which has been developed mainly by Ina Bornkessel-Schlesewsky and Matthias Schlesewsky, maintains that Broca's area—especially BA44—is sensitive to whether the linearization of utterances conforms to a variety of cross-linguistically common "prominence scales" that revolve around grammatically relevant semantic and pragmatic notions like actorhood, animacy, and referentiality (for reviews see Bornkessel-Schlesewsky & Schlesewsky, 2009a, 2009b, 2012). Some of the specific prominence scales that have been investigated are as follows

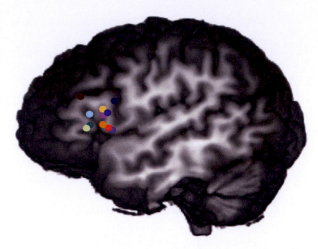

Figure 15.19 Activation peaks in Broca's area from 10 fMRI experiments on word order permutations in simple sentences. (From Bornkessel-Schlesewsky & Schlesewsky, 2012, p. 58.)

(note that ">" should be read as "is more prominent than"):

- nominative > dative > accusative (e.g., Obleser et al., 2011; see Figure 15.11 and the associated text);
- actor > undergoer (e.g., Bornkessel et al., 2005);
- animate > inanimate (e.g., Grewe et al., 2006);
- pronoun > non-pronominal argument (e.g., Grewe et al., 2005);
- proper noun > common noun (Bornkessel-Schlesewsky et al., 2009).

According to the hypothesis, sentences are easier to understand when words that are ranked higher on the various prominence scales precede words that are ranked lower. When the anticipated order is reversed, receptive processing becomes more difficult, and Broca's area is engaged to guide recovery and facilitate comprehension (Figure 15.19).

This proposal is theoretically well-motivated and empirically consistent with an impressive body of fMRI data. A potential challenge, however, that applies not only to it but also to the revised version of Friederici's hypothesis suggested above, comes from the neuropsychological literature. Both theories predict that damage to Broca's area should significantly disrupt the comprehension of semantically reversible sentences that have noncanonical word order—i.e., word order in which the undergoer NP precedes the actor NP, contrary to the second prominence scale listed above. We have already seen, though, that while the results of some lesion studies are in keeping with this prediction (e.g., Kinno et al., 2009), the results of many others are not (e.g., Dronkers et al., 2004; Caramazza et al., 2005; Thothathiri et al., 2012b).

Hypotheses that Emphasize Auditory–Verbal STM and Cognitive Control

It has long been suspected that the prefrontal cortex is crucially involved in most if not all forms of volitional, goal-directed thought and behavior, such as reasoning, planning, troubleshooting, multi-tasking, keeping information in an activated state, inhibiting impulses, regulating emotions, and interacting with other people in socially appropriate ways (e.g., Luria, 1966; Damasio, 1994; Miller & Cohen, 2001; Wood & Grafman, 2003; Fuster, 2008; see Chapter 1). These high-level capacities are sometimes referred to collectively as "executive" or "supervisory" functions, but such bureaucratic terms must always be interpreted metaphorically rather than literally, because no one really believes that a miniature CEO lives in the frontal lobes. Instead, the general consensus is that, through clever theoretical, experimental, and computational research, we will ultimately be able to decompose intelligence into smaller and smaller assemblies of interacting neurons (for an overview of recent progress in this endeavor, see Shallice & Cooper, 2011).

Given that Broca's area falls within what is sometimes called the ventrolateral portion of the prefrontal cortex, it is not surprising that some scholars have argued that the way in which it contributes to sentence comprehension reflects certain types of executive/supervisory operations. This family of hypotheses can be broken down further into two sets, one focusing on auditory–verbal STM, and the other focusing on cognitive control. The following discussion considers them in turn.

Earlier we observed that auditory–verbal STM (a.k.a. the phonological loop) has two components: first, a storage component that consciously represents the sounds of words "in the mind's ear," even in the absence of external auditory input; and second, a rehearsal component that continually refreshes those phonological forms in a top-down subvocal manner so that their activation levels remain high. We have already reviewed evidence that the storage component relies primarily on the pSTS and some adjacent regions. Now we are going to shine our spotlight on the rehearsal component, since numerous studies suggest that it draws heavily on articulatory mechanisms that reside mostly in Broca's area (neuropsychological evidence:

Vallar et al., 1997; Baldo & Dronkers, 2006; Newhart et al., 2012; functional neuroimaging evidence: Paulesu et al., 1993; Smith et al., 1998; D'Esposito et al., 1999; Henson et al., 2000; Hickok et al., 2003; see also Chapters 5 and 6).

Once again, the central issue concerns the potential role of auditory–verbal STM in sentence comprehension, only this time the focus is not on the storage component and the pSTS, but rather on the rehearsal component and Broca's area. The key question is this: Does Broca's area contribute to the comprehension of hard-to-understand sentences by using its articulatory mechanisms to actively "revivify" the auditory representations of the words, which reside back in the pSTS? The answer is by no means clear, but the available data suggest that even though auditory–verbal STM and sentence comprehension recruit some distinct patches of cortex in and near Broca's area (Amici et al., 2007; Makuuchi et al., 2009), they also share a great deal of neural "real estate" in that territory (Amici et al., 2007; Rogalsky et al., 2008b; see also Rogalsky & Hickok, 2011).

This is nicely illustrated by an fMRI experiment conducted by Rogalsky et al. (2008b). While their brain activity was being scanned, the subjects in this study listened to 90 sentences—45 involving subject-relatives (e.g., *The robber that stole the money was in the bank vault*) and 45 involving object-relatives (e.g., *The money that the robber stole was in the bank vault*). Their main task was to detect a small number of sentences that were semantically anomalous—six involving subject-relatives (e.g., *The money that stole the robber was in the bank vault*) and six involving object-relatives (e.g., *The robber that the money stole was in the bank vault*). What made the study especially interesting was that during some of the blocks of sentences, the subjects concurrently performed a secondary task. In one condition this additional task was to continuously whisper the sequence "ba da ga da," and in another condition it was to continuously tap out with the right hand the digit pattern "1 2 3 4 5 5 4 3 2 1," with 1 being the thumb, 2 being the index finger, etc. The articulatory task was intended to engage the same mechanisms that underlie the rehearsal component of auditory–verbal STM, and the finger-tapping task was meant to serve as a baseline to control for the effects of performing a secondary task while processing sentences. It is noteworthy that the neural correlates of these two tasks were also measured independently during trials that did not involve sentences.

What were the results? Behaviorally, the subjects were, overall, quite good at distinguishing between plausible and implausible sentences, but there was

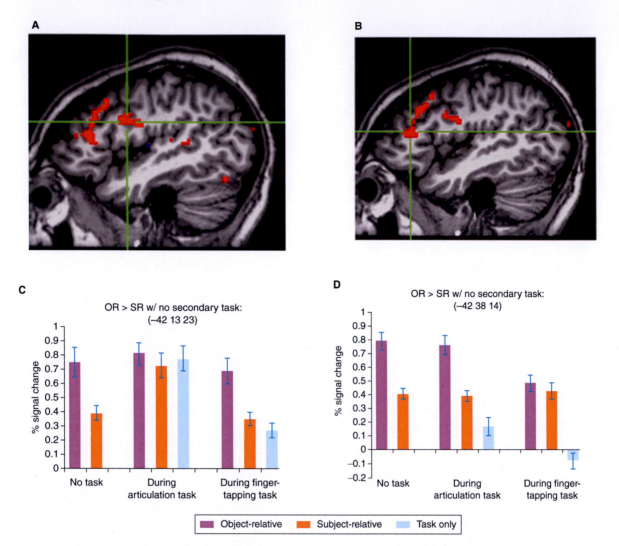

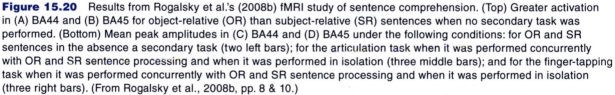

Figure 15.20   Results from Rogalsky et al.'s (2008b) fMRI study of sentence comprehension. (Top) Greater activation in (A) BA44 and (B) BA45 for object-relative (OR) than subject-relative (SR) sentences when no secondary task was performed. (Bottom) Mean peak amplitudes in (C) BA44 and (D) BA45 under the following conditions: for OR and SR sentences in the absence a secondary task (two left bars); for the articulation task when it was performed concurrently with OR and SR sentence processing and when it was performed in isolation (three middle bars); and for the finger-tapping task when it was performed concurrently with OR and SR sentence processing and when it was performed in isolation (three right bars). (From Rogalsky et al., 2008b, pp. 8 & 10.)

nevertheless an interaction between the two factors that were experimentally manipulated, these being the contrast between subject- and object-relatives and the contrast between articulatory and finger-tapping secondary tasks. Specifically, although the judgments for subject- and object-relatives were not significantly different from each other when the secondary task involved finger-tapping, the judgments for subject-relatives were significantly more accurate than those for object-relatives when the secondary task involved articulation. These findings invite the inference that the comprehension of object-relatives, but not

subject-relatives, depends on a cognitive resource that is also required for articulation, but not finger-tapping. And according to Rogalsky et al. (2008b), this resource may be the rehearsal component of auditory–verbal STM.

Importantly, the fMRI data support this interpretation. As shown in Figure 15.20, both parts of Broca's area (BAs 44 and 45) were engaged significantly more by object- than subject-relatives when no secondary task was being performed—an outcome that is consistent with other studies. The truly novel and theoretically valuable findings involve the remarkable ways in which this sentence complexity effect was, and was not, modulated by the two secondary tasks.

Focusing first on BA44 (see panels A and C in the figure), the concurrent articulatory task, but not the concurrent finger-tapping task, eliminated the complexity effect by raising the level of activation for subject-relatives up to the same level as for object-relatives. Moreover, essentially the same level of activation in BA44 was also attained when the articulatory task was performed by itself, but not when the finger-tapping task was performed by itself. Based on this intriguing response profile in BA44, Rogalsky et al. (2008b) concluded that the sentence complexity effect is due to the rehearsal component of auditory–verbal STM.

The logic of their interpretation has the following steps. (1) The data derived from the articulatory task by itself converge with other evidence that the rehearsal component relies on BA44. (2) When the articulatory task was performed concurrently with the judgment of sentences containing subject-relatives, the activation level in BA44 increased significantly. Why? Because even though the main sentence processing task did not require the rehearsal component, the secondary articulatory task did. (3) But when the articulatory task was performed concurrently with the judgment of sentences containing object-relatives, the activation level in BA44 did not increase very far beyond its already high magnitude. Why? Because—and this is really the crux of the matter—the main sentence processing task was, by inference, already drawing heavily on the rehearsal component, so that component did not have much capacity left to devote to the secondary articulatory task. As Rogalsky et al. (2008b, p. 11) put it, "processing complex sentences and performing articulatory rehearsal [share] the same pars opercularis [i.e., BA44] resources." (4) Finally, the fact that the sentence complexity effect in BA44 did not change when the concurrent task involved finger-tapping supports the view that the elimination of the effect by the articulatory task was due to the specific nature of that task, and not simply to the need to perform any sort of secondary task.

Shifting to the results for BA45 (see panels B and D in the figure), although the sentence complexity effect in this area was not modulated at all by the secondary articulatory task, it was completely eliminated by the secondary finger-tapping task, specifically by lowering the level of activation for object-relatives down to the same level as for subject-relatives. Rogalsky et al. (2008b) raise the possibility that

BA45 might implement some kind of domain-general sequence processing device that is recruited by both complex sentence comprehension and finger-tapping. But they acknowledge that while this interpretation can account for the elimination of the complexity effect, it cannot easily accommodate a separate finding—namely, that BA45 was not significantly engaged when the finger-tapping task was performed by itself. So the results for BA45 remain rather mysterious.

Still, it is worth emphasizing that the difficulty in fully explaining the results for BA45 does not detract from the theoretical implications of the results for BA44. As described above, those results provide strong evidence for the hypothesis that BA44 facilitates the processing of hard-to-understand sentences by using its articulatory mechanisms to subvocally replay the phonological forms of the words, thereby giving the listener another opportunity to determine "who's doing what to whom."

To be sure, this line of thinking has much to recommend it. At the same time, though, it also faces several challenges, especially from the neuropsychological literature. We have already encountered the two most worrisome problems, so they should come as no surprise. First, as indicated in the subsection focusing on the pSTS/BA39, there are a number of detailed case studies of brain-damaged patients who have severely reduced auditory–verbal STM capacities, but who are nevertheless able to process long and syntactically convoluted utterances fairly well (Butterworth et al., 1986; McCarthy & Warrington, 1987; Waters et al., 1991; Hanten & Martin, 2000; Friedmann & Gvion, 2003; Caplan et al., 2013). And second, as indicated earlier in this section, although damage to Broca's area sometimes impairs the ability to understand passives, object-relatives, object-clefts, and other types of complex sentences, several studies have failed to find such deficits (e.g., Dronkers et al., 2004; Caramazza et al., 2005; Thothathiri et al., 2012b; Newhart et al., 2012).

This brings us to the last set of hypotheses about the role of Broca's area in sentence comprehension. These proposals differ from each other in idiosyncratic ways, but they all have in common the core assumption that Broca's area contributes to receptive sentence processing by providing what is often called cognitive control. (For an example of how the cognitive control functions of Broca's area also contribute to speech production, see Figure 6.8 and the associated text in Chapter 6.) In a recent article devoted entirely to this topic, Novick et al. (2010, p. 907) unpack the central notion of cognitive control by pointing out that it applies not just to language, but also to a broad spectrum of other situations (for an opposing view see Fedorenko et al., 2011):

> Cognitive control refers to the mental ability to guide and adjust one's attention and actions in accordance with current goals. For example, consider an American pedestrian in London: using cognitive control, she must rein in her dominant bias to look left first before crossing the street. In the laboratory, the prototypical example of such prepotent response conflict comes from the Stroop task: naming the ink color of printed color words involves cognitive control because the instruction to attend to the perceptual stimulus conflicts with the well learned response to read the word; it is hard to utter "blue" when the word red appears in blue font. When individuals override such highly regularized or automatic behaviors, Broca's area . . . is recruited to promote a normally disfavored but presently appropriate response, in lieu of the most dominant one that initially comes to mind.

Within the realm of sentence comprehension, many researchers have argued that one of the ways in which Broca's area exerts cognitive control is by resolving conflicts between competing syntactic analyses (e.g., Novick et al., 2005, 2009, 2010; January et al., 2009; Ye & Zhou, 2009; Thothathiri et al., 2012a). This proposal should sound familiar because we considered it briefly in the subsection focusing on the pMTG, specifically in the context of the fMRI studies by Snijders et al. (2009) and Papoutsi et al. (2011) that explored the neural correlates of syntactic ambiguities.

To recapitulate, Snijders et al. (2009) found that when sentences containing noun/verb homophones like *bewijzen* ("proof"/"prove") were compared with sentences that did not contain such words, activation was observed not only in the pMTG but also in Broca's area (see Figure 15.8, Figure 15.9C, and the associated text). The basic explanation was that the pMTG represents multiple co-activated syntactic frames, and Broca's area intervenes to select the contextually appropriate one in a top-down manner.

Pursuing a closely related but somewhat different approach, Papoutsi et al.'s (2011) study involved ambiguous phrases like *bullying teenagers*, for which one analysis is favored or "dominant" (namely, treating *bullying* as an adjective and *teenagers* as an actor noun) and another analysis is disfavored or "subordinate" (namely, treating *bullying* as a verb and *teenagers* as an undergoer

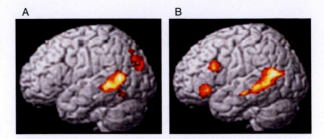

Figure 15.21 Results from Caplan et al.'s (2008a) fMRI study of sentence comprehension. (A) Greater activation in the pMTG for semantically constrained object-relative than subject-relative sentences. (B) Greater activation in both the pMTG and Broca's area for semantically unconstrained object-relative than subject-relative sentences. (From Caplan et al., 2008b, p. 647.)

noun). The researchers compared sentences in which the subordinate analysis was contextually appropriate (e.g., *The newspaper reported that bullying teenagers is bad for their self-esteem*) with sentences in which the dominant analysis was contextually appropriate (e.g., *The newspaper reported that bullying teenagers are a problem for the local school*), and once again they found activation not only in the pMTG but also in Broca's area (see Figure 15.10A and the associated text). They explained these results by arguing that Broca's area operates on the pMTG in a top-down fashion by suppressing that region's prepotent tendency to pick the dominant analysis and promoting instead its selection of the subordinate analysis. It is worth underscoring how similar this account is to Novick et al.'s (2010) description of the American pedestrian in London who must inhibit her inclination to look left before crossing the street and force herself to look right instead. According to Novick et al. (2010), Broca's area supplies the necessary forms of cognitive control in both situations.

Another interesting version of the cognitive control hypothesis has been offered by David Caplan and his colleagues at Massachusetts General Hospital (Caplan et al., 2008a, 2008b). According to this proposal, Broca's area enters into the receptive processing of sentences whenever it is necessary to "check" and/or "reanalyze" the initially determined linkages between NPs and participant roles. Some rather compelling evidence for this idea comes from a carefully designed fMRI experiment in which the subjects made plausibility judgments for four types of sentences that varied along two dimensions: first, whether they included subject- or object-relatives; and second, whether the actor and undergoer roles were semantically "constrained" (i.e., not easily reversed) or "unconstrained" (i.e., easily reversed) (Caplan et al., 2008b). Here are some examples:

(6) Constrained subject-relative: The policeman who arrested the thief watched the driver.

(7) Constrained object-relative: The thief who the policeman arrested watched the driver.

(8) Unconstrained subject-relative: The fireman who called the deputy saved the sailor.

(9) Unconstrained object-relative: The deputy who the fireman called saved the sailor.

As shown in Figure 15.21, the results revealed a striking interaction between the two factors. Although Broca's area was engaged significantly more for object- than subject-relatives when the sentences were semantically unconstrained, this complexity effect disappeared when the sentences were semantically constrained (see also Newman et al., 2010). Caplan et al. (2008a) developed a detailed interpretation of these and other findings, but we will limit our discussion to just two issues.

First, the results appear to threaten all three of the hypotheses that emphasize sequential and hierarchical aspects of sentence processing, these being the proposals formulated by Grodzinsky, Friederici, and Bornkessel-Schlesewsky and Schlesewsky. The basic problem is that those approaches predict, incorrectly, that Broca's area should be sensitive to the purely syntactic contrast between object- and subject-relatives, regardless of whether the actor/undergoer roles are semantically constrained or unconstrained. (It is notable, though, that in their recent work Bornkessel-Schlesewsky and Schlesewsky [2012] have begun to incorporate the notion of cognitive control into their theory.)

Second, although the results are compatible with the view that Broca's area contributes to the comprehension of complex sentences by subvocally repeating the phonological forms of the words, they point to a few ways in which that view could be refined. For one thing, the data suggest that subvocal repetition may not be needed for all kinds of complex sentences; instead, it may be most useful for sentences that have both noncanonical word order and semantically reversible participant roles. In addition, and even more importantly, it is quite possible that, as Caplan et al. (2008b) maintain, Broca's area does not merely replay the sound structures of such hard-to-understand sentences, but also "checks" and/or "reanalyzes" the linkages between NPs and participant roles to ensure that they are grammatically appropriate. Indeed, these sorts of operations fall squarely under the rubric of cognitive control, as it is generally conceived.

This hypothesis clearly has many virtues. But like all of the other proposals that we have considered, it has trouble accounting for the contradictory findings in the neuropsychological literature. If the "checking"/"reanalysis" functions that Broca's area putatively performs are essential for determining "who's doing what to whom" in syntactically noncanonical and semantically reversible sentences, then the disruption of those functions by lesions affecting Broca's area should reliably interfere with the comprehension of those sentences. As we have noted several times, however, several group studies have shown that damage to Broca's area does not consistently cause such deficits (e.g., Dronkers et al., 2004; Thothathiri et al., 2012b; Newhart et al., 2012).

Summary

The possible contributions of Broca's area to sentence comprehension have been investigated intensively for several decades, but they are still poorly understood. One set of hypotheses focuses on various ways in which Broca's area might extract the hierarchical structures of sentences as they unfold in time. Another set of hypotheses focuses on how Broca's area might facilitate the understanding of spoken sentences through articulatory rehearsal and cognitive control. Both of these general approaches, and all of their specific manifestations, have theoretical and empirical strengths, but none of them can account for all of the available data. Each individual theory faces its own unique set of challenges, but one particularly daunting obstacle looms over all of them. This is the frustratingly recalcitrant neuropsychological evidence that damage to Broca's area has highly inconsistent effects on sentence comprehension. In some cases, dysfunction in this region profoundly impairs the person's ability to understand sentences, but in many other cases, it does not. Perhaps these different outcomes have something to do with the recent discovery that there is substantial variability across the normal population in the degree to which Broca's area is engaged during the receptive processing of complex sentences (Prat et al., 2007; Prat & Just, 2011). The contradictory lesion data may also reflect the dynamic interplay of a host of other causal factors, such as the physiopathological nature of the disturbance (infarction, tumor, atrophy, or hypometabolism), the stage of the disease, the network of other regions that are also affected, the amount of functional–anatomical reorganization that has occurred, the specific types of sentences that are used as stimuli, the specific types of tasks that patients are asked to perform with those stimuli, and the patients' knowledge of the relevant kinds of action concepts (for a discussion of the contribution of Broca's area to action concepts, see Chapter 11). Needless to say, exploring all of these possible influences, among others, will undoubtedly keep the research community busy for several decades to come, at the very least.

Summary

The comprehension of spoken sentences is accomplished by a large-scale network of tightly interconnected cortical areas that operate synergistically to transform incoming strings of words into syntactically and semantically integrated messages. It is not yet known exactly how each node in this network contributes to the overall goal of understanding multi-word utterances, but the rough outlines of the functional architecture are slowly beginning to emerge (see also Box 15.2). At the very outset of this section, we previewed the major hypotheses about the most likely roles of each region, in order to get an initial sense of the big picture. Now that we have gone through all the key ideas in considerable detail, it's time to wrap up by briefly recapitulating the basic points:

- The pMTG seems to underlie one of the earliest stages of sentence comprehension—namely, retrieving the semantic and syntactic properties of perceived words. For example, suppose we were having a casual conversation, and you heard me say *My favorite musician has got to be Chuck Prophet, but I'm also a big fan of Eliane Elias*. Inside your brain, the phonological form of each word would be recognized in the pSTG/pSTS, and those signals would then be sent to the pMTG, which would in turn call up the corresponding semantic and syntactic specifications: *My* is a first-person possessive pronoun; *favorite* is an adjective meaning "most liked"; *musician* is a singular noun meaning "a person who plays music"; and so on. Now, if you're not familiar with either Chuck Prophet or Eliane Elias, their names would simply be registered as proper nouns designating potentially interesting individuals who you might want to Google. Regardless of that, however, what's most important in the current context is this: Whereas the semantic features of all the words in the utterance are most likely distributed across multiple cortical regions, there is growing evidence that their syntactic features are stored, at least to some extent, directly within the pMTG.

- Taking as input the lexical–syntactic information activated in the pMTG, the aSTG may work in concert with the adjacent portion of the temporal pole (BA38) to compute the hierarchical organization of sentences. Continuing with the example given above, this cortical territory may subserve the analysis of *My favorite musician* as an NP, the analysis of *has got to be* as a VP, the analysis of *Chuck Prophet* as another NP, the analysis of all three consecutive consituents as a clause, and so on. In addition, the immediately inferior region—specifically, the region comprising the aSTS, aMTG, and adjacent portions of the temporal pole (BA38)—may implement an integrative system that joins together not only the syntactic but also the semantic pieces of multi-word expressions to yield composite representations. A caveat, though, is that, nothwithstanding the data from Dronkers et al. (2004), damage to these anterior superior/lateral temporal areas does not always impair sentence comprehension.

- During online receptive sentence processing, the phonological forms of the words constituting utterances may be temporarily held in an activated state in the storage component of auditory–verbal STM, which seems to rely on the pSTS and some adjacent regions, most notably the pSTG and angular gyrus (BA39). Maintaining such verbatim records of spoken sentences is adaptive for several reasons. For one thing, it allows listeners to prevent important information from fading away (don't forget that name: Chuck Prophet!) In addition, by consulting the internal echo of what was said, listeners can verify that they understood it accurately, or, if necessary, they can correct their initial analysis. It should be borne in mind, however, that a severe reduction of auditory–verbal STM capacity does not invariably disrupt the ability to decipher long and convoluted sentences. Moreover, there is increasing evidence that, beyond its contribution to auditory–verbal STM, the angular gyrus (BA39) may be critically involved in a different function—namely, establishing correspondences between NPs and participant roles, especially for sentences that are liable to be misunderstood because they are semantically reversible and/or have noncanonical word order.

- Finally, the most controversial node in the large-scale network for sentence comprehension is Broca's area. Some researchers have proposed that it is involved in computing various aspects of the sequential and hierarchical structures of sentences. In contrast, other researchers have proposed that it facilitates comprehension through certain kinds of executive/supervisory operations, like using the articulatory component of auditory–verbal STM to refresh the phonological representations in the storage

Box 15.2 Subcortical Contributions to Sentence Comprehension

Although the lion's share of research on the neural substrates of sentence comprehension has concentrated on the large-scale cortical network that is the main focus of this chapter, there is also evidence for the involvement of certain subcortical structures, most notably the basal ganglia. In Parkinson's disease (PD) the dopamine supply to the basal ganglia gradually diminishes, and this interrupts several circuits that project from the basal ganglia to specific regions of the frontal lobes, causing not only movement problems such as tremor and rigidity, but also a variety of cognitive deficits. Roughly 20 percent of PD patients develop a dementia, and another 60 percent or so suffer from intellectual difficulties that are restricted mainly to executive/supervisory functions (for reviews see Taylor & Saint-Cyr, 1995; McNamara, 2011). Many of the patients in the latter group also display significant sentence comprehension impairments, especially for sentences that are both semantically reversible and syntactically noncanonical, like *The reporter who the senator attacked admitted the error*. The precise nature of these comprehension impairments is, however, controversial, since at least three different types of underlying disorder have been postulated:

- parsing (e.g., Lieberman et al., 1990, 1992; Natsopoulos et al., 1991, 1993);
- working memory capacity, including both auditory–verbal STM and strategic attention (e.g., Grossman et al., 1992, 2000, 2001, 2002a, 2002b; McNamara et al., 1996; Kemmerer, 1999);
- information processing speed (e.g., Grossman et al., 2002b; Lee et al., 2003).

On balance, the available data suggest that the sentence comprehension deficits displayed by nondemented PD patients can be attributed more to the second and third types of disorder than to the first. It remains unclear, however, exactly how the basal ganglia interact with the frontal lobes to facilitate the understanding of complex utterances (for an attempt to devise a computational model see Dominey & Inui, 2009; and for a different perspective see Lieberman, 2002).

component, and guiding the process of checking and/or re-analyzing the linkages between NPs and participant roles in unusually hard-to-understand sentences. Although all of these hypotheses have some merits, none of them can account for the full range of data. For example, one of the most serious challenges for future work will be to explain the inconsistencies in the neuropsychological literature, since there is substantial evidence that damage to Broca's area sometimes does and sometimes doesn't lead to debilitating sentence comprehension deficits.

Major ERP Components Associated with Sentence Comprehension

So far we have concentrated on delineating the anatomical and functional aspects of the large-scale neural network for sentence comprehension. Now we are going to shift our focus to the dynamic millisecond-by-millisecond timecourse of online sentence processing, which is tracked in exquisite detail by electrophysiological studies that measure event-related potentials

(ERPs). In Chapter 2 we noted that ERPs vary along four dimensions: polarity, latency, amplitude, and scalp distribution. During the past 30 years or so, research on language-related ERPs has uncovered several distinct types of responses that are characterized in terms of these four dimensions, and that seem to be triggered by certain phonological, semantic, and syntactic factors (for broad overviews see Kutas et al., 2006; Kaan, 2007; Swaab et al., 2012). The following survey highlights three of the most intensively investigated ERP effects that have been associated with specific aspects of sentence comprehension: the N400, which reflects the incremental build-up of multi-word meanings; the P600, which reflects combinatorial syntactic processing as well as interactions between syntactic and semantic information; and early and sustained negativities, which reflect working memory load.

The N400

Among all of the language-related ERP components, the N400 has, without a doubt, received the most attention; in fact, it has been the topic of over 1,000 articles (for reviews see Kutas & Federmeier, 2000, 2011; Hagoort, 2008; Lau et al., 2008; Baggio &

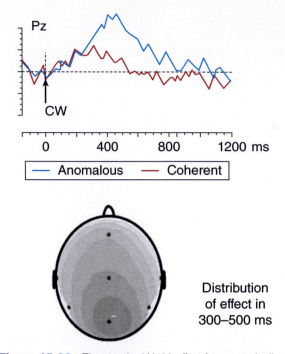

Figure 15.22 The standard N400 effect for semantically anomalous vs. coherent sentences. CW = critical word; Pz = central parietal electrode site. (From Hagoort & van Berkum, 2007, p. 802.)

Hagoort, 2011). This component was first discovered in 1980 by Marta Kutas and Steven Hillyard at the University of California, San Diego. In their groundbreaking study, subjects read sentences that were presented one word per second. Most of the sentences were quite ordinary (e.g., *I like my coffee with cream and sugar*), but some of them ended with a word that was contextually bizarre (e.g., *I like my coffee with cream and dog*). Compared with the normal sentences, the odd sentences elicited a pronounced "N400 effect." As shown in Figure 15.22, this consisted of a negative-going deflection of the waveform that began about 250 ms after the appearance of the critical word and peaked at around 400 ms, with the strongest amplitude manifested over central and parietal electrode sites (see also Figure 2.29 in Chapter 2).

Shortly after the N400 effect was discovered, researchers found that it does not index just any surprising properties of printed sentences, since it is not triggered by either orthographic changes (e.g., *She put on her high-heeled SHOES*) or grammatical errors (e.g., *All turtles have four leg*). Instead, it seems to be a signature of semantic processing. Further evidence for this view comes from studies showing that the effect is independent of input modality, being generated by semantic deviations not only in printed sentences but

also in spoken sentences (as well as signed sentences; see Grosvald et al., 2012). Moreover, the effect extends well beyond language, being induced, albeit with somewhat different scalp topographies, by violations of conceptual associations in several other kinds of stimuli, including the following:

- line drawings (Nigam et al., 1992; Holcomb & McPherson, 1994; Ganis et al., 1996; Federmeier & Kutas, 2001);
- comic strips (Cohn et al., 2012);
- photographs (McPherson & Holcomb, 1999);
- faces (Barrett & Rugg, 1989; Bobes et al., 1994; Jemel et al., 1999);
- actions (Sitnikova et al., 2003, 2008; Amoruso et al., 2013);
- sounds (Van Petten & Rheinfelder, 1995; Plante et al., 2000; Orgs et al., 2008);
- odors (Grigor et al., 1999; Sarfarazi et al., 1999).

In the domain of sentence comprehension, the amplitude, but not the timing, of the N400 is strongly modulated by semantic expectations. This is illustrated by the example given above, since it is easy to imagine someone saying *I like my coffee with cream and sugar*, but very hard to suppose that anyone would seriously say *I like my coffee with cream and dog*, and as shown in Figure 15.22, the final word in the latter sentence evokes a larger N400 than the final word in the former sentence. The influence of expectation can be formally measured in terms of **cloze probability**, which is the proportion of individuals who provide a particular word as the most likely continuation of a particular sentence fragment in a paper and pencil test. And beginning with Kutas and Hillyard's (1980) seminal study, numerous ERP experiments have demonstrated that the amplitude of the N400 elicited by a word is inversely related to that word's cloze probability in the given context. Against this background, it makes sense that as normal sentences unfold word by word, the N400s usually get progressively smaller (Figure 15.23). After all, as the semantic content of a sentence is gradually assembled in the receiver's brain, the interpretive constraints become stronger and it therefore becomes easier to fit incoming words into the overall message.

Further support for this idea comes from an ERP study that Federmeier and Kutas (1999) conducted

Cloze probability The percentage of individuals who would continue a sentence fragment with a specific word.

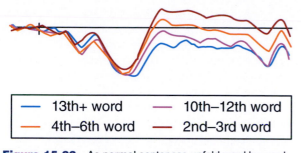

Figure 15.23 As normal sentences unfold word by word, the N400s usually get progressively smaller. (From Kutas & Federmeier, 2000, p. 465.)

13th+ word   10th–12th word
4th–6th word   2nd–3rd word

"They wanted to make the hotel look more like a tropical resort. So along the driveway they planted rows of ..."

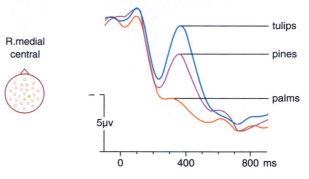

R.medial
central

tulips
pines
palms

5μv

0   400   800 ms

Figure 15.24 Results of Federmeier and Kutas's (1999) ERP study of N400 effects. Data are presented from a representative electrode site over the right medio-central part of the head, indicated by the filled circle on the iconic head. Relative to expected words like *palms* (orange line), within-category violations like *pines* (purple line) elicited smaller N400s than between-category violations like *tulips* (blue line), presumably because the former violations shared more semantic features with the correct words than latter violations did. (From Kutas & Federmeier, 2000, p. 466.)

using materials like the following: *They wanted to make the hotel look more like a tropical resort, so along the driveway they planted rows of palms/pines/tulips.* As this example shows, the critical sentence-final words included (1) the correct word (e.g., *palms*), (2) an incorrect word that belonged to the same conceptual category as the correct word (e.g., *pines*), and (3) an incorrect word that belonged to a different conceptual category than the correct word (e.g., *tulips*). A separate rating experiment showed that both types of incorrect words were in fact inappropriate, and the ERP experiment showed that both types also evoked robust N400s, relative to the control condition. What is most interesting and theoretically relevant, however, is that the N400s generated by the within-category violations were significantly smaller than those generated by the between-category violations, as depicted in Figure 15.24. This amplitude difference presumably reflects the fact that, compared to the words in the between-category condition, those in the within-category condition had more semantic features in common with the words in the control condition. For example, *tulips* does not have much conceptual overlap with *palms*, but both *pines* and *palms* refer to trees that are tall, green all year, have slender leaves in clusters, and drop things to the ground.

These different degrees of similarity between the three word meanings are part of the context-independent organization of long-term semantic memory, but they nevertheless have a measurable impact on how our brains process sentences in real time. Indeed, the ERP patterns suggest that when people are presented with a sentence context involving a hotel that is intended to look like a tropical resort, they predict that the scene will include palms, and this prediction causes the semantic features of *palms* to be pre-activated. If either *pines* or *tulips* is encountered instead, an N400 occurs in response to the deviation, but the amplitude of the

effect is much smaller for *pines* than *tulips* because the former word shares more pre-activated semantic features with *palms* than the latter word (see also Van Petten et al., 1999; DeLong et al., 2005; Federmeier, 2007; Kutas et al., 2011). More generally, the upshot is that the amplitude of the N400 increases systematically as a function of the number of semantic features that are initially anticipated but then suddenly violated in a particular sentence context (see also Li et al., 2006).

Importantly, the N400 is sensitive not only to the relationships between word meanings, but also to world knowledge outside the realm of language. This was demonstrated by an ERP study that Hagoort et al. (2004) conducted with Dutch speakers. Have you ever been to The Netherlands? If so, you probably know that the trains there are modern, fast, efficient, and very yellow (Figure 15.25). In designing their experiment, the researchers capitalized on such real-world facts by creating three conditions: (1) correct sentences like *The Dutch trains are yellow and very crowded;* (2) sentences that were semantically plausible but factually wrong like *The Dutch trains are white and very crowded;* and (3) sentences that were semantically implausible like *The Dutch trains are sour and very crowded* (note that the original stimuli were in Dutch). As shown in Figure 15.26, compared to the control condition, both of the violation conditions generated N400 effects that were identical in onset

Figure 15.25   A Dutch train.

and peak latency as well as quite similar in amplitude and topographic distribution. These findings indicate that both intra-linguistic semantic information and extra-linguistic world knowledge are recruited and integrated within the same time interval during on-line sentence comprehension, starting about 250 ms post word-onset. From a theoretical perspective, this outcome is significant because it challenges the hypothesis that when we understand sentences we engage in a two-step process of first determining the meaning and then determining whether that meaning is true or false (Forster, 1989). As Hagoort et al. (2004, p. 440) point out, the ERP results show that "it does not take any longer to discover that a sentence is untrue than to detect that it is semantically anomalous."

Now that we have considered the major factors that drive the N400 effect, we can briefly address its underlying neural correlates. Although the N400 effect has not yet been precisely localized in the brain, studies using magnetoencephalography (a technique with superb spatial and temporal resolution) and direct intracranial recording suggest that it reflects the coordinated activity of a number of mostly left-lateralized temporal and frontal areas (for reviews see Van Petten & Luka, 2006, and Lau et al., 2008). This activity seems to take the form of a "wave" that begins in the left pSTG and pMTG about 250 ms post word-onset, then spreads to inferior and anterior temporal regions by about 365 ms, and finally spreads to the frontal lobe between 370 and 500 ms. The functional aspects of these physiological changes remain to be seen, but the data appear to be consistent with some of the hypotheses discussed earlier. Specifically, the pMTG may implement a "lexical interface" that promotes access to the syntactic and semantic properties of perceived words; the ATL may contain an amodal "semantic hub" as well as a "combinatorial syntactic–semantic network"; and the ventrolateral prefrontal cortex (i.e., Broca's area and some adjacent regions) may subserve various executive/supervisory operations that guide the top-down regulation of receptive sentence processing. Much more research will be required, however, to work out exactly how these proposals relate to the unique characteristics of the N400 effect.

In summary, the N400 tracks the steady accumulation of semantic content over the course of sentence processing. As the overall message of a sentence is gradually assembled word by word, the progressive increase of information serves to constrain, and in some cases pre-activate, the meanings of forthcoming words. Hence, the richer the context becomes, the easier it is to assimilate expected words, and the harder it is to handle unexpected ones. This variation in the degree of ease or difficulty of semantic integration is precisely what the amplitude of N400 reflects. Kutas and Federmeier (2011, p. 641) capture this point as follows: "The N400 window thus provides a temporally delimited electrical snapshot of the intersection of a feedforward flow of stimulus-driven activity with a state of the distributed, dynamically active neural landscape that is semantic memory."

The P600

Another language-related ERP effect that has received a great deal of attention is the P600 (for reviews see Hagoort et al., 1999; Osterhout et al., 2004; Kuperberg, 2007; Bornkessel-Schlesewsky & Schlesewsky, 2008, 2009a; Van de Meerendonk et al., 2009). It is characterized by a positive-going deflection of the waveform that usually starts between 500 and 600 ms after the onset of the critical word, lasts for at least 500 ms, and is strongest over centroparietal sites. The P600 effect was first reported in the early 1990s by two research teams: Lee Osterhout and Phillip Holcomb at Tufts University (1992); and Peter Hagoort, Colin Brown, and Jolanda Groothusen at the Max Planck Institute for Psycholinguistics (1993). Unlike the N400 effect, this one seems to be more sensitive to syntactic than semantic integration during sentence processing, which is why Hagoort et al. (1993) originally called it the "syntactic positive shift (SPS)." As we will see, however, some of the situations that give rise to robust P600s seem to involve interactions between syntax and semantics.

First of all, it is well established that large P600s are elicited by syntactic violations in both printed and

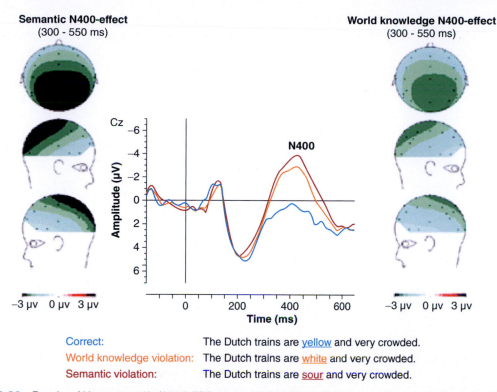

Semantic N400-effect
(300 - 550 ms)

World knowledge N400-effect
(300 - 550 ms)

−3 μv   0 μv   3 μv

−3 μv   0 μv   3 μv

Correct: The Dutch trains are <u>yellow</u> and very crowded.
World knowledge violation: The Dutch trains are <u>white</u> and very crowded.
Semantic violation: The Dutch trains are <u>sour</u> and very crowded.

Figure 15.26   Results of Hagoort et al.'s (2004) ERP study of N400 effects. Relative to correct words like *yellow* (blue line), both semantic violations like *sour* (brown line) and world knowledge violations like *white* (orange line) elicited significant N400s with equivalent temporal profiles and scalp distributions as well as similar amplitudes (but somewhat weaker for semantic than world knowledge violations). Cz = central electrode site. (From Hagoort et al., 2004, p. 439.)

spoken sentences. For example, Hagoort et al. (1993) found that such responses are triggered by errors involving subject–verb agreement, as exemplified by the contrast between *The spoiled child threw the toys on the floor* and ** The spoiled child throw the toys on the floor* (note that the original stimuli were in Dutch). And in a subsequent study Hagoort and Brown (1994) discovered that essentially the same responses are also generated by agreement violations in nonsense sentences that lack semantic and pragmatic constraints. This is illustrated in Figure 15.27, which shows that relative to the correctly inflected verb *smokes* in *The boiled watering can smokes the telephone in the cat*, the incorrectly inflected verb *smoke* in ** The boiled watering can smoke the telephone in the cat* evokes a large P600 (again, the original stimuli were in Dutch). Other studies have documented similar effects for a variety of other kinds of syntactic violations, including the following:

- Phrase structure (e.g., Neville et al., 1991; Hagoort et al., 1993; Friederici et al., 1996):
  - Correct: Bill admired Susan's picture of the park.
  - Incorrect: Bill admired Susan's of picture the park.
- Subcategorization (e.g., Osterhout et al., 1994; Ainsworth-Darnell et al., 1998):
  - Correct: The doctor hoped the patient was lying.
  - Incorrect: The doctor forced the patient was lying.
- Pronoun case (e.g., Coulson et al., 1998):
  - Correct: The plane took us to paradise and back.
  - Incorrect: The plane took we to paradise and back.
- Pronoun gender (e.g., Osterhout & Mobley, 1995; Münte et al., 1997):
  - Correct: The successful woman congratulated herself on the promotion.
  - Incorrect: The successful woman congratulated himself on the promotion.
- Verb tense (e.g., Osterhout & Nicol, 1999):
  - Correct: The expensive ointment will cure all forms of skin disease.
  - Incorrect: The expensive ointment will curing all forms of skin disease.
- Question formation (e.g., Neville et al., 1991; McKinnon & Osterhout, 1996):

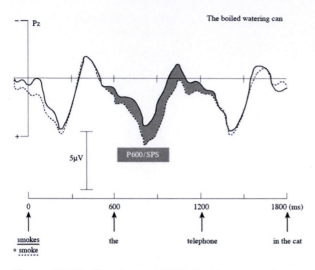

Figure 15.27 The standard P600 effect for grammatically ill-formed vs. well-formed sentences. Pz = central parietal electrode site; SPS = syntactic positive shift. (From Hagoort, 2008, p. 1058.)

○ Correct: Was a sketch of the landscape admired by the man?
○ Incorrect: What was a sketch of admired by the man?

Taken together, these sorts of results suggest that large P600s may index difficulties in syntactic unification. It is noteworthy, however, that similar effects have also been observed in response to violations of structure-dependent combinatorial rules in several non-linguistic domains, including music (Besson & Macar, 1987; Janata, 1995; Patel et al., 1998), mathematics (Núñez-Peña & Honrubia-Serrano, 2004), abstract sequences (Lelekov et al., 2000; Lelekov-Boissard & Dominey, 2002), and videoclips of actions (Sitnikova et al., 2003, 2008). Hence it is possible that the P600 component is the electrophysiological fingerprint of structure-building processes more generally.

Another important point is that, under certain circumstances, large P600s can be evoked by sentences that do not, strictly speaking, contain any outright syntactic violations whatsoever. One such situation involves the critical "red flag" word in so-called **garden path sentences**—i.e., sentences that lead the reader or listener "down the garden path" because they contain inconspicuous syntactic ambiguities that initially favor

> **Garden path sentence** A sentence that contains a temporary syntactic ambiguity that initially favors a simple analysis but later requires a more complex one.

a simple analysis but later require a more complex one, thereby forcing a sudden shift of processing strategies. This is nicely illustrated by an ERP study that Kaan and Swaab (2003) conducted using sentences like those in (10) and (11):

(10) The man is painting the house but the garage is already finished.
(11) The man is painting the house and the garage is already finished.

Both sentences are grammatically well-formed, but the second one contains a temporary syntactic ambiguity that the first one lacks. In particular, at the point in (11) when the NP *the garage* occurs, two distinct analyses are possible: one that treats it as a conjoined direct object of *painting*, on the same level as *the house*; and another that treats it as the subject of a second clause. Because the former analysis is simpler, the processing system adopts it by default. But then the subsequent verb *is* occurs, and this forces the system to abandon its initial analysis and rapidly build a new one that is compatible with the input. These abrupt computational reactions to the unexpected *is* in (11) are reflected by the generation of a robust P600, relative to the comparable instance of *is* in (10). Similar results have been obtained in other studies that have also investigated the electrophysiological correlates of the types of syntactic reanalyses that are required by garden path sentences (e.g., Osterhout & Holcomb, 1992, 1993; Osterhout et al., 1994; Mecklinger et al., 1995).

Another situation in which grammatically well-formed sentences elicit significant P600s involves syntactic complexity. This was first demonstrated by Kaan et al. (2000), who employed sentences like those in (12) and (13):

(12) Emily wondered whether the performer in the concert had imitated a pop star for the audience's amusement.
(13) Emily wondered who the performer in the concert had imitated for the audience's amusement.

In both sentences, when the verb *imitated* is encountered, its actor role is assigned to the NP *the performer*. In (13), however, another linking operation is also performed during the same time interval—specifically, the undergoer role is assigned to the NP *who*, which is separated from the verb by several words. What Kaan et al. (2000) found is that, relative to the verb in (12), the verb in (13) elicits a large P600, presumably reflecting the additional

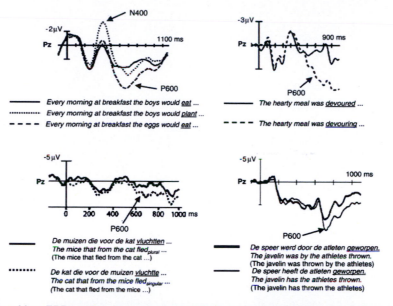

Figure 15.28 Results of four ERP studies demonstrating P600s that are elicited by the verb in grammatically well-formed sentences with the following special characteristics: The meanings of the NPs and the verb lead the reader/hearer to expect an arrangement of participant roles that would be plausible in the real world, but the syntactic cues dictate that the opposite arrangement actually applies, and this arrangement is semantically anomalous. (A) Kuperberg et al. (2003). (B) Kim & Osterhout (2005), Experiment 1. (C) Kolk et al. (2003). (D) Hoeks et al. (2004). Pz = central parietal electrode site. (From Kuperberg, 2007, p. 27.)

processing step that is necessary. This outcome lends further support to the notion that the P600 effect is the signature of syntactic integration difficulty.

Finally, P600s are usually evoked by the verb in grammatically well-formed sentences with the following special characteristics: The meanings of the NPs and the verb lead the reader/hearer to expect an arrangement of participant roles that would be plausible in the real world, but the syntactic cues dictate that the opposite arrangement actually applies, and this arrangement is semantically anomalous. For example, in one of the first studies that obtained such results, Kuperberg et al. (2003) found a very small, non-significant N400 but a very large, robust P600 for verbs like *eat* in sentences like *Every morning at breakfast the eggs would eat . . .*, relative to the same verbs in sentences like *Every morning at breakfast the boys would eat . . . .* These patterns are illustrated in Figure 15.28 together with similar observations that other researchers have reported using similar materials.

Several attempts have been made to explain these rather puzzling P600 effects (for reviews see Kuperberg, 2007; Bornkessel-Schlesewsky & Schlesewsky, 2008; Van de Meerendonk et al., 2009). According to one account, the effects index a repair process that disregards the syntactic cues and switches the participant role(s) of the NP(s) so that the expression makes sense

(Kim & Osterhout, 2005). But while this proposal can handle the data shown in Figure 15.28, it cannot accommodate a different finding—specifically, that P600s are also generated by the verb in sentences that are not amenable to such a repair process, as in *To make good documentaries cameras must interview . . .* (Kuperberg et al., 2006). Another hypothesis is that the P600s reflect the continued computation of syntactic–semantic correspondences after a conflict has been detected between an interpretation that is based primarily on word meanings and an interpretation that is based primarily on grammatical structures (Kuperberg, 2007). This explanation has much to recommend it, but it faces some challenges from cross-linguistic data, as pointed out by Bornkessel-Schlesewsky and Schlesewsky (2008). Yet another proposal is that the P600 effects shown in Figure 15.28 reflect a reanalysis process that (1) is initiated when one's expectations conflict with the input, (2) is geared toward determining whether the input was processed correctly, (3) is a form of cognitive control, and (4) is not unique to language (Van de Meerendonk et al., 2009). This account has been gaining support in recent years, but it seems to require further elaboration, especially regarding the relationship between the P600 and the N400. Much more could be said about these and other attempts to explain the data, but delving even deeper into the

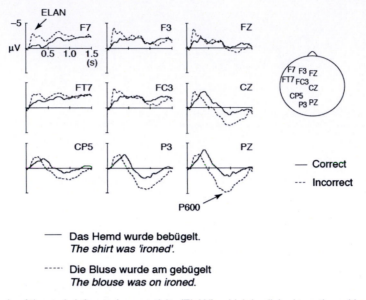

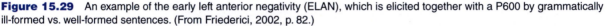

— Das Hemd wurde bebügelt.
The shirt was 'ironed'.

---- Die Bluse wurde am gebügelt
The blouse was on ironed.

Figure 15.29 An example of the early left anterior negativity (ELAN), which is elicited together with a P600 by grammatically ill-formed vs. well-formed sentences. (From Friederici, 2002, p. 82.)

details would take us too far afield. Suffice it to say that this general line of inquiry has uncovered some highly intriguing aspects of the P600 that will no doubt continue to receive close attention from neurolinguists for many years to come.

What are the neural sources of the P600? Unfortunately, this topic is poorly understood. Current data point to important roles for the pMTG, inferior frontoparietal cortices, and basal ganglia (Friederici et al., 1999; Frisch et al., 2003; Kwon et al., 2005; Service et al., 2007; Kuperberg et al., 2008). But these findings are only a beginning.

In summary, the amplitude of the P600 reflects the degree of difficulty of syntactic integration during sentence processing, but it also appears to be sensitive to certain aspects of the syntax–semantics interface. Significant P600 effects are triggered not only by a wide range of blatant syntactic violations, but also by at least three different classes of grammatically well-formed expressions: garden path sentences that require rapid reanalyses; complex sentences that require extra computations; and sentences in which the most plausible arrangement of participant roles is not syntactically licensed.

Early and Sustained Negativities

Although it is well established that syntactic violations elicit large P600s, it is also clear that these effects emerge rather late, peaking over half a second after the onset of the critical word. For this reason, it is natural to ask whether syntactic violations leave any earlier traces in the electrophysiological waveforms that are recorded during sentence processing. The answer is most definitely yes; however, the proper explanation for these early effects is controversial.

According to an influential model proposed by Friederici (2002, 2011), syntactic violations often give rise to a "biphasic" (i.e., two-component) ERP pattern. The first phase is an early left anterior negativity (ELAN) that is most prominent over left frontal electrode sites about 100–300 ms post-word-onset and that is thought to index the initial, automatic detection of the error. The second phase is a P600, which is thought to index a more strategic process of syntactic revision. This biphasic pattern is illustrated in Figure 15.29, which depicts the contrasting waveforms evoked by the German verb *gebügelt* ("ironed") in the well-formed sentence *Das Hemd wurde gebügelt* ("The shirt was ironed") and in the ill-formed sentence *Die Bluse wurde am gebügelt* ("The blouse was on ironed"). (Note that we discussed the same pair of sentences in the subsection of this chapter that deals with the aSTG.) When the latter sentence is perceived, the preposition *am* sets up an expectation for a noun, but because the verb *gebügelt* occurs instead, this expectation is disconfirmed, and the immediate electrophysiological effect is an ELAN, which is then rapidly followed by a P600.

The neurolinguistic literature seems to contain a wealth of solid ELAN data, but the reliability, validity,

Table 15.7   Experimental Conditions in Hastings and Kotz's (2008) ERP Study of Syntactic Violations

Condition	Agreement	Phrase Structure
Correct (1)	*er kegelt* (he bowls)	*er kegelt* (he bowls)
Incorrect (1)	**er kegelst* (*he bowl)	**er Kegel* (*he cone)
Correct (2)	*du kegelst* (you bowl)	*ein Kegel* (a cone)
Incorrect (2)	**du kegelt* (*you bowls)	**ein kegelt* (*a bowls)

Source: Hastings & Kotz (2008, p. 1210).

and functional significance of these findings have recently been questioned, most forcefully by Steinhauer and Drury (2012). These researchers describe many serious problems in detail, but here we will focus on just one. This particular issue has to do with the nature of the relationship between the ELAN and the P600. In a nutshell, a number of studies suggest that the ELAN is not really a brief effect at all, but is rather a "sustained negativity," the early part of which is always visible, as in Figure 15.29, but the later part of which is often "cancelled out" by the opposite polarity of the subsequent P600.

Some striking evidence for this phenomenon comes from an elegant ERP study by Hastings and Kotz (2008). As shown in Table 15.7, their stimuli consisted of several sets of auditorily presented two-word expressions that were phonologically quite similar, with the very end of the second word in each expression indicating whether it was grammatically well-formed, contained a subject–verb agreement error, or contained a phrase structure error. The investigators conducted two experiments with these stimuli. In the "attended" condition the subjects performed a grammaticality task, whereas in the "unattended" condition they ignored the expressions and concentrated instead on watching a silent movie. The ERP analyses, which were time-locked to the critical information at the end of each expression, yielded some fascinating findings.

Considering first the attended condition, both types of syntactic violations evoked an ELAN that was immediately followed by a P600 (Figure 15.30A). Although the magnitude of the P600 effect was significant for the agreement violations, it was not significant for the phrase structure violations; however, the authors argue that the latter result should not really concern us, since it may have been due to the fact that the phrase structure violations occurred in incomplete rather than complete sentences. Turning now to the unattended condition, both types of syntactic violations evoked a negative-going deflection of the

waveform that was quite similar to the ELAN in both temporal onset and scalp topography, but that, instead of being followed by a P600, was sustained for nearly 700 ms (Figure 15.30B).

What do these differences between the two experimental outcomes mean? One implication is that, in keeping with Friederici's (2002, 2011) model, the P600 reflects parsing operations that are under deliberate, strategic control, being recruited only when people pay close attention to the linguistic input. A much more interesting implication, though, is that, contrary to Friederici's (2002, 2011) model, the ELAN does not appear to be an discrete ERP component, but instead looks more like the first part of a sustained negativity, the second part of which tends to be "masked" by the subsequent P600 when subjects process the stimuli in a conscious manner. Steinhauer and Drury (2012, p. 147) even go so far as to make the following claim:

> We hypothesize that [syntactic] violations in auditory studies *always* elicit sustained negativities and no local ELANs. Whenever an ELAN looks like a local (transient) effect, this is likely to be due to a concurrent P600 component cancelling out the later part of the negativity . . . If our hypothesis is true, there may be no need to account for any local ELAN effects between 100 and 300 ms (as suggested by Friederici's model), but there is a need to explain sustained negativities with a remarkably early onset.

How, then, should these early and sustained negativities be interpreted? Based on a review of the relevant literature, Steinhauer and Drury (2012) suggest that they reflect increased working memory demands, especially when representations of incoming linguistic material must be kept active in an unintegrated format. This account is consistent with evidence that such ERP effects are associated not only with syntactic violations, but also with a variety of other situations,

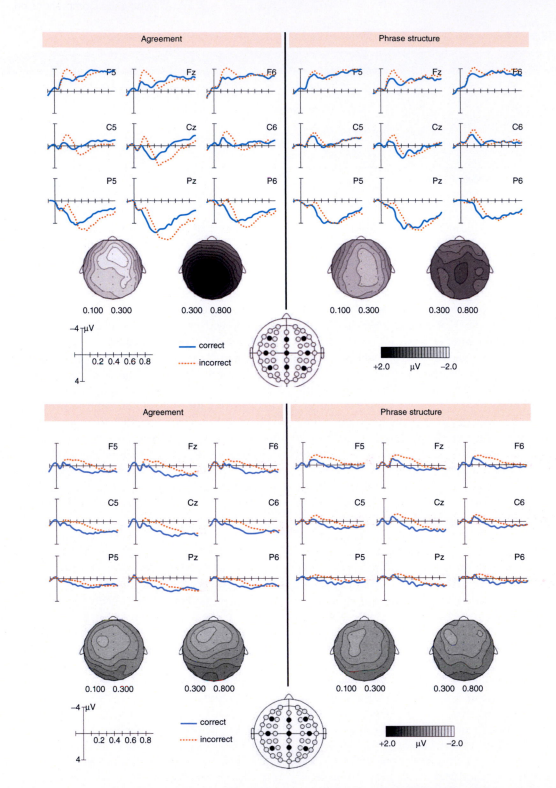

Figure 15.30 Results of Hastings and Kotz's (2008) ERP study of responses generated by grammatical vs. ungrammatical expressions that are either attended or unattended. Waveforms from nine electrode sites are shown together with topographic maps from two temporal windows, 100–300 ms and 300–800 ms. (A) ELAN-P600 combinations were elicited by subject–verb agreement and phrase structure violations when the task was to make explicit grammaticality judgments. (B) Sustained negativities were elicited by subject–verb agreement and phrase structure violations when the task was to ignore the expressions and concentrate instead on a silent movie. See the main text for details. (From Hastings & Kotz, 2008, pp. 1213–1214.)

including the following: (1) violations involving temporal relationships, mood, and modality (Münte et al., 1998; Dwivedi et al., 2006); (2) subvocal rehearsal (Ruchkin et al., 1992); (3) long-distance dependencies between NPs and verbs (Kluender & Kutas, 1993; King & Kutas, 1995; Fiebach et al., 2001, 2002; Phillips et al., 2005); and (4) establishing relationships between lexical–semantic and discourse-level representations (van Berkum et al., 2007; Steinhauer et al., 2010). Further research is needed, however, to verify and refine the working memory account of early and sustained negativities.

Summary

The ERP technique is ideal for tracking the rapidly changing neurodynamics of online sentence comprehension. Studies using this method have disclosed a number of language-related ERP components, three of which are as follows: the N400, which indexes the gradual assembly of multi-word meanings; the P600, which indexes syntactic unification and some aspects of the syntax–semantics interface; and early and sustained negativities, which index working memory load.

Summary and Key Points

- Understanding spoken sentences is a complex process that requires many different kinds of computational operations and processing resources that are collectively subserved by a large-scale neural network residing primarily in the left hemisphere.
- The key cortical components of this network are as follows:

  - the pMTG;
  - the aSTG;
  - the pSTS/BA39;
  - most of BA47;
  - part of BA46;
  - Broca's area (BAs 44 and 45).

- These regions are structurally interconnected by several white matter fiber tracts. Those involving the pMTG, which is a major "neural epicenter," are as follows:

  - The middle longitudinal fasciculus interconnects the pMTG and aSTG.
  - The inferior occipito-frontal fasciculus interconnects the pMTG and BA47.
  - The long segment of the arcuate fasciculus interconnects the pMTG and Broca's area.
  - The short segment of the arcuate fasciculus interconnects the pMTG and the pSTS/BA39.
  - The tapetum interconnects the pMTG in the left hemisphere with its twin in the right hemisphere.

- According to recent theoretical and empirical work, the cortical components of the network may contribute to sentence comprehension in the following ways:

  - The pMTG may be essential for retrieving the semantic and syntactic properties of incoming words. It may also represent the competing syntactic frames of category-ambiguous words.
  - The aSTG may play a central role in grouping words into hierarchically organized phrases and clauses, based largely on the syntactic specifications accessed by the pMTG. In addition, the inferiorly adjacent lateral sector of the left ATL may implement a "combinatorial network" that integrates the syntactic and semantic aspects of sentences to yield composite message-level representations.
  - The pSTS/BA39, together with the neighboring pSTG, may implement the storage component of auditory–verbal STM. Moreover, this region may also be necessary for linking NPs like subject and object with participant roles like actor and undergoer, especially in sentences that are semantically reversible and/or syntactically noncanonical.
  - The inferior frontal gyrus, including Broca's area, may facilitate sentence comprehension by subserving certain types of sequential and hierarchical processing and/or by subserving other sorts of mental resources, most notably the rehearsal component of auditory–verbal STM and various forms of cognitive control. However, the precise contribution of this region to sentence comprehension is highly controversial.

- ERP studies have begun to illuminate the millisecond-by-millisecond timecourse of online sentence processing. Three language-related ERP components are as follows:

  - The N400 seems to reflect the incremental build-up of multi-word meanings.
  - The P600 seems to reflect combinatorial syntactic processing as well as interactions between syntactic and semantic information.
  - Early and sustained negativities seem to reflect working memory load.

Recommended Reading

- Friederici, A.D. (2011). The brain basis of language processing: From structure to function. *Physiological Reviews, 91*, 1357–1392. An overview of one of the most influential models of the neural substrates of sentence comprehension, written by a leading figure in the field.
- Swaab, T.Y., LeDoux, K., Camblin, C.C., & Boudewyn, M.A. (2012). Language-related ERP components. In S.J. Luck & E.S. Kappenman (Eds.), *The Oxford handbook of event-related potential components* (pp. 397–439). Oxford, UK: Oxford University Press. An outstanding, up-to-date survey of ERP components related to sentence comprehension.
- Osterhout, L., Kim, A., & Kuperberg, G.R. (2012). The neurobiology of sentence comprehension. In M. Spivey, M. Joannisse, & K. McRae (Eds.), *The Cambridge Handbook of Psycholinguistics* (pp. 365–389). Cambridge, UK: Cambridge University Press. A promising approach that highlights multiple parallel and interacting streams of processing, emphasizing their neurobiological, genetic, and evolutionary foundations.

Discourse

16

Introduction

Having discussed how our brains process simple words, complex words, and entire sentences, we are now ready to move even closer to naturalistic, real-world language use by addressing the neural substrates of discourse. Many different definitions of discourse have been proposed, but all of them share the core idea that it comprises *language above and beyond the sentence* (Gee & Handford, 2012). Such a broad characterization has the advantage of embracing all of the multifarious forms of discourse, including ordinary conversational dialogue, play-by-play sports coverage, political speeches, religious texts, academic books and papers, newspaper articles, cooking recipes, song lyrics, poems, fables, myths, and novels. Despite this tremendous diversity, however, the vast majority of neuroscientific research on discourse has focused on a single genre, albeit a very large one—namely narratives, or to put it more colloquially, stories.

This is by no means an accident, since stories have played a central role in all cultures throughout recorded history and may even be woven into the very fabric of human psychology (Sarbin, 1986; Bruner, 1991; McAdams, 1997; Hutto, 2007; Mar & Oatley, 2008; Boyd, 2009; Gottschall, 2012). From Homer's *The Iliad* to Shakespeare's *Hamlet*, Dr. Seuss's *The Cat in the Hat,* and J.K. Rowling's *Harry Potter and the Sorcerer's Stone*, good narratives compress and coordinate a wealth of information about the world, including the causal relations between sequences of events, the emotional vicissitudes of life in certain environments, and the dynamic intentions of multiple interacting agents. In addition, by gravitating toward morally charged conflicts and enticing readers or listeners to imagine them from the alternative vantage points of different characters, well-crafted stories serve the valuable function of exercising people's perspective-taking and empathizing abilities. In fact, recent studies have shown that, independent of personality differences, individuals who consume a lot of fiction tend to have higher empathy scores than those who prefer nonfiction (Mar et al., 2006, 2009). One experiment even demonstrated that the more deeply people immerse themselves in a compassion-inducing story, the more likely they are to subsequently help others and perceive subtle expressions of fear in their faces (Johnson, 2012).

Such findings lend some support to the proposal that the Humanitarian Revolution—that is, the period extending from the 17th century through the 19th century when socially sanctioned forms of violence like slavery, superstitious killing, and sadistic punishment were systematically challenged and gradually abolished—was influenced in part by the increasing availability of poignant memoirs and novels describing the mistreatment of victims (Hunt, 2007; Pinker, 2011). To take an especially vivid example, in Harriet Beecher Stowe's famous novel *Uncle Tom's Cabin*, which appeared in 1852, there are many heartbreaking scenes in which slaves are flogged and children are taken from their mothers. These graphic portrayals of unwarranted suffering gripped people's hearts and minds so strongly that the book sold over 300,000 copies in the first year alone and helped catalyze the movement to end slavery. As Pinker (2011, p. 155) points out, "According to legend, when Abraham Lincoln met Stowe in 1862, he said, 'So you're the little woman who started this great war.'" Lincoln was exaggerating, of course, but his statement clearly attests to the power of narrative to change people's attitudes and galvanize them into action.

The purpose of this chapter is to present some of the highlights of recent research in cognitive neuroscience that has begun to illuminate the cortical networks that underlie the processes necessary to produce and understand stories—processes like establishing coherent relationships between sentences, imagining real or fictitious situations, adopting different points of view, and attributing mental states to protagonists. Here at the outset, it is important to note that, largely because of the sheer complexity of narrative discourse, this area of inquiry is not nearly as advanced as many of the other areas discussed in previous chapters. Nevertheless, some impressive and exciting findings have emerged, especially during the past decade or so, and the pace of progress has been accelerating (for reviews see Mar, 2004, 2011; Mason & Just, 2006, 2013; Ferstl, 2007, 2010; van Berkum, 2012; Willems, forthcoming). The chapter is organized in two main parts, the first of which focuses on story production, and the second of which focuses on story comprehension. The second part is more detailed than the first, but this simply reflects an inherent imbalance in the literature, since more has been learned about the neural systems that allow us to decipher stories than about those that allow us to generate them.

Story Production

Among the many "macrolinguistic" mental operations that are required to tell a tale, those that have received the most attention in the cognitive neuroscience literature are geared toward the creation of **discourse coherence**, which has to do with the conceptual connections—logical, causal, chronological, etc.—that relate utterances to each other over the course of a story, thereby tying all the ideas together into a unified whole. Such connections must be formed at two different structural levels—local and global. At the local level, the speaker must build coherence by ensuring that the meanings of consecutive sentences fit together cohesively so that the narrative has a smooth, continuous flow, without abrupt interruptions or erratic shifts in topic. And at the global level, the speaker must build coherence by keeping track of the overarching plot and preserving the thematic thread so that the major segments of the story are linked together from beginning to end.

Achieving both types of coherence clearly requires top-down, goal-directed planning abilities as well

> **Discourse coherence**   The conceptual connections—logical, causal, chronological, etc.—that relate sentences to each other over the course of a story. Such connections must be formed at both local and global levels.

as substantial working memory resources. These sorts of organizational processes fall squarely under the rubric of what we have referred to in previous chapters as executive/supervisory functions, and because those functions are known to depend primarily on various prefrontal areas of the brain, one would expect those areas to be heavily recruited whenever a person recounts a story. Given that the organizational processes that are necessary to assemble a coherent narrative are concerned mainly with the relationships between utterances, it seems likely that they transcend, and hence are dissociable from, the more lexically and syntactically oriented operations that are involved in producing single sentences. At the same time, however, it is reasonable to suppose that at least some of these processes are not unique to narrative construction, but are also used to regulate the performance of other kinds of cognitively demanding, multi-step tasks, such as preparing a meal. All of these predictions have been supported by a variety of studies employing neuropsychological and functional neuroimaging techniques (Kaczmarek, 1984; Sirigu et al., 1998; Crozier et al., 1999; Allain et al., 1999, 2001; Braun et al., 2001; Coelho, 2002; Davis & Coelho, 2004; Ash et al., 2006, 2012; Troiani et al., 2008; Ditman & Kuperberg, 2010; Marini et al., 2011; Coelho et al., 2012). Here, however, we will restrict our attention to a few studies that have explored these issues by focusing on an especially well-constrained type of narrative discourse commonly referred to, at least by researchers in this corner of academia, as frog stories.

Frog Stories: A Window onto the Neural Substrates of Narrative Coherence

Mercer Mayer is a prolific author and artist who was among the first professional illustrators to create wordless picture books for children—that is, books that relay stories entirely through drawings. Some of his most successful publications in this genre revolve around a little boy and his cute animal friends, and one of them is called *Frog, Where Are You?* It consists of a sequence of 24 black-and-white drawings that portray the boy's adventures as he and his dog wander through a forest searching for his pet frog who escaped from a jar during the night while he was sleeping (see Figure 16.1 for a sample of drawings). This particular book stands out from all the others in Mayer's oeuvre because it is beloved not only by the children it was originally intended for, but also by countless researchers who have used it to elicit

Figure 16.1 Seven of the 24 drawings comprising Mercer Mayer's *Frog, Where Are You?* (From Berman & Slobin, 1994, pp. 647–654.)

oral narratives, affectionately called frog stories, from people varying greatly in age and background. In fact, such verbal renderings of the short picture book have been recorded from speakers of over 70 languages worldwide, and meticulous analyses of these stories have led to many interesting discoveries about the nature of narrative discourse (Berman & Slobin, 1994; Strömqvist & Verhoeven, 2004; an example

of a complete frog story produced by a healthy adult English speaker is provided in Box 16.1).

In the current context, what matters most is that frog stories have also been elicited from individuals suffering from different types of brain damage, as well as from normal people undergoing fMRI scanning, in order to explore the neural bases of the organizational processes that are necessary to generate well-structured

Box 16.1   A Normal Frog Story

Once upon a time there was a little boy who had a frog and a dog. And after he and his doggie went to sleep one night, the frog got out of the jar and escaped. When he woke up in the morning, he saw that the frog was gone, and he was very sad. He looks in his boots and the doggie looked in the jar. Oops! The doggie got his head caught in the jar. They looked out the window and the doggie fell out of the window, but the jar broke off his head, so he didn't have his head stuck in the jar anymore. The boy and the doggie went looking for the froggie all over the place. The dog found a beehive and the little boy went and looked in a hole for the frog. The boy found a gopher, and the dog played with the beehive some more. That was a really dangerous thing to play with. And pretty soon, well, the little boy went and looked in the hole in the tree, he better be careful, looking in all those holes. Oops! An owl flew out of the hole in the tree and knocked him down out of the tree, and the bees chased the dog. (That boy better let those bees alone.) But the owl kept bothering the little boy, but then he left him alone. The little boy went and climbed up on a big rock and called his froggie. And the dog was really sad and he didn't like all those bees bothering him. But oops! The little boy was holding onto a branch which turned out to be the antlers of a deer, and then the deer went running off with the little boy, and the doggie ran alongside because he didn't want to get separated from his master. And then the deer threw the doggie off the edge of a tiny cliff and the doggie fell off too, because he didn't know the cliff was coming, and they fell in some water. And when they looked up they were fine, and they heard some frogs chirping. And they were very quiet so they could sneak up on the frogs and catch their froggie. But when they looked over the log trying to catch the frog, they found two frogs and they found some little baby frogs. They took one of the froggies away from his family of frogs and they went home.

(Berman & Slobin, 1994, pp. 77–78)

narratives. There are several reasons why Mayer's picture book provides an excellent set of stimuli for this sort of research. For one thing, in contrast to free conversation, which is poorly constrained, the drawings constitute stable anchors for evaluating the accuracy of each subject's discourse. Moreover, in contrast to familiar fairytales like "Cinderella," which may be overlearned for some subjects, the telling of *Frog, Where Are You?* is less likely to be influenced by long-term memory. Finally, in contrast to single scenes like the Cookie Theft picture, which is not very rich (see Figure 3.4 in Chapter 3), the plot of Mayer's book has enough detail to recruit the brain mechanisms that are essential to build narrative coherence. Keeping these points in mind, let's look now at some of the findings that have emerged from the elicitation and examination of frog stories in neuropsychological and functional neuroimaging studies.

Ash et al.'s (2006) Neuropsychological Study

To gain insight into the brain regions that are critical for generating narrative coherence, Ash et al. (2006) elicited frog stories from 35 patients with frontotemporal dementia and 10 healthy age-matched adults.

The patients with frontotemporal dementia fell into three subgroups. First, 10 patients were classified as having progressive nonfluent aphasia (PNFA), which, as noted in previous chapters, involves an impairment of grammar due to atrophy centered in the left ventrolateral prefrontal cortex, including Broca's area. Second, 13 patients were classified as having semantic dementia (SD), which, as also noted in previous chapters, involves an impairment of conceptual knowledge due to atrophy centered in the anterior temporal lobes of both hemispheres, although usually with some leftward asymmetry. And third, 12 patients were classified as having a non-aphasic syndrome characterized by an impairment of social comportment and executive functions (SOC/EXEC) due to the gradual deterioration of predominantly right-hemisphere frontotemporal regions (e.g., Rosen et al., 2002; Grossman et al., 2004; Williams et al., 2005; Seeley et al., 2009; this disorder is referred to as the behavioral variant of frontotemporal dementia [bvFTD] in Wilson et al.'s [2010b] neuropsychological study of sentence production, which is summarized in Chapter 14 [see Figure 14.8 and the associated text]).

As the investigators expected, the PNFA patients produced frog stories in a very slow and effortful manner that was marked by abundant grammatical errors and many inaccurate, incomplete, or missing descriptions of salient features in the drawings. Because some of the events in the drawings were simply not reported by the PNFA patients, their narratives tended to be rather impoverished. When these patients did describe consecutive events, however, they usually indicated how those events were semantically connected. Indeed, the quantitative analysis of this discourse dimension yielded a score of 93 percent. Thus, the patients succeeded in generating relatively normal local coherence. In addition, when they came to the 22nd picture, which is near the end of the book (see Figure 16.1), 70 percent of the patients explicitly mentioned that the boy and his dog had at long last found the frog they had been searching for. This suggests that, for the most part, their capacity to create global coherence was also preserved. From a neuroanatomical perspective, these results are consistent with the view that the brain region most severely affected in PNFA—namely, the left ventrolateral prefrontal cortex—plays an important role in the syntactic encoding of sentences, but is not critical for the generation of narrative coherence.

Shifting to the SD patients, the researchers anticipated that they would produce frog stories lacking in semantic specificity, and this prediction was robustly confirmed. The patients in this subgroup experienced significant word-finding difficulties, and as a consequence they often resorted to generic terms like *animal* to refer to both the dog and the frog. They also had a tendency to use imprecise expressions, like saying *got his head in the bottle* instead of *got his head stuck in the bottle* (see picture 4 in Figure 16.1). Furthermore, they succumbed to outright uncertainty far more than the normal control subjects did, as revealed by frequent uses of uninformative phrases like *whatever it's called*. Thus, largely because of their profound conceptual disturbances, the SD patients generated narratives with a paucity of appropriate content, and, not surprisingly, these semantic shortcomings reduced the coherence of their stories. It is important to note, however, that these deficiencies in narrative structure were not very severe. Nearly 80 percent of the consecutive events that the patients described were locally connected by various discourse devices, and well over half (62 percent) of the patients achieved global coherence by correctly stating toward the end of the book that the boy and his dog ultimately found the frog they had been seeking. Taken together, these results suggest that the cortical areas that are most atrophic in SD—namely, the anterior temporal lobes bilaterally—are vital parts of the neural architecture of semantic knowledge,

but contribute only moderately to the formation of discourse coherence during storytelling.

Finally, with regard to the non-aphasic SOC/EXEC patients, Ash et al. (2006) predicted that they would produce frog stories with fairly good lexical and grammatical structure but very poor narrative coherence, and these expectations were fulfilled. On the one hand, at the "microlinguistic" level of lexical and grammatical structure, the SOC/EXEC patients outperformed the PNFA and SD patients by generating a greater proportion of long, fluent, and well-formed utterances without major word-finding difficulties. On the other hand, at the "macrolinguistic" level of discourse structure, the SOC/EXEC patients performed much worse than the PNFA and SD patients, and their errors significantly affected both local and global coherence.

In terms of local coherence, these patients only pointed out the conceptual connections between consecutive events about three-quarters of the time. Their frequent failure to indicate how these events were related to each other, and hence to convey the forward flow of the story, is revealed by the extracts in (1), which are taken from the narrative of a patient who is talking about pictures 2 and 3 (see Figure 16.1). Not only does the patient completely ignore the key actions—specifically, the frog's escape from the jar during the night, and the boy's surprise and dismay the next morning—but he also neglects to link the two successive pictures in ways that express how they are elements of a larger plot. Instead, the patient just describes the objects and characters in each drawing.

(1) a. Picture 2: The boy is asleep in his bed. The frog is in a jar. And his [chuckle] . . . his . . . his boots are on the floor, nex-next to his uh . . . next to his shirt.
   b. Picture 3: Boy's in bed . . . next to his dog. His boots are on the floor. And so are his sandals . . . and an empty jar, and his shirt.

As for global coherence, only one quarter of the SOC/EXEC patients stated, at the climax of the story, that the boy and his dog found the frog that was with them at the outset. The difficulties that these patients experienced in recognizing and/or communicating this pivotal aspect of the story are revealed by the extracts in (2), which are taken from the narrative of a patient who is talking about pictures 22 and 23 (see Figure 16.1). Because the patient does not make any connections whatsoever between these drawings and those at the beginning of the book, it is tempting to conclude that he simply doesn't understand the overarching logic of the story.

(2) a. Picture 22: Dog—or boy's . . . over the log. Dog's over the log too. Um . . . they're on the log. See two frogs. See the mom and . . . dad and a mom frog.
    b. Picture 23: And you got one, two, three, four, five . . . seven little—eight little toads.

Ash et al. (2006) argue that the poor narrative coherence displayed by the SOC/EXEC patients can be attributed primarily to a general impairment of higher-order organizational processes. To support this account, they present additional experimental data showing that the SOC/EXEC patients, but not the PNFA or SD patients, exhibited significant correlations between, first, the two measures of narrative coherence described above (local and global), and second, a separate measure of executive/supervisory functions that required an internally directed mental search (specifically, producing within 1 minute as many words as possible that begin with a predetermined letter). Further support for the researchers' account comes from other studies showing that SOC/EXEC patients have trouble judging the order of events in familiar scripts such as "going fishing" or "making a sandwich" (Cosentino et al., 2006; Farag et al., 2010).

Lastly, with respect to neuroanatomical considerations, Ash et al. (2006) conducted an imaging analysis that involved 9 of the 12 SOC/EXEC patients, and the results revealed a significant relationship between reduced local coherence in the frog stories and reduced cortical volume in several anterior right-hemisphere regions (Figure 16.2; recall that the disease afflicting these patients targets primarily right-lateralized frontotemporal areas). Importantly, the critical regions included several prefrontal areas that are essential for, as the researchers put it,

> carrying out a multitude of routine actions which involve deciding on a goal, determining the steps needed to accomplish the goal, taking into account the necessary order of the steps, and then following through with carrying out the steps, keeping track of the steps themselves and the progress from step to step until the conclusion is reached.
> (Ash et al., 2006, p. 1411)

Such organizational processes are obviously required not only to craft a well-connected narrative, but also to accomplish many other types of complex tasks in daily life.

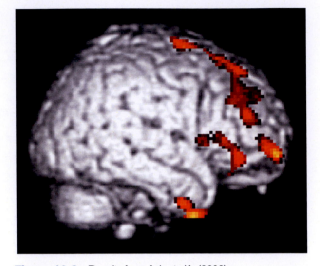

Figure 16.2   Results from Ash et al.'s (2006) neuropsychological study. The lateral view of the right hemisphere shows areas of cortical atrophy in SOC/EXEC patients that were significantly related to reduced local connectedness in their frog stories. (From Ash et al., 2006, p. 1410.)

Overall, this study provides valuable information about the cognitive and neural resources that are necessary to tell a coherent story. First, the results indicate that the ability to connect the parts of a story both locally and globally can be disrupted independently of the ability to present the parts themselves. Second, the results suggest that the organizational processes that are called upon to assemble a story also contribute to the management of other complex, multi-step activities. And third, the results show that these organizational processes depend, to some degree, on certain prefrontal regions of the right hemisphere.

Troiani et al.'s (2008) fMRI Study

With the aim of expanding on Ash et al.'s (2006) findings about the neural substrates of storytelling, Troiani et al. (2008) carried out an fMRI study in which a group of neurologically normal subjects produced frog stories while their brain activity was being recorded. This investigation did not use the conventional form of fMRI that measures BOLD signals, however; instead, it used a different type of fMRI called arterial spin labeling. The name of the technique is, to be sure, rather daunting, but for present purposes we only need to know the following aspects of it (for more information see Borogovac & Asllani, 2012). Like in PET, it monitors the distribution of a tracer through the vascular system of the brain. Unlike in PET, though, the tracer is not a radioactive isotope that is invasively injected into the bloodstream; rather, it consists of endogenous water molecules in the bloodstream that are magnetically "labeled" by altering their proton spins as they pass through the carotid arteries on their way up to the brain. Thus, at every voxel in the brain it is possible to calculate changes in blood flow, and hence changes in neural activity, by comparing the amount of labeled water with the amount of unlabeled water. This approach has several advantages over BOLD fMRI, one of which is that it is not vulnerable to signal distortion or dropout in areas near tissue–air boundaries, such as the anterior temporal and orbitofrontal regions, which are close to the sinuses. This benefit is especially relevant to Troiani et al.'s (2008) study, since one of their goals was to determine whether some of those regions are engaged during the generation of narrative coherence.

The experiment included several blocks, only two of which are discussed here. In both of these blocks, all 24 drawings from *Frog, Where Are You?* were shown one by one, with each picture displayed during a 9-second sequence that had the following structure (see Figure 16.3). First, a cross (+) was flashed for 100 ms to alert the subject. Then a picture was presented for 2,600 ms, during which time the subject was supposed to inspect it and begin planning a verbal description. Next, a green screen was shown for 200 ms, indicating that the subject should begin speaking, and immediately after that the same picture appeared again and remained visible for 5,300 ms, providing a stable basis for the subject's description. Then a red screen was shown for 400 ms, indicating that the subject should stop speaking. And finally, a blank screen was shown for 400 ms, during which time the researchers acquired brain data. The reason the researchers waited until the end of the speaking period to acquire brain data was because they wanted to avoid any artifacts due to head movement. It is important to note, however, that they timed the imaging period to coincide quite well with the peak of the hemodynamic response curve that was triggered by the beginning of the speaking period, when the subject started to talk about the characters, objects, and events portrayed in the drawing.

The two blocks that we will focus on differed in clever ways that allowed the researchers to isolate the linguistic dimension of narrative coherence both behaviorally and neurally. In the first block, the pictures were presented in a random order that was carefully designed to prevent the subject from inferring the plot of the story. The instructions specified that the subject should simply describe each picture with a sentence or two, starting when the green screen flashed and stopping when the red screen flashed. In the second block, however, the pictures were presented in the

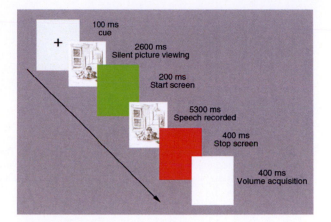

Figure 16.3 Timeline of stimulus presentation in Troiani et al.'s (2008) fMRI study. (From Troiani et al., 2008, p. 934.)

correct order so that the plot of the story was apparent. The instructions informed the subject ahead of time that the series of pictures constituted a story; moreover, they specified that the subject's task was to narrate the story as if telling it to a child, and that the green and red screens would serve again as start and stop cues for describing each picture.

When the researchers analyzed the behavioral results, they found that the spoken responses elicited by the two blocks were comparable in terms of the total number of words and the syntactic complexity of the sentences. As expected, however, the responses elicited by the second (correctly ordered) block had significantly greater narrative coherence than those elicited by the first (randomly ordered) block, as measured by the frequency of references to elements not shown in the current picture. In order to identify the neural correlates of this behavioral difference, the researchers contrasted the activation map associated with the second (correctly ordered) block against the one associated with the first (randomly ordered) block. As shown in Figure 16.4, this subtraction revealed significant activation in the lateral, ventral, and medial portions of the orbitofrontal cortices in both hemispheres. In addition, a marginally significant effect emerged in the left lateral prefrontal region.

These findings build nicely on those reported by Ash et al. (2006), and they also converge fairly well with several other studies of story production (most notably Kaczmarek, 1984; Sirigu et al., 1998; Crozier et al., 1999; Allain et al., 1999, 2001; Coelho et al., 2012). Taken together, the available data support the hypothesis that the ability to formulate a well-structured narrative—that is, one in which all the parts are conceptually connected—depends on

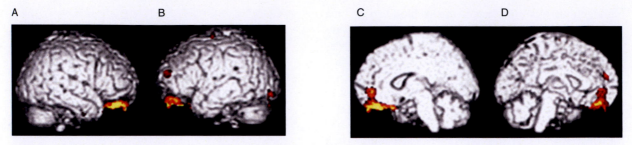

Figure 16.4   Results from Troiani et al.'s (2008) fMRI study. The panels show areas that were activated significantly more when subjects described the drawings of *Frog, Where Are You?* in the correct order than when they described them in a random order. (A) Right lateral view. (B) Left lateral view. (C) Right medial view. (D) Left medial view. (From Troiani et al., 2008, p. 936.)

the executive/supervisory functions of the frontal lobes in both hemispheres. The orbitofrontal and lateral prefrontal cortices appear to be particularly important, and, based on previous evidence about their different specializations (e.g., Miller & Cohen, 2001; Buchsbaum et al., 2005a; Zald & Andreotti, 2010; Stuss, 2011; Gläscher et al., 2012), it is reasonable to suppose that they may contribute to successful storytelling in the following ways.

The orbitofrontal cortices may underlie the kinds of value-based decision-making processes that are needed to choose the most relevant and potentially rewarding bits of information to include in the narrative, taking into account a variety of contextual factors that involve not only the development of the discourse itself, but also its presumed effects on the audience's state of mind. The lateral prefrontal cortices, on the other hand, may be more involved in the kinds of cognitive control operations that are needed to organize the main events of the story and present them in the proper sequence, with smooth transitions that maintain a cohesive dramatic arc. These proposals about the division of discourse labor in the frontal lobes have a solid foundation, but they are still quite speculative and pitched at a very general level of description, leaving many questions unanswered. Much more research is clearly needed to explore the neural substrates of story production in greater detail.

Story Comprehension

In a fascinating book called *The storytelling animal*, Jonathan Gottschall draws attention to the fact that people are easily entranced by good stories (p. 3): "Human minds yield helplessly to the suction of story. No matter how hard we concentrate, no matter how deep we dig in our heels, we just can't resist the gravity of alternate worlds." Now, he's talking here about the truly bewitching power of exceptionally well-wrought narratives, but even the ordinary little tales that we

tell each other every day can induce a special form of interpersonal alignment that cognitive neuroscientists have recently begun to describe as "brain-to-brain coupling" (Hasson et al., 2012).

For example, in an fMRI study by Stephens et al. (2010), the brain activity of a woman was measured while she told an unrehearsed real-life story about an experience she had as a freshman in high school. Then the brain activity of several other individuals was measured while they listened to an audio recording of that story. And finally the listeners completed a questionnaire that evaluated the degree to which they understood the story. Using an analytic tool called inter-subject correlation, the investigators showed that, as the narrative unfolded over time, the neural patterns in numerous areas of the listeners' brains—from core language regions like Broca's and Wernicke's areas to higher-order frontal and parietal cortices—tended to mirror the neural patterns in the corresponding areas of the speaker's brain. In many areas, these mirroring responses were slightly delayed, which supports the notion that they were driven and shaped by the perceived speech signals. In a few other areas, however, especially in the frontal lobes, the listeners' brain activity actually preceded the speaker's analogous brain activity, which suggests that the listeners were so immersed in the story that they predicted the speaker's upcoming utterances. On average, as the listeners' comprehension increased, so did their mirroring responses, and this positive relationship between communicative success and brain-to-brain coupling was most pronounced for the anticipatory responses in the frontal lobes. Overall, these findings demonstrate that when narrative discourse is most efficient, it effectively binds together the brains of speaker and hearer so that their dynamic patterns of activity are tightly coordinated, "ticking together" as they represent the unfolding events of the story. (Such neural coupling also occurs in several domains of nonverbal social collaboration, as discussed by Hasson et al., 2012.)

The aim of this section is to survey some of the most salient empirical findings and theoretical ideas in the recent literature on the neural substrates of story comprehension. We will begin by looking at a few ERP studies that indicate—in keeping with the data described above from Stephens et al.'s (2010) fMRI study—that during receptive narrative processing, people integrate the meaning of each consecutive word into their "situation model" of the story extremely quickly, sometimes even using the global discourse context to overcome local processing difficulties. Then we will consider the results of a meta-analysis of 12 functional neuroimaging studies of the comprehension of coherent versus incoherent narratives. As we will see, these results suggest that understanding stories relies on what Evelyn Ferstl calls "the extended language network"—a set of bilaterally distributed cortical areas that appear to perform such functions as integrating semantic information, establishing and updating situation models, drawing inferences, and attributing thoughts to protagonists (Ferstl et al., 2008; Ferstl, 2010; see also Mason & Just, 2009; Mar, 2011).

Electrophysiological Evidence for the Rapid Incorporation of Words into the Discourse Context

Based on the previous chapters, it is clear that when we listen to people talk, a huge amount of phonological, conceptual, and grammatical processing is necessary just to recognize each incoming word and fit it into the evolving framework of the immediate sentence. Hence one might assume that additional time-consuming computations are required to determine how the major content-bearing words should be assimilated into the wider context of the entire discourse. A growing body of literature, however, suggests that this is not the case. On the contrary, there is mounting evidence that it usually doesn't take any longer to incorporate a particular word into the relatively complex representation of the global discourse than it does to incorporate it into the relatively simple representation of the local sentence. Both types of semantic integration appear to take place more or less simultaneously, and, as mentioned above, the discourse context can even exert a beneficial top-down influence on comprehension by allowing the listener to anticipate what the speaker is likely to say next. Some of the strongest experimental support for these ideas comes from a series of influential ERP studies by Jos van Berkum and his colleagues at the Max Planck Institute for Psycholinguistics in Nijmegen, The Netherlands (e.g., van Berkum et al.,

1999, 2003, 2005; Niewland & van Berkum, 2006; Otten & van Berkum, 2008). We will restrict our attention here to just two of them.

In one study, van Berkum et al. (2003) recorded subjects' ERPs while they listened to short Dutch narratives. For each narrative there were two versions that differed only with respect to a single critical word in the final sentence. In both cases the critical word was completely natural within the narrow semantic framework of the final sentence taken by itself; however, while in one case it was also congruent with the scenario described in the preceding discourse, in the other case it was not. An example, translated into English, is shown below, with the critical word (congruent/anomalous) highlighted in italics:

> As agreed upon, Jane was to wake her sister and her brother at five o'clock in the morning. But her sister had already washed herself, and her brother had even got dressed. Jane told her brother that he was exceptionally *quick/slow.*

Altogether, the researchers created 80 miniature narratives like this, each of which had two alternative endings, one discourse-congruent and the other discourse-anomalous. During the experiment, two separate lists were used, each for half of the subjects. The lists were counterbalanced so that each included 40 discourse-congruent trials and 40 discourse-anomalous trials randomly intermixed with 160 "filler" trials. Each story occurred only once per list. The subjects were not instructed to produce any overt responses, but were asked to listen carefully to each story and process it for meaning.

The main results are depicted in Figure 16.5. As can be seen, relative to their discourse-congruent counterparts, the discourse-anomalous critical words elicited a significant N400 effect—that is, a negative-going deflection of the waveform that emerged roughly 200 ms post-word-onset, peaked at about 400 ms, lasted for about 800–1,000 ms, and had maximal amplitude over central and parietal scalp sites. In the last part of Chapter 15, we noted that when people process sentences in isolation—that is, without a wider discourse context—a robust N400 indexes difficulty integrating the meaning of a word into its local context. We also saw that such effects are triggered not only by words that violate intra-linguistic semantic knowledge, like *sour* in the sentence *The Dutch trains are sour and very crowded,* but also by words that violate extra-linguistic world knowledge, like *white* in the sentence *The Dutch trains are white and very crowded* (see Figures 15.26–27 and the associated text in

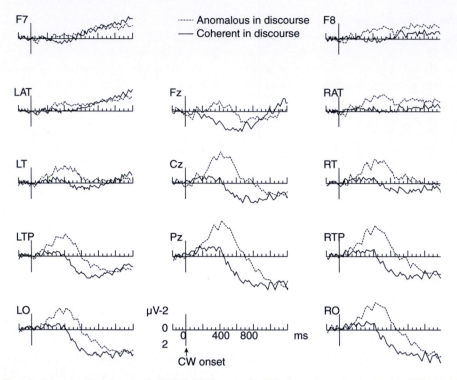

Figure 16.5 Results from van Berkum et al.'s (2003) ERP study. (Left) Left-hemisphere electrodes. (Middle) Midline frontal, central, and parietal electrodes; CW = critical word. (Right) Right-hemisphere electrodes. (From van Berkum et al., 2003, p. 705.)

Chapter 15). These findings indicate that during the online comprehension of isolated sentences, both types of constraints are simultaneously imposed on the analysis of each word. Against this background, what the results from van Berkum et al.'s (2003) study demonstrate is that when people process sentences that are embedded within a larger discourse, they also use the context of that discourse to constrain the processing of each word during the very same temporal window. Thus, starting about a quarter of a second after a word in an unfolding sentence has been encountered, it makes contact not only with sentence-level semantic specifications and more general world knowledge, but also with discourse-level contextual information. All three sources of interpretive constraints are employed in parallel.

Interestingly, however, in a subsequent ERP study Nieuwland and van Berkum (2006) showed that, in certain circumstances, discourse-level contextual information can actually take the upper hand in guiding the listener's analysis of the individual words of a story, exerting a top-down influence that is powerful enough to overrule sentence-level semantic anomalies. In this experiment Dutch-speaking subjects listened to short narratives that consisted of exactly six sentences, and for each narrative there were two minimally different versions—one in which a woman had a conversation with another person, and another in which she had the very same conversation with an inanimate entity. An example, translated into English, is shown below, with the sentences numbered and the critical words (animate/inanimate) highlighted in italics:

(1) Once upon a time, a psychotherapist was consulted in her home office by a *sailor/yacht* with emotional problems. (2) The *sailor/yacht* confided in her that everything in life had gone wrong and started crying. (3) The psychotherapist consoled the *sailor/yacht* by stating that everybody experiences these kinds of troubles every now and then. (4) But the *sailor/yacht* doubted whether to continue outlining his problems to her. (5) The psychotherapist advised the *sailor/yacht* to be honest not only with her, but also with himself. (6) At that moment the *sailor/yacht* cried out that he was absolutely terrified of water.

The researchers created a total of 60 stories like this, 30 in which the woman's interlocutor was animate, and 30 in which it was inanimate. As in van Berkum et al.'s (2003) study, the subjects were split into two groups, each of which received a separate list of stories, half from the animate condition and half from the inanimate condition, randomly intermixed with 90 "filler" stories and arranged so that each story occurred only once.

The subjects were instructed to simply listen to all the stories for comprehension.

When the researchers looked at the results, they focused on the critical animate/inanimate words in the first, third, and fifth sentence of each story. The chief outcomes are portrayed in Figure 16.6. In the first sentence the inanimate words (e.g., *yacht*) evoked a significant N400 effect relative to the animate words (e.g., *sailor*)—a finding that was, of course, fully expected (see Figure 16.6A). By the third sentence, however, this classic electrophysiological signature of anomaly detection had completely disappeared, and it remained absent in the fifth sentence as well (see Figures 16.6B, C). These results indicate that the interpretive influence of contextual appropriateness is strong enough to "neutralize" the processing difficulties induced by local anomalies, even when those anomalies involve a semantic feature as fundamental as animacy. Apparently, listeners have no trouble "bracketing" their real-world knowledge of the distinction between living and nonliving things in order to understand cartoonlike stories of the kind used in the study. Perhaps, though, this is not really so surprising, since one of the main purposes of stories is, after all, to trade reality for fantasy.

A Meta-Analysis of 12 PET and fMRI Studies of the Comprehension of Coherent Versus Incoherent Narratives

Having explored some of the fine-grained temporal aspects of discourse comprehension, we turn now to anatomical issues. Unfortunately, the neuropsychological literature on this topic is rather limited, since very few studies have documented reliable relationships between particular types of comprehension deficits and particular sites of brain damage. On the bright side, however, a growing number of functional neuroimaging studies have begun to illuminate the widely distributed set of cortical areas that collectively subserve discourse comprehension. With the aim of pooling the available data in a systematic way, Ferstl et al. (2008) conducted a meta-analysis of 23 PET and fMRI studies, 12 of which focused on the activation patterns elicited by coherent (i.e., conceptually well-connected) versus incoherent narratives. The results of this contrast revealed 10 clusters of voxels that presumably contribute to different aspects of the coherence-building process. All of these clusters are illustrated in Figure 16.7, but we will concentrate on the likely functions of just the following regions: the anterior temporal lobes; the medial parietal cortex; the dorsomedial prefrontal cortex; and the temporoparietal junction.

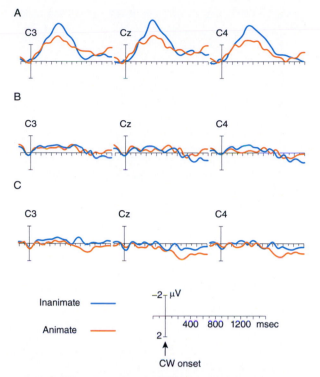

Figure 16.6 Results from Nieuwland and van Berkum's (2006) ERP study. (A) Animate/inanimate words (e.g., *sailor/yacht*) in first sentence; (B) in third sentence; (C) in fifth sentence. C3 = left-central electrode; Cz = midline-central electrode; C4 = right-central electrode; CW = critical word. (From Nieuwland & van Berkum, 2006, pp. 1102–1104.)

The Anterior Temporal Lobes: Integrating Semantic Information

The left and right anterior temporal lobes (ATLs) are labeled C1 and C2 in Figure 16.7. These hot spots should look familiar, since we have encountered variants of them many times in previous chapters. Specifically, in Chapters 5 and 15, we noted that in the left hemisphere the lateral ATL may implement a "combinatorial syntactic–semantic network" for understanding individual sentences; and in Chapters 10–12, we noted that the ATLs in both hemispheres may implement a "semantic hub" that represents amodal conceptual knowledge. Given these considerations, it is quite interesting that regions in more or less the same anatomical territory emerged in Ferstl et al.'s (2008) meta-analytic contrast between coherent and incoherent stories. Although this finding can be accounted for in several ways, perhaps the most parsimonious approach is to assume that, as just suggested, the ATLs are bilaterally involved in integrating semantic information. From this perspective, it makes sense that the regions respond more to coherent than incoherent stories, since the former

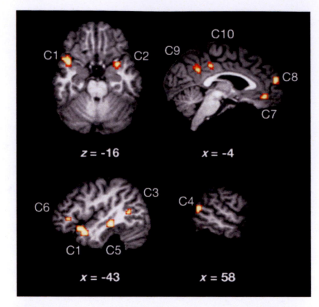

Figure 16.7 Results from Ferstl et al.'s (2008) meta-analysis of 12 PET and fMRI studies focusing on the comprehension of coherent versus incoherent narratives. Each "C" indicates a cluster of activated voxels. C1 = left anterior temporal lobe; C2 = right anterior temporal lobe; C3 = left temporoparietal junction; C4 = right temporoparietal junction; C5 = mid portion of left middle temporal gyrus; C6 = orbital portion of left inferior frontal gyrus; C7 = left ventromedial prefrontal cortex; C8 = left dorsomedial prefrontal cortex; C9 = left precuneus; C10 left posterior cingulate. (From Ferstl et al., 2008, p. 587.)

allow more conceptual connections to be made than the latter (see also Crinion et al., 2006, and Spitsyna et al., 2006). This line of explanation also fits well with the electrophysiological data described in the previous section, since the ATLs appear to be among the principal neural generators of the N400 component (Van Petten & Luka, 2006; Lau et al., 2008; for further discussion see Chapter 15).

The Medial Parietal Cortex: Establishing and Updating Situation Models

The meta-analytic contrast between coherent and incoherent stories also revealed significant activation in the medial parietal cortex, especially the precuneus and posterior cingulate, which are labeled C9 and C10 in Figure 16.7. These regions are extensively interconnected with sensory association cortices, anterior temporal cortices, and premotor/prefrontal cortices, an anatomical arrangement that allows them to "hold highly disparate sets of background activity in a coherent pattern," according to Damasio (2010, p. 229).

More specifically, several lines of evidence suggest that the medial parietal cortex plays a pivotal role in

constructing the private world of imagined experience or "virtual reality." First, it is a key node in the brain's so-called **default network**, which is active whenever a person is not effortfully attending to some external stimulus or task, but is instead simply resting quietly in a manner conducive to daydreaming (Buckner et al., 2008; Andrews-Hanna, 2012). Second, it is engaged during the contemplation of alternative scenarios, such as when one recalls past experiences, envisions future experiences, or thinks about the inner lives of other people (Buckner & Carroll, 2007; Hassabis & Maguire, 2007; Spreng et al., 2009). And third, it appears to be an important part of the brain's semantic system, which stands to reason, since the kind of imagination that is employed in daydreaming and conjuring up alternative scenarios necessarily involves abundant conceptual processing (Binder et al., 1999, 2009).

In light of all these points, it should come as no surprise that several researchers have recently proposed that the medial parietal cortex may contribute to narrative comprehension by using personal and real-world knowledge to transform text-based representations, supported in part by the ATLs, into full-fledged situation models—that is, multifaceted mental displays in which the characters, events, and settings of the story are richly elaborated and sometimes viewed in the mind's eye from particular visuospatial vantage points (for further details about the nature of story-based situation models, see van Dijk & Kintsch, 1983; Zwaan & Radvansky, 1998; Zwaan, 2004). Consistent with this account, fMRI studies have shown that the medial parietal cortex is highly responsive not only at the very beginning of a story, which is when a situation model must first be established (Xu et al., 2005; Yarkoni et al., 2008), but also at salient event boundaries, which is when the current situation model must be updated or even replaced (Speer et al., 2007, 2009; Whitney et al., 2009).

The role of the medial parietal cortex in revising situation models after narrative shifts is nicely illustrated by an fMRI study reported by Speer et al. (2007). In this experiment, the subjects' brains were scanned while they read four extracts from the book *One Boy's Day* (Barker & Wright, 1951), which recounts in a story-like style the activities of a 7-year-old boy named Raymond

Default network A set of cortical areas that are jointly active whenever a person is not effortfully attending to some external stimulus or task, but is instead simply resting quietly in a manner conducive to daydreaming. This network overlaps substantially with the one that supports the understanding of other people's minds, and it includes three of the four areas discussed here in connection with story comprehension: the medial parietal cortex, the dorsomedial prefrontal cortex, and the temporoparietal junction.

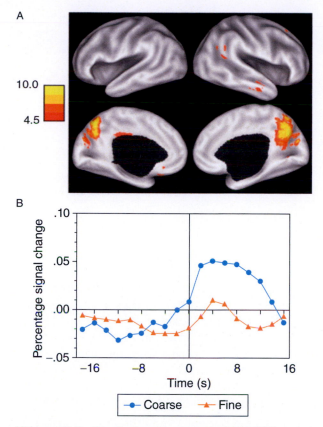

Figure 16.8 Results from Speer et al.'s (2007) fMRI study. (A) Regions exhibiting increased activation in response to narrative event boundaries. Inflated brain images are shown from the left lateral view (top left), right lateral view (top right), left medial view (bottom left), and right medial view (bottom right). (B) The average time-course of activation across all of the areas highlighted in (A), with separate plots for coarsely and finely segmented events. The vertical line indicates the point where an event boundary was identified. (From Speer et al., 2007, p. 452.)

Birch during a single day in the late 1940s. The four scenes that were chosen describe Raymond getting up and eating breakfast, playing with his friends on the school grounds, carrying out an English assignment in school, and participating in a class music lesson. Each extract was presented one word at a time in a separate block lasting between 8.5 and 10.9 minutes. Four days after the scanning session, each subject returned to the lab and read all four extracts again, only this time they were instructed to perform two tasks. In the *coarse-segmentation task*, they identified the largest units of activity that seemed natural and meaningful, and in the *fine-segmentation task*, they identified the smallest units of activity that seemed natural and meaningful.

When the researchers analyzed these behavioral responses, they found that both types of event boundaries were reliably associated with changes

involving the characters, their locations, their goals, and their interactions with objects, as well as with causal and temporal factors. With regard to the imaging data, the researchers picked out, for each individual subject, the words that the subject marked as indicating event boundaries in the coarse- or fine-segmentation task, and used them to define the centers of 36-second windows that stretched 18 seconds in each direction on the timeline. These windows then served as the frames within which BOLD signals were analyzed. As shown in Figure 16.8, the results revealed that the brain region that was most heavily modulated by the boundaries of narrated activities was the medial parietal cortex bilaterally. Signal strength in this territory increased significantly right after the occurrence of words that indicated shifts between events, with the boost being especially great for coarse-grained (i.e., large-scale) shifts and somewhat weaker for fine-grained (i.e., small-scale) shifts. Thus, the results demonstrate that even when a person reads a story without paying close attention to the various episodic changes, his or her medial parietal cortex efficiently tracks those changes so that the situation model can be appropriately updated.

The Dorsomedial Prefrontal Cortex: Drawing Inferences

Yet another region that turned out to be engaged significantly more by coherent than incoherent stories in Ferstl et al.'s (2008) meta-analysis was the dorsomedial prefrontal cortex (dmPFC), especially in the left hemisphere. This area is labeled C8 in Figure 16.7. Like the medial parietal cortex, it is part of the default network that is dominant during the conscious resting state (Buckner et al., 2008). In addition, it has been strongly implicated in "theory-of-mind" or "mentalizing" tasks—that is, tasks that require reasoning about the beliefs, desires, plans, intentions, etc., of other individuals (Amodio & Frith, 2006; Van Overwalle, 2009). For this reason, one might suppose that the dmPFC facilitates story comprehension by helping the reader or listener interpret the behaviors of the main characters in psychological terms. There is certainly some support for this view; however, there is also growing evidence that during discourse processing the dmPFC fulfills a more general function, since it seems to be involved in drawing inferences not only about people's mental states, but also about purely physical situations (e.g., Ferstl & von Cramon, 2002; Saxe & Powell, 2006; Sieböger et al., 2007; Friese et al., 2008).

This was first demonstrated in a compelling way by Ferstl and von Cramon (2002), who conducted an fMRI

Table 16.1 Experimental Conditions in Ferstl and von Cramon's (2002) fMRI Study

	Coherent	Incoherent
Part A: Theory-of-mind	Mary's exam was about to begin. Her palms were sweaty.	Mary's exam was about to begin. Some friends had remembered her birthday.
	Laura got a lot of mail today. Some friends had remembered her birthday.	Laura got a lot of mail today. Her palms were sweaty.
Part B: Logic	Sometimes a truck drives by the house. That's when the dishes start to rattle.	Sometimes a truck drives by the house. The car doesn't start.
	The car lights have been on since last night. The car doesn't start.	The car lights have been on since last night. That's when the dishes start to rattle.

Adapted from Ferstl & von Cramon (2002, p. 1601).

study consisting of two parts, A and B (see Table 16.1; although the examples are in English, the original stimuli were in German). In each part, the subjects were presented with audio recordings of 120 sentence pairs. In part A ("theory-of-mind"), all of the sentence pairs described human situations, and the instructions were as follows:

> Your task is to identify with the people mentioned. You should try to put yourself in their shoes, i.e., to understand their motivations, feelings, and actions. After the second sentence, please press the YES key if you succeeded, and the NO key if you did not.
> (Ferstl & von Cramon, 2002, p. 1603)

In part B ("Logic"), all of the sentence pairs described purely physical situations without any human protagonists, and the instructions were to indicate whether the second sentence in each pair was logically related to the first. In each part, half of the trials were coherent and half were not; moreover, the incoherent trials were created by switching the context sentences of two coherent trials. Finally, a control condition was included that consisted of 32 sentence pairs in which all of the content words were replaced with pseudowords. In half of the trials both sentences either did or did not include real function words, whereas in the other half only one of the two sentences did. The task was to indicate whether the "artificial language" was the same or different for the two sentences in each pair.

The subjects performed all of the tasks well, and the imaging results are depicted in Figure 16.9. As shown in the top two rows, the two critical contrasts—namely, the "theory-of-mind" condition minus the control condition, and the "logic" condition minus the control condition—yielded remarkably similar patterns of widespread bilateral activity. We needn't discuss all of the areas that were engaged, though, because what

matters most is that one particular region showed up in both subtractions, this being the left dmPFC, which is labeled "1" in the figure. In follow-up analyses, the researchers contrasted the coherent trials against the incoherent trials in each part of the experiment. No significant activations emerged in the "theory-of-mind" condition, which suggests that the neural mechanisms underlying mentalizing processes were recruited to roughly the same degree in both types of trials. However, several regions did emerge in the "logic" condition, including, most importantly, a large portion of the left dmPFC, as shown in the bottom row of Figure 16.9. This finding clearly suggests that the region is involved in discerning the conceptual connections between consecutive sentences, even when those connections are completely unrelated to the psychological aspects of human behavior.

Overall, then, Ferstl and von Cramon's (2002) fMRI study provides powerful evidence that the left dmPFC contributes to narrative comprehension not only when inferences must be made about the mental states of characters, but also when they must be made about purely physical situations. Although it is difficult to pinpoint the common denominator of these two kinds of reasoning, Ferstl and von Cramon (2002) emphasize that they both involve cognitive processes that are voluntarily initiated and sustained. As they point out, this account is consistent with neuropsychological studies showing that patients with damage in the vicinity of the left dmPFC often exhibit apathy, a lack of ideas, and a reduction of self-guided thought (see also Box 6.6 in Chapter 6, which is about akinetic mutism, a disorder of willful behavior that frequently results from bilateral damage to the dmPFC). Hopefully, future research with such patients will begin to explore the specific ways in which their comprehension of stories is and is not affected.

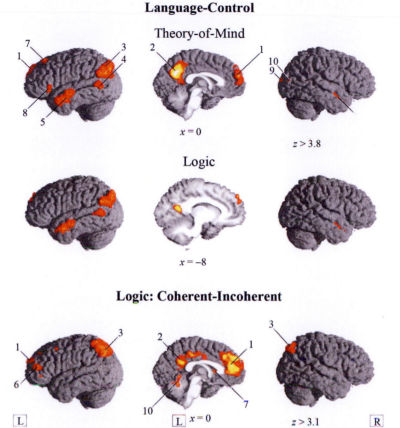

Figure 16.9 Results from Ferstl and von Cramon's (2002) fMRI study. (Top row) Contrast between "theory-of-mind" condition and control condition. (Middle row) Contrast between "logic" condition and control condition. (Bottom row) Contrast between coherent and incoherent narratives in "logic" condition. In each row the left brain image shows the left lateral view, the middle one shows the left medial view, and the right one shows the right lateral view. The most relevant brain region in the current context—namely, the dorsomedial prefrontal cortex—is designated "1." (From Ferstl & von Cramon, 2002, p. 1606.)

The Temporoparietal Junction: Attributing Thoughts to Protagonists

Among the many brain areas that Ferstl et al.'s (2008) meta-analysis revealed to be engaged more by coherent than incoherent stories, the last ones that we will discuss are located bilaterally near the posterior end of the superior temporal sulcus in a territory often referred to as the temporoparietal junction (TPJ). These areas, one in each hemisphere, are labeled C3 and C4 in Figure 16.7. They have received a great deal of attention in recent years, largely because, together with the two previous regions that we have considered, they participate in the default network and also assist in attributing thoughts to other people. Interestingly, the manner in which they contribute to such mentalizing operations may involve projecting oneself into the situation that the "target" individual happens to be in (Waytz & Mitchell, 2011). Some support for

this view comes from studies that have implicated the very same regions in video-gamers' identification with avatars (Corradi-Dell'Acqua et al., 2008) and in the strange phenomena known as out-of-body experiences, i.e., experiences in which one sees the world from an extra-corporeal, usually elevated, visuospatial perspective (Blanke & Arzy, 2005; Blanke, 2012). The most important evidence, however, comes from studies that have directly investigated mentalizing abilities, and in the current context it is quite fortuitous that many of these studies have employed miniature stories as stimuli, thereby bolstering the notion that during narrative comprehension the TPJ may be the key cortical structure that enables readers and listeners to put themselves in the positions of imagined protagonists.

In the fMRI study by Ferstl and von Cramon (2002) that we reviewed above, we can already see some relevant data, since the right TPJ, which is designated "10" in Figure 16.9 (top row), was activated in the

Table 16.2 Experimental Conditions in Saxe and Kanwisher's (2003) fMRI Study

A. Experiment 1	
1 Theory-of-mind (ToM) sample story	A boy is making a papier mâché project for his art class. He spends hours ripping newspaper into even strips. Then he goes out to buy flour. His mother comes home and throws all the newspaper strips away.
2 Mechanical inference (MI) sample story	Jane is walking to work this morning through a very industrial area. In one place the crane is taking up the whole sidewalk. To get to her building, she has to take a detour.
B. Experiment 2	
1 False belief (FB) sample story	John told Emily that he had a Porsche. Actually, his car is a Ford. Emily doesn't know anything about cars, though, so she believed John. *Probe:* When Emily sees John's car, she thinks it's a {Porsche/Ford}.
2 False photograph (FP) sample story	A photograph was taken of an apple hanging on a tree branch. The film took half an hour to develop. In the meantime, a strong wind blew the apple to the ground. *Probe:* The developed photograph shows the apple on the {ground/branch}.
3 Desire sample story	For Susie's birthday, her parents decided to have a picnic in the park. They wanted ponies and games on the lawn. If it rained, the children would have to play inside. *Probe:* Susie's parents wanted to have her birthday {inside/outside}.
4 Nonhuman description sample story	Nine planets and their moons, plus various lumps of debris called asteroids and comets, make up the sun's solar system. The earth is one of four rocky planets in the inner solar system. *Probe:* The solar system has {four/nine} planets.
5 Physical people sample story	Emily was always the tallest kid in her class. In kindergarten she was already over four feet tall. Now that she is in college she is 6'4". She is a head taller than the others. *Probe:* In kindergarten Emily was over {four/six} feet tall.

Adapted from Saxe & Kanwisher (2003, p. 1841).

contrast between the "theory-of-mind" condition and the control condition, but not in the contrast between the "logic" condition and the control condition. A number of other studies, however, have generated much more impressive and illuminating results (for reviews see Mar, 2011, and Mason & Just, 2009).

An excellent example is an influential fMRI study by Saxe and Kanwisher (2003) that included two closely related experiments. In Experiment 1, the subjects read two types of short narratives (see Table 16.2A for samples):

- "theory-of-mind" (ToM) stories, which require reasoning about people's intentions;
- "mechanical inference" (MI) stories, which require reasoning about inanimate objects.

In addition, during separate scans the subjects were shown pictures of both human bodies and inanimate objects. As shown in Figure 16.10A, the TPJ responded much more robustly in both hemispheres to the ToM stories than to the MI stories, and although it was also

activated to some extent in just the right hemisphere for pictures of both bodies and objects, its level of engagement for those stimuli was far below its level of engagement for the ToM stories. These findings strongly suggest that the TPJ underpins the process of attributing thoughts to verbally described characters, and the results of the next part of the study reinforce this conclusion.

In Experiment 2, the subjects once again read short narratives, only this time there were five types, and after each one the subjects were asked to complete a statement by selecting one of two words. The different kinds of stories were as follows (see Table 16.2B for samples):

- "false belief" (FB) stories, which describe characters whose beliefs conflict with reality;
- "false photograph" (FP) stories, which describe photos that no longer represent reality;
- "desire" stories, which describe characters' wishes;
- "nonhuman description" stories, which describe inanimate objects;
- "physical people" stories, which describe characters' physical traits.

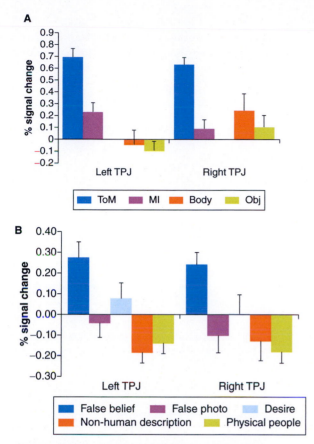

A

B

Figure 16.10 Results from Saxe and Kanwisher's (2003) fMRI study. (A) Experiment 1. (B) Experiment 2. See main text for details. (From Saxe & Kanwisher, 2003, pp. 1838 & 1840.)

that they enrich our social awareness by inviting us to imagine, in considerable detail, the inner lives of other people (Mar & Oatley, 2008). For example, if you read Herman Melville's famous novel, *Moby-Dick*, you have an extraordinary opportunity to transport yourself into not only the unique physical realm of an early 19th-century whaling ship, but also the equally if not more intriguing mental worlds of its various crew-members, including most notably the following individuals: Ahab, the obsessive captain who is hell-bent on hunting down and destroying the ferocious white whale that bit off one of his legs during an earlier encounter; Starbuck, the thoughtful first mate who believes Ahab is insane; Queequeg, the half-savage harpooner from the fictional island of Kokovoko; and Ishmael, the charismatic narrator and sole survivor of the amazing voyage that he describes. As you immerse yourself deeper and deeper into the plot, you will become increasingly familiar with all of these characters and increasingly capable of explaining and predicting their behaviors on the basis of what you assume to be their beliefs, desires, goals, plans, intentions, emotions, and so on. This process of attributing mental states to story protagonists may involve putting yourself in their positions, and according to neuroscientific experiments like those reported by Saxe and Kanwisher (2003), it may depend primarily on the efficient operation of the TPJ in both hemispheres. Still, this functional–anatomical hypothesis remains just that—a hypothesis—and further work is needed to both elaborate its specific claims and test them in various ways.

Summary

In recent years, research in cognitive neuroscience has gradually been delineating the large-scale network of cortical areas that collaboratively subserve story comprehension. The greatest progress has been made by PET and fMRI studies, and in an attempt to synthesize a substantial amount of data, Ferstl et al. (2008) conducted a meta-analysis of 12 investigations that focused on the activation patterns evoked by coherent versus incoherent narratives. A number of brain regions emerged as being significantly involved in the receptive processing of coherent (i.e., conceptually well-connected) stories. We restricted our attention, however, to just four areas and their likely functions. First, the anterior temporal lobes may contribute to the comprehension process by integrating semantic information. Second, the medial parietal cortex may combine linguistic cues with personal and real-world

As shown in Figure 16.10B, the magnitude of activation in the TPJ bilaterally was much greater for the FB stories than for the conceptually similar but non-psychological FP stories. The area was also engaged significantly above baseline for the "desire" stories, albeit only in the left hemisphere and not as intensely as for the FB stories. Last but not least, the area actually displayed decreased activity in both hemispheres during the "nonhuman description" stories as well as the "physical people" stories. Taken together, these findings extend those from Experiment 1 by demonstrating that the TPJ allows readers and listeners to reason specifically about the mental states of the characters described in narratives (for convergent neuropsychological data see Samson et al., 2004).

In the Introduction to this chapter, we observed that one of the most valuable functions of well-crafted stories—not the simplistic, artificial stories that are used for laboratory purposes, but the complex, finely woven ones that leave lasting impressions—is knowledge to establish and update full-fledged situation models. Third, the dorsomedial prefrontal cortex may help determine discourse coherence by drawing inferences that relate consecutive sentences to each other. And fourth, the temporoparietal junction may be essential for attributing thoughts to story protagonists, thereby treating them as plausible human beings with minds of their own.

Summary and Key Points

- Discourse comprises language above and beyond the sentence.
- Most of the neuroscientific research on discourse has focused on stories, also known as narratives.
- When people tell stories, they must strive for coherence at both local and global levels. Discourse coherence involves the conceptual connections—logical, causal, chronological, etc.—that relate sentences to each other over the course of a narrative.
- Achieving coherence requires top-down, goal-directed planning abilities and working memory resources. Data from neuropsychological studies with brain-damaged patients and fMRI studies with healthy subjects support the following hypotheses about the neural underpinnings of these organizational processes:

  o They dissociate from the mechanisms involved in programming single sentences.
  o They overlap with the mechanisms involved in programming complex, multi-step actions in non-linguistic domains (e.g., preparing a meal).
  o They include the orbitofrontal and lateral prefrontal cortices in both hemispheres.

- When people read or listen to stories, they integrate the meaning of each consecutive word into their situation model extremely quickly. Evidence comes from ERP studies showing that the N400 evoked by individual words can be modulated by the discourse context in the following complementary ways:

  o If a word is congruent with the immediate sentential context but incongruent with the wider discourse context, the N400 is significantly enhanced.
  o If a word is incongruent with the immediate sentential context but congruent with the wider discourse context, the N400 is not significantly enhanced.

- According to a meta-analysis of 12 PET and fMRI studies, the comprehension of coherent versus incoherent narratives is associated with activation in a broadly distributed network of brain regions. Some of these regions, and their potential contributions to discourse processing, are as follows:

  o The anterior temporal lobes: integrating semantic information.
  o The medial parietal cortex: establishing and updating situation models.
  o The dorsomedial prefrontal cortex: drawing inferences.
  o The temporoparietal junction: attributing thoughts to protagonists.

Recommended Reading

- Mar, R.A. (2004). The neuropsychology of narrative: Story comprehension, story production, and their interaction. *Neuropsychologia, 42,* 1414–1434. A valuable review of the early neuropsychological literature on narrative processing.
- Ferstl, E.C. (2010). Neuroimaging of text comprehension: Where are we now? *Italian Journal of Linguistics, 22,* 61–88. An insightful review of neuroimaging studies conducted since the meta-analysis reported by Ferstl et al. (2008).
- van Berkum, J.J.A. (2012). The electrophysiology of discourse and conversation. In M.J. Spivey, K. McRae, & M.F. Joanisse (Eds.), *The Cambridge handbook of psycholinguistics* (pp. 589–614). Cambridge, UK: Cambridge University Press. A highly informative survey of electrophysiological studies of discourse comprehension.

References

Aasland, W.A., & Baum, S.R. (2003). Temporal parameters as cues to phrasal boundaries: A comparison of processing by left- and right-hemisphere brain-damaged individuals. *Brain and Language, 87*, 385–399.

Abel, S., Dressel, K., Bitzer, R., Kümmerer, D., Mader, I., Weiller, C., & Huber, W. (2009). The separation of processing stages in a lexical interference fMRI paradigm. *NeuroImage, 44*, 1113–1124.

Aboitiz, F. (2012). Gestures, vocalizations, and memory in language origins. *Frontiers in Evolutionary Neuroscience, 4*, Article 2.

Abrams, D.A., Nicol, T., Zecker, S., & Kraus, N. (2008). Right-hemisphere auditory cortex is dominant for coding syllable patterns in speech. *Journal of Neuroscience, 28*, 3958–3965.

Abrams, D.A., Ryali, S., Chen, T., Balaban, E., Levitin, D.J., & Menon, V. (2013). Multivariate activation and connectivity patterns discriminate speech intelligibility in Wernicke's, Broca's, and Geschwind's areas. *Cerebral Cortex, 23*, 1703–1714.

Ackerman, D. (2011). *One hundred names for love: A stroke, a marriage, and the language of healing.* New York: W.W. Norton & Co.

Ackerman, F., & Moore, J. (2001). *Proto-properties and grammatical encoding: A correspondence theory of argument selection.* Stanford, CA: CSLI Publications.

Ackermann, H., Vogel, M., Peterson, D., & Poremba, M. (1992). Speech deficits in ischaemic cerebellar lesions. *Neurology, 239*, 223–227.

Ackermann, H., & Riecker, A. (2010). The contribution(s) of the insula to speech production: A review of the clinical and functional imaging literature. *Brain Structure and Function, 214*, 419–433.

Ackermann, H., & Ziegler, W. (2010). Brain mechanisms underlying speech motor control. In W.J. Hardcastle, J. Laver, & F.E. Gibbon (Eds.), *The handbook of phonetic sciences*, 2nd edition (pp. 202–250). Malden, MA: Wiley-Blackwell.

Acosta-Cabronero, J., Patterson, K., Fryer, T.D., Hodges, J.R., Pengas, G., Williams, G.B., & Nestor, P.J. (2011). Atrophy, hypometabolism, and white matter abnormalities in semantic dementia tell a coherent story. *Brain, 134*, 2025–2035.

Adlam, A.L.R., Patterson, K., Rogers, T.T., Nestor, P.J., Salmond, C.H., Acosta-Cabronero, J., & Hodges, J.R. (2006). Semantic dementia and fluent primary progressive aphasia: Two sides of the same coin? *Brain, 129*, 3066–3080.

Adolphs, R. (2010a). Emotion. *Current Biology, 20*, R549–R552.

Adolphs, R. (2010b). What does the amygdala contribute to social cognition? *Annals of the New York Academy of Sciences, 1191*, 42–61.

Adolphs, R., Damasio, H., & Tranel, D. (2002). Neural systems for recognition of emotional prosody: A 3–D lesion study. *Emotion, 2*, 23–51.

Adolphs, R., Damasio, H., & Tranel, D., Cooper, G., & Damasio, A.R. (2000). A role for somatosensory cortices in the visual recognition of emotion as revealed by 3–D lesion mapping. *Journal of Neuroscience, 20*, 2683–2690.

Adolphs, R., & Tranel, D. (1999). Intact recognition of emotional prosody following amygdala damage. *Neuropsychologia, 37*, 1285–1292.

Aggujaro, S., Crepaldi, D., Pistarini, C., Taricco, M., & Luzzatti, C. (2006). Neuroanatomical correlates of impaired retrieval of verbs and nouns: Interaction of grammatical class, imageability and actionality. *Journal of Neurolinguistics, 19*, 174–194.

Aikhenvald, A.Y. (2003). *Classifiers: A typology of noun categorization devices.* Oxford, UK: Oxford University Press.

Aikhenvald, A.Y., & Dixon, R.M.W. (Eds.) (2006). *Serial verb constructions: A cross-linguistic typology.* Oxford, UK: Oxford University Press.

Ainsworth-Darnell, K., Shulman, H.G., & Boland, J.E. (1998). Dissociating brain responses to syntactic and semantic anomalies: Evidence from event-related potentials. *Journal of Memory and Language, 38*, 112–130.

Alario, F.X., Chainay, H., Lehéricy, S., & Cohen, L. (2006). The role of the supplementary motor area (SMA) in word production. *Brain Research, 1076*, 129–143.

Albert, M.L., & Bear, D. (1974). Time to understand: A case study of word deafness with reference to the role of time in auditory comprehension. *Brain, 97*, 373–384.

Albright, A., & Hayes, B. (2003). Rules vs. analogy in English past tenses: A computational/experimental study. *Cognition, 90*, 119–161.

Aleman, A., Formisano, E., Koppenhagen, H., Hagoort, P., de Haan, E., & Kahn, R. (2005). The functional neuroanatomy of metrical stress evaluation of perceived and imagined spoken words. *Cerebral Cortex, 15*, 221–228.

Alexander, M.P. (2002). Aphasia I: Clinical and antomical issues. In M.J. Farah & T.E. Feinberg (Eds.), *Patient-based approaches to cognitive neuroscience*, 2nd edition (pp. 181–198). Cambridge, MA: MIT Press.

Alexander, M.P., & Annett, M. (1996). Crossed aphasia and related anomalies of cerebral organization: Case reports and a genetic hypothesis. *Brain and Language, 55*, 213–239.

Allain, P., Le Gall, D., Etcharry-Bouyx, F., Aubin, G., & Emile, J. (1999). Mental representation of knowledge following frontal-lobe lesion: Dissociations on tasks using scripts. *Journal of Clinical and Experimental Neuropsychology, 21*, 643–665.

Allain, P., Le Gall, D., Etcharry-Bouyx, F., Forgeau, M., Mercier, P., & Emile, J. (2001). Influence of centrality and distinctiveness of actions on script sorting and ordering in patients with frontal lobe lesions. *Journal of Clinical and Experimental Neuropsychology, 23*, 465–483.

Allen, P., Aleman, A., & McGuire, P. (2007). Inner speech models of auditory verbal hallucinations: Evidence from behavioral and neuroimaging studies. *International Review of Psychiatry, 19*, 407–415.

Allison, T., Puce, A., & McCarthy, G. (2000). Social perception from visual cues: Role of the STS region. *Trends in Cognitive Sciences, 4*, 267–278.

Allman, J.M., Tetreault, N.A., Hakeem, A.Y., Manaye, K.F., Semendeferi, K., Erwin, J.M., Park, S., Goubert, V., & Hof, P.R. (2010). The von Economo neurons in frontoinsular and anterior cingulate cortex in great apes and humans. *Brain Structure and Function, 214*, 495–517.

Allman, J.M., Watson, K.K., Tetreault, N.A., & Hakeem, A.Y. (2005). Intuition and autism: A possible role for Von Economo neurons. *Trends in Cognitive Sciences, 9*, 367–373.

Allport, D.A. (1985). Distributed memory, modular subsystems, and dysphasia. In S.K. Newman & R. Epstein (Eds.), *Current perspectives on dysphasia* (pp. 207–244). New York: Churchill Livingstone.

Almeida, D., & Poeppel, D. (in press). Word-specific repetition effects revealed by MEG and the implications for lexical access. *Brain and Language.*

Almor, A., Kempler, D., Andersen, E.S., McDonald, M.C., Hayes, U.L., & Hintiryan, H. (2002). The production of regularly and irregularly inflected nouns and verbs in Alzheimer's and Parkinson's patients. *Brain and Language, 83*, 149–151.

Altmann, L.J.P., Saleem, A., Kendall, D., Heilman, K.M., & Rothi, L.J.G. (2006). Orthographic directionality and thematic role illustration in English and Arabic. *Brain and Language, 97*, 306–316.

Álvarez, S.G., Novo, M.L., & Fernández, F.D. (2009). Naming faces: A multidisciplinary and integrated review. *Psicothema, 21*, 521–527.

Amici, S., Gorno-Tempini, M.L., Ogar, J.M., Dronkers, N.F., & Miller, B.L. (2006). An overview of primary progressive aphasia. *Behavioral Neurology, 17*, 77–87.

Amici, S., Ogar, J.M., Brambati, S.M., Miller, B.L., Neuhaus, J., Dronkers, N.F., & Gorno-Tempini, M.L. (2007). Performance in specific language tasks correlates with regional volume changes in progressive aphasia. *Cognitive and Behavioral Neurology, 20*, 203–211.

Amodio, D.M., & Frith, C.D. (2006). Meeting of minds: The medial frontal cortex and social cognition. *Nature Reviews Neuroscience, 7*, 268–277.

Amoruso, L., Gelormini, C., Aboitiz, F., González, M.A., Manes, F., Cardona, J.F., & Inanez, A. (2013). N400 ERPs for actions: Building meaning in context. *Frontiers in Human Neurosciences, 7*, Article 57.

Amunts, K., Malikovic, A., Mohlberg, H., Schormann, T., & Zilles, K. (2000). Brodmann's areas 17 and 18 brought into sterotaxic space: Where and how variable? *NeuroImage, 11*, 66–84.

Amunts, K., Schleicher, A., Bürgel, U., Mohlberg, H., Uylings, H.B.M., & Zilles, K. (1999). Broca's area revisited: Cytoarchitecture and inter-subject variability. *Journal of Comparative Neurology, 412*, 319–341.

Amunts, K., & Zilles, K. (2012). Architecture and organizational principles of Broca's region. *Trends in Cognitive Sciences, 16*, 418–426.

Anderson, A.K., & Phelps, E.A. (1998). Intact recognition of vocal expressions of fear following bilateral lesions of the human amygdala. *NeuroReport, 9*, 3607–3613.

Anderson, S.W., Damasio, A.R., & Damasio, H. (1990). Troubled letters but not numbers: Domain-specific cognitive impairments following focal damage in frontal cortex. *Brain, 113*, 749–766.

Andres, M., Seron, X., & Olivier, E. (2007). Contribution of hand motor circuits to counting. *Journal of Cognitive Neuroscience, 19*, 563–576.

Andrews, M., Vigliocco, G., & Vinson, D. (2009). Integrating experiential and distributional data to learn semantic representations. *Psychological Review, 116*, 463–498.

Andrews-Hanna, J.R. (2012). The brain's default network and its adaptive role in internal mentation. *The Neuroscientist, 18*, 251–270.

Ansorge, U., Kiefer, M., Khalid, S., Grassi, S., & König, P. (2010). Testing the theory of embodied cognition with subliminal words. *Cognition, 116*, 303–320.

Aravena, P., Hurtado, E., Riveros, R., Cardona, J.F., Manes, F., & Ibáñez, A. (2010). Applauding with closed hands: Neural signature of action-sentence compatibility effects. *PLoS ONE, 5*, e11751.

Arbib, M. (in press). Neurolinguistics. In B. Heine & H. Narrog (Eds.), *The Oxford handbook of linguistic analysis*, 2nd edition. Oxford, UK: Oxford University Press.

Arévalo, A., Baldo, J.V., & Dronkers, N.F. (2012). What do brain lesions tell us about theories of embodied semantics and the human mirror neuron system? *Cortex, 48*, 242–254.

Arévalo, A., Perani, D., Cappa, S.F., Butler, A., Bates, E., & Dronkers, N. (2007). Action and object processing in aphasia: From nouns and verbs to the effect of manipulability. *Brain and Language, 100*, 79–94.

Aristei, S., Melinger, A., & Rahman, R.A. (2011). Electrophysiological chronometry of semantic context effects in language production. *Journal of Cognitive Neuroscience, 23*, 1567–1586.

Armony, J.L., & Dolan, R.J. (2002). Modulation of spatial attention by fear-conditioned stimuli: An event-related fMRI study. *Neuropsychologia, 40*, 817–826.

Ash, S., McMillan, C., Gunawardena, D., Avants, B., Morgan, B., Khan, A., Moore, P., Gee, J., & Grossman, M. (2010). Speech errors in progressive non-fluent aphasia. *Brain and Language, 113*, 13–20.

Ash, S., Moore, P., Antani, S., McCawley, G., Work, M., & Grossman, M. (2006). Trying to tell a tale: Discourse impairments in progressive aphasia and frontotemporal dementia. *Neurology, 66*, 1405–1413.

Ash, S., Moore, P., Vesely, L., Gunawardena, D., McMillan, C., Anderson, C., Avants, B., & Grossman, M. (2009).

Non-fluent speech in frontotemporal lobar degeneration. *Journal of Neurolinguistics, 22*, 370–383.

Ash, S., Xie, S.X., Gross, R.G., Dreyfuss, M., Boller, A., Camp, E., Morgan, B., O'Shea, J., & Grossman, M. (2012). The organization and anatomy of narrative comprehension and expression in Lewy body spectrum disorders. *Neuropsychology, 26*, 368–384.

Ashby, F.G. (2011). *Statistical analysis of fMRI data*. Cambridge, MA: MIT Press.

Atkinson, J., Marshall, J., Woll, B., & Thacker, A. (2005). Testing comprehension abilities in users of British Sign Language following CVA. *Brain and Language, 94*, 233–248.

Atran, S., & Medin, D. (2008). *The native mind and the cultural construction of nature*. Cambridge, MA: MIT Press.

Auerbach, S.H., Allard, T., Naeser, M., Alexander, M.P., & Albert, M.L. (1982). Pure word deafness: Analysis of a case with bilateral lesions and a defect at the prephonemic level. *Brain, 105*, 271–300.

Austin, P., & Bresnan, J. (1996). Non-configurationality in Australian Aboriginal languages. *Natural Language and Linguistic Theory, 14*, 215–268.

Axer, H., Klingner, C.M., & Prescher, A. (2013). Fiber anatomy of dorsal and ventral language streams. *Brain and Language, 127*, 192–204.

Aziz-Zadeh, L., Wilson, S.M., Rizzolatti, G., & Iacoboni, M. (2006). Congruent embodied representations for visually presented actions and linguistic phrases describing actions. *Current Biology, 16*, 1818–1823.

Baars, B.J. (1980). The competing plans hypothesis: A heuristic viewpoint on the causes of errors in speech production. In H.W. Dechert & M. Raupach (Eds.), *Temporal variables in speech* (pp. 13–19). The Hague: Mouton.

Baars, B.J., & Gage, N.M. (2010). *Cognition, brain, and consciousness: Introduction to cognitive neuroscience*, 2nd edition. San Diego, CA: Academic Press.

Bach, D.R., Grandjean, D., Sander, D., Herdener, M., Strik, W.K., & Seifritz, E. (2008). The effect of appraisal level on processing of emotional prosody in meaningless speech. *NeuroImage, 42*, 919–927.

Bach, D.R., Hurlemann, R., & Dolan, R.J. (2013). Unimpaired discrimination of fearful prosody after amygdala lesion. *Neuropsychologia, 51*, 2070–2074.

Badecker, W., & Caramazza, A. (1985). On considerations of method and theory governing the use of clinical categories in neurolinguistics and cognitive neuropsychology: The case against agrammatism. *Cognition, 20*, 97–125.

Badecker, W., & Caramazza, A. (1986). A final brief in the case against agrammatism: The role of theory in the selection of data. *Cognition, 24*, 277–282.

Badecker, W., & Caramazza, A. (1991). Morphological composition in the lexical output system. *Cognitive Neuropsychology, 8*, 335–367.

Badets, A., Pesenti, M., & Olivier, E. (2010). Response-effect compatibility of finger-numerical configurations in arithmetical context. *Quarterly Journal of Experimental Psychology, 63*, 16–22.

Badre, D., Poldrack, R.A., Pare-Blagoev, J., Insler, R.Z., & Wagner, A.D. (2005). Dissociable controlled retrieval and generalized selection mechanisms in ventrolateral prefrontal cortex. *Neuron, 47*, 907–918.

Badre, D., & Wagner, A.D. (2007). Left ventrolateral prefrontal cortex and the cognitive control of memory. *Neuropsychologia, 45*, 2883–2901.

Baggio, G., & Hagoort, P. (2011). The balance between memory and unification in semantics: A dynamic account of the N400. *Language and Cognitive Processes, 26*, 1338–1367.

Bahlmann, J., Schubotz, R.I., & Friederici, A.D. (2009a). Hierarchical artificial grammar processing engages Broca's area. *NeuroImage, 42*, 525–534.

Bahlmann, J., Schubotz, R.I., Mueller, J.L., Koester, D., & Friederici, A.D. (2009b). Neural circuits of hierarchical visuospatial sequence processing. *Brain Research, 1298*, 161–170.

Bak, T.H., & Hodges, J.R. (2003). Kissing and dancing—A test to distinguish the lexical and conceptual contributions to noun/verb and action/object dissociation: Preliminary results in patients with frontotemporal dementia. *Journal of Neurolinguistics, 16*, 169–181.

Bak, T.H., & Hodges, J.R. (2004). The effects of motor neurone disease on language: Further evidence. *Brain and Language, 89*, 354–361.

Bak, T.H., O'Donovan, D.G., Xuereb, J.H., Boniface, S., & Hodges, J.R. (2001). Selective impairment of verb processing associated with pathological changes in Brodmann areas 44 and 45 in the motor neurone disease-dementia-aphasia syndrome. *Brain, 124*, 103–120.

Baker, C.I, Liu, J., Wald, L.L., Kwong, K.K., Benner, T., & Kanwisher, N. (2007). Visual word processing and experiential origins of functional selectivity in human extrastriate cortex. *Proceedings of the National Academy of Sciences, 104*, 9087–9092.

Baker, E., Blumstein, S.E., & Goodglass, H. (1981). Interaction between phonological and semantic factors in auditory comprehension. *Neuropsychologia, 19*, 1–15.

Balaguer, R.D.D., Costa, A., Sebastian-Galles, N., Juncadella, M., & Caramazza, A. (2004). Regular and irregular morphology and its relation with agrammatism: Evidence from two Spanish-Catalan bilinguals. *Brain and Language, 91*, 212–222.

Balaguer, R.D.D., Rodríguez-Fornells, A., Rotte, M., Bahlmann, J., Heinze, H.J., & Münte, T.F. (2006). Neural circuits subserving the retrieval of stems and grammatical features in regular and irregular verbs. *Human Brain Mapping, 27*, 874–888.

Balan, A., & Gandour, J.T. (1999). Effect of sentence length on the production of linguistic stress by left- and right-hemisphere-damaged patients. *Brain and Language, 67*, 73–94.

Baldo, J.V., Arevalo, A., Patterson, J.P., & Dronkers, N.F. (2013). Grey and white matter correlates of picture naming: Evidence from a voxel-based lesion analysis of the Boston Naming Test. *Cortex, 49*, 658–667.

Baldo, J.V., & Dronkers, N.F. (2006). The role of inferior frontal and inferior parietal cortex in working memory. *Neuropsychology, 20*, 529–538.

Baldo, J.V., Katseff, S., & Dronkers, N.F. (2012). Brain regions underlying repetition and auditory-verbal short-term memory deficits in aphasia: Evidence from voxel-based lesion-symptom mapping. *Aphasiology, 26*, 338–354.

Baldo, J.V., Wilkins, D.P., Ogar, J., Willock, S., & Dronkers, N.F. (2011). Role of the precentral gyrus of the insula in complex articulation. *Cortex, 47*, 800–807.

Bandettini, P.A. (2012). Functional MRI: A confluence of fortunate circumstances. *NeuroImage, 61*(2), A3–A11.

Bangert, B., Peschel, T., Schlaug, G., Rotte, M., Drescher, D., Hinrichs, H. Heinze, H.-J., & Altenmüller, E. (2006). Shared networks for auditory and motor processing in professional pianists: Evidence from fMRI conjunction. *NeuroImage, 30,* 917–926.

Banich, M.T., & Compton, R.J. (2011). *Cognitive neuroscience*, 3rd edition. Belmont, CA: Wadsworth.

Banissy, M.J., Sauter, D.A., Ward, J., Warren, J.E., Walsh, V., & Scott, S.K. (2010). Suppressing sensorimotor activity modulates the discrimination of auditory emotions but not speaker identity. *Journal of Neuroscience, 30*, 13552–13557.

Barber, H., Otten, L.J., Kousta, S.T., & Vigliocco, G. (2013). Concreteness in word processing: ERP and behavioral effects in a lexical decision task. *Brain and Language, 125*, 47–53.

Bardin, J. (2012). Making connections. *Nature, 483*, 394–396.

Barker, A.T., Jalinous, R., & Freeston, I.L. (1985). Non-invasive magnetic stimulation of human motor cortex. *Lancet, 1*, 1106–1107.

Barker, R.G., & Wright, H.F. (1951). *One boy's day: A specimen record of behavior.* New York: Harper & Brothers.

Baron-Cohen, S. (2003). *The essential difference: The truth about the male and female brain.* New York: Basic Books.

Barrett, S.E., & Rugg, M.D. (1989). Event-related potentials and the semantic matching of faces. *Neuropsychologia, 27*, 913–922.

Barrós-Loscertales, A., González, J., Pulvermüller, F., Ventura-Campos, N., Bustamante, J.C., Costumero, V., Parcet, A., & Ávila, C. (2012). Reading *salt* activates gustatory brain regions: fMRI evidence for semantic grounding in a novel sensory modality. *Cerebral Cortex, 22*, 2554–2563.

Barsalou, L.W. (1999). Perceptual symbol systems. *Behavioral and Brain Sciences, 22*, 577–660.

Barsalou, L.W. (2008). Grounded cognition. *Annual Review of Psychology, 59*, 617–645.

Barsalou, L.W., Santos, A., Simmons, W.K., & Wilson, C.D. (2008). Language and simulation in conceptual processing. In M. DeVega, A.M. Glenberg, & A.C. Graesser (Eds.), *Symbols and embodiment* (pp. 245–283). Oxford, UK: Oxford University Press.

Bartley, A.J., Jones, D.W., & Weinberger, D.R. (1997). Genetic variability of human brain size and cortical gyral patterns. *Brain, 120*, 257–269.

Bartoli, E., D'Ausilio, A., Berry, J., Badino, L., Bever, T., & Fadiga, L. (in press). Listener-speaker perceived distance predicts the degree of contribution to speech perception. *Cerebral Cortex.*

Barwood, C.H., Murdoch, B.E., Whelan, B.M., Lloyd, D., Riek, S., O'Sullivan, J.D., Coulthard, A., & Wong, A. (2011). Improved language performance subsequent to low-frequency rTMS in patients with chronic non-fluent aphasia post-stroke. *European Journal of Neurology, 18*, 935–943.

Basso, A., Casati, G., & Vignolo, L.A. (1977). Phonemic identification defects in aphasia. *Cortex, 13*, 84–95.

Bastiaanse, R., & Thompson, C.K. (Eds.) (2012). *Perspectives on agrammtism.* New York: Psychology Press.

Bates, E., Wilson, S.M., Saygin, A.P., Dick, F., Sereno, M.I., Knight, R.T., & Dronkers, N.F. (2003). Voxel-based lesion-symptom mapping. *Nature Neuroscience, 6*, 448–450.

Bates, E., & Wulfeck, B. (1989). Crosslinguistic studies of aphasia. In B. MacWhinney & E. Bates (Eds.), *The crosslinguistic study of sentence processing* (pp. 328–371). Cambridge, UK: Cambridge University Press.

Bauby, J.-D.(1997). *The Diving Bell and the Butterfly.* New York: Alfred A. Knopf.

Bauer, J.J., Mittal, J., Larson, C.R., & Hain, T.C. (2006). Vocal responses to unanticipated perturbations in voice loudness feedback: An automatic mechanism for stabilizing voice amplitude. *Journal of the Acoustical Society of America, 119*, 2363–2371.

Bauer, R.M., & McDonald, C.R. (2006). Auditory agnosia and amusia. In M.J. Farah & T.E. Feinberg (Eds.), *Patient-based approaches to cognitive neuroscience*, 2nd edition (pp. 133–146). Cambridge, MA: MIT Press.

Baum, S.R. (1998). The role of fundamental frequency and duration in the perception of linguistic stress by individuals with brain damage. *Journal of Speech and Hearing Research, 41*, 31–40.

Baum, S.R., & Dwivedi, V.D. (2003). Sensitivity to prosodic structure in left- and right-hemisphere-damaged individuals. *Brain and Language, 87*, 278–289.

Baum, S.R., Kelsch Daniloff, J., Daniloff, R., & Lewis, J. (1982). Sentence comprehension by Broca's aphasics: Effects of some suprasegmental variables. *Brain and Language, 17*, 261–271.

Baum, S.R., & Pell, M.D. (1997). Production of affective and linguistic prosody by brain-damaged patients. *Aphasiology, 11*, 177–198.

Baum, S.R., & Pell, M.D. (1999). The neural bases of prosody: Insights from lesion studies and neuroimaging. *Aphasiology, 13*, 581–608.

Baum, S.R., Pell, M.D., Leonard, C.L., & Gordon, J.K. (1997). The ability of right- and left-hemisphere damaged individuals to produce and interpret prosodic cues marking phrasal boundaries. *Language and Speech, 40*, 313–330.

Bavelier, D., Corina, D., Jezzard, P., Clark, V., Karni, A., Lalwani, A., Rauscheker, J.P., Braun, A., Turner, R., & Neville, H. (1998a). Hemispheric specialization for English and ASL: Left invariance-right variability. *NeuroReport, 9*, 1537–1542.

Bavelier, D., Corina, D., & Neville, H. (1998b). Brain and language: A perspective from sign language. *Neuron, 21*, 275–278.

Baxter, D.M., & Warrington, E.K. (1985). Category-specific phonological dysgraphia. *Neuropsychologia, 23*, 653–666.

Baxter, D.M., & Warrington, E.K. (1987). Transcoding sound to spelling: Single or multiple sound unit correspondence? *Cortex, 23*, 11–28.

Beauchamp, M.S., Haxby, J.V., Jennings, J.E., & DeYoe, E.A. (1999). An fMRI version of the Farnsworth-Munsell 100–Hue Test reveals multiple color-selective areas in human ventral occipito-temporal cortex. *Cerebral Cortex, 9*, 257–263.

Beauchamp, M.S., Haxby, J.V., Rosen, A.C., & DeYoe, E.A. (2000). A functional MRI case study of acquired cerebral dyschromatopsia. *Neuropsychologia, 38*, 1170–1179.

Beauchamp, M.S., & Martin, A. (2007). Grounding object concepts in perception and action. *Cortex, 43*, 461–468.

Beauchamp, M.S., Nath, A.R., & Pasalar, S. (2010). fMRI-guided transcranial magnetic stimulation reveals that the superior temporal sulcus is a cortical locus of the McGurk effect. *Journal of Neuroscience, 30*, 2414–2417.

Beaucousin, V., Lacheret, A., Turbelin, M.R., Morel, M., Mazoyer, B., & Tzourio-Mazoyer, N. (2007). fMRI study of emotional speech comprehension. *Cerebral Cortex, 17*, 339–352.

Beauvois, M.F., & Dérouesné, J. (1979). Phonological alexia: Three dissociations. *Journal of Neurology, Neurosurgery, and Psychiatry, 42*, 1115–1124.

Beauvois, M.F., & Dérouesné, J. (1981). Lexical or ortho-graphic agraphia. *Brain, 104*, 21–49.

Bechtel, W., & Abrahamsen, A. (1991). *Connectionism and the mind: An introduction to parallel processing in net-works*. Oxford, UK: Basil Blackwell.

Beck, J., Rohrer, J.D., Campbell, T., Isaacs, A., Morrison, K.E., Goodall, E.F., Warrington, E.K., Stevens, J., Revesz, T., Holton, J., Al-Sarraj, S., King, A., Scahill, R., Warren, J.D., Fox, N.C., Rossor, M.N., Collinge, J., & Mead, S. (2008). A distinct, clinical, neuropsychological and radiological phenotype is associated with progranulin gene mutations in a large UK series. *Brain, 131*, 706–720.

Bedny, M., Caramazza, A., Grossman, E., Pascual-Leone, A., & Saxe, R. (2008). Concepts are more than percepts: The case of action verbs. *Journal of Neuroscience, 28*, 11347–11353.

Bedny, M., Caramazza, A., Pascual-Leone, A., & Saxe, R. (2012). Typical neural representations of action concepts develop without vision. *Cerebral Cortex, 22*, 286–293.

Bedny, M., Hulbert, J.C., & Thompson-Schill, S.L. (2007). Understanding words in context: The role of Broca's area in word comprehension. *Brain Research, 1146*, 101–114.

Behrens, S. (1988). The role of the right hemisphere in the production of linguistic stress. *Brain and Language, 33*, 104–127.

Behrens, S. (1989). Characterizing sentence intonation in a right-hemisphere-damaged population. *Brain and Language, 37*, 181–200.

Behrmann, M., & Bub, D. (1992). Surface dyslexia and dysgraphia: Dual routes, single lexicon. *Cognitive Neuropsychology, 9*, 209–251.

Behrmann, M., Nelson, J., & Sekuler, E. (1998). Visual complexity in letter-by-letter reading: "Pure" alexia is not so pure. *Neuropsychologia, 36*, 1115–1132.

Behrmann, M., & Plaut, D.C. (in press). Bilateral hemispheric processing of words and faces: Evidence from word impairments in prosopagnosia and face impairments in pure alexia. *Cerebral Cortex*.

Beilock, S.L., Lyons, I.M., Mattarella-Micke, A., Nusbaum, H.C., & Small, S.L. (2008). Sports experience changes the neural processing of action language. *Proceedings of the National Academy of Sciences, 105*, 13269–13273.

Belin, P. (2006). Voice processing in human and nonhuman primates. *Philosophical Transactions of the Royal Society, B, Biological Sciences, 361*, 2091–2107.

Belin, P., & Zatorre, R.J. (2003). Adaptation to speaker's voice in right anterior temporal lobe. *NeuroReport, 16*, 2105–2109.

Belin, P., Zatorre, R.J., Lafaille, P., Ahad, P., & Pike, B. (2000). Voice-selective areas in human auditory cortex. *Nature, 403*, 309–312.

Bell, A.H., Malecek, N.J., Morin, E.L., Hadj-Bouziane, F., Tootell, R.B.H., & Ungerleider, L.G. (2011). Relationship between functional magnetic resonance imaging-identified regions and neuronal category selectivity. *Journal of Neuroscience, 31*, 12229–12240.

Bellgowan, P.S.F., Saad, Z.S., & Bandettini, P.A. (2003). Understanding neural system dynamics through task modulation and measurement of functional MRI amplitude, latency, and width. *Proceedings of the National Academy of Sciences, 100*, 1415–1419.

Bemis, D.K., & Pylkkänen, L. (2011). Simple composition: A magnetoencephalography investigation into the comprehension of minimal linguistic phrases. *Journal of Neuroscience, 31*, 2801–2814.

Bemis, D.K., & Pylkkänen, L. (2013). Basic linguistic composition recruits the left anterior temporal lobe and left angular gyrus during both listening and reading. *Cerebral Cortex, 23*, 1859–1873.

Bennett, P.R. (1974). Tone and the Nilotic case system. *Bulletin of the School of Oriental and African Studies, 37*, 19–28.

Ben-Shachar, M., Dougherty, R.F., Deutsch, G.K., & Wandell, B.A. (2007). Differential sensitivity to words and shapes in ventral occipito-temporal cortex. *Cerebral Cortex, 17*, 1604–1611.

Benson, D.F., & Ardila, A. (1996). *Aphasia: A clinical introduction*. Oxford, UK: Oxford University Press.

Benson, R.R., Richardson, M., Whalen, D.H., & Lai, S. (2006). Phonetic processing areas revealed by sinewave speech and acoustically similar non-speech. *NeuroImage, 31*, 342–353.

Benton, A. (1992). Gerstmann's syndrome. *Archives of Neurology, 49*, 445–447.

Benton, A., & Anderson, S.W. (1998). Aphasia: Historical perspectives. In M.T. Sarno (Ed.), *Acquired aphasia*, 3rd edition (pp. 1–24). San Diego, CA: Academic Press.

Beretta, A., Campbell, C., Carr, T.H., Huang, J., Schmitt, L.M., Christianson, K., & Cao, Y. (2003). A ER-fMRI investigation of morphological inflection in German reveals that the brain makes a distinction between regular and irregular forms. *Brain and Language, 85*, 67–92.

Berker, E.A., Berker, E.H., & Smith, A. (1986). Translation of Broca's 1865 report: Localization of speech in the third frontal convolution. *Archives of Neurology (Chicago), 43*, 1065–1072.

Berlingeri, M., Crepaldi, D., Roberti, R., Scialfa, G., Luzzatti, C., & Paulesu, E. (2008). Nouns and verbs in the brain: Grammatical class and task specific effects as revealed by fMRI. *Cognitive Neuropsychology, 25*, 528–558.

Berman, R.A., & Slobin, D.I. (1994). *Relating events in narrative*. Hillsdale, NJ: Erlbaum.

Bernal, B., & Ardila, A. (2009). The role of the arcuate fasciculus in conduction aphasia. *Brain, 132*, 2309–2316.

Berndt, R.S. (1987). Symptom co-occurrence and dissociation in the interpretation of agrammatism. In M. Coltheart, G. Sartori, & R. Job (Eds.), *The cognitive neuropsychology of language*. Hillsdale, NJ: Lawrence Erlbaum.

Berndt, R.S. (2001). Sentence production. In B. Rapp (Ed.), *The handbook of cognitive neuropsychology: What deficits reveal about the human mind* (pp. 375–396). Philadelphia: Psychology Press.

Berndt, R.S., Haendiges, A.N., Mitchum, C.M., & Sandson, J. (1997a). Verb retrieval in aphasia. 2. Relationship to sentence processing. *Brain and Language, 56*, 68–106.

Berndt, R.S., Mitchum, C.M., & Haendiges, A.N. (1996). Comprehension of reversible sentences in "agrammatism": A meta-analysis. *Cognition, 58*, 289–308.

Berndt, R.S., Mitchum, C.M., Haendiges, A.N., & Sandson, J. (1997b). Verb retrieval in aphasia. 1. Characterizing single word impairments. *Brain and Language, 56*, 107–137.

Berthier, M.L., Lambon Ralph, M.A., Pujol, J., & Green, C. (2012). Arcuate fasciculus variability and repetition: The left sometimes can be right. *Cortex, 48*, 133–143.

Besson, M., & Macar, F. (1987). An event-related potential analysis of incongruity in music and other non-linguistic contexts. *Psychophysiology, 24*, 14–25.

Bhatia, K.P., & Marsden, C.D. (1994). The behavioural and motor consequences of focal lesions of the basal ganglia in man. *Brain, 117*, 859–876.

Bhatnagar, S.C. (2002). *Neuroscience for the study of communicative disorders*, 2nd edition. Philadelphia: Lippincott, Williams & Wilkins.

Bi, Y., Han, Z., & Zhang, Y. (2009). Reading does not depend on writing, even in Chinese. *Neuropsychologia, 47*, 1193–1199.

Bierwisch, M., & Schreuder, R. (1992). From concepts to lexical items. *Cognition, 42*, 23–60.

Bikel, D.M. (2002). Design of a multi-lingual, parallel-processing statistical parsing engine. In *Proceedings of the second international conference on human language technology research* (pp. 178–182). San Francisco: Morgan Kaufmann.

Binder, J.R. (2007). Effects of word imageability on semantic access: Neuroimaging studies. In J. Hart, Jr., & M.A. Kraut (Eds.), *Neural basis of semantic memory* (pp. 149–181). Cambridge, UK: Cambridge University Press.

Binder, J.R., & Desai, R.H. (2011). The neurobiology of semantic memory. *Trends in Cognitive Sciences, 15*, 527–536.

Binder, J.R., Desai, R.H., Graves, W.W., & Conant, L.L. (2009). Where is the semantic system? A critical review and meta-analysis of 120 functional neuroimaging studies. *Cerebral Cortex, 19*, 2767–2796.

Binder, J.R., Frost, J.A., Hammeke, T.A., Bellgowan, P.S.F., Rao, S.M., & Cox, R.W. (1999). Conceptual processing during the conscious resting state: A functional MRI study. *Journal of Cognitive Neuroscience, 11*, 80–93.

Binder, J.R., Frost, J.A., Hammeke, T.A., Bellgowan, P.S.F., Springer, J.A., Kaufman, J.N., & Possing, E.T. (2000). Human temporal lobe activation by speech and nonspeech sounds. *Cerebral Cortex, 10*, 512–528.

Binder, J.R., McKiernan, K.A., Parsons, M.E., Westbury, C.F., Possing, E.T., Kaufman, J.N., & Buchanan, L. (2003). Neural correlates of lexical access during visual word recognition. *Journal of Cognitive Neuroscience, 15*, 372–393.

Binder, J.R., Medler, D.A., Westbury, C.F., Liebenthal, E., & Buchanan, L. (2006). Tuning of the human left fusiform gyrus to sublexical orthographic structure. *NeuroImage, 33*, 739–748.

Binkofski, F., & Buccino, G. (2004). Motor functions of Broca's area. *Brain and Language, 89*, 362–369.

Binney, R.J., Embleton, K.V., Jeffries, E., Parker, G.J.M., & Lambon Ralph, M.A. (2010). The ventral and infero-lateral aspects of the anterior temporal temporal lobe are crucial in semantic memory: Evidence from a novel direct comparison of distortion-corrected fMRI, rTMS, and semantic dementia. *Cerebral Cortex, 20*, 2728–2738.

Binney, R.J., Parker, G.J.M., & Lambon Ralph, M.A. (2012). Convergent connectivity and graded specialization in the rostral human temporal lobe as revealed by diffusion-weighted imaging probabilistic tractography. *Journal of Cognitive Neuroscience, 24*, 1998–2014.

Bird, H., Lambon Ralph, M.A., Patterson, K., & Hodges, J.R. (2000). The rise and fall of frequency and imageability: Noun and verb production in semantic dementia. *Brain and Language, 73*, 17–49.

Bird, H., Lambon Ralph, M.A., Seidenberg, M.S., McClelland, J.L., & Patterson, K. (2003). Deficits in phonology and past tense morphology: What's the connection? *Journal of Memory and Language, 48*, 502–526.

Bisiacchi, P.S., Cipolotti, L., & Denes, G. (1989). Impairment in processing meaningless verbal material in several modalities: The relationship between short-term memory and phonological skills. *Quarterly Journal of Experimental Psychology, 41A*, 293–319.

Blakemore, S.J., Fonlupt, P., Pachot-Clouard, M., Darmon, C., Boyer, P., Meltzoff, A.N., Segebarth, C., & Decety, J. (2001). How the brain perceives causality: An event-related fMRI study. *NeuroReport, 12*, 3741–3746.

Blakemore, S.J., Wolpert, D.M., & Frith, C.D. (2002). Abnormalities in the awareness of action. *Trends in Cognitive Sciences, 6*, 237–242.

Blanke, O. (2012). Multisensory brain mechanisms of bodily self-consciousness. *Nature Reviews Neuroscience, 13*, 556–571.

Blanke, O., & Arzy, S. (2005). The out-of-body experience: Disturbed self-processing at the temporo-parietal junction. *The Neuroscientist, 11*, 16–24.

Blazely, A., Coltheart, M., & Casey, B. (2005). Semantic impairment with and without surface dyslexia: Implications for models of reading. *Cognitive Neuropsychology, 22*, 695–717.

Blonder, L.X., Gur, R.E., & Gur, R.C. (1989). The effects of right and left hemiparkinsonism on prosody. *Brain and Language, 36*, 193–207.

Blumenfeld, H. (2010). *Neuroanatomy through clinical cases*, 2nd edition. Sunderland, MA: Sinauer Associates.

Blumstein, S.E., Cooper, W.E., Zurif, E.B., & Caramazza, A. (1977). The perception and production of voice-onset time in aphasia. *Neuropsychologia, 15*, 371–383.

Blumstein, S.E., & Goodglass, H. (1972). The perception of stress as a semantic cue in aphasia. *Journal of Speech and Hearing Research, 15*, 800–806.

Blundo, C., Ricci, M., & Miller, L. (2006). Category-specific knowledge deficit for animals in a patient with herpes simplex encephalitis. *Cognitive Neuropsychology, 23*, 1248–1268.

Boatman, D., Gordon, B., Hart, B., Selnes, O., Miglioretti, D., & Lenz, F. (2000). Transcortical sensory aphasia: Revisited and revised. *Brain, 123*, 1634–1642.

Boatman, D., Hall, C., Goldstein, M.H., Lesser, R., & Gordon, B. (1997). Neuroperceptual differences in consonant and vowel discrimination: As revealed by direct cortical electrical interference. *Cortex, 33*, 83–98.

Boatman, D., Lesser, R., & Gordon, B. (1995). Auditory speech processing in the left temporal lobe: An electrical interference study. *Brain and Language, 51*, 269–290.

Bobes, M.A., Valdés-Sosa, M., & Olivares, E. (1994). An ERP study of expectancy violation in face perception. *Brain and Cognition, 26*, 1–22.

Bock, J.K., & Levelt, W.J.M. (1984). Language production: Grammatical encoding. In M. Gernsbacher (Ed.), *Handbook of psycholinguistics* (pp. 945–984). San Diego: Academic Press.

Boemio, A., Fromm, S., Braun, A., & Poeppel, D. (2005). Hierarchical and asymmetric temporal sensitivity in human auditory cortices. *Nature Neuroscience, 8*, 389–395.

Bögels, S., Schriefers, H., Vonk, W., & Chwilla, D.J. (2011). Prosodic breaks in sentence processing investigated by event-related potentials. *Language and Linguistics Compass, 5*, 424–440.

Bogen, J.E., & Bogen, G.M. (1976). Wernicke's region—where is it? *Annals of the New York Academy of Sciences, 280*, 834–843.

Bohland, J.W., & Guenther, F.H. (2006). An fMRI investigation of syllable sequence production. *NeuroImage, 32*, 821–841.

Bohland, J.W., Guenther, F.H., & Bullock, D. (2010). Neural representations and mechanisms for the performance of simple speech sequences. *Journal of Cognitive Neuroscience, 22*, 1504–1529.

Bolger, D.J., Perfetti, C.A., & Schneider, W. (2005). Cross-cultural effect on the brain revisited: Universal structures plus writing system variation. *Human Brain Mapping, 25*, 92–104.

Bolognini, N., & Ro, T. (2010). Transcranial magnetic stimulation: Disrupting neural activity to alter and assess brain function. *Journal of Neuroscience, 30*, 9647–9650.

Bonilha, L., & Fridriksson, J. (2009). Subcortical damage and white matter disconnection associated with non-fluent speech. *Brain, 132*, 1–2.

Bonner, M.F., & Grossman, M. (2012). Gray matter density of auditory association cortex relates to knowledge of sound concepts in primary progressive aphasia. *Journal of Neuroscience, 32*, 7986–7991.

Bonner, M.F., Peelle, J.E., Cook, P.A., & Grossman, M. (2013). Heteromodal conceptual processing in the angular gyrus. *NeuroImage, 71*, 175–186.

Bonner, M.F., Vesely, L., Price, C., Anderson, C., Richmond, L., Farag, C., Avants, B., & Grossman, M. (2009). Reversal of the concreteness effect in semantic dementia. *Cognitive Neuropsychology, 26*, 568–579.

Booth, J.R., Burman, D.D., Meyer, J.R., Gitelman, D.R., Parrish, T.R., & Mesulam, M.M. (2002). Functional anatomy of intra- and cross-modal lexical tasks. *NeuroImage, 16*, 7–22.

Borchers, S., Himmelbach, M., Logothetis, N., & Karnath, H.O. (2012). Direct electrical stimulation of human cortex—the gold standard for mapping brain functions? *Nature Reviews Neuroscience, 13*, 63–70.

Bornkessel, I., & Schlesewsky, M. (2006). The Extended Argument Dependency Model: A neurocognitive approach to sentence comprehension across languages. *Psychological Review, 113*, 787–821.

Bornkessel, I., Zysset, S., Friederici, A.D., von Cramon, D.Y., & Schlesewsky, M. (2005). Who did what to whom? The neural basis of argument hierarchies during language comprehension. *NeuroImage, 26*, 221–233.

Bornkessel-Schlesewsky, I., & Schlesewsky, M. (2008). An alternative perspective on "semantic P600" effects in language comprehension. *Brain Research Reviews, 59*, 55–73.

Bornkessel-Schlesewsky, I., & Schlesewsky, M. (2009a). *Processing syntax and morphology: A neurocognitive perspective*. Oxford, UK: Oxford University Press.

Bornkessel-Schlesewsky, I., & Schlesewsky, M. (2009b). The role of prominence information in the real-time comprehension of transitive constructions: A cross-linguistic approach. *Language and Linguistics Compass, 3*, 19–58.

Bornkessel-Schlesewsky, I., & Schlesewsky, M. (2012). Linguistic sequencing and the prefrontal cortex. *The Open Medical Imaging Journal, 6*, 47–61.

Bornkessel-Schlesewsky, I., Schlesewsky, M., & von Cramon, D.Y. (2009). Word order and Broca's region: Evidence for a supra-syntactic perspective. *Brain and Language, 111*, 125–139.

Borod, J.C., Welkowitz, J., Alpert, M., Brozgold, A.Z., Martin, C., Peselow, E., & Diller, L. (1990). Parameters of emotional processing in neuropsychiatric disorders: Conceptual issues and a battery of tests. *Journal of Communication Disorders, 23*, 247–271.

Borogovac, A., & Asllani, I. (2012). Arterial spin labeling (ASL) fMRI: Advantages, theoretical constraints, and experimental challenges in neurosciences. *International Journal of Biomedical Imaging*, Article ID 818456.

Boronat, C.B., Buxbaum, L.J., Coslett, H.B., Tang, K., Saffran, E.M., Kimberg, D.Y., & Detre, J.A. (2005). Distinctions between manipulation and function knowledge of objects: Evidence from functional magnetic resonance imaging. *Cognitive Brain Research, 23*, 361–373.

Borovsky, A., Saygin, A.P., Bates, E., & Dronkers, N. (2007). Lesion correlates of conversational speech production deficits. *Neuropsychologia, 45*, 2525–2533.

Borreggine, K.L., & Kaschak, M.P. (2006). The action-sentence compatibility effect: It's all in the timing. *Cognitive Science, 30*, 1097–1112.

Bouchard, K.E., Mesgarani, N., Johnson, K., & Chang, E.F. (2013). Functional organization of human sensorimotor cortex for speech articulation. *Nature, 495*, 327–332.

Boukrina, O., & Graves, W.W. (2013). Neural networks underlying contributions from semantics in reading aloud. *Frontiers in Human Neuroscience, 7*, Article 518.

Boulenger, V., Hauk, O., & Pulvermüller, F. (2009). Grasping ideas with the motor system: Semantic somatotopy in idiom comprehension. *Cerebral Cortex, 19*, 1905–1914.

Boulenger, V., Roy, A.C., Paulignan, Y., Deprez, V., Jeannerod, M., & Nazir, T.A. (2006). Cross-talk between language processes and overt motor behavior in the first 200 ms of processing. *Journal of Cognitive Neuroscience, 18*, 1607–1615.

Boulenger, V., Silber, B.Y., Roy, A.C., Paulignan, Y., Jeannerod, M., & Nazir, T.A. (2008). Subliminal display of action words interferes with motor planning: A combined EEG and kinematic study. *Journal of Physiology, Paris, 102*, 130–136.

Boutonnet, B., Dering, B., Viñas-Guasch, N., & Thierry, G. (2013). Seeing objects through the language glass. *Journal of Cognitive Neuroscience, 25*, 1702–1710.

Bouvier, S.E., & Engel, S.A. (2006). Behavioral deficits and cortical damage loci in cerebral achromatopsia. *Cerebral Cortex, 16*, 183–191.

Bowerman, M. (2011). Linguistic typology and first language acquisition. In J.J. Song (Ed.), *The Oxford handbook of linguistic typology* (pp. 591–617). Oxford, UK: Oxford University Press.

Bowerman, M., & Brown, P. (Eds.) (2008). *Crosslinguistic perspectives on argument structure*. New York: Lawrence Erlbaum.

Boyd, B. (2009). *On the origin of stories: Evolution, cognition, and fiction*. Cambridge, MA: Harvard University Press.Bozeat, S., Lambon Ralph, M.A., Graham, K.S., Patterson, K., Wilkin, H., Rowland, J., Rogers, T.T., & Hodges, J.R. (2003). A duck with four legs: Investigating the structure of conceptual knowledge using picture drawing in semantic dementia. *Cognitive Neuropsychology, 20*, 27–47.

Bozeat, S., Lambon Ralph, M.A., Patterson, K., Garrard, P., & Hodges, J.R. (2000). Non-verbal semantic impairment in semantic dementia. *Neuropsychologia, 38*, 1207–1215.

Bozic, M., & Marslen-Wilson, W.D. (2010). Neurocognitive contexts for morphological complexity: Dissociating inflection and derivation. *Language and Linguistics Compass, 4*, 1063–1073.

Bozic, M., Marslen-Wilson, W.D., Stamatakis, E.A., Davis, M.H., & Tyler, L.K. (2007). Differentiating morphology, form, and meaning: Neural correlates of morphological complexity. *Journal of Cognitive Neuroscience, 19*, 1464–1475.

Bozic, M., Tyler, L.K., Su, L., Wingfield, C., & Marslen-Wilson, W.D. (2013). Neurobiological systems for lexical representation and analysis in English. *Journal of Cognitive Neuroscience, 25*, 1678–1691.

Braak, H., & Braak, E. (1996). The evolution of the neuropathology of Alzheimer's disease. *Acta Neurologica Scandinavica, Supplement, 165*, 3–12.

Bradshaw, J.L. (2001). *Developmental disorders of the frontostriatal system*. Philadelphia, PA: Taylor and Francis.

Brådvik, B., Dravins, C., Holtås, S., Rosén, I., Ryding, E., & Ingvar, D. (1990). Do single right hemisphere infarcts or transient ischaemic attacks result in aprosody? *Acta Neurologica Scandinavica, 81*, 61–70.

Brådvik, B., Dravins, C., Holtås, S., Rosén, I., Ryding, E., & Ingvar, D. (1991). Disturbances of speech prosody following right hemisphere infarcts. *Acta Neurologica Scandinavica, 84*, 114–126.

Braun, A.R., Guillemin, A., Hosey, L., & Varga, M. (2001). The neural organization of discourse: An $H_2^{15}O$-PET study of narrative production in English and American Sign Language. *Brain, 124*, 2028–2044.

Breedin, S.D., & Martin, R.C. (1996). Patterns of verb impairment in aphasia: An analysis of four cases. *Cognitive Neuropsychology, 13*, 51–91.

Breedin, S.D., & Saffran, E.M. (1999). Sentence processing in the face of semantic loss: A case study. *Journal of Experimental Psychology: General, 128*, 547–562.

Breedin, S.D., Saffran, E.M., & Coslett, H.B. (1994). Reversal of the concreteness effect in a patient with semantic dementia. *Cognitive Neuropsychology, 11*, 617–660.

Breese, E.L., & Hillis, A.E. (2004). Auditory comprehension: Is multiple choice really good enough? *Brain and Language, 89*, 3–8.

Breitenstein, C., Daum, I., & Ackermann, H. (1998). Emotional processing following cortical and subcortical brain damage: Contribution of the fronto-striatal circuitry. *Behavioral Neurology, 11*, 29–42.

Breitenstein, C., Lancker, D.V., Daum, I., & Waters, C.H. (2001). Impaired perception of vocal emotions in Parkinson's disease: Influence of speech time processing and executive functioning. *Brain and Cognition, 45*, 277–314.

Breiter, H.C., Gollub, R.L., Weisskroff, R.M., Kennedy, D.N., Makris, N., Berke, J.D., Goodman, J.M., Kantor, H.L., Gastfriend, D.R., Riorden, J.P., Matthew, R.T., Rosen, B.R., & Hyman, S.E. (1997). Acute effects of cocaine on human brain activity and emotion. *Neuron, 19*, 591–611.

Brennan, J., Nir, Y., Hasson, U., Malach, R., Heeger, D.J., & Pylkkänen, L. (2012). Syntactic structure building in the anterior temporal lobel during natural story listening. *Brain and Language, 120*, 163–173.

Brennan, J., & Pylkkänen, L. (2012). The time-course and spatial distribution of brain activity associated with sentence processing. *NeuroImage, 60*, 1139–1148.

Brentari, D. (1998). *A prosodic model of sign language phonology*. Cambridge, MA: MIT Press.

Brentari, D. (Ed.) (2010). *Sign languages*. Cambridge, UK: Cambridge University Press.

Brentari, D., & Eccarius, P. (2010). Handshape contrasts in sign language phonology. In D. Brentari (Ed.), *Sign languages* (pp. 284–311). Cambridge, UK: Cambridge University Press.

Bressler, S.L., & Menon, V. (2010). Large-scale brain networks in cognition: Emerging methods and principles. *Trends in Cognitive Sciences, 14*, 277–290.

Brickner, R.M. (1940). A human cortical area producing repetitive phenomena when stimulated. *Journal of Neurophysiology, 3*, 128–130.

Bright, P., Moss, H.E., Longe, O., Stamatakis, E.A., & Tyler, L.K. (2007). Conceptual structure modulates anteromedial temporal involvement in processing verbally presented object properties. *Cerebral Cortex, 17*, 1066–1073.

Bright, P., Moss, H.E., Stamatakis, E.A., & Tyler, L.K. (2008). Longitudinal studies of semantic dementia: The relationship between structural and functional changes over time. *Neuropsychologia, 46*, 2177–2188.

Britton, B., Blumstein, S.E., Myers, E.B., & Grindrod, C. (2009). The role of spectral and durational properties on hemispheric asymmetries in vowel perception. *Neuropsychologia, 47*, 1096–1106.

Broadbent, W.H. (1878). A case of peculiar affection of speech with commentary. *Brain, 1*, 484–503.

Broks, P. (2003). *Into the silent land: Travels in neuropsychology*. New York: Grove Press.

Brown, A.S. (2008). Putting thoughts into action. *Scientific American Mind, 19*(5), 50–57.

Brown, K., & Miller, J. (Eds.) (1996). *Concise encyclopedia of syntactic theories*. New York: Elsevier.

Brown, P. (2001). Learning to talk about motion UP and DOWN in Tzeltal: Is there a language-specific bias for verb learning? In M. Bowerman & S.C. Levinson (Eds.), *Language acquisition and conceptual development* (pp. 512–543). Cambridge, UK: Cambridge University Press.

Brown, P. (2006). A sketch of the grammar of space in Tzeltal. In S.C. Levinson & D. Wilkins (Eds.), *Grammars of space: Explorations in cognitive diversity* (pp. 230–272). Cambridge, UK: Cambridge University Press.

Brown, S., Ingham, R.J., Ingham, J.C., Laird, A.R., & Fox, P.T. (2005). Stuttered and fluent speech production: An ALE meta-analysis of functional neuroimaging studies. *Human Brain Mapping, 25*, 105–117.

Brown, S., Laird, A.R., Pfordresher, P.Q., Thelen, S.M., Turkeltaub, P., & Liotti, M. (2009). The somatotopy of speech: Phonation and articulation in the human motor cortex. *Brain and Cognition, 70*, 31–41.

Brück, C., Kreifelts, B., Kaza, E., Lotze, M., & Wildgruber, D. (2011). Impact of personality on the cerebral processing of emotional prosody. *NeuroImage, 58*, 259–268.

Bruner, J. (1991). The narrative construction of reality. *Critical Inquiry, 18*, 1–21.

Bryan, K. (1989). Language prosody and the right hemisphere. *Aphasiology, 3*, 285–299.

Bub, D., & Kertesz, A. (1982a). Deep agraphia. *Brain and Language, 17*, 146–165.

Bub, D., & Kertesz, A. (1982b). Evidence of lexicographic processing in a patient with preserved written over oral single word naming. *Brain, 105*, 697–717.

Buccino, G., Binkofski, F., Fink, G.R., Fadiga, L., Fogassi, L., Gallese, V., Seitz, R.J., Zilles, K., Rizzolatti, G., & Freund, H.J. (2001). Action observation activates premotor and parietal areas in a somatotopic manner: An fMRI study. *European Journal of Neuroscience, 13*, 400–404.

Buchanan, T.W., Lutz, K., Mirzazade, S., Specht, K., Shah, N.J., Zilles, K., & Jancke, L. (2000). Recognition of emotional prosody and verbal components of spoken language: An fMRI study. *Cognitive Brain Research, 9*, 227–238.

Buchman, A.S., Garron, D.C., Trost-Cardamone, J.E., Wichter, M.D., & Schwartz, M. (1986). Word deafness: One hundred years later. *Journal of Neurology, Neurosurgery, and Psychiatry, 49*, 489–499.

Buchsbaum, B. (2013). The role of consciousness in the phonological loop: Hidden in plain sight. *Frontiers in Psychology, 4*, Article 496.

Buchsbaum, B., Baldo, J., Okada, K., Berman, K.F., Dronkers, N., D'Esposito, M., & Hickok, G. (2011). Conduction aphasia, sensory-motor integration, and phonological short-term memory—An aggregate analysis of lesion and fMRI data. *Brain and Language, 119*, 119–128.

Buchsbaum, B., & D'Esposito, M. (2008). The search for the phonological store: From loop to convolution. *Journal of Cognitive Neuroscience, 20*, 762–778.

Buchsbaum, B., Greer, S., Chang, W.L., & Berman, K.F. (2005a). Meta-analysis of neuroimaging studies of the Wisconsin Card Sorting Task and component processes. *Human Brain Mapping, 25*, 35–45.

Buchsbaum, B., Hickok, G., & Humphries, C. (2001). Role of left posterior superior temporal gyrus in phonological processing for speech perception and production. *Cognitive Science, 25*, 663–678.

Buchsbaum, B., Olsen, R.K., Koch, P., & Berman, K.F. (2005b). Human dorsal and ventral auditory streams subserve rehearsal-based and echoic processes during verbal working memory. *Neuron, 48*, 687–697.

Buchsbaum, B., Olsen, R.K., Koch, P., Kohn, P., Kippenhan, J.S., & Berman, K.F. (2005c). Reading, hearing, and the planum temporale. *NeuroImage, 24*, 444–454.

Buckner, R.L., Andrews-Hanna, J.R., & Schacter, D.L. (2008). The brain's default network: Anatomy, function, and relevance to disease. *Annals of the New York Academy of Sciences, 1124*, 1–38.

Buckner, R.L., & Carroll, D.C. (2007). Self-projection and the brain. *Trends in Cognitive Sciences, 11*, 49–57.

Buckner, R.L., Sepulcre, J., Talukdar, T., Krienen, F.M., Liu, H., Hedden, T., Andrews-Hanna, J.R., Sperling, R.A., & Johnson, K.A. (2009). Cortical hubs revealed by intrinsic functional connectivity: Mapping, assessment of stability, and relation to Alzheimer's disease. *Journal of Neuroscience, 29*, 1860–1873.

Bullmore, E., & Sporns, O. (2012). The economy of brain network organization. *Nature Reviews Neuroscience, 13*, 336–349.

Butterworth, B., Campbell, R., & Howard, D. (1986). The uses of short-term memory: A case study. *Quarterly Journal of Experimental Psychology, 38A*, 705–737.

Butti, C., Santos, M., Uppal, N., & Hof, P.R. (2013). Von Economo neurons: Clinical and evolutionary perspectives. *Cortex, 49*, 312–326.

Buxbaum, L.J., & Saffran, E.M. (2002). Knowledge of object manipulation and object function: Dissociations in apraxic and nonapraxic subjects. *Brain and Language, 82*, 179–199.

Buxhoeveden, D.P., & Casanova, M.F. (2002). The minicolumn hypothesis in neuroscience. *Brain, 125*, 935–951.

Bybee, J.L., & Slobin, D.I. (1982). Rules and schemas in the development and use of the English past tense. *Language, 58*, 265–289.

Caccappolo-van Vliet, E., Miozzo, M., & Stern, Y. (2004a). Phonological dyslexia: A test case for reading models. *Psychological Science, 15*, 583–590.

Caccappolo-van Vliet, E., Miozzo, M., & Stern, Y. (2004b). Phonological dyslexia without phonological impairment? *Cognitive Neuropsychology, 21*, 820–839.

Cai, S., Ghosh, S.S., Guenther, F.H., & Perkell, J.S. (2011). Focal manipulations of formant trajectories reveal a role of auditory feedback in the online control of both within-syllable and between-syllable speech timing. *Journal of Neuroscience, 31*, 16483–16490.

Calvo, M.G., & Beltrán, D. (2013). Recognition advantage of happy faces: Tracing the neurocognitive processes. *Neuropsychologia, 51*, 2051–2061.

Campanella, F., D'Agostini, S., Skrap, M., & Shallice, T. (2010). Naming manipulable objects: Anatomy of a category-specific effect in left temporal tumours. *Neuropsychologia, 48*, 1583–1597.

Campbell, R., MacSweeney, M., Surguladze, S., Calvert, G., McGuire, P., Suckling, J., Brammer, M.J., & David, A. (2001). Cortical substrates for the perception of face actions: An fMRI study of the specificity of activation for seen speech and for meaningless lower-face acts (gurning). *Cognitive Brain Research, 12*, 233–243.

Campbell, R., MacSweeney, M., & Waters, D. (2007). Sign language and the brain: A review. *Journal of Deaf Studies and Deaf Education, 13*, 3–20.

Cancelliere, A.E., & Kertesz, A. (1990). Lesion localization in acquired deficits of emotional expression and comprehension. *Brain and Cognition, 13*, 133–147.

Caño, A., Hernández, M., Ivanova, I., Juncadella, M., Gascón-Bayarri, J., Reñe, R., & Costa, A. (2010). When one can say SALTO as noun but not as verb: A grammatical category-specific, modality-specific deficit. *Brain and Language, 114*, 26–42.

Canolty, R.T., Soltani, M., Dalal, S.S., Edwards, E., Dronkers, N.F., Nagarajan, S.S., Kirsch, H.E., Barbaro, N.M., & Knight, R.T. (2007). Spatiotemporal dynamics of word processing in the human brain. *Frontiers in Neuroscience, 1*, 185–196.

Cantlon, JF., Platt, M.L., & Brannon, E.M. (2009). Beyond the number domain. *Trends in Cognitive Sciences, 13*, 83–91.

Capek, C.M., Bavelier, D., Corina, D., Newman, A.J., Jezzard, P., & Neville, H.J. (2004). The cortical organization of audio-visual sentence comprehension: An fMRI study at 4 Tesla. *Cognitive Brain Research, 20*, 111–119.

Capek, C.M., Waters, D., Woll, B., MacSweeney, M., Brammer, M.J., McGuire, P.K., David, A.S., & Campbell, R. (2008). Hand and mouth: Cortical correlates of lexical processing in British Sign Language and speechreading English. *Journal of Cognitive Neuroscience, 20*, 1220–1234.

Capek, C.M., Woll, B., MacSweeney, M., Waters, D., McGuire, P.K., David, A.S., Brammer, M.J., & Campbell, R. (2010). Superior temporal activation as a function of linguistic knowledge: Insights from deaf native signers who speechread. *Brain and Language, 112*, 129–134.

Capitani, E., & Laiacona, M. (2011). Facts and hypotheses relevant for contrasting animal and plant life semantics: A comment on Gainotti (2010). *Cortex, 47*, 259–264.

Capitani, E., Laiacona, M., Mahon, B., & Caramazza, A. (2003). What are the facts of semantic category-specific deficits? A critical review of the clinical literature. *Cognitive Neuropsychology, 20*, 213–261.

Capitani, E., Laiacona, M., Pagani, R., Capasso, R., Zampetti, P., & Miceli, G. (2009). Posterior cerebral artery infarcts and semantic category dissociations: A study of 28 patients. *Brain, 132*, 965–981.

Caplan, D. (1987). *Neurolinguistics and linguistic aphasiology: An introduction*. Cambridge, UK: Cambridge University Press.

Caplan, D. (2006). fMRI studies of syntactic processing. *Current Medical Imaging Reviews, 2*, 443–451.

Caplan, D. (2009). The neural basis of syntactic processing. In M.S. Gazzaniga (Ed.), *The cognitive neurosciences*, 4th edition (pp. 805–817). Cambridge, MA: MIT Press.

Caplan, D., Chen, E., & Waters, G. (2008a). Task-dependent and task-independent neurovascular responses to syntactic processing. *Cortex, 44*, 257–275.

Caplan, D., DeDe, G., & Brownell, H. (2006a). Effects of syntactic features on sentence-picture matching in Broca's aphasics: A reply to Drai and Grodzinsky. *Brain and Language, 96*, 129–134.

Caplan, D., DeDe, G., & Michaud, J. (2006b). Task-independent and task-specific syntactic deficits in aphasic comprehension. *Aphasiology, 20*, 893–920.

Caplan, D., Gow, D., & Makris, N. (1995). Analysis of lesions by MRI in stroke patients with acoustic-phonetic processing deficits. *Neurology, 45*, 293–298.

Caplan, D., & Hanna, J.E. (1998). Sentence production by aphasic patients in a constrained task. *Brain and Language, 63*, 184–218.

Caplan, D., Michaud, J., & Hufford, R. (2013). Short-term memory, working memory, and syntactic comprehension in aphasia. *Cognitive Neuropsychology, 30*, 77–109.

Caplan, D., Stanczak, L., & Waters, G. (2008b). Syntactic and thematic constraint effects on blood oxygenation level dependent signal correlates of comprehension of relative clauses. *Journal of Cognitive Neuroscience, 20*, 643–656.

Caplan, D., & Waters, G. (1999). Verbal short-term memory and sentence comprehension. *Behavioral and Brain Sciences, 22*, 77–126.

Caplan, D., Waters, G., DeDe, G., Michaud, J., & Reddy, A. (2007a). A study of syntactic processing in aphasia I: Behavioral (psycholinguistic) aspects. *Brain and Language, 101*, 103–150.

Caplan, D., Waters, G., Kennedy, D., Alpert, N., Makris, N., DeDe, G., Michaud, J., & Reddy, A. (2007b). A study of syntactic processing in aphasia II: Neurological aspects. *Brain and Language, 101*, 151–177.

Cappa, S.F., Perani, D., Messa, C., Miozzo, A., & Fazio, F. (2006). Varieties of progressive non-fluent aphasia. *Annals of the New York Academy of Sciences, 777*, 243–248.

Cappelletti, M., Butterworth, B., & Kopelman, M. (2001). Spared numerical abilities in a case of semantic dementia. *Neuropsychologia, 39*, 1224–1239.

Cappelletti, M., Fregni, F., Shapiro, K., Pascual-Leone, A., & Caramazza, A. (2008). Processing nouns and verbs in the left frontal cortex: A transcranial magnetic stimulation study. *Journal of Cognitive Neuroscience, 20*, 707–720.

Caramazza, A. (1984). The logic of neuropsychological research and the problem of patient classification in aphasia. *Brain and Language, 21*, 9–20.

Caramazza, A. (1986). On drawing inferences about the structure of normal cognitive systems from the analysis of patterns of impaired performance: The case for single-patient studies. *Brain and Cognition, 5*, 41–66.

Caramazza, A. (1992). Is cognitive neuropsychology possible? *Journal of Cognitive Neuroscience, 4*, 80–95.

Caramazza, A. (1997). How many levels of processing are there in lexical access? *Cognitive Neuropsychology, 14*, 177–208.

Caramazza, A., & Badecker, W. (1989). Patient classification in neuropsychological research. *Brain and Cognition, 10*, 256–295.

Caramazza, A., & Badecker, W. (1991). Clinical syndromes are not God's gift to cognitive neuropsychology: A reply to a rebuttal to an answer to a response to the case against syndrome-based research. *Brain & Cognition, 16*, 211–227.

Caramazza, A., & Berndt, R.S. (1985). A multicomponent deficit view of agrammatic Broca's aphasia. In M.L. Kean (Ed.), *Agrammatism* (pp. 27–64). Orlando, FL: Academic Press.

Caramazza, A., Berndt, R.S., & Basili, A.G. (1983). The selective impairment of phonological processing: A case study. *Brain and Language, 18*, 128–174.

Caramazza, A., Capasso, R., Capitani, E., & Miceli, G. (2005). Patterns of comprehension performance in agrammatic Broca's aphasia: A test of the Trace Deletion Hypothesis. *Brain and Language, 94,* 43–53.

Caramazza, A., Capitani, E.,, Rey, A., & Berndt, R.S. (2001). Agrammatic Broca's aphasia is not associated with a single pattern of comprehension performance. *Brain and Language, 76,* 158–184.

Caramazza, A., & Coltheart, M. (2006). *Cognitive Neuropsychology* twenty years on. *Cognitive Neuropsychology, 23,* 3–12.

Caramazza, A., & Hillis, A.E. (1989). The disruption of sentence production: Some dissociations. *Brain and Language, 36,* 635–650.

Caramazza, A., & Hillis, A.E. (1990). Where do semantic errors come from? *Cortex, 26,* 95–122.

Caramazza, A., & Hillis, A.E. (1991). Lexical organization of nouns and verbs in the brain. *Nature, 349,* 788–790.

Caramazza, A., & Mahon, B.Z. (2003). The organization of conceptual knowledge: The evidence from category-specific semantic deficits. *Trends in Cognitive Sciences, 7,* 354–361.

Caramazza, A., & Mahon, B.Z. (2006). The organization of conceptual knowledge in the brain: The future's past and some future directions. *Cognitive Neuropsychology, 23,* 13–38.

Caramazza, A., & McCloskey, M. (1988). The case for single-patient studies. *Cognitive Neuropsychology, 5,* 517–527.

Caramazza, A., & Miceli, G. (1990). The structure of graphemic representations. *Cognition, 37,* 243–297.

Caramazza, A., & Miceli, G. (1991). Selective impairment of thematic role assignment in sentence processing. *Brain and Language, 41,* 402–436.

Caramazza, A., Miceli, G., Villa, G., & Romani, C. (1987). The role of the graphemic buffer in spelling: Evidence from a case of acquired dysgraphia. *Cognition, 26,* 59–85.

Caramazza, A., & Miozzo, M. (1998). More is not always better. A response to Roelofs, Meyer, and Levelt. *Cognition, 69,* 231–241.

Caramazza, A., & Shelton, J.R. (1998). Domain-specific knowledge systems in the brain: The animate-inanimate distinction. *Journal of Cognitive Neuroscience, 10,* 1–34.

Caramazza, A., & Zurif, E.B. (1976). Dissociation of algorithmic and heuristic processes in language comprehension. *Brain and Language, 3,* 572–582.

Cardin, V., Orfanidou, E., Rönnberg, J., Capek, C.M., Rudner, M., & Woll, B. (2013). Dissociating cognitive and sensory neural plasticity in human superior temporal cortex. *Nature Communications, 4,* 1473.

Carota, F., Moseley, R., & Pulvermüller, F. (2012). Body-part-specific representations of semantic noun categories. *Journal of Cognitive Neuroscience, 24,* 1492–1509.

Carroll, J.B., & White, M.N. (1973). Word frequency and age-of-acquisition as determiners of picture naming latency. *Quarterly Journal of Experimental Psychology, 25,* 85–95.

Casasanto, D. (2009). Embodiment of abstract concepts: Good and bad in right- and left-handers. *Journal of Experimental Psychology: General, 138,* 351–367.

Casasanto, D. (2011). Different bodies, different minds: The body-specificity of language and thought. *Current Directions in Psychological Science, 20,* 378–383.

Casasanto, D., & Chrysikou, E.G. (2011). When left is "right": Motor fluency shapes abstract concepts. *Psychological Science, 22,* 419–422.

Casasanto, D., & Henetz, T. (2012). Handedness shapes children's abstract concepts. *Cognitive Science, 36,* 359–372.

Casasanto, D., & Jasmin, K. (2010). Good and bad in the hands of politicians. *PloS ONE, 5,* e11805.

Caspers, S., Geyer, S., Schleicher, A., Mohlberg, H., Amunts, K., & Zilles, K. (2006). The human inferior parietal cortex: Cytoarchitectonic parcellation and interindividual variability. *NeuroImage, 33,* 430–448.

Castner, J.E., Chenery, H.J., Copland, D.A., Coyne, T.J., Sinclair, F., & Silburn, P.A. (2007). Semantic and affective priming as a function of stimulation of the subthalamic nucleus in Parkinson's disease. *Brain, 130,* 1395–1407.

Catani, M., Dell'Acqua, F., Bizzi, A., Forkel, S., Williams, S., Simmons, A., Murphy, D., & de Schotten, M.T. (2012). Beyond cortical localisation in clinico-anatomical correlation. *Cortex, 48,* 1262–1287.

Catani, M., & Mesulam, M.M. (2008). The arcuate fasciculus and the disconnection theme in language and aphasia: History and current state. *Cortex, 44,* 953–961.

Catani, M., Mesulam, M.M., Jakobsen, E., Malik, F., Martersteck, A., Wieneke, C., Thompson, C.K., de Schotten, M.T., Dell'Acqua, F., Weintraub, S., & Rogalski, E. (2013). A novel frontal pathway underlies verbal fluency in primary progressive aphasia. *Brain, 136,* 2619–2628.

Caviness, V., Makris, N., Montinaro, E., Sahin, N., Bates, J., Schwamm, L., Caplan, D., & Kennedy, D.N. (2002). Anatomy of stroke, part I: An MRI-based topographic and volumetric system of analysis. *Stroke, 33,* 2549–2556.

Chainay, H., Alario, F.X., Kainik, A., Duffau, H., Capelle, L., Volle, E., Cohen, L., & Lehéricy, S. (2009). Motor and language deficits before and after surgical resection of mesial frontal tumour. *Clinical Neurology and Neurosurgery, 111,* 39–46.

Chan, A.M., Baker, J.M., Eskandar, E., Schomar, D., Ulbert, I., Marinkovic, K., Cash, S.S., & Halgren, E. (2011). First-pass selectivity for semantic categories in human anteroventral temporal lobe. *Journal of Neuroscience, 31,* 18119–18129.

Chan, A.M., Dykstra, A.R., Jayaram, V., Leonard, M.K., Travis, K.E., Gygi, B., Baker, J.M., Eskandar, E., Hochberg, L.R., Halgren, E., & Cash, S.S. (in press). Speech-specific tuning of neurons in human superior temporal gyrus. *Cerebral Cortex.*

Chandrasekaran, B., & Kraus, N. (2010). The scalp-recorded brainstem response to speech: Neural origins and plasticity. *Psychophysiology, 47,* 236–246.

Chang, E.F., Rieger, J.W., Johnson, K., Berger, M.S., Barbaro, N.M., & Knight, R.T. (2010). Categorical speech perception in human superior temporal gyrus. *Nature Neuroscience, 13,* 1428–1432.

Chang, F, Dell, G.S., & Bock, K. (2006). Becoming syntactic. *Psychological Review, 113,* 234–272.

Chang, F., & Fitz, H. (in press). Computational models of sentence production: A dual-path approach. In M. Goldrick, V. Ferreira, & M. Miozzo (Eds.), *Oxford handbook of language production.* Oxford, UK: Oxford University Press.

Chang, S.E., Horwitz, B., Ostuni, J., Reynolds, R., & Ludlow, C.L. (2011). Evidence of left inferior frontal-premotor structural and functional connectivity deficits in adults who stutter. *Cerebral Cortex, 21,* 2507–2518.

Chang, S.E., Kenney, M.K., Loucks, T.M.J., Poletto, C.J., & Ludlow, C.L. (2009). Common neural substrates support speech and non-speech vocal tract gestures. *NeuroImage, 47,* 314–325.

Changizi, M.A., & Shimojo, S. (2005). Character complexity and redundancy in writing systems over human history. *Proceedings of the Royal Society B: Biological Sciences, 272,* 267–275.

Changizi, M.A., Zhang, Q., Ye, H., & Shimojo, S. (2006). The structures of letters and symbols throughout human history are selected to match those found in objects in natural scenes. *American Naturalist, 167,* E117–139.

Chanraud, S., Zahr, N., Sullivan, E.V., & Pfefferbaum, A. (2010). MR diffusion tensor imaging: A window into white matter integrity of the working brain. *Neuropsychology Review, 20,* 209–225.

Chao, L.L., Haxby, J.V., & Martin, A. (1999). Attribute-based neural substrates in temporal cortex for perceiving and knowing about objects. *Nature Neuroscience, 2,* 913–919.

Chao, L.L., & Martin, A. (2000). Representation of manipulable man-made objects in the dorsal stream. *NeuroImage, 12,* 478–484.

Chao, L.L., Weisberg, J., & Martin, A. (2002). Experience-dependent modulation of category-related cortical activity. *Cerebral Cortex, 12,* 545–551.

Chatterjee, A. (2008). The neural organization of spatial thought and language. *Seminars in Speech and Language, 29,* 226–238.

Chatterjee, A. (2010). Disembodying cognition. *Language and Cognition, 2,* 79–116.

Chatterjee, A., Maher, L., Gonzalez-Rothi, L.J., & Heilman, K.M. (1995a). Asynctactic thematic role assignment: The use of a temporal-spatial strategy. *Brain and Language, 49,* 125–139.

Chatterjee, A., Maher, L., & Heilman, K.M. (1995b). Spatial characteristics of thematic role representation. *Neuropsychologia, 33,* 643–648.

Chatterjee, A., Southwood, M.H., & Basilico, D. (1999). Verbs, events, and spatial representations. *Neuropsychologia, 37,* 395–402.

Chen, C.H., Gutierrez, E.D., Thompson, W., Panizzon, M.S., Jernigan, T.L., Eyler, L.T., Fennema-Notestine, C., Jak, A.J., Neale, M.C., Franz, C.E., Lyons, M.J., Grant, M.D., Fischl, B., Seidman, L.J., Tsuang, M.T., Kremen, W.S., & Dale, A.M. (2012). Hierarchical genetic organization of human cortical surface area. *Science, 335,* 1634–1636.

Chen, E., Widick, P., & Chatterjee, A. (2008). Functional-anatomical organization of predicate metaphor processing. *Brain and Language, 107,* 194–202.

Chen, H., Zhang, T., Guo, L., Li, K., Yu, X., Li, L., Hu, X., Han, J., Hu, X., & Liu, T. (2013). Coevolution of gyral folding and structural connection patterns in primate brains. *Cerebral Cortex, 23,* 1208–1217.

Chevillet, M., Riesenhuber, M., & Rauschecker, J.P. (2011). Functional correlates of the anterolateral processing hierarchy in human auditory cortex. *Journal of Neuroscience, 31,* 9345–9352.

Cho, H., Rapcsak, S.Z., & Beeson, P.M. (2009). Evidence for a common neural substrate of orthographic processing during reading and spelling. Presented at the Neurobiology of Language Conference, Chicago, IL.

Cholin, J., Levelt, W.J.M., & Schiller, N.O. (2006). Effects of syllable frequency in speech production. *Cognition, 99,* 205–235.

Cholin, J., Schiller, N.O., & Levelt, W.J.M. (2004). The preparation of syllables in speech production. *Journal of Memory and Language, 50,* 47–61.

Chomsky, N., & Halle, M. (1968). *The sound pattern of English.* New York: Harper and Row.

Cho-Reyes, S., & Thompson, C.K. (2012). Verb and sentence production and comprehension in aphasia: Northwestern Assessment of Verbs and Sentences (NAVS). *Aphasiology, 26,* 1250–1277.

Chouinard, P.A., & Goodale, M.A. (2010). Category-specific neural processing for naming pictures of animals and naming pictures of tools: An ALE meta-analysis. *Neuropsychologia, 48,* 409–418.

Christen, H.J., Hanefeld, F., Kruse, E., Imhauser, S., Ernst, J.P., & Finkenstaedt, M. (2000). Foix-Chavany-Marie (anterior operculum) syndrome in childhood: A reappraisal of Worster-Drought syndrome. *Developmental Medicine and Child Neurology, 42,* 122–132.

Christoffels, I.K., Formisano, E., & Schiller, N.O. (2007). Neural correlates of verbal feedback processing: An fMRI study employing overt speech. *Human Brain Mapping, 28,* 868–879.

Chumbley, J.I., & Balota, D.A. (1984). A word's meaning affects the decision in lexical decision. *Memory and Cognition, 12,* 590–606.

Cipolotti, L., Butterworth, B., & Denes, G. (1991). A specific deficit for numbers in a case of dense acalculia. *Brain, 114,* 2619–2637.

Cipolotti, L., & Warrington, E.K. (1995). Semantic memory and reading abilities: A case report. *Journal of the International Neuropsychological Society, 1,* 104–110.

Civier, O., Tasko, S.M., & Guenther, F.H. (2010). Overreliance on auditory feedback may lead to sound/syllable repetitions: Simulations of stuttering and fluency-inducing conditions with a neural model of speech production. *Journal of Fluency Disorders, 35,* 246–279.

Clark, A. (1989). *Microcognition: Philosophy, cognitive science, and parallel distributed processing.* Cambridge, MA: MIT Press.

Clark, A. (2013). Whatever next? Predictive brains, situated agents, and the future of cognitive science. *Behavioral and Brain Sciences, 36,* 181–253.

Clark, H.H. (1996). *Using language.* Cambridge, UK: Cambridge University Press.

Clark, H.H., & Clark, E.V. (1977). *Psychology and language: An introduction to psycholinguistics.* New York: Harcourt College Publishers.

Clark, J.M., & Paivio, A. (2004). Extensions of the Paivio, Yuille, and Madigan (1968) norms. *Behavioral Research Methods, Instruments, and Computers, 36,* 371–383.

Clerget, E., Winderickx, A., Fadiga, L., & Olivier, E. (2009). Role of Broca's area in encoding sequential human actions: A virtual lesion study. *NeuroReport, 20,* 1496–1499.

Cloutman, L., Gingis, L., Newhart, M., Davis, C., Heidler-Gary, J., Crinion, J., & Hillis, A.E. (2009). A neural network critical for spelling. *Annals of Neurology, 66,* 249–253.

Coelho, C. (2002). Story narratives of adults with closed head injury and non-brain-injured adults: Influence of socioeconomic status, elicitation task, and executive functioning. *Journal of Speech, Language, and Hearing Research, 45,* 1232–1248.

Coelho, C., Le, K., Mozeiko, J., Krueger, F., & Grafman, J. (2012). Discourse production following injury to the dorsolateral prefrontal cortex. *Neuropsychologia, 50,* 3564–3572.

Cogan, G.B., & Poeppel, D. (2011). A mutual information analysis of neural coding of speech by low frequency MEG phase information. *Journal of Neurophysiology, 106,* 554–563.

Cohen, L., & Dehaene, S. (2004). Specialization within the ventral stream: The case for the visual word form area. *NeuroImage, 22,* 466–476.

Cohen, L., Dehaene, S., Naccache, L., Lehéricy, S., Dehaene-Lambertz, G., Hénaff, M.A., & Michel, F. (2000). The visual word form area: Spatial and temporal characterization of an initial stage of reading in normal subjects and posterior split-brain patients. *Brain, 123,* 291–307.

Cohen, L., Jobert, A., Le Bihan, D., & Dehaene, S. (2004). Distinct unimodal and multimodal regions for word processing in the left temporal cortex. *NeuroImage, 23,* 1256–1270.

Cohen L., Lehéricy, S., Chochon, F., Lemer, C., Rivaud, S., & Dehaene, S. (2002). Language-specific tuning of visual cortex? Functional properties of the Visual Word Form Area. *Brain, 125,* 1054–1069.

Cohen, L., Martinaud, O., Lemer, C., Lehéricy, S., Samson, Y., Obadia, M., Slachevsky, A., & Dehaene, S. (2003). Visual word recognition in the left and right hemispheres: Anatomical and functional correlates of peripheral alexias. *Cerebral Cortex, 13,* 1313–1333.

Cohen Kadosh, R., & Walsh, V. (2009). Numerical representation in the parietal lobes: Abstract or not abstract? *Behavioral and Brain Sciences, 32,* 313–373.

Cohn, N., & Paczynski, M. (2013). Prediction, events, and the advantage of agents: The processing of semantic roles in visual narrative. *Cognitive Psychology, 67,* 73–97.

Cohn, N., Paczynski, M., Jackendoff, R., Holcomb, P.J., & Kuperberg, G.R. (2012). (Pea)nuts and bolts of visual narrative: Structure and meaning in sequential image comprehension. *Cognitive Psychology, 65,* 1–38.

Cole, R.A., & Jakimik, J. (1980). A model of speech perception. In R.A. Cole (Ed.), *Perception and production of fluent speech.* Hillsdale, NJ: Erlbaum.

Collins, D., Neelin, P., Peters, T., & Evans, A. (1994). Automatic 3D intersubject registration of MR volumetric data in standardized Talairach space. *Journal of Computer Assisted Tomography, 18,* 192–205.

Coltheart, M. (1981). The MRC psycholinguistic database. *Quarterly Journal of Experimental Psychology, 33,* 497–505.

Coltheart, M. (2006). Acquired dyslexias and the computational modeling of reading. *Cognitive Neuropsychology, 23,* 96–109.

Coltheart, M., & Funnell, E. (1987). Reading and writing: One lexion or two? In D.A. Allport, D.G. Mackay, W. Prinz, & E. Scheerer (Eds.), *Language perception and production: Shared mechanisms in listening, reading, and writing.* London: Academic Press.

Coltheart, M., Patterson, K., & Marshall, J.C. (Eds.) (1980). *Deep dyslexia.* London: Routledge & Kegan Paul.

Coltheart, M., Rastle, K., Perry, C., Langdon, R., & Ziegler, J. (2001). DRC: A dual route cascaded model of visual word recognition and reading aloud. *Psychological Review, 108,* 204–256.

Coltheart, M., Tree, J.J., & Saunders, S.J. (2010). Computational modeling of reading in semantic dementia: Comment on Woollams, Lambon Ralph, Plaut, and Patterson (2007). *Psychological Review, 117,* 256–272.

Comrie, B. (1989). *Language universals and linguistic typology,* 2nd edition. Chicago: University of Chicago Press.

Comrie, B., & Polinsky, M. (1998). The great Daghestanian case hoax. In A Siewierska & J.J. Song (Eds.), *Case, typology, and grammar* (pp. 95–114). Amsterdam: John Benjamins.

Conant, D., Bouchard, K.E., & Chang, E.F. (in press). Speech map in the human ventral sensory-motor cortex. *Current Opinion in Neurobiology.*

Connell, L., & Lynott, D. (2012). Strength of perceptual experience predicts word processing performance better than concreteness and imageability. *Cognition, 125,* 452–465.

Conway, B.R., & Tsao, D.Y. (2009). Color-tuned neurons are spatially clustered according to color preference within alert macaque posterior inferior temporal cortex. *Proceedings of the National Academy of Sciences, 106,* 18034–18039.

Cook, R., Bird, G., Catmur, C., Press, C., & Heyes, C. (in press). Mirror neurons: From origin to function. *Behavioral and Brain Sciences.*

Cooke, A., Grossman, M., DeVita, C., Gonzalez-Atavales, J., Moore, P., Chen, W., Gee, J., & Detre, J. (2006). Large-scale neural network for sentence processing. *Brain and Language, 96,* 14–36.

Cooper, W., Soares, C., Nicol, J., Michelow, D., & Goloskie, S. (1984). Clausal intonation after unilateral brain damage. *Language and Speech, 27,* 17–24.

Coppens, P., Hungerford, S., Yamaguchi, S., & Yamadori, A. (2002). Crossed aphasia: An analysis of the symptoms, their frequency, and a comparison with left-hemisphere aphasia symptomatology. *Brain and Language, 83,* 425–463.

Corballis, M.C., Badzakova-Trajkov, G., & Häberling, I.S. (2012). Right hand, left brain: Genetic and evolutionary bases of cerebral asymmetries for language and manual action. *WIREs Cognitive Science, 3,* 1–17.

Corbett, G.G. (1991). *Gender.* Cambridge, UK: Cambridge University Press.

Corina, D.P., Gibson, E.K., Martin, R., Poliakov, A., Brinkley, J., & Ojemann, G.A. (2005). Dissociation of action and object naming: Evidence from cortical stimulation mapping. *Human Brain Mapping, 24,* 1–10.

Corina, D.P., Lawyer, L.A., & Cates, D. (2013). Cross-linguistic differences in the neural representation of human language: Evidence from users of signed languages. *Frontiers in Psychology, 3,* Article 587.

Corina, D.P., Loudermilk, B.C., Detwiler, L., Martin, R.F., Brinkley, J.F., & Ojemann, G. (2010). Analysis of naming errors during cortical stimulation mapping: Implications for models of language representation. *Brain and Language, 115*, 101–112.

Corina, D.P., & McBurney, S.L. (2001). The neural representation of language in users of American Sign Language. *Journal of Communication Disorders, 34*, 455–471.

Corina, D.P., McBurney, S.L., Dodrill, C., Hinshaw, K., Brinkley, J., & Ojemann, G. (1999). Functional roles of Broca's area and supramarginal gyrus: Evidence from cortical stimulation mapping in a deaf signer. *NeuroImage, 10*, 570–581.

Corina, D.P., Poizner, H., Bellugi, U., Feinberg, T., Dowd, D., & O'Grady-Batch, L. (1992). Dissociation between linguistic and non-linguistic gestural systems: A case for compositionality. *Brain and Language, 43*, 414–447.

Corina, D.P., San Jose-Robertson, L., Guillemin, A., High, J., & Braun, A.R. (2003). Language lateralization in a bimanual language. *Journal of Cognitive Neuroscience, 15*, 718–730.

Corina, D.P., & Spotswood, N. (2012). Neurolinguistics. In R. Pfau, M. Steinbach, & B. Woll (Eds.), *Sign language: An international handbook* (pp. 739–761). Berlin: Mouton de Gruyter.

Corkin, S. (2013). *Permanent present tense: The unforgettable life of the amnesic patient H.M.* New York: Basic Books.

Corradi-Dell'Acqua, C., Ueno, K., Ogawa, A., Cheng, K., Rumiati, R.I., & Iriki, A. (2008). Effects of shifting perspective of the self: An fMRI study. *NeuroImage, 40*, 1902–1911.

Cosentino, S., Chute, D., Libon, D.J., Moore, P., & Grossman, M. (2006). How does the brain support script comprehension? A study of executive processes and semantic knowledge in dementia. *Neuropsychology, 20*, 307–318.

Coslett, H.B., Brashear, H.R., & Heilman, K.M. (1984). Pure word deafness after bilateral primary auditory cortex infarcts. *Neurology, 34*, 347–352.

Cotelli, M., Borroni, B., Manenti, R., Alberici, A., Calabria, M., Agosti, C., Arévalo, A., Ginex, V., Ortelli, P., Binetti, G., Zanetti, O., Padovani, A., & Cappa, S.F. (2006). Action and object naming in frontotemporal dementia, progressive supranuclear palsy, and corticobasal degeneration. *Neuropsychology, 20*, 558–565.

Coulmas, F. (1989). *The writing systems of the world.* Oxford, UK: Basil Blackwell.

Coulson, S., King, J., & Kutas, M. (1998). Expect the unexpected: Event-related brain responses to morphosyntactic violations. *Language and Cognitive Processes, 13*, 21–58.

Cowie, R.I., & Douglas-Cowie, E. (1983). Speech production in profound post-lingual deafness. In M.E. Lutman & M.P. Haggard (Eds.), *Hearing science and hearing disorders* (pp. 183–231). New York: Academic Press.

Craig, A.D. (2002). How do you feel? Interoception: The sense of the physiological condition of the body. *Nature Reviews: Neuroscience, 3*, 655–666.

Craig, A.D. (2009). How do you feel—now? The anterior insula and human awareness. *Nature Reviews: Neuroscience, 10*, 59–70.

Craig, A.D. (2010). Once an island, now the focus of attention. *Brain Structure and Function, 214*, 395–396.

Crepaldi, D., Berlingeri, M., Paulesu, E., & Luzzatti, C. (2011). A place for nouns and a place for verbs? A critical review of neurocognitive data on grammatical class effects. *Brain and Language, 116*, 33–49.

Creutzfeldt, O., Ojemann, G.A., & Lettich, E. (1989a). Neuronal activity in the human lateral temporal lobe. 1. Responses to speech. *Experimental Brain Research, 77*, 451–475.

Creutzfeldt, O., Ojemann, G.A., & Lettich, E. (1989b). Neuronal activity in the human lateral temporal lobe. 2. Responses to the subject's own voice. *Experimental Brain Research, 77*, 476–489.

Crinion, J.T., Warburton, E.A., Lambon Ralph, M.A., Howard, D., & Wise, R.J.S. (2006). Listening to narrative speech after aphasic stroke: The role of the left anterior temporal lobe. *Cerebral Cortex, 16*, 1116–1125.

Crisp, J., & Lambon Ralph, M.A. (2006). Unlocking the nature of the phonological-deep dyslexia continuum: The keys to reading aloud are in phonology and semantics. *Journal of Cognitive Neuroscience, 18*, 348–362.

Critchley, H., & Seth, A. (2012). Will studies of macaque insula reveal the neural mechanisms of self-awareness? *Neuron, 74*, 423–426.

Crocker, M.W., Knoeferle, P., & Mayberry, M.R. (2010). Situated sentence processing: The coordinated interplay account and a neurobehavioral model. *Brain and Language, 112*, 189–201.

Croft, W. (1991). *Syntactic categories and grammatical relations.* Chicago: University of Chicago Press.

Croft, W. (2012). *Verbs: Aspect and argument structure.* Oxford, UK: Oxford University Press.

Crozier, S., Sirigu, A., Lehéricy, S., van de Moortele, P.F., Pillon, B., Grafman, J., Agid, Y., Dubois, B., & LeBihan, D. (1999). Distinct prefrontal activations in processing sequence at the sentence and script level: An fMRI study. *Neuropsychologia, 37*, 1469–1476.

Crutch, S.J. (2006). Qualitatively different semantic representations for abstract and concrete words: Further evidence from the semantic reading errors of deep dyslexic patients. *Neurocase, 12*, 91–97.

Crutch, S.J., & Warrington, E.K. (2003). The selective impairment of fruit and vegetable knowledge: A multiple channels account of fine-grain category specificity. *Cognitive Neuropsychology, 20*, 355–372.

Crutch, S.J., & Warrington, E.K. (2005). Abstract and concrete concepts have structurally different representational frameworks. *Brain, 128*, 615–627.

Crutch, S.J., & Warrington, E.K. (2007). Semantic priming in deep-phonological dyslexia: Contrasting effects of association and similarity upon abstract and concrete word reading. *Cognitive Neuropsychology, 24*, 583–602.

Crutch, S.J., & Warrington, E.K. (2010). The differential dependence of abstract and concrete words upon associative and similarity-based information: Complementary semantic interference and facilitation effects. *Cognitive Neuropsychology, 27*, 46–71.

Curio, G., Neuloh, G., Numminen, J., Jousmäki, V., & Hari, R. (2000). Speaking modifies voice-evoked activity in the human auditory cortex. *Human Brain Mapping, 9*, 183–191.

Da Costa, S., van der Zwaag, W., Marques, J.P., Frackowiak, R.S.J., Clarke, S., & Saenz, M. (2011). Human primary auditory cortex follows the shape of Heschl's gyrus. *Journal of Neuroscience, 31*, 14067–14075.

Damasio, A.R. (1989a). Concepts in the brain. *Mind and Language, 4*, 24–28.

Damasio, A.R. (1989b). Time-locked multiregional retroactivation: A systems level proposal for the neural substrates of recall and recognition. *Cognition, 33*, 25–62.

Damasio, A.R. (1994). *Descartes' error.* New York: Grosset/Putnam.

Damasio, A.R. (1998). Signs of aphasia. In M.T. Sarno (Ed.), *Acquired aphasia*, 3rd edition (pp. 25–42). San Diego, CA: Academic Press.

Damasio, A.R. (1999). *The feeling of what happens.* New York: Harcourt Brace & Co.

Damasio, A.R. (2010). *Self comes to mind.* New York: Pantheon.

Damasio, A.R., Bellugi, U., Damasio, H., Poizner, H., & Van Gilder, J. (1986). Sign language aphasia during left-hemisphere Amytal injection. *Nature, 322*, 363–365.

Damasio, A.R., & Damasio, H. (1994). Cortical systems for retrieval of concrete knowledge: The convergence zone framework. In C. Koch & J.L. Davis (Eds.), *Large-scale neuronal theories of the brain* (pp. 71–74). Cambridge, MA: MIT Press.

Damasio, A.R., Damasio, H., & Tranel, D. (2013). Persistence of feelings and sentience after bilateral damage of the insula. *Cerebral Cortex, 23*, 833–846.

Damasio, H. (1998). Neuroanatomical correlates of the aphasias. In M.T. Sarno (Ed.), *Acquired aphasia*, 3rd edition (pp. 43–70). San Diego, CA: Academic Press.

Damasio, H. (2005). *Human brain anatomy in computerized images*, 2nd edition. Oxford, UK: Oxford University Press.

Damasio, H., Grabowski, T.J., Tranel, D., Hichwa, R.D., & Damasio, A.R. (1996). A neural basis for lexical retrieval. *Nature, 380*, 499–505.

Damasio, H., Tranel, D., Grabowski, T.J., Adolphs, R., & Damasio, A.R. (2004). Neural systems behind word and concept retrieval. *Cognition, 92*, 179–229.

Daniels, P.T., & Bright, W. (Eds.) (1996). *The world's writing systems.* Oxford, UK: Oxford University Press.

Danley, M., Cooper, W.E., & Shapiro, B. (1983). Fundamental frequency, language processing, and linguistic structure in Wernicke's aphasia. *Brain and Language, 19*, 1–24.

Danley, M., & Shapiro, B. (1982). Speech prosody in Broca's aphasia. *Brain and Language, 16*, 171–190.

Dara, C., Monetta, L., & Pell, M.D. (2008). Vocal emotion processing in Parkinson's disease: Reduced sensitivity to negative emotions. *Brain Research, 1188*, 100–111.

D'Ausilio, A., Bufalari, I., Salmas, P., Busan, P., & Fadiga, L. (2011a). Vocal pitch discrimination in the motor system. *Brain and Language, 118*, 9–14.

D'Ausilio, A., Jarmolowska, J., Busan, P., Bufalari, I., & Craighero, L. (2011b). Tongue corticospinal modulation during attended verbal stimuli: Priming and coarticulation effects. *Neuropsychologia, 49*, 3670–3676.

D'Ausilio, A., Pulvermüller, F., Salmas, P., Bufalari, I., Begliomini, C., & Fadiga, L. (2009). The motor somatotopy of speech perception. *Current Biology, 19*, 381–385.

Davis, C., Heidler-Gary, J., Gottesman, R.F., Crinion, J., Newhart, M., Moghekar, A., Soloman, D., Rigamonti, D., Cloutman, L., & Hillis, A.E. (2010). Action versus animal naming fluency in subcortical dementia, frontal dementias, and Alzheimer's disease. *Neurocase, 16*, 259–266.

Davis, C., Kleinman, J.T., Newhart, M., Gingis, L., Pawlak, M., & Hillis, A.E. (2008). Speech and language functions that require a functioning Broca's area. *Brain and Language, 105*, 50–58.

Davis, G.A., & Coelho, C.A. (2004). Referential cohesion and logical coherence of narration after closed head injury. *Brain and Language, 89*, 508–523.

Davis, M.H., & Johnsrude, I.S. (2003). Hierarchical processing in spoken language comprehension. *Journal of Neuroscience, 23*, 3423–3431.

De Araujo, I.E., Rolls, E.T., Kringelbach, M.L., McGlone, F., & Phillips, N. (2003). Taste-olfactory convergence, and the representation of the pleasantness of flavour, in the human brain. *European Journal of Neuroscience, 18*, 2059–2068.

De Bleser, R., Schwarz, W., & Burchert, F. (2006). Quantitative neurosyntactic analyses: The final word? *Brain and Language, 96*, 143–146.

Dediu, D., & Ladd, D.R. (2007). Linguistic tone is related to the population frequency of the adaptive haplogroups of two brain size genes, *ASPM* and *Microcephalin*. *Proceedings of the National Academy of Sciences, 104*, 10944–10949.

Deen, B., & McCarthy, G. (2010). Reading about the actions of others: Biological motion imagery and action congruency influence brain activity. *Neuropsychologia, 48*, 1607–1615.

DeFilipe, J. (2009). *Cajal's butterflies of the soul.* Oxford, UK: Oxford University Press.

Dehaene, S. (2009). *Reading in the brain: The science and evolution of a human invention.* New York: Viking.

Dehaene, S., & Cohen, L. (2007). Cultural recycling of cortical maps. *Neuron, 56*, 384–398.

Dehaene, S., & Cohen, L. (2011). The unique role of the visual word form area in reading. *Trends in Cognitive Sciences, 15*, 254–262.

Dehaene, S., Cohen, L., Sigman, M., & Vinckier, F. (2005). The neural code for written words: A proposal. *Trends in Cognitive Sciences, 9*, 335–341.

Dehaene, S., Jobert, A., Naccache, L., Ciuciu, P., Poline, J.B., Le Bihan, D., & Cohen, L. (2004). Letter binding and invariant recognition of masked words: Behavioral and neuroimaging evidence. *Psychological Science, 15*, 307–313.

Dehaene, S., Le Clec'H, G., Poline, J.B., Le Bihan, D., & Cohen, L. (2002). The visual word form area: A prelexical representation of visual words in the fusiform gyrus. *NeuroReport, 13*, 321–325.

Dehaene, S., Naccache, L., Cohen, L., Le Bihan, D., Mangin, J.F., Poline, J.B., & Riviere, D. (2001). Cerebral mechanisms of word masking and unconscious repetition priming. *Nature Neuroscience, 4*, 752–758.

Dehaene, S., Pegado, F., Braga, L.W., Ventura, P., Filho, G.N., Jobert, A., Dehaene-Lambertz, G., Kolinsky, R., Morais, J., & Cohen, L. (2010). How learning to read changes the cortical networks for vision and language. *Science, 330*, 1359–1364.

Dehaene-Lambertz, G., Pallier, C., Serniclaes, W., Sprenger-Charolles, L., Jobert, A., & Dehaene, S. (2005). Neural correlates of switching from auditory to speech perception. *NeuroImage, 24*, 21–33.

Dejerine, J., & Sérieux, P. (1897). Un cas de surdité verbale pure terminée par aphasie sensorielle, suivie d'autopsie. *Comptes Rendues des Séanses de la Société de Biologie (Paris), 49*, 1074–1077.

DeLeon, J., Gesierich, B., Besbris, M., Ogar, J., Henry, M.L., Miller, B.L., Gorno-Tempini, M.L., & Wilson, S.M. (2012). Elicitation of specific syntactic structures in primary progressive aphasia. *Brain and Language, 123*, 183–190.

DeLeon, J. Gottesman, R.F., Kleinman, J.T., Newhart, M., Davis, C., Heidler-Gary, J., Lee, A., & Hillis, A.E. (2007). Neural regions essential for distinct cognitive processes underlying picture naming. *Brain, 130*, 1408–1422.

Dell, G.S. (1995). Speaking and misspeaking. In L.R. Gleitman & M. Liberman (Eds.), *Language: An invitation to cognitive science, Vol. 1* (pp. 183–208). Cambridge, MA: MIT Press.

Dell, G.S., Lawler, E.N., Harris, H.D., & Gordon, J.K. (2004). Models of errors of omission in aphasic naming. *Cognitive Neuropsychology, 21*, 125–145.

Dell, G.S., Schwartz, M.F., Martin, N., Saffran, E.M., & Gagnon, D.A. (1997). Lexical access in aphasic and nonaphasic speakers. *Psychological Review, 104*, 801–838.

Dell, G.S., Schwartz, M.F., Martin, N., Saffran, E.M., & Gagnon, D.A. (2000). The role of computational models in neuropsychological investigations of language: Reply to Ruml and Caramazza (2000). *Psychological Review, 107*, 635–645.

Dell'Aqua, F., & Catani, M. (2012). Structural human brain networks: Hot topics in diffusion tractography. *Current Opinion in Neurology, 25*, 375–383.

DeLong, K.A., Urbach, T.P., & Kutas, M. (2005). Probabilistic word pre-activation during language comprehension inferred from electrical brain activity. *Nature Neuroscience, 8*, 1117–1121.

Denes, G., & Semenza, C. (1975). Auditory modality-specific anomia: Evidence from a case of pure word deafness. *Cortex, 11*, 401–411.

den Ouden, D.B., Fix, S., Parrish, T.B., & Thompson, C.K. (2009). Argument structure effects in action verb naming in static and dynamic conditions. *Journal of Neurolinguistics, 22*, 196–215.

de Quadros, R.M., & Lillo-Martin, D. (2010). Clause structure. In D. Brentari (Ed.), *Sign languages* (pp. 225–251). Cambridge, UK: Cambridge University Press.

de Ruiter, J.P., Mitterer, H., & Enfield, N.J. (2006). Projecting the end of a speaker's turn: A cognitive cornerstone of conversation. *Language, 82*, 515–535.

Desai, R., Binder, J.R., Conant, L.L., & Seidenberg, M.S. (2010). Activation of sensory-motor areas in sentence comprehension. *Cerebral Cortex, 20*, 468–478.

Desai, R., Conant, L.L., Waldron, E., & Binder, J.R. (2006). fMRI of past tense processing: The effects of phonological complexity and task difficulty. *Journal of Cognitive Neuroscience, 18*, 278–297.

Desai, R., Liebenthal, E., Waldron, E., & Binder, J.R. (2008). Left posterior temporal regions are sensitive to auditory categorization. *Journal of Cognitive Neuroscience, 20*, 1174–1188.

de Schotten, M.T., Ffytche, D., Bizzi, A., Dell'Acqua, F., Allin, M., Walshe, M., Murray, R., Williams, S., Murphy, D.G.M., & Catani, M. (2011). Atlasing location, asymmetry, and inter-subject variability of white matter tracts in the human brain with MR diffusion tractography. *NeuroImage, 54*, 49–59.

Desgranges, B., Matuszewski, V., Piolino, P., Chetelat, G., Mezenge, F., Landeau, B., De la Sayette, V., Belliard, S., & Eustache, F. (2007). Anatomical and functional alterations in semantic dementia: A voxel-based MRI and PET study. *Neurobiology of Aging, 28*, 1904–1913.

Desmurget, M., Song, Z., Mottolese, C., & Sirigu, A. (2013). Re-establishing the merits of electrical brain stimulation. *Trends in Cognitive Sciences, 17*, 442–449.

D'Esposito, M., Postle, B.R., Ballard, D., & Lease, J. (1999). Maintenance versus manipulation of information held in working memory: An event-related fMRI study. *Brain and Cognition, 41*, 66–86.

Devlin, J.T., Jamison, H.L., Gonnerman, L.M., & Matthews, P.M. (2006). The role of the posterior fusiform gyrus in reading. *Journal of Cognitive Neuroscience, 18*, 911–922.

Devlin, J.T., Rushworth, M.F.S., & Matthews, P.M. (2005). Category-related activation for written words in the posterior fusiform is task specific. *Neuropsychologia, 43*, 69–74.

Devlin, J.T., Russell, R.P., Davis, M.H., Price, C.J., Wilson, J., Moss, H.E., Matthews, P.M., & Tyler, L.K. (2000). Susceptibility-induced loss of signal: Comparing PET and fMRI on a semantic task. *NeuroImage, 11*, 589–600.

Devlin, J.T., & Watkins, K.E. (2007). Stimulating language: Insights from TMS. *Brain, 130*, 610–622.

Devlin, J.T., & Watkins, K.E. (2008). Investigating language organization with TMS. In E.M. Wassermann, C.M. Epstein, U. Ziemann, V. Walsh, T. Paus, & S.H. Lisanby (Eds.), *The Oxford handbook of transcranial magnetic stimulation* (pp. 479–500). Oxford, UK: Oxford University Press.

DeWitt, I., & Rauschecker, J.P. (2012). Phoneme and word recognition in the auditory ventral stream. *Proceedings of the National Academy of Sciences, 109*, E505–E514.

de Zubicaray, G.I., & McMahon, K.L. (2009). Auditory context effects in picture naming investigated with event-related fMRI. *Cognitive, Affective, and Behavioral Neuroscience, 9*, 260–269.

de Zubicaray, G.I., Rose, S.E., & McMahon, K.L. (2011). The structure and connectivity of semantic memory in the healthy older adult brain. *NeuroImage, 54*, 1488–1494.

Dhanjal, N.S., Handunnetthi, L., Patel, M.C., & Wise, R.J.S. (2008). Perceptual systems controlling speech production. *Journal of Neuroscience, 28*, 9969–9975.

Dick, A.S., & Tremblay, P. (2012). Beyond the arcuate fasciculus: Consensus and controversy in the connectional anatomy of language. *Brain, 135*, 3529–3550.

Dick, F., Saygin, A.P., Galati, G., Pitzalis, S., Bentrovato, S., D'Amico, S., Wilson, S., Bates, E., & Pizzamiglio, L. (2007). What is involved and what is necessary for complex linguistic and non-linguistic auditory processing: evidence from fMRI and lesion data. *Journal of Cognitive Neuroscience, 19*, 799–816.

Diessel, H. (2006). Demonstratives, joint attention, and the emergence of grammar. *Cognitive Linguistics, 17*, 463–489.

Dinner, D.S., & Lüders, H.O. (1995). Human supplementary sensorimotor area: Electrical stimulation and movement-related potential studies. *Advances in Neurology, 66*, 261–269.

Ditman, T., & Kuperberg, G.R. (2010). Building coherence: A framework for exploring the breakdown of links across clause boundaries in schizophrenia. *Journal of Neurolinguistics, 23,* 254–269.

Dixon, R.M.W. (2000). A typology of causatives: Form, syntax, and meaning. In R.M.W. Dixon & A.Y. Aikhenvald (Eds.), *Changing valency* (pp. 30–83). Cambridge, UK: Cambridge University Press.

Dixon, R.M.W. (2010a). *Basic linguistic theory. Vol. 1: Methodology.* Oxford, UK: Oxford University Press.

Dixon, R.M.W. (2010b). *Basic linguistic theory. Vol. 2: Grammatical topics.* Oxford, UK: Oxford University Press.

Dixon, R.M.W. (2012). *Basic linguistic theory. Vol. 3: Further grammatical topics.* Oxford, UK: Oxford University Press.

Domahs, F., Nagels, A., Domahs, U., Whitney, C., Wiese, R., & Kircher, T. (2012). Where the mass counts: Common cortical activation for different kinds of nonsingularity. *Journal of Cognitive Neuroscience, 24,* 915–932.

Domanski, C.W. (2013). Mysterious "Monsieur Leborgne": The mystery of the famous patient in the history of neuropsychology is explained. *Journal of the History of the Neurosciences, 22,* 47–52.

Dominey, P.F., Hoen, M., & Inui, T. (2006). A neurolinguistic model of grammatical construction processing. *Journal of Cognitive Neuroscience, 18,* 2088–2107.

Dominey, P.F., & Inui, T. (2009). Cortico-striatal function in sentence comprehension: Insights from neurophysiology and modeling. *Cortex, 45,* 1012–1018.

Donohue, M., & Wichmann, S. (Eds.) (2008). *The typology of semantic alignment.* Oxford, UK: Oxford University Press.

Dowty, D. (1991). Thematic roles and argument selection. *Language, 67,* 547–619.

Drai, D., & Grodzinsky, Y. (2006a). A new empirical angle on the variability debate: Quantitative neurosyntactic analyses of a large data set from Broca's aphasia. *Brain and Language, 96,* 117–128.

Drai, D., & Grodzinsky, Y. (2006b). The variability debate: More statistics, more linguistics. *Brain and Language, 96,* 157–170.

Dronkers, N. (1996). A new brain region for coordinating speech articulation. *Nature, 384,* 159–161.

Dronkers, N.F., & Baldo, J. (2009). Language: aphasia. In L.R. Squire (Ed.), *Encyclopedia of Neuroscience, Vol. 5* (pp. 343–348). Oxford, UK: Academic Press.

Dronkers, N.F., Plaisant, O., Iba-Zizen, M.T., & Cabanis, E.A. (2007). Paul Broca's historic cases: High-resolution MR imaging of the brains of Leborgne and Lelong. *Brain, 130,* 1432–1441.

Dronkers, N.F., Redfern, B.B., & Ludy, C.A. (1995). Lesion localization in chronic Wernicke's aphasia. *Brain and Language, 51,* 62–65.

Dronkers, N.F., Wilkins, D.P., Van Valin, R.D., Redfern, B.B., & Jaeger, J.J. (2004). Lesion analysis of the brain areas involved in language comprehension. *Cognition, 92,* 145–177.

Druks, J. (2006). Morpho-syntactic and morpho-phonological deficits in the production of regularly and irregularly inflected verbs. *Aphasiology, 20,* 993–1017.

Dryer, M.S. (2005a). Order of subject, object, and verb. In M. Haspelmath, M.S. Dryer, D. Gil, & B. Comrie (Eds.), *The world atlas of language structures* (pp. 30330–30333). Oxford, UK: Oxford University Press.

Dryer, M.S. (2005b). Polar questions. In M. Haspelmath, M.S. Dryer, D. Gil, & B. Comrie (Eds.), *World atlas of language structures* (pp. 470–473). Oxford, UK: Oxford University Press.

Duff, M.C., & Brown-Schmidt, S. (2012). The hippocampus and the flexible use and processing of language. *Frontiers in Human Neuroscience, 6,* Article 69.

Duffau, H. (2008). The anatomo-functional connectivity of language revisited: New insights provided by electrostimulation and tractography. *Neuropsychologia, 46,* 927–934.

Duffau, H., Bauchet, L., Lehéricy, S., & Capelle, L. (2001). Functional compensation of the left dominant insula for language. *NeuroReport, 12,* 2159–2163.

Duffy, J.R. (2005). *Motor speech disorders: Substrates, differential diagnosis, and management,* 2nd edition. St. Louis, MI: Mosby.

Dujardin, K., Blairy, S., Defebvre, L., Duhem, S., Noël, Y., Hess, U., & Destée, A. (2004). Deficits in decoding emotional facial expressions in Parkinson's disease. *Neuropsychologia, 42,* 239–250.

Dwivedi, V., Phillips, N.A., Lague-Beauvais, M., & Baum, S.R. (2006). An electrophysiological study of mood, modal context, and anaphora. *Brain Research, 1117,* 135–153.

Eckers, C., Kröger, B.J., Sass, K., & Heim, S. (2013). Neural representation of the sensorimotor speech-action-repository. *Frontiers in Human Neuroscience, 7,* Article 121.

Eggert, G.H. (1977). *Wernicke's work on aphasia: A sourcebook and review.* The Hague: Mouton.

Eichenbaum, H. (2013). What H.M. taught us. *Journal of Cognitive Neuroscience, 25,* 14–21.

Eickhoff, S.B., Heim, S., Zilles, K., & Amunts, K. (2009). A systems perspective on the effective connectivity of overt speech production. *Philosophical Transactions of the Royal Society, A, Mathematical, Physical & Engineering Sciences, 367,* 2399–2421.

Eimas, P.D., Siqueland, E.R., Jusczyk, P., & Vigorito, J. (1971). Speech perception in infants. *Science, 171,* 303–306.

Eisenstein, M. (2009). Putting neurons on the map. *Nature, 461,* 1149–1152.

Eliades, S.J., & Wang, X. (2008). Neural substrates of vocalization feedback monitoring in primary auditory cortex. *Nature, 453,* 1102–1106.

Embick, D., & Marantz, A. (2005). Cognitive neuroscience and the English past tense: Comments on the paper by Ullman et al. *Brain and Language, 93,* 243–247.

Emmorey, K. (1987). The neurological substrates for prosodic aspects of speech. *Brain and Language, 30,* 305–320.

Emmorey, K. (2002). *Language, cognition, and the brain: Insights from sign language research.* Mahwah, NJ: Lawrence Erlbaum Associates.

Emmorey, K. (Ed.) (2003). *Perspectives on classifier constructions in sign languages.* Mahwah, NJ: Lawrence Erlbaum Associates.

Emmorey, K., Damasio, H., McCullough, S., Grabowski, T.J., Ponto, L.L.B., Hichwa, R., & Bellugi, U. (2002). Neural systems underlying spatial language in American Sign Language. *NeuroImage, 17,* 812–824.

Emmorey, K., Grabowski, T.J., McCullough, S., Damasio, H., Ponto, L.L.B., Hichwa, R., & Bellugi, U. (2003). Neural systems underlying lexical retrieval for sign language. *Neuropsychologia, 41*, 85–95.

Emmorey, K., Grabowski, T.J., McCullough, S., Damasio, H., Ponto, L.L.B., Hichwa, R., & Bellugi, U. (2004). Motor-iconicity of sign language does not alter the neural systems underlying tool and action naming. *Brain and Language, 89*, 27–37.

Emmorey, K., Grabowski, T.J., McCullough, S., Ponto, L.L.B, Hichwa, R., & Damasio, H. (2005). The neural correlates of spatial language in English and American Sign Language: A PET study with hearing bilinguals. *NeuroImage, 24*, 832–840.

Emmorey, K., McCullough, S., Mehta, S., Ponto, L.L.B., & Grabowski, T.J. (2011a). Sign language and pantomime production differentially engage frontal and parietal cortices. *Language and Cognitive Processes, 26*, 878–901.

Emmorey, K., McCullough, S., Mehta, S., Ponto, L.L.B., & Grabowski, T.J. (2013). The biology of linguistic expression impacts neural correlates for spatial language. *Journal of Cognitive Neuroscience, 25*, 517–533.

Emmorey, K., Mehta, S., & Grabowski, T.J. (2007). The neural correlates of sign versus word production. *NeuroImage, 36*, 202–208.

Emmorey, K., Xu, J., & Braun, A. (2011b). Neural responses to meaningless pseudosigns: Evidence for sign-based phonetic processing in superior temporal cortex. *Brain and Language, 117*, 34–38.

Engel, A.K., Moll, C.K.E., Fried, I., & Ojemann, G.A. (2005). Invasive recordings from the human brain: Clinical insights and beyond. *Nature Reviews Neuroscience, 6*, 35–47.

Epelbaum, S., Pinel, P., Gaillard, R., Delmaire, C., Perrin, M., Dupont, S., Dehaene, S., & Cohen, L. (2008). Pure alexia as a disconnection syndrome: New diffusion imaging evidence for an old concept. *Cortex, 44*, 962–974.

Epley, N., & Waytz, A. (2009). Mind perception. In S.T. Fiske, D.T. Gilbert, & G. Lindzey (Eds.), *The Handbook of Social Psychology*, 5th edition (pp. 498–541). New York: Wiley.

Epstein, R., DeYoe, E.A., Press, D.Z., Rosen, A.C., & Kanwisher, N. (2001). Neuropsychological evidence for a topographical learning mechanism in parahippocampal cortex. *Cognitive Neuropsychology, 18*, 481–508.

Epstein, R., & Kanwisher, N. (1998). A cortical representation of the local environment. *Nature, 392*, 598–601.

Erickson, T.C., & Woolsey, C.N. (1951). Observations on the supplementary motor area of man. *Transactions of the American Neurological Association, 56*, 50–56.

Ethofer, T., Anders, S., Wiethoff, S., Erb, M., Herbert, C., Saur, R., Grodd, W., & Wildgruber, D. (2006). Effects of prosodic emotional intensity on activation of associative auditory cortex. *NeuroReport, 17*, 249–253.

Ethofer, T., Bretscher, J., Gschwind, M., Kreifelts, B., Wildgruber, D., & Vuilleumier, P. (2012). Emotional voice areas: Anatomic location, functional properties, and structural connections revealed by combined fMRI/DTI. *Cerebral Cortex, 22*, 191–200.

Ethofer, T., Bretscher, J., Wiethoff, S., Bisch, J., Schlipf, S., Wildgruber, D., & Kreifelts, B. (2013). Functional responses and structural connections of cortical areas for processing faces and voices in the superior temporal sulcus. *NeuroImage, 76*, 45–56.

Ethofer, T., Kreifelts, B., Wiethoff, S., Wolf, J., Grodd, W., Vuilleumier, P., & Wildgruber, D. (2008). Differential influences of emotion, task, and novelty on brain regions underlying the processing of speech melody. *Journal of Cognitive Neuroscience, 21*, 1255–1268.

Etkin, A., Egner, T., & Kalisch, R. (2011). Emotion processing in anterior cingulate and medial prefrontal cortex. *Trends in Cognitive Sciences, 15*, 85–93.

Evans, N. (1995). *A grammar of Kayardild*. Berlin: Mouton de Gruyter.

Evans, N. (2010). *Dying words: Endangered languages and what they have to tell us*. Chichester, UK: Wiley-Blackwell.

Evans, N. (2011). Semantic typology. In J.J. Song (Ed.), *The Oxford handbook of linguistic typology* (pp. 504–533). Oxford, UK: Oxford University Press.

Evans, N., & Levinson, S.C. (2009). The myth of language universals: Language diversity and its importance for cognitive science. *Behavioral and Brain Sciences, 32*, 429–492.

Evans, S., Kyong, J.S., Rosen, S., Golestani, N., Warren, J.E., McGettigan, C., Mourão-Miranda, J., Wise, R.J.S., & Scott, S.K. (in press). The pathways for intelligible speech: Multivariate and univariate perspectives. *Cerebral Cortex*.

Evrard, H.C., Forro, T., & Logothetis, N.K. (2012). Von Economo neurons in the anterior insula of the macaque monkey. *Neuron, 74*, 482–489.

Fadiga, L., Craighero, L., Buccino, G., & Rizzolatti, G. (2002). Speech listening specifically modulates the excitability of tongue muscles: A TMS study. *European Journal of Neuroscience, 15*, 399–402.

Fadiga, L., Craighero, L., & D'Ausilio, A. (2009). Broca's area in language, action, and music. *Annals of the New York Academy of Sciences, 1169*, 448–458.

Fairhall, S.L., & Caramazza, A. (2013). Brain regions that represent amodal conceptual knowledge. *Journal of Neuroscience, 33*, 10552–10558.

Farag, C., Troiani, V., Bonner, M., Powers, C., Avants, B., Gee, J., & Grossman, M. (2010). Hierarchical organization of scripts: Converging evidence from fMRI and frontotemporal degeneration. *Cerebral Cortex, 20*, 2453–2463.

Farah, M.J., & Rabinowitz, C. (2003). Genetic and environmental influences on the organization of semantic memory in the brain: Is "living thing" an innate category? *Cognitive Neuropsychology, 20*, 401–408.

Farah, M.J., Stowe, R.M., & Levinson, K.L. (1996). Phonological dyslexia: Loss of a reading-specific component of the cognitive architecture? *Cognitive Neuropsychology, 13*, 849–868.

Faroqi-Shah, Y. (2007). Are regular and irregular verbs dissociated in non-fluent aphasia? A meta-analysis. *Brain Research Bulletin, 74*, 1–13.

Fazio, P., Cantagallo, A., Craighero, L., D'Ausilio, A., Roy, A.C., Pozzo, T., Calzolari, F., Granieri, E., & Fadiga, L. (2009). Encoding of human action in Broca's area. *Brain, 132*, 1980–1988.

Fecteau, S., Belin, P., Joanette, Y., & Armony, J.L. (2007). Amygdala responses to nonlinguistic emotional vocalizations. *NeuroImage, 36*, 480–487.

Federmeier, K.D. (2007). Thinking ahead: The role and roots of prediction in language comprehension. *Psychophysiology, 44*, 491–505.

Federmeier, K.D., & Kutas, M. (1999). A rose by any other name: Long-term memory structure and sentence processing. *Journal of Memory and Language, 41*, 469–495.

Federmeier, K.D., & Kutas, M. (2001). Meaning and modality: Influences of context, semantic memory organization, and perceptual predictability on picture processing. *Journal of Experimental Psychology: Learning, Memory, and Cognition, 27*, 202–224.

Fedorenko, E., Behr, M.K., & Kanwisher, N. (2011). Functional specificity for high-level linguistic processing in the human brain. *Proceedings of the National Academy of Sciences, 108*, 16428–16433.

Fedorenko, E., Duncan, J., & Kanwisher, N. (2012a). Language-selective and domain-general regions lie side by side within Broca's area. *Current Biology, 22*, 2059–2062.

Fedorenko, E., Hsieh, P.J., Nieto-Castañón, A., Whitfield-Gabrieli, S., & Kanwisher, N. (2010). A new method for fMRI investigations of language: Defining ROIs functionally in individual subjects. *Journal of Neurophysiology, 104*, 1177–1194.

Fedorenko, E., & Kanwisher, N. (2009). Neuroimaging of language: Why hasn't a clearer picture emerged? *Language and Linguistics Compass, 3*, 839–865.

Fedorenko, E., Nieto-Castañón, A., & Kanwisher, N. (2012b). Syntactic processing in the human brain: What we know, what we don't know, and a suggestion for how to proceed. *Brain and Language, 120*, 187–207.

Feinstein, J.S., Adolphs, R., Damasio, A.R., & Tranel, D. (2010). The human amygdala and the induction and experience of fear. *Current Biology, 21*, 34–38.

Fellbaum, C. (1998). A semantic network of English verbs. In C. Fellbaum (Ed.), *Wordnet* (pp. 69–104). Cambridge, MA: MIT Press.

Fernandino, L., & Iacoboni, M. (2010). Are cortical motor maps based on body parts or coordinated actions? Implications for embodied semantics. *Brain and Language, 112*, 44–53.

Ferreira, F., & Engelhardt, P.E. (2006). Syntax and production. In M.J. Traxler & M.A. Gernsbacher (eds.), *Handbook of psycholinguistics*, 2nd edition (pp. 61–92). San Diego, CA: Academic Press.

Ferreira, V.S. (2010). Language production. *Wiley Interdisciplinary Reviews: Cognitive Science, 1*, 834–844.

Ferreira, V.S., & Slevc, L.R. (2007). Grammatical encoding. In G. Gaskell (Ed.), *Oxford handbook of psycholinguistics* (pp. 453–470). Oxford, UK: Oxford University Press.

Ferstl, E.C. (2007). The functional neuroanatomy of text comprehension: What's the story so far? In F. Schmalhofer & C.A. Perfetti (Eds.), *Higher level language processes in the brain* (pp. 53–102). Mahwah, NJ: Erlbaum.

Ferstl, E.C. (2010). Neuroimaging of text comprehension: Where are we now? *Italian Journal of Linguistics, 22*, 61–88.

Ferstl, E.C., Neumann, J., Bogler, C., & von Cramon, D.Y. (2008). The extended language network: A meta-analysis of neuroimaging studies on text comprehension. *Human Brain Mapping, 29*, 581–593.

Ferstl., E.C., & von Cramon, D.Y. (2002). What does the frontomedian cortex contribute to language processing: Coherence or Theory of Mind? *NeuroImage, 17*, 1599–1612.

Fiebach, C.J., Schlesewsky, M., & Friederici, A.D. (2001). Syntactic working memory and the establishment of filler-gap dependencies: Insights from ERPs and fMRI. *Journal of Psycholinguistic Research, 30*, 321–338.

Fiebach, C.J., Schlesewsky, M., & Friederici, A.D. (2002). Separating syntactic memory costs and syntactic integration costs during parsing: The processing of German WH-questions. *Journal of Memory and Language, 47*, 250–272.

Fiebach, C.J., & Schubotz, R.I. (2006). Dynamic anticipatory processing of hierarchical sequential events: A common role for Broca's area and ventral premotor cortex across domains? *Cortex, 42*, 499–502.

Fiez, J.A., Tranel, D., Seager-Frerichs, D., & Damasio, H. (2006). Specific reading and phonological processing deficits are associated with damage to the left frontal operculum. *Cortex, 42*, 624–643.

Fillimon, F., Nelson, J.D., Hagler, D.J., & Sereno, M.I. (2007). Human cortical representations for reaching: Mirror neurons for execution, observation, and imagery. *NeuroImage, 37*, 1315–1328.

Fillmore, C. (1967). The grammar of hitting and breaking. In R. Jacobs & P. Rosenbaum (Eds.), *Readings in English transformational grammar* (pp. 120–133). Waltham, MA: Ginn.

Finocchiaro, C., Basso, G., Giovenzana, A., & Caramazza, A. (2010). Morphological complexity reveals verb-specific prefontal engagement. *Journal of Neurolinguistics, 23*, 553–563.

Finocchiaro, C., Fierro, B., Brighina, F., Giglia, G., Francolini, M., & Caramazza, A. (2008). When nominal features are marked on verbs: A transcranial magnetic stimulation study. *Brain and Language, 104*, 113–121.

Fischer, M.H. (2008). Finger counting habits modulate spatial-numerical associations. *Cortex, 44*, 386–392.

Fitch, W.T. (2000). The evolution of speech: A comparative review. *Trends in Cognitive Sciences, 4*, 258–267.

Fitz, H. (2009). *Neural syntax*. Amsterdam: ILLC Publication Series.

Fletcher, P.C., Shallice, T., & Dolan, R.J. (2000). "Sculpting the response space"—An account of left prefrontal activation at encoding. *NeuroImage, 12*, 404–417.

Flinker, A., Chang, E.F., Barbaro, N.M., Berger, M.S., & Knight, R.T. (2011). Sub-centimeter language organization in the human temporal lobe. *Brain and Language, 117*, 103–109.

Flinker, A., Chang, E.F., Kirsch, H.E., Barbaro, N.M., Crone, N.E., & Knight, R.T. (2010). Single-trial speech suppression of auditory cortex in humans. *Journal of Neuroscience, 30*, 16643–16650.

Flores d'Arcais, G.B. (1994). Order of strokes writing as a cue for retrieval in reading Chinese characters. *European Journal of Cognitive Psychology, 6*, 337–355.

Fodor, J.A. (1975). *The language of thought*. Cambridge, MA: Harvard University Press.

Fogassi, L., & Ferrari, P.F. (2011). Mirror systems. *Wiley Interdisciplinary Reviews: Cognitive Science, 2*, 22–38.

Foley, W.A. (2007). A typology of information packaging in the clause. In T. Shopen (Ed.), *Language typology and syntactic description, Vol. 1: Clause structure* (pp. 362–446). Cambridge, UK: Cambridge University Press.

Ford, M. (1983). A method for obtaining measures of local parsing complexity throughout sentences. *Journal of Verbal Learning and Verbal Behavior, 22,* 203–2118.

Formisano, E., De Martino, F., Bonte, M., & Goebel, R. (2008). "Who" is saying "what"? Brain-based decoding of human voice and speech. *Science, 322,* 970–973.

Foroni, F., & Semin, G.R. (2009). Language that puts you in touch with your bodily feelings: The multimodal responsiveness of affective expressions. *Psychological Science, 20,* 974–980.

Forster, K.I. (1989). Levels of processing and the structure of the language processor. In W.E. Cooper & C.T. Walker (Eds.), *Sentence processing* (pp. 27–85). Hillsdale, NJ: Erlbaum.

Foxe, J.J., Wylie, G.R., Martinez, A., Schroeder, C.E., Javitt, D.C., Guilfoyle, D., Ritter, W., & Murray, M.M. (2002). Auditory-somatosensory multisensory processing in auditory association cortex: An fMRI study. *Journal of Neurophysiology, 88,* 540–543.

Freedman, M., Alexander, M.P., & Naeser, M.A. (1984). Anatomic basis of transcortical motor aphasia. *Neurology, 34,* 409–417.

Freud, S. 1891/1953). *On aphasia* (E. Stengel, Trans.). New York: International University Press.

Fridriksson, J., Kjartansson, O., Morgan, P.S., Hjaltason, H., Magnusdottir, S., Bonilha, L., & Rorden, C. (2010). Impaired speech repetition and left parietal lobe damage. *Journal of Neuroscience, 30,* 11057–11061.

Fridriksson, K., Holland, A., Coull, B.M., Plante, E., Trouard, T.P., & Beeson, P. (2002). Aphasia severity: Association with cerebral perfusion and diffusion. *Aphasiology, 16,* 859–872.

Friederici, A.D. (1982). Syntactic and semantic processes in aphasic deficits: The availability of prepositions. *Brain and Language, 15,* 249–258.

Friederici, A.D. (2002). Towards a neural basis of auditory sentence processing. *Trends in Cognitive Sciences, 6,* 78–84.

Friederici, A.D. (2009). Pathways to language: Fiber tracts in the human brain. *Trends in Cognitive Sciences, 13,* 175–181.

Friederici, A.D. (2011). The brain basis of language processing: From structure to function. *Physiological Reviews, 91,* 1357–1392.

Friederici, A.D. (2012). The cortical language circuit: From auditory perception to sentence comprehension. *Trends in Cognitive Sciences, 16,* 262–268.

Friederici, A.D., Bahlmann, J., Heim, S., Schubotz, R.I., & Anwander, A. (2006a). The brain differentiates human and non-human grammars: Functional localization and structural connectivity. *Proceedings of the National Academy of Sciences, 103,* 2458–2463.

Friederici, A.D., Fiebach, C.J., Schlesewsky, M., Bornkessel, I., & von Cramon, D.Y. (2006b). Processing linguistic complexity and grammaticality in the left frontal cortex. *Cerebral Cortex, 16,* 1709–1717.

Friederici, A.D., & Gierhan, S.M.E. (2013). The language network. *Current Opinion in Neurobiology, 23,* 250–254.

Friederici, A.D., Hahne, A., & Mecklinger, A. (1996). Temporal structure of syntactic parsing: Early and late event-related brain potential effects. *Journal of Experimental Psychology: Learning, Memory, and Cognition, 22,* 1219–1248.

Friederici, A.D., Kotz, S.A., Scott, S.K., & Obleser, J. (2010). Disentangling syntax and intelligibility in auditory language comprehension. *Human Brain Mapping, 31,* 448–457.

Friederici, A.D., Makuuchi, M., & Bahlmann, J. (2009). The role of the posterior superior temporal cortex in sentence comprehension. *NeuroReport, 20,* 563–568.

Friederici, A.D., Meyer, M., & von Cramon, D.Y. (2000). Auditory language comprehension: An event-related fMRI study of the processing of syntactic and lexical information. *Brain and Language, 74,* 289–300.

Friederici, A.D., Rüschemeyer, S.A., Hahne, A., & Fiebach, C.J. (2003). The role of left inferior frontal and superior temporal cortex in sentence comprehension: Localizing syntactic and semantic processes. *Cerebral Cortex, 13,* 170–177.

Friederici, A.D., Schönle, P., & Garrett, M. (1982). Syntactically and semantically based computations: Processing of prepositions in agrammatism. *Cortex, 19,* 133–166.

Friederici, A.D., von Cramon, D.Y., & Kotz, S.A. (1999). Language related brain potentials in patients with cortical and subcortical left hemisphere lesions. *Brain, 122,* 1033–1047.

Friederici, A.D., & Weissenborn, J. (2007). Mapping sentence form onto meaning: The syntax-semantics interface. *Brain Research, 1146,* 50–58.

Friedman, R.B., Beeman, M., Lott, S.N., Link, K., Grafman, J., & Robinson, S. (1993). Modality-specific phonological alexia. *Cognitive Neuropsychology, 10,* 549–568.

Friedmann, N., & Gvion, A. (2003). Sentence comprehension and working memory limitation in aphasia: A dissociation between semantic-syntactic and phonological reactivation. *Brain and Language, 86,* 23–39.

Friese, U., Rutschmann, R., Raabe, M., & Schmalhofer, F. (2008). Neural indicators of inference processes in text comprehension: An event-related functional magnetic resonance imaging study. *Journal of Cognitive Neuroscience, 20,* 2110–2124.

Frisch, S., Kotz, S.A., von Cramon, D.Y., & Friederici, A.D. (2003). Why the P600 is not just a P300: The role of the basal ganglia. *Clinical Neurophysiology, 114,* 336–340.

Friston, K.J. (1997). Imaging cognitive anatomy. *Trends in Cognitive Sciences, 1,* 21–27.

Friston, K.J. (2011). Functional and effective connectivity: A review. *Brain Connectivity, 1,* 13–36.

Frith, C.D., & Frith, U. (2006). The neural basis of mentalizing. *Neuron, 50,* 531–534.

Frith, U, & Frith, C.D. (2010). The social brain: Allowing humans to boldly go where no other species has been. *Philosophical Transactions of the Royal Society, B, Biological Sciences, 365,* 165–176.

Fromkin, V.A. (1971). The non-anomalous nature of anomalous utterances. *Language, 47,* 27–52.

Fromkin, V.A. (1973). Introduction. In V.A. Fromkin (Ed.), *Speech errors as linguistic evidence* (pp. 11–45). The Hague: Mouton.

Frühholz, S., Ceravolo, L., & Grandjean, D. (2012). Specific brain networks during explicit and implicit decoding of emotional prosody. *Cerebral Cortex, 22,* 1107–1117.

Fu, C.H., Vythelingum, G.N., Brammer, M.J., Williams, S.C.R., Amaro Jr., E., Andrew, C.M., Yáguez, L. van Haren, N.E.M.,

Matsumoto, K., & McGuire, P.K. (2006). An fMRI study of verbal self-monitoring: Neural correlates of auditory verbal feedback. *Cerebral Cortex, 16*, 969–977.

Fu, K.M., Johnston, T.A., Shah, A.S., Arnold, L., Smiley, J., Hackett, T.A., Garraghty, P.E., & Schroeder, C.E. (2003). Auditory cortical neurons respond to somatosensory stimulation. *Journal of Neuroscience, 23*, 7510–7515.

Fulton, J.F. (1928). Observations upon the vascularity of the human occipital lobe during visual activity. *Brain, 51*, 310–320.

Fushimi, T., Komori, K., Ikeda, M., Patterson, K., Ijuin, M., & Tanabe, H. (2003). Surface dyslexia in a Japanese patient with semantic dementia: Evidence for similarity-based orthography-to-phonology translation. *Neuropsychologia, 41*, 1644–1658.

Fuster, J.M. (2008). *The prefrontal cortex*, 4th edition. New York: Academic Press.

Fuster, J.M. (2009). Cortex and memory: Emergence of a new paradigm. *Journal of Cognitive Neuroscience, 21*, 2047–2072.

Gage, N., & Hickok, G. (2005). Multiregional cell assemblies, temporal binding, and the representation of conceptual knowledge in cortex: A modern theory by a "classical" neurologist, Carl Wernicke. *Cortex, 41*, 823–832.

Gaillard, R., Naccache, L., Pinel, P., Clemenceau, S., Volle, E., Hasboun, D., Dupont, S., Maulac, M., Dehaene, S., Adam, C., & Cohen, L. (2006). Direct intracranial, fMRI, and lesion evidence for the causal role of left inferotemporal cortex in reading. *Neuron, 50*, 191–204.

Gainotti, G. (2006). Anatomical, functional, and cognitive determinants of semantic memory disorders. *Neuroscience and Biobehavioral Reviews, 30*, 577–594.

Gainotti, G. (2010). The influence of anatomical locus of lesion and of gender-related familiarity factors in category-specific semantic disorders for animals, fruits and vegetables: A review of single-case studies. *Cortex, 46*, 1072–1087.

Gainotti, G. (2011). Are the representations of animals and plant life subsumed by quite different cortical networks within the temporal lobe? A reply to Capitani & Laiacona (2011). *Cortex, 47*, 265–270.

Gainotti, G., Ciaraffa, F., Silveri, M.C., & Marra, C. (2009). Mental representation of normal subjects about the sources of knowledge in different semantic categories and unique entities. *Neuropsychology, 23*, 803–812.

Gainotti, G., Micelli, G., Silveri, M.C., & Villa, G. (1982). Some anatomo-clinical aspects of phonemic and semantic comprehension disorders in aphasia. *Acta Neurologica Scandinavica, 66*, 652–665.

Gainotti, G., Spinelli, P., Scaricamazza, E., & Marra, C. (2013). The evaluation of sources of knowledge underlying different conceptual categories. *Frontiers in Human Neuroscience, 7*, Article 40.

Galaburda, A., & Sanides, F. (1980). Cytoarchitectonic organization of the human auditory cortex. *Journal of Comparative Neurology, 190*, 597–610.

Galantucci, B., Fowler, C.A., & Turvey, M.T. (2006). The motor theory of speech perception reviewed. *Psychonomic Bulletin and Review, 13*, 361–377.

Galantucci, S., Tartaglia, M.C., Wilson, S.M., Henry, M.L., Filippi, M., Agosta, F., Dronkers, N.F., Henry, R.G.,

Ogar, J.M., Miller, B.L., & Gorno-Tempini, M.L. (2011). White matter damage in primary progressive aphasias: A diffusion tensor tractography study. *Brain, 134*, 3011–3029.

Gallegos, D.R., & Tranel, D. (2005). Positive facial affect facilitates the identification of famous faces. *Brain and Language, 93*, 338–348.

Galton, C.J., Patterson, K., Graham, K., Lambon Ralph, M.A., Williams, G., Antoun, N., Sahakian, B.J., & Hodges, J.R. (2001). Differing patterns of temporal atrophy in Alzheimer's disease and semantic dementia. *Neurology, 57*, 216–225.

Gammon, S.A., Smith, P.J., Daniloff, R.G., & Kim, C.W. (1971). Articulation and stress-juncture production under oral anesthetization and masking. *Journal of Speech and Hearing Research, 14*, 271–282.

Gandour, J.T. (1998). Aphasia in tone languages. In P. Coppens, Y. Lebrun, & A. Basso (Eds.), *Aphasia in atypical populations* (pp. 117–141). Hillsdale, NJ: Lawrence Erlbaum.

Gandour, J.T. (2006). Tone: Neurophonetics. In K. Brown (Ed.), *Encyclopedia of language and linguistics*, 2nd edition, *Vol. 12* (pp. 751–760). Oxford, UK: Oxford University Press.

Gandour, J.T., Akamanon, C., Dechongkit, S., Khunadorn, F., & Boonklam, R. (1994). Sequences of phonemic approximations in a Thai conduction aphasic. *Brain and Language, 46*, 69–95.

Gandour, J.T., & Dardarananda, R. (1983). Identification of tonal contrasts in Thai aphasic patients. *Brain and Language, 18*, 98–114.

Gandour, J.T., & Dechongkit, S. (1992). Aphasia in a Thai speaking patient with a hemorrhagic lesion in the left basal ganglia. *Ramathibodi Medical Journal (Thailand), 15*, 111–116.

Gandour, J.T., Ponglorpisit, S., Potisuk, S., Khunadorn, F., Boongird, P., & Dechongkit, S. (1997). Interaction between tone and intonation in Thai after unilateral brain damage. *Brain and Language, 58*, 174–196.

Gandour, J.T., Potisuk, S., Ponglorpisit, S., Dechongkit, S., Khunadorn, F., & Boongird, P. (1996). Tonal coarticulation in Thai after unilateral brain damage. *Brain and Language, 52*, 505–535.

Gandour, J.T, Tong, Y., Wong, D., Talavage, T., Dzemidzic, M., Xu, Y., Li, X., & Lowe, M. (2004). Hemispheric roles in the perception of speech prosody. *NeuroImage, 23*, 344–357.

Gandour, J.T, Wong, D., Dzemidzic, M., Lowe, M., Tong, Y., & Li, X. (2003). A cross-linguistic fMRI study of perception of intonation and emotion in Chinese. *Human Brain Mapping, 18*, 149–157.

Gandour, J.T, Wong, D., Hsieh, L., Weinzapfel, B., Van Lancker, D., & Hutchins, G. (2000). A cross-linguistic PET study of tone perception. *Journal of Cognitive Neuroscience, 12*, 207–222.

Gandour, J.T, Wong, D., & Hutchins, G. (1998). Pitch processing in the human brain is influenced by language experience. *NeuroReport, 9*, 2115–2119.

Ganis, G., Kutas, M., & Sereno, M.I. (1996). The search for "common sense": An electrophysiological study of the comprehension of words and pictures in reading. *Journal of Cognitive Neuroscience, 8*, 89–106.

Garcea, F.E., Dombovy, M., & Mahon, B.Z. (2013). Preserved tool knowledge in the context of impaired action knowledge: Implications for models of semantic memory. *Frontiers in Human Neuroscience, 7,* Article 120.

Garell, P.C., Bakken, H., Greenlee, J.D.W., Volkov, I., Reale, R.A., Oya, H., Kawasaki, H., Howard, M.A., & Brugge, J.F. (2013). Functional connection between posterior superior temporal gyrus and ventrolateral prefrontal cortex in humans. *Cerebral Cortex, 23,* 2309–2321.

Garnham, A., Shillock, R.C., Brown, G.D.A., Mill, A.I.D., & Cutler, A. (1981). Slips of the tongue in the London-Lund corpus of spontaneous conversation. *Linguistics, 19,* 805–817.

Garrett, M.F. (1975). The analysis of sentence production. In G.H. Bower (Ed.), *The psychology of learning and motivation* (pp. 133–175). San Diego: Academic Press.

Garrett, M.F. (1976). Syntactic processes in sentence production. In R.J. Wales & E.C.T. Walker (Eds.), *New approaches to language mechanisms* (pp. 231–255). Amsterdam: North Holland.

Garrett, M.F. (1980). Levels of processing in sentence production. In B. Butterworth (Ed.), *Language production, Vol. 1, Speech and talk* (pp. 177–220). London: Academic Press.

Garrett, M.F. (1982). Production of speech: Observations from normal and pathological language use. In A.W. Ellis (Ed.), *Normality and pathology in cognitive functions* (pp. 19–76). London: Academic Press.

Garrett, M.F. (1988). Processes in language production. In F.J. Newmeyer (Ed.), *Linguistics: The Cambridge survey: Vol. 3, Psychological and biological aspects* (pp. 69–96). Cambridge, UK: Cambridge University Press.

Garrod, S., & Pickering, M.J. (2004). Why is conversation so easy? *Trends in Cognitive Sciences, 8,* 8–11.

Gaser, C., & Schlaug, G. (2003). Brain structures differ between musicians and non-musicians. *Journal of Neuroscience, 23,* 9240–9245.

Gazzaniga, M.S. (2000). Cerebral specialization and inter-hemispheric communication: Does the corpus collosum enable the human condition? *Brain, 123,* 1293–1326.

Gazzaniga, M.S. (2005). Forty-five years of split-brain research and still going strong. *Nature Reviews Neuroscience, 6,* 653–659.

Gazzaniga, M.S., Ivry, R.B., & Mangun, G. (1998). *Cognitive neuroscience: The biology of the mind,* 1st edition. New York: Norton.

Gazzaniga, M.S., Ivry, R.B., & Mangun, G. (2009). *Cognitive neuroscience: The biology of the mind,* 3rd edition. New York: Norton.

Gee, J.P., & Handford, M. (Eds.) (2012). *The Routledge handbook of discourse analysis.* New York: Routledge.

Geigenberger, A., & Ziegler, W. (2001). Receptive prosodic processing in aphasia. *Aphasiology, 15,* 1169–1188.

Gendron, M., Lindquist, K.A., Barsalou, L.W., & Barrett, L.F. (2012). Emotion words shape emotion percepts. *Emotion, 12,* 314–325.

Gennari, S.P. (2012). Representing motion in language comprehension: Lessons from neuroimaging. *Language and Linguistics Compass, 6,* 67–84.

Gentner, D. (2003). Why we're so smart. In D Gentner & S. Goldin-Meadow (Eds.), *Language in mind* (pp. 195–236). Cambridge, MA: MIT Press.

Gentner, D., & Boroditsky, L. (2001). Individuation, relativity, and early word learning. In M. Bowerman & S.C. Levinson (Eds.), *Language acquisition and conceptual development* (pp. 215–256). Cambridge, UK: Cambridge University Press.

Gentner, D., & Goldin-Meadow, S. (Eds.) (2003). *Language in mind.* Cambridge, MA: MIT Press.

George, M.S., Parekh, P.I., Rosinsky, N., Ketter, T.A., Kimbrell, T.A., Heilman, K.M., Herscovitch, P., & Post, R.M. (1996). Understanding emotional prosody activates right hemisphere regions. *Archives of Neurology, 53,* 665–670.

Gerfo, E.L., Oliveri, M., Torriero, S., Salerno, S., Koch, G., & Caltagirone, C. (2008). The influence of rTMS over prefrontal and motor areas in a morphological task: Grammatical vs. semantic effects. *Neuropsychologia, 46,* 764–770.

Gerhand, S. (2001). Routes to reading: A report of a non-semantic reader with equivalent performance on regular and irregular words. *Neuropsychologia, 39,* 1473–1484.

Gerstmann, J. (1940). Syndrome of finger agnosia, disorientation for right and left, agraphia, and acalculia. *Archives of Neurology and Psychiatry, 44,* 398–407.

Geschwind, N. (1965). Disconnection syndromes in animals and man. *Brain, 88,* 237–294 and 585–644.

Geschwind, N. (1969). Problems in the anatomical understanding of aphasia. In A.L. Benton (Ed.), *Contributions of clinical neuropsychology.* Chicago: University of Chicago Press.

Geschwind, N., Quadfasel, F.A., & Segarra, J.M. (1968). Isolation of the speech area. *Neuropsychologia, 6,* 327–340.

Gesierich, B., Jovicich, J., Riello, M., Adriani, M., Monti, A., Bentari, V., Robinson, S.D., Wilson, S.M., Fairhall, S.L., & Gorno-Tempini, M.L. (2012). Distinct neural substrates for semantic knowledge and naming in the temporoparietal network. *Cerebral Cortex, 22,* 2217–2226.

Ghazanfar, A.A. (2010). The unity of the senses in primate vocal communication. In M.J. Murray & M.Wallace (Eds.), *Frontiers in the neural bases of multisensory processes.* New York: Taylor & Francis.

Ghitza, O. (2011). Linking speech perception and neurophysiology: Speech decoding guided by cascaded oscillators locked to the input rhythm. *Frontiers in Psychology, 2,* Article 130.

Ghosh, S.S., Tourville, J.A., & Guenther, F.H. (2008). A neuroimaging study of premotor lateralization and cerebellar involvement in the production of phonemes and syllables. *Journal of Speech, Language, and Hearing Research, 51,* 1183–202.

Gibbs, R.W. (2006). *Embodiment and cognitive science.* Cambridge, UK: Cambridge University Press.

Gibson, E. (1998). Linguistic complexity: Locality of syntactic dependencies. *Cognition, 68,* 1–76.

Gierhan, S.M.E. (in press). Connections for auditory language in the human brain. *Brain and Language.*

Gilaie-Dotan, S., Kanai, R., Bahrami, B., Rees, G., & Saygin, A.P. (2013). Neuroanatomical correlates of biological motion detection. *Neuropsychologia, 51,* 457–463.

Giraud, A.-L., Kleinschmidt, A., Poeppel, D., Lund, T.E., Frackowiak, R.S.J., & Laufs, H. (2007). Edogenous cortical rhythms determine cerebral specialization for speech production and perception. *Neuron, 56,* 1127–1134.

Gläscher, J., Adolphs, R., Damasio, H., Bechara, A., Rudrauf, D., Calamia, M., Paul, L.K., & Tranel, D. (2012). Lesion mapping of cognitive control and value-based decision making in the prefrontal cortex. *Proceedings of the National Academy of Sciences, 109*, 14681–14686.

Glasser, M.F., & Rilling, J.K. (2008). DTI tractography of the human brain's language pathways. *Cerebral Cortex, 18*, 2471–2482.

Glezer, L.S., Jiang, X., & Riesenhuber, M. (2009). Evidence for highly selective neuronal tuning to whole words in the "Visual Word Form Area." *Neuron, 62*, 199–204.

Glezer, L.S., & Riesenhuber, M. (2013). Individual variability in location impacts orthographic selectivity in the "Visual Word Form Area." *Journal of Neuroscience, 33*, 11221–11226.

Goehl, H., & Kaufman, D.K. (1984). Do the effects of adventitious deafness include disordered speech? *Journal of Speech and Hearing Disorders, 49*, 58–64.

Goense, J., Whittingstall, K., & Logothetis, N.K. (2011). Neural and BOLD responses across the brain. *Wiley Interdisciplinary Reviews: Cognitive Science, 3*, 75–86.

Gold, B.T., Balota, D.A., Jones, S.J., Powell, D.K., Smith, C.D., & Anderson, A.H. (2006). Dissociation of automatic and strategic lexical-semantics: Functional magnetic resonance imaging evidence for differing roles of multiple frontotemporal regions. *Journal of Neuroscience, 26*, 6523–6532.

Goldberg, A.E. (1995). *Constructions: A construction grammar approach to argument structure*. Chicago: University of Chicago Press.

Goldberg, A.E. (2006). *Constructions at work: The nature of generalization in language*. Oxford, UK: Oxford University Press.

Goldberg, R.F., Perfetti, C.A., & Schneider, W. (2006a). Distinct and common cortical activations for multimodal semantic categories. *Cognitive, Affective, and Behavioral Neuroscience, 6*, 214–222.

Goldberg, R.F., Perfetti, C.A., & Schneider, W. (2006b). Perceptual knowledge retrieval activates sensory brain areas. *Journal of Neuroscience, 26*, 4917–4921.

Goldenberg, G. (2009). Apraxia and the parietal lobes. *Neuropsychologia, 47*, 1449–1459.

Goldin-Meadow, S. (2003). *The resilience of language*. New York: Psychology Press.

Goldman, A.I., & Sripada, C.S. (2005). Simulationist models of face-based emotion recognition. *Cognition, 94*, 193–213.

Goldrick, M., & Rapp, B. (2002). A restricted interaction account (RIA) of spoken word production: The best of both worlds. *Aphasiology, 16*, 20–55.

Golestani, N., Price, C.J., & Scott, S.K. (2011). Born with an ear for dialects? Structural plasticity in the expert phonetician. *Journal of Neuroscience, 31*, 4213–4220.

Golfinopoulos, E., Tourville, J.A., Bohland, J.W., Ghosh, S.S., Nieto-Castanon, A., & Guenther, F.H. (2011). fMRI investigation of underlying somatosensory feedback perturbation during speech. *NeuroImage, 55*, 1324–1338.

Golfinopoulos, E., Tourville, J.A., & Guenther, F.H. (2010). The integration of large-scale neural network modeling and functional brain imaging in speech motor control. *NeuroImage, 52*, 862–874.

Gonzalez, C.L.R., & Goodale, M.A. (2009). Hand preference for precision grasping predicts language lateralization. *Neuropsychologia, 47*, 3182–3189.

Gonzalez, J., Barros-Loscertales, A., Pulvermüller, F., Meseguer, V., Sanjuan, A., Belloch, V., & Avila, C. (2006). Reading *cinnamon* activates olfactory brain regions. *NeuroImage, 32*, 906–912.

Goodale, M.A. (2008). Action without perception in human vision. *Cognitive Neuropsychology, 7–8*, 891–919.

Goodale, M.A., & Milner, A.D. (2004). *Sight unseen: An exploration of conscious and unconscious vision*. Oxford, UK: Oxford University Press.

Goodglass, H. (1993). *Understanding aphasia*. San Diego, CA: Academic Press.

Goodglass, H., & Berko, J. (1960). Agrammatism and inflectional morphology in English. *Journal of Speech and Hearing Research, 3*, 257–267.

Goodglass, H., & Kaplan, E. (1983). *The assessment of aphasia and related disorders*, 2nd edition. Malvern, PA: Lea & Febiger.

Goodglass, H., Kaplan, E., & Barresi, B. (2001). *Boston Diagnostic Aphasia Examination*, 3rd edition. Philadelphia: Lippincott, Williams & Wilkins.

Goodglass, H., Klein, B., Carey, P., & Jones, K.J. (1966). Specific semantic word categories in aphasia. *Cortex, 2*, 74–89.

Goodglass, H., & Wingfield, A. (1997). Word-finding deficits in aphasia: Brain-behavior relations and clinical symptomology. In H. Goodglass & A. Wingfield (Eds.), *Anomia: Neuroanatomical and cognitive correlates* (pp. 3–30). New York: Academic Press.

Goodglass, H., Wingfield, A., Hyde, M.R., & Theurkauf, J. (1986). Category-specific dissociations in naming and recognition by aphasic patients. *Brain and Language, 36*, 411–419.

Goodman, R.A., & Caramazza, A. (1986). Aspects of the spelling process: Evidence froom a case of acquired dysgraphia. *Language and Cognitive Processes, 1*, 263–296.

Gopnik, A. (2010). Mind reading. *The New York Times Book Review*, January 3, p. BR15.

Gorno-Tempini, M.L., Brambati, S.M., Ginex, V., Ogar, J., Dronkers, N.F., Marcone, A., Perani, D., Garibotto, V., Cappa, S.F., & Miller, B.L. (2008). The logopenic/phonological variant of primary progressive aphasia. *Neurology, 71*, 1227–1234.

Gorno-Tempini, M.L., Dronkers, N.F., Rankin, K.P., Ogar, J.M., Phengrasamy, L., Rosen, H.J., Johnson, J.K., Weiner, M.W., & Miller, B.L. (2004). Cognition and anatomy in three variants of primary progressive aphasia. *Annals of Neurology, 55*, 335–346.

Gorno-Tempini, M.L., Hillis, A.E., Weintraub, S., Kertesz, A., Mendez, M., Cappa, S.F., Ogar, J.M., Rohrer, J.D., Black, S., Boeve, B.F., Manes, F., Dronkers, N.F., Vandenberghe, R., Rascovsky, K., Patterson, K., Miller, B.L., Knopman, D.S., Hodges, J.R., Mesulam, M.M., & Grossman, M. (2011). Classification of primary progressive aphasia and its variants. *Neurology, 76*, 1006–1014.

Gorno-Tempini, M.L., Ogar, J.M., Brambati, S.M., Wang, P., Jeong, J.H., Rankin, K., Dronkers, N.F., & Miller, B.L. (2006). Anatomical correlates of early mutism in progressive nonfluent aphasia. *Neurology, 67*, 1849–1851.

Gottschall, J. (2012). *The storytelling animal: How stories make us human*. New York: Houghton Mifflin Harcourt.

Gough, P.M., Nobre, A.C., & Devlin, J.T. (2005). Dissociating linguistic processes in the left inferior frontal cortex with transcranial magnetic stimulation. *Journal of Neuroscience, 25*, 8010–8016.

Grabenhorst, F., & Rolls, E.T. (2011). Value, pleasure, and choice in the ventral prefrontal cortex. *Trends in Cognitive Sciences, 15*, 56–67.

Grabowski, T.J., Damasio, H., Tranel, D., Ponto, L.L.B., Hichwa, R.D., & Damasio, A.R. (2001). A role for left temporal pole in the retrieval of words for unique entities. *Human Brain Mapping, 13*, 199–212.

Grabski, K., Lamalle, L., Vilain, C., Schwartz, J.L., Vallée, N., Tropres, I., Baciu, M., Le Bas, J.F., & Sato, M. (2012). Functional MRI assessment of orofacial articulators: Neural correlates of lip, jaw, larynx, and tongue movements. *Human Brain Mapping, 33*, 2306–2321.

Graham, N.L., Patterson, K., & Hodges, J.R. (2000). The impact of semantic memory impairment on spelling: Evidence from semantic dementia. *Neuropsychologia, 38*, 143–163.

Grainger, J., Rey, A., & Dufau, S. (2008). Letter perception: From pixels to pandemonium. *Trends in Cognitive Sciences, 12*, 381–387.

Grandjean, D., Sander, D., Pourtois, G., Schwartz, S., Seghier, M.L., Scherer, K.R., & Vuilleumier, P. (2005). The voices of wrath: Brain responses to angry prosody in meaningless speech. *Nature Neuroscience, 8*, 145–146.

Gratton, C., Nomura, E.M., Pérez, F., & D'Esposito, M. (2012). Focal brain lesions to critical locations cause widespread disruption of the modular organization of the brain. *Journal of Cognitive Neuroscience, 24*, 1275–1285.

Graves, W.W., Desai, R., Humphries, C., Seidenberg, M.S., & Binder, J.R. (2010). Neural systems for reading aloud: A multiparametric approach. *Cerebral Cortex, 20*, 1799–1815.

Graves, W.W., Grabowski, T.J., Mehta, S., & Gordon, J. (2007). A neural signature of phonological access: Distinguishing the effects of word frequency from familiarity and length in overt picture naming. *Journal of Cognitive Neuroscience, 19*, 617–631.

Graves, W.W., Grabowski, T.J., Mehta, S., & Gupta, P. (2008). Left posterior superior temporal gyrus participates specifically in accessing lexical phonology. *Journal of Cognitive Neuroscience, 20*, 1698–1710.

Graziano, M.S.A. (2009). *The intelligent movement machine: An ethological perspective on the primate motor system.* Oxford, UK: Oxford University Press.

Graziano, M.S.A., & Aflalo, T.N. (2007). Mapping behavioural repertoire onto the cortex. *Neuron, 56*, 239–251.

Grefkes, C., & Fink, G.R. (2011). Reorganization of cerebral networks after stroke: New insights from neuroimaging with connectivity approaches. *Brain, 134*, 1264–1276.

Grewe, T., Bornkessel, I., Zysset, S., Wiese, R., von Cramon, D.Y., & Schlesewsky, M. (2005). The emergence of the unmarked: A new perspective on the language-specific function of Broca's area. *Human Brain Mapping, 26*, 178–190.

Grewe, T., Bornkessel, I., Zysset, S., Wiese, R., von Cramon, D.Y., & Schlesewsky, M. (2006). Linguistic prominence and Broca's area: The influence of animacy as a linearization principle. *NeuroImage, 32*, 1395–1402.

Grewe, T., Bornkessel-Schlesewsky, I., Zysset, S., Wiese, R., von Cramon, D.Y., & Schlesewsky, M. (2007). The role of the superior temporal sulcus in the processing of unmarked transitivity. *NeuroImage, 35*, 343–352.

Griffiths, J.D., Marslen-Wilson, W.D., Stamatakis, E.A., & Tyler, L.K. (2013). Functional organization of the neural language system: Dorsal and ventral pathways are critical for syntax. *Cerebral Cortex, 23*, 139–147.

Griffiths, T.D., & Warren, J.D. (2002). The planum temporale as a computational hub. *Trends in Neurosciences, 25*, 348–353.

Grigor, J., Van Toller, S., Behan, J., & Richardson, A. (1999). The effect of odour priming on long latency visual evoked potentials of matching and mismatching objects. *Chemical Senses, 24*, 137–144.

Grill-Spector, L., Hensen, R., & Martin, A. (2006). Repetition and brain: Neural models of stimulus-specific effects. *Trends in Cognitive Sciences, 10*, 14–23.

Grindrod, C.M., Bilenko, N.Y., Myers, E.B., & Blumstein, S.E. (2008). The role of the left inferior frontal gyrus in implicit semantic competition and selection: An event-related fMRI study. *Brain Research, 1229*, 167–178.

Grodzinsky, Y. (1986). Language deficits and the theory of syntax. *Brain and Language, 27*, 135–159.

Grodzinsky, Y. (1989). Agrammatic comprehension of relative clauses. *Brain and Language, 31*, 480–499.

Grodzinsky, Y. (1990). *Theoretical perspectives on language deficits.* Cambridge, MA: MIT Press.

Grodzinsky, Y. (2000). The neurology of syntax: Language use without Broca's area. *Behavioral and Brain Sciences, 23*, 1–71.

Grodzinsky, Y., & Amunts, K. (Eds.) (2006). *Broca's region.* Oxford, UK: Oxford University Press.

Grodzinsky, Y., & Santi, A. (2008). The battle for Broca's region. *Trends in Cognitive Sciences, 12*, 474–480.

Grosbras, M.H., Beaton, S., & Eickhoff, S.B. (2012). Brain regions involved in human movement perception: A quantitative voxel-based meta-analysis. *Human Brain Mapping, 33*, 431–454.

Grossman, E.D. (2006). Evidence for a network of brain areas involved in perception of biological motion. In G. Knoblich, I.M. Thornton, M. Grosjean, & M. Shiffrar (Eds.), *Human body perception from the inside out* (pp. 361–386). Oxford, UK: Oxford University Press.

Grossman, M. (2010). Primary progressive aphasia: Clinicopathological correlations. *Nature Reviews: Neurology, 6*, 88–97.

Grossman, M. (2012). The nonfluent/agrammatic variant of primary progressive aphasia. *Lancet Neurology, 11*, 545–555.

Grossman, M., Anderson, C., Khan, A., Avants, B., Elman, L., & McCluskey, L. (2008). Impaired action knowledge in amyotrophic lateral sclerosis. *Neurology, 71*, 1396–1401.

Grossman, M., & Ash, S. (2004). Primary progressive aphasia: A review. *Neurocase, 10*, 3–18.

Grossman, M., Carvell, S., Stern, M.B., Gollomp, S., & Hurtig, H.I. (1992). Sentence comprehension in Parkinson's disease: The role of attention and memory. *Brain and Language, 42*, 347–384.

Grossman, M., Gloser, G., Kalmanson, J., Morris, J., Stern, M.B., & Hurtig, H.I. (2001). Dopamine supports sentence comprehension in Parkinson's disease. *Journal of the Neurological Sciences, 184*, 123–130.

Grossman, M., Kalmanson, J., Bernhardt, N., Morris, J., Stern, M.B., & Hurtig, H.I. (2000). Cognitive resource limitations during sentence comprehension in Parkinson's disease. *Brain and Language, 73*, 1–16.

Grossman, M., Lee, C., Morris, J., Stern, M.B., & Hurtig, H.I. (2002a). Assessing resource demands during sentence processing in Parkinson's disease. *Brain and Language, 80*, 603–616.

Grossman, M., McMillan, C., Moore, P., Ding, L., Glosser, G., Work, M., & Gee, J. (2004). What's in a name: Voxel-based morphometric analyses of MRI and naming difficulty in Alzheimer's disease, frontotemporal dementia, and corticobasal degeneration. *Brain, 127*, 628–649.

Grossman, M., Mickanin, J., Onishi, K., Hughes, E., D'Esposito, M., Ding, X.S., Alavi, A., & Reivich, M. (1996). Progressive nonfluent aphasia: Language, cognitive, and PET measures contrasted with probable Alzheimer's disease. *Journal of Cognitive Neuroscience, 8*, 135–154.

Grossman, M., & Moore, P. (2005). A longitudinal study of sentence comprehension difficulty in primary progressive aphasia. *Journal of Neurology, Neurosurgury, and Psychiatry, 76*, 644–649.

Grossman, M., Powers, J., Ash, S., McMillan, C., Burkholder, L., Irwin, D., & Trojanowski, J.Q. (2013). Disruption of large-scale neural networks in nonfluent/agrammatic variant primary progressive aphasia associated with frontotemporal degeneration pathology. *Brain and Language, 127*, 106–120.

Grossman, M., Rhee, J., & Antiquena, P. (2005). Sentence processing in frontotemporal dementia. *Cortex, 41*, 764–777.

Grossman, M., Zurif, E., Lee, C., Prather, P., Kalmanson, J., Stern, M.B., & Hurtig, H.I. (2002b). Information processing speed and sentence comprehension in Parkinson's disease. *Neuropsychology, 16*, 174–181.

Grosvald, M., Gutiérrez Sigut, E., Hafer, S., & Corina, D. (2012). Dissociating linguistic and non-linguistic gesture processing: Electrophysiological evidence from American Sign Language. *Brain and Language, 121*, 12–24.

Guenther, F.H. (1994). A neural network model of speech acquisition and motor equivalent speech production. *Biological Cybernetics, 72*, 43–53.

Guenther, F.H. (1995). Speech sound acquisition, coarticulation, and rate effects in a neural network model of speech production. *Psychological Review, 102*, 594–621.

Guenther, F.H., Brumberg, J.S., Wright, E.J., Nieto-Castanon, A., Tourville, J.A., Panko, M., Law, R., Siebert, S.A., Bartels, J.L., Andreasan, D.S., Ehirim, P., Mao, H., & Kennedy, P.R. (2009). A wireless brain-machine interface for real-time speech synthesis. *PloS One, 4*, 38218.

Guenther, F.H., Ghosh, S.S., & Tourville, J.A. (2006). Neural modeling and imaging of the cortical interactions underlying syllable production. *Brain and Language, 96*, 280–301.

Guenther, F.H., & Vladusich, T. (2012). A neural theory of speech acquisition and production. *Journal of Neurolinguistics, 25*, 408–422.

Gvion, A., & Friedmann, N. (2012). Does phonological working memory impairment affect sentence comprehension? A study of conduction aphasia. *Aphasiology, 26*, 494–535.

Hadjikhani, N., Liu, A.K., Dale, A.M., Cavanaugh, P., & Tootell, R.B.H. (1998). Retinotopy and color sensitivity in human visual cortical area V8. *Nature Neuroscience, 1*, 235–241.

Haggard, P. (2008). Human volition: Towards a neuroscience of will. *Nature Reviews: Neuroscience, 9*, 934–946.

Hagoort, P. (2008). The fractionation of spoken language understanding by measuring electrical and magnetic brain signals. *Philosophical Transactions of the Royal Society, B, Biological Sciences, 363*, 1055–1069.

Hagoort, P., & Brown, C.M. (1994). Brain responses to lexical ambiguity resolution and parsing. In C. Clifton, Jr., L. Frazier, & K. Rayner (Eds.), *Perspectives on sentence processing* (pp. 45–80). Hillsdale, NJ: Erlbaum.

Hagoort, P., Brown, C.M., & Groothusen, J. (1993). The syntactic positive shift (SPS) as an ERP measure of syntactic processing. *Language and Cognitive Processes, 8*, 439–483.

Hagoort, P., Brown, C.M., & Osterhout, L. (1999). The neurocognition of syntactic processing. In C.M. Brown & P. Hagoort (Eds.), *The neurocognition of language* (pp. 273–316). Oxford, UK: Oxford University Press.

Hagoort, P., Hald, L., Bastiaansen, M., & Petersson, K.M. (2004). Integration of word meaning and world knowledge in language comprehension. *Science, 304*, 438–441.

Hagoort, P., & van Berkum, J. (2007). Beyond the sentence given. *Philosophical Transactions of the Royal Society, B. Biological Sciences, 362*, 801–811.

Hakes, B., Evans, J., & Brannon, L. (1976). Understanding sentences with relative clauses. *Memory and Cognition, 4*, 283–296.

Hale, K.L. (1983). Warlpiri and the grammar of non-configurational languages. *Natural Language and Linguistic Theory, 1*, 5–47.

Hale, K.L., Laughren, M., & Simpson, J. (1995). Warlpiri. In J. Jacobs, A. von Stechow, W. Sternefeld, & T. Vennemann (Eds.), *Syntax. Ein internationales Handbuch zeitgenössicher Forschung* [*An international handbook of contemporary research*] (pp. 1430–1451). Berlin: Walter de Gruyter.

Halle, M., & Mohanan, K.P. (1985). Segmental phonology of modern English. *Linguistic Inquiry, 16*, 57–116.

Haller, S., Radue, E.W., Erb, M., Grodd, W., & Kircher, T. (2005). Overt sentence production in event-related fMRI. *Neuropsychologia, 43*, 807–814.

Hallett, M. (2007). Transcranial magnetic stimulation: A primer. *Neuron, 55*, 187–199.

Halpern, C., Clark, R., Moore, P., Antani, S., Colcher, A., & Grossman, M. (2004). Verbal mediation of number knowledge: Evidence from semantic dementia and corticobasal degeneration. *Brain and Cognition, 56*, 107–115.

Hamamé, C.M., Szwed, M., Sharman, M., Vidal, J.R., Perrone-Bertolotti, M., Kahane, P., Bertrand, O., & Lachaux, J.P. (2013). Dejerine's reading area revisited with intracranial EEG: Selective responses to letter strings. *Neurology, 80*, 602–603.

Hamberger, M.J., McClelland, S., McKhann, G.M., Williams, A.C., & Goodman, R.R. (2007). Distribution of auditory and visual naming sites in nonlesional temporal lobe epilepsy patients and patients with space-occupying temporal lobe lesions. *Epilepsia, 48*, 531–538.

Hamilton, A.C., & Coslett, H.B. (2008). Refractory access disorders and the organization of concrete and abstract semantics: Do they differ? *Neurocase, 14,* 131–140.

Hanson, S.J., & Bunzl, M. (Eds.) (2010). *Foundational issues in human brain mapping.* Cambridge, MA: MIT Press.

Hanten, G., & Martin, R.C. (2000). Contributions of phonological and semantic short-term memory to sentence processing: Evidence from two cases of closed head injury in children. *Journal of Memory and Language, 43,* 335–361.

Harciarek, M., & Kertesz, A. (2011). Primary progressive aphasias and their contribution to the contemporary knowledge about the brain-language relationship. *Neuropsychology Review, 21,* 271–287.

Hare, M., Elman, J., & Daugherty, K. (1995). Default generalization in connectionist networks. *Language and Cognitive Processes, 10,* 601–630.

Hargreaves, I.S., Leonard, G.A., Pexman, P.M., Pittman, D.J., Siakaluk, P.D., & Goodyear, B.G. (2012). The neural correlates of the body-object interaction effect in semantic processing. *Frontiers in Human Neuroscience, 6,* Article 22.

Harm, M.W., & Seidenberg, M.S. (2001). Are there orthographic impairments in phonological dyslexia? *Cognitive Neuropsychology, 18,* 71–92.

Harrison, K.D. (2007). *When languages die.* Oxford, UK: Oxford University Press.

Harrison, N.A., Singer, T., Rotshtein, P., Dolan, R.J., & Critchley, H.D. (2006). Pupillary contagion: Central mechanisms engaged in sadness processing. *Social, Cognitive, and Affective Neuroscience, 1,* 5–17.

Hart, J., & Gordon, B. (1990). Delineation of single-word semantic comprehension deficits in aphasia, with anatomical correlation. *Annals of Neurology, 27,* 226–231.

Hashimoto, Y., & Sakai, K.L. (2003). Brain activations during conscious self-monitoring of speech production with delayed auditory feedback: An fMRI study. *Human Brain Mapping, 20,* 22–28.

Haspelmath, M. (2010). Framework-free grammatical theory. In Heine, B., & Narrog, H. (Eds.), *The Oxford handbook of grammatical analysis* (pp. 341–365). Oxford, UK: Oxford University Press.

Haspelmath, M., & Sims, A.D. (2010). *Understanding morphology,* 2nd edition. Oxford, UK: Oxford University Press.

Hassabis, D., & Maguire, E.A. (2007). Deconstructing episodic memory with construction. *Trends in Cognitive Sciences, 11,* 299–306.

Hasson, U., Ghazanfar, A.A., Galantucci, B., Garrod, S., & Keysers, C. (2012). Brain-to-brain coupling: A mechanism for creating and sharing a social world. *Trends in Cognitive Sciences, 16,* 114–121.

Hasson, U., Levy, I., Behrmann, M., Hendler, T., & Malach, R. (2002). Eccentricity bias as an organizing principle for human higher-order object areas. *Neuron, 34,* 479–490.

Hastings, A.S., & Kotz, S. (2008). Speeding up syntax: On the relative timing and automaticity of local phrase structure and morphosyntactic processing as reflected in event-related brain potentials. *Journal of Cognitive Neuroscience, 20,* 1207–1219.

Hatfield, F.M., & Patterson, K.E. (1983). Phonological spelling. *Quarterly Journal of Experimental Psychology, 35A,* 451–458.

Hauk, O., Davis, M.H., Kherif, F., & Pulvermüller, F. (2008a). Imagery or meaning? Evidence for a semantic origin of category-specific brain activity in metabolic imaging. *European Journal of Neuroscience, 27,* 1856–1866.

Hauk, O., Johnsrude, I., & Pulvermüller, F. (2004). Somatotopic representation of action words in human motor and premotor cortex. *Neuron, 41,* 301–307.

Hauk, O., & Pulvermüller, F. (2004). Neurophysiological distinction of action words in the fronto-central cortex. *Human Brain Mapping, 21,* 191–201.

Hauk, O., & Pulvermüller, F. (2011). The lateralization of motor cortex activation to action words. *Frontiers in Human Neuroscience, 5,* Article 149.

Hauk, O., Shtyrov, Y., & Pulvermüller, F. (2008b). The time course of action and action-word comprehension in the human brain as revealed by neurophysiology. *Journal of Physiology, Paris, 102,* 50–58.

Hauk, O., & Tschentscher, N. (2013). The body of evidence: What can neuroscience tell us about embodied semantics? *Frontiers in Psychology, 4,* Article 50.

Havas, D.A., Glenberg, A.M., Gutowski, K.A., Lucarelli, M.J., & Davidson, R.J. (2010). Cosmetic use of botulinum toxin-A affects processing of emotional language. *Psychological Science, 21,* 895–900.

Havas, D.A., Glenberg, A.M., & Rinck, M. (2007). Emotion simulation during language comprehension. *Psychonomic Bulletin & Review, 14,* 436–441.

Hawkins, J.A. (1994). *A performance theory of order and constituency.* Cambridge, UK: Cambridge University Press.

Hawkins, J.A. (2011). Processing efficiency and complexity in typological patterns. In J.J. Song (Ed.), *The Oxford handbook of linguistic typology* (pp. 206–226). Oxford, UK: Oxford University Press.

Haxby, J.V. (2012). Multivariate pattern analysis of fMRI: The early beginnings. *NeuroImage, 62,* 852–855.

Haxby, J.V., Gobbini, M.I., & Montgomery, K. (2004). Spatial and temporal distribution of face and object representations in the human brain. In M.S. Gazzaniga (Ed.), *The cognitive neurosciences III* (pp. 889–904). Cambridge, MA: MIT Press.

Haynes, J.D., & Rees, G. (2006). Decoding mental states from brain activity in humans. *Nature Reviews Neuroscience, 7,* 523–534.

Head, H. (1926). *Aphasia and kindred disorders of speech.* New York: Macmillan.

Healy, A.F., & Miller, G.A. (1970). The verb as the main determinant of sentence meaning. *Psychonomic Science, 20,* 372.

Heilman, K., Bowers, D., Speedie, L., & Coslett, H. (1984). Comprehension of affective and nonaffective prosody. *Neurology, 34,* 917–921.

Hein, G., & Knight, R.T. (2008). Superior temporal sulcus— It's my area, or is it? *Journal of Cognitive Neuroscience, 20,* 2125–2136.

Heine, B. (1997). *Cognitive foundations of grammar.* Oxford, UK: Oxford University Press.

Heine, B., & Kuteva, T. (2002). *World lexicon of grammaticalization.* Cambridge, UK: Cambridge University Press.

Henry, M.L., Beeson, P.M., Alexander, G.E., & Rapcsak, S.Z. (2012). Written language impairments in primary progressive aphasia: A reflection of damage to central semantic and phonological processes. *Journal of Cognitive Neuroscience, 24,* 261–275.

Henry, M.L., Beeson, P.M., Stark, A.J., & Rapcsak, S.Z. (2007). The role of left perisylvian cortical regions in spelling. *Brain and Language, 100,* 44–52.

Henry, M.L., & Gorno-Tempini, M.L. (2010). The logopenic variant of primary progressive aphasia. *Current Opinion in Neurology, 23,* 633–637.

Henson, R.N., Burgess, N., & Frith, C.D. (2000). Recoding, storage, rehearsal, and grouping in verbal short-term memory: An fMRI study. *Neuropsychologia, 38,* 426–440.

Herculano-Houzel, S. (2009). The human brain in numbers: A linearly scaled-up primate brain. *Frontiers in Human Neuroscience, 3,* Article 31.

Herman, A.B., Houde, J.F., Vinogradov, S., & Nagarajan, S.S. (2013). Parsing the phonological loop: Activation timing in the dorsal speech stream determines accuracy in speech reproduction. *Journal of Neuroscience, 33,* 5439–5453.

Herrmann, B., Obleser, J., Kalberlah, C., Haynes, J.D., & Friederici, A.D. (2012). Dissociable neural imprints of perception and grammar in auditory functional imaging. *Human Brain Mapping, 33,* 584–595.

Hesling, I., Clément, S., Bordessoules, M., & Allard, M. (2005a). Cerebral mechanisms of prosodic integration: Evidence from connected speech. *NeuroImage, 24,* 937–947.

Hesling, I., Dilharreguy, B., Clement, S., Bordessoules, M., & Allard, M. (2005b). Cerebral mechanisms of prosodic sensory integration using low-frequency bands of connected speech. *Human Brain Mapping, 26,* 157–169.

Hickok, G. (2009a). The cortical organization of phonological processing. In M.S. Gazzaniga (Ed.), *The cognitive neurosciences,* 4th edition (pp. 767–776). Cambridge, MA: MIT Press.

Hickok, G. (2009b). The functional neuroanatomy of language. *Physics of Life Reviews, 6,* 121–143.

Hickok, G. (2012). Computational neuroanatomy of speech production. *Nature Reviews Neuroscience, 13,* 135–145.

Hickok, G., & Bellugi, U. (2001). The signs of aphasia. In R.S. Berndt (Ed.), *Handbook of neuropsychology,* 2nd edition, *Vol. 3* (pp. 31–50). Amsterdam: Elsevier.

Hickok, G., Bellugi, U., & Klima, E.S. (1996a). The neurobiology of sign language and its implications for the neural basis of language. *Nature, 381,* 699–702.

Hickok, G., Bellugi, U., & Klima, E.S. (1998a). The neural organization of language: Evidence from sign language aphasia. *Trends in Cognitive Sciences, 2,* 129–136.

Hickok, G., Bellugi, U., & Klima, E.S. (1998b). What's right about the neural organization of sign language? A perspective on recent neuroimaging results. *Trends in Cognitive Sciences, 2,* 465–468. (See also the accompanying response from Corina et al.)

Hickok, G., Buchsbaum, B., Humphries, C., & Muftuler, T. (2003). Auditory-motor interaction revealed by fMRI: Speech, music, and working memory in area Spt. *Journal of Cognitive Neuroscience, 15,* 673–682.

Hickok, G., Costanzo, M., Capasso, R., & Miceli, G. (2011a). The role of Broca's area in speech perception: Evidence from aphasia revisted. *Brain and Language, 119,* 214–220.

Hickok, G., Holt, L.L., & Lotto, A.J. (2009a). Response to Wilson: What does motor cortex contribute to speech perception? *Trends in Cognitive Sciences, 13,* 330–331.

Hickok, G., Houde, J., & Rong, F. (2011b). Sensorimotor integration in speech processing: Computational basis and neural organization. *Neuron, 69,* 407–422.

Hickok, G., Kirk, K., & Bellugi, U. (1998c). Hemispheric organization of local- and global-level visuospatial processes in deaf signers and its relation to sign language aphasia. *Brain and Language, 65,* 276–286.

Hickok, G., Love-Geffen, T., & Klima, E.S. (2002). Role of the left hemisphere in sign language comprehension. *Brain and Language, 82,* 167–178.

Hickok, G., Okada, K., Barr, W., Pa, J., Rogalsky, C., Donnelly, K., Barde, L., & Grant, A. (2008). Bilateral capacity for speech sound processing in auditory comprehension: Evidence from Wada procedures. *Brain and Language, 107,* 179–184.

Hickok, G., Okada, K., & Serences, J.T. (2009b). Area Spt in the human planum temporale supports sensory-motor integration for speech processing. *Journal of Neurophysiology, 101,* 2725–2732.

Hickok, G., Pickell, H., Klima, E.S., & Bellugi, U. (2009c). Neural dissociation in the production of lexical versus classifier signs in ASL: Distinct patterns of hemispheric asymmetry. *Neuropsychologia, 47,* 382–387.

Hickok, G., & Poeppel, D. (2000). Towards a funtional neuroanatomy of speech perception. *Trends in Cognitive Sciences, 4,* 131–138.

Hickok, G., & Poeppel, D. (2004). Dorsal and ventral streams: A framework for understanding aspects of the functional anatomy of language. *Cognition, 92,* 67–99.

Hickok, G., & Poeppel, D. (2007). The cortical organization of speech processing. *Nature Reviews Neuroscience, 8,* 393–402.

Hickok, G., Say, K., Bellugi, U., & Klima, E.S. (1996b). The basis of hemispheric asymmetries for language and spatial cognition: Clues from focal brain damage in two deaf native signers. *Aphasiology, 10,* 577–591.

Hilgetag, C.C., Theoret, H., & Pascual-Leone, A. (2001). Enhanced visual spatial attention ipsilateral to rTMS-induced "virtual lesions" of human parietal cortex. *Nature Neuroscience, 4,* 953–957.

Hillier, A., Beversdorf, D.Q., Raymer, A.M., Williamson, D.J.G., & Heilman, K.M. (2007). Abnormal emotional word ratings in Parkinson's disease. *Neurocase, 13,* 81–85.

Hillis, A.E. (1993). The role of models of language processing in rehabilitation of language impairments. *Aphasiology, 7,* 5–26.

Hillis, A.E. (2001). The organization of the lexical system. In B. Rapp (Ed.), *The handbook of cognitive neuropsychology* (pp. 185–210). Philadelphia, PA: Psychology Press.

Hillis, A.E. (2002). Models of the reading process. In A.E. Hillis (Ed.), *The handbook of adult language disorders* (pp. 3–14). Philadelphia, PA: Psychology Press.

Hillis, A.E. (2007a). Aphasia: Progress in the last quarter of a century. *Neurology, 69,* 200–213.

Hillis, A.E. (2007b). Magnetic resonance perfusion imaging in the study of language. *Brain and Language, 102,* 165–175.

Hillis, A.E., Boatman, D., Hart, J., & Gordon, B. (1999a). Making sense out of jargon: A neurolinguistic and computational account of jargon aphasia. *Neurology, 53,* 1813–1824.

Hillis, A.E., & Caramazza, A. (1991). Category-specific naming and comprehension impairment: A double dissociation. *Brain, 114,* 2081–2094.

Hillis, A.E., Heidler-Gray, J., Newhart, M., Chang, S., Ken, L., & Bak, T.H. (2006). Naming and comprehension in primary progressive aphasia: The influence of grammatical word class. *Aphasiology, 20*, 246–256.

Hillis, A.E., Newhart, M., Heidler, J., Barker, P., Herskovits, E., & Degaonkar, M. (2005). The roles of the "visual word form area" in reading. *NeuroImage, 24*, 548–559.

Hillis, A.E., Oh, S., & Ken, L. (2004a). Deterioration of naming nouns versus verbs in primary progressive aphasia. *Annals of Neurology, 55*, 268–275.

Hillis, A.E., & Rapp, B.C. (2004). Cognitive and neural substrates of written language: Comprehension and production. In M.S. Gazzaniga (Ed.), *The cognitive neurosciences III* (pp.775–787). Cambridge, MA: MIT Press.

Hillis, A.E., Rapp, B.C., & Caramazza, A. (1999b). When a rose is a rose in speech but a tulip in writing. *Cortex, 35*, 337–356.

Hillis, A.E., Tuffiash, E., & Caramazza, A. (2002a). Modality-specific deterioration in naming verbs in nonfluent primary progressive aphasia. *Journal of Cognitive Neuroscience, 14*, 1099–1108.

Hillis, A.E., Tuffiash, E., Wityk, R.J., & Barker, P.B. (2002b). Regions of neural dysfunction associated with impaired naming of actions and objects in acute stroke. *Cognitive Neuropsychology, 19*, 523–534.

Hillis, A.E., Wityk, R.J., Barker, P.B., & Caramazza, A. (2003). Neural regions essential for writing verbs. *Nature Neuroscience, 6*, 19–20.

Hillis, A.E., Work, M., Barker, P.B., Jacobs, M.A., Breese, E.L., & Maurer, K. (2004b). Re-examining the brain regions crucial for orchestrating speech articulation. *Brain, 127*, 1479–87.

Hocking, J., McMahon, K., & de Zubicaray, G. (2010). Semantic interference in object naming: An fMRI study of the postcue naming paradigm. *NeuroImage, 50*, 796–801.

Hodges, J.R., Graham, N., & Patterson, K. (1995). Charting the progression in semantic dementia: Implications for the organization of semantic memory. *Memory, 3*, 463–495.

Hodges, J.R., Martinos, M., Woollams, A.M., Patterson, K., & Adlam, A.L.R. (2008). Repeat and point: Differentiating semantic dementia from progressive non-fluent aphasia. *Cortex, 44*, 1265–1270.

Hodges, J.R., Mitchell, J., Dawson, K., Spillantini, M.G., Xuereb, J.H., McMonagle, P., Nestor, P.J., & Patterson, K. (2010). Semantic dementia: Demography, familial factors, and survival in a consecutive series of 100 cases. *Brain, 133*, 300–306.

Hodges, J.R., & Patterson, K. (1996). Nonfluent progressive aphasia and semantic dementia: A comparative neuropsychological study. *Journal of the International Neuropsychological Society, 2*, 511–524.

Hodges, J.R., & Patterson, K. (2007). Semantic dementia: A unique clinicopathological syndrome. *Lancet Neurology, 6*, 1004–1014.

Hodges, J.R., Patterson, K., Oxbury, S., & Funnell, F. (1992). Semantic dementia: Progressive fluent aphasia with temporal lobe atrophy. *Brain, 115*, 1783–1806.

Hodges, J.R., Patterson, K., & Tyler, L.K. (1994). Loss of semantic memory: Implications for the modularity of mind. *Cognitive Neuropsychology, 11*, 505–542.

Hoekert, M., Vingerhoets, G., & Aleman, A. (2010). Results of a pilot study on the involvement of bilateral inferior frontal gyri in emotional prosody perception: An rTMS study. *BMC Neuroscience, 11*, Article 93.

Hoenig, K., Sim, E.-J., Bochev, V., Herrnberger, B., & Kiefer, M. (2008). Conceptual flexibility in the human brain: Dynamic recruitment of semantic maps from visual, motor, and motion-related areas. *Journal of Cognitive Neuroscience, 20*, 1799–1814.

Hoffman, P., Jeffries, E., & Lambon Ralph, M.A. (2010). Ventrolateral prefrontal cortex plays an executive regulation role in comprehension of abstract words: Convergent neuropsychological and repetitive TMS evidence. *Journal of Neuroscience, 30*, 15450–15456.

Hoffman, P., Jones, R.W., & Lambon Ralph, M.A. (2012a). The degraded concept representation system in semantic dementia: Damage to pan-modal hub, then visual spoke. *Brain, 135*, 3770–3780.

Hoffman, P., Jones, R.W., & Lambon Ralph, M.A. (2013). Be concrete and be comprehended: Consistent imageability effects in semantic dementia for nouns, verbs, synonyms, and associates. *Cortex, 49*, 1206–1218.

Hoffman, P., & Lambon Ralph, M.A. (2011). Reverse concreteness effects are not a typical feature of semantic dementia: Evidence for the Hub-and-Spoke Model of conceptual representation. *Cerebral Cortex, 21*, 2103–2112.

Hoffman, P., & Lambon Ralph, M.A. (2013). Shapes, scents and sounds: Quantifying the full multi-sensory basis of conceptual knowledge. *Neuropsychologia, 51*, 14–25.

Hoffman, P., Meteyard, L., & Patterson, K. (in press). Broadly speaking: Vocabulary in semantic dementia shifts toward general, semantically diverse words. *Cortex.*

Hoffman, P., Pobric, G., Drakesmith, M., & Lambon Ralph, M.A. (2012b). Posterior middle temporal gyrus is involved in verbal and non-verbal semantic cognition: Evidence from rTMS. *Aphasiology.*

Hoffman, P., Rogers, T.T., & Lambon Ralph, M.A. (2011). Semantic diversity accounts for the "missing" word frequency effect in stroke aphasia: Insights using a novel method to quantify contextual variability in meaning. *Journal of Cognitive Neuroscience, 23*, 2432–2446.

Hoffman, T., & Trousdale, G. (Eds.) (2013). *The Oxford handbook of construction grammar.* Oxford, UK: Oxford University Press.

Hofstadter, D.R. (2001). Epilogue: Analogy as the core of cognition. In D. Gentner, K.J. Holyoak, & B.N. Kokinov (Eds.), *The analogical mind* (pp. 499–538). Cambridge, MA: MIT Press.

Holcomb, P.J., Kounios, J., Anderson, J.E., & West, W.C. (1999). Dual-coding, context-availability, and concreteness effects in sentence comprehension: An electrophysiological investigation. *Journal of Experimental Psychology: Learning, Memory and Cognition, 25*, 721–742.

Holcomb, P.J., & McPherson, W.B. (1994). Event-related brain potentials reflect semantic priming in an object decision task. *Brain and Cognition, 24*, 259–276.

Holmes, V.M., & O'Regan, J.K. (1981). Eye fixation patterns during the reading of relative clause sentences. *Journal of Verbal Learning and Verbal Behavior, 20*, 417–430.

Hornak, J., Bramham, J., Rolls, E.T., Morris, R.G., O'Doherty, J., Bullock, P.R., & Polkey, C.E. (2003). Changes in emotion after circumscribed surgical lesions of the orbitofrontal and cingulate cortices. *Brain, 126*, 1691–1712.

Hornak, J., Rolls, E.T., & Wade, D. (1996). Face and voice expression identification in patients with emotional and behavioral changes following ventral frontal lobe damage. *Neuropsychologia, 34,* 247–261.

Horwitz, B., Amunts, K., Bhattacharyya, R., Patkin, D., Zilles, K., & Braun, A.R. (2003). Activation of Broca's area during the production of spoken and signed language: A combined cytoarchitectonic mapping and PET analysis. *Neuropsychologia, 41,* 1868–1876.

Hotopf, W.H.N. (1983). Lexical slips of the pen and tongue. In B. Butterworth (Ed.), *Language production, Vol. 2.* San Diego: Academic Press.

Houde, J.F., & Jordan, M.I. (1998). Sensorimotor adaptation in speech production. *Science, 279,* 1213–1216.

Hsieh, L., Gandour, J., Wong, D., & Hutchins, G. (2001). Functional heterogeneity of inferior frontal gyrus is shaped by linguistic experience. *Brain and Language, 76,* 227–252.

Hsu, N.S., Frankland, S.M., & Thompson-Schill, S.L. (2012). Chromaticity of color perception and object color knowledge. *Neuropsychologia, 50,* 327–333.

Hsu, N.S., Kraemer, D.J.M., Oliver, R.T., Schichting, M.L., & Thompson-Schill, S.L. (2011). Color, context, and cognitive style: Variations in color knowledge retrieval. *Journal of Cognitive Neuroscience, 23,* 2544–2557.

Huettel, S.A. (2012). Event-related fMRI in cognition. *NeuroImage, 62,* 1152–1156.

Huettel, S.A., Song, A.W., & McCarthy, G. (2004). *Functional magnetic resonance imaging,* 1st edition. Sunderland, MA: Sinauer.

Huettel, S.A., Song, A.W., & McCarthy, G. (2009). *Functional magnetic resonance imaging,* 2nd edition. Sunderland, MA: Sinauer.

Humphreys, G.F., & Gennari. S.P. (2014). Competitive mechanisms in sentence processing: Common and distinct production and reading comprehension networks linked to the prefrontal cortex. *NeuroImage, 84,* 354–366.

Humphreys, G.F., Newling, K., Jennings, C., & Gennari, S.P. (2013). Motion and actions in language: Semantic representations in occipito-temporal cortex. *Brain and Language, 125,* 94–105.

Humphries, C., Binder, J.R., Medler, D.A., & Liebenthal, E. (2006). Syntactic and semantic modulation of neural activity during auditory sentence comprehension. *Journal of Cognitive Neuroscience, 18,* 665–679.

Humphries, C., Buchsbaum, B., & Hickok, G. (2001). Role of anterior temporal cortex in auditory sentence comprehension: An fMRI study. *NeuroReport, 12,* 1749–1752.

Humphries, C., Love, T., Swinney, D., & Hickok, G. (2005). Response of anterior temporal cortex to syntactic and prosodic manipulations during sentence processing. *Human Brain Mapping, 26,* 128–138.

Hunt, L. (2007). *Inventing human rights.* New York: Norton.

Hutto, D. (2007). *Folk psychological narratives.* Cambridge, MA: MIT Press.

Hwang, K., Palmer, E.D., Basho, S., Zadra, J.R., & Müller, R.-A. (2009). Category-specific activations during word generation reflect experiential sensorimotor modalities. *NeuroImage, 48,* 717–725.

Iggesen, O.A. (2005). Number of cases. In M. Haspelmath, M.S. Dryer, D. Gil, & B. Comrie (Eds.), *The world atlas of language structures* (pp. 202–205). Oxford, UK: Oxford University Press.

Indefrey, P. (2011). The spatial and temporal signatures of word production components: A critical update. *Frontiers in Psychology, 2,* Article 255.

Indefrey, P., Brown, C.M., Hellwig, F., Amunts, K., Herzog, H., Seitz, R.J., & Hagoort, P. (2001). A neural correlate of syntactic encoding during speech production. *Proceedings of the National Academy of Sciences, 98,* 5933–5936.

Indefrey, P., Hellwig, F., Herzog, H., Seitz, R.J., & Hagoort, P. (2004). Neural responses to the production and comprehension of syntax in identical utterances. *Brain and Language, 89,* 312–319.

Indefrey, P., & Levelt, W.J.M. (2000). The neural correlates of language production. In M. Gazzaniga (Ed.), *The new cognitive neurosciences* (pp. 845–865). Cambridge, MA: MIT Press.

Indefrey, P., & Levelt, W.J.M. (2004).The spatial and temporal signatures of word production components. *Cognition, 92,* 101–144.

Ionnides, A.A. (2007). Magnetoencephalography as a research tool in neuroscience: State of the art. *The Neuroscientist, 12,* 524–544.

Ischebeck, A.K., Friederici, A.D., & Alter, K. (2008). Processing prosodic boundaries in natural and hummed speech: An fMRI study. *Cerebral Cortex, 18,* 541–552.

Ishibashi, R., Lambon Ralph, M.A., Saito, S., & Pobric, G. (2011). Different roles of lateral anterior temporal lobe and inferior parietal lobule in coding function and manipulation tool knowledge: Evidence from an rTMS study. *Neuropsychologia, 49,* 1128–1135.

Ishitobi, M., Nakasato, N., Suzuki, K., Nagamatsu, K., Shamoto, H., & Yoshimoto, T. (2000). Remote discharges in the posterior language area during basal temporal stimulation. *Neuroreport, 11,* 2997–3000.

Jackendoff, R. (2007). A parallel architecture perspective on language processing. *Brain Research, 1146,* 2–22.

Jackendoff, R., & Pinker, S. (2005). The nature of the language faculty and its implications for the evolution of language. *Cognition, 97,* 211–225.

Jackson, J.H. (1878 & 1879). On affections of speech from diseases of the brain (2 parts). *Brain, 1,* 304–330; *Brain, 2,* 202–222.

Jaeger, J., Lockwood, A., Kemmerer, D., Van Valin, R.D., Jr., Murphy, B., & Khalak, H. (1996). A positron emission tomography study of regular and irregular verb morphology in English. *Language, 72,* 451–497.

Jaeger, J., Lockwood, A., Van Valin, R.D., Jr., Kemmerer, D., Murphy, B., & Wack, D. (1998). Sex differences in brain regions activated by grammatical and reading tasks. *NeuroReport, 9,* 2803–2807.

Jaeger, J.T., & Norcliffe, E.J. (2009). The cross-linguistic study of sentence processing. *Language and Linguistics Compass, 3,* 866–887.

James, C.T. (1975). The role of semantic information in lexical decisions. *Journal of Experimental Psychology: Human Perception and Performance, 1,* 130–136.

Janata, P. (1995). ERP measures assay the degree of expectancy violation of harmonic contexts in music. *Journal of Cognitive Neuroscience, 7,* 153–164.

Jancke, L., Wustenberg, T., Scheich, H., & Heinze, H.J. (2002). Phonetic perception and the temporal cortex. *NeuroImage, 15,* 733–746.

Jantunen, T., & Takkinen, R. (2010). Syllable structure in sign language phonology. In D. Brentari (Ed.), *Sign languages* (pp. 312–331). Cambridge, UK: Cambridge University Press.

January, D., Trueswell, J.C., & Thompson-Schill, S.L. (2009). Co-localization of Stroop and syntactic ambiguity resolution in Broca's area: Implications for the neural basis of sentence processing. *Journal of Cognitive Neuroscience, 21,* 2434–2444.

Jefferies, E. (2013). The neural basis of semantic cognition: Converging evidence from neuropsychology, neuroimaging and TMS. *Cortex, 49,* 611–625.

Jefferies, E., Bateman, D., & Lambon Ralph, M.A. (2005). The role of the temporal lobe semantic system in number knowledge: Evidence from late-stage semantic dementia. *Neuropsychologia, 43,* 887–905.

Jefferies, E., & Lambon Ralph, M.A. (2006). Semantic impairment in stroke aphasia versus semantic dementia: A case-series comparison. *Brain, 129,* 2132–2147.

Jefferies, E., Patterson, K., Jones, R.W., & Lambon Ralph, M.A. (2009). Comprehension of concrete and abstract words in semantic dementia. *Neuropsychology, 23,* 492–499.

Jefferies, E., Sage, K., & Lambon Ralph, M.A. (2007). Do deep dyslexia, dysphasia, and dysgraphia share a common phonological impairment? *Neuropsychologia, 45,* 1553–1570.

Jemel, B., Geore, N., Olivares, E., Fiori, N., & Renault, B. (1999). Event-related potentials to structural familiar face incongruity processing. *Psychophysiology, 36,* 437–452.

Jenkins, W., & Merzenich, M. (1987). Reorganization of neocortical representations after brain injury: A neurophysiological model of the bases of recovery from stroke. *Progress in Brain Research, 71,* 249–266.

Jescheniak, J.D., & Levelt, W.J.M. (1994). Word frequency effects in speech production: Retrieval of syntactic information and of phonological form. *Journal of Experimental Psychology: Learning, Memory, and Cognition, 20,* 824–843.

Jezzini, A., Caruana, F., Stoianov, I., Gallese, G., & Rizzolatti, G. (2012). Functional organization of the insula and inner perisylvian regions. *Proceedings of the National Academy of Sciences, 109,* 10077–10082.

Joanette, Y. (1990). Aphasia in left-handers and crossed aphasia. In F. Boller & J. Grafman (Eds.), *Handbook of neuropsychology, Vol. 2* (pp. 173–184). Amsterdam: Elsevier.

Joanisse, M.F., & Gati, J.S. (2003). Overlapping neural regions for processing rapid temporal cues in speech and nonspeech signals. *NeuroImage, 19,* 64–79.

Joanisse, M.F., & Seidenberg, M.S. (1999). Impairments in verb morphology after brain injury: A connectionist model. *Proceedings of the National Academy of Sciences, 96,* 7592–7597.

Joanisse, M.F., & Seidenberg, M.S. (2005). Imaging the past: Neural activation in frontal and temporal regions during regular and irregular past-tense processing. *Cognitive, Affective and Behavioral Neuroscience, 5,* 282–296.

Jobard, G., Crivello, F., & Tzouri-Mazoyer, N. (2003). Evaluation of the dual route theory of reading: A meta-analysis of 35 neuroimaging studies. *NeuroImage, 20,* 693–712.

Johansen-Berg, H., Rushworth, M.F.S. (2009). Using diffusion imaging to study human connectional anatomy. *Annual Review of Neuroscience, 32,* 75–94.

Johnson, D.R. (2012). Transportation into a story increases empathy, prosocial behavior, and perceptual bias toward fearful expressions. *Personality and Individual Differences, 52,* 150–155.

Johnson-Frey, S.H. (2004). The neural bases of complex tool use in humans. *Trends in Cognitive Sciences, 8,* 71–78.

Jonas, S. (1981). The supplementary motor area and speech emission. *Journal of Communication Disorders, 14,* 349–373.

Jones, E.G. (2000). Microcolumns in the cerebral cortex. *Proceedings of the National Academy of Sciences, 97,* 5019–5021.

Jones, J.A., & Munhall, K.G. (2005). Remapping auditory-motor representations in voice production. *Current Biology, 15,* 1768–1772.

Jones, O.P., Seghier, M.L., Duncan, K.J.K., Leff, A.P., Green, D.W., & Price, C.J. (2013). Auditory-motor interactions for the production of native and non-native speech. *Journal of Neuroscience, 33,* 2376–2387.

Jonkers, R., & Bastiaanse, R. (1996). The influence of instrumentality and transitivity on action naming in Broca's and anomic aphasia. *Brain and Language, 55,* 37–39.

Jonkers, R., & Bastiaanse, R. (1997). Verb retrieval in isolation and sentence context in Broca's aphasics: The effect of transitivity. *Brain and Language, 60,* 33–36.

Jonkers, R., & Bastiaanse, R. (1998). How selective are selective word class deficits? Two case studies of action and object naming. *Aphasiology, 12,* 245–256.

Joseph, J.E., Gathers, A.D., & Piper, G.A. (2003). Shared and dissociated cortical regions for object and letter processing. *Cognitive Brain Research, 17,* 56–67.

Josephs, K.A., Duffy, J.R., Strand, E.A., Whitwell, J.L., Layton, K.F., Parisi, J.E., Hauser, M.F., Witte, R.J., Boeve, B.F., Knopman, D.S., Dickson, D.W., Jack, C.R., & Petersen, R.C. (2006). Clinicopathological and imaging correlates of progressive aphasia and apraxia of speech. *Brain, 129,* 1385–1398.

Joynt, R.J., & Benton, A.L. (1964). The memoir of Marc Dax on aphasia. *Neurology, 14,* 851–854.

Juch, H., Zimine, I., Seghier, M.L., Lazeyras, F., & Fasel, J.H.D. (2005). Anatomical variability of the lateral frontal lobe surface: Implication for intersubject variability in language neuroimaging. *NeuroImage, 24,* 504–514.

Jung, R.E., & Haier, R.J. (2007). The parieto-frontal integration theory (P-FIT) of intelligence: Converging neuroimaging evidence. *Behavioral and Brain Sciences, 30,* 135–187.

Jürgens, U. (2002). Neural pathways underlying vocal control. *Neuroscience and Biobehavioral Reviews, 26,* 235–258.

Just, M., Carpenter, P., & Keller, T.A. (1996a). The capacity theory of comprehension: New frontiers of evidence and arguments. *Psychological Review, 103,* 773–780.

Just, M., Carpenter, P., Keller, T.A., Eddy, W.F., & Thulborn, K.R. (1996b). Brain activation modulated by sentence comprehension. *Science, 274,* 114–116.

Kaan, E. (2007). Event-related potentials and language processing: A brief introduction. *Language and Linguistics Compass, 1,* 571–591.

Kaan, E., Harris, A., Gibson, E., & Holcomb, P.J. (2000). The P600 as an index of syntactic integration difficulty. *Language and Cognitive Processes, 15,* 159–201.

Kaan, E., & Swaab, T.Y. (2002). The brain circuitry of syntactic comprehension. *Trends in Cognitive Sciences, 6,* 350–356.

Kaan, E., & Swaab, T.Y. (2003). Electrophysiological evidence for serial sentence processing: A comparison between non-preferred and ungrammatical continuations. *Cognitive Brain Research, 17,* 621–635.

Kable, J.W., Kan, I.P., Wilson, A., Thompson-Schill, S.L., & Chatterjee, A. (2005). Conceptual representations of action in the lateral temporal cortex. *Journal of Cognitive Neuroscience, 17,* 1855–1870.

Kable, J.W., Lease-Spellmeyer, J., & Chatterjee, A. (2002). Neural substrates of action event knowledge. *Journal of Cognitive Neuroscience, 14,* 795–805.

Kaczmarek, B.L.J. (1984). Neurolinguistic analysis of verbal utterances in patients with focal lesions of frontal lobes. *Brain and Language, 21,* 52–58.

Kadyamusuma, M.R., De Bleser, R., & Mayer, J. (2011). Lexical tone disruption in Shona after brain damage. *Aphasiology, 25,* 1239–1260.

Kan, I.P., Barsalou, L.W., Solomon, K.O., Minor, J.K., & Thompson-Schill, S.L. (2003). Role of mental imagery in a property verification task: fMRI evidence for perceptual representations. *Cognitive Neuropsychology, 20,* 525–540.

Kan, I.P., Kable, J.W., Van Scoyoc, A., Chatterjee, A., & Thompson-Schill, S.L. (2006). Fractionating the left frontal response to tools: Dissociable effects of motor experience and lexical competition. *Journal of Cognitive Neuroscience, 18,* 267–277.

Kandel, E. (2006). *In search of memory.* New York: Norton.

Kanwisher, N., & Yovel, G. (2006). The fusiform face area: A cortical region specialized for the perception of faces. *Philosophical Transactions of the Royal Society, B, 361,* 2109–2128.

Kappenman, E.S., & Luck, S.J. (2012). ERP components: The ups and downs of brainwave recordings. In S.J. Luck & E.S. Kappenman (Eds.), *The Oxford handbook of event-related potential components* (pp. 3–30). Oxford, UK: Oxford University Press.

Karow, C.M., Marquardt, T.P., & Marshall, R.C. (2001). Affective processing in left and right hemisphere brain-damaged subjects with and without subcortical involvement. *Aphasiology, 15,* 715–729.

Kassubek, J., Hickok, G., & Erhard, P. (2004). Involvement of classical anterior and posterior language areas in sign language production, as investigated by 4T functional magnetic resonance imaging. *Neurocience Letters, 364,* 168–172.

Katzev, M., Tüscher, O., Hennig, J., Weiller, C., & Kaller, C.P. (2013). Revisiting the functional specialization of left inferior frontal gyrus in phonological and semantic fluency: The crucial role of task demands and individual ability. *Journal of Neuroscience, 33,* 7837–7845.

Kayser, C., Petkov, C.I., Augath, M., & Logothetis, N.K. (2005). Integration of touch and sound in auditory cortex. *Neuron, 48,* 373–384.

Kean, M.L. (Ed.) (1985). *Agrammatism.* Orlando, FL: Academic Press.

Kellenbach, M.L., Brett, M., & Patterson, K. (2001). Large, colorful, or noisy? Attribute- and modality-specific activations during retrieval of perceptual attribute knowledge. *Cognitive, Affective, and Behavioral Neuroscience, 1,* 207–221.

Keller, T.A., Carpenter, P.A., & Just, M.A. (2001). The neural bases of sentence comprehension: An fMRI examination of syntactic and lexical processing. *Cerebral Cortex, 11,* 223–237.

Kemmerer, D. (1999). Impaired comprehension of raising-to-subject constructions in Parkinson's disease. *Brain and Language, 66,* 311–328.

Kemmerer, D. (2000). Grammatically relevant and grammatically irrelevant features of verb meaning can be independently impaired. *Aphasiology, 14,* 997–1020.

Kemmerer, D. (2003). Why can you *hit someone on the arm* but not *break someone on the arm*? A neuropsychological investigation of the English body-part possessor ascension construction. *Journal of Neurolinguistics, 16,* 13–36.

Kemmerer, D. (2005). The spatial and temporal meanings of English prepositions can be independently impaired. *Neuropsychologia, 43,* 797–806.

Kemmerer, D. (2006a). Action verbs, argument structure constructions, and the mirror neuron system. In M. Arbib (Ed.), *Action to language via the mirror neuron system* (pp. 347–373). Cambridge, UK: Cambridge University Press.

Kemmerer, D. (2006b). The semantics of space: Integrating linguistic typology and cognitive neuroscience. *Neuropsychologia, 44,* 1607–1621.

Kemmerer, D. (2010a). A neuroscientific perspective on the linguistic encoding of categorical spatial relations. In V. Evans & P. Chilton (Eds.), *Language, cognition, and space: The state of the art and new directions* (pp. 139–168). London: Equinox.

Kemmerer, D. (2010b). How words capture visual experience: The perspective from cognitive neuroscience. In B. Malt & P. Wolff (Eds.), *Words and the mind: How words capture human experience* (pp. 289–329). Oxford, UK: Oxford University Press.

Kemmerer, D. (2012). The cross-linguistic prevalence of SOV and SVO word orders reflects the sequential and hierarchical representation of action in Broca's area. *Language and Linguistics Compass, 6,* 50–66.

Kemmerer, D. (2014). Word classes in the brain: Implications of linguistic typology for cognitive neuroscience. *Cortex, 58,* 27–51.

Kemmerer, D., Chandrasekaran, B., & Tranel, D. (2007). A case of impaired verbalization but preserved gesticulation of motion events. *Cognitive Neuropsychology, 24,* 70–114.

Kemmerer, D., & Eggleston, A. (2010). Nouns and verbs in the brain: Implications of linguistic typology for cognitive neuroscience. *Lingua, 120,* 2686–2690.

Kemmerer, D., & Gonzalez Castillo, J. (2010). The two-level theory of verb meaning: An approach to integrating the semantics of action with the mirror neuron system. *Brain and Language, 112,* 54–76.

Kemmerer, D., Gonzalez Castillo, J., Talavage, T., Patterson, S., & Wiley, C. (2008). Neuroanatomical distribution of five semantic components of verbs: Evidence from fMRI. *Brain and Language, 107,* 16–43.

Kemmerer, D., Manzel, K., & Tranel, D. (2005). An exaggerated effect for proper nouns in a case of superior written over spoken naming. *Cognitive Neuropsychology, 22*, 3–27.

Kemmerer, D., Rudrauf, D., Manzel, K., & Tranel, D. (2012). Behavioral patterns and lesion sites associated with impaired processing of lexical and conceptual knowledge of actions. *Cortex, 48*, 826–848.

Kemmerer, D., & Tranel, D. (2000). Verb retrieval in brain-damaged subjects: 1. Analysis of stimulus, lexical, and conceptual factors. *Brain and Language, 73*, 347–392.

Kemmerer, D., & Tranel, D. (2003). A double dissociation between the meanings of action verbs and locative prepositions. *Neurocase, 9*, 421–435.

Kemmerer, D., & Tranel, D. (2008). Searching for the elusive neural substrates of body part terms: A neuropsychological study. *Cognitive Neuropsychology, 25*, 601–629.

Kemmerer, D., & Wright, S.K. (2002). Selective impairment of knowledge underlying *un*- prefixation: Further evidence for the autonomy of grammatical semantics. *Journal of Neurolinguistics, 15*, 403–432.

Kertesz, A. (1982). *Western aphasia battery*. New York: Grune & Stratton.

Kertesz, A., Davidson, W., McCabe, P., Takagi, K., & Munoz, D. (2003). Primary progressive aphasia: Diagnosis, varieties, and evolution. *Journal of the International Neuropsychological Society, 9*, 710–709.

Kertesz, A., & Munoz, D. (2004). Relationship between frontotemporal dementia and corticobasal degeneration/progressive supranuclear palsy. *Dementia and Geriatric Cognitive Disorders, 17*, 282–286.

Kertesz, A., Sheppar, A., & MacKenzie, R. (1982). Localization in transcortical sensory aphasia. *Archives of Neurology, 39*, 475–478.

Kherif, F., Josse, G., & Price, C.J. (2011). Automatic top-down processing explains common left occipito-temporal responses to visual words and objects. *Cerebral Cortex, 21*, 103–114.

Kho, K.H., Indefrey, P., Hagoort, P., van Veelen, C.W.M., van Rijen, P.C., & Ramsey, N.F. (2008). Unimpaired sentence comprehension after anterior temporal cortex resection. *Neuropsychologia, 46*, 1170–1178.

Kiefer, M., & Pulvermüller, F. (2012). Conceptual representations in mind and brain: Theoretical developments, current evidence and future directions. *Cortex, 48*, 805–825.

Kiefer, M., Sim, E.-J., Herrnberger, B., & Hoenig, K. (2008). The sound of concepts: Four markers for a link between auditory and conceptual brain systems. *Journal of Neuroscience, 28*, 12224–12230.

Kiefer, M., Trumpp, N., Herrnberger, B., Sim, E.J., Hoenig, K., & Pulvermüller, F. (2012). Dissociating the representation of action- and sound-related concepts. *Brain and Language, 122*, 120–125.

Kielar, A., Milman, L., Bonakdarpour, B., & Thompson, C.K. (2011). Neural correlates of covert and overt production of tense and agreement morphology: Evidence from fMRI. *Journal of Neurolinguistics, 24*, 183–201.

Kim, A., & Osterhout, L. (2005). The independence of combinatory semantic processing: Evidence from event-related potentials. *Journal of Memory and Language, 52*, 205–225.

Kim, M., & Thompson, C.K. (2000). Patterns of comprehension and production of nouns and verbs in agrammatism: Implications for lexical organization. *Brain and Language, 74*, 1–25.

Kim, M., & Thompson, C.K. (2004). Verb deficits in Alzheimer's disease and agrammatism: Implications for lexical organization. *Brain and Language, 88*, 1–20.

Kimura, D. (1981). Neural mechanisms in manual signing. *Sign Language Studies, 33*, 291–312.

King, J., & Kutas, M. (1995). Who did what when? Using word- and clause-level ERPs to monitor working memory usage in reading. *Journal of Cognitive Neuroscience, 7*, 376–395.

Kinno, R., Muragaki, Y., Hori, T., Maruyama, T., Kawamura, M., & Sakai, K.L. (2009). Agrammatic comprehension caused by a glioma in the left frontal cortex. *Brain and Language, 110*, 71–80.

Kirshner, H.S., Alexander, M., Lorch, M.P., & Wertz, R.T. (1999). *Disorders of speech and language*. Baltimore: Lippincott, Williams & Wilkins.

Kirshner, H.S., Tanridag, O., Thurman, L., & Whetsell, W.O., Jr. (1987). Progressive aphasia without dementia: Two cases with focal, spongiform degeneration. *Annals of Neurology, 22*, 527–532.

Kiss, K. (2000). Effect of verb complexity on agrammatic aphasics' sentence production. In R. Bastiaanse & Y. Grodzinsky (Eds.), *Grammatical disorders in aphasia: A neurolinguistic perspective* (pp. 152–170). London: Whurr.

Klein, D., Zatorre, R.J., Milner, B., & Zhao, V. (2001). A cross-linguistic PET study of tone perception in Mandarin Chinese and English speakers. *NeuroImage, 13*, 646–653.

Klein, R., & Harper, J. (1956). The problem of agnosia in the light of a case of pure word deafness. *Journal of Mental Science, 102*, 112–120.

Kleinschmidt, A., Lee, B.B., Requardt, M., & Frahm, J. (1996). Functional mapping of color processing by magnetic resonance imaging of responses to selective P- and M-pathway stimulation. *Experimental Brain Research, 110*, 279–288.

Kluender, R., & Kutas, M. (1993). Bridging the gap: Evidence from ERPs on the processing of unbounded dependencies. *Journal of Cognitive Neuroscience, 5*, 196–214.

Knecht, S., Deppe, M., Drager, B., Bobe, L., Lohmann, H., Ringelstein, E., & Henningen, H. (2000a). Language lateralization in healthy right-handers. *Brain, 123*, 74–81.

Knecht, S., Drager, B., Deppe, M., Bobe, L., Lohmann, H., Floel, A., Ringelstein, E., & Henningen, H. (2000b). Handedness and hemispheric language dominance in healthy humans. *Brain, 123*, 2512–2518.

Knibb, J.A., & Hodges, J.R. (2005). Semantic aphasia and primary progressive aphasia: A problem of categorization? *Alzheimer's Disease and Associated Disorders, 19*, S7–S14.

Knibb, J.A., Woollams, A.M., Hodges, J.R., & Patterson, K. (2009). Making sense of progressive non-fluent aphasia: An analysis of conversational speech. *Brain, 132*, 2734–2746.

Knoblich, G., Seigerschmidt, E., Flach, R., & Prinz, W. (2002). Authorship effects in the prediction of handwriting strokes: Evidence for action simulation during action perception. *Quarterly Journal of Experimental Psychology, 55*, 1027–1046.

Koechlin, E., & Jubault, T. (2006). Broca's area and the hierarchical organization of human behavior. *Neuron, 50*, 963–974.

Koenigs, M., Acheson, D., Barbey, A., Solomon, J., Postle, B.R., & Grafman, J. (2011). Areas of left perisylvian cortex mediate auditory-verbal short-term memory. *Neuropsychologia, 49*, 3612–3619.

Kohen, F., Milsark, G., & Martin, N. (2011). Effects of syntactic and semantic argument structure on sentence repetition in agrammatism: Things we can learn from particles and prepositions. *Aphasiology, 25*, 736–747.

Kolk, H.H., Van Grunsven, M.J.F., & Keyser, A. (1985). On parallelism between production and comprehension in agrammatism. In M.L. Kean (Ed.), *Agrammatism* (pp. 165–206). Orlando, FL: Academic Press.

Kosslyn, S.M., Pascual-Leone, A., Felician, O., Camposano, S., Keenan, J.P., Thompson, W.L., Ganis, G., Sukel, K.E., & Alpert, N.M. (1999). The role of area 17 in visual imagery: Convergent evidence from PET and rTMS. *Science, 284*, 167–170.

Kosslyn, S.M., Thompson, W.L., & Ganis, G. (2006). *The case for mental imagery.* Oxford: Oxford University Press.

Kotz, S.A., Kalberlah, C., Bahlmann, J., Friederici, A.D., & Haynes, J.D. (2013). Predicting vocal emotion expressions from the human brain. *Human Brain Mapping, 34*, 1971–1981.

Kotz, S.A., Meyer, M., Alter, K., Besson, M., von Cramon, D.Y., & Friederici, A.D. (2003). On the lateralization of emotional prosody: An event-related functional MR investigation. *Brain and Language, 86*, 366–376.

Kotz, S.A., Meyer, M., & Paulmann, S. (2006). Lateralization of emotional prosody in the brain: An overview and synopsis on the impact of study design. *Progress in Brain Research, 156*, 285–294.

Kotz, S.A., & Paulmann, S. (2011). Emotion, language, and the brain. *Language and Linguistics Compass, 5*, 108–125.

Kotz, S.A., & Schwartze, M. (2010). Cortical speech processing unplugged: A timely subcortico-cortical framework. *Trends in Cognitive Sciences, 14*, 392–399.

Kounios, J., & Holcomb, P.J. (1994). Concreteness effects in semantic processing: ERP evidence supporting dual-coding theory. *Journal of Experimental Psychology: Learning, Memory and Cognition, 20*, 804–823.

Kousta, S.T., Vigliocco, G., Vinson, D.P., Andrews, M., & Del Campo, E. (2011). The representation of abstract words: Why emotion matters. *Journal of Experimental Psychology: General, 140*, 14–34.

Kraemer, D.J., Macrae, C.N., Green, A.E., & Kelley, W.M. (2005). Musical imagery: Sound of silence activates auditory cortex. *Nature, 434*, 158.

Krainik, A., Lehericy, S., Duffau, H., Capelle, L., Chainay, H., Cornu, P., Cohen, L., Boch, A.L., Mangin, J.F., Le Bihan, D., & Marsault, C. (2003). Postoperative speech disorder after medial frontal surgery. *Neurology, 60*, 587–594.

Kranjec, A., & Chatterjee, A. (2010). Are temporal concepts embodied? A challenge for cognitive neuroscience. *Frontiers in Psychology, 1*, Article 240.

Kriefelts, B., Ethofer, T., Huberle, E., Grodd, W., & Wildgruber, D. (2010). Association of trait emotional intelligence and individual fMRI-activation patterns during the perception of social signals from voice and face. *Human Brain Mapping, 31*, 979–991.

Krieger-Redwood, K., Gaskell, M.G., Lindsay, S., & Jefferies, B. (in press). The selective role of premotor cortex in speech perception: A contribution to phoneme judgments but not speech comprehension. *Journal of Cognitive Neuroscience.*

Kriegeskorte, N. (2010). Interpreting brain images: Reflections on an adolescent field. *Trends in Cognitive Sciences, 14*, 475–476.

Krishnan, A., & Gandour, J.T. (2009). The role of the auditory brainstem in processing linguistically relevant pitch patterns. *Brain and Language, 110*, 135–148.

Kroll, J.F., & Merves, J.S. (1986). Lexical access for concrete and abstract words. *Journal of Experimental Psychology: Learning, Memory & Cognition, 12*, 92–107.

Kümmerer, D., Hartwigsen, G., Kellmeyer, P., Glauche, V., Mader, I., Klöppel, S., Suchan, J., Karnath, H.O., Weiller, C., & Saur, D. (2013). Damage to ventral and dorsal language pathways in acute aphasia. *Brain, 136*, 619–629.

Kuperberg, G. (2007). Neural mechanisms of language comprehension: Challenges to syntax. *Brain Research, 1146*, 23–49.

Kuperberg, G., Caplan, D., Sitnikova, T., Eddy, M., & Holcomb, P.J. (2006). Neural correlates of processing syntactic, semantic, and thematic relationships in sentences. *Language and Cognitive Processes, 21*, 489–530.

Kuperberg, G., McGuire, P.K., Bullmore, E.T., Brammer, M.J., Rabe-Hesketh, S., Wright, I.C., Lythgoe, D.J., Williams, S.C.R., & David, A.S. (2000). Common and distinct neural substrates for pragmatic, semantic, and syntactic processing of spoken sentences: An fMRI study. *Journal of Cognitive Neuroscience, 12*, 321–341.

Kuperberg, G., Sitnikova, T., Caplan, D., & Holcomb, P.J. (2003). Electrophysiological distinctions in processing conceptual relationships within simple sentences. *Cognitive Brain Research, 17*, 117–129.

Kuperberg, G., Sitnikova, T., & Lakshmanan, B. (2008). Neuroanatomical distinctions within the semantic system during sentence comprehension: Evidence from functional magnetic imaging. *NeuroImage, 40*, 367–388.

Kuperman, V., Stadhagen-Gonzalez, H., & Brysbaert, M. (2012). Age-of-acquisition ratings for 30 thousand English words. *Behavior Research Methods, 44*, 978–990.

Kuraoka, K., & Nakamura, K. (2007). Responses of single neurons in monkey amygdala to facial and vocal emotions. *Journal of Neurophysiology, 97*, 1379–1387.

Kutas, M., DeLong, K.A., & Smith, N.J. (2011). A look around at what lies ahead: Prediction and predictability in language processing. In M. Bar (Ed.), *Predictions in the brain* (pp. 190–207). Oxford, UK: Oxford University Press.

Kutas, M., & Federmeier, K.D. (2000). Electrophysiology reveals semantic memory use in language comprehension. *Trends in Cognitive Sciences, 4*, 463–470.

Kutas, M., & Federmeier, K.D. (2011). Thirty years and counting: Finding meaning in the N400 component of the event-related brain potential (ERP). *Annual Review of Psychology, 62*, 621–647.

Kutas, M., & Hillyard, S.A. (1980). Reading senseless sentences: Brain potentials reflect semantic incongruity. *Science, 207*, 203–205.

Kutas, M., van Petten, C.K., & Kluender, R. (2006). Psycholinguistics electrified II. In M.J. Traxler & M.A. Gernsbacher (Eds.), *Handbook of psycholinguistics*, 2nd edition (pp. 659–724). San Diego: Academic Press.

Kwon, H., Kuriki, S., Kim, J.M., Lee, Y.H., Kim, K., & Nam, K. (2005). MEG study on neural activities associated with syntactic and semantic violations in spoken Korean sentences. *Neuroscience Research, 51,* 349–357.

Laeng, B., Chabris, C.F., & Kosslyn, S.M. (2003). Asymmetries in encoding spatial relations. In K. Hugdahl & R. Davidson (Eds.), *The asymmetrical brain* (pp. 303–339). Cambridge, MA: MIT Press.

Laiacona, M., Barbarotto, R., & Capitani, E. (1993). Perceptual and associative knowledge in category-specific impairment of semantic memory: A study of two cases. *Cortex, 727–740.*

Laiacona, M., Barbarotto, R., & Capitani, E. (2006). Human evolution and the brain representation of semantic knowledge: Is there a role for sex differences? *Evolution and Human Behavior, 27,* 158–168.

Laiacona, M., & Caramazza, A. (2004). The noun/verb dissociation in language production: Varieties of causes. *Cognitive Neuropsychology, 21,* 103–123.

Laine, M., & Martin, N. (2006). *Anomia: Theoretical and clinical aspects.* Hove, UK: Psychology Press.

Lakoff, G., & Johnson, M. (1980). *Metaphors we live by.* Chicago: University of Chicago Press.

Lambon Ralph, M.A., Cipolotti, L., Manes, F., & Patterson, K. (2010a). Taking both sides: Do unilateral anterior temporal lobe lesions disrupt semantic memory? *Brain, 133,* 3243–3255.

Lambon Ralph, M.A., Ehsan, S., Baker, G.A., & Rogers, T.T. (2012). Semantic memory is impaired in patients with unilateral anterior temporal lobe resection for temporal lobe epilepsy. *Brain, 135,* 242–258.

Lambon Ralph, M.A., Ellis, A.W., & Franklin, S. (1995). Semantic loss without surface dyslexia. *Neurocase, 1,* 363–369.

Lambon Ralph, M.A., Graham, K.S., Ellis, A.W., & Hodges, J.R. (1998). Naming in semantic dementia: What matters? *Neuropsychologia, 36,* 775–784.

Lambon Ralph, M.A., Graham, K.S., Patterson, K., & Hodges, J.R. (1999). Is a picture worth a thousand words? Evidence from concept definitions by patients with semantic dementia. *Brain and Language, 70,* 309–335.

Lambon Ralph, M.A., Howard, D., Nightingale, G., & Ellis, A.W. (1998). Are living and nonliving category-specific deficits causally linked to impaired perceptual or associative knowledge? Evidence from a category-specific double dissociation. *Neurocase, 4,* 311–338.

Lambon Ralph, M.A., Lowe, C., & Rogers, T.T. (2007). Neural basis of category-specific semantic deficits for living things: Evidence from semantic dementia, HSVE, and a neural network model. *Brain, 130,* 1127–1137.

Lambon Ralph, M.A., & Patterson, K. (2008). Generalization and differentiation in semantic memory. *Annals of the New York Academy of Sciences, 1124,* 61–76.

Lambon Ralph, M.A., Patterson, K., Garrard, P., & Hodges, J.R. (2003). Semantic dementia with category specificity: A comparative case-series study. *Cognitive Neuropsychology, 20,* 307–326.

Lambon Ralph, M.A., Pobric, G., & Jefferies, E. (2009). Conceptual knowledge is underpinned by the temporal pole bilaterally: Convergent evidence from rTMS. *Cerebral Cortex, 19,* 832–838.

Lambon Ralph, M.A., Sage, K., Jones, R.W., & Mayberry, E.J. (2010b). Coherent concepts are computed in the anterior temporal lobes. *Proceedings of the National Academy of Sciences, 107,* 2717–2722.

Lametti, D.R., Nasir, S.M., & Ostry, D.J. (2012). Sensory preference in speech production revealed by simultaneous alteration of auditory and somatosensory feedback. *Journal of Neuroscience, 32,* 9351–9358.

Landau, B., & Jackendoff, R. (1993). "What" and "where" in spatial language and spatial cognition. *Behavioral and Brain Sciences, 16,* 217–238.

Langacker, R.W. (2008). *Cognitive grammar: A basic introduction.* Oxford, UK: Oxford University Press.

Laplane, D., Talairach, J., Meininger, V., Bancaud, J., & Orgogozo, J.M. (1977). Clinical consequences of corticectomies involving the supplementary motor area in man. *Journal of the Neurological Sciences, 34,* 301–314.

Lapointe, S.G. (1985). A theory of verb form use in the speech of agrammatic aphasics. *Brain and Language, 24,* 100–155.

Lapointe, S.G., & Dell, G.S. (1989). A synthesis of some recent work in sentence production. In G.N. Carlson & M.K. Tanenhaus (Eds.), *Linguistic structure in language processing.* Dordrecht: Kluwer.

LaPolla, R.J., Kratochvíl, F., & Coupe, A.R. (2011). On transitivity. *Studies in Language, 35,* 469–491.

Lau, E.F., Phillips, C., & Poeppel, D. (2008). A cortical network for semantics: (de)constructing the N400. *Nature Reviews Neuroscience, 9,* 920–933.

Leaver, A.M., & Rauschecker, J.P. (2010). Cortical representation of natural complex sounds: Effects of acoustic features and auditory object category. *Journal of Neuroscience, 30,* 7604–7612.

Le Ber, I., Camuzat, A., Hannequin, D., Pasquier, F., Guedj, E., Rovelet-Lecrux, A., Hahn-Barma, V., van der Zee, J., Clot, F., Bakchine, S., Puel, M., Ghanim, M., Lacomblez, L., Mikol, J., Deramecourt, V., Lejeune, P., de la Sayette, V., Belliard, S., Vercelletto, M., Meyrignac, C., Van Broeckhoven, C., Lambert, J.C., Verpillat, P., Campion, D., Habert, M.O., & Dubois, B. (2008). Phenotype variability in progranulin mutation carriers: A clinical, neuropsychological, imaging, and genetic study. *Brain, 131,* 732–746.

Lee, C., Grossman, M., Morris, J., Stern, M.B., & Hurtig, H.I. (2003). Attentional resource and processing speed limitations during sentence processing in Parkinson's disease. *Brain and Language, 85,* 347–356.

Leech, R., & Saygin, A.P. (2011). Distributed processing and cortical specialization for speech and environmental sounds in human temporal cortex. *Brain and Language, 116,* 83–90.

Leff, A.P., Crewes, H., Plant, G.T., Scott, S.K., Kennard, C., & Wise, R.J.S. (2001). The functional anatomy of single-word reading in patients with hemianopic and pure alexia. *Brain, 124,* 510–521.

Leff, A.P., Schofield, T.M., Crinion, J.T., Seghier, M.L., Grogan, A., Green, D.W., & Price, C.J. (2009). The left superior temporal gyrus is a shared substrate for auditory short-term memory and speech comprehension: Evidence from 210 patients with stroke. *Brain, 132,* 3401–3410.

Lehtonen, M., Monahan, P.J., & Poeppel, D. (2011). Evidence for early morphological decomposition:

Combining masked priming with magnetoencephalography. *Journal of Cognitive Neuroscience, 23*, 3366–3379.

Lehtonen, M., Vorobyev, V.A., Hugdahl, K., Tuokkola, T., & Laine, M. (2006). Neural correlates of morphological decomposition in a morphologically rich language: An fMRI study. *Brain and Language, 98*, 182–193.

Leinonen, L., Hyvarinen, J., & Sovijarvi, A.R.A. (1980). Functional properties of neurons in the temporo-parietal association cortex of awake monkey. *Experimental Brain Research, 39*, 203–215.

Leitman, D.I., Wolf, D.H., Ragland, D., Laukka, P., Loughead, J., Valdez, J.N., Javitt, D.C., Turetsky, B.I., & Gur, R.C. (2010). "It's not what you say, but how you say it": A reciprocal temporo-frontal network for affective prosody. *Frontiers in Human Neuroscience, 4*, Article 19.

Lelekov, T., Franck, N., Dominey, P.F., & Georgieff, N. (2000). Dissociable ERP profiles for processing rules vs. instances in a cognitive sequencing task. *NeuroReport, 11*, 2145–2149.

Lelekov-Boissard, T., & Dominey, P.F. (2002). Human brain potentials reveal similar processing of non-linguistic abstract structure and linguistic syntactic structure. *Clinical Neurophysiology, 32*, 72–84.

Lenneberg, E.H. (1962). Understanding language without the ability to speak: A case report. *Journal of Abnormal Social Psychology, 65*, 419–425.

Levelt, W.J.M. (1989). *Speaking: From intention to articulation*. Cambridge, MA: MIT Press.

Levelt, W.J.M. (1992). Accessing words in speech production: Stages, processes, and representations. *Cognition, 42*, 1–22.

Levelt, W.J.M. (1999a). Models of word production. *Trends in cognitive sciences, 3*, 223–232.

Levelt, W.J.M. (1999b). Producing spoken language: A blueprint of the speaker. In C.M. Brown & P. Hagoort (Eds.), *The neurocognition of language* (pp. 83–122). Oxford, UK: Oxford University Press.

Levelt, W.J.M. (2001). Spoken word production: A theory of lexical access. *Proceedings of the National Academy of Sciences, 98*, 13464–13471.

Levelt, W.J.M., Roelofs, A., & Meyer, A.S. (1999). A theory of lexical access in speech production. *Behavioral and Brain Sciences, 22*, 1–75.

Levelt, W.J.M., Schriefers, H., Vorberg, D., Meyer, A.S., Pechmann, T., & Havinga, J. (1991). The time course of lexical access in speech production: A study of picture naming. *Psychological Review, 98*, 122–142.

Levelt, W.J.M., & Wheeldon, L. (1994). Do speakers have access to a mental syllabary? *Cognition, 50*, 239–269.

Levin, B. (1993). *English verb classes and alternations*. Chicago: University of Chicago Press.

Levin, B., & Rappaport Hovav, M. (2005). *Argument realization*. Cambridge, UK: Cambridge University Press.

Levinson, S.C. (2003). *Space in language and cognition: Explorations in cognitive diversity*. Cambridge, UK: Cambridge University Press.

Levinson, S.C., & Wilkins, D. (2006). *Grammars of space: Explorations in cognitive diversity*. Cambridge, UK: Cambridge University Press.

Levy, B.J., & Wagner, A.D. (2011). Cognitive control and right ventrolateral prefrontal cortex: Reflexive reorienting, motor inhibition, and actiton updating. *Annals of the New York Academy of Sciences, 1224*, 40–62.

Levy, J., Pernet, C., Treserras, S., Boulanouar, K., Aubry, F., Démonet, J.F., & Celsis, P. (2009). Testing the Dual-Route Cascade reading model in the brain: An fMRI effective connectivity account of an efficient reading style. *PLoS ONE, 4*, e6675.

Levy, J., Pernet, C., Treserras, S., Boulanouar, K., Berry, I., Aubry, F., Démonet, J.F., & Celsis, P. (2008). Piecemeal recruitment of left lateralized brain areas during reading: A spatio-functional account. *NeuroImage, 43*, 581–591.

Lewis, J.W. (2006). Cortical networks related to human use of tools. *The Neuroscientist, 12*, 211–231.

Lewis, J.W., Wightman, F., Brefczynski, J.A., Phinney, R.E., Binder, J.R., & DeYoe, E.A. (2004). Human brain regions involved in recognizing environmental sounds. *Cerebral Cortex, 14*, 1008–1021.

Leyton, C.E., Villemagne, V.L., Savage, S., Pike, K.E., Ballard, K.J., Piguet, O., Burrell, J.R., Rowe, C.C., & Hodges, J.R. (2011). Subtypes of progressive aphasia: Application of the international consensus criteria and validation using beta-amyloid imaging. *Brain, 134*, 3030–3043.

Li, X., Gandour, J., Talavage, T., Wong, D., Dzemidzic, M., Lowe, M., & Tong, Y. (2003). Selective attention to Chinese tones recruits left dorsal frontoparietal network. *NeuroReport, 14*(17), 2263–2266.

Li, X., Shu, H., Liu, Y., & Li, P. (2006). Mental representation of verb meaning: Behavioral and electrophysiological evidence. *Journal of Cognitive Neuroscience, 18*, 1774–1787.

Liang, J., & Heuven, V.J. (2004). Evidence for separate tonal and segmental tiers in the lexical specification of words: A case study of a brain-damaged Chinese speaker. *Brain and Language, 91*, 282–293.

Liberman, A.M., Cooper, F.S., Shankweiler, D.P., & Studdert-Kennedy, M. (1967). Perception of the speech code. *Psychological Review, 74*, 431–461.

Libon, D.J., Rascovsky, K., Powers, J., Irwin, D.J., Boller, A., Weinberg, D., McMillan, C.T., & Grossman, M. (2013). Comparative semantic profiles in semantic dementia and Alzheimer's disease. *Brain, 136*, 2497–2509.

Lichtheim, L. (1885). On aphasia. *Brain, 7*, 433–484.

Lichtman, J.W., Livet, J., & Sanes, J.R. (2009). A technicolour approach to the connectome. *Nature Reviews Neuroscience, 9*, 417–422.

Liddell, S., & Johnson, R.E. (1989). American Sign Language: The phonological base. *Sign Language Studies, 64*, 197–277.

Liebenthal, E., Binder, J.R., Spitzer, S.M., Possing, E.T., & Medler, D.A. (2005). Neural substrates of phonemic perception. *Cerebral Cortex, 15*, 1621–1631.

Liebenthal, E., Desai, R., Ellingson, M.M., Ramachandran, B., Desai, A., & Binder, J.R. (2010). Specialization along the left superior temporal sulcus for auditory categorization. *Cerebral Cortex, 20*, 2958–2970.

Lieberman, P. (2002). *Human language and our reptilian brain: The subcortical bases of speech, syntax, and thought*. Cambridge, MA: Harvard University Press.

Lieberman, P., Friedman, J., & Feldman, L. (1990). Syntax comprehension in Parkinson's disease. *Journal of Nervous and Mental Disease, 178*, 360–366.

Lieberman, P., Kako, E., Friedman, J., Tajchman, G., Feldman, L., & Jiminez, E. (1992). Speech production, syntax comprehension, amd cognitive deficits in Parkinson's disease. *Brain and Language, 43,* 169–189.

Liégeois-Chauvel, C., de Graf, J.B., Laguitton, V., & Chauvel, P. (1999). Specialization of left auditory cortex for speech perception in man depends on temporal coding. *Cerebral Cortex, 9,* 484–496.

Lightman, A. (1993). *Einstein's Dreams.* New York: Pantheon.

Lin, L., Chen, G., Kuang, H., Wang, D., & Tsien, J.Z. (2007). Neural encoding of the concept of nest in the mouse brain. *Proceedings of the National Academy of Sciences, 104,* 6066–6071.

Lin, N., Lu, X., Fang, F., Han, Z., & Bi, Y. (2011). Is the semantic category effect in the lateral temporal cortex due to motion property differences? *NeuroImage, 55,* 1853–1864.

Linden, D.E.J., Thornton, K., Kuswanto, C.N., Johnston, S.J., van de Ven, V., & Jackson, M.C. (2011). The brain's voices: Comparing nonclinical auditory hallucinations and imagery. *Cerebral Cortex, 21,* 330–337.

Lindquist, K.A., Wager, T.D., Kober, H., Bliss-Moreau, E., & Barrett, L.F. (2012). The brain basis of emotion: A meta-analytic review. *Behavioral and Brain Sciences, 35,* 121–202.

Lissauer, H. (1890/1988). A case of visual agnosia with a contribution to theory (M. Jackson, Trans.). *Cognitive Neuropsychology, 5,* 157–192.

Liu, C., Zhang, W.T., Tang, Y.Y., Mai, X.Q., Chen, H.C., Tardif, T., & Luo, Y.J. (2008). The visual word form area: Evidence from an fMRI study of implicit processing of Chinese characters. *NeuroImage, 40,* 1350–1361.

Liu, W., Miller, B.L., Kramer, J.H., Rankin, K., Wyss-Coray, C., Gearhart, R., Phengrasamy, L., Weiner, M., & Rosen, H.J. (2004). Behavioral disorders in the frontal and temporal variants of frontotemporal dementia. *Neurology, 62,* 742–748.

Locatelli, M., Gatti, R., & Tettamanti, M. (2012). Training of manual actions improves language understanding of semantically related action sentences. *Frontiers in Psychology, 3,* Article 547.

Logothetis, N.K. (2008). What we can do what we cannot do with fMRI. *Nature, 453,* 869–878.

Loiselle, M., Rouleau, I., Nguyen, D.K., Dubeau, F., Macoir, J., Whatmough, C., Lepore, F., & Joubert, S. (2012). Comprehension of concrete and abstract words in patients with selective anterior temporal lobe resection and in patients with selective amygdalo-hippocampectomy. *Neuropsychologia, 50,* 630–639.

Londei, A., D'Ausilio, A., Basso, D., Sestieri, C., Del Gratta, C., Romani, G.-L., & Belardinelli, M.O. (2010). Sensory-motor brain network connectivity for speech comprehension. *Human Brain Mapping, 31,* 567–580.

Longcamp, M., Anton, J.L., Roth, M., & Velay, J.L. (2003). Visual presentation of single letters activates a premotor area involved in writing. *NeuroImage, 19,* 1492–1500.

Longcamp, M., Anton, J.L., Roth, M., & Velay, J.L. (2005a). Premotor activations in response to visually presented single letters depend on the hand used to write: A study in left-handers. *Neuropsychologia, 43,* 1801–1809.

Longcamp, M., Boucard, C., Gilhodes, J.C., & Velay, J.L. (2006). Remembering the orientation of newly learned characters depends on the associated writing knowledge: A comparison between handwriting and typing. *Human Movement Science, 25,* 646–656.

Longcamp, M., Boucard, C., Gilhodes, J.C., Anton, J.L., Roth, M., Nazarian, B., & Velay, J.L. (2008). Learning through hand- or typewriting influences visual recognition of new graphic shapes: Behavioral and functional imaging evidence. *Journal of Cognitive Neuroscience, 20,* 802–815.

Longcamp, M., Zerbato-Poudou, M.T., & Velay, J.L. (2005b). The influence of writing practice on letter recognition in preschool children: A comparison between handwriting and typing. *Acta Psychologica, 119,* 67–79.

Longe, O., Randall, B., Stamatakis, E.A., & Tyler, L.K. (2007). Grammatical categories in the brain: The role of morphological structure. *Cerebral Cortex, 17,* 1812–1820.

Longworth, C.E., Keenan, S.E., Barker, R.A., Marslen-Wilson, W.D., & Tyler, L.K. (2005a). The basal ganglia and rule-governed language use: Evidence from vascular and degenerative conditions. *Brain, 128,* 584–596.

Longworth, C.E., Marslen-Wilson, W.D., Randall, B., & Tyler, L.K. (2005b). Getting to the meaning of the regular past tense: Evidence from neuropsychology. *Journal of Cognitive Neuroscience, 17,* 1087–1097.

Lorenzen, B., & Murray, L.L. (2008). Bilingual aphasia: A theoretical and clinical review. *American Journal of Speech Language Pathology, 17,* 299–317.

Lotto, A.J., Hickok, G.S., & Holt, L.L. (2009). Reflections on mirror neurons and speech perception. *Trends in Cognitive Sciences, 13,* 110–114.

Lotze, M., Seggewies, G., Erb, M., Grodd, W., & Birbaumer, N. (2000). The representation of articulation in the primary sensorimotor cortex. *NeuroReport, 11,* 2985–2989.

Lucas, T.H., McKhann, G.M., & Ojemann, G.A. (2004). Functional separation of languages in the bilingual brain: A comparison of electrical stimulation in language mapping in 25 bilingual patients and 117 monolingual patients. *Journal of Neurosurgery, 101,* 449–457.

Luce, P.A., & Pisoni, D.B. (1998). Recognizing spoken words: The neighborhood activation model. *Ear and Hearing, 19,* 1–36.

Luck, S.J. (2005). *An introduction to the event-related potential technique.* Cambridge, MA: MIT Press.

Lueck, C.J., Zeki, S., Friston, K.J., Deiber, M.P., Cope, P., Cunningham, V.J., Lammertsma, A.A., Kennard, C., & Frackowiak, R.S. (1989). The color centre in the cerebral cortex of man. *Nature, 340,* 386–389.

Lukatela, G., & Turvey, M.T. (1994a). Visual lexical access is initially phonological: I. Evidence from associative priming by words, homophones, and pseudohomophones. *Journal of Experimental Psychology: General, 123,* 107–128.

Lukatela, G., & Turvey, M.T. (1994b). Visual lexical access is initially phonological: I. Evidence from phonological priming by homophones and pseudohomophones. *Journal of Experimental Psychology: General, 123,* 331–353.

Luo, H., & Poeppel, D. (2007). Phase patterns of neuronal responses reliably discriminate speech in human auditory cortex. *Neuron, 54,* 1001–1010.

Luo, H., & Poeppel, D. (2012). Cortical oscillations in auditory perception and speech: Evidence for two temporal windown in human auditory cortex. *Frontiers in Psychology, 3*, Article 170.

Luria, A.R. (1966). *Higher cortical functions in man*. New York: Basic Books.

Luria, A.R. (1970). *Traumatic aphasia*. The Hague: Mouton.

Luria, A.R., & Tsvetkova, L. (1967). Towards the mechanisms of "dynamic aphasia." *Acta Neurologica et Psychiatrica Belgica, 67*, 1045–1057.

Luzzatti, C., Raggi, R., Zonca, G., Pistarini, C., Contardi, A., & Pinna, G.D. (2002). Verb-noun double dissociation in aphasic lexical impairments: The role of word frequency and imageability. *Brain and Language, 81*, 432–444.

Luzzi, S., Snowden, J.S., Neary, D., Coccia, M., Provinciali, L., & Lambon Ralph, M.A. (2007). Distinct patterns of olfactory impairment in Alzheimer's disease, semantic dementia, frontotemporal dementia, and corticobasal degeneration. *Neuropsychologia, 45*, 1823–1831.

Lyons, I.M., Mattarella-Micke, A., Cieslak, M., Nusbaum, H.C., & Small, S.L. (2010). The role of personal experience in the neural processing of action-related language. *Brain and Language, 112*, 214–222.

Maass, A., & Russo, A. (2003). Directional bias in the mental representation of spatial events: Nature or culture? *Psychological Science, 14*, 296–301.

Maassen, B., & van Lieshout, P.H.H.M. (Eds.) (2010). *Speech motor control: New developments in basic and applied research*. Oxford: Oxford University Press.

MacDonald, M.C. (2013). How language production shapes language form and comprehension. *Frontiers in Psychology, 4*, Article 226.

MacDonald, M.C., & Seidenberg, M.S. (2006). Constraint satisfaction accounts of lexical and sentence comprehension. In M.J. Traxler & M.A. Gernsbacher (Eds.), *Handbook of psycholinguistics*, 2nd edition (pp. 581–612). San Diego: Academic Press.

MacGregor, L.J., Pulvermüller, F., van Casteren, M., & Shtyrov, Y. (2012). Ultra-rapid access to words in the brain. *Nature Communications, 3*, Article 711.

Machery, E. (2007). Concept empiricism: A methodological critique. *Cognition, 104*, 19–46.

Machulda, M.M., Whitwell, J.L., Duffy, J.R., Strand, E.A., Dean, P.M., Senjam, M.L., Jack, C.R., & Josephs, K.A. (in press). Identification of an atypical variant of logopenic progressive aphasia. *Brain and Language*.

MacKay, D.G. (1970). Spoonerisms: The structure of errors in the serial order of speech. *Neuropsychologia, 8*, 323–350.

Macoir, J. (2009). Is a plum a memory problem? Longitudinal study of the reversal of the concreteness effect in a patient with semantic dementia. *Neuropsychologia, 47*, 518–535.

MacSweeney, M., Campbell, R., Woll, B., Giampietro, V., David, A.S., McGuire, P.K., Calvert, G.A., & Brammer, M.J. (2004). Dissociating linguistic and nonlinguistic gestural communication in the brain. *NeuroImage, 22*, 1605–1618.

MacSweeney, M., Capek, C.M., Campbell, R., & Woll, B. (2008). The signing brain: The neurobiology of sign language. *Trends in Cognitive Sciences, 12*, 432–440.

MacSweeney, M., Woll, B., Campbell, R., Calvert, G.A., McGuire, P.K., David, A.S., Simmons, A., & Brammer, M.J. (2002b). Neural correlates of British Sign Language comprehension: Spatial correlates of topographic language. *Journal of Cognitive Neuroscience, 14*, 1064–1075.

MacSweeney, M., Woll, B., Campbell, R., McGuire, P.K., David, A.S., Williams, S.C.R., Suckling, J., Calvert, G.A., & Brammer, M.J. (2002a). Neural systems underlying British Sign Language and audiovisual English processing in native users. *Brain, 125*, 1583–1593.

MacWhinney, B. (2005). Commentary on Ullman et al. *Brain and Language, 93*, 239–242.

MacWhinney, B. (2008). How mental models encode embodied linguistic perspectives. In R.L. Katzky, B. MacWhinney, & M. Behrmann (Eds.), *Embodiment, ego-space, and action* (pp. 369–409). New York: Psychology Press.

MacWhinney, B., & Leinbach, J. (1991). Implementations are not conceptualizations: Revising the verb learning model. *Cognition, 40*, 121–157.

Maddieson, I. (2005a). Consonant inventories. In M. Haspelmath, M.S. Dryer, D. Gil, & B. Comrie (Eds.), *World atlas of language structures* (pp. 10–13). Oxford, UK: Oxford University Press.

Maddieson, I. (2005b). Tone. In M. Haspelmath, M.S. Dryer, D. Gil, & B. Comrie (Eds.), *World atlas of language structures* (pp. 58–61). Oxford, UK: Oxford University Press.

Maddieson, I. (2005c). Vowel quality inventories. In M. Haspelmath, M.S. Dryer, D. Gil, & B. Comrie (Eds.), *World atlas of language structures* (pp. 14–17). Oxford, UK: Oxford University Press.

Madhavan, A., Whitwell, J.L., Weigand, S.D., Duffy, J.R., Strand, E.A., Machulda, M.M., Tosakulwong, N., Senjam, M.L., Gunter, J.L., Lowe, V.J., Petersen, R.C., Jack, C.R., & Josephs, K.A. (2013). FDG PET and MRI in logopenic primary progressive aphasia versus dementia of the Alzheimer's type. *PLOS One, 8*, e62471.

Maguire, E.A., Gadian, D.G., Johnsrude, I.S, Good, C.D., Ashburner, J., Frackowiak, R.S., & Frith, C.D. (2000). Navigation-related structural change in the hippocampus of taxi drivers. *Proceedings of the National Academy of Sciences, 97*, 4398–4403.

Maher, L., Chatterjee, A., Gonzalez-Rothi, L., & Heilman, K. (1995). Agrammatic sentence production: The use of a temporal-spatial strategy. *Brain and Language, 49*, 105–124.

Mahon, B.Z. (in press). Missed connections: A connectivity constrained account of the representation and organization of object concepts. In E. Margolis & S. Laurence (Eds.), *Concepts: New directions*. Cambridge, MA: MIT Press.

Mahon, B.Z., Anzellotti, S., Schwarzbach, J., Zampini, M., & Caramazza, A. (2009). Category-specific organization in the human brain does not require visual experience. *Neuron, 63*, 397–405.

Mahon, B.Z., & Caramazza, A. (2003). Constraining questions about the organization and representation of conceptual knowledge. *Cognitive Neuropsychology, 20*, 433–450.

Mahon, B.Z., & Caramazza, A. (2005). The orchestration of the sensory-motor system: Clues from neuropsychology. *Cognitive Neuropsychology, 22*, 480–494.

Mahon, B.Z., & Caramazza, A. (2008). A critical look at the embodied cognition hypothesis and a new proposal for grounding conceptual content. *Journal of Physiology, Paris, 102*, 59–70.

Mahon, B.Z., & Caramazza, A. (2009). Concepts and categories: A cognitive neuropsychological perspective. *Annual Review of Psychology, 60*, 27–51.

Mahon, B.Z., & Caramazza, A. (2011). What drives the organization of object knowledge in the brain? *Trends in Cognitive Sciences, 15*, 97–103.

Mahon, B.Z., Milleville, S., Negri, G.A.L., Rumiati, R.I., Caramazza, A, & Martin, A. (2007). Action-related properties of objects shape object representations in the ventral stream. *Neuron, 55*, 507–520.

Maieron, M., Fabbro, F., & Skrap, M. (2013). Seeking a bridge between language and motor cortices: A PPI study. *Frontiers in Human Neuroscience, 7*, Article 249.

Majid, A., Boster, J.S., & Bowerman, M. (2008). The cross-linguistic categorization of everyday events: A study of cutting and breaking. *Cognition, 109*, 235–250.

Makris, N., & Pandya, D.N. (2009). The extreme capsule in humans and rethinking of the language circuitry. *Brain Structure and Function, 213*, 343–358.

Makuuchi, M., Bahlmann, J., Anwander, A., & Friederici, A.D. (2009). Segregating the core computational faculty of human language from working memory. *Proceedings of the National Academy of Sciences, 106*, 8362–8367.

Makuuchi, M., Kaminaga, T., & Sugishita, M. (2005). Brain activation during ideomotor praxis: Imitation and movements executed by verbal command. *Journal of Neurology, Neurosurgery, and Psychiatry, 76*, 25–33.

Malikovic, A., Amunts, K., Schleicher, A., Mohlberg, H., Eickhoff, S.B., Wilms, M., Palomero-Gallagher, N., Armstrong, E., & Zilles, K. (2007). Cytoarchitectonic analysis of the human extrastriate cortex in the region of V5/MT+: A probabilistic, stereotaxic map of area hOc5. *Cerebral Cortex, 17*, 562–574.

Malt, B.C., Gennari, S., Imai, M., Ameel, E., Tsuda, N., & Majid, A. (2008). Talking about walking: Biomechanics and the language of locomotion. *Psychological Science, 19*, 232–240.

Malt, B.C., & Majid, A. (2013). How thought is mapped into words. *WIREs Cognitive Science, 4*, 583–597.

Malt, B.C., Sloman, S.A., & Gennari, S. (2003). Universality and language-specificity in object naming. *Journal of Memory and Language, 49*, 20–42.

Malt, B.C., Sloman, S.A., Gennari, S., Shi, M., & Wang, Y. (1999). Knowing vs. naming: Similarity and the linguistic categorization of artifacts. *Journal of Memory and Language, 40*, 230–262.

Malt, B.C., & Wolff, P. (Eds.) (2010). *Words and the mind: How words capture human experience.* Oxford, UK: Oxford University Press.

Mandonnet, E., Winkler, P.A., & Duffau, H. (2010). Direct electrical stimulation as an input gate into brain functional networks: Principles, advantages, and limitations. *Acta Neurochirurgica, 152*, 185–193.

Mani, J., Diehl, B., Piao, Z., Schuele, S.S., LaPresto, E., Liu, P., Nair, D.R., Dinner, D.S., & Lüders, H.O. (2008). Evidence for a basal temporal visual language center: Cortical stimulation producing pure alexia. *Neurology, 71*, 1621–1627.

Mar, R.A. (2004). The neuropsychology of narrative: Story comprehension, story production, and their interaction. *Neuropsychologia, 42*, 1414–1434.

Mar, R.A. (2011). The neural bases of social cognition and story comprehension. *Annual Review of Psychology, 62*, 103–134.

Mar, R.A., & Oatley, K. (2008). The function of fiction is the abstraction and simulation of social experience. *Perspectives in Psychological Science, 3*, 173–192.

Mar, R.A., Oatley, K., Hirsh, J, Paz, J., & Peterson, J.B. (2006). Bookworms versus nerds: Exposure to fiction versus nonfiction, divergent associations with social ability, and the simulation of fictional social worlds. *Journal of Research in Personality, 40*, 694–712.

Mar, R.A., Oatley, K., & Peterson, J.B. (2009). Exploring the link between reading fiction and empathy: Ruling out individual differences and examining outcomes. *Communications, 34*, 407–428.

Marangolo, P., & Piras, F. (2010). Language and its interacting components: The right hemisphere hypothesis in derivational morphology. *Brain Research, 1320*, 114–122.

Marcus, G.F., Pinker, S., Ullman, M., Hollander, M., Rosen, T.J., & Xu, F. (1992). Overregularization in language acquisition. *Monographs of the Society for Research in Child Development, 57* (Serial No. 228).

Margulies, D.S., & Petrides, M. (2013). Distinct parietal and temporal connectivity profiles of ventrolateral frontal areas involved in language. *Journal of Neuroscience, 33*, 16846–16852.

Marini, A., Galetto, V., Zampieri, E., Vorano, L., Zettin, M., & Carlomagno, S. (2011). Narrative language in traumatic brain injury. *Neuropsychologia, 49*, 2904–2910.

Marshall, J. (2006). Jargon aphasia: What have we learned? *Aphasiology, 20*, 387–210.

Marshall, J., Atkinson, J., Smulovitch, E., Thacker, A., & Woll, B. (2004). Aphasia in a user of British Sign Language: Dissociation between sign and gesture. *Cognitive Neuropsychology, 21*, 537–554.

Marshall, J., Pring, T., Chiat, S., & Robson, J. (1996). Calling a salad a federation: An investigation of semantic jargon. 1. Nouns. *Journal of Neurolinguistics, 9*, 237–250.

Marslen-Wilson, W.D. (2007). Morphological processes in language comprehension. In G. Gaskell (Ed.), *Oxford handbook of psycholinguistics* (pp. 175–193). Oxford, UK: Oxford University Press.

Marslen-Wilson, W.D., & Tyler, L.K. (1997). Dissociating types of mental computation. *Nature, 387*, 592–594.

Marslen-Wilson, W.D., & Tyler, L.K. (1998). Rules, representations, and the English past tense. *Trends in Cognitive Sciences, 2*, 428–435.

Marslen-Wilson, W.D., & Tyler, L.K. (2007). Morphology, language and the brain: The decompositional substrate for language comprehension. *Philosophical Transactions of the Royal Society, B, Biological Sciences, 362*, 823–836.

Martin, A. (2007). The representation of object concepts in the brain. *Annual Review of Psychology, 58*, 25–45.

Martin, A. (2009). Circuits in mind: The neural foundations for object concepts. In M.S. Gazzaniga (Ed.), *The cognitive neurosciences*, 4th edition (pp. 1031–1046). Cambridge, MA: MIT Press.

Martin, N., Dell, G.S., Saffran, E.M., & Schwartz, M.F. (1994). Origins of paraphasias in deep dysphasia: Testing the consequences of a decay impairment to an interactive spreading activation model of lexical retrieval. *Brain and Language, 47*, 609–660.

Martin, N., Gagnon, D.A., Schwartz, M.F., Dell, G.S., & Saffran, E.M. (1996). Phonological facilitation of semantic errors in normal and aphasic speakers. *Language and Cognitive Processes, 11*, 257–282.

Martin, R.C. (2006). The neuropsychology of sentence processing: Where do we stand? *Cognitive Neuropsychology, 23*, 74–95.

Martin, R.C., & Blossom-Stach, C. (1986). Evidence of syntactic deficits in a fluent aphasic. *Brain and Language, 28*, 196–234.

Mason, R.A., & Just, M.A. (2006). Neuroimaging contributions to the understanding of discourse processes. In M. Traxler & M.A. Gernsbacher (Eds.), *Handbook of psycholinguistics* (pp. 765–799). Amsterdam: Elsevier.

Mason, R.A., & Just, M.A. (2009). The role of the Theory-of-Mind cortical network in the comprehension of narratives. *Language and Linguistics Compass, 3*, 157–174.

Mason, R.A., & Just, M.A. (2013). Identifying component discourse processes from their fMRI time course signatures. In M.A. Britt, S.R. Goldman, & J.F. Rouet (Eds.), *Reading: From works to multiple texts*. New York: Routledge.

Masterman, D.L., & Cummings, J.L. (1997). Frontal-subcortical circuits: The anatomic basis of executive, social, and motivated behaviors. *Journal of Psychopharmacology, 11*, 107–114.

Mathur, G., & Rathmann, C. (2010). Verb agreement in sign language morphology. In D. Brentari (Ed.), *Sign languages* (pp. 173–196). Cambridge, UK: Cambridge University Press.

Matsumoto, R., Nair, D.R., LaPresto, E., Najm, I., Bingman, W., Shibasaki, H., & Lüders, H.O. (2004). Functional connectivity in the human language system: A cortico-cortical evoked potential study. *Brain, 127*, 2316–2330.

Matthews, P.H. (1981). *Syntax*. Cambridge, UK: Cambridge University Press.

Mätzig, S., Druks, J., Masterson, J., & Vigliocco, G. (2009). Noun and verb differences in picture naming: Past studies and new evidence. *Cortex, 45*, 738–758.

Max, L., Guenther, F.H., Gracco, V.L., Ghosh, S.S., & Wallace, M.E. (2004). Unstable or insufficiently activated internal models and feedback-biased motor control as sources of dysfluency: A theoretical model of stuttering. *Contemporary Issues in Communication Science and Disorders, 31*, 105–122.

Mayberry, E.J., Sage, K., & Lambon Ralph, M.A. (2011). At the edge of semantic space: The breakdown of coherent concepts in semantic dementia is constrained by typicality and severity but not modality. *Journal of Cognitive Neuroscience, 23*, 2240–2251.

Mayer, E., Martory, M.D., Pegna, A.J., Landis, T., Delavelle, J., & Annoni, J.M. (1999). A pure case of Gerstmann syndrome with a subangular lesion. *Brain, 122*, 1107–1120.

Mayka, M.A., Corcos, D.M., Leurgans, S.E., & Vaillancourt, D.E. (2006). Three-dimensional locations and boundaries of motor and premotor cortices as defined by functional brain imaging: A meta-analysis. *NeuroImage, 31*, 1453–1474.

Mazoyer, B.M., Tzourio, N., Frak, V., Syrota, A., Murayama, N., Levrier, O., Salamon, G., Dehaene, S., Cohen, L., & Mehler, J. (1993). The cortical representation of speech. *Journal of Cognitive Neuroscience, 5*, 467–479.

McAdams, D.P. (1997). *The stories we live by*. New York: Guilford.

McCandliss, B.D., Cohen, L., & Dehaene, S. (2003). The visual word form area: Expertise for reading in the fusiform gyrus. *Trends in Cognitive Sciences, 7*, 293–299.

McCarthy, R.A., & Warrington, E.K. (1987). Understanding: A function of short-term memory? *Brain, 110*, 1565–1578.

McClelland, J.L., & Patterson, K. (2002a). Rules or connections in past-tense inflections: What does the evidence rule out? *Trends in Cognitive Sciences, 6*, 465–472.

McClelland, J.L., & Patterson, K. (2002b). "Words *or* Rules" cannot exploit the regularity in exceptions. *Trends in Cognitive Sciences, 6*, 464–465.

McClelland, J.L., & Rogers, T.T. (2003). The parallel distributed processing approach to semantic cognition. *Nature Reviews: Neuroscience, 4*, 310–322.

McClelland, J.L., Rogers, T.T., Patterson, K., Dilkina, K., & Lambon Ralph, M. (2009). Semantic cognition: Its nature, its development, and its neural basis. In M.S. Gazzaniga (Ed.), *The cognitive neurosciences*, 4th edition (pp. 1047–1066). Cambridge, MA: MIT Press.

McClelland, J.L., Rumelhart, D.E., & the PDP Research Group (Eds.) (1986). *Parallel distributed processing: Explorations in the microstructure of cognition, Vol. 2. Psychological and biological models*. Cambridge, MA: MIT Press.

McCloskey, M., & Caramazza, A. (1988). Theory and methodology in cognitive neuropsychology: A response to our critics. *Cognitive Neuropsychology, 5*, 583–623.

McFarland, D.H. (2001). Respiratory markers of conversational interaction. *Journal of Speech, Language, and Hearing Research, 44*, 128–143.

McGettigan, C., & Scott, S.K. (2012). Cortical asymmetries in speech perception: What's wrong, what's right, and what's left? *Trends in Cognitive Sciences, 16*, 269–276.

McGregor, W. (2002). *Verb classification in Australian languages*. Berlin: Mouton de Gruyter.

McGuire, P., Silbersweig, D., Murray, R., David, A., Frackowiak, R., & Frith, C. (1996). Functional anatomy of inner speech and auditory verbal imagery. *Psychological Medicine, 26*, 29–38.

McGurk, H., & MacDonald, J. (1976). Hearing lips and seeing voices. *Nature, 264*, 746–748.

McKinnon, R., & Osterhout, L. (1996). Constraints on movement phenomena in sentence processing: Evidence from event-related brain potentials. *Language and Cognitive Processes, 11*, 495–523.

McNamara, P. (2011). *The cognitive neuropsychiatry of Parkinson's disease*. Cambridge, MA: MIT Press.

McNamara, P., O'Quin, K., Krüger, M., & Durso, R. (1996). Frontal lobe function and sentence comprehension in Parkinson's disease: A comparison with Broca's aphasia. *International Journal of Neuroscience, 86*, 151–166.

McPherson, W.B., & Holcomb, P.J. (1999). An electrophysiological investigation of semantic priming with pictures of real objects. *Psychophysiology, 36*, 53–65.

Mechelli, A., Sartori, G., Orlandi, P., & Price, C.J. (2006). Semantic relevance explains category effects in medial fusiform gyri. *NeuroImage, 30*, 992–1002.

Mecklinger, A., Schriefers, H., Steinhauer, K., & Friederici, A.D. (1995). Processing relative clauses varying on syntactic and semantic dimensions: An analysis with event-related potentials. *Memory and Cognition, 23*, 477–494.

Meier, J.D., Aflalo, T.N., Kastner, S., & Graziano, M.S.A. (2008). Complex organization of human primary motor cortex: A high-resolution fMRI study. *Journal of Neurophysiology, 100,* 1800–1812.

Meir, I., Padden, C., Aronoff, M., & Sandler, W. (2007). Body as subject. *Journal of Linguistics, 43,* 531–563.

Meir, I., Sandler, W., Padden, C., & Aronoff, M. (2010). Emerging sign languages. In M. Marschark & P. Spencer (Eds.), *Oxford handbook of deaf studies, language, and education, Vol. 2* (pp. 267–280). Oxford, UK: Oxford University Press.

Meister, I.G., Krings, T., Foltys, H., Boroojerdi, B., Muller, M., & Topper, R. (2004). Playing piano in the mind: An fMRI study on music imagery and performance in pianists. *Brain Research, 19,* 219–228.

Meister, I.G., Wilson, S.M., Deblieck, C., Wu, A.D., & Iacoboni, M. (2007). The essential role of premotor cortex in speech perception. *Current Biology, 17,* 1692–1696.

Méligne, D., Fossard, M., Belliard, S., Moreaud, O., Duvignau, K., & Démonet, J.F. (2011). Verb production during action naming in semantic dementia. *Journal of Communicative Disorders, 44,* 379–391.

Meltzer-Asscher, A., Schuchard, J., den Ouden, D.B., & Thompson, C.K. (2013). The neural substrates of complex argument structure representations: Processing "alternating transitivity" verbs. *Language and Cognitive Processes, 28,* 1154–1168.

Mendez, M., Clark, D.G., Shapira, J.S., & Cummings, J.L. (2003). Speech and language in progressive nonfluent aphasia compared with early Alzheimer's disease. *Neurology, 61,* 1108–1113.

Mendez, M.F., & Geehan, G.R., Jr. (1988). Cortical auditory disorders: Clinical and psychoacoustic features. *Journal of Neurology, Neurosurgery, and Psychiatry, 51,* 1–9.

Menenti, L., Geirhan, S.M.E., Segaert, K., & Hagoort, P. (2011). Shared language: Overlap and segregation of the neuronal infrastructure for speaking and listening revealed by functional MRI. *Psychological Science, 22,* 1173–1182.

Menenti, L., Petersson, K.M., & Hagoort, P. (2012). From reference to sense: How the brain encodes meaning for speaking. *Frontiers in Psychology, 2,* Article 384.

Menn, L., & Obler, L.K. (Eds.) (1990a). *Agrammatic aphasia: A cross-language narrative sourcebook.* 3 vols. Amsterdam: John Benjamins.

Menn, L., & Obler, L.K. (1990b). Cross-language data and theories of agrammatism. In Menn, L., & Obler, L.K. (Eds.), *Agrammatic aphasia: A cross-language narrative sourcebook, Vol. 2* (pp. 1369–1389). Amsterdam: John Benjamins.

Menn, L., O'Connor, M., Obler, L.K., & Holland, A. (1995). *Nonfluent aphasia in a multilingual world.* Amsterdam: John Benjamins.

Menon, R.S., Luknowsky, D.C., & Gati, J.S. (1998). Mental chronometry using latency-resolved functional MRI. *Proceedings of the National Academy of Sciences, 95,* 10902–10907.

Mesulam, M.M. (1982). Slowly progressive aphasia without generalized dementia. *Annals of Neurology, 11,* 592–598.

Mesulam, M.M. (1987). Primary progressive aphasia: Differentiation from Alzheimer's disease. *Annals of Neurology, 22,* 533–534.

Mesulam, M.M. (1990). Large-scale neurocognitive networks and distributed processing for attention, language, and memory. *Annals of Neurology, 28,* 597–613.

Mesulam, M.M. (1998). From sensation to cognition. *Brain, 121,* 1013–1052.

Mesulam, M.M. (2000). Behavioral neuroanatomy: Large-scale networks, association cortex, frontal syndromes, the limbic system, and hemispheric specialization. In M.M. Mesulam (Ed.), *Principles of behavioral and cognitive neurology* (pp. 1–120). Oxford, UK: Oxford University Press.

Mesulam, M.M. (2001). Primary progressive aphasia. *Annals of Neurology, 49,* 425–432.

Mesulam, M.M. (2003). Primary progressive aphasia—A language-based dementia. *New England Journal of Medicine, 349,* 1535–1542.

Mesulam, M.M. (2007). Primary progressive aphasia: A 25-year retrospective. *Alzheimer's Disease and Associated Disorders, 21,* S8–S11.

Mesulam, M.M. (2008). Representation, inference, and transcendental encoding in neurocognitive networks of the human brain. *Annals of Neurology, 64,* 367–378.

Mesulam, M.M., Grossman, M., Hillis, A., Kertesz, A., & Weintraub, S. (2003). The core and halo of primary progressive aphasia and semantic dementia. *Annals of Neurology, 54,* S11–S14.

Mesulam, M.M., Johnson, N., Krefft, T.A., Gas, J.M., Cannon, A.D., Adamson, J.L., Bigio, E.H., Weintraub, S., Dickson, D.W., Hutton, M.L., & Graff-Radford, N.R. (2007). Progranulin mutations in primary progressive aphasia. *Archives of Neurology, 64,* 43–47.

Mesulam, M.M., Rogalski, E., Wieneke, C., Cobia, D., Rademaker, A., Thompson, C., & Weintraub, S. (2009a). Neurology of anomia in the semantic variant of primary progressive aphasia. *Brain, 132,* 2553–2565.

Mesulam, M.M., & Weintraub, S. (2008). Primary progressive aphasia and kindred disorders. In C. Duyckaerts & I. Litvan (Eds.), *Handbook of clinical neurology, Vol. 89* (pp. 579–593).

Mesulam, M.M., Wieneke, C., Hurley, R., Rademaker, A., Thompson, C., Weintraub, S., & Rogalski, E.J. (2013). Words and objects at the tip of the left temporal lobe in primary progressive aphasia. *Brain, 136,* 601–618.

Mesulam, M.M., Wieneke, C., Rogalski, E., Cobia, D., Thompson, C., & Weintraub, S. (2009b). Quantitative template for subtyping primary progressive aphasia. *Archives of Neurology, 66,* 1545–1551.

Meteyard, L., Cuadrado, S.R., Bahrami, B., & Vigliocco, G. (2012). Coming of age: A review of embodiment and the neuroscience of semantics. *Cortex, 48,* 788–804.

Meteyard, L., & Patterson, K. (2009). The relation between content and structure in language production: An analysis of speech errors in semantic dementia. *Brain and Language, 110,* 121–134.

Meteyard, L., Price, C.J., Woollams, A.M., & Aydelott, J. (2013). Lesions impairing regular versus irregular past tense production. *NeuroImage Clinical, 3,* 438–449.

Meyer, A.S. (1990). The time course of phonological encoding in language production: The encoding of successive syllables of a word. *Journal of Memory and Language, 29,* 524–545.

Meyer, A.S. (1991). The time course of phonological encoding in language production: Phonological encoding inside a syllable. *Journal of Memory and Language, 30,* 69–89.

Meyer, K., & Damasio, A.R. (2009). Convergence and divergence in a neural architecture for recognition and memory. *Trends in Neurosciences, 32,* 376–382.

Meyer, L., Obleser, J., Anwander, A., & Friederici, A.D. (2012a). Linking ordering in Broca's area to storage in left temporo-parietal regions: The case of sentence parsing. *NeuroImage, 62,* 1987–1998.

Meyer, L., Obleser, J., Kiebel, S.J., & Friederici, A.D. (2012b). Spatiotemporal dynamics of argument retrieval and reordering: An fMRI and EEG study of sentence processing. *Frontiers in Psychology, 3,* Article 523.

Meyer, M., Alter, K., & Friederici, A.D. (2003). Functional MR imaging exposes differential brain responses to syntax and prosody during auditory sentence comprehension. *Journal of Neurolinguistics, 16,* 277–300.

Meyer, M., Steinhauer, K., Alter, K., Friederici, A.D., & von Cramon, D.Y. (2004). Brain activity varies with modulation of dynamic pitch variance in sentence melody. *Brain and Language, 89,* 277–289.

Miceli, G., Benvegnu, B., Capasso, R., & Caramazza, A. (1997). The independence of phonological and orthographic lexical forms: Evidence from aphasia. *Cognitive Neuropsychology, 14,* 35–70.

Miceli, G., & Capasso, R. (2006). Spelling and dysgraphia. *Cognitive Neuropsychology, 23,* 110–134.

Miceli, G., & Caramazza, A. (1988). Dissociation of inflectional and derivational morphology. *Brain and Language, 35,* 24–65.

Miceli, G., Fouch, E., Capasso, R., Shelton, J.R., Tomaiuolo, F., & Caramazza, A. (2001). The dissociation of color from form and function knowledge. *Nature Neuroscience, 4,* 662–667.

Miceli, G., Gainotti, G., Caltagirone, C., & Masullo, C. (1980). Some aspects of phonological impairment in aphasia. *Brain and Language, 11,* 159–169.

Miceli, G., Mazzucchi, A., Menn, L., & Goodglass, H. (1983). Contrasting cases of Italian agrammatic aphasia without comprehension disorder. *Brain and Language, 19,* 65–97.

Miceli, G., Silveri, M.C., Romani, C., & Caramazza, A. (1989). Variation in the pattern of omissions and substitutions of grammatical morphemes in the spontaneous speech of so-called agrammatic patients. *Brain and Language, 36,* 447–492.

Miceli, G., Turriziani, P., Caltagirone, C., Capasso, R., Tomaiuolo, F., & Caramazza, A. (2002). The neural correlates of grammatical gender: An fMRI investigation. *Journal of Cognitive Neuroscience, 14,* 618–628.

Miller, B.L., Ponton, M., Benson. D.F., Cummings, J.L., & Mena, I. (1996). Enhanced artistic creativity with temporal lobe degeneration. *Lancet, 348,* 1744–1745.

Miller, E.K., & Cohen, J.D. (2001). An integrative theory of prefrontal cortex function. *Annual Review of Neuroscience, 24,* 167–202.

Miller, G.A. (1956). The magical number seven, plus-or-minus two: Some limits on our capacity for processing information. *Pychological Review, 101,* 343–352.

Millman, R.E., Woods, W.P., & Quinlan, P.T. (2011). Functional asymmetries in the representation of noise-vocoded speech. *NeuroImage, 54,* 2364–2373.

Milner, A.D., & Goodale, M.A. (2006). *The visual brain in action,* 2nd edition. Oxford, UK: Oxford University Press.

Mion, M., Patterson, K., Acosta-Cabronero, J., Pengas, G., Izquierdo-Garcia, D., Hong, Y.T., Fryer, T.D., Williams, G.B., Hodges, J.R., & Nestor, P.J. (2010). What the left and right anterior fusiform gyri tell us about semantic memory. *Brain, 133,* 3256–3268.

Miozzo, M. (2003). On the processing of regular and irregular forms of verbs and nouns: Evidence from neuropsychology. *Cognition, 87,* 101–127.

Miozzo, M., Fischer-Baum, S., & Postman, J. (2010). A selective deficit for inflection production. *Neuropsychologia, 48,* 2427–2436.

Mitchell, J.P. (2009). Inferences about mental states. *Philosophical Transactions of the Royal Society, B, Biological Sciences, 364,* 1309–1316.

Mitchell, R.L.C. (2006). How does the brain mediate interpretation of incongruent auditory emotions? The neural response to prosody in the presence of conflicting lexico-semantic cues. *European Journal of Neuroscience, 24,* 3611–3618.

Mobbs, D., Yu, R., Rowe, J.B., Eich, H., FeldmanHall, O., & Dalgleish, T. (2010). Neural activity associated with monitoring the oscillating threat value of a tarantula. *Proceedings of the National Academy of Sciences, 107,* 20582–20586.

Mohr, J.P., Pessin, M.S., Finkelstein, S., Funkenstein, H.H., Duncan, G.W., & Davis, K.R. (1978). Broca aphasia: Pathologic and clinical. *Neurology, 28,* 311–324.

Möller, J., Jansma, B.M., Rodriguez-Fornells, A., & Münte, T.F. (2007). What the brain does before the tongue slips. *Cerebral Cortex, 17,* 1173–1178.

Monetta, L., Cheang, H.S., & Pell, M.D. (2008). Understanding speaker attitudes from prosody by adults with Parkinson's disease. *Journal of Neuropsychology, 2,* 415–430.

Montant, M., & Behrmann, M. (2000). Pure alexia. *Neurocase, 6,* 265–294.

Moody, C.L., & Gennari, S.P. (2010). Effects of implied physical effort in sensory-motor and prefrontal cortex during language comprehension. *NeuroImage, 49,* 782–793.

Moore, B., Tyler, L., & Marslen-Wilson, W. (Eds.) (2010). *The perception of speech: From sound to meaning.* Oxford, UK: Oxford University Press.

Morford, J., & MacFarlane, J. (2003). Frequency characteristics of American Sign Language. *Sign Language Studies, 3,* 213–225.

Morris, H.H., Lüders, H., Lesser, R.P., Dinner, D.S., & Hahn, J. (1984). Transient neuropsychological abnormalities (including Gerstmann's syndrome) during cortical stimulation. *Neurology, 34,* 877–883.

Morris, J.S., Frith, C.D., Perrett, D.I., Rowland, D., Young, A.W., Calder, A.J., & Dolan, R.J. (1996). A differential responsein the human amygdala to fearful and happy facial expressions. *Nature, 383,* 812–815.

Morris, J.S., Scott, S.K., & Dolan, R.J. (1999). Say it with feeling: Neural responses to emotional vocalizations. *Neuropsychologia, 37,* 1155–1163.

Morrison, C.M., Ellis, A.W., & Quinlan, P.T. (1992). Age of acquisition, not word frequency, affects object naming, not object recognition. *Memory and Cognition, 17,* 1146–1160.

Moseley, R.L., Pulvermüller, F., & Shtyrov, Y. (2013). Sensorimotor semantics on the spot: Brain activity dissociates between conceptual categories within 150 ms. *Scientific Reports, 3,* Article 1928.

Moser, D., Fridriksson, J., Bonilha, L., Healy, E.W., Baylis, G., Baker, J.M., & Rorden, C. (2009). Neural recruitment for the production of native and novel speech sounds. *NeuroImage, 46,* 549–557.

Moss, H.E., Abdallah, S., Fletcher, P.C., Bright, P., Pilgrim, L.K., Acres, K., & Tyler, L.K. (2005). Selecting among competing alternatives: Selection and retrieval in the left inferior frontal gyrus. *Cerebral Cortex, 15,* 1723–1735.

Moss, H.E., Tyler, L.K., Durrant-Peatfield, M., & Bunn, E.M. (1998). "Two eyes of a see-through": Impaired and intact semantic knowledge in a case of selective deficit for living things. *Neurocase, 4,* 291–310.

Motley, M.T., & Baars, B.J. (1976). Laboratory induction of verbal slips: A new method for psycholinguistic research. *Communication Quarterly, 24,* 28–34.

Möttönen, R., Calvert, G.A., Jaaskelainen, I.P., Matthews, P.M., Thesen, T., Tuomainen, J., & Sams, M. (2006). Perceiving identical sounds as speech or non-speech modulates activity in the left posterior superior temporal sulcus. *NeuroImage, 30,* 563–569.

Möttönen, R., Dutton, R., & Watkins, K.E. (2013). Auditory-motor processing of speech sounds. *Cerebral Cortex, 23,* 1190–1197.

Möttönen, R., & Watkins, K.E. (2009). Motor representations of articulators contribute to categorical perception of speech sounds. *Journal of Neuroscience, 29,* 9819–9825.

Mountcastle, V.B. (1997). The columnar organization of the neocortex. *Brain, 120,* 701–722.

Münte, T.F., Heinze, H.J., Matzke, M., Wieringa, B.M., & Johannes, S. (1998). Brain potentials and syntactic violations revisited: No evidence for specificity of the syntactic positive shift. *Neuropsychologia, 36,* 217–226.

Münte, T.F., Matzke, M., & Johannes, S. (1997). Brain activity associated with syntactic incongruities in words and pseudowords. *Journal of Cognitive Neuroscience, 9,* 318–329.

Mur, M., Bandettini, P.A., & Kriegeskorte, N. (2009). Revealing representational content with pattern-information fMRI—an introductory guide. *Social, Cognitive, and Affective Neuroscience, 4,* 101–109.

Murakami, T., Restle, J., & Ziemann, U. (2011). Observation-execution matching and action inhibition in human primary motor cortex during viewing of speech-related lip movements or listening to speech. *Neuropsychologia, 49,* 2045–2054.

Murdoch, B.E. (2010). The cerebellum and language: Historical perspective and review. *Cortex, 46,* 858–868.

Murphey, D.K., Yoshor, D., & Beauchamp, M.S. (2008). Perception matches selectivity in the human color center. *Current Biology, 18,* 216–220.

Murray, R., Koenig, P., Antani, S., McCawley, G., & Grossman, M. (2007). Lexical acquisition in progressive aphasia and frontotemporal dementia. *Cognitive Neuropsychology, 24,* 48–69.

Myers, E.B., & Blumstein, S.E. (2008). The neural bases of the lexical effect: An fMRI investigation. *Cerebral Cortex, 18,* 278–288.

Näätänen, R., Lehtokoski, A., Lennes, M., Cheour, M., Huotilainen, M., Iivonen, A., Vainio, M., Alku, P., Ilmoniemi, R.J., Luuk, A., Allik, J., Sinkkonen, J., & Alho, K. (1997). Language-specific phoneme representations revealed by electric and magnetic brain responses. *Nature, 385,* 432–434.

Nachev, P., Kennard, C., & Husain, M. (2008). Functional role of the supplementary and pre-supplementary motor areas. *Nature Reviews: Neuroscience, 9,* 856–869.

Nadeau, S.E., & Gonzalez Rothi, L.J. (1992). Morphologic agrammatism following a right hemisphere stroke in a dextral patient. *Brain and Language, 43,* 642–667.

Naeser, M.A., Martin, P.I., Theoret, H., Kobayashi, M., Fregni, F., Nicholas, M., Tormos, J.M., Steven, M.S., Baker, E.H., & Pascual-Leone, A. (2011). TMS suppression of right pars triangularis, but not pars opercularis, improves naming in aphasia. *Brain and Language, 119,* 206–213.

Naeser, M.A., Martin, P.I., Treglia, E., Ho, M., Kaplan, E., Bashir, S., Hamilton, R., Coslett, H.B., & Pascual-Leone, A. (2010). Research with rTMS in the treatment of aphasia. *Restorative Neurology and Neuroscience, 28,* 511–529.

Naeser, M.A., Palumbo, C.L., Helm-Estabrooks, N., Stiassny-Eder, D., & Albert, M.L. (1989). Severe nonfluency in aphasia: Role of the medial subcallosal fasciculus and other white matter pathways in recovery of spontaneous speech. *Brain, 112,* 1–38.

Næss, A. (2007). *Prototypical transitivity.* Amsterdam: John Benjamins.

Nagao, M., Takeda, K., Komori, T., Isozaki, E., & Hirai, S. (1999). Apraxia of speech associated with an infarct in the precentral gyrus of the insula. *Neuroradiology, 41,* 356–357.

Nakamura, K., Kuo, W.J., Pegado, F., Cohen, L., Tzeng, O.J.L., & Dehaene, S. (2012). Universal brain systems for recognizing word shapes and handwriting gestures during reading. *Proceedings of the National Academy of Sciences, 109,* 20762–20767.

Namasivayam, A.K., van Lieshout, P.H.H.M., McIlroy, W.E., & De Nil, L.F. (2009). Sensory feedback dependence hypothesis in persons who stutter. *Human Movement Science, 28,* 688–707.

Narain, C., Scott, S.K., & Wise, R.J.S. (2003). Defining a left-lateralized response specific to intelligible speech using fMRI. *Cerebral Cortex, 13,* 1362–1368.

Narrog, H., & Heine, B. (2011). *The Oxford handbook of grammaticalization.* Oxford, UK: Oxford University Press.

Nasir, S.M., & Ostry, D.J. (2006). Somatosensory precision in speech production. *Current Biology, 16,* 1918–1923.

Nasir, S.M., & Ostry, D.J. (2008). Speech motor learning in profoundly deaf adults. *Nature Neuroscience, 11,* 1217–1222.

Nasir, S.M., & Ostry, D.J. (2009). Auditory plasticity and speech motor learning. *Proceedings of the National Academy of Sciences, 106,* 20470–20475.

Natsopoulos, D., Grouios, G., Bostantzopoulos, S., Mentanopoulos, G., Kastarou, Z, & Logothetis, J. (1993). Algorithmic and heuristic strategies in comprehension of complement clauses by patients with Parkinson's disease. *Neuropsychologia, 31,* 951–964.

Natsopoulos, D., Kastarou, Z, Bostantzopoulos, S., Grouios, G., Mentanopoulos, G., & Logothetis, J. (1991). Strategies in comprehension of relative clauses in Parkinsonian patients. *Cortex, 27,* 255–268.

Nazir, T.A., Boulenger, V., Roy, A., Silber, B., Jeannerod, M., & Paulignan, Y. (2008). Language-induced motor perturbations during the execution of a reaching movement. *Quarterly Journal of Experimental Psychology, 61*, 933–943.

Neary, D., Snowden, J.S., Gustafson, L., Passant, U., Stuss, D., Black, S., Freedman, M., Kertesz, A., Robert, P.H., Albert, M., Boone, K., Miller, B.L., Cummings, J., & Benson, D.F. (1998). Frontotemporal lobar degeneration: A consensus on clinical diagnostic criteria. *Neurology, 51*, 1546–1554.

Negri, G.A.L., Rumiati, R.I., Zadini, A., Ukmar, M., Mahon, B.Z., & Caramazza, A. (2007). What is the role of motor simulation in action and object recognition? Evidence from apraxia. *Cognitive Neuropsychology, 24*, 795–816.

Neidle, C., Kegl, J., MacLaughlin, D., Bahan, B., & Lee, R.G. (2000). *The syntax of American Sign Language: Functional categories and hierarchical structure.* Cambridge, MA: MIT Press.

Nespoulous, J.L., Dordain, M., Perron, C., Ska, B., Bub, D., Caplan, D., Mehler, J., & Lecours, A.R. (1988). Agrammatism in sentence production without comprehension deficits: Reduced availability of syntactic structures and/or grammatical morphemes? A case study. *Brain and Language, 33*, 273–295.

Nestor, P.J., Fryer, T.D., & Hodges, J.R. (2006). Declarative memory impairments in Alzheimer's disease and semantic dementia. *NeuroImage, 30*, 1010–1020.

Nestor, P.J., Graham, N.L., Fryer, T.D., Williams, G.B., Patterson, K., & Hodges, J.R. (2003). Progressive non-fluent aphasia is associated with hypometabolism centered on the left anterior insula. *Brain, 126*, 2406–2416.

Neville, H.J., Bavelier, D., Corina, D., Rauschecker, J., Karni, A., Lalwani, A., Braun, A., Clark, V., Jezzard, P., & Turner, R. (1998). Cerebral organization for language in deaf and hearing subjects: Biological constraints and effects of experience. *Proceedings of the National Academy of Sciences, 95*, 922–929.

Neville, H.J., Nicol, J.L., Barss, A., Forster, K.I., & Garrett, M.F. (1991). Syntactically based sentence processing classes: Evidence from event-related brain potentials. *Journal of Cognitive Neuroscience, 3*, 151–165.

Newcombe, P.I., Campbell, C., Siakaluk, P.D., & Pexman, P.M. (2012). Effects of emotional and sensorimotor knowledge in semantic processing of concrete and abstract nouns. *Frontiers in Human Neuroscience, 6*, Article 275.

Newhart, M., Trupe, L.A., Gomez, Y., Cloutman, L., Molitoris, J.J., Davis, C., Leigh, R., Gottesman, R.F., Race, D., & Hillis, A.E. (2012). Asyntactic comprehension, working memory, and acute ischemia in Broca's area versus angular gyrus. *Cortex, 48*, 1288–1297.

Newman, A.J., Bavelier, D., Corina, D., Jezzard, P., & Neville, H.J. (2002). A critical period for right hemisphere recruitment in American Sign Language processing. *Nature Neuroscience, 5*, 76–80.

Newman, S., Ikuta, T., & Burns, T. (2010). The effect of semantic relatedness on syntactic analysis. *Brain and Language, 113*, 51–58.

Nie, J., Guo, L., Li, K., Wang, Y., Chen, G., Li, L., Chen, H., Deng, F., Jiang, X., Zhang, T., Huang, L., Faraco, C., Zhang, D., Guo, C., Yap, P.T., Hu, X., Li, G., Lv, J., Yuan, Y., Zhu, D., Han, J., Sabatinelli, D., Zhao, Q.,

Miller, L.S., Xu, B., Shen, P., Platt, S., Shen, D., Hu, X., & Liu, T. (2012). Axonal fiber terminations concentrate on gyri. *Cerebral Cortex, 22*, 2831–2839.

Niedenthal, P.M. (2007). Embodying emotion. *Science, 316*, 1002–1005.

Nieder, A., & Dehaene, S. (2009). Representation of number in the brain. *Annual Review of Neuroscience, 32*, 185–208.

Nieto-Castañón, A., & Fedorenko, E. (2012). Subject-specific functional localizers increase sensitivity and functional resolution of multi-subject analyses. *NeuroImage, 63*, 1646–1669.

Nieuwland, M.S., & van Berkum, J.J.A. (2006). When peanuts fall in love: N400 evidence for the power of discourse. *Journal of Cognitive Neuroscience, 18*, 1098–1111.

Nigam, A., Hoffman, J.E., & Simons, R.F. (1992). N400 to semantically anomalous pictures and words. *Journal of Cognitive Neuroscience, 4*, 15–22.

Nishimura, H., Hashikawa, K., Doi, K., Iwaki, T., Watanabe, Y., Kusuoka, H., Nishimura, T., & Kubo, T. (1999). Sign language "heard" in the auditory cortex. *Nature, 397*, 116.

Niziolek, C.A., Nagarajan, S.S., & Houde, J.F. (2013). What does motor reference copy represent? Evidence from speech production. *Journal of Neuroscience, 33*, 16110–16116.

Noel, M.P. (2005). Finger gnosia: A predictor of numerical abilities in children? *Child Neuropsychology, 11*, 413–430.

Nolan, K.A., & Caramazza, A. (1983). An analysis of writing in a case of deep dyslexia. *Brain and Language, 20*, 305–328.

Noppeney, U., Josephs, O., Kiebel, S., Friston, K.J., & Price, C.J. (2005). Action selectivity in parietal and temporal cortex. *Cognitive Brain Research, 25*, 641–649.

Noppeney, U., Patterson, K., Tyler, L.K., Moss, H., Stamatakis, E.A., Bright, P., Mummery, C., & Price, C.J. (2007). Temporal lobe lesions and semantic impairment: A comparison of herpes simplex virus encephalitis and semantic dementia. *Brain, 130*, 1138–1147.

Noppeney, U., Price, C.J., Penny, W.D., & Friston, K.J. (2006). Two distinct neural mechanisms for category-selective responses. *Cerebral Cortex, 16*, 437–445.

Nota, Y., & Honda, K. (2003). Possible role of the anterior insula in articulation. In S. Palethorpe & M. Tabain (Eds.), *Proceedings of the sixth international seminar on speech production* (pp. 191–194). Sydney.

Novick, J.M., Kan, I.P., Trueswell, J.C., & Thompson-Schill, S.L. (2009). A case for conflict across multiple domains: Memory and language impairments following damage to ventrolateral prefrontal cortex. *Cognitive Neuropsychology, 26*, 527–567.

Novick, J.M., Trueswell, J.C., & Thompson-Schill, S.L. (2005). Cognitive control and parsing: Re-examining the role of Broca's area in sentence comprehension. *Cognitive, Affective, and Behavioral Neuroscience, 5*, 263–281.

Novick, J.M., Trueswell, J.C., & Thompson-Schill, S.L. (2010). Broca's area and language processing: Evidence for the cognitive control connection. *Language and Linguistics Compass, 4*, 906–924.

Numminen, J., & Curio, G. (1999). Differential effects of overt, covert, and replayed speech on vowel-evoked responses of the human auditory cortex. *Neuroscience Letters, 272*, 29–32.

Numminen, J., Salmelin, R, & Hari, R. (1999). Subjects' own speech reduces reactivity of the human auditory cortex. *Neuroscience Letters, 265*, 119–122.

Núñez-Peña, M.I., & Honrubia-Serrano, M.L. (2004). P600 related to rule violation in an arithmetic task. *Cognitive Brain Research, 18*, 130–141.

Oberman, L.M., Winkielman, P., & Ramachandran, V.S. (2007). Face to face: Blocking expression-specific muscles can selectively impair recognition of emotional faces. *Social Neuroscience, 2*, 167–178.

Obler, L.K, & Gjerlow, K. (1999). *Language and the brain*. Cambridge, UK: Cambridge University Press.

Obleser, J., Leaver, A.M., Van Meter, J., & Rauschecker, J.P. (2010). Segregation of vowels and consonants in human auditory cortex: Evidence for distributed hierarchical organization. *Frontiers in Psychology, 1*, Article 232.

Obleser, J., Meyer, L., & Friederici, A.D. (2011). Dynamic assignment of neural resources in auditory comprehension of complex sentences. *NeuroImage, 56*, 2310–2320.

Ogar, J., Baldo, J.V., Wilson, S.M., Brambati, S.M., Miller, B.L., Dronkers, N.F., & Gorno-Tempini, M.L. (2011). Semantic dementia and persisting Wernicke's aphasia: Linguistic and anatomical profiles. *Brain and Language, 117*, 28–83.

Ogar, J., Dronkers, N.F., Brambati, S.M., Miller, B.L., & Gorno-Tempini, M.L. (2007). Progressive nonfluent aphasia and its characteristic motor speech deficits. *Azheimer's Disease and Associated Disorders, 21*, S23–S30.

Ogar, J., Slama, H., Dronkers, N., Amici, S., & Gorno-Tempini, M.L. (2005). Apraxia of speech: An overview. *Neurocase, 11*, 427–432.

Ogar, J., Willock, S., Baldo, J., Wilkins, D., Ludy, C., & Dronkers, N. (2006). Clinical and anatomical correlates of apraxia of speech. *Brain and Language, 97*, 343–350.

Oh, T.M., Tan, K.L., Ng, P., Berne, Y.I., & Graham, S. (2011). The past tense debate: Is phonological complexity the key to the puzzle? *NeuroImage, 57*, 271–280.

Ojemann, G.A., Fried, I., & Lettich, E. (1989a). Electrocorticographic (EcoG) correlates of language: I. Desynchonization in temporal language cortex during object naming. *Electroencephalography and Clinical Neurophysiology, 73*, 453–463.

Ojemann, G.A., Ojemann, J., Lettich, E., & Berger, M. (1989b). Cortical language localization in left, dominant hemisphere. *Journal of Neurosurgery, 71*, 316–326. (Reprinted in 2008 in the *Journal of Neurosurgery, 108*, 411–421.)

Okada, K., & Hickok, G. (2006a). Identification of lexical-phonological networks in the superior temporal sulcus using fMRI. *NeuroReport, 17*, 1293–1296.

Okada, K., & Hickok, G. (2006b). Left posterior auditory-related cortices participate both in speech perception and speech production: Neural overlap revealed by fMRI. *Brain and Language, 98*, 112–117.

Okada, K., Rong, F., Venezia, J., Matchin, W., Hsieh, I.-H., Saberi, K., Serences, J.T., & Hickok, G. (2010). Hierarchical organization of human auditory cortex: Evidence from acoustic invariance in the response to intelligible speech. *Cerebral Cortex, 20*, 2486–2495.

Oldfield, R.C., & Wingfield, A. (1965). Response latencies in naming objects. *The Quarterly Journal of Experimental Psychology, 17*, 273–281.

Olson, I.R., McCoy, D., Klobusicky, E., & Ross, L.A. (2013). Social cognition and the anterior temporal lobes: A review and theoretical framework. *Social, Cognitive, and Affective Neuroscience, 8*, 123–133.

Op de Beeck, H., Haushofer, J., & Kanwisher, N. (2008). Interpreting fMRI data: Maps, modules, and dimensions. *Nature Reviews: Neuroscience, 9*, 123–135.

Orban, G.A., Van Essen, D., & Vanduffel, W. (2004). Comparative mapping of higher visual areas in monkeys and humans. *Trends in Cognitive Sciences, 8*, 315–324.

Orgs, G., Lange, K., Dombrowski, J.H., & Heil, M. (2008). N400–effects to task-irrelevant environmental sounds: Further evidence for obligatory conceptual processing. *Neuroscience Letters, 436*, 133–137.

O'Shea, J., & Walsh, V. (2006). Transcranial magnetic stimulation. *Current Biology, 17*, R196–R199.

Osnes, B., Hugdahl, K., & Specht, K. (2011). Effective connectivity analysis demonstrates involvement of premotor cortex during speech perception. *NeuroImage, 54*, 2437–2445.

Osterhout, L., & Holcomb, P.J. (1992). Event-related brain potentials elicited by syntactic anomaly. *Journal of Memory and Language, 31*, 785–806.

Osterhout, L., & Holcomb, P.J. (1993). Event-related potentials and syntactic anomaly: Evidence of anomaly detection during the perception of continuous speech. *Language and Cognitive Processes, 8*, 413–437.

Osterhout, L., Holcomb, P.J., & Swinney, D.A. (1994). Brain potentials elicited by garden path sentences: Evidence of the application of verb information during parsing. *Journal of Experimental Psychology: Learning, Memory, and Cognition, 20*, 786–803.

Osterhout, L., Kim, A., & Kuperberg, G.R. (2012). The neurobiology of sentence comprehension. In M. Spivey, M. Joannisse, & K. McRae (Eds.), *The Cambridge handbook of psycholinguistics* (pp. 365–389). Cambridge, UK: Cambridge University Press.

Osterhout, L., McLaughlin, J., Kim, A., Greenwald, R., & Inoue, K. (2004). Sentences in the brain: Event-related potentials as real-time reflections of sentence comprehension and language learning. In M. Carreiras & C. Clifton, Jr. (Eds.), *The on-line study of sentence comprehension* (pp. 271–308). New York: Psychology Press.

Osterhout, L., & Mobley, L.A. (1995). Event-related brain potentials elicited by failure to agree. *Journal of Memory and Language, 34*, 739–773.

Osterhout, L., & Nicol, J. (1999). On the distinctiveness, independence, and time course of the brain responses to syntactic and semantic anomalies. *Language and Cognitive Processes, 14*, 283–317.

Otten, L.J., & Rugg, M.D. (2005). Interpreting event-related brain potentials. In T.C. Handy (Ed.), *Event-related potentials: A methods handbook* (pp. 3–16). Cambridge, MA: MIT Press.

Otten, M., & van Berkum, J.J.A. (2008). Discourse-based word anticipation during language processing: Prediction of priming? *Discourse Processes, 45*, 464–496.

Ouellette, G., & Baum, S. (1994). Acoustic analysis of prosodic cues in left- and right-hemisphere-damaged patients. *Aphasiology, 8*, 157–283.

Pa, J., & Hickok, G. (2008). A parietal-temporal sensory-motor integration area for the human vocal tract: Evidence from an fMRI study of skilled musicians. *Neuropsychologia, 46*, 362–368.

Packard, J. (1986). Tone production deficits in nonfluent aphasic Chinese speech. *Brain and Language, 29*, 212–223.

Padden, C., Meir, I., Aronoff, M., & Sandler, W. (2010). The grammar of space in two new sign languages. In D. Brentari (Ed.), *Sign languages* (pp. 570–592). Cambridge, UK: Cambridge University Press.

Paivio, A. (1971). *Imagery and verbal processes*. New York: Holt, Rinehart & Winston.

Paivio, A. (1986). *Mental representations: A dual coding approach*. Oxford, UK: Oxford University Press.

Paivio, A. (1991). Dual coding theory: Retrospect and current status. *Canadian Journal of Psychology, 45*, 255–287.

Paivio, A. (2007). *Mind and its evolution: A dual coding theoretical approach*. Mahwah, NJ: Lawrence Erlbaum.

Paivio, A., Yuille, J.C., & Madigan, S.A. (1968). Concreteness, imagery, and meaningfulness values for 925 nouns. *Journal of Experimental Psychology, 76*, 1–25.

Pallier, C., Devauchelle, A.D., & Dehaene, S. (2011). Cortical representation of the constituent structure of sentences. *Proceedings of the National Academy of Sciences, 108*, 2522–2527.

Palti, D., Shachar, M.B., Hendler, T., & Hadar, U. (2007). Neural correlates of semantic and morphological processing of Hebrew nouns and verbs. *Human Brain Mapping, 28*, 303–314.

Panksepp, J. (1998). *Affective neuroscience: The foundations of human animal emotions*. Oxford, UK: Oxford University Press.

Pannekamp, A., Toepel, U., Alter, K., Hahne, A., & Friederici, A.D. (2005). Prosody-driven sentence processing: An event-related brain potential study. *Journal of Cognitive Neuroscience, 17*, 407–421.

Papagno, C., Capasso, R., & Miceli, G. (2009). Reversed concreteness effect for nouns in a subject with semantic dementia. *Neuropsychologia, 47*, 1138–1148.

Papagno, C., Cecchetto, C., Reati, F., & Bello, L. (2007). Processing syntactically complex sentences relies on verbal short-term memory: Evidence from a short-term memory patient. *Cognitive Neuropsychology, 24*, 2292–311.

Papathanasiou, I., Filipovic, S.R., Whurr, R., Rothwell, J.C., & Jahanshahi, M. (2004). Changes in corticospinal motor excitability induced by non-motor linguistic tasks. *Experimental Brain Research, 154*, 218–225.

Papeo, L., & Hochmann, J.R. (2012). A cross-talk between brain-damaged patients and infants on action and language. *Neuropsychologia, 50*, 1222–1234.

Papeo, L., Negri, G.A.L., Zadini, A., & Rumiati, R.I. (2010). Action performance and action-word understanding: Evidence of double dissociations in left-damaged patients. *Cognitive Neuropsychology, 27*, 428–461.

Papeo, L., Vallesi, A., Isaja, A., & Rumiati, R.I. (2009). Effects of TMS on different stages of motor and non-motor verb processing in primary motor cortex. *PLoS ONE, 4*, e4508.

Papoutsi, M., de Zwart, J.A., Jansma, J.M., Pickering, M.J., Bednar, J.A., & Horwitz, B. (2009). From phonemes to articulatory codes: An fMRI study of the role of Broca's area in speech production. *Cerebral Cortex, 19*, 2156–2165.

Papoutsi, M., Stamatakis, E.A., Griffiths, J., Marslen-Wilson, W.D., & Tyler, L.K. (2011). Is left fronto-temporal connectivity essential for syntax? Effective connectivity, tractography and performance in left-hemisphere damaged patients. *NeuroImage, 58*, 656–664.

Paradis, M. (1989). Bilingualism and polyglot aphasia. In F. Boller & J. Grafman (Eds.), *Handbook of neuropsychology, Vol. 2* (pp. 117–140). Amsterdam: Elsevier.

Paradis, M. (1998). Acquired aphasia in bilingual speakers. In M.T. Sarno (Ed.), *Acquired aphasia*, 3rd edition (pp. 531–550). San Diego, CA: Academic Press.

Pardo, J.S. (2006). On phonetic convergence during conversational interaction. *Journal of the Acoustical Society of America, 119*, 2382–2393.

Parkinson, J., Dyson, B.J., & Khurana, B. (2010). Line by line: ERP correlates of stroke order priming in letters. *Experimental Brain Research, 201*, 575–586.

Parkinson, J., & Khurana, B. (2007). Temporal order of strokes primes letter recognition. *Quarterly Journal of Experimental Psychology, 60*, 1265–1274.

Pascual-Leone, A., & Hamilton, R. (2001). The metamodal organization of the brain. *Progress in Brain Research, 134*, 427–445.

Patel, A.D., Gibson, E., Ratner, J., Besson, M., & Holcomb, P.J. (1998). Processing syntactic relations in language and music: An event-related potential study. *Journal of Cognitive Neuroscience, 10*, 717–733.

Patterson, K. (1986). Lexical but nonsemantic spelling? *Cognitive Neuropsychology, 3*, 341–367.

Patterson, K., & Hodges, J.R. (1992). Deterioration of word meaning: Implications for reading. *Neuropsychologia, 30*, 1025–1040.

Patterson, K., & Lambon Ralph, M.A. (2006). Selective disorders of reading? *Current Opinion in Neurobiology, 9*, 235–239.

Patterson, K., Lambon Ralph, M.A., Hodges, J.R., & McClelland, J.L. (2001). Deficits in irregular past-tense verb morphology associated with degraded semantic knowledge. *Neuropsychologia, 39*, 709–724.

Patterson, K., Lambon Ralph, M.A., Jefferies, E., Woollams, A., Hodges, J.R., & Rogers, T.T. (2006). "Presemantic" cognition in semantic dementia: Six deficits in search of an explanation. *Journal of Cognitive Neuroscience, 18*, 169–183.

Patterson, K., Nestor, P.J., & Rogers, T.T. (2007). Where do you know what you know? The representation of semantic knowledge in the brain. *Nature Reviews: Neuroscience, 8*, 976–987.

Paulesu, E., Frith, C., & Frackowiak, D. (1993). The neural correlates of the verbal component of working memory. *Nature, 362*, 342–345.

Paulesu, E., & Mehler, J. (1998). Right on in sign language. *Nature, 392*, 233–234.

Paulmann, S., Ott, D.V.M., & Kotz, S.A. (2011). Emotional speech perception unfolding in time: The role of the basal ganglia. *PLoS ONE, 6*, e17694.

Paulmann, S., & Pell, M.D. (2010). Dynamic emotion processing in Parkinson's disease as a function of channel availability. *Journal of Clinical and Experimental Neuropsychology, 32*, 822–835.

Paulmann, S., Pell, M.D., & Kotz, S.A. (2009a). Comparative processing of emotional prosody and semantics following basal ganglia infarcts: ERP evidence of selective impairments for disgust and fear. *Brain Research, 1295*, 159–169.

Paulmann, S., Seifert, S., & Kotz, S.A. (2009b). Orbitofrontal lesions cause impairment during late but not early emotional prosodic processing. *Social Neuroscience, 5,* 59–75.

Payabvash, S., Souza, L.C.S., Wang, Y., Schaefer, P.W., Furie, K.L., Halpern, E.F., Gonzalez, R.G., & Lev, M.H. (2011). Regional ischemic vulnerability of the brain to hypoperfusion: The need for location specific computed tomography perfusion thresholds in acute stroke patients. *Stroke, 42,* 1255–1260.

Pecher, D., Boot, I., & Van Dantzig, S. (2011). Abstract concepts: Sensory-motor grounding, metaphors, and beyond. In B. Ross (Ed.), *The psychology of learning and motivation, Vol. 54* (pp. 217–248). Burlington, VT: Academic Press.

Pecher, D., & Zwaan, R.A. (Eds.) (2005). *Grounding cognition.* Cambridge, UK: Cambridge University Press.

Peelen, M.V., Bracci, S., Lu, X., He, C., Caramazza, A., & Bi, Y. (2013). Tool selectivity in left occipitotemporal cortex develops without vision. *Journal of Cognitive Neuroscience, 25,* 1225–1234.

Peelen, M.V., & Caramazza, A. (2012). Conceptual object representations in human anterior temporal cortex. *Journal of Neuroscience, 32,* 15728–15736.

Peelen, M.V., & Downing, P.E. (2007). The neural basis of visual body perception. *Nature Reviews: Neuroscience, 8,* 636–648.

Peelen, M.V., Romagno, D., & Caramazza, A. (2012). Is verb selectivity in left posterior temporal cortex related to conceptual action knowledge? *Journal of Cognitive Neuroscience, 24,* 2096–2107.

Peelle, J.E., Cooke, A., Moore, P., Vesely, L., & Grossman, M. (2007). Syntactic and thematic components of sentence processing in progressive nonfluent aphasia and nonaphasic frontotemporal dementia. *Journal of Neurolinguistics, 20,* 482–494.

Peelle, J.E., Troiani, V., Gee, J., Moore, P., McMillan, C., Vesely, L., & Grossman, M. (2008). Sentence comprehension and voxel-based morphometry in progressive nonfluent aphasia, semantic dementia, and nonaphasic frontotemporal dementia. *Journal of Neurolinguistics, 21,* 418–432.

Peeva, M.G., Guenther, F.H., Tourville, J.A., Nieto-Castanon, A., Anton, J.L., Nazarian, B., & Alario, F.X. (2010). Distinct representations of phonemes, syllables, and supra-syllabic sequences in the speech production network. *NeuroImage, 50,* 626–638.

Pell, M.D. (1996). On the receptive prosodic loss in Parkinson's disease. *Cortex, 32,* 693–704.

Pell, M.D. (2006a). Cerebral mechanisms for understanding emotional prosody in speech. *Brain and Language, 96,* 221–234.

Pell, M.D. (2006b). Judging emotion and attitudes from prosody following brain damage. *Progress in Brain Research, 156,* 303–317.

Pell, M.D., & Baum, S.R. (1997). The ability to perceive and comprehend intonation in linguistic and affective contexts by brain-damaged adults. *Brain and Language, 57,* 80–99.

Pell, M.D., & Leonard, C.L. (2003). Processing emotional tone from speech in Parkinson's disease: A role for the basal ganglia. *Cognitive, Affective, and Behavioral Neuroscience, 3,* 275–288.

Pell, M.D., Monetta, L., Paulmann, S., & Kotz, S.A. (2009). Recognizing emotions in a foreign language. *Journal of Nonverbal Behavior, 33,* 107–120.

Penfield, W., & Boldrey, E. (1937). Somatic motor and sensory representation in the cerebral cortex of man as studied by electrical stimulation. *Brain, 60,* 389–443.

Penfield, W., & Rasmussen, T. (1949). Vocalization and speech arrest. *Archive of Neurology and Psychiatry, 61,* 21–27.

Penfield, W., & Rasmussen, T. (1950). *The cerebral cortex of man: A clinical study of localization of function.* New York: Macmillan.

Penfield, W., & Roberts, L. (1959). *Speech and brain-mechanisms.* Princeton, NJ: Princeton University Press.

Penfield, W., & Welch, K. (1951). The supplementary motor area of the cerebral cortex: A clinical and experimental study. *Archive of Neurology and Psychiatry, 66,* 289–317.

Penke, M., Janssen, U., & Krause, M. (1999). The representation of inflectional morphology: Evidence from Broca's aphasia. *Brain and Language, 68,* 225–232.

Peper, J.S., Brouwer, R.W., Boomsma, D.I., Kahn, R.S., & Hulshoff Poll, H.E. (2007). Genetic influences on human brain structure: A review of brain imaging studies in twins. *Human Brain Mapping, 28,* 464–473.

Perani, D., Cappa, S., Schnur, T., Tettamanti, M., Collina, S., Rosa, M., & Fazio, F. (1999). The neural correlates of verb and noun processing—a PET study. *Brain, 122,* 2337–2344.

Perfetti, C.A. (1997). The psycholinguistics of spelling and reading. In C.A. Perfetti & L. Rieben (Eds.), *Learning to spell: Research, theory, and practice across languages.* Mahwah, NJ: Lawrence Erlbaum.

Perfetti, C.A., Bell, L.C., & DeLaney, S.M. (1988). Automatic (prelexical) phonetic activation in silent word reading: Evidence from backward masking. *Journal of Memory and Language, 27,* 59–70.

Perkell, J.S. (2012). Movement goals and feedback and feedforward control mechanisms in speech production. *Journal of Neurolinguistics, 25,* 382–407.

Perkins, J.M., Baran, J.A., & Gandour, J. (1996). Hemispheric specialization in processing intonation contours. *Aphasiology, 10,* 343–362.

Perner, J., & Leekam, S. (2008). The curious incident of the photo that was accused of being false: Issues of domain specificity in development, autism, and brain imaging. *Quarterly Journal of Experimental Psychology, 61,* 76–89.

Perniss, P., Thompson, R.L., & Vigliocco, G. (2010). Iconicity as a general property of language: Evidence from spoken and signed languages. *Frontiers in Psychology, 1,* Article 227.

Perrone-Bertolotti, M., Kujala, J., Vidal, J.R., Hamame, C.M., Ossandon, T., Bertrand, O., Minotti, L., Kahane, P., Jerbi, K., & Lachaux, J.P. (2012). How silent is silent reading? Intracerebral evidence for top-down activation of temporal voice areas during reading. *Journal of Neuroscience, 32,* 17554–17562.

Perry, C., Ziegler, J., & Zorzi, M. (2007). Nested incremental modeling in the development of computational theories: The CDP+ model of reading aloud. *Psychological Review, 114,* 273–315.

Pessoa, L., & Adolphs, R. (2010). Emotion processing and the amygdala: From a "low road" to "many roads" to biological significance. *Nature Reviews Neuroscience, 11,* 773–783.

Petitto, L.A., Zatorre, R.J., Gauna, K., Nikelski, E.J., Dostie, D., & Evans, A.C. (2000). Speech-like cerebral activity in profoundly deaf people processing signed languages: Implications for the neural basis of human language. *Proceedings of the National Academy of Sciences, 97,* 13961–13966.

Petkov, C.I., Logothetis, N.K., & Obleser, J. (2009). Where are the human speech and voice regions, and do other animals have anything like them? *The Neuroscientist, 15,* 419–429.

Pfau, R., & Quer, J. (2010). Nonmanuals: Their grammatical and prosodic roles. In D. Brentari (Ed.), *Sign languages* (pp. 381–402). Cambridge, UK: Cambridge University Press.

Pfau, R., Steinbach, M., & Woll, B. (Eds.) (2012). *Sign language: An international handbook.* Berlin: Mouton de Gruyter.

Pflugshaupt, T., Gutbrod, K., Wurtz, P., von Wartburg, R., Nyffeler, T., de Haan, B., Karnath, H.O., & Mueri, R.M. (2009). About the role of visual field defects in pure alexia. *Brain, 132,* 1907–1917.

Philipose, L.E., Gottesman, R.F., Newhart, M., Kleinman, J.T., Herskovits, E.H., Pawlak, M.A., Marsh, E.B., Davis, C., Heidler-Gary, J., & Hillis, A.E. (2007). Neural regions essential for reading and spelling of words and pseudowords. *Annals of Neurology, 62,* 481–492.

Phillips, C., Kazanina, N., & Abada, S.H. (2005). ERP effects of the processing of syntactic long-distance dependencies. *Cognitive Brain Research, 22,* 407–428.

Pichon, S., & Kell, C.A. (2013). Affective and sensorimotor components of emotional prosody generation. *Journal of Neuroscience, 33,* 1640–1650.

Pick, A. (1892). Ueber die Beziehungen der senilen Hirnatrophie zur Aphasie. *Prager Medizinsche Wochenschrift, 17,* 165–167.

Pick, A. (1913). *Die agrammatischen Sprachstorungen. Studien zur psychologischen Grundlegung der Aphasielehre.* Berlin: Springer.

Pickering, M.J., & Garrod, S. (2007). Do people use language production to make predictions during language comprehension? *Trends in Cognitive Sciences, 11,* 105–110.

Pickering, M.J., & van Gompel, R.P.G. (2006). Syntactic parsing. In M.J. Traxler & M.A. Gernsbacher (Eds.), *Handbook of psycholinguistics,* 2nd edition (pp. 455–504). San Diego: Academic Press.

Pickering-Brown, S.M., Rollinson, S., Du Plessis, D., Morrison, K.E., Varma, A., Richardson, A.M.T., Neary, D., Snowden, J.S., & Mann, D.M.A. (2008). Frequency and clinical characteristics of progranulin mutation carriers in the Manchester frontotemporal lobar degeneration cohort: Comparison with patients with *MAPT* and no known mutations. *Brain, 121,* 721–731.

Pillon, A., & d'Honincthun, P. (2010). The organization of the conceptual system: The case of the "object versus action" dimension. *Cognitive Neuropsychology, 27,* 587–613.

Ping, R.M., Dhillon, S., & Beilock, S.L. (2009). Reach for what you like: The body's role in shaping preferences. *Emotion Review, 1,* 140–150.

Pinker, S. (1989). *Learnability and cognition: The acquisition of argument structure.* Cambridge, MA: MIT Press.

Pinker, S. (1991). Rules of language. *Science, 253,* 530–535.

Pinker, S. (1994). *The language instinct: How the mind creates language.* New York: Morrow.

Pinker, S. (1995). Why the child holded the baby rabbits: A case study in language acquisition. In L.R. Gleitman & M. Liberman (Eds.), *Language: An invitation to cognitive science, Vol. 1* (pp. 107–134). Cambridge, MA: MIT Press.

Pinker, S. (1999). *Words and rules: The ingredients of language.* New York: Basic Books.

Pinker, S. (2007). *The stuff of thought: Language as a window into human nature.* New York: Viking.

Pinker, S. (2011). *The better angels of our nature: Why violence has declined.* New York: Viking.

Pinker, S., & Bloom, P. (1990). Natural language and natural selection. *Behavioral and Brain Sciences, 13,* 707–784.

Pinker, S., & Prince, A. (1988). On language and connectionism: Analysis of a parallel distributed processing model of language acquisition. *Cognition, 28,* 73–193.

Pinker, S., & Ullman, M. (2002a). The past and future of the past tense. *Trends in Cognitive Sciences, 6,* 456–463.

Pinker, S., & Ullman, M. (2002b). Combination and structure, not gradedness, is the issue. *Trends in Cognitive Sciences, 6,* 472–474.

Pirog Revill, K., Aslin, R.A., Tanenhaus, M.K., & Bavelier, D. (2008). Neural correlates of partial lexical activation. *Proceedings of the National Academy of Sciences, 105,* 13111–13115.

Pitcher, D., Garrido, L., Walsh, V., & Duchaine, B.C. (2008). Transcranial magnetic stimulation disrupts the perception and embodiment of facial expressions. *Journal of Neuroscience, 28,* 8929–8933.

Piwnica-Worms, K.E., Omar, R., Hailstone, J.C., & Warren, J.D. (2010). Flavour processing in semantic dementia. *Cortex, 46,* 761–768.

Plante, E., Creusere, M., & Sabin, C. (2002). Dissociating sentential prosody from sentence processing: Activation interacts with task demands. *NeuroImage, 17,* 401–410.

Plante, E., Van Petten, C., & Senkfor, A.J. (2000). Electrophysiological dissociation between verbal and nonverbal semantic processing in learning disable adults. *Neuropsychologia, 38,* 1669–1684.

Planton, S., Jucla, M., Roux, F.E., & Demonet, J.F. (in press). The "handwriting brain": A meta-analysis of neuroimaging studies of motor versus orthographic processes. *Cortex.*

Plaut, D.C., & Behrmann, M. (2011). Complementary neural representations for faces and words: A computational exploration. *Cognitive Neuropsychology, 28,* 251–275.

Plaut, D.C., & Shallice, T. (1993). Deep dyslexia: A case study in connectionist neuropsychology. *Cognitive Neuropsychology, 10,* 377–500.

Pobric, G., Jefferies, E., & Lambon Ralph, M.A. (2007). Anterior temporal lobes mediate semantic representation: Mimicking semantic dementia by using rTMS in normal participants. *Proceedings of the National Academy of Sciences, 104,* 20137–20141.

Pobric, G., Jefferies, E., & Lambon Ralph, M.A. (2009). The role of the anterior temporal lobes in the comprehension of concrete and abstract words: rTMS evidence. *Cortex, 45,* 1104–1110.

Pobric, G., Jefferies, E., & Lambon Ralph, M.A. (2010a). Amodal semantic representations depend on both anterior temporal lobes: Evidence from repetitive transcranial magnetic stimulation. *Neuropsychologia, 48*, 1336–1342.

Pobric, G., Jefferies, E., & Lambon Ralph, M.A. (2010b). Category-specific versus category-general semantic impairment induced by transcranial magnetic stimulation. *Current Biology, 20*, 964–968.

Poeppel, D. (2001). Pure word deafness and the bilateral processing of the speech code. *Cognitive Science, 25*, 679–691.

Poeppel, D. (2003). The analysis of speech in different temporal integration windows: Cerebral lateralization as "asymmetric sampling in time." *Speech Communication, 41*, 245–255.

Poeppel, D., Idsardi, W.J., & van Wassenhove, V. (2008). Speech perception at the interface of neurobiology and linguistics. *Philosophical Transactions of the Royal Society, B, Biological Sciences, 363*, 1071–1086.

Poizner, H., & Battison, R. (1980). Cerebral asymmetry for sign language: Clinical and experimental evidence. In H. Lane & F. Grosjean (Eds.), *Recent perspectives on American Sign Language* (pp. 79–101). Hillsdale, NJ: Lawrence Erlbaum.

Poizner, H., Klima, E.S., & Bellugi, U. (1987). *What the hands reveal about the brain.* Cambridge, MA: MIT Press.

Poldrack, R.A., Mumford, J.A., & Nichols, T.E. (2011). *Handbook of functional MRI data analysis.* Cambridge, UK: Cambridge University Press.

Posner, M.I., & Raichle, M.E. (1994). *Images of mind.* New York: Scientific American Library.

Postle, N., McMahon, K.L., Ashton, R., Meredith, M., & de Zubicaray, G.I. (2008). Action word meaning representations in cytoarchitectonically defined primary and premotor cortices. *NeuroImage, 43*, 634–644.

Postma, A. (2000). Detection of errors during speech production: A review of speech monitoring models. *Cognition, 77*, 97–131.

Postma, A., & Laeng, B. (Eds.) (2006). Special issue: New insights in categorical and coordinate processing of spatial relations. *Neuropsychologia, 44*, 1513–1621.

Pouratian, N., Cannestra, A.F., Bookheimer, S.Y., Martin, N., & Toga, A.W. (2004). Variability of intraoperative electrocortical stimulation mapping parameters across and within individuals. *Journal of Neurosurgery, 101*, 458–466.

Prabhakaran, R., Blumstein, S.E., Myers, E.B., Hutchison, E., & Britton, B. (2006). An event-related fMRI investigation of phonological-lexical competition. *Neuropsychologia, 44*, 2209–2221.

Prat, C.S., & Just, M.A. (2011). Exploring the neural dynamics underpinning individual differences in sentence comprehension. *Cerebral Cortex, 21*, 1747–1760.

Prat, C.S., Keller, T.A., & Just, M.A. (2007). Individual differences in sentence comprehension: A functional magnetic resonance imaging investigation of syntactic and lexical processing demands. *Journal of Cognitive Neuroscience, 19*, 1950–1963.

Price, C.J. (2010). The anatomy of language: A review of 100 fMRI studies published in 2009. *Annals of the New York Academy of Sciences, 1191*, 62–88.

Price, C.J. (2012). A review and synthesis of the first 20 years of PET and fMRI studies of heard speech, spoken language and reading. *NeuroImage, 62*, 816–847.

Price, C.J. (2013). Current themes in neuroimaging studies of reading. *Brain and Language, 125*, 131–133.

Price, C.J., Crinion, J.T., & MacSweeney, M. (2011). A generative model of speech production in Broca's and Wernicke's areas. *Frontiers in Psychology, 2*, Article 237.

Price, C.J., & Devlin, J.T. (2003). The myth of the visual word form area. *NeuroImage, 19*, 473–481.

Price, C.J., & Devlin, J.T. (2011). The Interactive Account of ventral occipitotemporal contributions to reading. *Trends in Cognitive Sciences, 15*, 246–253.

Price, C.J., & Friston, K.J. (1997). Cognitive conjunction: A new approach to brain activation experiments. *NeuroImage, 5*, 261–270.

Pulvermüller, F. (2005). Brain mechanisms linking language and action. *Nature Reviews: Neuroscience, 6*, 576–582.

Pulvermüller, F. (2008). Brain embodiment of category-specific semantic memory circuits. In G.R. Semin & E.R. Smith (Eds.), *Embodied grounding: Social, cognitive, affective, and neuroscientific approaches* (pp. 71–97). Cambridge, UK: Cambridge University Press.

Pulvermüller, F. (2013). How neurons make meaning: Brain mechanisms for embodied and abstract-symbolic semantics. *Trends in Cognitive Sciences, 17*, 458–470.

Pulvermüller, F., Cooper-Pye, E., Dine, C., Hauk, O., Nestor, P.J., & Patterson, K. (2009a). The word processing deficit in semantic dementia: All categories are equal, but some categories are more equal than others. *Journal of Cognitive Neuroscience, 22*, 2027–2041.

Pulvermüller, F., Härle, M., & Hummel, F. (2001). Walking or talking? Behavioral and neurophysiological correlates of action verb processing. *Brain and Language, 78*, 143–168.

Pulvermüller, F., Hauk, O., Nikulin, V., & Ilmoniemi, R. (2005a). Functional links between motor and language systems. *European Journal of Neuroscience, 21*, 793–797.

Pulvermüller, F., Huss, M., Kherif, F., Moscoso del Prado Martin, F., Hauk, O., & Shtyrov, Y. (2006). Motor cortex maps articulatory features of speech sounds. *Proceedings of the National Academy of Sciences, 103*, 7865–7870.

Pulvermüller, F., Kherif, F., Hauk, O., Mohr, B., & Nimmo-Smith, I. (2009b). Distributed cell assemblies for general lexical and category-specific semantic processing as revealed by fMRI cluster analysis. *Human Brain Mapping, 30*, 3837–3850.

Pulvermüller, F., Shtyrov, Y., & Ilmoniemi, R. (2003). Spatiotemporal patterns of neural language processing: An MEG study using minimum-norm current estimates. *NeuroImage, 20*, 1020–1025.

Pulvermüller, F., Shtyrov, Y., & Ilmoniemi, R. (2005b). Brain signatures of meaning access in action word recognition. *Journal of Cognitive Neuroscience, 17*, 884–892.

Purcell, D.W., & Munhall, K.G. (2006). Adaptive control of vowel formant frequency: Evidence from real-time formant manipulation. *Journal of the Acoustical Society of America, 120*, 966–977.

Purcell, J.J., Napoliello, E.M., & Eden, G.F. (2011a). A combined fMRI study of typed spelling and reading. *NeuroImage, 55*, 750–762.

Purcell, J.J., Turkeltaub, P.E., Eden, G.F., & Rapp, B. (2011b). Examining the central and peripheral processes of written word production through meta-analysis. *Frontiers in Psychology, 2*, Article 239.

Purves, D., Brannon, E.M., Cabeza, R., Huettel, S.A., LaBar, K.S., Platt, M.L., & Woldorff, M.G. (2008). *Principles of cognitive neuroscience.* Sunderland, MA: Sinauer.

Pylyshyn, Z. (1984). *Computation and cognition.* Cambridge, MA: MIT Press.

Qiao, E., Vinckier, F., Szwed, M., Naccache, L., Valabregue, R., Dehaene, S., & Cohen, L. (2010). Unconsciously deciphering handwriting: Subliminal invariance for handwritten words in the visual word form area. *NeuroImage, 49,* 1786–1799.

Quiroga, R.Q. (2012). Concept cells: The building blocks of declarative memory functions. *Nature Reviews Neuroscience, 13,* 587–597.

Quiroga, R.Q., Kraskov, A., Koch, C., & Fried, I. (2009). Explicit encoding of multimodal percepts by single neurons in the human brain. *Current Biology, 19,* 1308–1313.

Rabinovici, G.D., Jagust, W.J., Furst, A.J., Ogar, J.M., Racine, C.A., Mormino, E.C., O'Neil, J.P., Lal, R.A., Dronkers, N.F., Miller, B.L., & Gorno-Tempini, M.L. (2008). Ab amyloid and glucose metabolism in three variants of primary progressive aphasia. *Annals of Neurology, 64,* 388–401.

Raettig, T., Frisch, S., Friederici, A.D., & Kotz, S.A. (2010). Neural correlates of morphosyntactic and verb-argument structure processing: An EfMRI study. *Cortex, 46,* 613–620.

Raizada, R.D.S., Tsao, F.M., Liu, H.M., & Kuhl, P.K. (2010). Quantifying the adequacy of neural representations for a cross-language phonetic discrimination task: Prediction of individual differences. *Cerebral Cortex, 20,* 1–12.

Rapcsak, S.Z., & Beeson, P.M. (2002). Neuroanatomical correlates of spelling and writing. In A. Hillis (Ed.), *Handbook of adult language disorders* (pp. 71–100). New York: Psychology Press.

Rapcsak, S.Z., & Beeson, P.M. (2004). The role of left posterior inferior temporal cortex in spelling. *Neurology, 62,* 2221–2229.

Rapcsak, S.Z., Beeson, P.M., Henry, M.L., Leyden, A., Kim, E., Rising, K., Andersen, S., & Cho, H. (2009). Phonological dyslexia and dysgraphia: Cognitive mechanisms and neural substrates. *Cortex, 45,* 575–591.

Rapcsak, S.Z., Gonzalez Rothi, L.J., & Heilman, K.M. (1987). Phonological alexia with optic and tactile anomia: A neuropsychological and anatomical study. *Brain and Language, 31,* 109–121.

Rapcsak, S.Z., Ochipa, C., Anderson, K.C., & Poizner, H. (1995). Progressive ideomotor apraxia: Evidence for a selective impairment of the action production system. *Brain and Cognition, 27,* 213–236.

Raposo, A., Moss, H.E., Stamatakis, E.A., & Tyler, L.K. (2009). Modulation of motor, premotor cortices by actions, action words, and action sentences. *Neuropsychologia, 47,* 388–396.

Rapp, B. (Ed.) (2001). *The handbook of cognitive neuropsychology.* Philadelphia, PA: Psychology Press.

Rapp, B., Benzing, L., & Caramazza, A. (1997). The autonomy of lexical orthography. *Cognitive Neuropsychology, 14,* 71–104.

Rapp, B., & Caramazza, A. (1997). From graphemes to abstract letter shapes: Levels of representation in written spelling. *Journal of Experimental Psychology: Human Perception and Performance, 23,* 1130–1152.

Rapp, B., & Caramazza, A. (1998a). A case of selective difficulty in writing verbs. *Neurocase, 4,* 127–139.

Rapp, B., & Caramazza, A. (1998b). Lexical deficits. In M.T. Sarno (Ed.), *Acquired aphasia,* 3rd edition (pp. 187–228). San Diego: Academic Press.

Rapp, B., & Caramazza, A. (2002). Selective difficulties with spoken nouns and written verbs: A single case study. *Journal of Neurolinguistics, 15,* 373–402.

Rapp, B., & Dufor, O. (2011). The neurotopography of written word production: An fMRI investigation of the distribution of sensitivity to word length and frequency. *Journal of Cognitive Neuroscience, 23,* 4067–4081.

Rapp, B., Folk, J., & Tainturier, M.J. (2001). Word reading. In B. Rapp (Ed.), *The handbook of cognitive neuropsychology* (pp. 233–262). Philadelphia, PA: Psychology Press.

Rapp, B., & Goldrick, M. (2000). Discreteness and interactivity in spoken word production. *Psychological Review, 107,* 460–499.

Rapp, B., & Goldrick, M. (2004). Feedback by any other name is still interactivity: A reply to Roelofs' comment on Rapp and Goldrick (2000). *Psychological Review, 111,* 573–578.

Rapp, B., & Goldrick, M. (2006). Speaking words: Contributions of cognitive neuropsychological research. *Cognitive Neuropsychology, 23,* 39–73.

Rapp, B., & Lipka, K. (2011). The literate brain: The relationship between reading and spelling. *Journal of Cognitive Neuroscience, 23,* 1180–1197.

Rappaport Hovav, M., Doron, E., & Sichel, I. (Eds.) (2009). *Lexical semantics, syntax, and event structure.* Oxford, UK: Oxford University Press.

Rauschecker, J.P., Bowen, R.F., Parvizi, J., & Wandell, B.A. (2012). Position sensitivity in the visual word form area. *Proceedings of the National Academy of Sciences, 109,* 9244–9245.

Rauschecker, J.P., & Scott, S.K. (2009). Maps and streams in the auditory cortex: Nonhuman primates illuminate human speech processing. *Nature Neuroscience, 12,* 718–724.

Recchia, G., & Jones, M.N. (2012). The semantic richness of abstract concepts. *Frontiers in Human Neuroscience, 6,* Article 315.

Redcay, E. (2008). The superior temporal sulcus performs a common function for social and speech perception: Implications for the emergence of autism. *Neuroscience and Biobehavioral Reviews, 32,* 123–142.

Reddy, L., & Kanwisher, N. (2006). Coding of visual objects in the ventral stream. *Current Opinion in Neurobiology, 16,* 408–414.

Reich, L., Szwed, M., Cohen, L., & Amedi, A. (2011). A ventral visual stream reading center independent of visual experience. *Current Biology, 21,* 363–368. (Erratum in 2012 paper.)

Reich, L., Szwed, M., Cohen, L., & Amedi, A. (2012). A ventral visual stream reading enter independent of visual experience. *Current Biology, 22,* 350–352. (Erratum for 2011 paper.)

Reilly, J., Rodriguez, A.D., Peelle, J.E., & Grossman, M. (2011). Frontal lobe damage impairs process and content in semantic memory: Evidence from category-specific effects in progressive nonfluent aphasia. *Cortex, 47,* 645–658.

Repetto, C., Colombo, B., Cipresso, P., & Riva, G. (2013). The effects of rTMS over the primary motor cortex: The link between action and language. *Neuropsychologia, 51*, 8–13.

Rhee, J., Antiquena, P., & Grossman, M. (2001). Verb comprehension in frontotemporal degeneration: The role of grammatical, semantic, and executive components. *Neurocase, 7*, 173–184.

Rice, S. (1998). Giving and taking in Chipewyan: The semantics of THING-marking classificatory verbs. In J. Newman (Ed.), *The linguistics of giving* (pp. 97–134). Amsterdam: John Benjamins.

Richardson, F.M., Ramsden, S., Ellis, C., Burnett, S., Megnin, O., Catmur, C., Schofield, T.M., Leff, A.P., & Price, C.J. (2011). Auditory short-term memory capacity correlates with gray matter density in the left posterior STS in cognitively normal and dyslexic adults. *Journal of Cognitive Neuroscience, 23*, 3746–3756.

Richardson, F.M., Thomas, M.S.C., & Price, C.J. (2009). Neuronal activation for semantically reversible sentences. *Journal of Cognitive Neuroscience, 22*, 1283–1298.

Richardson, J.D., Fillmore, P., Rorden, C., LaPointe, L.L., & Fridriksson, J. (2012). Re-establishing Broca's initial findings. *Brain and Language, 123*, 125–130.

Riecker, A., Brendel, B., Ziegler, W., Erb, M., & Ackermann, H. (2008). The influence of syllable onset complexity and syllable frequency on speech motor control. *Brain and Language, 107*, 102–113.

Righi, R., Blumstein, S.E., Mertus, J., & Worden, M.S. (2010). Neural systems underlying lexical competition: An eye tracking and fMRI study. *Journal of Cognitive Neuroscience, 22*, 213–224.

Rimol, L.M., Specht, K., Wes, S., Savoy, R., & Hugdahl, K. (2005). Processing of sub-syllabic speech units in the posterior temporal lobe: An fMRI study. *NeuroImage, 26*, 1059–1067.

Rinaldi, M.C., & Pizzamiglio, L. (2006). When space merges into language. *Neuropsychologia, 44*, 556–565.

Rissman, J., Eliassen, J.C., & Blumstein, S.E. (2003). An event-related fMRI investigation of implicit semantic priming. *Journal of Cognitive Neuroscience, 15*, 1160–1175.

Rizzolatti, G., & Sinigaglia, C. (2010). The functional role of the parieto-frontal mirror circuit: Interpretations and misinterpretations. *Nature Reviews: Neuroscience, 11*, 264–274.

Roberts, D.J., Woollams, A.M., Kim, E., Beeson, P.M., Rapcsak, S.Z., & Lambon Ralph, M.A. (2013). Efficient visual object and word recognition relies on high spatial frequency coding in the left posterior fusiform gyrus: Evidence from a case-series of patients with ventral occipito-temporal cortex damage. *Cerebral Cortex, 23*, 2568–2580.

Robinson, G., Shallice, T., Bozzali, M., & Cipolotti, L. (2013). The differing roles of the frontal cortex in fluency tests. *Brain, 135*, 2202–2214.

Robson, H., Sage, K., & Lambon Ralph, M.A. (2012). Wernicke's aphasia reflects a combination of acoustic-phonological and semantic control deficits: A case-series comparison of Wernicke's aphasia, semantic dementia, and semantic aphasia. *Neuropsychologia, 50*, 266–275.

Rochon, E., Kavé, G., Cupit, J., Jokel, R., & Winocur, G. (2004). Sentence comprehension in semantic dementia: A longitudinal case study. *Cognitive Neuropsychology, 21*, 317–330.

Rochon, E., Saffran, E.M., Berndt, R.S., & Schwartz, M.F. (2000). Quantitative analysis of aphasic sentence production: Further development and new data. *Brain and Language, 72*, 193–218.

Rodd, J.M., Davis, M.H., & Johnsrude, I.S. (2005). The neural mechanisms of speech comprehension: fMRI studies of semantic ambiguity. *Cerebral Cortex, 15*, 1261–1269.

Rodd, J.M., Longe, O.A., Randall, B., & Tyler, L.K. (2010). The functional organization of the fronto-temporal language system: Evidence from syntactic and semantic ambiguity. *Neuropsychologia, 48*, 1324–1335.

Rodríguez-Fornells, A., Münte, T.F., & Clahsen, H. (2002). Morphological priming in Spanish verb forms: An ERP repetition priming study. *Journal of Cognitive Neuroscience, 14*, 443–454.

Roelofs, A. (1992). A spreading-activation theory of lemma retrieval in speaking. *Cognition, 42*, 107–142.

Roelofs, A. (1997a). A case for non-decomposition in conceptually driven word retrieval. *Journal of Psycholinguistic Research, 26*, 33–67.

Roelofs, A. (1997b). The WEAVER model of word-form encoding in speech production. *Cognition, 64*, 249–284.

Roelofs, A. (2003). Modeling the relation between the production and recognition of spoken word forms. In N.O. Schiller & A.S. Meyer (Eds.), *Phonetics and phonology in language comprehension and production: Differences and similarities* (pp. 115–158). Berlin: Mouton de Gruyter.

Roelofs, A. (2004a). Error biases in spoken word planning and monitoring by aphasic and nonaphasic speakers: Comment on Rapp and Goldrick (2000). *Psychological Review, 111*, 561–572.

Roelofs, A. (2004b). Comprehension-based versus production-internal feedback in planning spoken words: A rejoinder to Rapp and Goldrick (2004). *Psychological Review, 111*, 579–580.

Roelofs, A. (2005). Spoken word planning, comprehending, and self-monitoring: Evaluation of WEAVER++. In R.J. Hartsuiker, R. Bastiaanse, A. Postma, & F. Wijnen (Eds.), *Phonological encoding and monitoring in normal and pathological speech* (pp. 42–63). Hove, UK: Psychology Press.

Roelofs, A. (2008). Attention to spoken word planning: Chronometric and neuroimaging evidence. *Language and Linguistics Compass, 2/3*, 389–405.

Roelofs, A., Meyer, A.S., & Levelt, W.J.M. (1998). A case for the lemma/lexeme distinction in models of speaking: Comment of Caramazza and Miozzo (1997). *Cognition, 69*, 219–230.

Roeltgen, D.P., & Heilman, K.M. (1984). Lexical agraphia: Further support for the two-system hypothesis of linguistic agraphia. *Brain, 107*, 811–827.

Roeltgen, D.P., & Heilman, K.M. (1985). Review of agraphia and a proposal for an anatomically-based neuropsychological model of writing. *Applied Psycholinguistics, 6*, 205–229.

Roeltgen, D.P., Rothi, L.G., & Heilman, K.M. (1986). Linguistic semantic agraphia: A dissociation of the lexical spelling system from semantics. *Brain and Language, 27*, 257–280.

Roeltgen, D.P., Sevush, S., & Heilman, K.M. (1983). Phonological agraphia: writing by the lexical-semantic route. *Neurology, 33*, 755–765.

Rogalski, E., Cobia, D., Harrison, T.M., Wieneke, C., Thompson, C.K., Weintraub, S., & Mesulam, M.M. (2011). Anatomy of language impairments in primary progressive aphasia. *Journal of Neuroscience, 31*, 3344–3350.

Rogalsky, C., & Hickok, G. (2009). Selective attention to semantic and syntactic features modulates sentence processing networks in anterior temporal cortex. *Cerebral Cortex, 19*, 786–796.

Rogalsky, C., & Hickok, G. (2011). The role of Broca's area in sentence comprehension. *Journal of Cognitive Neuroscience, 23*, 1664–1680.

Rogalsky, C., Matchin, W., & Hickok, G. (2008b). Broca's area, sentence comprehension, and working memory: An fMRI study. *Frontiers in Human Neuroscience, 2*, 14.

Rogalsky, C., Pitz, E., Hillis, A.E., & Hickok, G. (2008a). Auditory word comprehension impairment in acute stroke: Relative contribution of phonemic and semantic factors. *Brain and Language, 107*, 167–169.

Rogers, T.T., Lambon Ralph, M.A., Garrard, P., Bozeat, S., McClelland, J.L., Hodges, J.R., & Patterson, K. (2004). The structure and deterioration of semantic memory: A neuropsychological and computational investigation. *Psychological Review, 111*, 205–235.

Rogers, T.T., & McClelland, J.L. (2004). *Semantic cognition: A parallel distributed processing approach.* Cambridge, MA: MIT Press.

Rohrer, J.D., Caso, F., Mahoney, C., Henry, M., Rosen, H.J., Rabinovici, G., Rossor, M.N., Miller, B., Warren, J.D., Fox, N.C., Ridgway, G.R., & Gorno-Tempini, M.L. (2013). Patterns of longitudinal brain atrophy in the logopenic variant of primary progressive aphasia. *Brain and Language, 127*, 121–126.

Rohrer, J.D., Knight, W.D., Warren, J.E., Fox, N.C., Rossor, M.N., & Warren, J.D. (2008). Word-finding difficulty: A clinical analysis of the progressive aphasias. *Brain, 131*, 8–38.

Rohrer, J.D., Ridgway, G.R., Crutch, S.J., Hailstone, J., Goll, J.C., Clarkson, M.J., Mead, S., Beck, J., Mummery, C., Ourselin, S., Warrington, E.K., Rossor, M.N., & Warren, J.D. (2010). Progressive logopenic/phonological aphasia: Erosion of the language network. *NeuroImage, 49*, 984–993.

Rohrer, J.D., Rossor, M.N., & Warren, J.D. (2009a). Neologistic jargon aphasia and agraphia in primary progressive aphasia. *Journal of the Neurological Sciences, 15*, 155–159.

Rohrer, J.D., Warren, J.D., Modat, M., Ridgeway, G.R., Douiri, A., Rossor, M.N., Ourselin, S., & Fox, N.C. (2009b). Patterns of cortical thinning in the language variants of frontotemporal lobar degeneration. *Neurology, 72*, 1562–1569.

Rolheiser, T., Stamatakis, E.A., & Tyler, L.K. (2011). Dynamic processing in the human language system: Synergy between the arcuate fascicle and extreme capsule. *Journal of Neuroscience, 31*, 16949–16957.

Romani, C., McAlpiine, S., & Martin, R.C. (2007). Concreteness effects in different tasks: Implications for models of short-term memory. *Quarterly Journal of Experimental Psychology, 61*, 292–323.

Romanski, L.M., & Averbeck, B.B. (2009). The primate cortical auditory system and neural representation of conspecific vocalizations. *Annual Review of Neuroscience, 32*, 15–46.

Romero Lauro, L.J., Reis, J., Cohen, L.G., Cecchetto, C., & Papagno, C. (2010). A case for the involvement of the phonological loop in sentence comprehension. *Neuropsychologia, 48*, 4003–4011.

Rorden, C., & Karnath, H.O. (2004). Using human brain lesions to infer function: A relic from a past era in the fMRI age? *Nature Reviews Neuroscience, 5*, 813–819.

Rosci, C., Chiesa, V., Liacona, M., & Capitani, E. (2003). Apraxia is not associated with a disproportionate naming impairment for manipulable objects. *Brain and Cognition, 53*, 412–415.

Rosen, H.J., Allison, S.C., Ogar, J.M., Amici, S., Rose, K., Dronkers, N., Miller, B.L., & Gorno-Tempini, M.L. (2006). Behavioral features in semantic dementia vs. other forms of progressive aphasia. *Neurology, 67*, 1752–1756.

Rosen, H.J., Gorno-Tempini, M.L., Goldman, W.P., Perry, R.J., Schuff, N., Weiner, M., Feiwell, R., Kramer, J.H., & Miller, B.L. (2002). Patterns of brain atrophy in frontotemporal dementia and semantic dementia. *Neurology, 58*, 198–208.

Rosen, S. (1992). Temporal information in speech: Acoustic, auditory and linguistic aspects. *Philosophical Transactions of the Royal Society, B, Biological Sciences, 336*, 367–373.

Rosen, S., Wise, R.J.S., Chadha, S., Conway, E.J., & Scott, S.K. (2011). Hemispheric asymmetries in speech perception: Sense, nonsense, and modulations. *PLoS ONE, 6*, e24672.

Ross, E.D. (1981). The aprosodias: Functional-anatomic organization of the affective components of language in the right hemisphere. *Archives of Neurology, 38*, 561–569.

Ross, E.D. (2000). Affective prosody and the aprosodias. In M.M. Mesulam (Ed.), *Principles of behavioral and cognitive neurology* (pp. 316–331). Oxford, UK: Oxford University Press.

Ross, E.D., Edmondson, J.A., Seibert, G.B., & Homan, R.W. (1988). Acoustic analysis of affective prosody during right-sided Wada test: A within subjects verification of the right hemisphere's role in language. *Brain and Language, 33*, 128–145.

Ross, E.D., & Monnot, M. (2008). Neurology of affective prosody and its functional-anatomic organization in right hemisphere. *Brain and Language, 104*, 51–74.

Ross, E.D., Thompson, R.D., & Yenkosky, J.P. (1997). Lateralization of affective prosody in brain and the collosal integration of hemispheric language functions. *Brain and Language, 56*, 27–54.

Ross, J.R. (1967). *Constraints on variables in syntax.* Doctoral dissertation, MIT.

Rostomily, R.C., Berger, M.S., Ojemann, G.A., & Lettich, E. (1991). Postoperative deficits and functional recovery following removal of tumors involving the dominant hemisphere supplementary motor area. *Journal of Neurosurgery, 75*, 62–68.

Rottenberg, D.A., & Hochberg, F.H. (1977). *Neurological classics in modern translation.* New York: Hafner Press.

Roux, F.E., Boetto, S., Sacko, O., Chollet, F., & Trémoulet, M. (2003). Writing, calculating, and finger recognition in the region of the angular gyrus: A cortical stimulation study of Gerstmann syndrome. *Journal of Neurosurgery, 99*, 716–727.

Roux, F.E., Dufor, O., Giussani, C., Wamain, Y., Draper, L., Longcamp, M., & Démonet, J.F. (2009). The graphemic/motor frontal area: Exner's area revisited. *Annals of Neurology, 66*, 537–545.

Rubin, D.C. (1980). 51 properties of 125 words: A unit analysis of verbal behavior. *Journal of Verbal Learning and Verbal Behavior, 19*, 736–755.

Ruchkin, D.S., Johnson, R., Grafman, J., Canoune, JH.L., & Ritter, W. (1992). Distinctions and similarities among working memory processes: An event-related potential study. *Cognitive Brain Research, 1*, 53–66.

Rueschemeyer, S.A., & Bekkering, H. (2012). Embodied lexical relations: Flexible tools for predicting the future. In Y. Coello & A. Bartolo (Eds.), *Language and action in cognitive neuroscience* (pp. 111–125). London: Psychology Press.

Rueschemeyer, S.-A., Brass, M., & Friederici, A.D. (2007). Comprehending prehending: Neural correlates of processing verbs with motor stems. *Journal of Cognitive Neuroscience, 19*, 855–865.

Rueschemeyer, S.A., Glenberg, A.M., Kaschak, M.P., Mueller, K., & Friederici, A.D. (2010a). Top-down and bottom-up contributions to understanding sentences describing objects in motion. *Frontiers in Psychology, 1*, 1–11.

Rueschemeyer, S.A., van Rooij, D., Lindemann, O., Willems, R., & Bekkering, H. (2010b). The function of words: Distinct neural correlates for words denoting differently manipulable objects. *Journal of Cognitive Neuroscience, 22*, 1844–1851.

Rumelhart, D.E., & McClelland, J.L. (1986). On learning the past tenses of English verbs. In J.L. McClelland, D.E. Rumelhart, and the PDP Research Group (Eds.), *Parallel distributed processing: Explorations in the microstructure of cognition, Vol. 2. Psychological and biological models* (pp. 216–271). Cambridge, MA: MIT Press.

Rumelhart, D.E., McClelland, J.L., & the PDP Research Group (Eds.) (1986). *Parallel distributed processing: Explorations in the microstructure of cognition, Vol. 1. Foundations.* Cambridge, MA: MIT Press.

Rumiati, R.I., Zanini, S., Vorano, L., & Shallice, T. (2001). A form of ideational apraxia as a selective deficit of contention scheduling. *Cognitive Neuropsychology, 18*, 617–642.

Ruml, W., & Caramazza, A. (2000). An evaluation of a computational model of lexical access: Comment on Dell et al. (1997). *Psychological Review, 107*, 609–634.

Ruml, W., Caramazza, A., Shelton, J.R., & Chialant, D. (2000). Testing assumptions in computational theories of aphasia. *Journal of Memory and Language, 43*, 217–248.

Rusconi, E., Pinel, P., Dehaene, S., & Kleinschmidt, A. (2010). The enigma of Gerstmann's syndrome revisited: A telling tale of the viscissitudes of neuropsychology. *Brain, 133*, 320–332.

Rusconi, E., Pinel, P., Eger, E., LeBihan, D., Thirion, B., Dehaene, S., & Kleinschmidt, A. (2009). A disconnection account of Gerstmann syndrome: Functional neuroanatomy evidence. *Archives of Neurology, 66*, 654–662.

Rusconi, E., Walsh, V., & Butterworth, B. (2005). Dexterity with numbers: rTMS over left angular gyrus disrupts finger gnosis and number processing. *Neuropsychologia, 43*, 1609–1624.

Ryalls, J., & Reinvang, I. (1986). Functional lateralization of linguistic tones: Acoustic evidence from Norwegian. *Language and Speech, 29*, 389–398.

Sabsevitz, D.S., Medler, D.A., Seidenberg, M., & Binder, J.R. (2005). Modulation of the semantic system by word imageability. *NeuroImage, 27*, 188–200.

Saccuman, M.C., Cappa, S.F., Bates, E.A., Arevalo, A., Rosa, P.D., Danna, M., & Perani, D. (2006). The impact of semantic reference on word class: An fMRI study of action and object naming. *NeuroImage, 32*, 1865–1878.

Sach, M., Seitz, R., & Indefrey, P. (2004). Unified inflectional processing of regular and irregular verbs: A PET study. *NeuroReport, 15*, 533–537.

Sacks, O. (1995). The case of the colorblind painter. In O. Sacks, *An anthropologist on Mars* (pp. 3–41). New York: Vintage.

Sacks, O. (2010). A man of letters. In O. Sacks, *The mind's eye* (pp. 53–81). New York: Knopf.

Sadoski, M., Goetz, E.T., & Rodriguez, M. (2000). Engaging texts: Effects of concreteness on comprehensibility, interest, and recall in four text types. *Journal of Educational Psychology, 92*, 85–95.

Saffran, E.M., Berndt, R.S., & Schwartz, M.F. (1989). The quantitative analysis of agrammatic production: Procedure and data. *Brain and Language, 37*, 440–479.

Saffran, E.M., Marin, O.S., & Yeni-Komshian, G.H. (1976). An analysis of speech perception in word deafness. *Brain and Language, 3*, 209–228.

Saffran, E.M., Schwartz, M.F., & Marin, O.S.M. (1980a). Evidence from aphasia: Isolating the components of a production model. In B. Butterworth (Ed.), *Language production, Vol. 1.* London: Academic Press.

Saffran, E.M., Schwartz, M.F., & Marin, O.S.M. (1980b). The word order problem in agrammatism II: Production. *Brain and Language, 10*, 263–280.

Saffran, E.M., & Sholl, A. (1999). Clues to the functional and neural architecture of word meaning. In C.M. Brown & P. Hagoort (Eds.), *The neurocognition of language* (pp. 241–271). Oxford, UK: Oxford University Press.

Sahin, N.T., Pinker, S., Cash, S.S., & Halgren, E. (2009). Sequential processing of lexical, grammatical, and phonological information within Broca's area. *Science, 326*, 445–449.

Sahin, N.T., Pinker, S., & Halgren, E. (2006). Abstract grammatical processing of nouns and verbs in Broca's area: Evidence from fMRI. *Cortex, 42*, 540–562.

Sajjadi, S.A., Patterson, K., Arnold, R.J., Watson, P.C., & Nestor, P.J. (2012a). Primary progressive aphasia: A tale of two syndromes and the rest. *Neurology, 78*, 1670–1677.

Sajjadi, S.A., Patterson, K., Tomek, M., & Nestor, P.J. (2012b). Abnormalities of connected speech in the non-semantic variants of primary progressive aphasia. *Aphasiology, 26*, 1219–1237.

Sakai, K.L., Tatsuno, Y., Suzuki, K., Kimura, H., & Ichida, Y. (2005). Sign and speech: Amodal commonality in left hemisphere dominance for comprehension of sentences. *Brain, 128*, 1407–1417.

Sammler, D., Kotz, S.A., Eckstein, K., Ott, D.V.M., & Friederici, A.D. (2010). Prosody meets syntax: The role of the corpus collosum. *Brain, 133*, 2643–2655.

Samson, D., Apperly, I.A., Chiavarino, C., & Humphreys, G.W. (2004). Left temporoparietal junction is necessary for representing someone else's belief. *Nature Neuroscience, 7*, 499–500.

Samson, D., & Pillon, S. (2003). A case of impaired knowledge for fruits and vegetables. *Cognitive Neuropsychology, 20*, 373–400.

Sanai, N., Mirzadeh, Z., & Berger, M.S. (2008). Functional outcome after language mapping for glioma resection. *New England Journal of Medicine, 358*, 18–27.

Sander, D., Grafman, J., & Zalla, T. (2003). The human amygdala: An evolved system for relevance detection. *Reviews in the Neurosciences, 14*, 303–316.

Sander, D., Grandjean, D., Pourtois, G., Schwartz, S., Seghier, M.L., Scherer, K.R., & Vuilleumier, P. (2005). Emotion and attention interactions in social cognition: Brain regions involved in processing anger prosody. *NeuroImage, 28*, 848–858.

Sandler, W. (1989). *Phonological representation of the sign*. Dordrecht: Foris.

Sandler, W. (2005). Sign language: Overview. In K. Brown (Ed.), *Encyclopedia of language and linguistics*, 2nd edition (pp. 328–338). Oxford, UK: Elsevier.

Sandler, W. (2009). Symbiotic symbolization by hand and mouth in sign language. *Semiotica, 174*, 241–275.

Sandler, W., & Lillo-Martin, D. (2006). *Sign language and linguistic universals*. Cambridge, UK: Cambridge University Press.

Sandler, W., Padden, C., & Aronoff, M. (2005). The emergence of grammar: Systematic structure in a new language. *Proceedings of the National Academy of Sciences, 102*, 2661–2665.

Sandrini, M., Umilta, C., & Rusconi, E. (2011). The use of transcranial magnetic stimulation in cognitive neuroscience: A new synthesis of methodological issues. *Neuroscience and Biobehavioral Reviews, 35*, 516–536.

San José-Robertson, L., Corina, D.P., Ackerman, D., Guillemin, A., & Braun, A.R. (2004). Neural systems for sign language production: Mechanisms supporting lexical selection, phonological encoding, and articulation. *Human Brain Mapping, 23*, 156–167.

Santi, A., Servos, P., Vatikiotis,-Bateson, E., Kuratate, T., & Munhall, K. (2003). Perceiving biological motion: Dissociating visible speech from walking. *Journal of Cognitive Neuroscience, 15*, 800–809.

Santiago, J., Román, A., & Ouellet, M. (2011). Flexible foundations of abstract thought: A review and a theory. In T.W. Schubert & A. Maass (Eds.), *Spatial dimensions of social thought* (pp. 39–108). Berlin: Mouton de Gruyter.

Santos, A., Chaigneau, S.E., Simmons, W.K., & Barsalou, L.W. (2011). Property generation reflects word association and situated simulation. *Language and Cognition, 3*, 83–119.

Sanz, M., Laka, I., & Tanenhaus, M.K. (Eds.) (2013). *Language down the garden path: The cognitive and biological basis for linguistic structures*. Oxford: Oxford University Press.

Sapolsky, D., Bakkour, A., Negreira, A., Nalipinski, P., Weintraub, S., Mesulam, M.M., Caplan, D., & Dickerson, B.C. (2010). Cortical neuroanatomic correlates of symptom severity in primary progressive aphasia. *Neurology, 75*, 358–366.

Sarbin, T.R. (1986). *Narrative psychology*. Wesport, CT: Praeger.

Sarfarazi, M., Cave, B., Richardson, A., Behan, J., & Sedgwick, E.M. (1999). Visual event related potentials modulated by contextually relevant and irrelevant olfactory primes. *Chemical Senses, 24*, 145–154.

Sato, M., Cattaneo, L., Rizzolatti, G., & Gallese, V. (2007). Numbers within our hands: Modulation of corticospinal excitability of hand muscles during numerical judgment. *Journal of Cognitive Neuroscience, 19*, 684–693.

Sato, M., Tremblay, P., & Gracco, V. (2009). A mediating role of the premotor cortex in phoneme segmentation. *Brain and Language, 111*, 1–7.

Saur, D., Kreher, B.W., Schnell, S., Kümmerer, D., Kellmeyer, P., Vry, M.-S., Umarova, R., Musso, M., Glauche, V., Abel, S., Huber, W., Rijntjes, M., Hennig, J., & Weiller, C. (2008). Ventral and dorsal pathways for language. *Proceedings of the National Academy of Sciences, 105*, 18035–18040.

Saur, D., Schlelter, B., Schnell, S., Kratochvil, D., Küpper, H., Kellmeyer, P., Kümmerer, D., Klöppel, S., Glauche, V., Lange, R., Mader, W., Feess, D., Timmer, J., & Weiller, C. (2010). Combining functional and anatomical connectivity reveals brain networks for auditory language comprehension. *NeuroImage, 49*, 3187–3197.

Savill, N., Lindell, A., Booth, A., West, G., & Thierry, G. (2011). Literate humans sound out words during silent reading. *NeuroReport, 22*, 116–120.

Saxe, R. (2006). Uniquely human social cognition. *Current Opinion in Neurobiology, 16*, 235–239.

Saxe, R., & Kanwisher, N. (2003). People thinking about people: The role of the temporo-parietal junction in "theory of mind." *NeuroImage, 19*, 1835–1842.

Saxe, R., & Powell, L. (2006). It's the thought that counts: Specific brain regions for one component of theory of mind. *Psychological Science, 17*, 692–699.

Saygin, A.P. (2012). Sensory and motor brain areas supporting biological motion perception: Neuropsychological and neuroimaging studies. In K. Johnson & M. Shiffrar (Eds.), *People watching: Social, perceptual, and neurophysiological studies of body perception* (pp. 371–389). Oxford, UK: Oxford University Press.

Saygin, A.P., Dick, F., Wilson, S.M., Dronkers, N.F., & Bates, E. (2003). Neural resources for processing language and environmental sounds: Evidence from aphasia. *Brain, 126*, 928–945.

Saygin, A.P., Leech, R., & Dick, F. (2010a). Nonverbal auditory agnosia with lesion to Wernicke's area. *Neuropsychologia, 47*, 3275–3278.

Saygin, A.P., McCullough, S., Alac, M., & Emmorey, K. (2010b). Modulation of the BOLD response in motion sensitive lateral temporal cortex by real and fictive motion sentences. *Journal of Cognitive Neuroscience, 22*, 2480–2490.

Scahill, V.L., Hodges, J.R., & Graham, K.S. (2005). Can episodic memory tasks differentiate semantic dementia from Alzheimer's disease? *Neurocase, 11*, 441–451.

Scherer, K.R., Banse, R., Wallbott, H.G., & Goldbeck, T. (1991). Vocal cues in emotion encoding and decoding. *Motivation and Emotion, 15*, 123–148.

Schiller, N.O., Schmitt, B.M., Peters, J., & Levelt, W.J.M. (2006). Monitoring metrical stress in polysyllabic words. *Language and Cognitive Processes, 21*, 112–140.

Schirmer, A., Escoffier, N., Li, Q.Y., Li, H., Strafford-Wilson, J., & Li, W.-I. (2008a). What grabs his attention but not hers? Estrogen correlates with neurophysiological measures of vocal change detection. *Psychoneuroendocrinology, 33*, 718–727.

Schirmer, A., Escoffier, N., Zysset, S., Koester, D., Striano, T., & Friederici, A.D. (2008b). When vocal processing gets emotional: On the role of social orientation in relevance detection by the human amygdala. *NeuroImage, 40*, 1402–1410.

Schirmer, A., & Kotz, S.A. (2003). ERP evidence for a gender-specific Stroop effect in emotional speech. *Journal of Cognitive Neuroscience, 15*, 1135–1148.

Schirmer, A., & Kotz, S.A. (2006). Beyond the right hemisphere: Brain mechanisms mediating vocal emotional processing. *Trends in Cognitive Sciences, 10*, 24–30.

Schirmer, A., Kotz, S.A., & Friederici, A.D. (2005). On the role of attention for the processing of emotions in speech: Sex differences revisited. *Cognitive Brain Research, 24*, 442–452.

Schirmer, A., Zysset, S., Kotz, S.A., & von Cramon, D.Y. (2004). Gender differences in the activation of inferior frontal cortex during emotional speech perception. *NeuroImage, 21*, 1114–1123.

Schmahmann, J.D. (2010). The role of the cerebellum in cognition and emotion: Personal reflections since 1982 on the dysmetria of thought hypothesis, and its historical evolution from theory to therapy. *Neuropsychology Review, 20*, 236–260.

Schnur, T.T., Schwartz, M.F., Kimberg, D.Y., Hirshorn, E., Coslett, H.B., & Thompson-Schill, S.L. (2009). Localizing interference during naming: Convergent neuroimaging and neuropsychological evidence for the function of Broca's area. *Proceedings of the National Academy of Sciences, 106*, 322–327.

Schock, J., Cortese, M.J., & Khanna, M.M. (2012). Imageability estimates for 3,000 disyllabic words. *Behavior Research Methods, 44*, 374–379.

Schonwiesner, M., Rubsamen, R., & von Cramon, D.Y. (2005). Hemispheric asymmetry for spectral and temporal processing in the human antero-lateral auditory belt cortex. *European Journal of Neuroscience, 22*, 1521–1528.

Schoonover, C. (2010). *Portraits of the mind: Visualizing the brain from antiquity to the 21st century.* New York: Abrams.

Schroeder, C.E., Lindsley, R.W., Specht, C., Marcovici, A., Smiley, J.F., & Javitt, D.C. (2001). Somatosensory input to auditory association cortex in the macaque monkey. *Journal of Neurophysiology, 85*, 1322–1327.

Schroeter, M.L., Raczka, K., Neumann, J., von Cramon, D.Y. (2007). Towards a nosology for frontotemporal lobar degenerations: A meta-analysis involving 267 subjects. *NeuroImage, 36*, 487–510.

Schultze-Berndt, E. (2006). Sketch of a Jaminjung grammar of space. In S.C. Levinson & D. Wilkins (Eds.), *Grammars of space: Explorations in cognitive diversity* (pp. 63–114). Cambridge, UK: Cambridge University Press.

Schurmann, M., Caetano, G., Hlushchuk, Y., Jousmaki, V., & Hari, R. (2006). Touch activates human auditory cortex. *NeuroImage, 30*, 1325–1331.

Schwanenflugel, P. (1991). Why are abstract concepts hard to understand? In P.J. Schwanenflugel (Ed.), *The psychology of word meanings* (pp. 223–250). Hillsdale, NJ: Lawrence Erlbaum.

Schwanenflugel, P., Harnishfeger, K.K., & Stowe, R.W. (1988). Context availability and lexical decisions for abstract and concrete words. *Journal of Memory and Language, 27*, 499–520.

Schwanenflugel, P., & Shoben, E. (1983). Differential context effects in the comprehension of abstract and concrete verbal materials. *Journal of Experimental Psychology: Learning, Memory and Cognition, 9*, 82–102.

Schwanenflugel, P., & Stowe, R.W. (1989). Context availability and the processing of abstract and concrete words in sentences. *Reading Research Quarterly, 24*, 114–126.

Schwartz, J.L., Basirat, A., Ménard, L., & Sato, M. (2012a). The Perception-for-Action-Control Theory (PACT): A perceptuo-motor theory of speech perception. *Journal of Neurolinguistics, 25*, 336–354.

Schwartz, M.F. (1984). What the classical aphasia categories can't do for us and why. *Brain and Language, 21*, 3–8.

Schwartz, M.F., Faseyitan, O., Kim, J., & Coslett, H.B. (2012b). The dorsal stream contribution to phonological retrieval in object naming. *Brain, 135*, 3799–3814.

Schwartz, M.F., Linebarger, M.C., & Saffran, E.M. (1985). The status of the syntactic deficit theory of agrammatism. In M.L. Kean (Ed.), *Agrammatism* (pp. 83–124). Orlando, FL: Academic Press.

Schwartz, M.F., Saffran, E.M., & Marin, O.S.M. (1980). Fractionating the reading process in dementia: Evidence for word-specific print-to-sound associations. In M. Coltheart, K. Patterson, & J.C. Marshall (Eds.), *Deep dyslexia* (pp. 259–269). London: Routledge & Kegan Paul.

Schwartzkopf, D.S., & Rees, G. (2011). Pattern classification using functional magnetic resonance imaging. *Wiley Interdisciplinary Reviews: Cognitive Science, 2*, 568–579.

Scorolli, C., Binkofski, F., Buccino, G., Nicoletti, R., Riggio, L., & Borghi, A.M. (2011). Abstract and concrete sentences, embodiment, and language. *Frontiers in Psychology, 2*, Article 227.

Scorolli, C., & Borghi, A.M. (2007). Sentence comprehension and action: Effector specific modulation of the motor system. *Brain Research, 1130*, 119–124.

Scott, S.K., Blank, C.C., Rosen, S., & Wise, R.J.S. (2000). Identification of a pathway for intelligible speech in the left temporal lobe. *Brain, 123*, 2400–2406.

Scott, S.K., & Johnsrude, I.S. (2003). The neuroanatomical and functional organization of speech perception. *Trends in Neurosciences, 26*, 100–107.

Scott, S.K., McGettigan, C., & Eisner, F. (2009). A little more conversation, a little less action—Candidate roles for the motor cortex in speech perception. *Nature Review Neuroscience, 10*, 295–302.

Scott, S.K., Young, A.W., Calder, A.J., Hellawell, D.J., Aggleton, J.P., & Johnson, M. (1997). Impaired auditory recognition of fear following bilateral amygdala lesions. *Nature, 385*, 254–257.

Seeley, W.W., Crawford, R.K., Zhou, J., Miller, B.L., & Greicius, M.D. (2009). Neurodegenerative diseases target large-scale human brain networks. *Neuron, 62*, 42–52.

Seeley, W.W., Matthews, B.R., Crawford, R.K., Gorno-Tempini, M.L., Foti, D., Mackenzie, I.R., & Miller, B.L. (2008). Unravelling Boléro: Progressive aphasia, transmodal creativity, and the right posterior neocortex. *Brain, 131*, 39–49.

Seeley, W.W., Merkle, F.T., Gaus, S.E., Craig, A.D. (Bud), Allman, J.M., & Hof, P.R. (2012). Distinctive neurons of the anterior cingulate and frontoinsular cortex: A historical perspective. *Cerebral Cortex, 22*, 245–250.

Segaert, K., Menenti, L., Weber, K., Petersson, K.M., & Hagoort, P. (2012). Shared syntax in language production and language comprehension—an fMRI study. *Cerebral Cortex, 22*, 1662–1670.

Seghier, M.L. (2013). The angular gyrus: Multiple functions and multiple subdivisions. *The Neuroscientist, 19*, 43–61.

Seghier, M.L., Fagan, E., & Price, C.J. (2010). Functional subdivisions in the left angular gyrus where the semantic system meets and diverges from the default network. *Journal of Neuroscience, 30*, 16809–16817.

Seghier, M.L., Lee, H.L., Schofield, T., Ellis, C.L., & Price, C.J. (2008). Inter-subject variability in the use of two different neuronal networks for reading aloud familiar words. *NeuroImage, 42*, 1226–1236.

Sehm, B., Schnitzler, T., Obleser, J., Groba, A., Ragert, P., Villringer, A., & Obrig, H. (2013). Facilitation of inferior frontal cortex by transcranial direct current stimulation induces perceptual learning of severely degraded speech. *Journal of Neuroscience, 33*, 15868–15878.

Semenza, C., & Mondini, S. (2006). The neuropsychology of compound words. In G. Libben & G. Jarema (Eds.), *The representation and processing of compound words* (pp. 71–95). Oxford, UK: Oxford University Press.

Semin, G.R., & Smith, E.R. (Eds.) (2008). *Embodied grounding: Social, cognitive, affective, and neuroscientific approaches*. Cambridge, UK: Cambridge University Press.

Senft, G. (Ed.) (2000). *Systems of nominal classification*. Cambridge, UK: Cambridge University Press.

Senghas, A., Kita, S., & Özyürek, A. (2004). Children creating core properties of language: Evidence from an emerging sign language in Nicaragua. *Science, 305*, 1779–1782.

Sérieux, P. (1893). Sur un cas de surdité verbale pure. *Revue de Medecine, 13*, 733–750.

Service, E., Helenius, P., Maury, S., & Salmelin, R. (2007). Localization of syntactic and semantic brain responses using magnetoencephalography. *Journal of Cognitive Neuroscience, 19*, 1193–1205.

Seshadri, V. (2004). Aphasia. *The New Yorker*, April 12.

Shallice, T. (1981). Phonological agraphia and the lexical route in writing. *Brain, 104*, 413–429.

Shallice, T. (1988). *From neuropsychology to mental structure*. Cambridge, UK: Cambridge University Press.

Shallice, T., & Cooper, R.P. (2011). *The organization of mind*. Oxford, UK: Oxford University Press.

Shapiro, B., & Danley, M. (1985). The role of the right hemisphere in the control of speech prosody in propositional and affective contexts. *Brain and Language, 25*, 19–36.

Shapiro, K.A., & Caramazza, A. (2003a). Grammatical processing of nouns and verbs in left frontal cortex? *Neuropsychologia, 41*, 1189–1198.

Shapiro, K.A., & Caramazza, A. (2003b). The representation of grammatical categories in the brain. *Trends in Cognitive Sciences, 7*, 201–206.

Shapiro, K.A., & Caramazza, A. (2009). Morphological processes in language production. In M.S. Gazzaniga (Ed.), *The cognitive neurosciences*, 4th edition (pp. 777–788). Cambridge, MA: MIT Press.

Shapiro, K.A., Moo, L.R., & Caramazza, A. (2006). Cortical signatures of noun and verb production. *Proceedings of the National Academy of Sciences, 103*, 1644–1649.

Shapiro, K.A., Moo, L.R., & Caramazza, A. (2012). Neural specificity for grammatical operations is revealed by content-independent fMR adaptation. *Frontiers in Psychology, 3*, Article 26.

Shapiro, K.A., Pascual-Leone, A., Mottaghi, F.M., Gangitano, M., & Caramazza, A. (2001). Grammatical distinctions in the left frontal cortex. *Journal of Cognitive Neuroscience, 13*, 713–720.

Shapiro, K.A., Shelton, J., & Caramazza, A. (2000). Grammatical class in lexical production and morphological processing: Evidence from a case of fluent aphasia. *Cognitive Neuropsychology, 17*, 665–682.

Shapiro, L. (2010). *Embodied cognition*. New York: Routledge.

Sharma, A., & Dorman, M. (2000). Neurophysiologic correlates of cross-language phonetic perception. *Journal of the Acoustical Society of America, 107*, 2697–2703.

Sharp, D.J., Scott, S.K., & Wise, R.J.S. (2004). Retrieving meaning after temporal lobe infarction: The role of the basal language area. *Annals of Neurology, 56*, 836–846.

Shattuck-Hufnagel, S. (1979). Speech errors as evidence for a serial-order mechanism in sentence production. In W.E. Cooper & E.C.T. Walker (Eds.), *Sentence processing: Psycholinguistic studies presented to Merrill Garrett* (pp. 295–342). Hillsdale, NJ: Erlbaum.

Shen, H. (2013). See-through brainis clarify connections. *Nature, 496*, 151.

Shergill, S., Brammer, M., Williams, S., Murray, R., & McGuire, P. (2000). Mapping auditory hallucinations in schizophrenia using functional magnetic resonance imaging. *Archives of General Psychiatry, 57*, 1033–1038.

Shibatani, M. (2006). On the conceptual framework for voice phenomena. *Linguistics, 44*, 217–269.

Shmuelof, L., & Zohary, E. (2007). Watching others' actions: Mirror representations in the parietal cortex. *The Neuroscientist, 13*, 667–672.

Shopen, T. (Ed.) (2007). *Language typology and syntactic description, Vol. II: Complex constructions*. Cambridge, UK: Cambridge University Press.

Shtyrov, Y., Hauk, O., & Pulvermüller, F. (2004). Distributed neuronal networks for encoding category-specific semantic information: The mismatch negativity to action words. *European Journal of Neuroscience, 19*, 1083–1092.

Shuster, L.I. (2009). The effect of sublexical and lexical frequency on speech production: An fMRI investigation. *Brain and Language, 111*, 66–72.

Shuster, L.I., & Lemieux, S.K. (2005). An fMRI investigation of covertly and overtly produced mono- and multisyllabic words. *Brain and Language, 93*, 20–31.

Sidtis, J.J., & Van Lancker Sidtis, D. (2003). A neurobehavioral approach to dysprosody. *Seminars in Speech and Language, 24*, 93–105.

Sieber, H.R., Hartwigsen, G., Kassuba, T., & Rothwell, J.C. (2009). How does transcranial magnetic stimulation modify neuronal activity in the brain? Implications for studies of cognition. *Cortex, 45*, 1035–1042.

Siebörger, F.T., Ferstl, E.C., & von Cramon, D.Y. (2007). Making sense of nonsense: An fMRI study of task induced inference processes during discourse comprehension. *Brain Research, 1166,* 77–91.

Sigman, M., Jobert, A., Lebihan, D., & Dehaene, S. (2007). Parsing a sequence of brain activations at psychological times using fMRI. *NeuroImage, 35,* 655–668.

Simmons, W.K., & Barsalou, L.W. (2003). The similarity-in-topography principle: Reconciling theories of conceptual deficits. *Cognitive Neuropsychology, 20,* 451–486.

Simmons, W.K., Hamann, S.B., Harenski, C.N., Hu, X.P., & Barsalou, L.W. (2008). fMRI evidence for word association and situated simulation in conceptual processing. *Journal of Physiology, Paris, 102,* 106–119.

Simmons, W.K., Martin, A., & Barsalou, L.W. (2005). Pictures of appetizing foods activate gustatory cortices for taste and reward. *Cerebral Cortex, 15,* 1602–1608.

Simmons, W.K., Ramjee, V., Beauchamp, M.S., McRae, K., Martin, A., & Barsalou, L.W. (2007). A common neural substrate for perceiving and knowing about color. *Neuropsychologia, 45,* 2802–2810.

Simmons, W.K., Rapuano, K.M., Ingeholm, J.E., Avery, J., Kallman, S., Hall, K.D., & Martin, A. (in press). The ventral pallidum and orbitofrontal cortex support food pleasantness inferences. *Brain Structure and Function.*

Sirigu, A., Cohen, L., Zalla, T., Pradat-Diehl, P., Van Eeckhout, P., Grafman, J., & Agid, Y. (1998). Distinct frontal regions for processing sentence syntax and story grammar. *Cortex, 34,* 771–778.

Sirigu, A., Duhamel, J.R., & Poncet, M. (1991). The role of sensorimotor experience in object recognition: A case of multimodal agnosia. *Brain, 114,* 2555–2573.

Sitnikova, T., Holcomb, P.J., Kiyonaga, K.A., & Kuperberg, G. (2008). Two neurocognitive mechanisms of semantic integration during the comprehension of visual real-world events. *Journal of Cognitive Neuroscience, 20,* 1–21.

Sitnikova, T., Kuperberg, G., & Holcomb, P.J. (2003). Semantic integration in videos of real-world events: An electrophysiological investigation. *Psychophysiology, 40,* 160–164.

Skipper, J.I., Nusbaum, H.C., & Small, S.L. (2005). Listening to talking faces: Motor cortical activation during speech perception. *NeuroImage, 25,* 76–89.

Skipper, J.I., Nusbaum, H.C., & Small, S.L. (2006). Lending a helping hand to hearing: Another motor theory of speech perception. In M.A. Arbib (Ed.), *Action to language via the mirror neuron system* (pp. 250–285). Cambridge, UK: University of Cambridge Press.

Slevc, L.R., Martin, R.C., Hamilton, A.C., & Joanisse, M.F. (2011). Speech perception, rapid temporal processing, and the left hemisphere: A case study of unilateral pure word deafness. *Neuropsychologia, 49,* 216–230.

Slobin, D.I. (1996). From "thought and language" to "thinking for speaking." In J.J. Gumperz & S.C. Levinson (Eds.), *Rethinking linguistic relativity* (pp. 70–96). Cambridge, UK: Cambridge University Press.

Slobin, D.I. (2000). Verbalized events: A dynamic approach to linguistic relativity and determinism. In S. Niemeier & R. Dirven (Eds.), *Evidence for linguistic relativity* (pp. 107–138). Amsterdam: John Benjamins.

Slobin, D.I. (2003). Language and thought online: cognitive consequences of linguistic relativity. In D. Gentner & S. Goldin-Meadow (Eds.), *Language in mind: Advances*

in the study of language and thought (pp. 157–192). Cambridge, MA: MIT Press.

Small, D.M., Bender, G., Veldhuizen, M.G., Rudenga, K., Nachtigal, D., & Felsted, J. (2007). The role of the human orbitofrontal cortex in taste and flavor processing. *Annals of the New York Academy of Sciences, 1121,* 136–151.

Small, D.M., & Prescott, J. (2005). Odor/taste integration and the perception of flavor. *Experimental Brain Research, 166,* 345–357.

Smith, A. (1992). The control of orofacial movements in speech. *Critical Reviews in Oral Biology and Medicine, 3,* 233–267.

Smith, E.E. (1978). Theories of semantic memory. In W.K. Estes (Ed.), *Handbook of learning and cognitive processes, Vol. 6.* Hillsdale, NJ: Erlbaum.

Smith, E.E., Jonides, J., Marshuetz, C., & Koeppe, R.A. (1998). Components of verbal working memory: Evidence from neuroimaging. *Proceedings of the National Academy of Sciences, 95,* 876–882.

Smith, K. (2013). Reading minds. *Nature, 502,* 428–430.

Snijders, T.M., Vosse, T., Kempen, G., van Berkum, J.A., Petersson, K.M., & Hagoort, P. (2009). Retrieval and unification of syntactic structure in sentence comprehension: An fMRI study using word-category ambiguity. *Cerebral Cortex, 19,* 1493–1503.

Snodgrass, J.G., & Yuditsky, T. (1996). Naming times for the Snodgrass and Vanderwart pictures. *Behavioral Research Methods, Instruments, and Computers, 28,* 516–536.

Snowden, J.S., Bathgate, D., Varma, A., Blackshaw, A., Gibbons, Z.C., & Neary, D. (2001). Distinct behavioural profiles in frontotemporal dementia and semantic dementia. *Journal of Neurology, Neurosurgery, and Psychiatry, 70,* 323–332.

Snowden, J.S., Goulding, P.J., & Neary, D. (1989). Semantic dementia: A form of circumscribed cerebral atrophy. *Behavioral Neurology, 2,* 167–182.

Snowden, J.S., Neary, D., & Mann, D.M.A. (Eds.) (1996). *Frontotemporal lobar degeneration.* London: Churchill Livingstone.

Snowden, J.S., Pickering-Brown, S.M., Mackenzie, I.R., Richardson, A.M.T., Varma, A., Neary, D., & Mann, D.M.A. (2006). Progranulin gene mutations associated with frontotemporal dementia and progressive non-fluent aphasia. *Brain, 129,* 3091–3102.

Snyder, H.R., Banich, M.T., & Munakata, Y. (2011). Choosing our words: Retrieval and selection processes recruit shared neural substrates in left ventrolateral prefrontal cortex. *Journal of Cognitive Neuroscience, 23,* 3470–3482.

Söderfeldt, B., Rönnberg, J., & Risberg, J. (1994). Regional cerebral blood flow in sign language users. *Brain and Language, 46,* 59–68.

Sörös, P., Bose, A., Sokoloff, L.G., Graham, S.J., & Stuss, D.T. (2011). Age-related changes in the functional neuroanatomy of overt speech production. *Neurobiology of Aging, 32,* 1505–1513.

Sörös, P., Sokoloff, L.G., Bose, A., McIntosh, A.R., Graham, S.J., & Stuss, D.T. (2006). Clustered functional MRI of overt speech production. *NeuroImage, 32,* 376–387.

Specht, K., & Reul, J. (2003). Functional segregation of the temporal lobes into highly differentiated subsystems for auditory perception: An auditory rapid event-related fMRI task. *NeuroImage, 20,* 1944–1954.

Speer, N.K., Reynolds, J.R., Swallow, K.M., & Zacks, J.M. (2009). Reading stories activates neural representations of visual and motor experiences. *Psychological Science, 20,* 989–999.

Speer, N.K., Reynolds, J.R., & Zacks, J.M. (2007). Human brain activity time-locked to narrative event boundaries. *Psychological Science, 18,* 449–455.

Spitsyna, G., Warren, J.E., Scott, S.K., Turkheimer, F.E., & Wise, R.J.S. (2006). Converging language streams in the human temporal lobe. *Journal of Neuroscience, 26,* 7328–7336.

Sporns, O., Tononi, G., & Kötter, R. (2005). The human connectome: A structural description of the human brain. *PLoS Computational Biology, 1*(4), e42.

Spreng, R.N., Mar, R.A., & Kim, A.S.N. (2009). The common neural basis of autobiographical memory, prospection, navigation, theory of mind, and the default mode: A quantitative meta-analysis. *Journal of Cognitive Neuroscience, 21,* 489–510.

Sprengelmeyer, R., Young, A.W., Mahn, K., Schroeder, U., Woitalla, D., Büttner, T., Kuhn, W., & Przuntek, H. (2003). Facial expression recognition in people with medicated and unmedicated Parkinson's disease. *Neuropsychologia, 41,* 1047–1057.

Squire, L.R., & Wixted, J.T. (2011). The cognitive neuroscience of human memory since H.M. *Annual Review of Neuroscience, 34,* 259–288.

Stamatakis, E.A., Marslen-Wilson, W.D., Tyler, L.K., & Fletcher, P.C. (2005). Cingulate control of fronto-temporal integration reflects linguistic demands: A three-way interaction in functional connectivity. *NeuroImage, 28,* 115–121.

Starkstein, S.E., Federoff, J.P., Price, T.R., Leiguarda, R.C., & Robinson, R.G. (1994). Neuropsychological and neuroradiologic correlates of emotional prosody comprehension. *Neurology, 44,* 515–522.

Starrfelt, R., & Behrmann, M. (2011). Number reading in pure alexia: A review. *Neuropsychologia, 49,* 2283–2298.

Starrfelt, R., & Gerlach, C. (2007). The visual what for area: Words and pictures in the left fusiform gyrus. *NeuroImage, 35,* 334–342.

Starrfelt, R., Habekost, T., & Leff, A.P. (2009). Too little, too late: Reduced visual span and speed characterize pure alexia. *Cerebral Cortex, 19,* 2880–2890.

Stefanatos, G.A. (2008). Speech perceived through a damaged temporal window: Lessons from word deafness and aphasia. *Seminars in Speech and Language, 29,* 239–252.

Stefanatos, G.A., Gershkoff, A., & Madigan, S. (2005). On pure word deafness, temporal processing, and the left hemisphere. *Journal of the International Neuropsychological Society, 11,* 456–470.

Steinhauer, K., Alter, K., & Friederici, A.D. (1999). Brain potentials indicate immediate use of prosodic cues in natural speech processing. *Nature Neuroscience, 2,* 191–196.

Steinhauer, K., & Drury, J.E. (2012). On the early left anterior negativity (ELAN) in syntax studies. *Brain and Language, 120,* 135–162.

Steinhauer, K., Drury, J.E., Portner, P., Walenski, M., & Ullman, M.T. (2010). Syntax, concepts, and logic in the temporal dynamics of language comprehension: Evidence from event-related potentials. *Neuropsychologia, 48,* 1525–1542.

Steinhauer, K., & Friederici, A.D. (2001). Prosodic boundaries, comma rules, and brain responses: The closure positive shift in ERPs as a universal marker for prosodic phrasing in listeners and readers. *Journal of Psycholinguistic Research, 30,* 267–295.

Stephens, G.J., Silbert, L.J., & Hasson, U. (2010). Speaker-hearer neural coupling underlies successful communication. *Proceedings of the National Academy of Sciences, 107,* 14425–14430.

Stepniewska, I., Friedman, R.M., Gharbawie, O.A., Cerkevich, C.M., Roe, A.W., & Kaas, J.H. (2011). Optical imaging in galagos reveals parietal-frontal circuits underlying motor behavior. *Proceedings of the National Academy of Sciences, 108,* E725–E732.

Stewart, L., Walsh, V., Frith, U., & Rothwell, J.C. (2001). TMS produces two dissociable types of speech disruption. *NeuroImage, 13,* 472–478.

Stivers, T., Enfield, N.J., Brown, P., Englert, C., Hayashi, M., Heinemann, T., Hoymann, G., Rossano, F., de Ruiter, J.P., Yoon, K.-E., & Levinson, S.C. (2009). Universals and cultural variation in turn-taking in conversation. *Proceedings of the National Academy of Sciences, 106,* 10587–10592.

Stockall, L., & Marantz, A. (2006). A single route, fully decompositional model of morphological complexity. *The Mental Lexicon, 1,* 85–123.

Stokoe, W., Casterline, D., & Croneberg, C. (1965). *A dictionary of American Sign Language.* Washington, DC: Gallaudet University Press.

Stowe, L.A. (2005). Rethinking the neurological basis of language. *Lingua, 115,* 997–1042.

Stowe, L.A., Paans, A.M.J., Wijers, A.A., Zwarts, F., Mulder, G., & Vaalburg, W. (1999). Sentence comprehension and word repetition: A positron emission tomography investigation. *Psychophysiology, 36,* 786–801.

Striem-Amit, E., Cohen, L., Dehaene, S., & Amedi, A. (2012). Reading with sounds: Sensory substitution selectively activates the visual word form area in the blind. *Neuron, 76,* 640–652.

Strömqvist, S., & Verhoeven, L. (Eds.) (2004). *Relating events in narrative, Vol. 2.* Mahwah, NJ: Erlbaum.

Stuss, D.T. (2011). Functions of the frontal lobes: Relation to executive functions. *Journal of the International Neuropsychological Society, 17,* 759–765.

Suh, M., Bahar, S., Mehta, A.D., & Schwartz, T.H. (2006). Blood volume and hemoglobin oxygenation response following electrical stimulation of human cortex. *NeuroImage, 31,* 66–75.

Surmeier, D.J. (2013). To go or not to go. *Nature, 494,* 178–179.

Swaab, T.Y., LeDoux, K., Camblin, C.C., & Boudewyn, M.A. (2012). Language-related ERP components. In S.J. Luck & E.S. Kappenman (Eds.) *The Oxford handbook of event-related potential components* (pp. 397–439). Oxford, UK: Oxford University Press.

Sweet, R.A., Dorph-Petersen, K.A., & Lewis, D.A. (2005). Mapping auditory core, lateral belt, and parabelt cortices in the human superior temporal gyrus. *Journal of Comparative Neurology, 491,* 270–289.

Szwed, M., Dehaene, S., Kleinschmidt, A., Eger, E., Valabregue, R., Amadon, A., & Cohen, L. (2011).

Specialization for written words over objects in the visual cortex. *NeuroImage, 56*, 330–344.

Tainturier, M.J., & Rapp, B. (2001). The spelling process. In B. Rapp (Ed.), *The handbook of cognitive neuropsychology* (pp. 263–290). Philadelphia, PA: Psychology Press.

Takac, M., Benuskova, L., & Knott, A. (2012). Mapping sensorimotor sequences to word sequences: A connectionist model of language acquisition and sentence generation. *Cognition, 125*, 288–308.

Talairach, J., & Tournoux, P. (1988). *A co-planar stereotactic atlas of the human brain.* Stuttgart: Thieme Verlag.

Tan, L.H., Spinks, J.A., Eden, G.F., Perfetti, C.A., & Siok, W.T. (2005). Reading depends on writing in Chinese. *Proceedings of the National Academy of Sciences, 102*, 8781–8785.

Tanaka, K. (2003). Columns for complex visual object features in the inferotemporal cortex: Clustering of cells with similar but slightly different stimulus selectivities. *Cerebral Cortex, 13*, 90–99.

Tanenhaus, M.K. (2007). Spoken language comprehension: Insights from eye movements. In M.G. Gaskell (Ed.), *The Oxford handbook of psycholinguistics* (pp. 309–326). Oxford, UK: Oxford University Press.

Taylor, A., & Saint-Cyr, J. (1995). The neuropsychology of Parkinson's disease. *Brain and Cognition, 28*, 281–296.

Taylor, K.I., Moss, H.E., Stamatakis, E.A., & Tyler, L.K. (2006). Binding crossmodal object features in perirhinal cortex. *Proceedings of the National Academy of Sciences, 103*, 8239–8244.

Taylor, K.I., Moss, H.E., & Tyler, L.K. (2007). The conceptual structure account: a cognitive model of semantic memory and its neural instantiation. In J. Hart, Jr., & M.A. Kraut (Eds.), *Neural basis of semantic memory* (pp. 265–301). Cambridge, UK: Cambridge University Press.

Taylor, K.I., Stamatakis, E.A., & Tyler, L.K. (2009). Crossmodal integration of object features: Voxel-based correlations in brain-damaged patients. *Brain, 132*, 671–683.

Taylor, L.J., & Zwaan, R.A. (2008). Motor resonance and linguistic focus. *Quarterly Journal of Experimental Psychology, 61*, 896–904.

Taylor, L.J., & Zwaan, R.A. (2009). Action in cognition: The case of language. *Language and Cognition, 1*, 45–58.

Taylor, L.J., & Zwaan, R.A. (2012). Fault tolerant comprehension. In Y. Coello & A. Bartolo (Eds.), *Language and action in cognitive neuroscience* (pp. 145–158). London: Psychology Press.

Ter Doest, L., & Semin, G.R. (2005). Retrieval contexts and the concreteness effect: Dissociations in memory for concrete and abstract words. *European Journal of Cognitive Psychology, 17*, 859–881.

Tettamanti, M., Buccino, G., Saccuman, M.C., Gallese, V., Danna, M., Scifo, P., Fazio, F., Rizzolatti, G., Cappa, S.F., & Perani, D. (2005). Listening to action-related sentences activates fronto-parietal motor circuits. *Journal of Cognitive Neuroscience, 17*, 273–281.

Tettamanti, M., Rotondi, I., Perani, D., Scotti, G., Fazio, F., Cappa, S.F., & Moro, A. (2009). Syntax without language: Neurobiological evidence for cross-domain syntactic computations. *Cortex, 45*, 825–838.

Thompson, C.K., Ballard, K.J., Tait, M.E., Weintraub, S., & Mesulam, M.M. (1997a). Patterns of language decline in non-fluent primary progressive aphasia. *Aphasiology, 11*, 297–331.

Thompson, C.K., Bonakdarpour, B., Fix, S.C., Blumenfeld, H.K., Parrish, T.B., Gitelman, D.R., & Mesulam, M.M. (2007). Neural correlates of verb argument structure processing. *Journal of Cognitive Neuroscience, 19*, 1753–1767.

Thompson, C.K., & Faroqi-Shah, Y. (2002). Models of sentence production. In A.E. Hillis (Ed.), *The handbook of adult language disorders: Integrating cognitive neuropsychology, neurology, and rehabilitation* (pp. 311–330). New York: Psychology Press.

Thompson, C.K., Lange, K., Schneider, S., & Shapiro, L. (1997b). Agrammatic and non-brain-damaged subjects' verb and verb argument structure production. *Aphasiology, 11*, 473–490.

Thompson, C.K., Lukic, S., King, M.C., Mesulam, M.M., & Weintraub, S. (2012). Verb and noun deficits in stroke-induced and primary progressive aphasia: The Northwestern Naming Battery. *Aphasiology, 26*, 632–655.

Thompson, C.K., Meltzer-Asscher, A., Cho, S., Lee, J., Wieneke, C., Weintraub, S., & Mesulam, M.M. (2013). Syntactic and morphosyntactic processing in stroke-induced and primary progressive aphasia. *Behavioral Neurology, 26*, 35–54.

Thompson, P.M., Hayashi, K.M., de Zubicaray, G., Janke, A.L., Rose, S.E., Semple, J., Herman, D., Hong, M.S., Dittmer, S.S., Doddrell, D.M., & Toga, A.W. (2003). Dynamics of gray matter loss in Alzheimer's disease. *Journal of Neuroscience, 23*, 994–1005.

Thompson-Schill, S.L. (2005). Dissecting the language organ: A new look at the role of Broca's area in language processing. In A. Cutler (Ed.), *Twenty-first century psycholinguistics* (pp. 173–190). Mahwah, NJ: Erlbaum.

Thompson-Schill, S.L., Kan, I.P., & Oliver, R.T. (2006). Functional neuroimaging of semantic memory. In R. Cabeza & A. Kingstone (Eds.), *Handbook of functional neuroimaging of cognition* (pp. 149–190). Cambridge, MA: MIT Press.

Thompson-Schill, S.L., Swick, D., Farah, M.J., D'Esposito, M., Kan, I.P., & Knight, R.T. (1998). Verb generation in patients with focal frontal lesions: A neuropsychological test of neuroimaging findings. *Proceedings of the National Academy of Sciences, 26*, 14792–14797.

Thothathiri, M., Kim, A., Trueswell, J.C., & Thompson-Schill, S.L. (2012a). Parametric effects of syntactic-semantic conflict in Broca's area during sentence processing. *Brain and Language, 120*, 259–264.

Thothathiri, M., Kimberg, D.Y., & Schwartz, M.F. (2012b). The neural basis of reversible sentence comprehension: Evidence from voxel-based lesion-symptom mapping in aphasia. *Journal of Cognitive Neuroscience, 24*, 212–222.

Thothathiri, M., Schwartz, M.F., & Thompson-Schill, S.L. (2010). Selection for position: The role of the left ventrolateral prefrontal cortex in sequencing language. *Brain and Language, 113*, 28–38.

Tian, X., & Poeppel, D. (2010). Mental imagery of speech and movement implicates the dynamics of internal forward models. *Frontiers in Psychology, 1*, Article 166.

Tillotson, S.M., Siakaluk, P.D., & Pexman, P.M. (2008). Body-object interaction ratings for 1,618 monosyllabic nouns. *Behavioral Research Methods, 40*, 1075–1078.

Tissot, R., Mounin, G., & Lhermitte, F. (1973). *L'Agrammatisme*. Brussels: Dessart.

Tomasello, M. (1999). *The cultural origins of human cognition*. Cambridge, MA: Harvard University Press.

Tomasino, B., & Rumiati, R.I. (2013). At the mercy of strategies: The role of motor representations in language understanding. *Frontiers in Psychology, 4*, Article 27.

Tong, F., & Pratte, M.S. (2012). Decoding patterns of human brain activity. *Annual Review of Psychology, 63*, 483–509.

Tourville, J.A., Reilly, K., & Guenther, F.H. (2008). Neural mechanisms underlying auditory feedback control of speech. *NeuroImage, 39*, 1429–1443.

Tovar-Spinoza, Z.S., Ochi, A., Rutka, J.T., Go, C., & Otsubo, H. (2008). The role of magnetoencephalography in epilepsy surgery. *Neurosurgical Focus, 25*, E16.

Toyomura, A., Koyama, S., Miyamaoto, T., Terao, A., Omori, T., Murohashi, H., & Kuriki, S. (2007). Neural correlates of auditory feedback control in humans. *Neuroscience, 146*, 499–503.

Tranel, D. (2006). Impaired naming of unique landmarks is associated with left temporal polar damage. *Neuropsychology, 20*, 1–10.

Tranel, D. (2009). The left temporal pole is important for retrieving words for unique concrete entities. *Aphasiology, 23*, 867–884.

Tranel, D., Adolphs, R., Damasio, H., & Damasio, A.R. (2001). A neural basis for the retrieval of words for actions. *Cognitive Neuropsychology, 18*, 655–670.

Tranel, D., Damasio, H., & Damasio, A.R. et al. (1997a). A neural basis for the retrieval of conceptual knowledge. *Neuropsychologia, 35*, 1319–1327.

Tranel, D., Damasio, H., Eichhorn, G.R., Grabowski, T.J., Ponto, L.L.B., & Hichwa, R.D. (2003a). Neural correlates of naming animals from their characteristic sounds. *Neuropsychologia, 41*, 847–854.

Tranel, D., Grabowski, T.J., Lyon, J., & Damasio, H. (2005). Naming the same entities from visual or from auditory stimulation engages similar regions of left inferotemporal cortices. *Journal of Cognitive Neuroscience, 17*, 1293–1305.

Tranel, D., & Kemmerer, D. (2004). Neuroanatomical correlates of locative prepositions. *Cognitive Neuropsychology, 21*, 719–749.

Tranel, D., Kemmerer, D., Adolphs, R., Damasio, H., & Damasio, A.N. (2003b). Neural correlates of conceptual knowledge of actions. *Cognitive Neuropsychology, 20*, 409–432.

Tranel, D., Logan, C.G., Frank, R.J., & Damasio, A.R. (1997b). Explaining category-related effects in the retrieval of conceptual and lexical knowledge for concrete entities: Operationalization and analysis of factors. *Neuropsychologia, 35*, 1329–1339.

Tranel, D., Manzel, K., Asp, E., & Kemmerer, D. (2008). Naming static and dynamic actions: Neuropsychological evidence. *Journal of Physiology, Paris, 102*, 80–94.

Tranel, D., Martin, C., Damasio, H., Grabowski, T.J., & Hichwa, R. (2005). Effects of noun-verb homonymy on the neural correlates of naming concrete entities and actions. *Brain and Language, 92*, 288–299.

Traxler, M.J. (2011). Parsing. *Wiley Interdisciplinary Reviews: Cognitive Science, 2*, 353–364.

Tree, J.J., & Kay, J. (2006). Phonological dyslexia and phonological impairment: An exception to the rule? *Neuropsychologia, 44*, 2861–2873.

Tremblay, P., Deschamps, I., & Gracco, V.L. (2013). Regional heterogeneity in the processing and the production of speech in the human planum temporale. *Cortex, 49*, 143–157.

Tremblay, S, Shiller, D.M., & Ostry, D.J. (2003). Somatosensory basis of speech production. *Nature, 423*, 866–869.

Trimmer, C.G., & Cuddy, L.L. (2008). Emotional intelligence, not music training, predicts recognition of emotional speech prosody. *Emotion, 8*, 838–849.

Troiani, V., Fernández-Seara, M.A., Wang, Z., Detre, J.A., Ash, S., & Grossman, M. (2008). Narrative speech production: An fMRI study using continuous arterial spin labeling. *NeuroImage, 40*, 932–939.

Trumpp, N.M., Kliese, D., Hoenig, K., Haarmeier, T., & Kiefer, M. (2013). Losing the sound of concepts: Damage to auditory association cortex impairs the processing of sound-related concepts. *Cortex, 49*, 474–486.

Trumpp, N.M., Traub, F., Pulvermüller, F., & Kiefer, M. (in press). Unconscious automatic brain activation of acoustic and action-related conceptual features during masked repetition priming. *Journal of Cognitive Neuroscience*.

Tsapkini, K., Jarema, G., & Kehayia, E. (2002). A morphological processing deficit in verbs but not nouns: A case study in a highly inflected language. *Journal of Neurolinguistics, 15*, 265–288.

Tsapkini, K., & Rapp, B. (2010). The orthography-specific functions of the left fusiform gyrus: Evidence of modality and category specificity. *Cortex, 46*, 185–205.

Tucker, D., Watson, R., & Heilman, K. (1977). Discrimination and evocation of affectively intoned speech in patients with right parietal disease. *Neurology, 27*, 947–950.

Turkeltaub, P.E., & Coslett, H.B. (2010). Localization of sublexical speech perception components. *Brain and Language, 114*, 1–15.

Turken, A.U., & Dronkers, N.F. (2011). The neural architecture of the language comprehension network: Converging evidence from lesion and connectivity analyses. *Frontiers in Systems Neuroscience, 5*, Article 1.

Tyler, L.K. (1992). *Spoken language comprehension*. Cambridge, MA: MIT Press.

Tyler, L.K., Bright, P., Fletcher, P., & Stamatakis, E.A. (2004). Neural processing of nouns and verbs: The role of inflectional morphology. *Neuropsychologia, 42*, 512–523.

Tyler, L.K., Cheung, T.P.L., Devereux, D., & Clarke, A. (2013a). Syntactic computations in the language network: Characterizing dynamic network properties using representational similarity analysis. *Frontiers in Psychology, 4*, Article 271.

Tyler, L.K., Chiu, S., Zhuang, J., Randall, B., Devereux, B.J., Wright, P., Clarke, A., & Taylor, K.I. (2013b). Objects and categories: Feature statistics and object processing in the ventral stream. *Journal of Cognitive Neuroscience, 25*, 1723–1735.

Tyler, L.K., deMornay-Davies, P., Anokhina, R., Longworth, C., Randall, B., & Marslen-Wilson, W.D. (2002a). Dissociations in processing past tense morphology: Neuropathology and behavioral studies. *Journal of Cognitive Neuroscience, 14*, 79–94.

Tyler, L.K., & Marslen-Wilson, W.D. (1997). Dissociating types of mental computation. *Nature, 387,* 592–594.

Tyler, L.K., Marslen-Wilson, W.D., Randall, B., Wright, P., Devereux, B.J., Zhuang, J., Papoutsi, M., & Stamatakis, E.A. (2011). Left inferior frontal cortex and syntax: Function, structure and behaviour in patients with left hemisphere damage. *Brain, 134,* 415–431.

Tyler, L.K., Marslen-Wilson, W.D., & Stamatakis, E.A. (2005a). Differentiating lexical form, meaning and structure in the neural language system. *Proceedings of the National Academy of Sciences, 102,* 8375–8380.

Tyler, L.K., Randall, B., & Marslen-Wilson, W.D. (2002b). Phonology and neuropsychology of the English past tense. *Neuropsychologia, 40,* 1154–1166.

Tyler, L.K., Stamatakis, E.A., Post, B., Randall, B., & Marslen-Wilson, W.D. (2005b). Temporal and frontal systems involved in speech processing: An fMRI study of the past tense processing. *Neuropsychologia, 43,* 1963–1974.

Tzourio, N., Nkanga-Ngila, B., & Mazoyer, B. (1998). Left planum temporale surface correlates with functional dominance during story listening. *NeuroReport, 9,* 829–833.

Ueno, T., Saito, S., Rogers, T.T., & Lambon Ralph, M.A. (2011). Lichtheim 2: Synthesizing aphasia and the neural basis of language in a neurocomputational model of the dual dorsal-ventral language pathways. *Neuron, 72,* 385–396.

Ullman, M.T. (2004). Contributions of memory circuits to language: The declarative/procedural model. *Cognition, 92,* 231–270.

Ullman, M.T., Corkin, S., Coppola, M., Hickok, G., Growdon, J.H., Koroshetz, W.J., & Pinker, S. (1997). A neural dissociation within language: Evidence that the mental dictionary is part of declarative memory, and that grammatical rules are processed by the procedural system. *Journal of Cognitive Neuroscience, 9,* 289–299.

Ullman, M.T., Pancheva, R., Love, T., Yee, E., Swinney, D., & Hickok, G. (2005). Neural correlates of lexicon and grammar: Evidence from the production, reading, and judgment of inflection in aphasia. *Brain and Language, 93,* 185–238.

Ullman, M.T., & Walenski, M. (2005). Moving past the past tense. *Brain and Language, 93,* 248–252.

Underwood, E. (2013). Tissue imaging method makes everything clear. *Science, 340,* 131–132.

Ure, J., Faccio, E., Videla, H., Caccuri, R., Giudice, F., Ollari, J., & Diez, M. (1998). Akinetic mutism: A report of three cases. *Acta Neurologica Scandinavica, 98,* 439–444.

Vaden, K.I., Jr., Muftuler, L.T., & Hickok, G. (2010). Phonological repetition-suppression in bilateral superior temporal sulci. *NeuroImage, 49,* 1018–1023.

Vallar, G., & Baddeley, A. (1984). Phonological short-term store, phonological processing, and sentence comprehension. *Cognitive Neuropsychology, 1,* 121–141.

Vallar, G., Di Betta, A.M., & Silveri, C. (1997). The phonological short-term store-rehearsal system: Patterns of impairment and neural correlates. *Neuropsychologia, 35,* 795–812.

van Berkum, J.J.A. (2012). The electrophysiology of discourse and conversation. In M.J. Spivey, K. McRae, & M.F. Joanisse (Eds.), *The Cambridge handbook of psycholinguistics* (pp. 589–614). Cambridge, UK: Cambridge University Press.

van Berkum, J.J.A., Brown, C.M., Zwitserlood, P., Kooijman, V., & Hagoort, P. (2005). Anticipating upcoming words in discourse: Evidence from ERPs and reading times. *Journal of Experimental Psychology: Learning, Memory, and Cognition, 31,* 443–467.

van Berkum, J.J.A., Hagoort, P., & Brown, C.M. (1999). Semantic integration in sentences and discourse: Evidence from the N400. *Journal of Cognitive Neuroscience, 11,* 657–671.

van Berkum, J.J.A., Koornneef, A.W., Otten, M., & Nieuwland, M.S. (2007). Establishing reference in language comprehension: An electrophysiological perspective. *Brain Research, 1146,* 158–171.

van Berkum, J.J.A., Zwitserlood, P., Hagoort, P., & Brown, C.M. (2003). When and how do listeners relate a sentence to the wider discourse? Evidence from the N400 effect. *Cognitive Brain Research, 17,* 701–718.

Van Bezooijen, R., Otto, S.A., & Heenan, T.A. (1983). Recognition of vocal expressions from emotion. *Journal of Cross-Cultural Psychology, 14,* 387–406.

Van de Meerendonk, N., Kolk, H.H.J., Chwilla, D.J., & Vissers, C.T.W.M. (2009). Monitoring in language perception. *Language and Linguistics Compass, 3,* 1211–1224.

Vandenberghe, R., Nobre, A.C., & Price, C.J. (2002). The response of left temporal cortex to sentences. *Journal of Cognitive Neuroscience, 14,* 550–560.

Van de Ven, V., Esposito, F., & Christoffels, I.K. (2009). Neural network of speech monitoring overlaps with overt speech production and comprehension networks: A sequential spatial and temporal ICA study. *NeuroImage, 47,* 1982–1991.

Van Dijk, T.A., & Kintsch, W. (1983). *Strategies of discourse comprehension.* New York: Academic Press.

Van Elk, M., Van Shie, H.T., Zwaan, R.A., & Bekkering, H. (2010). The functional role of motor activation in language processing: Motor cortical oscillations support lexical-semantic retrieval. *NeuroImage, 50,* 665–677.

Van Essen, D.C., Glasser, M.F., Dierker, D.L., Harwell, J., & Coalson, T. (2012). Parcellations and hemispheric asymmetries of human cerebral cortex analyzed on surface-based atlases. *Cerebral Cortex, 22,* 2241–2262.

Van Galen, G.P. (1991). Handwriting: Issues for a psychomotor theory. *Human Movement Science, 10,* 165–191.

Vanier, M., & Caplan, D. (1990). CT-scan correlates of agrammatism. In L. Menn & L.K. Obler (Eds.), *Agrammatic aphasia: A cross-language narrative sourcebook, Vol. 1* (pp. 37–115). Amsterdam: John Benjamins.

van Kemenade, B., Muggleton, N., Walsh, V., & Saygin, A.P. (2012). The effects of TMS over STS and premotor cortex on the perception of biological motion. *Journal of Cognitive Neuroscience, 24,* 896–904.

Van Lancker Sidtis, D., Pachana, N., Cummings, J.L., & Sidtis, J.J. (2006). Dysprosodic speech following basal ganglia insult: Toward a conceptual framework for the study of the cerebral representation of prosody. *Brain and Language, 97,* 135–153.

Vann, S.D., Aggleton, J.P., & Maguire, E.A. (2009). What does the retrosplenial cortex do? *Nature Reviews: Neuroscience, 10,* 792–802.

Van Orden, G.C. (1987). A ROWS is a ROSE: Spelling, sound, and reading. *Memory and Cognition, 15,* 181–198.

Van Orden, G.C., Jansen op de Haar, M.A., & Bosman, A. (1997). Complex dynamic systems also predict dissociations, but they do not reduce to autonomous components. *Cognitive Neuropsychology, 14*, 131–165.

Van Overwalle, F. (2009). Social cognition and the brain: A meta-analysis. *Human Brain Mapping, 30*, 929–858.

Van Petten, C., Coulson, S., Rubin, S., Plante, E., & Parks, M. (1999). Time course of word identification and semantic integration in spoken language. *Journal of Experimental Psychology: Learning, Memory, and Cognition, 25*, 394–417.

Van Petten, C., & Luka, B.J. (2006). Neural localization of semantic context effects in electromagnetic and hemodynamic studies. *Brain and Language, 97*, 279–293.

Van Petten, C., & Rheinfelder, H. (1995). Conceptual relationships between spoken words and environmental sounds: Event-related brain potential measures. *Neuropsychologia, 33*, 485–508.

Van Rijn, S., Aleman, A., van Diessen, E., Berckmoes, C., Vingerhoets, G., & Kahn, R.S. (2005). What is said or how it is said makes a difference: Role of the right frontoparietal operculum in emotional prosody as revealed by repetitive TMS. *European Journal of Neuroscience, 21*, 3195–3200.

Van Riper, C. (1982). *The nature of stuttering* (2nd edition). Englewood Cliffs, NJ: Prentice-Hall.

van Schie, H.T., Toni, I., & Bekkering, H. (2006). Comparable mechanisms for action and language: Neural systems behind intentions, goals, and means. *Cortex, 42*, 495–498.

van Schie, H.T., Wijers, A.A., Mars, R.B., Benjamins, J.S., & Stowe, L.A. (2005). Processing of visual semantic information to concrete words: Temporal dynamics and neural mechanisms indicated by event-related brain potentials. *Cognitive Neuropsychology, 22*, 364–386.

Van Turennout, M., Hagoort, P., & Brown, C.M. (1997). Electrophysiological evidence on the time course of semantic and phonological processes in speech production. *Journal of Experimental Psychology: Learning, Memory, and Cognition, 23*, 787–806.

Van Valin, R.D., Jr. (2006). Some universals of verb semantics. In R. Mairal & J. Gil (Eds.), *Linguistic universals* (pp. 155–178). Cambridge, UK: Cambridge University Press.

Van Valin, R.D., Jr., & LaPolla, R. (1997). *Syntax: Structure, meaning, and function*. Cambridge, UK: Cambridge University Press.

Velay, J.L., & Longcamp, M. (2013). Motor skills and written language perception: Contribution or writing knowledge to visual recognition of graphic shapes. In Y. Coello & A. Bartolo (Eds.), *Language and action in cognitive neuroscience* (pp. 161–176). New York: Psychology Press.

Venezia, J.H., & Hickok, G. (2009). Mirror neurons, the motor system, and language: From the motor theory to embodied cognition and beyond. *Language and Linguistics Compass, 3*, 1–14.

Vigliocco, G., Antonini, T., & Garrett, M.F. (1997). Grammatical gender is on the tip of Italian tongues. *Psychological Science, 8*, 314–317.

Vigliocco, G., Kousta, S., Della Rosa, P.A., Vinson, D.P., Tettamanti, M., Devlin, J.T., & Cappa, S.F. (2014). The neural representation of abstract words: The role of emotion. *Cerebral Cortex, 24*, 1767–1777.

Vigliocco, G., Kousta, S., Vinson, D., Andrews, M., & Del Campo, E. (2013). The Representation of abstract words: What matters? Reply to Paivio's (2013) comment on Kousta et al. (2011). *Journal of Experimental Psychology: General, 142*, 288–291.

Vigliocco, G., Meteyard, L., Andrews, M., & Kousta, S. (2009). Toward a theory of semantic representation. *Language and Cognition, 1*, 219–240.

Vigliocco, G., Vinson, D.P., Druks, J., Barber, H., & Cappa, S.F. (2011). Nouns and verbs in the brain: A review of behavioural, electrophysiological, neuropsychological, and imaging studies. *Neuroscience and Biobehavioral Reviews, 35*, 407–426.

Vigliocco, G., Vinson, D.P., Lewis, W., & Garrett, M.F. (2004). Representing the meanings of objects and action words: The feature and unitary semantic space hypothesis. *Cognitive Psychology, 48*, 422–488.

Vigneau, M., Beaucousin, V., Hervé, P.Y., Duffau, H., Crivello, F., Houdé, O., Mazoyer, B., & Tzourio-Mazoyer, N. (2006). Meta-analyzing left hemisphere language areas: Phonology, semantics, and sentence processing. *NeuroImage, 30*, 1414–1432.

Vincent, J.L., Kahn, I., Snyder, A.Z., Raichle, M.E., & Buckner, R.L. (2008). Evidence for a frontoparietal control system revealed by intrinsic functional connectivity. *Journal of Neurophysiology, 100*, 3328–3342.

Vinckier, F., Dehaene, S., Jobert, A., Dubus, J.P., Sigman, M., & Cohen, L. (2007). Hierarchical coding of letter strings in the ventral stream: Dissecting the inner organization of the visual word-form system. *Neuron, 55*, 143–156.

Vinson, D.P., Ponari, M., & Vigliocco, G. (in press). How does emotional content affect lexical processing? *Cognition and Emotion*.

Vinson, D.P., & Vigliocco, G. (2008). Semantic feature production norms for a large set of objects and events. *Behavior Research Methods, 40*, 183–190.

Visser, M., Embleton, K.V., Jefferies, E., Parker, G.J., & Lambon Ralph, M.A. (2010). The inferior, anterior temporal lobes and semantic memory clarified: Novel evidence from distortion-corrected fMRI. *Neuropsychologia, 48*, 1689–1696.

Visser, M., Jefferies, E., Embleton, K.V., & Lambon Ralph, M. (2012). Both the middle temporal gyrus and the ventral anterior temporal area are crucial for multimodal semantic processing: Distortion-corrected fMRI evidence for a double gradient of information convergence in the temporal lobes. *Journal of Cognitive Neuroscience, 24*, 1766–1778.

Visser, M., Jefferies, E., & Lambon Ralph, M. (2009). Semantic processing in the anterior temporal lobes: A meta-analysis of the functional neuroimaging literature. *Journal of Cognitive Neuroscience, 22*, 1083–1094.

Vitevitch, M.S. (2003). The influence of sublexical and lexical representations on the processing of spoken words in English. *Clinical Linguistics and Phonetics, 17*, 487–499.

Vitevitch, M.S., & Luce, P.A. (1999). Probabilistic phonotactics and neighborhood activation in spoken word recognition. *Journal of Memory and Language, 40*, 374–408.

Vitevitch, M.S., & Rodríguez, E. (2005). Neighborhood density effects in spoken word recognition in Spanish.

Journal of Multilingual Communication Disorders, 3, 64–73.

von Kriegstein, K., Eger, E., Kleinschmidt, A., & Giraud, A. (2003). Modulation of neural responses to speech by directing attention to voices or verbal content. *Cognitive Brain Research, 17,* 48–55.

Vouloumanos, A., Kiehl, K.A., Werker, J.F., & Liddle, P.F. (2001). Detection of sounds in the auditory stream: Event-related fMRI evidence for differential activation to speech and nonspeech. *Journal of Cognitive Neuroscience, 13,* 994–1005.

Vuilleumier, P. (2005). How brains beware: Neural mechanisms of emotional attention. *Trends in Cognitive Sciences, 9,* 585–594.

Wada, J., & Rasmussen, T. (1960). Intracarotid injection of sodium amytal for the lateralization of cerebral speech dominance. *Journal of Neurosurgery, 17,* 266–282.

Walker, G.M., Schwartz, M.F., Kimberg, D.Y., Faseyitan, O., Brecher, A., Dell, G.S., & Coslett, H.B. (2011). Support for anterior temporal involvement in semantic error production in aphasia: New evidence from VLSM. *Brain and Language, 117,* 110–122.

Walker, J.P., Daigle, T., & Buzzard, M. (2002). Hemispheric specialization in processing prosodic structures: Revisited. *Aphasiology, 16,* 1155–1172.

Walker, J.P., Fongemie, K., & Daigle, T. (2001). Prosodic facilitation in the resolution of syntactic ambiguities in subjects with left and right hemisphere damage. *Brain and Language, 78,* 169–196.

Wallentin, M. (2009). Putative sex differences in verbal abilities and language cortex: A critical review. *Brain and Language, 108,* 175–183.

Wallentin, M., Lund, T.E., Ostergaard, S., Ostergaard, L., & Roepstorff, A. (2005). Motion verb sentences activate left posterior middle temporal cortex despite static context. *NeuroReport, 16,* 649–652.

Wallentin, M., Nielson, A.H., Vuust, P., Dohn, A., Roepstorff, A., & Lund, T.E. (2011). BOLD response to motion verbs in left posterior middle temporal gyrus during story comprehension. *Brain and Language, 119,* 221–225.

Wamain, Y., Tallet, J., Zanone, P.G., & Longcamp, M. (2012). Brain responses to handwritten and printed letters differentially depend on the activation state of the primary motor cortex. *NeuroImage, 63,* 1766–1773.

Wandell, B.A. (2011). The neurobiological basis of seeing words. *Annals of the New York Academy of Sciences, 1224,* 63–80.

Wandell, B.A., Dumoulin, S.O., & Brewer, A.A. (2007). Visual field maps in human cortex. *Neuron, 56,* 366–383.

Wang, J., Baucom, L.B., & Shinkareva, S.V. (2013a). Decoding abstract and concrete concept representations based on single-trial fMRI data. *Human Brain Mapping, 34,* 1133–1147.

Wang, J., Conder, J.A., Blitzer, D.N., & Shinkareva, S.V. (2010). Neural representation of abstract and concrete concepts: A meta-analysis of neuroimaging studies. *Human Brain Mapping, 31,* 1459–1468.

Wang, X., Han, Z., He, Y., Caramazza, A., & Bi, Y. (2013b). Where color rests: Spontaneous brain activity of bilateral fusiform and lingual regions predicts object color knowledge performance. *NeuroImage, 76,* 252–263.

Ward, J. (2010). *The student's guide to cognitive neuroscience,* 2nd edition. New York: Psychology Press.

Warren, J.E., Wise, R.J.S., & Warren, J.D. (2005). Sounds do-able: Auditory-motor transformations and the posterior temporal plane. *Trends in Neurosciences, 28,* 636–643.

Warrington, E.K. (1975). The selective impairment of semantic memory. *Quarterly Journal of Experimental Psychology, 27,* 635–657.

Warrington, E.K., & McCarthy, R. (1983). Category specific access dysphasia. *Brain, 106,* 859–878.

Warrington, E.K., & McCarthy, R. (1987). Categories of knowledge: Further fractionations and an attempted integration. *Brain, 110,* 1273–1296.

Warrington, E.K., & Shallice, T. (1984). Category specific semantic impairments. *Brain, 107,* 829–854.

Wassermann, E.M., Epstein, C.M., Ziemann, U., Walsh, V., Paus, T., & Lisanby, S.H. (Eds.) (2008). *The Oxford handbook of transcranial magnetic stimulation.* Oxford, UK: Oxford University Press.

Waters, G., Caplan, D., & Hildebrandt, N. (1991). On the structure of verbal short-term memory and its functional role in sentence comprehension: Evidence from neuropsychology. *Cognitive Neuropsychology, 8,* 81–126.

Watkins, K.E., Strafella, A.P., & Paus, T. (2003). Seeing and hearing speech excites the motor system involved in speech production. *Neuropsychologia, 41,* 989–994.

Watson, C.E., Cardillo, E.R., Ianni, G.R., & Chatterjee, A. (2013). Action concepts in the brain: An activation-likelihood estimation meta-analysis. *Journal of Cognitive Neuroscience, 25,* 1191–1205.

Waytz, A., & Mitchell, J.P. (2011). Two mechanisms for simulating other minds: Dissociations between mirroring and self-projection. *Current Directions in Psychological Science, 20,* 197–200.

Webster, J., Franklin, S., & Howard, D. (2004). Investigating the subprocesses involved in the production of thematic structure: An analysis of four people with aphasia. *Aphasiology, 18,* 47–68.

Webster, J., Franklin, S., & Howard, D. (2007). An analysis of thematic and phrasal structure in people with aphasia: What more can we learn from the story of Cinderella? *Journal of Neurolinguistics, 20,* 363–394.

Weekes, B., Coltheart, M., & Gordon, E. (1997). Deep dyslexia and right hemisphere reading: A regional cerebral blood flow study. *Aphasiology, 11,* 1139–1158.

Wei, T., Liang, X., He, Y., Zang, Y., Han, Z., Caramazza, A., & Bi, Y. (2012). Predicting conceptual processing capacity from spontaneous neuronal activity of the left middle temporal gyrus. *Journal of Neuroscience, 32,* 481–489.

Weiduschat, N., Thiel, A., Rubi-Fessen, I., Hartmann, A., Kessler, J., Merl, P., Kracht, L., Rommel, T., & Heiss, W.D. (2011). Effects of repetitive transcranial magnetic stimulation in aphasic stroke: A randomized controlled pilot study. *Stroke, 42,* 409–415.

Weintraub, S., Mesulam, M.M., & Kramer, L. (1981). Disturbances in prosody: A right hemisphere contribution to language. *Archives of Neurology, 38,* 742–744.

Weintraub, S., Rubin, N.P., & Mesulam, M.M. (1990). Primary progressive aphasia: Longitudinal course, neuropsychological profile, and language features. *Archives of Neurology, 47,* 1329–1335.

Wepman, J.M. (1951). *Recovery from aphasia.* New York: Ronald.

Wernicke, C. (1874). *Der aphasische symptomenkomplex.* Breslau: Cohn und Weigert.

Wertz, R.T., LaPointe, L.L., & Rosenbek, J.C. (1984). *Apraxia of speech: The disorder and its management.* New York: Grune and Stratton.

West, W.C., & Holcomb, P.J. (2000). Imaginal, semantic, and surface-level processing of concrete and abstract words: An electrophysiological investigation. *Journal of Cognitive Neuroscience, 12,* 1024–1037.

Wheatley, T., Weisberg, J., Beauchamp, M.S., & Martin, A. (2005). Automatic priming of semantically related words reduces activity in the fusiform gyrus. *Journal of Cognitive Neuroscience, 17,* 1871–1885.

Wheeldon, L.R., & Levelt, W.J.M. (1995). Monitoring the time course of phonological encoding. *Journal of Memory and Language, 34,* 311–334.

Wheeldon, L.R., & Morgan, J.L. (2002). Phoneme monitoring in internal and external speech. *Language and Cognitive Processes, 17,* 503–535.

Wheeler, M.E., Petersen, S.E., & Buckner, R.L. (2000). Memory's echo: Vivid remembering reactivates sensory-specific cortex. *Proceedings of the National Academy of Sciences, 97,* 11125–11129.

Whitney, C., Huber, W., Klann, J., Weis, S., Krach, S., & Kircher, T. (2009). Neural correlates of narrative shifts during auditory story comprehension. *NeuroImage, 47,* 360–366.

Whitwell, J.L. (2009). Voxel-based morphometry: An automated technique for assessing structural changes in the brain. *Journal of Neuroscience, 29,* 9661–9664.

Whitwell, J.L., Avula, R., Senjem, M.L., Kantarci, K., Weigand, S.D., Samikoglu, A., Edmonson, H.A., Vemuri, P., Knopman, D.S., Boeve, B.F., Petersen, R.C., Josephs, K.A., & Jack, C.R. (2010). Gray and white matter water diffusion in the syndromic variants of frontotemporal dementia. *Neurology, 74,* 1279–1287.

Whitworth, A., Webster, J., & Howard, D. (2005). *A cognitive neuropsychological approach to assessment and intervention in aphasia: A clinician's guide.* Hove, UK: Psychology Press.

Wicker, B., Keysers, C., Plailly, J., Royet, J.P., Gallese, V., & Rizzolatti, G. (2003). Both us disgusted in *my* insula. *Neuron, 40,* 655–664.

Wiethoff, S., Wildgruber, D., Grodd, W., & Ethofer, T. (2009). Response and habituation of the amygdala during processing of emotional prosody. *NeuroReport, 20,* 1356–1360.

Wiethoff, S., Wildgruber, D., Kriefelts, B., Becker, H., Herbert, C., Grodd, W., & Ethofer, T. (2008). Cerebral processing of emotional prosody—influence of acoustic parameters and arousal. *NeuroImage, 39,* 885–893.

Wilbur, R. (2010). The semantics-phonology interface. In D. Brentari (Ed.), *Sign languages* (pp. 355–380). Cambridge, UK: Cambridge University Press.

Wildgruber, D., Ackermann, H., Kriefelts, B., & Ethofer, T. (2006). Cerebral processing of linguistic and emotional prosody: fMRI studies. *Progress in Brain Research, 156,* 249–268.

Wildgruber, D., Ethofer, T., Grandjean, D., & Kriefelts, B. (2009). A cerebral network model of speech prosody comprehension. *International Journal of Speech-Language Pathology, 11,* 277–281.

Wildgruber, D., Hertrich, I., Riecker, A., Erb, M., Anders, S., Grodd, W., & Ackermann, H. (2004). Distinct frontal regions subserve evaluation of linguistic and emotional aspects of speech intonation. *Cerebral Cortex, 14,* 1384–1389.

Wildgruber, D., Riecker, A., Hertrich, I., Erb, M., Grodd, W., Ethofer, T., & Ackermann, H. (2005). Identification of emotional intonation evaluated by fMRI. *NeuroImage, 24,* 1233–1241.

Wilkins, R.H. (1964). Neurosurgical classics XI. *Journal of Neurosurgery, 21,* 424–431.

Willems, R. (Ed.) (forthcoming). *Towards a cognitive neuroscience of natural language use.* Cambridge, UK: Cambridge University Press.

Willems, R., & Hagoort, P. (2009). Broca's region: Battles are not won by ignoring half of the facts. *Trends in Cognitive Sciences, 13,* 101.

Willems, R., Hagoort, P., & Casasanto, D. (2010a). Body-specific representations of action verbs: Neural evidence from right- and left-handers. *Psychological Science, 21,* 67–74.

Willems, R., Toni, I., Hagoort, P., & Casasanto, D. (2010b). Neural dissociations between action verb understanding and motor imagery. *Journal of Cognitive Neuroscience, 22,* 2387–2400.

Williams, G.B., Nestor, P.J., & Hodges, J.R. (2005). Neural correlates of semantic and behavioral deficits in fronto-temporal dementia. *NeuroImage, 24,* 1042–1051.

Willms, J.L., Shapiro, K.A., Peelen, M.V., Pajtas, P.E., Costa, A., Moo, L.R., & Caramazza, A. (2011). Language-invariant verb processing regions in Spanish-English bilinguals. *NeuroImage, 57,* 251–261.

Wilson, M., & Wilson, T.P. (2005). An oscillator model of the timing of turn-taking. *Psychonomic Bulletin and Review, 12,* 957–968.

Wilson, S. (1999). *Coverbs and complex predicates in Wagiman.* Stanford, CA: CSLI Publications.

Wilson, S.M., Brambati, S.M., Henry, R.G., Handwerker, D.A., Agosta, F., Miller, B.L., Wilkins, D.P., Ogar, J.M., & Gorno-Tempini, M.L. (2009a). The neural basis of surface dyslexia in semantic dementia. *Brain, 132,* 71–86.

Wilson, S.M., Dronkers, N.F., Ogar, J.M., Jang, J., Growden, M.E., Agosta, F., Henry, M.L., Miller, B.L., & Gorno-Tempini, M.L. (2010a). Neural correlates of syntactic processing in the nonfluent variant of primary progressive aphasia. *Journal of Neuroscience, 30,* 16845–16854.

Wilson, S.M., Galantucci, S., Tartaglia, M.C., Rising, K., Patterson, D.K., Henry, M.L., Ogar, J.M., DeLeon, J., Miller, B.L., & Gorno-Tempini, M.L. (2011). Syntactic processing depends on dorsal language tracts. *Neuron, 72,* 397–403.

Wilson, S.M., Henry, M.L., Besbris, M., Ogarm, J.M., Dronkers, N.F., Jarrold, W., Miller, B.L., & Gorno-Tempini, M.L. (2010b). Connected speech production in three variants of primary progressive aphasia. *Brain, 133,* 2069–2088.

Wilson, S.M., & Iacoboni, M. (2006). Neural responses to non-native phonemes varying in producibility: Evidence for the sensorimotor nature of speech perception. *NeuroImage, 33*, 316–325.

Wilson, S.M., Isenberg, A.L., & Hickok, G. (2009b). Neural correlates of word production stages delineated by parametric modulation of psycholinguistic variables. *Human Brain Mapping, 30*, 3596–3608.

Wilson, S.M., Rising, K., Stib, M.T., Rapcsak, S.Z., & Beeson, P.M. (2013). Dysfunctional visual word form processing in progressive alexia. *Brain, 136*, 1260–1273.

Wilson, S.M., Saygin, A.P., Sereno, M.I., & Iacoboni, M. (2004). Listening to speech activates motor areas involved in speech production. *Nature Neuroscience, 7*, 701–702.

Wilson-Mendenhall, C.D., Barrett, L.F., Simmons, W.K., & Barsalou, L.W. (2011). Grounding emotion in situated conceptualization. *Neuropsychologia, 49*, 1105–1127.

Wilson-Pauwels, L., Akesson, E.J., Stewart, P.A., & Spacey, S.D. (2002). *Cranial nerves in health and disease*, 2nd edition. London: BC Decker.

Wingfield, A. (1968). Effects of frequency on identification and naming of objects. *American Journal of Psychology, 81*, 226–234.

Winston, J.S., Vuilleumier, P., & Dolan, R.J. (2003). Effects of low-spatial frequency components of fearful faces on fusiform cortex activity. *Current Biology, 13*, 1824–1829.

Witteman, J., van Heuven, V.J.J.P., & Schiller, N.O. (2012). Hearing feelings: A quantitative meta-analysis of the neuroimaging literature on emotional prosody perception. *Neuropsychologia, 50*, 2752–2763.

Witteman, J., van Ijzendoorn, M.H., van de Velde, D., van Heuven, V.J.J.P., & Schiller, N.O. (2011). The nature of hemispheric specialization for linguistic and emotional prosodic perception: A meta-analysis of the lesion literature. *Neuropsychologia, 49*, 3722–3738.

Wittforth, M., Schröder, C., Schardt, D.M., Dengler, R., Heinze, H.J., & Kotz, S.A. (2010). On emotional conflict: Interference resolution of happy and angry prosody reveals valence-specific effects. *Cerebral Cortex, 20*, 383–392.

Wolff, A.B., Sass, K.J., & Keiden, J. (1994). Case report of an intracarotid amobarbital procedure performed on a deaf patient. *Journal of Clinical and Experimental Neuropsychology, 16*, 15–20.

Wolman, D. (2012). A tale of two halves. *Nature, 483*, 260–263.

Wolpert, D.M., & Flanagan, J.R. (2001). Motor prediction. *Current Biology, 11*, R729–R732.

Wolpert, D.M., & Kawato, M. (1998). Multiple paired forward and inverse models for motor control. *Neural Networks, 11*, 1317–1329.

Wong, C., & Gallate, J. (2012). The function of the anterior temporal lobe: A review of the empirical evidence. *Brain Research, 1449*, 94–116.

Wong, P.C.M. (2002). Hemispheric specialization of linguistic pitch patterns. *Brain Research Bulletin, 56*, 83–95.

Wong, P.C.M., Chandrasekaran, B., & Zheng, J. (2012). The derived allele of *ASPM* is associated with lexical tone perception. *PLoS ONE, 7*, e34243.

Wong, P.C.M., & Diehl, R.L. (1999). The effect of reduced tonal space in Parkinsonian speech on the perception of Cantonese tones. Paper presented at the 2nd convention of the European Acoustics Association, Berlin, Germany.

Wong, P.C.M., Parsons, L.M., Martinez, M., & Diehl, R.L. (2004). The role of the insular cortex in pitch pattern perception: The effect of linguistic contexts. *Journal of Neuroscience, 24*, 9153–9160.

Wong, P.C.M., Perrachione, T.K., Gunasekera, G., & Chandrasekaran, B. (2009). Communication disorders in speakers of tone languages: Etiological bases and clinical considerations. *Seminars in Speech and Language, 30*, 162–173.

Wong, P.C.M., Warrier, C.M., Penhune, V.B., Roy, A.K., Sadehh, A., Parrish, T.B., & Zatorre, R.J. (2008). Volume of left Heschl's gyrus and linguistic pitch learning. *Cerebral Cortex, 18*, 828–836.

Wood, J.N., & Grafman, J. (2003). Human prefrontal cortex: Processing and representational perspectives. *Nature Reviews Neuroscience, 4*, 139–147.

Woods, D.L., Herron, T.J., Cate, A.D., Kang, X., & Yund, E.W. (2011). Phonological processing in human auditory cortical fields. *Frontiers in Human Neuroscience, 5*, Article 42.

Woollams, A.M. (2012). Apples are not the only fruit: The effects of concept typicality on semantic representation in the anterior temporal lobe. *Frontiers in Human Neuroscience, 6*, Article 85.

Woollams, A.M., Lambon Ralph, M.A., Plaut, D.C., & Patterson, K. (2007). SD-squared: On the association between semantic dementia and surface dyslexia. *Psychological Review, 114*, 316–339.

Woollams, A.M., Lambon Ralph, M.A., Plaut, D.C., & Patterson, K. (2010). SD-squared revisited: Reply to Coltheart, Tree, and Saunders (2010). *Psychological Review, 117*, 273–283.

Woollams, A.M., & Patterson, K. (2012). The consequences of progressive phonological impairment for reading aloud. *Neuropsychologia, 50*, 3469–3477.

Woolsey, C.N., Erickson, T.C., & Gilson, W.E. (1979). Localization in somatic sensory and motor areas of human cerebral cortex as determined by direct recording of evoked potentials and electrical stimulation. *Journal of Neurosurgery, 51*, 476–506.

Wright, N.D., Mechelli, A., Noppeney, U., Veltman, D.J., Rombouts, S.A., Glenman, J., Haynes, J.D., & Price, C.J. (2008). Selective activation around the left occipito-temporal sulcus for words relative to pictures: Individual variability or false positives? *Human Brain Mapping, 29*, 986–1000.

Wright, P., Randall, B., Marslen-Wilson, W.D., & Tyler, L.K. (2011). Dissociating linguistic and task-related activity in the left inferior frontal gyrus. *Journal of Cognitive Neuroscience, 23*, 404–413.

Wu, C.Y., Ho, M.H.R., & Chen, S.H.A. (2012). A meta-analysis of fMRI studies on Chinese orthographic, phonological, and semantic processing. *NeuroImage, 63*, 381–391.

Wu, D.H., Waller, S., & Chatterjee, A. (2007). The functional neuroanatomy of thematic and locative relational knowledge. *Journal of Cognitive Neuroscience, 19*, 1542–1555.

Xu, J., Kemeny, S., Park, G., Frattali, C., & Braun, A. (2005). Language in context: Emergent features of word, sentence, and narrative comprehension. *NeuroImage, 25*, 1002–1015.

Xu, Y., Gandour, J., Talavage, T., Wong, D., Dzemidzic, M., Tong, Y., et al. (2006). Activation of the left planum temporale in pitch processing is shaped by language experience. *Human Brain Mapping, 27*(2), 173–183.

Yarkoni, T., Speer, N.K., & Zacks, J.M. (2008). Neural substrates of narrative comprehension and memory. *NeuroImage, 41*, 1408–1425.

Ye, Z., & Zhou, X. (2009). Conflict control during sentence comprehension: fMRI evidence. *NeuroImage, 48*, 280–290.

Yeh, W., & Barsalou, L.W. (2006). The situated nature of concepts. *American Journal of Psychology, 119*, 349–384.

Yi, H.A., Moore, P., & Grossman, M. (2007). Reversal of the concreteness effect for verbs in semantic dementia. *Neuropsychology, 21*, 9–19.

Yip, J.T.H., Lee, T.M.C., Ho, S.H., Tsang, K.L., & Li, L.S. (2003). Emotion recognition in patients with idiopathic Parkinson's disease. *Movement Disorders, 18*, 1115–1122.

Yip, M. (2003). *Tone.* Cambridge, UK: Cambridge University Press.

Yiu, E., & Fok, A. (1995). Lexical tone disruption in Cantonese aphasic speakers. *Clinical Linguistics and Phonetics, 9*, 79–92.

Yoncheva, Y.N., Zevin, J.D., Maurer, U., & McCandliss, D. (2010). Auditory selective attention to speech modulates activity in the visual word form area. *Cerebral Cortex, 20*, 622–632.

Zaehle, T., Wustenberg, T., Meyer, M., & Jancke, L. (2004). Evidence for rapid auditory perception as the foundation of speech processing: A sparse temporal sampling fMRI study. *European Journal of Neuroscience, 20*, 2447–2456.

Zaidel, E. (1985). Language in the right hemisphere. In D.F. Benson & E. Zaidel (Eds.), *The dual brain: Hemispheric specialization in humans* (pp. 205–231). New York: Guilford Press.

Zald, D.H., & Andreotti, C. (2010). Neuropsychological assessment of the orbital and ventromedial prefrontal cortex. *Neuropsychologia, 48*, 3377–3391.

Zannino, G.D., Perri, R., Pasqualetti, P., Paola, M.D., Caltagirone, C., & Carlesimo, G.A. (2006). The role of semantic distance in category-specific impairments for living things: Evidence from a case of semantic dementia. *Neuropsychologia, 44*, 1017–1028.

Zatorre, R.J., & Gandour, J.T. (2008). Neural specializations for speech and pitch: Moving beyond the dichotomies. *Philosophical Transactions of the Royal Society, B, Biological Sciences, 363*, 1087–1104.

Zatorre, R.J., Halpern, A.R., Perry, D.W., Meyer, E., & Evans, A.C. (1996). Hearing in the mind's ear: A PET investigation of musical imagery and perception. *Journal of Cognitive Neuroscience, 8*, 29–46.

Zeki, S. (1990). A century of achromatopsia. *Brain, 113*, 1721–1777.

Zeki, S. (1991). Cerebral akinetopsia (visual motion blindness): A review. *Brain, 114*, 811–824.

Zeki, S., & Bartels, A. (1999). The clinical and functional measurement of cortical (in)activity in the visual brain, with special reference to the two subdivisions (V4 and V4α) of the human color centre. *Philosophical Transactions of the Royal Society, B, 354*, 1371–1382.

Zeki, S., Watson, J.D.G., Lueck, C.J., Friston, K.J., Kennard, C., & Frackowiak, R.S.J. (1991). A direct demonstration of functional specialization in human visual cortex. *Journal of Neuroscience, 11*, 641–649.

Zempleni, M.Z., Renken, R., Hoeks, J.C., & Hoogduin, J.M., & Stowe, L.A. (2007). Semantic ambiguity processing in sentence context: Evidence from event-related fMRI. *NeuroImage, 34*, 1270–1279.

Zentner, J., Meyer, B., Stangl, A., & Schramm, J. (1996). Intrinsic tumors of the insula: A prospective surgical study of 30 patients. *Journal of Neurosurgery, 85*, 263–271.

Zheng, Z.Z. (2009). The functional specialization of the planum temporale. *Journal of Neurophysiology, 102*, 3079–3081.

Zheng, Z.Z., Munhall, K.G., & Johnsrude, I.S. (2010). Functional overlap between regions involved in speech perception and in monitoring one's own voice during speech production. *Journal of Cognitive Neuroscience, 22*, 1770–1781.

Zhou, J., Gennatas, E.D., Kramer, J.H., Miller, B.L., & Seeley, W.W. (2012). Predicting regional neurodegeneration from the healthy brain functional connectome. *Neuron, 73*, 1216–1227.

Zhuang, J., Tyler, L.K., Randall, B., Stamatakis, E.A., & Marslen-Wilson, W.D. (in press). Optimally efficient neural systems for processing spoken language. *Cerebral Cortex.*

Ziegler, D. (1952). Word deafness and Wernicke's aphasia. *Archives of Neurological Psychology, 67*, 323–331.

Ziegler, J.C., & Goswami, U. (2005). Reading acquisition, developmental dyslexia, and skilled reading across languages: A psycholinguistic grain size theory. *Psychological Bulletin, 131*, 3–29.

Zihl, J.D., Von Cramon, N., Mai, N., & Schmid, C.H. (1991). Disturbance of movement vision after bilateral posterior brain damage. *Brain, 114*, 2235–2252.

Zilles, K., & Amunts, K. (2010). Centenary of Brodmann's map: Conception and fate. *Nature Reviews Neuroscience, 11*, 139–145.

Zilles, K., & Amunts, K. (2012). Architecture of the cerebral cortex. In J.K. Mai & G. Paxinos (Eds.), *The human nervous system*, 3rd edition (pp. 826–885). San Diego, CA: Academic Press.

Zimmer, C. (2004). *Soul made flesh: The discovery of the brain, and how it changed the world.* New York: Free Press.

Zwaan, R.A. (2004). The immersed experiencer: Toward an embodied theory of language comprehension. In B.H. Ross (Ed.), *The psychology of learning and motivation, Vol. 44* (pp. 35–62). New York: Academic Press.

Zwaan, R.A., & Radvansky, G.A. (1998). Situation models in language comprehension and memory. *Psychological Bulletin, 123*, 162–185.

Zwaan, R.A., & Taylor, L.J. (2006). Seeing, acting, understanding: Motor resonance in language comprehension. *Journal of Experimental Psychology: General, 135*, 1–11.

Author Index

Note: Italics indicate that the name is located in the list of references.

Subject Index

Note: "F" after a page number indicates a figure; "t" indicates a table.

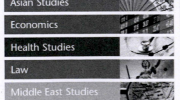
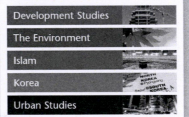